ARBA Guide to
Library Science Literature
1970-1983

ARBA Guide to Library Science Literature 1970-1983

Edited by
DONALD G. DAVIS, JR.
University of Texas at Austin
and
CHARLES D. PATTERSON
Louisiana State University

LIBRARIES UNLIMITED, INC.
Littleton, Colorado
1987

Ref
Z
666
.A73
1987

LIBRARIES UNLIMITED, INC.
P.O. Box 263
Littleton, Colorado 80160-0263

Library of Congress Cataloging-in-Publication Data

ARBA guide to library science literature, 1970-1983.

    Includes index.
    1. Library science--Book reviews. 2. Library
science--Bibliography. I. Davis, Donald G., Jr.
II. Patterson, Charles D., 1928-   . III. American
reference books annual.
Z666.A73 1987   016.02   86-27712
ISBN 0-87287-585-7

Libraries Unlimited books are bound with Type II nonwoven material that meets and exceeds National
Association of State Textbook Administrators' Type II nonwoven material specifications Class A
through E.

Contents

Introduction ix
Contributors xi
Publications Cited xix

Part 1
GENERAL WORKS

1 — INTRODUCTORY WORKS 3

2 — PROCEEDINGS, SYMPOSIA, AND
ESSAYS 8

3 — COMMUNICATION OF SCIEN-
TIFIC AND TECHNICAL
INFORMATION 12

4 — CURRENT ISSUES 15

5 — THEORETICAL FOUNDATIONS 21

Part 2
REFERENCE WORKS

6 — GENERAL WORKS 25

7 — BIBLIOGRAPHIES 34

8 — INDEXES 40

9 — DICTIONARIES AND
ENCYCLOPEDIAS 42

10 — HANDBOOKS AND MANUALS 46

11 — ANNUALS AND YEARBOOKS 53

12 — DIRECTORIES 56

13 — SELECTION AIDS 61

14 — LIBRARY HOLDINGS —
SURVEYS AND GUIDES 68
Comprehensive 68
Regional Studies 76
Individual Libraries and Subjects 79

15 — BIOGRAPHICAL WORKS 81
Comprehensive 81
Specific Groups 82

16 — FESTSCHRIFTEN 86
Indexes 86
Individual Authors 86

17 — COLLECTED WRITINGS 93
Bibliographies 93
Individual Authors 94

Part 3
TYPES OF LIBRARIES

18 — COLLEGE AND RESEARCH
LIBRARIES 99
Academic Librarianship 99
College and Community Libraries 103
Statistics 107

19 — PUBLIC LIBRARIES 109

20 — SCHOOL LIBRARY MEDIA
CENTERS 116
General Works 116
Reference Works 124

21 — SPECIAL LIBRARIES 127
General Works 127

21 – SPECIAL LIBRARIES – *Continued*
  Reference Works....................130
  Business and Industrial Libraries......131
  Government Libraries................133
  Health Sciences Libraries...........134
  Library of Congress.................137
  Map Libraries......................139
  Religious Libraries.................141
  Other Types of Special Libraries......142

Part 4
LIBRARY SERVICES AND
SPECIFIC TOPICS

22 – ARCHITECTURE, FACILITIES,
  AND EQUIPMENT................151

23 – ARCHIVES AND SPECIAL
  COLLECTIONS 160

24 – AUDIOVISUAL AND OTHER
  MEDIA 164
  General Works.....................164
  Reference Works...................166
  Collection Development............168
  Organization and Bibliographic
    Control 169
  Types of Libraries.................170
    Academic Libraries.............170
    Public Libraries................171
    School Libraries................171
  Specific Media....................173
    Ephemera and Bulletin Boards....173
    Films, Prints, and Pictures.......174
    Maps 177
    Music.........................178
    Video.........................178

25 – AUTOMATION AND NEW
  TECHNOLOGIES 180
  General Works before 1976..........180
  General Works since 1976...........185
  Reference Works...................194
  Microcomputers...................195
  Minicomputers....................198
  Programming Languages............199

26 – BIBLIOGRAPHIC CONTROL
  AND BIBLIOGRAPHY.............202
  General Works.....................202
  Proceedings, Symposia, and Essays....203
  Specific Topics....................205

27 – BIBLIOTHERAPY.................207

28 – CATALOGING AND
  CLASSIFICATION 210
  General Works.....................210

  Reference Works....................211
  Introductory Texts and Manuals......212
  Audiovisual Materials...............217
  Authority Control..................219
  Research 221
  Serials 222
  Descriptive Cataloging..............223
    General Works..................223
    Introductory Texts and Manuals..224
    AACR2 227
  Classification 235
    General Works..................235
    Introductory Texts and Manuals..237
    Bliss 238
    Dewey Decimal Classification....239
    Library of Congress
      Classification 243
    UDC 250
    Book Numbers.................251
    Other Classification Schemes.....252
  Subject Headings..................255
    General Works..................255
    Reference Works................255
    Introductory Texts and Manuals..256
    LC Subject Headings and
      Related Works.............256
    Sears List.....................259
    Other Types of Subject Headings..259
  Catalog Maintenance................261
    General Works..................261
    Filing 263
  Online Cataloging and Automation....266
    General Works..................266
    MARC......................269
    OCLC 270
    Other Systems.................271

29 – CENSORSHIP AND
  INTELLECTUAL FREEDOM.......273

30 – COLLECTION DEVELOPMENT....281
  General Works.....................281
  Reference Works...................283
  Introductory Texts and Manuals......284
  Acquisitions 286
    General Works..................286
    Reference Works................288
    Introductory Texts and Manuals..289
    Approval Plans.................289
    Foreign Materials...............290
    Gifts and Exchanges............291
    Nonbook Materials.............292
  Selection Process..................293
    General Works..................293
    College and University Libraries..294
    School Libraries and Media
      Centers 295
    Other Topics..................296

Selection Aids......................298
   College and Research Libraries...298
   Public Libraries................300
   School Libraries and Media
      Centers 300

31 – COMPARATIVE AND INTER-
   NATIONAL LIBRARIANSHIP......305
   General Works.....................305
   Reference Works..................309
   Information Systems and
      Networks.....................311
   Specific Regions and Countries......312
      Africa.......................312
      Asia 313
      Australia, New Zealand, and
         Related Areas..............314
      Canada 316
      Developing Countries..........317
      Europe and the USSR..........320
      Latin America.................324

32 – CONSERVATION AND
   PRESERVATION...................325
   General Works.....................325
   Reference Works..................330
   Proceedings and Seminars...........332

33 – COPYRIGHT AND
   REPROGRAPHY...................334
   General Works.....................334
   Reference Works..................336
   Essays 337
   Copyright 337

34 – EDUCATION 343
   General Works.....................343
   Reference Works..................345
   Proceedings and Symposia..........347
   Continuing Education...............348
   Curriculum Studies.................351
   School Media Personnel............352

35 – EMPLOYMENT 354

36 – GOVERNMENT PUBLICATIONS...358
   General Works.....................358
   Reference Works..................363
   Proceedings.......................365

37 – HISTORY.......................368
   General Works.....................368
   Reference Works..................374
   Proceedings.......................375
   Biography 376
   College and University Libraries......384
   Public Libraries...................386
   Private and Special Libraries........391

Library Education..................395
Other Topics......................397

38 – HUMOR 399

39 – INDEXING AND ABSTRACTING...400
   General Works.....................400
   Reference Works..................403
   Other Topics......................405

49 – INFORMATION MANAGEMENT...410
   General Works.....................410
   Reference Works..................413
   Proceedings, Symposia, and Essays....413

41 – LEGISLATION, PUBLIC POLICY,
   AND FUNDING...................421
   Legislation and Public Policy.........421
   Funding...........................424

42 – LIBRARY INSTRUCTION.........426
   General Works.....................426
   Reference Works..................429
   Proceedings, Symposia, and Essays....429
   College and University..............432
   School Libraries and Media Centers...436
   Other Topics......................437

43 – LIBRARY ORIENTATION
   GUIDES 439
   General Works.....................439
   Precollege Level...................446
   College Level.....................451

44 – MANAGEMENT 453
   General Works.....................453
   Reference Works..................457
   Proceedings, Symposia, and Essays....457
   Functions.........................459
      Budgeting and Finance..........459
      Evaluating and Measurement.....463
      Planning and Decision-making
         Systems 467
      Staffing and Personnel..........469
   Types of Libraries..................477
      College and Research Libraries...477
      Public Libraries...............485
      School Library Media Centers....491
      Special Libraries...............498

45 – MARKETING AND PROMOTION..503

46 – MICROFORMS 514

47 – NETWORKING AND
   RESOURCE SHARING.............520
   General Works.....................520
   Reference Works..................525

47 – NETWORKING AND
 RESOURCE SHARING – *Continued*
 Proceedings, Symposia, and Essays 526
 Interlibrary Loan 528
 International Developments 529

48 – ONLINE SEARCHING 532
 General Works 532
 Reference Works 535
 Proceedings 538

49 – PROFESSIONAL STATUS 540
 General Works 540
 Paraprofessionals 544
 School Library Media Personnel 545
 Women 546

50 – PUBLIC SERVICES 549
 General Works 549
 Circulation Systems 551
 Community Services and
   Information 552
 User Studies 554

51 – REFERENCE SERVICES 556
 General Works 556
 Reference Works 561
 Introductory Texts and Manuals 561
 Proceedings and Essays 565
 Reference Strategies 566
 Research Studies 566
 Subject Approaches 567
 Other Topics 570

52 – RESEARCH 573
 General Works 573
 Statistical Approaches 576

53 – RETRIEVAL SYSTEMS 578
 General Works before 1976 578
 General Works since 1976 580

 Reference Works 585
 Proceedings and Symposia 588
 Other Topics 589

54 – SERIALS 592
 General Works 592
 Proceedings, Symposia, and Essays 594
 Acquisitions 595
 Automation 597
 Other Topics 599

55 – SPECIAL USER GROUPS 602
 Adult Education 602
 Children 603
   General Works 603
   Reference Works 607
   Proceedings, Symposia,
     and Essays 607
   Media Skills and Curriculum
     Enrichment 608
   Storytelling 610
 Disabled Users 612
   General Works 612
   Reference Works 617
   Blind and Physically
     Handicapped 618
   Children and Young Adults 620
 Disadvantaged Users 623
 Ethnic Minorities 624
 Older Adults 627
 Prisoners 628
 Reading 629
 Young Adults 630
   General Works 630
   Reference Works 632
   Proceedings and Symposia 633

56 – TECHNICAL SERVICES 636

Author/Title Index 639
Subject Index 675

Introduction

During the early 1980s, the professional library community began to act to solve a problem that many had noted for many years. That is, while the profession had carefully monitored, evaluated, and gathered into bibliographic form the literature of other fields, it had not done so with its own material. To be sure, periodical literature received attention through the general and specialized indexing services. Several attempts to provide a bibliography of books and other materials in specific subfields of librarianship have been published within the past decade. Examples of these include Marjorie E. Murfin and Lubomyr R. Wynar's *Reference Service: An Annotated Bibliographic Guide* (Libraries Unlimited, 1977) and Rose Mary Magrill and Constance Rinehart's *Library Technical Services: A Selected, Annotated Bibliography* (Greenwood Press, 1977). The appearance of Gary R. Purcell and Gail Ann Schlachter's *Reference Sources in Library and Information Services: A Guide to the Literature* (ABC-Clio, 1984) marked a new level in bibliographical coverage of reference works.

Since 1970 *American Reference Books Annual* (*ARBA*) has presented yearly reviews of reference works published and distributed in the United States. It also, until 1985, evaluated on a broader scope all books appearing in library science—both reference and nonreference works. The present compilation of *ARBA* reviews in library science from the 1970-1984 volumes represents an attempt to provide a bibliography of library science for the years 1970 through 1983. This work provides a foundation for the coverage which *Library Science Annual*, devoted to book reviews along with other bibliographical surveys, has continued from 1985 onward. It also constitutes the first step in a retrospective bibliography. The second step anticipates a work that reviews the literature of library science from the nineteenth century to 1970. When this is complete, the profession will have done for itself what it has long done, and encouraged, for others.

The arrangement of this work generally follows the pattern that *ARBA* has developed over the years. Because of the number of entries and the dynamic change in the profession, several categories of special topics have been added, modified, or incorporated with others. Four broad categories form the basic outline: general works, reference works, works dealing with types of libraries, and works dealing with library services and special topics. General works include titles dealing with such a wide range of topics that further differentiation is not possible or useful. In the last two sections, major headings are alphabetically arranged, as are the entries themselves within the various subheadings. The subheadings in the library services and special topics section are those that arrange the existing literature in a logical manner.

The editors have placed entries where they think users expect to find them, but, as always, users may have to search in two or three places for exhaustive coverage. The author/title and limited subject indexes will provide assistance. Most of the signed reviews of the original volumes appear under the names of the original reviewers. They are listed in the list of contributors. Unsigned reviews were prepared by various editors or by the editors of this volume and their assistants.

Several adjustments make the present compilation something other than a mere republication of library science entries from *ARBA*. About 275 entries were excluded because they fell into the following categories: (1) general reference guides to and bibliographies of general reading, periodicals, and book reviews; (2) reference books on a type of literature; (3) general library selection aids, unless continuing standard works; (4) works in related fields, such as communication, computer science, and education; (5) works described better as "general" than as "library science"; (6) annual reports of library associations and agencies; (7) proceedings and minutes of annual meetings or conferences; (8) new periodical titles; (9) individual periodical issues unless special editions; and (10) miscellaneous and ephemeral works.

In order to consolidate the reviews, nearly 200 individual entries were deleted by substituting descriptive summary reviews for several serial or annual reference publications and by presenting reviews of only the most recent edition of multi-edition titles (chiefly reference works and textbooks) with references to earlier editions. Reprints are included only selectively.

Recognizing that the early years of *ARBA* were less than complete for its own scope, the editors have added entries for over 80 titles that appeared between 1970 and 1973. The result of this editing is a comprehensive, though not exhaustive, evaluative listing of over 1,700 works in library science published in the fourteen years from 1970 to 1983. As is natural in a retrospective work of this nature, some reviewers' remarks represent conditions at the time the review was written rather than the current situation.

In addition to modifying the selection of entries for the compilation, the editors have cited additional reviews for items that did not have them in *ARBA*. These were drawn from *Book Review Index*, with coverage through February 1986. The list of source periodicals for all cited reviews appears with the abbreviations used in the list of publications cited. At the insistence of the publisher, bibliographic, in-print, and price information was verified when possible in *Books in Print* in the first half of 1986. Although the coverage of this work is through 1983, major titles have been updated to the most recent edition, since the publisher feels this information will be more useful for these important works. Updating does not reflect some recent changes in distribution of British materials; for example, Library Association publications are no longer distributed by Oryx Press, but by the American Library Association.

The editors wish to express appreciation to their respective deans and their institutions for research assistance that speeded this project along. The John P. Commons Teaching Fellowship at Texas in spring 1986 brought the manuscript to fruition. Barbara Mercer, Fang-Wan Yang, Pimonpan Raper, and David Morrow helped at the University of Texas at Austin, and Cindy Rooks helped at Louisiana State University, Baton Rouge. E. B. Jackson at Texas was an encouragement at critical junctures. The decisions for overall selection, arrangement and organization, however, were those of the editors.

Donald G. Davis, Jr.
Charles D. Patterson

Contributors

Donald C. Adcock, Director of Library Services, Glen Ellyn District 41, Ill.

Richard G. Akeroyd, Jr., Asst. City Librarian and Director of Public Services, Denver Public Library, Colo.

Christopher Albertson, City Librarian, Tyler Public Library, Tex.

Ann Allan, Assoc. Professor, School of Library Science, Kent State Univ., Ohio.

Walter C. Allen, Assoc. Professor, Graduate School of Library and Information Science, Univ. of Illinois, Urbana.

Brian Alley, Univ. Librarian and Assoc. Dean, Sangamon State Univ., Springfield, Ill.

Rao Aluri, Asst. Professor, Division of Librarianship, Emory Univ., Atlanta, Ga.

Mohammed M. Aman, Dean and Professor, School of Library Science, Univ. of Wisconsin, Milwaukee.

Saul J. Amdursky, Administrator, Racine County Library System, Racine, Wis.

Frank J. Anderson, Librarian Emeritus, Sandor Teszler Library, Wofford College, Spartanburg, S.C.

James D. Anderson, Assoc. Dean and Professor, School of Communication, Library, and Information Studies, Rutgers Univ., New Brunswick, N.J.

Margaret Anderson, Assoc. Professor, Faculty of Library and Information Science, Univ. of Toronto, Ont.

Charles R. Andrews, Dean of Library Services, Hofstra Univ., Hempstead, N.Y.

Theodora Andrews, Pharmacy, Nursing, and Health Sciences Librarian, Purdue Univ., West Lafayette, Ind.

Pauline V. Angione, Asst. Professor, Graduate School of Library and Information Science, Rosary College, River Forest, Ill.

Andy Armitage, Chief Librarian, Owen Sound Public Library, Ont.

Robert Balay, Head, Reference Dept., Yale Univ. Library, New Haven, Conn.

Doris H. Banks, Public Services Librarian, Whitworth College, Spokane, Wash.

Pierre P. Barrette, Coordinator of Audiovisual Methods, Dept. of Curriculum, Instruction and Media, Southern Illinois Univ., Carbondale.

Linda S. Batty, Librarian, Northfield-Mt. Hermon School, East Northfield, Mass.

Barbara L. Bell, Documents/Reference Librarian, College of Wooster, Ohio.

JoAnn H. Bell, Director, Health Sciences Library, East Carolina Univ., Greenville, N.C.

Bruce C. Bennion, Asst. Professor, School of Library Science, Univ. of Southern California, Los Angeles.

Stephen J. Bensman, Social Science Bibliographer, Middleton Library, Louisiana State Univ., Baton Rouge.

Robert A. Berk, Director, Medical Library, School of Medicine, Southern Illinois Univ., Springfield.

Irene Berkey, Foreign and International Law Librarian, Northwestern Univ., Chicago.

Charles L. Bernier, Professor, School of Information and Library Studies, State Univ. of New York, Buffalo.

Robert C. Berring, Law Librarian and Professor, Univ. of California, Berkeley.

Julie Bichteler, Assoc. Professor, Graduate School of Library and Information Science, Univ. of Texas, Austin.

Fay M. Blake, School of Library and Information Science, Univ. of California, Berkeley.

Marty Bloomberg, Head of Library Operations, California State College, San Bernardino.

Marjorie E. Bloss, Asst. Director, Technical Services and Automation, Illinois Institute of Technology, Chicago.

Martha Boaz, Dean Emerita, Graduate School of Library and Information Sciences, Univ. of Southern Calif., Los Angeles.

James E. Bobick, Head of Collection Development, Central Library System, Temple Univ., Philadelphia.

George S. Bobinski, Dean, School of Information and Library Studies, State University of New York, Buffalo.

Sharon C. Bonk, Head of Acquisitions, Univ. Library, State Univ. of New York, Albany.

Peggy Clossey Boone, Librarian, Joseph A. Leonard Jr. High School, Old Town, Me.

Anindya Bose, Library School, Kent State University, Ohio.

William Brace, Assoc. Professor, Graduate School of Library Science, Rosary College, River Forest, Ill.

Carol June Bradley, Music Librarian, State Univ. of New York, Buffalo.

Deborah Jane Brewer, Editor, *State Legislatures*, Denver, Colo.

Barbara E. Brown, Head, General Cataloging Section, Library of Parliament, Ottawa, Ont.

David W. Brunton, Acting Assoc. Director, Arapahoe Regional Library, Englewood, Colo.

E. T. Bryant, Manchester School of Librarianship, England.

Richard M. Buck, Asst. to the Chief, Performing Arts Research Center, New York Public Library, Lincoln Center.

Dwight F. Burlingame, Director of Univ. Libraries, Bowling Green State Univ., Ohio.

Lois Buttlar, Asst. Director, Instructional Resources Center, and Asst. Professor, Dept. of Educational Psychology, Administration, Technology, and Foundations, Kent State Univ., Ohio.

Greg Byerly, Coordinator of Library Automation, Kent State Libraries, Kent State Univ., Ohio.

Hans E. Bynagle, Director, Cowles Memorial Library, Whitworth College, Spokane, Wash.

Heather Cameron, formerly Staff, Libraries Unlimited.

Jerry Cao, Asst. Library Director, Woodbury Univ., Los Angeles, Calif.

Jennifer Cargill, Assoc. Librarian, Texas Tech Univ. Library, Lubbock.

Jackson H. Carter, Reference Librarian, Los Alamos National Library, N. Mex.

Susan Dedmond Casbon, Teacher-Librarian, Ananda Schools, Nevada City, Calif.

Jefferson D. Caskey, Professor of Library Science and Instructional Media, Western Kentucky Univ., Bowling Green.

Ching-chih Chen, Professor and Assoc. Dean, Graduate School of Library and Information Science, Simmons College, Boston, Mass.

Frances Neel Cheney, Professor Emerita, Dept. of Library Science, George Peabody College for Teachers, Vanderbilt Univ., Nashville, Tenn.

Boyd Childress, Reference Librarian, Auburn Univ., Ala.

Mary Clotfelter, Instructor, Library Science, Eastern New Mexico Univ., Portales.

Harriette M. Cluxton, formerly Director of Medical Library Services, Illinois Masonic Medical Center, Chicago.

Pauline Atherton Cochrane, Professor, School of Information Studies, Syracuse Univ., N.Y.

William L. Cohn, Asst. Professor, School of Library Science, Univ. of Wisconsin, Milwaukee.

John P. Comaromi, Chief, Decimal Classification Division, Library of Congress, Washington, D.C.

Charles Wm. Conaway, School of Library Science, Florida State Univ., Tallahassee.

Barbara Conroy, Educational Consultant, Santa Fe, N. Mex.

C. Donald Cook, Professor, Faculty of Library and Information Science, Univ. of Toronto, Ont.

M. Kathy Cook, Asst. Education/Psychology Librarian, Morris Library, Southern Illinois Univ., Carbondale.

Judith Ann Copler, Head, Interlibrary Services, Indiana Univ., Bloomington.

Bill J. Corbin, Lecturer in Library and Information Science, Vanderbilt Univ., Nashville, Tenn.

Paul B. Cors, Music Cataloger, Univ. of Wyoming Library, Laramie.

Keith M. Cottam, Director, University of Wyoming Libraries, Laramie.

Caroline M. Coughlin, Asst. Director, Drew Univ. Library, Madison, N.J.

Richard J. Cox, Head, Governmental Records Division, Alabama Dept. of Archives and History, Montgomery.

Jennie B. Cross, Documents Librarian and Asst. Professor, Kresge Library, Oakland Univ., Rochester, Mich.

Milton H. Crouch, Asst. Director for Reader Services, Bailey/Howe Library, Univ. of Vermont, Burlington.

Elizabeth Crowell, Assoc. Professor, College of Social Professions, Univ. of Kentucky, Lexington.

Katherine Cveljo, Assoc. Professor, School of Library and Information Sciences, North Texas State Univ., Denton.

Jay E. Daily, Professor Emeritus, Graduate School of Library and Information Science, Univ. of Pittsburgh, Pa.

Doris Cruger Dale, Professor, Dept. of Curriculum, Instruction, and Media, Southern Illinois Univ., Carbondale.

William J. Dane, Supervising Art and Music Librarian, Newark Public Library, N.J.

Melinda D. Davis, formerly Asst. Professor and Cataloger, Univ. of Tennessee, Knoxville.

Dominique-René de Lerma, Professor of Music and Graduate Music Coordinator, Morgan State Univ., Baltimore, Md.

Roberta J. Depp, Asst. County Librarian, Eagle County Public Library, Colo.

Mary Alice Deveny, Youth Librarian, Venice Area Public Library, Fla.

Judith W. Devine, Supervisor, Reference Dept., St. Paul Public Library, Minn.

Robert K. Dikeman, Asst. Professor, Division of Library Science, San Jose State Univ., Calif.

Peter Doiron, Woodbridge Public Library, N.J.

Mary Kay Donahue, Resource Development Librarian, Texas A & M Univ. Library, College Station.

G. Kim Dority, formerly Staff, Libraries Unlimited.

Paul Z. DuBois, Director, Trenton State College Library, N.J.

Susan Ebershoff-Coles, Supervisor of Technical Services, Indianapolis-Marion County Public Library, Ind.

Neal L. Edgar (deceased), Assoc. Curator, Special Collections, Kent State Univ., Ohio.

Michael B. Eisenberg, Coordinator of Field Work/School Media, School of Information Studies, Syracuse Univ., N.Y.

Marie Ellis, English and American Literature Bibliographer, Univ. of Georgia Libraries, Athens.

Claire England, Assoc. Professor, Faculty of Library and Information Science, Univ. of Toronto, Ont.

Jonathon Erlen, Curator, History of Medicine, Univ. of Pittsburgh, Pa.

Leigh Estabrook, Dean, Graduate School of Library and Information Science, Univ. of Illinois, Urbana-Champaign.

G. Edward Evans, Librarian of Tozzer Library, Harvard Univ., Cambridge, Mass.

Shelley Ewing, formerly Staff, Libraries Unlimited.

George H. Fadenrecht, Professor of Librarianship and Reference Librarian, Central Washington Univ., Ellensburg.

Joyce Duncan Falk, Data Services Coordinator and Reference Librarian, Library of Univ. of California, Irvine.

Josephine Riss Fang, Professor of Library Science, Simmons College, Boston, Mass.

John Farley, Professor, School of Library and Information Science, State Univ. of New York, Albany.

Jean W. Farrington, Asst. Head of Circulation, Van Pelt Library, Univ. of Pennsylvania, Philadelphia.

Adele M. Fasick, Professor, Faculty of Library and Information Science, Univ. of Toronto, Ont.

Valmai Fenster (deceased), Asst. Professor, Library School, Univ. of Wisconsin, Madison.

Eleanor Ferrall, Reference Librarian and Subject Specialist, Criminal Justice/Public Affairs, Arizona State Univ., Tempe.

Mary K. Fetzer, Documents/Reference Librarian, Alexander Library, Rutgers Univ., New Brunswick, N.J.

P. William Filby, formerly Director, Maryland Historical Society, Baltimore.

Ralph J. Folcarelli, Professor of Library Science, Palmer Graduate School, C. W. Post Center, Long Island Univ., Greenvale, N.Y.

Linda L. Folck, Library Director, East Liverpool Campus, Kent State Univ., East Liverpool, Ohio.

Donald D. Foos, formerly Staff, Libraries Unlimited.

Norman Frankel, Asst. Professor and Librarian, Western Michigan Univ., Kalamazoo.

Susan J. Freiband, Independent Consultant, Library and Information Services, Arlington, Va.

Juan R. Freudenthal, Assoc. Professor, Graduate School of Library and Information Science, Simmons College, Boston, Mass.

Elizabeth Frick, Assoc. Professor, School of Library Service, Dalhousie Univ., N.S.

Stephen M. Fry, Head, Music Library, Schoenberg Hall, Univ. of California, Los Angeles.

Sherrilynne Shirley Fuller, Director, Bio-Medical Library, Univ. of Minnesota, Minneapolis.

Ahmad Gamaluddin, Professor, School of Library Science, Clarion State College, Pa.

Betty Gay, Central Library Director, Los Angeles Public Library, Calif.

Mary Ardeth Gaylord, Reference Librarian, Kent State Univ., Ohio.

James W. Geary, Asst. Professor of Library Administration, Kent State Univ., Ohio.

Marilyn Gell, Library Projects Manager, Washington Metropolitan Council of Governments, Washington, D.C.

Mary W. George, Head, General Reference Division, Princeton Univ., N.J.

Ray Gerke, Assoc. Librarian, Reference, Wessell Library, Tufts Univ., Medford, Mass.

Ruth I. Gordon, Director, IMC-Library Services, Lassen County, Calif.

Frank Wm. Goudy, Assoc. Professor, Univ. Libraries, Western Illinois Univ., Macomb.

M. Ruth Graham, Resource Consultant, Gifted/Talented Programs, Grand Rapids Public Schools, Mich.

Richard A. Gray, formerly Staff, Libraries Unlimited.

Helen Gregory, Reference Librarian, Grosse Pointe Public Library, Mich.

Lawrence Grieco, formerly Consultant/Librarian, Colorado State Library, Denver.

Laurel Grotzinger, Graduate Dean and Chief Research Officer, Western Michigan Univ., Kalamazoo.

Leonard Grundt, Professor, Library Dept., Nassau Community College, Garden City, N.Y.

Ann E. Hagedorn, Research and Development Librarian, New York Univ. Libraries.

Nabil Hamdy, Assoc. Professor, Graduate School of Librarianship, Univ. of Denver, Colo.

Malcolm C. Hamilton, Head Librarian, John F. Kennedy School of Government, Harvard Univ., Cambridge, Mass.

Donald P. Hammer, Executive Secretary, Information Science and Automation Division, American Library Association, Chicago, Ill.

Thomas S. Harding, Librarian Emeritus, Washburn Univ. of Topeka, Kans.

Roberto P. Haro, Asst. Vice Chancellor, Univ. of California, Berkeley.

Patricia C. Harpole, Chief of the Reference Library, Minnesota Historical Society, St. Paul.

Jessica L. Harris, Assoc. Professor, Division of Library and Information Science, St. John's Univ., N.Y.

Michael H. Harris, Professor, College of Library and Information Science, Univ. of Kentucky, Lexington.

Ann Hartman, formerly Staff, Libraries Unlimited.

John F. Harvey, International Library and Information Science Consultant, Lyndonville, Vt.

Ann J. Harwell, formerly Staff, Libraries Unlimited.

Robert J. Havlik, Univ. Engineering Librarian, Univ. of Notre Dame, Ind.

Mary Anne Heaphy, Director, Baldwinsville Public Library, N.Y.

Rosemary Henderson, Director of Library Services, Coffeyville Community College, Kans.

Peter Hernon, Assoc. Professor, Graduate Library School, Univ. of Arizona, Tucson.

Mark Y. Herring, Director, E. W. King Memorial Library, King College, Bristol, Tenn.

Shirley B. Hesslein, Assoc. Health Sciences Librarian, State Univ. of New York, Buffalo.

Joe A. Hewitt, Assoc. Univ. Librarian for Technical Services, Univ. of North Carolina, Chapel Hill.

Shirley A. Hibbeln, Librarian, Herrick Junior High School, Downers Grove, Ill.

Doralyn J. Hickey, Professor, School of Library and Information Sciences, North Texas State Univ., Denton.

Charles L. Hinkle, Professor of Business and Administration, Univ. of Colorado, Colorado Springs.

George V. Hodowanec, Director, William Allen White Library, Emporia State Univ., Kans.

Marjorie P. Holt, Director of Reference and Research, Brooklyn Public Library, N.Y.

Shirley L. Hopkinson, Professor, Dept. of Library Science, San Jose State Univ., Calif.

John Phillip Immroth (deceased), Assoc. Professor, Graduate School of Library and Information Science, Univ. of Pittsburgh, Pa.

Janet R. Ivey, Head of Support Services, Boynton Beach City Library, Fla.

Clara O. Jackson, Assoc. Professor, School of Library Science, Kent State Univ., Ohio.

E. B. Jackson, Professor Emeritus, Graduate School of Library and Information Science, Univ. of Texas, Austin.

Miles M. Jackson, Professor, Graduate School of Library Studies, Univ. of Hawaii, Honolulu.

Sidney L. Jackson (deceased), Professor, School of Library Science, Kent State Univ., Ohio.

Zena Jacobs, Head, Reference Dept., Polytechnic Institute of New York, Brooklyn.

Gerald Jahoda, Professor, School of Library Science, Florida State Univ., Tallahassee.

Lola Januskis, Ibero-American Bibliographer, Samuel Paley Library, Temple Univ., Philadelphia.

Casper L. Jordan, Central Librarian, Atlanta Public Library, Ga.

E. J. Josey, Professor, School of Library and Information Science, Univ. of Pittsburgh, Pa.

Ivan L. Kaldor, Columbus, Ohio.

Thomas A. Karel, Asst. Director for Public Services, Shadek-Fackenthal Library, Franklin and Marshall College, Lancaster, Pa.

Ruth M. Katz, Assoc. Director of Library Services, East Carolina Univ., Greenville, N.C.

Linda S. Keir, Reference Librarian, Univ. of Dayton, Ohio.

Dean H. Keller, Assoc. Director of Public Service and Collection Development, Kent State Libraries, Kent State Univ., Ohio.

Rosemary Henderson Keller, Director of Library Services, Coffeyville Community Junior College, Kans.

Patrick J. Kenrick, Head of Readers Services, Library, Indiana Univ. Southeast, New Albany.

Joel S. Kent, Asst. Director for Member Services, OHIONET, Columbus, Ohio.

John E. Kephart, Geneseo, N.Y.

Michael Keresztesi, Professor, Library Science, Wayne State Univ., Detroit, Mich.

Philip H. Kitchens, Reference Librarian, U.S. Army Missile Command, Redstone Scientific Information Center, Huntsville, Ala.

Susan Kohlman, formerly Staff, Libraries Unlimited.

Larissa Kolody, formerly Staff, Libraries Unlimited.

Mary Larsgaard, Map Librarian, Arthur Lakes Library, Colorado School of Mines, Golden.

Mildred Knight Laughlin, Assoc. Professor, School of Library Science, Univ. of Iowa, Iowa City.

Hwa-Wei Lee, Director of Libraries and Professor, Ohio Univ., Athens.

Donald J. Lehnus, Assoc. Professor, Graduate School of Library and Information Sciences, Univ. of Mississippi, University.

Dorothy E. Litt, Flushing, N.Y.

Robert D. Little, Chair and Professor, Dept. of Library Science, Indiana State Univ., Terre Haute.

David W. Littlefield, Subject Cataloging Division, Processing Dept., Library of Congress, Washington, D.C.

Janet H. Littlefield, Mayer, Brown & Platt, Denver, Colo.

Catherine R. Loeb, Asst. to the Women's Studies Librarian-at-Large, Univ. of Wisconsin System, Madison.

Koert C. Loomis, Jr., Denver, Colo.

Amy Gische Lyons, Senior Asst. Librarian, Health Sciences Library, State Univ. of New York, Buffalo.

Sara R. Mack, Professor Emerita, Kutztown Univ., Pa.

Theodore Manheim, Head, Education Library, Wayne State Univ., Detroit, Mich.

H. Robert Malinowsky, Chicago, Ill.

Guy A. Marco, Washington, D.C.

Joan K. Marshall, Assoc. Librarian for Technical Services, Brooklyn College Library, N.Y.

John David Marshall, Univ. Bibliographer/Professor, Middle Tennessee State Univ., Murfreesboro.

Lorraine Mathies, formerly Head, Education and Psychology Library, Univ. of California, Los Angeles.

David E. Matthews, Computer Consultant, Compuware, Houston, Tex.

Theresa Maylone, formerly Staff, Libraries Unlimited.

Kathryn McChesney, Asst. Professor, School of Library Science, Kent State Univ., Ohio.

Kathleen McCullough, Bibliographer, Humanities, Social Sciences and Education Library, Purdue Univ., West Lafayette, Ind.

Joseph McDonald, Drexel Univ., Philadelphia, Pa.

Laura H. McGuire, Documents Librarian, Eastern New Mexico Univ. Library, Portales.

Margaret McKinley, Head, Serials Dept., Univ. Library, Univ. of California, Los Angeles.

Haynes McMullen, Professor Emeritus, School of Library Science, Univ. of North Carolina, Chapel Hill.

Gil McNamee, Head, Business Library, San Francisco Public Library, Calif.

Constance Mellott, Asst. Professor, School of Library Science, Kent State Univ., Ohio.

Philip A. Metzger, Curator of Special Collections, Lehigh Univ., Bethlehem, Pa.

Shirley Miller, Reference Librarian, Kalamazoo Public Library, Mich.

Paula Montgomery, Chief, School Library Media Services, Maryland State Dept. of Education, Baltimore.

Joe Morehead, Assoc. Professor, School of Library and Information Sciences, State Univ. of New York, Albany.

P. Grady Morein, Univ. Librarian, Univ. of Evansville, Ind.

Walter L. Newsome, Documents Librarian, Univ. of Virginia Library, Charlottesville.

Gail M. Nichols, International and Foreign Documents Librarian, Univ. of California, Berkeley.

Robert J. Nissenbaum, Reference Librarian, Tarlton Law Library, Univ. of Texas, Austin.

Danuta A. Nitecki, Assoc. Director for Public Services, Univ. of Maryland Libraries, College Park.

Margaret Norden, Reference Librarian, Falk Library, Univ. of Pittsburgh, Pa.

O. Gene Norman, Head, Reference Dept., Indiana State Univ. Library, Terre Haute.

Marilyn Strong Noronha, Reference Dept., Univ. of Connecticut, West Hartford.

Dennis North, Boston, Mass.

Judith E. H. Odiorne, Library Consultant, Oxford, Conn.

Jeanne Osborn, Professor Emerita, School of Library Science, Univ. of Iowa, Iowa City.

Harry S. Otterson, Jr., Senior Librarian, Attica Correctional Facility, N.Y.

Joseph W. Palmer, Assoc. Professor, School of Information and Library Studies, State Univ. of New York, Buffalo.

Richard Palmer, Assoc. Professor, School of Library Science, Simmons College, Boston, Mass.

Judith M. Pask, Asst. Management and Economics Librarian, Krannert Library, Purdue Univ., West Lafayette, Ind.

Anna Grace Patterson, Staff, Libraries Unlimited.

Annette Pekarek, formerly Staff, Libraries Unlimited.

Daniel F. Phelan, Head, Audio Visual Dept., North Bay Public Library, Ont.

Kathleen Phillips, Undergraduate Librarian, Univ. of Tennessee Undergraduate Library, Knoxville.

Hannah Pickworth, Head Librarian, Sayre School, Lexington, Ky.

George Piternick, Professor Emeritus, School of Library, Archival, and Information Studies, Univ. of British Columbia, Vancouver.

Gloria Palmeri Powell, formerly Staff, Libraries Unlimited.

Ann E. Prentice, Director, Graduate School of Library and Information Science, Univ. of Tennessee, Knoxville.

Emanuel T. Prostano, Professor and Dean of Library Science and Instructional Technology, Southern Connecticut State Univ., New Haven.

Gary R. Purcell, Professor, Graduate School of Library and Information Science, Univ. of Tennessee, Knoxville.

Johnnie Ann Ralph, Asst. Head, Library Operations, California State College, San Bernardino.

F. W. Ramey, formerly Staff, Libraries Unlimited.

Ronald Rayman, Rayman Americana, San Diego, Calif.

Bernard D. Reams, Jr., Assoc. Professor of Law and Law Librarian, Washington Univ. School of Law, St. Louis, Mo.

Alan M. Rees, Professor Emeritus, School of Library Science, Case Western Reserve Univ., Cleveland, Ohio.

Mary Reichel, Senior Reference Librarian, Undergraduate Library, State Univ. of New York, Buffalo.

James Rettig, Reference Librarian, Univ. of Illinois, Chicago.

John V. Richardson, Jr., Assoc. Professor, Graduate School of Library and Information Science, Univ. of Calif., Los Angeles.

Edward A. Richter, Reference Librarian, Eastern New Mexico Univ., Portales.

Donald L. Roberts, Audiovisual Librarian, Hennepin County Library, Edina, Minn.

Ilene F. Rockman, Assoc. Librarian, California Polytechnic State Univ., San Luis Obispo.

Antonio Rodriguez-Buckingham, Professor, School of Library Service, Univ. of Southern Mississippi, Hattiesburg.

A. Robert Rogers (deceased), Dean, School of Library Science, Kent State Univ., Ohio.

JoAnn V. Rogers, Assoc. Professor, College of Library Science, Univ. of Kentucky, Lexington.

Jim Roginski, Brooklyn, N.Y.

Judith K. Rosenberg, formerly Children's Librarian, Ayers Branch, Akron Public Library, Ohio.

Samuel Rothstein, Professor Emeritus, School of Library, Archival, and Information Studies, Univ. of British Columbia, Vancouver.

Linda Running, Audiovisual Cataloger, Hennepin County Library, Edina, Minn.

William Saffady, Assoc. Professor, Graduate School of Library and Information Science, Pratt Institute, Brooklyn, N.Y.

Edmund F. SantaVicca, Humanities Reference Bibliographer, Cleveland State Univ. Libraries, Ohio.

Pat R. Scales, Library Media Specialist, Greenville Middle School, S.C.

William Z. Schenck, Head, Acquisitions Dept., Wilson Library, Univ. of North Carolina, Chapel Hill.

Nancy P. Schneider, Community Services Librarian, Kern County Library System, Bakersfield, Calif.

Alan Edward Schorr, Univ. Librarian, California State Univ., Fullerton.

Candy Schwartz, Asst. Professor, Graduate School of Library and Information Science, Simmons College, Boston, Mass.

Eleanor Elving Schwartz, Coordinator, Library/Media Program, and Assoc. Professor, Kean College of New Jersey, Union.

LeRoy Schwarzkopf, formerly Government Documents Librarian, Univ. of Maryland, College Park.

Ralph L. Scott, Assoc. Professor, East Carolina Univ., Greenville, N.C.

Lillian L. Shapiro, School Library Consultant, New York, N.Y.

Ravindra Nath Sharma, Asst. Director for Public Services, Univ. Libraries, Univ. of Wisconsin, Oshkosh.

Patricia Tipton Sharp, Asst. Professor of Library Science, Baylor Univ., Waco, Tex.

Avery T. Sharp, Music Librarian, Baylor Univ., Waco, Tex.

Thomas W. Shaughnessy, Director of Libraries, Univ. of Missouri, Columbia.

Ward Shaw, Executive Director, Colorado Alliance of Research Libraries, Denver.

Jean Crosby Shearer, Lexington, Ky.

Jesse H. Shera (deceased), Dean Emeritus, School of Library Science, Case Western Reserve Univ., Cleveland, Ohio.

Sherrilynne Shirley, Assoc. Director, Norris Medical Library, Univ. of Southern California, Los Angeles.

Bruce A. Shuman, Reference Librarian, Johnson Free Public Library, Hackensack, N.J.

John Sigwald, Director, Unger Memorial Library, Plainview, Tex.

Timothy W. Sineath, Dean, College of Library and Information Science, Univ. of Kentucky, Lexington.

Mary R. Sive, Pearl River, N.Y.

Stanley J. Slote, Library Consultant, White Plains, N.Y.

Barbara E. Smith, Government Documents Librarian, Skidmore College Library, Saratoga Springs, N.Y.

Natalia Sonevytsky, Head, Reference Dept., Barnard College Library, New York, N.Y.

Paul H. Spence, Univ. College Librarian, Mervyn H. Sterne Library, Univ. of Alabama, Birmingham.

Barbara Sproat, Librarian, Denver Public Libraries, Colo.

Joseph W. Sprug, Chief Librarian, St. Edward's Univ., Austin, Tex.

Jerry E. Stephens, Assoc. Law Librarian, Univ. of Kansas, Lawrence.

Norman D. Stevens, Univ. Librarian, Univ. of Connecticut, Storrs.

Robert D. Stevens, Professor Emeritus, Graduate School of Library Science, Univ. of Hawaii, Manoa.

Rolland E. Stevens, Professor Emeritus, Graduate School of Library and Information Science, Univ. of Illinois, Urbana.

Esther F. Stineman, formerly Teaching Fellow for Yale Univ., Women's Studies and American Studies Programs, New Haven, Conn.

Leon J. Stout, Univ. Archivist, Pennsylvania State Univ. Libraries, University Park.

Robert D. Stueart, Dean, Graduate School of Library and Information Science, Simmons College, Boston, Mass.

Louise Stwalley, formerly Staff, Libraries Unlimited.

Peggy A. Sullivan, Dean, Graduate Studies, Northern Illinois Univ., DeKalb.

Elaine Svenonius, Professor of Library and Information Science, Univ. of California, Los Angeles.

Arthur W. Swarthout, Pastor, St. John United Methodist Church, Scott Depot, W. Va.

James H. Sweetland, Head Librarian, State Historical Society of Wisconsin, Madison.

Norman E. Tanis, Director of Libraries, California State Univ., Northridge.

Arlene Taylor, Assoc. Professor, School of Library Service, Columbia Univ., New York, N.Y.

Rebecca L. Thomas, Elementary School Library/Media Specialist, Onaway Elementary School, Shaker Heights, Ohio.

Johanna W. Thompson, Serials and Documents Librarian, Washington and Lee Univ. Law Library, Lexington, Va.

Marilyn Thompson, Director of Library Services, George Williams College, Downers Grove, Ill.

Andrew G. Torok, Assoc. Professor, Dept. of Library Science, Northern Illinois Univ., DeKalb.

Joanne Troutner, Media Specialist, Klondike Jr. High School, West Lafayette, Ind.

Dean Tudor, Professor, School of Journalism, Ryerson Polytechnical Institute, Toronto, Ont.

Frederick Van Antwerp, Reference Dept., Patee Library, Pennsylvania State Univ., University Park.

Sarah K. Vann, Professor Emerita, Graduate School of Library Studies, Univ. of Hawaii, Honolulu.

Phyllis J. Van Orden, Professor and Assoc. Dean, School of Library Science, Florida State Univ., Tallahassee.

Fritz Veit, Director of Libraries Emeritus, Chicago State Univ., Ill.

Carol J. Veitch, Librarian, Currituck County Library, Barco, N.C.

Carole Franklin Vidali, Syracuse, N.Y.

Kathleen J. Voigt, Head, Reference Dept., Carlson Library, Univ. of Toledo, Ohio.

Mary Jo Walker, Univ. Archivist and Special Collections Librarian, Eastern New Mexico Univ., Portales.

Terry L. Weech, Assoc. Professor, Graduate School of Library and Information Science, Univ. of Illinois, Urbana-Champaign.

Lillian Biermann Wehmeyer, Asst. Superintendent of Instruction for Curriculum, Riverside Unified School District, Calif.

Jean Riddle Weihs, Course Director, Library Techniques, Seneca College of Applied Arts & Technology, North York, Ont.

Darlene E. Weingand, Asst. Professor, Library School, Univ. of Wisconsin, Madison.

Ina J. Weis, Asst. to the Director for Special Projects, Univ. of Toledo Libraries, Ohio.

Erwin K. Welsch, Social Studies Bibliographer, Memorial Library, Univ. of Wisconsin, Madison.

Lucille Whalen, Assoc. Dean and Professor, School of Library and Information Science, State Univ. of New York, Albany.

John Robert Wheat, Archivist, Barker Texas History Center, Univ. of Texas, Austin.

Jeanne Wieckert, Media Specialist, Denver Public School System, Colo.

Wayne A. Wiegand, Assoc. Professor, College of Library and Information Science, Univ. of Kentucky, Lexington.

Constance D. Williams, formerly Staff, Libraries Unlimited.

Robert V. Williams, Assoc. Professor, College of Librarianship and Information Science, Univ. of South Carolina, Columbia.

Wiley J. Williams, Professor, School of Library Science, Kent State Univ., Ohio.

Paul A. Winckler, Professor of Library Science, Palmer Graduate School, Long Island Univ., C. W. Post Center, Greenvale, N.Y.

Alice J. Wittig, District Librarian, Mendocino Unified School District, Calif.

Glenn R. Wittig, Asst. Professor, School of Library Science, Univ. of Southern Mississippi, Hattiesburg.

Francis J. Witty, Professor, Dept. of Library Science, Catholic Univ. of America, Washington, D.C.

Judith Wolfe, Coordinator of Library Resources, Missouri State Library, Jefferson City.

Marda Woodbury, Research Ventures, Berkeley, Calif.

Joyce Wright, Head, Asia Collection, Univ. of Hawaii Library, Honolulu.

Kieth C. Wright, Professor, Univ. of North Carolina, Greensboro.

Anna Wynar, Certified Rehabilitation Counselor, Ravenna, Ohio.

Bohdan S. Wynar, Editor-in-Chief, Libraries Unlimited.

Lubomyr R. Wynar, Professor, School of Library Science, and Director, Program for the Study of Ethnic Publications in the United States, Kent State Univ., Ohio.

A. Neil Yerkey, Asst. Professor, School of Information and Library Studies, State Univ. of New York, Buffalo.

Arthur P. Young, Dean of Libraries, Univ. of Rhode Island, Kingston.

Publications Cited

A Arch	American Archivist
AB	AB Bookman's Weekly
ABC	American Book Collector
AL	American Libraries
BC	Book Collector
BL	Booklist
BSA−P	Bibliographical Society of America−Papers
C&RL	College & Research Libraries
Choice	Choice
CLW	Catholic Library World
DLQ	Drexel Library Quarterly
Emerg Lib	Emergency Librarian
Gov Pub R	Government Publications Review
Indexer	Indexer
IRLA	Information Retrieval & Library Automation
JAL	Journal of Academic Librarianship
JLH	Journal of Library History
LJ	Library Journal
LQ	Library Quarterly
LR	Library Review
LRTS	Library Resources & Technical Resources
RBB	Reference Books Bulletin
RQ	RQ
RSR	Reference Services Review
SBF	Science Books & Films
Ser R	Serials Review
SL	Special Libraries
SLJ	School Library Journal
SLMQ	School Library Media Quarterly/School Media Quarterly

TN   Top of the News

Unesco   Unesco Bulletin for Libraries/Unesco Journal
                        of Information Science, Librarianship &
                        Archives

VOYA   Voice of Youth Advocates

WLB   Wilson Library Bulletin

Part 1
GENERAL WORKS

1 Introductory Works

1. Atkinson, Frank. **Librarianship: An Introduction to the Profession.** Hamden, Conn., Linnet Books and Clive Bingley, 1974. 112p. illus. index. o.p. LC 74-164289. ISBN 0-208-01351-2.

This subjective and highly personal account of librarianship in England (with only occasional references to other countries) presents, with verve and humor, an account of what the profession involves. The book has two major objectives, to enlighten the uninitiated on the significance of librarianship, and to inspire enthusiasm for the profession among those who might be recruited to it. Because the author is animated by a sincere dedication to and affection for the profession, his goals are likely to be achieved.

Atkinson, who was on the staff of the City of London libraries, covers, in broad brush strokes, such topics as the unity of librarianship; the choices it offers as a career; the patron; physical equipment; nonbook materials; publicity; the education of the librarian; professional associations; occupational mobility, both within the United Kingdom and beyond; and library publications. At the appropriate points in the text two essays have been introduced: one on special librarianship, by B. C. Bloomfield, librarian, School of Oriental and African Studies, University of London; and the other on academic librarianship, by P. G. New, principal lecturer, Polytechnic of North London. The volume concludes with a gracefully written essay on the author and his work by Bernard I. Palmer, Education Officer of the Library Association.

Because the book is written primarily—one might say exclusively—for an English audience, its value to librarians on this side of the Atlantic will be limited. Nevertheless, there is much in it that American librarians, as well as the uninitiated, can read with profit. Atkinson has written a wise and entertaining little book. [R: LJ, 15 Sept 74, p. 2135; AL, July/Aug 74, p. 367]

Jesse H. Shera

2. Gates, Jean Key. **Introduction to Librarianship.** 2nd ed. New York, McGraw-Hill, 1976. 288p. bibliog. index. (McGraw-Hill Series in Library Education). o.p. LC 75-42316. ISBN 0-07-022977-5.

The first edition of this work was published in 1968, and we assume that this second edition will continue to be used as a required or supplementary text for undergraduate courses in library science. Part 1, appropriately entitled "The Story of Libraries," provides, in a popular style and with generalizations that are occasionally rather simplistic, sufficient background information on historical library development. Beginning with antiquity, it ends up with a description of the major trends in American librarianship during the nineteenth century. This section constitutes a major portion of the book. Part 2, "Librarianship as a Profession," is rather skimpy, devoting some 30 pages to professional organizations and library education. Part 3, "Kinds of Libraries and Library Services," devotes five to seven pages each to such topics as state responsibility for library service, the municipal public library, academic libraries, research libraries, etc. There is also a 10-page section on automation in libraries. All in all, this is a satisfactory book for the unsophisticated reader, collecting well-known facts in one handy volume. [R: LJ, 1 Oct 76, p. 2020]

Bohdan S. Wynar

3. Harrison, Colin, and Rosemary Beenham. **The Basics of Librarianship.** 2nd ed.

London, Clive Bingley; distr., Hamden, Conn., Shoe String Press, 1985. 240p. index. $17.50. ISBN 0-85157-370-3.

To librarians in the United States the library profession in Great Britain is truly foreign. The "basics," however, vary little, and the functions, management, organization, and the routines of British libraries have much in common with similar practices in this country.

The Basics of Librarianship is a text aimed at the paraprofessional in British libraries. It is designed for support staff positions as prescribed by the Business Education Council of the City and Guilds of London Institute. The brief book is divided into twelve chapters, each treating a different aspect of library work. Each chapter is informative and provides an overview and concludes with sample assignments — both practical and written — about its subject. An example is found in the chapter on classification. The student is assigned to visit the local public library and locate reference works, the fiction collection, and circulating nonfiction. One of the written assignments is to list the ten main classes of the Dewey system.

The volume goes beyond its single purpose of education. It introduces British librarianship in much the same way as a standard text. It is a valuable little volume even though targeted for a limited audience.   Boyd Childress

4.   Hulbert, James A. **An Introduction to Library Service: A Textbook.** New York, Exposition Press, 1971. 140p. o.p. LC 72-146909. ISBN 0-682-47225-5.

The author of this text, who spent more than six years as the Director of Library Service of the United States Information Service Library in East Pakistan, apparently originally conceived of this book as an aid to his students in Pakistan. This text was prepared for librarians who have to start "from scratch," since this unfortunately is the most typical situation in many underdeveloped countries. We think it will serve its audience, describing in simple terms such problems as libraries — their growth and significance; organization of reader services; technical services; administration; etc. The publisher's blurb advertises this text as "a practical guidebook which will prove of immense value to students and teachers of librarianship in America as well." However, in this country it will offer nothing even for undergraduate students, not to mention teachers or library school students. In addition, for a text to be used even in underdeveloped countries there is a need for an index, especially in view of the many topics discussed in this book. The author also is not familiar with recent library literature. For

example, for him Aker's book is still in its second edition, published in 1949; Carter and Bank's *Building Library Collections* is in its 1959 edition, etc. Many standard titles published in the 1960s are simply not listed. A director of library service should know better.

Bohdan S. Wynar

5.   Kumar, Krishan. **Library Manual.** New Delhi, India, Vikas Publishing; distr., New York, Advent Books, 1982. 386p. index. $32.50. ISBN 0-7069-2292-1.

Kumar, an experienced and well-known author, has written another book, this one for the benefit of paraprofessionals working in all types of libraries and for those who are interested in becoming librarians. The purpose of this book is to give an overview of the library and its procedures. Kumar has succeeded in his mission.

Library Manual has been divided into six parts. In part 1, "The Library and Society," the author deals with the different types of libraries, i.e., school, college, university, public, and special, and the laws of library science. Part 2 deals with administration and management, including staffing, budgets, book selection, book orders, circulation, periodicals, annual reports, etc. Part 3 has chapters on classification including the Dewey Decimal and Colon classifications, with brief introductions of Library of Congress, Universal Decimal, and Bibliographic classification. Part 4 has a chapter on the theory of cataloging with examples of entries according to AACR and Classified Catalog Code. Part 5 deals with bibliography and book selection. The sixth and final part discusses the types of reference services and books in brief.

The lists of further readings at the end of each chapter are very short, and Kumar has not dealt with the role of computers in all parts of libraries, e.g., circulation, acquisitions, catalogs, and reference and bibliographic services. In spite of this drawback the book gives a good overview in brief and should be helpful to paraprofessionals and prospective library school students, especially those in the developing countries.   Ravindra Nath Sharma

6.   Lock, R. Northwood, ed. **Manual of Library Economy: A Conspectus of Professional Librarianship for Students and Practitioners.** London, Clive Bingley; Hamden, Conn., Linnet Books, 1977. 447p. illus. index. $25.00. LC 77-5034. ISBN 0-85157-226-X(Bingley); 0-208-01538-8(Linnet).

The purpose of this collection of essays is to contribute to an understanding of the essential unity of librarianship, and in particular to help offset the growing tendency of the discipline to fragment into a variety of more or less independent areas. The contributing authors seek to set forth what a practicing librarian should know of his or her craft—not the detailed routines appropriate to a staff manual, but expositions of current practice in a variety of library types and activities. The book emphasizes those aspects which are likely to be of most value to library school students and younger staff, while at the same time including some new material that may be of value to the experienced practitioner.

The collection itself is composed of 20 essays (by 18 contributors), divided into four parts: "Libraries for All," "Buildings and Books," "Books and People," and "Libraries and Librarians." All subjects treated in the individual essays cover a wide range in the spectrum of librarianship, including national, academic, and public libraries; buildings and equipment; sources of material; acquisition policies; reference services; children's libraries; library cooperation; library publicity; professional education and training; library organizations; and professional literature. Each chapter is written by a librarian in a senior position who has been chosen for his or her particular competence in his or her area.

Since librarians on this side of the Atlantic are confronted by much the same problems in preserving disciplinary unity, this anthology will be useful to librarians in the United States as well as the United Kingdom.

Lock's compilation makes an admirable companion volume to D. A. Kemp's *The Nature of Knowledge: An Introduction for Librarians*, issued by the same publisher. From these two volumes the experienced librarian, as well as the newly initiated, can learn much concerning the nature of his profession. [R: CLW, Apr 78, p. 405]   Jesse H. Shera

7. Maidment, William R. **Librarianship.** North Pomfret, Vt., David & Charles, 1975. 151p. bibliog. index. (Professions Series). o.p. LC 75-17. ISBN 0-7153-6897-4.

Librarianship is one in this publisher's series on the professions. Though written by a professional (chartered, in Great Britain) librarian—Maidment is the Director of Libraries in the London borough of Camden—the book is addressed neither to librarians nor to library school students but to youth who may be looking to librarianship as a possible career. Primarily concerned with public libraries, the author's own field of expertise, the book consists of eight chapters with titles like "A Librarian's Day," "Behind the Scenes," and "Ideals

and Realities." Since all of its examples, models, standards, and statistics are British, the book unfortunately will have no direct relevance to young Americans in search of a career. This is unfortunate because it is quite charmingly written, better than any American counterpart that has come to my attention. An example of the author's prose: "King George V once described the public library system as a national university that all may attend and none need ever leave. A notable comment this, just the kind of thing chief librarians like to quote in their annual reports." [R: AL, Jan 76, p. 64; LJ, 1 Mar 76, p. 675]   Richard A. Gray

8. Shera, Jesse H. **Introduction to Library Science: Basic Elements of Library Service.** Littleton, Colo., Libraries Unlimited, 1976. 208p. illus. bibliog. index. (Library Science Text Series). $20.00. LC 76-21332. ISBN 0-87287-173-8.

The purpose of this textbook is to provide a point of entry for those for whom librarianship, as an anticipated career, is only a beginning. Each of the eight chapters addresses a major area or problem of librarianship. The opening chapter, "Up the Centuries from Sumer," is a succinct survey of the key events, places, people, and movements that contributed to the development of libraries from ancient times to the present. "The Library and Society," chapter 2, examines the role of the public library in a democratic setting. Former dean Shera introduces chapter 2 with this explanation: "to understand what the library has been, is, and may be expected to become, one must first look at the nature of society itself and the cultural and value systems that operate within it" (p. 42). The concept of library service is the topic of chapter 3, "Knowing Men and Books." It engages the student in an examination of this complex and basic function of librarianship.

La Vahn Overmeyer contributed chapter 4, "*Deus ex Machina*," which deals with library automation. Following a thorough survey of the technological developments in the field of information retrieval, Overmeyer describes the current uses of automation in libraries and the challenges facing present and future librarians due to these new technologies.

The remaining four chapters of the book deal with the professional and scholarly issues of librarianship. Chapter 5, "Librarianship in a New Key," discusses the librarian's responsibilities in organizing materials for the scholar, where the emphasis is on special problems of bibliography and information science. Librarianship and its professional organizations are the topic of chapter 6, in which the basic structures of the associations are sketched and the literature of librarianship is surveyed. Shera devotes chapter 7 to a review of library education and research in the field.

Margaret Anderson contributed the final chapter, "Library and Information Services: Components in Planning for National Development." In this survey, Anderson examines problems facing library service in developing nations and in industrialized countries of the world. Each chapter includes notes and selected readings. [R: C&RL, Mar 77, p. 164; JAL, Jan 77, p. 307; JLH, Spring 77, p. 190; LJ, 1 Jan 77, p. 82; LQ, Oct 77, p. 470]   Ann Hartman

9. Thompson, James. **A History of the Principles of Librarianship.** London, Clive Bingley; Hamden, Conn., Linnet Books, 1977. 236p. index. $20.00. LC 77-3335. ISBN 0-85157-241-3(Bingley); 0-208-01661-9(Linnet).

This book, by a librarian at the University of Reading, purports to examine the historical basis of librarianship in order to delineate a set of principles that can be applied to "professional existence." It is, then, a continued examination of the themes opened up in his *Library Power*. The main body of the work is a superficial retelling of library history from antiquity to the present, and, from a historical perspective, it touches on such topics as size of library collections, responsibility for conservation, access, the purposes of the library, the arrangement and design of libraries, and the role of the librarian.

From this hasty survey, the author derives 17 principles of librarianship that he regards as being supported by the historical record — libraries are created by society; libraries are conserved by society; libraries are for the storage and dissemination of knowledge; libraries are centers of power; libraries are for all; libraries must grow; a national library should contain all national literature with some representation of other national literatures; every book is of use; the librarian must be a person of education; the librarian is an educator; the librarian's role can only be an important one if it is fully integrated into the social and political system; a librarian needs training "and/or" apprenticeship; it is the librarian's duty to increase the stock of his or her library; a library must be arranged in some kind of order and a list of its contents provided; since libraries are storehouses of knowledge, they should be arranged according to subject; a library must have a subject catalog. No great critical sense is required to see that these "principles," which remind one vaguely of Ranganathan's "Five Laws," are either platitudinous or debatable, and their elucidation does not justify the library's existence through the historical

transcript. [R: C&RL, Mar 78, p. 151; JAL, Jan 78, p. 352; LJ, 1 Sept 78, p. 1575]
                                             Jesse H. Shera

10. Thompson, James. **Library Power: A New Philosophy of Librarianship.** Hamden, Conn., Linnet Books and Clive Bingley, 1974. 111p. o.p. LC 74-6330. ISBN 0-208-01379-2.

The author of this book, a librarian at the University of Reading, has written a polemic for what he regards as "a new philosophy of librarianship." It is his belief that libraries exert more power in society than librarians generally believe. This power derives, first, from the fact that since its inception the library has been the repository of the records of the human adventure and, second, because the library supports the educational and cultural forces in the society in which it flourishes. The library's contribution to education, he argues, and its power in preserving cultural continuity, have made libraries places for the preservation of intellectual freedom and hence "enemies of dictatorial pressures." However, before the librarians' professional potential can be realized, there must be a "complete restructuring of library staffing," a rethinking of library duties, and "a new approach to the library's relation to society."

Because the author believes that librarians have devoted an excessive amount of attention to their technology and clerical tasks, he would see developed in the profession an elite corps of truly professional librarians who are well educated and thoroughly committed to the transmission of knowledge to all segments of society. This elite corps must be "democratically structured" and the tasks they perform should be limited to those that can be truly regarded as librarianship.

One finds it difficult to see why Thompson regards his ideas as being either new or innovative. In the United States they go back at least to the 1930s, if not before, and many of his arguments were the battle cry of the young activists in librarianship during the 1960s. He is, however, right in urging the restructuring of librarians' tasks and the formation of an elite corps of librarians that will return to the profession its once proud scholarly tradition. [R: JLH, Oct 75, p. 371; LR, Winter 74/75, p. 358; SL, Nov 75, p. 556]   Jesse H. Shera

11. Urquhart, Donald. **The Principles of Librarianship.** Metuchen, N.J., Scarecrow, 1981. 98p. bibliog. index. $10.00pa. LC 81-13563. ISBN 0-8108-1470-6.

This sturdy polemic by the founder of the National Lending Library for Science and Technology (now part of the British Library

Lending Division) delivers a "kick in the pants" to contemporary British librarianship, reminiscent of the shock waves sent through American librarianship by Butler and others on the faculty of the Graduate Library School of the University of Chicago in the 1930s. In his insistence that librarianship is an "experimental science" which should deal in facts rather than opinions and that librarians should be numerate as well as literate, Urquhart is unlikely to raise too many hackles on this side of the Atlantic. One thinks of quantitative studies by Kantor (also a physicist drawn into library research) and Buckland. Some comments about the "self-renewing library" are reminiscent of *Farewell to Alexandria* and other writings by our own *enfant terrible*, Daniel Gore. Occasionally, Urquhart's interest in the transmission of knowledge is reminiscent of Shera, and his propensity for enumerating "principles" and "laws" is suggestive of Ranganathan. Not that he has borrowed from any of these. Rather, he shares with them a propensity for getting to the fundamental questions of librarianship. Despite some repetition and undue disparagement of the social sciences, this is a book worth reading. [R: JAL, Mar 82, pp. 41-42]

A. Robert Rogers

2 Proceedings, Symposia, and Essays

12. Bonn, George S., and Sylvia Faibisoff, eds. **Changing Times: Changing Libraries.** Champaign, Ill., Graduate School of Library Science, University of Illinois, 1978. 166p. index. (Allerton Park Institute, No. 22). $8.00. LC 78-1283. ISBN 0-87845-047-5.

This volume includes the proceedings of a conference on possible social and technological changes occurring in the next quarter century. Futurologists delivered papers at the Allerton Park Institute on the cause of change (government, economic conditions, and science and technology), the results of change, and the means by which one creates conditions for change. Librarians responded to these presentations by indicating implications for libraries. The problem with this book is that the specialists' remarks were often quite mundane and/or disjointed. Of even less value were the responses, many of which were unbelievably poorly prepared. One librarian did not even read the speech before responding, but guessed what the specialist might have stated—and reacted to that. Unfortunately, she guessed incorrectly. Another respondent openly stated that his remarks would be disjointed and would not deal directly with the content of the futurologist's speech. There are other examples, but perhaps the best is the "response" to a paper which was not presented. This publication is definitely not recommended. [R: C&RL, Nov 78, p. 501; LJ, 15 Sept 78, p. 1709]

Alan Edward Schorr

13. Eastlick, John T., ed. **The Changing Environment of Libraries.** Chicago, American Library Association, 1971. 86p. (Papers delivered at the 1970-71 Colloquium Series, Graduate School of Librarianship, University of Denver). o.p. LC 79-176325. ISBN 0-8389-0113-1.

This volume includes five papers delivered by seasoned professionals at the University of Denver in 1971 that focus on the library in a changing environment, its present and its future. A sixth paper, written by the editor, deals with the changing environment of librarians. Uneven in quality and style, the papers offer no solutions, but summarize the need for both libraries and librarians to be prepared for change. [R: LJ, 15 June 72, p. 2162]

Charles D. Patterson

14. Gerard, David E., ed. **Libraries and the Arts: A Symposium of Papers and Discussions at the Seminar Held in the College of Librarianship, Wales, September 1-6, 1969.** London, Clive Bingley; distr., Hamden, Conn., Archon, 1970. 215p. o.p. ISBN 0-208-01057-2.

This volume contains a series of papers that pose questions about the role of the library in promoting cultural relations within the community and expanding the traditional custodial function. It stresses better relations of libraries with all cultural agencies and organizations, more attention to publicity, and development of new professions within the library. It provides the North American librarian with insight and understanding of the arts in Britain. [R: LJ, 15 Jan 71, p. 174]

Charles D. Patterson

15. **Information for the 1980's: Final Report of the White House Conference on Library and Information Services, 1979.** Washington, GPO, 1980. 808p. o.p. S/N 052-003-00764-9.

The first White House Conference on Library and Information Services occurred in 1979, some 20 years after the concept was suggested by a library trustee. In this final report, every aspect of the conference is covered, beginning with President Carter's opening remarks and concluding with a list of publications and media produced by the conference. In between are sections devoted to a national program, legislative outline, resolutions, proceedings, transcripts and speeches, open hearings, joint congressional hearing, participants, and appendices.

Sixty-four resolutions that were passed by the delegates form the core of the report. These were distilled from approximately 3,000 resolutions and recommendations received from the 58 conferences organized to provide ideas and suggestions for the main conference. Resolution topics include networking, postal rates, federal funding formulas, interlibrary cooperation, minority needs, and international copyright agreement, to name a few.

The bulk of the report is taken up with verbatim testimony of delegates, lists of delegates, transcripts of hearings, and written testimony submitted by groups and individuals. The major failing is the lack of an index. [R: BL, 15 Jan 81, p. 680; LJ, 15 Jan 81, p. 129]

Brian Alley

16. Josey, E. J., ed. **The Information Society, Issues and Answers: American Library Association's Presidential Commission for the 1977 Detroit Annual Conference.** Phoenix, Ariz., Oryx Press, 1978. 133p. index. (A Neal-Schuman Professional Book). $29.95. LC 78-17708. ISBN 0-912700-16-5.

This publication resulted from the president's program on "Issues and Answers" at the 1977 annual conference of the American Library Association. Seven speakers (five of them librarians) commented on various aspects of the post-industrial society, in which the dominant activity will be the provision of information and services, rather than the production of goods and food. While Rollin Marquis (who gave the lead-off address) and Frederick G. Kilgour were optimistic, other speakers were more cautious. Thomas R. Buckman warned of some of the impending economic changes in libraries, while Fay M. Blake cautioned against neglecting the current needs of today's library users.

Each address was followed by a "literature review" on the speaker's topic, compiled by another contributor. Bibliographies were compiled for the following topics: the impact of technology on libraries and librarians; the impact of social change on libraries; the impact of economic change on libraries; the new role of librarians as professionals; and problems of access in libraries. The bibliographies include both books and periodicals, but there is a preponderance of the latter because of the recency of most of the items cited. Finally, Joseph A.

Boisse and Carla J. Stoffle provide a comprehensive and panoramic view of the participants. This little book makes stimulating reading. [R: C&RL, Jan 79, p. 73; JAL, May 79, p. 99; JLH, Winter 79, p. 112; LJ, 1 Jan 79, p. 85; LQ, July 79, p. 325]

Thomas S. Harding

17. **Libraries and the Life of the Mind in America: Addresses Delivered at the Centennial Celebration of the American Library Association.** Chicago, American Library Association, 1977. 130p. $10.00. LC 77-3288. ISBN 0-8389-0238-3.

This volume, which draws its felicitous title from one of Perry Miller's books, is a collection of six addresses delivered during the centennial celebration of the American Library Association (ALA). Historian John Hope Franklin relates the problems of cultural diversity to public library development. Dan Lacy, publisher and friend of libraries, analyzes the growth of egalitarianism in America and relates the interplay of knowledge and power to national information policy. The early tensions within the library movement and the successes and failures of federal aid to libraries are perceptively recounted by Kathleen Molz. Herman Liebaers, former Royal Librarian of Belgium, in a rather impressionistic address, expounds on the achievements of American librarianship and the expanding internationalism of library organizations. Civil liberties lawyer Harriet F. Philpel summarizes recent trends regarding censorship and supports ALA's vigilant role. Daniel Boorstin, Librarian of Congress, challenges librarians to refurbish their founding principles of self-help, autonomy, and community in this age of technological confusion.

Although uneven in some respects, the volume is well worth reading. Awards for the most cerebral essays must go to Molz and Boorstin. Several errors were noted. Franklin's statement that Harvard College was founded to educate the clergy is not true, and Molz's claim that ALA first endorsed federal aid to libraries during the 1930s is equally inaccurate. The association testified before Congress in 1919 on behalf of the first bill (unsuccessful) which stipulated national library funding. [R: C&RL, Jan 78, p. 66; JAL, July 78, p. 162; JLH, Summer 78, p. 329; LQ, Apr 78, p. 212; RQ, Summer 78, p. 349]

Arthur P. Young

18. McClellan, A. W. **The Reader, the Library and the Book: Selected Papers 1949-1970.** London, Clive Bingley; distr., Hamden, Conn., Shoe String Press, 1973. 148p. index. o.p. ISBN 0-85157-164-6.

This is a collection of 12 articles and papers written between 1949 and 1970. Ten of them were previously published. McClellan is well known to British librarians, and his comments on the social role of libraries may still be valid for many European countries. Some of his observations (such as in the article "Professional Work for Professional Librarians") seem to be on the simplistic side. In this country, Shera said it not only much better but also much earlier. [R: LJ, 15 Nov 73, p. 3357]

19. National Inventory of Library Needs, 1975: Resources Needed for Public and Academic Libraries and Public School Library/ Media Centers. A study submitted by Boyd Ladd to the National Commission on Libraries and Information Science. Washington, GPO, 1977. 277p. bibliog. o.p. S/N 052-003-00328-7.

This report has been prepared at the request of the National Commission on Libraries and Information Science, partially as background material for the special state and national conferences now getting under way. The ALA *National Inventory of Library Needs, 1965* was used as a model (although this new report measures nine areas of library resources versus three in 1965). Data were provided by the National Center for Education Statistics from its 1974 and 1975 surveys of public, public school, and academic libraries. Quantitative data on their resources were then juxtaposed with current accepted standards (termed "indicators of needs") to arrive at specific national needs for each type of library. Data were collected for staff, collections, acquisitions, space, hours of service, and operating expenditures. Reports from individual libraries on their resources were also used.

Although many people in the profession may disagree with the standards applied or even with the method of determining "needs," this report does supply valuable information and is a good starting point for this kind of evaluation. The data and results can be viewed from many philosophical positions for application or interpretation in specific cases, but the report itself is intended as a generalization and not as a formula for individual libraries.

The report is organized into seven chapters, covering highlights of the results, the setting, explanation for "indicators of need," the three types of libraries (data), and a summary of national and state library needs. Four appendices present the methodology applied, a discussion of library standards, public library standards by state, and a bibliography. Charts and tables are liberally used throughout the report. From this presentation, we learn that five out of every six schools in the country had a school library/ media center in 1974 (which is an increase from the 1965 report showing only 56 percent of all schools), but that they generally fall far short of meeting collection needs. Public libraries, while expanding 26.5 percent in number, appear to suffer from lack of adequate space and are usually underfunded. Academic libraries have twice the professional staff that they had in 1963, and have more than doubled their collections. Two-year colleges, however, show a much greater gap between existing conditions and needs. This is a readable, well-organized report, one that all librarians should take the time to examine as we embark on a national effort to evaluate the current and future requirements necessary to serve our individual publics. [R: BL, 15 June 77, p. 1565; C&RL, Nov 77, p. 548]

Roberta J. Depp

20. Stueart, Robert D., ed. Information Needs of the 80s: Libraries and Information Services Role in "Bringing Information to People" Based on the Deliberations of the White House Conference on Library and Information Services. Greenwich, Conn., JAI Press, 1982. 192p. index. (Foundations in Library and Information Science, Vol. 15). $47.50. LC 82-9960. ISBN 0-89232-164-4.

The contributions of seven attendees to the 1979 White House Conference on Library and Information Services are presented with introductory remarks by Marilyn K. Gell, Executive Director of the White House Conference, and an epilog by Charles Benton, Chairman of the National Commission on Libraries and Information Science and Chairman of the White House Conference. Each contributor covers a different issue on how libraries are to bring information to the people: Margaret Knox Goggin, "Meeting Personal Needs"; Annette I. Hoage Phinazee, "Enhancing Lifelong Learning"; Donald R. King, "Library and Information Services for Improving Organizations and the Professions"; Richard L. Darling, "Effectively Governing Our Society: The Role of Information"; Jean E. Lowrie, "Increasing International Understanding: Tomorrow's Challenge"; Ching-chih Chen, "Citizens' Information Needs: A Regional Investigation"; and Ann Heidbreder Eastman, "A Citizen's View." Although books of this type can be very boring, this one is not. Each contribution is interestingly written for most readers. Daniel J. Boorstin's remarks to the conference are included in appendix 1. The resolutions passed by the delegates are in appendix 2, and appendix 3 is a reprint of *Citizen Information-Seeking Patterns: A New England Study*, an executive summary report published by the U.S. Office of Education. H. Robert Malinowsky

21. West, Celeste, Elizabeth Katz, et al., eds. **Revolting Librarians.** San Francisco, Calif., Booklegger Press; distr., Chicago, American Library Association, 1972. 158p. illus. o.p. LC 72-78317. ISBN 0-912932-01-5.

This is a potpourri of stories, poems, articles, and miscellaneous writings, which although uneven and at places poorly written, are informative and certainly entertaining. The volume is divided into various categories, including organization and administration, library literature, image of librarians, prospects for the future, recruiting, classification, and work with young adults. Each treats the reader to a waft of fresh air. [R: C&RL, Mar 73, p. 165; LJ, 15 Feb 73, p. 515]

Charles D. Patterson

22. **The White House Conference on Library and Information Services, 1979: Summary.** Washington, GPO, 1980. 101p. $4.00pa. S/N 040-000-000423-8.

The final report on the White House Conference on Library and Information Services requires 808 pages to tell the story. The summary does the job in 101 pages and contains all of the relevant information, eliminating hundreds of pages of testimony and transcripts of hearings. The 64 resolutions passed by the delegates form the core of the conference, and they are all included in the summary. In addition, the summary contains the proposed National Library and Information Services Act and the elements of a comprehensive national library and the Information Services Program: Legislative and Administrative Initiatives. The summary is a good investment for the library requiring some background material on WHCLIS. [R: C&RL, Mar 81, p. 174] Brian Alley

3 Communication of Scientific and Technical Information

23. Garvey, William D. **Communication, the Essence of Science: Facilitating Information Exchange among Librarians, Scientists, Engineers and Students.** New York, Pergamon Press, 1979. 332p. index. $19.50pa. LC 78-40530. ISBN 0-08-023344-9.

As a social psychologist, the author feels that librarians play an important role in the communication process. Nevertheless, they should be more aware of communication patterns and activities within certain specialized groups of scientists, suggesting among other things that librarians must more actively participate in scientific conferences and other professional activities. In doing so, librarians will become more knowledgeable participants in existing mechanisms of prepublication channels used by researchers. Probably the most interesting chapter is "The Librarian's Role as a Social Scientist," and this book will certainly help librarians to better understand the scientific communication channels of their constituency. Highly recommended as a supplementary text to all general orientation courses in library school curriculum. [R: C&RL, Mar 80, pp. 166-67]

Bohdan S. Wynar

24. King, Donald W., and others. **Telecommunications and Libraries: A Primer for Librarians and Information Managers.** White Plains, N.Y., Knowledge Industry Publications, 1981. 184p. illus. bibliog. index. (Professional Librarian Series). o.p. LC 81-6040. ISBN 0-914236-88-1; 0-914236-51-2pa.

Many librarians are bewildered by the rapid advances being made in telecommunications — modems, microwaves, COMSAT, teletext, optical discs. What do they all mean? And how is this going to affect librarianship? Both novices and those with some background will find answers in this enlightening and thought-provoking "primer." Various authors offer concise, lucid introductory overviews of such topics as: the basic terminology of telecommunications; how cable television is being used in American public libraries; and telefacsimile in libraries (with an emphasis on the TALINET Project). Particularly fine are the contributions by Rita G. Lerner (communications satellites), Kathleen Criner (a survey of teletext and viewdata projects), and Charles M. Goldstein (an examination of the potential impact of optical videodisc technology on digital information storage).

The whole book is given perspective and bite by articles by F. W. Lancaster and Donald W. King, which open and close the volume. Together, they offer a model for the information transfer spiral and outline how the library, through its activities, fits into the scheme. Lancaster provides an exhilarating and alarming essay, "The Future of the Library in the Age of Computers," which succinctly and impressively summarizes his well-known ideas on the subject. He sees a promising future for librarians, but doom by the year 2000 for print reference tools and research libraries. King follows this up with an analysis of some "roadblocks" that could prevent Lancaster's transition from happening quite that fast. A thoroughly worthwhile book and one that all librarians should read.

Joseph W. Palmer

25. McGarry, K. J. **Communication Knowledge and the Librarian.** London, Clive Bingley; Hamden, Conn., Linnet Books, 1975. 207p.

bibliog. index. o.p. LC 75-4864. ISBN 0-208-01369-5.

McGarry, a lecturer in the College of Librarianship, Wales, has prepared a textbook on communications that apparently is used in his school and could be used in other library schools. It must be understood at the outset that McGarry conceives communications to be *the* necessary foundation study for librarianship. Despite the phrase "and the librarian" in his title, his book actually impinges on librarianship only in a peripheral way.

In this book he has quite enough to do to make conceptual sense of the many different strands of influence and tradition that make up the study of communications. In eight chapters, the author attempts to interrelate cybernetics, man-machine models, the sociology of knowledge, behaviorist psychology, the theory of games, transformational grammar, and many more disparate schools of thought in a reasonably coherent synthesis. The task he has set for himself, however, simply cannot be done within the compass of a book of 200 pages. [R: C&RL, Mar 76, p. 182; JAL, Jan 76, p. 26; LJ, 1 Sept 76, p. 1717; LQ, Apr 76, p. 199; LR, Autumn 75, p. 132]   Richard A. Gray

26. McGarry, K. J., ed. **Mass Communications: Selected Readings for Librarians.** London, Clive Bingley; distr., Hamden, Conn., Linnet Books, 1972. 255p. index. bibliog. o.p. ISBN 0-8515-7217-6.

According to the editor, this collection of essays by leading British and American authorities illustrates that librarians have many of the problems of the professional communicator. These essays cover, for example, the nature of the communications process, cultural problems of the media, the audience, and problems of media content. The short and excellent bibliographic essays emphasize British materials and are therefore not altogether appropriate for American library students. [R: LJ, Aug 73, p. 2251]   Charles D. Patterson

27. Orr, J. M. **Libraries as Communication Systems.** Westport, Conn., Greenwood Press, 1977. 220p. index. (Contributions in Librarianship and Information Science, No. 17). $27.50. LC 76-8739. ISBN 0-8371-8936-5.

This work has been restructured from its original form as a dissertation written for the University of Strathclyde. To Orr, director of the School of Librarianship at Robert Gordon's Institute of Technology at Aberdeen, Scotland, "it is especially pleasing that it is to be included in the Contributions in Librarianship and Information Science series because it is offered

exactly as that—a contribution—and no more. There are no sensational disclosures to be found in this book. Rather it is a new look at, and construction of, many well-discussed topics" (preface). The author is right. There is nothing new here. Orr provides no pattern or foundation for a general philosophy of librarianship based on the "general systems theory." Instead, we find 17 essays covering certain aspects of such diverse subjects as pornography and obscenity, fragments (quite repetitive) on the history of books and printing, some comments on the holdings of major British libraries, and, indeed, something on publishing (or rather the history of publishing), which makes little sense to this reader. This is a disappointing book, one that, at best, serves as an incomplete attempt to incorporate rather sophisticated elements of systems theory with trivia of ill-defined "facts" and historical "happenings." [R: C&RL, Sept 77, pp. 439-40; JAL, Nov 77, pp. 292-93; JAL, July 77, p. 179; LJ, July 77, p. 1469]
          Bohdan S. Wynar

28. **Papers: Communication's Changing Face —The Challenge to Libraries.** London, Library Association; distr., Phoenix, Ariz., Oryx Press, 1983. 91p. index. (The Library Association Conference, Blackpool 1982). o.p. ISBN 0-85365-845-5.

This book reproduces, apparently unedited, the brief proceedings of a recent Library Association (British) conference. It provides a cursory and generally uncritical survey of the information or communication revolution's effects on libraries, with little material that is new to us in the United States.

On the occasion of British Information Technology Year, calling attention to recent communication mode changes, the conference sought to heighten awareness of the many aspects of these changes with an extremely varied series of talks. British publishers, librarians, computer service managers, professors, and a member of Parliament constituted the distinguished roster of speakers.

This paperback's 10 chapters deal with the communication revolution's recent computer and telecommunication developments, their impact on work, the impact of electronic publishing on readers, new horizons for community service, school training developments, library education implications, and impact on leisure and on individual privacy. A brief index and a vita section are provided but neither a bibliography nor a useful appendix. Several speakers make bold predictions for the future and project well past the year 2000. Occasionally, attention is paid to the situation of developing countries. With a few exceptions, the presentations are chatty and vague. [R: JAL, Nov 83, p. 305]   John F. Harvey

29.   Waldhart, Thomas J., and Enid S. Waldhart. **Communication Research in Library and Information Science: A Bibliography on Communication in the Sciences, Social Sciences, and Technology.** Littleton, Colo., Libraries Unlimited, 1975. 168p. index. o.p. LC 75-5551. ISBN 0-87287-111-8.

This is specifically a bibliography for the years 1964 to 1973. In the introductory statement the Waldharts include a Research Information Cycle chart developed by Redmond, Sinclair, and Brown, which portrays those aspects of the communication system that they have considered in scope. They say "only those studies whose subjects were scientists, social scientists, or technologists were selected for inclusion, while the analysis, design, and operation of information storage and retrieval systems, although important to the overall communication process, were considered outside the scope of this bibliography." Nevertheless, their arrangement of the bibliography highlights the fact that more than 600 references (half of the list) deal with just those aspects, if "system" includes primary publication, secondary and tertiary services. The main sections are: "General" (bibliographies, methods of study, etc.); "Structures of Communication"; "Discipline-Oriented Studies"; "Communication Barriers"; and "Communication Innovations."

The bibliography is organized on a topical basis, with other access via separate author and subject indexes. Referring to the subject "Gatekeepers in Agriculture," entry 1032 is found under the section "Discipline-Oriented Studies — Technology — Agriculture." Throughout the bibliography, the 1,288 citations provide basic bibliographic information, except for "mini-indicators," bracketed descriptive phrases that enable the user to establish the scope or emphasis of the reference. An asterisk marks those references of high quality that provide surveys helpful to users generally unfamiliar with the field.

A list of the 40 journals, five abstracting services, and two critical bibliographies scanned is included. The usual procedure of tracing references in previously identified documents was also followed.

A model bibliography, useful to the intended audience in the library and information science community as well as to individuals in the specific substantive disciplines. [R: LQ, Jan 76, p. 108; RQ, Winter 75, p. 185]

Pauline Atherton Cochrane

4 Current Issues

30. Coughlin, Caroline M., ed. **Recurring Library Issues: A Reader.** Metuchen, N.J., Scarecrow, 1979. 521p. $22.50. LC 79-14966. ISBN 0-8108-1227-4.

Caroline Coughlin has compiled an anthology of articles and excerpts from monographs focusing on the primary issues that continually face American librarianship. The 40 selections are grouped in seven categories: United States library environment; government regulation; management goals and standards; creative library services; human resources; philosophical questions; and the changing boundaries of librarianship. Inasmuch as 85 percent of the selections originally appeared in the 1970s, there is a void of library classics published prior to this period. Though one may argue the merits of including or excluding certain selections, there are many very good articles in this book which address the major issues of librarianship; for example, excellent selections by Jesse Shera, Mary Jo Lynch, Tom Galvin, Harold Goldstein, and Vannevar Bush. *Recurring Library Issues* is a useful instructional aid primarily for library science students. [R: C&RL, July 80, pp. 360-61; JAL, May 80, p. 101]

Alan Edward Schorr

31. Dunkin, Paul S. **Tales of Melvil's Mouser; or Much Ado about Libraries.** New York, R. R. Bowker, 1970. 182p. illus. o.p. LC 74-131911. ISBN 0-8352-0467-7.

These satirical sketches about libraries, librarianship, and librarians are a response to what the author considers our failure to come to grips with the real issues and needs of librarianship. The tales draw upon the author's intimate observations extending over many years as a librarian, author, editor, teacher, and active participant in professional affairs. A book to stimulate, irritate, and most certainly entertain. [R: BL, 15 May 71, p. 758; C&RL, Jan 72, p. 58; LJ, 1 Apr 71, p. 1200]

Charles D. Patterson

32. Estabrook, Leigh, ed. **Libraries in Post-Industrial Society.** Phoenix, Ariz., Oryx Press, 1977. 337p. illus. bibliog. index. (A Neal-Schuman Professional Book). o.p. LC 77-8928. ISBN 0-912700-00-9.

This volume is not a ready reference book, since it is not organized for fast retrieval of information and since I hardly believe reference desks are going to be besieged by users avid for predigested information about libraries in post-industrial society. This volume may not even be a book. It is, perhaps, a manufactured artifact, prepared and marketed because "booksellers now see the post-industrial label as a way to sell books," as Peter Stearns, one of the contributors, points out. Librarians have taken the post-industrial society to their bosoms because the concept of an information society seems to enhance the social value of librarians. So for librarians who want to explore what or whether post-industrial society is, the articles collected here are a once-over-lightly capsule to be taken three times a day before meals. Although there's a whole section on libraries, only one article in the book was written by a librarian. Most of the material is by professors and is, consequently, academic in bias and language. Ordinary people will need to have some of the material translated into English. Most of the articles have bibliographies of their own, and there is an extensive general bibliography as well. Taken in small doses along with concentrated doses of healthy skepticism, the articles in this collection can lead librarians to question generally accepted assumptions about their role in a society which still looks very much like an industrial society, only more so. [R: C&RL, Nov 77, pp. 544-45; JAL, Nov 77, pp. 294-95]

Fay M. Blake

33. Gerard, David, ed. **Libraries in Society: A Reader.** London, Clive Bingley; distr., New York, K. G. Saur, 1978. 163p. bibliog. o.p. ISBN 0-85157-260-X.

This rich anthology draws on articles from the British and U.S. press, over one-half of them written by individuals who are not librarians. Each in some way deals with the library's social value and utility to the community of which it is a part. Gerard's selections reveal his belief that the ideology of library service must be seen as evolutionary—moving from traditional nineteenth-century liberalism to present-day conflict in values. Social and political factors, he believes, shape the direction of library services. Introductions that place each article in a historical context, and a partially annotated, selective bibliography enhance the value of this work for the general reader or as a supplementary text in library education. [R: LJ, 1 Dec 79, p. 2549] Leigh Estabrook

34. Hammer, Donald P., ed. **The Information Age: Its Development, Its Impact.** Metuchen, N.J., Scarecrow, 1976. 275p. index. o.p. LC 76-10603. ISBN 0-8108-0945-1.

A breezy introduction by Donald Hammer leads off this collection of papers dealing with the development of the library and information fields. The collection focuses on the decade from 1965 to 1975, but the contributing authors were not limited to this time frame in their discussions. In Hammer's words, their charge was to "examine the happenings of the period, evaluate them, and consider their possible impact on the future of the information sciences."

The authors, all of whom have been directly involved in the field, have combined their knowledge and experiences into a readable overview of the information science field. Individual papers range from general history or background discussions to specific aspects of concern, such as standards to be employed and the effect of commercialization of information services. Terms are defined, examples given, and theoretical questions explored. Anyone involved in the field will recognize many familiar names and will find this a useful summary of developments. For those new to librarianship or information science, this collection provides an excellent introduction. Bibliographic references at the end of most papers will aid the reader seeking further information. [R: C&RL, July 77, p. 342; JAL, May 77, p. 122; JLH,

Summer 77, p. 299; LJ, 1 Jan 77, p. 82]

Roberta J. Depp

35. Hug, William E. **Strategies for Change in Information Programs.** New York, R. R. Bowker, 1974. 373p. index. o.p. LC 73-20269. ISBN 0-8352-0695-5.

This anthology consists of 24 articles on a timely subject, reprinted from a variety of sources. Only four of the articles are by librarians: Wasserman's "Professional Adaptation," McAnally and Downs's "The Changing Role of Directors of University Libraries," Pauline Atherton's "Putting Knowledge to Work," and Jesse Shera's "Documentation into Information Science." The other articles, written by educators, social scientists, and computer technologists, are rather uneven—many of them are simply disappointing. We have enough oratory in our own professional literature without borrowing from other fields. There are, of course, a few articles that are interesting (such as Robert Gagne's or Victor Thompson's). On the other hand, Bob F. Steere's "Ex-Innovators as Barriers to Change" amounts to nothing, and Hug's claim that the article is "thought-provoking" does a disservice to the library profession. Librarians today are less naive than they used to be, and they will no longer be fooled by the large doses of jargon found in many articles written by nonlibrarians. They remain unimpressed with rhetoric alone, and they look for something more substantial. Unfortunately, this anthology is not substantial fare at all; in our opinion Hug did not make the best possible selection of articles. General educational theory, management, behavioral psychology, systems analysis, media technology, and the other topics represented in this anthology can be better examined if one goes directly to sources, since many articles included here are not representative of current thinking. [R: AL, June 74, pp. 299-300; C&RL, Sept 74, pp. 376-77; LJ, 15 Apr 74, p. 1107] Bohdan S. Wynar

36. Lancaster, F. Wilfrid, ed. **The Role of the Library in an Electronic Society.** Champaign, Ill., University of Illinois, Graduate School of Library Science, 1980. 200p. index. (Proceedings of the 1979 Clinic on Library Applications of Data Processing). $9.00. LC 79-19449. ISBN 0-87845-053-X.

The first clinic was held in 1963, when libraries were being introduced to the use of data processing equipment to automate clerical routines. Most of the papers in those early clinics were prosaic descriptions of "how we use the computer." At first they were exciting, but the newness soon wore off. This clinic is different, and recaptures some of that early excitement, giving us a fascinating, but sometimes frightening, picture of how the computer will change the way we go about obtaining information. Instead of focusing on library automation, the 1979 clinic dovetailed with NSF-sponsored research by Lancaster on the paperless society and the library of the future (see Lancaster's *Toward Paperless Information Systems*, Academic Press, 1978).

The first essay, "Happiness Is a Warm Librarian," by D. J. deS. Price, is a fine account of how humans throughout history have invented mechanisms to cope with ever-expanding knowledge. Price predicts that secondary literatures (which have never been very satisfactory) will no longer be needed when we computerize primary literature and move away from systems of linear sequential indexes to a "new encyclopedism." The final essay, by F. W. Lancaster, et al., is a provocative but likely scenario of the library in the paperless society. Libraries will be smaller in physical size and staff and will devote an increasing portion of their budgets to purchasing online access to information, on-demand rather than in anticipation of use. Libraries will become switching centers, and librarians will become information consultants rather than archivists. Between these two thoughtful essays are others, of mixed quality and relevance—some by leaders outside the field of librarianship. They address such topics as the online journal (several of the participants agree that the printed journal is on the way out); the use of computers in newspapers; the impact of the computer on library processes; problems and prospects of machine-readable databases; online intelligence information; and electronic mail and conferencing.

In all, this is an extremely interesting and provocative volume which presents a challenge to librarians and information scientists to develop the outlook necessary to cope with these changes. It should be required reading for all library school students and faculty, for when the library of the year 2000 deals with online knowledge rather than with indexed knowledge, we will need librarians who are equipped to talk to people and to machines at the same time, and to lead the people through the information labyrinth that the communication/information revolution has spread before them. [R: BL, 15 Oct 80, p. 304; C&RL, Sept 80, pp. 460-61; JAL, Nov 80, p. 292]   A. Neil Yerkey

37. Mathews, Virginia H. **Libraries for Today and Tomorrow: How Do We Pay for Them? Who Uses Them? Who Staffs Them? What Are Their Services?** Garden City, N.Y.,

Doubleday, 1976. 228p. index. o.p. LC 75-25440. ISBN 0-385-05564-1.

In her brief opening chapter, the author sketches the social history of the United States to show how and why we as a people have become a nation of information users. The history of American libraries is briefly told in two further chapters, which show how these institutions have fulfilled the needs of these information users from colonial times through the late 1960s. After a chapter describing many typical and special services of individual libraries as examples of what libraries do for their users, a narrative of the recent harrowing experiences of budget restrictions beginning with the federal government brings the account of library history from 1968 up through 1975. In her brief final chapter, the author presents a wide-ranging survey of possible future directions for library service. Statistical tables and a chart of federal programs appear as appendices. A short index completes this succinct review of where our libraries have come from and what they have come through. There are no footnotes citing quotation sources and no bibliographies. Valuable for most librarians, students, and general readers, despite its heavy public library emphasis. [R: SLJ, May 76, p. 41]

Dennis North

38. McCrimmon, Barbara. **American Library Philosophy: An Anthology.** Hamden, Conn., Shoe String Press, 1975. 248p. illus. bibliog. index. (Contributions to Library Literature Series). $17.50. LC 75-9544. ISBN 0-208-01503-5.

"Everyman his own anthologizer." This appears to be the motto of an increasing number of librarians, and the result has been the appearance of numerous collections of readings over the past ten years or so. Generally speaking, these collections are welcome, since they bring together in a convenient and inexpensive format a number of scattered works dealing with special topics. McCrimmon's anthology is no exception to this rule. However, upon examination of the 19 selections included, one is struck by two related concerns. First is the general question of what materials to include. It is obvious that, to different readers, the selection of items for inclusion will appear faulty in some respect. Such a problem is common with any anthology. A more serious criticism is related to McCrimmon's criteria for selecting and organizing her material. She appears to have adopted the rather simpleminded, and all too frequently used, view that library philosophy can be boiled down to the two extremes of those who love books (to the detriment of users) and those who love the pragmatics of library management (often to the detriment of collection development). To this reviewer such a superficial view must be combated, because it excludes from consideration much of the most constructive thinking ever done relative to the role of the library in society. For instance, where does one find a place within this framework for the representation of the views of that large group of librarians and public library trustees who have written articulately and at length about the library's role as a stabilizing and conservative force in society? Further, it leaves little room for the debate over whether the library should serve as the "guardian of the people's right to know" or as a radical and authoritarian force for social change. These debates, it seems to me, deserve a good deal more attention than the question of whether librarians should "love" books or not. Despite this serious conceptual shortcoming, McCrimmon's collection does contain some of the best thinking yet done on "library philosophy," and librarians and educators should be able to use it profitably as background for their professional endeavors. [R: BSA-P, July 76, p. 438; JLH, Apr 76, p. 177; LQ, July 76, p. 345]   Michael H. Harris

39. Moon, Eric, and Karl Nyren, eds. **Library Issues: The Sixties.** New York, R. R. Bowker, 1970. 400p. o.p. LC 71-103618. SBN 8352-0297-6.

This work consists of the editorials published in *Library Journal*, presumably all of them without change since there is no editorial statement to the contrary. They have been grouped together under predictable headings, such as "Federal Aid: Progress and Program," "State of the Art," and "Identity of the Librarian." Each of these groups has a one-paragraph introduction, and the general subject of each editorial is indicated, though only in the table of contents, since few of the titles themselves are indicative of anything in particular. The whole is prefaced by a short introductory essay. That is all there is to the work; there is no index, no updating of individual editorials, no elucidation of now obscure allusions. It does provide a composite document on the state of the American library profession during the last decade, its alarums and discursions, as seen from the offices of Bowker, and, in Eric Moon's contributions, in particular, a sprinkling of fact. [R: C&RL, Jan 71, p. 50]   Dennis North

40. Penland, Patrick R., and Aleyamma Mathai. **The Library as a Learning Service Center.** New York, Marcel Dekker, 1978. 237p. bibliog. index. (Books in Library and Information Science, Vol. 24). o.p. LC 78-13491. ISBN 0-8247-6750-0.

New concepts for the library profession are needed, and Penland and Mathai challenge librarians to find new directions and become involved with innovative and unaccustomed procedures. They expect librarians to become active political forces for community improvement. Such a role for librarians is neither new nor noncontroversial, but as described by the authors, having librarians spend unlimited time with any one client is unrealistic. In addition, many of the other concepts are poorly, ineffectively, and incoherently presented.

Much of what Penland says in this latest book can be traced, through his other publications, to his 1960 dissertation; and in the interval he has said little, if anything, new. Whole paragraphs are lifted from earlier works, sometimes with slight rewording, sometimes not. Usually no citation is offered, and the material is usually not even indicated as a quotation. The format is supposed to be clever with its charts, boxed aphorisms, flow charts, and questionnaires; but the organization is confusing and fuzzy. Some of this is syntax: "a profile has the connotation of a formula" and "get on the bandwagon of an idea whose time has come." Some of this is psycho-babble: what is "cognitive content mapping"? The attempt to appear learned results in a superior attitude glossed by a flow of pseudo-sociological gobbledygook. There is little documentation and inadequate citation practice. There are no footnotes, and the bibliography contains errors (e.g., Nancy Polette is listed as Lancy Poletti). Many will be offended by statements like: "Until the appearance of this publication, the role of the librarian as a possible helping professional had not been given much if any sustained consideration." This might be expected of educators insulated from day-to-day practical problems. The authors seem to have forgotten the reader's advisor of the 1930s and offer the same concept dressed in fancy language. This volume is not a contribution to librarianship and is best forgotten and unpurchased. [R: JAL, Mar 79, p. 35; LJ, 1 Feb 79, p. 360]   Neal L. Edgar

41. Plotnik, Arthur. **Library Life—American Style: A Journalist's Field Report.** Metuchen, N.J., Scarecrow, 1975. 220p. illus. $15.00. LC 75-16280. ISBN 0-8108-0852-8.

This book is a joyful celebration of American librarianship—grass roots librarianship, as Plotnik would say. Subtitled "a journalist's field report," the volume contains Plotnik's impressionistic portrait of American librarianship from the Bronx to West Virginia, from Illinois to California. Throughout these essays, first written from 1971 to 1974, the author strives mightily, and in most cases successfully, to tread the thin line between "healthy optimism" and "polyanna-ism." In total the book must be considered an enormously insightful and positive assessment of "Library Life U.S.A." in the late 1960s and early 1970s. Through it all Plotnik sees strength, commitment, and intelligence in the library scene. And while one is prone to question the exuberant tenor of his book, especially in these dark times for libraries, one must also conclude that *Library Life—American Style* represents one of the most significant "travel accounts" ever addressed to the library community. We predict that it will be widely read by librarians today, and that tomorrow it will be analyzed by historians trying to understand the complex evolution of library service in America during the halcyon days Plotnik so articulately describes. [R: LJ, 1 Apr 76, p. 872]

Michael H. Harris

42. Pratt, Allan D. **The Information of the Image.** Norwood, N.J., Ablex Publishing, 1982. 117p. illus. index. (Libraries and Librarianship Series). $22.50. LC 81-15075. ISBN 0-89391-055-4.

This book is a welcome addition to the growing number of publications concerned with the scope, boundaries, and future of librarianship and information science. The role of libraries and librarians in the human communication process is discussed, and classic concepts, such as the nature of information, are briefly summarized. More important, the work focuses on the future of libraries in society.

Libraries are treated as social systems which act as critical intermediaries in graphic-records communication processes. Librarians create meta-records which maximize the "social utility of graphic records." Librarianship is a profession because it stresses individualized service, but at the expense of research. Information science provides the research methodology for identifying the broader characteristics and general properties of graphic records and record users, but is in need of new conceptual tools to measure how graphic records are used and dispersed.

Libraries are compared to other social systems, termed CPOD (collection, preservation, organization, and dissemination), with library-like functions. These systems may exert more control over graphic records, and thus pose a danger to the future of libraries. Librarians need mathematical and statistical tools to study these systems and need to be more aggressive in the area of information resource management. The author makes recommendations for changes needed at the practicing professional level and in library schools.

While no new ground is broken, the book provides the framework for redefining the role of librarians and library educators in the communication process. Stimulating and provocative reading for librarians, educators, library science students, and information scientists. [R: JAL, May 82, p. 120; LJ, 1 Sept 82, p. 1623]

Andrew G. Torok

43. **The Right to Read and the Nation's Libraries.** Edited by the Right to Read Committee of the American Association of School Librarians, Children's Services Division, and The Public Library Association, American Library Association. Chicago, American Library Association, 1974. 109p. o.p. LC 74-12075. ISBN 0-8389-0193-X.

In 1969, Commissioner of Education James E. Allen, Jr., delivered a speech in which he called for "a total national commitment to and involvement in the achievement of the 'right to read' goal." The goal, simply stated, was to eradicate illiteracy as soon as humanly possible. Allen had in mind the bicentennial year of 1976 as a viable target date for achievement of that goal. This slender paperbound volume is designed to give a state-of-the-project report as of late summer, 1974. At a time less than two years away from the hoped-for date, a number of gratifying (and not-so-gratifying) stories are here detailed, with a dozen or so commentaries from practitioners of library-based "Adult Reading Academies."

The shocking facts come first. By Allen's reckoning, fully 25 percent of adults in America are "functionally illiterate," which carries the sense of being unable to comprehend fully the information necessary to cope with an increasingly complex society. During the five years after that statistic was reported, libraries and other social agencies, such as YMCAs, made modest inroads into illiteracy. These brief papers document the who, the where, and the how of reading programs for adults up to 1974, with analysis of success or failure. Success seems to be a function of planning and funding. As most nonliterate Americans are of "disadvantaged" minorities, programs rich in ethnic content and staffing seem to work best. When failure must be recorded, it is normally attributed to an absence of these factors, together with staff inability or unwillingness to obtain and use multimedia materials.

In format, the volume is somewhat unsatisfying. The pages suffer from a variable printing job: now lighter, now darker. A few black and white photographs do not do much to punctuate the narratives. All told, there's not much to criticize here. It chronicles a commendable goal, and will provide to the reader a useful series of practical do's and don'ts in attempting to involve the library in an adult reading program. Useful appendix of references for further reading. Recommended for purchase. [R: BL, 1 Feb 75, p. 534] Bruce A. Shuman

44. Schuman, Patricia Glass, comp. and ed. **Social Responsibilities and Libraries: A Library Journal/School Library Journal Selection.** New York, R. R. Bowker, 1976. 402p. index. o.p. LC 76-27894. ISBN 0-8352-0952-0.

This anthology reprints 51 articles from *Library Journal* and *School Library Journal*, spanning the years 1968 to 1976—years that were characterized by campus unrest and an organized movement for social responsibility within the library profession. The Social Responsibilities Round Table was officially incorporated as a unit of ALA in 1969. The articles are grouped under six categories: "Advocacy and Action," "Women and Minorities," "Service to the Community," "Service to Youth," "Service to Students and Faculty," and "Inventing the Future." The authors reflect on the library as an agent for change and stress a service function in addition to the library's responsibility for the conservation of the graphic record. The library should not only serve its present clientele but should identify and address the needs of those who would benefit from its services.

The anthology would have benefited from a broader perspective, taking articles from other journals on subjects such as outreach librarianship and a comparison between American librarianship and that in other countries. In spite of these shortcomings, the collection of essays serves as an introductory reader and suggests changes that might redefine certain library positions, thereby underscoring the need for those engaged in library operations to participate in continuing education activities. [R: JAL, May 77, p. 122; RQ, Summer 77, p. 360]

Peter Hernon

45. Wasserman, Paul. **The New Librarianship: A Challenge for Change.** New York, R. R.

Bowker, 1972. 287p. index. o.p. LC 72-8621. ISBN 0-8352-0604-1.

This is a highly personal, carefully researched commentary on librarians and librarianship. Although highly opinionated and, at times arrogant, it is a statement that compels attention due to the author's perception of reality. A work that is at once controversial yet necessary. [R: C&RL, Sept 73, p. 284; LJ, 15 Apr 73, p. 1256; RQ, Spring 74, p. 219]

46. Withers, F. N. **Standards for Library Service: An International Survey.** Paris, UNESCO; distr., New York, UNIPUB, 1974. 421p. $19.75pa. ISBN 92-3-101177-4.

The present survey is a revision and updating of a previous study published in 1970. Both were completed by F. N. Withers (Polytechnic of North London School of Librarianship) as a result of contracts between UNESCO and IFLA. The study includes not only standards officially promulgated as such by professional associations but also pertinent legislation and surveys that make specific recommendations for improvement of library service.

The book consists of separate chapters on standards for national, university and college, special, public, and school libraries. There is a concluding chapter on model standards for developing countries. The author's method is to open each chapter with a comparative overview, followed by summaries of standards from various countries. In the case of public libraries, some very useful comparative tables have been added.

The coverage appears to be thorough and complete within the guidelines and time frame. The situation is dynamic. Since the author's cut-off date, two major new American standards have appeared: *Media Programs: District and School* (Chicago, ALA, 1975) and "Standards for College Libraries" (*College & Research Libraries News* 36, Oct 75, 277-79, 290-301). Furthermore, at the time of writing, Withers could not possibly have known of the ACRL's recent appointment of a committee to develop quantitative standards to go with its 1972 *Guidelines for Two-Year College Learning Resource Programs*. [R: LJ, Aug 75, p. 72]

A. Robert Rogers

5 Theoretical Foundations

47. Batty, David, ed. **Knowledge and Its Organization.** College Park, Md., College of Library and Information Services, University of Maryland, 1976. 145p. illus. bibliog. (Student Contribution Series, No. 8). $8.75pa. LC 76-620022. ISBN 0-911808-12-4.

This is a collection of papers by several University of Maryland students; the purpose of the papers was to identify and outline the major typologies of knowledge. There are five major sections: "The Nature and Growth of Knowledge," "Knowledge and Society," "The Origins of Ideas," "Organization and Expression," and "Applications of Knowledge." These are followed by "The Organization of Knowledge: An Outline Bibliography." Kemp's *The Nature of Knowledge: An Introduction for Librarians* presents a rather interesting sequel to this reading. [R: LJ, 15 Oct 76, p. 2152]

48. Kemp, D. A. **The Nature of Knowledge: An Introduction for Librarians.** London, Clive Bingley; Hamden, Conn., Linnet Books, 1976. 199p. illus. bibliog. index. o.p. LC 76-28343. ISBN 0-85157-216-2(Bingley); 0-208-01528-0 (Linnet).

This book is an attempt to identify several components of knowledge and the lineaments of its communication between people — in particular, the different ways in which communication is absorbed and interpreted. The material is presented in 11 chapters, such as "The Nature of Knowledge," "Philosophy and Knowledge," "Psychology and Knowledge," "The Philosophy of Science and Social Knowledge," etc. It is primarily intended for students in library schools in Great Britain. [R: LJ, 1 Apr 77, p. 778]

49. Shera, J. H. **Sociological Foundations of Librarianship.** New York, Asia Publishing House, 1970. 195p. index. o.p. SBN 210-22283-2.

This is a series of five lectures by one of the most prominent educators in the field of library science, with a concluding chapter by S. R. Ranganathan. The following topics are covered: library and individual, library and society, library and knowledge, transition and change, and education of the librarian. [R: LJ, 1 Jan 72, p. 46]

50. Shores, Louis. **The Generic Book: What It Is and How It Works.** Norman, Okla., Library-College Associates, 1977. 164p. bibliog. (Learning for Living Series). o.p. LC 77-22891. ISBN 0-917706-02-1.

This is one in the series of titles published to "meet a special need that continually appears in the growing literature on the Library-College." The term "generic book" dates from the 1960s and is usually defined as representing "the total number of ways which men have of communicating with each other." Shores argues, and proceeds to demonstrate, that it must be considered as a fundamental construct in library-college thought. The work is divided into seven chapters, the first entitled "Of Media and Men," with the next three dealing with the subject, level, and format dimensions of the generic book, respectively. The fifth covers print and graphic materials, the sixth discusses human and environmental media, and the final chapter, appropriately enough, "puts it all together." The focus is on learning through the library-college, rather than on prescriptive teaching, although the work does offer a number of suggestions as to how teachers might use various materials to stimulate the learning process. Both the learner and tools of communication receive the bulk of the author's attention. This is a reasonably considered discussion of a currently popular topic. [R: C&RL, Jan 78, p. 68; JAL, Jan 78, p. 352]

Jesse H. Shera

51. Wilson, Patrick. **Second-Hand Knowledge: An Inquiry into Cognitive Authority.** Westport, Conn., Greenwood Press, 1983. 210p. index. (Contributions in Librarianship and Information Science, No. 44). $29.95. LC 82-21069. ISBN 0-313-23763-8.

A work that suggests and inspires further thinking, rather than presenting "scientific" facts and conclusions, *Second-Hand Knowledge* discusses the many facets of cognitive authority as they pertain to those people involved in the creation, validation, processing, and dissemination of information. An opening essay, "First-Hand and Second-Hand Knowledge," sets the tone for the remaining chapters as it analyzes the nature and variability factors associated with perspective and perception.

Wilson follows this exercise with an analysis of cognitive authority, distinguishing the nuances of authority, influence, and credibility. He also presents a coherent explanation of differences between knowledge and opinion, spheres of authority, degrees of authority, bases of authority, and expertise and authority. Although his arguments are flawed in places, he succeeds in presenting a base from which to argue subsequent points.

Of two chapters concerned with the knowledge industry, the first attempts to profile the quality and fashion of the industry through an industry analysis, as well as giving the author's thoughts on knowledge production and quality control, fashion and intellectual taste, and fashion in the knowledge industry. The subsequent chapter on the knowledge industry discusses institutional authority, authority in the sciences, authority in the social sciences, and critical authority. In succeeding chapters, the author analyzes the nature of cognitive authority in everyday life and the relationships between information retrieval and cognitive authority.

The work concludes, of necessity, with a brief bibliographical essay that explains the lack of any solid body of literature on the subject of cognitive authority and mentions key sources that the author found useful.

As a whole, Wilson's work is to be commended. An attempt to understand the nature of authority, the reliability of information, and the importance of these issues to the information handler, *Second-Hand Knowledge* vacillates between the theoretical and the practical, between the esoteric and the mundane. Although this may at first appear to be a liability, it assures as successful a means as any for the author's discussion of the topic.

The information professional may have varying reactions to the work — a behavior that will support many of Wilson's ideas. And there may be many counterarguments from other spheres of authority. But the author presents a platform that should inspire debate and that could force professionals to an understanding and resolution of cognitive authority issues on an individual — if not a collective — level. [R: LJ, 15 June 83, p. 1238; WLB, Dec 83, pp. 302-3]

Edmund F. SantaVicca

Part 2

REFERENCE WORKS

6 General Works

52. England, Claire, ed. **Guide to Basic Reference Materials for Canadian Libraries.** 7th ed., rev. and enlarged. With contributions by Patricia Fleming and others. Buffalo, N.Y., published for the Faculty of Library and Information Science by University of Toronto Press, 1984. 309p. index. $25.00pa. ISBN 0-8020-6581-3.

This is the seventh edition of a work first published only 16 years ago. Obviously the guide well satisfies a real need; its relevance and quality can be taken as proven.

The present edition is some 15 percent larger (insofar as size can be determined by a simple page count) than its 1980 predecessor. The principal additions are in the fields of library and information science, government documents, and publications from international organizations. The basic structure and composition remain, however, much as before: a listing (usually with descriptive annotations) of the some 2,000 titles considered to constitute the "basic reference materials for Canadian libraries." Canadian libraries need a broad range of general and "subject" reference books as well as special strength in reference publications relating specifically to Canada. The guide presents a well-chosen selection from both kinds of reference stock — a combination which is available in no other reference guide.

Unfortunately, the publisher of this guide has not done well by the compilers. The typographical layout, with its plethora of uppercase, is confusing and unattractive; the perfect binding is too weak for such a large volume; worst of all, the index (produced by computer?) is inexplicably limited to titles plus a handful of author entries. At $25.00 for a paperback, one might justifiably have expected more.

Samuel Rothstein

53. McCormick, Mona. **The New York Times Guide to Reference Materials.** rev. ed. New York, Times Books/Random House, 1985. 242p. illus. index. $15.95. LC 84-40109. ISBN 0-8129-1127-X.

This guide was first published in hardcover as *Who-What-When-Where-How-Why Made Easy* (Quadrangle Books, 1971). The paperback edition, titled *The New York Times Guide to Reference Materials* (Popular Library, 1971), was updated in 1977. This revised edition, like its predecessors, is "intended to assist students and general readers in their search for information by offering a strategy for searching and an *introduction* [author's emphasis] to basic reference sources" (p. ix). In all editions the author has been Mona McCormick, formerly a reference librarian at *The New York Times* and now associate librarian, University Research Library, UCLA.

The arrangement of the work is simple and orderly, forming a logical progression. Part 1, "Finding Information," briefly discusses search strategy (i.e., orderly sifting through information for the pertinent and the best materials), library and online catalogs, terms and abbreviations used in reference materials, and computerized searching, including a selected list of more than one hundred databases. Part 2 introduces in six chapters reference books by type: almanacs and atlases, bibliography, biography, dictionaries, encyclopedias, newspapers, and magazines. The structure of each chapter follows a fairly uniform format: overview of the type of reference material under consideration, description (and sometimes comparisons and facsimile illustrations) of selected titles, and a bibliography of titles just described. Part 3 — the largest section — applies the part 2 format to subject reference sources in twenty-two areas (e.g., art;

books and literature; business, economics, and statistics; quotations; science and technology). Two areas—minorities and women's studies—are new to the edition. The fourth part is a chapter on critical thinking as applied to the research process. McCormick here announces (1) that "*finding* the information is not the most important part of research; what you *do* with it is" and (2) that certain attitudes are requisite to critical thinking: intellectual curiosity, personal honesty and objectivity, open-mindedness and respect for the viewpoints of others, flexibility, skepticism, persistence and orderliness. She concludes the chapter with the (a) cornerstones of evaluation of reference materials (authority, purpose, scope, audience) and (b) primary/secondary sources. The fifth part—"Organizing and Communication Information"—introduces researchers to (a) writing guides (Safire's *What's the Good Word?*, Strunk and White's *Elements of Style*, etc.) and publishing/marketing guides (e.g., *Literary Market Place, Writer's Market, Writer's Handbook*), (b) style manuals, (c) footnotes and bibliography, and (d) a sample term paper. The guide concludes with a selected bibliography of titles for further study and an A-Z index of authors, titles, and subjects of the more than five hundred sources treated. The index does not, however, include the databases cited earlier.

All in all, this guide generally succeeds in its stated purpose. And while no cutoff date is given, the volume lists a number of 1983 and 1984 editions/titles. A sampling of various sections does suggest the need for citing later editions and/or additional titles. Oxford companions (p. 86) to American literature, classical literature, and English literature are available in later editions (1983, 1984, 1985, respectively). There is a 1981 edition of *Random House Dictionary* (p. 45). Perhaps the entries for native Americans (pp. 128-29) should add the Smithsonian Institution's projected twenty-volume set, *Handbook of North American Indians* (1978-). *Survey of Current Business* (p. 98) has been the responsibility since its inception (1921) of the Bureau of Foreign and Domestic Commerce and now of the Bureau of Economic Analysis—but *not* of the Bureau of the Census as mentioned. The third edition of *McGraw-Hill Dictionary of Modern Economics* (p. 95) appeared in 1983. Another McGraw-Hill publication, *Encyclopedia of Economics* (1982), merits consideration for inclusion on the same page. Not mentioned (p. 94) is that a revised edition of Daniells's *Business Information Sources* (1976), in progress for a number of years, was published in 1985. The twelve-volume *Guide to American Law: Everyone's Legal Encyclopedia*

(1983-1985) is surely a candidate for inclusion in the chapter on politics, government, and current events. [R: LJ, 15 Apr 85, p. 66]

Wiley J. Williams

54. Sheehy, Eugene P., comp. **Guide to Reference Books.** 9th ed. With the assistance of Rita G. Keckeissen and Eileen McIlvaine. Chicago, American Library Association, 1976. 1015p. index. $30.00. LC 76-11751. ISBN 0-8389-0205-7.

Finally, after several years of preparation, the new edition of *Guide to Reference Books* is available; the eighth edition was published in 1967. Eugene P. Sheehy, head of the Reference Department at Columbia University Libraries, is the new compiler, and he was assisted by Rita Keckeissen and Eileen McIlvaine. Several other staff members from Columbia and a small number of other librarians are mentioned in the acknowledgments.

Some 10,000 entries are included—an increase of 2,500 over the eighth edition. As the press release for the book indicates, the new work is the "net product not only of many added entries but also the withdrawal of those less current." Most entries in this edition conform to those appearing on Library of Congress printed cards, and Library of Congress class marks are supplied with the entries when these appeared on the printed cards. There are also a few changes in arrangement and coverage. The "Societies" section has been eliminated, and much of the material from this section has been absorbed into the subsection "Associations, Societies, and Academies" under "Social Sciences." In the "Literature" section individual author bibliographies and concordances are less extensively covered, being limited now only to major literary figures. This change is justified in the preface by mention of today's proliferation of both types of reference works.

For all practical purposes the cut-off date is 1973, and the compiler notes that "the total number of 1974 items included is disappointingly small" (p. x). Sheehy also indicates that "with Miss Winchell's gracious permission, much of the text of the previous edition is used without alteration. Although additions and changes have been made wherever they were necessary or deemed helpful, many of the annotations have been carried forward unchanged from the eighth edition and its supplements" (p. ix). No special search was made for reprint editions, which means that "reprints are listed if they are in the collections of the Columbia University Libraries or if Library of Congress cards for reprint editions were encountered in the verification process" (p. x).

To these general introductory comments provided in the preface, we might add that this new edition omits citations to reviews, although there is no explanation of why this practice was dropped. So much for that.

What will probably be disappointing to many users is the fact that this standard and very well known guide is so much behind schedule; for all practical purposes, at least two and a half years of reference book production are not represented here. It is hoped that the first supplement will be published soon, because currency in this type of work is rather important.

Equally disturbing is the fact that a significant number of annotations and bibliographical citations carry over errors from previous supplements or the eighth edition. Of course, one also occasionally finds new errors, an exclusive property of the ninth edition. A few examples may illustrate this. Entry AD 711: This etymological dictionary of the Ukrainian language is not in the "2d rev. ed." and it started in 1962, not in 1966. Bound volumes simply incorporate parts published separately, a well-known German practice for certain encyclopedic works. There are also errors in the annotation. The bound volume 1 consists of parts 1-11 (letters A-G) and not of parts 1-5 (A-Voro). It was issued not in 1966 but in 1972. The next entry (AD 712) contains the term "Slovnik." This is incorrect. The Ukrainian word for dictionary is "Slovnyk," as correctly used in entry AD 710.

Since we have begun examining Ukrainian material, it is worth noting that there is an entry (AC 88) for the *Ukrainian Soviet Encyclopedia* published in Ukrainian in Kiev in 1959-68. Why are other multivolume encyclopedic works omitted? Examples are *Radians'ka entsyklopedia istorii Ukrainy* (Kiev, 1969-1972, 4v.), *Ukrains'ka sil's'kohospodars'ka entsyklopediia* (Kiev, 1970-1072, 3v.) or *Entsykiopediia narodnoho hospodarstva Ukrains'koi RSR* (Kiev, 1969-1971, 3v.), to mention only three encyclopedias pertaining to history, agriculture, and national economy of Ukraine. Instead, the reader will find here Korduba's old and now obsolete historiographical survey published in French in 1938 and unnecessarily reprinted in 1972 in Germany (DC 362). A much better work on this subject (not to mention any Soviet works here) is *A Survey of Ukrainian Historiography*, by D. Doroshenko and O. Ohloblyn, published by the Ukrainian Academy of Arts and Sciences in 1957. But why go into such details if the Ukrainian national bibliography is not even listed? This work, published for many years, serves as an equivalent to *Knizhnaia letopis'* (AA 868).

Obviously, the random selection of Ukrainian reference works is a deficiency that is not unique to that group of materials; it pertains also to Russian works, in spite of the fact that for obvious reasons they are much better represented. Thus, in the section on history, under "dictionaries, outlines, tables" (?) one finds a few recent and several obsolete historical encyclopedias and dictionaries—e.g., DA 39 or DA 40 (good choice), and DA 38 or DA 41, two rather obsolete chronologies. But why not include *Sovetskaia istoricheskaia entsiklopediia* (Soviet Historical Encyclopedia), one of the most comprehensive works of its kind (Moscow, 1961- , 15v. In progress)? Why not include *Teatral'naia entsiklopediia* (Encyclopedia of the Theatre) published in Moscow (1964-1967, 5v. and bibliographical supplement)? This omission is particularly glaring in view of the fact that such a substandard work as *The Penguin Dictionary of the Theatre* (BG 35) is included, albeit in its old edition (the new revised edition of this work was published in 1970).

Instead of continuing, let us simply say that errors in fact or interpretation pertaining to foreign works are rather numerous and that the selection policy of the guide in this area leaves much to be desired. The lack of editorial attention, however, is not limited to foreign reference books. Probably one of the best examples of somewhat embarrassing negligence is the entry for *Books in Print* (AA 473). Among other things, the entry repeats an old subtitle—"an author-title-series index to the Publishers' trade list annual." No, not any longer. BIP no longer serves as an index to PTLA, and this subtitle no longer appears on the title page. In addition, this fact was discussed in some depth in library literature, including *Library Journal*. The annotation remains unchanged from the old edition (AA 348) and the "fact" that BIP is an index to PTLA is again stated in the annotation. Added to the annotation in the ninth edition is a paragraph about *Books in Print Supplement, 1972-73. Caveant consules.*

In our review of the third supplement (*ARBA* 73, entry 5) we examined the section on philosophy. It might be appropriate to take a look at this section in the new edition. The field of philosophy is of a manageable size because there are simply not too many reference works published. Not counting entries for individual philosophers (BA 72-BA 93), this section contains 71 entries, 29 in English and 42 in other languages. Of the 29 English-language titles, 23 were published in this country. Considering the fact that so few books exist in this area, one might imagine that the editor had an easy task.

Apparently not. A few examples will illustrate some of the deficiencies in selection criteria; since we examined the selection of Soviet works earlier in this review, we will continue this approach. The only Soviet entry pertaining to philosophy is BA 62, Rozental' and Iudin's *Dictionary of Philosophy*, published in 1963 and translated into English by Progress Publishers (Moscow) in 1967. Its only claim to fame is probably this rather poor translation; though Soviet philosophical dictionaries are not numerous, this particular work is not only rather obsolete but it also shows a stronger than usual Soviet bias. No such criticism is indicated in the accompanying "annotation" of eight words. More substantial works, however, have been omitted, such as the comprehensive *Filosofskaiia entsiklopediia* (Philosophical Encyclopedia. Moscow, 1960-1970, 5v.) or even *Istoriia filosofii v SSSR* (History of Philosophy in the Soviet Union, Moscow, 1968-1971, 4v.). This is not a ready reference work but a comprehensive history; however, *Guide to Reference Books* includes such histories as Ueberweg's *Grundriss* (BA 67). We have searched in vain for at least one work on Marxist philosophy. Nothing, unless we want to count John Lachs's *Marxist Philosophy: A Bibliographical Guide* (CJ 241), which we found purely by accident in the political science section under "Communism and Socialism." Granted, Henry Thomas's *Biographical Encyclopedia of Philosophy* (Doubleday, 1965) was probably excluded because of its uneven treatment, but one would be hard pressed to find justification for exclusion of such standard works as *Philosophical Books* (1960- , a quarterly British reviewing service limited to books in English) or *Philosophischer Anzeiger* (1949/50- , a German reviewing journal that provides international coverage of current literature).

The coverage of dictionaries and encyclopedias in philosophy is no better. Among other things, there is no indication that the well-known *Encyclopedia of Philosophy* (BA 54) is now available also in a four-volume edition (at a much reduced price) and, here again, omissions of standard foreign works are numerous. Thus, one does not find here the standard Italian dictionary, Abbagnano's *Dizionario di filosofia* (Turin, 1961) or the monumental German work, Schmidt's *Philosophisches Wörterbuch*, first published in 1961 and now in its sixteenth edition. A smaller German work, namely Brugger's *Philosophisches Wörterbuch* (BA 48) is cited here but in its old fourth edition. To our knowledge, the eighth edition of this work was published in 1961. German contributions in philosophy are rather important, especially in the area

of reference sources. Since there is nothing here on Marxist philosophy, we might recommend for possible inclusion one of the best dictionaries on this subject, namely G. Klaus and M. Buhr's *Philosophisches Wörterbuch* (Leipzig, 1970, 2v.), now in its seventh edition. More recent works exist, but the coverage in *Guide to Reference Books* stops for all practical purposes with the year 1973, so it would be unfair to cite them.

Examining the coverage of individual philosophers shows a similar pattern. Out of the total of 22 works cited (a rather small number), several have been superseded by more recent works, and the number of philosophers represented is not exactly impressive (nothing on Hegel, Leibnitz, Locke, Sartre, Voltaire, etc.).

One final, more general comment, since we can assume that other reviewers will examine other sections of this new edition in detail. In our review of the second supplement (*ARBA* 71, entry 7), we indicated that most annotations are brief; they are descriptive but seldom critical. We also said that many titles listed in the main volume of Winchell are of only sentimental value and could be safely removed to an "historical volume." This comment seems even more valid with respect to this new edition. Apparently in order to accommodate more titles, many of the annotations are brief—sometimes to the point of being meaningless. They are also occasionally somewhat misleading. *Pro domo sua*, we may quote part of the annotation for *ARBA* (AA 380): "Offers descriptive and evaluative notes (many of them signed by contributors)...." In *ARBA* 76 the average length of these "notes" is approximately 250 words; but never mind this. It is a good place to stop.

In summation re this new edition: the paper is of good quality, margins are wide, and the book lies flat when opened. We also found no errors in the index. Sheehy's edition adequately maintains the long tradition of *Guide to Reference Books*, and this work can be safely recommended for libraries of all types. It will probably serve the uninitiated rather well. [R: LJ, 15 Dec 76, p. 2560]   Bohdan S. Wynar

55. Sheehy, Eugene P., ed. **Guide to Reference Books, Supplement.** 9th ed. With the assistance of Rita G. Keckeissen, and others. Chicago, American Library Association, 1980. 305p. index. $15.00pa. LC 79-20541. ISBN 0-8389-0294-4.

The main volume of this work, reviewed in *ARBA* 77 (entry 14), indicated that for all practical purposes the cut-off date was 1973. This supplement concentrates on works published between fall 1974 and fall 1978, including a number of earlier imprints as well as a few works published after fall 1978. According to the preface, "no attempt was made to set strict numerical limits for the individual sections of the *Supplement*, and a few categories may appear disproportionately long in relation to corresponding sections of the parent work. However, the great number of recently published volumes relating to women, ethnic groups, blacks, energy, and cinema studies, and the many publications inspired by our nation's bicentennial celebration have made inevitable a certain weighting of relevant sections" (p. vii). Over 3,000 entries are included (10,000 in the main volume), with a separate section on "Data Bases" new to this work. What probably will be disappointing to many users is again the fact that this standard work is so much behind schedule and at least two years of reference production are not represented here. Substantially improved are the sections on pure and applied sciences, compiled by Richard J. Dionne, Elizabeth E. Ferguson, and Robert C. Michaelson, all from Yale University. Apparently in order to accommodate more titles, many of the annotations are brief; they are descriptive but seldom critical. In general, the text is free of misspellings, although occasionally they occur in foreign languages. Thus, in entry AD 102 we find two errors (both in transliteration) – "Anhloukrains'ky" and "Kiiv." The following entry (AD 103) provides correct transliteration of "Kyiv."

In reviewing the main set we examined a number of topics and sections, among them philosophy. It might be appropriate to take a look at this section again. The field of philosophy is of a manageable size because there are simply not too many reference works published. In the supplement, this section contains 14 entries, 12 in English and 2 in other languages. Here we found under individual philosophers Gunter's work on Henry Bergson (BA 12) but not Lapointe's on Jean-Paul Sartre (both published by the Philosophy Documentation Center at Bowling Green University). Also omitted is Erickson's *Aristotle's Rhetoric*, published by Scarecrow in 1975. One of the most important publications in this field is *The American Philosophical Society Year Book* (see *ARBA* 76, entry 1105). In recent years this publication incorporated a number of very useful features, among them references to lengthy biographical memoirs of scholars who recently died, awards and prizes, and descriptive reports of significant research. This yearbook of the American Philosophical Society (founded in 1743 by Benjamin Franklin) is probably one of the most important reference sources in

philosophy, and it is somewhat disappointing not to see all updated information about this annual in the supplement. Apparently, in such a well-defined field as philosophy, it is almost impossible to provide a well-balanced coverage in such a general reference source as Sheehy's *Guide to Reference Books*. There are simply too many reference books published each year, and in order to cover them, one has to publish the guide in several volumes. As it is, the guide and its supplement adequately maintain the long tradition of Winchell and will serve rather well the uninitiated reader. [R: BL, 15 Apr 80, pp. 1177-78; LJ, July 80, p. 1502; WLB, Sept 80, p. 65]   Bohdan S. Wynar

56.   Sheehy, Eugene P., ed. **Guide to Reference Books, Second Supplement.** 9th ed. Chicago, American Library Association, 1982. 243p. index. $15.00pa. LC 82-1719. ISBN 0-8389-0361-4.

The first supplement to *Guide to Reference Books* was published in 1980 and reviewed in *ARBA* 81 (entry 3). The main volume was reviewed at some length in *ARBA* 77 (entry 14). The first supplement concentrated on works published between fall 1974 and fall 1978 (some 3,000 entries included). The second lists nearly 2,100 entries, most of them published during the 1978-80 period. According to the preface, "No attempt was made to assign 'quotas' to the individual sections or to balance the number of items in a given section of this supplement against that of a corresponding section of the 1980 volume. Rather, we have intended to make inclusion a matter of merit" (p. vii). *Sapienta sat.* Indeed, this is a long-standing policy of Winchell and now Sheehy, and enough was already said about some inconsistencies of this policy in our previous reviews. Here let me simply concentrate on positive things.

First of all, the time lag so evident in the publication of the main volume and the first supplement is now being significantly closed. A two-year gap is much better than a four- or six-year gap. Bibliographic accuracy is constantly improving and is really quite remarkable if one cares to compare Sheehy with Walford, especially the condensed version of Walford reviewed in the previous volume of *ARBA*. With few exceptions, form of entry corresponds to that found on Library of Congress printed cards or in MARC records. As in earlier editions, prices are provided in local currency, and occasionally only in United States dollars. As was done previously, annotations are brief and descriptive, containing numerous quotations from prefaces or listing partial tables of contents. On some occasions, short references to published reviews are provided, i.e., *Academic American Encyclopedia*, and hopefully this practice will be more fully developed in future editions. All in all, Sheehy reflects some of our best practices in compiling general bibliographic guides, and this supplement is a must purchase for all libraries that have the main volume.

Bohdan S. Wynar

57. Walford, A. J., ed. **Guide to Reference Material: Volume 3, Generalities, Languages, the Arts and Literature.** 3rd ed. London, Library Association; distr., Chicago, American Library Association, 1977. 710p. index. o.p. ISBN 0-85365-409-3.

The publication of this third volume completed the set in its third edition. The third edition of *Generalia, Language and Literature, the Arts* contains main entries for some 5,000 books, plus several hundred subsumed entries—"a total increase of about 15% on the 2nd edition of v.2 (1970), even allowing for excisions.... To help provide more critical annotations, comments from an increasing variety of reviewing journals, both general and special, have been added" (introduction, p. v).

The second edition of volume 3 (not volume 2, as indicated in this introduction) was reviewed at some length in *ARBA* 72 (entry 6). At that time, we indicated that the second edition constituted a 50 percent increase in corresponding sections of the first edition and its supplement. The total for the third edition, for all practical purposes, shows no net increase for titles covered. Indeed, some titles were added and others deleted, but most remain unchanged. Occasionally, this proves to be embarrassing. See, for example, the entry for *Books in Print* (p. 40), which indicates that this is "an author-title-series index" to the PTLA. All libraries in this country are well aware that this is no longer the case. Unfortunately, many of these "retained" annotations contain factual errors, occasionally even typographical errors—e.g., the entry for the most important Polish retrospective bibliography, Estreicher's *Bibliografia polska* (p. 24, error in imprint).

In examining several sections of the third volume, it appears that Walford covers practically the same number of American imprints as Sheehy (see *ARBA* 77, entry 14), but his coverage of British and European imprints is stronger. To some extent, this is even true of non-European titles, especially reference books published by developing countries. Walford's section on the Soviet Union (see "Russian Literature," pp. 610-14) provides more complete coverage than does Sheehy (20 titles). On the other hand, Sheehy's work is more accurate and provides a better index. Thus, it can be said that Sheehy and Walford's works supplement and complement each other. The quality of the third volume of *Guide to Reference Material* is somewhat disappointing compared with that of previous volumes, but we hope that this will be remedied in the next edition.

The fourth edition of this volume is scheduled for late 1986 (768p. $80.00).

Bohdan S. Wynar

58. Walford, A. J., ed. **Walford's Concise Guide to Reference Material.** London, Library Association; distr., Phoenix, Ariz., Oryx Press, 1981. 434p. index. $50.00. ISBN 0-85365-882-X.

The *Concise Guide* reduces Walford's three-volume *Guide to Reference Material* to one-sixth of its size in response to demand for a more portable version. Some 2,560 main entries and several hundred subsumed entries are included, with some items being listed for the first time. (Walford states that the cut-off date for inclusion was 29 March 1980.) Entries are arranged by the Universal Decimal Classification, and emphasize English-language and British publications. Size constraints made it necessary to eliminate all entries for "men of letters" with the exception of Shakespeare. In most cases, annotations remain their original length, although some of the very long descriptions have been condensed. Prices have been verified, whenever possible, in *British Books in Print, 1980* and *Books in Print, 1980-81*. (Prices appear in both pounds and dollars when available.) A thorough author, title, and subject index provides page references.

Because of the British bias of the *Concise Guide*, there are only 10 entries for U.S. history, compared to some 50 entries for British, Irish, and Scottish history. The "Political Parties" listing includes four titles on British parties and one on American politics. The British bias is visible throughout the volume: "Economics" comprises primarily British (and European) titles; "Government Publications" lists six British works and three American titles. This orientation is not unexpected, nor is it a fault—the user simply should be aware that it exists. (The introduction states the fact plainly.)

American users will probably continue to favor the three-volume set of *Guide to Reference Material* to access the full range of titles on the United States. However, *Best Reference Books 1970-1980* (Libraries Unlimited, 1981) presents 920 titles selected from *American Reference Books Annual*, providing substantial coverage of titles of particular concern to American audiences.

Janet H. Littlefield

59. Walford, A. J., ed. **Walford's Guide to Reference Material: Volume 1, Science & Technology.** 4th ed. With the assistance of Anthony P. Harvey and H. Drubba. London, Library Association; distr., Chicago, American Library Association, 1980. 697p. index. $55.00. ISBN 0-8389-3243-6.

Walford's *Guide*, a standard and well-known source to all librarians, was reviewed in some detail in previous volumes of *ARBA*. The third edition of the *Science & Technology* volume shows a somewhat better balance in terms of works covered than Sheehy's *Guide to Reference Books*, and it is certainly more comprehensive. A total of 4,300 items was included, plus a further 700 subsumed entries. The cutoff date for the third edition was April 1972.

The present edition covers about 5,000 entries, of which over 1,000 are subsumed. Among many new subjects and topics included in this edition, one should mention enlarged sections on biochemistry, environmental pollution, alternative technology, and microcomputers. The cutoff date for this edition was March 1979, and consequently, it provides more recent coverage in comparison to the main volume of *Guide to Reference Books*, compiled by Sheehy (cutoff date is 1973). In comparison to *Guide to Reference Books* and its supplement, Walford's guide contains longer and more evaluative annotations and is certainly much stronger not only for British titles but for other primarily Western European languages. Many annotations contain brief references to published reviews, with occasional notes to related titles. The index in this new edition is also somewhat improved, especially in terms of title entries. Occasional typographical errors or even omissions of certain standard titles should not detract from the overall usefulness of this standard work, which retains its well-established tradition and should be highly recommended for all academic institutions and special libraries in this country.

Bohdan S. Wynar

60. Walford, A. J., ed. **Walford's Guide to Reference Material: Volume 2, Social & Historical Sciences, Philosophy & Religion.** 4th ed. London, Library Association; distr., Chicago, American Library Association, 1982. 812p. index. $74.50. ISBN 0-85365-564-2.

This is the second volume of the fourth edition; the final volume, which completes the set, should be published in 1986. Volume 2 contains main entries for some 5,000 titles, plus approximately 2,000 subsumed entries. According to the introduction, this represents an increase of about 10 percent over the third edition of volume 2, published in 1975. Some of the sub-

jects highlighted are: minorities, industrial relations, women and society, social services, the European Economic Community, Parliament, education, aspects of less-developed countries, primary historical sources, and British local history. The guide is international in scope, but with an English-language emphasis. Reprints of older reference material, announcements of forthcoming works or volumes, "hidden" bibliographies appearing in periodicals or as parts of books, and entries for leading review journals continue to find a place in the fourth edition.

Bibliographical citations in Walford include UDC numbers and prices. Prices were taken from *Books in Print 1980/81*, *British Books in Print 1980*, and the French and German equivalents. United States prices and distributors are cited for the first time in the fourth edition. For other languages, prices are usually omitted. Annotations include helpful comments from a variety of reviewing journals, both general and special.

This volume contains a number of cross-references to volume 1, and volume 3 will probably use the same procedure, cross-referencing to volumes 1 and 2. Volume 3 will also contain an author, title, and subject index for all three volumes. The cut-off date for inclusion in this volume was April 1981, though a very few titles with later imprints were inserted at proof stage. Entries in Walford are not numbered, so the index is not as easy to use as that in its American counterpart. Because index references are to page numbers, the reader must spend a considerable amount of time trying to locate a needed item on a given page. It is particularly difficult to scan for the entries that are mentioned within annotations.

We examined the coverage of the religion section of this volume which consists of three parts: religion, Christianity, and non-Christian religions (pp. 31-79). According to our sample, there are about 360 main entries. Sheehy's edition of the guide contains 408 entries. Thus, allowing for subsumed entries in Walford, the number of entries is about the same in the two works. In terms of imprints, about one third of the titles in this section were published in Great Britain, about 15 percent were published in the United States, and the rest were published jointly or in other countries. This appears to be consistent with the rest of the volume.

How much does Walford overlap with Sheehy? We examined the area of philosophy, specifically encyclopedias and dictionaries, listed in Walford on pp. 4-6. A total of 18 dictionaries and encyclopedias are listed here with the following breakdown: nine titles in English

(American and British), three in German, two in French, and the balance in other languages. Sheehy's main volume lists 19 titles, 8 in English. Both volumes cover essential works, e.g., *The Encyclopedia of Philosophy* (1967 in 8v.) or Ritter's *Historisches Wörterbuch der Philosophie* (in progress). Sheehy omits a very important Soviet work, *Filosofskaiia entsiklopediia* (Moscow, 1960-70, 5v.) and both authors omit such works as Grooten's *New Encyclopedia of Philosophy*, an English translation from the Dutch, or Nauman's *Dictionary of Asian Philosophers* (1978). Walford shows a stronger coverage for European literature and longer annotations; Sheehy is better in providing bibliographical history of a given work, but seldom refers to related works.

As we said before, the index to Walford is not as useful as it should be. Although the introduction does not explicitly say so, there are no title entries in the index except for title main entries. A given author's works are listed under the author entry, but there is no actual title access. This very much limits the value of the index—a limitation that is reinforced by the sketchiness of the subject indexing. A cumulative subject index is projected for volume 3. It might be useful if a cumulative title index were also provided.

All in all, Walford's guide is a useful work, and the fact that most of the editorial work was done by one man is impressive.

Bohdan S. Wynar

61. Wynar, Bohdan S., ed. **American Reference Books Annual 1984. Volume 15.** Anna Grace Patterson and Carol Rasmussen, assistant eds. Littleton, Colo., Libraries Unlimited, 1984. 793p. index. $65.00. LC 75-120328. ISBN 0-87287-426-5; ISSN 0065-9959.

The appearances of the fifteenth volume of *ARBA* and of the third of the five-year cumulative indexes (1980-1984) provide a suitable occasion for some historical assessment a well as comment on the most recent issue.

There have been more than 25 reviews of *ARBA* since its first appearance in 1970. Some have been critical, but most have been favorable. Among the early accolades was inclusion in "Reference Books of 1970" (*LJ*, 15 Apr 71, p. 1326). Several of the early reviewers noted that *ARBA* complements, but does not replace, such standard sources as Winchell/Sheehy and Walford. The reviewer of *ARBA* 70 in *RQ* (Winter 70, p. 183) questioned the value of such a publication, on the grounds that reference books were reviewed elsewhere in a more timely fashion. By contrast, Frances Neel Cheney thought that it would be heavily used for selec-

tion and certain types of reference questions (*LQ*, Jan 71, pp. 73-74). In a generally favorable review praising *ARBA* 70 for its scope and timeliness (*LJ*, 15 Nov 70, p. 3887), William Katz complained about the two-volume format and the indexing. In his review of *ARBA* 71 (*LJ*, 1 Nov 71, p. 3581), Katz noted that both deficiencies had been corrected and recommended *ARBA* "without reservation." In a similar vein, Cheney noted improvements in *ARBA* 71 and called attention to the number of reference books reviewed only in *ARBA* (*WLB*, Sept 71, p. 83). In a short annotation in the *Papers* of the Bibliographical Society of America (July 71, p. 340), hope was expressed that the coverage would be expanded to other countries and languages. The first three volumes of *ARBA* were reviewed together in *Booklist* (15 Jan 73, pp. 453-54). Mention was made of the lack of a definition of reference books and the inclusion of some titles that might not really qualify as well as some titles too specialized for most libraries. Favorable mention was made of *ARBA*'s comprehensiveness of coverage, fullness of bibliographical description, accuracy of indexing, and citation of other reviews. However, the reviewer felt that *ARBA*'s annotations "do not necessarily provide accurate appraisals." By contrast, the review of *ARBA* 73 in *RSR* (July 73, p. 11) disagreed with the somewhat "lukewarm" review in *Booklist*, contending that the reviews in *ARBA* "more often than not give accurate evaluations" and arguing that the inclusiveness of *ARBA* was a strength rather than a weakness. In reviewing volumes 1-4, Bonnie Collier (*RSR*, Oct 74, p. 56) noted substantial improvements, but expressed concern about the placement of some titles within the classification system. Annotations in *Choice* for *ARBA* 72 (Mar 73, p. 55) and *ARBA* 74 (Sept 74, p. 907) were both favorable, though note was made in the latter that some citations to *Choice* reviews had been missed, perhaps because they appeared in subject sections. *ARBA* 74 and the 1970-1974 index were reviewed together in *Booklist* (15 July 75, pp. 1196-97), with concern still expressed about lack of a statement of criteria and the "unevenness in character and quality of annotations," though the latter concern was modified by the statement: "For the major subject fields, reviews are signed by contributors, and the majority of these annotations are very competently prepared and informative." Expansion of the list of journals from which reviews were cited was praised and the five-year index was assessed as "well executed."

By the mid-1970s, *ARBA* had established a solid reputation as a comprehensive source of reviews of American reference books. Expanded coverage of librarianship was noted in a review of *ARBA* 75 (*LQ*, Oct 75, p. 459). In reviewing *ARBA* 76 (*JAL*, Jan 77, pp. 3326-27), Judith Mistichelli noted the addition of ethnic studies as a positive feature and commented favorably on the indexing and completeness of bibliographic data. Although she thought the reviews had improved, she considered that too many were "purely descriptive annotations." While generally praising the thoroughness of coverage, she noted some omissions (e.g., *American Humanities Index*) and suggested that the editors "might also attempt to increase contact with university presses and research centers." In reviewing *ARBA* 79 (*JAL*, Jan 80, p. 348), Mistichelli mentioned "a noticeable increase in the critical tone of reviews, in regard to both favorable and unfavorable commentary" and praised the effort to match books with reviewers' expertise. Noting the omission of G. K. Hall publications, she raised the issue of whether reviewers might be asked to seek these out in libraries if the publisher chose not to supply review copies. She repeated her earlier suggestion about increased contact with university presses, research centers, and small presses and added a new suggestion—"the review of computerized bibliographic data bases and microfiche-film sources." The most recent review in *Booklist* (1 June 83, p. 1296) is primarily a description of *ARBA* 82 but concludes that *ARBA* "provides comprehensive coverage of reference books published in the U.S. and offers critical evaluations by known reviewers."

ARBA 84 exhibits the characteristics of its immediate predecessors, with reviews of 1,534 reference books in 43 subject categories and a combination of form and subject subdivisions. (The total number of reference titles reviewed since *ARBA* began in 1970 is 25,349.) *ARBA* 84 includes a new chapter, "Automation and Data Processing," devoted to reviews of print sources (not databases) and including sections on software and microcomputers. There is a need for more comprehensive reviewing of databases than *RQ* has thus far been able to provide. Should *ARBA* undertake this new task—or continue to do what it now does so well?

A. Robert Rogers

7 Bibliographies

62. American Society for Information Science and ERIC Clearinghouse on Library and Information Sciences. **Library and Information Sciences: An ERIC Bibliography.** New York, CCM, 1972. 487p. index. $11.50. LC 72-82741. SBN 8409-0334-0.

Lists the acquisitions of the Clearinghouse on Library and Information Sciences since its inception in 1967. The 3,000 annotated entries cover documents announced in *Research in Education* (*RIE*) from 1968 to 1971, as well as journal articles indexed in *Current Index to Journals in Education* (*CIJE*) from 1969 to 1971. The arrangement is by ED accession number sequence. The bibliography consists of four main parts: ERIC documents, ERIC journal articles, subject index, and author index. Ordering instructions for ERIC documents are included in the introductory pages.

63. Barr, Larry J., Haynes McMullen, and Steven G. Leach, comps. **Libraries in American Periodicals before 1876: A Bibliography with Abstracts and an Index.** Jefferson, N.C., McFarland, 1983. 426p. index. $65.00. LC 83-780. ISBN 0-89950-066-8.

This bibliography includes articles in periodicals about libraries in the world, the United States, Europe, and other countries and areas. It extends Harry Cannons's *Bibliography of Library Economy from 1876 to 1920* (1920; B. Franklin, 1971, repr. ed.) backward, as far as periodicals published in the United States are concerned. The individual bibliographic entries contain titles of periodicals used in the *Union List of Serials*, and an abstract is written for every article. Very few illustrations are included in the articles, but when they are present they are noted in the abstracts and in the separate list of illustrations. A few articles have been included that are not about libraries or librarians;

these are the texts or summaries of lectures given before members of library associations. Six kinds of entries in a single alphabet are included in the index: authors; types of libraries; cities or other places; names of individual libraries; librarians, donors, and other persons prominently mentioned in the articles; and a few ideas (the educational value of libraries) or events (fires in libraries). A very valuable reference tool for larger libraries. [R: JAL, Nov 83, p. 298]

Ina J. Weis

64. Besterman, Theodore. **Bibliography, Library Science, and Reference Books: A Bibliography of Bibliographies.** Totowa, N.J., Rowman & Littlefield, 1971. 271p. (Besterman World Bibliographies). o.p. LC 70-29437. ISBN 0-87471-041-3.

This is one of several works derived from the author's *World Bibliography of Bibliographies* (5v., 4th ed., Lausanne: Societas Bibliographica, 1965-1966) and released by the publisher as subject bibliographies. The work consists of brief entries for a comprehensive list of separately published, library science oriented bibliographies from many countries and languages. The number of entries included in each cited work is noted.

65. Ducote, Richard L. **Learning Resource Centers: Best of ERIC; A Selected, Annotated Bibliography.** Syracuse, N.Y., ERIC Clearinghouse on Information Resources, 1977. 70p. o.p.

This bibliography updates *The Best of ERIC: Learning Resources Centers* (March 1973) by annotating 192 selected titles on the topic that have been produced since 1972. Entries are grouped under four major categories—elementary and secondary schools, colleges and universities, personnel and training, and special listings—and subdivided by topical headings. Full bibliographical data, ED number, and an abstract are given for each entry.

66. Dyer, Esther R., and Pam Berger. **Public, School, and Academic Media Centers: A Guide to Information Sources.** Detroit, Gale, 1981. 237p. index. (Books, Publishing, and Libraries Information Guide Series, Vol. 3; Gale Information Guide Library). $60.00. LC 74-11554. ISBN 0-8103-1286-7.

This volume provides excellent entry into the literature of the years 1970-78 that pertains to planning, management, services, collection development, architecture, and equipment in media centers. Quality, uniqueness, currency, and accessibility are said to have served as criteria for admission to this roster of some 500 books, periodicals, and other sources. Brief annotations clearly pinpoint the usefulness of each entry. They are grouped in 24 sections, among which copyright, cable regulations, budgeting and funding (private and public), program evaluation, equipment evaluation, and intellectual freedom are particularly noteworthy.

The trouble is not with content, which is fine, but with a publishing process that introduces a two-year gap between compilation of data and their publication. As a result, some information is dated (e.g., *Audiovisual Instruction* changed its name to *Instructional Innovator*, EPIE changed its address, *Media Mix* ceased publication); some authors are represented by their earlier works only (e.g., Wehmeyer, J. Brown); and some subjects are neglected (e.g., microcomputers). But the work does provide the tools for overcoming that lag with a listing of over 100 periodicals that cover all or some aspects of media center operation. Other handy features are glossaries of terms applicable to audio, film, overhead projection, filmstrips, and slides, a list of abbreviations, and one of media organizations. A few typos and omissions in indexing were noted. [R: BL, 1 Sept 82, p. 67; Emerg Lib, Sept 81, p. 21]

Mary R. Sive

67. **FID Publications: An 80 Year Bibliography, 1895-1975.** The Hague, International Federation for Documentation, 1975. 94p. index. (FID, No. 531). o.p. ISBN 92-66-00531-2.

The present edition updates the previous cumulation for 1895-1970. It includes 67 additional items published in the intervening five years. The bibliography inventories a total of 587 titles ranging from the various national editions of the Universal Decimal Classification (UDC) schemes, to bibliographies, reports, yearbooks, and directories brought out under the aegis of FID and its specialized committees. The material is organized in a sequence of five-year periods without any specific order, which makes it almost useless as a finding tool. An effort was made in the present issue to facilitate its use by means of a reasonably detailed subject index and a personal author index. A separate committee index helps identify the publications emanating from the organization's eight specialized subsidiary bodies, each having its own headquarters and publishing program. For the first time, an index to UDC publications and a selected list of unnumbered FID publications has been added. Of the total 587 entries, some 160 titles are listed in the *FID Publications Catalogue* currently on sale.

This bibliography is significant as a document reflecting the concerns, activities, and accomplishments of FID in the past 80 years. It belongs in the libraries of schools of library and information science, as well as in collections devoted to international organizations.

Michael Keresztesi

68. **International Bibliography of the Book Trade and Librarianship, 1976-1979.** 12th ed. Munich, New York, K. G. Saur; distr., Detroit, Gale, 1981. 692p. index. (Handbook of International Documentation and Information, Vol. 2). $95.00. ISBN 3-598-20516-3; ISSN 0071-3627.

This book contains 9,000 titles, attempting to cover as comprehensively as possible all the new literature (1976-1979) on the history of script and printing, including bibliographies, manuscript listings, and catalogs; the history of the book trade, including the study of reading habits and bibliophily; professional literature on all aspects of the book manufacturing industries, publishing, and the retail book trade and its history; commemorative volumes produced by publishers and booksellers; and the major booktrade catalogs and "books-in-print" listings. Publications on librarianship and related fields, particularly in the field of information science and archives, are selectively included.

This bibliography covers only monographs, although some small brochures, mimeographed publications, and other nontrade materials are included. The entries are arranged first according to continent: Europe, Africa, the Americas, Asia, and Australia and Oceania. Over one-half of the book is devoted to European entries. Almost one-half of the rest of the book covers titles in the United States. Under the continents, the book is further divided by country, alphabetically according to the English spelling. Under each country, the titles are entered according to a systematic subject arrangement, which is outlined under the directions on how to use the book. Finally, the titles are arranged alphabetically under each subject heading.

Many of the non-European countries have only one or two entries, mainly a general bibliography or catalog. Each title is entered under the country in which it was published or reprinted, except if the material is a library catalog published or reprinted by a publisher outside of the country of the library. Then it is regarded as a publication of the country of that publisher.

There are no cross-references, and each title is listed only once. An index of authors and editors and a limited subject index in English are provided.

Each entry contains full bibliographic information, including ISBN or ISSN and the approximate price. Additional information is provided for multivolume works. There are descriptive translations of the title in either German or English for material in the lesser-known languages. The Yugoslav titles were not translated, even though Serbo-Croatian is generally considered a lesser-known language. The entries under the other Slavic-speaking countries did have translations for the titles.

Mohammed M. Aman

69. Jordan, Anne Harwell, and Melbourne Jordan, eds. **Cannons' Bibliography of Library Economy, 1876-1920: An Author Index with Citations.** Metuchen, N.J., Scarecrow, 1976. 473p. o.p. LC 76-3711. ISBN 0-8108-0918-4.

For the period from 1876 through 1920, H. G. T. Cannons's *Bibliography of Library Economy* is the major "classified index to professional periodical literature in the English language" for these 44 years. It includes "articles published in the leading periodicals devoted to librarianship in the United States and Great Britain, as well as a few monographs." *Cannons's* presents the citations in a subject or classified arrangement, and within each grouping the material is arranged chronologically by date of publication. This was a useful arrangement for historians, but for others it meant that checking through *Cannons's* was a painstaking and laborious task.

Anne and Melbourne Jordan have prepared *An Author Index with Citations* to *Cannons's*, a supplementary publication that serves "to provide further access to this material." Their work is arranged in two major units: (1) a list of publications indexed and (2) an alphabetical list by author's surname. Thus, the writings of Putnam, Dewey, Billings, Dana, Cutter, Spofford, Williamson, and other "historically

figures in librarianship" are now more easily accessible to students and researchers. Each entry contains the following data: author's surname, initials, title of article or monograph, name of periodical, volume number, and pagination. It would have been helpful if the date of issue had been included in these citations. However, this is a useful reference tool for librarians, library educators, library school students, and library historians.

John Burke states in the introduction that "the Jordans have improved upon the indexing of this important bibliography. Corrections were made, whenever possible, to the existing material appearing in *Cannons'*, and a considerable number of incomplete and blind entries were rescued with appropriate changes. This book as a result, is a genuine supplement to Cannons' *Bibliography of Library Economy*, as well as a tool which makes Cannons' indexing accessible to the profession." [R: LJ, 15 Nov 76, p. 2152] Paul A. Winckler

70. Kilgour, Frederick G. **The Library and Information CumIndex.** Los Altos, Calif., R&D Press, 1976. 722p. (The Information Access Series, Vol. 7). o.p. LC 72-86076. ISBN 0-88274-006-7.

This computer-produced cumulation of more than 90,000 back-of-the-book index entries from 96 selected English-language books on library and information science provides single-source access to works covering all aspects of librarianship. Books were chosen for their accuracy, scope, and depth of information. Unindexed volumes were, of course, excluded.

Alphabetical lists of the indexed books appear inside the front and back covers, and following the index is a list of books giving author, title, edition, place of publication, publisher, date, and Library of Congress call number, arranged by book code used in the *CumIndex*.

This book is volume seven of a series of 14 indexes; other volumes cover statistics and probability, the Civil War, operations research and management science, public health, computer science, econometrics, and applied mechanics. They furnish single-source access to the literature of these fields, within the boundaries noted above. [R: C&RL, Jan 77, p. 72]

Richard Palmer

71. Lilley, Dorothy B., and Rose Marie Badough. **Library and Information Science: A Guide to Information Sources.** Detroit, Gale, 1982. 151p. bibliog. index. (Books, Publishing, and Libraries Information Guide Series, Vol. 5;

Gale Information Guide Library). $60.00. LC 82-962. ISBN 0-8103-1501-7.

The authors of this guide to information sources in library and information science state their purposes of compiling it in the "Summary and Epilogue": "1) to alert library and information science scholars to new developments that affect search strategy, 2) to offer examples of steps in the search process that assist an individual in conducting economical, systematic searches, 3) to provide a listing of information sources by form, and 4) to provide a listing of information sources by type of work." The book is organized into four parts, according to these four purposes or objectives. One wishes that the statement of purpose had appeared at the beginning rather than at the end of the book, so that the reader could quickly grasp the authors' general approach.

Part 1 offers several short overviews of new developments affecting search strategy, including bibliometrics, citation indexes, and online retrieval. Part 2 discusses search strategy models as outlined in the literature. Parts 3 and 4 describe specific reference tools useful in searching out information, first by form (e.g., research studies, periodicals, books, and government publications), and then by type (e.g., guides to the literature; indexing, abstracting, and database services; annuals and other serials; reviewing sources; and bibliographies). Included are more than 100 titles, each briefly annotated, which, according to the authors "are needed to maintain bibliographic control of the literature."

This guide is fairly successful in covering the major bibliographical tools which permit access to library science literature, and in providing a basic orientation to research techniques and innovations. It will be most useful to the neophyte, who would benefit most from this book by treating it as a research guide rather than a guide to the literature. [R: JAL, July 82, p. 186; LJ, Aug 82, p. 1391; RQ, Summer 82, p. 419]   Heather Cameron

72. MacCafferty, Maxine, comp. **Library-Information Science: Bibliographies, Guides, Reviews, Surveys.** London, Aslib, 1976. 104p. index. (Aslib Bibliography, No. 3). o.p. ISBN 0-85142-087-7.

This selective guide contains 484 annotated references on bibliographies, guides, reviews, and surveys in librarianship and information science, drawn from 80 English-language monographs, periodicals, or reports and covering the period from July 1973 through December 1975. Topics covered are education in library and information science, library and information

workers, library and information science, libraries, subject specialisms, other specialisms, and 40 subtopics under these major headings. Third in a series of Aslib bibliographies compiled by Maxine MacCafferty, this publication has both an author index and a subject index. Most of the references are to materials held in the Aslib library and are available for loan.

Richard Palmer

73. Magnotti, Shirley. **Library Science Research, 1974-1979.** Troy, N.Y., Whitston Publishing, 1983. 140p. $15.00. LC 75-8232. ISBN 0-87875-235-8.

A continuation of the author's previous lists (1975, 1976) of library science theses issued by the same publisher — *Master's Theses in Library Science, 1960-1969* (see *ARBA* 76, entry 126) and *Master's Theses in Library Science, 1970-1974* (see *ARBA* 78, entry 130) — this latest compilation has been expanded to include some 200 thesis titles and about 550 research reports accepted in lieu of theses. Altogether some 4,000 unannotated titles are now available in the three works. Arranged alphabetically by author's last name, the entries include the title of the work, the institution that accepted it, and the date. Part 2 is a subject index that is arranged by broad subject categories assisted by liberal use of *see* references. The institutions, some 40 for all volumes, from which the items were drawn appear in an appendix. This work will be of some use for institutions requiring an exhaustive approach to formal, academic research in library science. [R: LJ, 15 Sept 83, p. 1777]

Donald G. Davis, Jr.

75. Schlachter, Gail A., and Dennis Thomison. **Library Science Dissertations, 1973-1981: An Annotated Bibliography.** Littleton, Colo., Libraries Unlimited, 1982. 414p. index. (Research Studies in Library Science, No. 18). $50.00. LC 82-17172. ISBN 0-87287-299-8.

This is the supplement to *Library Science Dissertations, 1925-1972: An Annotated Bibliography* (Libraries Unlimited, 1974, o.p.). At the time it was published, the base volume represented the most significant increase in access to library science dissertations as well as to library science-related dissertations (e.g., education, communications, information services) to appear in over a decade. After systematically compiling 660 entries by drawing upon listings in *Library Science Dissertations, 1925-1959: An Annotated Bibliography of Doctoral Studies, Dissertation Abstracts International, Library Literature, Library Quarterly,* and *Doctoral Dissertations in Library Science* (a University

Microfilms pamphlet), the authors initiated a survey of the dissertations' authors. Questionnaires were sent in order to obtain information that could be used to prepare informative annotations.

In this supplement more than 1,000 doctoral dissertations in library science and related fields, which were accepted by academic institutions in the United States and Canada, have been annotated. Entries are arranged chronologically by year of acceptance, following the format established in the base volume. Additional access is provided by author and subject indexes. Annotations are generally included for each entry, detailing purpose, procedures used, findings, conclusions, and recommendations. Bibliographic information provides the author's name, degree received, degree-granting institution, year of acceptance, and complete title of the study. In addition, the number of pages and the University Microfilms order number are specified where available. Completing the volume is a statistical description of the dissertations, encompassing the sex of the author, year completed, degree received, institution attended, and research methodology employed. [R: JAL, July 83, p. 172]   Susan Kohlman

76.   Schutze, Gertrude. **Information and Library Science Source Book: A Supplement to Documentation Source Book.** Metuchen, N.J., Scarecrow, 1972. 492p. index. $18.00. LC 72-1157. ISBN 0-8108-0466-2.

In 1965 Scarecrow published *Documentation Source Book*, covering organization and management of libraries, technical services, information services, etc. This supplement, with a similar structure, adds some 2,000 books, articles, and reports published from mid-1964 through 1969. All entries are annotated, and there is a subject and author index. Like the main volume, it is a practical guide to materials pertaining to management of libraries and should be of some assistance to the uninitiated. [R: BL, 15 Jan 73, p. 455; CLW, Apr 73, p. 555; C&RL, July 73, p. 318; LJ, 1 Jan 73, p. 53]

77.   Stevens, Norman D., and Nora B. Stevens, eds. **Author's Guide to Journals in Library & Information Science.** New York, Haworth Press, 1982. 183p. index. (Author's Guide to Journals in Library and Information Science). $24.95. LC 80-20964. ISBN 0-917724-13-5.

The main section of this book contains detailed information about some 150 major American, Canadian, British, and international library and information science journals. Forty-

seven separate pieces of information (e.g., editorial policy and review process; audience; publication time lag; reprint policy; etc.) were gathered from a questionnaire. There is also a separate section that lists names and addresses only for approximately 50 journals for which no questionnaires were returned. All entries are arranged alphabetically by title with an association, keyword, and subject index. In addition, the Stevenses have included brief but quite useful comments on how to write a journal article and have outlined the publication process.

At least two comparable works have been published: Peter Hernon's *Library and Library-related Publications* (Libraries Unlimited, 1973), which is now outdated, and Mary Ann Bowman's *Library and Information Science Journals and Serials* (Westport, Conn., Greenwood Press, 1985). These works are useful directories for the librarian interested in getting articles published. However, for most libraries the *Directory of Publishing Opportunities in Journals and Periodicals* (5th ed., Marquis Academic Media, 1981), which includes similar information for all academic disciplines, including library and information science, is a more prudent purchase. [R: JAL, Sept 82, p. 247; LJ, July 82, p. 1305; RQ, Fall 82, p. 88]

Alan Edward Schorr and Annette Pekarek

78.   Taylor, Peter J., ed. **Library and Information Studies in the United Kingdom and Ireland, 1950-1974: An Index to Theses.** London, Aslib, 1976. 69p. index. o.p. ISBN 0-85142-085-0.

This useful index compiles, in one list, all theses in professional education for librarianship and information science which have been accepted for higher degrees (masters, doctorate, and the research bachelors) by library schools or other departments of the universities in the United Kingdom. The two major sources used in the compilation were Aslib's *Index to Theses* and the *Library Association Yearbook*. Other sources of information included the *Library Association Record, Library and Information Bulletin,* and domestic lists of dissertations and theses published by individual universities.

The index is valuable as a source of information about completed studies, as a basis for future work, and as a guide to avoid unnecessary duplication of research effort. Arranged chronologically by date of completion, entries include author, institution, title, degree awarded, and year of award. The index does not list any theses completed after 1974, since that year marks the beginning of the *RADIALS Bulletin*, which systematically assembles information

about research in an effort to provide bibliographic control of research in librarianship and
information studies. Martha Boaz

79. Wasserman, Paul, ed. **Library Bibliographies and Indexes: A Subject Guide to Resource
Material Available from Libraries, Information
Centers, Library Schools and Library Associations in the United States and Canada.** Detroit,
Gale, 1975. 301p. $80.00. LC 74-26741. ISBN
0-8103-0390-6.

This book's progenitor was Ireland's *Local
Indexes in American Libraries* (Boston, Faxon,
1947). That little book was very serviceable for
several years after its publication. Its clear and
eminently reasonable purpose was to call to the
attention of librarians myriad locally produced
bibliographies and indexes that were totally
lacking in bibliographic control. In adapting the
Ireland idea to the 1970s, Wasserman et al. have
swollen it out of all recognition to the original.

Questionnaires were sent to "more than
12,000 libraries and information centers, library
schools and library associations in the U.S. and
Canada," asking each to identify "their
separately issued bibliographies and indexes and
any continuing series or continuations devoted
exclusively or primarily to bibliographic contributions." Among the libraries and information centers canvassed were the National
Library of Medicine, all of the ERIC Clearinghouses, the Library of Congress, the Institute
for Scientific Information, and the National
Agricultural Library. The bibliographic series of
all of these august institutions are duly entered
repeatedly throughout the book under various
subject headings.

Here the abrupt departure from the clear
and simple Ireland model is most evident.
Ireland was concerned with bringing to
librarians' awareness truly obscure but potentially important near-print or manuscript bibliographic compilations. The Library of Congress
and the ERIC Clearinghouses hardly qualify as
"local institutions." They have excellent
"presses" and fine announcement and distribution channels.

Further difficulties stem from the system of
subject analysis that is used. There are insufficient cross-references and detailed subject
breakdowns, with the result that some entries
are retrievable only with great difficulty.

Finally, a brief note on the typography is in
order. The margins and the internal spacing are
overly generous, suggesting that a visually
more agreeable compression could have been
achieved. [R: Choice, Nov 75, p. 1146; RQ, Fall
75, pp. 83-84; WLB, Sept 75, p. 77]

Richard A. Gray

8 Indexes

80. **Library Literature: An Index to Library and Information Science.** New York, H. W. Wilson, 1936- . Bimonthly with annual cumulation. Sold on service basis. LC 36-27468. ISSN 0024-2373.

H. W. Wilson's *Library Literature* was first published in 1936, indexing library literature for the period 1933-1935. Actually *Library Literature* has a much longer tradition: it began as a continuation of indexing efforts by ALA published during 1921-1932 under the same title that, in turn, was a continuation (supplement) of H. G. T. Cannons's *Bibliography of Library Economy* covering the years 1876-1920. Along with *Information Science Abstracts* (1966-) and *Library and Information Science Abstracts* (1969-), *Library Literature* provides rather comprehensive coverage of library and information science materials and is familiar to and used by most professional librarians and information specialists.

As one would expect, at first the coverage of professional literature in this indexing service was probably not adequate (e.g., 20 to 30 periodicals in the 1940s and 60 to 70 in the 1960s). This problem was discussed at the Albany conference on bibliographic control (19-20 April 1968) sponsored by the Library Education Division of ALA and at a number of subsequent meetings. By the 1970s, the coverage of library and information science materials in *Library Literature* was fairly impressive. In addition to over 200 periodicals including many foreign titles, it covered books and other monographic material, pamphlets, library theses and dissertations, films, filmstrips, microfilms, microcards, and a significant number of research papers. Now, on the average, about 600 books and pamphlets are indexed in *Library Literature* each year. Accessions of the ERIC/CIR (Clearinghouse on Information Resources of the Educational Resources Information Center), however, have been dropped since 1976.

The coverage of periodicals in library science is complete, including more important announcements, letters to the editor, obituaries, and significant appointments. The format of entry closely follows that of other Wilson indexes. All titles are provided with full bibliographical citations—and translations if the title is foreign. Only nonlibrary science periodicals included in other Wilson indexing services are covered more selectively. The 1983 cumulation indexes 211 titles, including 130 domestic (61.6 percent) and 81 foreign. The time lag evident in indexing periodicals seems to be significant primarily for foreign titles. Thus, for example, according to our sampling, nationally known periodicals published in this country (*Library Journal, American Libraries,* or *Wilson Library Bulletin*) have a time lag of only one to two months. Regional publications or subject-oriented periodicals (published in the United States) show a somewhat greater time lag, averaging between three and seven months. Significant time lag is shown with foreign periodicals averaging from one to three years, sometimes four (*Bogens Verden* and *Bibliotekar'*).

Entries for book and nonbook material are arranged in one alphabet by author and specific subject headings, with adequate cross-references. There is a "Checklist of Monographs Cited for the First Time in *Library Literature*," which is published in bimonthly issues but unfortunately not in the cumulative editions. A useful feature in *Library Literature* is a separate listing of book reviews by main entry, with the name of reviewer indicated. Reviews of audiovisual materials and periodicals are not separately listed and appear only in the main body of the index.

Generally speaking, *Library Literature* is a comprehensive and well-executed indexing service. With the exception of some new and many regional periodicals and newsletters, it indexes the most important periodicals published in this country and abroad. The coverage of monographic material is somewhat weaker. Probably only about 60 percent of books and pamphlets published in this country are indexed here, as indicated by some samplings we did in comparing the coverage of *Library Literature* with materials reviewed in *American Reference Books*

Annual. The coverage of foreign material is less than adequate: approximately 10 percent of the books published in Western Europe and only a token coverage of developing countries and Eastern Europe. Nevertheless, the impressive number of 10,000 citations each year is quite encouraging and with constant progress in automation, *Library Literature* in its online version will continue to serve our profession well, providing timely and accurate information.

Bohdan S. Wynar

9 Dictionaries and Encyclopedias

81. **ALA World Encyclopedia of Library and Information Services.** Robert Wedgeworth, ed.; Joel Lee, associate ed. Chicago, American Library Association, 1980. 601p. illus. $95.00. LC 80-10912. ISBN 0-8389-0305-3.

From "Academic Libraries" to "Zimbabwe Rhodesia," the *ALA World Encyclopedia of Library and Information Services* proposes to "inform and educate" students, practitioners, and the public about the field of librarianship at the international level. Following the inception of the *ALA Yearbook*, first published in 1976, the yearbook editorial staff sought an international perspective, but considered that the breadth and scope of such coverage demanded knowledge of history as well as the present status and condition of libraries, archives, and other information services in many countries. For these reasons, the new encyclopedia was conceived in 1976 and published in 1980.

This reference tool includes 452 articles, 700,000 words, 364 contributors from 145 countries, 33 editorial advisers, 300 (black and white) illustrations, and 144 statistical tables. Articles on librarianship in various countries of the world, on major historical periods, on the library as an institution, on the theory and practice of librarianship, and biographies are covered in average lengths of more than 1,000 words. Contributors were "selected for their knowledge, experience, and professional or scholarly achievements [that] lend impressive authority to the *ALA Encyclopedia*." A weakness of the encyclopedia is the differing levels of contributors' expertise. As an example, articles on library education: comparative; curriculum; history; and specialization (pp. 320-30), written by four different authors, vary in documentation and treatment. Two are well written and

scholarly in nature, while the other two are speculative, superficial in nature, and cursory in content.

The outline of contents is organized in five principal divisions: the library in society; the library as an institution; theory and practice of librarianship; education and research; and international library, information, and bibliographic organizations. Fritz Milkau's *Handbuch der Bibliothekswissenschaft, The Encyclopedia of Library and Information Science*, edited by Kent, Lancour, and Daily, and *The Dictionary of American Library Biography*, published by Libraries Unlimited, are mentioned for assistance in planning and setting standards for publishing the encyclopedia. A "Parallel Index" in the margins throughout the volume accompanies articles and provides the reader with other references.

As a new single-volume encyclopedia in the field of librarianship, this is a selectively needed item in any reference collection. The price may prohibit purchase by small libraries with limited budgets. Larger libraries may also have Thomas Landau's *Encyclopedia of Librarianship* (3rd rev. ed., Hafner Publishing, 1966, 484p.), now somewhat dated. The emphasis in this work is definitely on Great Britain. Most entries vary from one sentence to several pages, depending on the relative importance of a given topic. [R: C&RL, Sept 80, pp. 450-54; Choice, Sept 80, p. 61; JAL, Sept 80, pp. 227-29]

Donald D. Foos and Bohdan S. Wynar

82. Clason, W. E., comp. **Elsevier's Dictionary of Library Science, Information and Documentation.** rev. ed. Amsterdam, New York, Elsevier Scientific Publishing, 1977. 708p. $103.75. ISBN 0-444-41475-4.

Clason prefaces the dictionary with a rather vague discussion of his criteria for inclusion: "If one takes the position that a document is an object that carries information and thus that the term covers not only the clay tablets of antiquity but also the most modern encyclopedia, then clearly the inclusion of the various fields in this dictionary is completely justified. For this reason, the author has taken the somewhat unusual step of listing specific documents." There are 5,439 English/American entries number-keyed to French, Spanish, Italian, Dutch, German, and Arabic entries. Among the terms chosen are 14 advertising-related entries, parts of speech, computer logic, kinds of languages, complex grammatical terms, and a wide-ranging choice of other items, e.g., *sell* (to) by auction, census, and casebook (the latter defined as "a book containing the names of patients treated in a hospital and their treatment"). Some of the definitions are unusual: *compilator* is glossed as "the person who compiles a work"; *compiler, compiling program* (US), *compiling programme* (GB) is "a program(me) designed to transform program(me)s expressed in terms of one language into equivalent program(me)s expressed in terms of a computer language or a language of similar form." *Compile* (to) is "to construct a written or printed work out of materials collected from various sources." Thus, caution is advisable in using the definitions of English/American terms, but the dictionary will serve a useful function as a multilingual thesaurus. [R: AB, 8 Sept 80, p. 1332]

Deborah Jane Brewer

83. Encyclopedia of Library and Information Science. Allen Kent, Harold Lancour, and others, eds. New York, Marcel Dekker, 1968-83. 35v. $65.00/vol. **Supplements.** 1983- . LC 68-31232.

Originally *Encyclopedia of Library and Information Science* was projected to comprise 18 olumes, with the first volume published in 1968. This projection was revised several times; finally the main set was completed in 35 volumes in 1983, including a competently produced two-volume author and subject index. Beginning with 1983, two supplementary volumes have been published, with each volume arranged in a separate alphabet. Now it is projected that two supplementary volumes will be issued every year to update articles already published and to discuss new topics not included in the main set. According to the title page of the supplementary volumes, Jay E. Daily no longer serves as an executive editor and Allen Kent, who started this encyclopedia with the late Harold Lancour, assumes the position of sole executive editor. It

probably should be noted that Allen Kent was also one of three executive editors of *Encyclopedia of Computer Science and Technology*, also published by Marcel Dekker (16v., 1975-81). As is well known, the *Encyclopedia of Library and Information Science* has a long history of preparation, with 32 prominent librarians on an advisory board and several hundred contributors, practically from all over the world, including the Soviet Union, Western Europe, and developing countries. This encyclopedia was reviewed or annotated in *ARBA* on several occasions. The set was favorably received by our profession at large. Some criticism made earlier may still be valid today and in this review we will try to summarize some of the major points.

The purpose of the encyclopedia is clearly stated in the preface to the first volume: "The emphasis has been, throughout, on depth of treatment. While contributors were urged to stress basic information, they were likewise encouraged to express their evaluative opinions as well, wherever possible, to suggest and indicate future trends as they saw them.... The editors are ... committed to a 'one world' concept of their science. To this end, the approach has been strongly international.... A more accurate description of the basic editorial policy would be that this work is not so much inter-national as it is non-national although, admittedly, this has not been easy to accomplish." In general, the editors kept their promise. There is an impressive number of foreign contributors, a number of good articles on individual countries, the reporting of specific libraries and institutions and library operations is very good, if not outstanding. Most biographical sketches are also competent, occasionally somewhat subjective, as in the case of Harold Lancour, or (especially) of Sidney Jackson.

Nevertheless, it seems that material is of uneven quality. Articles vary in length, not necessarily reflecting the relative importance of a given topic. Some articles are quite chatty, others provide only a minimum of factual data and occasionally read like some observations made by tourists visiting libraries in some strange countries. This is, unfortunately, not limited to articles on libraries in Botswana, British West Indies, or the Panama Canal area. Good examples of this treatment are found in a long article on the National Library of Austria and in an article on libraries in Bulgaria that contains, in addition to other things, a number of factual errors (regarding, for example, the founding of Ivan Vazov National Library and Sofia University Library). Obviously most articles dealing with foreign countries are very good; for example, "French National Bibliography," "Yugoslavia Libraries and Librarianship," and "Moslem Libraries (Medieval)."

How is the "home front"? Much better indeed. Most important libraries are adequately described, with some outstanding contributions (e.g., on Harvard, Yale, and the Library of Congress). Most existing (and some now not existing) library schools have good descriptive articles. The same is true of major library operations or activities, state agencies, etc. Unfortunately, again, there are some exceptions. As was indicated in one of our previous reviews, an article on bookmobiles takes 57 pages and, by contrast, an article on bibliography only 12 pages. We do not understand this kind of editorial policy. Obviously, one measures the value of material not only in terms of printed pages; in other respects, too, the article on bibliography is rather disappointing: there are many familiar names, even more titles, but hardly anything worthwhile about major theoretical concepts or important historical contributions. By contrast, an article on historical bibliography (published in *Supplement 1*) is very good. Thus, some editorial attention to allocation of space or a little more guidance in providing a proper framework for a given topic would be helpful.

Somewhat more understandable is the problem of currency in several articles. It is only to be expected that in the work which has taken one and a half decades to produce, there will be articles of this sort. The impact of technology on library services in the last ten years is well known to all of us. How will this problem be resolved by using supplements? It is fairly easy to update an article on Canada and this was successfully done in *Supplement 1*—"Canada, Libraries in, 1970-1979." But how about the range of articles in the area of technical services or, as a matter of fact, reference services that employ now not only new sophisticated technology, but have changed so dramatically in terms of their philosophical concepts? Printed material in those areas may now serve as a kind of historical "background" that needs not only updating but more important, complete rethinking, taking into consideration realities of today and future projections. Our vote is simply for a new edition of this important work, one that would condense some of the existing material and bring forward a kind of synthesis that any excellent encyclopedia can use. In the humble opinion of this reviewer, the major objective of an encyclopedia is to educate, second to inform, and last to analyze and provide a frame of reference so any given information can be evaluated in a proper perspective. Allen Kent might be right that many of the articles still stand the test of time. But we are not sure that producing supplementary volumes will "catch up" obvious "gaps." This methodological approach may solve some of the secondary problems, but the educational value of this massive and impressive work may quickly diminish.

Bohdan S. Wynar

84. Harrod, Leonard Montague. **The Librarians' Glossary of Terms Used in Librarianship, Documentation and the Book Crafts, and Reference Book.** 4th rev. ed. Boulder, Colo., Westview Press, 1977; repr., Lexington, Mass., Lexington Books, 1982. 903p. o.p. LC 76-52489. ISBN 0-89158-727-6.

This dictionary first appeared in 1938 with the title *The Librarians' Glossary, Terms Used in Librarianship and the Bookcrafts.* The third edition of *The Librarians' Glossary* was characterized as "a handbook of British terminology ... for a British audience" (*ARBA* 72, entry 88). The fourth edition of the glossary provides well-written definitions of library terms for American as well as British librarians. New terms in the fourth edition include: "Information science," glossed by Hal Borko; "PRECIS," defined by Derek Austin; and in the supplement, *Williams & Wilkins v. the United States* discussed under the term "Fair use." The British orientation is evident in the discussion of "Cataloguing in Source," which describes the CIP program at the Library of Congress, though not by name. On the other hand, "Centralized processing" only refers to developments in the United States.

The third edition defined 784 pages of terms. In this new edition, 690 terms have been added and 310 expanded, to give a total of 903 pages. It would be useful to know the number and kinds of terms that have been dropped, and the policy for such revisions (i.e., obsolescence, terminology change, etc.). The major and peripheral areas of librarianship are adequately covered, including printing, information science, bibliography, professional associations and awards (British and American), the larger library institutions, and the functional areas of acquisitions, cataloging, reference, and, to a lesser degree, management. *The Librarians' Glossary*, fourth edition, makes the effort to reach an American audience. Since American libraries have accepted "catalogue" in AACR2, perhaps an "Anglo-American" glossary accords well with a developing trend of linguistic cooperation. [R: JAL, March 78, p. 49; LJ, 15 June 78, p. 1238]   Deborah Jane Brewer

85. Tayyeb, R., and K. Chandna, comps. **A Dictionary of Acronyms and Abbreviations in**

Library and Information Science. 2nd ed. Ottawa, Canadian Library Association, 1985. 279p. $20.00pa. ISBN 0-88802-195-X.

If the AAAAAA had been more active, compilers Tayyeb and Chandna would not have had to record so many widely ranging entries. For this acronym, third entry in the new edition of this dictionary, stands for Association for the Alleviation of Asinine Abbreviations and Absurd Acronyms. The new edition attempts to include as many French and Canadian abbreviations as possible. The number of abbreviations and acronyms is also expanded. Related entries range widely from reference book titles (e.g., *Grove, DAB*) to such miscellaneous entries as *SIG*, "Special Interest Group" and *KISS*, "Keep it simple, Sir/Stupid." Although many of the entries will be found in other dictionaries of acronyms and abbreviations, this dictionary can be recommended for its well-searched contents, arrayed in such readable form. It will be helpful to those using the literature of library and information science.   Frances Neel Cheney

86. Wersig, Gernot, and Ulrich Neveling, comps. **Terminologie de la documentation: A Selection of 1,200 Basic Terms Published in English, French, German, Russian and Spanish.** Paris, UNESCO; distr., New York, UNIPUB, 1976. 274p. bibliog. index. $32.50. ISBN 92-3-001232-7.

This work is not only a multilingual dictionary for documentation (English, French, German, Russian, and Spanish), but a technical vocabulary as well, defining in English each of the 1,200 terms included. Arrangement is in broad classes, and terms are alphabetical within each class. A UDC index provides access by UDC notations.

The entry words (in English) are in boldface type, followed by the French, German, Russian, and Spanish equivalents for the term. Definitions are numbered (the entry words themselves are not). If a word used in a definition is itself defined elsewhere in the dictionary, it is printed in italics, and the entry number for that definition is given. There are cross-references to broader, narrower, opposite, and related terms, where appropriate. In addition to

the UDC index, there is an index for each language.

A bibliography, subdivided by language, lists the sources used in compiling the dictionary. In scope, the dictionary covers linguistic problems, documentary languages, systems analysis, and general concepts of electronic data processing. Its aim is to provide "specialists in information and documentation with a work which will enable them to participate in the technical communications of their field" (p. 14). As a means of fostering international cooperation and as a reference work for organizations and individuals working in the areas of documentation and information processing, this dictionary will be a useful tool.

87. Young, Heartsill, ed., with the assistance of Terry Belanger and others. **The ALA Glossary of Library and Information Science.** Chicago, American Library Association, 1983. 245p. bibliog. $50.00. LC 82-18512. ISBN 0-8389-0371-1.

Putting together a glossary of terms that pertain to library and information science was the goal of the editor of this book. The book includes definitions "of terms that relate to the provision of access to recorded information by libraries and similar information agencies, individually and collectively, and to the functions and activities performed by those agencies." In addition to terms from library and information science, there are terms from associated fields: printing and publishing, including paper, typography, composition, and binding; graphic arts, including photography; computer science; telecommunications; reprography, including micrographics; educational technology; administrative science; and archives administration. The names of persons and corporate bodies are excluded, as are names of commercial products, systems, and services. There are *see* and *compare with* references to aid the user in seeing the full picture. Twenty-five sources were consulted to arrive at the definitions that were used, which, with the form of spelling of the terms, should become the accepted definitions for the library community. [R: JAL, Nov 83, p. 297; LJ, 1 Dec 83, p. 2228; WLB, Nov 83, p. 222]
                  H. Robert Malinowsky

10 Handbooks and Manuals

88. Allardyce, Alex. **Letters for the International Exchange of Publications: A Guide to Their Composition in English, French, German, Russian and Spanish.** Peter Genzel, ed. New York, K. G. Saur, 1978. 148p. (IFLA Publications, 13). o.p. LC 78-13489. ISBN 0-89664-113-9; ISSN 0344-6891.

Published under the auspices of the IFLA Section on the Exchange of Publications, this book is designed to help exchange librarians write simple letters to their foreign counterparts in five languages without other assistance. The basic text was written in English by Alex Allardyce of the British Library Lending Division and translated into French by Jacques Lethève, into German by Maria Razumovsky, into Russian by Boris P. Kanyevsky, and into Spanish by Adolfo Rodriguez. This work does not include sample letters for various purposes or lists of useful words and phrases. Instead, it furnishes an assembly kit with five sets of parts—each set in its own self-contained section by language—from which, it is hoped, routine correspondence may be composed. Each set contains identical pieces for letters of inquiry, responses, claims, cancellations, etc. To keep this manual as short as possible, each piece appears only once and is later referred to, rather than repeated in context.

This publication can be used as a guide to composing exchange correspondence only by those with an elementary knowledge of the language employed, a definite message in mind, and patience to follow where the guide leads in search of the right framework and the right phrase. Even so, the final product would be inferior to a letter written by someone familiar with the chosen language. Also, the manual contains many typographical errors, and an American may have difficulty with some British expressions used. It seems that any library large enough to engage in international exchanges would have access to specialists in European languages and would not need this book.

Leonard Grundt

89. Allen, C. G. **A Manual of European Languages for Librarians.** New York, R. R. Bowker, 1975. 803p. o.p. LC 73-6062. ISBN 0-85935-028-2.

This is a remarkably comprehensive and extremely useful manual which treats, from the librarian's point of view, some 36 European languages including ancient and modern Latin and Greek. Certainly the lack of personnel who know foreign languages is felt particularly in the college, university, and other research libraries, especially in the United States, where foreign language training in the schools (when it exists at all) is often inadequate and sometimes ridiculous. The present volume will be of particular interest to the technical services librarians, who often would be delighted to have at least "title-page Russian, German, etc." in order to give at least summarily adequate treatment to the volumes they must record, identify, search, etc. Allen's treatment is much fuller than what can be found in von Ostermann.

A classified pattern of treatment has been adopted for all the languages to which this uniform approach can be applied. The general characteristics (e.g., history, order of words) are described; then there follows a section called "Bibliolinguistics," which deals with those elements of particular interest to librarians (names, title entries, editions, periodicals, etc.). This is followed by a grammatical treatment of the parts of speech. Each section devoted to a language ends with a glossary of bibliographic terms and a grammatical index. The author is described as having a "life-long addiction" to foreign languages and was only recently retired after many years in the library profession. But in addition to the careful work of the author, each language section has been reviewed by a native speaker or similar expert. In fact, the reviewer was unable to find even a misprint in the treatment of the eight languages he felt competent enough to examine critically. It should be added that even the vagaries of consonantal variation that occur in the Celtic languages are explained with remarkable clarity and conciseness.

To give some idea of the languages covered: the Germanic group also includes Afrikaans and Icelandic; the Latin-Romance has Catalan and Rumanian. Irish, Welsh, Greek, Albanian, Maltese, Turkish, Basque, and Esperanto appear, along with the many languages included under Slavonic, Baltic, and Finno-Ugrian headings.

The manual is truly comprehensive and a "must" for every library that acquires material in the foreign languages of Europe. The reviewer found only one minor usage that detracted from clarity in the general treatment of the Germanic languages: the use of the abbreviations "De" for German (*Deutsch*) and "Da" for Danish (*Dansk*); these abbreviations had not been included in the list of abbreviations and apparently occur nowhere else in the work. The binding is serviceable and the typography clear and tastefully chosen. [R: LJ, 1 Dec 76, p. 2461]
Francis J. Witty

90. Borchardt, D. H., and J. D. Thawley. **Guide to the Availability of Theses: Compiled for the Section of University Libraries and Other General Research Libraries.** Munich, New York, K. G. Saur; distr., Hamden, Conn., Shoe String Press, 1981. 443p. index. (IFLA Publications, No. 17). $38.00. ISBN 3-598-20378-0; ISSN 0344-6891.

The title is very exact. This is not a bibliography of theses or a bibliography of bibliographies of theses. Instead, it is a guide which provides information about the bibliographic control of dissertations and theses in 85 countries, based on questionnaire replies from 698 institutions. The arrangement is alphabetical by country and then by institution. Where possible, information is given at the beginning of each country's section about coverage in such sources as national bibliographies or national thesis bibliographies, followed by institutional listings with information about the manner in which theses are handled (e.g., deposited in a university library, available or not available for interlibrary loan, microform availability, etc.).

As explained in the preface, this is the second worldwide survey. The first, by Marc Chauveinc, was published as *Guide on the Availability of Theses* by IFLA in 1978. Coverage is much more extensive in this edition (only 296 institutions were included in the first). Coverage would have been even better had librarians from all 1,498 institutions in 126 countries replied to the questionnaires. There are curious inclusions and omissions. For example, the only listing for Egypt is Minia University, and the only two for Italy are the University of Siena and the Luigi Bocconi Commercial University in Milan. For the Soviet Union, only Tartu State University is included. There are no listings for Iran. Coverage, not surprisingly, is best for Western Europe, Canada, the United States, and Australia. Even here, there are some unfortunate omissions, such as Kent State University. (The University of Akron, Bowling Green State University, Cleveland State University, The Ohio State University, and Ohio University are included but not the University of Cincinnati, Miami University, or Youngstown State University.) On balance, we should be grateful for what the compilers have achieved and hope that there will be a further survey in which more librarians in more countries will respond to the questionnaires.
A. Robert Rogers

91. **Handbook of Black Librarianship.** E. J. Josey and Ann Allen Shockley, comps. and eds. Littleton, Colo., Libraries Unlimited, 1977. 392p. index. o.p. LC 77-21817. ISBN 0-87287-179-7.

The *Handbook of Black Librarianship*, compiled and edited by two distinguished librarians, defines black Americans' contributions to American libraries in the past and present. The handbook contains 37 topical essays and resource lists, arranged in seven major sections: "Pioneers and Landmark Episodes"; "Early Library Organization"; "Contemporary Black Librarianship"; "Vital Issues in Black Librarianship"; "Significant Books and Periodicals for Black Collections"; "African Resources"; "Afro-American Resources." Seven directories follow the main part of the text: "Undergraduate Library School Departments in Predominantly Black Colleges and Universities"; "Predominantly Black Graduate Library Schools"; "Libraries of Public Library Systems Serving Predominantly Black Communities"; "Black Academic Libraries"; "Additional Libraries Named for Afro-Americans"; "Selective List of Black-Owned Bookstores"; "Black Book Publishers."

Historical material in the first two sections includes, among the eight articles, a chronology of events in black librarianship, 1808-1977; a history of the Hampton Institute Library School; and descriptions of five early black library organizations.

Contemporary black librarianship is well covered by 11 articles encompassing topics such as the Black Caucus of ALA, statistics on black libraries and librarians, and library services to black Americans.

A special feature of the handbook is the identification and description of resources for African and Afro-American studies. Here are found lists of reference books and periodicals reflecting the black experience and several articles dealing with black authors, bestsellers, and black librarians as writers. Black resources in U.S. libraries, archives, oral history programs, and museums are also discussed and described. [R: BL, 15 May 78, p. 1519; C&RL, May 78, p. 223; JAL, Sept 78, p. 229; JLH, Summer 78, p. 304]   Ann Hartman

92. International Handbook of Contemporary Developments in Librarianship. Miles M. Jackson, ed. Westport, Conn., Greenwood Press, 1981. 619p. bibliog. index. $75.00. LC 80-27306. ISBN 0-313-21372-0.

Intended to "present an overview of the major developments and most significant trends in librarianship since 1945" (preface), this collection offers 34 original articles on libraries and librarianship in 65 countries throughout the world. Although the editor, Miles M. Jackson, states that "the book is not intended as a work of comparative library studies" (preface), it will certainly be of use to researchers and scholars working in this area.

The handbook is organized by regions of the world and then by countries within the region. An introduction to each region provides a general statement on the history, sociological composition, and status of libraries within that particular area. The articles generally offer a brief history and the geographic and political background on each country, followed by a discussion of the library associations, library education, the national library, and academic, special, school, and public libraries. Bibliographies are included at the end of most articles. Although contributors sometimes differ on the amount of coverage they give to their topics, the unevenness which is usually so apparent in a work of this nature is, for the most part, absent. It is evident from the thorough coverage of each country and the familiarity with which each contributor addresses the topic, that the articles are written by either natives of the country or by individuals who have had extensive experience with libraries in the country under discussion.

One area which was only generally addressed in the preface is the criteria used to select countries for inclusion in the work. According to the editor, "countries that are presented here as representative have library developments that are significant and more pronounced than those found in other countries. Many of the countries selected have made advances over the past thirty years which require detailed analysis of basic processes" (preface). However, these criteria do not explain why Mexico is the only country representing Latin American nations, nor why Europe, Denmark, and Hungary were selected, yet Sweden, Norway, and Spain were not. In spite of this limitation, the handbook, which brings together a variety of information on international librarianship, makes a valuable contribution to the literature. [R: C&RL, Sept 82, pp. 414-17; JAL, May 82, p. 104; LJ, 1 Apr 82, p. 694]   Ann Hartman

93. Kent, Rosalind. Reading the Russian Language: A Guide for Librarians and Other Professionals. New York, Marcel Dekker, 1974. 229p. index. (Books in Library and Information Science, Vol. 9). o.p. LC 74-81799. ISBN 0-8247-6236-3.

Walker's *Russian for Librarians* (Linnet Books, 1973) was a welcome addition to the meager literature on this subject, in spite of its deficiencies; in *ARBA* 74 (entry 130), this reviewer indicated that such a book was rather overdue. Kent's work is different in both scope and purpose. It is a self-study manual of common Russian phrases found in books, designed to enable the student or practicing librarian to read a Russian book "technically" and to catalog Russian materials. The introduction indicates that "the objective of this book is to teach Russian to librarians who have never tried to learn the language or why have tried and given up" (p. ix). The material consists of 14 chapters that discuss common principles of Russian grammar. Practical illustrations are included of words or phrases encountered in a typical cataloging situation. It is difficult for this reviewer, who knows Russian, to judge whether or not the manual will help those who "have never tried to learn the language or who have tried and given up." Courses in Russian are offered on practically any college campus and in many high schools; this book does not claim to be a substitute for a beginning Russian course. The manual is the result of an interesting experiment at the School of Library and Information Sciences at the University of Pittsburgh, an experiment in teaching foreign vocabulary of interest to librarians. It will certainly supplement Walker's work. Although reproduced from a typescript, the manual is quite easy to read and seems to be virtually free of typographical errors. Bohdan S. Wynar

94. Kim, Choong H. **Books by Mail: A Handbook for Libraries.** Westport, Conn., Greenwood Press, 1977. 416p. illus. bibliog. index. $39.95. LC 76-15335. ISBN 0-8371-9029-0.

This is an important tool for librarians who are interested in providing clients with books by mail service. It is more than a compilation of data about library book mail programs in the United States and Canada. Part 1 is a descriptive manual that effectively lays out step by step the approaches that can be used in types of libraries. It covers such topics as reading interest of books-by-mail users, preparation of mail catalogs, developing the book collection for this service, details on operations, procedures and practices, and cost-effectiveness analysis.

Part 2, which consists of case studies, gives practical views and experiences from nine libraries. In addition to views from the perspective of an administrator, there are also descriptions of a statewide program and rural and institutional programs.

Part 3 is a thoroughly prepared descriptive directory giving facts about 75 programs in the United States and Canada.

Overall, this is a worthwhile investment for the library contemplating extending its services to a wider clientele. [R: JAL, July 77, p. 172; LJ, 15 Oct 77, p. 2143] Miles M. Jackson

95. Ladenson, Alex, ed. **American Library Laws.** 5th ed. Chicago, American Library Association, 1983. 2009p. index. $110.00. LC 83-21543. ISBN 0-8389-0400-9.

American Library Laws first appeared in 1930 and was compiled for the League of Library Commissions by Milton J. Ferguson under a financial grant of the Carnegie Corporation of New York. It has been issued in succeeding editions with various supplements.

This fifth edition contains all federal and state library laws in effect 31 December 1982. It supersedes the fourth edition, published in 1973, and its three supplements. A conservative estimate is that 30 percent of the material is new or revised.

The text begins with a section listing all the library laws of the federal government and follows it with a roll call of state library laws. Within each section laws are arranged by agency, type of library, and subject. There is also a modest subject index which seems to rely on the keywords in the titles of the laws as its base. Using the index, under "Fees" one finds that the majority of entries discuss fees levied to support

county court libraries or filing fees for certification exams. Only one state law which empowers a public library to charge fees can be accessed through the index. Therefore, to answer the question of whether other states are truly silent on this issue one would have to supplement the text with counsel from state library staff and Association of State and Cooperative Library Agencies publications.

It should be understood that only laws are included; any regulations developed by executive agencies to support legislation are excluded. Also important to remember is the organic nature of legislation. New laws cancel or change old laws regularly, and occaasional supplements may not be sufficiently timely.

Recommended for all state agency, law, and library school collections. [R: LJ, 15 June 84, p. 1228] Caroline M. Coughlin

96. **Library Resources Market Place: LRMP 1980.** New York, R. R. Bowker, 1980. 248p. index. o.p. ISBN 0-8352-1290-4; ISSN 0000-0442.

Joining the other popular Market Place handbooks, here for the first time is one specifically geared to a librarian's workaday world. Library-related products and services, personnel, and organizations which can be found in a variety of reference sources are here condensed and consolidated into a single volume for easy, one-step question answering. Need a step stool? See the suppliers section, classified by equipment and materials. Over 400 suppliers are included. Need to contact a wholesaler or jobber? Over 700 U.S. and Canadian firms are listed and, of course, cross-indexed. Some 450 library and information science periodicals (U.S. and Canadian) can be found here, including regional and state publications, and 95 AV producers and distributors are listed. Library and information science publishers, braille and large-type publishers, and micropublishers listed number 200, 70, and 170, respectively. Names of importers, antiquarians, back issue dealers, and auctioneers with address and phone number are available.

The list of 225 U.S. and Canadian library and information science associations includes national, regional, state, provincial, special, school, media, and a few international associations. Address, phone number, and personnel names are provided. State supervisors of school library and media agencies are here. Book and AV trade associations, state library agencies, U.S. regional depository libraries, grant-awarding foundations, networks and consortia, library schools, consultants, online vendors, employment services, and library awards are gathered here (selectively in some cases) with address, phone number, and personnel names given. The names and numbers directory, typical of this series, indexes the 4,500 organizations and people found in the text.

Obviously, this product is a gathering of information from, for the most part, other Bowker reference works. Sectional introductions direct the reader to these, or other publishers' works, as sources of further information, e.g., *Literary Market Place, Large Type Books in Print, Audiovisual Market Place, American Book Trade Directory, Library Journal, The Bowker Annual of Library & Book Trade Information,* and *American Library Directory.* Convenience could justify the purchase of this compilation if the other sources were already owned. If they are not, this should prove an indispensable first acquisition to current library resources.   Mary Alice Deveny

97. Lyman, Helen Huguenor. **Literacy and the Nation's Libraries.** Chicago, American Library Association, 1977. 212p. bibliog. index. $15.00. LC 77-4450. ISBN 0-8389-0244-8.

The purpose of this manual, as enunciated by Robert Wedgeworth in the introduction, is "to guide librarians in their efforts to assist people of all ages and all reading levels to become competent, habitual, and independent readers" (p. xi). The work succeeds in fulfilling this objective because it includes practical guidelines for the development of a successful literacy program. The appendices are particularly valuable, for they include a community analysis checklist, a list of "real world" materials, resources such as federal and state funding agencies, literacy programs and organizations, handbooks for tutor training, six reports of successful library literacy projects, two summaries of national literacy studies, a list of acronyms, a glossary, and a general bibliography. Although the title page lists Helen Huguenor Lyman as the author, Don A. Brown wrote chapter 8, "The Nature of Reading and Reading Instruction," and according to the introduction, eight units of ALA contributed to planning and writing this manual. The members of the Literacy Manual Project Advisory Board are listed in the acknowledgments as having a deep and continuing involvement in the development of this manual; however, their involvement is not clearly defined. It was the board that made the decision to eliminate footnotes—a mistake, considering the audience for which the manual was designed. Footnotes would have made it far easier to check references for further information. Chapter 9, "Questions and Answers," could have been omitted or the information could have been absorbed in the other chapters. In spite of

these minor criticisms, the manual is extremely valuable in bringing to the attention of librarians the extent of the literacy problem in the United States, along with suggestions and ideas to guide them in starting literacy programs. [R: JAL, Nov 77, p. 302]   Doris Cruger Dale

98. Montgomery, A. C., comp. and ed. **Acronyms & Abbreviations in Library & Information Work: A Reference Handbook of British Usage.** 2nd ed. London, Library Association; distr., Phoenix, Ariz., Oryx Press, 1982. 97p. $15.50pa. ISBN 0-85365-904-4.

According to its editor, "the purpose of this handbook is to provide a quick reference listing of the acronyms and abbreviations encountered in the general English language literature of librarianship and information work." The handbook lives up to this purpose with its entries arranged in alphabetical order, letter by letter, and covering projects; organizations; associations; information resources and services; technical terms; and abstracting, indexing, and professional services and journals from all over the world. Foreign-language expansions are translated where an official or semiofficial English translation has been found, and an English interpretation is supplied in brackets where known, even if the full foreign expansion is not available. The country of origin or application is given if known and not observable from the expansion. This is a useful book for identifying those acronyms that are constantly being created in the library profession. [R: JAL, Jan 83, p. 363]   H. Robert Malinowsky

99. Murphy, Marcy, and Claude J. Johns, Jr. **Handbook of Library Regulations.** New York, Marcel Dekker, 1977. bibliog. index. (Books in Library and Information Science, Vol. 20). o.p. LC 76-19994. ISBN 0-8247-6498-6.

The purpose of this volume, as stated by the authors, is "to provide a state-of-the-art report on internal regulations which are in effect in U.S. and some few Canadian libraries." It discusses these regulations for public, research, special, and state libraries but not for school library/media centers nor for computerized information retrieval systems.

A very ingenious approach is taken to the discussion of each type of library. The authors lead into the rules and regulations by first discussing the type of library in its broad, historical development, and bringing it up-to-date by indicating current trends. Regulations are then discussed, based on a questionnaire return, as they apply to users, circulation, resources, interlibrary loan and reprography, and administration. Each chapter lists the libraries that responded to the questionnaire, ranging from 16 special libraries to a high of 35 public libraries. The background information for each chapter is well documented with extensive footnotes. An important addition is chapter 2, which covers users and their access to the library, including analysis of data on who can use the library, when access may be gained, and how the collections are arranged.

This well-organized and authoritatively presented volume should allow each library to compare its regulations with those of other libraries, particularly when new rules and regulations are being contemplated or deleted. It also sets the stage for more detailed analysis of particular areas of regulations—such as administration. [R: C&RL, Sept 77, p. 440; JAL, Sept 77, p. 245; LJ, 15 June 77, p. 1356]

Robert D. Stueart

100. Taylor, L. J. **A Librarian's Handbook.** London, Library Association; distr., Syracuse, N.Y., Gaylord Professional Publications, 1976-1980. 2v. LC 77-362108. ISBN 0-85365-079-9 (vol. 1); 0-85365-651-7 (vol. 2).

These two volumes contain everything you could want to know about British libraries and the Library Association's standards and policies. Volume 1 is divided into seven parts and covers a wide range of topics—British government policy relating to libraries; statements, policies, and documents of the Library Association (this section is 300 pages long); standards for library programs from non-Library Association organizations (UNESCO, IFLA, School Library Association, etc.). There is a section called "Professional Aids: Documents," which consists of such items as British Library reference division regulations, British Publishers Association's policies and regulations, Library Association regulations for professional certification, etc. Also included are a section on book trade statistics; an extensive directory of vendors of library materials and services (binderies, jobbers, office supplies, mobile units, furniture, even prefabricated buildings); and a 58-page bibliography in which most of the references deal with British standards (e.g., "presentation of bibliographical information in printed music; presentation of translations; and recommendations for the documentation of computer-based systems"). The extensive table of contents and the very complete index provide easy access to the material contained in this large volume.

Volume 2 of this handbook is arranged by subject into two parts. Part 1 includes 17 chapters of introductory material covering subjects such as national, academic, school, and public libraries; cooperation; special users; special materials; library research; library education; censorship; copyright; and book trade. Part 2 contains related documents, and is organized by subject, corresponding to the subjects covered in part 1. The reader is referred from part 1 to related documents contained in the second half of the handbook. In addition, statistical tables of librarianship and book trade are included at the end of the text, as well as names and addresses of more than 1,000 library- or book-related organizations and companies (e.g., information systems and services, picture suppliers, bookbinders, audiovisual organizations, etc.). In areas where no new statistical information was available, the table was eliminated from this second volume, but the reader is referred to volume 1 of the handbook. The second volume contains numerous cross-references and a general index to both volumes.

Volume 1 covers information through the mid-1970s, while volume 2 covers more current source material, some of which is difficult to find elsewhere. The scope of *A Librarian's Handbook* is far more extensive than anything published in the United States on the same subject. If an American counterpart is ever published, it will be a must for every library in the country. [R: LR, Winter 80, p. 299]

G. Edward Evans and Ann Hartman

101. Thompson, Enid T. **Local History Collections: A Manual for Librarians.** Nashville, Tenn., American Association for State and Local History, 1978. 99p. bibliog. index. $8.95pa. LC 77-28187. ISBN 0-910050-33-3.

In addition to a good bibliography, this book contains eight major sections on topics ranging from collecting local history to special projects. Of these, the most useful is the one on training volunteers. As to other aspects, this work should generally prove of use to individuals who need "some helpful ideas" (p. 10) in building and sustaining a local history collection. By and large, the author's advice is sound. For example, the discussion of the need for developing policy statements on what an institution will accept or reject should be followed closely (p. 36).

This book would be of more value, however, had the author made at least some mention of some basic principles of arrangement, such as that of provenance. Such would be essential in the processing of a fairly well organized, but large, collection. Also missing is some treatment of inventories and calendars as alternatives to the cataloging of individual items. The use of inventories is especially crucial for processing a massive collection. Further, the practice of keeping "together" the negative and positive prints of a photograph (p. 24) is not necessarily the best to follow from the standpoint of preservation. In this area as well, one should consider the desirability of photocopying newspaper clippings on good quality paper rather than attaching the original clipping to a piece of acid-free paper (p. 31).

The book is nevertheless a good beginning point for librarians who are either faced with or interested in a local history collection. However, it should be used in conjunction with those works that include examples of inventories or that discuss arrangement and description. Such works would include Ruth M. Bordin and Robert M. Warner's *The Modern Manuscript Library* (New York, Scarecrow Press, 1966) and Lucile M. Kane's *A Guide to the Care and Administration of Manuscripts* (Nashville, Tenn., The American Association for State and Local History, 1966). [R: LJ, 15 Sept 78, p. 1710]

James W. Geary

102.   Walker, Gregory. **Russian for Librarians and Russian Books in Libraries.** 2nd rev. ed. London, Clive Bingley; distr., Hamden, Conn., Shoe String Press, 1983. 120p. index. $22.50. ISBN 0-85157-359-2.

A revised and expanded version of a book first published in 1973. Primarily intended for the technical services non-Russian-speaking librarian, this guide will be helpful to any English-speaking person dealing with Russian books. The first section is a very useful, succinct, self-instructional course in the rudiments of Russian grammar (with exercises) followed by sections on transliteration, bibliographies, and vocabulary all with emphasis on library usage and problems. An entirely new section on the present-day Soviet publishing industry and book trade has been added. Russian-English vocabulary, Russian abbreviations commonly encountered in bibliographic work, and a list of principal Soviet publishing houses end this very useful handbook.

All librarians dealing with acquisitions and cataloging of Russian books will want to keep this book on their desks for ready reference.

Natalia Sonevytsky

103.   Weber, Olga S., and Stephen J. Calvert, eds. **Literary and Library Prizes.** 10th ed. New York, R. R. Bowker, 1980. 651p. index. $26.95. LC 59-11370. ISBN 0-8352-1249-1; ISSN 0075-9880.

The first edition of this work appeared in 1935 and in the intervening years has been issued in succeeding revised and enlarged editions. Four major sections divide this tenth edition: international prizes, American prizes, British prizes, and Canadian prizes. The international section lists major awards made to writers of any nationality. American prizes are subdivided into general, publishers, juvenile, poetry, drama, short story, and library prizes. Within these categories, entries are arranged alphabetically by name of award. Information on each award includes a brief history; a description of the form of the award (scroll, plaque, medal, etc.), and if cash, the amount; requirements for eligibility; and methods for selecting winners. Also included is the roster of winning books and/or authors from the prize's inception through 1979, where available. Awards discontinued since the last edition (1976) are indicated, with the past winners listed. A general index, alphabetically listing awards, recipients, and donors, is provided. Other discontinued awards are noted in the index, with year of the edition in which they last appeared. British and Canadian prizes are arranged alphabetically by name of award, e.g., "James Tait Black Memorial Prizes: (British prizes)" is considered a "B" entry and is listed in the index as "Black, James Tait, Memorial prizes, 465." Names of original publishers are provided, but no attempt is made to determine whether or not the book is in print. This should be a necessary reference tool for any type of library. (See *ARBA* 77, entry 178 for a review of the ninth edition.)

Donald D. Foos

11 Annuals and Yearbooks

104. **Advances in Librarianship.** Vol. 1- . New York, Academic Press, 1970- . annual. $32.00. LC 79-86675. ISSN 0065-2830.

Advances in Librarianship does not attempt comprehensive annual coverage on a worldwide basis—an undertaking no longer possible, as the Library Association discovered more than a decade ago. Rather, the editor chooses a few key topics and invites experts to prepare comprehensive essays which review current developments in the light of past trends. The latest volume opens with Charles McClure's "Management Information for Library Decision Making," continues with Nancy Williamson's "Subject Access in the On-Line Environment," and concludes with C. D. Hurt's "Important Literature Identification in Science." In between are essays on community information services (Joan Durrance), IFLA (Robert Vosper), Latin America (Marietta Daniels Shepard), and two studies on collection development (Marcia Pankake, Paul H. Mosher).

Methods of trying to identify important literature are explored and the difficulty of predicting future usage is noted, but with an awareness of the value of community analysis and user studies in enhancing predictability of use. Reference features include a detailed table of contents, lengthy bibliographies, and a brief index. Generally, the writing is clear and enjoyable to read. The volume in hand can serve as a summary, a stimulus, and a guide. [R: C&RL, Sept 85, p. 449; C&RL, July 82, p. 386; C&RL, Mar 80, p. 147; JAL, Sept 81, p. 238; JAL, Mar 81, p. 40; LJ, 15 May 81, p. 1052; LJ, 1 May 80, p. 1052; LQ, July 80, p. 394; LR, Summer 80, p. 126] A. Robert Rogers

105. **Advances in Library Administration and Organization: A Research Annual.** Greenwich, Conn., JAI Press, 1982- . annual. price varies. ISSN 0732-0671.

Each volume of this annual publication provides the reader with a dozen or so articles on a wide variety of topics. In the fourth volume (1985) these topics range from public library unions and academic library service, to disabled students (an annotated bibliography), to satisfaction in library systems and the impacts of automation and technology. Among the twelve authors or co-authors there are five library school faculty members, five academic library administrators, and two representatives of library networks.

The articles are generally well written, and contain useful ideas and information. The subtitle, "A Research Annual," is not completely accurate, since a number of the articles are descriptive or opinion pieces or summaries of the literature. There are valuable author and subject indexes to all of the articles.

In summary, this series continues to provide important contributions to the literature of library administration and organization, but at a very high per-volume cost. [R: JAL, Nov 83, p. 313; JAL, Mar 83, p. 38; JAL, May 82, p. 122; LJ, 15 Nov 83, p. 2144; LJ, 1 June 82, p. 1076; LQ, July 84, p. 305; SLMQ, Fall 83, p. 68] George S. Bobinski

106. **The ALA Yearbook of Library and Information Services: A Review of Library Events.** Vol. 1- . Edited by Robert Wedgeworth. Chicago, American Library Association, 1976- . annual. price varies. LC 76-647548. ISSN 0364-1597.

A long overdue annual review volume, this work was begun during the centennial of the American Library Association in 1976. The 140-150 liberally illustrated articles per year deal with various divisions, round tables, and committees within ALA; state chapters; other national associations and coordinating bodies; and general topics of interest to the library community. Approximately a dozen feature articles each year highlight topics warranting special focus or holding unique interest. Noteworthy features include biographical sketches of persons reaching professional prominence and obituaries of those making significant contributions to the profession. Since publication of the *ALA World Encyclopedia of Library and Information Services* in 1978, the *ALA Yearbook* has served as a supplement. Various individual volumes have been reviewed in *ARBA* 77 (entry 188), *ARBA* 78 (entry 139), *ARBA* 79 (entry 170), *ARBA* 80 (entry 136), *ARBA* 82 (entry 151), and *ARBA* 83 (entry 122).

Donald G. Davis, Jr.

107. **Annual Review of Information Science and Technology.** Vol. 1- . White Plains, N.Y., Published for the American Society for Information Science by Knowledge Industry, 1966- . annual. price varies. LC 79-88675. ISSN 0066-4200.

As noted in past *ARBA* reviews, the annual review of information science and technology should be essential reading for anyone seriously interested in keeping abreast of trends in information science and technology. The thoroughness, balance, timeliness, and scholarship characteristic of each volume are evident.

The eight to ten entries in each volume follow a long-range plan whereby some topics receive more frequent reviews than others, but each bibliographic essay systematically evaluates the literature on the topic since the last review and includes complete references at the end.

Following the basic plan for the entire series, volume 18 (1983), for example, is divided into four parts. Part 1, "Basic Techniques and Technologies," includes review articles on videotex and teletext, human factors in interactive computer dialog, and bibliography and information-processing standards. A substantial section on applications (part 2) follows, including chapters on the scholarly communication process, primary publication systems and scientific text processing, secondary information systems and services, toxicological information, and energy information systems and services. Manfred Kochen contributed a provocative piece on information and society in part 3, "The Profession." For the first time, the special topics section (part 4) focuses entirely on Asia, and especially on Japan, where, in its author's view, the developing information infrastructure

is well on the way to becoming the envy of the world.

Considering the range of issues addressed, their timeliness, and the lasting reference value of each volume, *ARIST* is a bargain. Various volumes have been reviewed in *ARBA* 70 (vol. 1, p. 18), *ARBA* 78 (entry 141), *ARBA* 79 (entry 171); *ARBA* 81 (entry 146), and *ARBA* 83 (entries 123-24). [R: C&RL, July 83, p. 296; IRLA, Mar 83, p. 8; WLB, Mar 83, p. 604]

Donald G. Davis, Jr.

108. **The Bowker Annual of Library & Book Trade Information.** New York: R. R. Bowker, 1966- . annual. price varies. LC 55-12434. ISSN 0068-0540.

Preceded by an earlier title that began in 1956, this standard reference work has earned a reputation for being a good source for ready reference information, current articles, and statistics on topics of timely interest. Though content has varied over its span of existence, some categories have remained somewhat constant. Broad divisions of recent volumes include reports from the field; legislation, funding, and grants; library education, placement, and salaries; research and statistics; international reports and statistics; reference information; and a directory of organizations. Various volumes have been reviewed in *ARBA* 71 (entry 73), *ARBA* 77 (entry 190), *ARBA* 79 (entry 172), and *ARBA* 82 (entry 152). [R: AB, 5 July 82, p. 87; BL, 15 Mar 82, p. 979; CLW, Feb 83, p. 272; SLJ, Jan 83, p. 14]

Donald G. Davis, Jr.

109. Katz, Bill, and others. **Library Lit: The Best of....** Vol. 1- . Metuchen, N.J., Scarecrow, 1971- . annual. price varies. LC 78-15482. ISSN 0085-2767.

With the aid of a jury of a half-dozen authorities in the field of librarianship and library-related publishing, the authors annually select about thirty articles which have appeared in the year of coverage. These are reprinted in full and arranged under broad headings such as "Libraries and Librarians," "Technical Services/Readers' Services," "Communication and Education," and "The Social Prerogative." The volumes will be especially useful in the smaller library that cannot subscribe to the array of publications from which "the best" have come. Various volumes have been reviewed in *ARBA* 72 (entry 64), *ARBA* 73 (entry 66), *ARBA* 74 (entry 119), *ARBA* 75 (entry 142), *ARBA* 76 (entry 113), *ARBA* 77 (entry 158), *ARBA* 79 (entry 173), *ARBA* 80 (entry 138), *ARBA* 81 (entry 150), *ARBA* 83 (entry 127), and

ARBA 84 (entry 98). [R: JAL, Jan 84, p. 354; LJ, 1 Sept 83, p. 1667; WLB, Nov 83, p. 223]

Donald G. Davis, Jr.

110. **LIST: Library and Information Services Today: An International Registry of Research and Innovation.** Paul Wasserman, ed. Detroit, Gale, 1971-75. annual. (Vol. 4, 1974, 548p.; vol. 5, 1975, 633p.). $80.00/per vol. LC 71-143963. ISSN 0075-9821.

Five volumes of *LIST* were published from 1971 to 1975 to list and describe research projects in progress during the years of coverage. Information was solicited by questionnaires from directors of programs, deans, departmental chairpersons, and others holding key positions in institutions where research in library science was thought likely to be in progress. Projects are listed under more than two hundred subject headings, ranging from abstracting to zoology. Some representative headings are: "Information Use," "Microforms," "Preservation of Materials," and "Computer Memory." Volume 4 lists 1,362 projects, and volume 5 lists 1,335.

In five years, this series progressively expanded its database and improved its reporting techniques and its indexing. As of 1976, libraries with a need for current information on library research in progress indicated a standing order for this series; however, it was discontinued after only five volumes were published. Volumes 4 and 5 were listed in the publisher's catalog through spring 1985. Volumes 1-3, under the title *Library and Information Science Today*, have long been out-of-print.

Richard A. Gray and Annette Pekarek

12 Directories

111. **American Library Directory.** Edited by Jaques Cattell Press. New York, R. R. Bowker, 1923- . biennial until 1978, then annual. (38th ed., 1985, $119.95). LC 23-3581. ISSN 0065-910X.

The standard directory for all types of libraries (except school) in the United States and Canada, this work lists and describes more than thirty thousand libraries by state, region, or province, then by city, and finally by institution name. Most of the book consists of statistical information on public, academic, government, and special libraries, including name and address of the library, names of key personnel, and information on the library's holdings. In addition, budget, expenditures, subject interests, special collections, automation, and publications are frequently noted within each entry. Data were obtained from each library to provide accuracy.

A "Library Information" section concludes the work, including information on consortia, library schools, library systems, libraries for the handicapped, public library agencies, state school library agencies, interlibrary loan codes, U.S. Armed Forces overseas libraries, and U.S. Information Agency centers. An index listing libraries by name provides access to the library profiles. This work continues to be a useful purchase for all libraries.   Gloria Palmeri Powell

112. Burwell, Helen P., comp. and ed. **Directory of Fee Based Information Services.** Houston, Tex., Burwell Enterprises, 1984. 203p. index. $18.95 spiralbound. LC 76-55469. ISBN 0-936288-02-7.

Since this publication was last reviewed (see *ARBA* 82, entry 145), it has grown from 89 to 203 pages, increased its coverage from 257 to 334 listings, and escalated in price from $6.95 (paper) to $18.95 (spiralbound). Information consulting is a profession growing in both popularity and profitability, it would seem.

The current edition of *Directory of Fee Based Information Services* conforms to the format of previous editions: entries are arranged alphabetically by states within the U.S. section, by countries (seventeen) in the international section. Each entry is numbered, and includes individual or company name, address, telephone and telex number, former name (if appropriate), key individuals, branches, date founded, areas of specialization, information services offered, and a brief statement submitted by the organization describing the firm and its services. Four indexes — company name, key personnel, subject, and service — provide handy access by entry number to the data contained in the text. Information is current as of January 1984.

The directory has several limitations. It is not comprehensive (nor does it claim to be so). A cursory check of Colorado's nine entries revealed the omission of at least two major information consulting companies. Furthermore, no price or price range information for services has been included, nor the number of employees per firm, both areas that might be determining factors in deciding which of several companies to contact. In addition, the brief descriptive paragraphs submitted by each firm occasionally lapse into useless hornblowing (e.g., "They know what to do—and what NOT to do—when bringing new ideas to bear on real world library problems"). Overall, however, this is a helpful, well-organized source that can be of use to both the library staff and their patrons in public and academic libraries. [R: BL, 1 Feb 85, p. 762; RBB, 1 Feb 85, p. 762]

G. Kim Dority

113. **Directory of Library Associations in Canada.** 3rd ed. Ottawa, Library Documentation Centre, National Library of Canada, 1977. 1v. (unpaged). index. free. spiralbound. ISSN 0380-1187.

The Library Documentation Centre has been collecting all observable data on the Canadian library community since 1970. One of its spinoff publications is this directory, first issued in 1974 (see *ARBA* 75, entry 160). Essentially, it is an alphabetical listing of 123 identified groups, containing data on name, acronym, mailing address, telephone, founding date, objectives, numbers of members, meetings, officers and their terms, committees, publications, and constitution. A liberal definition of "association" also includes alumni groups, archivists, and national advisory committees but excludes publishers' groups, library unions, and staff associations. As data collection is by osmosis (indexes, clippings, surveys, phone, mailings, contacts, tips, etc.), there are still gaps (I can think of a half dozen groups not yet listed), and for this reason a revision sheet is attached. There are three useful indexes (acronyms, geography, and subject orientation), and the English section is duplicated in French (or vice versa). [R: LJ, 15 Sept 77, p. 1827]   Dean Tudor

114. **Encyclopedia of Information Systems and Services: An International Descriptive Guide to Approximately 3,300 Organizations, Systems, and Services Involved in the Production and Distribution of Information in Electronic Form ..., 1985-86.** 6th ed. Detroit, Gale, 1985. 2v. index. $325.00/set. LC 82-18359. ISBN 0-8103-1537-8.

The sixth edition of this standard resource on the electronic information industry describes some thirty-three hundred organizations—approximately 35 percent of which are new to this edition—that provide bibliographic, full-text, numeric, and other types of computer-processed information. Because of the vast increase in material over the previous edition, the directory is now published in two volumes: *International*, listing more than eleven hundred foreign organizations from fifty-nine countries, and *United States*, with the latter volume including a combined master index to entries contained in both volumes. Each volume may be purchased separately. Other changes new to this edition include expanded and more detailed information being provided for each entry, especially in the area of publications; inclusion of brief or partial entries for organizations for which complete information was not available (in previous editions, only those organizations submitting a completed questionnaire were listed); inclusion of the address or code through which an organization can be contacted through public electronic mail networks; and several indexing enhancements.

Entries describing such categories of information as videotex/teletext information services, abstracting and indexing services, magnetic tape providers, library and information networks, information-on-demand services, document delivery services, research projects, and electronic mail applications are arranged alphabetically by name of the parent organization. Twenty-two indexes, each introduced by a scope note, provide access to organizations by function (e.g., community information and referral, online/host services, personal computer-oriented services) and to specific subject, personnel, geographic location, database names, publications, and software.

Supplemented by the periodic *New Information Systems and Services*, the encyclopedia continues to be a valuable information resource. However, given the high price of this set, smaller libraries may want to consider purchasing only the U.S. volume ($190.00).

G. Kim Dority

115. Fang, Josephine Riss, and Alice H. Songe. **International Guide to Library, Archival, and Information Science Associations.** 2nd ed. New York, R. R. Bowker, 1980. 448p. index. $32.50. LC 80-21721. ISBN 0-8352-1285-8.

The preliminary edition of this work was published in 1973, with the subsequent first edition in 1976 reviewed in *ARBA* 77 (entry 176). As we pointed out in our review of the first edition, the information provided for certain countries was not complete. This situation is partially remedied in the second edition, which covers 178 countries, 77 more than the last edition.

The format remains basically the same—two separate sections comprise the main text, an alphabetical listing of the international associations and a geographical listing for the national associations. In most cases, a typical entry provides the following: official name with an acronym (if any), address, names and titles of executive officers, staff, language used, plus a brief description of major fields of interest, goals, activities, membership information, etc. In reviewing the first edition, we pointed out a number of deficiencies. Some of them remain in the second edition. Thus, for example, there is only one entry for the Soviet Union describing the activities of the USSR Library Council. This obviously is not adequate. Using this reasoning, one might expect to find only one entry under the United States of America—namely, the Council of National Library Associations, since the CNLA serves the same purpose as the USSR Library Council. Each Soviet republic has its own national association, not to mention special groups, equivalent to our Special Library Association. Most of them should have been listed, as was done, for example, for Uganda — Uganda Special Library Association (ULA), Uganda School Library Association (USLA), and Uganda Special Library Association (pp. 281-82). Nevertheless, such omissions can be expected in a work of this type, which required a tremendous volume of correspondence and the use of many secondary sources, especially library directories produced by individual countries.

On the plus side, one should mention a number of useful features that enhance this edition, e.g., a general bibliography covering the years 1975-1980, a list of official journals, a roster of chief officers of the associations, etc. All in all, it is a competent work on this subject of special interest to all librarians working in the area of comparative librarianship or active in IFLA and similar organizations. [R: JAL, Mar 81, p. 43; LJ, 15 Jan 81, p. 129]

Bohdan S. Wynar

116. Hernon, Peter, Maureen Pastine, and Sara Lou Williams. **Library and Library-Related Publications: A Directory of Publishing Opportunities in Journals, Serials, and Annuals.** Littleton, Colo., Libraries Unlimited, 1973. 216p. index. o.p. LC 73-84183. ISBN 0-87287-068-5.

This directory lists details of publishing opportunities in all major library-oriented periodicals and serials. Publications are listed by title; information provided for each includes: type of articles accepted, style requirements, approximate length of manuscript, time required for evaluation, royalties (if any), characteristics of typical contributions, and a brief description of the general editorial orientation. Address, subscription rate, circulation, frequency, and editor are also given for each entry.

Entries are arranged in three main sections: "Library Periodicals"; "Annuals, Irregular Series, Monographic Series"; and "Library-Related Periodicals." Appendix 1 contains information about additional monographic series, and appendix 2 lists some out-of-print publications. A subject index and a separate title index provide access to materials in all sections of the directory. [R: RSR, Jan 74, p. 26]

117. **IFLA Directory 1980/81.** The Hague, International Federation of Library Associations and Institutions, 1980. 193p. index. ISSN 0074-6002.

On 1 January 1980, IFLA had more than 950 members and affiliates in 110 countries. In addition to the names and addresses of these members and affiliates, the *IFLA Directory 1980/81* contains the names and addresses of IFLA officers and key information on the personnel, committee members, and terms of reference (goals) for its divisions, sections, and roundtables. The directory also contains general information on IFLA: membership requirements, past and future sessions of the council, and a list of IFLA publications. There have been some changes with this issue of the directory. It does not contain the statutes and rules of procedure. A separate brochure with the text of the statutes and rules may be requested free of charge from the IFLA Secretariat. This directory serves for the years 1980/81. With the restructuring of IFLA, councils are held in odd years only, so that it is not necessary to publish the directory annually. New members will be listed regularly in the *IFLA Journal.*

118. Lengenfelder, Helga, ed. **World Guide to Libraries.** 6th ed. Munich, New York, K. G. Saur, 1983. 1186p. index. (Handbook of International Documentation and Information, Vol. 8). $158.00. ISBN 3-598-20523-6; ISSN 0000-0221.

In reaction to suggestions and criticism regarding the previous edition (see *ARBA* 82, entry 146), the editors have attempted to improve their product once again. Undoubtedly, some librarians will approve of the changes; others will disapprove.

The quantity of entries is up only slightly. This volume includes 42,700 libraries in 167 countries, reflecting the inclusion of 2,150 new listings and the deletion of 1,600 out-of-date listings. Criteria for inclusion remain the same. National, federal, state, college, public, university, and other academic libraries must have had a minimum of thirty thousand volumes to be included; while special, parliamentary, government, religious, and business libraries must have holdings of at least three thousand volumes.

Organization and arrangement of the volume remain unchanged, beginning with the division of libraries by major geographical area: Europe, America, Africa, Asia, Oceania. Within each of these divisions, subdivision is first alphabetical by country, then by type of library, and finally, alphabetical by city (not first by state). It is this final subdivision which at first appears to have no logic. However, once the arrangement is mastered, access improves.

Nine categories of library are used: "National," "General Research," "University and

College," "Professional and School," "Government," "Religious," "Corporate and Business," "Special," and "Public." Somewhat misleading may be the category of school libraries, since this includes primarily junior and community colleges, trade schools, and academies.

Each entry provides standard directory information, including telephone number; telex number, telegram address; name of director; date of founding; special collections; statistics of holdings; and indication of participation in data networks, interlibrary loan programs, and professional organizations above the local and state level.

The subject index used in the previous edition has been replaced by an alphabetical index by name of institution, keyed with an entry number. This should help alleviate librarian or patron frustration in locating a specific institution. However, we are now at a loss for access to special collections by subject. To rectify this the editors plan a separate publication.

For any library in the United States, this work cannot replace the *American Library Directory*. However, its strength comes from its comprehensive scope and its coverage of libraries around the world. Until there may be a suitable title to replace this work, it remains recommended for large academic and public libraries, and for special libraries with subject scope and user need that demand the information it contains. [R: RQ, Summer 84, p. 481]

Edmund F. SantaVicca

120. Vaillancourt, Pauline M. **International Directory of Acronyms in Library, Information and Computer Sciences.** New York, R. R. Bowker, 1980. 518p. index. $50.00. LC 80-18352. ISBN 0-8352-1152-5.

As used in this book, the term *acronym* includes both true acronyms and initialisms. An acronym is a word formed from the initial letters or syllables of other words, as in LAMA for Library Administration and Management Association. The *International Directory of Acronyms in Library, Information and Computer Sciences* was compiled to provide an integrated listing of the acronymic vocabularies of these fields.

Of the more than fifty-five hundred acronyms listed, approximately two thousand are international or foreign in origin or use. Nine categories of acronyms are represented: associations, societies and organizations in the library, information and computer sciences; commonly used terms from these fields; meetings, conferences, and workshops of a continuing nature; publications, including books, journals, and data tapes; libraries and information centers;

information-related government agencies; commercial firms; consortia, networks, and systems; and research or experimental projects and services. Acronyms from related disciplines are selectively included, as are some historically important acronyms still in use.

Entries contain three parts: acronym, full name of acronym, and a brief annotation. Some use of *see* references refers the reader to one main entry. In some entries, dates of establishment are provided. Not all entries are similar; in some cases additional information is provided for an association, etc., including full address, establishment date, former names (when applicable), and annotation, while others are not completely described. Some entries are misleading, e.g., "SLA" (page 208) refers to six library associations, including the Southeastern Library Association (SELA) and the Southwestern Library Association (SWLA). Under "SELA" (page 203) we find "Southeastern Library Association" without a *see* reference to "SLA"; and under "SWLA" (page 217) we find "Southwestern Library Association. See SLA." Further, under "SMART" (page 209), "Salton's Magical Automatic Retrieval of Texts" is found, but the "System for the Mechanical Analysis and Retrieval of Text" is not mentioned. An extensive index is provided, but without instructions is difficult to use, as all entries are not indexed and the indexing scheme related to keywords and phrases, extracted from the full names of the acronyms (e.g., "Southwestern" refers to "Southwestern Library Association, SLA," and "Southwestern Library Interstate Cooperative Endeavor, SLICE," but not to "SWLA"), is again misleading.

The compiler of this edition is to be commended on the amount of work and energy involved in this gigantic task. Hopefully, the revised editions will be more detailed and informative. [R: JAL, Nov 80, p. 312; LJ, 1 Nov 80, p. 2318]   Donald D. Foos

121. **World Guide to Technological Information and Documentation Services. Guide mondial des centres de documentation et d'information techniques.** Paris, UNESCO; distr., New York, UNIPUB, 1969. 287p. $11.00pa.

Described in this companion volume to the *World Guide to Science Information and Documentation Services* are 273 centers in seventy-three countries and territories which provide technical information services. The centers responded to a questionnaire survey about their history, address and telephone, staff, subject specialties, library collection, bibliographic, abstracting, reprographic, and translating services. Payments, if any are charged, are explained.

Because the guide is not complete (only thirteen centers in the United States are described), its use would be extremely limited were it not for the references to national and regional directories. The subjects most adequately represented are agriculture, architecture, building, chemical engineering, chemistry, electrical engineering, forestry, geology, industrial management, mechanical engineering, metallurgy, nuclear physics and chemistry, nutrition, physics, textiles and water. Twenty subjects are listed in the subject index as being covered by only one center (e.g., clocks, computer technology, etc.). Such as it is, this subject index, based on information provided by the institution, leaves much to be desired. The basic arrangement of the guide is in alphabetical order by country, preceded by a listing of fourteen international centers. An alphabetical list of institutions is asterisked to show the sixty repeats which appear in the earlier guide. The guide would be of use for referral and as a starting point. [R: LJ, 15 Sept 70]   Pauline Atherton Cochrane

13 Selection Aids

122. Bell, Marion V., and Eleanor A. Swidan. **Reference Books: A Brief Guide.** 8th ed. Baltimore, Enoch Pratt Free Library, 1978. 179p. index. $5.00pa. ISBN 0-910556-11-3.

The seventh edition of this handy guide for smaller libraries, containing 815 titles, was published in 1970 and reviewed in *ARBA* 71 (entry 6). This edition includes annotations for 933 titles and, following the arrangement for earlier editions, is divided into two main sections: "Reference Books General in Scope" (encyclopedias, almanacs, dictionaries, etc.) and "Reference Books in Special Subjects" (humanities, arts, sciences, and social sciences). It is unfortunate that within certain categories—for example, "Art, architecture, and minor arts" (pp. 92-100), entries are listed at random rather than simply in alphabetical order. All entries provide adequate bibliographical descriptions and annotations, but prices are not listed, a notable deletion since many small libraries use this book for selection purposes. All in all, this is a useful compilation. Bohdan S. Wynar

123. **Best Reference Books, 1970-1980: Titles of Lasting Value Selected from** *American Reference Books Annual.* Susan Holte and Bohdan S. Wynar, eds. Littleton, Colo., Libraries Unlimited, 1981. 480p. index. o.p. LC 81-5788. ISBN 0-87287-255-6.

Best Reference Books, 1970-1980 provides a selection of 920 reference titles determined by the editors to be of lasting value to libraries of all types. These titles were selected from the 20,553 titles reviewed in the twelve volumes of *American Reference Books Annual* published from 1970 to 1981. Works appearing in this selection include those of a specialized nature, which will be of particular value to larger libraries, as well as those of wider appeal, which will

be useful to smaller as well as large and medium-sized libraries. This volume was designed to be used as a selection tool for existing libraries looking for gaps in their collections and for new libraries just beginning to build a reference collection.

Reviews for the titles included in this volume were prepared by 290 subject specialists throughout the United States and Canada who review for *ARBA*. Editorial notes have been added to many of these reviews to indicate new editions, added volumes, and other changes since the original review was published. Many reviews have been re-edited or completely rewritten to reflect a title's value in view of other publications in that subject area. Complete bibliographic and ordering information is provided for each title. References to reviews published in periodicals (e.g., *Library Journal, Wilson Library Bulletin,* etc.) are appended to the reviews. [R: Choice, Dec 81, p. 484; JAL, Nov 81, p. 299; LJ, 1 Sept 81, p. 1622; WLB, Sept 81, p. 59]

124. **Children's Catalog, 1981.** 14th ed. Edited by Richard H. Isaacson and Gary L. Bogart. New York, H. W. Wilson, 1981. 1277p. index. (Standard Catalog Series). $54.00. LC 81-7550. ISBN 0-8242-0662-2.

The twelfth edition of the *Children's Catalog* was reviewed in *ARBA* 72 (entry 164). This title is familiar to librarians, as it has been a valuable selection tool since the first edition of 1909. In preparing this edition, the company had the benefit of an advisory committee of seven librarians. Titles in the previous edition were reexamined and new titles were proposed. The list was then sent to sixteen children's librarians in the United States, who elected the titles for inclusion.

This edition includes 5,901 titles and 11,256 analytical entries of books for children from preschool through sixth grade. Out-of-print books have been excluded. The general features of the last edition have been retained, except that only the first book in a series is given in full; the others are listed briefly with no annotations. The use of uniform titles begun in the previous edition has been continued. The arrangement of the entries is similar to previous editions and consists of three parts: (1) the classified catalog, (2) author, title, subject, and analytical index, and (3) directory of publishers and distributors. The introduction "How to Use Children's Catalog" is clear and well written. Some of the subjects which reflect the cultural style of this decade include: bilingual books (French-English and Spanish-English only), blacks, physically handicapped children, old age, death, divorce, and women (with many subheadings). This should be a priority purchase for all libraries. [R: BL, 1 Dec 81, p. 504; RSR, July 82, p. 69]

Doris Cruger Dale

125.   Deveny, Mary Alice, ed. **Recommended Reference Books in Paperback.** Littleton, Colo., Libraries Unlimited, 1981. 317p. index. $25.00; $19.50pa. LC 81-15638. ISBN 0-87287-269-6; 0-87287-279-3pa.

Recommended Reference Books in Paperback is an annotated bibliography of 950 currently available, high-quality reference books published in paperback format at a moderate price. Bibliographies, dictionaries, handbooks, guides, directories, one-volume encyclopedias, and other information sources are listed with complete bibliographic information and an evaluative annotation, often with comparisons to other similar paperback or hardbound works. Citations to other reviews in nine library media, including *Booklist, Choice,* and *School Library Journal*, are part of the annotations. In addition to general reference works, the wide range of subjects covered in the thirty-six chapters includes business, crafts, education, fine arts, genealogy, history, literature, psychology, religion, statistics, and theater. *Recommended Reference Books in Paperback* is a convenient one-volume guide to the selection and use of these economical means of keeping a reference collection current.

126.   **Fiction Catalog, 1980.** 10th ed. Edited by Juliette Yaakov and Gary L. Bogart. New York, H. W. Wilson, 1981. 803p. (Standard Catalog Series). $70.00 (base volume and suppls.). LC 81-43101. ISBN 0-8242-0660-6.

The format and general arrangement of this part of the Standard Catalog Series remain the same as in the last edition: the bulk of the volume is devoted to entries for specific titles, arranged by author, then title, giving basic bibliographic information, a brief annotation, and, usually, one or two excerpts from reviews. Entries include references to Nobel prizes, occasionally to several in-print editions, and, for short story and similar collections, contents notes.

The main entry section is followed by a title/subject index including analytics for novellas and similar parts of collective works, but not most short stories. (These are presumably handled by references to *Short Story Index* in the text.) Subject headings and general arrangement are similar to most Wilson products, but the index includes some very broad headings, notably for genres and ethnic groups. This index is followed by a directory of publishers, giving full addresses and names for the abbreviated versions used in the text.

The *Fiction Catalog* has three main uses. First, it is a companion to the *Public Library Catalog* (Wilson, 1978), giving the "best fiction" in English and in English translations, as determined by a representative group of public library systems. Second, it continues to provide a larger collection of plot summaries and descriptions of fiction than do, for example, the *Readers' Advisor*, volume 1 (see *ARBA* 75, entry 1314) or the *Thesaurus of Book Digests* (1st ed., Crown Publishers, 1949; *1950-1980*, Crown Publishers, 1981). Third, given the continued neglect of subject cataloging for fiction in most libraries, it provides a means of meeting the need for such.

It is clear that much care is given the selections. Roughly one-fourth of the titles are changed from the ninth edition, and an even larger proportion of annotations and review excerpts have been modified. It is an obviously difficult task to retain the "classics" while adding new titles, and the panel of selectors appears to do a good job. Unfortunately, since no criteria are listed, it is not possible for the user to judge how good a job. One does note, however, an apparently increasing number of short story collections, as well as a larger proportion of out-of-print titles in successive editions. There also appears to be a tendency to judge multivolume series as a whole, but then to treat each title separately — sequels, on the other hand, seem to be treated separately, and thus are less likely to be included.

In practice, the main use of this tool is for its subject index, and this meets the usual high Wilson standards. However, a number of improvements in this could be made. Many of the genre and geographic headings are very long; the reader could be better served with more subheadings. There are also occasional omissions in series entries, and some lapses in subject consistency. For example, Leinster's *First Contact*, definitely a short story, gets full analytical treatment, while most stories of such length do not.

Although most larger libraries will have many of the specialized bibliographies, they, as well as smaller ones, will still find this catalog useful for most general reference work in fiction. One major improvement would be full access to the entire text, including the annotations.   James H. Sweetland

127.   Galin, Saul, and Peter Spielberg. **Reference Books: How to Select and Use Them.** New York, Random House, 1969. 312p. o.p. LC 69-16443.

Bibliographic guide to 217 reference books, selected primarily for high school and undergraduate students. The first part of the book covers general reference works arranged by form, providing descriptions of their contents, method of organization, and potential use, with references to related works. Other parts dealing with humanities, social sciences, and physical sciences are arranged by title with similar information. In the last chapter the authors provide information on how to use library resources and write papers. Several critical comments can be made. The authors attempt to provide a rather detailed description of a given reference book, and at the same time fail to indicate pagination for monographic works, not to mention other important bibliographical details. Quite frequently old editions are used for a description, even in the case of well-known annuals, such as *Europa Year Book*, and new editions of some other equally well-known books, such as *Van Nostrand Scientific Encyclopedia* (4th ed., 1968) are not noted. In general, the coverage in the area of science and technology is quite weak (some twenty-five titles described) and probably this area should be omitted unless it is more fully treated. The index is quite detailed but, unfortunately, there are misleading references and the alphabetical sequence is not always consistent. Finally, the authors include hardly any bibliographic guides. This is true even in such areas as education. Obviously, bibliographic guides are very helpful for students interested in comprehensive coverage for a given area. Despite such flaws, this book will be a handy reference guide. As the paper edition indicates, it is intended for a mass market. [R: LJ, Jan 69; RQ, Fall 69]

128.   **Junior High School Library Catalog, 1980.** 4th ed. Edited by Gary L. Bogart and Richard H. Isaacson. New York, H. W. Wilson, 1980. 939p. (Standard Catalog Series). $62.00 (base vol. and suppls.). LC 80-53462. ISBN 0-8242-0652-5.

The fourth edition of this bibliographic guide which first appeared in 1965, annotates 3,775 books, in-print at the time of cataloging, considered appropriate for the seventh, eighth, and ninth grades. Preliminary evaluation is done by an advisory committee, and the resulting list is submitted to a group of consultants who vote on those to be included. The books are arranged according to the *Abridged Dewey Decimal Classification*. Fiction and short story collections are included. Complete bibliographical information, including price, ISBN, LC card number, suggested subject headings based on *Sears List of Subject Headings*, and an annotation are given for each book. The annotation usually includes one or more quoted evaluations from published reviews. The books can be accessed through a detailed 450-page author, title, subject, and analytical index. There are 9,061 analytical entries, with subject analytics providing access to those parts of books not covered by the general subject, and author/title analytics accessing the contents of collections of plays, short stories, etc. Part 3 is a directory of the publishers and distributors found in part 1.

Inadequacies in the coverage of the modern history of foreign countries noted in the review of the third edition (see *ARBA* 76, entry 159) have, for the most part, been remedied. More titles are noted in this edition for Scandinavia, Greece, Africa, and India. Coverage in political science, however, seems somewhat scanty, especially for our four most recent presidents. *Books in Print* lists numerous titles for Nixon, Ford, Carter, and Reagan, several of which were published before 1980 and would be suitable for junior high level readers. No entries are found in the index under Iran concerning the hostage situation.

As the reviewer in 1976 noted, despite these shortcomings, this is a valuable acquisitions and reference tool for junior high school librarians and teachers. [R: JAL, Jan 82, p. 379]

Louise Stwalley

129.   **Magazines for Libraries.** 4th ed. Bill Katz and Linda Sternberg Katz, eds. New York, R. R. Bowker, 1982. 958p. index. $75.00. LC 81-21769. ISBN 0-8352-1495-8.

Like its previous editions, the fourth edition of *Magazines for Libraries* seeks to identify and describe the "best and most useful" magazines for the "average primary or secondary school, public, academic or special library." Over one hundred consultants in different subject areas selected and annotated some sixty-five hundred titles from among over sixty-five thousand possibilities. Bill Katz and his co-editor, Linda Sternberg Katz, provided the consultants with basic guidelines and acted as overall evaluators of all sections and individual titles. However, the individual style and approach of each contributor are evident, making this work very much a collaborative effort.

As in the previous editions, entries are organized by subject and coded according to the appropriate audience. Titles of indexing and abstracting services covering each magazine follow the full bibliographical description. The annotations show purpose, scope, and audience with some evaluation provided. Each subject section begins with a short introduction and a recommended list of core periodicals essential for a basic collection.

The editors claim that this edition represents a "total revision," with 30 percent of titles being listed for the first time and carry-over entries from the third edition being revised. Like its predecessors, this edition will be an enormously useful tool for collection building and reference work for almost all kinds of libraries. [R: JAL, Sept 82, pp. 245-46; WLB, Sept 82, p. 75]   Heather Cameron

130. McLean, Isabel, comp. **Canadian Selection: Books and Periodicals for Libraries, 1977-1979 Supplement.** Buffalo, N.Y., University of Toronto Press, 1980. 398p. index. $35.00. ISBN 0-8020-4593-6.

The base book was reviewed in *ARBA 79* (entry 181). From the introduction to the supplement, the purpose is still the same: "to meet the need for a selective guide to significant English language books and periodicals for adults, published in Canada, about Canada, or written by Canadians at home and abroad. The choice has been made with the small and medium-sized public libraries in mind, but school and college libraries may find some sections useful."

The base book contained forty-three hundred listings plus 275 periodicals, all published through 1976. The supplement has 1,856 new listings with 35 new periodicals, and an occasional book from before the time frame of 1977-79. References are made to the base book for earlier editions of newly revised books. In addition, there appears to be a special, enlarged emphasis on legal materials. Once again, there are

bibliographic descriptions, suggested Dewey numbers and subject headings, plus signed annotations.

There have been some changes since the publication of the base book. More annotations are signed; the index has been improved (but still lacks cross-references); and the physical appearance is now in line with other such bibliographic tools available from the University of Toronto Press. However, this supplement covers only English-language materials. It is unfortunate that no French-Canadian items are included (except for those available in English translation) or items in any other language spoken in Canada.   Dean Tudor

131. **Public Library Catalog, 1983.** 8th ed. Gary L. Bogart and John Greenfieldt, eds. New York, H. W. Wilson, 1984. 1442p. index. $140.00 (price includes 4 suppls. for 1984-1987). LC 84-3508. ISBN 0-8242-0702-5.

This work originally appeared in 1928 under the title *Standard Catalog for Public Libraries.* Since then it has been issued in succeeding editions, with intervening supplements, and its title has changed.

The *Public Library Catalog* is a traditional collection development tool for public libraries and undergraduate colleges. The 7,777 titles, all of which are in print, are arranged by Dewey Decimal Classification, and each entry includes complete bibliography and cataloging information plus current price and an annotation or evaluation from an identified source. The author, title, and subject index accesses 12,815 analytical entries. The full name and address for the publisher and distributor of each title listed form the third part of the volume.

The catalog has sometimes been labelled traditional, conservative, and out-of-step with the times. In order to test this, two subject areas, the 320s ("Political Science") and the 610s ("Medicine") were reviewed in the 1973, 1978, and the present 1983 edition to determine how much change had taken place. Political science entries were reduced by half over the decade. Classics such as Machiavelli and Locke were retained but concerns for civil rights and political action by currently noteworthy authors were well represented. In international relations, more than half the titles changed every five years and the newer entries reflect recent concerns such as disarmament. Books on medicine doubled in number over the decade with only about a third to a quarter of the titles repeated from one edition to the next. Emphasis on fitness and physical self-awareness increased markedly in the titles selected. In each of these samples, the catalog reflects current concerns, and entries change as concerns change. It is a carefully crafted reference tool, definitely not unresponsive to the world around us. Appreciation for the catalog increases with use.

Ann E. Prentice

132. Reference and Subscription Books Reviews. Prepared by the American Library Association Reference and Subscription Books Review Committee. Helen K. Wright, ed. Beth A. Nickels, comp. Chicago, American Library Association, 1970- . biennial until 1974, then annual. $20.00. LC 73-159565. ISSN 0080-0430.

This annual publication is a compilation of evaluations produced by the American Library Association's Reference and Subscription Books Review Committee and published in *Reference Books Bulletin* (formerly *Reference and Subscription Books Reviews*), a separate periodical contained within ALA's twice-monthly *Booklist*. The book is intended to serve primarily as a selection tool for acquisitions librarians of small and medium-sized public and college libraries, and secondarily as an aid to laypersons who choose reference works for their homes and businesses.

All of the committee's evaluations are prepared as a team effort, rendering collective and perhaps less biased opinions. The reviews focus on content in terms of the book's audience and use as well as the importance of its subject to the profession. They also consider packaging: the appeal of the cover, the quality of printing and binding, and so forth. It is the committee's policy to state price without commenting upon it, but the group nonetheless plays the role of consumers' advocate by not recommending or not reviewing expensive works that contribute little to the literature.

In the past, these reviews were considered to be the best and most reliable to be found. However, they have also been roundly criticized for the time lag — as much as nine months — resulting from the lengthy process of preparing each review. Beginning in 1983, the committee attempted to ameliorate this situation by introducing the short and superficial signed "News Notes," a compromise of the committee's tradition of detailed analysis.

The value of *Reference and Subscription Books Reviews* is that it gathers a year of the committee's evaluations into one convenient source; however, it would be a practical purchase for only the largest libraries of the book's target audience. Smaller libraries that already subscribe to *Booklist* can get the same

information there and make purchasing decisions on a semimonthly basis.

Shelley Ewing and Annette Pekarek

133. Reference Sources for Small and Medium-sized Libraries. 4th ed. Compiled by the Ad Hoc Committee for the Fourth Edition of *Reference Sources for Small and Medium-sized Libraries.* Edited by Jovian P. Lang and Deborah C. Masters. Chicago, American Library Association, 1984. 252p. index. $20.00pa. LC 84-6513. ISBN 0-8389-3293-2.

Reference services have changed greatly in the past five years, largely because of increasing use of computerized database searching to find both bibliographic and "hard" data. ALA has changed the name of its *Reference Books for Small and Medium-sized Libraries* to reflect the growing use of databases as well as microforms. Although most of the sources are in print, some important out-of-print works have been included. The expanded text of this fourth edition (there is an 80 percent increase in the number of entries) also includes reference books useful for children and young adults or for librarians who work with them (e.g., *The Dinosaur Dictionary*). Such sources are noted with a "J" for juvenile or "Y" for young adults in the annotations. Each entry includes bibliographic information, frequency of publication if applicable, current price, ISBN or ISSN number, and an annotation. Superintendent of Documents numbers are given when appropriate. Entries are listed by twenty-two major subject areas and are further subdivided both by subject and by type of source. This edition contains separate chapters for encyclopedias and psychology and adds law to political science. It omits "contemporary social concerns," moving those sources to appropriate places in other chapters.

ALA has done an excellent job of including the fundamental works in each subject area. The annotations are concise but useful. This book will be appreciated and used by those smaller libraries which are committed to keeping up with the latest developments in the delivery of reference and information services. It will also be useful for larger libraries wishing to evaluate their ready-reference collections. [R: LJ, Aug 84, p. 1430; WLB, Nov 84, pp. 226-27]

Linda S. Keir

134. Senior High School Library Catalog. 12th ed. Gary L. Bogart and Richard H. Isaacson, eds. New York, H. W. Wilson, 1982. 1299p. index. (Standard Catalog Series). $70.00. LC 82-15974. ISBN 0-8242-0677-0.

This work began in 1926 as *Standard Catalog for High School Libraries.* This edition of

Senior High School Library Catalog continues the work's long tradition as a source of recommended books for a core collection for senior high school libraries. Experienced librarians from all sections of the country selected the books included in this edition. With 5,056 titles, it is smaller by 225 titles than the eleventh edition and has 15,530 analytic entries compared to 17,587 in the eleventh.

According to the preface, one of the problems the committee encountered in compiling the list was the rapidity with which many books go out-of-print. Items known to be out-of-print were excluded, so the coverage on certain subjects is necessarily restricted.

Like previous editions, the twelfth edition has a classified catalog; author, title and subject, and analytical indexes; and a directory of publishers and distributors. Except for entries in the directory, the type size and typeface make entries easy to read. The publishers and distributors list, however, should have an accompanying magnifying glass.

Most entries in the classified catalog have one or two brief quotations from reviews of the book and include the name of the review source. For some books, however, a quotation from the book's preface is used or a short annotation is supplied.

In general, the selections are well made, with due concern for quality literature and information. One inclusion was a surprise. *The New Grove Dictionary of Music and Musicians* is an outstanding reference source, but its cost will keep many school libraries from purchasing the set. After being omitted from the eleventh edition, *The Adventures of Huckleberry Finn* is back in the twelfth, but Thomas Hardy's *The Mayor of Casterbridge* is not included. Six Jane Austen titles are listed in the twelfth; only four were in the eleventh.

A helpful list of published editions for works of fiction both provides a guide to the range of publishers of a work and includes each book's hardbound and paperbound editions. [R: BL, 15 Dec 83, pp. 623-24]

Patricia Tipton Sharp

135. Stevens, Rolland E., and Donald G. Davis, Jr. **Reference Books in the Social Sciences and Humanities.** 4th ed. Champaign, Ill., Stipes, 1977. 189p. index. $6.80pa. ISBN 0-87563-140-1.

The third edition of this work, published in 1971, was written as a teaching aid for courses in the social sciences and humanities. This edition is substantially enlarged, covering 584 titles "of the most useful books in these subject fields" (preface, p. iii). Approximately 225 titles have

been added and 185 dropped from the previous edition. It is probably not fair to discuss selection criteria for such a uniquely selective listing since both authors obviously have their own preferences. Apart from this, it seems to us that there is occasional misinformation given—for example, the implication that there is a Russian counterpart to Sheehy or Walford (p. 2), and the *Annual Register of Grant Support* (p. 23) was not only published in 1969 but in several subsequent years (and its scope has changed substantially since 1973). All annotations are descriptive, and the authors occasionally provide helpful comments on certain strengths or weaknesses of a particular title. [R: WLB, Sept 77, p. 90]

Bohdan S. Wynar

136. Wynar, Bohdan S., ed. **Recommended Reference Books for Small and Medium-sized Libraries and Media Centers 1984.** Littleton, Colo., Libraries Unlimited, 1984. 287p. index. $27.50. LC 81-12394. ISBN 0-87287-435-4; ISSN 0277-5948.

Like its predecessors, the fourth issue of this annual identifies new reference books and selected reference serials appropriate for consideration by small college, public, and school libraries. The editor selected the 506 titles reviewed from the 1,534 reviewed in *ARBA 84*. Their arrangement into forty-one topical chapters is almost identical to *ARBA*'s. Although school, public, and college libraries are the target audience, librarians working in these types of libraries are underrepresented in the group of over two hundred reviewers, top-heavy with university librarians. The reviews were writen for *ARBA* and its very broad audience made up of all types of libraries of all sizes. The effect of these factors is inconsistency among the reviews; not all of them address the question of a book's suitability for the target audience libraries. Code letters assigned to the reviews to indicate the type of library or libraries for which each is recommended help compensate for this inconsistency.

Although all 506 titles are recommended favorably, many reviews point out faults or errors in the books. Because the reviewers use their special knowledge of a subject, of reference works, or of both in evaluating the books, selectors can place considerable confidence in their judgments. When in doubt, selectors can easily consult another review in one or more of ten other reference review media whose reviews are cited, in the style of *ARBA*.

This annual continues to prove its value to small and medium-sized libraries which want an annual review of new reference works geared to their needs. It offers them convenience and economy. Needless to say, large libraries which (as they should) subscribe to *ARBA* do not need to duplicate a third of it with this.

James Rettig

14 Library Holdings— Surveys and Guides

COMPREHENSIVE

137. Collier, Clifford, and Pierre Guilmette. **Dance Resources in Canadian Libraries.** Ottawa, Ont., National Library of Canada, 1982. 1v. (various paging). (Research Collections in Canadian Libraries: Special Studies, No. 8). $21.30pa. ISBN 0-660-51022-7.

This book is not only a survey of dance research and education in Canada but also a description of "the state-of-the-art in the field of library resources for dance studies" and an "aid in developing and improving existing collections or starting new ones." The edition is bilingual (English/French), which probably accounts for its relatively steep cost for a paperbound volume, but it is a model of scholarship, expertly researched, organized, and written, and will be of interest outside as well as within the country.

The main text consists of five parts: a brief introduction and discussion of methodology used in the study; a historical overview; a statistical summary with three tables, the first two indicating the approximate size of monograph and serial collections, the third noting the existence of nonbook materials (vertical files, picture files, ballet programs, manuscripts, microforms, slides, and films) in Canadian libraries; more detailed descriptions of major individual collections by province with access and type of classification system noted; and observations and suggestions for the future. These are followed by a brief page of footnotes and bibliography, four appendices, and an index.

Appendix A, I lists and locates dance serials (titles and holdings) available in Canada; A, II lists dance serials not found in Canadian libraries. Both lists are alphabetically arranged and give publication date and place. Both current and retrospective titles are included; these range from The American Dance Therapy Association's *Newsletter* to *Mixed Pickles: The Magazine of Folk Dance, Folklore and Related Folk Arts* to a large number of classical dance journals. Appendix B lists reference works related to dance; appendix C cites postsecondary institutions in Canada which grant diplomas or offer instruction in dance; and appendix D lists collections (by province) which include books, journals, notations, and set/costume designs together with the approximate number of holdings of each.

Carole Franklin Vidali

138. Downs, Robert B. **American Library Resources: A Bibliographic Guide. Supplement 1971-1980.** Chicago, American Library Association, 1981. 209p. index. $30.00. LC 51-11156. ISBN 0-8389-0342-8.

The introduction to *American Library Resources, 1971-1980* states "the purpose of the present work is to offer a bibliographical guide to all the resources of U.S. libraries. The intention is to record all published library catalogs; all checklists of specialized collections in libraries; calendars of manuscripts and archives; exhibition catalogs; articles descriptive of library collections; guides to individual libraries and their holdings; directories of libraries; union lists of periodicals, newspapers, and other serials; and any other records, descriptive, analytical or critical, that may guide the scholar, research worker, or advanced student in finding significant materials." The 1971-1980 supplement is the third (previous supplements covered 1951-1960, published in 1962, and 1961-1970, published in 1972); the original volume of *American Library Resources: A Bibliographical Guide* appeared in 1951 and covered information available from 1870 to 1950.

American Library Resources functions as a bibliography of bibliographies, rather than as a description of specific library resources. Arranged by subject, using the Dewey Decimal Classification as a guide, the work presents bibliographic descriptions of works, regardless of length, that describe library holdings. The number of published guides to library resources has been growing with each supplement: the 1951-1960 work covered 2,818 items; 3,241 titles were included in the 1961-1970 supplement; and some 4,250 items appear in the 1971-1980 volume. This fact makes it apparent that research libraries wish to publicize their collections and share their resources. However, it must be recognized that not every library has a published collection guide. *American Library Resources*, nonetheless, continues to be an important work for librarians and scholars in the United States.   Janet H. Littlefield

139. Downs, Robert B. **British and Irish Library Resources: A Bibliographical Guide.** rev. ed. Assisted by Elizabeth C. Downs. London, Mansell; distr., New York, H. W. Wilson, 1981. 427p. index. $62.00. ISBN 0-7201-1604-X.

This work, a revised and updated edition of the author's *British Library Resources* (1973), is considerably expanded over its predecessor, containing 6,731 entries, one-third more than the earlier edition's 5,039. Like the earlier edition, this one attempts to collect library catalogs, checklists of special collections, calendars of manuscripts and archives, exhibition catalogs, articles describing library collections, guides or directories of libraries, union lists, or any other publication that may assist the scholar or student in locating materials of interest in libraries of the United Kingdom or Eire. The altered title probably reflects changing politics, since the earlier work also listed publications describing libraries in Eire.

A few reservations must be noted. No work of this kind will claim to be complete, and a random check of twenty titles taken from Stephen Roberts's *Research Libraries and Collections in the United Kingdom* (1978), which Downs includes as his item 156, found two omitted (W. L. Davies's *The National Library of Wales: A Survey of Its History, Its Contents and Its*

Activities, 1937; and R. Datta's *Union Catalogue of the Government of Pakistan Publications Held by Libraries in London, Oxford and Cambridge*, 1967). It is disconcerting to search Downs's indexes for the *Catalogue of the Comparative Education Library* of the University of London (1971; *Supplement*, 1974) and find it unlisted except with the five pages of entries for education; it would have helped to include institutional headings with the author/compiler/editor index. Also, it would have relieved the eye and assisted in picking entries from the page to vary the typeface, perhaps by using boldface for main entries and smaller type size for annotations, in the manner of Sheehy's *Guide to Reference Books*.

These, however, are minor complaints against a work that has proven its value over several years and that reference librarians have found repeatedly useful in advising readers who are planning research projects that will take them to British or Irish libraries. The arrangement, by a subject classification based on the Dewey classification, will be familiar to librarians and recognized by scholars and students. Indexes are carefully prepared, and the subject index gives access to topics that escape the classification scheme. Reference librarians will want to use Downs jointly with the one by Roberts mentioned above; the latter lists publications describing a library's collections together with the entry for the institution, an approach that Downs lacks. Particularly useful in Downs is the final section, the individual bibliography, which identifies collections relating to individual writers, musicians, politicians, etc.

In finding important collections in British and Irish libraries, this book has no rival, and it will be wanted in every college or research library.   Robert Balay

140. Foster, Janet, and Julia Sheppard. **British Archives: A Guide to Archive Resources in the United Kingdom.** Detroit, Gale, 1982. 533p. bibliog. index. $65.00. ISBN 0-8103-1126-7.

British Archives is a major reference work that every researcher needing to use such records and manuscripts will want to consult. This volume includes a description of 708 institutions, which have been arranged by geographic area (these locations are listed alphabetically). Each institution's description consists of its address, telephone number, the name of the individual to contact, hours of operation, access, historical background, acquisitions policy, major collections, nonmanuscript material, available finding aids, reading room facilities, and publications. *British Archives* also includes a select bibliography of published references and general subject indexes.

This publication seems to be a handy reference work, although its real value can only be tested by those researchers endeavoring to use it. The reference could have been strengthened, however, with the inclusion of a map or maps of the repository locations; explanation for the selection of references in the concluding bibliography, with some annotations to the more important works; and some greater detail in the description of the holdings (the formula entry for local government records is explained but is still annoying for a researcher wanting to know more precisely their holdings). None of these criticisms should, however, deter use of this guide.

British Archives is recommended for all institutions with strong European history and genealogy collections. [R: BL, 1 Dec 83, pp. 549-50; LJ, 15 Apr 83, p. 816]

Richard J. Cox

141. Gebhardt, Walther, comp. **Special Collections in German Libraries: Federal Republic of Germany Incl. Berlin (West).** By commission of Deutsche Forschungsgemeinschaft. New York, Walter de Gruyter, 1977. 739p. index. $59.20. LC 77-22288. ISBN 3-11-005839-1.

This volume, the results of a project underwritten by the Deutsche Forschungsgemeinschaft, is an attempt to list all of the special collections in German libraries. These include not only libraries in the Federal Republic of Germany, but other "federal collections abroad," such as collections in Istanbul, Athens, and Florence. East German collections are not included.

The criteria used for listing the 877 special collections are that of (1) size of collection, and (2) usefulness as source materials for researchers. Categories of the collections included are traditional literature, printed graphics, portraits, leaflets, posters, maps, printed music, and some esoteric collections such as emergency money (*Notgeld*) and ration cards. The collections are found not only in special libraries, public libraries, and institute and seminar libraries in universities, but also in archives, museums, associations, and some private collections.

Separate listings include a classification scheme for the collections, a subject heading list, and an extensive index. Each entry includes the address of the holder and the telephone number, as well as additional information (on size, depth, and subject) that could be gleaned from the questionnaire returned. The entries are

uneven in their treatment because of the questionnaire responses.

The author admits that "much more remains to be done in a later edition as far as institute and private libraries are concerned." Certainly it would be a more useful volume if all special collections of German libraries could be included. Even with these limitations, though, it is a monumental work, well documented, with a good format. It should be an invaluable aid for scholars and librarians in pursuing research interests and interlibrary borrowing. [R: C&RL, May 78, p. 236; LJ, 1 Apr 78, p. 725]

Robert D. Stueart

142. Grimsted, Patricia Kennedy. **Archives and Manuscript Repositories in the USSR: Estonia, Latvia, Lithuania, and Belorussia.** Princeton, N.J., Princeton University Press, 1981. 929p. bibliog. index. (Columbia University. Studies of the Russian Institute; Harvard Ukrainian Research Institute. Harvard Ukrainian Series). $60.00. LC 79-15427. ISBN 0-691-05279-4.

The accolades that greeted Patricia Grimsted's first volume, *Archives and Manuscript Repositories in the USSR: Moscow and Leningrad*, apply equally to the present guide of archival materials in Estonia, Latvia, Lithuania, and Belorussia. This handbook is a model of logical organization, expedient arrangement, clear description of material, and inclusion of additional relevant matter. Not only does Grimsted provide excellent descriptions of holdings of central state archives, Communist Party archives, and manuscript collections of all major libraries, but she also provides the user with a bibliography of general reference works, finding aids for related materials, charts and historical maps, and tables of geographical names for each republic. One should also emphasize the usefulness of the first-rate historical survey essays preceding each descriptive section.

This guide will be useful not only to scholars and researchers planning a trip to the Soviet Union, but to all who have a scholarly interest in the Baltic republics and Belorussia. A catalog of finding aids on microfiche put out by the Inter Documentation Company in Switzerland and correlated with Grimsted's volume is available.

Natalia Sonevytsky

143. Howell, J. B., ed. **Special Collections in Libraries of the Southeast.** Jackson, Miss., published for the Southeastern Library Association by Howick House, 1978. 423p. index. o.p.

Intended to partially update Robert B. Downs's *Resources of Southern Libraries* (American Library Association, 1937), this volume lists 2,022 special collections in 10 states (Alabama, Florida, Georgia, Kentucky, Mississippi, North Carolina, South Carolina, Tennessee, Virginia, and West Virginia). Each state section, compiled by a librarian of that state, is subdivided by towns. Each entry provides the name and address of the library and a brief description of each of its major special collections. For smaller libraries (historical society or public), annotations are basically general statements of content and purpose of the total collection. Most entries supply some indication of the size of the collection.

Collections with restricted access are noted; however, no information is provided on where to apply for admission to a restricted collection, if access is possible. No personal names or telephone numbers are given, so a researcher must spend extra time locating this information. Geographic, corporate, and general (subject) indexes are included. If this volume is used in conjunction with other reference tools, such as P. M. Hamer's *Guide to Archives and Manuscripts in the United States* (Yale University Press, 1961), L. Ash's *Subject Collections* (6th ed., R. R. Bowker, 1985), and the Downs title mentioned above, the researcher will have access to a fairly complete representation of the major special collections in the Southeast. [R: C&RL, May 79, p. 288; LJ, 1 Apr 79, p. 807; WLB, Mar 79, p. 527]   G. Edward Evans

144. Jackson, William Vernon. **Resources of Research Libraries: A Selected Bibliography.** Pittsburgh, Pa., University of Pittsburgh Book Center, 1969. 65p. o.p.

This work is a selected list of 487 references for those interested in library resources and "seeking orientation for a program of reading." Although entries are not annotated, they are arranged under topical headings (e.g., "Spatial and Financial Aspects of Library Resources" and "Description and Evaluation of Library Resources"), with some subdivisions (a total of 20 sections). Thus the bibliography serves a purpose quite different from the comprehensive listing found in Robert B. Downs's *American Library Resources: A Bibliographical Guide* (American Library Association, 1951), and its supplements. Despite its date, it is still useful for its classified approach. There is an author/title index at the end.

Donald G. Davis, Jr.

145. Keller, Clara D., comp. **American Library Resources: Cumulative Index, 1870-1970.** Chicago, American Library Association, 1981. 89p. $25.00. LC 81-12788. ISBN 0-8389-0341-X.

The cumulative index to *American Library Resources* identifies by subject and library all special collections acquired by American libraries from 1870 through 1970. It has been published at the same time as *American Library Resources: A Bibliographical Guide, Supplement 1971-1980* (American Library Association, 1981) and must be used in conjunction with the index to this supplement to discover the full range of publications relating to the resources of libraries in the United States. Structure of the cumulative index is straightforward: entries are followed by a Roman numeral and an Arabic number. The Roman numeral refers to the main volume or supplements of *American Library Resources* (through 1970), and the Arabic number identifies the entry number with the volume cited. Libraries possessing *American Library Resources* will find the index a time-saving device.   Janet H. Littlefield

146. Lewanski, Richard C., comp. **Subject Collections in European Libraries.** 2nd ed. New York, R. R. Bowker, 1978. 495p. index. $57.00. ISBN 0-85935-011-8.

Intended as a companion volume to Lee Ash's *Subject Collections* (see *ARBA* 80, entry 122), this work is somewhat improved and substantially enlarged (12,000 entries) in comparison to the first edition published in 1965 (8,000 entries). It is arranged by subject, using the Dewey Decimal Classification, and the information is based on a questionnaire mailed to some 10,000 libraries selected from national and local library directories and other sources. According to the preface, only about 25 percent of the libraries answered the questionnaire; consequently, most of the information included in this volume is based on secondary sources. Each entry includes the following data: name of institution, address, director (when given), year established, special items, size of collection, and restrictions in use, if any. This new edition occasionally includes hours of service, availability of photocopying facilities, and types of catalogs or periodicals published by a given institution. The volume concludes with a rather inadequate subject index, which serves as a kind of alphabetical key to the classification scheme.

The listing for Ukrainian literature (p. 362) includes 11 entries. The largest library in Ukraine, Tsentral'na Naukova Biblioteka of the Academy of Sciences of the Ukrainian SSR in Kiev, is listed; however, the information provided is not always accurate. Some of the errors were probably made in typing or copying from the rather obsolete directory, *Biblioteky Ukrains'koi SSR. Dovidnyk* [*Libraries of Ukrainian SSR. Directory*] (Kharkiv, 1969). Thus, much of the information is taken word for word from the above-mentioned source (e.g., name of the director (now deceased), quantity of mss., music scores, picture prints, patents, etc.). Lewanski indicates general holdings of this library as 4 million items (should be 6 million, according to *Biblioteky Ukrains'koi SSR. Dovidnyk*, and is now actually over 7 million). Interestingly enough, the same library is listed again under Ukrainian history (p. 449); this entry lists the library's holdings as 5 million and mostly repeats the information provided in the section under literature.

If Lewanski correctly lists some of the special collections for leading literary figures (e.g., Kotsiubyns'kyi) under literature, it is unnecessary to list them again in the historical section. Instead, special collections of prominent Ukrainian historians (e.g., Lazarevs'kyi or M. Hrushevs'kyi) should be listed only in the historical section. Of the 11 entries given for Ukrainian literature, some are simply not pertinent. Thus, Knyzhkova Palata Ukrains'koi SSR (Ukrainian Book Chamber) is an equivalent to the All-Union Book Chamber in Moscow, specializing in bibliographical work (primarily preparing Ukrainian national bibliographies as well as some trade bibliographies). The same is true of some smaller libraries, for example, libraries of certain institutes of education listed by the compiler. Most large university libraries are not listed (e.g., Kiev, Odessa, etc.). As a matter of fact, Lenin Library in Moscow, the largest Soviet library, contains a rather significant collection of Ukrainian literature, as do other libraries in the Soviet Union outside of Ukraine.

Such errors in fact or interpretation can be found in other subjects, which simply illustrates the difficulty in executing a project of this magnitude. These difficulties notwithstanding, the work provides a beginning point from which to locate special collections. It should be recommended to all academic libraries. [R: C&RL, July 79, p. 391; JAL, May 79, p. 111; LJ, 1 June 79, p. 1231]   Bohdan S. Wynar

147. **Music Resources in Canadian Collections.** Ottawa, Ont., National Library of Canada, 1980. 1v. (various paging). bibliog. index. (Research Collections in Canadian Libraries, Vol. 7). $21.30. ISBN 0-660-50451-0.

This volume, a directory of music holdings in Canadian libraries, is the seventh report in the National Library of Canada's series Research Collections in Canadian Libraries. The informa-

tion was collected by questionnaire and visits by staff members of the Music Division of the National Library of Canada. The book's most important aspect as a reference tool is the directory section. For each of 142 libraries there are addresses, phone numbers, hours of service, and sigla reflecting services and facilities, as well as descriptions of holdings in terms of number of titles, subscriptions, items, or linear feet. There is also a section devoted to the holdings of small collections and those to which access is restricted, as well as a list of nonpublic music collections in Canada. This directory aspect of the volume complements international efforts to describe the world's music collections. Of more parochial value are a historical statement, statistical tables, and an appraisal of musical Canadiana within Canadian libraries.

There is a very complex index of names which refers to page rather than entry number. In the directory part of the volume, this slows down the user because there are several entries per page. In fact, the preponderance of Arabic numerals within the directory is in itself slowing. The various components of each entry are numbered, and the sigla which describe services and facilities are also numbered. There is some differentiation in typeface among the three sets of numbers, but the use of boldface entry numbers in the index and alphabetical characters for the various components of each entry would have made reference use faster and easier.

The volume is in two paginations, one in English, the other in French. It will be an essential acquisition for all Canadian libraries and American research music collections.

An earlier report in this series was published in 1978 as a directory of fine arts holdings in Canadian libraries. The structure is basically the same as in this report, but the fine arts report was published in two volumes.

Carol June Bradley

148. National Library of Canada. **Research Collections in Canadian Libraries: I, Universities; 1, Prairie Provinces.** Ottawa, Ont., National Library of Canada, 1972. 136p. $1.00pa.

This report is Part 1, volume 1 of *Research Collections in Canadian Libraries*, an ongoing series undertaken by the National Library to report statistically by subject the collections of the universities offering graduate studies in the humanities and the social sciences. This is the outgrowth of two surveys of academic libraries in Canada—the *Downs Report* and the *Williams Report*. This volume surveys the five universities in the three prairie provinces of Saskatchewan, Alberta, and Manitoba. Arranged by LC class number, this census gives some indication of the resources available to support graduate studies in the region. All indications show poor support levels, but these statistics are badly out-of-date. The National Library has promised, however, that the statistics will be kept up and that they will be augmented by further surveys of federal government libraries, special libraries, and large public libraries and by the extension of these surveys to include science and other collections. A remarkable statistical reporting plan and an important addition to the literature of the field. [R: UNESCO, Jan/Feb 73, p. 48]

Andy Armitage

149. Nelson, Bonnie R. **A Guide to Published Library Catalogs.** Metuchen, N.J., Scarecrow, 1982. 342p. index. $17.50. LC 81-16558. ISBN 0-1808-1477-3.

After examining this guide carefully, one will be struck anew by the great diversity in both form and content of published library catalogs. Nelson's labor of love describes 429 such catalogs published within the last 20 years. They are arranged into 33 subject categories such as ancient and classical studies, the American West, women's studies, performing arts, psychology, Middle East, labor, business, English and American literature, medical sciences, and the like. The description of each catalog includes: subjects covered, languages included, types of materials (books, periodicals, government documents, theses, nonprint materials, etc.), presence of analytical entries for journal articles, the types of subject headings used, and the classification system.

The use of a printed library catalog to a researcher is obvious. Published catalogs can also be helpful in collection development, compilation of subject bibliographies, verification of a citation, or location of a known title. Librarians, scholars, and researchers will welcome this new well-annotated and clearly arranged guide. [R: JAL, July 82, p. 187; LJ, 1 Sept 82, p. 1623]

Natalia Sonevytsky

150. **Research Collections in Canadian Libraries. II, Special Studies. 1, Theatre Resources in Canadian Collections.** By Heather McCallum. Ottawa, Ont., National Library of Canada; distr., Ottawa, Ont., Information Canada, 1973. 113p. illus. index. $1.00pa.

This report is intended "to locate and assess theatre resources in Canadian collections in order to meet a growing need for such information by librarians, university faculty and scholars, educators, researchers, theatre personnel, students and members of the general public" (p. 1). The basic information section

contains a somewhat evaluative entry on materials in each of some 114 institutions in 10 categories ranging from federal government to special, private, and cinema collections. Five major archives outside Canada are listed, the only one in the United States being the Theater Collection of The New York Public Library at Lincoln Center.

Because of the nature of theater source materials, emphasis is rightly placed on nonbook materials of various types. The great value of this information is its usefulness for finding the small, special collection of particular materials that cannot be found in the large theater collections in the United States. Of course, such treasures can be found only through the subject index or by scanning the entire information section for the subject of one's interest. Since this means looking through only 72 pages, it would be no great problem for the serious researcher of, say, the Empire Theatre in Toronto, to find the McNeil collection of photographs in the University of Toronto Library listed on page 25, although this important collection is not brought out in the index. (McNeil's *name* is in the index for that entry, but the researcher would have to know that he had been the manager of the Empire to assume the collection would be of interest to his research.)

Following the inventory of the collections, the author assesses the resources of and recommends cooperation among the libraries and other institutions, especially the setting up of a committee to "work toward the establishment of a decentralized theatre information service for the whole of Canada" (p. 89). At the time of publication (1973) collecting policy was haphazard and disorganized, but this little volume does help as a guide and should be added to theater collections in the United States that make any kind of referrals at all.

The 10 pages of rather poorly reproduced photographs of material from collections neither add to nor detract from the reference value of the volume.

Richard M. Buck

151. **Research Collections in Canadian Libraries: II, Special Studies; 2, Federal Government Libraries.** Report of the Collections Team, Federal Government Library Survey. Ottawa, Ont., National Library of Canada, 1975. 231p. bibliog. $1.50pa. ISSN 0316-0319.

For a six-month period over the winter of 1972-1973, there was an investigation of collections, personnel, policies, and practices in the libraries of the federal government of Canada. Of the 199 libraries, 101 were visited and 98 were not. The appendices detail all the forms used, plus a subject and regional breakdown for the main interests of the collections of all 199 libraries. Included in the terms of reference was a mandate to make assessments and recommendations (e.g., strengths, weaknesses, overlaps, collection development, and planning), with a view to library cooperation, concepts of networks, and sharing of a scarcity of resources. Forty-three major recommendations are made and substantiated, most of them of the nature of nonphysical consolidation. Of particular interest to researchers are pages 67-100 (detailing special and unique collections by library, language, and subject) and appendix G (special and unique collections of government publications and technical reports).   Dean Tudor

152. Roberts, Stephen, Alan Cooper, and Lesley Gilder, comps. **Research Libraries and Collections in the United Kingdom: A Selective Inventory and Guide.** London, Clive Bingley; Hamden, Conn., Linnet Books, 1978. 285p. index. $25.00. ISBN 0-208-01667-8.

This book was published to meet the need for a one-volume reference to British libraries and research collections. A total of 247 institutions are listed, including national, specialist, public, and university libraries in the United Kingdom, and polytechnic libraries in England and Wales, with a separate listing of Scottish central institutions. There are three indexes—subject, name, and geographical—for comprehensive coverage. Preceding the list of libraries are two useful bibliographies: one of guides to libraries and collections; the second of archives and manuscripts in libraries.

For each entry, much useful information is provided in compressed form. In addition to such basic information as the number of books, periodicals, and audiovisual materials, the guide indicates the classification used (many British university libraries have turned to either the Dewey Decimal or the Library of Congress system), availability to users, and opening hours.

Inevitably, the volume will be compared to *The World of Learning* (see *ARBA* 76, entry 617). A check of the 1977-1978 edition of the latter disclosed that a total of eight libraries and 43 universities and colleges are duplicated in *Research Libraries and Collections.* However, the two publications may be considered complementary. *The World of Learning* has a broader coverage, but the new guide provides more detailed information on each institution, as well as new material on polytechnic libraries. This publication should be useful in meeting its declared objective: to be a point of departure for more detailed exploration. It is recommended for this purpose. [R: C&RL, July 79, p. 391;

JAL, May 79, p. 101; LJ, 1 May 79, p. 1018]
                                        Thomas S. Harding

153. **Special Collections in Children's Literature.** Carolyn W. Field, ed. Chicago, American Library Association, 1982. 257p. index. $18.00. LC 81-20565. ISBN 0-8389-0345-2.

The editor notes in her introduction that there has been a growing awareness among scholars and librarians of the importance of children's literature. This survey is designed to update and expand the 1969 *Subject Collections in Children's Literature.* It was prepared by the National Planning for Special Collections Committee, Association for Library Service to Children (ALA), with consultants Margaret N. Coughlan, Library of Congress, and Sharyl C. Smith, Nightingale Bamford School for Girls.

This work includes an introduction, a brief discussion of children's special collections, "Collections and Collectors of Children's Books," by Peggy Sullivan, a main section, "Collections by Subject"; another main section, "Directory of Collections"; two appendices, "Reference to Collections," and "Authors and Illustrators in Major Collections Not Listed in Body of Work"; and an index. In the introduction, the criteria for items are clearly defined: all formats of material for research relating to children's literature, series, comic books, unique collections, bibliographies, and oral and visual histories are included. The work does not include private collections, general browsing collections, parent-teacher collections, general collections in colleges and universities for the study of children's literature courses, or collections in examination centers or pedagogical libraries. This index does identify authors, illustrators, countries, genre, and format type. Under each subject entry is listed the place, collection, and information on the collection. The directory identifies the address, telephone number, and subject categories. It should be noted that the illustrations are taken from books in the Rare Books Department at the Free Library of Philadelphia. This volume will be of use mainly to those scholars who are interested in further special research in literature for children, and would be of assistance to large academic or special libraries only. [R: BL, July 82, p. 1452; Choice, Sept 82, pp. 58-60; JAL, July 82, p. 173; RQ, Summer 82, pp. 420-21; SLJ, Nov 82, p. 36]
                                        Paula Montgomery

154. Steele, Colin. **Major Libraries of the World: A Selective Guide.** New York, R. R. Bowker, 1976. 479p. illus. o.p. ISBN 0-85935-012-6.

In defining the major purpose of this book—to identify 300 major libraries of the world—Steele did not set himself an easy task. Assistant librarian at the Bodleian Library, Oxford, he admits in his preface that "the final responsibility for the selection of the libraries lies firmly with the author, who realises any such selection is invariably subjective. A small number of libraries were excluded because they did not reply either to the questionnaire on which *the Guide is based* [italics added] or to subsequent letters.... A general library of 400,000 volumes may not rank very highly in the United States or Europe but in Africa or Asia the impact of such a collection can be completely different" (preface, p. xv). Unfortunately, Steele defines neither his criteria for selection nor the term "major libraries." Is this compilation based entirely on a questionnaire and follow-up correspondence? On holdings? On the impact of a given library on the cultural development of the country or region? We do not know.

To confuse this matter even a little more, Steele points out in his brief preface that "certain libraries have been included as being representative of 'special libraries', e.g., the Lyndon Baines Johnson Library at Austin." What is meant by "representative"? Under the United States, 39 libraries are listed, one of which is a presidential library. Why is the Lyndon Baines Johnson Library "representative"? Another question: Why is the Detroit Public Library included but not the Cleveland Public Library? Numerous puzzles of this nature spring to mind immediately—and this reviewer's guess will be as good as that of any other reviewer. The criteria for selection are not explained—but such an explanation is an essential prerequisite for a work of this type.

What do we have in this book? There is a listing of 300 "major libraries," arranged alphabetically by country and then city. The author attempts to describe the history of each (in one or two brief paragraphs), and this is followed by another paragraph on special collections ("its treasures") and directory-type information: the library address and telephone number; exhibition areas, if any; hours when open; transport (we assume this means location of the library and how to get there); parking facilities; admission; sales and gift shops; facilities for copying; etc. All this is very nice, and most of this information was probably taken from the questionnaire or secondary sources. Yet, there is something else. In many cases the reader will find here a small photograph of the library's exterior and an illustration of a "special item" from the library's collection. The libraries and librarians

who supplied Steele with these photographs are acknowledged on page xvii. The photographs are of poor quality, and the selection of "special items" seems to have been done at random, serving at times simply to point out how little the author knows about a particular library, its history, and its holdings.

For what kind of audience was this book written? As a simple guide to 300 libraries (many selected at random), this directory probably will do; it might be of some assistance to the tourist. It is not a serious contribution to professional library literature, and its author showed considerable courage in publishing this book under such a pretentious title. [R: AB, 28 Mar 77, p. 1907; BL, 15 July 77, p. 1749; Choice, July 77, p. 662; LJ, Aug 77, p. 1584; WLB, Mar 77, p. 604]   Bohdan S. Wynar

155. Subject Collections: A Guide to Special Book Collections and Subject Emphases as Reported by University, College, Public, and Special Libraries and Museums in the United States and Canada. 6th ed. rev. and enl. Lee Ash, William G. Miller, and Barbara J. McQuitty, comps. New York, R. R. Bowker, 1985. 2v. index. $165.00/set. ISBN 0-8352-1917-8.

The sixth edition of *Subject Collections* provides access to the special collections of over 11,000 libraries and museums in the United States and Canada. As was true of the previous edition, "virtually all libraries included in this book are listed in the *American Library Directory*." Libraries not listed are omitted because they did not return their questionnaires or because their replies were unusable. In addition, the entries for museums have increased. The editors continue to urge museums to report their holdings more explicitly, as they "are often unique ... and should be part of the corpus of research materials available...." Editorial policy continues to emphasize efforts to collect this information. The result of this continuing effort to collect more and better information is a work that has become a standard purchase for most libraries. *See* references are plentiful in the work, though not one *see also* was found. One hopes that users will consult the Library of Congress Subject Heading list in order to make full use of available entries. This one criticism aside, *Subject Collections* is an extremely laudable and much-needed work.   Constance D. Williams

156. Suffolk Parochial Libraries: A Catalogue. London, Mansell, on behalf of St. Edmundsbury and Ipswich Diocesan Parochial Libraries Committee; distr., Salem, N.H., Mansell, 1977. 129p. o.p. ISBN 0-7201-0704-0.

The English parish or "parochial" library is a precursor of the public library and largely a phenomenon of the seventeenth and eighteenth centuries. In that era of growing literacy, these libraries frequently provided the only reading matter readily available for rural Englishmen. Their collections were, not unexpectedly, theological; however, over time, classical writers and histories became more prevalent. The decay and near-demise of the parish library makes this volume particularly welcome, for it assures us that by consolidation and attempts to refurbish, some of these collections survive intact.

This volume catalogs the holdings of eight libraries, three *in situ* and five preserved in St. Edmundsbury Cathedral. This is Mansell's second venture into the field, the first having covered Shropshire's parochial libraries (appropriately, since Dr. Thomas Bray, eighteenth-century champion of parish libraries, was a Shropshire native). The 1,850 volumes are listed alphabetically by author, with title, imprint, pagination, size, and (frequently) binding, marginalia, and "bound with" notes. Cross-references are interspersed; however, there is no index. Abbreviations indicate each item's owning libraries and its Wing number and Pollard and Redgrave numbers. The layout is clean and workmanlike, and the cataloging appears to be accurate.

One would wonder at this book's usefulness in America, as it is specifically a finding aid. It is also, of course, raw material for social and intellectual history of late seventeenth- and eighteenth-century England. As one would expect, Erasmus's *Paraphrases*, Foxe's *Book of Martyrs*, and Bishop Jewel's *Apologie* are represented. Three-fourths of the volumes listed are English imprints, with about one-third of the 1,850 represented in the *Short-Title Catalogues*. The libraries' declines show up in the fact that one-third of the titles are eighteenth century and only perhaps one-twentieth, nineteenth century. The historical introduction indicates a "number of previously unrecorded titles" for STC revisions. It would have been useful to know how many, as a sample of 10 percent of the titles indicated that the number might be fewer than one dozen. However, a harvest of even that size is a boon to bibliographers.   Leon J. Stout

157. Tait, J. A. **Library Resources in Scotland.** Glasgow, Scotland, Scottish Library Association; distr., New York, State Mutual Books, 1981. 151p. index. $45.00. ISBN 0-900649-19-4.

In 1968 the Scottish Library Association published the first edition of this directory. The present volume, which has been substantially restructured, omits the small collections that are of little interest to the general public. Also, as a matter of general editorial policy, school libraries, private libraries, and libraries engaged in profit-making have been excluded. The following information is provided for each institution: name and address, name of the librarian, number of library staff members, holdings (books and periodicals), classification used, hours the library is open, and services that the library provides.

REGIONAL STUDIES

158. Association for Asian Studies. Committee on South Asian Libraries and Documentation. **South Asian Library Resources in North America: Papers from the Boston Conference, 1974.** Edited by Maureen L. P. Patterson and Martin Yanuck. Zug, Switzerland, Inter Documentation, 1975; distr., Columbia, Mo., South Asia Books, 1976. 362p. (Bibliotheca Asiatica, 11). o.p. ISBN 3-85750-010-7(Inter Documentation); 0-88386-797-4(South Asia).

This work not only covers the problems of collecting South Asian library materials but also includes a list of libraries that maintain and develop collections from the countries in question: India, Pakistan, Ceylon, Bangladesh, and Nepal. The papers are written to include a survey of materials available, linguistic and other problems, and a general approach to the state of publication and librarianship within the area. These areas are rationally considered as parts of a whole region rather than separate, if not disparate, entities in themselves. The result is a work that is much more for reference purposes than for casual reading. Papers from a conference are always difficult to read, and surveys of library holdings are among the most useful of reference aids, but the book is aimed at scholars rather than those whose interests have not already been awakened to the expansion of cultural activity in South Asia. Along with the diffuse nature of such works, the typography presents further difficulties. However, the scholar in need of information or eager to read about the area and language of his particular effort will not be distracted or disappointed. The authors are experts in their own right and the whole work bears the stamp of reliability and authority.

     Jay E. Daily

159. **Directory of Libraries and Special Collections on Eastern Europe and the U.S.S.R.** Gregory Walker, ed. Hamden, Conn., Archon, 1971. 159p. index. o.p. SBN 258-96837-0.

This directory describes materials found in British libraries on the following countries: Albania, Bulgaria, Czechoslovakia, East Germany, Greece, Hungary, Yugoslavia, Poland, Romania, and the Soviet Union. Most of the information for individual libraries was obtained by means of a questionnaire administered in June 1970. The material is arranged in two parts. Part 1, the main body of the directory, lists libraries in alphabetical order by location subdivided by the name of the library. With some variations, the usual information includes the name of the chief librarian, the person in charge of the special collection, a brief description of holdings, admission requirements, services provided, etc. Part 2 lists names, addresses, and telephone numbers only of other sources of information defined as nonconventional libraries (e.g., news agencies, embassies, etc.). As specialists in this area are aware, Mostecky's work was published many years ago. We do not now have anything similar to Walker's guide for American libraries, and it is hoped that Slavicists in this country will take advantage of this handy source. [R: CLW, Feb 72, p. 311; LJ, 1 Mar 72, p. 849]

160. East Central and Southeast Europe: A Handbook of Library and Archival Resources in North America. Paul L. Horecky, chief ed. Santa Barbara, Calif., ABC-Clio, 1976. 467p. index. (Joint Committee on Eastern Europe Publication Series, No. 3). o.p. LC 76-28392. ISBN 0-87436-214-8.

Paul Horecky, chief of the Slavic and Eastern European Division at the Library of Congress, needs no introduction. He is the author or editor of several excellent bibliographies on the Soviet Union and Eastern Europe, among them *East Central Europe: A Guide to Basic Publications* and *Southeastern Europe: A Guide to Basic Publications*, both published by the University of Chicago Press. According to the foreword, "the present volume is intended to provide scholars, librarians, students, and researchers with a basic reference tool for the study of the essential collections available in major libraries, archives, and research institutions in the United States and Canada, by outlining the profiles of these collections and offering broad guidance to their subject and area contents" (p. ix). Emphasizing the humanities and the socioeconomic and political sciences, the handbook covers the following countries: Albania, Bulgaria, Czechoslovakia, East Germany, Greece, Hungary, Poland, Romania, and Yugoslavia. Forty participating research libraries, archives, and special institutions are described in this handbook. Chapters, ranging

in length from 2,000 to 5,000 words, were contributed by librarians or scholars from the particular institutions—for example, the holdings of the University of California at Berkeley are described by Rudolf Lednicky, those of the University of Chicago by Václar Laška. Most of the contributions to the handbook were received in late 1972 and the first half of 1973, and they reflect the state of the collections and services as of that period.

All in all, this is an excellent general orientation guide for students and faculty. [R: Choice, Sept 77, p. 828; RQ, Summer 77, p. 347] Bohdan S. Wynar

161. Hannam, Harry, ed. The SCOLMA Directory of Libraries and Special Collections on Africa in the United Kingdom and Western Europe. 4th rev. and expanded ed. Munich, New York, Hans Zell/K. G. Saur; distr., Detroit, Gale, 1983. 183p. index. $42.00. ISBN 3-598-10502-9.

This small and expensive directory is designed to help researchers and librarians locate material on Africa. The Standing Conference on Library Materials on Africa (SCOLMA) was founded 20 years ago to assist in coordinating research library acquisitions and interlibrary loan activities supporting university area studies programs. It has 100 members, an active publication program, and a general area specialization scheme.

For this edition, coverage was extended to Western European libraries and a special effort was made to include media holdings. The book lists 142 African collections in the United Kingdom and 133 collections in Western Europe. It is arranged alphabetically by country, then city, then institution, but the United Kingdom precedes other countries. The following information is given for most libraries: name, address, telephone number, librarian's name, and hours of opening. A paragraph describes the collection, including conditions of access and useful publications. A detailed index concludes the volume.

Obviously, to reach a fourth edition, this directory has been useful and unique. However, considerable upgrading will be needed before it can be called a first-rate reference title. Its most glaring weakness is the lack of exact information on each library's holdings. Most entries fail to give a clear idea of the African collection's size or depth, subject or country coverage. Nor does the directory clarify the collection's strength in items published in Africa versus items published about Africa in other countries. Many vague phrases are used. Often the total collection size is given and then followed by a note that Africa is well represented in the collection. Most descriptions are 3 to 15 lines long. The compiler's introduction warns that library coverage leaves much to be desired, particularly outside the United Kingdom, since information was collected by a mailed questionnaire. Western European collection descriptions are even shorter and more vague than those for the United Kingdom. In addition, to serve continental scholars, the book should be published in French, German, Spanish, and Italian.

John F. Harvey

162. Lewanski, Richard C. **Eastern Europe and Russia/Soviet Union: A Handbook of West European Archival and Library Resources.** New York, Munich, K. G. Saur, 1981. 317p. $50.00. ISBN 3-598-08012-3.

This handbook is a directory and inventory of the principal research resources in non-Communist Europe that pertain to the Slavic and Eastern European countries. It lists some 1,000 repositories – institutions of higher learning, libraries, archives, and museums – in 22 countries, also encompassing East Germany because of the German tradition for Slavic and Eastern European scholarship. The main subject focus is on the humanities and social sciences in the broadest sense, including the history of the natural sciences and technology.

The handbook is arranged alphabetically by country, within country by locality, and within locality by institution. For each repository the following information is provided where possible: address, director and/or Eastern European specialist, year established, subject profile and special holdings, type of catalog, photoduplication services, hours, circulation policy, and a list of publications issued about or sponsored by the institution. Moreover, the handbook contains other bibliographic materials on the surveyed repositories, such as union catalogs and general bibliographies concerning the repositories as a group or those of a given country or locality. The data relate to 1977, when the survey was completed.

Compiled by the noted bibliographer Richard C. Lewanski (see *ARBA* 76, entry 215 and *ARBA* 80, entry 133), this handbook is part of a series of bibliographic guides sponsored by the American Council of Learned Societies, the Social Science Research Council, and their Joint Committee on Eastern Europe in Support of Slavic and Eastern European Studies. As such it represents a companion volume to *East Central and Southeast Europe: A Handbook of Library and Archival Resources in North America*, edited by Paul L. Horecky (see *ARBA* 77, entry 192). Although the handbook could have been

strengthened as a reference source by the provision of an institutional index and a more specific subject index, the information in it will be of great value to librarians and research scholars. [R: BL, 1 Nov 81, p. 401; RQ, Fall 81, p. 94]

Stephen J. Bensman

163. **The United States: A Guide to Library Holdings in the UK.** Peter Snow, comp. Westport, Conn., Meckler Publishing, 1982. 717p. index. $45.00. ISBN 0-930466-45-4.

This guide is an excellent aid to the identification and location of holdings relating to the United States in over 350 libraries of the United Kingdom. Its scope encompasses printed, microform, and audiovisual materials in the arts, the humanities, the social sciences, and, to a lesser degree, the sciences. The guide provides the Americanist with information on the resources of an institution or area; on the conditions and facilities to be found in an institution, including such useful information as library hours and the availability of photographic and photocopying services; or holdings on particular subjects, periods, or individuals; and on the location of specific collections of large works. The guide includes an appendix listing over 1,800 microforms and multivolume works, with symbols indicating their location in about 30 major centers. Periodical holdings are excluded from the location lists since the *Union Catalogue of American Studies Periodicals*, by C. Deering, will include them in full. The guide is an excellent companion to J. Raimo's *A Guide to Manuscripts Relating to America in Great Britain and Ireland* (Meckler Publishing, 1979), and to the Institute of Advanced Legal Studies's *Union List of the United States Law Literature in Oxford, Cambridge and London* (1967).

This work is especially recommended for academic, research, and special libraries with interest in American studies, American history, and/or American-British relations. While the guide is intended to be used exclusively as a research tool, it is important to note that many of the holdings of the libraries listed are accessible to Americanists through the excellent services of the British Library Lending Division. [R: JAL, Sept 82, p. 253]

Antonio Rodriguez-Buckingham

164. **Workshop for Japanese Collection Librarians in American Research Libraries, August 28-30, 1978, Washington, D.C.** Washington, D.C., Association of Research Libraries, Office of Management Studies, 1979. 111p. illus. $12.50pa. ISBN 0-318-16140-0.

This publication results from a workshop, sponsored by the Japan-U.S. Friendship

Commission and coordinated by the Office of Management Studies of ARL, which brought together 26 Japanese collection librarians and curators to identify issues and problems of importance to the future of Japanese collections in the United States and to propose solutions, all of this in the context of the need to rationalize Japanese resources nationwide, given increasing fiscal pressures. Problems identified in these papers and recommendations for action relate to the development, use, and support of Japanese collections, their management and organization, and resource sharing.

The opening paper, "The Current Status and Directions of Japanese Studies," by M. Jansen of Princeton, describes the environment within which most Japanese collections exist. Papers by librarians include "Collections in Support of Japanese Studies: Current Status" (H. Kaneko, Yale), which, supported by statistics, assesses collections in terms of holdings, acquisitions, funding, geographical distribution, and bibliographical control. It concludes that there is a decided imbalance between the volume of Japanese publishing and the libraries' coverage of it. "Book Market in Japan and LC's Acquisition Program" (H. Matsumoto, Library of Congress), whose author is a former head of the LC Tokyo office, describes the Japanese book trade, with emphasis on uniquely Japanese practices which differ markedly from those in the United States. "Emerging Issues in National Resource Sharing: The Case of Japanese Collections" (W. Tsuneishi, Library of Congress) outlines some issues that require attention before rational distribution of resources can be effected nationally. These include the need for a study of the actual and potential clientele and its use of Japanese resources; for qualitative assessments of collections and guides to their contents; for in-depth collection analysis as a prelude to coordinated acquisitions; and problems related to access, to cooperative collection development, and to participation in national networks. Two other papers discuss resource sharing from the viewpoint of the smaller collection (S. Matsuda, Indiana) and at the regional level (P. Yampolsky, Columbia).

"Organization and Management of Japanese Collections" (L. Martin, Harvard), by a research library director who must weigh competing collection demands, provides a different perspective, as does "Japanese Libraries for Japanese Studies" (N. Fukuda, University of Michigan), which focuses mainly on literature and history collections in Japan. An appendix, "Results and Recommendations," sets forth some short- and long-term projects to deal with the issues and problems raised.

These papers, the first such compilation, should serve as a valuable guide for general library administrators, students, area specialists, and others who seek information about Japanese collections in the United States. They are essential reading for librarians who work with Japanese materials or who have any responsibility for them, and for administrators of libraries that include Japanese among their collections. It should be noted that, although the factual material relates to Japanese collections, much of the information about issues in relation to future developments is transferable to East Asian collections. This book should remain useful for a long time since, despite many workable recommendations, the problems presented will not soon disappear.

Joyce Wright

INDIVIDUAL LIBRARIES AND SUBJECTS

165. Melville, Annette, comp. **Special Collections in the Library of Congress: A Selective Guide.** Washington, D.C., Library of Congress; distr., Washington, D.C., GPO, 1980. 464p. index. $17.00. LC 79-607780. ISBN 0-8444-0297-4; S/N 030-001-00092-3.

Anyone engaged in serious research at the Library of Congress will probably find a knowledgeable staff member to offer guidance to the vast resources available. But a scholar may sometimes wish to have some awareness of the scope of materials in a special area before making a trip to the Library of Congress. The present volume offers overviews of holdings in 269 collections of books, pamphlets, drawings, films, manuscripts, maps, music, musical instruments, prints, photographs, sound recordings, videotapes, and other nonbook items. It replaces the 1949 publication *A Guide to the Special Book Collections in the Library of Congress,* which covered 140 collections.

Arrangement is alphabetical by collection name, with a detailed index to personal/corporate names and subjects. An appendix gives brief descriptions of the LC divisions and their holdings. One need not be a scholar to be intrigued by some of the collections. Consider the 1,350 tapes and 1,900 transcription discs which carry jazz and swing performances from the 1940s through the 1960s—recordings not otherwise accessible; or the stereoscopic photographs of California and Nevada in the mid-nineteenth century; or the 5,000 pieces of French graphic art relating to World War I; or the 2,300 comic books; or the 1,550 volumes on cryptography from the seventeenth century.

All libraries will want this attractive, inexpensive volume—not only as a guide for scholars, but as a fascinating testimony to the splendors of the Library of Congress and the art of collection development. [R: LJ, 1 Sept 81, p. 1607; RQ, Fall 81, pp. 102-3]

Guy A. Marco

166. National Agricultural Library Catalog: Indexes for 1971-1975. Totowa, N.J., Rowman and Littlefield, 1978. 2v. $115.00/set. ISBN 0-8476-6093-1.

A cumulation of annual indexes that appear in the December issues of the *National Agricultural Library Catalog*, this two-volume set must be used with the *NAL Catalog* to obtain full bibliographic information. Books, periodicals, and serials (but not individual articles) are accessed by four separate indexes: personal author, corporate author, title, and subject. Each entry in the index contains only the indexing name or word and the citation number for the item in the monthly issue of the *NAL Catalog*. Entries under an existing term are arranged alphabetically, except in the subject index, where multiple listings are arranged by ascending citation number within each year. The National Agricultural Library changed to Library of Congress subject headings in 1972, so the user should read the section on cataloging, and be prepared to use several subject terms to access all the material. Librarians who frequently use the *NAL Catalog* will find this cumulated index useful. [R: Choice, Apr 79, p. 206; RQ, Spring 79, pp. 312-13]

167. Williams, Sam P., comp. **Guide to the Research Collections of the New York Public Library.** Chicago, American Library Association, 1975. 336p. index. o.p. LC 75-15878. ISBN 0-8389-0125-5.

This title replaces Karl Brown's *Guide to the Reference Collections of the New York*

Public Library, published by the library in 1941, but it differs enough in arrangement to be considered a new work, not merely a revision of Brown's guide. Brown presented materials in the same arrangement in which they appeared on the shelves, while Williams uses a hierarchical subject arrangement that brings together collections on related topics whether or not the materials are actually kept in the same area of the NYPL. Four major categories (general materials, humanities, social sciences, and pure and applied sciences) are divided into 64 subject classes, most of which are further subdivided unless the total holdings in a class are very small. For each class there is a statement of scope and collection policy and a brief history of the development of the library's holdings (often but not invariably including the approximate number of volumes); detailed descriptions of the collection follow, though only rarely are notable individual titles mentioned. The terms used to measure collections vary in precision: "exhaustive," "comprehensive," "selective," and "representative" are carefully quantified in the work's introductory matter, but more subjective terms like "strong," "rich," "adequate" (for whom?), and "small but significant" also appear, and may not convey the same meanings to all readers. The data are accurate as of December 1969. Appendices include a bibliography of published catalogs of NYPL's collections and a location guide (as of April 1975) to the library's buildings; there is a good index of subjects and named collections. Because the New York Public Library is a research resource of international significance, this guide will be useful to scholars everywhere. [R: C&RL, July 76, pp. 373-74; Choice, Sept 76, p. 802; RQ, Summer 76, pp. 364-65]

Paul B. Cors

15 Biographical Works

COMPREHENSIVE

168. Dictionary of American Library Biography. George S. Bobinski, Jesse Hauk Shera, and Bohdan S. Wynar, eds. Littleton, Colo., Libraries Unlimited, 1978. 596p. index. $85.00. LC 77-28791. ISBN 0-87287-180-0.

The publication of *Dictionary of American Library Biography* marks the culmination of five years of planning, research, writing, and editorial work by the editorial board of *DALB*, over 200 contributors throughout the library community, and the staff of Libraries Unlimited. *DALB*, the first scholarly dictionary of past American library leaders, contains thoroughly researched, original biographical sketches of 301 outstanding men and women who, in large measure, founded and built this country's libraries, professional associations, and library education programs, and who developed basic bibliographic tools and information networks.

Selected for inclusion in *DALB* were those individuals who made contributions of national significance to American library development, whose writings influenced library trends and activities, who held positions of national importance, who made major achievements in special fields of librarianship, or who affected American libraries through their significant scholarly, philanthropic, legislative, or governmental support or activity. To insure proper historical perspective, only those people deceased as of 30 June 1976 are included. Probably the first biographical dictionary of its kind for any profession in the United States, *DALB* is a significant contribution to library history, making it possible to gain the historical perspective necessary to better interpret the profession's present resources and their origins. [R: C&RL, Sept 78, p. 403; LJ, 1 Sept 78, p. 1575; WLB, Sept 78, p. 89]

169. Librarians Phone Book, 1981. Edited by Jaques Cattell Press. New York, R. R. Bowker, 1979, c1980. 531p. o.p. ISBN 0-8352-1321-8; ISSN 0195-332X.

Designed to be a companion to the *American Library Directory*, the *Librarians Phone Book* is an alphabetical list of over 55,000 librarians throughout the United States and Canada. Included are librarians, heads of library networks and consortia, and faculty of library science programs. There is no doubt that this is a handy source for finding phone numbers of libraries—entries list name, position, place of employment, and phone number. To find an address one must refer to the *American Library Directory*.

No criteria for inclusion are provided; spot checking revealed many omissions with no discernible pattern. School librarians are not listed; many special librarians are. Assistant librarians and assistant professors are not well represented. A director of a local library was found in the 1980 edition, but was omitted from the 1981 edition; she has not changed jobs. Cross-checking indicates that her name was also omitted from the thirty-third edition of the *American Library Directory*. This suggests that the *ALD* was used as the source for the names included in the *Phone Book*, but this is not stated. The editors welcome reports of omissions and errors, so future editions may be more accurate. The *Librarians Phone Book* is an easy first reference, but it does not contain all the names one might be interested in finding. [R: BL, 1 Nov 80, p. 415; RQ, Summer 80, pp. 394-95]

Janet H. Littlefield

170. Who's Who in Librarianship and Information Science. Edited by T. Landau. 2nd ed.

London, Abelard-Schuman; distr., New York, Intext, 1973. 311p. o.p. LC 70-184398. ISBN 0-200-71871-1.

This directory of British librarians includes the following information for each person: name, highest degree earned, association memberships, title and current place of employment, home address, year and place of birth, marital status, schools attended (including high schools), previous positions, and special interests (e.g., hobbies). There is no preface or introduction, so there is no way to know what criteria were used for selection of people listed.

171. **Who's Who in Library and Information Services.** Joel M. Lee, ed. Chicago, American Library Association, 1982. 559p. $150.00. LC 81-20480. ISBN 0-8389-0351-7.

The need for an update to *A Biographical Directory of Librarians in the United States and Canada* (1970) has been evident for quite some time. According to the editor, this new work is intended to fill that gap.

Each entry includes the biographer's name, birthdates, employment history, education, organizational memberships, honors and awards, principal publications, professional activities, and mailing address. Included for coverage are librarians, as well as information scientists, archivists, and other individuals in fields such as publishing whose primary activity relates to librarianship and information fields. To accomplish this task, 36 national association membership lists were merged and questionnaires were mailed to 55,000 people with extensive follow-up conducted.

However, when important individuals in the information science field, such as Samuel Beatty, executive director of ASIS, are excluded, it appears that the emphasis is most definitely on library science. Admittedly, however, it is difficult to determine who was excluded as an oversight and who actually requested that they not be included.

Although the editors and advisory committee sought to develop a directory which would be selective, "including the most significant members of the library and information community according to a set of eligibility guidelines" (editor's introduction, p. vi), the qualifications according to these guidelines seem quite vague, for example, "substantial experience as a practitioner or educator," and "active participation in professional, educational, and service organizations ..." (user's guide, p. ix). Does simply being a current member of ALA make one eligible for inclusion?

In spite of the questionable selection criteria, lack of coverage of the information

industry, and hefty price, this biographical directory will offer some assistance to librarians in making connections with others in the profession. [R: RQ, Fall 82, pp. 99-100; WLB, Sept 82, pp. 77-78]

Ann Hartman

SPECIFIC GROUPS

172. Cummings, Cynthia S. **A Biographical-Bibliographical Directory of Women Librarians.** Madison, Wis., Library School Women's Group, University of Wisconsin, 1976. 1v. (unpaged). index. o.p.

This valuable little booklet needs and deserves a second edition, and this reviewer hopes that such may be forthcoming. The present product is very informative, presenting as it does a condensed biographical sketch of each subject followed by a bibliography of writings about her (mostly from library-related journals), including biographical directories and dictionaries. To qualify for inclusion, each woman had to have completed her official career (if still active, then to have "retired" at some point) and she also had to be or have been a member of the American Library Institute or be listed in *Women in the Library Profession*. Indexes link each biographee with her area of specialization, then group the various biographees under the specialties, to provide a clearer idea of areas of concern and relationships therein.

The second edition is needed to correct errors and to add a few names to the list. The *Dictionary of American Library Biography* would be a source for a few more names worthy of inclusion. As to errors, Minerva Amanda Sanders comes out Saunders (but at least consistently). Esther June Piercy was a cataloger at the University of New Mexico, not Minnesota (a typo from NM to MN would explain that). Finally, the biography of Ernestine Rose by Yuri (not Uri) Suhl actually concerns a Polish feminist labor organizer who only lived in the United States from 1836 to 1869; librarianship's Rose lived from 1880 to 1961 and worked primarily in Harlem during the Negro renaissance.

However, if citations are checked thoroughly, this would be an invaluable help in researching library history. We need more!

Koert C. Loomis, Jr.

173. **Directory of Ethnic Studies Librarians.** Beth J. Shapiro, comp. Chicago, American Library Association, Office for Library Service to the Disadvantaged, 1976. 104p. index. o.p. ISBN 0-8389-5487-1.

This directory lists approximately 250 librarians in the United States and Canada designated as ethnic studies librarians. Information about each librarian includes name, address, place of employment, position held, and area of responsibility or interest. Arrangement is alphabetical by name of the librarian. An area of employment index lists librarians under the following categories: American Library Association, colleges and universities, federal agencies, public libraries, publishing, schools, special libraries and museums, and state agencies. A geographic index lists ethnic studies librarians alphabetically by state. An institution index is an alphabetical listing of the school, college, library, or other institution employing the librarians. The subject index is primarily a listing of the ethnic groups or area of studies with which the librarians are concerned or in which they have expressed an interest. Other topics in this alphabetical listing include bilingual outreach, ethnology, ethnomusicology, foreign language collection development, oral history, and women.

This directory provides a helpful start for the scholar who wishes to make contacts that might further his or her research. However, a more comprehensive listing could probably have been compiled by using a questionnaire survey rather than depending on announcements in selected library media. Also, no distinction is made between librarians who work with collections that deal with a particular group's history, experience, contributions, etc., in America, as opposed to librarians of foreign-language collections. However, the author makes no claim "to weed out those individuals 'not really ethnic studies librarians.' "

It is hoped that the planned revised edition will be more useful in that the list of ethnic studies librarians will be more comprehensive and will provide more specific information about the extent (number of volumes; linear or cubic feet of archives; number of films, etc.) of the ethnic collections with which the ethnic studies librarians are working.   Lois Buttlar

174. **Directory of Library Consultants.** John N. Berry, III, comp. New York, R. R. Bowker, 1969. 141p. index. o.p. LC 75-79425. SBN 8352-0210-0.

The first edition, compiled by the editor of *Library Journal*, provides biographical data on some 500 American and Canadian library consultants in such areas as architecture and buildings; collections; technical processing; automation; personnel and public relations; community, regional, and state planning; etc. The infor-

mation includes address, birthdate, educational background, area of specialization, publications, and important consultant services rendered in the past several years. In a few cases there is some padding of information, which is understandable if one takes into consideration that the information was primarily based on a questionnaire submitted to the biographee. In general, this is a useful directory with subject specialty and geographic indexes appended. [R: BSA-P, Apr 70, p. 262; C&RL, Mar 70, p. 123; WLB, Feb 70, p. 661]

175. **Directory of the Black Caucus of the American Library Association.** 2nd ed. Chicago, American Library Association, Black Caucus, 1978. 140p. $10.00 spiralbound. ISBN 0-686-14255-1.

This publication, first compiled and published by the late Louise Giles in 1973, represented an attempt to provide information on members of the Black Caucus of the American Library Association. The volume is not a who's who among blacks in librarianship; it's only a record of those librarians who actively participate in Black Caucus activities.

Names of members are arranged under four sections: alphabetical with home addresses, alphabetical giving library addresses, clarified by type of library, and clarified by geographical location. One of the problems connected with publishing a directory is that it is out-of-date on the day of publication. There have been many changes in positions that are not reflected in the listing. Of course if members did not return questionnaires, the editors obviously decided to retain information on the person from the early edition. It is hoped that this will be corrected in future editions.

Information on Black Caucus members is not duplicated in any other source. As a matter of fact, there is more identification of black librarians in this directory than can be found anywhere, including *Who's Who among Black Americans* (see *ARBA* 77, entry 438). Libraries may wish to acquire the volume for reference collections or black collections, and it is indispensable for library science collections. It must be used with caution in regard to current addresses for some of those listed.   E. J. Josey

176. Engelbarts, Rudolf. **Librarian Authors: A Bibliography.** Jefferson, N.C., McFarland, 1981. 276p. index. $21.95. LC 80-28035. ISBN 0-89950-007-2.

Rudolf Engelbarts has produced an excellent compilation for librarians and library school students. Although it has the title of

Librarian Authors, his work includes a number of benefactors and friends of libraries, including Sir Thomas Bodley, Thomas Bray, Andrew Carnegie, Richard Rogers Bowker, and Halsey W. Wilson.

Engelbarts lists names and publications of 109 men and women who were outstanding both as librarians and as authors. Most of these librarian-authors were American or English, with a scattering of Europeans. The book has been divided somewhat arbitrarily into three sections: part 1, the period from 1600 to 1800, when librarianship in its modern theory and practice had not yet evolved; part 2, the period from 1800 to 1950, which saw the proliferation of libraries and the emergence of modern librarianship; and part 3, the contemporary period from 1950 to 1980, featuring a selection of librarians who are still active or have recently terminated their activities. Among the living librarians cited are Robert B. Downs and Lawrence Clark Powell.

The bulk of this volume consists of vignettes of librarians and library benefactors, with a listing of their principal works. Not all the published works were on librarianship: Randolph G. Adams, William Frederick Poole, and Justin Winsor were also historians, and John Shaw Billings was a physician. There are three bibliographies: one on publications in librarianship; the second on librarians as authors; and the third a special bibliography of the 109 librarians and benefactors with a list of their principal works, as well as their biographies.

There are a few minor flaws. Page iii of the preface lists a total of 108 librarians or library benefactors, while on page 162 the number drops to 105. The actual count is 109. On page 57, the death date of Charles Ammi Cutter is given as 1907 instead of 1903. On page 86, Herbert Putnam is reported to have succeeded Ainsworth Rand Spofford as Librarian of Congress, ignoring the administration of John Russell Young. On page 276, the index lists no pages for Louis Round Wilson, whose contributions are described on page 161. However, these errors are not sufficient to detract from a comprehensive and thoroughly researched volume. Engelbarts's book deserves a place on the shelf of every librarian and library school teacher. [R: AB, 5 July 82, p. 88; JAL, Jan 82, p. 371]
Thomas S. Harding

177.   Josey, E. J., ed. **The Black Librarian in America (Edited and Introduced by E. J. Josey).** Metuchen, N.J., Scarecrow, 1970. 336p. bibliog. index. o.p. LC 79-17850. ISBN 0-8108-0362-3.

A collection of provocative autobiographical essays by 25 prominent black librarians representing a cross section of librarianship and library service. The profiles are written with candor and relate the reasons for choosing a library career, the difficulties encountered, the subject's unfaltering determination, and encouragement received from other blacks. A moving statement of endeavor for justified recognition, acceptance, and equality, it is an important contribution to American social history and librarianship. [R: BL, 1 July 71, p. 879; C&RL, July 71, p. 322; LJ, 15 Mar 71, p. 937]
Charles D. Patterson

178.   **SHARE, a Directory of Feminist Library Workers.** 3rd ed. Berkeley, Calif., Women Library Workers, 1978. 58p. index. o.p.

This directory first appeared in 1975 under the titles *Sisters Have Sources Everywhere*. The second edition, with the current title, was reviewed in *ARBA* 77 (entry 183).

The third edition of *SHARE* (*Sisters Have Resources Everywhere*) is the last biennial. *SHARE* follows the same format as previous editions. The members of Women Library Workers (WLW) are listed, geographically, with home address and phone number. Work, skills, interests, and memberships are listed in a short paragraph, along with random comments under the heading "Other." A name index, subject index, organizations index, and publications index complete the directory. While *SHARE* is interesting to browse, it has little reference value to anyone except WLW members. Although a membership application for WLW is included, the directory does not include a statement of WLW's goals or activities. Since it is basically a "consciousness-raising" tool for feminist library workers, and not a particularly valuable reference tool, *SHARE* will appeal only to a limited audience.
Janet H. Littlefield

179.   Trejo, Arnulfo D., ed., with the assistance of Kathleen L. Lodwick. **Quien Es Quien: A Who's Who of Spanish Heritage Librarians in the United States.** Tucson, Ariz., College of Education, University of Arizona, 1976. 29p. (Graduate Library School Monograph, No. 5). o.p.

This small pamphlet, containing an alphabetical list of 245 "Spanish-heritage librarians in the U.S." and "librarians in Puerto Rico," will serve as an excellent nucleus for a more comprehensive edition of Spanish-speaking librarians in the future. Although it must be acknowledged that the difficulties of compiling such a list are overwhelming, this directory woefully fails to list many librarians qualified for inclusion (including this reviewer). Each entry includes general biographical data and the current position. An attempt was made to indicate the "ethnic group" to which each belongs, but for many persons, including this reviewer, it is difficult to comprehend the difference between "Chicano" and "Mexican-American," or "Spanish-American" and "Ibero-American" of Spanish heritage. The introduction proclaims the need for Spanish-speaking librarians in the United States, and certainly such a need does exist; however, one must not confuse the terms "Spanish-speaking" and "Spanish-heritage," since they are not synonymous! A directory of Spanish-speaking librarians would be much more valuable than a listing of those librarians whose ancestors spoke the language.

Donald J. Lehnus

16 Festschriften

INDEXES

180. Danton, J. Periam, and Jane F. Pulis, with the assistance of Patiala Khoury Wallman. **Index to Festschriften in Librarianship 1967-1975.** New York, K. G. Saur; distr., New York, R. R. Bowker, 1979. 354p. $49.50. ISBN 3-598-07034-9.

The first volume of *Index to Festschriften in Librarianship* was published in 1970 (see *ARBA* 71, entry 88), and covered 3,300 articles appearing in 283 *Festschriften* between 1864 and 1966. The second volume brings under bibliographic control nearly twice as many articles (ca. 6,000) from half as many sources (136) published between 1967 and 1975 in 26 countries — an indication of the renascence of homage publishing during this period.

The intent of these volumes is to provide access to articles by author, title, subject, and individual contribution in the field of librarianship. As the editors point out in their comprehensive introduction, many indexes to *Festschriften* exist, but for the library researcher are deficient either in scope or in breadth and depth of indexing. The present volume is deficient in none of these. In addition, full bibliographic citations to review articles of *Festschrift* volumes consulted are given in the front matter.

Certainly the specialized usefulness and thoroughness of the contents justify the nearly fourfold increase in price of the second volume over the first — at least to the research collections that will acquire it. It is unfortunate, however, that the quality of book production is not equal to that of content: this reviewer's copy has already begun to show signs of pages becoming detached from their perfect binding. [R: RQ, Winter 79, p. 182]   Theresa Maylone

INDIVIDUAL AUTHORS

181. Barr, Keith, and Maurice Line, eds. **Essays on Information and Libraries: Festschrift for Donald Urquhart.** London, Clive Bingley; Hamden, Conn., Linnet Books, 1975. 211p. illus. bibliog. $12.50. ISBN 0-208-01370-9.

In 1974, Donald Urquhart, one of England's most prominent librarians and the man behind the amazing rise of the National Lending Library for Science and Technology, retired. He had taken the NLL, now part of the new British Library, to a point that it was considered the most innovative and efficient of its kind. These essays range across a variety of topics related to British librarianship, and also give considerable attention to Urquhart's role in the development of British libraries during his tenure at the NLL.

The 14 papers included vary in quality and depth of treatment, focusing on the British library scene. Papers treat such subjects as contemporary special libraries, the emerging consensus relative to the value and significance of the NLL, the design of academic library buildings, library education, and the organization of scientific and technical information; one deals with interlibrary loan service in the United States. A bibliography of Urquhart's published work is also included. This is a handsomely produced book that will certainly prove useful to the European library community and to those librarians in America with an interest in comparative librarianship. [R: C&RL, May 76, p. 275; LQ, Oct 76, p. 464]

Michael H. Harris

182. Comparative Librarianship: Essays in Honor of Professor D. N. Marshall. Edited by N. N. Gidwani. New Delhi, Vikas Publishing House; distr., Portland, Ore., International Scholarly Book Services, 1974. 245p. illus. index. $10.50. ISBN 0-7069-0233-5.

The book is an appropriate *Festschrift* to commemorate the sixty-fifth birthday of Professor Dara N. Marshall, a renowned Indian librarian, library educator, and leader in the profession. Twelve essays have been contributed by internationally known librarians and bibliographers, many of whom are friends and admirers of D. N. Marshall. The essays range in scope from a description of libraries and librarianship in Australia, by D. H. Borchardt, to bibliographical comments in a collection of Fatimid manuscripts, by Asaf A. Fayzee. As in all *Festschriften*, the unifying element of the essays is the span of interests of the person in whose honor the volume is brought out.

Marshall has been associated with Bombay University for over 40 years and has served as its librarian and the head of its library school for 20 years. His primary interest, as one gathers from examining this volume, is in the bibliothecal and bibliographical fields. As Pearson puts it, "He ranks among the greatest of non-Muslims who have contributed to Islamic bibliography" (p. 199).

It is strange, however, to discover that the volume does not include a single essay on library education, a subject that would seem very appropriate for the occasion, since Marshall has served as head of the Bombay Library School for two decades.

The 13 chapters are of approximately equal length. The first essay, by Dongerkery, compares university libraries in Great Britain, India, and the United States; the second, by K. Metcalf, enumerates 18 reasons for the wide variety of basic plans that have been used in recent years and their inevitable influence on the future; the third essay, by Borchardt, describes recent developments in Australian university libraries.

Two essays are concerned with special libraries, present and past. The first describes the search for and acquisition of transcripts which now form the treasures of the Indian office; the second article describes the life and works of Bhaskaracharya, a medieval Indian astrologer and mathematician, and throws some light on his research library.

Two well-written essays deal with early Indian imprints: "Lucknow Printers, 1820-1850," by K. S. Diehl, and "Indian Incunabula," by A. K. Priolkar. Four articles may interest the student of South Asian bibliography: "Portuguese Sources for the History of India: A Bibliographical Note," by B. Anderson; "Towards a Bibliography of the Sikhs and the Punjab," by K. Navalani; "Towards a Retrospective Bibliography of Books in Indian Languages: Case Study of Kannada Publications," by K. S. Deshpande; and "Documentation on India," by N. N. Gidwani. Those interested in Islamic bibliography will find the essay "Notes on Islamic Bibliography," by J. D. Pearson, to be interesting reading on the making of two major bibliographies: his *Index Islamicus* and Giuseppe Gabrieli's *Manuale di bibliographia Musulmana.* For those who are wondering why *Index Islamicus* has not been computerized, Pearson's remarks may provide the answer. "A Collection of Fatimid Manuscripts," by Asaf A. Fayzee, describes in brief some of the remaining manuscripts in his private collection.

The two presidential addresses of D. N. Marshall provide some good general background on library development in India in 1964 and 1969. They were delivered by Marshall at the Conference of the Indian Library Association and the Indian Association of Special Libraries and Information Centers. [R: LJ, 15 Dec 74, p. 3187]   Mohammed M. Aman

183. Farber, Evan Ira, and Ruth Walling, eds. **The Academic Library: Essays in Honor of Guy R. Lyle.** Metuchen, N.J., Scarecrow, 1974. 171p. bibliog. $15.00. LC 74-2098. ISBN 0-8108-0712-2.

Guy R. Lyle, who retired as director of the library at Emory University, had a long and varied career of distinguished service to academic libraries. His best-known work, *Administration of the College Library*, has long been essential reading for those aspiring to administrative careers in college and university libraries.

This *Festschrift*, with its contributions from friends and colleagues in a variety of academic institutions, exemplifies Lyle's own wise and human approach to the world of readers and books. There is a minimum of the managementese that too often characterizes library "literature." Among the well-known contributors are Jerrold Orne, David Kaser, Jack Dalton, Paul Bixler, and Eldred Smith.

Several of the essays are sparkling and provocative—and none more so than Evan Farber's "College Librarians and the University-Library Syndrome," an incisive analysis of the key differences between college and university libraries. Farber's co-editor, Ruth Walling, contributes an interesting biographical sketch of Lyle as well as the customary bibliography—a bibliography that fully reveals the range of Lyle's remarkable career.

Jack Dalton gives the reader some new insights into the uneasy truce between libraries and library schools; Jerrold Orne speculates, in an amusing and instructive manner, on theories X, Y, O, and P of library administration; and Paul Bixler, in reviewing the evolution of the core collection, ruminates on the capture of the library-college movement by the educationists. Finally, Turner Cassity, a poet and serials librarian, contributes a spirited albeit rambling defense of the nonscholarly journal.

This is a lively *Festschrift*, which Lyle's own literary favorite, Christopher Morley, would perhaps have enjoyed—and that is high praise, indeed. [R: AL, Oct 74, p. 497; LJ, 15 Oct 74, p. 2587]   Paul Z. DuBois

184.   Galvin, Thomas J., Margaret Mary Kimmel, and Brenda H. White, eds. **Excellence in School Media Programs.** Chicago, American Library Association, 1980. 228p. $15.00. LC 79-26944. ISBN 0-8389-3239-8.

A collection of pieces by 20 authors, this *Festschrift* celebrates the dynamism and professional commitment of Elizabeth T. (Betty) Fast, who was prematurely felled by cancer in 1977. Nine of her own articles and 18 original essays treat four themes: the child, the school media center, the community, and the future. The latter two topics include, in addition to more immediately obvious subjects, library school training, professional associations, and accreditation. The contributors knew Betty Fast personally and are themselves well-known writers and leaders in the school library field.

The essays vary markedly in tone. Morton Schindel has contributed an inspirational "letter to Betty" on the development of Weston Woods. In much the same vein Peggy Sullivan discusses the use of power to improve media programs, with Betty Fast as an example. Clara Jackson's review of heightening awareness of children's needs from 1962 on has a bibliographic emphasis. Alice E. Fite's account of the development of standards for school media programs, Patricia B. Pond's review of AASL membership and activities in the last two decades, and Thomas Hart's discussion of accreditation of elementary schools all offer detailed information. Cosette N. Kies's article provides procedures and an instrument for a communications audit.

Some controversial issues are exposed: inconsistency in selection standards by Lillian N. Gerhardt, the rights and needs of children and parents by Margaret Mary Kimmel, difficulties in professional training and field work by Jane Anne Hannigan and Kay E. Vandergrift. Other contributors have written more generalized articles: Virginia M. Crowe (on media production by children), Blanche Woolls (evaluation techniques), Richard L. Darling (district services), Evelyn H. Daniel (professionalism), D. Philip Baker (federal legislation), Phyllis Land (networking), Bernard Schlessinger and Patricia Jensen (continuing education).

Library schools and system-level professional collections in school districts or county offices of education will want to purchase this volume. [R: BL, 15 June 80, p. 1541]
                    Lillian Biermann Wehmeyer

185.   Gleaves, Edwin S., and John Mark Tucker. **Reference Services and Library Education: Essays in Honor of Frances Neel Cheney.** Lexington, Mass., Lexington Books/ D. C. Heath, 1983. 306p. index. $31.50. LC 81-48266. ISBN 0-669-05320-1.

Friends, colleagues, and former students of Cheney have produced an exceptional *Festschrift*. Cheney is perhaps best known for her column "Current Reference Books" in the *Wilson Library Bulletin*, which ran for 30 years, but she was also an outstanding teacher and a member of the faculty of Peabody Library School for nearly 34 years.

The broad scope of the *Festschrift* is indicated by its title. There are four sections. Part 1 is a personal tribute to Cheney that includes a chronology. Part 2 deals with current trends in reference services and the characteristics of selected reference books. The essays in part 3 deal with the historical development of library education in Cheney's region and with key issues in the library profession. Finally, part 4 is a bibliography of works by and about Cheney from 1936 to 1982, with approximately 400 items by Cheney alone. (This total is, however, deceptive, since the entry for "Current Reference Books" represents reviews of 5,819 titles.)

All the essays are of high quality. Special mention should be made of the articles by Bill Katz on reading reference books, Robert S. Burgess on computer-assisted reference service, and Edward G. Holley on the history of library education in the South.

This is an outstanding publication. It belongs in the working collection of every reference librarian and on the shelves of every library school library. [R: C&RL, May 83, pp. 268-69; JAL, Mar 83, p. 42; July 83, p. 167; LJ, 15 May 83, p. 984; RQ, Summer 83, p. 438]

Thomas S. Harding

186. Jeffreys, Alan, ed. **The Art of the Librarian: A Collection of Original Papers from the Library of the University of Newcastle upon Tyne.** Newcastle upon Tyne, England, Oriel Press; distr., Boston, Routledge & Kegan Paul, 1974. 190p. $9.50. ISBN 0-85362-151-9.

Upon the retirement of Joan M. Gladstone as head of the order department at the University of Newcastle upon Tyne Library in England, more than a dozen individuals, all of whom were associated at one time or another with that academic institution, collaborated in producing this *Festschrift* to honor her. It contains 11 essays, mostly by librarians, covering such diverse subjects as library acquisition policies, new media in libraries, education for librarianship, quantitative measurement of collections, French libraries in the seventeenth century, library use, and automation. Since the University of Newcastle upon Tyne has been a pioneer in the application of computers to library operations, it is not surprising that five articles deal with aspects of that topic. The emphasis in all but one of the papers in this volume is on current practices in British libraries. Many of the essays are of the "how I run my library good" variety. Some, such as Maurice B. Line's "Local Acquisition Policies in a National Context," Brian Enright's "New Media and the Library," and Alistair Elliot's "Special Collections Computing in Newcastle University Library" make especially interesting reading for American librarians. While this book will not win any awards, it is nevertheless valuable for its information regarding the functioning of academic libraries on the other side of the Atlantic. [R: LJ, 1 Nov 74, pp. 2822-23]

Leonard Grundt

187. Lee, Joel M., and Beth A. Hamilton, eds. **As Much to Learn as to Teach: Essays in Honor of Lester Asheim.** Hamden, Conn., Linnet Books, 1979. 273p. bibliog. index. $17.50. LC 78-11313. ISBN 0-208-01751-4.

This collection of essays is presented as a tribute to Lester Asheim's impressive career, first as dean of the Graduate Library School of the University of Chicago, subsequently as a member of the staff of the American Library Association, and then as the holder of a named professorship at the School of Library Science of the University of North Carolina. The volume opens with an appreciation of Asheim by Grace T. Stevenson, followed by a biographical sketch prepared by Ruth French Carnovsky, who was a member of the Chicago faculty at the time of Asheim's deanship. The substantive articles begin with an excellent presentation of the historical roots and possible future trends of the major library issues of the 1970s. In this brilliant essay, Edward G. Holley demonstrates that the major problems that aroused the concern of the profession during the decade were actually reconsiderations of problems that had bothered librarianship for many years and were likely to do so in the years ahead.

Other essays follow in order: "Asheim's Work on Intellectual Freedom," by David K. Berninghausen; "American Librarians and the Pursuit of Happiness," by Haynes McMullen; "Librarians and the Political Process," by Alice B. Ihrig; "Adult Education and the Public Library," by Cyril O. Houle; "The Library as Change Agent," by Roderick G. Swartz; "Professional Education," by Kathleen M. Heim; "Library Education," by Irving Lieberman; "Changing Trends in Academic Libraries," by Robert Downs; "The Literature of International Librarianship," by Boyd Rayward; and "Asheim Confronts the Catalog," by Joel M. Lee. The volume concludes with a bibliography of Asheim's writings. This collection, distinguished for its excellence, is, on the whole, better than the majority of such occasional compilations. [R: C&RL, May 79, pp. 292-93; JAL, May 79, p. 100; LJ, July 79, p. 1432]

Jesse H. Shera

188. McIlwaine, Ia, John McIlwaine, and Peter G. New, eds. **Bibliography and Reading: A Festschrift in Honour of Ronald Staveley.** Metuchen, N.J., Scarecrow, 1983. 172p. $15.00. LC 82-21489. ISBN 0-8108-1601-6.

Staveley, senior lecturer and director of library studies at the School of Library, Archive and Information Studies at University College London, retired in 1979. This work is a collection of essays in subject bibliography and reading studies, areas of librarianship in which Staveley has special expertise. This work consists of a tribute to Staveley, a comprehensive bibliography of his works by the editors, and 11 essays. There are essays on bibliographical planning in the United Kingdom and in Japan; language, classification, and reading in intellectual development; the place of the antiquarian in the library; reference books published in Britain from 1870 to 1914; and bibliography and scientists, among other subjects. The editors are well known in the U.S. library world, as are the other contributors: Peter Hoare, Tamiko

Matsumura, Dorothy Anderson, Douglas Foskett, Sylva Simsova, Mary Piggott, Chris Needham, Roy Stokes, Edward Dudley, and Brian Vickery. [R: JAL, Nov 83, p. 291; LJ, 15 Apr 83, p. 803]

Antonio Rodriguez-Buckingham

189. Milne, A. T., ed. **Librarianship and Literature: Essays in Honour of Jack Pafford.** London, University of London, Althone Press; distr., New York, Oxford University Press, 1970. 141p. o.p. ISBN 0-485-11117-9.

An important and cohesive collection of eight essays on topics of interest to Pafford written by notable authors in their respective fields, each of which constitutes a significant contribution to the literature, and a conspectus of library trends in the last quarter century. Contributors include Sir Frank Francis, Raymond Irwin, S. P. L. Filon, Joseph W. Scott, Roser Thomas, Arthur Brown, Harold F. Brooks, and Francis Wormald. [R: C&RL, Sept 71, p. 394; LJ, Aug 70, p. 2640]   Charles D. Patterson

190. Mitchell, P. M. **Halldór Hermannsson.** Ithaca, N.Y., Cornell University Press, 1978. 167p. bibliog. index. (Islandica XLI). $29.95. LC 77-14665. ISBN 0-8014-1085-1.

Published to commemorate the centenary of the birth of Halldór Hermannsson, the first curator of the Fiske Icelandic Collection in the Cornell University Libraries (1905-1948), this book is volume 41 of Islandica, a series begun by Hermannsson himself in 1908. Written by one of Hermannsson's students, P. M. Mitchell, who was the first Cornell undergraduate to take his degree in Scandinavian, the book reviews Hermannsson's life as a scholar and bibliographer. In addition, Mitchell provides a critical resume of each of Hermannsson's books and his many articles over a period of more than 60 years, from 1897 to 1958.

The turning point in Hermannsson's life came in 1899, when he met Willard Fiske, who had served as Cornell's first librarian. With Hermannsson's assistance, Fiske assembled collections in several fields, including Icelandic books and periodicals, during his later years. Before Fiske died in 1904, he bequeathed his books to Cornell University and established an Icelandic collection. On Fiske's recommendation, Hermannsson was appointed curator of the collection.

Mitchell's work has two themes. One is the story of a dedicated bibliographer who devoted 43 years to building up Fiske's basic Iceland collection both in quantity and quality. To publicize the contents of the collection, Her-

mannsson published three catalogs between 1914 and 1943, showing his concern that it should become available to researchers. The second theme deals with Hermannsson's career as a productive scholar. He excelled in both breadth and depth in the fields of old Icelandic literature, bibliography, cartography and manuscripts, and modern Icelandic; delved into the historic voyages to Vinland; and offered courses in Scandinavian languages and literature. His official retirement as curator did not end his activity; instead, his publications continued until his death ten years later. (Readers unfamiliar with Icelandic culture and literature may find this part of Mitchell's work somewhat beyond their depth.) While this is a scholarly monograph rather than a reference book, it should command interest as the story of a dedicated scholar-librarian who worked tirelessly to achieve his ideal of a useful and historically valuable special collection.

Thomas S. Harding

191. Orne, Jerrold, ed. **Research Librarianship: Essays in Honor of Robert B. Downs.** New York, R. R. Bowker, 1971. 162p. o.p. LC 78-163902.

Not many librarians are honored with a *Festschrift*; certainly Downs, a former dean at the University of Illinois, well deserves this fine recognition. Ably edited by Jerrold Orne, this volume contains a good biography of Downs by Robert Delzell, a bibliography of his numerous publications by Clarabelle Gunning, and an interesting article on library surveys by William V. Jackson. All in all, a worthwhile volume that should be of interest to a large library audience. [R: WLB, Mar 72, p. 656]

Bohdan S. Wynar

192. Poole, Herbert, ed. **Academic Libraries by the Year 2000: Essays Honoring Jerrold Orne.** New York, R. R. Bowker, 1977. 205p. bibliog. index. o.p. LC 77-81880. ISBN 0-8352-0993-8.

A *Festschrift* honoring Jerrold Orne is certain to cover nearly every aspect of academic librarianship, reflecting Orne's numerous and varied activities over a span of four decades. His comprehensive views and the range of his interests are shown in the wide scope of the articles themselves and in the credentials of the authors, most of whom are either academic library administrators or teachers in library schools, representing two of Orne's major contributions to the library profession.

The 13 articles themselves show a wide variation. A short biography by Herbert Poole offers a good summary of Orne's varied career as administrator and teacher. In the keynote essay, "What Lies Ahead for Academic Libraries?" Edward G. Holley surveys historical developments in academic libraries since the early 1960s, and then raises several questions on their future when confronted with the prospect of declining enrollments and restricted finances. Other essays range from the brilliant article "The Effect of the Revolution of 1969-1970 on University Library Administration," by David Kaser, to the highly technical account "Operations Research and the Academic Library," by Herbert Poole and Thomas H. Mott, Jr. However, all of these essays have one common theme: each offers a substantial, data-supported description of some aspect or trend in academic librarianship.

This volume is recommended for all academic librarians, teachers in library schools, and others who wish to be well informed on the current status and future prospects of academic libraries in the final quarter of the twentieth century. [R: LQ, Jan 79, p. 83]

Thomas S. Harding

193. Rawski, Conrad H., ed. **Toward a Theory of Librarianship: Papers in Honor of Jesse Hauk Shera.** Metuchen, N.J., Scarecrow, 1973. 564p. index. o.p. LC 72-5764. ISBN 0-8108-0535-9.

This *Festschrift* in honor of one of the most prominent librarians in this country will significantly contribute to the understanding of Shera's thinking about our profession. It contains a well-prepared bibliography of his writings, a good introduction by Conrad H. Rawski, and 24 articles by such authors as Vickery, Foskett, Richmond, Metcalfe, Tauber, Menzel, Harlow, and Ranganathan. The foreword was written by the late Verner W. Clapp. The format and technical execution of the book are not as outstanding as the contents. [R: C&RL, Jan 74, p. 57; CLW, Feb 74, p. 348; LQ, July 74, p. 253; LRTS, Summer 74, p. 311]

194. **The Service Imperative for Libraries: Essays in Honor of Margaret E. Monroe.** Gail A. Schlachter, ed. Littleton, Colo., Libraries Unlimited, 1982. 215p. index. $28.50. LC 82-8991. ISBN 0-87287-272-6.

The essays contained in this volume commemorate the career of Margaret E. Monroe, an outstanding library educator, author, lecturer, innovator, and promoter of library outreach services. Written by her former students, employees, and colleagues, these original essays address a theme which is implicit in Monroe's

writings—that service, imperative in successful library operations, consists of four elements: information, instruction, guidance, and stimulation.

Eliza T. Dresang begins this work with her essay entitled "The Service Paradigm: An Introduction." The four fundamental components of library public service are addressed in the essays in part 2 of this work: "Information," by Mary Jo Lynch; "Instruction," by Carolyn A. Kirkendall and Carla J. Stoffle; "Guidance," by Rhea Joyce Rubin; and "Stimulation," by Kathleen H. Heim. Education and evaluation are the topics covered in part 3, with contributions by F. William Summers, "Education for Reference Service," and Ellen Altman, "Assessment of Reference Services." The final section of the work is a comprehensive, annotated bibliography by Miriam Pollack of Monroe's writings— 102 publications consisting of books, articles, chapters, speeches, reviews, and reports, as well as citations for reviews of works by Margaret Monroe and articles about her. [R: BL, 15 Jan 83, p. 657; JAL, May 83, p. 94; RQ, Spring 83, p. 322; WLB, Mar 83, p. 604]

195. Stevens, Norman D., ed. **Essays for Ralph Shaw.** Metuchen, N.J., Scarecrow, 1975. 212p. o.p. LC 75-6664. ISBN 0-8108-0815-3.

All royalties earned by this *Festschrift* are being donated to the Ralph R. Shaw Visiting Scholar Fund at Rutgers University, and the editor and contributors were either students or colleagues of Shaw's at Rutgers during his tenure there. All the ex-students but one earned their doctorates at the Rutgers Graduate School of Library Service, and these essays constitute a tribute to his influence upon them. Sentimentality has been eschewed in the preparation of this volume; the editor owns that contact with Shaw often left scars among the other deep impressions.

The first section, on Shaw the person, consists of a dreadful unattributed portrait frontispiece, an introduction by Stevens, a short tribute by Lowell Martin, and an essay "Shaw and the Machine" by Theodore Hines. An amusing selection of 50 or so of Shaw's aphorisms and *bons mots* concludes the volume.

Between are the contributions themselves, arranged in the three groups reflecting Shaw's major library interests. The projects and experiments section includes papers by R. F. Clarke, R. M. Dougherty, I. W. Harris, Peter Hiatt, and M. L. Jones. The papers on scientific management and statistics are by Fred Heinritz, T. S. Huang, C. H. Kim, and Henry Voos. The part on theory and philosophies is made up of essays by Susan Artandi, Leonard Grundt, D. J. Hickey, and Stevens.

The quality of the individual contributions is quite uneven, as is typical of all such works, and the group headings imply more unity among the papers than actually exists. But most are readable, and some are interesting and thought-provoking. [R: C&RL, Nov 75, pp. 515-16]

George Piternick

196. Venkatappaiah, V., general ed. **March of Library Science: Kaula Festschrift, Papers Presented in Honour of Prof. P. N. Kaula.** C. V. Subba Rao and Amitabha Chatterjee, executive eds. New Delhi, Vikas Publishing House; distr., New York, Advent Books, 1979. 626p. $40.00. ISBN 0-7069-0482-6.

In this *Festschrift* honoring the Indian library science educator, P. N. Kaula, its editor assembled a rather wide range of topics, with an international cast of authors. The volume is divided into parts A-N (62 articles) covering (usually rather briefly) the philosophy of library science, comparative librarianship, organization of knowledge, cataloging of documents and cataloging in Sri Lanka, document procurement, bibliographical organization, information transfer, scientific management, library education, problems in reading, as well as a number of articles on university, research, and school libraries.

As one would expect, not all contributions are of the same quality, and some are rather disappointing, for example, "Library Science—A Laboratory Science?" by Günther Reichardt, a rather pedestrian "Obscured and Duplicated Information," by Danal Roth, or "The Future of Cataloguing," by B. Guha, which tells practically nothing in its 10 pages. Among better contributions we find a translation from Russian on "Social Problems of Reading," by O. S. Chubarian, "Costing in University Libraries," by K. W. Humphreys, "American University Libraries Organization and Administration," by Edward Holley, and the witty "Of Peacocks, Elephants, and the Philosophy of Librarians," by Jesse Shera.

Unfortunately, this is not a "monumental volume," as was indicated in the review published in *College and Research Libraries*, but rather a "mixed bag" of brief, one-to-three-page articles and several well-written essays—in other words, a typical *Festschrift* which tells us a few things about practically everything, including the progress of library science in India and some other countries. This volume will be useful to students in library schools and librarians interested in comparative librarianship. [R: C&RL, Nov 80, pp. 555-56]   Bohdan S. Wynar

17 Collected Writings

BIBLIOGRAPHIES

197. Marshall, John David, comp. **Louis Shores, Author-Librarian: A Bibliography.** Tallahassee, Fla., Gamma Chapter, Beta Phi Mu, School of Library Science, Florida State University, 1979. 77p. illus. o.p.

An updated version of *Louis Shores: A Bibliography*, compiled by Marshall in 1964, this book carries the record of Shores's writings down to 1978. Prepared to honor his seventy-fifth birthday, the listing subdivides his various writings by type, including two recorded discussions, one a videotape. Two brief biographical sketches are included, one from the 1964 edition, and the second covering the years since. Also supplied is some factual information about Shores — his awards, and references to other bibliographies and to biographical sketches. Two samples of Shores's own writing are appended; one, entitled "Library Literature," is reprinted from the 1964 edition, and the second, presumed to be Shores's first published work, is a short story from his university paper (the University of Toledo).

While the compiler points out, quite correctly, that several items not included in the 1964 edition have since been collected and tabulated for inclusion here, recent arrivals on the library scene would profit from the addition of brief descriptive annotations by being able to appreciate a monograph's significance at the appropriate time. For example, *Reference as the Promotion of Free Inquiry*, listed as appearing in 1976 (Littleton, Colo., Libraries Unlimited), is actually a collection of essays on this topic written much earlier. A minor point perhaps, but worth noting nonetheless. [R: JLH, Summer 80, p. 364] Jesse H. Shera

198. Szigethy, Marion C. **Maurice Falcolm Tauber: A Bibliography, 1934-1973.** Published for Beta Phi Mu, Nu Chapter, Columbia University School of Library Service. Metuchen, N.J., Scarecrow, 1974. 136p. index. o.p. LC 74-7401. ISBN 0-8108-0725-4.

Maurice Tauber is among the select group of a very few library educators whose contributions and writings have changed the course of librarianship — not only in this country, but throughout the world. His contributions, whether in textbook form, surveys, monographs, or articles, cover a wide variety of topics, such as college and university librarianship, library administration, technical services, book catalogs, cataloging and classification, documentation, and other related subjects.

The volume presents a comprehensive record of Tauber's contributions to librarianship. Marion Szigethy, one of Tauber's doctoral students, divides her work into three main parts: (1) bibliographical appreciations dealing with Tauber's career as scholar, teacher, colleague, administrator, and friend; (2) an essay by Tauber on the "Survey Method in Approaching Library Problems"; and (3) the bibliography, which lists Tauber's writings and writings about him from 1934 to 1973. It totals 539 entries, some of which are composite. Materials are arranged in nine chapters: papers; monographs; contributions to other works; forewords to other works; library surveys; contributions to conferences, institutes and meetings; course outlines, essays, and book reviews; and materials about Maurice F. Tauber. The secondary arrangement is chronological by publication date and alphabetical within each year.

The indexes include subjects, names of persons and institutions mentioned in the entries, and titles of books.

While the volume is a valuable tool for identifying and reviewing many of Tauber's writings, the lack of annotations for all entries lessens its value somewhat. A careful examination of entries shows that some of Tauber's major surveys and writings are missing. The compiler comforts us by promising a future supplement that will include omissions from this bibliography as well as works by Tauber now in preparation. [R: C&RL, May 75, p. 231]

Mohammed M. Aman

INDIVIDUAL AUTHORS

199. Basler, Roy P. **The Muse and the Librarian.** Westport, Conn., Greenwood Press, 1974. 207p. (Contributions in American Studies, No. 10). $29.95. LC 72-780. ISBN 0-8371-6134-7.

That Roy Basler, the prominent Lincoln scholar and chief of the Manuscript Division of the Library of Congress, should bring these previously published essays together in one volume will come as no surprise to Americanists. The studies reprinted here are articulate and perceptive assessments of American literary life, and especially modern American poetry.

But why review such a book in a section devoted to new publications in library science? The explanation lies in the title essay, "The Muse and the Librarian," which traces in glorious detail the origins and evolution of the "chair of poetry" at the Library of Congress. Library historians will welcome this essay for the insights it provides into the management of one small, but important, aspect of the National Library's program. [R: AL, Dec 74, p. 612]

Michael H. Harris

200. Ellsworth, Ralph E. **Ellsworth on Ellsworth.** Metuchen, N.J., Scarecrow, 1980. 163p. illus. bibliog. index. $15.00. LC 80-12656. ISBN 0-8108-1311-4.

This interesting volume on one of the best-known librarians traces the evolution of American academic librarianship over a period of 45 years, starting with 1931 — "the year library science and I discovered each other." The tone of this informal autobiography is properly set with the following excerpt from the preface. "This is not a normal autobiography. If it were, I should have had to write about myself and my family and the social milieu in which I have lived. And, lest I cheat my readers out of some choice morsel, I should have had to wait

until nearer the end. Instead, the book is an attempt to comment on the ways of the library profession in response to the infusion of a new concept — the scientific spirit — as introduced by the University of Chicago Graduate Library School in the early 1930s.... And, like a properly conducted funeral, the account attempts to cover the subject but not be too darned serious about it" (p. vii). Indeed, Ellsworth's comments and involvement with many of the events and developments in university libraries, for example, his role in the expansion of the National Union Catalog or the development of a Library Bill of Rights and the ACRL and ARL, constitute some of the most interesting and stimulating reading, so seldom found in other autobiographical essays. [R: AB, 22 June 81, p. 4940; C&RL, Mar 81, p. 155; JAL, May 81, p. 99; LJ, 15 Feb 81, p. 434]

Bohdan S. Wynar

201. Gore, Daniel. **To Know a Library: Essays and Annual Reports, 1970-1976.** Westport, Conn., Greenwood Press, 1978. 379p. index. (New Directions in Librarianship, No. 1). $35.00. LC 77-84769. ISBN 0-8371-9881-X.

The first one-third of *To Know a Library* consists of ten enjoyable essays, three previously unpublished, by one of the best known and most controversial contemporary American library writers; the last two-thirds of the book consists of six annual reports covering the period 1970/1971-1975/1976, that Gore wrote in his role as library director at Macalester College. Gore is a remarkably skillful writer who forcefully and intelligently presents his ideas in a manner that, at least in the essays, is a delight to read even when one disagrees with them. Unfortunately, even so skillful a writer is unable to breathe enough life into annual reports to warrant their rescue from the decent obscurity that they normally receive and deserve. Skimmed in small doses (as they arrive sporadically and free at a library), annual reports are bearable. Sometimes, they contain some useful information; but to read six at one sitting in an expensive book is absolutely unbearable. If this book has any merit, it is that, taken as a whole, it shows how the ideas of the major spokesman for the emerging "no-growth" school of academic library thought have developed specifically from his experiences with the severe financial and space problems of a single library supplemented by limited, selective use of other material. Testimony, it must be recognized, may as well be the source of error as of truth, and this book helps reveal the inadequate underpinning of Gore's ideas. They appear, when examined in detail, to be little more than a sophisticated version of the all-too-familiar "how I run my library good" story. [R: BL, 15 May 78, p. 1479; C&RL, Nov 78, p. 504; LJ, 1 Oct 78, p. 1930]   Norman D. Stevens

202. Hoole, William Stanley. **Scholar-Librarian and Literary Maverick.** University, Ala., University of Alabama Press, 1973. 341p. o.p. LC 74-148688. ISBN 0-8137-7102-8.

A selection of 46 essays drawn from previously published articles, speeches, books and reviews written by the author between 1930 and 1970 which reflect his personal philosophy about libraries, librarianship, and library education. Includes an autobiographical sketch but lacks an index. [R: JAL, July 75, p. 34; JLH, Jan 75, p. 81; LJ, 1 Nov 73, p. 3237]
          Charles D. Patterson

203. MacLeish, Archibald. **Champion of a Cause: Essays and Addresses on Librarianship.** Chicago, American Library Association, 1971. 284p. $65.50pa. LC 70-150577. ISBN 0-8389-0091-7.

A collection of 19 papers consisting of official reports, addresses, and articles written between 1939 and 1967 by MacLeish, whose appointment as Librarian of Congress was highly controversial. Although not a librarian by profession, his tenure in that office is recognized and remembered as distinguished and outstanding. [R: BL, 15 Sept 71, p. 68; LJ, 1 Jan 72, p. 45]   Charles D. Patterson

204. Oboler, Eli M. **Ideas and the University Library: Essays of an Unorthodox Academic Librarian.** Westport, Conn., Greenwood Press, 1977. 203p. bibliog. index. (Contributions in Librarianship and Information Science, Vol. 20). $27.50. LC 77-11. ISBN 0-8371-9531-4.

At once, the name Eli Oboler conjures up the impression of acute thinking, nimble wit, and intelligent but bombastic criticism. Ever since his first letter appeared in *Library Journal* in 1950, he has been on the national library scene prompting us to use our common sense, or chastising us if we hadn't. It should come as no surprise to anyone that a collection of his works would reveal his insightful but barbed posture.

Ideas and the University Library is a collection of reprinted articles, talks, letters, verse, and other writings that seem to be a good representation of Oboler's prolific output. His ideas, fundamental and often unique, are just as current as the problems he has addressed over his 35-year writing history. The book includes a complete bibliography of his works (unfortunately in chronological order) and a serious omission: the article "The Vectors of Tolerance" (pp. 19-27), is not listed in the acknowledgments, and curiously enough, not in the bibliography either. It seems unfortunate, also, that each acknowledgment is not listed along with each article.

Oboler's ideas are often refreshingly original, stimulating, and always controversial. [R: LJ, 1 Nov 77, p. 2221]
          Frederick Van Antwerp

205. Shera, Jesse H. **"The Complete Librarian" and Other Essays.** Cleveland, Ohio, Case Western Reserve University Press, 1971. 183p. o.p. LC 73-99236. ISBN 0-8295-0193-2.

A collection of 49 essays, most of which were previously published (*Wilson Library Bulletin, Library Journal*), that seemingly touch on all topics concerning libraries, librarians, and librarianship. Always intelligent, urbane, and articulate, Shera is not only a scholar but a remarkably readable librarian. [R: LJ, 1 June 71, p. 1942]   Charles D. Patterson

206. Shera, Jesse H. **Knowing Books and Men; Knowing Computers, Too.** Littleton, Colo., Libraries Unlimited, 1973. 363p. o.p. LC 73-85553. ISBN 0-87287-073-1.

The title of this collection of 29 essays traces the perimeters of Jesse H. Shera's investigations into the foundations of librarianship. Together the writings present a comprehensive picture of his professional thinking as it has developed over nearly 40 years of work as a librarian, a researcher, and an educator of international acclaim. The collection contains essays written between 1931 and 1973. Many of the essays have been revised. The classic piece on American library history has been updated and expanded to twice its original length. The essays are arranged in six groups: philosophy of librarianship, library history, reference librarianship, documentation, academic libraries, and library education. [R: AL, Jan 74, p. 38; BL, 1 Feb 74, p. 555; LJ, 1 June 74, p. 1525; RSR, Jan 74, p. 27]

207. Thompson, Lawrence S. **Books in Our Time: Essays by Lawrence S. Thompson.** Washington, D.C., Consortium Press, 1971. 356p. illus. o.p. ISBN 0-8434-0452-3.

A collection of essays written between 1941 and 1970. Arrangement is under three broad categories—"The Humanistic Librarian," "World Library Resource," and "The Spell of the Book." The introduction is by Lawrence Clark Powell. The critical points of the *Library Journal* review are well taken: this could be a booby trap for unwary readers. [R: LJ, 15 Dec 71, p. 3975]

208. Thompson, Lawrence S. **Essays in Hispanic Bibliography.** Hamden, Conn., Shoe String Press, 1970. 117p. o.p. LC 75-96729. ISBN 0-208-00978-7. [Available from Books on Demand. ISBN 0-8357-9583-7. $32.30.]

A collection of nine essays, all previously published, which reflect the wide and diverse areas of interest of this scholar. Although not all essays can be considered "Hispanic," they do provide all-too-brief but informative and enjoyable reading. [R: LJ, 15 Apr 71, p. 1340]

Charles D. Patterson

Part 3

TYPES OF LIBRARIES

18   College and Research Libraries

ACADEMIC LIBRARIANSHIP

209. **Academic Librarianship: Yesterday, Today, and Tomorrow.** Robert Stueart, ed. New York, Neal-Schuman, 1982. 273p. bibliog. index. $29.95. LC 81-18866. ISBN 0-918212-52-9.

This title, dedicated to Ralph Ellsworth, is a collection of 13 essays on the "yesterday, today, and tomorrow" of academic librarianship. While a number of diverse topics are covered, there is a lack of a clearly defined focus to this work. No real attempt is made to unify the writings into a coherent view of where libraries and librarians are headed in the future, and there are very few new insights on existing or past practices. For instance, the area of automation is dealt with rather superficially. Certainly, there are passages on its role in such chapters as "Centralized Cataloging," "Interlibrary Cooperation," and "Collection Development." However, each of these essays provides only a passing reference to potential future developments of automated hardware and software systems and their impact on information dissemination and collection building practices and policies.

We are experiencing the effects of growing economic restriction for academic institutions, including their libraries. Again, there is a dearth of analysis on how libraries can cope with the personnel, service, and material problems that must be planned for "today" and managed "tomorrow." This work would be most useful to new students entering library school and is of limited value to those who already possess experience and a firm knowledge of academic librarianship. [R: LJ, 1 Sept 82, p. 1623]

— Frank Wm. Goudy

210. Breivik, Patricia Senn. **Open Admissions and the Academic Library.** Chicago, American Library Association, 1977. 131p. illus. bibliog. $10.00. LC 77-5816. ISBN 0-8389-3195-2.

This modest monograph provides both a review of the problems created for academic libraries by the movement toward "open admissions" in public institutions of higher education and a report of an experiment with a small group of students enrolled in the Brooklyn College division of the City University of New York. The work opens with a section summarizing the history of open admissions programs, coupled with something of a polemic against academic librarians for failing to prepare for the influx of students occasioned by such programs.

Although there is little doubt that academic libraries were poorly prepared to offer the special assistance needed by large and extremely heterogeneous student bodies, they are perhaps castigated more than might be necessary to document the author's point—namely, that the history of the success of library instruction programs in academic settings is a bleak one. Although Breivik notes that academic librarians have argued that they could do nothing "heroic" without additional funds, she also maintains that these same librarians have failed to insist upon or qualify for a collegial role with the faculty, which would allow them to acquire development monies or engage in team efforts to meet the varied needs of open admission students.

The more interesting section of the volume deals with the details of a cooperative experiment between the author, who was supported by members of the Department of Educational Services at Brooklyn College, and two professors of English at the college. Although the test and control groups were small, the resulting statistics are meaningfully interpreted. It is clear not only that the cooperative effort between faculty and librarians improved student performance in preparing research papers but also that traditional library instruction actually worsened performance. [R: C&RL, May 78, p. 225; CLW, Apr 78, p. 404; JAL, Sept 78, p. 226; LJ, 1 Apr 78, p. 726; LQ, July 78, p. 345; RQ, Summer 78, p. 348]   Doralyn J. Hickey

211. Bryan, Harrison. **University Libraries in Britain: A New Look.** London, Clive Bingley; distr., Hamden, Conn., Linnet Books, 1976. 192p. index. o.p. ISBN 0-85157-218-9(Bingley); 0-208-01532-9(Linnet).

This book resulted from a survey of university libraries in Great Britain undertaken by Bryan, a librarian at the University of Sydney, Australia, in the second half of 1975. The survey was a follow-up study to an earlier survey undertaken by the author — *A Critical Survey of University Libraries and Librarianship in Great Britain* (1966). For the new study, the author visited 61 libraries, and he presents the results in 18 brief chapters, under such headings as finance, staff, technical services, services to readers, and other aspects of the library in the university setting. Part 2 of the book provides capsule descriptions of different types of libraries starting with "Oxbridge" (three pages for Cambridge, four pages for Oxford). The text is quite readable and will be of assistance to the beginning student of comparative librarianship. [R: C&RL, Sept 77, p. 438; JAL, July 77, p. 159; LJ, 1 May 77, p. 561; LQ, Oct 77, p. 490; LR, Spring 77, p. 51]

212. Christ, John M. **Toward a Philosophy of Educational Librarianship.** Littleton, Colo., Libraries Unlimited, 1972. 154p. (Research Studies in Library Science, No. 7). index. o.p. LC 72-79887. ISBN 0-87287-048-0.

University, college, and school libraries for years have sought academic identification. What is the present status of the profession? As Christ indicates, "the practical, applied approach common to librarians and library systems is the main orientation supported and used in their day-to-day operations. Administrative and technical duties form the main element in the librarian's identity rather than academic activities." In fact, librarians in academic settings have not fully accepted as part of their professional activities the pedagogical and intellectual pursuits — research, publishing, or even advanced degrees — common to the faculties in academic institutions.

The author's comparison of library science with other social science disciplines reveals some interesting dissimilarities. The librarian's nontheoretical attitude toward his or her field is stressed, within the framework of general communication theory. Such familiar topics as "the crisis of theory and philosophy in library science" and "the concept of service versus operational library functions" are covered in the book's 12 chapters. In addition, there is an extensive review of theoretical and historical generalizations as expressed in library literature.

213. Fussler, Herman H. **Research Libraries and Technology: A Report to the Sloan Foundation.** Chicago, University of Chicago Press, 1974. 91p. index. (The University of Chicago Studies in Library Science). $10.00. LC 73-81481. ISBN 0-226-27558-2.

This report was originally produced as one of a series of state-of-the-art studies commissioned by the Sloan Foundation to help develop its program in educational technology, which was inaugurated in 1970. It is focused on large research libraries (which have the greatest service and processing problems) and the technologies that may be brought to bear upon these problems in the immediate future, on the assumption that significant improvements realized for these libraries will be of direct or indirect benefit to all libraries.

Fussler's report is not therefore addressed primarily to librarians. The first two chapters give a broad overview of research library operations, trends, and problems, with a discussion of present technologies and their possible roles in libraries. Chapter 3 deals more specifically with problems of bibliographic control; chapter 4 with methods of increasing resource availability: collection sharing, photographic miniaturization, and facsimile transmission. Chapters 5 and 6 review the use of computers in library operations, with a detailed description of selected important current applications. The final chapter is given over to Fussler's general observations and conclusions.

A large amount of useful information is packed into this small volume. Fussler is neither hidebound traditionalist nor doctrinaire visionary; his observations and conclusions are sensible, sound, and convincing. [R: C&RL, Sept 74, pp. 375-76; LJ, July 74, p. 1783]

George Piternick

214. Galvin, Thomas J., and Beverly P. Lynch, eds. **Priorities for Academic Libraries.** San Francisco, Calif., Jossey-Bass, 1982. 106p. bibliog. index. (New Directions for Higher Education, No. 39; Paperback Sourcebooks in the Jossey-Bass Higher Education Series). $8.95. LC 81-48572. ISBN 0-87589-897-1; ISSN 0271-0560.

This slender volume is not designed for librarians, though they and library school students will find it a useful summary of current issues. Rather, it is planned for presidents, academic vice presidents, and others in the higher education community who are seeking a better understanding of both the problems and the possibilities of college and university libraries. An administrator's view is presented by Robert M. O'Neil, president of the University of Wisconsin system. This is followed by chapters from other academic administrators as well as librarians. Most of the topics are familiar: user expectations, financing, collection development, resource sharing, preservation, productivity, and the role of new technologies. William Moffett's chapter, "What the Academic Librarian Wants from Administrators and Faculty," discusses a topic less often covered in the professional literature than the other subjects. The book is mercifully free from jargon, and the individual authors present informed views on contemporary issues. There are differences of emphasis and relatively few solutions. What does emerge is what the editors desired: a better understanding of the problems and prospects of academic libraries. [R: AL, Apr 83, p. 204; JAL, May 83, p. 97]   A. Robert Rogers

215. Higham, Norman. **The Library in the University: Observations on a Service.** Boulder, Colo., Westview Press, 1980. 205p. index. $22.50. LC 80-51340. ISBN 0-86531-053-X.

Norman Higham undertakes to survey the state of the art with respect to academic libraries. His is a thoughtful, thought-provoking approach meant to be read by those looking for an overview of the aims and objectives of academic libraries. Higham examines the library in relation to the university, exploring library finance, acquisitions, selection, and processing as well as a number of other aspects of academic librarianship including staffing, interlibrary loan, and computer applications. For each topic he reviews the basic principles, points out problems, renders opinions, and offers advice. His well-stated, personal point of view constitutes sound examples of good judgment and reveals a thorough knowledge of his subject. Although the book is intended primarily for a British audience, the author consistently includes references to American academic libraries and cites American practice.

This is an enjoyable, well-organized book in which the author not only examines the subject in detail, but also shares with the reader his views and opinions based on his 25 years as a librarian. [R: LR, Winter 80, p. 290]
Brian Alley

216. Josey, E. J., ed. **New Dimensions for Academic Library Service.** Metuchen, N.J., Scarecrow, 1975. 349p. index. o.p. LC 74-30062. ISBN 0-8108-0786-6.

The central issue linking the 25 original essays that make up this book is the new patterns emerging in academic libraries in response to social, political, and technological developments. The volume is divided into four parts, plus an epilogue: part 1, "The Library: A Vital Component in Higher Education"; part 2, "New Approaches in Solving Academic Library Problems"; part 3, "Unscrambling Critical Academic Library Issues"; part 4, "Patterns of Library Information Systems, Networks, and Consortia"; and "Providing Information and Library Services to Academic Library Users." Essays, for the most part, were written by practicing academic librarians. Bibliographies are included at the end of each chapter. Recommended reading for academic librarians and administrators. [R: C&RL, Sept 75, pp. 426-27; LJ, 15 Dec 75, p. 2308]   Zena Jacobs

217. Lyle, Guy R. **The Librarian Speaking: Interviews with University Librarians.** Athens, Ga., University of Georgia Press, 1970. 206p. illus. index. o.p. LC 71-119553. ISBN 0-8203-0254-6.

Informal exploration of academic librarianship, its past, present, and future, as expressed by 16 noted librarians answering questions posed by the author. Questions touch upon many problems which continue to plague academic libraries, and although interviews have their limitations, the volume is important as a permanent record documenting individuals' opinions. An interesting book for academic librarians and useful as a supplement for an academic librarianship course. [R: C&RL, July 71, p. 323; LJ, July 70, p. 2435]
Charles D. Patterson

218. **Options for the 80s: Proceedings of the Second National Conference of the Association of College and Research Libraries.** Michael D. Kathman and Virgil F. Massman, eds. Greenwich, Conn., JAI Press, 1982. 2v. index.

(Foundations in Library and Information Science, Vol. 17). $125.00/set. LC 82-7721. ISBN 0-89232-276-4.

The Second National Conference of the Association of College and Research Libraries held in Minneapolis on 1-4 October 1981, generated a total of 60 formal presentations and one panel discussion. Of the 60 presentations, 5 were theme papers dealing with problems in higher education. The 55 contributed papers cover a variety of topics, including management, bibliographic control, bibliographic instruction, collection development, special collections, the role of the librarian, and technological implications. The panel discussion was an attempt to summarize the theme papers.

The first volume, part A, includes a list of contributors, a brief introduction, the theme papers, and 26 contributed papers. The second volume, part B, contains the balance of the contributed papers, a transcript of the panel discussion, an author and a subject index, and a brief ACRL who's who. The excellent subject index will make this volume useful for research purposes. Recommended for library school collections. Brian Alley

219. Stirling, John F., ed. **University Librarianship**. London, Library Association; distr., Phoenix, Ariz., Oryx Press, 1981. 229p. index. $32.50. ISBN 0-85365-621-5.

Although the contributors are librarians associated with various British universities, this collection is intended to serve as a general text to academic librarianship. It also describes some of the techniques currently used in British university libraries.

In 9 of the 10 chapters, a broad discussion of a topic is presented, followed by a case study at a specific library. The final chapter, "Library Planning in an Era of Financial Constraint," gives an overview of the problems British libraries will be confronting in the immediate future. The implications of the controversial Atkinson Report (which advocated strict limits to the growth of libraries) are also considered here. Yet, the librarians writing in this handbook are not inordinately concerned with fiscal crises. John F. Stirling's chapter on library administration and organization stresses the importance of flexibility, both in staffing and in the management of resources. He also describes the political environment of British universities within which the library must operate. In this context, the University Library Committee plays an important advisory role in setting policy for the library. R. F. Eatwell, writing on reader services, emphasizes user instruction and access to

information. C. K. Balmforth's discussion of management information systems is especially helpful for library administrators. Other topics treated in this collection are rather predictable: resource sharing, nonbook materials, acquisitions policies, ordering procedures, special collections, and the impact of automation. Notes and references accompany each chapter, citing American as well as British publications. The case studies provide good insights into the operation of academic libraries in Great Britain and may suggest some new approaches to handling library problems or procedures.

Despite some uniquely British terminology and acronyms, this is an introductory work that American librarians can find quite useful. It is comprehensive, up-to-date, and well written. As Stirling points out in his introduction, "the fundamental problems of academic librarianship are common to all and ... apparent dissimilarities are often merely differences of emphasis." [R: C&RL, July 82, p. 356; LR, Spring 82, p. 56] Thomas A. Karel

220. Stone, Walter Clarence, comp. **Academic Change and the Library Function: Papers Delivered at a Meeting of the College and Research Division, Pennsylvania Library Association, October, 1969**. Pittsburgh, Pa., Pennsylvania Library Association, 1970. 50p. o.p. LC 71-120169.

Three papers presented at a meeting of the College and Research Division of the Pennsylvania Library Association on 3 October 1969 in Pittsburgh by two educators and one computer-oriented librarian, whose aim is the encouragement of academic librarians to use media as well as books in their libraries. Nothing new or startling but does form a record of the conference. [R: LJ, 15 Oct 70, p. 3453] Charles D. Patterson

221. Stueart, Robert D., and Richard D. Johnson, eds. **New Horizons for Academic Libraries: Papers Presented at the First National Conference of the Association of College and Research Libraries, Boston, Massachusetts, November 8-11, 1978**. New York, K. G. Saur, 1979. 583p. illus. maps. $50.00. LC 79-12059. ISBN 0-89664-093-0.

The seven invited "theme" papers and the 66 contributed papers delivered at the first national conference of ACRL are here presented in full, but without transcription of ensuing questions and discussion. The theme papers are concerned with the future of higher education in the United States, ways and means of managing academic libraries, the influence of technology in the modern library, network development, the library's function as an information "broker," the future of collection-sharing and overall bibliographical control, and the changing role of the university librarian. The contributed papers are grouped under the headings of administration and management, bibliographical control and automation, bibliographical instruction, cooperation, economic aspects, the librarian's role, resources, and services.

The theme papers together stress the importance and magnitude of the changes in academic librarianship taking place at the present time and those expected in the near future. By and large, they are well done and stimulating. The contributed papers, generally much shorter and devoted to more specific topics, are the usual mixed bag, ranging from the trivial to the useful. Overall, their quality appears well above average for conference papers of this kind. It is the rare academic librarian who will fail to find material of interest and value in this group of papers.

The publisher has managed to include very many words in a volume that is not bulky. Although the type is small, it is readable; and the paper and binding are adequate. The editors and the publisher deserve credit for bringing out a publication of this size and complexity so rapidly. The reviewer's copy found its way to him scarcely 10 months after the conference itself was held. [R: AB, 23 June 80, p. 4903; JAL, Mar 80, p. 42; LJ, 15 May 80, p. 1143]
George Piternick

222.   Taylor, Robert S. **The Making of a Library: The Academic Library in Transition.** New York, Becker and Hayes, 1972. 230p. index. (A Wiley-Becker-Hayes Publication; Hampshire College Working Paper, No. 2). o.p. LC 71-180245. ISBN 0-471-84831-X.

This volume describes "an intellectual and operational 'marriage' between the sometimes disparate educational requirements of the *academic library* and its *academic context.* The discussion centers around the decision-making that went into the building design, the systems planning, and the experimental style of the Hampshire College Library Center in Amherst, Massachusetts" (publisher's statement). [R: LJ, Aug 72, p. 2550]

223.   **Use, Mis-Use and Non-Use of Academic Libraries.** Edited by the Committee on Requirements of the Academic Library User. Woodside, N.Y., College and University Libraries Section, New York Library Association, 1970. 129p. o.p.

Proceedings of a conference whose participants included library directors, professors, students, and library school deans who, through speeches and panel discussions, effectively examine many aspects of academic librarianship. Concerns include ways to make the library more meaningful in the educational process, better understanding of clientele and their needs, the nonlibrary user, strengthening public relations, and role of the librarian and the library in teaching. Conclusions are optimistic. [R: LJ, 1 Dec 70, p. 4140]
Charles D. Patterson

COLLEGE AND COMMUNITY LIBRARIES

224.   Allen, Kenneth. **Use of Community College Libraries.** Hamden, Conn., Linnet Books, 1971. 159p. bibliog. o.p. LC 74-132001. ISBN 0-208-01143-9.

A rewritten dissertation with the following objectives: to identify student and faculty attitudes toward the community college library, and to determine faculty and student use of the community college library. [R: C&RL, Mar 72, p. 145]

225.   Braden, Irene A. **The Undergraduate Library.** Chicago, American Library Association, 1970. 158p. illus. index. bibliog. (ACRL Monograph, No. 31). o.p. LC 75-80834. ISBN 0-8389-3097-2.

This volume is based on the author's 1967 University of Michigan doctoral dissertation, and examines the objectives and mission of the undergraduate libraries at Cornell, Harvard, Indiana, Michigan, South Carolina, and Texas. As the first full-length study of the subject it is very useful to those planning such facilities, but it lacks details of the unique academic and physical circumstances of the six libraries examined. Additional updated material could have been added between presentation of the dissertation and its publication. [R: C&RL, Nov 70, p. 417; LJ, 1 June 70, p. 2105; RQ, Winter 70, p. 178]
Charles D. Patterson

226.   Branscomb, Harvie. **Teaching with Books: A Study of College Libraries.** Chicago, Association of American Colleges, 1940; repr., Hamden, Conn., Shoe String Press, 1974. 239p. index. o.p. LC 64-17332.

This issue of *Teaching with Books* requires little in the way of summary or evaluation; it is, of course, one of the earliest, most influential, and most frequently cited bibles of the "Library-College" movement, as well as a complete and perceptive study of American college libraries of the 1930s. First published in 1940, this issue constitutes its second unaltered reprinting; the first appeared in 1964 and has been out-of-print for some years. The 34 years that have passed since first publication have seen many changes and developments in college librarianship, and some chapters, notably that on costs of library service, are hopelessly out of date. Other aspects of modern college librarianship—audiovisual materials and services, for instance—are barely touched. Conceptually, however, *Teaching with Books* remains fresh and readable; it is an indispensable item in any collection of writings on librarianship.

George Piternick

227.   Burlingame, Dwight F., Dennis C. Fields, and Anthony C. Schulzetenberg. **The College Learning Resource Center.** Littleton, Colo., Libraries Unlimited, 1978. 176p. index. o.p. LC 78-13716. ISBN 0-87287-189-4.

The text focuses upon the organization and administration of college learning resource centers and assists in the development of a sound learning resources program. Although the emphasis is on establishing and maintaining learning resource centers in four-year colleges and universities, the principles set forth apply as well to graduate degree-granting institutions and other post-secondary centers of learning. The text covers administrative organization; resources and information (collection development, access to the collection, and physical facilities); instructional technology services (graphics, photography, television, etc.); instructional development and faculty development; technical services; and management, personnel, and finance. Each of these chapters synthesizes goals and procedures for individual units, all within the framework of learning resources philosophy and considered as part of the program in its entirety. [R: C&RL, Mar 79, p. 177; JAL, May 79, p. 95; LJ, 1 Feb 79, p. 360]

228.   **College Learning Resources Programs: A Book of Readings.** Washington, D.C., Association for Educational Communications and Technology, 1977. 80p. illus. $6.95pa. ISBN 0-89240-005-6.

This book of readings is an outgrowth of a committee of AECT which addressed itself to the development of guidelines for college and university learning resources programs. The term "learning resources" is used to mean several different things in today's educationese. This work is no exception. It is readily apparent

that AECT and ALA need to agree upon common definitional meanings for "college learning resources." Eight authors offer their viewpoints on such topics as "The Production Function," "The Utilization Function," the "ID Function," etc. Because of the time lag in publication, several of the readings suffer from a lack of recent references. Much of the material has appeared earlier in other sources. In the final analysis, this book falls short of its purpose and would more appropriately be entitled "College Educational Communications/Technology Programs." [R: JAL, Sept 77, p. 231; LJ, 1 Dec 77, p. 2413]   Dwight F. Burlingame

229.   **College Libraries: Guidelines for Professional Service and Resource Provision.** 3rd ed. London, Library Association; distr., Phoenix, Ariz., Oryx Press, 1982. 64p. bibliog. index. $12.00pa. ISBN 0-85365-635-5.

The product of two years' work (beginning January 1980) on the part of the Colleges of Further and Higher Education Group (CoFHE) of the Library Association, this work is the new edition of *College Libraries: Recommended Standards of Library Provision in Colleges of Technology* ... (1971). It was prepared in the light of heavy demands made on college libraries with respect to such things as "changes in government policy, economic circumstances, legislation, staff-student ratios, learning and teaching methodology, and increases in the nature, level, and diversity of courses" (preface). The *Guidelines* are based on a wide spectrum of professional opinion and experience, and are aligned with the Library Association's published policy on the staffing of nonuniversity academic libraries.

While the new edition discusses many of the same topics as were covered by the 1971 edition—stock, scope and philosophy, services, user education, and staffing—the compilers tell us that new papers have been prepared in each case, that they have not indulged in simple updating, and a comparison of the second and third editions indicates that this is the case. New to this edition are a section on "The Library's Relationships with the Parent College and External Bodies" and an appendix giving "Recommended Salary Grades and Conditions of Service for Staff in Non-University Academic Libraries." The latter is the official policy statement of the Library Association.

While "guidelines" are, of course, intended only to "guide," one might expect to find, particularly in the light of declining funding for education in Britain, more specific figures on costs (the tendency is to refer to other lists published elsewhere) and perhaps some minimum set of figures for collection sizes— one is given this for journals, but not really for monographic or audiovisual materials, where percentages of book budgets are all that is mentioned. The guidelines do set out, for both college librarians and administrators, all the main points to be considered if these libraries are to continue to serve the college students and staff, and as such, deserve serious consideration. [R: JAL, Sept 82, p. 241]   Margaret Anderson

230. Cowley, John, ed. **Libraries in Higher Education: The User Approach to Service.** London, Clive Bingley; Hamden, Conn., Linnet Books, 1975. 163p. illus. bibliog. o.p. ISBN 0-208-01371-7.

The title of this collection of essays misleads; it is actually a discussion of most aspects of reader services and staff development as practiced in British polytechnic colleges. The editor and contributors are all librarians at The Polytechnic of North London; their essays provide a view of current theory and practice at that institution and at the other British polytechnics in the two main areas of providing library use and subject specialization.

Following an interesting and lucid history of the development of polytechnics (and their libraries) by the editor, successive chapters in the first section deal with reader services, public relations and publicity, nonprint media, and teaching library use. In the section on subject specialization, essays on book selection, information services for academic staff, planning library instruction, and professional awareness follow an introduction and survey of the section.

The collection will be interesting to North American librarians, who will discern significant similarities between the British polytechnics and North American community colleges, and other likenesses between the libraries serving them, their problems, and the ways in which these problems are approached. [R: C&RL, May 76, p. 277; JAL, May 76, p. 92; LJ, 15 Feb 76, p. 596; LR, Autumn 75, p. 132; RQ, Spring 76, p. 283]

George Piternick

231. Davidson-Arnott, Frances, comp. **Policies and Guidelines Developed for Community and Technical College Libraries.** Ottawa, Canadian Library Asasociation, 1983. 277p. index. $25.00pa. ISBN 0-88802-171-2.

This work consists mainly of reprinted policies and guidelines developed for 16 Canadian community and technical college libraries. According to the compiler, the two basic

purposes for this manual are "to provide models of, the formats of, and topics covered by, various libraries' policies" and to provide "the actual content of these policies to use in the development of one's own policies."

The contents are divided into 12 topical sections, covering all aspects of library service as well as audiovisual software, hardware, and production; library archives; collection development; copyright; and personnel and professional development. Each section contains from 2 to 11 samples of policies or guidelines concerning a subject. They range in length from single paragraphs to many pages. Similarly varied are the aspects, details, and situations covered in each example. All the documents are in English, and several are presented in both French and English.

Each of the sections is prefaced with a brief narrative and a list of sources for additional reading. The lists are particularly helpful for an overview of the existing literature on policies, guidelines, and standards, especially for those issued by the American Library Association. The index is brief and could be more detailed; as it is, a user must peruse an entire section or a lengthy policy to find a sample treatment of a very specific aspect of a topic. For example, such subjects as pathfinders, desk lock-ups, and fire alarms are not mentioned in the index, although they are treated in the text.

The documents, of course, were created to address general, as well as unique, situations at the institutions that developed them. They are nevertheless handy as samples because of their format, their style, and certainly their general content. This compilation should prove useful as a guide in smaller academic libraries that need to create or update their current operational policies.   Linda L. Folck

232. Jefferson, George, and G. C. K. Smith-Burnett, eds. **The College Library: A Collection of Essays.** London, Clive Bingley; Hamden, Conn., Linnet Books, 1978. 208p. index. o.p. ISBN 0-208-01665-1.

This collection of eight essays relates almost exclusively to British libraries, with its focus upon the development and growth of the British technical, or "polytechnical," colleges and their libraries over the past two decades. Despite the significant, highly interesting aspects of British college libraries, this work offers little new information pertinent to the college library beyond that already covered in comparable American sources. Predictable essays on development, government and finance, organization, staffing, services, library usage, the learning resource center, and library cooperation and coordination are included; they are, with the single exception of the essay that examines "organisational structures," uniformly uninteresting and, lamentably, they plow wellworn ground once again. This book might have been salvaged with the implementation of some sort of different emphasis, but unfortunately, the "college library" topic is so very much discussed that a new work, even from the British point of view, seems redundant. This collection of essays is of limited usage in the United States for all but the largest academic and library school libraries. [R: LJ, 1 Nov 78, p. 2175]

Ronald Rayman

233. Miller, William, and D. Stephen Rockwood, eds. **College Librarianship.** Metuchen, N.J., Scarecrow, 1981. 284p. $17.00. LC 80-25546. ISBN 0-8108-1383-1.

The editors claim to present practical, comparative, and theoretical articles that "provide a sense of where the college library now stands and where it is going." Perhaps as many as 6 of the 15 original articles are practical or thoughtful; those concerned with user instruction (Hopkins), with government documents (Heim and Moody), and with library buildings (Poole) are especially good. One of the two management articles (Maurer) and those describing the parameters of equal employment opportunity (Guy) and the establishment of archives (Counihan) are well written and contain good advice, although the information presented is neither new nor uniquely oriented to college library situations.

Several of the articles are of very limited usefulness. One is a descriptive survey of college libraries that presents 1978 data and offers the conclusion that there is "a great deal of diversity among college libraries in the United States"; one is about budgetary trends in small private liberal arts colleges in Ohio; and one is a slightly revised version of a previously published article on collection development. Few of the articles in the anthology are supported by extensive references to the literature, and the book is not indexed.

The book has limited value both for reference and for staff development purposes. Librarians or library educators considering purchase should first review the extent to which they believe college libraries are different from other academic libraries. Too many of the articles in this collection make the assumptions that (a) nearly all librarians and educators continue to perceive the college library as a small, university library, and (b) college libraries are so

unique as to require a separate literature base. The contents of this book indicate that these are false assumptions. [R: LJ, Aug 81, pp. 1510-11]

Ruth M. Katz

234. Platt, Peter, ed. **Libraries in Colleges of Education.** 2nd ed. London, Library Association; distr., Detroit, Gale, 1972. 409p. illus. index. o.p. ISBN 0-85365-335-6.

The first edition of this work was published in 1966 under the title *Library Practice for Colleges of Education.* This new edition has been completely restructured. The 14 articles, written by a number of authors, are grouped under four broad subject categories: colleges of education and their libraries; the essentials of library practice; the college of education library and its relationships with other libraries; and college of education libraries overseas, which also contains an article on the United States. This book will be of interest to administrators in some of the larger academic libraries. [R: RSR, Oct 73, p. 18]

235. Veit, Fritz. **The Community College Library.** Westport, Conn., Greenwood Press, 1975. 221p. illus. index. (Contributions in Librarianship and Information Science, No. 14). $27.50. LC 72-843. ISBN 0-8371-6412-5.

This book is a survey of what the author considers to be the distinctive elements of library facilities serving community colleges. It covers the history of the community college learning resource personnel, administrative organization, technical services, microforms, user services, materials and equipment, cooperation, standards, and building planning. An index and several illustrations (i.e., charts and figures) facilitate the use of this work. At times, because the author states and restates the obvious and covers familiar details, the book becomes heavy going. Additionally, the material is dated with respect to the place and thrust of the community college in higher education today. For organization and administration of the learning resources center, Kenneth and Lorin Allen's work, *Organization and Administration of the Learning Resources Center in the Community College*, is still the best available work. In fact, although it was published in 1973, this reviewer finds it a more progressive work than the 1975 publication by Veit. Despite the shortcomings of Veit's work, it would still be a helpful tool to the student of the community college learning resources center. Although Veit prefers the shorter title of "College Library," it would seem to this author more appropriate and consistent with the standards that his book be be titled "The Community College Learning Resources Center." [R: C&RL, Mar 76, p. 183; Choice, Feb 76, p. 1557; CLW, Feb 76, p. 306; JAL, May 76, p. 85; LJ, 15 Feb 76, p. 596; LQ, Oct 76, p. 450; RQ, Spring 76, p. 284]

Dwight F. Burlingame

236. Wilkinson, Billy R., ed. **Reader in Undergraduate Libraries.** Englewood, Colo., Information Handling Services, 1978. 447p. bibliog. index. (Readers in Librarianship and Information Science, 25). o.p. LC 78-9504. ISBN 0-910972-76-1.

Unlike many of the readers in this series, this volume contains a number of hard-to-locate and previously unpublished papers. Four of the unpublished papers (those by John Haak, Patricia Knapp, Melvin Voight, and Billy Wilkinson) resulted from a 1970 summer institute at the University of California-San Diego and cover the issues in evaluating undergraduate libraries. Another three previously unpublished items from a 1971 preconference program of the Association of College and Research Libraries provide some insight into the problems of defining appropriate and effective service programs in undergraduate libraries.

Of the 33 articles, only two were written after 1972 (one in 1973 and a short 1977 piece by Ellsworth Mason on the UBC undergraduate library building). The book does provide a good historical review of the topic, as 15 of the articles were written in the 1950s. Wilkinson divides the papers into the following sections: library service for undergraduates in the late nineteenth and early twentieth centuries; Lamont Library; symposia on library service to undergraduate students, 1952 and 1955; the early 1960s and 1970s; Institute on Training for Service in Undergraduate Libraries, 1970; Institute on Training for Service on the Undergraduate Environment, 1971; and a critical overview of undergraduate libraries. Certainly, the authors of the papers could be listed on an honor roll of advocates of the undergraduate libraries: Keyes Metcalf, Edwin Williams, William Dix, Billy Wilkinson, Norah Jones, Patricia Knapp, James Davis, and Irene Braden, to name but a few. Both an adequate index and a list of suggested readings add to the value of the volume.

No book is completely flawless, and this volume is no exception. For the last four to five years, extended debates about the future of the undergraduate library have been raging. Although the question has not been resolved, Wilkinson fails to include any discussion of this critical debate. The *Reader* is an interesting collection of historical essays but is totally inadequate as a review of the current situation and future prospects of the undergraduate library. [R: C&RL, Sept 79, pp. 471-72]

G. Edward Evans

STATISTICS

237. Baumol, William J., and Matityahu Marcus. **Economics of Academic Libraries.** Prepared for the Council on Library Resources by Mathematica, Inc. Washington, D.C., American Council on Education, 1973. 98p. illus. bibliog. o.p. LC 73-10244. ISBN 0-8268-1257-0.

The Council on Library Resources has sponsored a study attempting to provide statistical data that will be helpful in long-range library planning. It should be welcomed by library administrators. Two major areas are explored: growth rates of libraries and cost trends of library materials and operations.

Growth rates are based on data for two decades collected from a special group of research libraries. While growth rates were high and relatively consistent throughout the period, they were not high in relation to other institutional costs or to size of the student body. Staff size declined in relation to number of students served and the size of collections serviced. Cost trends are based on statistics gathered from 678 colleges and universities. The volume of acquisitions was found to be directly related to the size of the collection, size of enrollment, and educational expenditure per student.

The direct application of the study's findings to budget preparation and long-range planning is discussed thoroughly. It can be expected that the results of this study will be reflected in a more analytical approach to library budget preparation by an application of the mathematical formulas developed. [R: AL, Mar 74, p. 143; BL, 1 Jan 74, p. 458; LJ, 15 Feb 74, p. 466]

Paul Spence

238. Beazley, Richard M. **Library Statistics of Colleges and Universities, 1976 Institutional Data.** Washington, D.C., U.S. Department of Health, Education, and Welfare; distr., Champaign, Ill., University of Illinois, 1979. 183p. (University of Illinois. Graduate School of Library Science. Monograph No. 16). $5.00pa. ISBN 0-87845-061-0.

The importance of this series of continuing information on American libraries cannot be overestimated. It has become, in addition to the statistical information issued by other agencies such as ARL, the standard source for data.

They are presented as uniformly as reporting standards permit and are important in delineating the standards and activities of American libraries, including everything from volumes held to FTE rates per professional staff member. This is an important work being issued through the University of Illinois, with data provided by the National Center for Educational Statistics.   Erwin K. Welsch

239. Library Statistics of Colleges and Universities: Summary Data 1979. Chicago, Association of College and Research Libraries, American Library Association, 1982. 68p. $13.00 spiralbound; $10.00 spiralbound (ACRL members).

This volume presents the results of a previously unpublished survey, funded by the U.S. Department of Health, Education, and Welfare and made available from the National Center for Educational Statistics. Although individual institutions are not identified, basic statistical information is provided on over 3,000 public and private institutions in 50 states and the District of Columbia. U.S. armed forces schools and those in outlying areas, such as Puerto Rico, are also included to a limited degree. Statistics are limited to basic measures of central tendency and aggregate data. Variables for which data are provided include: full- and part-time employees, circulation, interlibrary loan, reference transactions, hours open per week, financial information relating to personnel and operating costs, holdings information, institution size, location by state, and book stock. Further information on the above variables is provided in some cases. The survey instrument is appended.

The volume is a welcome addition to the growing amount of descriptive data available on a large scale. Academic libraries, library schools, and library researchers will benefit the most from it. [R: JAL, July 83, p. 175]
          Andrew G. Torok

240. Library Statistics of Colleges and Universities, 1982 Institutional Data. Data gathered by the National Center for Education Statistics, U.S. Department of Education. Chicago, Association of College and Research Libraries,

American Library Association, 1984. 177p. $16.00pa.; $12.00pa. (ACRL members). ISBN 0-8389-6640-3.

After a lapse of three years, the annual National Center of Education Statistics (NCES) Higher Education General Information Survey (HEGIS) collection for academic libraries has been published again. Apparently, this edition was compiled, analyzed, and printed by NCES and published by ACRL. It is very welcome since this data collection is available nowhere else, but it contains not only many of the good features but also many of the problems of earlier editions.

The book's data categories, divided into three tables, are (1) collections; (2) expenditures; and (3) fall 1982 enrollment, analyses of expenditures per student and per faculty member and a a percent of general educational expenditures, bookstock per student, and students per staff member. Data are shown by state and by institution. Explanatory footnotes conclude each table. In addition, the book contains a contents table, classification of institutions, and brief foreword.

Each edition of these statistics has produced its own unique features and this one is no exception. Publication by ACRL for the first time is an example, but we can add the lack of raw personnel data and of public service data. Certain data categories are added to the previous list; the full table of data analyses is new, for example. Other categories are dropped out.

Certain curious facts emerge from the collection; for instance, (1) several libraries report no current periodical subscriptions (including Princeton University, Louisiana State University, and the University of Missouri, St. Louis); (2) several institutions report no library facilities; and (3) a number of institutions have a library but report data for it incompletely or not at all.

It is too bad also that no city could be given in most cases to fix institutional location, no national grand total or decile totals could be provided for each data column (even in the computer age!), and no list of previous NCES statistics publications could be provided. And it is too bad that such a valuable report series cannot be available annually.

          John F. Harvey

19 Public Libraries

241. Berelson, Bernard, with the assistance of Lester Asheim. **The Library's Public: A Report of the Public Library Inquiry.** New York, Columbia University Press, 1949; repr., Westport, Conn., Greenwood Press, 1976. bibliog. $24.75. LC 75-31430. ISBN 0-8371-8499-1.

A classic in its own right, this volume of the Public Library Inquiry was originally published in 1948 under the title *The Public Library and the People.* It was subsequently reprinted by Columbia under the current title. Greenwood Press has made a wise choice in reprinting it again. Most library school students should read at least this volume, which includes the findings and a summary of the survey.

242. Broadus, Robert N., ed., with the assistance of Brian Nielsen. **The Role of the Humanities in the Public Library: Proceedings of a Conference Sponsored by the School of Library Science, University of North Carolina at Chapel Hill, March 5-7, 1978.** Chicago, American Library Association, 1979. $20.00. LC 79-24117. ISBN 0-8389-0297-9.

Funded by a grant from the National Endowment for the Humanities, the conference included six papers, followed by comments from two respondents for each paper and then by general discussion. Papers, responses, and highlights of the discussion are reported.

A short review cannot do justice to the individual chapters, but can only indicate the wealth of intellectual stimulation. Dan Lacy's paper, from a publisher's viewpoint, defines the humanities very broadly to include all works that deal with basic questions about the nature and destiny of humanity. (Several other speakers also stress that quality of mind, rather than subject content, which is what makes a book humanistic.) R. Kathleen Molz reviews the history of the American public library, with particular emphasis on the debate between those who believe a library should stock only "useful" books, and those who find value in works of creative imagination. Charles Frankel stresses the need for "disciplined self-criticism and self-examination" of society's institutions. Louis R. Heckler, dissenting from the emphasis placed by previous speakers on books, stresses the role of television, especially the potential of cable television and home videocassette usage. E. Laurence Chalmers, Jr., describes the efforts of the Art Institute of Chicago to reach new audiences. Ronald Williams evaluates the successes and failures of public libraries and urban universities. The book concludes with a masterful summation by Lester Asheim.

This work makes a far more enduring contribution to the literature of librarianship than do most conference proceedings. There are several reasons why this is so. The issues are timely—but also perennial, the speakers were thoughtful and lucid, the discussants were incisive in their comments, and the editing was done with care and discretion. The result is a book that adds a significant chapter to the debate and invites the entire profession to grapple with issues of long-standing concern as we continue to attempt to articulate a philosophy of librarianship. [R: BL, 15 Apr 80, p. 1177; C&RL, Sept 80, pp. 485-86]   A. Robert Rogers

243. Bundy, Mary Lee. **Helping People Take Control: The Public Library's Mission in a Democracy.** College Park, Md., Urban Information Interpreters, 1980. 236p. bibliog. $14.95.

The author is a crusader for those deprived of power. She has written an angry attack on those in power who control our society and on those she perceives as doing nothing to counteract the excesses of the empowered. Public libraries, library associations, and librarians are her particular focus. She sets forth the role of the public library as an institution responsible for raising social consciousness and for informing the information deprived. She then states that librarians have missed their opportunity to serve their advocacy role and blames library education, professional associations, and all the organized information groups for failing to support those wishing to serve as information advocates. In addition to her strongly worded attack, the author includes listings of sources and resources helpful in developing collections related to social concerns and in developing I & R services. This is the most useful aspect of the book.

Bundy's message that today's public libraries and librarians are doing too little for the information deprived is one of the believer championing a cause with some fact and much passion. Its message would be appropriate to the megaphone of 1969 and shouted to the crowd. A decade later, the issues she raises still exist and merit our concern, but the megaphone style is out of date. [R: LJ, 1 Dec 80, p. 2480]

Ann E. Prentice

244.   Campbell, H. C. **Public Libraries in the Urban Metropolitan Setting.** Hamden, Conn., Linnet Books, 1973. 298p. illus. index. (The Management of Change: Studies in the Evolution of Library Systems). $22.50. LC 73-6518. ISBN 0-208-01193-5.

The author makes a number of useful comparisons—in terms of social, urban, and administrative settings—between metropolitan library systems in the New York area and in Washington, Detroit, Chicago, Denver, Los Angeles, Montreal, Toronto, and Vancouver. He also provides somewhat briefer information on metropolitan public libraries in Great Britain, West Germany, Denmark, Sweden, France, Australia, and Japan. The study is well documented and should be useful to all library administrators. [R: BL, 15 Jan 74, p. 501; LJ, 1 Jan 74, p. 36]

245.   Conant, Ralph W., and Kathleen Molz, eds. **The Metropolitan Library.** Cambridge, Mass., MIT Press, 1972. 333p. bibliog. index. o.p. LC 72-4338. ISBN 0-262-03041-1.

Contains 18 essays (written by librarians, educators, urban planners, and communication specialists) that attempt to describe essential developmental problems facing public libraries in metropolitan areas. Among the authors the reader will find Dan Lacy ("The Dissemination of Print"), Jesse Shera ("The Public Library in Perspective"), Kathleen Molz ("The Urban Public Library: A Perspective"), and Lowell A. Martin ("The Role and Structure of Metropolitan Libraries"). An annotated bibliography of pertinent writings is provided by Leonard Grundt. [R: LJ, 1 June 73, p. 1789; RQ, Spring 73, p. 313]

246.   Getz, Malcolm. **Public Libraries: An Economic View.** Baltimore, Md., Johns Hopkins University Press, 1980. 214p. bibliog. index. $21.00. LC 80-10651. ISBN 0-8018-2395-1.

Getz is an economist at Vanderbilt University who attempts to use traditional economic concepts and techniques and apply them in a library environment. The effort is based upon data gathered from 31 of the 50 largest public library systems in the country, with a wide range of statistical data and analysis provided on these selected libraries. For example, in chapter 2 Getz measures library operations in terms of activities, services, and their costs. Additional chapters consider labor costs, efficiency in public service, and innovations in technical systems. In ecah case, the focus of the study centers on the basic choices in public services of how many facilities to operate, of how many materials to purchase and retain, and of how many hours to operate the library. Regressional analysis is heavily used to consider the various policy alternatives, although political considerations are not forgotten in an attempt to reduce all decisions to simple math.

Overall, this is an interesting effort that provides a fresh perspective which is badly needed in library decision-making models. A major disappointment, however, is the scant attention paid to federal and state sources of income. While LSCA, CETA, and General Revenue Sharing are mentioned, a more fully developed examination of the impact that these revenues have made on library finances would have greatly enhanced this research. Appendices include a summary of the library system data collected, an explanation of the statistical methods used, and a review of the literature on evaluating library services. This title would be of most benefit to scholars and practitioners of public library administration. [R: BL, 15 Jan 81, p. 669; C&RL, May 81, p. 261; LJ, 1 Jan 81, p. 39]

Frank Wm. Goudy

247. International Federation of Library Associations. Section of Public Libraries. **Standards for Public Libraries.** Munich, Verlag Dokumentation; distr., Totowa, N.J., Rowman & Littlefield, 1973. 53p. o.p. ISBN 3-7940-4310-3.

Seventeen years after the IFLA Council formulated minimum recommendations and three years after the announcement of the UNESCO Public Library Manifesto, a guideline to standards for public libraries was generally available. This guide suggests basic standards for administration and general services, collections, staff, and physical plant. Standards are necessarily generalized but are in all cases formulated on the size and nature of the population served. The committee makes specific recommendations for size and emphasis of collections, staff and floorspace appropriate for various collections, and type of administrative unit needed. A separate section treats the needs of special groups—including children, hospitalized persons, and prisoners. The discussion in each section is specific and helpful, but because of the complexities involved, the recommendations on costs of service are very generalized. These guidelines will prove invaluable to local and national administrators concerned with creating, maintaining, or upgrading public library service. [R: AL, Jan 74, p. 38; LJ, 1 June 74, p. 1525]   Nancy P. Schneider

248. Martin, Lowell A., assisted by Terence Crowley and Thomas Shaughnessy. **Library Response to Urban Change: A Study of the Chicago Public Library.** Chicago, American Library Association, 1969. 313p. index. $12.00. LC 76-104040. SBN 8389-0077-1.

This is a very detailed report of the survey made on all aspects of the Chicago Public Library. Probably no public library has been so thoroughly scrutinized as this one; this is the third extensive survey made in this century. The other two are the library's own report, *A Library Plan for the Whole City* (Chicago Public Library, 1916) and Joeckel and Carnovsky's *A Metropolitan Library in Action* (University of Chicago Press, 1940). This new survey includes an analysis of Chicago's present and probable future population and in view of this the objectives and principles behind the library's very existence are examined with many proposals made for immediate and future planning. Martin has left no stones unturned and no sacred cows untouched as he recommends and sets priorities that need to be carried through. He has looked into every detail of the library's policies and practices concerning personnel, the

book collection, physical facilities, location of branches and work units, as well as operations of acquisitions and technical services, reference and circulation. These recommendations for improvement, revitalization and modernization are quite sound, and there is no doubt that other cities also need serious and comprehensive studies of their library systems. Even though there are many ideas brought out here which could be just as applicable to other library systems, the ones put forth here should only serve as stimuli to other libraries to investigate and analyze their own policies and operations. [R: C&RL, May 70, p. 203; DLQ, July 70, p. 346; JLH, Oct 70, p. 375; LQ, Apr 70, p. 269; LR, Spring 70, p. 281; LR, Summer 70, p. 314; WLB, June 70, p. 1067]   Donald J. Lehnus

249. Palmini, Cathleen. **Better Libraries Create Better Cities: A Study of Urban Library Needs.** Urbana, Ill., Graduate School of Library Science, University of Illinois, 1972. 47p. (Prepared for the Urban Library Trustees Council by the Library Research Center). o.p. NUC 75-112003.

This report provides a review of general trends in larger U.S. cities and is fundamentally a statistical summary interspaced with textual comments and citations from various sources demonstrating both demographically and financially the collective status of public libraries in urban America. Does not address a number of important concerns, including (1) the inability of libraries to adjust their programs to new populations, (2) outside funding of city libraries to support noncity users, and (3) the need for specific recommendations for funding. Of limited value beyond a summary of urban trends. [R: LJ, 15 Nov 73, p. 3358]
          Charles D. Patterson

250. Price, Paxton P., ed. **Future of the Main Urban Library.** Las Cruces, N. Mex., Urban Libraries Council, 1979. 107p. o.p.

Library directors, trustees, library educators, and government officials met in Chicago in October 1978 to discuss their concerns about the past and future of the urban main library in light of problems caused by lack of funding and decline in users, and in relation to its role in the national network. Three papers, with commentary by urban library directors, deal with the urban main library's historical role (Molz), its future role (Martin), and its role in networking (Avram).

Molz provides insights into urban library development that extend and expand the New England library history model. She describes the urban public library as an agency that "just grew" and grew to serve specific client groups with specific collections. Urban library policies shaped by this nineteenth-century legacy of unplanned growth are a major cause of our present confusion as to what the urban library should do or be.

Martin's paper meshes well with Molz's presentation, carrying many of her insights into the present and then shaping them into future directions. He identifies the functions, not the alternatives, of the urban library to be those of resource center, metropolitan information center, research center, and educational and culture center. As the clienteles of the urban library move from the city, it is "left with residues of former publics and it has not established a new constituency." These functions plus the library's need to move beyond them to become a partner in information networking will provide the outline for the future. Martin states, and the library directors responding concur, that the way in which this is accomplished will vary according to the library's historical and present role.

Avram provides a good summary of the role of the national network and the role of the urban library as a partner in that network. Asheim ties the presentation together, with his usual perceptive wit, to provide an appropriate summary. The entire report is well worth reading, and Molz's article should be required reading for those concerned with the beginnings of public library service in the United States. [R: LJ, 1 May 79, p. 1018]   Ann E. Prentice

251. Public Librarianship: A Reader. By Jane Robbins-Carter. Littleton, Colo., Libraries Unlimited, 1982. 555p. $35.00. LC 81-14313. ISBN 0-87287-246-7.

A variety of points of view and concepts concerning issues in public librarianship are presented in 49 original and reprinted readings by librarians and other professionals. The editor's intent is to provide "a conception both of the unique contribution the public library has made to American culture and of the direction in which this potentially pivotal institution must develop to remain a contributor to contemporary American society." Among the topics discussed are historical development of public libraries; purpose of the public library; standards for public library service; planning; user studies; legislation, politics, and public relations; and governance. [R: SBF, Nov/Dec 82, p. 60]

252. Public Libraries and New Directions for Adult Services: An Institute in Honor of Rose Vainstein, Margaret Mann Professor of Library Science: Proceedings. Joan C. Durrance and Rose Vainstein, eds. Ann Arbor, Mich., School of Library Science, University of Michigan, 1981. 73p. illus. bibliog. $7.50pa.

It is fitting that an Institute on Public Libraries and New Directions for Adult Services was held in honor of Rose Vainstein, professor in the School of Library Science at the University of Michigan, for she worked tirelessly for many years to make adult library service effective and dynamic. Although the main part of the booklet contains the papers and discussions of the institute, there are also a number of thoughtful tributes to the work of Rose Vainstein and an earlier paper of hers, *An Historic Perspective on Adult Services in American Public Libraries*, which presents an excellent summary of adult services, by whatever title, as they evolved in the American public library.

The institute's presentations are divided into three main sessions: (1) "The Public Library Setting—Community Profiles and What the 80s and 90s Will Bring," presented by Roger Greer; (2) "The NOW Scene—Diversity in Adult Services and Programming," presented by a series of speakers; and (3) "The Future Scene—Opportunities and New Directions for Adult Services in the American Public Library," by Margaret Monroe. The thoughtful, well-prepared papers describe different types of programs and their relationships to other agencies in addition to factors influencing the future direction of adult library services. Summaries of the discussion, particularly questions relating to public image and the current budget crisis, are included.

The booklet provides a good overview of how adult services developed and where such programs are going. Copies of worksheets useful in planning and a well-selected bibliography help to make this a useful tool for anyone interested in the varied programs being developed in public libraries today.

Lucille Whalen

253. Public Library Policy: Proceedings of the IFLA/Unesco Pre-Session Seminar, Lund, Sweden, August 20-24, 1979. K. C. Harrison, ed. Munich, New York, K. G. Saur; distr., Hamden, Conn., Shoe String Press, 1981. 152p. illus. (IFLA Publications, No. 19). $15.00. ISBN 3-598-20380-2; ISSN 0344-6891.

Usually devoted to the circumstances of public libraries in the Third World, the pre-IFLA Conference seminar from which these proceedings were gleaned was planned by its organizers to have a "wider applicability than just that of solving developing country situations." The 12 selections in this slim volume are the record of presentations by such diverse figures as public librarians from Sweden and the United States, directors of national library services for Tanzania and Singapore, and library researchers from Denmark and the Netherlands. Their aim was to "isolate general principles of public library policy"—that term referring, of course, to the larger issue of public library goals and objectives and national policy for library development rather than policy as the administrative rules and regulations of individual libraries (selection policies, etc.).

Within that framework the participants of this conference managed to address many facets of such policy including literacy programs, service to minorities, and the general purpose of public libraries. Much of this material, however, is narrative in nature, describing activities and programs in various locales rather than getting to the heart of a rationale for the existence of public libraries and a need for a national policy on libraries in the life of a nation. Although some of the presentations do raise interesting and legitimate issues concerning the determination of the purpose of public libraries in a changing world, nothing here is unique or pertinent enough to warrant the expenditure by other than those library schools desiring to have a complete collection of IFLA proceedings. [R: JLH, Spring 83, p. 226; LQ, Oct 82, p. 416; LR, Summer 83, p. 164]   Christopher Albertson

254.   Rayward, W. Boyd, ed. **The Public Library: Circumstances and Prospects.** Chicago, University of Chicago Press, 1978. 162p. (University of Chicago Studies in Library Science). $10.00. LC 78-19604. ISBN 0-226-70585-4.

The public library, as we all known, is in a state of change. This volume, which contains 11 papers presented at the thirty-ninth conference of the Graduate Library School (published earlier in the October 1978 issue of the *Library Quarterly*), discusses some of the factors that have contributed to the change and some of the directions the public library might take in the future. W. Boyd Rayward provides the introduction to the conference. Gordon Stevenson reviews current communication studies and comments on their relevance to the public library's role in society. Kathleen Molz discusses the development of financial support for the

public library. Kenneth Dowlin discusses computers, microforms, and video applications in "The Technological Setting of the Public Library." Genevieve Casey covers cooperation and networking, with an emphasis on the New York and Illinois systems, and Thomas Childers concentrates on "Information and Referral" in his discussion of reference and information services. Mary Jo Lynch covers adult services, Mary Chelton comments on young adult services, and Mae Benne reviews services for children. Lorna Paulin presents an overview of public library services in the United Kingdom. Robert Wedgeworth wraps things up with "Prospects for and Effecting Change in the Public Library," in which he suggests that continuing education is the appropriate means to obtain change.

The quality of the articles is variable; some concentrate on trends and issues, while others call for action and solutions. Although not a collection that is likely to change the course of the public library, this volume contains some lively and interesting papers. The issues raised by Mary Chelton regarding the provision of services to young adults and the education of young adult librarians especially deserve attention. [R: JAL, Nov 79, p. 290]

Terry L. Weech

255.   Seymour, Whitney North, Jr., and Elizabeth N. Layne. **For the People: Fighting for Public Libraries.** New York, Doubleday, 1979. 189p. bibliog. o.p. LC 78-14657. ISBN 0-385-14359-1.

Defined by the authors as a citizen's manual to be used to assure the future of public libraries, this readable, attractive book has greater scope than that purpose might suggest. It is an argument in favor of libraries, as well as a source of ideas for services, approaches, and marketing techniques for present-day public libraries. Using vignettes about library users and concisely written notes about library services now available, the authors, both associated with the National Citizens Emergency Committee to Save Our Libraries, have followed a simple outline: a brief history and chapters on various kinds of library users, concluding with a resounding argument in favor of public libraries in a time of austerity, and appendices that include texts of the draft of the Public Library Association mission statement, the Library Bill of Rights, and a bibliography. Access to the contents could have been improved with an index. Nevertheless, the book certainly serves the purpose for which it was written, and it is hoped it will be a part of library collections on citizens' advocacy, rather than buried among materials on librarianship. [R: BL, 15 May 79, p. 1406; LJ, 15 June 79, p. 1325]   Peggy Sullivan

256. Standards for Public Libraries. 2nd ed. Munich, Verlag Dokumentation; distr., New York, K. G. Saur, 1977. 53p. (IFLA Publications, 9). $6.40pa.; $4.60 (members). ISBN 3-7940-4429-0.

IFLA's *Standards for Public Libraries* was originally published in 1973. A third edition was published in 1984 (ISBN 3-598-20391-8). However, the concept of internationally accepted standards for public libraries originated in 1956 with the formulation of standards that were never officially published. As with the unpublished, but widely circulated 1956 standards, the second edition discusses five major areas: books and other materials, staff, availability, facilities and amenities, and library premises. The revision of the 1973 standards is necessary because of the growing library reliance on nonbook materials, which was not discussed in detail in the first edition. In addition to 119 standards, the volume includes the "Unesco Public Library Manifesto," principles drawn from it, and a discussion of the need for standards. The book will be valuable not only to library administrators but to anyone interested in the basic concepts of public librarianship.

257. A Strategy for Public Library Change: Proposed Public Library Goals — Feasibility Study. By Allie Beth Martin, Project Coordinator for the Public Library Association, American Library Association. Chicago, American Library Association, 1972. 84p. o.p. LC 72-000062. ISBN 0-8389-3106-5.

This study was sponsored by the Public Library Association, American Library Association and funded jointly by the Council on Library Resources and the National Endowment for the Humanities. The Project Advisory Committee included ten members, among them noted librarians and library educators.

This small volume contains in its 84 pages much provocative material. It examines the societal factors affecting the public library; studies the development of the public library in the past 20 years from 1950 through 1970; reports on the current status of the public library in terms of major strengths and weaknesses; and makes recommendations for the next phase of "public library change" leaving the actual direction this will take up to the library profession. The study contains a discussion of the critical problems facing public libraries relating to finance, public relations, staff,

society, management, technology, and objectives. Each problem area is discussed "in regards to its effect on the public library's attempt to perform needed community functions."

This is certainly "required reading" for all public librarians, library educators, and library school students who are interested in the public library. It is also a useful source for library research projects. Much of the material provides excellent points for further discussion in trying to provide "direction for public libraries." A useful annotated bibliography lists over 175 publications. [R: LJ, 15 Nov 72, p. 3690]

Paul A. Winckler

258. Sykes, Paul. **The Public Library in Perspective: An Examination of Its Origins and Modern Role.** London, Clive Bingley; distr., New York, K. G. Saur, 1979. 184p. bibliog. index. $15.00. ISBN 0-85157-284-7.

The author, who has served in public libraries for nearly 30 years and has directed three, presents a provocative and soundly argued tract for the times aimed at the British library establishment. He seeks to answer the questions: "During a period of intensive social and political upheaval when, ostensibly, the public library was emerging as a device which could be manipulated by the reformer or the demagogue, why did its potential pass largely unnoticed? And why did this new and hard-won facility fail to excite widespread public interest?" (p. 7). The answers to these questions have, the author maintains, serious implications for the plight of public libraries in Britain today; the roots of current lack of enthusiasm for public library support go back more than a century, eluding only those who refuse to take the trouble to understand the record.

Basing his study on printed primary sources including biographical material, social-economic histories, and professional literature, the author feels that attitudes have changed little in the past century and that fundamental rethinking of the public library role in society is needed to save the institution from slow extinction. Following a discouraging survey of nineteenth-century reform leaders, who virtually ignored libraries, and an analysis of the public record of the past century and a half, the author deals with present realities (stemming in part from the Local Government Act of 1972) which, within consolidations of governing authorities, have limited the apparent relevance of public libraries by identifying them with the educational rather than leisure/recreational agencies. Sykes, in much fuller fashion, provides a goad for British audiences similar to that wielded by Michael Harris in the United States during the 1970s. [R: LJ, 1 Dec 79, p. 2548]

Donald G. Davis, Jr.

259. Weingand, Darlene E. **Reflections of Tomorrow: Lifelong Learning and the Public Library.** Madison, Wis., DERBy Associates, 1980. 270p. bibliog. (A Delphi Study). $24.95. ISBN 0-9604692-0-6.

This volume raises significant speculation regarding public libraries as part of the articulated lifelong learning process in the United States. Although it specifically addresses whether public libraries "can or will be one of the nonformal providers of lifelong learning in the State of Minnesota," the report of the findings can be extrapolated beyond that scope. It serves to raise more questions than it answers as it examines the relationship between libraries and other parts of the educational system.

Part 1 reviews in 30 pages the history of public library involvement. It reveals not only the progress made and innovative instances where lifelong learning has been a public library focus, but also barriers such as the low awareness of library services by the public and the lack of status accorded adult education.

Part 2, by far the bulk of the book, reports a 1979 Delphi study of 42 Minnesota libraries and citizens. These findings are in the areas of social and economic change, work and leisure, technological advances, information-based society, education and governance, and funding. Statistics in percentages are reported; a scenario based on the responses is described, and implications are drawn for libraries. This study was the author's doctoral work.

Part 3, a bare 17 pages, presents an overview of the total scenario from 1980 to 2000, together with the author's conclusions and recommendations. Extensive appendices and a bibliography complete the volume.

The basic assumption of the book is that the study is likely to be applicable to what may happen in the future, pointing out the possibilities rather than making predictions. This, in turn, can enable decision makers to formulate direction and policy to meet future possibilities. This assumption can be questioned on at least two grounds. A Delphi study gathers opinions on specific topics from a series of mailed inquiries. This Delphi panel of respondents was not representative in terms of education (50 percent have master's degrees) or ethnic background (2 percent black) or occupation (2 percent laborers). And, the implications for libraries drawn appear based on what exists in library literature more than on insights gained from the findings. The book is photoreproduced typewritten pages, relatively easy to read, except for the forms and statistics and appendices, which are not clear. [R: LJ, 1 Feb 81, p. 315]

Barbara Conroy

20 School Library Media Centers

GENERAL WORKS

260. Aaron, Shirley L. **A Study of Combined School-Public Libraries.** Chicago, American Association of School Librarians, American Library Association, 1980. 107p. bibliog. (School Media Centers: Focus on Trends and Issues, No. 6). $7.00pa. LC 80-19785. ISBN 0-8389-3247-9.

This sixth volume in ALA's School Media Centers: Focus on Trends and Issues series presents five elements responsible for the renewed interest in the combined school/public library in recent years—need for better use of tax monies; broader acceptance of the community school concept and expansion of its media center services to the whole community; increasing perception of the roles of public and school libraries as parallel; and growing demand for access to the nonprint resources of information available in school media centers. The monograph is divided into three phases. Phase 1 is a framework for analyzing past and present merger attempts to indicate the extent to which combination libraries may be practical. Phase 2 is a comprehensive study of merged school and public libraries in Florida. Phase 3 is a checklist, used by the Florida State Library, designed to help a community make its decision on which option to pursue. Appendices A-F may be considered as step-by-step directions for those wishing to consider the feasibility of combining a school/public library. Wilma Wooland's book, *Combined School/Public Libraries: A Study with Conclusions and Recommendations* (Scarecrow, 1980; see *ARBA* 81, entry 196), could be used as a companion volume to Aaron's study. Both are recommended reading for those who wish to consider the concept of combined libraries in their communities. [R:

BL, 1 Jan 81, p. 628; JAL, Jan 81, p. 362; LQ, July 81, p. 346] Donald D. Foos

261. Anderson, Pauline H. **The Library in the Independent School.** Boston, National Association of Independent Schools, 1980. 55p. $7.75pa. LC 79-29701. ISBN 0-934338-43-4.

Although a slight volume, this updated version of a 1968 publication contains some well-presented approaches to library issues. Nearly half the space is devoted to thoughtful questions designed to stimulate discussion and expedite communication between library, faculty, and administration. The section titled "The Library in the School" uses the method of setting forth a statement and following it with specific questions to that point. The library self-evaluation questions are selected for attention by the head of the school or by the librarian. A brief opening chapter presents the unique position of the library in an independent secondary school. The section following clearly presents a variety of current concerns, such as censorship and security systems, in a very brief manner. The explanation in an appendix of the meanings of a selection of library acronyms adds to the usefulness of this booklet. The purpose stated by the author in the foreword, of giving "administrators, librarians and teachers a starting point for continuing discussions of libraries and library programs," has been well met. [R: SLJ, Dec 80, p. 35] Alice J. Wittig

√262. Case, Robert N., and Anna Mary Lowrey. **Curriculum Alternatives: Experiments in School Media Education.** Chicago, American Library Association, 1974. 254p. o.p. LC

74-12070. ISBN 0-8389-3154-5. (Available from Ann Arbor, Mich., Books on Demand, $63.30).

In 1963 a grant from the Knapp Foundation enabled the American Association of School Librarians-ALA to conduct a project aimed at demonstrating the interrelatedness of excellent school media service and quality education. That project was described in *Realization*, edited by Peggy Sullivan. A second Knapp-funded project, the School Library Manpower Project, carried investigation into the area of training personnel for the new services required in school library media programs. Directed by Robert N. Case and Anna Mary Lowrey, SLMP has issued *Occupational Definitions for School Library Media Personnel* and *Behavioral Requirements Analysis Checklist*. Now, in phase 2 of the project, *Curriculum Alternatives* describes the programs undertaken in six schools of library education ranging from undergraduate programs (as in Millersville State College in Pennsylvania) to postgraduate education directed toward training district school media personnel at the University of Denver. The other programs tool place at Arizona State University at Tempe, Auburn University in Alabama, Mankato State College in Minnesota, and the University of Michigan at Ann Arbor. Included in each school's report in *Curriculum Alternatives* are descriptions of the institutions, program goals and components, procedures structured to attain their objectives, and sample forms and questionnaires. The identification of similar program components in the six programs (e.g., emphasis on field work and internship) is valuable. In spite of the educational jargon that marks some of the writing, this presentation is a useful addition to professional literature. [R: JAL, May 75, p. 23; LR, Summer 75, p. 74]

Lillian L. Shapiro

263. Cook, John, ed. **School Librarianship.** New York, Pergamon Press, 1981. 260p. index. $28.00; $17.50pa. ISBN 0-08-024814-4; 0-08-024813-6pa.

School Librarianship is a collection of articles on various aspects of school librarianship in Australia. It is intended to serve as a basic introductory text and a practical handbook, and to offer a description and analysis of the present state of school library development in Australia and New Zealand.

The book consists of 12 chapters contributed by prominent Australian school librarians. Topics covered include the history of school librarianship in Australia and New Zealand, the educational role of the school library, selection and acquisition of print and nonprint materials, reference work, cataloging and classification, management, and others.

Although the editor claims that "much of the content of the British and American texts is not relevant to conditions here," one is impressed more by the similarities in the offerings of the British and American texts and this Australian one than the differences. See, for example, Prostano's *School Library Media Center*, 3rd ed. (*ARBA* 83, entry 159) and Herring's *School Librarianship* (*ARBA* 83, entry 207). Indeed, the reliance upon U.S. materials is evident, particularly in bibliographic references accompanying each chapter. Nevertheless, Cook's publication will be an important contribution to the Australian professional community and also of interest to American librarians who take an interest in the international professional scene.

Heather Cameron

264. Corrigan, John T., ed. and comp. **The Relationship of the Library to Instructional Systems.** Haverford, Pa., Catholic Library Association, 1978. 58p. (Catholic Library Association, Studies in Librarianship, No. 2). $3.00pa. ISBN 0-87507-006-X.

The introduction to these four papers delivered at the 1977 CLA San Francisco convention pinpoints their purpose: to help librarians relate the media center's program to the school's teaching program by exploring their ability to apply principles of learning and learning theory to informational objectives.

James W. Brown handled "Media Center Goals in the Educational Program." In the hope of having "people who comprehend all types of media and can use it to the fullest," Michael McKibbin's "The Media Center's Function in Alternative Learning Environments" includes experiences as a media resource teacher in an alternative learning environment, and encourages the development of a "repertoire of strategies" for the media specialist.

Emmett Corry's "The English Teacher and the Library Media Program—An Example of Relationship" describes his 1976 study (with illustrative tables), showing the use made of all educational materials by English teachers, which proved that those in grant-receiving exemplary schools (New York State high schools which received ESEA Title II special purpose grants) made more use of a greater variety of educational media than colleagues in schools not receiving grants. With accompanying notes and suggested readings, Lillian Wehmeyer's "The Library and Independent Study" stresses the organization of the total environment "to facilitate gradual and successful moves toward self-directed learning."

Whatever the school setting, these papers — with their underlying philosophy and occasional checklist features — are useful for individual examination of the media specialist's role, and for those involved with related training programs.

Clara O. Jackson

265. Davies, Ruth Ann. **The School Library Media Program: Instructional Force for Excellence.** 3rd ed. New York, R. R. Bowker, 1979. 580p. bibliog. index. $18.50. LC 79-20358. ISBN 0-8352-1244-0.

The first edition of this textbook appeared in 1969 under the title *The School Library: A Force for Educational Excellence.* Reflecting the changes and critical challenges that will face those in school media centers in the 1980s, this timely revision and augmentation of the 1974 edition, *The School Media Center* (see *ARBA* 75, entry 194) is an appropriate learning resource for those preparing to be school media specialists. It also provides much valuable resource material for practicing librarians trying to define their role in the context of the "emerging social, economic, and political trends" of the 1980s. A major emphasis is that of the curriculum support role which the school librarian plays. Many of the chapters relate the activities of the media specialist to those of the classroom teacher. Gathered in several hundred pages of appendices are articles, reports, how-to guides, and other documents drawn from a variety of sources, many from the field of education. Missing from this section and from the index is any reference to the inclusion of school library media centers in the national library network. Many of the issues addressed in the revised first sections of the text should be related to the participation of school libraries in single-type school library networks and in multitype library networks, which will be the pattern of the future.

The 1978 report sponsored by the National Commission on Libraries and Information Science, *The Role of the School Library Media Program in Networking*, which is not discussed, may lead to the cure for the "anemia of the spirit" which the author fears may result from the lack of confidence experienced by today's educators. This should be the document used to reshape the thinking of the profession rather than the 1960 standards which the author suggests should be used as a blueprint for the future revision of the current standards. Even with this significant shortcoming, this volume includes a wealth of material well presented. [R: BL, 15 Apr 80, pp. 1196-97; SLJ, Mar 80, p. 146]

JoAnn V. Rogers

266. Gillespie, John T., and Diana L. Spirt. **Creating a School Media Program.** New York, R. R. Bowker, 1973. 236p. bibliog. index. $11.50. LC 77-164032. ISBN 0-8352-0484-7. (Available from Ann Arbor, Mich., Books on Demand, ISBN 0-8357-9039-8, $61.50).

John Gillespie and Diana Spirt have once again combined their talents in the preparation of a practical and useful book for school media specialists. The authors concentrate on basic principles and practices involved in creating, organizing, and administering an individual school media center. The focus is on practical considerations, especially in regard to problems to be anticipated in converting a school library to a media center.

Part 1 is a very brief history of the development of the school media center concept; part 2 discusses the nature, elements, and evaluation of media programs; and part 3 concentrates on specific aspects of management of a media center — budget, staff, facilities, selection, and acquisition and organization. The four well-chosen appendices provide selection policies and specific criteria for selecting media and equipment. A list of readings and an index complete the work. The whole book is noteworthy for its precise text with no unnecessary verbiage, its illustrations, and its lists. The principles and practices presented are clearly and succinctly stated. Topics that are adequately treated in other texts (for example, technical services) are covered here only briefly. This is a handy and informative manual for school media centers. [R: RSR, Apr 74, p. 20]

Christine Gehrt Wynar

267. Glogau, Lillian, Edmund Krause, and Miriam Wexler. **Developing a Successful Elementary School Media Center.** West Nyack, N.Y., Parker, 1972. 287p. illus. index. o.p. LC 74-164897. ISBN 0-13-205096-X.

The aim of this book is to "show educators that the most humble elementary school facility can be rearranged, reorganized, or restructured to encompass the media center concept" (p. 5). It is essentially a very practical how-to-do-it handbook based on the authors' experiences in elementary schools. The 10 chapters touch on all aspects of planning, organizing, and operating a media center. Two of the authors are school principals and one is a media specialist. The first four chapters describe how a school can organize a media center, using a three-phase plan. Methods of scheduling use of the center, curriculum goals for the center, and techniques for involving teachers in the media center are discussed. The next five chapters (the major part of the book) describe techniques for implementing the goals, providing sample lessons, activities, games, etc., to use at various grade levels. The last chapter presents suggestions for designing a media center in a new building and includes sample floor plans.

As a practical guide for administrators who want to introduce a media center into their schools, this is certainly a helpful book. However, one would have hoped for even more detail on planning the center. The text speeds along so enthusiastically that little forewarning is given of the inevitable pitfalls and oversights that occur with new media centers. While basing their planning recommendations on situations familiar to them, the authors err in not making it clear that a basic list of equipment and resources will vary depending on a large number of factors. They also fail to note that, oftentimes, more than one procedure, technique, or standard is available. On the other hand, one strong point the authors make is that without the cooperation of the teachers, a successful media program is a myth. Some suggestions, obviously based on experience, are offered on this topic.

School librarians who like to use snappy, ready-made lesson sheets and quizzes will find a lot of samples in this book. Unfortunately, no bibliographies or references to other books or articles are given. Consequently, some unwary educators may be led to believe that this book contains "everything you need to make the media center the hub of your school program" (jacket), or that little else is available on the subject. This is an interesting book, but it does not provide all the answers for developing elementary school media centers. [R: SLMQ, Winter 74, p. 153] Christine Gehrt Wynar

268. Herring, James E. **School Librarianship.** London, Clive Bingley; distr., Hamden, Conn., Shoe String Press, 1982. 116p. bibliog. index. $13.00. ISBN 0-85157-347-9.

School librarianship in the United Kingdom, as James E. Herring frequently points out, began later and has not advanced as far as school librarianship in the United States. Although only 3 percent of professional librarians in the United Kingdom work in schools, there is a movement within the profession to increase school library services during the 1980s.

Herring's book, which concentrates on secondary school libraries, provides a brief survey of present practices and future directions for British school libraries. Topics covered include library education, management, provision and organization of materials, user education, and the librarian's relationships with teachers and pupils.

In the 101 pages of basic text, the author can only skim the surface of principles and problems. Herring attempts to overcome space limitations by including copious references from British and American sources. Many chapters provide interesting contrasts. Library Association standards suggest having a professional librarian in all secondary schools, a desirable but difficult goal. A stock of 13 items per pupil for students under 16 years and 19 per pupil for older students contrasts sharply with the ALA standards, which suggest approximately 40 items per pupil as part of the basic collection.

Because of the lower expectations of British school librarians, this book is not likely to be useful to many practicing librarians in North America. Library schools may want to buy it for historical purposes and for courses in comparative librarianship. Adele M. Fasick

269. Hug, William E. **Instructional Design and the Media Program.** Chicago, American Library Association, 1975. 148p. illus. bibliog. $9.00pa. LC 75-40425. ISBN 0-8389-0207-3.

The stated purpose of this title is to "assist school and district media professionals, school administrators, and teachers in their efforts to conceptualize and build media programs as an integral part of the school curriculum." Hug starts from a springboard that describes the relationship between information and the mission of education, and proceeds with definitions of curriculum movements (e.g., subject-organized, social processes, broad fields, core, humanistic, et al.). The author's philosophy of school media programming stems from that which is delineated in *Media Programs: District and School* (American Library Association, 1975). Thus, it addresses itself to the four functions that the national document considers basic: management and administration, design, information, and consultation. The final chapter, "Technology as Means," tries valiantly to find an equilibrium between two points of view, the way of behavioral objectives and the way that leans more toward humanism.

The book is obviously intended as a text for library schools (and, perhaps, teacher-training institutions), since each chapter closes with problems for research and a sample "minimodule." Reading lists are also included.

One cannot fault the author for his expressed desire to move administrators toward a more comprehensive view of the media program. What does sit uneasily on the minds of those who value grace and clarity in language is the educational jargon that weaves through the book, with emphasis on "input," "interfacings," and systems analysis. Diagrams that obfuscate more than they explain (an apparent *sine qua non* for the educationist) are another minus. A reviewer who has spent long years in the *practice* of the profession senses in books such as this one a too-long absence from the arena where it is all happening—the school itself. [R: RQ, Summer 76, p. 356]   Lillian L. Shapiro

270. Leopold, Carolyn Clugston. **School Libraries Worth Their Keep: A Philosophy Plus Tricks.** Metuchen, N.J., Scarecrow, 1972. 349p. illus. index. o.p. LC 72-7494. ISBN 0-8108-0503-0.

One doubts whether a description of the contents of this book would serve any purpose. Yes, there are chapters such as "The Librarian as a Professional," "Specific Library Skills," or even "Reading Pictures." But the seven-page bibliography is a revealing picture of the author's own skills. See the entry for *Current Index to Journals in Education* (open entry?), or observe the lack of consistency in style for the Arthur Koestler entry (pp. 327-28). It is not exactly clear what this "bibliography" is supposed to cover, but perhaps this is not important, since the book deals with "philosophy plus tricks." Indeed, there are plenty of tricks—the author's style, for one. Leopold has a propensity for clichéd expressions which one assumes are intended to add color to her writing. However, when she speaks of bringing the library "out of the darkness of disuse and noncomprehension" into "the light of full library power," we may suspect her evangelical zeal of being slightly overstated. Jargon, that shortcut to communication so rampant in the trade, is in use throughout. "Multimedia experience," "input," "output," and "feedback" contrast strangely with those lyrical passages through which Leopold tells us of her own personal experiences, and with such pithy, colorful words as "paydirt" which she uses to describe the catalog's subject approach. Such attempts to span the whole spectrum of language inevitably lead to trouble in the form of mixed metaphors. Thus, we "weave a fabric" of lesson plans to "unlock the expensive museum library," and

library specifications are written out "in bricks, courses, and mortar." Lillian Gerhardt, in her interesting article "A Modest Proposal for the Very Worst Children's Book Award Ever" (see *SLJ*, 15 May 71, pp. 1136-37), suggests calling such an award for children's books the "Huckleberry Finn Pin." Something similar is badly needed for books like Leopold's in the area of professional library literature. [R: AL, Mar 73, p. 149; CLW, Apr 73, p. 556; RSR, Apr 73, p. 26]   Ann J. Harwell

271. Lowrie, Jean Elizabeth. **Elementary School Libraries.** 2nd ed. Metuchen, N.J., Scarecrow, 1970. 238p. $15.00. LC 71-9962. ISBN 0-8108-0305-4.

Presented 10 years after the original study of the same title, this new edition reflects the uneven yet tremendous growth in elementary school library functioning, approaches and attitudes as embodied in the "total Media Center." The author has included "a broad spectrum of schools," stressing services for the disadvantaged. Based on much visitation, keen observation, and intense discussion with librarians in charge and the internal materials they use, the chapters first introduce the elementary school library philosophy, scope, and services. Examples of curriculum-supportive experiences in the middle grades (including reading guidance, library instruction and reference work), early elementary library experience, the teacher and the school librarian, the role of the school administrator, auxiliary features, community relations, pointing up that elementary school libraries are indeed realities, and advancing recommendations for further development, are included. It is regrettable that the volume suffers from an average format, lacks illustrations which might animate many of the varied activities described, and lacks full bibliographical citations for the core of books appended. But the references following each chapter and the record of visitations offer a rich base for further research.   Clara O. Jackson

272. Pearson, Neville P., and Lucius A. Butler, eds. **Learning Resource Centers: Selected Readings.** Minneapolis, Minn., Burgess, 1973. 249p. illus. index. o.p. LC 72-78260. ISBN 0-8087-1632-8.

There is much confusion with regard to terminology in the library media field today, since a number of names are applied to the facility that serves the school or college in the area of instructional materials. According to the preface, the compilers of this volume define "learning resource centers" as collections of materials, both print and nonprint, that deal with a particular subject and that are located adjacent to that department "to meet individual needs — when the individual feels a need."

From the title and the above definition, the reader is led to assume that the readings contained in this volume are concerned solely with establishing and operating such centers. Not so! Almost half of the 55 articles deal not with subject collections but with instructional materials centers (the main facility, which includes print and nonprint materials and services in all subject areas); in this respect, the book seems to be a continuation of the editors' former volume, *Instructional Materials Centers: Selected Readings* (Burgess, 1969).

Those articles, however, that deal with learning resource centers have been carefully selected from 33 different educational journals. They exemplify the increasing number of such facilities that are being established on every educational level to meet the needs of every conceivable type of student.

This anthology has value not only for teachers (in training or in service) but also for educators in the library media field, practicing media specialists, and school and college administrators who are searching for theoretical and practical means of providing for the teaching/learning needs of teachers and students. [R: C&RL, Jan 74, p. 58; SLMQ, Winter 74, p. 156]

Sara R. Mack

273. Ray, Colin. **Library Service to Schools and Children.** Paris, UNESCO; distr., New York, UNIPUB, 1979. 137p. illus. (Documentation, Libraries and Archives: Studies and Research, 10). $7.00pa. ISBN 93-3-101640-7.

"This handbook aims at giving basic knowledge of design and administration of children's and school libraries." As are many of the other UN library publications, this is really a how-to primer designed to encourage and assist underdeveloped nations to start or improve library services — in this case, to children. As a basic and simplistic tool, it could be of great value to people having little knowledge in the field of children's librarianship. It covers almost every important aspect of library function in enough practical detail to help the inexperienced to get such library services underway, and lists basic standards, information sources, and much more hard information. This is an impressive, useful, simplified work by a careful, knowledgeable, and experienced author. [R: LQ, Jan 80, p. 162]

Stanley J. Slote

274. Ray, Sheila G. **Library Service to Schools.** 3rd ed. London, Library Association; distr., Phoenix, Ariz., Oryx Press, 1982. 64p. bibliog. (Library Association Pamphlet, No. 32). o.p. ISBN 0-85365-953-2.

Since the publication of the second edition of this work in 1972, there have been many changes in library service to schools in Great Britain, and this third edition reflects those changes. Intended for librarians who may find themselves in positions of support for school libraries, the book aims to promote understanding of school libraries and their functions in the education process.

A brief history of the development of school libraries is followed by chapters focusing on libraries in the primary and the secondary school. Sources of help are treated briefly in Chapter 4, and the remaining two chapters cover school library services. A detailed bibliography completes the book. [R: JAL, Mar 83, p. 45; SLMQ, Fall 83, p. 69]

275. Rossoff, Martin. **The School Library and Educational Change.** Littleton, Colo., Libraries Unlimited, 1971. 113p. index. (Library Science Text Series). o.p. LC 71-178876. ISBN 0-87287-037-5.

This work, by the author of *Using Your High School Library*, summarizes recent trends in school library development. Particular attention is paid to the parallels between these recent trends and trends in educational thinking. [R: CLW, May 72, p. 526; LJ, 15 Feb 72, p. 753; LQ, Apr 72, p. 271]

276. Rowell, John, and M. Ann Heidbreder. **Educational Media Selection Centers: Identification and Analysis of Current Practices.** Chicago, American Library Association, 1971. 178p. (ALA Studies in Librarianship, No. 1). o.p. LC 75-140213. SBN 8389-0088-7.

The results of phase 1 of this project funded by the U.S. Office of Education are presented in this publication in the form of some 80 tables with explanations of the findings, plus appendices containing samples of the questionnaires. The project surveyed facilities and examined programs which introduce librarians and teachers to educational media at state, regional, and local levels. Questionnaires sent to some 440 education media selection centers and on-site surveys of 50 selected centers were used to gather data for the study. The study disclosed that few, if any, centers performed functions and carried out responsibilities as originally conceived by the investigators. Among other things which the investigators learned is the fact that a center's major function is not that of a static depository but a service unit. Other surprising discoveries include the need to establish more centers and improve the existing ones. The conclusions point up the need for an accepted definition of a center and the preparation of guidelines for a variety of models, not a single model. [R: AL, June 71, p. 650]

Christine Gehrt Wynar

277. Saunders, Helen E. **The Modern School Library.** 2nd ed., completely rev. by Nancy Polette. Metuchen, N.J., Scarecrow, 1975. 237p. index. bibliog. $15.00. LC 75-20377. ISBN 0-8108-0864-1.

Nancy Polette has done a thorough revision of Saunders's *The Modern School Library.* The table of contents shows that the author intends to cover every aspect of organizing and operating a school library media center. When the author writes about school LMCs, she has in mind the secondary level. Chapters cover definition of a media program; the librarian as a member of the instructional team; services to academic departments; reference; selection, acquisition, and processing materials; circulation; facilities; personnel; and evaluation. The four appendices contain a sample handbook for teachers, sample specifications for a media center, selection tools, and selected readings. A brief index is appended. Most of the sections checked in the text appeared to be up-to-date (e.g., the "1975 Standards" are described). Covering all of these topics in only 181 pages of text demands that most topics be given only brief attention. Text space is diminished further by inclusion of an abundance of lists, sample forms, charts, and outlines. Most of these are pertinent, and this aspect is not overdone here, as it is in Davis's *The School Library Media Center: A Force for Educational Excellence* (2nd ed., Bowker, 1974); nevertheless, the result is that the textual discussion concentrates primarily on how-to aspects. Polette offers sound practical guidance on library practice, but not enough attention is given to theoretical considerations, especially administrative. Undergraduate programs intent on training students for typical tasks performed in media centers will find such clear and no-nonsense information quite useful. Graduate level students will need more analytical material, which would provide thorough discussion of the problems, not merely the recommended practices. Another weakness of the text is the tendency to describe only one method of operation or procedure,

ignoring the basic elements to be considered in designing a procedure. The short discussion of circulation procedures for books is an example of this. In addition, examples of practices should be extended beyond the author's Missouri schools. Interlibrary loan is such a case. The new Illinois statewide program includes schools in its interlibrary loan system and could be noted as a contrast to the arrangement in the Parkway School District (Missouri). The cataloging section sounds a warning note concerning acceptance of LC subject headings on printed cards, but, unfortunately, the text does not explain the roots of the problem. Further total silence is maintained on ISBD. Numerous topics examined reveal similar deficiencies. The selection tools and readings listed in the appendices are well chosen, although many more could be added. Peggy Sullivan's *Problems in School Media Management* is one candidate for inclusion. Under tools for selecting reference materials neither this reviewer's *Guide to Reference Books for School Media Centers* nor Peterson's *Reference Books for Elementary and Junior High Schools* is mentioned. *School Media Quarterly* is now available by subscription as well as membership. Hardgrove's *Mathematics Library: Elementary and Junior High School* was issued in a new edition in 1973, and so on. There is a subject index but no access is provided to authors and titles of materials listed in the book.

In summary, it is a useful handbook of library practice for undergraduates within the limitations mentioned. [R: SLMQ, Spring 76, p. 248]

Christine Gehrt Wynar

278. Thomason, Nevada Wallis. **The Library Media Specialist in Curriculum Development.** Metuchen, N.J., Scarecrow, 1981. 278p. bibliog. index. $16.00. LC 81-50. ISBN 0-8108-1406-4.

Nevada Wallis Thomason's anthology of 32 professional journal articles is a needed resource. The editor limits the scope of the book to the school library media specialist's role in curriculum development, and she has chosen articles by media specialists and library educators published in the past two decades. The subjects range from the media specialist as an educational change agent to curriculum involvement through professional relationships. The section on research has only two articles, a reflection of the unfortunate state of reported research on curriculum and the library media program.

Numerous articles not readily available are in this collection, and a bibliography of over 150 books, articles, and theses provides for further research. A subject index is also included. The format of the book is acceptable, with adequate margins, clear type, and easily read charts and diagrams.

The book provides a concise introduction to some of the crucial questions which library media specialists confront in the area of curriculum. It is especially useful for courses in media center administration and for practitioners who are looking for succinct articles (the average length is eight pages) about curriculum involvement. [R: BL, 1 Sept 81, p. 53; SLJ, Oct 81, p. 107]   Patricia Tipton Sharp

279. Turner, Philip M. **Handbook for School Media Personnel.** 2nd ed. Littleton, Colo., Libraries Unlimited, 1980. 132p. illus. bibliog. index. $13.50. LC 80-21152. ISBN 0-87287-225-4.

Designed specifically for the person charged with administering the school audiovisual center, this new edition of Philip Turner's popular handbook is a compendium of practical information for handling everyday organization and operation. The topics covered include faculty communication; equipment selection, maintenance, and distribution; local production of audiovisual instructional materials by both the media staff and students; use of student helpers; software selection, arrangement, and distribution; and inservice training for the teaching faculty in equipment operation and software production.

The second edition has been updated and revised to include many suggestions made by practicing media personnel. Highlighting the text are sample forms for equipment maintenance procedures, equipment distribution, materials requests, and materials evaluation. Prepurchase checklists of factors to consider in general hardware and specific types of equipment selection help the inexperienced media person to make wise choices. In-house production techniques and tips are illustrated for enlargement/reduction of illustrations and for slide and filmstrip production. The bibliography of further resources for media personnel is grouped to correspond to chapter subjects. [R: VOYA, Feb 81, p. 50]   Susan Kohlman

280. Vandergrift, Kay E. **The Teaching Role of the School Media Specialist.** Chicago, American Association of School Librarians, American Library Association, 1979. 56p. (School Media Centers: Focus on Trends and Issues, No. 3). $6.00pa. LC 78-27401. ISBN 0-8389-3222-2.

This 56-page monograph is part of a new series in which all of the items to date have been less than 100 pages. Obviously, the editors plan to reach an audience that wants some form of brief, personal, continuing education experiences at the cost of less than $10.00 a half hour. The cost is reasonable, but the content of this essay could use some strengthening.

Vandergrift has developed the outline of what was probably a standard classroom lecture and expanded it slightly. However, there is no significant research base in the work, and this lack weakens the entire essay. Various opinions about why librarians are or are not comfortable in a teaching role and what should be done so that librarians welcome teaching responsibilities and are welcomed in a teaching role are mentioned throughout the essay. At times, a sentence offers a challenging idea, but most often the ideas are familiar. What the essay lacks is a powerful theory or evidence based on previous research. The lack is significant for this reviewer, but new school librarians should find comfort and challenge in this essentially encouraging pamphlet. [R: JAL, July 79, p. 169]
                    Caroline M. Coughlin

281. Ward, Pearl L., and Robert Beacon, comps. **The School Media Center: A Book of Readings.** Metuchen, N.J., Scarecrow, 1973. 299p. illus. index. o.p. LC 73-4901. ISBN 0-8108-0618-5.

The 40 articles chosen for this reader discuss a wide range of topics relating to the development, administration, organization, and use of media centers. Articles on media evaluation and selection are included, but there is nothing on topics such as reading, reference work, or literature for children or young adults. Many of the reprints were originally published in *School Libraries* and *Audiovisual Instruction.* The compilers were obviously trying to develop a general overview of IMCs, but the effort, for the most part, was unsuccessful. The quality of the articles is uneven, and many of the brief pieces add little substance. Concentration on fewer topics might have brought better results. [R: AL, Mar 74, p. 144; LJ, 15 May 74, p. 1460]   Christine Gehrt Wynar

282. Wehmeyer, Lillian Biermann. **The School Library Volunteer.** Littleton, Colo., Libraries Unlimited, 1975. 123p. illus. bibliog. index. o.p. LC 75-12586. ISBN 0-87287-110-X.

This is an excellent introduction to the purposes and routines of the multi-media school library. Although it is addressed specifically to the parent volunteer, it will also be of use to school librarians who work with volunteers and to new librarians who want a quick review of basic library routines. An introductory chapter explains the school library program and its goals and the part that the volunteer can play in helping to achieve the goals. Another chapter outlines the basic library routines and procedures in which the volunteer may expect to participate. The illustrations of circulation forms are clear and easy to understand. Clever examples of overdue notices and posters could easily be copied for use in the library. Everything that the volunteer needs to know is well presented. The last two-thirds of the book is devoted to two programmed learning units, one on sorting and shelving both fiction and nonfiction materials, the other on filing in the card catalog. Call numbers, shelf arrangement, the Dewey Decimal System, the arrangement of biographies, kinds of catalog cards and headings, and basic filing rules are all presented within the programmed texts. There is also an index to filing rules. A section on sources and resources lists publishers, library supply companies, books that will be particularly helpful, and associations and organizations that can supply information on library materials and processes. [R: SLMQ, Summer 76, p. 336]

Shirley L. Hopkinson

283. Woolard, Wilma Lee Broughton. **Combined School/Public Libraries: A Survey with Conclusions and Recommendations.** Metuchen, N.J., Scarecrow, 1980. 184p. index. o.p. LC 80-36742. ISBN 0-8108-1335-1.

The original study that preceded this book was completed by the author in spring 1977 as a master of science degree thesis at Illinois State University. It is on file with the ERIC Clearinghouse on Information Resources at Syracuse University. Summaries of the study were published in January and February 1978 in *American Libraries* and *Library Journal*. This book, in a revised form, was developed in response to the original study and to the published articles. Findings in the study are based on information collected from over 130 combined libraries in the United States.

The survey was designed to identify advantages and benefits of combining school and public libraries; problems, weaknesses, and limitations; how matters of governance are determined; and what pre-existing conditions within schools and communities appear to be conducive to effecting combined facilities. Chapters 2-4 provide background reading, studies, surveys, and representative programs. Chapter 5, "Conclusions and Recommendations," will be very useful to the reader, in that the author provides some excellent considera-

tions for others who may wish to examine the concept of combined libraries in their communities (e.g., "The results of this study would seem to indicate that the optimum environment would be communities with 5,000 residents or fewer"). The "Bibliography with Annotations" is current and definitive, with pertinent entries (e.g., Shirley Aaron's three-phase study, "A Study of the Combined School Public Library," 1977-1978). Appendix B provides the user with a state-by-state "Directory of Combined School/Public Libraries in the United States as Confirmed by This Survey." Appendix C, "Statements of Agreements, Policies, Letters of Intent, Articles of Incorporation, etc.," provides many excellent examples for those needing source materials to form a combined school/public library.

This book, especially in view of existing national economic problems in funding public libraries, should be considered as recommended reading. [R: JAL, Mar 81, p. 49; LJ, 1 Jan 81, p. 39]

Donald D. Foos

REFERENCE WORKS

284. Carroll, Frances Laverne. **Recent Advances in School Librarianship.** New York, Pergamon Press, 1981. 249p. bibliog. index. (Recent Advances in Library and Information Services, Vol. 1). $33.00. ISBN 0-08-026084-5.

In a field such as school librarianship, which is changing so rapidly and which has such an impact on the education of the world's youth, a work which addresses advances in this area from an international perspective could have significant value to researchers and practitioners. Unfortunately, *Recent Advances in School Librarianship* is so poorly written and exhibits so little editorial assistance that it is difficult to actually evaluate its content.

Although there is no preface or introduction, it is assumed that the author's intent is to provide an international perspective on the progress of school librarianship during the past decade. In chapter 1 she states: "This book is considered the first in what may be a series of books on recent advances in school librarianship in the world which could be written for each decade or suitable period of time hereafter" (p. 4).

Covering topics such as the growth and development of school libraries; cooperation and planning, including networking and school-public library cooperation; the educational role of the school librarian; and education for school librarians, the work focuses primarily on achievements and growth in the United States, with only a brief reference to these topics in other countries. It is not until the final chapter, "School Library Development in Other Countries," that other nations, such as Nigeria, Iran, Tasmania, Scotland, and Hong Kong, are addressed in any detail. Why certain countries were selected for coverage while others were omitted remains a mystery. Except for the article on Scotland, which presumably was written by the author, the articles in this final chapter were contributed by individuals involved in libraries in their respective countries. The unevenness of topics covered from country to country and the imbalance in this chapter are extremely distressing. For example, in the eight-page article on school libraries in Nigeria, Virginia W. Dike, lecturer in school librarianship at the University of Nigeria, discusses such topics as the history and present status of school libraries, physical accommodations, staffing, legislation and funding, significant developments, and professional associations, while the article on Hong Kong, written by Laibing Kan, a university librarian at Chinese University of Hong Kong, is a mere half-page in length and conveys very little about school librarianship there.

The references provided at the end of each chapter and the works cited throughout the text are current and fairly comprehensive, leading the reader to sources of information which may provide better insight into the topic than the book itself. Although the author appears to have an understanding of her topic, the lack of editorial control and the difficulty one has in reading this typescript work make it inaccessible. [R: Emerg Lib, Jan 82, p. 28]

Ann Hartman

285. Freeman, Patricia. **Index to Research in School Librarianship, 1960-1974.** Washington, D.C., U.S. Department of Health, Education and Welfare, National Institute of Education; distr., Arlington, Va., Computer Microfilm International, 1976. 50p. (ERIC Reports; ED 119 741; IR 003 222). o.p.

A guide to research studies on school librarianship from 1960 to 1974, this is the first work to attempt a comprehensive bibliography of the literature. "Included are U.S. and Canadian studies about school libraries and directly concerned with school libraries that were published or accepted as theses or dissertations 1960-1974 and dissertations announced in *School Media Quarterly* before 1975. Studies on the schools, on the library field, and on educational media are included only when the

school library is identified as a major object of the research" (preface). The bibliography is organized by topics; entries are not annotated, but citations to abstracts and reviews are given. The table of contents lists the topics used. There are an author index and a subject and methodology index. Few of the studies listed have been published, but many are available in microform, some can be obtained through interlibrary loan, and some can only be read at the holding library. This bibliography brings together abstracts, reviews, and listings that had been scattered in over 400 volumes.

Janet Littlefield

286. Haglund, Elaine J., and Marcia L. Harris. **On This Day: A Collection of Everyday Learning Events and Activities for the Media Center, Library, and Classroom.** Littleton, Colo., Libraries Unlimited, 1983. 470p. illus. bibliog. index. $27.50. LC 82-13960. ISBN 0-87287-345-5.

This work contains a chronology of events for every day of the year, suggesting activities, lessons, and exhibit ideas to help teachers, media specialists, and librarians develop learning strategies for both small groups and independent learners. Intended to serve as a source for motivating students to learn how to learn, the book is designed to encourage initiative and resourcefulness in the student who is trying to acquire skills in locating and gathering educational materials. The first of the book's five parts chronologically lists selected events, both significant and seldom acknowledged, for each day of the month. Entries include historical events and important dates related to famous persons, discoveries, and inventions. Following each listing are suggested ways for presenting the information and cross-references to other activity sections of the book. Additional techniques for using the information in part 1 are offered in part 2, "The Extra-Know-How Section." The remaining sections provide: task cards, offering numerous activities that can be used either separately or in conjunction with the entries in part 1; reproducible worksheets and diagrams, arranged in numerical order corresponding to the entries in part 1; and student folders, enabling teachers to develop an individualized, contract-based program. [R: BL, 1 June 83, p. 1280; RQ, Summer 83, p. 427]

Susan Kohlman

287. Marshall, Faye Dix. **School Librarian's Encyclopedic Dictionary.** West Nyack, N.Y., Parker, 1979. 248p. index. o.p. LC 79-10365. ISBN 0-13-793679-6.

The publisher's claim that this volume contains information on all vital areas of school librarianship is a great exaggeration. The approximately 230 entries, with 2 or 3 per page, cover a variety of terms related to techniques, procedures, and routine library operations. Most are simple definitions of terms used in technical processing, including cataloging, classification, processing, and circulation. Quite a few terms related to the history of books and printing, not particularly central to school librarianship, are also included.

Access to information is poor. Selection tools, for example, are listed under "Book Aids for the Librarian's Bookshelf" and do not appear in the very limited index under either *selection* or *acquisition*, two terms which appear neither in the text nor in the index.

More useful definitions of cataloging terms can be found in glossaries of cataloging codes and guides, and basic terms related to books and printing can be found in texts. Although the book is intended as a practical aid, few of the definitions are detailed enough to be of much use. [R: BL, 15 June 80, p. 1569]

JoAnn V. Rogers

288. Martin, Betty, and Ben Carson. **The Principal's Handbook on the School Library Media Center.** Hamden, Conn., Shoe String Press, 1981. 212p. bibliog. index. $14.50. LC 78-1957. ISBN 0-208-01912-X.

Collaboration by two individuals with expertise as a school media services consultant and as a school administrator in the southeastern United States, respectively, has resulted in a handy reference guide to the school media center especially for the principal, a key figure in its development and use. "It offers a more comprehensive approach that assures broad utilization of all materials in the center by providing a better understanding of role implications for principals, teachers, superintendents and the media specialists."

Of its three parts, the first covers the media program as a component of the school program, with three chapters devoted to the goals and objectives of the media program, the difference between a traditional library and a media center, and the relation of the media program to the school program. In its six chapters, part 2 defines the roles of the principal, teacher, media specialist, and district media director. Part 3 deals with the operation of the center, highlighting its services, techniques of administration, facilities and equipment, desirable community involvement, and evaluation. Throughout are charts, figures, lists, and summaries, and each chapter concludes with a "scenario" and several questions.

The appendices include: 100 representative media center tasks, selected references on library networks and centralized cataloging, and several assessment instruments. A 42-item bibliography and index are provided. Despite a slip like "Salient" for SALINET (p. 159), this compact volume can be a reference companion, most especially for its primary audience but also for others with roles linked to the media center, enabling them "to find the specific information needed or to answer one or more questions which serve as chapter headings." [R: SLJ, Feb 79, p. 31; SLMQ, Summer 79, p. 284]

Clara O. Jackson

289. **School Library Media Annual 1985.** Volume Three. Shirley L. Aaron and Pat R. Scales, eds. Littleton, Colo., Libraries Unlimited, 1985. 525p. index. $40.00. ISBN 0-87287-475-3; ISSN 0739-7712.

Volume 3 of the *School Library Media Annual* maintains the structure of the first two volumes. Part 1 deals with events and issues; part 2 deals with programs and collections; part 3 deals with research and development; and part 4 deals with trends and forecasts. Some changes have been made in this edition. For example, the subsection in part 1 formerly entitled "Intellectual Freedom" has been renamed "Access to Information" in order to reflect a broader approach to the topics related to this area, and now includes such topics as copyright.

This annual contains articles written by nationally known practitioners in the field with a wide variety of backgrounds. These articles covering topics of continuing interest to school library media professionals are interspersed with lists of award-winning materials, state-level school media staffs, library school faculty members, and addresses of organizations related to all aspects of the profession. Of particular interest in the edition are the examination of copyright; a survey of the struggle surrounding censorship and intellectual freedom; a review of trends in vocational education programming and library media service to gifted young adults; and an examination of the uses of microcomputers, interactive video, and telecommunications in school library media programs. This volume continues to meet the editors' stated purpose of "helping library media professionals at all levels to examine important events, issues, practices, and trends relevant to the field." [R: WLB, Oct 85, p. 76]

Donald C. Adcock

21 Special Libraries

GENERAL WORKS

290. Anthony, L. J., ed. **Handbook of Special Librarianship and Information Work.** 5th ed. London, Aslib, 1982. 416p. illus. index. £23.00; £19.50 (members); £14.50pa.; £12.50pa. (members). ISBN 0-85142-160-1; 0-85142-161-Xpa.

Like its predecessors, the fifth edition of Aslib's *Handbook of Special Librarianship* is an exceptionally useful tool for keeping up with developments in special librarianship. It covers the period from 1975—the publication date of the fourth edition—to 1982. This is a period during which the application of sophisticated information management techniques acquired great importance in the library operations of highly industrialized countries. The current edition covers the major technological achievements known in the United Kingdom and the United States. Separate chapters, written by various authorities, deal with subjects such as system design and planning; audiovisual materials; computer-based housekeeping systems; indexing languages; computer-based information retrieval systems; and library and information networks. While the orientation of the work is, by definition, British, the information and principles in it are applicable to any highly developed, technological milieu.

The book is essential for practitioners, teachers, and students of special librarianship. It is highly recommended for academic libraries with special collections or bibliographic strength in business, economics, the sciences, and engineering. It is equally recommended for library school libraries. [R: IRLA, Feb 83, p. 9; LR, Summer 83, p. 162]

Antonio Rodriguez-Buckingham

291. Ashworth, Wilfred. **Special Librarianship.** London, Clive Bingley; distr., New York, K. G. Saur, 1979. 120p. index. (Outlines of Modern Librarianship). $12.00. ISBN 0-85157-277-4.

This book's purpose is to introduce, but not provide an in-depth treatment of, those things that make special libraries special. The author's definition of a special library is rather provocative in that he describes it as one established to obtain and exploit specialized information for the private advantage of an organization. Based on this definition, the book proceeds to explore the special library's function and ways of working, highlighting those aspects that make it different from public, academic, and other libraries. It presents a general overview of special librarianship: definition and purpose, the place of the special library in an organization, special information sources and services, and how to evaluate services. It does not describe routines, nor does it describe the administration and activities of the myriad types of special libraries. Detailed routines and administration of various types are covered in scores of other books.

Since *Special Librarianship* presents nothing really new and its intent is to lead the reader to those other sources, it is unfortunate that the references themselves are not adequate for this purpose: almost all are from the United Kingdom, they barely scratch the surface, and there is no general bibliography. Examples, references, philosophy, and practices are British, and rarely are practices outside the United Kingdom described. Even so, the book is well written and the ideas universal enough (albeit rather conventional) to provide a springboard. Although a good first book for students interested in special libraries, it is unfortunate that it does not lead the reader to other sources more systematically and thoroughly. [R: JAL, Mar 80, p. 48]   A. Neil Yerkey

292. Campbell, D. J. **Small Technical Libraries: A Guide for Librarians without Technological Training.** Paris, UNESCO; distr., New York, UNIPUB, 1973. 40p. bibliog. o.p. ISBN 92-3-101088-3.

Small technical libraries, as defined in this book, are found in technical colleges, in research organizations of various kinds, and in industry. Most of these libraries deal with scientific subjects, and the truth of the matter is that most librarians in charge are inadequately trained for the task. This small volume was written as a practical guide for librarians who have come into technical work with a variety of qualifications and training, none of it technical. It was originally published in the September/October and November/December 1972 issues of the *UNESCO Bulletin for Libraries.* D. J. Campbell, who has a Ph.D. in chemistry, has served as information officer at the Pressed Steel Fisher Ltd. in Oxford, England, and as librarian of the Institute of Cancer Research at the University of London.

Campbell's introduction, which deals with the need for technical knowledge, the technical librarian's job, and the librarian's status, and his chapter on the relations with management and administration contain sound advice not only for new librarians but also for old hands who may need a reminder that blind adherence to rules is not consistent with good service. The later chapters, which deal with library materials and their special processing, reveal some of the author's personal preferences for solving problems of classification, indexing, and filing periodicals. In general, however, his opinions are based on sound and practical experience. Probably his best advice is that any library with a staff of six or fewer will not justify its own use of machine or electronic methods and that a thorough "systems analysis" will reap greater benefits. Although the text refers to much British equipment, materials, and practice, the bibliography presents a broad international view. The nearly 100 references listed would provide an excellent background for any core course in technical libraries, special librarianship, and information work. [R: Unesco, Nov/Dec 73, p. 353]

Robert J. Havlik

293. Halm, Johan van. **The Development of Special Libraries as an International Phenomenon.** New York, Special Libraries Association, 1978. 626p. index. (SLA State-of-the-Art Review, No. 4). o.p. LC 78-13188. ISBN 0-87111-245-0. (Available from Books on Demand, ISBN 0-317-30410-0, $159.50).

This study was undertaken for two reasons: to gather sufficient data on which to base recommendations to SLA for an international policy, and to aid special librarians in studying library development during investigative trips outside the United States. This is an awesome compilation, and would appear to satisfy the aims intended.

The first part of the study provides a context — historical and definitional — for the country reports which follow. The methodology of data collection included literature searches, reports from experts on library developments in individual countries, correspondence with other individuals and associations, visits to international conferences, and questionnaires.

The country reports are grouped alphabetically within continent divisions, and focus on special libraries, librarianship, and documentation, although valuable information on professional education and international cooperation becomes part of the presentation. An absolutely essential inclusion is the index of associations, bibliographic centers, and abbreviations. The index of countries is adequate, given the arrangement of the volume itself.

The Development of Special Libraries as an International Phenomenon makes an excellent contribution to the literature in terms of its concentration on special librarianship. In addition, the volume will be valuable to students of international librarianship as a starting point for further research. [R: LJ, 1 Mar 80, p. 590; LQ, Oct 80, p. 514]   Theresa Maylone

294. Jackson, Eugene B., ed. **Special Librarianship: A New Reader.** Metuchen, N.J., Scarecrow, 1980. 759p. index. $35.00. LC 80-11530. ISBN 0-8108-1295-9.

Arranged under headings ("The Past, Present and Future of Special Libraries"; "The Special Librarian as an Individual"; "The Special Librarian — Managed and Managing"; "Host-Organization-Related"; "Public Relations-Related"; "Tool/Format-Related"; and "The special Librarian as Information Scientist"), this reader is an anthology of 70 readings intended especially for the new professional in special librarianship. Unlike its predecessor, Harold Sharp's *Readings in Special Librarianship* (Scarecrow, 1963), the new reader favors original, specially written chapters over reprints. Half of the papers included were written specifically for this volume. Heavily revised versions of materials previously available but reworked for the beginning professional are represented in 11 chapters. Twenty-four are reprints of classics of the literature of the 1970s, as nominated by instructors of special librarianship in North American library schools and/or SLA division officers. Higher royalty requests led to the exclusion of some items for this reader. Jackson lists special chapters that were not included because of unsuccessful efforts in locating "competent, available authors." Subject and name indexes are included. A very much needed addition to the literature has been provided by Jackson. [R: LJ, 15 Dec 80, p. 2554]   Donald D. Foos

295. Jobin, Pamela, and Marcy Murphy, comps. **Issues and Involvement: Alberta L. Brown Lectures in Special Librarianship 1978-1980.** New York, Special Libraries Association, 1983. 94p. $10.50pa. LC 82-19479. ISBN 0-87111-292-2.

This volume contains an interesting collection of papers that were presented as a part of the special libraries course at Western Michigan University. The title of the book and the publisher's description might lead one to believe that the volume consists of theoretical or philosophical discussions of special librarianship. Indeed, "Closing the Gap" by William Hubbard is an excellent discussion of the basis for special librarianship. To some degree, Alberta Brown's essay also provides a general philosophical approach to the practice of special librarianship. Other essays in this category include Joseph Dagnese's overview of the interface of special libraries with selected national programs and David Bender's discussion of the factors that must be taken into account as special librarianship moves into the future. These four essays provide a good perspective on issues of interest to special librarians. The remaining essays are primarily descriptions of a few special libraries. One can glean from them, by implication, some of the issues of interest to the profession; but the essays do not make any particular attempt to illustrate how the operation of these libraries relates to larger issues in the field.   Jo Ann H. Bell

296. Mount, Ellis. **Special Libraries and Information Centers: An Introductory Text.** New York, Special Libraries Association, 1983. 194p. bibliog. index. $25.00pa. LC 83-571. ISBN 0-87111-282-5.

The instructor who teaches a general course on special librarianship has a difficult task in locating general information about special libraries, their collections, and management. Numerous articles are available focusing on a single aspect, but no single book has been written that presents the basic background information needed by a student. Mount, an assistant professor at the Columbia University School of Library Service, has written an introductory text that is intended to help both the instructor and the student. He has outlined the information in 26 chapters divided into 7 sections: overview, management, user services, technical services, collections, relationships with other organizations, and library facilities and equipment. The chapters are brief, three to five pages, and include references. It would have been useful to include some of these chapter references in the appendix, "Selected Books on Special Librarianship." Another appendix briefly profiles 12 types of special libraries, including association, law, business, finance, science-technology, publishing, communications, art, graphic, and museum. This is not a detailed treatise on special librarianship and the management of a special library. It is an overview that can provide the basis for more detailed texts covering special library management and research by students. As a beginning text, this should be useful to the student who knows very little about special libraries and their management. [R: JAL, Nov 83, p. 302]   H. Robert Malinowsky

297. Musiker, Reuben. **Special Libraries: A General Survey with Particular Reference to South Africa.** Metuchen, N.J., Scarecrow, 1970. 215p. index. bibliog. o.p. LC 72-12733. ISBN 0-8108-0310-0.

A survey of special libraries providing background information including definition, history, and standards, followed by a lengthy section on South Africa, which receives more emphasis than any other country in the world. Helpful information on the user, services, bookstock, special collection, and staff. [R: LJ, 15 Jan 71, p. 175]   Charles D. Patterson

298. **A Sampler of Forms for Special Libraries.** By Social Science Group, Washington, D.C. Chapter, Special Libraries Association. New York, Special Libraries Association, 1982. 211p. index. $26.00 spiralbound. LC 81-8747. ISBN 0-87111-262-0.

The advantages of this "sampler of forms" are obvious. In its published form, this compilation is an outgrowth of a project of the SLA Social Science Group, which project consisted of collecting and evaluating diverse forms and letters developed and used by a variety of libraries. The collected forms were carefully weeded and edited by two committees of librarians representing a diversity of organizations, and then compiled into a notebook for circulation in the Washington, D.C. area. Its success warranted its publication for wider distribution. In this respect, it will be found most useful in any type of library.

The contents range from forms used in acquisitions, extending to forms designed for cataloging, circulation, interlibrary loan, reference, periodicals control, general library statistics, to budgeting forms. Each section is preceded by a description of the forms and their utilization, and the index in its arrangement reflects these sections. The selected, annotated bibliography represents references from both library and business literature. The section "Mechanics of Forms Design" (reprinted from *Forms Design and Control*, by J. B. Kaiser) provides guidelines in designing forms and/or adapting them for practical usage. This is a much-needed compilation and as such will be found to be a great time-saver in any type of library. [R: JAL, Sept 82, pp. 240-41]   Katherine Cveljo

299. SLA Triennial Salary Survey. New York, Special Libraries Association, 1983. 74p. $20.00pa. LC 83-595. ISBN 0-87111-302-3.

Since 1959 the Special Libraries Association has conducted periodic surveys of members' salaries in the United States and Canada. It has undertaken these on a triennial schedule since 1967, with annual updates since 1980.

The sixth *SLA Triennial Salary Survey* summarizes information received from 3,255 members employed on a full-time basis. Data for the United States and Canada are presented separately in 78 tables from a variety of perspectives, including historical figures as well as those current as of 1 April 1982. Salary distributions are indicated by percentiles as well as by mean and median averages, stratified by types of organizations and geographical locations. (The organizations covered include, among others, manufacturing and transportation companies, medical and legal services, government agencies, and academic and public libraries. The geographical locations used correspond with the nine major U.S. census regions or, in some cases, with Standard Metropolitan Statistical Areas.) Within this basic structure, the tables compare salaries according to such factors as age, sex, ethnic group, educational level, major subject specialization, job title, total years of working experience, years in one particular position, level of administrative and supervisory responsibility, and budget ranges for the kinds of organizations covered. Preliminary graphs compare median annual salaries from 1965 to 1982 with rises in the Consumer Price Index.

The survey should have many uses. It establishes a data bank concerning salaries of special librarians and information personnel, provides systematic information for those engaged in hiring and recruitment activities or planning library careers, and facilitates accurate comparisons by a variety of variables. Modestly priced, it shows careful organization and may well serve as a model for others undertaking similar surveys. [R: JAL, July 83, p. 174]

Mary Jo Walker

REFERENCE WORKS

300. Anderson, Beryl L., comp. Special Libraries and Information Centres in Canada: A Directory. rev. ed. Ottawa, Ont., Canadian Library Association, 1970. 168p. indexes. o.p. LC 72-197100. ISBN 0-88802-030-9.

An expanded edition of the earlier work, this volume includes subject departments in public and university libraries. Data were collected by questionnaires, and the work is understandably uneven in coverage and reporting. Arrangement is alphabetical by special library/information center or institution. Has subject index, geographic index, and personal name index. [R: LJ, 1 Feb 71, p. 453]

301. Codlin, Ellen M., ed. Aslib Directory, Volume 2: Information Sources in the Social Sciences, Medicine and the Humanities. 4th ed. London, Aslib, 1980. 871p. index. $135.00. ISBN 0-85142-130-X.

This is a directory of over 3,600 organizations, including libraries, in the United Kingdom which make information available by subscriptions, publications, or as consultants. They are listed alphabetically, with references from changed or alternative names. For the first time, a key index of abbreviations has been included. A geographical approach to finding organizations is difficult because towns or counties of location are not consistently listed in the index. Each organization is assigned an entry number, and for each organization the address, telephone number, type (public library, company, government, professional association, etc.), person to whom enquiries should be directed, subject coverage, special collections, and publications, where applicable, are given.

Subject access is provided by the index, which gives better subject than geographic coverage, although the names of special collections are not indexed. Volume 1 (4th ed., 1977) of the directory covers science, technology, and commerce. These volumes would be useful not only to those doing research in the United Kingdom but to those doing research about it as well. [R: BL, 1 June 82, p. 1324]   Louise Stwalley

302. **Directory of Special Libraries and Information Centers.** 9th ed. Brigitte T. Darnay, ed. Detroit, Gale, 1985. 3v. index. $320.00/vol. 1; $265.00/vol. 2; $275.00/vol. 3. LC 82-6068. ISBN 0-8103-1881-1 (vol. 1); 0-8103-1889-X (vol. 2); 0-8103-0281-0 (vol. 3).

The ninth edition of this guide to special and research libraries, archives, and information centers in the United States and Canada contains over 17,000 entries. More than 1,000 new entries have been added, and all entries have been fully revised and updated and reset in new, modern typography. Again published in a multivolume format, volume 1 is the directory part of the work, arranged alphabetically by sponsoring institution. The numbered entries include name of sponsoring institution, name of library or information center, the major subject or type of material represented by the collection, address, phone number, head of the library or information center, founding date, staff size, special collections, holdings, subscriptions, services, automated library operations, networks, publications issued, special catalogs and indexes, former and/or alternative names, and names of principal staff members. Over 5,000 cross-references are included to direct the user. The appendices include information about computerized services and a listing of over 700 networks and consortia. Volume 1 includes a subject index.

Volume 2 contains geographic and personnel indexes which provide access to volume 1. The geographic index lists all the institutions described in volume 1 by state or province; the personnel index lists alphabetically all the library personnel mentioned in volume 1. The third volume, *New Special Libraries*, is published as an inter-edition supplement in order to keep the user up-to-date on newly formed libraries and information facilities. This is a valuable guide, but because of the steep price, librarians will need to carefully evaluate their need to add this directory to their collections. [R: BL, July 84, p. 1532; IRLA, Mar 84, p. 12]

Ann L. Hartman and Annette Pekarek

303. **Who's Who in Special Libraries 1985-86.** Washington, D.C., Special Libraries Association, 1985. 196p. index. $25.00pa. ISSN 0278-842X.

The always useful directory of the members of the Special Libraries Association (SLA) — the preeminent body of special librarians in North America — was apparently a partial victim of the move of SLA's headquarters from New York to Washington, D.C. This work is less complete than last year's. Furthermore, the paper seems to be newsprint quality.

However, a plus is the reversion from last year's experimental main listing by subject divisions with alphabetical index of members' names and a chapter approach. This year there is an alphabetical main (and only) listing of members' names.

Statistically, it is noted that SLA's current membership of 11,775 is concentrated, with 1,386 members in the New York chapter, 856 in the Washington, D.C., chapter, and in Illinois, 657. The South Carolina provisional chapter is smallest, at 23 members. The SLA divisions are subject-based and are important for program emphasis. Business and finance leads with 2,366 members; information technology has 2,005; library management has 1,541; and science-technology has 1,496. Trailing is physics-mathematics astronomy, with 142 members.

The usual strategy when searching for a special librarian is to look first in whichever is newer: this work or the "Personnel Index" to Gale's *Directory of Special Libraries and Information Centers.* This year they are about equal, with the Gale work being distributed in October and SLA's in December. Gale does have more librarians in the subspecialties, such as law, medicine, and music. Gale's ninth edition lists 28,875 names from 17,476 institutions.

E. B. Jackson

BUSINESS AND INDUSTRIAL LIBRARIES

304. Calderhead, Patricia, ed. **Libraries for Professional Practice.** London, Architectural Press; distr., New York, Crane-Russak, 1972. 127p. illus. o.p. ISBN 0-85139-565-1.

The editor of this volume was formerly librarian of the *Architects' Journal* in Great Britain, and some of the articles included in this book were originally published in the journal. It covers the basic principles involved in establishing a company library, including information on budget, equipment, floor plans, etc. It should be noted that most specifications pertain to practice in Great Britain. [R: LJ, 1 Dec 72, p. 3878]

305. Campbell, Malcolm J., ed. **Manual of Business Library Practice.** London, Clive Bingley; distr., Hamden, Conn., Linnet Books, 1975. 186p. bibliog. index. o.p. LC 75-20223. ISBN 0-85157-178-8(Bingley); 0-208-01359-8 (Linnet).

According to the introduction, this book was prepared on the premise that library schools lack adequate texts for the teaching of courses in special librarianship. The work contains 12 chapters written by eight contributors. Representative chapter titles are "The Structure of Commercial Library Information," "Directories of Company Information Sources," "Statistics and Market Research Resources—Bibliographies," and "Special Sources of Business Libraries."

The chapters, which are both expositional and bibliographic, are strong on UK and European Economic Community sources but relatively weak on U.S. materials. Although certainly of some interest to special business libraries in this country, the book's preponderant emphasis on British models, sources, and standards diminishes its value.

The second edition was published in 1985, and will be reviewed in the third volume of *Library Science Annual* (Libraries Unlimited, 1987). [R: C&RL, Sept 76, p. 473; LJ, 15 June 76, p. 1397; LQ, July 76, p. 333]

Richard A. Gray

306. Ladendorf, Janice M. **The Changing Role of the Special Librarian in Industry, Business, and Government.** New York, Special Libraries Association, 1973. 29p. (SLA State-of-the-Art Review, No. 1). o.p. LC 73-6683. ISBN 0-87111-219-1.

In 1972 the SLA Research Committee commissioned a series of state-of-the-art reviews to provide definitive statements on selected problems and issues of major importance to special libraries. Ladendorf was assigned the first review, the purpose of which is to examine the changing role of the special librarian, with particular emphasis on the impact of networks and information science. The review was to be prepared in two parts: (1) summarizing existing research, and (2) identifying needed research. As she explains in her preface, she discovered that practically no scientifically controlled research has been done that relates to the assigned topics. She also found, as have many

others, that there are no adequate definitions to distinguish special librarianship from other forms of librarianship and from information science. The author resolved the problem by first writing a background essay that discusses special libraries in terms of a classic problem in overload theory and that stresses the librarian's need to adopt a whole new range of skills. This is followed in part 2 by pleas for research on the role definition of the librarian and user and for evaluation of library and information services using research and theories developed by other disciplines. The use of the idea of overload is an interesting one, and the author plausibly demonstrates how the formation of networks is a symptom of overload in a communications system. In part 2 the author further suggests research possibilities in the study of the impact of information science, information flow research, and relevance and the user. She is more specific in her outline of recommendations, which lists five nonresearch recommendations directed to ways SLA may help the situation and 11 research recommendations that would make excellent projects for any graduate student or researcher. The references used are all recent, and the work is very readable and absorbing. [R: LJ, 1 Jan 74, p. 36]

Robert J. Havlik

307. Slater, Margaret. **The Neglected Resource: Non-Usage of Library-Information Services in Industry and Commerce.** London, Aslib, 1981. 68p. bibliog. (British Library Research and Development Report, No. 5628; Aslib Occasional Publication, No. 25). £12.50pa.; £10.00 (members). ISBN 0-85142-145-8.

This study attempts to redress an alleged imbalance between the considerable time, effort, and money that have been invested in studies to identify the needs and wants of users of library/information systems and the comparatively little effort put into study of nonusers. By design, the study was a small-scale exploratory one within specified limitations: the sample consisted entirely of industrial/commercial services on the current mailing list of Aslib membership. In June 1980, 460 questionnaires were distributed to the library/information managers (*not* to the nonusers themselves); of these, 173 usable replies were received. Both the questionnaire and its covering letter are appended. "Non-use" was defined to include "underuse, misuse, in fact any kind of sub-optimal usage" (p. 62). This report includes the incidence, causes, and cures of non- and underusage as perceived by library/information managers, some of whom are anonymously quoted. Further studies of the under-exploitation of industrial and commercial library/information services are planned. The brief reading list concluding this volume is about equally divided between British and American sources. [R: LR, Summer 82, p. 133]

Wiley J. Williams

GOVERNMENT LIBRARIES

308. **Canadian Library Directory: Volume 1, Federal Government Libraries. Volume 2, University, College and Special Libraries.** Ottawa, Ont., National Library of Canada, Information Canada, 1974-76. 2v. index. o.p./vol. 1; $6.00/vol. 2. ISBN 0-660-00668-5 (vol. 2).

Each of the two volumes in this directory is arranged in one alphabet, with the exception of the National Library of Canada, which is listed first. The information was gathered by means of a questionnaire. For each library are given the name and address, person in charge, hours the library is open, conditions for use, special services, staff (professional and nonprofessional), collection (volumes, titles of periodicals, etc.), subjects covered, special collections, and library publications, if any. There are also four supplementary indexes: an index to automated operations, a geographic index, a personal name index, and a subject index. All this information is provided twice, first in English and then in French.

309. Grolier, Éric de. **The Organization of Information Systems for Government and Public Administration.** Paris, UNESCO; distr., New York, UNIPUB, 1979. 163p. (Documentation, Libraries and Archives: Studies and Research, No. 8). $10.00pa. ISBN 92-3-101595-8.

This eighth volume in a series of UNESCO studies is a concise, superb handbook covering the special characteristics of information systems for government and public administration (ISGPA). It deals with the flow of information in these systems, offers some case studies of a number of national ISGPAs, including the United States, France, Federal Republic of Germany, United Kingdom, as well as Eastern Bloc countries, and addresses the special problems of developing countries. Particularly effective is its discussion of the problems and requirements for developing effective information systems. A number of topics covered here are not dealt with in Pauline Atherton's *Handbook for Information Systems and Services* (UNESCO, 1978). It offers models, presents development plans,

describes technical, economic, and legislative requirements, outlines development plans, priorities, and pilot projects, and is unusual in its frank discussion of training and staffing problems for these systems as well as the difficulties in providing appropriate training of users.

While the work has no index or bibliography, it is richly footnoted with excellent citations, and the detailed table of contents, together with its brevity, permits the serious reader to locate topics of interest. [R: C&RL, May 80, pp. 263-65; LJ, 1 Mar 80, p. 590]

Richard Palmer

310. **World Directory of Administrative Libraries: A Guide of Libraries Serving National, State, Provincial, and Länder-Bodies, Prepared for the Sub-Section of Administrative Libraries.** Edited by Otto Simmler. Munich, Verlag Dokumentation; distr., New York, UNIPUB, 1976. 475p. illus. index. (IFLA Publications 7). o.p. ISBN 3-7940-4427-4.

This directory, based on a questionnaire administered by the IFLA Sub-Section for Administrative Libraries, lists over 300 administrative or governmental libraries—that is, libraries designed to "serve the state on governmental level" (p. 47). The Sub-Section has published this information in the hope of eliciting "future international cooperation" from other administrative libraries (p. 24).

Arrangement is alphabetical by country, with institutions arranged by size under each country. To facilitate access to institutions, the following indexes are provided: index of librarians, index of the libraries (arranged alphabetically under each country), "comparative list of the official and English names," topographic index (with libraries arranged alphabetically under city). At some point during the production of the book, however, an error was perpetrated that renders the indexes almost useless. Apparently the indexes were prepared before the front matter of the book was typeset, and no allowance was made for the pagination of front matter. Thus, an index reference to page 1 should actually be to page 75 (which is the first page of the directory proper). This error extends through all the indexes. In order to find any entry, the user must add "74" to the page number given in the index. This is less than convenient. One additional caveat: Albania is called "Albany" whenever reference is made to it.

Entries give official name of the library, English translation, telephone and telex numbers, type of collections, description of inventory, number of personnel, director of library, and special services.

All in all, this directory represents a long-term effort by the Sub-Section to create a listing of the administrative libraries in IFLA member countries. It is hoped that the next edition will not only improve its coverage but will also revise the indexes so that the reader can locate entries without using a calculator.　　Ann J. Harwell

311. **Worldwide Directory of Federal Libraries.** Judith Bettelheim, ed., and the staff of Academic Media. Orange, N.J., Academic Media, 1973. 411p. index. o.p. LC 72-75955. ISBN 0-87876-029-6.

This lists only libraries of the U.S. government, both domestic and overseas. "A broad definition of the word 'library' has been used" (introduction) to include information centers, media centers, reference collections, etc. Data were compiled from information supplied by either the libraries listed or the various governing agencies. Entries are arranged by branch of government and then by major department or agency, followed by the divisions thereof. A full entry includes the following information: name of major department, agency name, library name, address, and telephone number, data on professional and nonprofessional staff, librarian's name, major subject of holdings, numbers of books and periodicals, annual budget for books and periodicals and salaries, services available, and special features. A library name index and a geographic index complete the volume.

HEALTH SCIENCES LIBRARIES

312. **Annual Statistics of Medical School Libraries in the United States and Canada.** 4th ed. Richard Lyders, ed. Houston, Tex., Association of Academic Health Sciences Library Directors, Texas Medical Center Library, Houston Academy of Medicine, 1981. 1v. (various paging). index. $65.00pa.; $40.00pa. (members of AAHSLD). ISSN 0196-6448.

Earlier editions of this statistical work were published by the University of Texas Health Science Center Library at Dallas (see *ARBA 80*, entry 176). This fourth edition continues to be a useful statistical source and information management tool for medical school library administrators and librarians. The 54 tables, compiled from data from 123 medical libraries in the United States and Canada, are organized into five groups: (1) library characteristics tables, (2) summary tables which tabulate by library the responses to various questions (this section contains 20 tables summarizing information on

collections, personnel, services, and significant detail for expenditures in categories ranging from binding to travel and education), (3) rank order tables, which show in descending order the values of significant variables, with each library's rank indicated (this section contains 25 tables covering such variables as total number of primary users, number of journal subscriptions, number of hours open each week, total number of database accesses, etc.), (4) rank order summaries by library, and (5) salary tables by position and region. Appendix 1 gives the names and addresses of responding libraries, and appendix 2 is the questionnaire followed by an index.

The information is current, well organized, easily interpreted, and very complete for most of the 123 (out of 139) libraries that responded. This is an important tool for both medical school library administrators and medical library educators.　　James E. Bobick

313. Basler, Beatrice K., and Thomas G. Basler, eds. **Health Sciences Librarianship: A Guide to Information Sources.** Detroit, Gale, 1977. 186p. index. (Books, Publishing and Libraries Information Guide Series, Vol. 1; Gale Information Guide Library). $60.00. LC 74-11552. ISBN 0-8103-1284-0.

In the traditional sense of an annotated bibliography, this can be a useful tool, bringing together approximately 550 nonjournal entries of sources. A considerable number of titles (complete with their descriptive annotations) are duplicated in more than one section; for example, F. W. Lancaster's report and book appear on both page 48 and page 102.

The 13 section headings, assigned rather subjectively by the editors, are inadequate to cover all the major specific topics of interest to the practicing librarian. The assignment of several entries to a specific section was made rather arbitrarily, and therefore the entry could possibly be lost in the section. For example, Adam Scott's chapter "National Library of Medicine" was listed under section 1, "General Health Science Librarianship."

It is understood from the introduction that the book covers only monographic materials. Thus, it would probably be more accurate to subtitle the book "A Guide to Monographic Sources." However, this reviewer has further difficulty with the editors' definition of monographic materials, because, besides books, a great number of the 550+ entries are other types of materials, such as pamphlets, vertical file materials (under 10 pages), annual reports, technical reports, library serials lists, journal series, library or professional society newsletters, videotapes, cassettes, etc. Occasionally, one also can spot a few publications that appear in journals, such as the one from *Federation Proceedings* on page 47. Certain book chapters are also listed separately as individual entries throughout this book, such as the various chapters of the *Handbook of Medical Library Practice*. Thus, the coverage is not consistent with what the editors indicate in the introduction.

The editors claim that throughout this work, they have emphasized currently available materials. This reviewer took the liberty of checking the publication dates of all sources listed in the first 57 pages (one-third) of the book. It was found that of the 203 entries listed there, 81 were pre-1970 publications, 50 were published in 1970-1971, 56 in 1972-1973, 11 in 1974, and only 5 in 1975. This time lag is quite serious. Many monographs published since 1975 are essential to health sciences librarians but seem likely to be missed in this book! [R: JAL, Sept 77, p. 231]   Ching-chih Chen

314.   Bloomquist, Harold, and others. **Library Practice in Hospitals: A Basic Guide.** Cleveland, Ohio, Press of Case Western Reserve University, 1972. 344p. illus. bibliog. index. o.p. LC 79-175301. ISBN 0-8295-0227-0.

The hospital library is of growing importance both as a source of information for health professionals and as their access to national biomedical resources. This handbook for the person in charge of the hospital library is designed for use by the individual who has no library experience or no hospital experience, or the one who needs some brush-up. Three sections cover the field: "The Hospital and the Health Sciences," "Library Tools and Techniques," "System Coupling Networks." The 17 chapters, prepared by 23 experienced contributors, were reviewed by a total of 32 "readers" as critics. The vocabulary is nontechnical, but the coverage is complete — from what to do with gift books to how to get a grant.

The volume is designed to be read, to be dipped into, to be used as a reference tool. The excellent index and the bibliographies at the end of each chapter extend the usefulness of this guide. A fine and unusual continuing education tool, it will be treasured by many libraries, neophyte and experienced, in and out of hospitals. [R: LJ, 1 Jan 73, p. 53]

Shirley B. Hesslein

315.   Chen, Ching-chih. **Sourcebook on Health Sciences Librarianship.** Metuchen, N.J., Scarecrow, 1977. 307p. illus. index. o.p. LC 76-30263. ISBN 0-8108-1005-0.

Chen has performed an inestimable service for health science librarians by producing this unique and excellent sourcebook.

Part 1 reports her systematic study of the articles published in the *Bulletin of the Medical Library Association* from 1966 through 1975, with their citations. Subject scope, output of authors, frequency and dates of articles cited, relationship to trends in the field, and other data of professional interest are carefully documented statistically.

The much longer part 2 is a citation bibliography, arranged by broad subjects, of the BMLA articles for this 10-year period, plus the references cited. These 3,000 citations, necessarily retroactive and selective, refer to scientific or other books and journals that are related to librarians' interests but not readily retrievable from other sources, as well as to BMLA or library journal articles. Author and corporate author indexes complete the volume.

As a core compilation of key sources, based on the definitive journal in the field, this handy and timesaving little book should be exceptionally useful to teachers, students, speakers, authors, and practitioners of health science librarianship. Serious researchers will also need to consult *Library Literature, Hospital Literature Index, CIM*, etc., since no claim is made for comprehensiveness of literature coverage beyond the journal studied. [R: BL, 15 Oct 77, pp. 405-6; LJ, 15 Apr 77, p. 889]

Harriette M. Cluxton

316.   **Directory of Health Sciences Libraries in the United States, 1973.** Susan Crawford and Gary Dandurand, comps. and eds. Chicago, American Medical Association, 1974. 196p. illus. index. $15.00pa. LC 74-14292. ISBN 0-686-15429-0.

In 1973 the AMA, in cooperation with the Committee on Surveys and Statistics of the Medical Library Association, conducted a second survey of health sciences libraries in the United States to update the 1969 directory. Interestingly enough, 2,984 libraries were identified in 1973, as compared to 3,155 health science libraries in 1969. Entries are arranged alphabetically by state, then by city within the state. The following information is included: chief librarian, address and telephone number, type of institution, number of volumes and currently received serial titles, number of staff, and primary occupations of the users of the particular library. A useful directory for those needing this information.

Though still in print, this directory has been superseded by a new directory (*Directory of Health Sciences Libraries in the United States*, Alan M. Rees and Susan Crawford, comps. and eds., Chicago, Medical Library Association, 1980, $25.00).

Dwight F. Burlingame

317. Directory of Medical Libraries in the British Isles. 4th ed. Compiled by the Medical Section of the Library Association. London, Library Association; distr., New York, UNIPUB, 1976. 199p. index. o.p. ISBN 0-85365-049-7.

Libraries included in this edition were selected from the third edition, the *Directory of Postgraduate Medical Centres*, and recommendations from librarians in the field. The criterion for entry was that a library have holdings of at least 25 periodical titles. Entries are arranged alphabetically by locality but are numbered consecutively throughout to facilitate retrieval via the indexes. Information provided, when available, includes: name and address of the institution, director of individual in charge, number of staff, date of founding, hours, who may use the library, special collections, total holdings (broken down by type), classification system used, and publications of the library. Addenda include late entries and four indexes (personal name, institutional name, geographical, and special collections), which add to the usefulness of this directory. Of interest to their counterparts in the United States.

318. Key, Jack D., and Thomas E. Keys, eds. **Classics and Other Selected Readings in Medical Librarianship.** Huntington, N.Y., Robert E. Krieger Publishing, 1980. 744p. illus. $37.50. LC 78-9040. ISBN 0-88275-691-5.

Classics and Other Selected Readings in Medical Librarianship is intended for "practicing medical librarians, library school students, and physicians interested in libraries." It is an anthology of 61 articles which are considered "representative writings of persons who have influenced medical librarianship." Ten of the selected articles were Janet Doe lectures that were presented at the annual meetings of the Medical Association between 1967 and 1977. The remaining articles were arranged under six categories: the profession, the librarian, the ecology of medical libraries, innovations and services, technologies, and history of medicine and the library. Brief biographical sketches of 50 or so authors of the selections are appended. Nearly 75 percent of the selections appeared in the *Bulletin of the Medical Library Association*,

and more than half were published in the 1960s and 1970s.

Although *Classics* contains some excellent selections representing well-known medical librarians, one is struck by the lack of identifiable selection criteria. The compilers state that "selections are based on works of personalities that appealed to us." This, of course, is a rather ill-defined criterion. Another weakness is that a number of articles under the section on technologies do not deal with technology per se. In any case, *Classics* is not designed to be a reference source. However, medical librarians may want to acquire it for their personal collections. [R: JAL, Nov 80, pp. 301-2]　Rao Aluri

319. Lindberg, Donald A. B. **The Growth of Medical Information Systems in the United States.** Lexington, Mass., Lexington Books, a division of D. C. Heath, 1979. 194p. index. o.p. LC 79-1555. ISBN 0-669-02911-4.

The book is an outgrowth of the author's background paper, "The Development and Diffusion of a Medical Technology: Medical Information Systems," prepared in 1977 for the Committee on Technology and Health Care of the National Academy of Sciences. The author's charge was to describe the evolution of medical information systems (MISs) as an example of one form of medical technology. In the context of a national sense of urgency to reduce and control soaring health care costs, the author views MISs as a potential means to an immediate moderate saving in direct health care costs and also to get a handle on the whole process of hospital management. The purpose of this book is to assess the realism of these expectations.

Even though the Library of Congress Cataloging-in-Publication data for the book include "Information storage and retrieval systems—Medicine" as an index term, the book does not cover medical bibliographic database systems such as the National Library of Medicine's MEDLARS/MEDLINE, which is quite consistent with the definition of a medical information system used by the author: a set of formal arrangements by which facts concerning the health or health care of individual patients are stored and processed in computers. The book deals with the development of MISs in the United States only; however, the author provides a brief guide to the international literature in the field. The subject of the book includes two critical issues of our time—the skyrocketing cost of health care, and application of computer technology in the management process (in this case, health care management). The author has handled these and the other concerns of the book quite well. [R: LJ, 1 June 80, p. 1282]

Anindya Bose

320. Linton, W. D., comp. **Directory of Medical and Health Care Libraries in the United Kingdom and Republic of Ireland 1982.** 5th ed. London, Library Association; distr., Phoenix, Ariz., Oryx Press, 1982. 228p. index. $18.50pa. ISBN 0-85365-536-7.

Previous editions carried the title *Directory of Medical Libraries in the British Isles.* This edition, compiled by using a minicomputer, is also available as an electronic database. Growth in the health science library field is reflected in the increased number of entries.

Arrangement is alphabetical by city, then by institution. This necessitates separate indexes of institutions and counties for locating entries easily. Entries include address, phone, staff by name, type of library, users, stock, circulation policies, computer access, holdings, classification, publications, and network affiliation. There are indexes of personal names and special collections and a list of members of the NHS Regional Librarians Group.

United States library schools and professional organizations should find this directory useful. The closest U.S. parallel is A. M. Rees and S. Crawford's *Directory of Health Science Libraries in the United States, 1979* (Medical Library Association, 1980). [R: BL, 1 Dec 83, p. 552]

Harriette M. Cluxton

321. **Medical Librarianship.** Michael Carmel, ed. London, Library Association; distr., Phoenix, Ariz., Oryx Press, 1981. 359p. index. bibliog. (Handbooks on Library Practice). $36.00; $18.50pa. ISBN 0-85365-502-2; 0-85365-703-3pa.

While the emphasis is on medical librarianship in the United Kingdom, most of this book will interest librarians in health sciences fields in other countries, particularly the United States. The contributors are all British except two, one (from the United States) writing on recent developments in health science libraries in North America, and the other (from Brazil) writing on Third World medical libraries.

There are sections on the health care professions, including the medical specialties, dentistry, nursing, and supporting professions. Pharmacy is not mentioned except by occasional references to libraries in pharmaceutical industries. Drug information services, however, are discussed briefly. There is a chapter on serving patients and the public, topics often overlooked in books of this kind. Other chapters cover information networks, serials, books, audiovisuals, publicity, library planning, reference service, literature searching, current awareness services, document delivery, instructing users on library use, library management, library research, and continuing education for librarians.

The chapters covering the medical literature do not mention very many specific materials. Titles are provided usually as examples of types of literature only. Emphasis is on handling materials. Frequent references are made, however, to computerized databases of interest. Literature references follow each chapter.

The book is of high quality, well written, and adequate in its coverage. The Medical Library Association's *Handbook of Medical Library Practice* is similar and is likely to be preferred by librarians in the United States, although it is not so up-to-date. [R: AB, 26 Apr 82, p. 3302; LR, Autumn 81, p. 186]

Theodora Andrews

322. Sewell, Winifred, ed. **Reader in Medical Librarianship.** Westport, Conn., Greenwood Press, 1973. 340p. (Reader Series in Library and Information Science). $28.50. LC 72-86634. ISBN 0-313-24043-4.

This volume in the Reader Series presents a selection of reprinted articles and papers on the environment of medical libraries (10 articles), medical librarianship as a profession (2 articles), organization and administration (13 articles), various types of medical libraries (9 articles), and medical library networks (7 articles). [R: LJ, 15 Sept 73, p. 2528]

LIBRARY OF CONGRESS

323. Cole, John Y., ed. **The Library of Congress in Perspective: A Volume Based on the Reports of the 1976 Librarian's Task Force and Advisory Groups.** New York, R. R. Bowker, 1978. 281p. index. o.p. LC 78-5000. ISBN 0-8352-1055-3.

The "Report of the 1976 Librarian's Task Force on Goals, Organization, and Planning," transmitted to the Librarian of Congress on 28 January 1977, is the fifth comprehensive assessment of the Library of Congress. Earlier assessments were made in 1940, 1947, 1962, and 1967. These assessments are part of the history of the Library of Congress, which is presented in some detail by the editor of this volume in chapter 1 — "The Library of Congress, 1800-1975." Although the information in this chapter is available in other sources, the historical perspective is a necessary prelude to the 1976 study, which is published in full in chapter 2. As a result of the Task Force report, changes were made at LC in 1977, as reported by Charles A. Goodrum in three issues of the *Library of Congress Information Bulletin*. These articles are reprinted in the epilogue, which is chapter 3. The four lengthy appendices include supporting data: three background papers, two of the fourteen subcommittee reports, all eight advisory group reports, and a list of Task Force members, and the personnel of the subcommittees and advisory groups.

The report is a valuable document that includes 33 recommendations, including the appointment of a board of advisors, improvement of the basic book delivery service, establishment of a reader guidance service that begins at the door of the library, provision for an enlarged reference program, and the establishment of a career development plan of action. In order to gain a scholarly perspective on the Task Force and its recommendations, the historical chapter and the appendices need to be read before reading the actual report. For the library historian and the library school student, the remaining twelve subcommittee reports should be made available. The report, which is quite short (pp. 85-131), deserves wide dissemination. This reviewer was surprised not to find it listed in the spring 1978 Library of Congress *Publications in Print*. [R: C&RL, Nov 78, p. 502]

Doris Cruger Dale

324. Goodrum, Charles A., and Helen W. Dalrymple. **The Library of Congress.** 2nd ed. Boulder, Colo., Westview Press, 1982. 337p. illus. index. $32.00; $11.95pa. LC 82-8457. ISBN 0-86531-303-2; 0-86531-497-7pa.

Many second editions deserve no more than a brief review, but this book does not belong in that category. The first edition (see *ARBA 75*, entry 204) was an important contribution to the literature on the Library of Congress, and the second is also significant. The changes within the library itself have been major; their complexity is illustrated by the differences in the organizational charts in the two editions. Continuing technological advances have had additional impact on the Library of Congress and its influence on the library world.

The book covers the history of our national library, its internal operation, the problems and pressures facing the Library of Congress, and alternatives for future developments. The major difference in the second edition is, obviously, its emphasis on the Boorstin years. The authors conclude that the library now has two options

for tomorrow: the development of specialized library collections in a regional system, and the enhancements offered by computers and other forms of automation. Developments involving the automation of the Congressional Research Service in the last dozen years are only one example of the potential of the electronic library.

The authors, both of whom have worked in the Library of Congress, were criticized for using a too-popular writing style in the first edition. The style is the same in the second, but it does not present serious difficulties for general readership. Both the bibliography and the index have been expanded. [R: C&RL, Mar 83, pp. 184-86; JAL, July 83, p. 168; LJ, July 83, p. 1345; SBF, Nov 83, p. 64]　　　　Boyd Childress

325. Hu, Shu Chao. **The Development of the Chinese Collection in the Library of Congress.** Boulder, Colo., Westview Press, 1979. 259p. bibliog. index. (A Westview Replica Edition). o.p. LC 79-1741. ISBN 0-89158-552-4.

A study, based on the author's dissertation, of the development of the Chinese collection in the Orientalia Division (since 1979, Asian Division) of the Library of Congress, "the largest collection of its kind in the Western world," which began in 1869 and grew to over 430,000 volumes by 1977, including some 2,000 rare Chinese items. Not included are Chinese law materials in the Far Eastern Law Division. The author, a library school educator, investigates the social, cultural, and political forces which contributed to the building of this important collection. After an introductory chapter on the purpose, scope, and methods of this study, the book is arranged by broad chronological sections. The extensively documented narrative, containing many citations from original sources, covers the period up to about 1975, and concludes with summaries of the findings and recommendations for further studies, such as on the collection of Chinese law materials. A separate chronology provides brief, useful references to events and the people involved. Appendices include copies of historical correspondence and a list of acquisition policy statements, followed by an extensive bibliography of primary and secondary sources, and an adequate index.

The poor physical production in offset, low quality paper, and binding that does not allow the volume to lie flat, is supposed to make such types of scholarly publications possible at a moderate price in this Westview series. This first major study of the topic makes highly interesting reading for those concerned with U.S.-Chinese cultural relations and American library history, and provides a wealth of information and insight for the serious researcher. A substantial contribution to the history of the Library of Congress. [R: C&RL, May 80, p. 256] Josephine Riss Fang

326. **The Library of Congress as the National Bibliographic Center.** Washington, D.C., Association of Research Libraries, 1976. 58p. illus. $4.00pa. ISBN 0-686-75997-4.

Contains five brief articles describing major aspects of certain activities in the Library of Congress. Of special interest to a wider audience are an article by William Welsh and Henriette Avram, "Automation Activities of the Processing Department"; Lucia Rather's "The Core Bibliographic System"; and Henriette Avram's "The National Bibliographic System." Much of this information the reader will find in annual reports of the Library of Congress and, according to the foreword, the same material will appear in the *ARL Minutes*. [R: C&RL, Nov 76, p. 562]

327. **The Role of the Library of Congress in the Evolving National Network.** Washington, D.C., Library of Congress; distr., Washington, D.C., GPO, 1978. 141p. $3.25pa. LC 78-17012. ISBN 0-8444-0269-9. S/N 030-000-00102-8.

In 1975, the National Commission on Libraries and Information Science issued a position paper, *Toward a National Program for Library and Information Services: Goals for Action*, proposing several broad responsibilities to be assumed by the Library of Congress. As partial follow-up, it funded a survey of opinions and suggestions from 23 libraries and network centers. Under contract to the LC Network Development Office, two investigators from Inforonics explored the possibilities of broadening the National Program for Acquisitions and Cataloging (NPAC), increasing MARC coverage, distributing bibliographic data online, expanding a reference program, and establishing a center for personnel training in, and dissemination of information about, LC techniques and processes. The present document summarizes that study.

The book's first 36 pages describe the survey, with results and recommendations. Its primary thesis is that the Library of Congress should coordinate technical and standards-related efforts to link federal, multistate, state, and local systems into a national bibliographic network. It further suggests specific roles that the survey participants would like to see the LC assume. Two appendices identify the advisory committee for the study and the institutions

consulted. The 23 network centers are described in some detail. Summaries of their organization, services, financing, experiences, and future plans comprise well over one-half of the report, giving a useful review of bibliographic networking at the time of the survey (mid-1976 through early 1977). Readers of *The Library of Congress in Perspective* (see *ARBA* 79, entry 237) will be interested in this soberly optimistic outline of a distributed bibliographic processing system using the Library of Congress as a *primus inter pares*. [R: SLMQ, Summer 79, p. 242]
Jeanne Osborn

MAP LIBRARIES

328. Drazniowsky, Roman, comp. **Map Librarianship: Readings.** Metuchen, N.J., Scarecrow, 1975. 548p. illus. maps. index. o.p. LC 74-19244. ISBN 0-8108-0739-4.

Here is a collection of articles that have appeared in a variety of publications concerned with maps and map librarianship. The range of content is wide and the selection of articles is good. The titles of the units into which the book is divided reflect the content: "Introduction to Maps," "The Elements of Maps," "Map Classification and Use," "Map Processing and Cataloging," "Map Storage and Preservation," and "Map Librarianship/Map Collections." The readings are accompanied by a lengthy bibliography of additional references related to maps and map librarianship. The articles in the collection provide useful background information for the understanding of maps and map making as well as technical aspects of map librarianship. This collection will be useful for a student of cartography or a library science student planning on a career in map librarianship. In addition, it would serve as a good basic reference for map librarians. [R: C&RL, Sept 75, pp. 422-23; RQ, Fall 75, p. 85] Gary R. Purcell

329. Larsgaard, Mary. **Map Librarianship: An Introduction.** Littleton, Colo., Libraries Unlimited, 1978. 330p. bibliog. index. (Library Science Text Series). o.p. LC 77-28821. ISBN 0-87287-182-7.

Map Librarianship serves students preparing to enter the field or librarians who have been given specific responsibility for a map collection, without any special training, as part of a larger library unit. The emphasis is on practical aspects of both day-to-day and long-term work with maps in libraries, and with the people who use them. The book serves as a working manual and reference source as well as a classroom text.

It combines timely, pragmatic information, a survey of existing practices, and guidance in choosing specific procedures. The arrangement of the text parallels the actual steps in dealing with maps in libraries. The chapters cover map selection and acquisition; cataloging and computer applications; the care, storage, and repair of maps; public relations and reference services; and the administration of a map library. The text is followed by a bibliography and by fifteen appendices. These provide sample policy statements, accessions lists, forms, etc.; list working tools not in the scope of the bibliography; give addresses of producers of maps and globes; and supply a brief glossary of map terms. The text is indexed by subject. A second edition will be published in late 1986. [R: LJ, 1 Nov 78, p. 2175]

330. Nichols, Harold. **Map Librarianship.** 2nd ed. London, Clive Bingley; distr., Hamden, Conn., Shoe String Press, 1982. 272p. bibliog. index. $29.50. ISBN 0-85157-327-4.

Both the writing and the editing seem to be improved from the 1976 edition of the book of the same title. It remains primarily a handbook for British public libraries, with very little of interest — or rather, very little that is new — for college and university libraries and medium-to-large-sized public libraries in the United States, although a goodly amount of space is given to rare and old maps, and this material might indeed prove helpful to many libraries. The primary focus of the book seems to be local maps and old maps, with scarcely a whisper on cataloging of twentieth-century maps using automation — an area that is certainly a major focus of attention and interest in the United States today.

Nichols is very diligent about providing addresses, which makes the book handy for foreign acquisitions work, and it is, as the introduction states, an attempt to assist both the generalist librarian and the specialist curator (not, perhaps, so successfully for the latter), and an attempt to put forward a commonsense approach to working with maps in libraries. There are a few minor problems that could create a problem for a beginning cataloger: Winch's *International Maps and Atlases in Print* (any edition) is most definitely *not* a list of maps in print, but rather of the maps and atlases that Stanford had in stock at the time of publication; and there is a punctuation error in the section on cataloging — it should be 17--?, not 17-? for decade uncertain. Overall, Nichols is obviously very well read, and while there are some errors, they tend to be relatively minor. Still, libraries

with the previous edition of this book might want to examine this before they purchase it. [R: JAL, Sept 82, p. 240]   Mary Larsgaard

331. Ristow, Walter W. **The Emergence of Maps in Libraries.** Hamden, Conn., Linnet Books, 1980. 358p. $27.50. LC 80-12924. ISBN 0-208-01841-7.

Walter Ristow has long been the doyen of map librarians in the United States; this collection of some of his writings makes clear the reason why. Ristow is far too modest in his introduction when he says he "participated" in the "evolution and maturing of map librarianship." He molded, formed, and pushed it along, has certainly done considerably more than make "some few contributions" to the literature, and has been for many years one of the best and surely the most prolific of writers in the field of map libraries and map librarianship. It is indeed a pleasure to see one's favorite articles, such as "The Greening of Map Librarianship" and "The Emergence of Maps in Libraries," and even more enjoyable to discover articles that had been forgotten, or worse, missed. As the author states in his introduction, these papers "summarize much in the history of the development" of map librarianship. The articles are divided into seven subject parts — history and development; acquisitions and procurement; technical processes; reference; map library education; memorials for map librarians and cartobibliographers; and international map librarianship. Reading over these articles, one may observe the changes in the field, and, incidentally, in Ristow's writing style. His writings are must reading for all map librarians, and are appropriate for purchase by universities with library schools and any library with an interest in map collections, map librarianship, and map acquisitions. [R: C&RL, Mar 81, pp. 162-64; JAL, July 81, p. 176]   Mary Larsgaard

332. Wallis, Helen, and Lothar Zögner, eds. **The Map Librarian in the Modern World: Essays in Honour of Walter W. Ristow.** Munich, New York, K. G. Saur, 1979. 295p. illus. maps. index. $20.00pa. ISBN 3-598-10063-9.

This overview of map libraries and map librarians of the world will be a basic work for any map collection, although the price seems a bit stiff for a paperback that is not even offset print, with all the writing done by volunteer labor. By far the most valuable article for U.S. libraries is also the longest, just under 100 pages, and also the first; it deals at length with the Library of Congress's Geography and Map

Division, detailing the history of that very important collection. The rest of the papers, like the first, are by authors whose names read like a roll call of the important names in map librarianship. There is considerable emphasis on pre-1900 maps, and on large map collections, or on particularly important map collections. The articles are in English, French, or German. There is a brief index. Appropriate for academic libraries that support degrees in geography, and for libraries with map collections. [R: C&RL, Mar 80, p. 178; JAL, July 80, p. 163; LJ, 15 Feb 80, p. 489] Mary Larsgaard

RELIGIOUS LIBRARIES

333. Harvey, John F., ed. **Church and Synagogue Libraries.** Metuchen, N.J., Scarecrow, 1980. 279p. illus. index. $18.00. LC 80-11736. ISBN 0-8108-1304-1.

To describe church and synagogue libraries in the United States (estimated to number 25,300) and identify recent trends in their development is the purpose of this collection of 20 essays plus the editor's introductory piece, "The American Church and Synagogue Library World." The first four papers provide an overview of this very special field of librarianship—historical and demographic background, collection development, architecture (with some suggested floor plans included), and finances. Then follow three papers on Jewish libraries, two on Catholic libraries, eight on Protestant and other Christian libraries. The last three essays will especially appeal to American library history aficionados, dealing as they do with the Parish and Community Libraries Section of the Catholic Library Association, the Association of Jewish Libraries, and the Church and Synagogue Library Association. Titles of useful books, addresses of associations, and sources of materials/equipment cited in a number of the papers should prove useful to the tyro church librarians.

Thomas Bray once observed that "an excessive scarcity of money" would be the primary obstacle to the development of a library in each American Anglican parish. That observation is as valid today as it was in 1697—and not just for the church/synagogue library! The editor describes this work as "a pioneer volume" in one of "the library world's newest and least known fields." This it surely is. And *mirabile dictu* the format is more attractive than usual for a Scarecrow Press book. [R: LJ, 15 Nov 80, p. 2392] John David Marshall

334. McMichael, Betty. **The Library and Resource Center in Christian Education.** Chicago, Moody Press, 1977. 256p. illus. bibliog. index. o.p. LC 77-6722. ISBN 0-8024-4895-X.

This is one of the most comprehensive and professional manuals yet to appear that deals with the organization of a church library. The author recommends that those who are responsible for this type of library follow as closely as possible professional techniques and procedures. Too many similar manuals in the past have proposed abbreviated techniques that only cause problems as the library expands or others take over its management. This particular manual can be used for the established as well as beginning church library and includes all of the basics from philosophy, physical space, and funding, to acquisitions, cataloging, and circulation.

Of particular note is the inclusion in each section of information dealing with audiovisual materials. In fact, the library concept employed throughout the book is one of the media or resource center. The author does present alternatives within the limits of good professional practice that can be selected by individual libraries according to their own needs. An example of this is her discussion of the use of an accession book or the shelflist card for record keeping. Illustrations used throughout the manual are very clear and appropriately placed near corresponding text to demonstrate particular procedures or materials.

Appendices include: sample questionnaire from the library survey used to gather data for this work; a directory of suppliers; Dewey Decimal Classification outline and further selected numbers in the 200 series (religion); and a selected list of subject headings useful for church libraries. A bibliography and index further enhance the manual. *The Minister's Library* (see *ARBA* 77, entry 235) could be used as a selection aid along with this manual; and to supplement material in chapter 9, "Promoting the Library's Ministry," Ruth Smith's *Getting the Books Off the Shelves: Making the Most of Your Congregation's Library* (see *ARBA* 77, entry 241) might be useful. Recommended for all church library/resource centers. Roberta J. Depp

335. Newhall, Jannette E. **A Theological Library Manual.** With a foreword by Raymond P. Morris. London, Theological Education Fund; distr., Naperville, Ill., Alec R. Allenson, Inc., 1970. 162p. index. illus. bibliog. o.p. LC 70-594222. ISBN 0-9029-0300-4.

This volume consists of 15 chapters dealing with a wide range of topics essential to those who will establish the small special collection. In this case, the modest theological seminary library, particularly those in developing countries, would be included. Basics include administration, book selection, cataloging and classification, periodicals, rare books, and archives and library buildings. Also included are drawings and charts detailing library operations and a detailed index. [R: LJ, 1 Jan 71, p. 50]

Charles D. Patterson

OTHER TYPES OF SPECIAL LIBRARIES

336. Anderson, Elizabeth L., ed. **Newspaper Libraries in the U.S. and Canada: An SLA Directory.** 2nd ed. New York, Special Libraries Association, Newspaper Division, 1980. 321p. index. $18.50pa. LC 80-25188. ISBN 0-87111-265-5.

This directory contains information about 314 newspaper libraries in the United States and Canada. The 1976 edition was reviewed in *ARBA* 77 (entry 182). This edition includes 17 additional newspapers and updated information (mostly personnel changes), but differs little in format or information provided. Data were solicited by questionnaire from 558 newspapers with daily circulations of 25,000 or more. The response of 56 percent includes 95 percent of those newspapers with over 100,000 daily circulation.

The directory is arranged by U.S. state, then city, followed by 21 Canadian newspapers by province/city. There are indexes by city, newspaper group, and library personnel. There is also a listing of Washington, D.C. news bureaus. Each library is given one full page, which includes information about the newspaper: its name and address, telephone number, time of issue circulation, group with which affiliated, availability of indexes and microform editions. Many of the entries include a photo-reduction of the newspaper's banner. Library information includes the founding date, number of staff, name of the person in charge and assistants, hours, public access and limitations, holdings, special collections, internal indexes, automation efforts, and products for sale.

The value of this directory to newspaper librarians is obvious for interlibrary loan and other cooperative efforts. In addition, it provides some useful information about the newspapers themselves. In all, this is a well-organized, concise, and easy-to-use directory containing useful information for newspaper and nonnewspaper librarians. [R: JAL, Sept 81, p. 247]

A. Neil Yerkey

337. Blunt, Adrian. **Law Librarianship.** London, Clive Bingley; distr., Hamden, Conn., Shoe String Press, 1980. 126p. index. (Outlines of Modern Librarianship). $12.00. ISBN 0-85157-299-5.

Adrian Blunt's *Law Librarianship* is part of the Outlines of Modern Librarianship series, published by the Shoe String Press, designed to introduce the general reader to various specialty fields in librarianship. Blunt treats the subject of law librarianship in the United Kingdom in a readable, clearly expressed form. The book stands as more than an introduction to law and law libraries in Britain; it is also a short and simple introduction to the legal literature of the United Kingdom. It provides in its nine chapters looks at legislation, law reports, secondary materials, bibliographies and reference tools, etc. In addition, it provides quick glimpses of the other legal systems in the British Isles, the law of the European Economic Community, and international law. While the book is short, only 126 pages, and therefore cannot be a comprehensive treatment of any of these subjects, it provides an excellent first look for the novice. Many experienced American law librarians will find the capsule descriptions of British legal materials useful as well. This book seems to stand with Morris Cohen's *Legal Research in a Nutshell* (West Publishing, 1968) as the best kind of introduction to the literature of a country. The price makes the book especially appealing. Recommended for most collections, including those of the research variety. [R: JAL, Nov 81, p. 306]

Robert C. Berring

338. Bradley, Carol June, ed. **Reader in Music Librarianship.** Washington, D.C., Microcard Editions, 1973. 340p. bibliog. index. (Reader Series in Library and Information Science). $28.50. LC 73-82994. ISBN 0-910972-48-6.

This anthology has seven sections, of which the first ("General Survey") and third ("Bibliographical Services") have 13 and 20 articles, respectively. The other five sections (on bibliography, mechanical processes, phonograph records, buildings and equipment, and music librarianship) total 20 articles between them. There are 53 articles in all, three of them translations.

The editor claims that "this *Reader* reprints the classic articles ... and ... annotates those historical items which it does not reprint."

Indeed, the bibliographies that precede each section of the text are a most valuable feature. But the criterion of a periodical's unavailability as a basis for inclusion seems inconsistently applied. The editor writes that "there are several articles reprinted from *Notes* ... even though *Notes* itself is generally available.... *Fontes artis musicae* cannot be considered generally available and, therefore, quite a few articles are reprinted from its pages.... No articles are reprinted from *Library Trends*, all back numbers of which are in print."

Most contributions are prefaced by an editorial introduction, and one wishes that this had always been done, with a few words about the author (as in *The Academic Library* in this same series) for background. When the original article includes references, these have been retained, and the editor has gone to great trouble to correct, update, or amplify citations where necessary.

British references are sometimes misleading (e.g., it is ambiguous to describe J. D. Brown as "an English librarian"; he was a Scot in charge of a London library).

Of the specially written articles, one is on thematic catalogs. It is true that "such catalogues are generally organized chronologically, though some use other principles of organization," but one is astonished to read that "the first of these is illustrated by the Köchel catalogue of the works of Mozart, the Schmieder catalogue of the works of J. S. Bach, or the Hoboken catalogue of the works of Haydn, all catalogues which list the works in chronological order" (p. 186). The second original contribution is on copyright, but it duplicates many statements of fact found in another article from 1965, rather than simply complementing and updating.

The book is similar in format to others in this series. The page layout, with two columns of print, unjustified at the right-hand margins and divided by a heavy black rule down the page center, is unattractive. There are the apparently inevitable spelling mistakes (e.g., "supercedes" on p. 130; "concensus" on pp. 237, 243) and misprints ("scarecly," p. 79; "proscribed" for "prescribed" on p. 209 — a difference of one letter that makes nonsense of the sentence).

The bibliographical annotations of items vary both in length and in adequacy. That for the article by Riddle, quoted on page 22, appears to this reader to be quite misleading. In any case, it is difficult to understand why this reference is included in preference to any mention of the writings of Ernest A. Savage, an outstanding British public librarian of his day

and a man with strong (if unorthodox) views on the provision of music scores.

Nevertheless, despite the criticisms made here, it is clear that Bradley's anthology has been worth making and will be of real value to many readers. [R: LJ, July 74, p. 1783]

E. T. Bryant

339. Collins, Marcia, and Linda Anderson. **Libraries for Small Museums.** 3rd ed. Columbia, Miss., Museum of Anthropology, University of Missouri, 1977. 48p. bibliog. (Miscellaneous Publications in Anthropology, No. 4). $2.50pa. ISBN 0-913134-90-2.

This brief manual contains information on planning, financing, and organizing a small museum's library; ordering books; processing; cataloging; circulation; record keeping; and reference service. The experienced professional will discover nothing new, but the novice will welcome its assistance. The value of this publication is its advice on running a library with an extremely restricted budget, and heads of all small libraries — not just those connected with a museum — would do well to glance at it. In such a publication, it is not surprising to discover some mistakes in methodology. The statement that "archival materials, typescripts and photocopies of original manuscripts are also catalogued like books," for example, violates basic archival principles; those persons holding archival materials should obtain the new Basic Manual Series of the Society of American Archivists. Richard J. Cox

340. Fusonie, Alan, and Leila Moran, eds. **International Agricultural Librarianship: Continuity and Change: Proceedings of an International Symposium Held at the National Agricultural Library, November 4, 1977.** Westport, Conn., Greenwood Press, 1979. 127p. index. $29.95. LC 78-67916. ISBN 0-313-20640-6.

This text consists of the edited proceedings of a symposium in honor of Foster E. Mohrhardt, former director of the National Agricultural Library, that was held on 4 November 1977. Its purpose is to provide a comprehensive overview of the practical role of agricultural librarians, documentalists, and information specialists, offering substantive, well-documented information on the current state of the field of agricultural librarianship on an international level. Chapters range from broad international comparisons to discussions of the function of agricultural libraries in a particular country. For example, "Agricultural Libraries and the Spirit of Cooperation: A Continuing Process" outlines international cooperative organizations and their activities, while "International Agricultural Librarianship: The Differences" provides a succinct comparison of agricultural research activities in Brazil and the United States. This text comprehensively covers the practice of international librarianship, and will be particularly useful for those practicing in this area of the profession. [R: C&RL, Nov 79, pp. 560-61]   Betty Gay

341. The Impact of the Environmental Sciences & the New Biology on Law Libraries. Dobbs Ferry, N.Y., Glanville Publishers; distr., Dobbs Ferry, N.Y., Oceana, 1973. 174p. o.p.

This publication is the result of the Berkeley Summer Institute in Law Librarianship (1971). It is divided into four parts: (1) "Technology Assessment and the Law"; (2) "Life and Death—Their Social Definitions"; (3) "World Demographic Problems"; and (4) "Scientific Manipulation of Human Biology." "One of the most impressive annotated bibliographies on 'frontier' law ever produced" (*Library Journal*). [R: LJ, 15 Nov 73, p. 3358]

Charles D. Patterson

342. Lendvay, Olga. **Primer for Agricultural Libraries.** 2nd ed., rev. and enl. Wageningen, Netherlands, Centre for Agricultural Publishing and Documentation; distr., New York, UNIPUB, 1980. 91p. bibliog. $7.50pa. ISBN 90-220-0727-8.

The preliminary edition of this manual was published in 1967. Its stated purpose is to help people who must operate agricultural libraries but who lack sufficient specialized training. It includes brief sections on a wide variety of topics, from collection development, processing, organization, and maintenance, to library administration, reader services, public relations, doing an inventory, statistics and reports, planning new library buildings, library automation, and agricultural databases. Much of the material relates to library practice, although there is little detail since the text portion of the volume consists of only 47 pages. This section is followed by the bibliography and eight appendices, many of which list various types of publications in the field of agriculture, such as guides to the literature, bibliographies, and indexing and abstracting journals. Other appendices include form letters for exchange of publications and a EUR-AGRIS input sheet. There is a table of contents but no index. This work would be especially useful for agricultural libraries in developing countries and should be of interest as well to library science educators and students.   Constance Mellott

343. The Libraries, Museums & Art Galleries Yearbook, 1971. Edmund V. Corbett, comp. and ed. London, James Clarke; distr., New York, R. R. Bowker, 1971. 694p. index. o.p.

Begun in 1897, this four-part directory of public libraries, special libraries, museums and art galleries, including stately homes, is geographically arranged by type, each with a selective subject index to special collections. Three parts cover the United Kingdom more comprehensively with each annual volume. The very short part for the Republic of Eire lists no "stately homes" except Bunratty Castle and Yeats Tower, Thoor Ballylee. The usual directory information on hours of opening, admission charges, and staff is given for each, but descriptions of collections vary greatly, from a detailed listing of the Shakespeare Birthplace Trust properties to six lines for the collections of the British Museum. The harried compiler notes, "indeed it has required the patience of Job to decipher many questionnaires which have been completed in almost illegible handwriting," implying that some errors were inevitable. Nevertheless, it should be a very useful and relatively up-to-date directory for larger American libraries. [R: LJ, 15 Feb 72, p. 659; RQ, Spring 72, p. 271]   Frances Neel Cheney

344. Miller, George B., Jr., Janet S. Harris, and William E. Hannaford, Jr., comps. and eds. **Puppetry Library: An Annotated Bibliography Based on the Batchelder-McPharlin Collection at the University of New Mexico.** Westport, Conn., Greenwood Press, 1981. 172p. index. $29.95. LC 80-23474. ISBN 0-313-21359-3.

One of the world's largest puppetry libraries, the University of New Mexico's Batchelder-McPharlin Collection, claims 2,247 items in 21 languages, including books, periodicals, scores, illustrations, pamphlets, scripts, etc., on the aesthetics, uses, and craft of puppetry. When each scrap is counted, 2,247 items doesn't seem immense for a university collection, although it's excellent as McPharlin's own. Only 528 items are listed in this bibliography, which is devoted to monographs of 50 pages or more. Indexes include subject, personal, and organization name; adult puppet plays; and children's puppet plays. An introduction gives background on the McPharlins, and appendices cover a summary by type of the entire collection and a selective journal list (10 were listed, but there are only 19 different periodicals in the collection represented in 439 issues).

While it is easy to use this bibliography, and especially helpful due to succinct annotations, standard works of children's puppetry by such notables as Laura Ross and Bernice Carlson are missing. And despite comment in regard to a dearth of materials available on puppet manipulation, Larry Engler's fine book, *Making Puppets Come Alive* (Taplinger, 1973), is omitted.

The Russian collection, 51 titles listed separately and printed in the Cyrillic alphabet, is annotated in English and has author headings use the Latin alphabet, while titles remain Cyrillic and untranslated.

Overall, the work provides access to a significant, if not overwhelming, collection, and should be useful in research libraries and wherever puppets are serious business. [R: Choice, Sept 81, p. 52]   Helen Gregory

345. Mount, Ellis. **University Science and Engineering Libraries.** 2nd ed. Westport, Conn., Greenwood Press, 1985. 303p. bibliog. index. (Contributions in Librarianship and Information Science, No. 49). $35.00. LC 84-6530. ISBN 0-313-23949-5.

This book is intended for librarians employed in college and university sci-tech libraries as well as library science students and other librarians interested in these types of libraries. As in the earlier edition, health science libraries are not included. The volume is divided into six sections. The first section, consisting of one chapter, describes the general nature of academic sci-tech libraries. These are compared and contrasted with their public and special library counterparts. The second section, containing seven chapters, deals with management issues such as planning and budgeting, staff supervision, marketing, evaluation, and so on. The third and fourth sections deal with technical and user services respectively. The fifth section discusses collection development, and the sixth section addresses facilities and library equipment. These sections amount to an additional ten chapters. An appendix presents the survey instrument and results of interviews on sixteen campuses in 1983, which formed the basis for much of the information presented in this volume. Included among the seven illustrations are library layouts for Swarthmore College, the University of California at Berkeley, and Harvard University. A bibliography and index complete the volume.

This edition devotes more space to computer applications and networking, and omits much of the guide to literature found in the first volume. The work is a welcome addition to the growing publications about special libraries. [R: LJ, 1 May 85, p. 42; WLB, June 85, p. 699]
          Andrew G. Torok

346. Sherrod, John, and Alfred Hodina, eds. **Reader in Science Information.** Washington, D.C., Microcard Editions, 1973. 403p. (Reader Series in Library and Information Science). $28.50. LC 72-97713. ISBN 0-910972-20-6.

Another volume in this well-established series of readers prepared under the general editorship of Paul Wasserman. A total of 30 articles are arranged under five subject categories — science and society, nature and function of science information, primary information sources (SATCOM and COSATI reports, among other things), secondary information services (more SATCOM reports), and management of science information. Appendix B, "Guides to the Literature of Science and Technology," is a simple checklist of selected reference books that is not always up-to-date (e.g., the listings for mathematics). All in all, a useful publication. [R: RSR, Jan 74, p. 31]   Bohdan S. Wynar

347. Sloane, Richard, and Marie Wallace. **Private Law Library: 1980's and Beyond.** New York, Practicing Law Institute, 1979. 320p. (Patents, Copyrights, Trademarks and Literary Property, Course Handbook Series, No. 107). $35.00. LC 79-87893. ISBN 0-686-59557-2.

Providing essential information on all facets of private law libraries, this guide was prepared for distribution at a program sponsored by the Practicing Law Institute, a body that sponsors several series of continuing legal education programs for lawyers. The volume contains articles on space planning, design, information management, cost control, computer applications, and other relevant topics. The list of contributors is a roster of the most prominent law firm law librarians in the country. There are also a useful 16-page bibliography and three articles on coordinated research reprinted from the *New York Law Journal.* As with any assemblage of articles, the quality of the pieces varies, and the book suffers the format problems common to all PLI books — since they are prepared for distribution at the program, speed, and not consistency or ease of use, is emphasized. Still, *Private Law Library* is an important work and one that any institution which purports to collect in the areas of special libraries or collection management should have. [R: SL, Nov 79, p. 502]   Robert C. Berring

348. Special Libraries Association, Transportation Division, comp. **Transportation Libraries in the United States and Canada: An SLA Directory.** 3rd ed. New York, Special Libraries Association, 1978. 221p. index. o.p. LC 77-17615. ISBN 0-87111-233-7.

First published in 1968, the second edition of this work (1973, see *ARBA* 74, entry 176) appeared under the title *Directory of Transportation Libraries in the United States and Canada*. In its third edition, this is a useful information source as far as it goes, but it falls short of being a truly comprehensive guide to transportation collections in the United States and Canada. It is based on a questionnaire (a copy of which is appended to the text), but neither the basis for distributing this questionnaire nor the percentage of response is indicated. Most of the libraries listed are affiliated with businesses or governmental agencies dealing with transportation, with little coverage of special collections in public or academic libraries, so one may probably infer that the Division's membership roster was the basis of the mailing list. The 205 entries vary in completeness of response, but those that are complete include name; address; phone number; date of establishment; name of principal librarian; size of professional and clerical staff; network affiliations; detailed description of the collection, indicating both format and content of materials included; services available to unaffiliated users (including interlibrary loan policies); and a list of regularly issued publications. Arrangement is alphabetical by name of agency, with personal name, subject, and geographical indexes providing good access (it may be worth noting that "Pedestrians" rates as many index entries as "Motorcycles": two each). Researchers in the field (especially those concerned with current problems rather than historical development) and interlibrary loan departments will need to have this book available, despite its selective coverage. [R: LJ, July 78, p. 1363]

Paul B. Cors

349.   The State Library Agencies: A Survey Project Report, 1983. 6th ed. Compiled and edited by the ASCLA Headquarters Staff in cooperation with the Chief Officers of State Library Agencies. Chicago, Association of Specialized and Cooperative Library Agencies/American Library Association, 1983. 359p. $25.00pa.; $22.50pa. (members). LC 81-68269. ISBN 0-8389-6603-9.

An invaluable reference tool for librarians in any capacity, this work will find a specialized target audience with library administrators and planners. Providing succinct, up-to-date, and readable information supplied by respective state agencies—as well as useful summary appendices—*State Library Agencies* profiles the complexities and salient characteristics of each state agency. Of the 50 states, only 4—Hawaii, North Carolina, North Dakota, and Oregon—did not provide information. The remaining 47 agencies (2 from Massachusetts) responded with a wealth of information.

Basic directory information is provided for each state, as well as a descriptive statement regarding the place of that agency in the respective state government organization. A summary of the powers, duties, and purpose of the state library agency, as defined by the creating authority, is followed by a matrix of personnel distribution throughout the agency. This matrix is then amplified through a key staff roster that provides names, titles, addresses, phone numbers, and areas of responsibility for the administrative/planning staff of the agency.

Summary descriptive statements indicating specific advisory groups that work with the agency are included, followed by detailed statements of the major functional units of the state library agency. A description of the services, responsibilities, and functions of each unit, as well as an indication of who receives the services, is included. In addition, notable activities and major program emphases of each agency are briefly described, as are special services and special projects. Recurring publications of the agency, as well as recent publications (since January 1981), are listed, concluding with an organizational chart for the agency.

With a prefatory overview by F. William Summer and 15 summary appendices, *State Library Agencies* is arranged alphabetically by state. It remains unique in supplying so much necessary information regarding state library agencies. Public, academic, school, and special libraries could all avail themselves of the information in this volume and reap benefits from the profiles.   Edmund F. SantaVicca

350.   Whatmore, Geoffrey. The Modern News Library: Documentation of Current Affairs in Newspaper and Broadcasting Libraries. Syracuse, N.Y., Gaylord Professional Publications, 1978. 202p. illus. index. o.p. LC 78-16174. ISBN 0-915794-35-7.

Whatmore draws examples from his years of experience in a variety of British newspaper libraries to provide a general overview of the problems involved in developing, maintaining, and managing a newspaper library. The chapters are: "Library for News"; "Stock, Sources, and Selection"; "Intake, Issues, and Inquiries"; "Classification, Arrangement, and Order"; "Subject Organisation"; "The

Treatment of Location"; "Personality Aspect"; "Sequences for Special Subjects"; "Finding Aids"; "Files, Folders, and Furniture"; "New Technology"; and "Mainly for Management."

Although the book will be of some interest to American librarians, its British emphasis limits its application as a textbook or handbook for practice in the United States. G. Edward Evans

Part 4

LIBRARY SERVICES AND
SPECIFIC TOPICS

22 Architecture, Facilities, and Equipment

351. Bahr, Alice Harrison. **Book Theft and Library Security Systems, 1981-82.** White Plains, N.Y., Knowledge Industry Publications, 1981. 157p. illus. bibliog. index. (Professional Librarian Series). o.p. LC 80-26643. ISBN 0-914236-71-7.

In the new edition of her book, *Book Theft and Library Security Systems, 1981-82,* Alice Harrison Bahr discusses ways to achieve greater security for libraries. Electronic security systems such as Checkpoint, Sentronic, LPS International, 3M Company, Knogo, and Gaylord are described, with many photos included. Descriptions of each security system tell who sells the equipment, how it works, what it costs, what it protects, how it is installed, and special features of the system. The author discusses the cost effectiveness of security systems and analyzes the similarities and differences of the various systems. In addition to the descriptions, there is a short section of library users' reports on the effectiveness of systems in selected libraries. Only 21 libraries are queried concerning satisfaction with the systems used, but an appendix, although only a partial list, includes many libraries using electronic security systems. Separate chapters discuss methods of measuring book losses, alternatives to electronic systems, and protection of journals, nonprint materials, and special collections. For librarians contemplating the installation of a library security system, this book should be a useful resource. For a review of the 1978-79 edition, see *ARBA* 79 (entry 250). [R: LJ, 15 Nov 81, p. 2219]
Marilyn T. Thompson

352. Baumann, Charles H. **The Influence of Angus Snead MacDonald and the Snead Bookstack on Library Architecture.** Metuchen, N.J., Scarecrow, 1972. 307p. illus. index. $16.00. LC 74-171928. ISBN 0-8108-0390-9.

Baumann's revised doctoral dissertation is a well-written and interesting book which examines the proposition, "Angus Snead MacDonald ... was one of the principal forces responsible for the radical changes in library architecture after World War II" (p. 9). The text covers such topics as the development of American library architecture to 1941; a biography of MacDonald; a history of Snead and Company; MacDonald's theory of library planning and construction; a major section on module construction; and an analysis of other factors which influenced post-World War II library construction. The book is carefully documented and provides some useful insights into MacDonald's concept of library construction and the use of the module to achieve a highly flexible environment. As a reference book it will be of very limited value: the bibliography is selective, but rather long (25 pages), the survey of library buildings 1930-1960 is of little current planning value, and the floor plans which are included are of only historical interest.
G. Edward Evans

353. Brawne, Michael. **Libraries: Architecture and Equipment.** New York, Praeger, 1970. 188p. illus. index. bibliog. o.p. LC 73-89609. ISBN 0-269-02520-0.

This volume is the work of an English professor of architecture who is also a practicing architect. The volume is divided into three major categories: public libraries, research libraries, and national and large university libraries. Those included represent American, German, Italian and Scandinavian examples, with many interior and exterior illustrations, none of which is in color. There is also a chapter on library operations and services, necessary considerations in designing a library facility. Useful for both architects and librarians. [R: LJ, 1 June 70, p. 2106]   Charles D. Patterson

354. Cohen, Aaron, and Elaine Cohen. **Designing and Space Planning for Libraries: A Behavioral Guide.** New York, R. R. Bowker, 1979. 250p. illus. (part col.). bibliog. index. $32.50. LC 79-12478. ISBN 0-8352-1150-9.

Architect Aaron Cohen and behaviorist Elaine Cohen have put together an extremely readable and informative book on designing, building, or renovating a library and allocating space within it. Guidelines are given, listing the step-by-step procedures that should be followed when undertaking the project. A very helpful chapter on who does what describes the roles of the numerous professionals (consultants, architects, engineers, contractors, etc.) who come into play and how they might interact. Fees for these jobs are also discussed on a percentage-of-cost basis. The chapters "Acoustics" and "Lighting, Power and Energy" reflect the late 1970s time frame, especially the latter chapter and its acknowledgment of the energy situation.

The authors claim that human behavior should be on an equal footing with the physical planning that occurs in library design. Although they do discuss psychology of change and examine the behavioral aspects of space, the chapters concerning the library building itself and what goes into it predominate.

While this book can be viewed as a basic text on the subject, its value lies in the authors' ability to point out both the advantages and disadvantages of a variety of situations confronting those laypersons responsible for their library's design. The book is illustrated throughout with pictures, charts, and diagrams. A two-and-one-half-page bibliography is included. [R: BL, 15 Jan 80, p. 698; C&RL, Mar 80, p. 175; CLW, Sept 80, p. 92; JAL, July 80, p. 166; LJ, 1 Feb 80, p. 362; LQ, July 80, p. 386; LR, Summer 80, p. 132; SL, July 80, p. 331]
Marjorie E. Bloss

355. Draper, James, and James Brooks. **Interior Design for Libraries.** Chicago, American Library Association, 1979. 152p. illus. bibliog.

index. $10.00. LC 79-16635. ISBN 0-8389-0282-0.

After almost eight years in which no new books on library space planning appeared, during 1979 three new books on the subject were published. Each one (the Cohens's *Designing and Space Planning for Libraries* and Lushington and Mills's *Libraries Designed for Users*) has some special and useful features; however, this relatively small book has something to offer every type of library. Given the present economic conditions, very few libraries will have the luxury of getting a new building or even a major addition. Almost all libraries are presently or soon will be facing their limits of growth. Draper and Brooks are only concerned with the interior design problems of libraries. Their chapter titles, such as "Stepping Out," "Give Your Windows a Treat," or "Up against the Wall," are more indicative of their style of writing (light and very upbeat) than of content. They provide some background material on scale drawings, use of templates, and standard architectural symbols before addressing the major issues of effective/efficient interior design. Topics such as handling traffic flow (people and books); use of color and signs; furniture, fabrics, and finishes; wall and window treatments; storage and workroom spaces; along with some tips on budgeting and getting the most for your money are all given fairly detailed treatment.

The major lack is that there is no in-depth discussion on evaluating alternative interior design possibilities. Aside from that limitation, this is a fine book that deserves a place in all medium- and large-sized libraries. It may also be used as one of several textbooks in a library space planning class, as it has the most complete current coverage of interior design problems in libraries. [R: BL, 15 Apr 80, p. 1177; C&RL, May 80, pp. 275-76; JAL, Mar 80, p. 58; LJ, 1 May 80, p. 1052; SLJ, Nov 80, p. 48]
G. Edward Evans

356. Ellsworth, Ralph E. **Academic Library Buildings: A Guide to Architectural Issues and Solutions.** Boulder, Colo., Colorado Associated University Press, 1973. 530p. illus. index. o.p. LC 72-83499. ISBN 0-87081-042-1.

According to the preface, "this book attempts to present representative examples of successful architectural solutions to the important problems librarians and architects face in planning new college and university library buildings or in remodeling and enlarging existing structures" (p. xi). Ralph Ellsworth is one of the best-known consultants for library architecture in this country. The approach of this book, however, differs from the approach in the author's other works, *Planning the College and University Library Building* and *The School Library*. This one is actually an annotated pictorial record of 130 academic libraries, with some 1,500 photos. The text is kept to a minimum and, as the author admits, it does not attempt to make case study evaluation. Metcalf's *Planning Academic and Research Library Buildings* (McGraw-Hill, 1965) is now certainly dated, but it is still the best overall study on this subject. [R: C&RL, Sept 73, p. 286; LJ, 15 June 73, p. 1895] Bohdan S. Wynar

357. Ellsworth, Ralph E. **Planning Manual for Academic Library Buildings.** Metuchen, N.J., Scarecrow, 1973. 159p. illus. bibliog. index. o.p. LC 73-14896. ISBN 0-8108-0680-0.

Ralph Ellsworth is a person who would be able to get 60 miles per gallon while driving an Indianapolis "500" car through the Colorado mountains. His *Planning Manual for Academic Library Buildings* is an example of how many books he can produce on one topic. This is his eighth book on library building problems. It draws heavily on all of his previous publications and contains little new material. The purpose, however, is clearly stated in both the text and the publisher's statement. "This manual presents in a concise manner the information an institution would need in order to plan a library building. Aimed for librarians, campus planners, architects, trustees, and faculty committees who are *not* experienced in library planning, it briefly describes the best methods for planning academic buildings and discusses some of the typical problems encountered in the process."

Ellsworth succeeded in producing a concise *overview* of the methods and problems in planning academic library buildings. He does not, nor do I think he intended to, provide all "the information an institution would need in order to plan a library building." The book must be viewed as supplemental to other more comprehensive works, such as Metcalf's. Without question this book provides an excellent current overview for the inexperienced planning team, but that is all.

The most likely use for the *Planning Manual* will be in library school courses on building planning. The basic elements are discussed: the concept program; how to use existing knowledge and experience in writing a program; how to select the architect and planning consultant; the service plan; growth and expansion; audiovisual materials; building costs; units of measurement; and physical requirements of certain departments in the library. It does not provide *the* answer to the questions raised, although Ellsworth does say he is going to describe the *best* methods. Some people may expect to find the magic formula for the Instant Successful Academic Library Building; needless to say, they will (and should) be disappointed in what they find.

There are several reasons why the book will be used primarily in workshops and library school courses. First, most of the planning process is a matter of opinion, and here one has only Ellsworth's opinions as to what is best. When he discusses planning failures, he says one must be careful to distinguish between failures and differences of opinion; he is not always careful to note, however, when something is fact and when it is his opinion. He makes such a distinction in his other books, but—since this book is for inexperienced people—he should not assume that his readers are familiar with his other books.

A problem related to the confusion between fact and opinion stems from the way the book is referenced—or, rather, is *not* referenced. Since it is brief, introductory, and supplemental, one would expect to find a fairly extensive reference system; but this is not the case. One example of the problem is on page 31: "However, the basic studies that have been made of this method show that sending little-used books to a storage system does not save money and usually creates inconvenience and antagonism among the library's users (Rider, Ash, Fussler, Ellsworth, Shishko)." All these writers have written a number of books and articles; which ones are relevant? Do these writers have first names? The audience addressed by the book is broader than librarians, and even many librarians will not know Shishko. Also, there are other studies of this subject, which are not listed. Finally, the statement is really Ellsworth's opinion of the findings, rather than conclusions that the reader will find in the cited studies. The book simply does not provide the reader with enough leads to other literature. This is unfortunate; with a good reference system, this could have been an outstanding book. [R: RSR, Apr 74, p. 19]

G. Edward Evans

358. Hannigan, Jane Anne, and Glenn E. Estes, comps. and eds. **Media Center Facilities Design.** Chicago, American Library Association, 1978. 117p. illus. bibliog. index. $13.00pa. LC 78-9336. ISBN 0-8389-3212-6.

Reprints from *School Media Quarterly* issues for Spring 1974 and Summer 1976 and from other previously published documents are supplemented here by material expressly written for this publication. Easily the most readable among the latter are Peggy Sullivan's observations on how to live with what the architect has wrought. Neither architects nor media people can get much help from this volume, however. As in any anthology, there is much repetition in the total of 28 separate papers. A small number of illustrations does little to relieve page after page of unrelentingly closely spaced text. There are some useful tables and checklists but, astonishingly, only one floor plan. For the easy-to-use, well-illustrated reference that such a pragmatic subject requires, media center planners had better turn to *LJ Special Report No. 3: The Learning Resources Center* (64p., $3.95pa.). [R: BL, 1 Nov 78, p. 486]

Mary R. Sive

359. Holt, Raymond M., ed. **An Architectural Strategy for Change: Remodeling and Expanding for Contemporary Public Library Needs.** Proceedings of the Library Architectural Preconference Institute held at New York, N.Y., 4-6 July 1974 under the sponsorship of the Architecture for Public Libraries Committee, Buildings and Equipment Section, Library Administration Division, American Library Association. Chicago, American Library Association, 1976. 149p. illus. o.p. LC 76-7965. ISBN 0-8389-0210-3.

Published institute proceedings seldom provide the same impact as attending an institute. Certain types of institutes lend themselves more readily to a published format; architectural institutes are not among those types. The cost of publishing all the graphic material used in the presentations is too high to justify the procedure. As a result, an editor must select the most important items for inclusion, and the publication is never as good as the in-person presentation. This volume suffers from these problems; almost all of the sessions included graphics, and only a few could be published. Allie Beth Martin used a film as part of her keynote address, and some of her remarks assume that one viewed the film. Nevertheless, her address is the best section in the volume. Seven library buildings and their remodeling needs were discussed at the institute (Martin Luther King Memorial, Washington, D.C.; Rosenberg Library, Galveston, Texas; Tulsa City-County Library, Oklahoma; Tenzler Branch, Tacoma, Washington; Musser Library, Muscatine, Iowa; Skokie Public Library, Illi-

nois; and Richmond Public Library, Virginia). The format follows the typical ALA buildings institute form—a building presentation by an architect and/or librarian followed by a group discussion. Some buildings were also critiqued by a building consultant. Each session is reported and the critical graphics presented. There were also two workshop sessions—median and building plans—which were summarized by the workshop directors.

Anyone interested in remodeling problems will find a new idea or two but will have to go through material that is 90 to 98 percent familiar to find the new; there is no index. Despite the promise of new insights into the impact of media and new technologies on libraries, there is really very little on that topic in the volume. All in all, a book of limited value. [R: LQ, Oct 77, p. 493]

G. Edward Evans

360. Kaula, Prithvi N. **Library Buildings: Planning and Design.** New Delhi, Vikas Publications; distr., Dobbs Ferry, N.Y., Oceana, 1971. 237p. illus. index. bibliog. o.p. LC 76-917423. ISBN 0-379-00304-X.

This book is intended to guide those planning library facilities but it probably holds little appeal for American librarians. Contains chapters on the development of the library and other topics, the importance of which is most appropriate for a local situation in India. Three appendices deal with seating capacity, the Indian University Grants Commission Standard for Library Buildings, and standards for toilet facilities per hundred by sex. Illustrations consist of a series of floor plans. [R: LJ, 1 Apr 72, p. 1249]

Charles D. Patterson

361. Langmead, Stephen, and Margaret Beckman. **New Library Design: Guide Lines to Planning Academic Library Buildings.** New York, Wiley, 1970. 117p. illus. index. bibliog. o.p. LC 70-155107. SBN 471-51717-8.

This handbook, written in simple nontechnical language, was based primarily on activities connected with the McLaughlin Library, University of Guelph, in Canada. It covers such subjects as campus planning, collection of data, and library design and construction, and has a separate chapter on the McLaughlin Library. Illustrations are kept to a bare minimum, although there are some charts and statistical data, usually relating to Canadian standards. In general, this text might be of some assistance to the uninitiated. [R: LJ, 15 June 71, p. 2063]

362. Lushington, Nolan, and Willis N. Mills, Jr. **Libraries Designed for Users: A Planning**

Handbook. Syracuse, N.Y., Gaylord Professional Publications, 1979. 289p. illus. bibliog. index. $27.50. LC 78-27114. ISBN 0-915794-29-2.

A librarian and an architect have produced a useful overview of the process and particulars of planning a public library building for communities of up to 100,000 population. The guiding principle is user convenience in a library building that makes possible personalized service and efficient self-service, and enables a complex service organization to function on an intimate personal level.

The book is as valuable for its approach to the planning process as it is in offering checklists of service areas and processing requirements. Knowledge of the community, a library self-study of its physical needs and its function for the community, use of consultants on planning and selecting, and working with an architect are discussed. Sample cases for critiquing are offered to illustrate more technical points in the text.

Information is provided on lighting choice, energy conservation, graphics, facilities for handicapped users, parking, and site location. This information is not technical, but provides a framework for intelligent discussion of specific plans to be developed by the architect. Included are chapters on overall library organization for services, designing children's and adult service areas, and school library media center design.

Weaknesses include a lack of specific documentation to take the reader further into the technical aspects. Some informal citations are included in the text, but are not repeated in an appendix or in the bibliography. The bibliography reflects the book's more social, user-centered approach to design. The handbook will be useful to librarians and trustees who were introduced to planning in *Design of the Small Public Library* by Rolf Myller (R. R. Bowker, 1966) and who received more specific planning information not focused on the public library in *Planning and Design of Library Buildings* (see *ARBA* 79, entry 260). [R: LJ, 1 Nov 79, p. 2290]
Sharon C. Bonk

363. Mason, Ellsworth. **Mason on Library Buildings.** Metuchen, N.J., Scarecrow, 1980. 333p. illus. index. $35.00. LC 80-12029. ISBN 0-8108-1291-6.

This collection of Mason's writings has been put together to share with people planning new buildings all he has learned by planning and observing the building of academic, community college, and elementary and secondary school libraries over the last 20 years. Some of the chapters have been revised from earlier published format. Others, specifically the reviews of six library buildings, have not been readily accessible.

The author's purpose for bringing these writings together is his concern about the paucity of good current literature in this area, beyond the standard works of Metcalf and Ellsworth (Metcalf's *Planning Academic and Research Library Buildings*, McGraw-Hill, 1965, and Ellsworth's *Planning the College and University Library Building*, Pruett Press, 1968). Public library planners should also be aware of *Libraries Designed for Users* by N. Lushington (Gaylord Professional Publications, 1979; see *ARBA* 80, entry 162). The author is aware of the difficulty of doing a good job of planning because of all the details, people, and specialized knowledge needed. With this information before them, future library planners have solid ground from which to begin the "multifarious ... chaos-prone process."

The book has three sections. Part 1 is Mason's views on the planning process, lighting, air control systems, and interior design. Part 2, a detailed review of six major libraries, is most instructive in its detail. Appended are a model planning document for use in considering, analyzing, and reporting details of functions, space, and staffing to architects before they present their plans, and a summary evaluation of 105 other libraries. [R: LJ, Aug 80, p. 1612]
Sharon C. Bonk

364. Metcalf, Keyes D. **Library Lighting.** Washington, D.C., Association of Research Libraries, 1970. 99p. index. o.p. LC 76-141351.

Presents the results of a survey directed to 52 "professional" experts (architects, engineers, research scholars, interior designers, physicians, etc.) none of whom are librarians, who responded to 130 questions concerning lighting in academic libraries. The questions, answers, and the author's comments form the bulk of the book, which, although it contains much worthwhile information, lacks an index. Data on providing lighting according to need and function and concerning lighting cost are particularly useful. [R: C&RL, Sept 71, p. 393; LJ, 15 May 71, p. 1688]
Charles D. Patterson

365. Meyers, Gerald E. **Insurance Manual for Libraries.** Chicago, American Library Association, 1977. 64p. $7.00pa. LC 77-24524. ISBN 0-8389-0236-7.

Prepared by the Insurance for Libraries Committee of the Library Organization Management Section, Library Administration

Division, American Library Association, this "how-to-do-it" manual is an updating and expansion of an earlier manual prepared by six Illinois library systems for the use of their libraries. It is divided into nine chapters, each covering a particular aspect of library insurance problems (e.g., procedures for handling the insurance program, analysis of risks, appraisals and valuation of property, rates and premiums, claims, etc.). The insurance approach applied is that of "Risk Management," using information on the relative impact and probability of losses to determine whether risks should be covered by outside insurance or be self-insured. This manual is applicable to most libraries, and the appendices provide sample forms and checklists suitable for small and medium-sized, as well as larger, libraries. A short glossary of insurance terms is also provided.

366. Morris, John. Managing the Library Fire Risk. 2nd ed. Berkeley, Calif., University of California, Office of Risk Management, 1979. 147p. illus. (part col.). bibliog. $15.50. LC 78-22603. ISBN 0-9602278-1-4.

This is an expansion of the 1975 work (see *ARBA* 76, entry 118), which was published by the Office of Insurance and Risk Management of the University of California at Berkeley to update the existing guides. Since the first edition was not widely publicized or distributed through the book trade, and because of more recent testing and product development, this update was issued. It also includes information on user and staff safety and disaster preparedness. The photos of burning libraries, library ruins, and damaged books, as well as arson statistics and lists and accounts of recent and historic library fires, are bound to scare administrators into improving fire protection systems. The book serves well as a background guide, giving technical information in summary form, selected reprints from technical literature, and an extensive bibliography. The knowledge gained by the administrators is to be used in planning with fire protection engineers. It is not a do-it-yourself manual.   Sharon C. Bonk

367. Mount, Ellis, ed. Planning the Special Library. New York, Special Libraries Association, 1972. 122p. illus. (SLA Monograph, No. 4). $11.00pa. LC 72-85956. ISBN 0-87111-205-1.

This volume is intended for use by the special librarian who, when given the opportunity, is asked to participate in the planning, designing, or furnishing of the special library. Papers are by experienced librarians and cover

all aspects of the planning process and include selected examples of floor plans and other illustrations, checklists, and a bibliography of related literature. Too detailed for the novice and too elementary for the experienced librarian. [R: C&RL, July 73, p. 319; LJ, 1 Apr 73, p. 1096]   Charles D. Patterson

368. New Academic Library Buildings/II. Karl Nyren, ed. New York, R. R. Bowker, 1982. 72p. illus. (LJ Special Report, No. 23). $8.50pa. (prepaid); $10.00pa. (billed). ISBN 0-8352-1601-2; ISSN 0362-448X.

Like its predecessor (LJ Special Report No. 16, 1981), this *LJ*-format "volume" is based on a previous *LJ Architectural Issue*, in this case, that of 1 December 1979. Bare statistical and other basic data on 21 buildings are expanded to include statements by the responsible librarian and, usually, the architect. Coverage ranges from modest projects (Ramapo College, N.J.) to major buildings (University of Cincinnati), both new and remodeled. The editor notes specifically that this is not intended as a "top ten" selection, but as a cross-section. The volume would be far more useful if (a) there were floor plans, at least of one major floor of each building (there are none), and (b) the many and generally excellent illustrations were captioned (many are hard to interpret, since the text doesn't always identify the particular area shown). As it is, it will have limited reference use for students of library buildings and librarians engaged in building projects.
                    Walter C. Allen

369. New Library Buildings, 1974 Issue. Herbert Ward, ed. London, Library Association, 1974. 140p. illus. £8.00pa. ISBN 0-85365-397-6.

Sixty-five public, university, and special library buildings in England, Wales, and Scotland, built during 1971 and 1972, are assessed and illustrated in this second issue of *New Library Buildings*.

Each library is thoroughly described and evaluated on architectural style, functional performance, and building elements, such as sites, air-conditioning, floor plans, clockrooms, transportation and parking facilities, lighting, atmosphere, traffic patterns, accessibility to handicapped patrons, exhibition areas, staff rooms, auditoriums, views from windows, carpeting, color, not to mention the furniture and shelving, and much, much more.

Statistics of space, costs, volumes, mechanical services, special features, and population served, together with the names of architects and librarians, complete the library's profile. Good photographs and scale diagrams of floor plans give visual impact to the text.

Anyone planning to build a new library building or renovate an existing building would find this excellent work extremely informative. It will give answers to questions as yet unthought of, but worthy of advance contemplation. The book is also recommended for architectural collections as a prototype for standards of architectural evaluation. [R: LJ, 15 June 75, p. 1196] Patricia C. Harpole

370. Novak, Gloria, ed. **Running Out of Space—What Are the Alternatives?: Proceedings of the Preconference, June 1975, San Francisco.** Chicago, American Library Association, 1978. 160p. $15.00pa. LC 78-1796. ISBN 0-8389-3215-0.

This volume, the proceedings of an ALA preconference sponsored by the Buildings for College and University Libraries Committee, Building and Equipment Section of the Library Administration Division, is based on papers presented at the 1975 San Francisco Conference. This 160-page, typed photo-offset volume is divided into seven basic sections—book storage; microforms as a substitute; space utilization; cooperation; new buildings versus addition or renovation; funding; and, finally, a view of the situation from outside the profession. Each of the sections concludes with a question and answer/discussion session. Unfortunately, because the proceedings are evidently taken from transcribed tapes, some of the commentators are not identified at all and others by last name only.

Many of the papers are accounts of experiences that individual speakers have had with their own libraries—Harvard's and the University of Washington's experiences with storage facilities, MIT's work with project Intrex, the University of California's experience with regional planning, the University of British Columbia's underground addition, and the University of Texas's central library. There is no index and there is no list of conference attendees, both of which would have been helpful. This is a useful volume in that it does relate individual experiences and presents alternative solutions to the problem being explored. Although the conference was limited in scope, the volume is a useful supplement to standard works on library buildings. [R: C&RL, Sept 78, p. 412]

Robert D. Stueart

371. Pierce, William S. **Furnishing the Library Interior.** New York, Marcel Dekker, 1980.

288p. illus. index. (Books in Library and Information Science, Vol. 29). $55.00. LC 79-25569. ISBN 0-8247-6900-7.

Presenting insights from two decades of the author's consulting on library interiors, this work deals with space planning; housing of users; work stations for professional staff; outfitting of reception, map, rare book, and other special areas; storage of print and nonprint media; the selection, evaluation, and purchase of library furniture, equipment, and appointments; and the writing of specifications for library purchases. Generously illustrated with photographs taken by the author during visits to well over 200 libraries of successful and unsuccessful interiors, including lobbies, children's story areas, circulation and reference desks, audiovisual, micrographic, and computer equipment, carrels, shelving, seating, file cabinets, catalogs, etc., this volume should prove of some use to those involved in the planning of attractive and functional library space.

Displaying a strongly traditional orientation, this work devotes 27 pages to shelving, 11 pages to carrels, and less than a page to computer terminals and facilities. Because it touches too briefly on many essential aspects of library interior treatment, this work is no substitute for an up-to-date library consultant. Indexed, with no footnotes, and a highly selective 13-item bibliography. [R: C&RL, Sept 80, pp. 464-65; LJ, July 80, p. 1493] Richard Palmer

372. **Planning Barrier Free Libraries: A Guide for Renovation and Construction of Libraries Serving Blind and Physically Handicapped Readers.** Washington, D.C., Library of Congress, National Library Service for the Blind and Physically Handicapped, 1981. 61p. illus. free. pa. LC 80-607821. ISBN 0-8444-0352-0.

This guide to making library buildings free from barriers for the handicapped was prepared by Charles A. Moss, Jr., of an Alabama architectural firm, in consultation with a regional librarian, Miriam M. Pace. It serves both architects who are unfamiliar with library programs and librarians who do not know architects' information needs. Emphasis is on new buildings, although there is a final chapter on renovations. There are many illustrations of the architect's way of thinking—functional relationship design drawings, schematic designs, elevations, and material movement flow diagrams. Every page is idea-laden; for instance, topics covered include the fragrance garden, the tactile map floor plan, a recess for blind guide sticks with a break at each stopping point, changes in floor surfacing to differentiate area changes, and restroom adaptations. Appropriate standards and codes, as well as sources for more information, are identified.

Any librarian who is contemplating major, or even minor, building or renovation will find this an important reference. Construction of functional space for both workers and patrons is difficult enough; adding barrier-free environment spices up the challenge, as the authors assert.   Doris H. Banks

373. Pollet, Dorothy, and Peter C. Haskell, comps. and eds. **Sign Systems for Libraries: Solving the Wayfinding Problem.** New York, R. R. Bowker, 1979. 271p. illus. bibliog. index. $24.95. LC 79-11138. ISBN 0-8352-1149-5.

If you have entered a library, felt welcome, completed your task, and left feeling satisfied, it was not accidental but the result of an awareness on the part of building designers of how individuals relate to space and how they navigate within that space. If you have lost your way in the library, unable to find people or resources you were seeking, you do not need to be convinced of the importance of an appropriate, nonconfusing, legible sign system.

The editors-compilers have approached the subject of sign systems from the user's viewpoint as well as from that of the designer. Chapters on the way in which people approach public service environments and the way in which they develop wayfinding behavior are particularly well done, summarizing research from many disciplines, including psychology, anthropology, and geography. Steps in the design of a visual guidance system are described, and the needs of different clientele—among them, the child, the adult, the visually impaired—are indicated. Sign systems, meanings of symbols, and uses of architectural design to lead people from one location to another are discussed by experts in library and information science, architecture, psychology, and graphic design, and by users.

Additional chapters are devoted to a discussion of graphics appropriate to various situations, and case studies of sign system development are provided. Bibliographies with the chapters and at the book's end cover both the behavioral and the graphic aspects of sign systems. The book is well illustrated. Highly recommended for all individuals who are responsible for making libraries inviting and library resources easily available to the user. [R: BL, 15 Oct 79, p. 329; C&RL, Nov 79, pp. 568-69; LJ, 15 Nov 79, p. 2422]
                                      Ann E. Prentice

374. Schell, Hal B., ed. **Reader on the Library Building.** Westport, Conn., Greenwood Press, 1975. 359p. illus. index. (Reader Series in Library and Information Science). $28.50. LC 73-93967. ISBN 0-313-24049-3.

This reader, one of a long series issued by the publisher, assembles about 45 previously published writings under nine part headings, ranging from "The Past and Future of Library Buildings" to "Furnishings and Equipment." The other main topics are the use of consultants, building programs, selection of sites, staff spaces, mechanical spaces, and space requirements for computer equipment.

All of the well-known librarian-experts on library buildings are represented in this anthology, some of them repeatedly. Among the latter are Keyes Metcalf, Ellsworth Mason, and Martin Van Buren. The main and part introductions are exceedingly brief and add little to the book. [R: JAL, July 76, p. 140]
                                      Richard A. Gray

375. Thompson, Godfrey. **Planning and Design of Library Buildings.** 2nd ed. London, Architectural Press; distr., New York, Nichols, 1977. 189p. illus. bibliog. index. $75.00. LC 77-137. ISBN 0-89397-019-0.

This work is probably the best single source in English of information on planning new physical spaces for a library. It covers all types of libraries (public, academic, and industrial/special) and topics in more depth than any American title published at the same time. Library functions and the relationship of these functions to physical space requirements appear to be universal in nature; therefore, there is little difficulty in using this book in the United States.

The basic structure (chapter headings, format, and such special features as providing both metric and British Imperial measurements) remains the same as in the first edition (1974). However, this edition places more emphasis on remodeling and renovating old libraries rather than on constructing new buildings, thereby reflecting the economic situation. Thompson also devotes attention to the problems of energy conservation, but his treatment of energy conservation is the major weakness in the book. Given the nature of long-term energy problems, it would have been reasonable to prepare an entire chapter on this issue. As anyone who has attempted to work with this problem knows, it is complex and filled with alternative approaches. Librarians need some information on the pros and cons of the major trade-offs in this area (is it better to use more windows for maximum natural light and face a heat transfer problem because of the expanded fenestration or vice versa?). In the sections on space requirements, especially for storage of nonbook materials, Thompson has made a number of changes and provided expanded, detailed information based upon new data and first edition reader input. [R: BL, 15 May 78, p. 1479; JAL, Sept 78, p. 228]

G. Edward Evans

376. Trezza, Alphonse F., ed. **Library Buildings: Innovation for Changing Needs.** Chicago, American Library Association, Library Admin-

istration Division, 1972. 293p. illus. bibliog. (Proceedings of the Library Building Institute Conducted at San Francisco, California, June 22-24, 1967). o.p. LC 73-39011. ISBN 0-8389-3132-4.

This volume provides analysis of eight academic libraries as detailed in a series of institute papers that present a variety of problems faced by university libraries, college libraries, and the specialized library in an academic setting. It includes a good selection of libraries which represent a cross-section of various types. Excellent illustrations include floor plans for each, some facades of buildings, and a few site diagrams. [R: C&RL, May 73, p. 228; LJ, 1 Dec 72, p. 3878]

Charles D. Patterson

23 Archives and Special Collections

377. Cave, Roderick. **Rare Book Librarianship.** 2nd rev. ed. London, Clive Bingley, distr., Hamden, Conn., Shoe String Press, 1982. 162p. bibliog. index. $20.00. ISBN 0-85157-328-2.

Thorough, practical, sensible, and concise were words used to describe the first edition in 1976 (see *ARBA* 77, entry 191) and all remain true of this 1982 edition. The nature of rare books, why and how they are different, and what special treatment such materials should receive are all covered in a compact, straightforward manner in this now standard text for the field. Fortunately, the book is also sprinkled with dry wit gleaned from obviously long and deep experience.

The 11 chapters, covering background, acquisitions, cataloging, processing, care and restoration, organizing collections, publicity, and administrative aspects, are the same. The newer edition has 162 pages rather than 168, but most of this difference is an increase of four lines on a fully printed page. The text indicates considerable rewriting, polishing, and updating. Footnotes, bibliography, and textual references add new scope. At the same time, many passages remain word for word. But no reason exists to change material which is excellent and which needs no revision. It is also instructive to be introduced to doryphores, the marginal annotators of books, and to caoutchouc (unsewn) binding.

The viewpoint is British, but it is also broad, often considerate of the user. The treatment is comprehensive, even in such a brief text. The bibliography is a solid introduction, the index works, and the book production is solid. All librarians who want to know at least the basics in this field should study, savor, and appreciate this edition of Cave's work. [R: JAL, Jan 83, p. 367]   Neal L. Edgar

378. Clark, Robert L., Jr., ed. **Archive-Library Relations.** New York, R. R. Bowker, 1976. 218p. bibliog. index. o.p. LC 76-18806. ISBN 0-8352-0770-6.

Similarities and dissimilarities of the archival and library professions have often confused, amused, and plagued their respective practitioners for years. "This is the first comprehensive book dealing with the joint concerns and relationships of the two professions," announces the editor; this book opens a channel of communication between the professions. The volume includes essays by Robert L. Clark, Jr., Frank G. Burke, Miriam I. Crawford, Fraser G. Poole, Robert L. Brubaker, and Marietta Malzer on the general characteristics of the professions, materials and methodology, education, legislation, copyright and literary property rights, access and confidentiality, social responsibility, public relations and fund raising, collection building and acquisition policies, standardization and technology, preservation, and an annotated bibliography on archive-library related topics. While the essays rehash subjects very familiar to both archivists and librarians, this is an interesting, different presentation. The authors often go beyond mere recapitulations and make provocative suggestions regarding the future trends of these professions and the possibilities for cooperation. [R: C&RL, Mar 77, p. 169; JAL, Mar 77, p. 39; LJ, 15 Feb 77, p. 464; LQ, Oct 77, p. 519; RQ, Spring 77, p. 251]   Richard J. Cox

379. Gilbert, Karen Diane. **Picture Indexing for Local History Materials.** Monroe, N.Y., Library Research Associates, 1973. 36p. bibliog. index. $3.45pa. ISBN 0-912526-12-2.

Everywhere one senses an urgency to locate and collect local history archival materials.

Communities with sufficient funds have organized historical societies and museums whose purpose is to collect, organize, and make available booklets, souvenir programs, and other ephemera—as well as to establish oral history programs and to collect and organize old photographs. Those without funds usually delegate the job to a public or local university library. The attempts of overworked librarians to gain bibliographic control over these materials (photographic records, in particular) has been complicated by lack of nationally accepted standards for their arrangement and description. This lack is partially alleviated by Gilbert's *Picture Indexing*, a manual that describes a viable, easily adapted system devised by the Newark Public Library for cataloging and indexing photographs. Location symbols, main entries, tracings, and geographical and special subject headings are suggested and defined. Examples of main entry and added entry cards are given, and methods of storage and retrieval discussed. A bibliography of selected readings and an index complete the work. Although probably too elementary for trained archivists, Gilbert's manual should prove useful to any librarian faced with organizing and gaining bibliographic control of a burgeoning collection of graphic materials. [R: RSR, July 74, p. 33]

Mary Jo Walker

380. Hobbs, John L. **Local History and the Library.** 2nd rev. ed. by George A. Carter. London, Andre Deutsch; distr., New York, Academic Press, 1974. 344p. illus. bibliog. index. $11.50. LC 62-3034. ISBN 0-233-95615-8.

This second edition of a 1962 work by the late Borough Librarian of Shrewsbury has been thoroughly revised and partly rewritten by George Carter of the Warrington Municipal Library. Hobbs was a fellow of both the Library Association and the Royal Historical Society, and Carter is the author of a number of books on local history. The purpose of this work is to provide for the practicing librarian a manual on the collecting, custody, and servicing of local historical materials, to supplement whatever formal training he or she may have had in professional library education. In a sense, then, the volume bridges the gap between conventional librarianship and archival practice. Though the archivist will probably find little that is new, librarians, and particularly those in smaller communities, should find it extremely helpful.

The scope of the book is comprehensive. It begins with a consideration of the nature of local history and its importance today, followed by a discussion of the various types of records.

The author then turns his attention to the care and treatment of archival materials, extensions of service, exhibition techniques, and photographic procedures. This is followed by a discussion of the use of local records for research, and a consideration of the administrative organization of the local history department in the library, the staff, the cataloging and indexing of the collection, and its classification. The author concludes with an outline of a proposed classification scheme for various types of local materials. Among the appendices are a discussion of the place of archives and manuscripts in the field of librarianship, and a reprinted British government circular referring to the Local Government (Records) Act, 1962. There are an excellent 10-page bibliography, and, in addition to the general index, an index to special collections mentioned in the text.

The work is, of course, based on British practice, and much of it relates to the library scene (and local history scene) in Great Britain. These geographical limits, however, are not serious handicaps to its utility for American librarians, much of whose archival training is derived from British sources. The book is important for its treatment of archival problems from the librarian's point of view, and will be useful to the practicing librarian who is seriously concerned about expanding the library's services to meet the growing public interest in local history and genealogy.   Jesse H. Shera

381. Kemp, Edward C. **Manuscript Solicitation for Libraries, Special Collections, Museums, and Archives.** Littleton, Colo., Libraries Unlimited, 1978. 204p. bibliog. index. $25.00. LC 77-29015. ISBN 0-87287-183-5.

Kemp presents a practical approach to solicitation of gifts, especially manuscripts, including detailed planning before beginning a solicitation program. He points out some often overlooked potential collection sources for the librarian to consider and what types of materials are appropriate to solicit. He then details preliminary correspondence with the potential donor; visiting the donor and assessing the collection; the receipt, sorting, organization, description, and financial appraisal of the collection; and finally, maintaining donor interest. The author describes two examples of collection programs with which he was involved. Additional chapters deal with the book gift, professional and personal qualities desirable in a solicitor, and the benefits to be gained from a solicitation program. Appendices include sample letters, field notes, sample deeds, inventories, and files to be maintained during the course of a collection development program. At the end of the book are a useful bibliography, arranged by chapter headings, and a subject index. [R: C&RL, Nov 78, p. 510; LJ, 15 Dec 78, p. 2495]

382. Manual for Accessioning, Arrangement and Description of Manuscripts and Archives. 2nd ed. Seattle, Wash., University of Washington Libraries, University of Washington, 1982. 98p. illus. $10.00 (looseleaf).

Very frequently, directors of libraries, historical societies, and small archival institutions are faced with the necessity of educating and training new staff in the handling of archival and manuscript materials. In most instances these staff members have little or no experience with these kinds of materials and, in many cases, are only part-time or volunteer workers in the repository with no long-term commitment to the field. Nevertheless, in order to use these people in the most efficient and effective manner, it is necessary to give them basic training (and even some education) about the nature of archives and manuscript work. What these directors need is a good manual, with lots of examples, for these workers to use when problems arise. The University of Washington Libraries (primarily in the person of Richard C. Berner, head of the University Archives and Manuscripts Division) have provided such a work in the second edition of the manual used by their staff.

The manual, three-hole punched for easy insertion in a notebook, covers the "educational" basics of archival theory as well as the practical training needed to carry out the basic operations of accessioning, arrangement, and description. Part 1, "Theory," is a concise introduction to the basic principles, with adequate beginning-level treatment of how these principles relate to the actual day-to-day work. Part 2, "Practice," then provides basic "how we do it here" instructions for workers to follow at each stage. The second section is thoroughly illustrated with examples of forms and procedures that are used for accessioning, arrangement, and description. In both sections, the author managed effectively to weave into the text the differences between archival records and manuscript collections and the implications these have for the work to be done.

The manual is an excellent one, but it is not by any means the last word on the topic. In some ways it is too University of Washington-specific, and users should be aware that a variety of acceptable alternative practices are available to them in such areas as subject control, name authority control, preservation procedures, and level of collection description. Directors of archival and manuscript repositories will also want to be aware of and keep up with new developments in the cataloging/description of these materials as efforts are made to establish a national database. (See, for example, the *Archives, Personal Papers and Manuscripts: A Cataloging Manual* ..., Washington, D.C., Library of Congress, 1983, and the MARC format for manuscripts and archives.)   Robert V. Williams

383. Menzenska, Sister Mary Jane. **Archives and Other Special Collections: A Library Staff Handbook.** New York, Columbia University, School of Library Service, 1973. 87p. index. bibliog. o.p. LC 75-311894.

This work is intended for the beginner working in the small college library and has as its focus an emphasis upon archives and personal papers. Contains some useful material but also some that is out-of-date. It can be used as a text or training manual where the instructor or experienced librarian is at hand. [R: Choice, Nov 73, p. 1366; LJ, 1 Dec 73, p. 3532]
                                    Charles D. Patterson

384. Nichols, Harold. **Local Studies Librarianship.** London, Clive Bingley; distr., Munich, New York, K. G. Saur, 1979. 128p. bibliog. index. (Outlines of Modern Librarianship). $12.00. ISBN 0-85157-272-3.

This brief primer is an adequate introduction to the basics of local history libraries. Nichols comments on acquisitions, storage and preservation, classification and cataloging, indexing, reference service, publications, public relations, and exhibitions. The drawback of this work for Americans is its orientation to a British audience, which greatly limits its usefulness as a practical guide. Staffs of local historical libraries on this side of the Atlantic will do better to start with Enid T. Thompson's *Local History Collections: A Manual for Librarians* (see *ARBA* 79, entry 176), and Dorothy Weyer Creigh's *A Primer for Local Historical Societies* (American Association for State and Local History, 1976), and reserve Nichols for a comparative look. [R: LJ, 1 Apr 80, p. 790; LR, Winter 79, p. 275]   Richard J. Cox

385. Suelflow, August R. **Religious Archives: An Introduction.** Chicago, Society of American Archivists, 1980. 56p. illus. $7.00pa.; $5.00 (members). LC 80-17159. ISBN 0-913828-20-1.

The Society of American Archivists has published this work "as an acknowledgement of the recent surge in religious archival activity." The author, director of the Concordia Historical Institute, is a leader in this field. The content, appearing in two-column format on 8½x11-inch pages, is divided into 10 sections (covering history and place of archival work; basic requirements such as budget, facilities, and staff; the acquisition and processing of materials; reference service, exhibits, and publications), a bibliography (of 19 works and 5 serials), and three appendices (primarily examples of record forms). The text of this paper-covered manual, written in a clear, straightforward style, is easy to understand. On the negative side, the bibliography is brief and dated (items date between 1945 and 1977; Suelflow's own publications are from the period 1961-1969), and the illustrations, more decorative than illustrative, are overly dark. [R: C&RL, Jan 81, p. 88]   Glenn R. Wittig

24 Audiovisual and Other Media

GENERAL WORKS

386. Boyle, Deirdre, ed. **Expanding Media.** Phoenix, Ariz., Oryx Press, 1977. 343p. index. (A Neal-Schuman Professional Book). $35.00. LC 77-23335. ISBN 0-912700-03-3.

Original publication dates of the over 40 articles reprinted here range from 1969 to 1977, but only a few are earlier than 1973. It thus updates *Reader in Media, Technology and Libraries* (1975), which anthologized pre-1973 articles. Both the views of those who deplore audiovisual media and those of advocates are represented, in the section entitled "Why Media?" That section and the one on programming are the fullest, followed by selection and evaluation, equipment, standards and cataloging, production, education, and finally, "Media Politics," which deals in part with censorship problems. Drawn from a wide spectrum of professional publications, this collection presents a fair sample of what has been said recently on the subject in the library press, which has concerned media use in public libraries more than in school or academic settings. Of interest to media personnel in public libraries and to students. [R: JAL, Nov 77, p. 303]   Mary R. Sive

387. Brown, James W., ed. **Nonprint Media Information Networking: Status and Potentials.** Stanford, Calif., ERIC Clearinghouse on Information Resources, Stanford Center for Research and Development in Teaching, School of Education, Stanford University, 1976. 60p. $3.25pa.

The 16 brief papers reprinted here were prepared for an ERIC/IR-sponsored seminar on nonprint media information networking, which was held as a concurrent program element of the national convention of the AECT, 30 March 1976. The papers are grouped in four sections representing the viewpoints of different groups of nonprint users or producers: education/library users; U.S. government; entrepreneurial information organizations; and commercial publishers and data system suppliers. The papers were limited to 1,000 words. As might be expected, these papers are typical of conference presentations—brief and concerned mainly with "current" information. Most of the information is no longer current and is not presented in a way that suggests "lasting value." This booklet can be safely bypassed by most libraries.

Christine Gehrt Wynar

388. Burlingame, Dwight F., ed. **Library & Media: Marriage or Divorce.** Evansville, Ind., University of Evansville Press, 1977. 78p. o.p. LC 77-91273. ISBN 0-930982-00-2.

Seven papers from a November 1976 conference address the use and management of instructional technology in higher education. The subject of the title—whether print and nonprint media should be together or separate—is the subject of three of the papers, those by Burlingame (University of Evansville), David Crossman (University of Pittsburgh), and Leland Park (Davidson College). W. C. Meierhenry's opener presents a clear, well-organized overview of the history, present trends, and possible future of instructional technology. Park's contribution is particularly refreshing since he openly takes a "separatist" position, thus placing himself squarely against the then-prevailing views in the library profession (stated in this volume by Burlingame). A small liberal arts college with a low student-faculty ratio has less need for audiovisuals, states Park. But an even more telling argument, he says, is that separate book and audiovisual organizations can achieve higher budgets than a combined operation. Indeed, we learn in Crossman's paper that competition for funds between the library and the instructional technology division was one of the reasons that the University of Pittsburgh decided to split up that particular marriage after several years. In that case, the inherent conflict between the research orientation and the teaching functions in a large university caused the marriage to fail. Gerald Brong makes a case for program budgeting; Donald Ely, for competency based education of personnel; while Pearce Grove surveys existing bibliographic controls over media. Bibliographies are at the end of each chapter. [R: JAL, March 78, p. 41]

Mary R. Sive

389. Casciero, Albert J., and Raymond G. Roney. **Introduction to AV for Technical Assistants.** Littleton, Colo., Libraries Unlimited, 1981. 250p. index. (Library Science Text Series). $28.00; $20.00pa. LC 81-13690. ISBN 0-87287-232-7; 0-87287-281-5pa.

Casciero and Roney have prepared a handbook covering the basic organizational, administrative, and production techniques needed by the person involved in the day-to-day operation of an audiovisual center. Photographs, charts, and diagrams illustrate the general survey of materials, equipment, personnel, and facilities in part 1. Included are common procedures for the acquisition and organization of audiovisual software—selection aids, classification schemes, card catalogs, and storage systems. Parts 2 and 3 introduce current technology in the production and presentation of visual displays, still photography, audiorecordings, videotapes, graphics, and projected materials. The chapters are abundantly illustrated with photographs and line drawings throughout. A glossary of terms assists in familiarizing the reader with terminology. [R: JAL, Mar 82, p. 48; SLJ, May 82, p. 32]

390. Enright, B. J. **New Media and the Library in Education.** Hamden, Conn., Linnet Books, 1972. 162p. illus. index. o.p. ISBN 0-208-01175-7.

Concerned about the library as an educational institution and the role of the librarian as an educator, Enright tries, through a literature survey, to identify the problem areas facing libraries because of the introduction of these media, and to present them to the library profession for study, examination, and establishment of policies. Even though the book is not

"an operational handbook" and does not offer any solutions to the problems identified, it is an excellent addition to the literature of the library's role in relation to the new media and education. As the author points out, "It seems important to stimulate discussion of the library's role before attempts are made to devise and describe methods of organizing media materials by the library."

The author carefully leads the reader from a discussion of the new media and their role in education, through the arguments for and against library involvement, to the effects these media will have on the library. He offers evidence to support his conclusion that the arrival of the new media is far from being a "threat or irritant to libraries" and that it "promises to help, rather than hinder, libraries of all types to make an increasingly valuable contribution to the current and future needs of the community." [R: BL, 15 Feb 73, p. 539; CLW, Apr 73, p. 556; LJ, 15 May 73, p. 1560; LR, Spring 73, p. 27; SLMQ, Winter 73, p. 149]

Nabil Hamdy

391. Fothergill, Richard, and Ian Butchart. **Non-book Materials in Libraries: A Practical Guide.** 2nd ed. London, Clive Bingley; distr., Hamden, Conn., Shoe String Press, 1984. 308p. illus. bibliog. index. $23.00. ISBN 0-85157-345-2.

The second edition of this book like the first is written for the British practitioner. The authors indicated in the first edition that this "book may be used both as textbook on the librarianship of non-book materials and as a simple manual of practice." By the authors' definition, books, pamphlets, leaflets, manuscripts, maps, serials, and music scores are excluded from their coverage of nonbook materials. Areas covered in this guide, by chapter, are "The Background," "The User," "The Materials," "The User and the Materials," and "Management."

Except for the updating of the names of sources and resources, the only substantive additions to this edition are (1) the discussion of *Anglo-American Cataloguing Rules*, second edition, as the rules to the cataloging of nonbook materials and (2) microcomputers, viewdata, and teletext as new forms of nonbook materials. The definite British slant of the work is evidenced by a bibliography which contains few items from outside Great Britain, British terminology such as *backing store* and *datestore*, use of the British GMDs, and inclusion within the text of sources of supply, bibliographic organizations and databases, sources of cataloging information, and publications which would not be known to most practitioners outside that country.

In addition, the authors sometimes offer questionable advice, such as "The information given in Chapter 9 Machine-readable data files is not particularly helpful and should in the main be ignored: do not use this chapter as the cataloguing standard" (p. 232). Other weaknesses in this work include errors in the examples provided. In the discussion of GMDs, none are given in the example on page 209, and there is a discrepancy in the statement of responsibility given in figures 29 and 30 on page 202, both dealing with the cataloging of the same work. Finally, a great deal of space is devoted to long explanations of equipment operation which are nonspecific to a particular piece of equipment and therefore of little help (pages 142-56). This guide is too specific to be used as a text and too general to be used as a manual of practice and has little to commend it to American library schools and practitioners. [R: C&RL, Mar 79, p. 188; LR, Spring 79, p. 33]

Donald C. Adcock

392.   Jonassen, David H. **Nonbook Media: A Self-paced Instructional Handbook for Teachers and Library Media Personnel.** Hamden, Conn., Library Professional Publications/ Shoe String Press, 1982. 408p. illus. $42.50. LC 81-17211. ISBN 0-208-01891-3.

This unique work is a combination reference guide and how-to handbook. It summarizes the fundamentals of educational technology theory and provides instruction in audiovisual media production and equipment operation. There are chapters on the systems approach, behavioral objectives, communication models, graphics, transparencies, slides, filmstrips, audio media, film, video, programmed and computer-based instruction, games and simulations, and media selection. Actual discussion of these topics is brief, but each chapter cites relevant sections in a dozen educational technology texts and includes a fairly current bibliography of books, articles, and nonprint resources. Self-evaluative tests enable specialists to diagnose their need to consult the collateral readings. Noteworthy are the book's numerous excellent diagrams, flowcharts, and illustrations, which are especially useful in the audiovisual production techniques and equipment utilization sections. If the book has a shortcoming, it is that it is dated in spots. This is most noticeable in the section on selection aids. Many outdated titles and superseded editions

are listed while important works are missing. One also would like more detailed coverage of newer technological developments than the volume provides. This is a valuable book that fills a real need and — for the most part — does so very well. One hopes the author is already at work on an updated edition. [R: SLJ, Nov 82, p. 37]

Joseph W. Palmer

393.   Shores, Louis. **Audiovisual Librarianship: The Crusade for Media Unity, 1946-1969.** Littleton, Colo., Libraries Unlimited, 1973. 160p. bibliog. index. o.p. LC 73-85472. ISBN 0-87287-076-6.

To chronicle the crusade to achieve media unity, Shores has gathered together in this anthology most of his shorter writings relating to the great professional conversation on audiovisualism and librarianship. For anyone interested in the development of the media unity concept, this collection covers a variety of important writings. [R: AL, Jan 74, p. 36; LJ, 15 Mar 74, p. 874; RSR, Jan 74, p. 27]

REFERENCE WORKS

394.   Chisholm, Margaret E. **Media Indexes and Review Sources.** College Park, Md., School of Library and Information Services, University of Maryland; distr., College Park, Md., Student Supply Store, University of Maryland, 1972. 84p. index. o.p. LC 72-89575.

The purpose of Chisholm's work is to identify and describe the major indexing and reviewing services for nonprint media. Part 1 is an essay evaluating the reviewing media; part 2 is an alphabetical (by title) list of 103 reviewing journals and guides. This section presents bibliographic data for each entry plus comments on the media reviewed and the content of the evaluations. Part 3 contains a subject index and an index by type of media. [R: SLMQ, Spring 73, p. 227]

395.   Daniel, Evelyn H., with the assistance of Karen A. Stiles. **Media in the Library: A Selected, Annotated Bibliography.** Syracuse, N.Y., ERIC Clearinghouse on Information Resources, 1978. 93p. index. (IR-32). $5.25pa. ED 168 590.

About 100 of the reference materials on all aspects of operating a media center noted here are marked with an asterisk (*) as "particularly important." This smaller selection will be a service to the practicing media specialists, library school students, and educational technologists to whom this well-organized guide to nonprint is addressed. These titles and the remainder of the total of 496 entries are arranged in chapters comprising general works, selection of materials and equipment, managing the media center, operation and production, media in context, media and teaching, and research and special issues. The section on production is the briefest, that on selection the fullest, reflecting the "library" orientation of its authors and providing a welcome counterweight to other media guides that treat selection cursorily.

Subdivision of most chapters by format makes it easy to locate the appropriate book, article, document, or serial. Where the title is not self-explanatory, entries are briefly annotated with concise and to-the-point comments. Films, slides, audio and video recordings, and cable television are among the formats dealt with, and there is brief consideration, too, of oral history and music librarianship. Publication dates of 1970 to 1978 eliminate most, if not all,.dated titles. A good many of the entries are ERIC documents. Mary R. Sive

396. Rosenberg, Kenyon C., with the assistance of Paul T. Feinstein. **Dictionary of Library and Educational Technology.** 2nd ed., rev. and expanded. Littleton, Colo., Libraries Unlimited, 1983. 185p. bibliog. $24.50. LC 83-19641. ISBN 0-87287-396-X.

This completely revised and updated second edition of *Media Equipment: A Guide and Dictionary* (see *ARBA 77*, entry 658) is designed to aid both practicing and prospective teachers and media specialists who are involved with the acquisition and maintenance of media equipment. Every type of audiovisual hardware from motion picture projectors to tuners is covered, as is the equipment used for reprographics and micrographics. New to this edition is a thorough consideration of both computer hardware and computer software. The text is divided into three sections. The first offers an in-depth discussion of criteria for equipment selection. This section provides an invaluable orientation for those with little or no knowledge about the equipment that they may have to select or operate. After a complete, easy-to-understand technical description of each piece of equipment, there is an evaluation checklist to facilitate purchasing. The second, larger section of the text is an alphabetically arranged dictionary defining nearly 800 terms including acronyms and the names of equipment components,

supplies, procedures, and professional organizations. Following the dictionary is a selective bibliography, arranged by type of equipment.

397. Rufsvold, Margaret I. **Guides to Educational Media.** 4th ed. Chicago, American Library Association, 1977. 159p. index. $6.00pa. LC 77-5058. ISBN 0-8389-0232-4.

An update of the third edition (1971), this standard guide lists 245 educational media catalogs, indexes, and reviewing services for all subject areas and ages. It is larger than the previous edition by a third, and contains citations to guides published between 1972 and 1976. Excluded are trade and promotional catalogs, as well as audiovisual library collection catalogs. All entries are annotated; besides full bibliographic citation, each entry lists scope, arrangement, content of entries, and special features of the guide. The arrangement is alphabetical by title, with an index to provide access to subjects, authors, publishers, organizations, institutions, and types of media. The guides listed cover a wide range of subjects, and the age range is from kindergarten to post-graduate level. Rufsvold suggested intended audiences for each item, whenever possible. For a more comprehensive examination of instructional materials lists for grades K-12, see Sive's *Educators' Guide to Media Lists* (Libraries Unlimited, 1975). Janet H. Littlefield

398. Tarakan, Sheldon L. **Directory of Recorded Specialties.** 1982-1983 ed. Roslyn Heights, N.Y., Sound Advice Enterprises, 1982. 1v. (unpaged). index. (Tarakan Music Letter Guides for Libraries, No. 1). o.p. ISBN 0-943668-00-X.

The *Directory of Recorded Specialties* describes 180 specialty recording sources, including small ethnic music labels and business associations (Indian House, Amacom Cassettes), special-interest groups and governmental organizations (Cultural Guild, Smithsonian Collection), societies and foundations (American Bible Society, Sea Heritage Foundation), and health and educational services (Soundwords Health Library, Teach 'em, Inc.). Each entry begins with the company name, address, and telephone number. Each entry also provides a brief description of what the company produces, followed, in most cases, by ordering information, prices and discounts, payment terms, postage requirements, catalog availability, and other labels belonging to the same company.

The directory is meant to help librarians, media specialists, and collectors who wish to develop well-rounded or highly specialized recordings collections. Used as a resource for building a comprehensive collection of specialty company catalogs, it could be of substantial benefit. It is a useful companion and supplement to the recording company lists in the *Music Industry Directory* (7th ed., Marquis Who's Who, 1983) and the *Billboard's International Buyers' Guide* (Billboard Directories, 1958-). [R: LJ, 1 Dec 82, p. 2239; WLB, Dec 82, p. 362]   Avery T. Sharp

399. Weber, Olga S., comp., with the assistance of Deirdre Boyle. **North American Film and Video Directory: A Guide to Media Collections and Services.** New York, R. R. Bowker, 1976. 284p. o.p. LC 76-26748. ISBN 0-8352-0883-4; ISSN 0362-7802.

The film and video services offered by about 1,300 libraries and media centers across this country and Canada are listed here, with useful and detailed information about each. The directory is a revision and expansion of the Film Library Information Council's pioneering *Directory of Film Libraries in North America*, which appeared in 1971. The collections, facilities, equipment, loan policies and restrictions, services, even the annual budgets and expenditures of each center, all gleaned from detailed questionnaires, are recorded fully but concisely. The format, juxtaposing a variety of type styles, boldface and italics, is well designed for expedient use. Entries are arranged alphabetically by city within each state or Canadian province. Separate indexes of libraries and special film collections by topic, plus an annotated list of film circuits and cooperatives, have been added. This is a comprehensive and valuable guide to collections previously not well documented. [R: LJ, 15 Dec 76, p. 2560]   Stephen M. Fry

COLLECTION DEVELOPMENT

400. Cabeceiras, James. **The Multimedia Library: Materials Selection and Use.** 2nd ed. New York, Academic Press, 1982. 282p. illus. index. $29.00. LC 77-11209. ISBN 0-12-153950-4.

The subtitle of this work indicates its actual scope: it is a textbook for a materials selection course for any type of library. However, the approach is quite novel. The basic principle of the work is that today's library must contain works in many media, and that the medium selected in any given case should be geared to the requirements of both the information being presented and of the user for whom it is intended.

The opening chapters cover the philosophy summarized above, present and future trends in librarianship, selection aids, and the systems approach to materials selection. The author discusses several aspects of media selection including policy formulation, selection standards, media categories, utilization procedures, and each medium's applicability to specific tasks. He includes a chapter on local production of materials and concludes with information pertaining to copyrighted materials and a discussion of the librarian's obligation to ensure intellectual freedom.

The first edition of this work (1978, see *ARBA* 79, entry 224) was considered an important one because it was one of the first to take an effective multimedia approach without being limited to school media centers. Since this second edition also covers many forms of media which are new to librarianship, this work is valuable for students and librarians alike.

Jessica L. Harris and Annette Pekarek

401. Nadler, Myra, ed. **How to Start an Audiovisual Collection.** Metuchen, N.J., Scarecrow, 1978. 157p. index. $15.00. LC 78-1993. ISBN 0-8108-1124-3.

There are a number of guides to establishing and running media centers in schools, but this may be the only guide specifically addressed to audiovisual operations in public libraries. A good one it is, too. A collection of original papers by contributors of the stature of Laura Murray, Wesley Doak, and Helen Cyr, among others, it covers aspects of audiovisual library service from planning space to public relations.

Cyr's introductory chapter offers much good advice on selection, evaluation, and organization. She outlines six steps in selection, and directs the reader's attention to some not-very-well-known sources of audio- and videotapes and slides; she also makes some pithy observations about film evaluation by committee. One welcomes her stress on the archival function of the public library and the role of media in it but deplores her failure to mention that state laws may prohibit film lending to schools.

Leon Drolet's comments on equipment models and prices are based on 1976-1977 data and will become dated, but his pointers on factors to consider in hardware selection will remain useful. Murray's discussion of personnel is essentially based on ALA's 1975 *Recommendations for Audiovisual Materials and Services for Small and Medium-Sized Public Libraries.* A table showing the distribution of duties among available staff addresses the realities of staffing an audiovisual program with only professionals and pages, with the addition of a clerk and finally of a technician. It does not consider an operation without professional or even technician personnel. Patricia del Mar's chapter on space planning would have benefited from some sample plans, since without them, it remains somewhat general, as is William Sloan's discussion of services. Masha R. Porte's summary of publicity procedures and Doak's glossary complete the volume. [R: LJ, July 78, p. 1363]

Mary R. Sive

402. Sive, Mary Robinson. **Media Selection Handbook.** Littleton, Colo., Libraries Unlimited, 1983. 171p. illus. index. $22.50. LC 83-932. ISBN 0-87287-350-1.

This handbook assists the librarian in identifying the most essential selection tools for nonprint media (exclusive of films), describing the scope and limitations of each, and suggesting strategies for current and retrospective searches. Designed to be used by librarians building nonprint collections, from kindergarten through community college, this guide offers detailed directions for the identification of specific needs and available instructional media, and an assessment of the quality of the media in relation to cost and potential usage. Three separate sections compose this handbook. Topics such as the principles of media use, media selection, and instructional development are covered in part 1. Part 2 describes in detail the features of 15 selection tools, reproducing sample pages and offering specific directions for usage. These aids will assist in the selection of a variety of nonprint materials, such as filmloops, filmstrips (sound and silent), kits, pictorial and graphic items, simulation games, slides, sound recordings, transparencies, and videorecordings. Optimal paths for current and retrospective searches are suggested in part 3, with examples that demonstrate specific applications of the procedures offered in previous chapters. [R: JAL, Sept 83, p. 245]

ORGANIZATION AND BIBLIOGRAPHIC CONTROL

403. Chibnall, Bernard. **The Organisation of Media.** London, Clive Bingley; distr., Hamden, Conn., Linnet Books, 1976. 80p. bibliog. index. o.p. LC 75-37930. ISBN 0-85157-212-X(Bingley); 0-208-01525-6(Linnet).

According to the preface, "the purpose of this book is not to set out detailed instructions for the organisation of media ... [but] to try to develop the underlying principles behind the process of organisation, so that we may be better able to see the common purpose which the librarian, resource manager, producer or, for that matter, teacher should be trying to serve" (p. 7). The author provides some 70 pages of generalizations about such topics as the interrelationships between educational theories and communication, organizational pattern, staffing problems, facilities, etc. Much of this discussion is a rather simplistic combination of "common sense" and "hints," with the author's chatty observations added (see his discussion on how to choose equipment from many different manufacturers on page 49). We are not sure how Chibnall envisions the audience for this book, but it is certainly not our library schools.

Bohdan S. Wynar

404. Daily, Jay E. **Organizing Nonprint Materials: A Guide for Librarians.** New York, Marcel Dekker, 1972. 190p. bibliog. (Books in Library and Information Science, Vol. 3). $39.75. LC 72-87849. ISBN 0-8247-6044-1.

Discusses nonprint materials in all types of libraries. The author provides a number of helpful hints on differences in treatment of nonprint materials versus books. According to the author, most tasks in descriptive cataloging could be accomplished by nonprofessionals. While the first part of the book deals with this problem in general, the second part relates to practices at the University of Pittsburgh. The highly selective bibliography at the end of the book omits some important reference books on this subject. Like most books in this area, Daily's monograph is not going to provide all answers, but it is a step in the right direction. [R: LJ, 15 Mar 73, p. 849]

405. Grove, Pearce S., and Evelyn G. Clement, eds. **Bibliographic Control of Nonprint Media.** Chicago, American Library Association, 1972. 415p. index. o.p. LC 70-183706. ISBN 0-8389-0109-3.

The 68 papers, reports, and questions-and-answers resulting from a three-session institute (August 1969 and April 1970), were edited for publication in this volume. Papers, some only a page or two in length (excluding the transcripts of the discussion periods), were presented by 49 specialists at the institute. At the end of the volume are a bibliography of books and articles and an index. It is doubtful that this compilation will be of much lasting interest to anyone except researchers studying that phenomenon of the late 1960s — OEO institutes. [R: C&RL, May 73, p. 229; LRTS, Spring 73, p. 251; SLMQ, Winter 73, p. 150]

406.   Project Media Base. **Problems in Bibliographic Access to Non-Print Materials: Final Report.** Washington, D.C., National Commission on Libraries and Information Science; distr., Washington, D.C., GPO, 1979. 86p. o.p. LC 79-16600. S/N 052-003-00714-2.

This report presents the background and findings of a study originated by the Association for Educational Communications and Technology (AECT) and jointly funded by AECT and the National Commission on Libraries and Information Science (NCLIS). Its specific focus is on the bibliographic control of audiovisual resources. The report discusses why such control is important, indicates the status of efforts to develop such control, and presents some requirements for the future. The Project Media Base, consisting of four authors and an advisory committee of 13 librarians and other information professionals, was to test the hypothesis that "all the essential elements for a national bibliographic system for audiovisual information resources currently exist" and, given that this hypothesis was correct, define the functional specifications for such a network of audiovisual resources. To accomplish this, the study team undertook a historical survey of bibliographic control of audiovisual resources, an inventory of current operational systems, and a user needs assessment.

The report presents the historical survey, with important dates appended, and analyzes the response of 58 automated audiovisual database systems and the user needs assessment. Although the study group sought to define the functional specifications for such an integrated system of audiovisual resources, it found it was not possible to specify detailed functional specifications for as complex a system as would be needed to manage the audiovisual output of the United States. Therefore, a conceptual framework and general guidelines for such a national database are presented. Among the conclusions of the study group was the consensus that there are barriers to the development of such a system, but the essential elements do currently exist. The study team's final recommendations are summarized, including the recommendation that a proposal be developed and funding sought to provide for further study.

Louise Stwalley

407.   Weihs, Jean, with Shirley Lewis and Janet Macdonald. **Nonbook Materials: The Organization of Integrated Collections.** 2nd ed. Ottawa, Ont., Canadian Library Association; distr., Chicago, American Library Association, 1979. 134p. illus. bibliog. index. $10.00. ISBN 0-88802-130-5.

Developed as a companion volume for the use of the AACR2 code regarding the principles and fundamental rules for cataloging of nonbook materials, the authors of this manual prepared this second edition in consultation with the CLA/ALA/AECT/AMTEC Advisory Committee on the Cataloging of Nonbook Materials. It is written for all types of libraries and media centers which wish to have an "all-media catalogue, i.e., one in which the entries for all materials, both book and nonbook, are interfiled." This book presupposes a knowledge of book cataloging and basic cataloging principles. The catalog card format is used extensively in examples throughout the volume. The manual is divided into six parts: "Cataloging Policy for Nonbook Materials," "Cataloging Rules for Nonbook Materials," "References to Materials Not Listed in the Catalogue," "Glossary and Abbreviations," "Storage," and "Appendices." The glossary and abbreviations section is short but descriptive and useful, as is the included bibliography. The index makes this book a very handy manual. Well illustrated with many examples, this book should be a welcomed guide for those using AACR2 for the cataloging of nonbook materials.

Donald D. Foos

TYPES OF LIBRARIES

Academic Libraries

408.   Grove, Pearce S., ed. **Nonprint Media in Academic Libraries.** Chicago, American Library Association, 1975. 239p. bibliog. (ACRL Publications in Librarianship, No. 34). $11.00pa. LC 74-23972. ISBN 0-8389-0153-0.

The development of media or nonprint collections and services in academic libraries is moving so fast that this publication is left floundering in the wake. It cannot be used as a reference book. It is seriously lacking as a useful information source for other purposes. The book is the result of drawn-out committee work, which added several years to its production time. Further delays were apparently experienced, since the cut-off date for all footnotes and references is 1972, with the majority being pre-1970. It is a bad case of publication lag, and in the media field such a denial of instant availability is simply deadly. No mention is made of video technology. The information included on other subjects is not definitive and cannot be easily consulted for specific points of interest because there is no index. One must read an entire chapter to learn something of the characteristics and problems of managing recordings, slides, films, maps, or pictures. For some areas in the field the book will serve as a useful overview guide, or as a starting point for the initial stages of conducting further inquiry. The "Selected References ..." chapter, for example, will be of such value. Similarly, the footnotes for each chapter lend credibility to the description of historical perspective and "current" developments. [R: C&RL, Sept 75, pp. 430-31; LJ, Aug 75, p. 1392]   Keith M. Cottam

Public Libraries

409. Audiovisual Committee. Public Library Association. American Library Association. **Guidelines for Audiovisual Materials and Services for Large Public Libraries.** Chicago, American Library Association, 1975. 35p. index. o.p. ISBN 0-8389-3172-3.

This pamphlet is a revision of *Guidelines for Audiovisual Materials and Services for Public Libraries* (American Library Association, 1970). In this extension of that earlier work, large public libraries, defined as those serving a population base of 150,000, has been separated from small and medium-sized libraries, for which a companion pamphlet has been issued by the Audiovisual Committee of PLA. The emphasis throughout the *Guidelines* is on quantitative standards, which are set forth under the following headings: "Level of Responsibilities"; "Services"; "Materials"; "Personnel"; "Space and Equipment"; "Statistics." There is an initial section devoted to definitions of audiovisual terms. [R: RQ, Summer 76, p. 368]

410. Audiovisual Committee. Public Library Association. American Library Association. **Recommendations for Audiovisual Materials and Services for Small and Medium-Sized Public Libraries.** Chicago, American Library Association, 1975. 29p. index. o.p. ISBN 0-8389-3175-1.

This set of audiovisual guidelines for libraries under 150,000 population base is the companion piece to *Guidelines for Audiovisual Materials and Services for Large Public Librar-*

ies (American Library Association, 1975). For details on organization, see entry 409. [R: RQ, Summer 76, p. 368]

School Libraries

411. Hicks, Warren B., and Alma Tillin. **Developing Multi-Media Libraries.** New York, R. R. Bowker, 1970. 199p. o.p. LC 72-112397. SBN 8352-0265-8.

School librarians who are still running hard to catch up with the log jam of processing and reorganization to effectively integrate nonbook material into unified multimedia collections must be eagerly scanning the horizons for a good how-to-do-it book. Warren Hicks and his colleague have taken on a big task in their attempt to "offer guidelines for the evaluation, selection, acquisition, cataloging, and physical processing and storage of audiovisual materials in libraries of all types and sizes" (Bowker press release). Part 1 is an overview of all aspects and part 2 contains the practical procedures illustrated with cataloging and processing examples. The whole book is overloaded with photos plus 18 figures and forms. A little editorial skill could have eliminated some unnecessary illustrations. More important, deadwood should have been pruned from part 1 where a rehash of written selection policies is served up. And no doubt the authors would have appreciated some little editorial niceties accorded to them such as printing their first as well as last names on the title page. On the plus side is the presentation under one cover of one method of handling the ordering, processing and cataloging of a long list of multimedia. The forms reproduced for these jobs will be useful as well as some of the tables and flow charts. The cataloging procedures are based on the adoption of media symbols and color coding. Not all librarians agree on this approach. In fact, the Technical Services Committee of the Canadian Library Association found the use of the media code in the call number unworkable in field tests. Color coding was also found wanting. Hicks and Tillin provide much that is useful in their book, but it should be kept in mind that alternative methods of cataloging and processing are not discussed. [R: DLQ, Jan 71, p. 73; RQ, Spring 71, p. 269]

Christine Gehrt Wynar

412. Hicks, Warren B., and Alma M. Tillin. **Managing Multimedia Libraries.** New York, R. R. Bowker, 1977. 264p. illus. bibliog. index. $22.50. LC 76-49116. ISBN 0-8352-0628-9.

First, it should be stated that this is not a revision of the authors' earlier title, *Developing Multi-Media Libraries* (*ARBA* 71, entry 137), but an entirely different work presenting a system of management for an established multimedia library. Hicks and Tillin believe that the pressures of accountability require that library managers re-examine their past practices and consider new approaches, and that multimedia libraries in particular present unique situations and problems to the manager. Through the application of the systems approach to management (specifically, "management by objectives"), they attempt to demonstrate better solutions to the management concerns of multimedia libraries. Their approach to library management as a subsystem of general management theory is one also supported by Stueart and Eastlick in their *Library Management* (Libraries Unlimited, 1977), although the latter work doesn't address itself specifically to the multimedia library.

Managing Multimedia Libraries examines in three sections foundations, structures, and programs. "Foundations" addresses itself to the general philosophy and goals of multimedia libraries. "Structures" cover basic organization, management, and personnel; while "Programs" discusses such specific functions as resource selection, cataloging, circulation, and reference. The latter section also surveys future concerns that may affect the management of multimedia libraries, especially in the area of information technology.

Each chapter begins with an abstract of the subjects under discussion and concludes with a summary of its major points. Case studies are often used to reinforce particular issues, and the many charts and diagrams outline specific processes. Chapters vary in the degree of background knowledge required. Chapter 6, for example, presents a fairly sophisticated discussion of selection processes, while the chapter 8 explanation of library circulation is rather basic. Of special note in chapter 8, however, is the examination of reference services as applied in a multimedia environment. Too often reference is defined only in terms of print material, and this discussion of source alternatives is especially refreshing.

Although some basic background in libraries and media is assumed, this work would be useful to mid-program library students as well as working professionals needing a new approach to managerial techniques. An effort appears to have been made to remain within the context of a general multimedia library rather than outline application to one type of library,

such as school or public. There does seem to be some emphasis on educational situations, but this may be partially due to the current applications of multimedia rather than an intended bias. An excellent bibliography and an index contribute to the usefulness of this work. [R: C&RL, July 77, pp. 360-61; JAL, July 77, p. 186; LJ, 1 June 77, p. 1257]   Roberta J. Depp

413. Margrabe, Mary. **The "Now" Library Media Center: A Stations Approach with Teaching Kit.** rev. ed. Washington, D.C., Acropolis Books, 1975. 162p. illus. index. $9.95pa. LC 72-12395. ISBN 0-87491-343-8.

This work is aimed at school librarians and teachers who are interested in developing a child's media skills. The author has chosen 80 library skills such as the use of books, filmstrips, viewing and listening equipment, preparation of audiovisuals, knowledge of the arrangement and organization of the library, and use of the card catalog and reference books. Each station includes exercise sheets, and there are suggestions on administering the program, grouping stations, and recording progress. The stations can be adapted for grades K-12, with goals listed for each level. The plan is certainly worth examination by school librarians and teachers; however, one may guess that children will need much supplementary explanation and many additional exercises in order to master some of the more difficult skills.

Christine Gehrt Wynar and Annette Pekarek

414. **Planning and Operating Media Centers: Readings from Audiovisual Instruction—2.** Washington, D.C., Association for Educational Communications and Technology, 1975. 79p. illus. $3.95. ISBN 0-317-36879-6.

This second book of readings from *Audiovisual Instruction* attempts to provide an overview of the changes that the development of the media center concept brought to library service in the school community. Articles are grouped into four sections: (1) "The Media Center Concept," (2) "Designing the Media Center Program," (3) "Operating the Media Center Program," and (4) "The Media Center—Case Studies." A fifth section provides a directory of selected media centers throughout the country willing to share their experiences with others. By giving expression to different authors' viewpoints within a given section, this reader permits comparison of several approaches to the media center. Unfortunately, no criteria for selecting the articles are indicated. Primarily oriented to individual media center experiences (i.e., the "this is what we did" approach), the collection will appeal to those looking for practical examples rather than theory. [R: LQ, Oct 77, p. 496]   Roberta J. Depp

415. Prostano, Emanuel T. **Audiovisual Media and Libraries: Selected Readings.** Littleton, Colo., Libraries Unlimited, 1972. 276p. o.p. LC 72-89111. ISBN 0-87287-053-7.

Prostano has made a distinct contribution to the library and audiovisual fields in selecting articles dealing with philosophical considerations, traditional audiovisual forms and practices, major technological innovations, and evaluation and selection of media. The 44 articles are arranged in the following chapters: "A New Look at the Audiovisual Field"; "An Old Standby: 16mm Film"; "Media Mix: Utilization/Production"; "Microform Technology"; "Computer Technology"; "Video Technology"; "Remote Access: Audio/Video Technology"; "More Communications Technology"; "Media Evaluation." Prostano is the author of several books, including *The School Library Media Center* (Libraries Unlimited, 1971). [R: BL, 1 Apr 73, p. 727; LJ, 15 Mar 73, p. 848; RSR, Apr 73, p. 13]

SPECIFIC MEDIA

Ephemera and Bulletin Boards

416. Clinton, Alan. **Printed Ephemera: Collection Organisation and Access.** London, Clive Bingley; distr., Hamden, Conn., Shoe String Press, 1981. 125p. index. $15.00. ISBN 0-85157-337-1.

This book is a by-product of an investigative project which the author conducted in 1979 and 1980 under the sponsorship of the British Library Research and Development Department and the Bodleian Library, Oxford University. The project was titled "Preliminary Survey of Collections of Ephemera."

In his text, Clinton stresses that there is disagreement as to what constitutes ephemera. Therefore, he has chosen to concentrate upon content rather than form—"to think less in terms of 'ephemera,' and more in terms of collections and their subject matter." By focusing upon specific subject areas and specific collections, he hoped to arrive at an understanding of the state of the art and to develop recommendations for the future.

After a preliminary chapter on what Clinton calls "general ephemera collections," he devotes himself to nonbook printed materials selected from three contrasting fields: the historical area, the pictorial area, and the area of modern social problems. For his historical example, Clinton chose collections dealing with British postal history. The pictorial area is represented by collections containing pictures of domestic appliances. To reflect modern social problems, the author picked collections concerned with housing. For each of these special areas, Clinton outlines how material in the field can be found, and delineates the location and organization of the chief collections in the field. In each case, he supplements this descriptive material with a chapter on problems of acquisition, organization, or access which surfaced during the collection examination. It is obvious from Clinton's presentation that his concern is with collections of interest to serious students, historians, researchers, and collectors. A final chapter summarizes the author's conclusions, and presents his arguments for establishing a National Register of Collections.

This book was intended for British librarians, archivists, museum curators, and collectors. However, readers in our country will discover that British experiences and problems often parallel those in the United States. Clinton's observations and recommendations may have application here as well as in Great Britain. [R: JAL, Jan 82, p. 384; LR, Spring 82, p. 64]
                                Shirley Miller

417. Coplan, Kate, and Constance Rosenthal. **Guide to Better Bulletin Boards: Time and Labor-Saving Ideas for Teachers and Librarians.** Dobbs Ferry, N.Y., Oceana, 1970. 232p. $20.00. LC 76-102937. ISBN 0-379-00369-4.

Teachers are always eager to find new sources of bulletin board ideas, and this guide follows the old-fashioned tradition of giving directions on materials and colors to use and method of construction. Patterns for figures take up pages 174-214, and seven blank "Memo" pages are added at the back, presumably for the reader's creative patterns. The subjects cover a wide range but are mainly oriented to elementary schools. As can be expected, the quality of the selections varies, but science ideas seem weak and without content or imagination. It is startling to see only one example for shapes, and that isn't outstanding (it isn't even listed in the index). A lack of awareness of minority sensitivities is shown by inclusion of stereotyped "Little Indians." Because the illustrations are not arranged within any obvious categories and the index is incomplete, locating specific topics is not easy. The introductory section, "Bulletin Board Basics," is hardly informative and the reader would be better served in this area by Mona

Garvey's *Library Displays* (H. W. Wilson, 1969) or some of the older books and booklets on the subject.   Christine Gehrt Wynar

418.   Miller, Shirley. **The Vertical File and Its Satellites: A Handbook of Acquisition, Processing, and Organization.** 2nd ed. Littleton, Colo., Libraries Unlimited, 1979. 251p. illus. index. (Library Science Text Series). $22.50. LC 79-13773. ISBN 0-87287-164-9.

The second edition of this standard handbook for selecting and organizing vertical file materials and other supplementary resources has been thoroughly revised and updated. (For a review of the first edition, see *ARBA* 72, entry 124.) It introduces new products and techniques that have appeared since the first edition in 1971, and expands upon topics of that edition to provide a more thorough treatment of subjects such as photographs. Also included is information about vertical files and related resources in special libraries.

This volume has numerous tips on locating resources; lists of key publications and sources; techniques for labeling, filing, weeding, and circulating materials; and ideas on what to do with special collections of vocational material, local history items, maps, pictures, and information on local events. *The Vertical File and Its Satellites* will admirably serve as an organizational tool for those pamphlets, clippings, and other supplementary materials that are not found elsewhere in basic library collections but which often provide precise answers to reference questions. [R: BL, 15 Jan 80, p. 699]

Films, Prints, and Pictures

419.   Evans, Hilary. **Picture Librarianship.** Hamden, Conn., Shoe String Press, 1980. 136p. bibliog. index. (Outlines of Modern Librarianship). $12.00. ISBN 0-85157-294-4.

The growth of the heavily illustrated book, magazine, journal, and newspaper and the subsequent need for knowledgeable picture librarians and researchers capable of selecting and obtaining illustrations from a vast visual reservoir have brought picture librarianship into its own as a specialty. Evans has written a useful textbook to serve as an introduction to both library school students and practitioners. The author is a noted expert in this field and has produced several standard reference books, including *The Art of Picture Research* (David & Charles, 1979), *The Picture Researcher's Handbook* (Scribner's, 1979), and *Sources of Illustration*

1500-1900 (Hastings House, 1972), the last two titles co-authored with Mary Evans.

The picture library has been defined as one which collects all types of illustrations, from cave paintings to photographs, cinema stills, old master paintings, postcards, posters, newspaper clippings, and the like. The work of a variety of picture libraries is presented: public, archives, societies, professional bodies, commercial and industrial firms, press agencies, photo agencies, and historical reference archives. Although written for a British audience, the underlying themes of the nature, function, acquisition, care and maintenance, access and retrieval, classification and cataloging, and administration of picture libraries are discussed broadly enough and with enough common sense to be applicable almost anywhere. [R: SL, Oct 81, p. 410]
                                                    Juan R. Freudenthal

420.   **Film Cataloging.** Prepared by the Cataloging Commission, International Federation of Film Archives. New York, Burt Franklin, a division of Lennox Hill, 1979. 174p. illus. bibliog. o.p. LC 78-2769. ISBN 0-89102-076-4.

This publication is the culmination of studies by the Congress of the Federation International des Archives du Film committee resulting from the expansion in audiovisual mass media. The guide is a practical tome for film archives—not for libraries per se; it is advisory and presents various alternative methods that have been adopted. The advantages and disadvantages of the various methods are discussed.

One-third of the volume covers the structure of the film collection; the preservation; detailed information compiled for the cataloging systems, including the technical data and film movement records; and some practical recommendations. Detailed information recorded from the archive film, not from a copy of the film, is discussed as part of those records. Two-thirds of the work is devoted to appendices; forms of abbreviations suggested for use; numbering systems and acquisition records used in Belgrade, London, Wiesbaden, and Berlin; and technical data files. Also covered are the Universal Decimal Classification, lists of genre or film categories in current use, and subject classification methods for films at the Filmarchivum Magyar Filmtudomanyi Intezet, the Imperial War Museum, and the Filmoteka/Ceskoslovensky Filmovy Ustav. A list of definitions for animation techniques (compiled by the Library of Congress), serving as a guide for catalogers, concludes the work. An excellent, lengthy selected bibliography has been compiled.

Twenty-four pages of illustrations, not numbered, are in the back, showing catalog drawers and catalog and technical data cards used in film catalogs. There is no index, so one must rely on the table of contents. [R: LQ, Jan 81, p. 119]

Mary Clotfelter

421. Foster, Donald L. **Prints in the Public Library**. Metuchen, N.J., Scarecrow, 1973. 124p. index. o.p. LC 72-13056. ISBN 0-8108-0579-0.

Libraries and smaller museums will find helpful advice and information in this survey on the acquisition and handling of original works of graphic art in public collections. Definitely written for the amateur in this specialized field, the book contains basic advice on selection, cataloging, circulation, storage, and framing of prints. Major techniques are defined, and the text, which begins with a sweeping historical survey, concludes with a chapter on conservation, a glossary, and a list of reliable print dealers in a dozen large cities. There are myriad alternate procedures to those set down by the author, and collectors and print librarians for existing collections will find nothing new here. However, the collecting of fine prints is a library service that should be encouraged; new collectors, whether institutional or private, will find this publication to be a good, compact starting point. [R: LJ, 15 Sept 73, p. 2529]

William J. Dane

422. Harrison, Helen P. **Film Library Techniques: Principles of Administration**. New York, Hastings House, 1973. 277p. index. (Studies in Media Management; Communication Arts Books). $17.50. LC 73-5615. ISBN 0-8038-2294-4.

The author attempts to describe principles and techniques for organizing and administering film libraries. The 14 chapters nicely outline the major categories for such a guide (e.g., function, history and development of film libraries, selection principles, film handling, sequence listing, storage, cataloging, information retrieval, economics, and staffing, etc.). However, the presentation is simplistic in style and content. Only very general information is presented in most chapters. In addition, the text is written for British readers, which limits its value for American students. [R: C&RL, July 84, p. 302; LJ, 1 May 74, p. 1279; LR, Spring 74, p. 224; SL, Nov 73, p. 540]

423. Harrison, Helen P., ed. **Picture Librarianship**. Phoenix, Ariz., Oryx Press, 1981.

542p. illus. bibliog. index. $39.50; $29.50pa. LC 81-11291. ISBN 0-89774-011-4; 0-89774-013-0pa.

Viewing picture librarianship as different from art librarianship, this collection of essays in part 1 and the descriptions of picture libraries in part 2 emphasize the techniques and practices associated with collecting, organizing, and disseminating visual information found mainly in photographs and illustrations. In addition to the introduction, the editor has contributed two chapters on processing and administration. Others in part 1, approximately half of the volume, include essays about the history of photography, sources for acquisition, selection, preservation and storage, arranging and indexing, technological developments, microforms, dissemination, and copyright. Short descriptions of about 25 picture collections in national, government, special, public, school, and commercial picture libraries, and in the communications industry, plus an extensive bibliography, complete the volume.

Although much of the information in this book is applicable to picture librarianship in the United States or elsewhere, it should be noted that often the point of reference is that of libraries in the United Kingdom, the home of a large proportion of the contributors. Although some of the outstanding collections in the United States are discussed in part 2, its orientation is British, as is that of much of the material cited in the bibliography. Part 1 is generally relevant to library practice here and elsewhere but does fall short when addressing issues such as copyright in the United States, discussed on two pages.

The essays in part 1 vary in the number of detailed suggestions offered in methodology. The chapters on processing and on preservation and storage present good overviews of these areas. The chapter on arrangement and indexing also surveys different approaches, but gives little guidance on choice of a classification or indexing method. The chapter on recent technological developments mentions only briefly the use of automated systems for the bibliographic control of visual materials; a topic which promises to add an important new dimension to the challenge of providing access to pictorial information. Most of the chapters include in the text and in chapter references citations of materials for further study.

This book is not a manual for the practice of picture librarianship but does provide a good overview of different practices in the field. It is significantly different from those items aimed at picture researchers or those focusing on a single library function, and makes a significant contribution to the literature of nonbook librarianship. [R: LR, Summer 82, p. 137]

JoAnn V. Rogers

424.	Hill, Donna. **The Picture File: A Manual and a Curriculum-Related Subject Heading List.** 2nd ed., rev. and enl. Hamden, Conn., Linnet Books, 1978. 183p. illus. bibliog. index. o.p. LC 78-3728. ISBN 0-208-01745-3.

There has been a continuing, ever-growing interest in developing and handling manageable and responsive picture files, a fact that is reflected in the present revision. Tapping experience especially in the New York Public Library's Picture Collection and Hunter College's Teachers Central Laboratory, this work offers both practical perspectives and guidance to the potential user, the novice, the experienced, and, to some extent the experimenter.

As the preface notes, "new material in *Part One* MANUAL includes some suggestions for building a collection of pictures where funds do not permit the purchase of a dry mounting press, ..." for selecting and processing pictures, and for the circulation and maintenance of the collection. A newly designated part 2, "Uses of Pictures in Education," covers use for reference, research, and display in the library, the classroom, and in teaching specific subjects and concepts in general curricular areas. The "Subject Heading List," part 3, includes three chapters devoted to using the checklist (with some consideration given to the card catalog), together with suggestions for expanding the subject heading list and assigning headings. The checklist itself, "Subjects A-Z" (pp. 97-160), incorporates some scope notes as well as cross- and *see also* references. It is followed by "Geography," which provides an alphabetical list "intended to include history since the rise of modern nations" (also with tiny scope notes and cross- and *see also* references). The appendix covers "other uses of the dry mounting press," a short glossary, an updated bibliography highlighting the subject, and an index. It would be useful to apply, test, and then compare this information with a subject file more closely allied with the card catalog. [R: SL, July 79, p. 308; SLMQ, Summer 79, p. 282]	Clara O. Jackson

425.	Irvine, Betty Jo, with the assistance of P. Eileen Fry. **Slide Libraries: A Guide for Academic Institutions, Museums, and Special Collections.** 2nd ed. Littleton, Colo., Libraries Unlimited, 1979. 321p. illus. index. $30.00. LC 79-17354. ISBN 0-87287-202-5.

Irvine's pioneering work, *Slide Libraries* (see *ARBA* 75, entry 205), out-of-print and unavailable to slide curators, art librarians, and media professionals for several years, has been fully revised and enlarged in this second edition. Among the expanded topics are automation applications for slide collections, the development of standardized cataloging and classification applications, and sophisticated indexing techniques using both manual and machine systems. A section has been devoted to a subject that was only mentioned in the 1974 edition—environmental controls and preservation measures for slides.

Slide Libraries presents a comprehensive overview of the establishment and management of slide libraries: administration and staffing, classification and cataloging, use of standard library techniques and tools, equipment and supplies, storage and access systems, planning for physical facilities, projection systems, and acquisition, production methods, and equipment. The text is supplemented by a 35-page classified bibliography, a directory of distributors and manufacturers of equipment and supplies, and a directory of slide sources. Illustrating the volume are 50 figures, 29 diagrams, and 19 photographs. [R: C&RL, July 80, p. 358]

426.	**Public Library Subject Headings for 16mm Motion Pictures.** rev. ed. Prepared by Subject Headings Committee, Audio-Visual Chapter, California Library Association. Sacramento, Calif., California Library Association, 1974. 49p. o.p.

It is undoubtedly time for libraries to give serious consideration to cataloging procedures and subject headings for 16mm films, and the California Library Association could be the authoritative source for providing innovative and well-thought-out guidelines for public libraries to follow. In their attempt to compile a listing of subject headings, the CLA has used public library catalogs, Sears, and commonly accepted terminology; the CLA seems to be assuming, however, that film collections will be cataloged and housed separately from book collections. But there is evidence that some libraries (Hennepin County, for example) are integrating book and nonbook collections; therefore, the list should reflect subjects that would be appropriate for either method of collection arrangement. Such a premise necessitates the use of subject headings more akin to those assigned to book materials (i.e., more specific headings rather than the general ones collected by CLA). As an example, "Religions" is too broad a heading to include the 13 cross-reference not referring to the heading. The subject does not provide adequate information for the user seeking films on Taoism, for example, unless the title of the film contains the religion's name. "United States—History" is grossly inadequate to encompass the over 100 subject headings that LC has established for books on the same subject.

Concerning the subjects themselves: some old prejudices and biases are conspicuously evident and out of place in a 1974 publication. CLA could certainly develop a more sensitive approach to identifying social situations, instead of labeling blacks, Chicanos, Orientals (which Asian people refer to themselves as Orientals?), etc., and women as "Social Problems." Since the catalog of terms is totally in the context of 16mm films, the subjects beginning with "Motion pictures" are redundant. *All* the subjects are for motion pictures. Why not use "Animated motion pictures" or "Animated films," "Documentary films," "Feature films," etc., instead of the "Motion picture" forms?

If the committee insists on maintaining very general headings, more cross-references must be added or films will be lost to the public for whom the list is supposedly intended. Current terminology must be represented ("Gays. see Homosexuals," "Overpopulation. see Population," "Feminism. see Woman") and commonly requested kinds of public library films are worth noting (paralleling the CLA form "Foreign language films," there could be headings such as "Horror films," "Kinestasis films," "Melodramatic films," etc.). Linda Running

427. Rehrauer, George. **The Film User's Handbook: A Basic Manual for Managing Library Film Services.** New York, R. R. Bowker, 1975. 301p. illus. biblig. index. o.p. LC 75-15884. ISBN 0-8352-0659-9.

A practical handbook covering every aspect of the organization and administration of a library film service such as financing, staffing, selecting and acquiring films, cataloging and processing, using and programming, and evaluating. Sample forms and other useful illustrations abound. This much-needed book is without rivals; rather than a general reference book, it is a comprehensive text in the field. However, much that is included is of genuine quick reference value, such as a bibliography for film service, lists of film periodicals, associations and organizations, distributors, and film equipment manufacturers. There is also a useful glossary of film terms. Undoubtedly, this unique work will become a basic source for all

libraries offering or planning film services. [R: BL, 15 Mar 76, p. 1057; JAL, May 76, p. 92; LJ, 1 June 76, p. 1268; LQ, Oct 76, p. 455]
Ralph J. Folcarelli

428. Shaw, Renata V. **Picture Searching: Techniques and Tools.** New York, Special Libraries Association, 1973. 65p. illus. (SLA Bibliography No. 6). o.p. LC 72-13234. ISBN 0-87111-207-8. (Available from Books on Demand, $20.00, ISBN 0-317-09419-X).

Picture searching for publishers, film and television producers, and designers is a specialized and exacting profession; much of its success depends on efficient and informed search procedures. This bibliography was compiled to guide the searcher in planning a reference search and in gathering illustrations. Included are 500 entries for printed sources that may aid in the location or identification of pictures. Entries are arranged under 30 subject headings. Cross-references are provided, but there is no index. Thirty illustrations demonstrate the range of pictures that require a searcher's expertise. [R: RSR, Oct 74, p. 112]

Maps

429. Carrington, David K., and Richard W. Stephenson, comps. **Map Collections in the United States and Canada: A Directory.** 3rd ed. New York, Geography and Map Division, Special Libraries Association, 1978. 230p. index. o.p. LC 77-26685. ISBN 0-87111-243-4. (Available from Books on Demand, $60.00, ISBN 0-317-30406-2).

Even though the information in this third edition was three years old at date of publication, it is an invaluable tool for all map librarians and general reference sections. There is a considerable increase in coverage (745 map collections covered, a 23 percent increase over the 1970 edition, the introduction informs us). Not only are more map libraries included, but more information has been garnered for each. Staff, number of maps, books and other materials, annual accessions, area, subject and chronological specializations, special cartographic collections, cataloging and classification, depositories, public served, reproduction facilities, when established, interlibrary loan, name of map librarian, and telephone number are included when available. Information is presented alphabetically by state, and within states, alphabetically by city. Well presented and put together, this is irreplaceable. A detailed index is included. [R: LJ, 1 Sept 78, p. 1576]

Mary Larsgaard

Music

430. Daily, Jay E. **Cataloging Phonorecordings: Problems and Possibilities.** New York, Marcel Dekker, 1975. 172p. index. (Practical Library and Information Science Series, Vol. 1). $39.75. LC 73-90723. ISBN 0-8247-6196-0.

Unfortunately, AACR never provided a reasonable solution to the problem of cataloging audiovisual materials. Daily has published articles and books on this subject, among them his *Organizing Nonprint Materials* (Marcel Dekker, 1972), and his somewhat controversial views on title unit entry are well known to the profession. It should be made clear that this is not a "how-to" book, although the reader will find here a number of practical suggestions for solving certain problems in this area. For example, the author insists that the record label is the most important element in descriptive cataloging, rather than the jacket, which can be easily discarded. This is sound advice. It is hoped that some of the problem areas described in this book will receive proper attention and more discussion in library literature; certainly Daily is one of the few people qualified to provide such a stimulus. His book should be highly recommended to all professional collectors—again, with a clear understanding that the author does not "advocate a method of cataloging" but rather offers logical "means of understanding what the possibilities are." More books of this nature are needed in the professional literature. [R: C&RL, Sept 75, pp. 429-30; LJ, 1 Sept 75, p. 1484]

Bohdan S. Wynar

431. International Association of Music Libraries. United Kingdom Branch. **Phonograph Record Libraries: Their Organization and Practice.** 2nd ed. Henry F. J. Currall and A. Hyatt King, eds. Hamden, Conn., Archon, 1970. 303p. index. $22.50. SBN 208-00381-9.

Of the 26 articles which make up this compendium, very few have reference value. Indeed, very few have any value at all to the American reader. Some additions and changes have been made in the new edition (first was 1963), but much of the content has an archaic quality nonetheless. For instance, the impact of tape and cassette on libraries of phonorecords is ignored, or rather postponed, by Currall to "the editor of a future edition." Certain important publications issued since the first edition are not caught in the articles or in the bibliography

(e.g., the *Manual of Music Librarianship* of the Music Library Association, 1966).

The more useful contributions are: L. G. Lovell's statement on policies of public libraries relating to discs, E. T. Bryant's overview of cataloging problems, Eric Cooper's technical article on record manufacture, and David Williams's survey of the European record industry. Probably the best item in the book is a statistical fold-out which reveals the resources and practices of those British public libraries which answered a 1968 Library Association survey. Other pieces in the volume are for the most part brief, personal, and localized approaches to routine problems. The bibliography is weak. [R: WLB, Apr 71, p. 788]

Guy A. Marco

Video

432. Bahr, Alice Harrison. **Video in Libraries: A Status Report, 1979-80.** 2nd ed. White Plains, N.Y., Knowledge Industry Publications, 1980. 119p. illus. bibliog. index. $24.50pa. LC 79-25951. ISBN 0-914236-49-0.

The first edition (see *ARBA* 78, entry 248) of this report explored the role of libraries as collectors of videotape and cassette recordings, buyers of equipment, producers of videotaped shows of community events, and producers of programs for local CATV channels reaching local viewers. Based on information gathered from telephone interviews and a mail survey, this report presents pessimistic conclusions about the future of video in libraries due to the fast obsolescence of equipment, programming, and format.

This updated and expanded second edition includes information on video collection management, uses of video in libraries, profiles of a dozen libraries (including problems and procedures), and future implications of video technology. It also contains directories of U.S. public libraries involved in video, and programming suppliers and distributors. Reference to a nonexistent appendix D has been corrected in this edition, and a bibliography and illustrations have been added. The price of $24.50 is much more reasonable for this edition than it was for the first.

Anindya Bose and Annette Pekarek

433. Cherry, Susan Spaeth, ed. **Video Involvement for Libraries: A Current Awareness Package for Professionals.** Chicago, American Library Association, 1981. 83p. index. $6.00pa. LC 81-2337. ISBN 0-8389-0323-1.

The subtitle of this book is "A Current Awareness Package for Professionals," and it does seem to be more of a "package" of unrelated articles than a book. All of the articles, of course, deal with video technology in libraries, but they have the accidental relationship of a group of articles dropped into one folder of a vertical file rather than the intellectual relationship of a coherent approach to a particular subject. The editor of the book and several of the authors write for *American Libraries*, and many of the articles sound as though they were culled from the pages of that journal. We are shown glimpses of the citizens of Port Washington, New York, taping their community activities with the help of library equipment, two dedicated librarians in Pocatello, Idaho, delivering services via video, and patrons in St. Cloud, Minnesota, watching videodiscs in the library. All of these articles are brief and newsy. However, they raise more questions than they answer, since none goes into the nitty-gritty of expenses, evaluation, effect on other library services, or the objectives of video use.

Somewhat more informative are the technical articles such as "A Primer of Video Grammar" and "The New TV Information Systems," an overview of current available systems. Even this last article, however, the longest one in the book, is of course already out of date. This type of information, by its very nature, is most appropriately treated in a journal, where succeeding articles can update and expand the subject. Most librarians who keep up with their professional reading will know most of what is contained in this book already; others, who have suddenly become aware of video technology and want to start learning, will do better to find a book which treats the subject systematically and then to devote some time to reading current literature as it appears in journals. [R: BL, 15 Jan 82, p. 634]

Adele M. Fasick

434. Thomasen, Cora E., ed. **CATV and Its Implications for Libraries.** Urbana, Ill., Graduate School of Library Science, University of Illinois, 1974. 90p. index. (Allerton Park Institute, No. 19). $7.00. LC 74-620101. ISBN 0-87845-040-8.

This work presents the proceedings of the nineteenth Allerton Park Institute, covering the implications of cable television for libraries. Some of the papers of special interest are: "What the Industry Can Offer: The Next Community Network," by James S. Keller; "CATV as a Medium for Information Access," by Brigitte L. Kenny; and "Cable Television as an Information Tool," by Ken Dowlin. As always, these papers are well edited; unfortunately, the index is inadequate. [R: C&RL, Sept 75, p. 418; LJ, 1 June 75, p. 1100; LR, Summer 75, p. 74; RSR, Jan 75, p. 118]

25 Automation and New Technologies

GENERAL WORKS BEFORE 1976

435. Artandi, Susan. **An Introduction to Computers in Information Science.** 2nd ed. Metuchen, N.J., Scarecrow, 1972. 190p. index. $13.00. LC 72-1136. ISBN 0-8108-0485-9.

The first edition was published in 1968. This second edition has been somewhat revised, but its major objectives remain the same. Part 1 provides an overview of the field of information science and technology, and part 2 presents theoretical aspects of document retrieval, with an emphasis on the intellectual problems that apply to document organization on all levels. Other chapters cover processing of documents for input, the retrieval of documents, computer-based systems, and representative machine applications. Since all of this is in 190 pages, the coverage is somewhat superficial for most subjects. Suitable for beginning courses on an undergraduate level. [R: RSR, Apr 73, p. 20; SL, Apr 73, p. 216]

436. Balmforth, C. K., and N. S. M. Cox, eds. **INTERFACE: Library Automation with Special Reference to Computing Activity.** Cambridge, Mass., MIT Press, 1971. 251p. index. $27.50. LC 70-158649. ISBN 0-262-02084-X.

Papers from a Seminar on the Management of Computing Activity in Academic Libraries presented at Newcastle in January 1969, plus additional papers that supplement and update those. Intended for novice library administrators knowing nothing of computers, automation, or management. Somewhat condescending in tone and style. [R: LJ, 15 June 72, p. 2162]
Charles D. Patterson

437. Carroll, Dewey E., ed. **Clinic on Library Applications of Data Processing. 1969 Proceedings.** Urbana, Ill., University of Illinois Graduate School of Library Science, 1970. 149p. illus. $7.00. LC 65-1841. ISBN 0-87845-017-3.

This volume contains papers presented to the seventh annual clinic held in April 1969 at the University of Illinois and includes a description of the MARC Project and contributions from university and special libraries detailing accounts and analyses of operational use of various processing systems. Useful for the seasoned practitioner and beginning student alike. [R: BL, 1 Sept 70, p. 5; LJ, 15 Sept 70, p. 2891]
Charles D. Patterson

438. Clifton, Joe Ann, and Duane Helgeson, eds. **Computers in Information Data Centers.** Montvale, N.J., American Federation of Information Processing Societies, AFIPS Press, 1973. 109p. illus. o.p. LC 72-83728. ISBN 0-88283-001-8.

The 10 papers comprising this work were presented in December 1972 at the American Federation of Information Processing Societies Fall Joint Computer Conference at Anaheim, California. Under the general heading used as the title of this volume, the participants discussed a potpourri of subjects, including the historical impact of computers on libraries and information centers; computer software; a library online circulation system at Bucknell University; the University of Minnesota Bio-Medical Library Mini-Computer project; Project BALLOTS at Stanford; the information retrieval capabilities of the Environmental Protection Agency in Cincinnati, Ohio; the management of the ERIC database; human factors in online searching; automatic indexing; and the future prospects for interlibrary communications.

These papers furnish a mixture of data about and insights into the 1972 state-of-the-art of computer use in libraries. In an area where developments are continuous and rapid, reports such as this quickly become dated. However, they are of some use to librarians who wish to improve their understanding of the special problems connected with library computer systems.

Richard Palmer

439. Eyre, John, and Peter Tonks. **Computers & Systems: An Introduction for Librarians.** Hamden, Conn., Linnet Books, 1971. 127p. illus. index. o.p. ISBN 0-208-01073-4.

Another of the so-called introductory texts to this subject. Provides capsule information on the library use of computers, the methods of information input and output, etc. All this is obviously based on British practice. In a two-page bibliography appended to the text one finds a total of three books published in the United States, including Dougherty and Heinritz's *Scientific Management of Library Operations* (Scarecrow, 1966). To this one should add that *College & Research Libraries* should not be found among periodicals "frequently carrying articles on computer applications in libraries" (p. 124). *Journal of Library Automation—* yes. Of little value. [R: AL, June 72, p. 676; LJ, 1 May 72, p. 1681]

440. Fasana, Paul J., and Allen Veaner, eds. **Collaborative Library Systems Development.** Cambridge, Mass., MIT Press, 1971. 241p. illus. index. o.p. LC 71-165076. ISBN 0-262-06046-9.

In 1968 the National Science Foundation awarded a grant to support a project called "Collaborative Library Systems Development." Participants in the project were libraries of the University of Chicago, Columbia University, and Stanford University. Two of the more important objectives of the CLSD Project were: (1) to test certain technical assumptions, such as the feasibility of developing a mechanism to facilitate cooperative work and the possibility of developing compatible and transferable automated library systems; and (2) to communicate the findings and experience of the project group to the general library community. This volume contains all the major papers presented at the New York conference and a selection of papers presented at the Stanford conference, plus a paper describing CLSD experience from 1968 through 1970. [R: LJ, 15 May 72, p. 1186]

441. Hayes, Robert M., and Joseph Becker. **Handbook of Data Processing for Libraries.** 2nd ed. Sponsored by the Council on Library Resources. Los Angeles, Calif., Melville, 1974.

688p. illus. bibliog. index. (A Wiley-Becker & Hayes Series Book; Information Sciences Series). $63.50. LC 74-9690. ISBN 0-471-36483-5.

The first edition of this handbook appeared in 1970 (see *ARBA* 72, entry 141). This second edition of what is undoubtedly the best available handbook on data processing in library operations is organized into 20 chapters distributed over four sections. The section headings are "Introduction," "Management of Library Data Processing," "Data Processing Technology," and "Library Subsystems."

Those who remember the first edition will realize that there has been not only a substantial rearrangement of materials but an actual shrinkage of content, at least in number of pages. The first edition had 885 pages and five sections, the first three of which were the same as those listed above. What is called "Library Subsystems" in the second edition combines sections 4 and 5, "Library Clerical Processes" and "Library Intellectual Processes," of the first edition.

Although the authors do not say so explicitly, it is implied that the much greater familiarity with computerized applications on the part of librarians has relieved them of the obligation to explicate elementary considerations. An example is the first edition's chapter on "Information Science in Librarianship." This is entirely lacking in the second edition.

In view of the extraordinary development of computerized operations in libraries, a new edition was necessary if Hayes and Becker was to retain its value as a state-of-the-art review as well as an explicative handbook. The first edition, however, is not entirely superseded by the second; therefore, it should be retained for the fuller explanation of basic considerations which it contains. [R: LJ, Aug 75, p. 1392]

Richard A. Gray

442. Heiliger, Edward W., and Paul B. Henderson, Jr. **Library Automation: Experience, Methodology, and Technology of the Library as an Information System.** New York, McGraw-Hill, 1971. 333p. index. o.p. LC 77-137128. SBN 07-027888-1.

In essay form, the authors "provide an introductory exposition of automation in practice, in theory, and in prospect to those who are familiar with the objectives and purposes of the library." A glossary of terms and a suggested reading list are included after each of three parts of the book. An extensive bibliography of 1,029 items covers most of the pertinent literature through early 1970. This bibliography has a subject index separate from the book's index. Illustrations throughout the book, but especially in part 2 where the systems approach is discussed, are helpful in explaining the concepts involved. In part 2 the reader/librarian will find known experiences (e.g., technical processes, control processes, and administrative processes) discussed in such a way that efforts at automation in these areas appear to be the natural outgrowth of progressive developments. Although it uses a broad brush approach, it is a useful introduction. In the final part, the authors make some telling statements about the prospects for library automation in the 1970s.

Compared with the Hayes and Becker *Handbook of Data Processing for Libraries* (Wiley, 1970) it stands as an introductory essay, not as a comprehensive text, with the Hayes and Becker book being used for more study, in-depth, of specific processes, routines, or machine and data descriptions. There are many features of their handbook (e.g., inventory of available mechanized bibliographic databases) which do not appear in this book. There should be room on the library shelf for both titles.

Pauline Atherton

443.   Henderson, Kathryn L., ed. **Proceedings of the 1970 Clinic on Library Applications of Data Processing: MARC Uses and Users.** Urbana, Ill., Graduate School of Library Science, University of Illinois, 1971. 113p. index. o.p. LC 65-1841. ISBN 0-878-45019-X.

Papers presented at the 26-29 April 1970 clinic held at the University of Illinois. Topics covered include new technological developments, details of the MARC production system at the Library of Congress, summary of the distribution service provided by the Argonne National Laboratories, and details of MARC users' experiences with maintenance of catalogs. [R: LJ, 15 Dec 71, p. 4075]

Charles D. Patterson

444.   Henley, J. P. **Computer-Based Library and Information Systems.** 2nd ed. New York, Elsevier, 1972. 106p. illus. index. (Computer Monographs). o.p. LC 71-171221. ISBN 0-444-19584-X.

The aim of this introductory text is to bridge the gap between the librarian and the computer specialist. It discusses the limitations of the information retrieval field (as well as its opportunities), and the current hardware and software features. The first edition of this work appeared in 1969. This edition incorporates more information related to practices in this

country—a change that is reflected in the appended bibliography as well. [R: Choice, June 73, p. 652]

445.   Kaplan, Louis, ed. **Reader in Library Services and the Computer.** Westport, Conn., Greenwood Press, 1971. 239p. illus. bibliog. (Reader Series in Library and Information Science). $28.50. LC 70-149298. ISBN 0-313-24041-8.

Another volume in this Reader series, published under the general editorship of Paul Wasserman. Previous volumes were *Reader in Library Administration* (Greenwood Press, 1969), *Reader in Research Methods for Librarianship* (Greenwood Press, 1970), and *Reader in the Academic Library* (Greenwood Press, 1970). This volume includes some 25 articles, which hardly cover this subject, arranged under seven subject categories, including theory of management (one article) and catalogs and the computer (two articles). There is also a list of "additional readings," some 25 entries. It is interesting to note that bibliographical information in this "bibliography" is rather incomplete, to say the least. Why the editing was so poor, we don't know. As to the articles selected, one probably can question many inclusions as well as omissions. We do. But again, selection is the privilege and prerogative of the compiler. It will be useful in library schools as supplementary reading and will be favored by many who like shortcuts and have to stay within a budget. [R: LJ, 15 Oct 71, p. 3300]   Bohdan S. Wynar

446.   Kimber, R. T. **Automation in Libraries.** 2nd ed. New York, Pergamon Press, 1974. 240p. illus. index. (International Series of Monography in Library and Information Science, Vol. 10). $33.00. LC 74-13847. ISBN 0-08-017969-X.

The first edition of this textbook on library automation was published in 1968. Within six years there had been such an expansion in the state-of-the-art that a completely restructured revision of the original text became necessary.

The book is organized in 10 chapters. The first is a general introduction; the second considers the reasons for automating; the third and fourth deal with planning an automated system.

The fifth chapter, "Bibliographic Record Structures," is the most theoretical discussion in the book in that it presupposes some measure of mathematical knowledge. The other chapters detail the operations of specific library functions such as circulation control, serials control ordering, and acquisitions.

The author tends to draw most of his illustrative examples from British library practice but by no means exclusively so. Major U.S. projects such as MARC, Project BALLOTS, and OCLC are cited and discussed. The author writes simply and clearly and with a minimum of jargon. The book should be an effective textbook in library schools in both Britain and the United States. [R: JAL, July 76, p. 140; LJ, 15 Feb 76, p. 596; LQ, Apr 76, p. 183]

447. Markuson, Barbara Evans, and others. **Guidelines for Library Automation: A Handbook for Federal and Other Libraries.** Santa Monica, Calif., System Development Corp., 1972. 401p. bibliog. o.p.

This handbook is the result of a 1970 study on the status of federal library automation projects which was conducted under the auspices of the Federal Library Committee's Task Force on Automation. This survey was carried out by the System Development Corporation and funded by the U.S. Office of Education. It is one of two reports generated from the study data (the other report being *Automation and the Federal Library Community*).

The study consisted of a questionnaire survey of 2,104 federal libraries, 964 of which responded. Of that number, 57 libraries had one or more functions automated and 10 had one or more functions in various stages of development or planning.

The handbook purports to help the federal librarian answer the question: "Is it feasible to use automation for my library?" It attempts to do this by presenting step-by-step guidelines "from the initial feasibility survey through systems analysis and design to fully operational status." The reader is informed of the steps that should be considered with each aspect of automation development and, additionally, is informed of what others have previously done about each phase or problem. Much of this material is too general and too brief to do more than call the reader's attention to the fact that certain requirements must be met in the successful development of an automation project.

A large portion of the book is taken up with descriptions of automation projects in 59 federal libraries. Approaches have been provided to this survey material by automated application, form of publication, type of equipment used, and by the special features of each system. Surprisingly, there is no approach by name of library.

The final section of the book, a potpourri of information about nonfederal automation activities, is the weakest section of the volume. It includes a list of "automated libraries" that was published before and is very incomplete and poorly defined. Additionally, it only discusses databases, commercial ventures, microforms in libraries, and input/output hardware.

The final section is a selected bibliography. The items included range over the whole spectrum of library automation, and some items have nothing to do with automation at all. There is no index to the book as a whole, and a fair number of errors is present.

In summary, the book includes a limited amount of rather old information, most of which is available in other places in far greater detail. As a book of "guidelines" it does succeed in providing information in uncluttered and simplified form, but it is a very disappointing publication that leaves much to be desired both in substance and in organization. [R: C&RL, Jan 73, p. 71]   Donald P. Hammer

448. Martin, Susan K., and Brett Butler, eds. **Library Automation; The State of the Art II: Papers Presented at the Preconference Institute on Library Automation Held at Las Vegas, Nevada, June 22-23, 1973.** Chicago, American Library Association, 1975. 191p. bibliog. $9.00pa. LC 75-20168. ISBN 0-8389-3152-9.

The Las Vegas Preconference Institute was dedicated to an examination of the computerized library systems that had become operational since ISAD's first preconference institute held in 1967. In pursuit of that goal the first paper was Allen Veaner's review of progress from 1968 to 1973. This was followed by seven other papers: "Technology," by Deana Delaney; "User Services," by Lois M. Kershner; "Cataloging Systems," by Maurice Freedman; "Acquisitions Systems," by David L. Weisbrod; "Systems Personnel," by Pauline Atherton; "Innovative Strategies," by Walter Curley; and "Outlook for the Future," by Ralph Shoffner. The work concludes with a bibliography prepared by Martha W. West. [R: C&RL, July 76, p. 375; LJ, July 76, p. 1502]

449. Mitchell, Ruth K. **Information Science and Computer Basics: An Introduction.** Hamden, Conn., Linnet Books, 1971. 101p. index. $12.50. LC 70-142596. SBN 208-01118-8.

The major portion of this programmed text began as a thesis at the University of Wisconsin. It is divided into five parts, each of which is concerned with separate aspects—introduction to information science, information retrieval, advanced data processing, machine language translation, and "some directions," which provides a summary of the progress in the use of automation and mechanization. Appended to this text are a fairly adequate bibliography and a glossary of basic terms. Unfortunately, the coverage is not adequate, and in general this text is very disappointing. [R: LJ, 15 Sept 71, p. 2746]

450.   Pritchard, Alan. **A Guide to Computer Literature: An Introductory Survey of the Sources of Information.** 2nd ed., rev. and exp. Hamden, Conn., Linnet Books, 1972. 194p. index. o.p. ISBN 0-208-01182-X.

The first edition of this work was published in 1969 and reviewed in *ARBA* 70 (vol. 1, pp. 24-25). The second edition has been substantially enlarged (194 pages versus 130 pages in the first), with material added in several chapters (e.g., periodicals, date books, and directories) plus new chapters on software and hardware. [R: LR, Summer 73, p. 71; RSR, Apr 73, p. 19]

451.   Salmon, Stephen R., ed. **Library Automation. A State of the Art Review. Papers Presented at the Preconference Institute on Library Automation Held in San Francisco, California, June 22-24, 1967.** Chicago, American Library Association, 1969. 175p. bibliog. $7.50pa. LC 73-77283. ISBN 0-8389-3091-3. (Available from Books on Demand, $46.50, ISBN 0-317-29366-4).

The third printing of these proceedings sponsored by the Information Science and Automation Division of ALA was published in 1970. The dissemination of information about the new technology is a timely subject and it is only unfortunate that it took so long to see papers of this preconference published. Each of the 10 sessions of the institute was designed to concentrate on a particular area of automation activity: the future of library automation, library systems analysis and design, building implications of library automation, acquisitions, cataloging, book catalogs, the Library of Lawyers automation projects, serials, circulation, and trends affecting library automation. Most of the papers are well edited and a selective bibliography on automation concludes this volume. [R: BL, 1 Jan 70, p. 526]

Bohdan S. Wynar

452.   Salmon, Stephen R. **Library Automation Systems.** New York, Marcel Dekker, 1975. 291p. (Books in Library and Information Science, Vol. 15). $55.00. LC 75-25168. ISBN 0-8247-6358-0.

There is an abundance of literature on library automation. In 1975 alone, several books on this subject were published, including Kim-ber's *Automation in Libraries* (see *ARBA* 76, entry 231), Martin and Butler's *Library Automation* (see *ARBA* 76, entry 233), and Sherrod's *Information Systems and Networks* (see *ARBA* 76, entry 236). Solomon, using an historical approach, covers a number of pioneering systems but discusses only systems that have been implemented. Nonoperational (i.e., purely theoretical) systems are omitted. The scope of this work is limited to automation of technical services and circulation systems, omitting computerized information services. In conclusion, this is a good summation of the state-of-the-art. Within its limitations, Solomon's contribution will be helpful to the beginning as well as the advanced librarian who needs a readable text on this timely subject. [R: C&RL, July 76, pp. 374-75]

Bohdan S. Wynar

453.   Salton, Gerard. **Dynamic Information and Library Processing.** Englewood Cliffs, N.J., Prentice-Hall, 1975. 523p. illus. index. o.p. LC 74-31452. ISBN 0-13-221325-7.

Salton is well known for his work with the SMART system at Harvard and Cornell. That work provides the basic data for this book. He proposes "a dynamic environment for libraries and information centers" based on three main principles: "(a) A 'total' library system in which one basic input serves to initiate a chain of successive processing steps, the basic inputs undergoing successive modifications as a result of the various steps in the processing chain. (b) The widest possible use of cooperative and shared operations, including collaborative or centralized acquisitions policies, shared cataloging, and standardized library housekeeping operations. (c) An adaptive environment in which the user population influences the main intellectual processes such as the indexing vocabulary and practices, the storage organization, the search and retrieval operations, and finally the collection control necessitated by document growth and retirement" (p. 15).

Using these principles as the foundation, Salton provides the reader with a wealth of material to support his concept. Part 1 provides an excellent survey of theory and practice in information processing. Most of this section is understandable to a novice, if the person has a reasonable background in mathematics. Part 2 is an extended discussion of systems analysis and evaluation, while part 3 provides the details of "dynamic information processing." Both of these parts require very advanced knowledge of the field. It is almost as if he is writing only for the advanced researcher. Fortunately, most of the chapters in these two sections have introductory passages that allow the nonexpert a few insights into what Salton wants to say. One important missing element is a discussion of the impact copyright regulations will have on his proposed system. He makes two brief references to possible "legal problems" but does not explore the issue.

For the advanced researcher/student in information science, this is a valuable work. [R: JAL, Mar 76, p. 31; RQ, Winter 75, p. 185]

G. Edward Evans

454. Swihart, Stanley J., and Beryl F. Hefley. **Computer Systems in the Library: A Handbook for Managers and Designers.** Los Angeles, Calif., Melville, 1973. 338p. illus. index. (Information Sciences Series; A Wiley Becker & Hayes Series Book). o.p. LC 73-603. ISBN 0-471-83995-7. (Available from Books on Demand, $88.00pa., ISBN 0-317-10536-1).

A rather comprehensive treatment of such subjects as circulation activities, acquisitions, cataloging routines, serials, planning an automation program, etc. It covers only those library activities that can reasonably be automated today. Because of its clear presentation, it is probably one of the best books on this subject; library administrative personnel may find it essential. [R: LJ, 1 Sept 74, p. 2044; LR, Spring 74, p. 224]

GENERAL WORKS SINCE 1976

455. Adamovich, Shirley Gray, ed. **Reader in Library Technology.** Westport, Conn., Greenwood Press, 1976. 236p. illus. (Reader Series in Library and Information Science). $28.50. LC 75-8051. ISBN 0-910972-52-4.

Another in a long series of readers being issued by the publisher, this anthology organizes 51 previously published writings on library technical assistants or paraprofessionals under five part headings: "Library Technology," "Growth and Development"; "Policies and Criteria for Library Education"; "Definition and Debate"; "Education of Library Technical Assistant"; "The Library Technical Assistant at Work."

As in other readers in this series, the part introductions offer students little guidance in the interpretation of the criteria. [R: C&RL, Sept 76, p. 478; JAL, July 76, p. 140]

Richard A. Gray

456. Bidmead, Margaret, ed. **Use of Computers in Libraries and Information Centres: Proceedings of a Conference Held by Aslib with the** **Co-operation of the Aslib Computer Applications Group in London on 19-20 May 1975.** London, Aslib, 1976. 93p. illus. £4.50pa. ISBN 0-85142-084-2.

Twelve of the thirteen papers presented at the Aslib-Computer Applications Group Conference in London in May 1975 comprise this slim paperbound volume on the state-of-the-art in the use of computers in library and information centers. Focused on British applications, which generally follow U.S. developments, there is little new information; however, the emphasis given to the differing effectiveness for subject retrieval of the MARC record (for monographs) and database files (for periodicals, journals, etc.) directs the attention of U.S. professionals to a major problem requiring their investigation and solution.

Although the papers reflect unevenness in the vision and competency among library and information science professionals, the conference discussions are of better than average quality and utility. A few charts and figures; no list of participants; no index; and no bibliography.

Richard Palmer

457. **Books, Libraries and Electronics: Essays on the Future of Written Communication.** By Efrem Sigel and others. White Plains, N.Y., Knowledge Industry Publications, 1982. 139p. bibliog. $24.95. LC 82-15229. ISBN 0-86729-024-2.

Six authors discuss a variety of questions that center upon what will happen to books as more and more information is created or disseminated in electronic form. Robert Stueart writes of the changing nature of the library. Eric Barnouw, historian of broadcasting, describes the growth of video as a communications medium. Anthony Smith discusses the new nature of authorship in the computer age; and Dan Lacy shows how publishers are already being affected by the electronic technology. There is an essay on the future of the book by Efrem Sigel. A final chapter on video disc technology is by Lewis Branscomb. There is no index. The six essays are stimulating and interesting comment and speculation on coming developments in the information society, but the book has no discernible value as a reference work.

John Farley

458. **Buying New Technology.** New York, Library Journal/R. R. Bowker, 1978. 64p. illus. (LJ Special Report, No. 4). o.p. ISBN 0-8352-1062-6; ISSN 0362-448X.

Librarians considering the purchase of new equipment and services are likely to be disappointed with this slim volume. They might reasonably expect that this "Special Report" will provide them with guidance in areas new to them — perhaps a *Consumer Reports* approach, with attention given to general considerations of library technology, comparative tables of features, costs, services/repair performance charts, and suggestions on negotiating contracts. Unfortunately, this title does none of these things. Instead, it appears to be *Library Journal*'s expedient method of dealing with its "slush pile" of publishable articles relating in one way or another to library technology.

The individual articles themselves are not bad; indeed, the first three do present a useful overview of automated circulation systems and the factors involved in selecting them, and there is a good checklist of questions to consider in deciding whether to contract for online database searching in a given library. The majority of the other articles are of the "how-we-did-it" type, and cover such varied topics as automated materials storage systems, the use of audiotapes for current awareness for librarians, and the touch-a-matic telephone. Although there is no index, the article titles are usually descriptive, so the table of contents can be used instead. However, a typographical error in a page reference and a badly classified title reduce its usefulness. The other titles in the Special Report series are far superior to this one. [R: C&RL, Mar 79, pp. 168-71]   Charles Wm. Conaway

459. Changing Information Concepts and Technologies: A Reader for the Professional Librarian. White Plains, N.Y., Knowledge Industry Publications, 1982. 179p. illus. bibliog. (Professional Librarian Series). $34.50; $27.50pa. LC 82-166. ISBN 0-86729-028-5; 0-86729-027-7pa.

A compilation of eight chapters selected from four previously published works by the same publisher — *The Library and Information Manager's Guide to Online Services* (1980); *Microcomputers and Libraries: A Guide to Technology, Products and Applications* (1981); *Getting Ready for AACR 2: The Cataloger's Guide* (1980); and *Telecommunications and Libraries: A Primer for Librarians and Information Managers* (1981) — this latest addition to the Professional Librarian series should serve as a valuable introduction to changing information concepts and technologies as they relate to libraries and librarians. Each chapter is designed to provide basic introductory information on a particular aspect of the subject; and each includes a bibliography for further reading.

This volume should prove to be a handy ready-reference primer for anyone interested in the field, and in developing his or her professional skills and knowledge. Some of the language and concepts are, as necessary, technical. However, each of the authors provides sufficient explanation of terms used; and the work is far more readable and comprehensible for the beginner than a number of similar introductory works. Thirty-seven tables and figures, supplemented by photographs, are included to aid the learning process. [R: BL, 15 Oct 82, p. 292]

Edmond F. SantaVicca

460. Cline, Hugh F., and Loraine T. Sinnott. The Electronic Library: The Impact of Automation on Academic Libraries. Lexington, Mass., Lexington Books/D. C. Heath, 1983. 186p. bibliog. index. (The Lexington Books Special Series in Libraries and Librarianship). $20.00. LC 81-47871. ISBN 0-669-05113-6.

The authors have brought the discipline of sociology to the world of academic libraries to study the impact of automation on the organizational structure of those institutions. After a brief, but adequate, review of the nature and function of academic libraries and the history of library automation, they move to the heart of the book, which is based on four case studies conducted in 1979. The libraries studied, all major research centers, were the University of Chicago, Northwestern University, Stanford University, and the University of Oregon.

Data for the studies were collected through interviews, observations, and the study of pertinent reports and other documents. A total of approximately 220 librarians, predominantly from the middle-management strata, were interviewed. Interviewees were asked questions dealing with the organization and operation of their library, the history and function of the automated system(s), and the impact of the system(s) on procedures, attitudes, perceptions, communications, and so on. The data thus gathered were then analyzed to evaluate the impact of automation on four areas: organizational structure, information channels and dissemination, fiscal considerations, and personnel.

This work is well researched and written and should provide worthwhile information for the library administrator contemplating the implementation of an automated system or for the library science student preparing for a profession that will almost certainly require working with computers. [R: LQ, July 84, p. 314; RQ, Summer 84, p. 486]   Bill J. Corbin

461. Corbin, John. **Developing Computer-Based Library Systems.** Phoenix, Ariz., Oryx Press, 1981. 226p. bibliog. index. (A Neal-Schuman Professional Book). o.p. LC 81-1232. ISBN 0-912700-10-6.

More specific and more detailed than Matthews's *Choosing an Automated Library System: A Planning Guide* (see *ARBA* 82, entry 232), Corbin's *Developing Computer-Based Library Systems* is an in-depth look at the system development process and its management. Contents include an overview of the systems approach as applied in libraries, project planning and management, system requirements, system evaluation and comparison, writing specifications, requests for proposals, and system implementation. Appendices provide examples of most of the documents attendant to the system development process. A glossary and selected bibliography are included.

Corbin's and Matthews's books are among the first of their kind and among the best. Any librarian involved in developing an automated system will want to have one or both. The Matthews book is written perhaps more from the librarian's perspective, and Corbin's is more detailed and somewhat more technical. Both are highly recommended reading for librarians before they begin the development of a computer-based system. [R: LJ, 1 Dec 81, p. 2293]   Ward Shaw

462. **Current Trends in Library Automation: Papers Presented at a Workshop Sponsored by the Urban Libraries Council in Cooperation with the Cleveland Public Library, May 7-8, 1981.** Alex Ladenson, ed. Chicago, Urban Libraries Council, 1981. 106p. illus. $7.50pa.

Current Trends in Library Automation is a compilation of papers presented at a workshop sponsored by the Urban Libraries Council in conjunction with the Cleveland Public Library. The information contained in this publication is geared toward the managers of public libraries. This is not your common "how-to-do-it manual" — it is more a why to do it. Attempts have been made to cover automation applications of numerous facets of a public library's activities. Offered at the end of several talks are bibliographies suggesting further readings.

An important note stressed in the publication is that one should not automate first and think about it later. Plenty of thought should be given to what a library's needs are before any action is taken. The overall message seems to be

that the time has come for public libraries to actively pursue technological applications for library operations. Plunge carefully. Public library administrators would find this publication useful. [R: IRLA, Jan 83, p. 9]
          Amy Gische Lyons

463. Divilbiss, J. L., ed. **The Economics of Library Automation.** Urbana-Champaign, Ill., Graduate School of Library Science, University of Illinois, 1977. 164p. illus. index. $8.00. LC 77-075153. ISBN 0-87845-046-7; ISSN 0069-4789.

The Annual Clinics on Library Applications of Data Processing, sponsored by the Graduate School of Library Science, University of Illinois, are well known for the timeliness of the topics studied and the succinctness of the presentations. This volume, containing the papers presented at the thirteenth clinic (1976) on the economics of library automation, is in no way an exception. Some of the papers deal with specific library processes, such as circulation and book catalog production, while others look at the economics of conversion, whether as an independent system or in the realm of cooperative development. No magical formulas are offered as ways of reducing the costs of automation. Instead, very lucid and practical suggestions are made with regard to both the costs and the value of such efforts. This is a collection of very important and significant papers dealing with critical issues in library automation. [R: C&RL, Nov 77, pp. 533-34; JAL, Sept 77, p. 243]   Lorraine Mathies

464. Divilbiss, J. L., ed. **Negotiating for Computer Services.** Urbana-Champaign, Ill., Graduate School of Library Science, University of Illinois, 1978. 117p. index. (Proceedings of the 1977 Clinic on Library Applications of Data Processing). $9.00. LC 78-13693. ISBN 0-87845-048-3.

The general premise behind this work is that librarians in general do not know how to negotiate contracts, in particular contracts for computer-based services. This volume should serve as a handy aid for any librarians facing the necessity of learning to negotiate. All of the papers will be useful in situations to which they apply, but of particular value are Boss's "Negotiating an Automated Circulation System: The Librarian's Viewpoint"; Gurr's "Negotiating a Turnkey System: The Vendor's Viewpoint"; Dyer's "Data Processing Contracts: A Tutorial"; and Corey's "Negotiating Computer Services within an Organization." These four papers are worth the price of the book for the advice that they give, advice that is applicable to a variety of situations, but that also gets down to specific details. Other papers, useful in special situations, discuss network contracts with OCLC, innovative services, database service, and database sharing.   Jessica L. Harris

465. Divilbiss, J. L., ed. **Public Access to Library Automation.** Urbana-Champaign, Ill., Graduate School of Library and Information Science, University of Illinois, 1981. 128p. illus. index. (Proceedings of the 1980 Clinic on Library Applications of Data Processing). $10.00. LC 81-11685. ISBN 0-87845-065-3.

"Of the various trends in library automation today, public access is clearly one of the most difficult, complex, and potentially rewarding areas of development," says editor Divilbiss on page 1. Several of the following papers indicate that this public access is facilitated by the existence of user-centered, active information service facilities (such as were envisioned by ALA's "Library of the Future" at the New York World's Fair as long ago as 1964).

There seems to be agreement among the authors that the user is smarter and more involved than he or she was given credit for before—and further, that this affects the design process. One paper sees that process as involving this set of heuristics: describe and weigh acceptable characteristics of hardware, software, data, and interaction processes, then "cut and try," modify and improve, and then implement carefully but firmly. Another paper sees the role of the technical services function as being greatly affected by the change of the new code from the previous focus on the main entry to the "user-friendly" multi-access style of today. Readers appreciating practical papers are referred to Beckman's description of the University of Guelph's experiences, while those with a theoretical bent would prefer that by Hewett and Meadow. Nothing new is added by the paper on problems of the handicapped. Physician Levy's chapter on "Resistence to Technology" is a minor classic and heartening to a lonely project director needing to prepare a final report. Public access is or will become an issue at your institution so you *do* need access to this slim volume. [R: JAL, May 82, p. 98]
                                        E. B. Jackson

466. Fosdick, Howard. **Computer Basics for Librarians and Information Scientists.** Arlington, Va., Information Resources Press, 1981. 203p. bibliog. index. $22.50. LC 81-80539. ISBN 0-87815-034-X.

This volume actually deals with computer basics. Its strengths are its treatment of storage considerations, programming languages and their special characteristics and capabilities, internal methods of memory management, the technical computing principles of multiprogramming and virtual storage, and the essentiality of documentation. It deals with addressability, static-partition multiprogramming, dynamic-partition memory management, program relocation memory management, and virtual storage, including advantages and disadvantages of various options.

In addition to the above topics, the book provides a simple introduction to computing systems hardware, personnel requirements, storage mediums, operating systems and systems support software, database systems (of which there are now more than 900), and mini- and microcomputer systems.

While librarians may wish that the volume had been less brief and had covered the MARC communications format developed by the Library of Congress when discussing fixed-length records (blocked or unblocked) and variable-length blocked records, the latter discussion might have proved too extensive and complex for a work of this type.

The appendices include a helpful character code translation table, including ASCII and EBCDIC, a capacity table from the IBM 3330 Disk Reference Summary, and an outline of IBM operating systems development. Also included are a topical index, a regular index, and a selective, annotated bibliography. The major advantage of this work for librarians and information system personnel who are desirous of achieving a stronger technical mastery of the computer is that it provides technical information about computers in a form that they can comprehend. [R: BL, 15 Apr 82, p. 1066; LQ, July 82, p. 289]   Richard Palmer

467. Hagler, Ronald, and Peter Simmons. **The Bibliographic Record and Information Technology.** Chicago, American Library Association, 1982. 346p. illus. bibliog. index. $25.00. LC 82-14706. ISBN 0-8389-0370-3.

Although the preface of this work declares that it is intended to be a library school textbook on bibliographic information and its automated handling as well as on the development of coordinated systems of bibliographic control and the intelligent use of them, it is not a how-to manual. It is also more than a student's introduction to the complex world of computer hardware, software, and online bibliographic networks. Because of its lucid handling of everything from the purposes and methods of bibliography and the content and format of bibliographic records to the use of bibliographic files and the creating and sharing of bibliographic records in networks, it will serve as a basic reference work for library and information system personnel, even though it offers no bibliography and few footnotes. Readers are directed to extensive bibliographies in the *Annual Review of Information Science and Technology* and *Library Resources & Technical Services* (annual articles on "Year's Work") for more detailed treatment of topics covered in this text.

The appendix includes a detailed examination of the Canadian MARC format, with an index to MARC coding, and a useful discussion of alphanumeric arrangement, covering filing rules and filing by computer.

This textbook should help information professionals make better decisions about cataloging, classifying, and filing rules and their suitability in particular systems. It should also contribute to the development of better-quality bibliographic records for inclusion in computer systems and networks. [R: C&RL, Nov 83, pp. 491-92; JAL, May 83, p. 121; JAL, Sept 83, p. 232; LJ, 15 June 83, p. 1238; RQ, Summer 83, pp. 435-36] Richard Palmer

468. The Impact of New Technology on Libraries and Information Centres: Report of the Library Association Working Party 1981-2. London, Library Association; distr., Phoenix, Ariz., Oryx Press, 1982. 54p. bibliog. (Library Association Pamphlet, No. 38). $10.00pa. ISBN 0-85365-925-7.

This is the report of the Library Association Working Party on the New Technologies, whose purpose was to address the changing technology of information dissemination in libraries. In a very brief first section the establishment, scope, and methods of the Working Party are described. Next, the technologies applicable to library work are treated in a general way. The main part of the report is about the various effects of technological advances on the field itself, particularly in regard to the rapid change brought about by technology. How the professional librarian and the user can adapt to this change and what the problems are that will be encountered in the process are discussed and analyzed, and recommendations are given for arriving at solutions.

As Alvin Toffler pointed out in *Future Shock*, the future is here. This is especially evident in the computerization of library technical

and public services. This report is intended to minimize the shock. [R: C&RL, Nov 83, pp. 492-93; JAL, Mar 83, p. 59]

469. Information Technology: Critical Choices for Library Decision-Makers. Allen Kent and Thomas J. Galvin, eds. New York, Marcel Dekker, 1982. 477p. index. (Books in Library and Information Science, Vol. 40). $57.50. LC 82-14886. ISBN 0-8247-1737-6.

This volume presents papers and a summary of discussion from the Fourth Pittsburgh Conference, held in November 1981. The conference focused on electronic information technology and its impact on library and information services. The book is divided into seven sections that reflect the five major conference sessions and the materials distributed to participants. A paper discussing the impact of five key developments in information technology on libraries appears in section 1. The main sessions deal with technological directions for the future; managerial problems of choice of technology; implications of networking, especially from the viewpoint of the local library; effect of machines on people; and competition between tax-supported information agencies and the private sector. A presentation entitled "Libraries in Our Future: Federal Postures and Perceptions" and concluding statements are also included. An appendix contains a lengthy paper on current information technologies and a glossary of data processing terms. Short bibliographies are provided by a few authors, and the volume contains a comprehensive index.

The book is intended for those who were unable to attend the conference and for students and practitioners concerned with the future of libraries in a technological society. The information is both authoritative and current. There is surprisingly little duplication for a volume of this type, and continuity among the presentations is good. [R: BL, 15 Apr 83, p. 1074; C&RL, July 83, pp. 293-94; JAL, Mar 83, p. 59; JAL, Sept 83, p. 228; LJ, 15 Apr 83, p. 803] Andrew G. Torok

470. Lancaster, F. W. **Libraries and Librarians in an Age of Electronics.** Arlington, Va., Information Resources Press, 1982. 229p. illus. bibliog. index. $26.50. LC 82-081403. ISBN 0-87815-040-4.

If he is not actually a proponent of a paperless society, Lancaster has written extensively on the subject and the role of libraries in an ever more pervasive electronic environment. Can any book that talks about the "limited life expectancy" of libraries, refers to the "inevitable decline" of the library in the last two decades of this century, and includes a chapter entitled "The Disembodiment of the Library" offer hope to the library profession as a whole? To traditional librarians and for the traditional library, the answer is no. Lancaster concludes, however, that the "future of the professional information specialist appears very secure." This apparent contradiction can only be resolved if librarians reassess their roles. Librarians must become providers of information who are not tied, physically or mentally, to the traditional library and its internal materials.

Lancaster restates his opinions that electronic communications will eventually substitute for all other forms, that paper publishing will be replaced by electronic publications, and that libraries will become obsolete. This theme is a familiar one, and, indeed, several portions of this book have been published in other forms. As is stated in the preface, an attempt has been made in this book to "pull this and other material together and to present it as a coherent whole." This attempt is successful in that the book is highly readable and provides a cohesive overview of Lancaster's opinions. The work is indexed and has a lengthy unannotated bibliography. Recommended reading for all librarians, especially any still unfamiliar with Lancaster's views of a paperless society. [R: BL, 15 Jan 83, p. 657; C&RL, July 83, p. 294; RQ, Spring 83, pp. 319-20; WLB, Feb 83, pp. 518-19]

Greg Byerly

471.   Lancaster, F. Wilfrid, ed. **Library Automation as a Source of Management Information: Papers Presented at the 1982 Clinic on Library Applications of Data Processing, April 25-28, 1982.** Champaign, Ill., Graduate School of Library and Information Science, University of Illinois, 1983. 200p. index. $15.00. LC 83-9110. ISBN 0-87845-068-8.

This collection of 11 papers, presented at the nineteenth annual clinic on library applications of data processing, ostensibly focuses on the use of automated systems as sources of data for improving management and decision making. The volume includes three philosophical discussions, one tutorial on management information systems, and seven studies of the use of automated systems as sources of management data in such diverse settings as Bell Laboratories, the University of Arizona, OCLC, Pikes Peak Library District, State University of New York, Bibliographic Retrieval Services, and the University of California at Berkeley. The use studies are quite system specific; they are likely to be of marginal use in other systems or en-

vironments. The philosophical presentations cover the role of intuition, experience, and inference in using data, the likelihood of human distress and unrest under increasingly quantitative MIS systems, and the characteristics of managerial resistance to such systems.

Unfortunately, the very able editor, Lancaster, contributes only a half page of introduction and an index. What the work lacks in focus and coherence is probably indicative of the current state of the art in library management and administrators' fledgling contacts with library automation. The book should be of moderate interest to librarians and library school students.

Richard Palmer

472.   Lancaster, F. Wilfrid, ed. **Problems and Failures in Library Automation.** Urbana-Champaign, Ill., University of Illinois, Graduate School of Library Science, 1979. 109p. index. (Proceedings of the 1978 Clinic on Library Applications of Data Processing). $9.00. LC 78-31801. ISBN 0-87845-050-5.

Nine reports document experiences and lessons learned from library automation projects in various places and types of libraries. Turnkey computer systems and home-grown acquisition, circulation, and cataloging systems, as well as computer-based networks, are described. There is also one paper on the problems of teaching library automation at the University of Illinois. The papers are of uneven quality— some of them are merely reminiscences, while others are philosophical and didactic. A compilation of all the lessons learned or problem issues would have been helpful, but neither the editor nor the indexer saw fit to do such a synthesis, although they did compile a list of acronyms used by the individual authors. An unusual paper on the problems of library automation in *India* seems out of place, but is still appropriate because it includes a list of recommended improvements for library planners to consider; we could wish that the authors at this conference had been asked to do the same from their perspectives. Kunkel's paper on the Washington library network comes the closest to fulfilling this requirement by asking and answering questions about system characteristics, governance, financing, and computer technology. [R: C&RL, Sept 79, pp. 477-78; JAL, Nov 79, pp. 290-91; LJ, 15 Oct 79, p. 2177]

Pauline Atherton

473.   **Library Automation: Five Case Studies.** Maurice J. Freedman, ed. New York, Library Journal/R. R. Bowker, 1982. 56p. illus. (LJ Special Report, No. 22). $8.50pa. (prepaid);

$10.00pa. (billed). ISBN 0-8352-1537-7; ISSN 0362-448X.

Although the title would suggest that this collection of case studies covers the broad area of library automation, it is actually limited to accounts of the implementation of commercial circulation systems. The case studies detail the experiences of one university library and four public libraries as they installed systems provided by five different vendors. Although not all vendors which offer circulation systems are represented, those selected certainly compose a very large percentage of what is actually a specialized area of the automation market. The vendors included are: SCI (Systems Control Inc.), Gaylord, DataPhase, GEAC, and CLSI.

This collection is well edited and presented. As would be expected, the case studies cover such areas as planning, bidding, training, installation, acceptance, maintenance, and future development. The presentations are arranged in a fairly uniform style, which makes comparison relatively easy. However, *Library Automation* suffers from a malady common to all such works: the fact that so much of any experience is very much indigenous to the institution and is not applicable elsewhere. In addition, both the CLSI and GEAC installations occurred in the early corporate life of those companies. Therefore, many of the difficulties encountered by the two libraries have since been eliminated and would not likely be of concern to libraries now considering their systems. In spite of these problems, this work is must reading for any library considering the purchase of a circulation system. A careful reading could very well prevent many costly mistakes in what can be a very frustrating experience. [R: RQ, Winter 82, p. 213]   Bill J. Corbin

474. MacCafferty, Maxine, comp. **Fax & Teletext.** London, Aslib, 1977. 77p. index. (Aslib Bibliography, No. 5). £4.25pa. ISBN 0-85142-093-1.

This work is up to the usual standard of the Aslib Bibliographies and is in the same format. The 394 references, many annotated, range from popular lay items to technical discussions. In addition to books and journals, there are references to patents, newspapers, and the trade literature mostly from 1974 to 1976. References conform to the stated purpose: "to illustrate developments in the United Kingdom." While the technical coverage is worldwide (mostly English language), discussion of applications is limited to Britain, with some additions for other countries.

The American user will find this bibliography very useful for coverage of facsimile and related developments, in many of which the United Kingdom is considerably ahead of the United States. There are even references on do-it-yourself Teletext. Articles on Ceefax, Oracle, Viewdata, Postfax, and Confravision are included. Brief appendices give helpful information for learning more about these systems.
                    Jessica L. Harris

475. Matthews, Joseph R. **Choosing an Automated Library System: A Planning Guide.** Chicago, American Library Association, 1980. 119p. bibliog. index. $12.50pa. LC 80-17882. ISBN 0-8389-0310-X.

The acquisition and operation of computer-based systems to support internal library functions is no longer esoteric or avant-garde. Most of the barriers to this kind of activity — among them high cost and lack of availability — have fallen in the last several years, and all but the smallest libraries can expect to become involved in automated systems. But, how does the librarian go about choosing from among the many available options? Questions about which of the vendor systems to choose, whether to develop a system from scratch, how much it will cost, or how to evaluate its benefits are complex in themselves, and made more complex by the extraordinary mythology associated with computers.

Luckily, as the profession has gained more experience in this area, books are appearing which can provide guidance. Matthews's *Choosing an Automated Library System* is one of the best. A consultant, Matthews understands the different perspectives of the librarian and the computer specialist, and writes to bridge the gap between the two.

The work is essentially a how-to-do-it guide, presenting all kinds of useful information and suggestions from "how to begin" through needs analysis, considering alternatives, selection, contracting, installations, and implementation. Appendices present more detailed information about particular areas in the library that might be considered for automation. As a general guide to the process, this book will be hard to beat. For a more technical approach, see Corbin's *Developing Computer-Based Library Systems* (Oryx Press, 1981). Both are highly recommended. [R: BL, 15 Jan 81, p. 671; JAL, May 81, pp. 98-99]   Ward Shaw

476. **New Information Technologies — New Opportunities.** Linda C. Smith, ed. Urbana-Champaign, Ill., Graduate School of Library

Science, University of Illinois, 1982. 119p. bibliog. index. (Clinic on Library Application of Data Processing: 1981). $11.00. LC 82-10947. ISBN 0-87845-066-1.

This collection of 10 papers presented at the eighteenth annual clinic reflects the very substantial progress that has been made in using technological developments, such as microcomputers, word processors, videotext and videodisc systems, and improved input/output devices, in libraries and information systems. Over the years the clinics at the University of Illinois have provided a valuable and remarkably consistent forum for well-informed experts to present their views, findings, and recommendations on the shifting and expanding penetration of new technologies into the management of information in libraries and database services.

This year's volume includes offerings from two directors of research and development, one at a university library and one at an abstracting service, three faculty members at the host institution, two information consultants, one reference librarian, one technical information specialist, and one manager of information sciences at a research institute. Several papers describe technologies for information processing, several others describe technologies for information transmission, and several assess some of the problems and issues raised by technological innovation. One addresses the problems that have surfaced in providing copyright protection for computer software and databases, and one discusses the changing professional roles, identity, and status of librarians and information professionals as new technologies tend, in the popular mind, to give a "scientific" aura to the profession. A useful and penetrating state-of-the-art conference report.   Richard Palmer

477. Norman, Adrian R. D. **Electronic Document Delivery: The ARTEMIS Concept for Document Digitalisation and Teletransmission.** White Plains, N.Y., Knowledge Industry Publications, 1982. 226p. $45.00. LC 81-20774. ISBN 0-86729-011-0.

One of the major components of effective systems for access to information is electronic document delivery. Up to now, we have effectively invented systems to tell us where items are, but have been unable to crack the delivery nut. This report is one of a very few documents that begins to point the direction for solving this problem.

Electronic Document Delivery is a report of a study by Arthur D. Little, Inc., for The Directorate General Information Market and Innova-

tion of the Commission of the European Communities. It describes a proposed system of document delivery to supplement Euronet/Diane, the online European information service. The report is divided into two parts. The first outlines the ARTEMIS document delivery system as conceived by ADL, discussing objectives, problems, solutions, and probable legal and managerial issues raised. It also presents a helpful scheme for development. The analysis is of considerable general interest, although understandably specific to the European situation. The second part of the report consists of an extremely helpful review of the technology related to document delivery along with guesses about how the technology is likely to develop. It covers capture techniques for new material, conversion techniques for existing material, archival and other storage devices, intelligent copiers, printing terminals, text and image compression, document quality, telecommunications, and satellite communications. This second section is of considerable usefulness.

In spite of a bothersome format and a variety of irritating typographical errors, I strongly recommend this book for all library and information science collections. It is a first attempt to cover what will likely be the most important topic in the field a few years from now. [R: C&RL, Jan 83, p. 82]   Ward Shaw

478. Plaister, Jean M. **Computing in LASER (London and South Eastern Library Region): Regional Library Co-operation.** London, Library Association; distr., Phoenix, Ariz., Oryx Press, 1982. 55p. bibliog. (Case Studies in Library Automation). $15.00pa. ISBN 0-85365-954-0.

LASER, financed by its member libraries, is part of a nationwide system for regional library cooperation in London and southeastern England. This case study traces the development of LASER from its beginning in 1970 through 1982. Although it is a British system, the concepts and ideas used in the development of LASER are applicable to library systems throughout the world. This study highlights some of the concerns that many libraries have encountered, including the use of microfilm for interlibrary lending, the collective requirements of network members, and the development of a system on a small and tightly controlled budget. LASER is a success story that is well worth reading. [R: LR, Summer 83, p. 170]

H. Robert Malinowsky

479. **The Professional Librarian's Reader in Library Automation and Technology.** White

Plains, N.Y., Knowledge Industry Publications, 1980. 201p. illus. bibliog. (Professional Librarian Series). o.p. LC 80-11636. ISBN 0-914236-59-8.

In her introduction, Susan Martin reveals that this monograph is composed of selected chapters from earlier Knowledge Industry Publications volumes. An analysis of this list reveals that: all are from the Professional Librarian series, all were published between 1977 and 1979, several have been superseded or are second editions (which suggests the possibility of future updating), and several have been previously reviewed in *ARBA*. The analysis follows:

Alice Harrison Bahr — *Automated Library Circulation Systems 1979-80*, 2nd ed. (*ARBA* 80, entry 225); *Microforms: The Librarian's View 1978-79*, 2nd ed. (*ARBA* 79, entry 332); *Book Theft and Library Security Systems 1978-79* (*ARBA* 79, entry 250).

Susan K. Martin — *Library Networks, 1978-79*, 3rd ed. (*ARBA* 79, entry 150).

Pauline Atherton and Roger Christian — *Librarians and Online Services* (*ARBA* 79, entry 299).

Roger Christian — *The Electronic Library: Bibliographic Data Bases 1978-79*, 2nd ed. (*ARBA* 79, entry 261).

Audrey N. Grosch — *Minicomputers in Libraries, 1979-80* (*ARBA* 81, entry 294).

S. Michael Malinconico and Paul J. Fasana — *The Future of the Catalog: The Library's Choices* (*ARBA* 81, entry 242).

Selected chapters are usually general overviews of the topics covered.

Whereas the original volumes are useful and of good quality, the usefulness of this volume is suspect given the assumption that the promised later editions will provide in similarly selected chapters, information which will supersede that offered through this compilation. One also wonders why chapters from another of the series titles, *Library Manager's Guide to Automation* (1979), by Richard Boss, were not included. [R: LJ, 15 Oct 80, p. 2170]

Judith Wolfe

480.　Rowley, J. E. **Computers for Libraries.** London, Clive Bingley; distr., Hamden, Conn., Shoe String Press, 1980. 159p. index. (Outlines of Modern Librarianship). $12.00. ISBN 0-85157-298-7.

Rowley's work is an introduction to the computer and its library-related applications, suggested for use by library and information science students. It is an attempt to present a rather broad overview of a very rapidly expand-

ing field. Fundamental information is given on such topics as the design and function of computer hardware, the implementation of computerized systems, the storage and retrieval of information, and the use of computers in standard library operations. Numerous systems in Europe (especially Great Britain) and the United States are surveyed, with an emphasis placed on online databases, search services, and techniques.

Although it is less dated than earlier works, such as L. A. Tedd's *Introduction to Computer-Based Library Systems* (Heyden, 1977), Stanley J. Swihart's *Computer Systems in the Library* (Melville, 1973), or Stephen R. Salmon's *Library Automation Systems* (Marcel Dekker, 1975), Rowley's work suffers from a fragmentation caused by the author's overzealous attempt to survey far too many subjects in 159 pages. The average reader in the intended audience will come away with an information overload resulting from too many brief encounters with new concepts. Admittedly, the text is intended to be a springboard, but the majority of the chapter references are from British works of the mid-1970s. Few of these will prove useful resources today. The text, if used in a short course, will confuse students. In a full term, more in-depth coverage would be better suited.

The second edition (1986) was expanded to 250 pages to accommodate all the areas of librarianship in which computers are now used. Since this is practically every area, this work remains a condensed overview without much depth. [R: JAL, Nov 81, p. 297; LJ, 1 Oct 81, p. 1889]

Bill J. Corbin

481.　Rowley, J. E. **Mechanized In-House Information Systems.** London, Clive Bingley; distr., New York, K. G. Saur, 1979. 208p. illus. index. $20.50. ISBN 0-85157-259-6.

The aim of the book is to introduce students and others unfamiliar with computer-based information systems to the role of such systems and to develop a framework for understanding computer operations. Part 1, "Introduction to Basic Concepts," defines a mechanized in-house system, and discusses aspects of systems design and computer processing. Although considerable space is devoted to problems of input (bibliographic information, document numbers, abstracts, classification, thesauri, and instructions for formating output, etc.), it serves as a summary and is not a substitute for basic computer coursework and reading. An extensive bibliography follows part 1. Part 2, "Case Studies," provides an account of 12 representative systems operational during

1978—among them are ASSASSIN, ENLIST, LABSTAT, and SCORPIO. A bibliography of writings related to the specific systems follows each case. The book serves its intended purpose as a general introduction to computer-based information systems and is useful supplementary reading for students. [R: JAL, Nov 79, p. 307]

Christine Gehrt Wynar

482.   The Sourcebook of Library Technology: A Cumulative Edition of Library Technology Reports, 1965-1985. 1986 ed. Chicago, American Library Association, 1986. 1v. plus microfiche in pockets. $50.00 (looseleaf). ISBN 0-8389-5469-3.

This cumulative edition of one of the most important library publication projects must be a most welcome addition to our professional collection. For years librarians have relied on *LTR* in selecting and evaluating their equipment. The *Sourcebook*, published in a three-ring looseleaf binder, contains a title page, subscription information, an introduction with how-to-use-it instructions, and an 11-page index. The microfiche are stored in reinforced fiche pockets. *SLT* excludes "Abstracts," "Library Technology News" and "New Products," which is quite understandable in a retrospective cumulation.

Some of the material listed in *SLT* has been updated (e.g., addresses of manufacturers). Prices, however, have inexplicably *not* been updated. Also, the printed index does not include the titles of reports or the names of companies evaluating the project. Despite all this, *SLT* is an essential purchase for even the smallest libraries. [R: C&RL, Nov 76, pp. 558-61]

Bohdan S. Wynar

483.   Tedd, L. A. An Introduction to Computer-Based Library Systems. New York, Heyden, 1978. 208p. illus. index. (Heyden International Topics in Science). o.p. ISBN 0-85501-221-8.

This textbook, the outgrowth of a course taught at the College of Librarianship, Wales, provides in three major sections a nontechnical introduction to computers, to computer-based library housekeeping systems, and to computerized information retrieval systems. It deals with the advantages and disadvantages of computer systems in the library environment, the basic components of the computer, procedures in setting up computer systems, the nature of programming, with illustrations in BASIC, the characteristics of the MARC communications format, a variety of computer-produced indexes, the elements of SDI and retrospective search systems, and includes some helpful discussions on acquisitions and cataloging, circulation, and serials systems (with evaluations of them and their costs).

Each of the chapters concludes with references, and many chapters also list examples and suggestions for further reading. Some useful works published in the United States are not listed. Some illustrative material is provided. Figures include a punched card, a bar-coded label, a flow chart, a computer-generated book card, a search on the Dialog system, and an SDI system. Tables cover the date, size, source, and cost of a sample of databases; the name, supplier, language, and comments about software packages; and the printed source, database name, and producer of a short list of bibliographic databases. Three appendices cover binary arithmetic, a glossary of computer terms for librarians, and instructions on how to compute a check digit. The volume closes with acronym and subject indexes. This well-organized, British-oriented introductory textbook should prove useful in library schools in England and North America. A few explanations are less than transparent, and a skilled instructor will need to interpret.

A second edition (1984) has been published. [R: SL, Apr 81, p. 165]

Richard Palmer

484.   Thompson, James. The End of Libraries. London, Clive Bingley; distr., Hamden, Conn., Shoe String Press, 1982. 127p. index. $17.50. ISBN 0-85157-349-5.

Thompson examines the impact of technology on the libraries of the future and the future of libraries. He discusses in some detail machine-readable records, databases, electronic publishing, electronic storage of information, videotext systems, and the training that will be needed by future librarians and information specialists. That libraries and librarianship are changing goes without saying, whether for good or ill. A careful reading of Thompson's book will do much to alert librarians and others to what lies ahead in the next few years. A special merit of this attention-getting title is the author's ability to write about complex matters in a style that is both readable and informative. [R: JAL, May 83, p. 101; JAL, Sept 83, p. 227]

John David Marshall

REFERENCE WORKS

485.   Dewe, Ainslie, comp. An Annotated Bibliography of Automation in Libraries 1975-1978. London, Aslib, 1980. 76p. index.

£6.90pa. (Aslib members); £8.75 (non-members). ISBN 0-85142-132-6.

A continuation in the series of bibliographies on library automation by Aslib, this title surveys 732 references from 86 periodicals, providing brief annotations for most items. The emphasis is on library housekeeping operations. Materials describing commercially available information services have generally been included only where there is a discussion of procedures which have general application in the automation of libraries (e.g., automatic indexing). The Aslib Bibliography Series No. 8, *On-Line Information Retrieval 1965-1976* (and future editions), complements this volume.

The bibliography is divided into four sections: "General," "Housekeeping Routines," "Bibliographic Control," and "Information Work." Included are items in English as well as French and German, and most of the materials are available for loan from the Aslib library. An author index and subject index (terms are drawn mainly from titles and abstracts) complete the volume. [R: LR, Autumn 80, p. 195]

Sherrilynne Shirley

486. MacCafferty, Maxine, comp. **An Annotated Bibliography of Automation in Libraries and Information Systems, 1972-1975.** London, Aslib, 1976. 147p. index. £6.50pa. ISBN 0-85142-079-8.

This compilation of 813 items updates Tinker's *Annotated Bibliography of Library Automation 1968-1972* (Aslib, 1973). The range of topics is shown by the sections included: information processing and management, housekeeping routines, bibliographic control, and retrieval and search. All the references are in English, about equally divided between United States and British Commonwealth publications. There is also substantial coverage of international publications.

Coverage is thorough and the annotations are helpful. Author and subject indexes complete the work. The latter is better than many such but could be improved. Acronyms and names of systems are bountifully given, but concept coverage is more erratic. All in all, this is an excellent resource. [R: LQ, Oct 77, p. 519]

Jessica L. Harris

487. **Online Terminal/Microcomputer Guide & Directory, 1982-83.** 3rd ed. Weston, Conn., Online, 1982. 286p. $40.00 spiralbound. ISSN 0198-697X.

This third edition features, as the title would indicate with the inclusion of microcomputers, an expansion in scope over previous editions. The publisher's introductory note makes a good case for broadening the mission of this compendium in light of wider applications and as substitutes for dumb terminals. Four feature articles on terminal and microcomputer selection are technically solid and provide a sound base for further reading.

The guide begins with a limited glossary of terms most often found regarding printers (RO and KSR), video terminals, microcomputers, and modems. Next come a useful annotated bibliography and a couple of information matrices on databases and value-added telecommunication networks. The hardware listings are by manufacturer and model number. Each entry is in functional specification format and resembles an abbreviated product brief. At a quick glance these charts are helpful in comparing equipment. I do *not* recommend any decision to select or reject equipment be based solely on these entries, as there were several inaccuracies spotted on first reading and others noted upon closer investigation. The new section on microcomputers surveys 65 models of some 40 manufacturers. The entries range from the small home or personal class machines up to the larger business application micros.

The directory section lists names of firms, addresses, and phone numbers for U.S. sales, brokers, and service centers. Eighty countries are covered in the international sales/service section.

Joel S. Kent

MICROCOMPUTERS

488. Anthony, L. J., ed. **Microprocessors and Intelligence: Proceedings of an Aslib Seminar Held 14-15 May, 1979.** London, Aslib, 1979 (c1980). 62p. £6.90pa. ISBN 0-85142-126-1.

These proceedings of an Aslib seminar held in Slough, England, in May 1979, deal with advances in the technology of computers, word and image processing, and telecommunications, with special emphasis on microprocessors and microcomputers, their associated memories, and their rapidly decreasing costs. The sessions also addressed the problem of the increasing cost of developing software adequate to meet the ever-expanding complexity of modern information needs, as well as the problem of the substantial social, economic, and management adjustments inherent in the shift to electronic office information systems. Also included are some practical comments on difficulties experienced with both Prestel (ViewData) and Teletext.

In six papers and six discussion group reports, obviously well-informed and experienced experts discuss present and future information requirements, emerging trends in computer capabilities, and the question of whether the present education of information professionals is adequate to enable them to upgrade their activities from the processing of information to the interpretation and evaluation of information that advanced computer systems will require.

While some proceedings are limited in scope and utility, these brief, British-oriented reports provide penetrating insights highly useful to progressive management personnel, information professionals, and information science educators, not only in England but in the United States as well. Occasional footnotes and references, a list of participants, including their affiliations, but no index or bibliography.

Richard Palmer

489. Boss, Richard W. **Automating Library Acquisitions: Issues and Outlook.** White Plains, N.Y., Knowledge Industry Publications, 1982. 134p. bibliog. index. (Professional Librarian Series). $27.50pa. LC 82-8941. ISBN 0-86729-006-4.

Automating Library Acquisitions is a highly readable book that is useful for librarians and library school students. It provides a checklist of features of an ideal acquisitions system that librarians will find of value in comparing the various systems available in the market. Described in this book are 3 software packages available for purchase and 11 systems marketed by turnkey vendors such as CLSI, bibliographic utilities such as OCLC, and book distributors such as Baker and Taylor. Each description covers hardware, specific functions performed by the system, special features such as the handling of gifts and exchanges, serials, routing, types of reports generated, and cost of the system.

Although *Automating Library Acquisitions* is a useful publication, it should be kept in mind that the information contained in a book of this type dates quickly. For one thing, new systems are being regularly introduced into the marketplace. For another, older vendors tend to add new features to their established systems. In view of this, librarians should keep track of such additions and changes by such means as conference exhibits, publicity brochures, and word of mouth. Finally, this book does not include systems that are available on microcomputers. Such systems are of great help to smaller libraries, and one can expect more of those systems in the future. Similarly, the usefulness of this book would have been enhanced if the author had used a tabular format to compare the features of the systems he described. The inclusion of a model request for proposal also would have been of great help to practicing librarians. [R: LJ, 15 Jan 83, p. 114]

Rao Aluri

490. Costa, Betty, and Marie Costa. **A Micro Handbook for Small Libraries and Media Centers.** Littleton, Colo., Libraries Unlimited, 1983. 216p. illus. bibliog. index. $19.50. LC 83-11294. ISBN 0-87287-354-4.

This handbook will assist in the selection and implementation of microcomputer systems. Written in clear, nontechnical language, it provides the reader with the practical knowledge needed to evaluate software and hardware in terms of a library's or media center's specific, individual needs. It offers a brief survey of the history of computers and their role in libraries, an introduction to computer software, and a discussion of the basics of hardware (central processing unit, memory, input and output devices, and modems and other peripheral devices). Detailed coverage of a variety of specific types of software and applications for microcomputers in libraries comprises the bulk of this work. Library aplications for general-purpose software packages that handle word processing, spreadsheet programs, database management systems, and various library functions that lend themselves to microcomputer automation are discussed. The final chapters instruct the reader in selecting and implementing a computer system and offer an account of one of the author's experiences in using a microcomputer in the media center. An extensive selection of additional sources of information is provided in the appendices, which include lists of books, periodicals, newsletters, software dealers and packages, organizations, and individuals, as well as a glossary of terms, information on caring for the computer system, and sample evaluation charts. The second edition (1986) is now available. [R: AL, Sept 83, p. 565; BL, 15 Jan 84, p. 714; JAL, Nov 83, p. 305; RQ, Spring 84, p. 378; SLJ, Mar 84, p. 120; SLMQ, Summer 84, p. 311; TN, Winter 84, p. 217; VOYA, Feb 84, p. 350; WLB, Jan 84, p. 367]

491. **Microcomputers for Libraries: How Useful Are They?** Jane Beaumont and Donald Krueger, eds. Ottawa, Ont., Canadian Library Association, 1983. 123p. $12.00 spiralbound. ISBN 0-88802-170-4.

This book is composed of nine papers presented at a workshop held during the 1982 Canadian Library Association Annual Conference. The purpose of the workshop and this resulting publication was "to facilitate information exchange and document the usefulness of microcomputers in libraries and their unique role in information work." The first four papers discuss general applications of microcomputers in libraries. Howard Fosdick, the keynote speaker, presents a very useful and instructive technical overview of microcomputers. Certain selected topics are considered in more detail in the remaining five papers. These include guidelines for selecting application software, database management systems, microcomputer-based bulletin board systems, and potential uses of microcomputers in library research. Two appendices list sources of microcomputer information and present a checklist of microcomputer applications.

The information presented in these papers is accurate, informative, and potentially valuable to persons attempting to determine how useful microcomputers can be in libraries. The strength of the collected papers is their detailed explanations of how microcomputers can be and are being used in many different kinds of libraries. As in any published proceedings, however, the papers included are of uneven quality and necessarily cover a wide variety of topics. Even though some of the papers emphasize Canadian applications, this book compares quite favorably with two other books about microcomputers, Mark Rorvig's *Microcomputers and Libraries* (Knowledge Industry Publications, 1981) and Ching-chih Chen and Stacey E. Bressler's *Microcomputers in Libraries* (Neal-Schuman, 1982; see *ARBA* 83, entry 243). [R: JAL, Sept 83, p. 243; LJ, 1 June 83, p. 1114]
Greg Byerly

492. **Microcomputers in Libraries.** Ching-chin Chen and Stacey E. Bressler, eds. New York, Neal-Schuman, 1982. 259p. illus. bibliog. index. (Applications in Information Management and Technology Series). $27.95pa. LC 82-6493. ISBN 0-918212-61-8.

This work is a compilation of information given at a two-day Institute on Microcomputers in Libraries at Simmons College in 1982. There are 13 addresses which cover a broad spectrum of topics. Most of the chapters are geared toward the complete computer novice.

The book is divided into five major sections. Part 1 includes a general introduction into the world of microcomputers. A brief discussion of computer history is coupled with an under-standable section on computer hardware, software, and operation. Part 2 presents an in-depth look at hardware and software. The topics of evaluating and selecting the necessary hardware and peripheral devices, and administrative concerns about hardware acquisitions such as bids, site preparation, and security are also discussed. A selection on what is available in computer software for library management uses and how to evaluate the software is included. Part 3 deals with the area of applications. It begins with a general article which touches on all areas of computer application. This section is rounded out with articles on microcomputer applications for academic, public, school, and special libraries. Part 4 deals with the issue of staff development and training. Part 5 discusses how to conduct a needs assessment before jumping into the world of micros. Appendices contain a hardware comparison chart, a glossary of computer vocabulary, an extensive bibliography, as well as other items. The volume is indexed.

This work provides a beginning background for those who wish to use microcomputers for administrative and management functions in all types of libraries. It is a good introductory volume to have on the reference shelf. [R: BL, 15 Jan 83, p. 657; LJ, 1 Feb 83, p. 187; LR, Summer 83, p. 169; RQ, Winter 82, p. 213]
Joanne Troutner

493. Williams, H. L., ed. **Computerised Systems in Library and Information Services: Proceedings of a Conference of the Aslib Biological and Agricultural Sciences Group Held at the Commonwealth Institute, London, June 9, 1982.** London, Aslib, 1983. 76p. £9.50pa.; £8.00pa. (Aslib members). ISBN 0-85142-169-5.

These proceedings consist of five chapters summarizing the experiences of users of mainframe and microcomputer systems in information processing. Each contains bibliographic references. There is no index.

The chapters focus on giving advice "on what is available, how to make rational choices, and the strategy and tactics to adopt in bidding." They are addressed mainly to library and information center managers rather than to computer or systems people. Three papers discuss what can be done with computers and provide some ideas about systems analysis and managing change. One is a particularly useful presentation about what microcomputers can and cannot do. The book includes a well-organized list of references. A short paper discusses mainframe computers.

There is nothing new or very exciting in this volume, but it does draw together some practical advice to librarians embarking on computer projects. [R: JAL, Sept 83, p. 244]

A. Neil Yerkey

MINICOMPUTERS

494.   Boss, Richard W. **The Library Manager's Guide to Automation.** White Plains, N.Y., Knowledge Industry Publications, 1979. 106p. illus. bibliog. index. (Professional Librarian Series). o.p. LC 79-3057. ISBN 0-914236-33-4; 0-914236-38-5pa.

The book's intended purpose is to "describe the present state of automation, its value to libraries, future trends and the role of the library manager in the conversion process" as well as "all the steps in the process of making and carrying out the decision [to automate]." This ambitious goal requires more than the 85 pages of text actually devoted to it. The remaining pages are given to a brief "Glossary of Automation Terms," "Selected General Readings," "Sources for Automated Products and Services," "Bibliography," and an index. The volume is apparently intended for library directors of medium- to large-sized libraries, since the term "library manager" is not defined and most of the examples and discussion center around academic or large public library systems.

Although an authoritative work, the book is far from being a definitive guide to library automation. An expansion of some sections, such as the one on contract negotiations and other managerial decision areas, would have been more useful than the cursory discussion of hardware and software. The role of microcomputers in libraries is dismissed in favor of minicomputer applications. No specific mention is made of Data Base Management Systems (DBMS), although the major bibliographic utilities are briefly discussed. Topics presented in this book are covered in greater detail by other volumes in the Professional Librarian Series and other works, e.g., *Developing Computer-Based Library Systems* (Oryx Press, 1980).

The book will serve best as an executive summary of fairly recent library automation activity for the busy library manager. It will also prove useful as an outline of library automation for the beginning library science student. A second edition was published in 1984. [R: C&RL, July 80, pp. 372-74; JAL, Sept 80, p. 229]

Andrew G. Torok

495.   Grosch, Audrey N. **Distributed Computing and the Electronic Library: Micros to Superminis.** White Plains, N.Y., Knowledge Industry Publications, 1985. 205p. bibliog. index. (Professional Librarian Series). $36.50; $28.50pa. LC 85-7627. ISBN 0-86729-145-1; 0-86729-144-3pa.

This updated and expanded version of the tremendously successful 1982 work, *Minicomputers in Libraries*, is a basic source for librarians and information specialists who want information about the current state of the art of distributed systems for libraries and information centers. In a chapter on the state of the art of computer applications and plans for the future, Grosch presents the results of a questionnaire distributed to U.S. and foreign libraries. Chapters are also devoted to trends in library automation, to communications technology, and to hardware and software developments. One chapter describes and analyzes commercially available integrated library systems and another discusses systems software for specific applications. There is a directory of installed systems arranged by library which includes basic facts about each system. This directory has its own index. There are an additional directory of names and addresses of suppliers and a glossary.

This is a carefully prepared, sensible guide for the novice in computer applications in libraries, replete with vitally important advice for library decision makers. There are other software directories, but this is particularly useful because of Grosch's critical analysis of commercially available systems and recognition that an ideal system for one library may not suit another. While directed towards the tyro, this book should be a valuable resource and reference tool for those with much more experience.

Margaret McKinley

496.   Lancaster, F. Wilfrid, ed. **Applications of Minicomputers to Library and Related Problems: Papers Presented at the 1974 Clinic on Library Applications of Data Processing, April 28-May 1, 1974.** Urbana-Champaign, Ill., Graduate School of Library Science, University of Illinois, 1974. 195p. illus. index. o.p. LC 65-1841. ISBN 0-87845-041-6; ISSN 0069-4789.

The papers in these proceedings of the annual Illinois clinic present a wide range of applications of minicomputers to library operations. Included in the volume are papers on circulation control, cataloging, education and training, information retrieval, acquisitions, serials control, and other technical processes. In some applications the minicomputer is a stand-alone unit, in others it is a data collection and preparation device, and in still others it is an online terminal operating within a network. All of these configurations are represented in these proceedings.

Some of the papers are valuable for their instructional approach to the subject while others are useful for their description of operational systems. Additionally, the book includes "home-made" systems (e.g., the University of Maryland, Stanford's BALLOTS, and the University of Chicago's system) along with commercial systems (e.g., the IBM System 7, CLSI, and BIBNET).

The volume was not intended as a reference book and, therefore, is not designed for that use. Even though it is packed with information, there is no ready reference approach to it, except for a broad index. It is, however, an excellent examination of the use of minicomputers in the library. [R: C&RL, Nov 75, pp. 517-19]

Donald P. Hammer

497. Young, Micki Jo, with Frank A. Pezzanite and J. Chris Reisinger. **Introduction to Minicomputers in Federal Libraries.** Washington, D.C., Library of Congress; distr., Washington, D.C., GPO, 1978. 155p. bibliog. $3.25pa. LC 78-1652. S/N 030-000-00097-8.

Introduction to Minicomputers in Federal Libraries is primarily written for federal library administrators who have already conducted an internal needs assessment. Parts are suitable for middle managers and section heads at the federal level. It is assumed that the reader is already familiar with existing fundamental concepts of computers, computer peripherals, software, and systems analysis. A well-footnoted cursory review of these is given in the first three chapters.

Analysis of library applications of minicomputers begins in chapter 4, which is well thought out and organized. The reader is taken sequentially through a set of 38 possible minicomputer system design parameters. With the use of tables, each parameters is compared with the hardware and software impact that may be needed. Typical library functions are compared with operations, relationships, files, and inputs and outputs of a minicomputer system. A sample case study involving cooperative acquisitions among branch libraries illustrates the application of the design parameters and functions. Minicomputer systems are classified into five categories. This classification permits the formulation of three possible alternative minicomputer systems for the sample case study. Special considerations associated with cataloging, serials, circulation, interlibrary loan, reference, and information services are briefly

treated. This chapter alone makes the book an invaluable guide for any librarian who may be contemplating library automation.

Using the design model proposed in chapter 4, chapter 5 applies these considerations into formulating selection criteria for various minicomputer systems. New hardware and software cost data will necessarily have to replace the 1978 figures, and this trend is noted. The section "Evaluation," associated with preparing and evaluating an RFP, is particularly useful, with its direct reference to and use of a suggested LC weighting schedule supplied in the appendix. The formulation of a set of system specifications reflecting overall minicomputer systems requirements is well outlined in section F of the appendix. While the book does not include an index, it is well documented with extensive tables and readable charts that greatly assist organizing the complex topics in a cohesive, logical manner.

Pierre P. Barrette

PROGRAMMING LANGUAGES

498. Brophy, Peter. **COBOL Programming: An Introduction for Librarians.** London, Clive Bingley; distr., Hamden, Conn., Linnet Books, 1976. 153p. illus. index. o.p. LC 76-2022. ISBN 0-85157-215-4(Bingley); 0-208-01527-2(Linnet).

Given the fact that COBOL has become the computer language most commonly used in library procedures, and given the fact that the majority of librarians do not have training in computer techniques or languages, the author has seen fit to provide a bridge for that gap. COBOL is used for data manipulation rather than for calculation, and librarians involved in information retrieval, if only peripherally, will find that their jobs involve computers and computer languages to a greater extent every day. Thus, Brophy has created the first part of his book as a step-by-step tracing of a problem, introducing terms, telling how to prepare to write a COBOL program, and tracing the program through to its conclusion. The second section is a more formal presentation of COBOL as a specific language embodying assumptions, and it examines the ways in which the language works, as well as its characteristics in depth. A glossary of computer terms is provided, as in an appendix of COBOL "character sets" and "reserved words." Finally, the author cautions that his is not a programming manual, and that anyone desiring to enter programming must consult manuals keyed to the particular equipment being used, as these vary somewhat according to manufacturer. His approach of running through a problem and then becoming more technical might be very helpful to people who have no computer experience but who do not wish to remain entirely ignorant of the most significant development in the profession within recent years. [R: LJ, 1 Mar 77, p. 561; LR, Summer 77, p. 125] Koert C. Loomis, Jr.

499. Davis, Charles H., and Gerald W. Lundeen. **Illustrative Computer Programming for Libraries: Selected Examples for Information Specialists.** 2nd ed. Westport, Conn., Greenwood Press, 1981. 129p. illus. bibliog. index. (Contributions in Librarianship and Information Science, No. 39). $17.50. LC 81-1128. ISBN 0-313-22151-0; ISSN 0084-9243.

The first edition of this textbook appeared in 1974 (see *ARBA* 75, entry 275). Primarily an educational text rather than a reference work, this slender volume still has some use to novices as a handbook. The index provides clues to basic computing concepts and a subset of PL/I commands with examples to get started on. These samples are credible if not exemplary (e.g., one may code an in-core sort or a binary search in PL/I but the current state of software technology renders such unnecessary).

This is an introductory text—there is only a limited discussion of file access methods and real-time programming. In general, large-scale systems such as library applications lend themselves to the use of more sophisticated software. Modern Data Base/Data Communication interfaces to higher level languages, such as PL/I, which greatly simplify the programming task and enhance "user-friendliness" are not mentioned.

The book progresses from very simple exercises to moderately difficult projects, including a short discussion of the theory behind the computing principle and the PL/I examples. The beginner familiar with this text should be able to code simple programs, the first step to practical applications. [R: JAL, May 82, p. 119]
David E. Matthews

500. Fosdick, Howard. **Structured PL/I Programming for Textual and Library Processing.** Littleton, Colo., Libraries Unlimited, 1982. 304p. bibliog. index. $25.00. LC 82-8951. ISBN 0-87287-328-5.

Assuming no previous experience with computers or programming, this text is a totally nonmathematical introduction to computer programming for librarians and information scientists. It is self-instructional in guiding the reader towards a practical and proficient use of the PL/I programming language as a vehicle for the solution of library and textual processing problems, and contains numerous full programming examples.

The book is organized into three sections. The first section provides necessary background information on programming and leads the reader through simple programming examples. The second section explores the use of PL/I for textual processing. The final section is oriented towards library data processing, presenting several realistic library file processing systems.

Building upon previous works in this area, this text discusses new software technologies, including an orientation towards online programming, and an introduction to Virtual Storage access methods. It also covers entirely new areas, such as library data processing and the important topic of database systems. [R: C&RL, Nov 82, p. 370]

501. Hunter, Eric J. **The ABC of BASIC: An Introduction to Programming for Librarians.** London, Clive Bingley; distr., Hamden, Conn., Shoe String Press, 1982. 120p. illus. index. $16.00. ISBN 0-85157-355-X.

Part 1 of this primer is an introduction to programming in BASIC, an acronym for Beginners' All-purpose Symbolic Instruction Code. Part 2 includes sample programs. There is also a brief discussion of files and file management. BASIC is the most widely used programming language for personal computer systems, and there are several versions; but Hunter neglects to inform his readers of this. He scarcely mentions that any novice programmer must have an instruction manual for the system he or she is using, especially anyone interested in building files. The sample programs illustrate solutions to specific problems in data management in small libraries and may be helpful to some librarians. The instructional material contained in part 1 could also supplement a manufacturer's reference manual, but readers who anticipate writing programs successfully relying solely on instructions in this book will be disappointed. [R: JAL, Mar 83, p. 59]
Margaret McKinley

502. Mott, Thomas H., Jr., and Susan Artandi Leny Struminger. **Introduction to PL/I Programming for Library and Information Science.** New York, Academic Press, 1972. 321p. index. bibliog. (Library and Information Science Series). $37.50. LC 78-182675. ISBN 0-12-508750-0.

A readable textbook on PL/I programming which also includes basic concepts of Boolean algebra and logic, terms of library programming, samples of the logic of document retrieval systems, and practice exercises with their answers. Many illustrations and examples make it suitable to instruct the novice in fundamentals of a widely used programming language and basic information handling. [R: Choice, Jan 73, p. 1438; LJ, 15 Oct 73, p. 2983; SBF, Mar 73, p. 289]   Charles D. Patterson

26 Bibliographic Control and Bibliography

GENERAL WORKS

503. Davinson, Donald. **Bibliographic Control.** 2nd ed. London, Clive Bingley; distr., Hamden, Conn., Shoe String Press, 1981. 164p. index. $12.00. ISBN 0-85157-319-3.

Donald Davinson has revised and enlarged (an additional 39 pages) the first edition published in 1975 (see *ARBA* 76, entry 197). The second edition represents a considerable amount of added material. Chapters have been rewritten and expanded, and a new chapter, "Ephemera," and an author index have been added. Another improvement in the second edition is the manner in which references are listed at the end of each chapter. In the previous edition, references were scattered throughout the text. This is a useful reference guide to bibliographic sources, and has been sufficiently revised to warrant purchase by library schools and large university and public library collections. [R: LR, Winter 81, p. 253] Brian Alley

504. Dunkin, Paul S. **Bibliography: Tiger or Fat Cat?** Hamden, Conn., Archon Books, 1975. 120p. index. o.p. LC 75-5634. ISBN 0-208-01519-1.

Paul S. Dunkin's informative, witty, and readable book on analytical bibliography is rewarding reading for any librarian, especially catalogers and reference librarians. "Bibliographers" will find it instructive too. Dunkin discusses, among many other things, the transcription of title pages, collation by gathering and the statement of it, the use of skeleton forms in printing, press numbers, ornaments and printers' devices, and watermarks in paper, showing how bibliographers have used evidence derived from these and other aspects of printing to propose a theory, to describe a book and the circumstances under which it was printed, and to reach conclusions about the practice of printing in various periods. Often enough, bibliographers are in conflict over the meaning of evidence, have incomplete information upon which to draw conclusions, or are imprecise in stating their case, as Dunkin demonstrates in each of his sections. The book is compact, clearly written, and free of the jargon which Dunkin claims has crept into much of the writing on this subject. [R: LJ, 1 Nov 75, p. 2034]
Dean H. Keller

505. Harmon, Robert B. **Elements of Bibliography: A Simplified Approach.** Metuchen, N.J., Scarecrow, 1981. 253p. index. $15.00. LC 81-4687. ISBN 0-8108-1429-3.

This work seems best adapted for textbook use, although the author never states precisely the readership he seeks. Indeed, his preface appeals to "a wide body of users." A quartet of chapters introduces definitions, history, and a typology of bibliographers and their artifacts. There follow two discussions of the nature, uses, and techniques of enumerative, as distinct from analytical, bibliography, supplemented by an annotated list of references, and another of bibliographic periodicals. Other chapters treat the evaluation of bibliographies, and bibliography in the imminent paperless society. A list of accredited library schools, and one of training programs for publishing, printing, bookselling, the rare book trade, indexing/abstracting, and more specifically bibliographic skills, give suggestions for career opportunities. A glossary, a list of additional research sources, an extensive footnote section, and an index are available.

The style is discursive, rather than systematic. We are warned that this is "essentially the kind of book that depends on the work of many others." Quotations and citations are so numerous as to become obtrusive. Yet the overall effect is less of a distillation of primary sources than of a chatty handbook and directory. As a manual for would-be bibliographers, and for inquiring users of bibliography, it is comprehensive without becoming ponderous. [R: JAL, Jan 82, p. 371; LJ, 1 Jan 82, p. 45]

Jeanne Osborn

506. Loosjes, Th. P. **On Documentation of Scientific Literature.** London, Butterworths; distr., Hamden, Conn., Archon Books, 1973. 187p. illus. index. $17.50. ISBN 0-408-70429-2.

The first edition of this book, published in 1967, received favorable reviews in library literature. This edition has been substantially enlarged and updated. The author concentrates on theoretical problems of bibliographic control and information retrieval; discussing bibliographic control of articles in periodicals, serials, monographs, general design of retrieval systems, etc. In addition, the reader will find here a brief but adequate chapter on the use of bibliographic aids and problems of machine translation. The material is presented in a readable form and library school students will find this text very useful in their beginning courses dealing with the literature of science and technology. [R: LR, Fall 73, p. 124; SL, Jan 74, p. 47]

PROCEEDINGS, SYMPOSIA, AND ESSAYS

507. Afflerbach, Lois, and Marga Franck, eds. and comps. **The Emerging Field of Sociobibliography: The Collected Essays of Ilse Bry.** Westport, Conn., Greenwood Press, 1977. 251p. index. (Contributions in Librarianship and Information Science, No. 19). $35.00. LC 76-28644. ISBN 0-8371-9289-7.

This work consists of fourteen "editorials" that the late Ilse Bry published in the *Mental Health Book Review Index* from 1959 to 1972. Although these essays seemingly encompass a wide variety of topics such as "Is Bibliographic Standardization Possible?" and "Bibliographical Challenges in the Age of the Computer," they focus primarily on the problems of making all facets of a work in the behavioral sciences accessible to scholarly use. Toward this end, Bry employed the term "sociobibliography" or that which "focuses on issues of common concern to the social sciences and bibliography ... by merging methods of social and bibliographical research" (p. 237).

Among the contributions of this work, most significant is that of the methodology proposed for making materials accessible for interdisciplinary studies. Equally as important is the discussion of the types of studies that can result from knowing about pertinent publications in other fields. As such, the work has value not only for librarians who may want to improve their approach to bibliographical organization and access, but as a supplementary text in certain library science courses. Although it is not recommended for literature courses, since it does not cover basic titles to which a student should be exposed, it might prove useful in a research methods or a foundations course for familiarizing students with certain concepts. Thus, a student would learn about topics such as the use of historical method in the behavioral disciplines and how traditional bibliographical method is outmoded because it is based on academic divisions that are no longer valid.

There is one flaw in the arrangement of this work, however. In presenting the various essays, the editors followed a strict chronological pattern, which placed Bry's essay on "The Emerging Field of Sociobibliography" at the very end of the work. Despite the value of this approach for tracing the gradual development of a person's attitude toward an issue, this choice is nevertheless unfortunate, since a reader would gain a much clearer understanding of "sociobibliography" if introduced fully to this concept at the very beginning of the book. [R: JAL, Sept 77, p. 224]

James W. Geary

508. Brenni, Vito J., comp. and ed. **Essays on Bibliography.** Metuchen, N.J., Scarecrow, 1975. 552p. bibliog. index. $22.50. LC 75-14082. ISBN 0-8108-0826-9.

This anthology, put together by a sometime academic library administrator, reference librarian, and library educator, attempts to place within the hard covers of a single volume 50 articles touching "bibliography" in some way. Nine headings form rallying points for the material, from "Theory and History of Bibliography" (ten articles) to "Bibliographic Centers" (three articles). Other headings deal with bibliographic organization and control; national, author, and subject bibliography; analytical and textual bibliography; bibliographical research;

bibliographers; and bibliography and the library. Well-known authorities such as Collison, Shera, Downs, Shaw, Tanselle, and Butler are joined by others such as Stiles, whom the editor was unable to identify. The pieces date from 1919 to 1974, but only three appeared originally before 1950; nine were published in the 1970s. About 80 percent come from journal literature, the rest primarily from monographs and at least two from encyclopedias, which lead off the selections. While the editor had library science and English students in mind in his efforts, the anthology's breadth and lack of unity will prevent it from serving the needs of most curricula. The extremities in range of focus raise questions about exactly who will use it for other than an archival record. The volume cries out for some general interpretation and explanation. A "select bibliography" of some 700 items supplements the works actually selected for inclusion and is stronger in historical emphasis than the anthology proper. Identification of contributors concludes the volume. [R: LJ, 15 Oct 75, p. 1907]   Donald G. Davis, Jr.

509.   **Prospects for Change in Bibliographic Control: Proceedings of the Thirty-Eighth Annual Conference of the Graduate Library School, November 8-9, 1976.** Abraham Bookstein, Herman H. Fussler, and Helen F. Schmierer, eds. Chicago, University of Chicago Press, 1977. 138p. (The University of Chicago Studies in Library Science). $10.00. LC 77-23767. ISBN 0-266-06365-8.

The question of bibliographic control is one of the major concerns of librarianship. The publication of papers covering this topic during the 38th Annual Conference of the Graduate Library School of the University of Chicago is very timely. This volume contains the following papers: H. H. Fussler and K. Kocher, "Contemporary Issues in Bibliographic Control"; D. Hickey, "Theory of Bibliographic Control in Libraries"; W. J. Haas, "Organizational Structures to Meet Future Bibliographic Requirements"; R. L. Wigington and C. N. Costakos, "Technological Foundations for Bibliographic Control Systems"; S. M. Malinconico, "Technology and Standards for Bibliographic Control"; E. Svenonius and H. F. Schmierer, "Current Issues in the Subject Control of Information"; and H. D. Avram, "Production, Dissemination, and Use of Bibliographic Data and Summary of the Conference."

Most of the papers deal with the application of computer technology as it relates to bibliographic data. There is no question that bibliographical control of published and un-

published materials is undergoing dramatic changes in view of technological developments. This volume will provide a good starting point for discussion and critical analysis of bibliographic apparatus in the United States. [R: JAL, Sept 78, p. 227; LR, Summer 78, p. 117]
                    Lubomyr R. Wynar

510.   **Sources, Organization, Utilization of International Documentation: Proceedings of the International Symposium on the Documentation of the United Nations and Other Intergovernmental Organizations, Geneva, 21-23 August 1972.** The Hague, International Federation for Documentation, 1974. 586p. (FID Publication 506). o.p.

The deliberations and working papers in this volume represent the judgment on the present state and hopeful future of international documentation by some 260 experts. These experts were participants in a symposium jointly sponsored by the United Nations Institute for Training and Research, the Association of International Libraries, the International Federation of Library Associations, and the International Federation for Documentation. The 51 working papers, many of them written by librarians and documentalists employed by international intergovernmental organizations, present a variety of detail about the current practices of the United Nations and many of the specialized agencies in the production, distribution, indexing, and use of international documentation. The general picture that emerges is of a proliferation of documents, a lack of standardization and coordination, a deterioration of indexing services since 1963, and an underlying hope that intelligent use of the computer will solve some of the major problems. The 64 recommendations of the assembled experts cover a wide range of ameliorative measures including better coordination of programs as well as documentation within the UN family, improvements in series symbols as a means of distinguishing between documents intended for general and restricted distribution, distribution of documents in microform, use of International Standard Book Numbers, standardization of title pages, establishment of regional libraries and revision of the present network of depository libraries, provision of specialized training for documentalists and librarians, and analytical studies of the use and impact of international documents in contemporary society, especially in the developing countries. [R: LQ, Apr 76, p. 189]
                    Robert D. Stevens

SPECIFIC TOPICS

511. ISBD(A): International Standard Bibliographic Description for Older Monographic Publications (Antiquarian). London, IFLA International Office for UBC; distr., Ottawa, Ont., Canadian Library Association, 1980. 59p. $23.00pa. ISBN 0-903043-27-0.

The *ISBD(A)* specifies requirements for the description and identification of monographic publications issued before the year 1801, as well as for later publications when the items are produced by hand or by methods continuing the tradition of the hand-produced book. The purpose of special rules for older books is to provide expanded information on the extent of responsibility; edition; and basic details of originator and extent, especially if the description is in a language with which the cataloger or user is unfamiliar. The aim is "not only description of an antique, but the clarification of the transmission of the text and the 'points' which distinguish editions" (introduction). *ISBD(A)* departs in detail, but not in principle, from *ISBD(M)* (Monographic publications) chiefly in the three areas of title, imprint, and collation. "The ISBD(A) is intended to provide for the description of older books in *general* catalogues, bibliographies and databases containing records of approximately equal detail for books, and other library material, of all periods, and has been developed within the ISBD(G) (General) framework and its annotated text. It is not, therefore, a set of rules for the full bibliographical description of older books, nor is it presented as a definitive text to be used as it stands for specialized analytical bibliographies" (introduction). It allows for variation tailored to the needs of individual catalogs or bibliographies.

The guide begins with definitions of terms, outlines of the ISBD(G) and ISBD(A), and guidelines for punctuation, capitalization, and accents. It then proceeds step-by-step through the form for the elements of title and statement of responsibility area; edition area; material (or type of publication) specific area; publication, printing and distribution, date, etc., area; physical description area; series area; note area; fingerprint area; and multivolume publications. Examples illustrate the numbered rules. Selected examples of complete descriptions in English and five foreign languages are appended.

Louise Stwalley

512. ISBD(PM): International Standard Bibliographic Description for Printed Music. London, IFLA International Office for UBC; distr., Ottawa, Ont., Canadian Library Association, 1980. 53p. $23.00pa. ISBN 0-903043-26-2.

"The ISBD(PM) specifies requirements for the description and identification of printed music publications, assigns an order to the elements of the description, and specifies a system of punctuation for the description. The primary purpose of the ISBD(PM) is to aid the international communication of bibliographic information by 1) making records from different sources interchangeable, so that records produced in one country can be easily accepted in library catalogues or other bibliographic lists in any other country; 2) assisting in the interpretation of records across language barriers, so that records produced for users of one language can be interpreted by users of other languages; and 3) assisting in the conversion of bibliographic records to machine-readable form" (Scope, purpose, and use section).

The *ISBD(PM)* is based on the framework of the *ISBD(G)* (General) and its annotated text, and also makes use of the stipulations in the first revised edition of *ISBD(M)* (Monographic publications). It begins with definitions of terms, outlines of the ISBD(G) and the ISBD(PM), notes on punctuation, sources of information, language and script of the description, abbreviations, and capitalization. It then leads the cataloger step-by-step through the process of forming the elements of title, statement of responsibility, and edition; the printed music specific area; the publication, distribution, etc., area; the physical description area; the series area; the note area; the International Standard Number (or alternative) and plate number; and provisions for multivolume publications. Appended are a list of specific material designations and examples of full descriptions in English and four foreign languages.

Louise Stwalley

513. Whitby, Thomas J., and Tanja Lorković. Introduction to Soviet National Bibliography. Littleton, Colo., Libraries Unlimited, 1979. 229p. bibliog. index. o.p. LC 79-4112. ISBN 0-87287-128-2.

National bibliography is currently a vital area of concern in the issue of bibliographic control. In the USSR, a single organization, the All-Union Book Chamber, has been designated the center of national bibliography. A legal deposit system has effectively created a complete and current national bibliographic system in the Soviet Union.

Part 1 of *Introduction to Soviet National Bibliography* traces the development of Soviet national bibliography from its beginnings under tsarism to the present time, and describes the activities of the All-Union Book Chamber, the basic function of which is bibliographic registration in the organs of national bibliography. From these are derived the other important functions of research, statistics, cataloging, reference, publishing, archival deposit, and library collection building.

Part 2 is a translation by Tanja Lorković (as edited by Thomas J. Whitby) of the Russian *Gosudarstvennaia bibliografiia SSSR* [Guide to the Organs of National Bibliography in the USSR], second edition (1967). It includes descriptions of the publications of the All-

Union Book Chamber and of the individual book chambers of the union and autonomous republics. Book chamber publications are used for many purposes: providing information about new literature published, acquisition of library materials, compilation of indexes, bibliographic reference work, etc., much as the Library of Congress *National Union Catalog* is used in the United States. Useful appendices include a list of book chambers with addresses, a glossary of terms, and a bibliography. [R: C&RL, Nov 79, pp. 576-78; LJ, 1 Oct 79, p. 2085]

27 Bibliotherapy

514. Donohue, Joseph C. **Understanding Scientific Literatures: A Bibliometric Approach.** Cambridge, Mass., MIT Press, 1974. 101p. illus. bibliog. index. o.p. LC 72-10334. ISBN 0-262-04039-5.

Understanding Scientific Literatures is a much-needed addition to the literature of library and information science. Because it was originally the author's Ph.D. dissertation, much of the material addresses a fairly narrow topic — the study of the literature of information science as reflected in the publication of the AFOSR (Air Force Office of Scientific Research), Information Sciences Directorate, *Information Science—1967.* The importance of this work to librarians, however, lies in the description of various bibliometric techniques and the application of these techniques to a definitive subject literature. These bibliometric techniques include Bradford's law of scattering, Zipf's and Booth's relationships concerning word frequency, bibliographic coupling, citation tracing, and epidemic theory. The author concludes by showing how these techniques can be applied in a stepwise fashion to problems of library planning and material selection and retention. [R: AL, July/Aug 74, p. 368; LJ, 1 Sept 74, p. 2045; RQ, Fall 74, pp. 75-76] Robert K. Dikeman

515. Monroe, Margaret E., ed. **Reading Guidance and Bibliotherapy in Public, Hospital and Institution Libraries.** Madison, Wis., University of Wisconsin, Library School, 1971. 76p. bibliog. $3.00pa. LC 73-152326. ISBN 0-936442-02-6.

These are papers drawn from institutes presented between 1965 and 1968 which unite the concerns and points of view about the subject as expressed by public and institution librarians, an educator, an anthropologist, and a bibliotherapist. A blend of both theory and practice, the papers, through both implications and suggestions, are stimulating and thought provoking. [R: LJ, 15 Mar 72, p. 992]

Charles D. Patterson

516. Nicholas, David, and Maureen Ritchie. **Literature and Bibliometrics.** London, Clive Bingley; distr., Hamden, Conn., Linnet Books, 1978. 183p. $16.50. LC 77-20135. ISBN 0-208-01541-8(Linnet).

Not detailed enough to serve a professional who wishes to employ bibliometric techniques, this book is a useful introduction to statistical analysis of written communication. Use of bibliometrics is not limited to library and information science, but finds applications in the sciences, social sciences, and humanities, all of which are briefly discussed in this work; nor is bibliometrics in the library confined to the esoterics of citation analysis, but is useful in collection development and analysis, circulation studies, weeding, and staffing decisions.

The first part of the book includes definitions and a discussion of various uses of bibliographic elements in the analysis of literature. (Literature is used synonymously with written communication, in opposition to aural, pictorial, or electronic information.) The second section deals with specific applications of bibliometrics, and the final part of the book is a review of statistical methods, including sampling, computers, and graphic presentations. Many of the examples used involve the Design of Information in the Social Sciences (DISISS) project at the University of Bath, England. The book will be useful not only as a basic manual of bibliometric practices, but for its discussion of the findings of the DISISS project. [R: JAL, Nov 78, p. 415; LR, Winter 78, p. 253]

Janet H. Littlefield

517. Rubin, Rhea Joyce, ed. **Bibliotherapy Sourcebook**. Phoenix, Ariz., Oryx Press, 1978. 393p. index. (A Neal-Schuman Professional Book). $32.50. LC 78-939. ISBN 0-912700-04-1.

This anthology of important papers in the field of bibliotherapy should prove useful to both librarians and psychotherapists. The anthology is comprehensive in scope. Selections are grouped under four areas: (1) classic works from the period prior to 1947; (2) recent views on bibliotherapy by psychiatrists and other psychotherapists; (3) modern papers on the relationship between bibliotherapy and library science, written largely by medical librarians; and (4) papers reflecting foreign views of bibliotherapy. The volume concludes with a group of appendices, including a selective annotated bibliography of monographs, a list of theses and dissertations on bibliotherapy, and a descriptive inventory of people, resources, and organizations concerned with bibliotherapy. In addition to those that originally appeared in professional journals, several of the selections in this anthology originally appeared in dissertations that may be difficult for interested users to obtain. [R: BL, 1 Sept 79, p. 60; C&RL, Jan 79, p. 83; LJ, 1 Dec 78, p. 2395]   William Saffady

518. Rubin, Rhea Joyce. **Using Bibliotherapy: A Guide to Theory and Practice**. Phoenix, Ariz., Oryx Press, 1978. 245p. bibliog. index. (A Neal-Schuman Professional Book). $32.50. LC 78-9349. ISBN 0-912700-07-6.

The author attempts in this publication to "clarify the definition and history of bibliotherapy and to offer information on the dynamics and mechanics of the field." In the introduction, Rubin presents several concepts of bibliotherapy, including the characteristics of three types of bibliotherapy: institutional, clinical, and developmental. Chapter 1 is a history of the field; chapter 2, "Dynamics," discusses the objectives, effects, theories, and research associated with bibliotherapy, as well as attitudes and behavior and group dynamics. The third chapter, "Mechanics of Bibliography," considers the settings, clients, selection of materials, procedures, record keeping and evaluation of bibliotherapy programs. The final section of the main body (chapter 4) deals with education and training for bibliotherapists. A series of appendices includes: "Suggested Juvenile Materials for Bibliotherapy," an annotated list on such themes as contemporary problems,

death and old age, emotions, family, friends, identity and self-discovery, imagination and creativity, sexuality and love, etc. Another selected (but more briefly annotated) multimedia bibliography of materials for adults is provided in appendix 2 (compiled by Clara E. Lack) on such topics as anger, decision making, humor, man/woman relationships, and many others. Appendix 3 is "Certification and the St. Elizabeth's Hospital Bibliotherapy Training Program" (Arleen M. Hynes); appendix 3B is "Standards for Certification of Poetry Therapists and Related Matters: A Proposal" (Morris R. Morrison); appendix 3C, "Job Descriptions for Bibliotherapists"; and appendix 3D, "Synopsis of Certification (or Registration) Standards for Other Therapy Groups." A 15-page "Bibliography to Text" is also included; brief lists of references conclude each chapter.

Rubin's bibliography of juvenile materials is particularly useful in that it indicates both reading level and interest level of materials (elementary, intermediate, teen). Her work as a whole is comprehensive and well documented, and her analysis of bibliotherapy in the context of librarianship provides needed information on the topic for the student of literature and library science. [R: LJ, 1 Dec 78, p. 2395]

Lois Buttlar

519. Zaccaria, Joseph S., Harold A. Moses, and Jeff S. Hollowell. **Bibliotherapy in Rehabilitation, Educational, and Mental Health Settings: Theory, Research, and Practice**. Champaign, Ill., Stipes Publishing, 1978. 247p. bibliog. index. $8.80pa. ISBN 0-87563-149-5.

The authors of this work describe bibliotherapy as a powerful and effective technique, which practitioners can use in a wide variety of settings with many different types of individuals. It is a type of helping effort involving the use of various reading materials as a part of the intervention strategy of the practitioner. Reading a short story, a poem, or a book relating to a specific problem often can help to prepare a person to better understand situations and to consider alternative solutions to problems. The major thrust of this book is its advocacy of the use of bibliotherapy in remedial-rehabilitative situations. It is divided into two major parts. Part 1 is an attempt to provide the reader with an "understanding of the objectives, rationale, research, and implemental aspects of the bibliotherapeutic process." The authors are pertinacious in their attitude that the practitioner must develop a set of goals for each situation and, insofar as possible, must also plan the means to be used in attaining these desired ends.

They identify striking parallels between goals and the interventions of practitioners in both educational and rehabilitation settings. Bibliotherapy is used as a very effective technique in a variety of situations.

Part 2 consists of an extensive annotated bibliography organized according to problems associated with various types of disabilities. Both reading and interest levels are indicated by broad age groups. Although the list is considered to be comprehensive in coverage, it is not exhaustive either in its categorical assignments or in the reading and interest level notations. It is compiled for the use of persons engaged in various types of helping relationships, such as clergy, teachers, counselors, and others.

This unusual document should be regarded as an authoritative handbook for practitioners and others interested in using bibliotherapy. Although the rationale and practice of this technique tend to be justified in early psychological and philosophical concepts documenting the purposes of education, attention to the objectives and principles of using bibliotherapy is sound. The handbook includes an index of authors as well as publishers.

Lorraine Mathies

28 Cataloging and Classification

GENERAL WORKS

520. Berman, Sanford. **The Joy of Cataloging: Essays, Letters, Reviews, and Other Explosions.** Phoenix, Ariz., Oryx Press, 1981. 249p. index. $35.00; $27.50pa. LC 80-20525. ISBN 0-912700-51-3; 0-912700-94-7pa.

Forty-two short essays and two appendices comprise this collection of alternative views on library cataloging. They are grouped by topic, starting with two "manifestos." Three articles treat aspects of AACR2; three discuss periodicals cataloging; twenty emphasize linguistic problems of access, and fair treatment for controversial topics; three examine cataloging for juveniles; four discuss the Dewey Decimal System. There follow six book reviews and a final section presenting two research resumes not listed in the table of contents, plus a parody of "highly statistical, heavily footnoted, uniformly dull and usually irrelevant catalog-use studies." All but three of the forty-two articles are reprints: ten from *Library Journal*, twenty from the *Hennepin County Library Cataloging Bulletin*. An appended list of readings supplements the notes and citations accompanying several of the articles. A Model Authority File for Names, Subjects, and Dewey Numbers, and a general index complete the volume.

Concern for immediacy, ease, and equality of access is the familiar and fundamental tenet of this anthology. Busy catalogers are tempted to rely without challenge, or even much thought, on official pronouncements and authoritative examples. Berman hopes to counteract bureaucratic standardization by restoring to the local library catalog his vision of its true function as a unique catalyst for effective retrieval and reference service. [R: BL, 15 Oct 81, p. 283]   Jeanne Osborn

521. Dunkin, Paul Shaner. **How to Catalog a Rare Book.** 2nd ed., rev. Chicago, American Library Association, 1973. 105p. illus. index. o.p. LC 72-6515. ISBN 0-8389-0141-7. (Available from Books on Demand, $29.30pa., ISBN 0-317-30447-X).

In 1951 Dunkin published a rather skimpy manual (85 pages) on the cataloging of rare books. The reaction to it was mixed: there were some positive comments from librarians and some rather negative reviews from specialists such as Bowers. After 22 years there is now a new edition, but for all practical purposes it again provides a simplistic approach to a complex problem. The *Library Journal* review indicates that "this new edition has been updated, expanded, and, in some cases, reorganized," but it offers little evidence in support of the statement. In the preface to this new edition, however, Dunkin speaks for himself: "While I was writing the first edition of *How to Catalog a Rare Book*, Fredson Bowers' *Principles of Bibliographical Description* (1949) was published. In it Bowers endorsed a highly complicated collation formula to be used in printed bibliographies and in papers in bibliographical journals. I set forth in my book a much simpler collation formula for cataloging, and I still believe that it is practical. Meanwhile, somewhat to my surprise, many compilers of printed bibliographies and authors of papers in bibliographical journals have used the Bowers formula or some version of it" (p. ix). The material in this edition includes an explanation of Bowers's formula side-by-side with Dunkin's own (which remains unchanged from his first edition); apparently the rationale is that "although catalogers will never (I hope) use the

Bowers formula, they may often have to compare a book in hand with a Bowers-formula description in some printed bibliography or bibliographical journal" (p. ix). All this has made the new edition some 20 pages longer than the first edition. Needless to say, there is no bibliography and there are no footnotes in this manual. *Sapere aude*, poor cataloger! Dunkin said it all. [R: LJ, 15 Sept 73, p. 2528]

Bohdan S. Wynar

522. Foster, Donald L. **Managing the Catalog Department.** 2nd ed. Metuchen, N.J., Scarecrow, 1982. 236p. bibliog. index. $16.00. LC 81-16694. ISBN 0-8108-1486-2.

Foster has revised and updated the first 1975 edition (see *ARBA* 77, entry 254) of his basic introduction to management routines and responsibilities in cataloging departments. The bibliography, still limited to books, has been expanded from 43 to 63 titles published through 1981. The more detailed index indicates some increased attention to automation, although card catalogs and manual routines are still emphasized. Almost no mention is made of online public access catalogs.

The book is aimed at librarians who have had no management experience or training. The reader is even advised, for example, on the elements to include in a standard business letter. Separate chapters describe the functions of most cataloging departments; the department head and his [!] responsibilities; current issues in cataloging; staff selection and job assignments; staff orientation, training, and evaluation; relationships among staff; research and development (with little attention to the application of scientific research methods or statistical analysis); organizational structure; written and oral communication; and basic management tools (e.g., the budget, the computer, systems analysis—very briefly described). Throughout, upper management personnel are referred to as "he, him," while clerical staff are assigned "she, her."

This work should be useful for the librarian who has received her or his first management assignment. It is hoped that much of the information and advice given will not be new, but even the review of the basics of cataloging routines and the management of cataloging operations and staff should be helpful. [R: BL, Aug 82, p. 1506; LJ, Aug 82, pp. 1390-91]

James D. Anderson

523. Hickey, Doralyn J. **Problems in Organizing Library Collections.** New York, R. R.

Bowker, 1972. 206p. (Problem-Centered Approaches to Librarianship Series). o.p. LC 74-39692. ISBN 0-8352-0539-8.

This series is already known to library school students because of the previously published volumes. The present volume, the fourth in the series, includes 30 case studies covering all major types of libraries. There is no index, and the price might be rather high for library school students. [R: AL, Oct 72, p. 1020; LJ, 15 Dec 72, p. 3974]

524. Painter, Ann F., ed. **Reader in Classification and Descriptive Cataloging.** Westport, Conn., Greenwood Press, 1972. 320p. $28.50. LC 72-78204. ISBN 0-313-24035-3.

This anthology is similar in structure to other volumes in this series. The *Library Journal* reviewer complains that there are fewer than three pages on Lubetzky. And he is right. [R: LJ, 15 Dec 72, p. 3974]

REFERENCE WORKS

525. **Library of Congress Cataloging Service Bulletins 1-125, with a Comprehensive Subject Index.** Helen Savage, ed. Detroit, Gale, 1980. 2v. index. $165.00/set. LC 79-25343. ISBN 0-8103-1103-8.

Lives there a cataloger with soul so dead that he or she will not welcome this reprint? Most of us, or our libraries, are on the *Cataloging Service Bulletins* mailing list, but few of us were around when it first appeared in June 1945. Many did not start to read it faithfully until it began to announce and discuss official AACR rule additions and changes in 1967. It had, of course, offered a similar service since 1953 for the earlier "red book" and "green book" rules. Such material makes the earlier issues seem largely outdated and antiquarian, but an occasional announcement or definition gives useful insights into modern standardized practice, as affected by the paternalistic leadership of the Library of Congress. For instance, the initial issue gave news of certain LC-approved transliteration tables. Thenceforward, publication of what are now termed "Romanization tables" has regularly followed each LC adoption for a different non-Roman script.

The photo-reproductions are slightly reduced in size from their originals. Some pages of early issues show less than perfect visual quality, but it is nearly carping to say so, for all are completely legible. Growth in scope and coverage is implicit in the fitting of bulletins 1 through 106 (1945 to mid-1973) into volume 1, whereas bulletins 107 through 125 (December 1973 to spring 1978) comprise, with the 38-page index, an equally bulky volume 2. Tables of contents were inaugurated with bulletin 104 (May 1972) — a further evidence of increasing size and complexity. LC publication and distribution announcements were carried from the first. Local, national, and international committee and conference decisions, particularly those affecting descriptive practices (e.g., ISBD) are frequent. LC directives for applying both its own and the Dewey Decimal classifications have burgeoned, as have explanations and lists or tables of changes for LC subject headings and LC shelf-listing practices. The index includes both topical headings and rule-number entries.

This collection is sensibly limited to those issues published under the original form of the name. A "new" series took over in the summer of 1978, changing nothing of format and content, differing only in its addition of the word *Bulletin* to the title proper, and in its reversion to number "1" for its first issue. This purely technical change in bibliographic identification reflects the impact of AACR and the International Serials Data System on the form of the title entry. It was the logical time to provide catalogers full retrospective control of their much-thumbed, incomplete, unbound sets. Untidy shelves can be emptied to accumulate a second, continuingly useful, serial generation. [R: C&RL, Sept 80, pp. 469-72; LJ, 15 June 80, p. 1371]   Jeanne Osborn

526. Olson, Nancy B., comp. **Cataloging Service Bulletin Index: No. 1-16, Summer, 1978-Spring, 1982.** Lake Crystal, Minn., Soldier Creek Press, 1982. 55p. $10.00. ISBN 0-317-12929-5.

This is the latest publication of a work that began with the author's *Library of Congress Cataloging Service Bulletin Index* (1974) and the series of books entitled *Index to the Library of Congress Cataloging Service Bulletin* (see *ARBA* 78, entry 223 and *ARBA* 81, entry 247) and then *Index to the Cataloging Service Bulletin of the Library of Congress* (see *ARBA* 81, entry 248).

It would seem to most catalogers that an index of a cataloging periodical would be among the best. Who better to arrange and catalog subjects? Such is the *Cataloging Service Bulletin Index*, compiled by Nancy B. Olson.

The *Cataloging Service Bulletin*, which supersedes *Cataloging Service* as of 1978, serves as a "medium of occasional communication between the Library of Congress and the libraries,

institutions, agencies, firms, and individuals purchasing Library of Congress catalog cards." The *Cataloging Service Bulletin Index*, therefore, should serve as a reference tool for the cataloger. The index is arranged numerically by bulletin and page as well as alphabetically. Thus, librarians wanting articles on "Poland, Revised Headings" would have the information at their fingertips. It is for these reasons, and because *Cataloging Service Bulletin* is not indexed in any other source, that this reviewer recommends purchasing the index.   Janet R. Ivey

INTRODUCTORY TEXTS AND MANUALS

527. Aman, Mohammed M., ed. **Cataloging and Classification of Non-Western Material: Concerns, Issues and Practices.** Phoenix, Ariz., Oryx Press, 1980. 368p. index. (A Neal-Schuman Professional Book). $37.50. LC 80-16725. ISBN 0-912700-06-8.

Cataloging and Classification of Non-Western Material incorporates the contributions of 12 librarians with expertise in the problems of international librarianship and the organization of non-Western materials. Non-Western materials discussed include: Nigerian, Ghanian, Indian, Pakistanian, Chinese, Japanese, Southeast Asian, Slavic, Arabic, and Hebraic. The book is intended to introduce the Western world to some of the problems facing catalogers of non-Western materials. This objective is accomplished by discussion of the cataloging difficulties inherent in the cultures represented, as well as problems created by Western misconceptions and the imposition of artificial cataloging and classification rules. The author presents a non-Western perspective of Western classification systems and subject analysis commonly used for organization of non-Western materials despite recognized inadequacies and insufficient attention to the literature, culture, and politics of non-Western nations. For example, the LC subject headings continue to incorporate offensive, dated, and inauthentic headings for African subjects, and there are inadequacies in LC and Dewey systems for classification of newer subjects.

The writers clearly illustrate the barriers to effective bibliographic control on an international level. The problems outlined have few easy answers; therefore, the reader should expect to find food for thought rather than remedies. The necessity for cooperation among librarians to resolve the problems of transliteration; uniformity of personal names; rules of main entry (the more practical approach by title rather than author in many non-Western situations); adaptation of International Standard Bibliographic Description (ISBD), etc., is stressed throughout the work.

Bibliographies at the end of each article and relevant tables on topics such as transliteration, subject headings, and personal names appropriately complement the text. The index to *Cataloging and Classification of Non-Western Material* provides convenient access to the varied problems and opinions on issues common to catalogers of non-Western materials (e.g., transliteration, conversion tables, implementation of the ISBD, and bibliographic control).

This title bridges a knowledge gap in professional awareness of international cataloging problems. It is an important source for students and practitioners of international librarianship as well as for catalogers of both Western and non-Western materials. [R: IRLA, June 81, p. 10; JAL, Jan 81, p. 372; LQ, Oct 81, p. 464; LR, Summer 81, p. 113]

Ahmad Gamaluddin

528.   Bakewell, K. G. B. **A Manual of Cataloguing Practice.** New York, Pergamon Press, 1972. 298p. illus. index. (International Series of Monographs in Library and Information Science, Volume 14). $72.00. LC 73-171838. SBN 08-016697-0.

There are 16 chapters in this manual, from "The Nature of Catalogues" through chapters on the name catalog and the subject catalog, to the usual ending, "The Future of Cataloguing." The treatment of individual topics is rather brief (e.g., the description of major cataloging codes takes a little more than 20 pages, the history of catalogin 11 pages) but this manual will probably be of some assistance to undergraduate programs in Great Britain. Library school students in this country will not benefit much from this text, in view of its rather simplified presentation of practically all aspects of cataloging and classification. There are several better books on the subject published in this country and, as a matter of fact, in Great Britain as well. [R: LJ, 1 Nov 72, p. 3691]

Bohdan S. Wynar

529.   Chan, Lois Mai. **Cataloging and Classification: An Introduction.** New York, McGraw-Hill, 1981. 397p. illus. bibliog. index. (McGraw-Hill Series in Library Education). $29.95. LC 80-15695. ISBN 0-07-010498-0.

Written by an authority on Library of Congress Classification and LC subject headings, this introductory text introduces readers to the principles and procedures of library cataloging and classification. The first main section, on descriptive cataloging, has chapters on the development of cataloging codes, description, choice of access points and headings, and uniform title. A section on subject cataloging covers general principles, Library of Congress subject headings, *Sears List of Subject Headings*, and PRECIS. Various classification systems are discussed in the classification section, including Dewey Decimal, Library of Congress, Universal Decimal, and Colon. The last part is concerned with the production and organization of cataloging records. Each section has background and further reading lists. Emphasis throughout the text is on current practice. [R: LJ, 1 Jan 82, p. 45]

530.   Curley, Arthur, and Jana Varlejs. **Akers' Simple Library Cataloging.** 7th ed. Metuchen, N.J., Scarecrow, 1984. 375p. illus. index. $16.50. LC 83-14423. ISBN 0-8108-1649-0.

Susan Grey Akers, in the fifth edition of this book, stated that its purpose is "to teach the librarian of the small public, school, college, or special library who lacks professional training how to catalog a collection, and to serve as a textbook for short elementary courses in cataloging or as collateral reading in the early parts of basic cataloging courses." The sixth and seventh editions were revised by the two current authors, but the purpose remains the same.

The book gives the fundamental rules for using Dewey Decimal Classification tables as succinctly as possible, making no attempt to suggest new ways to catalog a small library. Illustrative title pages, sample catalog cards, and the like are used frequently. The discussions and examples in this edition reflect the second edition of *Anglo-American Cataloging Rules*, the eleventh edition of *Sears List of Subject Headings*, and the eleventh edition of the *Abridged Dewey Decimal Classification*.

However, this new edition is little more than an updating of familiar contents and approach. Format and organization are a low-key response to the rapid changes in cataloging theory and technique. Any new material is buried under time-honored terminology and arrangement of the chapters and their headings. For example, there is still no major section devoted to the revolutionary changes stemming from the creation and use of large automated databases.

Jeanne Osborn
and Annette Pekarek

531.   Dowell, Arlene Taylor. **Cataloging with Copy: A Decision-Maker's Handbook.** Littleton, Colo., Libraries Unlimited, 1976. 295p.

illus. bibliog. index. $22.50. LC 76-1844. ISBN 0-87287-153-3.

While the rapidly expanding membership of large and medium-sized libraries in OCLC and other similar bibliographic networks greatly reduces libraries' need to perform original cataloging, the responsibility for properly editing and revising the network-prepared copy is emerging as a major administrative problem. Cataloging copy prepared outside the particular institution's cataloging department can appear in the form of "hard copy," such as LC catalog cards or commercially prepared cards, or it can be viewed on a CRT screen.

Dowell describes the many types of problems arising from use of outside-prepared copy and provides specific examples to illustrate the decision-making processes required to resolve the problems. Each case is accompanied by one or more catalog cards that illustrate conflicts and demonstrate the action needed to eliminate them. The handbook deals with specific types of problems and examines the extent of alteration that can and should be undertaken in various kinds of library situations. The decision-making process is constantly related to the needs of catalog users and to the elimination of unnecessary barriers to retrieval of information.

The handbook acts as a manual for catalog-copy editors; it also serves as an administrative tool for catalog departments in determining appropriate guidelines for cataloging copy revision. Library administrators and systems analysts will find an explanation of the potential consequences, and in many cases the impossibility, of using outside copy exactly as it appears. Noncataloging librarians are given a glimpse of the complications that arise from a decision to alter outside copy. They are also shown why it takes time to integrate copy into a local catalog in such a way that the item can be found when needed.

Seven appendices list directory-type information about sources of supplies, equipment, card sets and processing services. A model training manual for copy catalogers is also included. [R: C&RL, Mar 77, p. 167; JAL, May 77, p. 121]

532. Downing, Mildred Harlow. **Introduction to Cataloging and Classification.** 5th ed., rev. and enl. in accordance with *AACR2* and the 19th ed. of the *Dewey Decimal Classification.* Jefferson, N.C., McFarland, 1981. 230p. illus. bibliog. index. $15.95. LC 80-20299. ISBN 0-89950-017-X.

In this fifth edition of her *Introduction to Cataloging and Classification*, Mildred Harlow

Downing, assistant professor at the School of Library Science, University of North Carolina, aims to provide a first course in cataloging and classification and to lay foundations for advanced work. J. Paul Bain collaborates with her in two chapters on Library of Congress classification and in presenting sample catalog cards. The 15 chapters cover bibliographic description, subject access, Dewey Decimal and Library of Congress Classification schemes, nonbook materials, and the shelf list. Review questions follow most chapters, and there are bibliographies of sources cited. Appendices contain 58 sample catalog cards and reference sources for establishing personal names.

Problems abound due to juxtapositions, materials that are included and omitted, and careless errors. Several points are separated which could have been usefully juxtaposed. For example, as discussion of "literary warrant," which is not indexed, occurs only in the chapter on LC classification, the reader may assume it is a concept unique to LC. Bain details methods of assigning LC author numbers, but does not include LC's Cutter Table until over 30 pages later. Downing, on the other hand, excludes discussion of author numbers in DDC and the shelf list. Consequently, this omission does not allow illustration of call numbers for specific authors or explanation of devices which manipulate related criticisms or translations to shelve in proximity with the works on which they are based. The concept of "chief source" is not discussed until chapter 14 on nonbook materials, and then only superficially, while "prescribed source" and "title proper" are never mentioned.

Too much detail leads to virtuosity in some sections, such as when verification of Agatha Christie's name takes seven pages to elucidate. Here a succinctly summarized search, without such close attention to the constraints of practice, would have clarified the objectives of authority work.

Haste in preparation has led to other glaring errors. In saying "if the copyright date differs from the date of printing, include both" (p. 17), Downing fails to differentiate between the functions of printing and publication and misrepresents *AACR2* 1.4F5. The footnote on page 17 incorrectly has information enclosed in brackets supplied "from a source outside the work" rather than from outside the "prescribed source" (*AACR2*, p. 14). Subject headings, we are told, must provide access from "all possible points of view" (p. 52), while later we are cautioned against double-posting "Mammals" and "Cats" for a work about cats (p. 55). Many of

Bain's sample cards, which purport to follow *AACR2*, will cause students to puzzle. For example, an author statement reads "by V. G. Dethier," while the entry heading is given according to *ALA* 1949 as "Dethier, Vincent Gaston, 1915- " (p. 187). If the catalog contained another author of the same name, or if the option to include the full name had been followed (*AACR2*.16A), the entry should read "Dethier, V. G. (Vincent Gaston), 1915- ," thus allowing both distinction in the file and access by the name commonly used (*AACR2* 22.1A). Three candidates for uniform titles fail to employ them, while the two examples that do, give no indication in the tracing of references which must be made from author and title proper in order to lead the user to the author and uniform title used in filing.

In addition to these conceptual errors and failures in communication between the authors, lack of access from the index, faulty proofreading, and errors in punctuation on sample cards will cause difficulty for students. Teachers should assign readings cautiously, bearing in mind the alternative texts, Wynar's *Introduction to Cataloging and Classification*, 7th edition (Libraries Unlimited, 1985), and Chan's *Cataloging and Classification: An Introduction* (McGraw-Hill, 1981). [R: C&RL, Sept 81, p. 504]

Valmai Fenster

533. Hoffman, Herbert H. **Small Library Cataloging.** Santa Ana, Calif., Headway Publications, 1977. 213p. index. o.p. ISBN 0-89537-003-4.

"This book was primarily written for all who find themselves in charge of a small library without having had the benefit of formal instruction in library cataloging" (p. v). To this end, the reader is given three tasks: (1) clean up and weeding, (2) organization and arrangement, and (3) cataloging, with the emphasis on the latter task. In order to circumvent the difficulties of professional library cataloging ("an esoteric specialty mastered by few"; p. v), the principle of title main entry is proposed for all types of publications. "This eliminates the traditional distinctions between author entry, title entry, uniform title entry, and mixed entry, with the attendant compilcations that have made standard cataloging rules so difficult to understand" (p. vi). But whether the *nontraditional* distinctions made between author added entries, title added entries, and so-called categorical and relational added entries, each of which are further subdivided (e.g., categorical added entries are broken down into subject headings, genre added entries, format added entries, and

tracings) are *simpler* to understand and "logically in no way inferior to standard (large) library cataloging" (p. vi) is open to question.

In the chapter on categorical added entries, the reader is given two contradictory sets of information. "If the cataloger lacks the subject knowledge and/or necessary experience and cannot enlist the help of an expert it is far better to defer the making of subject added entries ..." (p. 95). The onus for making an inexperienced person provide subject entries is placed upon library administrators ("being laymen as far as library work is concerned, [they] cannot be relied upon to appreciate the complexities of subject cataloging"; p. 96). A "compromise solution" is offered, whereby subject cataloging is covered in a six-step routine. In effect, *Small Library Cataloging* assumes the potential user is between the devil and the deep blue sea, misunderstood, and desperate for commands. Unresolved is the problem of a small library growing into a medium-sized library with an inadequate catalog that cannot easily be upgraded to professional cataloging standards. [R: JAL, Mar 78, p. 48; LJ, July 78, p. 1362]

Deborah Jane Brewer

534. Hunter, Eric J., and K. G. B. Bakewell. **Cataloguing.** London, Clive Bingley; distr., Hamden, Conn., Shoe String Press, 1979. 197p. illus. index. (Outlines of Modern Librarianship). $12.00. ISBN 0-85857-267-7.

Because cataloging is such a fast-moving field, the authors have expressed some apprehension about this work becoming dated. This feeling is somewhat justified by the apparent frustration caused by the postponement of the implementation of AACR2 by the Library of Congress and their lack of information about RLIN, which was organized shortly after the writing. The book is admirable, however, in that it takes into account not only the changes AACR2 will make on conventional cataloging but the impact that computers will have on all information indexing and retrieval systems and networks. The chronological chart on the history of cataloging is very interesting because it shows the developmental relationship between many cataloging and indexing systems we believe to be new. There is strong British emphasis in this book, but it demonstrates that the problem of cataloging information has no boundaries. All in all, this book is a good review of the current state of cataloging. A second edition (1983) is also in print. [R: C&RL, July 80, pp. 384-85]

Robert Havlik

535. Immroth, John Phillip, and Jay E. Daily. **Library Cataloging: A Guide for a Basic Course.** Metuchen, N.J., Scarecrow, 1971. 202p. index. bibliog. o.p. LC 72-147066. ISBN 0-8108-0396-8.

This guide is intended for use in a beginning catalog and classification course, most effectively in conjunction with a standard textbook. The guide is divided into two major sections: "Descriptive Analysis" and "Subject Analysis." Contains many examples including sample catalog cards, worksheets, and enrichment readings. [R: LJ, 1 Sept 71, p. 2607]

Charles D. Patterson

536. Manheimer, Martha L. **Cataloging and Classification: A Workbook.** 2nd ed., rev. and expanded. New York, Marcel Dekker, 1980. 148p. illus. (Books in Library and Information Science, Vol. 30). $13.50. LC 80-15039. ISBN 0-8247-1027-4.

Manheimer's text, *Cataloging and Classification*, is a workbook for beginning courses in cataloging and classification, and must be used in conjunction with *Anglo-American Cataloging Rules*, 2nd edition. The following works must also be available: *Dewey Decimal Classification and Relative Index, Edition 19*; *Library of Congress Subject Headings*; the Library of Congress classification schedules; and *Immroth's Guide to the Library of Congress Classification*, 2nd edition. The workbook consists of five sections. The first presents the elements of the International Standard Bibliographic Description as presented in *AACR2*. Also discussed are series, notes, and tracings. The second and third sections cover "choice of access points" (*AACR2*, chapter 21) and headings, uniform titles, and references. Part 4 examines the Library of Congress classification and subject headings; part 5 covers the Dewey Decimal Classification. The text is heavily illustrated with samples of catalog cards.

This workbook will be useful in most basic cataloging and classification classes, and can be used as a self-study tool. Those wanting in-depth examination of cataloging theory should refer to a text such as Wynar's *Introduction to Cataloging and Classification* (7th ed., Libraries Unlimited, 1985). Janet H. Littlefield

537. Miller, Rosalind E., and Jane C. Terwillegar. **Commonsense Cataloging: A Cataloger's Manual.** 3rd ed. New York, H. W. Wilson, 1983. 166p. illus. bibliog. index. $22.00. LC 83-1306. ISBN 0-8242-0689-4.

Commonsense Cataloging was originally issued in 1965, and has been revised by different people for each of its two subsequent editions. The second edition was little more than extensive duplication of the first edition with minor textual revisions.

This third edition shows a much greater attempt at revision. New chapter headings and text stress such topical matters as the history of cataloging, AACR2, problems and recent achievements in subject cataloging, and the impact of large-scale member-supported databases and microcomputers. However, as in past editions, professional activities have been greatly generalized while specific clerical routines have been stated in detail. This manual may be quite useful for its clear discussions of clerical routines, but both the professional librarian and the library school student will need to go elsewhere for an understanding of descriptive and subject cataloging and other professional activities.   John Phillip Immroth

and Jeanne Osborn

538. Needham, C. D. **Organizing Knowledge in Libraries: An Introduction to Information Retrieval.** 2nd rev. ed. New York, Seminar Press, 1971. 448p. index. (Grafton Library Science Series). o.p. LC 72-176298.

The first edition of this work was published in 1964. The second edition incorporates information on some of the new developments since the publication of the first edition (e.g., Anglo-American Cataloging Rules, ALA Filing Rules, MARC, etc.). The author's approach to cataloging and classification remains basically the same. It is practical and presents in a readable form all essential information required by the beginner.

539. Ranganathan, S. R. **Cataloguing Practice.** 2nd ed. New York, Asia Publishing House, 1975. 517p. bibliog. index. o.p. ISBN 0-210-22281-6.

Originally published in 1950 under the title *Library Catalogue: Fundamentals and Procedure*, this book presents a practical, step-by-step approach to teaching students the application of Ranganathan's *Classified Cataloging Code*, the CCC. Topics covered are fundamentals of cataloging and classification, problems of entries, series notes, and subjects. Part N lists amendments to the CCC. A closing section is devoted to problems with regard to the CCC and Indian documents worthy of pursuit, and a general discussion of various innovative measures such as cataloging in source and cooperative cataloging, which certainly show that Ranganathan was far in advance of his time.

This book, with its planned lessons corresponding to rules in the CCC, is intended for classroom use for teaching the application of Ranganathan's rules of cataloging and classification. Beyond that, it serves to initiate those who have more than a superficial interest in Ranganathan's method of teaching into how his system works. Marjorie K. Ho

540. Viswanathan, C. G. **Cataloguing: Theory and Practice.** 4th ed. New Delhi, India, Today and Tomorrow's Printers and Publishers; distr., Houston, Tex., Scholarly Publications, 1973. 359p. index. $7.50. ISBN 0-88065-207-1.

The first edition of this work was published in 1954, the present edition in 1970, with a distributor's imprint of 1973. The chapters on descriptive cataloging, cataloging code, and main entry have been restructured and revised in this fourth edition. In general, it is a clearly written book that serves as a beginning textbook for Indian library school students. The chapter on cost analysis of cataloging, however, is outdated; the author is apparently not familiar with the most recent literature on this subject.
Bohdan S. Wynar

541. Wynar, Bohdan S., and Arlene G. Taylor. **Introduction to Cataloging and Classification.** 7th ed. Littleton, Colo., Libraries Unlimited, 1985. 641p. illus. bibliog. index. (Library Science Text Series). $35.00; $21.50pa. LC 85-23147. ISBN 0-87287-512-1; 0-87287-485-0pa.

For over 20 years, successive editions of this text have appeared, and it is probable that a majority of those currently cataloging have had much of their basic training with "Wynar." The present, seventh edition is the second to be undertaken by Taylor, and the content, organization, and presentation continue to improve with each version.

The section on descriptive cataloging under AACR2 has been altered extensively to provide more discussion and explanation and less direct repetition of the rules themselves. LC rule interpretations have been incorporated in a number of cases, making it easier for students and practitioners to create records which conform to general national practice. MARC formats and some coding information have been included, although newcomers to the field probably would benefit from a more thorough treatment.

The section on the subject approach to information has been updated, but continues to be a considerably more summary presentation of both classification and subject headings than that for descriptive cataloging. In view of the increasing attention being given to subject access

of various kinds and in varying types of catalogs, an augmented discussion of this important aspect of cataloging is to be desired.

The emphasis on computer-based cataloging has increased, although students will need considerably more information than given here before they will be comfortable preparing cataloging information for input via a terminal—and the field has moved so rapidly that, despite the updating, there is no index entry for "microcomputers."

The typography and layout have been improved, and the book is easy to use. "Wynar" (or, increasingly, "Taylor") should continue as a frequently used textbook—while waiting for the eighth edition. C. Donald Cook

AUDIOVISUAL MATERIALS

542. Frost, Carolyn O. **Cataloging Nonbook Materials: Problems in Theory and Practice.** Arlene Taylor Dowell, ed. Littleton, Colo., Libraries Unlimited, 1983. 390p. bibliog. index. $28.50. LC 82-18711. ISBN 0-87287-329-3.

This book discusses the theoretical and practical issues that are associated with the organization of nonbook materials. Questions concerning the various cataloging codes are discussed, and detailed examples using *Anglo-American Cataloguing Rules*, edited by Michael Gorman and Paul Winkler (see *ARBA 80*, entry 204) and Jean Weihs's *Nonbook Materials: The Organization of Integrated Collections* (see *ARBA* 81, entry 250) are provided. Through these issues and questions, the basic theoretical principles of the codes are compared and examined, and the current codes for cataloging nonbook materials are placed in historical perspective. Following a survey of the development of the codes, the problems in applying bibliographic concepts, such as "author" and "edition," to nonbook items are discussed. Separate chapters on various categories of media offer complete bibliographic records, citation of rules (including those for main entry), and commentary to highlight theoretical and practical problems. The types of media discussed include cartographic materials, sound recordings, motion pictures, videorecordings, graphic materials, three-dimensional artifacts and realia, microforms, and kits as well as serials, manuscripts, and musical scores reproduced in audiovisual formats. [R: BL, 15 Oct 83, p. 326]

543. Horner, John. **Special Cataloguing with Particular Reference to Music, Films, Maps, Serials and the Multi-Media Computerised**

Catalogue. Hamden, Conn., Linnet Books, 1973. 327p. illus. index. o.p. LC 73-8787. ISBN 0-208-01189-7.

This brief discussion of special cataloging problems includes separate chapters on music, films, maps and atlases, serials, and the multimedia catalog as it relates to computer and machine-readable data. [R: LJ, 1 Oct 74, p. 2455; LR, Winter 73/74, p. 166; RSR, Jan 74, p. 26]

544.   Johnson, Jean Thornton, and others. **AV Cataloging and Processing Simplified.** Raleigh, N.C., Audiovisual Catalogers, 1971. 236p. illus. bibliog. o.p.

This is an audiovisual cataloging and processing manual for instructional media. It is "designed to be especially useful for the paraprofessional and the volunteer" (p. 5). It was developed by a committee of librarians from the Raleigh public schools.

The manual is arranged in 20 sections, one for each of the forms of media. These are tabbed for quick reference. There is also an appendix providing definitions, sample catalog cards, and bibliography. Masters for some worksheets are also grouped at the end in an unpaged section. Each section has a page defining the form (filmstrip) and outlining cataloging information and its location on the catalog card. Directions for accessioning, labeling, preparation of borrower's card, and pocket are illustrated. Also shown are sketches of storage and display equipment. A worksheet is given to illustrate the proper gathering of data. Catalog cards are reproduced in original size to show main entry, subject entry, added entry, shelf list, and federal inventory card.

For its intended purpose and audience, the manual is well executed. However, it is not aimed at the professional librarian. No discussion is offered to explain why certain procedures and methods were selected. The cataloging is a variant form differing in some aspects from both the well-accepted guide *Non-Book Materials: The Organization of Integrated Collections* (Canadian Library Association, 1970) and Hicks and Tillin's *Developing Multi-Media Libraries* (Bowker, 1970). Media designation appears above the call number but not in the body of the catalog card, and accessioning by year-code is used. If these practices are in use in a particular library, the manual may be a useful training tool for nonprofessionals.

545.   Olson, Nancy B. **Cataloging of Audiovisual Materials: A Manual Based on AACR2.** 2nd ed. Mankato, Minn., Minnesota Scholarly

Press, 1985. 306p. illus. bibliog. index. $34.50pa. ISBN 0-933474-38-5.

If one were to wait until all of the problems associated with cataloging nonprint materials and entering them into records of the bibliographic utilities were solved, catalogers would never have the opportunity to receive the help that this manual provides. The first edition of this work, which is about half the length of this second edition, focuses on a limited number of cataloging examples and provides short explanations of a few parts of the description for each. The most significant change in this second edition is the inclusion of much more extensive discussions of the reasons for choices made. Olson's approach in the second edition provides the cataloger with a generalizable learning experience in addition to a specific example. This is a great improvement, although the user may find it more time-consuming to use. Once the principles are learned, however, the cataloger will find that a better understanding of the process is more valuable than numerous examples from which one must infer the principle in order to catalog the item in hand. Library of Congress Rule Interpretations as well as other guidelines relevant to different types of materials also are well integrated into the text and discussions.

In addition to the expansion of chapters from the first edition, new chapters on microcomputer software and serials are added, along with a useful chapter dealing with general considerations applicable to most nonprint. This is a practical and useful guide for catalogers, containing enough new material to make purchase worthwhile. [R: JAL, Sept 85, p. 250; LJ, Aug 85, p. 71]   JoAnn V. Rogers

546.   Olson, Nancy B. **Cataloging of Audiovisual Materials: A Manual Based on AACR 2, Supplement: Coding and Tagging for OCLC.** Mankato, Minn., Minnesota Scholarly Press, 1985. 78p. $15.00pa. ISBN 0-933474-39-3.

Meant to accompany the second edition of *Cataloging of Audiovisual Materials*, this supplement is a collection of the catalog cards in that work, but in OCLC input form. The illustrations appear exactly as they would look on the screen of an OCLC terminal, complete with fixed and variable fields, codes, tags and delimiters, and full bibliographic information. Included are examples for three OCLC formats, *Sound Recordings*, *Audiovisual Media*, and *Machine-readable Data Files*. Brief comments follow some of the examples interpreting more difficult applications of the OCLC documentation. Also included is a valuable wall chart that displays the coding of the 007 field used to set forth the physical description of an item. Olson explains the relationship between elements, fields, and records along with the purpose of codes, tags, delimiters, and indicators. Two OCLC user groups are promoted.

The illustrations are arranged in the same sequence as in the main volume and contain page references to it at the top of each record. A table of contents or an index by type of material would have been helpful as would headings across the top of the pages. A separate sheet of corrections accompany the text and point out a major error made when the second and third lines of the fixed fields were reversed. For libraries that are OCLC members, this supplement will be useful to input operators and/or catalogers in their catalog departments, depending upon which group is responsible for tagging functions. It will also be of significant value to students when as a part of their curriculum, they must catalog nonbook materials and work in the OCLC format. [R: LJ, 15 Nov 85, p. 68]

Ann Allan

547. Rogers, JoAnn V. **Nonprint Cataloging for Multimedia Collections: A Guide Based on AACR 2.** Littleton, Colo., Libraries Unlimited, 1982. 198p. bibliog. index. $21.00. LC 82-8986. ISBN 0-87287-284-X.

Organized according to the mnemonic structure of AACR 2, this book offers information and provides suggestions to aid the cataloger in making judgments and decisions necessary in developing bibliographic descriptions for nonprint materials. The first chapter discusses bibliographic control of nonprint materials and the role of the new code in providing better bibliographic access than any previous method used for accessing these materials. Levels of description, various alternative methods for presenting descriptive information, and optional additions of information to the basic descriptions are discussed and illustrated with examples throughout. The physical characteristics of various nonprint formats are explained to assist the cataloger in dealing with these varied items. The author points out options applied by the Library of Congress and offers guidance in the use of alternative methods allowed in the rules. The appendices include lengthy bibliographies of additional sources of information. [R: JAL, Nov 82, p. 312; LRTS, July 83, p. 268]

548. Tillin, Alma M., and William J. Quinly. **Standards for Cataloging Nonprint Materials: An Interpretation and Practical Application.** 4th ed. Washington, D.C., Association for Educational Communications and Technology, 1976. 230p. illus. index. $8.95pa. LC 75-38605. ISBN 0-89240-000-5.

As national and international catalog code revision committees continue their efforts to develop and agree upon full standardization of cataloging rules for nonprint media, the Association for Educational Communications and Technology has continued its input into resolving some of the questions of standards and their applications to instructional audiovisual media. The need for this fourth edition is sufficient evidence, if any is required, of the increased concern for directing nonprint cataloging practices toward practical standardization. The AECT standards represent an attempt to stay current with the changes nationwide, such as the major revisions of *AACR* chapter 6 and chapter 12, and to incorporate wherever possible simplified or alternative practices that are compatible with the code. The work is not a manual or textbook, but some examples are used to illustrate certain rules. The main purpose is to present in section one a synthesis of basic cataloging rules, especially as controlled by *AACR* chapter 6. Section two deals with the cataloging of 18 specific media formats.

It is important to recognize that there are other interpretations and applications of AACR rules for some aspects of nonprint materials, especially those under revision by cataloging code committees. The authors also call attention to this fact in the preface: "There is not yet, however, complete agreement on every facet of nonbook cataloging. This volume attempts to reflect what the authors consider to be the thinking of the majority of those who have participated with them in the various discussions." Some adaptation of punctuation is made, for example, although it generally follows the ISBD format. The standards offer some useful guidance on nonprint cataloging, at least for the interim, while additional problems are being hammered out in AACR committees. An appendix contains some practical aids: physical description chart, glossary, abbreviations, state name abbreviations, metric equivalents, a rather sparse bibliography, and suggested designators and code for printed materials. [R: SLJ, Feb 77, p. 46]

Christine Gehrt Wynar

AUTHORITY CONTROL

549. **Authority Control: The Key to Tomorrow's Catalog; Proceedings of the 1979 Library and Information Technology Association Institutes.** Mary W. Ghikas, ed. Phoenix, Ariz.,

Oryx Press, 1982. 194p. illus. index. $32.50. LC 82-2088. ISBN 0-912700-85-8.

Authority Control contains the papers presented at the LITA Institute in Atlantic City in May 1979. The institute was repeated in Los Angeles in September of that year, with the addition of a paper by Sally McCallum. The speakers included Michael Gorman, Barry Burns, Ritvars Bregzis, and Michael Malinconco. Susan K. Martin and Brett Butler participated as official reactors.

The various problems concerning authority control were analyzed. The methods used by the various networks such as WLN and OCLC, as well as commercial bibliographic databases such as DIALOG, were discussed in some of the papers. The need for effective authority control with cross-references and automated transfer of records from the invalid heading to the accepted form was emphasized. Otherwise, the user will not find all the relevant records, as some will be linked to the variant form. The cost of verification and control is offset at least in part by the reduction in the number of discarded cards created under the invalid headings and the resulting need to generate replacement cards under the correct heading. The only solution offered is a great deal of hard work involving the expenditure of a large amount of time and money.

The pages are well laid out and easy to read. Each paper is accompanied by a bibliography, and a detailed index is provided at the end. This book is highly recommended to all those working with automated bibliographic systems. Even those using manually produced catalog card files will find it of some interest. [R: BL, 15 Oct 82, p. 292; JAL, Sept 82, pp. 247-48]　　　　　Barbara E. Brown

550.　Baecker, Edith K., and Dorothy C. Senghas. **A Little Brief Authority: A Manual for Establishing and Maintaining a Name Authority File.** Norwood, Mass., DeDoss Associates, 1978. 48p. illus. bibliog. index. o.p. LC 78-8699. (Publisher's address: 332 Railroad Ave., Norwood, MA 02062).

Every cataloging manual, from Dorcas Fellows's *Cataloging Rules* of the early 1920s to Bohdan Wynar's *Introduction to Cataloging and Classification*, seventh edition (Libraries Unlimited, 1985), extols the virtues of a well-kept authority file or files, and gives instructions for maintaining them. Until recently, however, most busy catalog departments honored such routines more in the breach than in the observance. Then name changes prescribed by the 1967 *Anglo-American Cataloging Rules* led to

the Library of Congress's abortive policy of superimposition. Soon after, the problems foreseen from the closing of various large card catalogs generated a feverish enthusiasm for authority records. In 1974, the Library of Congress started publication of its cumulated quarterly, *Name Headings with References.* Professional "how to" articles, as well as theoretical discussions, began to appear. The work in hand is part of that surge.

An elementary introduction to the purposes, guidelines, techniques, and formats of name authority files, this work's most sophisticated feature is its title, lifted from Shakespeare's *Measure for Measure.* Criteria are enunciated, step-by-step procedures are outlined, and dozens of 3x5-inch card examples are included. A list of bibliographic tools for establishing name headings, and a brief, but adequate, index close the discussion. Here is information that has been available, though generally in less detail, for decades. Perhaps the fresh format and the ABC approach will reassure timid practitioners that the advantages of keeping such an in-house file outweigh the burdens.　　　　　Jeanne Osborn

551.　**INIS: Authority List for Corporate Entries and Report Number Prefixes.** Vienna, International Atomic Energy Agency; distr., New York, UNIPUB, 1978. 416p. index. (INIS Reference Series). $16.00pa. ISBN 92-0-178378-7.

This report provides descriptive catalogers in the International Nuclear Information System with standard forms for recording the names of organizations as author affiliations and as corporate entries. The list of 18,500 entries is Revision 11, and supersedes Revision 10 and its supplements. The format for corporate entries is based on the recommendations of the United States Committee on Scientific and Technical Information (COSATI) in its *Standard for Descriptive Cataloging of Government Scientific and Technical Reports,* with some modifications by the International Atomic Energy Agency for use in an international system. Part 1 lists names of international societies and names of organizations by country. Part 2 is an alphabetical list of all corporate entries, followed by an authority list of report number prefixes that have appeared in the INIS *Atomindex* through 1977. An alphabetical index of country names is appended.

This report is part of the INIS Reference series, which documents the rules, standards, formats, codes, and authority lists on which the system is based. The authority list, however, has a wider application, and can serve as a reference tool for catalogers to supplement LC-established corporate entries; it is especially useful because of its frequent revision. The latest revision is the sixteenth (1983).

Deborah Jane Brewer

552. **Subject Authorities: A Guide to Subject Cataloging.** Prepared by the R. R. Bowker Department of Bibliography in collaboration with the Publications Systems Department. New York, R. R. Bowker, 1981. 3v. $150.00/set. ISBN 0-8352-1307-2.

Subject Authorities will make the work of a cataloger easier and more consistent. Presented are some 184,000 unique combinations of LC subject headings, DDC numbers, and LC classification numbers used in LC cataloging in the United States for the years 1973-1981. The *American Book Publishing Record* database was used as the authority, and all subject headings were verified as current in *LC Subject Headings*, ninth edition.

The three-volume work is composed of three separate indexes: the subject heading index, the Dewey Decimal Classification index, and the Library of Congress Classification index. *Subject Authorities* can be accessed through three different starting points: if a subject heading has been established, it can be located in the subject heading index (volume 1), and the user will be provided with both DDC and LC Classification numbers unique to that subject heading. For example: "Fish ponds" is a randomly selected heading—the appropriate DDC number is 639'.311, and the LC Classification number is SH159. Conversely, if one knows that a title is classified under 639'.311 and needs to know the heading for that classification, volume 2, the DDC index, will tell the user that "Fish ponds" is the heading used with that number. Locating SH159 in the LC Classification index, volume 3, will provide the same information. Of course, it will be necessary to verify the classification numbers in the schedules to insure that the proper number and subject heading have been selected. The heading "Fish ponds" applies to fish culture in natural and artificial ponds, according to DDC, not to indoor culture of ornamental fish or to culture of specific types of fish. The point is that *Subject Authorities* is not the final authority for classifying titles or providing subject headings, but it is a convenient and most welcome starting point.

The first volume, the subject heading index, also provides two special sections that will save time for the cataloger. A list of free-floating subdivisions is divided into three sections—"Most Commonly Used Subdivisions," "Table of Pattern Headings," and "Subdivisions Used under Place Names." Also provided is a "Table of Relocations of Dewey Decimal Classification Numbers (from Edition 18 to Edition 19)." *Subject Authorities* will find its major use in the cataloging department, but it can also be valuable to assist users of online bibliographic databases. A second edition (ISBN 0-8352-2053-2, $199.00/set) is in preparation. Publication date is not yet set. [R: BL, 15 Feb 83, p. 796]

Janet H. Littlefield

RESEARCH

553. Gorman, Michael. **The Concise AACR2: Being a Rewritten and Simplified Version of Anglo-American Cataloguing Rules, Second Edition.** Chicago, American Library Association, 1981. 164p. index. $8.00pa. LC 81-3496. ISBN 0-8389-0325-8.

The Concise AACR2 was originally envisioned as "a set of basic rules, stated in simple English, that could be used by relatively untrained personnel for relatively small and uncomplicated catalogues," mainly for use in Third World countries. However, the final work has much broader application, and will be appropriate for use in smaller libraries throughout the world and for teaching beginning cataloging students. Emphasized throughout *The Concise AACR2* is the idea that AACR2 is a coherent set of principles, not simply some 500 pages of specific rules: "This book is intended to convey the essence and basic principles of the second edition of the *Anglo-American Cataloguing Rules* (*AACR2*) without many of that comprehensive work's rules for out-of-the-way and complex materials." The rules have been rewritten, simplified, and often supplied with new examples; equivalent rules in the full text are cited in brackets. Monographic works are stressed, but serials and nonbook materials are also treated. Two appendices accompany the text: rules for capitalization, and a fairly extensive glossary of terms used in the text. An index concludes the work. Practicing librarians, library technicians, and cataloging students will appreciate *The Concise AACR2* for its ability to clear away the rarely used specific rules, and present a clear path to describing common library materials. [R: BL, 15 Jan 82, p. 633; Indexer, Apr 82, p. 69; LJ, 1 Feb 82, p. 237; LQ, July 82, p. 280; LR, Spring 82, p. 61]

Janet H. Littlefield

554.   Lehnus, Donald J. **Milestones in Cataloging: Famous Catalogers and Their Writings, 1835-1969.** Littleton, Colo., Libraries Unlimited, 1974. 137p. index. (Research Studies in Library Science, No. 13). o.p. LC 73-94030. ISBN 0-87287-090-1.

Utilizing the method of citation analysis, Lehnus has identified the more important writings in the area of cataloging for the period from 1835 to 1969. On the basis of this core literature, the author subsequently identifies the most influential catalogers of the period, studies the interrelationships between them (invisible colleges) and, by noting the duration of citations, nominates super-classics, classics, and potential classics in the field. An additional concern is to demonstrate the importance of a few libraries and related institutions, either because they published many of the important monographs or because they employed a significant number of these influential catalogers. Appendix 1 lists the 184 most frequently cited works, while appendix 2 presents the most often cited authors (141). Appendix 3 is a selective bibliography of citation analysis studies, arranged chronologically. A bibliography, a general index, and a personal name index conclude the volume. [R: LJ, 1 Jan 75, p. 35; LQ, Apr 75, p. 209; RSR, July 74, p. 34]

555.   Pope, S. Elspeth. **The Time-Lag in Cataloging.** Metuchen, N.J., Scarecrow, 1973. 209p. bibliog. index. $14.00. LC 72-8097. ISBN 0-8108-0551-0.

Based upon the author's University of Pittsburgh doctoral dissertation which asserts that time-lag increased between 1961 and 1969 and poses suggestions for coping with the problem: (1) discover if programs at the Library of Congress are sufficient to decrease the lag and (2) is it possible for the Library of Congress to accept bibliographical data as provided by publishers' catalogs? Forms a good basis for further research in this area. [R: C&RL, Nov 73, p. 490; LJ, 15 Oct 73, p. 2982]
                              Charles D. Patterson

556.   Tait, James A. **Authors and Titles: An Analytical Study of the Author Concept in Codes of Cataloging Rules in the English Language, from That of the British Museum in 1841 to the Anglo-American Cataloging Rules 1967.** Hamden, Conn., Archon, 1969. 154p. bibliog. index. $16.00. LC 78-8432. ISBN 0-208-00876-4.

A detailed, analytical investigation which focuses on choice of main entry. Although the work fails to mention important considerations

and is somewhat uneven and inconsistent, it is a worthwhile contribution which will become a standard source for teaching. [R: LJ, 15 May 70, p. 1818]
                              Charles D. Patterson

SERIALS

557.   Cannan, Judith Proctor. **Serial Cataloging: A Comparison of *AACR 1* and 2.** New York, New York Metropolitan Reference and Research Library Agency, 1980. 73p. illus. bibliog. (METRO Miscellaneous Publication, No. 28). o.p. ISSN 0076-7018.

Although a small work (73 pages), *Serial Cataloging: A Comparison of AACR 1 and 2* will be quite useful. Cannan has based this book on two presentations held in 1979 on the impact of AACR2 on serial cataloging. While not an official Library of Congress publication, the text and examples have been approved by the Library. *Serial Cataloging* is constructed to broadly follow the arrangement of *AACR2*, and provides detailed comparisons of *AACR1* and 2. Specific rules in both editions are cited. (The user must have access to both editions of the cataloging rules to use this book.) The use of ISBD-S punctuation is also discussed. *Serial Cataloging* concludes with nearly 20 pages of title pages illustrating the rule changes; title page reproductions are accompanied by sample catalog cards illustrating both *AACR1* and *AACR2* cataloging. Although the examples appear in a group as an appendix, the text refers to appropriate examples. There is no index, but the table of contents is quite detailed. *Serial Cataloging* is a useful instructional tool, not only for practicing librarians, but also for cataloging students. [R: JAL, May 81, p. 119; LRTS, Apr 81, p. 211; Ser R, Apr 81, p. 87]
                              Janet H. Littlefield

558.   Smith, Lynn S. **A Practical Approach to Serials Cataloging.** Greenwich, Conn., JAI Press, 1978. 424p. illus. bibliog. index. (Foundations in Library and Information Science, Vol. 2). $40.00. LC 77-25282. ISBN 0-89232-007-9.

Serials cataloging is a difficult art that has received relatively little treatment in library literature. A long-standing need has been for a comprehensive, detailed, and authoritative manual for serials catalogers. In this book, Smith meets these needs in many ways, professionally and with substance. The book has many strengths. Its arrangement is clear and developmental; it covers description, classification, and management; and it covers several new developments as they affect serials. The language is readable and flows evenly from idea to idea and concept to concept. The illustrations are apt and well selected. There is some wit and humor, which is light and does not detract from the purpose.

There are some faults, mostly minor. Some of the text and appendices treat too closely of local practice in one library. The edition of *ISBD(S)* that is discussed was superseded sometime before the book went to press. Also a few errors can be found in lists, and capitalization in citations should follow bibliographic, not cataloging, style.

Nonetheless, this book is an important one. Lynn Smith brings together, for the first time, a text on the organization and practice of serials cataloging. Recommended for all who are involved with serials in any way. [R: LJ, 1 Dec 78, p. 2395]   Neal L. Edgar

559. **Union Lists: Issues and Answers.** Dianne Ellsworth, ed. Ann Arbor, Mich., Pierian Press, 1982. 99p. bibliog. (Current Issues in Serials Management, No. 2). $24.50. LC 82-81471. ISBN 0-87650-141-2.

This book on the technical problems in creating union lists of serials appears at an opportune time when financial exigencies are forcing libraries to direct attention to resource sharing. It contains the proceedings – updated and supplemented by additional essays – of a 1979 workshop sponsored in San Francisco by the California Library Association Technical Services Chapter.

The keynote paper in this book is that of Elaine Woods, an independent consultant formerly with the Library of Congress. This paper surveys the state of the art in serials bibliographic control and proposes the development of a national location system for serials. The other essays in the book include descriptions of various serials projects in California and elsewhere, analyses of the implications of AACR2 for serials management and union listing, as well as a presentation on the use of a word processor to prepare a serials holding list. There are also the minutes of a workshop discussion group on the form of entry for serials. Among the authors in the book are representatives from such major bibliographic utilities as Blackwell North America, OCLC, and the Research Libraries Group. The book concludes with a glossary of serials terms and acronyms, a selected bibliography, and a list of contributors. [R: LRTS, July 83, p. 257]

Stephen J. Bensman

DESCRIPTIVE CATALOGING

General Works

560. Carpenter, Michael. **Corporate Authorship: Its Role in Library Cataloging.** Westport, Conn., Greenwood Press, 1981. 200p. bibliog. index. (Contributions in Librarianship and Information Science, No. 34). $29.95. LC 80-1026. ISBN 0-313-22065-4; ISSN 0084-9243.

This thoughtful, well-documented study of bibliographic authorship, particularly corporate authorship, critiques past definitions, and proposes new, more precisely reasoned ones. Part 1, "The Problem of Corporate Authorship," details the history of descriptive cataloging codes and their handling of corporate authorship from pre-Panizzi through AACR2, where provisions for that form of access have "substantial difficulties" according to the present analysis. A shorter part 2, "The Nature of Authorship," examines the terminology and typology of authorship by "Origination," by "Assumption of Responsibility," and by "Corporate Utterance." Problems of consensus, ratification, fraudulence, and ritual failure are examined, with solutions offered. The general thesis is that, while corporate authorship is a legitimate, useful function, a well-defined, sufficiently reliable theory is still lacking and urgently needed. A proposed operative definition states: "The textual content of a work must be represented as a corporate utterance of a corporate body in order for that body to be treated as its author."

There are descriptive notes on archival sources. A topical index follows the "Index of Works Cited," but may prove misleading, since the names of some, but by no means all, noted cataloging theorists are listed in both alphabets. [R: LJ, 15 Nov 81, p. 2219]

Jeanne Osborn

561. Hyman, Richard J. **Analytical Access: History, Resources, Needs.** Flushing, N.Y., Queens College, City University of New York, 1978. 68p. bibliog. (Queens College Studies in Librarianship, No. 2). $5.00pa. LC 78-18413. ISBN 0-930146-12-3; ISSN 0146-8677.

In this brief monograph, Hyman continues his history of attempts to provide access to books and bibliographic units within other works. The first monograph, *From Cutter to MARC: Access to the Unit Record* (1977), concentrated on access to complete units. In the present work, he traces the history of analytics from their eighteenth-century origins to the current interactive bibliographic systems. He gives most attention to the second half of the nineteenth century, wherein the theoretical and working foundations of today's AACR, book catalogs, and computer databases lie. (Today's goal of complete bibliographical control is but a twentieth-century restatement of the nineteenth-century ideal.) Throughout the work is the stated and implied concern of the author: the computer is not the total answer. Manual systems and printed sources still have an important place in the bibliographic chain of being, both for current access in nonautomated libraries and for retrospective access. For practicing librarians this is a given, but for those new to the field who have seen the computer touted as the future of all bibliographic events, this reminder is necessary.

The value of this work is that it provides a synthesis for those familiar with bibliographic theory and history and an introduction for students and others who have not before thought about the antecedents of today's computer-oriented cataloging and indexing. Since the work is aimed at students, it is richly supplemented by a glossary of terms that I am sure are rarely defined for students before they find themselves immersed in specialized concepts and jargon. Other appendices include a chronological outline of the events described in the text and somewhat superfluous lists of abstracting and indexing services and computer databases available from the three major vendors. Most helpful and in keeping with the topic of the paper is an *indexed* bibliography. This is definitely recommended for student reading lists. [R: C&RL, Mar 79, p. 174; LJ, 1 Apr 79, p. 806; LR, Summer 79, p. 110]　　　Sharon C. Bonk

562.　Verona, Eva. **Corporate Headings: Their Use in Library Catalogues and National Bibliographies.** London, IFLA Committee on Cataloguing; distr., Ottawa, Ont., Canadian Library Association, 1975. 224p. index. $18.00pa. ISBN 0-903043-05-X.

This work is the most significant contribution to date on the topic of corporate authorship as a kind of entry in bibliographies and library catalogs. A comparison of more than 70 different codes in languages ranging from Russian to Hungarian, from Spanish to Swedish, is used to explore the concept from every conceivable point of view. Verona refers to a wide range of theorists and concludes the concise but definitive review with a list of topics that can be the subject of further international meetings. Just what degree of standardization is possible, even though based on this peerless groundwork, is

less a matter of scholarship than of legislation. Certainly there will be no further excuse for ignorance of the topic as it appears in the cataloging and bibliographic codes that are essential to, and confirmed in, the principle of main entry. Title unit entry is summarily dismissed on page eight.

The work should be used with two cautionary reservations in mind. Verona tends to make pontifical but unsupported statements. This does not mean that Verona is always wrong, but simply that there is room for doubt, especially since she does not countenance anything beyond the parameters of codes she investigated. Similarly, this work is essentially a contribution to the history of cataloging theory. It was never intended as a bold new approach to anything, least of all cataloging procedures. Finding the common meeting ground among many divergent approaches is sufficient and too demanding a labor for anyone of less competence and persistence, which must include everybody. The Margaret Mann Citation, awarded in recognition of Verona's work, was never more honestly deserved. [R: C&RL, Sept 76, p. 480]
　　　　　　　　　　　　　　　Jay E. Daily

Introductory Texts and Manuals

563.　Boll, John J. **Introduction to Cataloging, Vol. I: Descriptive Cataloging and an Overview of Catalogs and Cataloging.** New York, McGraw-Hill, 1970. 400p. illus. index. (McGraw-Hill Series in Library Education). o.p. LC 73-87296. ISBN 0-07-006412-1.

This is the first of a series of volumes intended for use as an introduction to cataloging and designed to be used with AACR. Examples and text are clear but the latter is sometimes marred by errors and oversimplification of the obvious. Emphasis is on cataloging books with little attention given to other equally important formats. Primarily useful for undergraduate and extension students and as a supplementary text for graduate level students. [R: C&RL, May 71, p. 232; LJ, 1 Dec 70, p. 4148]
　　　　　　　　　　　　　Charles D. Patterson

564.　Boll, John J. **Introduction to Cataloging, Vol. II: Entry Headings with Emphasis on the Cataloging Process and on Personal Names.** New York, McGraw-Hill, 1974. 423p. illus. index. (McGraw-Hill Series in Library Education). $35.95pa. LC 73-87296. ISBN 0-07-006412-1.

The first volume of this manual, published in 1970, covered certain aspects of descriptive cataloging (e.g., title statement, author statement, imprint, collation, series statement, and notes). This volume covers such problems as choice and form of entry headings, plus fairly detailed coverage of personal names (surnames with prefixes, compound surnames, nobility, royalty, names in religion, etc.). In light of the revision of chapter 6 of *AACR*, dealing with separately published monographs, the first volume of this series has become somewhat obsolete. In order to make this series of manuals useful, the author and his associates should probably accelerate publication of all the volumes, incorporating the new revisions. On page 389, for example, it is stated that the Library of Congress "has adopted the policy of 'Superimposition' with respect to the form of the headings." There are developments in this area that the manual does not take into account. The volume is well illustrated, and each chapter has a number of helpful questions/exercises for self-study. [R: LJ, Aug 74, p. 1915]

Bohdan S. Wynar

565.   Escreet, P. K. **Introduction to the Anglo-American Cataloguing Rules.** London, Gower Publishing; distr., Lexington, Mass., Lexington Books, 1971. 384p. (Grafton Library Science Series). $18.00. LC 72-175030. ISBN 0-12-828850-7.

This book, like several other works published earlier, is designed to assist the cataloger in understanding and interpreting AACR. However, it is more comprehensive and it provides a detailed examination of the rules. In doing so, it has successfully shown many of the ambiguities, inconsistencies, and complexities of the rules.

In addition, the author, in his discussion of the rules, has shown many of the differences between the British and the North American texts of the *AACR*. Chapter 8 is completely devoted to these differences in the rules of entry and heading.

Excluded from the discussion is part 3 of the code, which covers the cataloging of non-book materials. Also, the reader of this book will not find any information on the implementation of AACR; as the author points out, this problem has been the subject of several other published papers.

In all, the book makes interesting reading and is recommended to catalogers as well as to students of cataloging. The reader, however, must be reminded, as the author indicates, that this study is only a supplement and can not be a substitute for studying the actual text of the rules. [R: LR, Summer 72, p. 243]

Nabil Hamdy

566.   Hoffman, Herbert H. **Descriptive Cataloging in a New Light: Polemical Chapters for Librarians.** Santa Ana, Calif., Rayline Press, 1976. 171p. illus. index. o.p.

There are 11 chapters in this little book covering procedural steps in descriptive cataloging. Probably most interesting is chapter 3, "The First Cataloging Decision: Description Principle." A few quotations may illustrate the author's thinking: "Catalog manuals in the past have all but ignored the difference between works, books, and sets. As a result, the importance of choice of unit to be cataloged has never been stressed in cataloging theory" (p. 41). The author further claims that "The question of the choice of unit has been overlooked mainly, I think, because the term 'work' was never unequivocally defined" (p. 41). Hoffman offers as his own solution "the Description Principle," and we recommend the reading of at least this chapter. One warning—in spite of some bragging and several promises, there are no "precise definitions" in this book. Instead, there are plenty of library folklore and some misconceptions (e.g., "Entry Principle," chapter 4). [R: LJ, 15 Mar 77, p. 692]   Bohdan S. Wynar

567.   Hunter, Eric J. **Anglo-American Cataloguing Rules 1967: An Introduction.** Hamden, Conn., Linnet Books, 1972. 1v. (unpaged). index. o.p. ISBN 0-208-00882-9.

Designed to promote self-teaching in Great Britain, this programmed text is similar in structure to other titles by this publisher, such as *An Introduction to Colon Classification*, by C. D. Batty (Archon, 1967), or *An Introduction to Sears List of Subject Headings*, by P. Corrigan (Archon, 1967). [R: CLW, May 73, p. 601; LJ, 1 Mar 73, p. 717; LR, Winter 72/73, p. 346]

568.   **INIS: Descriptive Cataloguing Samples.** Vienna, International Atomic Energy Agency; distr., New York, UNIPUB, 1978. 53p. illus. (INIS Reference Series). $2.25pa. ISBN 92-0-178278-0.

This third revision of *INIS: Descriptive Cataloguing Samples* illustrates, with examples, the application of the *INIS: Descriptive Cataloguing Rules*, Revision 4, to real documents. The samples were chosen to demonstrate the simplest, most concise way of cataloging the documents in the International Nuclear Information System without losing important information. Sample bibliographic and indexing worksheets are included for pieces of literature cataloged at each of the seven permitted bibliographic levels. There are also samples for related pieces of literature, translations, patents, and short communications. In each case, the sample is accompanied by the reproduced title page(s) or pages containing relevant information for the cataloger. Also included are samples of changed, revised, deleted, and withdrawn records.   Deborah Jane Brewer

569. Lehnus, Donald J. **A Comparison of Panizzi's 91 Rules and the AACR of 1967.** Urbana-Champaign, Ill., Graduate School of Library Science, University of Illinois, 1972. 39p. (Occasional Papers, No. 105). $2.00pa.

Lehnus provides a number of interesting insights for the two sets of rules. He points out some similarities in general approach.

570. Lehnus, Donald J. **How to Determine Author and Title Entries According to AACR: An Interpretive Guide with Card Examples.** Dobbs Ferry, N.Y., Oceana, 1971. 195p. index. $15.00. LC 70-165999. SBN 379-00058-X.

Intended as supplementary material to be used directly with the full text of the *Anglo-American Cataloging Rules*, this manual covers rules for determination of personal, corporate, and title entries, some aspects of descriptive cataloging, and special rules for nonbook materials which supplement rules from the other two parts of the code. A rather helpful part of this manual is the list of headings for U.S. government bodies determined according to AACR and a list of headings for governmental bodies of Great Britain as presented in *British National Bibliography* and determined by AACR. A list of references apparently used in preparation of this manual includes eleven entries. [R: BL, 1 Feb 72, p. 441; LJ, 1 May 72, p. 1680]

571. Sayre, John L., and Roberta Hamburger. **An Illustrated Guide to the Anglo-American Cataloging Rules.** Enid, Okla., Seminary Press, 1971. 150p. index. o.p.

This is another card "sampler" illustrating selected examples of AACR. It consists primarily of LC card reproductions (some typed cards are also included) plus brief quotation of pertinent rules. Unfortunately, there are many typographical errors and some inaccuracies in interpretation. For librarians interested in this type of publication we would rather recommend John J. Boll's *Introduction to Cataloging, Vol. 1, Descriptive Cataloging* (McGraw-Hill, 1970) or Lehnus's *How to Determine Author and Title Entries According to AACR* (see *ARBA* 72, entry 122). [R: LRTS, Winter 73, p. 107]

572. Sayre, John L., and Roberta Hamburger, comps. **An Illustrated Guide to the International Standard Bibliographic Description for Monographs.** corrected ed. Enid, Okla., Seminary Press, 1976. 85p. illus. index. o.p. ISBN 0-912832-12-6.

In 1971 these authors compiled an *Illustrated Guide to the Anglo-American Cataloging Rules* as a typical card sampler for a selected portion of AACR. By the end of 1975 at least 38 rules had been changed and three chapters totally revised. In 1974 the revised chapter 6, for separately published monographs (including photographic and other reproductions, formerly in chapter 9), was published, and in 1975 a revised chapter 12, for audiovisual media, was issued. Perhaps the most significant single change in descriptive cataloging has been the application of standards of bibliographic description based on International Standard Bibliographic Description (ISBD) for descriptive cataloging of monographs, audiovisual media, and special instructional materials. In this little pamphlet, the authors provide card illustrations to individual rules as found in chapter 6, in most cases quoting portions of the AACR code verbatim. They also apologize in advance "for those errors that inevitably have been included."   Bohdan S. Wynar

573. Tait, James A., and Douglas Anderson. **Descriptive Cataloguing: A Students' Introduction to the Anglo-American Cataloguing Rules.** 2nd ed. rev. and enl. Hamden, Conn., Linnet Books, 1971. 122p. illus. o.p. LC 76-31326. ISBN 0-208-01077-7.

Based on the British text of cataloging rules, this second edition is as simplistic as was the first. Half of the book contains 40 facsimile title pages (15 more than the first edition), followed by appropriate examples. Poorly indexed and, frankly, of little value to the practicing librarian in this country. Library school students may want to examine this little book. [R: AL, Apr 72, p. 432; LJ, 1 May 72, p. 1679]

574. Verona, Eva. **Statement of Principles Adopted at the International Conference on Cataloguing Principles, Paris, October 1961: Annotated Edition.** IFLA Committee on Cataloguing; distr., Chicago, American Library Association, 1971. 119p. o.p. LC 72-184471. ISBN 0-903043-00-9.

This volume is conveniently arranged into several sections including prefatory background material, a listing of codes mentioned in the commentary, and the statement itself (followed by commentary. A general bibliography and an index would have been especially useful. This annotated edition of the statement contains much helpful information for catalogers and cataloging instructors. [R: LJ, 1 June 72, p. 2056]   Charles D. Patterson

AACR2

575.   **AACR 2 Goes Public.** Tucson, Ariz., Art Libraries Society of North America, 1982. 64p. illus. bibliog. (Occasional Papers of the Art Libraries Society of North America, No. 1). $5.00pa. ISSN 0730-7160.

This is the first in a new series of Occasional Papers to be published by the Art Libraries Society of North America. The four papers in this volume were presented at the society's San Francisco conference held in February 1981.

In an article addressed to reference librarians, Daniel A. Starr contrasts the attitudes of reference librarians and catalogers toward the catalog and its purposes. Ferris Olin presents the results of his survey, conducted during the fall of 1980, of 77 academic, art school, museum, and public art libraries regarding their adoption of AACR2 and their plans for closing their catalogs. Seven pages of charts summarize the results of the survey. Olin also discusses alternatives available to libraries and problems that may result from various choices. Patricia J. Barnett discusses options in the design of catalogs: the split catalog with no links, the split catalog with links, one catalog with internal links, the unified catalog with modified links, and the combination catalog with interfiled, modified, and linked headings. Sample guide and reference cards illustrate this paper. Bonnie Postlethwaite examines the effect of changes in serials bibliographic records on the catalog user and the impact of the new rules on the creation and use of other serials access tools. The last two articles include bibliographies, and there is a short list of suggested readings appended to the collection. Although the articles are addressed to art librarians, they contain sufficient general information to make them of interest to the profession as a whole. [R: JAL, July 82, p. 183; LJ, July 82, p. 1305]

Shirley L. Hopkinson

576.   **AACR2 Headings: A Consolidated List of Heading Decisions Made by the Library of Congress.** San Jose, Calif., California Library

Authority for Systems and Services, 1982. 1v. (various paging). $19.00 looseleaf.

This list was produced by arranging into uniform alphabetical sequences the name authority decisions made by the Library of Congress in preparation for the conversion to AACR2 and published as current work progressed in the LC *Cataloging Service Bulletin* (nos. 6-11, 1979-1981). These decisions dealt with only those headings used most often (25 times or more) in the MARC bibliographic files. The list is divided into two sections: in the first the names are alphabetized by the old AACR form; in the second, by the new AACR2 form.

Founded in 1976, the producer of the list — the California Library Authority for Systems and Services (CLASS) — is a public agency serving libraries of all types not only in its own state but also in Nevada and Washington. The list is stored as a file in the CLASS computer for revision in accordance with future LC authority decisions, and the work's looseleaf format is well suited for rapid and coherent updating.

Stephen J. Bensman

577.   **Anglo-American Cataloguing Rules.** 2nd ed. Michael Gorman and Paul W. Winkler, eds. Ottawa, Ont., Canadian Library Association; distr., Chicago, American Library Association, 1978. 620p. index. $20.00; $15.00pa. LC 78-13789. ISBN 0-8389-3210-X; 0-8389-3211-8pa.

According to its preface, *AACR2* has "the same principles and underlying objectives as the first edition," although the rules are vastly different from those of 1967 in terms of content and presentation. Most significant is part 1 (chapters 1-13), which comprises the rules for description. The first, general chapter presents broad provisions that are applicable in many situations; chapters 2-13 provide rules for particular types of materials, or for specific conditions or patterns of publication. Since the rules recommend description made in terms of the item at hand, in order to describe a microform, for instance, the cataloger is instructed first to follow the rules in chapter 11. Then, when a rule for a particular area of this description does not differ from the general rule, the cataloger simply consults the corresponding rule in the general chapter to complete the description. This involves some turning of pages, but the mnemonic numbering of the rules facilitates the process.

Part 2 covers headings, uniform titles, and references. Many significant changes have occurred here as well. Much less emphasis has been placed on main entry, which reflects the opinion that if description is complete (at a chosen level of detail), the designating of one access point as the "main entry" is of secondary importance. Main entry under editor or compiler, for example, has been dropped, and now only a few categories of works are entered under the heading for corporate body. As a result, determining main entry should take less time, but deciding upon the form of heading will be more involved. A personal author, for instance, is to be entered under the name that is most "commonly known"; a corporate body, "under the name by which it is predominantly identified" (e.g., "W. K. Kellogg Arabian Horse Center" rather than "Kellogg (W. K.) Arabian Horse Center").

The rules are deliberately less prescriptive than those in *AACR1*. Rule examples follow the same principle; they are designed to "illuminate the provisions of the rule ... rather than to extend those provisions" (0.14, page 4). The rules provide three acceptable levels of detail in description, which encourages the cataloger to interpret the rules in light of the needs of the user. In addition, *AACR2* offers many "optional additions" to the description, which, again, provides for individualization of description for a particular collection. Options to be followed by the Library of Congress (see *Cataloging Service Bulletin*, Fall 1978) must be carefully studied by libraries, especially those which rely heavily on LC cataloging.

Implementation of *AACR2* will demand a great amount of planning, retraining of catalogers, costly file rearrangements, even the closing of existing catalogs. The rules are already expediting the computerization of authority files by the Library of Congress. The full impact of *AACR2* is yet to be realized in many areas, but it should encourage uniformity in cataloging of print and nonprint media, improve international bibliographic control, and encourage bibliographic networking. [R: C&RL, May 79, pp. 271-76; LJ, 15 Feb 79, p. 468; SLJ, Apr 79, pp. 30-31]   F. W. Ramey

578. **Anglo-American Cataloguing Rules: Revisions.** 2nd rev. ed. By the Joint Steering Committee for Revision of AACR. Chicago, American Library Association, 1984. 48p. $3.50pa. LC 83-21474. ISBN 0-8389-3300-9.

In 1978 descriptive catalogers fielded their second drastic code revision in 11 years. *AACR2* (see *ARBA* 80, entry 204) retained much of the *AACR1* content but altered and redirected the treatment of corporate headings, uniform titles, and fullness of names. Options were increased and presentation was reorganized, partly on

theoretical grounds but also to increase emphasis on nonbook formats. Even before its appearance, librarians were warned that perhaps it too would not pass away, but at least it would undergo further change as the requirements of automated, integrated catalogs, and the inadequacy or inefficiency of some decisions, were ascertained.

Here is the first slim collection of revisions. It omits the errata and corrigenda to the text, which were published in *Cataloging Service Bulletin* nos. 5-6 (Summer and Fall 1979), as well as the local LC rule interpretations appearing in subsequent issues of that serial. An introductory table of "Instructions and Contents" lists 35 specific rule, appendix B, and glossary locations. In part 1 ("Description"), 20 rules in chapters 1-3, 5-6, 8, and 11-12 are affected. The 11 changes in part 2 fall in chapters 21 ("Access Points"), 22 ("Headings for Persons"), and 25 ("Uniform Titles"). They comprise 13 additions, 10 deletions, and 14 revisions, 2 of which involve only punctuation. Nineteen changes are extensive enough to warrant separate insertion pages; the rest are merely cited to be done by hand. Fourteen of these involve changes in examples. Rule numbering is unaffected, for the most part, although four rules are entirely deleted, leaving gaps in the numbering, while one new rule number (8.7B22) inexplicably skips the unassigned number preceding it. No significant disruptions can be noted in this compendium, which rather incorporates clarification and adjustment. Future *AACR2* printings will include these revisions either in the text proper or in a supplemental section.

Jeanne Osborn

579. Blixrud, Julia C., and Edward Swanson. **A Manual of AACR2 Examples Tagged and Coded Using the MARC Format.** Lake Crystal, Minn., Soldier Creek Press, 1982. 116p. $12.50pa. ISBN 0-936996-13-7.

This is one of a series of manuals prepared by the Minnesota AACR2 Trainers to illustrate the cataloging of various materials according to the *Anglo-American Cataloguing Rules*, second edition. It specifically illustrates the transfer of cataloging data to a machine-readable format. Cataloging examples have been selected from manuals previously published by the Trainers, then transposed into the MARC format. Additional information has been supplied when needed for the fixed fields. Pages are set up with the cataloging copy on one side and the MARC format on the other. The book category contains the largest number of examples, 36. Main entry headings have been checked against the

Library of Congress's Name Authority File, and include examples of personal names, corporate names, and entries for the Bible. The section on serials has 18 examples; audiovisual media has 12. Sound recordings and microforms each have 8, while maps and music scores each have 6.

Some of the examples were prepared before the Library of Congress made decisions on the application of AACR2 rules, so they do not reflect current cataloging practice. On a few of the pages, the print is so light that it is difficult to read, and one of the examples is not decipherable. In spite of these minor weaknesses, the examples have been well chosen, and the manual will be very useful in library school courses and as a guide for technical services employees. [R: JAL, May 84, p. 112]

Shirley L. Hopkinson

580. Clack, Doris Hargrett, ed. **The Making of a Code: The Issues Underlying AACR2: Papers Given at the International Conference on AACR2 Held March 11-14, 1979, in Tallahassee, Florida, Sponsored by the School of Library Science, Florida State University.** Chicago, American Library Association, 1980. 256p. bibliog. index. $15.00pa. LC 80-17496. ISBN 0-8389-0309-6.

The information supplied by this series of papers is most useful. The writers were directly involved either in drafting *AACR2*, or in its early stages of practical application. They speak with authority, or with perceptive critical insight, not fearing to grapple with general theoretical questions which affect standardization and economical, effective development of library catalogs or machine-related bibliographic databases. On such issues they in no sense follow a party line. Differences of interpretation and opinion, with suggestions for future work, are expressed forcefully, but courteously, with every effort at equable coverage of all worthy points of view.

The 15 addresses are grouped under four broad headings. The first group ("Generalities") looks at political and bibliographic influences on the entire code. The second ("Description") and third ("Access Points") respectively address specific questions of format analysis, and choice of entry plus heading formulation. Two essays dealing with adoption of the code at the Library of Congress and outside the United States comprise group 4 ("Looking beyond the Rules"). Three appendices give (1) abbreviations used throughout the text, (2) a selected bibliography arranged chronologically from the year 1974, but not limited to footnote references, and (3) short professional sketches of the contributors.

The index supplies chapter number, rule number, and topical entries for both editions of *AACR*, as well as other important personal, corporate, and subject citations. It is easy to find fault with indexes. For instance, this one has no reference to discussions of designation of function. But such faults are relatively minor. Here is a reference tool which every serious descriptive cataloger should place alongside *AACR2* itself. [R: BL, 15 Jan 81, p. 669; JAL, July 81, p. 177; LJ, 1 May 81, p. 951; SLJ, Aug 81, p. 32]

Jeanne Osborn

581. Cook, C. Donald, comp., with the assistance of Glenna E. Stevens. **AACR 2 Decisions and Rule Interpretations.** 2nd ed. Ottawa, Ont., Canadian Library Association; distr., Chicago, American Library Association, 1982. 1v. (various paging). o.p. ISBN 0-88802-165-8.

This work consolidates the decisions and rule interpretations that the Library of Congress, the National Library of Canada, the British Library, and the National Library of Australia have composed governing their use of *Anglo-American Cataloguing Rules*, second edition.

It is intended to assist librarians who use cataloging that is influenced by any of the above-named groups, to aid librarians in interpreting the rules for their own use, and to guide catalog instructors in teaching the rules and how to apply them.

Published in looseleaf format and unbound, it may be interspersed with *AACR2* for convenience.

Where earlier decisions have been revised, only the most recent appears. When there is concurrence on decisions, only one resolution appears with an indication of agreement from the other agencies. Most of the decisions are linked to specific rules. The decisions and interpretations are current through 31 December 1981 (except for the Joint Steering Committee, which is current through May 1982). [R: BL, 15 Apr 83, p. 1073; JAL, July 83, p. 169; LJ, 1 June 83, p. 1114]

Anna Grace Patterson

582. Corrigan, John T., ed. and comp. **Anglo-American Cataloging Rules: One Year Later.** Haverford, Pa., Catholic Library Association, 1982. 61p. (Studies in Librarianship, No. 6). $8.00pa. ISBN 0-87507-023-X.

The impact of *AACR*, first and second editions (see *ARBA* 80, entry 204), has not yet run its full course. Its early shocks, and the strenuous endorsements of its advocates, have grown familiar with time. The present work belongs to a second wave of assessment, based on retrospective evaluation. It consists of five papers presented at a workshop held during the 1982 annual convention of the Catholic Library Association. All are written from the perspective of the academic librarian. The first, a typical comparison of *AACR1* and *AACR2*, is followed by an implementation report from a library where a retrospective conversion project was launched almost simultaneously. A third paper addresses the problems of choice and form of entry encountered in a full year's application of the new code. A fourth outlines the catalog maintenance problems encountered, and solutions developed, for a preexisting 500,000-record database in a large institution with many departmental library catalogs. The last describes the results of a general staff orientation and implementation plan in a medium-sized, long-established catalog department. These short, practical analyses of first-hand, first-year successes and failures permit readers to see not only that their problems and pet peeves are shared by colleagues, but that genuine progress is under way to make AACR a useful code for present and future cataloging purposes.   Jeanne Osborn

583. Dodd, Sue A. **Cataloging Machine-Readable Data Files: An Interpretive Manual.** Chicago, American Library Association, 1982. 247p. illus. index. $35.00pa. LC 82-11597. ISBN 0-8389-0365-7.

Expanding concepts of library materials directed considerable attention for over two decades to the problems of cataloging nonprint items. More recent concern has focused on specific questions related to machine-readable data file (MRDF) cataloging. *AACR2* (see *ARBA* 80, entry 204) made commendable efforts to apply its general precepts to the cataloging of various types of nonprint materials, including in its chapter 9 preliminary specifications for the MRDF. But data file librarians faced almost daily the need for more authoritative background knowledge and consensus than could be furnished by a code published before such a format, with its identifying features, was standardized.

Dodd's manual assumes a basic understanding of how to catalog by AACR2. It supplies a valuable supplement, giving basic orientation, theoretical analysis of needs and problems, instruction and interpretation of *AACR2* chapter 9, step-by-step examples, chapters on serial and time series dynamic databases, guidelines for bibliographic conventions and multilevel record-keeping, appendices on punctuating, checklisting, and worksheeting a

catalog record, and examples of card format and model records. Notes, a glossary, and an index complete the work. Important objectives include bridging the communications gap between data archives and traditional libraries, standardizing the bibliographic decisions and information sources of data file producers, and facilitating high-quality, shareable library catalog records, with their cognate services. This compendium of state-of-the-art expertise will be welcomed in all libraries with collections of machine-readable data files. [R: C&RL, Nov 83, p. 491; JAL, May 83, p. 114; JAL, July 83, pp. 168-69]   Jeanne Osborn

584. Dowell, Arlene Taylor. **AACR 2 Headings: A Five-Year Projection of Their Impact on Catalogs.** Littleton, Colo., Libraries Unlimited, 1982. 145p. bibliog. index. (Research Studies in Library Science, No. 17). $25.00. LC 82-9929. ISBN 0-87287-330-7.

With the implementation of AACR2, librarians have been faced with decisions of whether to attempt to change conflicting headings, provide *see also* cross-references, or begin new catalogs. The results of this analysis will assist in making such decisions. These projections are the result of a study of the catalogs of three academic libraries of varying sizes. Differences between pre-AACR2 and AACR2 headings are analyzed, and potential catalog conflicts over a five-year period examined. The effects of OCLC's machine conversion to AACR2 are discussed. Analysis is not limited to AACR2, however. Cataloging is also analyzed by type of material, place and date of publication, subject area, type of cataloging copy, and type of heading. [R: C&RL, Nov 82, p. 368]

585. Elrod, J. McRee. **Choice of Main and Added Entries: Updated for Use with AACR 2.** 3rd ed. Metuchen, N.J., Scarecrow, 1980. 82p. illus. (Modern Library Practices Series, No. 4). o.p. LC 80-23724. ISBN 0-8108-1339-4.

Fourth in the author's series, Modern Library Practices (see *ARBA* 81, entries 228-30 and 285), this workbook provides a basic introduction to the choice of main and added entries. This programmed unit must be used in conjunction with *Anglo-American Cataloguing Rules*, second edition, and the student should first complete the workbook, *Construction and Adaptation of the Unit Card* (Scarecrow, 1980). Elrod stresses that none of his self-instruction books are intended to replace formal course work, but are meant to be used by nonprofessional library workers to increase understanding of technical processing. The workbook consists of an alphabetically arranged series of learning sequences, from added entries and analytics to uniform titles and unit cards. Answers to the exercises appear after the problems. The program can be used by both nonprofessionals and library school students.

Janet H. Littlefield

586. Elrod, J. McRee, **Construction and Adaptation of the Unit Card: Updated for Use with AACR 2.** 3rd ed. Metuchen, N.J., Scarecrow, 1980. 72p. illus. (Modern Library Practices Series, No. 1). o.p. LC 80-18903. ISBN 0-8108-1336-X.

Construction and Adaptation of the Unit Card is number 1 of the Modern Library Practices Series (see *ARBA 81*, entries 227-29 and 285). It is a programmed unit intended as a workbook for nonprofessional technical processing workers, and should take about four to eight hours to complete. After completion of the unit, a person should be able to type a unit card, using a marked title page, and adapt it or a set of printed cards to make a full set of catalog cards. This edition has been updated to reflect changes caused by AACR2 and to introduce the International Standard Bibliographic Description. The program recognizes that individual libraries will follow divergent practices; specific learning sequences are noted so that changes can be made to reflect local practice. While intended for use by nonprofessionals, this programmed text could be equally useful for beginning cataloging students. Janet H. Littlefield

587. Hagler, Ronald. **Where's That Rule?: A Cross-Index of the Two Editions of the Anglo-American Cataloguing Rules.** Ottawa, Ont., Canadian Library Association, 1979. 127p. o.p. ISBN 0-88802-123-2.

This little book serves a very specific purpose for the uninitiated. In the tables which comprise the bulk of this work, each substantive part of each AACR rule is matched, in rule number sequence, against its corresponding AACR2 rule, and vice versa. Unfortunately, this publication is reproduced from a typescript, and on many pages the quality of reproduction is poor. The Canadian Library Association should have done a little better job, because this painstaking work merits a more professional execution. Hopefully, it can be reproduced in a better format by the American Library Association or a Canadian or American commercial publisher. Bohdan S. Wynar

588. Hoffmann, Christa F. B. **Getting Ready for AACR 2: The Cataloger's Guide.** White Plains, N.Y., Knowledge Industry Publications, 1980. 225p. illus. index. $24.50pa. LC 80-15168. ISBN 0-914236-64-4.

Getting Ready for AACR 2 is emphatically not a critique of the new code, nor is it a text for the beginning cataloging student. Hoffmann has written a manual for the practicing librarian who must implement the new code. Following an introduction that touches briefly on the controversial aspects of AACR2 and discusses the major changes caused by the new rules, Hoffmann discusses concepts new to AACR2 and presents a glossary of selected terms and acronyms. The general rules for description and punctuation are thoroughly examined, and examples contrasting AACR with AACR2 are presented. The major portion of the book, "Description: Cataloging Examples, Old and New," presents actual cataloging problems, illustrated with facsimiles of the source of information—title page, disc label, etc. Monographs are stressed, but music, sound recordings, microforms, and serials are treated. Choice of main entry and major changes in forms of names are discussed, reflecting changes recorded in *AACR2*, chapter 21, "Choice of Access Points." The manual concludes with a chapter of "Cataloger's Aids," an annotated bibliography of handbooks and manuals to supplement *AACR2*. The afterword briefly discusses sources necessary to keep up with changes instituted after publication of the code.

Getting Ready for AACR 2 is more than a manual of examples illustrating the new code; changes are explained and illustrated, then related to working situations. Tables are provided to allow the library to record decisions on optional matters. Catalogers will, of course, benefit most from this book, but it is not overly technical. *Getting Ready for AACR 2* will be of interest to administrators, reference librarians, and advanced students who need to understand the new rules. [R: AL, Jan 81, p. 50; JAL, Jan 81, p. 372; LJ, 1 May 81, p. 951; LRTS, Apr 81, p. 207] Janet H. Littlefield

589. Hunter, Eric J. **AACR 2: An Introduction to the Second Edition of Anglo-American Cataloguing Rules.** rev. ed. London, Clive Bingley; distr., Hamden, Conn., Linnet Books, 1979. 148p. index. o.p. LC 78-23933. ISBN 0-208-01684-8(Linnet).

This programmed text introduces the beginning student to the fundamentals of cataloging according to the *Anglo-American Cataloguing Rules*, second edition. An earlier edition introduced the original *AACR*. This edition, extensively revised, "is designed to teach the principles underlying *AACR 2*, rather than a detailed knowledge of the rules themselves" (p. 13).

The reader is guided step-by-step through the basics of describing library materials, choosing main and added access points, formulating headings for access points, and creating references from forms of headings not used. Analysis is touched on briefly, and there are a few complete examples at the end of the book.

A leaf of "errata and additional comments" is inserted. For the most part, the errata noted are relatively minor; nevertheless, this leaf should be consulted if the reader is not to be misled. In addition, there are occasional errors in the text that have not been corrected (e.g., in frames 21 and 39, the word "in" or a colon should be inserted between "Original" and "National" in the note "Original National Portrait Gallery, London"); but these, too, are minor and do not prevent the transmission of basic principles.

The presentation of textual material is in sequential order—not "scrambled" as in some programmed texts. This sequential feature allows reading or review of the commentary without having to answer correctly every question before proceeding. The examples are clear and contribute to an understanding of the principles.

The book is recommended as a supplementary text for beginning cataloging courses. It should also be purchased by libraries for immediate use as a basic introduction to AACR2 for their staffs and for on-going use by those libraries that give in-service training. [R: C&RL, Sept 79, pp. 481-82]	Arlene Taylor

590.	Hunter, Eric J., and Nicholas J. Fox. **Examples Illustrating AACR 2: Anglo-American Cataloguing Rules.** 2nd ed. London, Library Association; distr., Ottawa, Ont., Canadian Library Association, 1980. 184p. illus. o.p. ISBN 0-85365-951-6.

Examples Illustrating AACR 2 is exactly what it claims to be. "There is no intention in this work of presenting an official view of how particular rules in *AACR 2* are to be interpreted." The book is simply formatted: a "problem and general index" refers to the 383 numbered examples. A "rule index" follows, listing the numbered AACR2 rules with appropriate examples. The examples are arranged in one alphabetical sequence of main entries filed according to *ALA Rules for Filing Catalog Cards*, second edition (American Library Association, 1968). The book is designed to be used in three ways: to find examples illustrating

particular AACR2 rules; to find examples illustrating particular cataloging problems; and as a source for browsing to discover how AACR2 approaches various cataloging difficulties. Monographs are stressed, but sound recordings, microforms, and machine-readable data files are also illustrated. The examples follow a standard format. Source material (title page, label, etc.) is illustrated if pertinent, then the entry follows the pattern prescribed by AACR2: heading; title and statement of responsibility; edition; material (or type of publication) specific details; publication, distribution, etc.; physical description; series; notes; standard number; and added entries. The entry is then followed by a brief discussion of the cataloging difficulties presented by the item, referring to appropriate AACR2 rule numbers.

Examples Illustrating AACR 2 is loosely based on a 1973 book illustrating the 1967 edition of the British text of *AACR*. The earlier work contained 217 examples; half have been retained in the present work. *Examples* will be useful as a reference tool in the cataloging department, and as a teaching aid in cataloging courses. The emphasis is British, but American and foreign-language examples are not ignored. [R: Indexer, Oct 80, p. 105; LRTS, Apr 81, p. 207]	Janet H. Littlefield

591.	Manning, Ralph W., ed. **AACR2 Seminar Papers: From Presentations Given at "Evolution or Revolution," Ottawa, June, 1979, and "Cataloguing Using AACR2 in the Cooperative Environment," Vancouver, June, 1980.** Ottawa, Ont., Canadian Library Association, 1981. 146p. bibliog. $12.00. ISBN 0-88802-158-5.

The aim of these papers from two different workshops sponsored by the Technical Services Coordinating Group of the Canadian Library Association is "not to emphasize the implementation of AACR2 as such but to discuss this new development as only one, albeit a major one, of those developments affecting libraries, their catalogues, and their technical services ..., place the various developments in perspective and provide librarians with the information necessary to make the best decisions."

Although these papers were written before the implementation of AACR2, most of the information is still pertinent. The few out-of-date articles are interesting from a historical point of view. The topics include the history and future of library catalogs, the history of AACR and AACR2, the theoretical basis of AACR2, authority control systems, networks, the National Library of Canada's role in the technical service community, the library administrator's perspective on technical service change, and the effect of technological, economic, and social change on libraries.

Almost all collections suffer from an uneven quality in content and style. This collection has a larger number of readable articles with useful information than many other such books.

All 15 papers, with one exception, were contributed by Canadians. However, the Canadian content does not restrict the volume's use in other countries. Little of the material pertains solely to Canada, and the Canadian examples can be universally applied. The thoughtful analyses of experiences and historical background will be useful to libraries everywhere. The book ends with a nine-page bibliography on "Library Catalogues in Perspective."

Jean Riddle Weihs

592. Maxwell, Margaret F. **Handbook for AACR2: Explaining and Illustrating** *Anglo-American Cataloguing Rules, Second Edition.* Chicago, American Library Association, 1980. 463p. illus. index. $20.00pa. LC 80-17667. ISBN 0-8389-0301-0.

The introduction of AACR2 has brought confusion to many librarians and cataloging students; practicing catalogers face the necessity of learning new rules and unlearning old habits; students must thread a path through hundreds of unfamiliar rules. Maxwell, among others, has devised a guide to the new AACR code. Nearly as long as the code itself, Maxwell's handbook is "designed to assist library school students and cataloguers in the application of the most commonly used rules for description, choice of access points, and forms of headings as set forth in" AACR2. Unlike the examples used in *AACR2*, Maxwell presents catalog card entries as illustrations, since it is easier to understand examples appearing in the context of full entries.

Maxwell has wisely chosen not to reproduce each rule illustrated; the user of the *Handbook for AACR2* learns to use the code while locating examples for specific problems. The handbook follows *AACR2* format, citing rule numbers and headings. The work does not confine itself to providing illustrations, but also explains the purpose of specific rules and provides overall discussions of each *AACR2* chapter. Differences between *AACR1* and *AACR2* explained. In most cases, title page information is provided with the catalog card examples, although actual title pages are not reproduced.

The *Handbook for AACR2* is similar to several other works. Wynar's *Introduction to Cataloging and Classification*, seventh edition (Libraries Unlimited, 1985); contains similar explication of rules, but is far broader in scope than Maxwell, covering the entire cataloging and classification process. *Using AACR2: A Diagrammatic Approach*, by Malcolm Shaw and others (Oryx Press, 1981), takes a totally different approach to interpreting the code (see *ARBA* 82, entry 253). Slocum's *Sample Cataloguing Forms* (Scarecrow, 1980; see *ARBA* 82, entry 256) is less comprehensive than Maxwell. Hoffmann's *Getting Ready for AACR 2* (see *ARBA* 81, entry 235) is geared to the practicing librarian and deals mainly with the differences between *AACR1* and *AACR2*. Each of these titles is suited for slightly different audiences, but Maxwell's handbook is the closest to a rule-by-rule explanation of AACR2 and will be useful for the beginning student, as well as being a companion to the code for the practicing cataloger. [R: BL, 15 Jan 81, p. 671; C&RL, May 81, pp. 265-66; JAL, May 81, p. 98; LJ, 1 May 81, p. 951]   Janet H. Littlefield

593. Shaw, Malcolm, and others. **Using AACR2: A Diagrammatic Approach.** Phoenix, Ariz., Oryx Press, 1981. 199p. illus. index. $39.50. LC 80-26779. ISBN 0-912700-88-2.

For those who find the reading and interpretation of expository codes difficult, this British flowchart of *AACR2* chapters 21-25 ("Access Points," "Heading," and "Uniform Titles") offers an alternative strategy. Its gaming overtones can be stimulating, and its clues illuminating. No attempt is made to cover bibliographic description, which the authors say is not susceptible to this approach. After a brief review of author catalogs and cataloging, two basic algorithms (Number 1 for "Access Points"; Number 2 for "Forms of Heading") are extensively detailed, with ample cross-referencing and rule citations. Each is then reduced to a single-page display of its essential structure, with page references to the fuller version forming a kind of diagrammatic index. Thirty-two examples follow, with title pages reproduced, supplementary information supplied where needed, and an appendix of solutions and commentaries. Classroom students and cataloging apprentices will find them helpful for practice, self-testing, and review. An alphabetic index cites proper names from the examples, and a meticulous list of pertinent AACR2 rules and sections, as well as conceptual terms. [R: LJ, 15 Oct 81, p. 2001]   Jeanne Osborn

594. Simonton, Wesley, and Marilyn Jones McClaskey. **AACR 2 and the Catalog: Theory— Structure—Changes.** Littleton, Colo., Libraries Unlimited, 1981. 78p. index. $9.50pa. LC 81-11757. ISBN 0-87287-267-X.

This guide provides a basic introduction to the changes resulting from the adoption of AACR2 which affect the construction of the formal bibliographic description, whether on a card or a computer system. The authors explain the concept of authorship and how this is applied to the choice of main entry and the correct headings for persons, corporate bodies, geographic areas and names, and uniform titles in accordance with AACR2. Numerous examples illustrate the changes that have taken place, comparing the old form of an entry under AACR with the new form used with AACR2.

In discussing bibliographic description the authors clearly define the components and illustrate the form with several examples, showing the differences between main entry and added entry access points. Both card and computer displays are shown. The differences between first, second, and third levels of description are also explained.

There are three valuable appendices to this guide: (1) a glossary of terms selected from the official *AACR* glossary, (2) an explanation of the types of references and their uses, with numerous examples, and (3) a selected list of approximately 500 of the most often used headings for person, bodies, and uniform titles which have been revised with the adoption of AACR2, emphasizing those requiring a change in location within the catalog. [R: WLB, Dec 81, pp. 313-14]

595. Slocum, Robert B. **Sample Cataloguing Forms: Illustrations of Solutions to Problems of Descriptions.** 3rd ed. Metuchen, N.J., Scarecrow, 1980. 114p. illus. index. $17.50. LC 80-21507. ISBN 0-8108-1364-5.

In the day-to-day routine of a cataloger, there arise questions about application of rules and the proper placement of this or that. Such a situation is more certainly true in the aftermath of a new cataloging code. No stranger to the beleaguered cataloger is Robert Slocum, who has previously provided two editions of his *Sample Cataloguing Forms* to aid the cataloger in interpreting and applying the rules of the code. This third edition is most welcome.

The new code, with its many rules and the widespread use of optional provisions and its tripartite levels of cataloging fullness, requires catalogers to make many more decisions. Many more local options are available. Yet the cataloger must likewise keep an eye toward network requirements as well as the certain uniformity required by computerized databases. *Sample Cataloguing Forms* aids the cataloger in this decision making. Arranged similarly to *AACR2*, problems within each chapter are highlighted alphabetically with one or two sample cards given under each problem. The problem with which the sample card deals is underlined. The text uses abundant cross-references (e.g., from old to new terminology or to alternate treatment of a problem). Generous attention is given to optional provisions in *AACR2*. *Sample Cataloguing Forms* is enlightening and easy to use. It is of value to veteran and neophyte alike. [R: JAL, Mar 81, p. 57; LRTS, July 81, p. 290]

Harry S. Otterson

596. Swanson, Edward. **A Manual of AACR 2 Examples for Microforms.** Lake Crystal, Minn., published for the Minnesota AACR2 Trainers by Soldier Creek Press, 1982. 48p. illus. $10.00pa. ISBN 0-936996-09-9.

A manual of 32 examples of descriptive cataloging of microforms, each done according to *AACR2* chapter 11 and according to the Library of Congress "rule interpretation," which basically allows description based on a previously published original rather than the microform in hand, may be some help to the cataloger in seeing the application of the rules. Done by a representative of the Minnesota Historical Society, presumably a librarian, its original purpose is for use by the Minnesota AACR2 Trainers in workshops for catalogers. As a class syllabus it is marginal; as an offering to the library profession, it does little more than retrieving examples of cataloging of microforms from LC catalogs or tapes or from a bibliographic utility can do. And it has several serious problems, primarily illegibility of both the type in the examples and in the illustrations of the bibliographic information duplicated from the microform.

The idea is good as far as it goes, that is to give an illustration of the bibliographic information on the item in hand and descriptive cataloging for each example. Missing is any discussion of the rules or discussion of application of the rules to the examples. An index to rule numbers which the editor and author "specifically wished to illustrate" is of limited usefulness in trying to understand the cataloging applications. Catalogers would be better advised to look at cataloging of microforms in one of the basic cataloging texts or wait for a more complete and better-executed publication.

JoAnn V. Rogers

597. Swanson, Edward, and Marilyn H. Jones, eds. **A Manual of AACR2 Examples.** Compiled by the Minnesota AACR2 Trainers. Lake Crystal, Minn., Soldier Creek Press, 1980. 87p. illus. index. $7.50pa. ISBN 0-936996-01-3.

A Manual of AACR2 Examples was designed "for use at a series of workshops on AACR2 held in Minnesota in the spring of 1980." Each example (there are approximately 90) is chosen to illustrate a number of rules from AACR2. The examples generally contain an illustration of the source material (title page, etc.), and then illustrate the headings and body of entries and added entries. Then the pertinent rules are cited. Monographs receive more coverage than other materials. An index lists AACR2 rule numbers and brief descriptions of the rules, followed by page references. This is the basic manual of a series of manuals of AACR2 examples in specific library topics.

A second edition (1985) has been published.
Janet H. Littlefield

598. Tseng, Sally C., comp. **LC Rule Interpretations of AACR2, 1978-1982 Cumulated Edition. Update: CSB No. 17.** Metuchen, N.J., Scarecrow, 1983. 47p. $10.00 looseleaf. LC 82-10353. ISBN 0-8108-1572-9.

This edition is an expansion and update of an earlier, unpublished version prepared for use during 1980-1981 in conjunction with cataloging courses offered by the University of Toronto. In comparison to the first edition, published in 1981, the reader will find here a revised table of contents and rule index plus 47 pages of new material, incorporating the changes, interpretations, and revisions included in the *Cataloging Service Bulletin* (no. 17, Summer 1982). However, two other issues of *Cataloging Service Bulletin* (nos. 18 and 19, Fall and Winter 1982) are not incorporated in this update, which necessitates additional consultations. Appearing in the form of loose pages, original entries are reproduced full size and are quite legible, with clear instructions on how to replace pages. It is a welcome publication. [R: JAL, July 83, p. 169; LJ, Aug 83, p. 1458]   Bohdan S. Wynar

CLASSIFICATION

General Works

599. Brown, A. G., in collaboration with D. W. Langridge and J. Mills. **An Introduction to Subject Indexing.** 2nd ed. London, Clive Bingley; distr., Hamden, Conn., Shoe String

Press, 1982. 1v. (various paging). illus. index. $19.50. ISBN 0-85157-331-2.

All indexing (including, of course, cataloging and classification) consists of two processes: the analysis of the subject, form, and bibliographic characteristics of a document, and the translation of this analysis into particular indexing languages. Library education and textbooks in the United States tend to skim over the first process, with its intellectual challenges, and to concentrate on the technical aspects of translating subjects and forms into the Dewey Decimal or Library of Congress Classification and LC or Sears subject headings. This book is an antidote to this deficiency. Brown, with the help of two other British indexing experts, Langridge and Mills, has revised this introduction to subject analysis and translation, combining the original two volumes into one. Using a programmed format with frequent review questions and special guidance when the reader goes awry, the authors cover analysis into fundamental categories and constituent facets and focuses; introduce translation to faceted and semienumerative classifications, with V. Ranganathan's Colon and the Universal Decimal (UDC) Classifications as examples; move on to the construction of subject headings using chaining techniques; and conclude with postcoordinate indexing systems. The use of these "un-American" classifications prevents the student from getting bogged down in the intricacies of applied number building and, instead, stresses understanding of process. Access to the Abridged English Edition of the UDC is assumed, but the text can be read with considerable benefit even in its absence. The treatment of creating subject headings will lead, as well, to better understanding of existing lists. Altogether, an excellent book. Recommended especially for practicing catalogers who wonder what they are really doing. [R: Indexer, Apr 83, p. 211; IRLA, Aug 82, p. 9; LRTS, July 83, p. 275]
James D. Anderson

600. Elrod, J. McRee. **Classification: For Use with LC or Dewey.** 3rd ed. Metuchen, N.J., Scarecrow, 1980. 79p. illus. (Modern Library Practices Series, No. 3). o.p. LC 80-23718. ISBN 0-8108-1338-6.

Elrod's Modern Library Practices series consists of five workbooks (see *ARBA 81*, entries 227-28, 230, and 285); *Classification* is number 3. It is not intended as a substitute for a course in cataloging, but can serve as a self-instruction program for the nonprofessional library employee or as a workbook in a cataloging course. It is intended for use with either the

Library of Congress Classification or Dewey Decimal Classification, and the Cutter or Cutter-Sanborn author number tables. The program may also be broken down into units for students interested in particular sequences: general principles, classification numbers, book numbers, order of books on the shelf, serials and series, reclassification, and the classed catalog.   Janet H. Littlefield

601. General Classification Systems in a Changing World: Proceedings of the FID Classification Symposium Held in Commemoration of the Dewey Centenary, Brussels, November 1976. The Hague, International Federation for Documentation, 1978. 107p. (FID, 561). price not reported. pa. ISBN 92-66-00561-4.

A selection of papers presented at the symposium, General Classification Systems in a Changing World, is included in this volume. The symposium, honoring the Dewey Decimal Classification Centenary, was held in November 1976 in Brussels and sponsored by the International Federation for Documentation. Some 15 short papers discuss the Dewey Decimal and the Universal Decimal Classification systems, comparing them to each other and to other classifications currently in use. Responsiveness of classification systems to the needs of various nations and the future development of classification systems are considered. No summary is included, and, inexplicably, the introduction is in French. [R: LQ, Jan 80, p. 146]
                    Janet H. Littlefield

602. Langridge, D. W. Classification and Indexing in the Humanities. Boston, Butterworths, 1976. 143p. illus. index. $13.95. ISBN 0-408-70777-1.

This is a companion to *Classification and Indexing in Science*, by B. C. Vickery (3rd ed., Butterworths, 1975) and *Classification and Indexing in the Social Sciences*, by D. J. Foskett (2nd ed., Butterworths, 1975). In the first chapter, the author discusses the philosophical basis for the classification of knowledge. This is followed by separate chapters on the theory of bibliographic classification; a definition of the humanities; the classification of history and biography; the classification of philosophy, religion, and the occult; and the classification of arts, crafts, and entertainment. The last two chapters discuss the construction of special classification schemes in the humanities and the question of indexing in the humanities. [R: C&RL, Jan 77, p. 71; LJ, 15 Mar 77, p. 692; LQ, Oct 77, p. 486]

603. Maltby, Arthur, ed. Classification in the 1970's: A Discussion of Development and Prospects for the Major Schemes. Hamden, Conn., Linnet Books, 1972. 269p. index. o.p. ISBN 0-208-01170-6.

A number of short essays cover the following classification schemes: Bibliographic Classification, Colon, Dewey Decimal, Library of Congress, and Universal Decimal Classification. Other articles in the anthology cover such related topics as prospects for classification suggested by evaluation tests carried out from 1957 to 1970. Most studies are well documented, and this book will help library school students understand some of the basic principles of major classification schemes. For more in-depth coverage, however, the reader will have to look elsewhere. [R: AL, June 72, p. 675; LJ, July 72, p. 2361]

604. Maltby, Arthur, ed. Classification in the 1970s: A Second Look. rev. ed. London, Clive Bingley; distr., Hamden, Conn., Linnet Books, 1976. 262p. index. o.p. LC 76-43965. ISBN 0-85157-221-9(Bingley); 0-208-01533-7(Linnet).

The first edition of this work was published in 1972 and reviewed in *ARBA* 73 (entry 102). Some essays in this edition were updated, but only a few were completely revised. This is indicated by Maltby in his general introduction (which is itself substantially revised). D. Austin's paper, "CRG Research into a Freely Faceted Scheme" remains essentially unchanged except for an added discussion of PRECIS. The only new chapter is by Karen Sparck Jones on automatic classification. Some new information on bibliographic classification will be found in J. Mills's article, and Sarah Vann's contribution on "Dewey Decimal Classification" includes new material on the eighteenth edition. All articles are well documented, and this new edition should be considered by library schools as a good overview of this subject. [R: JAL, Sept 77, pp. 222, 250; LJ, 1 Oct 77, p. 2017]

605. Palmer, Bernard I. Itself an Education. (Six Lectures on Classification), 2nd ed., with Continuation by Derek Austin, "Two Steps Forward." London, Library Association, 1971. 115p. index. LC 72-180253.

These lectures were orginally published in 1962 and have been out-of-print since 1968. They deal with the background and development of classification, including the sociohistorical framework in which classification developed, the concept of main classes, notation, and the advocacy that classification is the foundation study for all librarians. Derek

Austin contributes a continuation stating how classification theory has been affected by developments in information storage and retrieval in the past ten years. [R: LJ, 1 Apr 72, p. 1248]

Charles D. Patterson

606. Russell, Keith W., comp. and ed. **Subject Access: Report of a Meeting Sponsored by the Council on Library Resources.** Washington, D.C., Council on Library Resources, 1982. 1v. (various paging). $10.00pa. LC 82-23563.

"The purpose of the meeting was to identify a set of long-term and short-term recommendations that could be acted upon by a variety of individuals and organizations to improve subject access in bibliographical databases for the user." In this case the "user" means the untutored library patron approaching the in-place online catalog for information.

For once, the conference attendance was held down to a small group with expert skills (25 persons), so that some confidence was justified in the emergence of a worthwhile result. Their 16 recommendations are largely in the areas of subject headings, classification, and databases.

Unsurprisingly, the conferees found that the Library of Congress *List of Subject Headings* will be the initial subject terminology employed; but, as nearly any reference librarian can testify, having fewer than two subject headings for monographs is insufficient. There needs to be a means to tie classification numbers to the subject headings, and a thesaurus discipline would greatly improve *LCSH*. (Fortunately, these points are forcefully made in the volume.) One quibble: the defined users would have been better served if a subject discipline-based person had contributed. [R: JAL, Sept 83, p. 243; JAL, July 83, p. 180]

E. B. Jackson

607. Swanson, Gerald L., comp. and ed. **Dewey to LC Conversion Tables.** New York, Macmillan, 1973. 188p. $32.00. LC 72-82737. ISBN 0-02-468400-7.

Intended to assist librarians in converting their collections from the Dewey Decimal system of classification to that of the Library of Congress. This is a computer printout in four columns, which makes it a little difficult to read. Pages 165 to 188 consist of an outline of the Library of Congress Classification—one wonders why? The first answer that comes to mind is that the outline is there to justify the rather steep price of this book. Libraries that might need it cannot afford it; larger libraries that have already been through the converting experience won't need it.

Bohdan S. Wynar

608. Wellisch, Hans (Hanan), and Thomas D. Wilson, eds. **Subject Retrieval in the Seventies, New Directions: Proceedings of an International Symposium Held at the Center of Adult Education, University of Maryland, College Park, May 14 to 15, 1971.** Published in conjunction with the School of Library and Information Services, University of Maryland. Westport, Conn., Greenwood Press, 1972. 180p. illus. index. (Contributions in Librarianship and Information Science, No. 3). $25.00. LC 70-183149. ISBN 0-8371-6322-6.

A collection of nine papers from a well-rounded conference on this topic of obvious interest. Special attention should be called to Richard Angell's "Library of Congress Subject Headings—Review and Forecast," Eric de Grolier's "Recent Research Trends in the Field of Information Retrieval Languages," and T. D. Wilson's "The Work of the British Classification Research Group." [R: Unesco, May/June 73, p. 178; LJ, 1 Apr 73, p. 1095]

Introductory Texts and Manuals

609. Foskett, A. C. **The Subject Approach to Information.** 4th ed. London, Clive Bingley; distr., Hamden, Conn., Linnet Books/Shoe String Press, 1982. 574p. index. $27.50; $18.50pa. ISBN 0-208-01934-0; 0-208-01970-7pa.

This popular textbook has been revised yet again (for reviews of the second edition, see *ARBA* 73, entry 99; for the third edition, see *ARBA* 79, entry 270). It is not by any means a brand new edition. The contents are basically the same as in the last edition, with only one new chapter, treating online searching in derived indexes, and two new illustrations, one to show search formulations for water pollution when truncation and Boolean operators are used and another to show the BSO (Broad System of Ordering) outline. Even though much of the content looks identical to that of the third edition, the bibliographies have been updated and remarks relating to each indexing system have been reviewed, somewhat revised, and updated, as of September 1981. The helpful list of abbreviations has also been augmented.

As valuable as this text is, it does not do justice to the online environment, where many indexing systems are being revised or altered considerably by the retrieval system enhancements, displays, and user feedback. The lack of coverage of developments in the United States is also evident, but the author should not be faulted too harshly for this, as a U.S. author of a similar book probably would not cover EPSILON or AUSINET.

The book is still required reading, at least as a supplemental text, in any course on subject analysis.   Pauline Atherton Cochrane

610. Henderson, Kathryn Luther, ed. **Major Classification Systems: The Dewey Centennial.** Urbana-Champaign, Ill., Graduate School of Library Science, University of Illinois, 1976. 182p. illus. index. (Allerton Park Institute, No. 21). $8.00. LC 76-026331. ISBN 0-87845-044-0.

Classification in the 1970's, edited by Arthur Maltby (Linnet Books, 1972; rev. ed., 1976), provides a good overview of major classification systems—Dewey Decimal Classification, Library of Congress Classification, Colon Classification, Bibliographic Classification, etc. It might be fair to say that, in comparison, *Major Classification Systems* is not as broad in scope but, nevertheless, is an essential book on this subject. Allerton Park Institute of the University of Illinois Graduate School of Library Science conducted, over the years, a number of successful conferences, and it was only fitting in the Dewey centennial year to concentrate on DDC since, as the editor rightly pointed out, Dewey's scheme has had a major impact on library classification throughout the world.

The volume consists of 10 well-edited essays on such topics as "Library Classification: One Hundred Years after Dewey" (David Batty), "The Historical Development of the Dewey Decimal Classification System" (Comaromi), "Dewey Today: An Analysis of Recent Editions" (Cockshutt), "Summary of a Survey of the Use of the Dewey Decimal Classification in the United States and Canada" (Michael), "Dewey Today: The British and European Scene" (Downing), "The Library of Congress Classification Scheme and Its Relationship to Dewey" (Stevenson). There are also four other essays covering the role of indexing and classification in subject retrieval; a comparative evaluation of DDC, UDC, and BSO; plus a rather weak essay by Peter Lewis, "Factors in the Selection of a Classification Scheme for a Large General Library." (The author, unfortunately, was not present at the conference.) All in all, it is a well-executed work that will be of special interest to library schools. [R: LQ, Oct 77, p. 483; LR, Summer 77, p. 134]
                                Bohdan S. Wynar

611. Langridge, Derek. **Approach to Classification: For Students of Librarianship.** Hamden, Conn., Linnet Books, 1973. 122p. index. o.p. LC 72-8181. ISBN 0-208-01184-6.

Although the author is a prominent British librarian, this slim volume provides only a simplistic approach to the subject. One assumes that the text may have some use in Great Britain in connection with correspondence courses—or as an introductory text for those new to the concept of classification. [R: CLW, Feb 74, p. 347]

Bliss

612. **Bliss Bibliographic Classification**, 2nd ed. J. Mills and Vanda Broughton, with the assistance of Valerie Lang. Boston, Butterworths. o.p.

Introduction and Auxiliary Schedules. 1977. 209p. index. o.p. ISBN 0-408-70821-2.

Class J: Education. 1977. 21p. index. o.p. ISBN 0-408-70829-8.

Class P: Religion, the Occult, Morals and Ethics. 1977. 43p. o.p. ISBN 0-408-70832-8.

Class Q: Social Welfare. 1977. 36p. index. o.p. ISBN 0-408-70833-6.

Class I: Psychology and Psychiatry. 1978. 62p. index. o.p. ISBN 0-408-70841-7.

These are the introduction and several schedules required by the effort to revise Bliss, described as "comprehensive and radical" in the *Journal of Documentation* in March 1973 (v. 29, p. 64). The main concerns are facet analysis and citation order.

Precisely how the changes affect the classification of library materials in Bliss libraries, and what influence they exert upon the development of other systems and non-Bliss institutions remains to be seen. It seems unlikely that they will do any more than the periodic improvements in the Dewey to reduce wasteful duplication between close or faceted classmarks and subject headings. Yet, we cannot fail to benefit from refreshing our acquaintance with Bliss's reasoning, in a world both favored and hampered by growing computerization.

The fifth volume (Class I) in the second edition of BC follows the format established for the earlier, individual class schedules. First and second outlines of the entire scheme precede a 12-page introduction to the new class. Then comes the class I outline, followed by the full development of the schedule. A subject index gives access to "elementary" class terms, but not to the many compound classes that the schedules are capable of specifying. Nor does it identify alternative locations, which are sometimes included in the schedules under preferred locations (e.g., "IHT PARA-PSYCHOLOGY. *Alternative* (not recommended) is to collocate with the Occult in PX").

Sidney L. Jackson and Jeanne Osborn

613. Maltby, Arthur, and Lindy Gill. **The Case for Bliss: Modern Classification Practice and Principles in the Context of the Bibliographic Classification.** London, Clive Bingley; distr., New York, Munich, K. G. Saur, 1979. 142p. index. $14.50. ISBN 0-85157-290-1.

The serial publication in England of individual class schedules for a second edition of the *Bliss Bibliographic Classification* (see *ARBA* 78, entries 224-27 and *ARBA* 80, entry 206) occasions renewed discussion of that admirable American scheme, and of its qualities vis-à-vis other well-known schemes. Here is a multipurpose treatise which: (1) sets the second edition within its historical and functional context, (2) provides a general bibliography, (3) analyzes strengths and weaknesses, (4) illustrates practical applications, and (5) suggests ways and means for future development. While the authors have devoted substantial parts of their professional careers to the rejuvenation and use of BC, they strive for, and achieve rather well, objectivity and balance in their critical comments. They hold that a study of Bliss, more than of any other general system, gives insights into the persistent issues which enliven modern discussions of subject analysis and retrieval.

There can never be a perfectly constructed, universally and permanently accepted shelf arrangement or indexing scheme. BC has long been recognized for its seminal influence on classification theory, although its adoption was largely limited to a few British libraries. Its inadequacies stemmed chiefly from its single authorship and its lack of continuous maintenance. This survey demonstrates the viability and advantages of the second edition without glossing over its inevitable problems. [R: C&RL, July 80, pp. 387-88]

Jeanne Osborn

Dewey Decimal Classification

614. Batty, C. D. **An Introduction to the Eighteenth Edition of the Dewey Decimal Classification.** Hamden, Conn., Linnet Books, 1971. 1v. (unpaged). index. (Programmed Texts in

Library and Information Science). o.p. LC 71-27514. ISBN 0-208-01067-X.

This small volume is a programmed text which serves to introduce the beginning student to the fundamentals of classifying with the Dewey Decimal Classification. This edition, extensively revised, is keyed specifically to the eighteenth edition of Dewey. Two earlier editions were keyed to the sixteenth and seventeenth editions of Dewey.

The reader is guided step-by-step from the selection of an index entry in the Decimal Classification to the assignment of a classification number. Some of the concepts covered in the text include: add devise (general and limited), areas notation, built-in geographical subdivision, double zero in standard subdivisions, geographical subdivision, historical subdivision (general and special), language class, physiographic features in area notation, specificity, standard subdivisions, and tables of procedure.

A "corrigenda" is included; unless it is used the reader will not reach the correct frames, which causes considerable confusion. It might have been advisable for Batty to await the publication of the eighteenth edition of Dewey rather than to work from the "final manuscript," as this was the cause of some errors. The corrigenda also corrects errors which appear in nearly 10 percent of the frames. These too might have been checked and corrected before being committed to print.

This should be a good supplementary text to help introduce the student to Dewey. The reviewer sees no particular virtues to the "scrambled" programmed text, but it may appeal to some readers. The author is successful in presenting the concepts of the Dewey Classification, and the examples are clear—although somewhat esoteric at times.

The book can be recommended for use as a supplementary text for classroom use. [R: AL, Apr 72, p. 432]

Marty Bloomberg

615. Batty, C. D. **An Introduction to the Nineteenth Edition of the Dewey Decimal Classification.** London, Clive Bingley; distr., Hamden, Conn., Shoe String Press, 1981. 1v. (unpaged). index. $12.00. ISBN 0-85157-303-7.

This is the fourth edition of a programmed text that Batty developed to teach building numbers with the Dewey Decimal Classification. Begun originally at the College of Librarianship, Wales, to test the suitability of the programmed text approach, it is used extensively by library science students as a companion volume to Dewey.

The student is led step-by-step through approximately 40 underlying concepts including add devices, centered headings, double synthesis, geographical subdivisions, historical subdivisions, language notation, scope notes, specificity, and synthesis. The concept is explained and examples are given, followed by a test question with several different alternative answers, one of which is right. Specifically how to build the number is left to the student.

The text stresses using the index volume of Dewey. This might conflict with some teaching approaches that emphasize determining the main topic through using the schedules and summaries and then proceeding hierarchically to the most specific aspect. Such an approach leaves learning the use of the index until after the student becomes familiar with the schedule arrangement.

This particular edition differs from its predecessors by including a seven-page essay on the origin and development of the scheme that nicely complements the editor's introduction found in Dewey. Eliminated are the problems that existed in the previous edition caused by going to press prior to the finalization of Dewey. The book is recommended as a supplementary text for students and staff wanting to build skills in classifying in Dewey. [R: IRLA, Nov 81, p. 9; LR, Spring 82, p. 63]

Ann Allan

616. Bloomberg, Marty, and Hans Weber. **An Introduction to Classification and Number Building in Dewey.** Edited by John Phillip Immroth. Littleton, Colo., Libraries Unlimited, 1976. 199p. bibliog. index. (Library Science Text Series). o.p. LC 76-26975. ISBN 0-87287-115-0.

The text is a concise and practical introduction to the basic principles and techniques of number building with Dewey Decimal Classification schedules and the Relative Index. The text is intended for library technical assistants, clerks, and paraprofessionals, and for library school students and librarians who have had little experience using Dewey schedules. The first chapter presents a general orientation to the Dewey Decimal Classification, covering the following topics: history of DDC; format of the eighteenth edition and the tenth abridged edition; general characteristics (hierarchical structure, decimal system, classification by discipline); specific characteristics (tables and mnemonic features, classification schedules— notes and instructions); segmentation of DDC numbers; sources of DDC numbers; principles of book classification. This key chapter presents

the essential structure and format of DDC and prepares the student for the intricate analysis of specific characteristics and problems encountered in number building, developed in the following ten chapters.

Each of chapters 2 through 11 treats a complete class of DDC. Each contains seven sections: introductory note; outline of the class; introduction to the class; details of the class; number building examples (with explanations); problems to solve; answers to problems. Each chapter surveys a class, serving as a "road map" to the schedules and pointing out the major contents, basic organization, and arrangement. The main portion of each chapter contains a carefully constructed sequence of number building examples, problems, and solutions. The text shows how to use the Relative Index correctly to find the appropriate location in the schedules, then how to build the correct number. The authors do clearly explain the number building process in both the schedules and the auxiliary tables. Chapter 12, "Book Numbers," discusses basic functions of these devices and the use of the three most widely used schemes: Cutter Tables, Library of Congress Author Numbers, and DDC Book Numbers. An appendix contains additional problems for the student to solve. A bibliography of basic books on classification and an index complete the text. [R: LQ, Jan 78, p. 82]

617. **A Classification and Subject Index for Cataloguing and Arranging the Books and Pamphlets of a Library.** Amherst, Mass., Melvil Dewey, 1876; repr., Albany, N.Y., Forest Press Division, Lake Placid Education Foundation, 1976. 44p. $59.95.

The first edition of Melvil Dewey's classification schedule was reprinted to celebrate the centennial of its original publication. The first edition of the classification consists of the following parts: preface; divisions, the original schedule; tables; subject index; explanations; and subject catalog.

This facsimile reprint will be a welcome addition to library science collections that do not have the original. [R: C&RL, Mar 77, pp. 161-62]

618. Dewey, Melvil. **Abridged Dewey Decimal Classification and Relative Index.** 11th ed. Edited under the direction of Benjamin A. Custer. Albany, N.Y., Forest Press Division, Lake Placid Education Foundation, 1979. 618p. index. $29.00. LC 78-12514. ISBN 0-910608-22-9.

The *Abridged Dewey Decimal Classification and Relative Index* is designed primarily for small general libraries, especially elementary and secondary schools and small public libraries. It is also intended to assist in the teaching of "the theory and practice of classification in general and of the DDC in particular." The previous edition, the tenth, was an adaptation of the unabridged edition 18. It assumed that libraries using the abridgment would not grow in size and would not have to expand their classification. This resulted in shorter, and sometimes slightly different, numbers because some of the more detailed structures of edition 18 were dropped.

Abridged edition 11, based on unabridged edition 19, is a "true abridgment" with topics appearing in the same basic number in each edition. This enables the smaller library to use Library of Congress cards and other bibliographic citation without fear of error. Further, several phoenix sections have been added to replace crowded numbers. A very thorough introduction explains the changes made since the last edition, and provides a basic introduction to the theory of classification. Small libraries and cataloging courses will find this edition helpful. [R: LQ, Oct 80, p. 483]

Janet H. Littlefield

619. Dewey, Melvil. **Dewey Decimal Classification: 301-307 Sociology Expanded Version Based on Edition 19.** John P. Comaromi, ed.; Margaret J. Warren, assistant ed. Albany, N.Y., Forest Press Division, Lake Placid Education Foundation, 1981. 52p. index. free to purchasers of Edition 19. LC 81-17531. ISBN 0-910608-33-4.

True to its promise in *DC&*, volume 4, number 1 (June 1980), Forest Press has expanded this most significant of the phoenix changes in *DDC19* for the benefit of all purchasers of that edition (see *ARBA* 80, entry 210). This revision was accepted for use on Library of Congress catalog records as of 1 January 1982. The brevity of the original phoenix 301-307 schedule was a matter of general concern to classifiers. Its new incarnation is approximately double the size, including centered headings, tables of precedence, do not use, and class here notes, as well as single numbers and sequences not previously available. Only section 301 is untouched. There are four relocations and one reinstatement, all summarized in the introduction. An index and a comparative table of *DDC18/DDC19* changes are familiar features, supplemented by 10 pages of instruction excerpted from the *Manual on the Use of the*

Dewey Decimal Classification (Forest Press Division, 1982).

Jeanne Osborn

620. Dewey, Melvil. **Dewey Decimal Classification and Relative Index.** 19th ed. Edited by Benjamin A. Custer. Albany, N.Y., Forest Press Division, Lake Placid Education Foundation, 1979. 3v. index. $37.00/vol.; $105.00/set. LC 77-27967. ISBN 0-910608-19-9 (v. 1); 0-910608-20-2 (v. 2); 0-910608-21-0 (v. 3), 0-910608-23-7 (set).

By shaving ¾-inch from its long-established height, and ½-inch from its customary width, this nineteenth edition of *DDC* seems physically less awkward than its predecessors without sacrificing visual effectiveness. One finds it hard to believe that the schedule actually contains nearly 13 percent more entries than the preceding edition (29,528 as compared with 26,141 in the eighteenth, and 22,355 in the seventeenth edition). Other matters than size affect ease of use, however. The editorial staff has worked hard to improve and simplify the presentations. The familiar three-volume format has changed very little, though, under its neat gray binding, trimmed in maroon.

Volume 1 is devoted primarily to the instructive "Editor's Introduction," with its supplemental glossary and index, and to the seven auxiliary tables, five of which were introduced as recently as edition 18, but all of which have been revised and updated. One of the three phoenix schedules of this edition is in the -41-42 (i.e., the British Isles) area notations of auxiliary table 2. Volume 1 also gives lists of relocations, schedule reductions, and changed numbers.

Volume 2 presents the schedules proper, with their traditional guides (running titles plus section numbers, differentiated type sizes and faces showing hierarchical progressions, left-hand margin adjustments for the same purpose, brief internal summary tables and centered headings to counteract the tyranny of the decimal notation, brackets to identify unassigned or optional numbers, and italics to show reassignments to recently vacated numbers). Its scope notes include definitions and examples, as well as class here (and class there) suggestions. Base numbers are spelled out as starting points for the numerous situations where asterisked footnotes say to add to as instructed under some number in a different location. The remaining two phoenix schedules of this edition are located in sections 301-307, where "Sociology" has been recast from the former 301, and in 324, where the "Political Process" has been recast from the former 324 and 329, eliminating the older bias toward U.S. political parties. Throughout the schedules, options are increased to accommodate favored languages, religions, and the like, in the interests of international use. The last of the few words remaining in edition 18 in simplified spelling (e.g., "divorst," "publisht," etc.) have disappeared for the same reason.

Volume 3 is devoted entirely to the relative index, prefaced by its list of abbreviations. It frequently offers numbers considerably longer than any found in the schedules, a kind of double-check on the number building instructions. Format features such as entries for "*s.s.* −," "*area* −," "*lit.sub.* −," etc., numbers from the auxiliary tables, cross-references to "other aspects," and the like are little altered from the eighteenth edition, although the terminology is of course updated.

There seems no reason to doubt that this modest milestone in the developmental history of the Dewey Decimal Classification will serve its objectives well. The final decision to omit a projected phoenix schedule for 560-590 ("Life Sciences") divisions is indicative of current efforts to make haste deliberately, using study and consultation before attempting numerous or revolutionary changes in any single edition. [R: LQ, Oct 80, p. 483]   Jeanne Osborn

621.   Manual on the Use of the Dewey Decimal Classification: Edition 19. John P. Comaromi, ed.; Margaret J. Warren, assistant ed. Albany, N.Y., Forest Press Division, Lake Placid Education Foundation, 1982. 3v. 551p. index. $37.00/vol.; $105.00/set. ISBN 0-910608-32-6.

This long-awaited guide to the use of *DDC19* (see *ARBA* 80, entry 210) is the first separately published official set of instructions and interpretations since the *Guide to the Use of Dewey Decimal Classification* (Forest Press Division, 1942). It has significant similarities to, as well as differences from, the format and content of *DDC19*. Its introduction, like the editor's introduction in *DDC19*, addresses questions of cataloging in general and DDC cataloging in particular and has its own index. Yet it supplements, rather than duplicates, the previously published information. Point-by-point coverage of auxiliary table and schedule numbers consists largely of definitions and various kinds of scope notes (e.g., class here, do not use, class elsewhere, etc.). Eight maps reminiscent of those in *LC Classification Schedule G* accompany the section on table 2 (areas). Few of the "Corrections, Changes and New Numbers" from *DC&*, volume 4, are reproduced. Those that are usually show alteration. (See, for example, the DDC 404.2 ["bilingualism"] note in the manual as contrasted with that

found in *DC&*, volume 4 [number 1, p. 17, June 1980].) Sample sections from the manual were reproduced in *DC&*, volume 4 (number 2, pp. 4-8, October 1981). The familiar relative index format is called an alphabetical index here, while another − numerical − index identifies some 3,000 discussions of interrelated table and schedule numbers but ignores numbers, such as 623.441 ("Weaponry of Pre-firearm Origin"), that carry no cross-classification hints. This work is clearly of value to every DDC cataloger and student. [R: LR, Summer 83, p. 172; LRTS, July 83, p. 275]   Jeanne Osborn

622.   Osborn, Jeanne. Dewey Decimal Classification, 19th Edition: A Study Manual. Littleton, Colo., Libraries Unlimited, 1982. 366p. bibliog. index. $27.50. LC 82-21. ISBN 0-87287-293-9.

Jeanne Osborn presents an introduction, review, and analysis of the *Dewey Decimal Classification*, nineteenth edition (1979). The first few chapters trace the history of DDC and discuss its current status and characteristics, as well as the modernization of DDC schedules, notation, and terminology. The major portion of the work describes and illustrates the notable changes that have been made in the auxiliary tables and in each main class. The detailed analysis of each class and its divisions includes comparisons between the eighteenth and nineteenth editions. Included at the ends of these chapters are numerous exercises in number analysis and synthesis. An examination of the eleventh abridged edition is followed by a final chapter which surveys book numbers, nonprint classification, the pros and cons of DDC, and the status of DDC numbers on Library of Congress bibliographic records. [R: BL, 15 Oct 82, p. 293]

623.   Sistema de Clasificación Decimal. Planeado originalmente por Melvil Dewey. Adapto y traducido bajo la dirección de Jorge Aguayo; indice por Donald J. Lehnus. Basado en la 18ª ed. con adiciones de la 19ª ed. Albany, N.Y., Forest Press Division, Lake Placid Education Foundation, 1980. 3v. index. $28.00/vol.; $81.00/set. LC 80-24527. ISBN 0-910608-26-1.

Librarians of the Spanish-speaking world will welcome the publication of *Sistema de Clasificación Decimal*, the second translation of the Dewey Decimal Classification into Spanish. The first *Sistema* (Forest Press Division, 1955) was based on edition 15 of the DDC, had 620 pages of schedules (the body of the classification), and 432 of index. This *Sistema* has 1,700 pages of schedules, 476 of index, and 497 of introduction and tables, the latter comprising tables for standard subdivisions, places, and so on. The schedules are almost three times fuller than those of the 1955 translation.

Though the *Sistema* is based on edition 18 with additions from edition 19, it is basically the same classification as edition 19. The only important divergences occur in the *Sistema*'s not having the expansion of 362-363 for social problems and social welfare that was developed for edition 19, and not making the relocation of management of an enterprise from 658.9 to standard subdivision 068. With increasing international exchange of information, such congruity is a decided strength.

Another major strength of the *Sistema* is the various adaptations made for Spanish culture. Believing that a straight translation of the DDC mis-serves non-Anglo-American cultures, Forest Press and the editor made the following adaptations: (1) the books of the Bible are organized according to the canon of the Catholic Church; (2) Spanish (460) is the model for languages rather than English (420); (3) the history and area numbers for Latin America have been expanded to considerable detail; and (4) the schedule from the 1955 *Sistema* on the law of Roman origin and its index have been appended to volume 1. Each adaptation provides sufficient detail and appropriate structure.

The editing of these volumes was ably done by Jorge Aguayo, an eminent scholar in American librarianship; the index by Donald Lehnus, a U.S. scholar of cataloging and classification. The three volumes are sturdy, lie flat when open, and are printed in the typed format familiar to the users of the Library of Congress Classification, though the print of the *Sistema* is larger and crisper.

Indispensable for DDC libraries in the Spanish-speaking world, the *Sistema* can also be useful in DDC libraries having a Spanish-speaking clientele (e.g., public libraries in the U.S. Southwest): the schedules (volume 2) explain what the numbers mean in Spanish, and the index (volume 3) indicates in Spanish where material on a subject can be found. All parties to the production of the *Sistema* are to be congratulated on this highly useful professional tool.　　　John P. Comaromi

Library of Congress Classification

624.　Chan, Lois Mai. **Immroth's Guide to the Library of Congress Classification.** 3rd ed. Littleton, Colo., Libraries Unlimited, 1980. 402p. illus. index. (Library Science Text Series). $33.00; $21.00pa. LC 80-16981. ISBN 0-87287-224-6; 0-87287-235-1pa.

Lois Chan's revision updates Immroth's *Guide to the Library of Congress Classification* (see *ARBA* 72, entry 120) by elucidating changes in policies and practices that have taken place since 1971 and by incorporating examples and instructive analysis of later published schedules and revisions of schedules. The text continues to provide students with a basic understanding of the characteristics of LC Classification, the arrangement within the classes, the format of the schedules and tables, and special problems of use and notation.

Chapter 1-4, completely reorganized and rewritten, treat the development and purpose of the classification, its general principles and characteristics, the notation (including Cutter number) applicable to the entire system, and the use of the tables. Chapter 5, which discusses individual classes, has been completely revised and enlarged; and chapter 6, on special types of library materials, is new to this edition.

Examples are included throughout. Many are new, and those retained from the second edition have been checked against the Library of Congress shelflist to ensure validity. Later writings on the classification have been added to the bibliographies at the ends of chapters. The appendix contains only those tables that are used throughout the system but printed in only a few of the schedules, and tables that have undergone significant change or revision. [R: JAL, Nov 80, p. 308]

625.　Dershem, Larry D., comp. **Library of Congress Classification: Class K, Subclass KF—Law of the United States Cumulative Index.** Littleton, Colo., published for the American Association of Law Libraries by Fred B. Rothman, 1982. 1v. (unpaged). (AALL Publications Series, No. 18). $35.00 looseleaf. LC 82-22987. ISBN 0-8377-0115-5.

This cumulative index of KF Library of Congress classification represents a long-desired aid for both technical and public service departments in law libraries of all varieties. Dershem provides a cumulation of Library of Congress noncumulative additions and changes to the KF schedule. This index precludes the need for catalogers to update KF schedules by hand or to rely on commercially prepared noncumulative supplements to the schedule. The looseleaf format permits easy supplementation of the index following the quarterly supplement of Library of Congress additions and changes. Further verification is possible since the compiler provides additions and changes list numbers behind each new term added to the original schedule.

Although primarily designed as a tool to assist catalogers, this index may have public service use. Often reference librarians are called upon to provide readers with general call numbers on a particular legal topic to permit readers to browse through available material. This index fosters an economical use of the reference librarian's services by providing a quick index to Library of Congress classification of numerous U.S. legal topics. This work is an admirable addition to the American Association of Law Libraries' publication series.

Robert J. Nissenbaum

626. Greenberg, Alan M. **An Author Index to Library of Congress Classification: Class P; Subclasses PN, PR, PS, PZ.** New York, Marcel Dekker, 1981. 80p. $19.75. LC 81-1698. ISBN 0-8247-1516-0.

This index lists, in alphabetical order, the author names in the Library of Congress class PR (English literature) and class PS (American literature). The entries are in the form in which they appear in the LC schedules. These forms are those usually appearing in LC card catalogs.

Since author names in the LC schedules are arranged in a number of chronological groupings, the classifier must know not only the writer's nationality but the original publication dates of his or her works in order to assign the proper class number. Variant names and pseudonyms are also included in the alphabetical listing. The class number is given with each form rather than requiring the classifier to follow cross-references to identify the number. All pseudonyms are enclosed in quotation marks to alert the user to the existence of another form of name.

The arrangement of names follows rules given in the second edition of the *ALA Rules for Filing Catalog Cards*. Some names in the index also appear in the LC Authority File on OCLC; others do not. Susan Ebershoff-Coles

627. Hamilton, Linda K., ed. **The Library of Congress Shelflist: A User's Guide to the Microfiche Edition, Volume One.** Ann Arbor, Mich., University Microfilms International, 1979. 57p. illus. o.p. LC 78-27249. ISBN 0-8357-0210-3.

This brief, pamphlet-sized volume contains a very readable and enlightening account of the theory and practice of shelflisting at the Library of Congress. Following instructions for using the guide and a brief description of the microfiche shelflist and the filming process, the work

provides two interesting articles. Mary K. D. Pietris's "History of the Library of Congress Shelflist" outlines the interrelationship between the Library of Congress Classification system and the growth and development of the shelflist. The recording of the LC Classification numbers, revisions in classification, and provision of alternate class numbers are all discussed as these affect the shelflist and its maintenance. The presentation is informative and clear.

Linda K. Hamilton demonstrates various uses of the microfiche shelflist for cataloging and interlibrary loan, bibliography, and networking. She offers many helpful suggestions which could be easily implemented by a creative and ingenious library staff. Moreover, she is quick to point out that other uses of the shelflist could readily be devised. In its totality, this 57-page pamphlet would be of interest to librarians and library educators alike, and could well be a required reading in a cataloging, classification, or Library of Congress Classification course. [R: C&RL, Jan 80, p. 94]

Harry S. Otterson, Jr.

628. Immroth, John Phillip. **A Guide to the Library of Congress Classification.** 2nd ed. Littleton, Colo., Libraries Unlimited, 1971. 335p. index. o.p. LC 75-178877. SBN 87287-039-1.

This second edition has been completely revised and reset. Basic principles of the organization of Library of Congress Classification are presented, and there are numerous examples to guide the reader through the complex processes of analyzing schedules and number-building with tables. After an introductory historical survey, the format and general principles of the schedules and tables are discussed. This is followed by individual treatment of the classes A-Z, covering the problems involved in working with each schedule. The appendix contains many examples of tables, and each chapter is followed by an extensive bibliography. [R: CLW, May 72, p. 527; LJ, 1 May 72, p. 1679; LRTS, Summer 72, p. 406]

629. **An Index to the Library of Congress Classification: With Entries for Special Expansions in Medicine, Law, Canadiana, and Nonbook Materials.** prelim. ed. J. McRee Elrod, Judy Inouye, and Ann Craig Turner, eds. Ottawa, Ont., Canadian Library Association, 1974. 1v. (various paging). o.p. ISBN 0-88802-100-3.

The LC list of subject headings is not adequate as an index to the LC Classification because many headings have no class numbers. James G. Williams's *Classified Library of*

Congress Subject Headings (Marcel Dekker, 1972) does not answer the need either, because it does not show class numbers for previously unclassified headings.

The technique used by the compilers of this work was to combine the indexes of the separate LC schedules, to which was added original indexing of these schedules without official LC indexing.

To further enrich the overall index, class numbers developed by several non-LC expansions have been added. Of these, the most important are those of the Quebec Bibliothèque Nationale, the Canadian National Archives, and the U.S. National Library of Medicine. Where class numbers used by these and other expansions differ from those of LC, they are listed in addition to the LC numbers.

The final result is a work that does answer a long-felt need of librarians. This volume is called a preliminary edition. As is common in preliminary editions, the typography leaves much to be desired. Many of the class numbers are so faint as to be illegible.

Richard A. Gray

630. Lang, Jovian P. **Your Search Key to L.C.: Library of Congress Classification.** student's ed. Bronx, N.Y., Fordham Publishing, 1979. 149p. illus. index. (Library Instruction Program IV; Enrichment through Research, No. 1). $9.95pa. LC 75-50688. ISBN 0-913308-06-2.

This program book by Jovian P. Lang is intended to help users "learn how to locate material in libraries using the Library of Congress Classification scheme." It is written for "overworked teachers and librarians" engaged in library instruction and for students who are interested in self-education. It may be used alone or with a teacher's edition.

There are three main sections, each of which has numerous flaws, such as appear in examples below. "Basic Assumptions" discusses the parts of a book and its relation to the description on a catalog record which may be encountered in card, book, or on-line catalogs. Access points via author, subject, title, and analytical entries are demonstrated, together with an explanation of filing methods. There is much unnecessary focus on details which will not interest a nonlibrarian, such as the difference between title main entry and other title access. The attempt to show a page from a computer-produced book catalog (p. 27) would have benefited from graphic presentation in printout format.

The second section describes historical development of the "Library of Congress Classification." It includes a 26-page summary of classes A-Z and an explanation of call number formation. But readers do not need to know the details of form division, or geographical and chronological tables. They are not inquisitive about the meaning of call numbers, requiring them merely for location. Lang states (pp. 28-29) that LC has "proved more valuable" and that its close classification and fine flexibility as well as the capacity of its mixed notation for greater expansion make it superior. With what is he comparing the scheme? Is he implying superiority over DDC? Assuming his readers are familiar with DDC, Lang attempts to compare the two schemes. On page 32, columns under the two schemes are visually, but not intellectually, matched. Confusion results, with HF ("Commerce") being parallel with 630 ("Agriculture"), and N ("Fine Arts") opposite 400 ("Language").

The third section, "Searching by Subject in LC," discusses the fallacy of browsing for material on different aspects of a subject that have been dispersed throughout the classification. Twenty-nine catalog searches are simulated in the sciences, humanities, and social sciences, and accompanying exercises require the reader to search in the home library subject catalog. Lang attempts to replicate the thought processes of a subject search by contriving to place the user inside his own mind. In some cases the initial search clue is obvious because it is a keyword from the title. In others, Lang resorts to hit and miss tactics, relying on association which "rings a bell" (p. 116) or on setting the mind "on a different turn" (p. 131). The reader will dispair of learning a systematic procedure. The section concludes with a bibliography, an index, and 11 blank pages for notes.

Lang's work is more ambitious than his title or preface conveys, for he attempts not only to explain the LC Classification but also to reconstruct the intricate thought processes involved in searching the subject catalog to find a class number. Fordham publishers failed to catch several spelling mistakes, an error in subject subdivision (p. 132), and a peculiar lapse regarding "complaints from any sizable group" (p. 129). Unfortunately, this work will be of questionable value for bibliographic instruction with any user group.

Valmai Fenster

631. Lang, Jovian P. **Your Search Key to L.C.: Library of Congress Classification.** teacher's ed. Bronx, N.Y., Fordham Publishing,

1979. 33p. illus. (Library Instruction Program IV; Enrichment through Research, No. 1). $9.95pa. LC 75-50688. ISBN 0-913308-06-1.

The teacher's edition of *Your Search Key to L.C.* is intended as an aid to librarians or teachers engaged in bibliographic instruction and is coordinated with a student manual. The first 11 pages contain brief background material that is intended to give the teacher an elementary understanding of such theoretical concepts as hierarchical classification, referential subdivision, specificity, and predominant subject. Unfortunately, like the student manual, this book suffers from poor editing. For example, Lang states that Charles Cutter's Expansive Classification (1891) was developed in the 1980s instead of the 1880s. In the same section on classification systems several footnotes are mismatched.

Half of the manual consists of copyrighted ditto masters containing exercises that are intended to test the students' use of the catalog and comprehension of the material in the seven sections of the student's edition: "The Book," "Library Catalogs," "Filing Rules," "Historical Development," "Description of L.C. Classification," "Formation of L.C. Call Numbers," and "Fundamentals of the L.C. Classification Scheme." At the outset, librarians should seriously question whether all the skills presented are necessary for students to learn. In addition, some questions are ambiguous and difficult to understand until the reader looks up the answer (e.g., "There is a certain advantage to keeping material on a large subject together in the catalog. What method is used to accomplish this?").

Although commercially prepared exercises may appeal to the busy librarian, surely a cardinal principle of responsible bibliographic instruction is to motivate catalog users by integrating problems that are tailored to the questions for which they need answers.

Valmai Fenster

632. Library of Congress Classification Schedules: A Cumulation of Additions and Changes, 1974-77. Helen Savage, ed. Detroit, Gale, 1978. 32v. o.p. ISBN 0-8103-0883-5.

The Library of Congress Classification schedules are frequently reviewed by committee to ensure that the system is adaptable to new subjects and flexible enough to admit changes in established subjects. Changes are published, as they occur, in the quarterly *Library of Congress Additions and Changes*. In 1974, Gale Research Company published *Library of Congress Classification Schedules: A Cumulation of Additions*

and Changes through 1973. The 32-volume set updated to December 1973 the latest editions of the 30 volumes of basic schedules. *Cumulation of Additions and Changes, 1974-77*, also in 32 volumes, supplements the 1973 publication. Although Gale had no official connection with LC in this project, LC cooperated whenever problems arose.

The advantages of the cumulations are obvious; the cataloger will no longer have to look through the many quarterly issues of *L.C. Additions and Changes* or spend time inserting changes into the original schedules. It will still be necessary to code the original schedule volumes to indicate the existence and location of a change. Apparently, costs prohibited the publication of additions and changes that include the previously issued changes to 1973. The cataloger must still use two volumes of changes along with the original schedule and any quarterly changes issued in the future. Two solutions come to mind that would relieve the cataloger of the need to search for additions and changes: to issue the schedules in looseleaf format and publish changes on replacement pages; or to develop a computer-stored system that would display the schedules on a CRT screen. Both ideas appear prohibitively expensive. Gale's cumulations are the best existing solution to the problem of maintaining a usable file of additions and changes. The type is legible, the format logical, and the volumes are bound in sturdy soft covers.   Janet H. Littlefield

633. Library of Congress Classification Schedules: Indexes to Class P Subclasses and to Their Additions and Changes through 1978. Helen Savage, ed. Detroit, Gale, 1982. 10v. $500.00pa./set. LC 82-47646. ISBN 0-8103-1607-2.

Two quite different supplements to the *L.C. Classification Schedules* come from Gale. One of these is the cumulation of additions and changes through 1981 made available in 34 separately published parts. The other one, which is of concern here, is the index to the "P" subclasses. The 10 volumes of this index cover: P-PA; PA Supplement; PB-PH; PG; PJ-PM; PR, PS, PZ; PQ (Part 1); PQ (Part 2); PT (Part 1); and PT (Part 2). The prices on these parts vary from $35.00 to $95.00.

The lists of authors' names in the LC Classification have increased in importance for catalogers and for reference work. This was for years especially true for the classical languages and literatures, whose lists were accepted by classicists as a first authority. Over the years, authors' names have been added in all the "P"s, but never has there been a consistent approach to this wealth of information. Now it exists, for the "P"s at least, through 1978 in this set of 10 indexes. Authors, titles of anonymous works, and comprehensive subject headings are all included in one alphabet. Usually only one number is given, since the individual author developments are not indexed. Neither are the tables indexed. But cross-references help a user locate terms and names.

These indexes must not be used to classify by themselves. Catalogers should use them in conjunction with the latest edition of the classification schedule and a copy of the appropriate cumulation of additions and changes. Each of these parts has the same two-page preface, which explains the basis for index construction and for the filing arrangement, with a brief example. The rationale for the division into 10 volumes is that each index can stand next to parallel schedules and cumulations of additions and changes. Each part is reproduced from typed copy on the recto only. The facing blank pages are convenient for notes and for further additions until such a time as another index is prepared. The slightly off-white paper is strong and opaque. The printing is even, and the type style is clear and open. While the spines are square, the pages are glued in signatures using a technique which seems strong enough for extended shelf life. The bindings are heavy coated paper.

The Library of Congress has no official connection with this publication. This editorial disclaimer is important because the index is not LC's publication and does not carry LC's approval, although the library's staff did cooperate with the work, answering questions whenever possible.

Helen Savage has made a major contribution with this work. The volumes will assist the cataloging process; also, many information questions can be answered using these indexes since, as one example, most names carry dates or some other identification. The price may mean that smaller libraries will hesitate to purchase, but libraries which do original cataloging or which are about to embark on reclassification will find this set a requirement.

Neal L. Edgar

634. Matthis, Raimund E., and Desmond Taylor. **Adopting the Library of Congress Classification System: A Manual of Methods and Techniques for Application or Conversion.** New York, R. R. Bowker, 1971. 209p. illus. index. o.p. LC 72-163906. ISBN 0-8352-0493-6.

This interesting book is especially recommended for small libraries wishing to convert to the LC Classification system (LCC). Matthis and Taylor encourage the use of LCC on the basis of its practical merits in relation to "the promise and prospects of centralized cataloging and classification," rather than on theoretical considerations.

The book incorporates valuable information on (1) cost considerations involved in a reclassification project, (2) some of the problems to be expected from using LCC, (3) procedures and techniques to be followed, and (4) description and evaluation of the various types of Xerox copiers.

On the other hand, the book is limited in scope. The discussion of the various problems of LCC schedules deals with very few classes; most of it is concerned with tables VIIIa and IXa of the "P" schedule. The section on equipment does not provide any choices other than the Xerox copiers. The reader, therefore, must be aware that the book only suggests some guidelines and is not to be considered as a manual of procedure, although this is implied in the title of the book.

Finally, an excellent feature of the book is chapter 5, which includes an extensive annotated bibliography on the subject of reclassification. [R: LJ, 1 May 72, p. 1680]

Nabil Hamdy

635. Olson, Nancy B., comp. **Author-Number Index to the Library of Congress Classification Schedules 1974, Volume 1.** Washington, D.C., United States Historical Documents Institute, 1975. 918p. (Combined Indexes to the Library of Congress Classification Schedules, 1974; Set I, Vol. 1). $1,145.00/set (15 volumes). LC 74-29322. ISBN 0-88222-050-0.

For years, users of the Library of Congress Classification schedules have been hampered by the lack of a comprehensive index that covers all of them. Classifiers have been forced to hand-search the individual indexes to each class or subclass with a great deal of uncertainty. Nancy Olson has compiled a set of indexes that should alleviate the difficult. Index 1 covers authors of literary works and their classification numbers; index 2, philosophers, musicians, historical figures, educators, scientists, etc.; index 3, materials from index 2 arranged by classification number with headings for classes, subgroups, and time periods when appropriate; index 4, geographical names; and index 5, a subject keyword to the entire Library of Congress system. The first volume of the set covers authors of literary works, A-K. A typical entry reads "PZ 3.B4193 Belloc, Hilaire, Full name: Joseph Hilaire Pierre Belloc, 1870-1953," with a symbol indicating the source of the information (e.g., the schedules, LC shelflist, etc.). Authors' names are arranged alphabetically. Entries are clear, and typesize is easily readable. A spot-check of about 100 entries revealed no errors. This important contribution to the tools of cataloging and classification will be of great interest to the neophyte cataloger, catalogers in small libraries, and those who must reclassify a collection from Dewey to LC. Reference librarians may also find the set helpful.

Harry S. Otterson, Jr.

636. Olson, Nancy B., comp. **Biographical Subject Index to the Library of Congress Classification Schedules 1974, Volume 1.** Washington, D.C., United States Historical Documents Institute, 1975. 815p. (Combined Indexes to the Library of Congress Classification Schedules, 1974; Set II, Vol. 1). $1,145.00/set (15 volumes). LC 74-29322. ISBN 0-88222-053-7.

This "Set II" of the computer-produced indexes to the Library of Congress Classification schedules consists of three volumes that provide an alphabetical listing of all biographees listed in the LC basic schedules, their additions and changes, the LC shelflist, and the publication *Books: Subjects.* Each name is accompanied by the LC call numbers under which the biography or bibliography was classified, as well as by a symbol indicating the source of the call number. Many biographees have more than one number, pointing out either the various fields to which the person has made contributions or the fact that LC often classifies literary persons in the PZ section as well as in other numbers of the "P" schedule. Cross-references are provided for pseudonyms and variant forms of names. In the foreword, it is stated that "libraries should find this compilation a useful source for aid in determining classification numbers, tracing Library of Congress current classification practices, and approaching subjects from an alternative point to subject headings," and that it "will increase the accessibility of all types of library collections which use the Library of Congress classification system" as well as "replace lengthy searches in the National Union Catalog and provide much useful information for libraries not accepting the PZ 3 and 4 numbers assigned by LC." It should prove to be quite useful to all libraries doing a great amount of original cataloging.

Donald J. Lehnus

637. Olson, Nancy B., comp. **Classified Index to Persons in the Library of Congress Classification Schedules 1974.** Washington, D.C., United States Historical Documents Institute, 1975. 3v. (Combined Indexes to the Library of Congress Classification Schedules, 1974; Set III). $1,145.00/set (15 volumes). LC 74-29322.

These computer-produced volumes are the third of five sets of *Combined Indexes to the Library of Congress Classification Schedules,* produced at Mankato State College under a grant from the United States Historical Documents Institute. A 1975 imprint, volume 1 of set 3 has just become available for review. According to the compiler's introduction, the *Classified Index* is a list, arranged in classification order, of personal names comprehended by the LC Classification—including the original schedules, the shelflist of the Library of Congress, *Books: Subjects,* and *Additions & Changes* to the published classification schedules. Sigla indicate the source of the name if it is not from the basic schedules. The compiler suggests that the *Classified Index* be maintained as an authority file for personal classification and Cutter numbers and that it be used by reference librarians as a guide to their own collections.

As a music librarian, I turned to classes ML and MT to evaluate the quality and quantity of the information provided in volume 1. Collating ML410.C against the SUNY at Buffalo shelflist, I found 22 LC names in that shelflist under the letter "C" that are not in the *Classified Index.* Although the compiler's introduction described the addition of the letter "E" to indicate the German umlaut in this computer-produced list, no instances of that usage were found in the ML list; Händel is printed Handel, Schütz as Schutz, etc. Yet, it is impossible to maintain a name authority file without accurate diacritical marks and current death dates. The *Classified Index* indicates that Stravinskii is still alive when, in fact, he died in 1971. Wieland Wagner, also without a death date, died in 1966. Such omissions are intolerable in volumes designed to be librarians' tools.

The compiler's introduction suggests that the *Classified Index* be used to locate the various LC numbers that represent an individual's work (e.g., the seven numbers appropriate to Albert Schweitzer). However, access to those seven numbers in a classified list requires an alphabetical index, which is set 2 of the fifteen-volume *Combined Indexes.* Similarly, a reference librarian would need the alphabetical approach to use any volume of the *Combined Indexes* as a guide to his or her own collection.

Given its limitations, the *Classified Index* might be useful in libraries that prepare a great deal of original cataloging and need to fit Cutter numbers into the LC schedules. For most libraries, however, the *Biographical Subject Index* (set 2) and the *Subject Keyword Index* (set 5) would seem more appropriate than the *Classified Index*. The compiler is preparing supplementary volumes to each set that will more consistently include information from the LC shelflists; if those supplementary volumes correct the defects noted above, the usefulness of the *Classified Index* will be enhanced. Meanwhile, purchase will probably be limited to library school libraries.   Carol June Bradley

638. Olson, Nancy B., comp. **Geographical Name Index to the Library of Congress Classification Schedules 1974.** Washington, D.C., United States Historical Documents Institute, 1974. 570p. (Combined Indexes to the Library of Congress Classification Schedules, 1974; Set IV). $1,145.00/set (15 volumes). LC 74-29322. ISBN 0-88222-058-6.

This geographic name index, compiled by the Computer Services staff of Mankato State College, Minnesota, is one of five computer-generated indexes to the Library of Congress Classification Schedules. It attempts to provide unified access to the 45,520 geographic entries dispersed in the indexes of 31 separately printed LC schedules and their supplements published through December 1973. Included are political jurisdictions and geographical regions and features, whether these occur as broad class divisions or as subdivisions under topics such as literature. Such integrated approaches are not available in the *LC Subject Heading List,* Williams's *Classified List of Subject Headings* (volume 2, 1972), or the Canadian Library Association's *Index* (1974), which give access only by broad classes.

In the permuted KWIC (Key Word in Context) index, context words precede the alphabetized keyword. Class numbers and the schedule edition or supplement from which they derive follow the keyword. Some supplement numbers are omitted. *See* references were taken directly from schedule indexes, and the danger of integrating these without editing is evident. Because many *see* references function as *see also* references, confusion often results. For example, both "Lappi Region, *see* Lapland," and "Lappi (Region), *see* Lapland" function as reciprocal *see also* references. Additional ambiguity results because the former reference is read from right (keyword) to left: "Lapland see

Lappi (Region)." The introduction's explanation of this procedure, with its model of "Dutch East Indies" and "Indonesia," is obscure, and not all of the compiler's examples could be found in the index.

Preceding the index are an introduction and a user's guide, a list of editions that were sources of data, and geographical tables for countries, the United States, states, and cities. The sources of these tables are omitted, but the first two may be found in the G Schedule (4th ed.). Each volume of the set contains G. A. Morgan's "L.C. Classification System, Its History and Development."

Such an index, though desirable, can never be really current. A computerized index, updated and online, would eliminate costly investment in quickly outdated book form indexes. Small libraries, which would benefit most from this integrated approach, will find the cost prohibitive. Catalogers in large research libraries will have sufficient bibliographic precedent in shelflists and subject files to find class numbers of formerly established names, but will need to verify post-1974 names and classes in more recent schedules and supplements.

Valmai Fenster

639. Olson, Nancy B., comp. **Subject Keyword Index to the Library of Congress Classification Schedules 1974, Volume 1.** Washington, D.C., United States Historical Documents Institute, 1974. 750p. (Combined Indexes to the Library of Congress Classification Schedules, 1974; Set V, Vol. 1). $1,145.00/set (15 volumes). LC 74-29322. ISBN 0-88222-059-4.

The volume at hand is the first of a collection of six containing a KWIC index to the various editions of the LC Classification schedules (LCC). The combined indexes, of which this is a part, encompass 15 volumes. That there is a need for an overall index to LCC is obvious; that there is also a need for uniformity in terminology in the subject headings and in the classification schedules of LC is even more obvious; and that, it goes without saying, is manifest in this work. The index is combinatory, as one expects with KWIC; but it has been carefully and, perhaps, lovingly compiled. It has included all additions, corrections, and supplements up to 1974. However, this reviewer has always suggested to his students that the LC *Subject Headings* list can certainly act as a "poor man's" index to LCC for those who cannot afford the price of this set; and in using the subject heading list, perhaps a better grasp of both classification and subject cataloging might be acquired than in the employment of a strictly "verbal" index, as we have here in the KWIC presentation.

Francis J. Witty

640.   Perkins, John W., et al. **Library of Congress Classification Adapted for Children's Books.** 2nd ed. Inglewood, Calif., Inglewood Public Library, 1972. 100p. index. o.p.

This edition reflects changes made in the work after the Inglewood Library's children's collection was reclassified and new titles were added. Changes in classification from the preliminary edition include (1) omitting three subclasses, (2) adding three new subclasses, (3) providing 41 new subclasses by expanding existing classes. The original introduction and the section on the number of subclasses have been revised. The index has been expanded and numerous changes made in the index headings arranged by classification. There are also some changes and modifications in the section concerning suggestions and recommendations for spine labels and special collections. Detailed notes concerning changes and modifications to the LC Classification and examples of titles illustrating classes and subclasses are omitted in this section.

A third edition (1976) was also published. It was not reviewed in *ARBA* and is also now out-of-print.

641.   Piper, Patricia Luster, and Cecilia Hing-Ling Kwan. **A Manual on KF: The Library of Congress Classification for Law of the United States.** South Hackensack, N.J., Fred B. Rothman, 1972. 135p. illus. bibliog. index. (American Association of Law Libraries Publications Series, No. 11). $22.50. LC 72-86471. ISBN 0-8377-0109-0.

This treatise gathers in one place highly relevant information on the theory and use of the Library of Congress subclass KF. Written by members of the professional staff of the law library at the University of California, Davis, this work reflects their pioneering experience in using the KF system since 1967. Application of the KF system is aptly illustrated by numerous examples of LC cards. The scope of this work covers all possible technical areas involved in law library cataloging, plus considerations to evaluate before adopting the "K" class, problems confronting KF users, and methods of handling non-KF materials. An essential item for law and library science collections.

Bernard D. Reams, Jr.

UDC

642.   **Bibliographical Survey of UDC Editions.** The Hague, International Federation of Documentation, 1982. 73p. (FID Publication 573). 45.00Dfl. ISBN 92-66-00573-8.

This bibliography is based on publications of the Universal Decimal Classification (UDC) held by the Secretariat of the International Federation of Documentation (FID) on 31 December 1980. The classification schedules are divided into groups according to the fullness of the editions (i.e., full, medium, abridged, and special subject editions). "Full edition" does not refer to a volume containing the numbers 000-999, but rather to a single number or a short series of classification numbers which are complete for that subject field. Medium editions contain about 25-30 percent of what is found in a full edition; abridged editions contain about 10 percent of the numbers. Entries vary in length because they are based on information found in the publication: generally, title, year of publication, number of pages, and the FID number of the publication. Under each section the publications are grouped by language. In addition to the index for special subject editions there are two appendices: (1) a list of 35 guides and textbooks on UDC, and (2) addresses of publishers in more than 20 countries who are responsible for the editions of UDC listed herein.

About the only American libraries that might be interested in this bibliography are library school libraries, or any other where there is an especial interest in classification. [R: JAL, Sept 82, p. 247]

Donald J. Lehnus

643.   **Computers and the UDC: A Decade of Progress 1963-1973.** Prepared by Malcolm Rigby. The Hague, International Federation for Documentation, 1974. 108p. 35.00Dflpa. ISBN 92-66-00523-1.

Tracing the merger of advanced technology and the Universal Decimal Classification (UDC) system during the decade 1963-1973, this incisive volume provides brief descriptions of about 60 experimental or operational computer applications in a dozen countries. The use of the computer for arranging, storing, retrieving, or displaying bibliographic data, classification schedules, vocabularies, or indexing in conjunction with UDC, as well as the activities of the FID/CCC-M (Subcommittee on Mechanization of UDC of the Central Classification Commission of the International Federation for

Documentation) are briefly described. Contrary to the opinion of some, this work argues that UDC and the computer are not incompatible and that their union will make substantial contributions in large heterogeneous or multilingual communities. In addition to a list of acronyms and abbreviations and some sample pages of printouts from computer systems, a 159-item bibliography is included. A good quick review of UDC-computer interaction.

Richard P. Palmer

644. Foskett, A. C. **The Universal Decimal Classification: The History, Present Status and Future Prospects of a Large General Classification Scheme.** Hamden, Conn., Linnet Books, 1973. 171p. index. o.p. LC 73-3041. ISBN 0-208-01195-1.

In recent years more has been written about UDC than about almost any other classification schedule. Foskett, author of several books pertaining to the theory and philosophy of classification (e.g., *The Subject Approach to Information*), is eminently qualified to provide a synthetic text on this subject. In this study he discusses the present status of UDC as well as its historical background, analyzing some of the significant work on the use of UDC in computerized information retrieval systems. [R: LJ, 15 Dec 73, p. 3615]

645. International Federation for Documentation. **Ten-Year Supplement to Abridged UDC Editions, 1958-1968.** The Hague, International Federation for Documentation; distr., New York, UNIPUB, 1969. 173p. o.p.

This German-English-French supplement updates the trilingual abridged edition of UDC of 1958 and other abridged UDC editions published during the last ten years. Extensions or revisions, including number and full text cancelled, text modified, and new number and text are appropriately identified. The alphabetical index includes all major new items. This work, designed for use with abridged UDC, provides guidance to additional publications needed by users employing the full tables of the Universal Decimal Classification.

Richard P. Palmer

646. Perreault, Jean. **An Introduction to UDC.** Hamden, Conn., Archon, 1969. 111p. o.p. SBN 208-00878-0.

Jean Perreault authors the fifth title in the series Programmed Texts in Library and Information Science. The treatment of UDC is presented by one of its major advocates in a simple and straightforward manner. The overall

design of series editor C. David Batty is generally followed by Perreault in this programmed text. It should be noted that this text is planned to be used only with the abridged English edition of UDC. [R: BSA-P, Apr 70, p. 258; LJ, 15 Feb 70, p. 643; LRTS, Summer 70, p. 471; RQ, Spring 70, p. 275]   John Phillip Immroth

647. Perreault, Jean M. **Towards a Theory for UDC; Essays Aimed at Structural Understanding and Operational Improvement.** Hamden, Conn., Archon, 1969. 241p. o.p. SBN 208-00874-8.

With the publication of this collection of essays Jean Perreault takes another step toward becoming one of the American classification theorists. This book is not a treatise on the Universal Decimal Classification, as Perreault carefully points out in his introduction. This is a collection of previously written and in some cases previously published essays related to and beginning the development of a basic philosophical theory for UDC. The seventeen essays are arranged into four categories: "General Theoretical Background," "Structure of UDC," "Problems of Display (Notation)," and "UDC and Reclassification." The collection of these essays into a single volume will prove most useful to both student and scholar. This book is a valuable contribution to classification theory in general as well as to UDC in particular. Perhaps the only criticism of Perreault's writing may be best expressed by Geoffrey Lloyd in his preface to this book: "This book will be read by thousands, because he writes on a subject of topical interest in a manner that is lively and sincere—if sometimes overlaid with philosophical phraseology and classification jargon, and because he has often some fresh view to put across or some new battle to fight." This book should be required reading for all students of classification theory and research. [R: BSA-P, Apr 70, p. 258; LJ, 15 Feb 70, p. 643; LQ, Apr 70, p. 273; LRTS, Summer 70, p. 471; RQ, Spring 70, p. 275]   John Phillip Immroth

Book Numbers

648. Comaromi, John P., ed. **Book Numbers: A Historical Study and Practical Guide to Their Use.** Littleton, Colo., Libraries Unlimited, 1981. 145p. index. $25.00. LC 81-13691. ISBN 0-87287-251-3.

Full treatment of the Library of Congress shelflisting methods and Bertha Barden's special schemes, as well as extensive coverage of Cutter numbers, is provided in this work. In addition,

John P. Comaromi traces the historical development of book numbers.

The historical survey chapters include discussions of the principles and purposes of shelflisting, the features of different classification schemes (Dewey Decimal Classification, Library of Congress Classification, and Universal Decimal Classification), accession catalogs and shelflists, and the early book numbers devised by Melvil Dewey, Jacob Schwartz, Charles Cutter, A. P. Massey, and Walter Stanley Biscoe.

The second half of the book is devoted to an explanation of the use of Cutter numbers, Bertha Barden's four special schemes for prolific authors, and the Library of Congress shelflisting methods. Extensive examples accompany the discussion of the application of Cutter and Cutter-Sanborn numbers, including the use of work marks, criticism marks, edition numbers, and copy numbers. This material is supplemented by appended reproductions of the instruction books for the three Cutter author tables. All types of works by and about an author, such as collected works, works in translation, criticism, and concordances, can be grouped logically using the methods outlined in the chapter on Barden's schemes. The chapter on Library of Congress shelflisting practice includes the full text of the latest revision of the LC book number tables, followed by an explanation, illustrated with examples, of their application to personal and corporate authors, editions, translations, and biographical/critical material. Variations employed by selected libraries illustrate use outside LC. [R: JAL, Jan 82, p. 378]

649. Lehnus, Donald J. **Book Numbers: History, Principles, and Application.** Chicago, American Library Association, 1980. 153p. bibliog. index. $8.00pa. LC 80-23100. ISBN 0-8389-0316-9.

Anyone interested in library cataloging and classification will find useful information in this work. Those who accept Library of Congress call numbers will find that part 1, "Historical Background," illuminates the esoteric practices involved in what LC calls "shelflisting." Biscoe time numbers, Olin biography tables, and of course the contributions of Dewey, Cutter, Sanborn, and others are thoroughly researched for the light they shed on current usage. Classifiers applying the Dewey Decimal Classification to extensive general or special collections can take part 2, "Guidelines and Principles for Assigning Book Numbers," as a manual of practice. The chapters on translations and other works related

to previous publications, on anonymous classics and voluminous authors, and on subject, rather than author, arrangement of biographies, autobiographies, and genealogies, are extensively illustrated with examples based on DDC, nineteenth edition (see *ARBA* 80, entry 210) and on the 1969 Swanson-Swift revision of the Cutter-Sanborn three-figure author table. A chronological bibliography from 1876 to 1978, and a comprehensive index complete this authoritative treatment of a little-discussed and poorly understood aspect of library organization. [R: LJ, 1 Nov 81, p. 2095] Jeanne Osborn

Other Classification Schemes

650. Chenhall, Robert G. **Nomenclature for Museum Cataloging: A System for Classifying Man-Made Objects.** Nashville, Tenn., American Association for State and Local History, 1978. 512p. bibliog. index. $25.00. LC 77-20097. ISBN 0-910050-30-9.

Chenhall, who has substantial experience with data banks and systems, has devised a remarkable classification scheme for man-made objects, one that should be of priority interest to museum workers and administrators. The scheme may be expanded, and it provides a splendid universal language for objects, thereby facilitating in-house use as well as use by people in the world of museums. This is a museum tool comparable to the Dewey Decimal Classification system for the discipline of library science; the system does not include natural history, which has already been classified by others. The two most intriguing sections of the book are the description of a logical system for naming things and a hierarchical listing of major artifact categories, classification terms, and the names of objects. The principal purpose of Chenhall's scheme, which was devised at the Strong Museum (Rochester, New York) is "to provide an authority file for the identification of man-made artifacts." Museum registrars and curators will find the concept absorbing as well as useful in bringing order and uniformity to museum catalogs. [R: LJ, 15 Oct 78, p. 2058]

William J. Dane

651. Chismore, W. Dale, and Quentin M. Hill. **A Classification of Educational Subject Matter.** Washington, D.C., National Center for Education Statistics; distr., Washington, D.C., GPO, 1978. 223p. bibliog. index. o.p. S/N 017-080-01876-4.

This classification was prepared for the National Center for Education Statistics (NCES) by Educational Management Services, Inc. (EMS), Minneapolis. "The primary reason for developing the Classification was to provide a single, standardized scheme which will facilitate the recording, reporting, and exchange of data about subject matter" (p. 2) at all levels of instruction. It is not intended to replace either the *Standard Terminology for Curriculum and Instruction in Local and State School Systems* (Handbook VI of the State Educational Records and Report Series, 1971), or *A Taxonomy of Instructional Programs in Higher Education* (HEGIS Taxonomy, 1971). The classification is to be applied only to subject matter and should not be used for instructional programs. The developers anticipate its applications to extend from its basic use in reporting data in a uniform manner, to uses relating to longitudinal studies of students' academic pursuits and for transferring students' subject matter experience records from one educational setting to another.

The subject matter elements are presented in a hierarchical array, beginning with 22 first-order subject matter areas and disaggregated into second, third, and fourth-level orders. The eight-digit coding structure uses two digits for each order in the classification: 03 ("Arts, Visual and Performing" [first level]); 03.03 ("Music" [second order]); 03.03 02 ("Music Studies" [third order]); 03.03 02 03 ("Music Theory" [fourth order]). The instructions in appendix E provide ways to classify aggregate subject matter (a combination of two or more subject matter elements) and multiple subject matter (combinations within subject matter areas and interdisciplinary combinations). Four other appendices (A-D) give codes for difficulty level of subject matter, level of subject matter instruction, organization providing instruction, and type of instructional program. Instructions on using these additional dimensional codes are not given; their application will depend on individual reporting requirements and procedures.

The classification has provision for expansion, but nothing is said about use of this feature or evaluation of the classification once it has been put into practical application. [R: BL, 15 Jan 79, p. 799]　　　Christine Gehrt Wynar

652. ILO Thesaurus: Labour, Employment and Training Terminology. 3rd ed. Washington, D.C., International Labour Office, 1985. 463p. $42.75. ISBN 92-2-003850-1.

The second edition of this book replaced *ILO's Thesaurus of Descriptors Used for Information Processing in the ILO Library*. This third edition contains the English, French, and Spanish terminology used by the ILO to index

and retrieve information about documents recorded in the ILO's International Science Information Service system. The scope (e.g., narrow term, related term, prescribed term) of each item is indicated, and in some cases an explanation of the term is given. Major subject areas have been updated; specific fields such as rural development, vocational rehabilitation, law, and human rights have been expanded; and international collaboration has caused adaptation of the terminology to modern usage. The format of the book has also been changed: descriptors are now arranged by subject in three columns, one for each language. This was designed to permit the use of the thesaurus as a multilingual glossary and to facilitate the international exchange of information. This thesaurus is highly specialized, but for those researchers retrieving information from the ILO's database of abstracts it is a necessity.

Elizabeth Crowell and Annette Pekarek

653. McKeon, Donald Bruce, tr. The Classification System of Jacques-Charles Brunet. Baton Rouge, La., Louisiana State University, 1976. 109p. illus. (Louisiana State University, Graduate School of Library Science Occasional Papers, No. 1). o.p.

Presented here in part 1 are a foreword, in which general editor Francis L. Miksa introduces the series, a preface annotating the table of contents, seven pages about Brunet and his classification system, and a list of Brunet's published writings. Part 2, the body of the work (pp. 15-100), comprises Brunet's *Introduction and Schedules* (5th ed., 1864), followed by McKeon's depiction (in six pie charts) of the allocation of space in that edition (appendix). The place of Brunet in the history of classification is touched on only lightly. The reader is referred to La Montagne's *American Library Classification* (Shoe String Press, 1961).

Probably most valuable is the attention that McKeon's labors draw to Brunet's philosophy of book classification. If re-reading the 1876 report always reminds us that good thinking antedates the invention of the computer, Brunet's explanations of his decisions, and other reflections, testify that our library founding fathers also had excellent models to learn from. ("Books are classified according to their most obvious feature.... We know that this system cannot satisfy everyone"; p. 25.)

How many of those attracted to library history need a translation from French? Brunet's sentences are cumbersome but clear. McKeon has not improved on *successivement* (Brunet, VI: Col. viii) by writing "in sequitur"

(McKeon, p. 21). But in general he has done well and may serve the convenience of investigators who increasingly and regrettably these days are comfortable only in English. In any case, Miksa might consider aiding us all with cheap editions, even if only reprints of the French, of figures like Archard, Parent l'aîné, Peignot, and Petit-Radel. [R: LQ, July 78, p. 372; WLB, Nov 77, p. 200]

Sidney L. Jackson

654. Moulds, Michael. **FIAF Classification Scheme for Literature on Film and Television.** London, Aslib, 1980. 85p. index. £10.50pa.; £8.75 (Aslib members). ISBN 0-85142-131-8.

The introduction states: "This classification was produced out of a need for a comparatively simple scheme which would be suitable for use in newly created archives throughout the world"; therefore the authors have produced this classification scheme based on the abridged English edition of the Universal Decimal Classification, 1961 edition. The system is designed for archival material about film and television with prefixes to designate the two subjects. Two versions of the scheme are given in parallel pages. The full version is on the right-hand page, and the abridged is on the left-hand page facing the full version. Detailed breakdown is presented in the full version. Should the full version be too detailed for the particular book collections in the library, the user can instantly refer from the full version to the abridged on the opposite page.

A brief outline of the auxiliaries and symbols is presented, practical classification hints are included for the nonprofessional librarian, and some 180 examples of the use of the classification are listed after the schedules, along with notes on alternative approaches to some problems. The majority of the examples are for books and periodicals. The detailed alphabetical index is comparable to that of the DDC or UDC, and the cataloger should consult the schedules to locate the most appropriate position for classification of a work about film or television.   Mary Clotfelter

655. **National Library of Medicine Classification: A Scheme for the Shelf Arrangement of Books in the Field of Medicine and Its Related Sciences.** 4th ed. Washington, D.C., National Library of Medicine; distr., Washington, D.C., GPO, 1978. 390p. index. (DHEW Publication, No. (NIH) 78-1535). $9.50. LC 78-56040. S/N 017-052-00193-1.

The *National Library of Medicine Classification* was developed in 1951 and covers the field of medicine and related sciences, using the QS-QZ and W schedules, which were permanently excluded from Library of Congress Classification. The 1978 edition of the *NLM Classification* is a complete revision of the third edition that was published in 1964 and reprinted in 1969. Although few classification numbers have been changed, many have been expanded and new concepts added. This edition includes modernization of headings and integration of all possible form numbers into each schedule, as well as an index with more than 17,000 entries. [R: LJ, 1 Nov 78, p. 2176]

656.   Vernon, K. D. C., and Valerie Lang. **The London Classification of Business Studies: A Classification and Thesaurus for Business Libraries.** 2nd ed. Revised by K. G. B. Bakewell and David A. Cotton. London, Aslib, 1979. 253p. index. price not reported. pa. ISBN 0-85142-124-5.

This second edition is highlighted by several improvements, additions, and changes. With approximately nine years of working experience, visits to user libraries, testing against the literature of business, and input from librarians and others, the editors have issued a more usable and practical scheme. Hierarchical notation has been abandoned to provide better hospitality; alternative locations have been provided to accommodate compounds; schedule arrangement has been restructured in several areas; and the layout has been rearranged in such a manner that the scheme can be used both for classification of library materials and as a thesaurus.

Based on literary warrant, the terms are taken from the literature of business and related disciplines and arranged according to principles of facet analysis, allowing specification of several aspects of a subject and reducing the possibility of cross-classification. The notation is basically simple, primarily using capital letters; however, application of auxiliary tables that consist of integral numbers leads to a mixed notation, depending on the needs of the user. A facet indicator (/) is provided for compound subjects. The introduction is clear both in outlining philosophical considerations that underlie the system and in directions for use. The index is well done. The instructions for use indicate a "preferred order" for classification, although the user is free to employ any citation order desired. This could be a drawback in this day of shared resources and computerized networks.

Business libraries should find this classification scheme/thesaurus very serviceable.

American users may have to adapt some terminology. [R: LR, Autumn 80, p. 201]

Harry S. Otterson, Jr.

SUBJECT HEADINGS

General Works

657.   Christ, John M. **Concepts and Subject Headings: Their Relation in Information Retrieval and Library Science.** Metuchen, N.J., Scarecrow, 1972. 174p. o.p. LC 72-2093. ISBN 0-8108-0491-3.

The purpose of this book was to compare the main index headings from the *International Encyclopedia of the Social Sciences* with the seventh edition of *Library of Congress Subject Headings*. The author came to the conclusion that a wide conceptual gulf exists between the terminology used in the social sciences and that used in library science. [R: C&RL, July 73, p. 318; CLW, Apr 73, p. 556; LJ, 1 Apr 73, p. 1096; RQ, Spring 73, p. 312]

Reference Works

658.   Atkins, Thomas V., ed. **Cross-Reference Index.** 2nd ed. New York, R. R. Bowker, 1985. 368p. $49.95. LC 73-23066.

Cross-Reference Index lists 8,000 subject indexing terms from the following sources: *Library of Congress, Sears List, Readers' Guide to Periodical Literature, New York Times Index, Public Affairs Information Service Bulletin, Business Periodicals Index, Psychological Abstracts,* and *Educational Resources Information Center.* Subject headings are arranged alphabetically, with three types of entries. A *see* reference directs users to a "main term" entry because that subject heading is not used by any of the six sources. A "use" entry means that the subject heading is used by one of the eight sources, and the researcher is directed to one or more of the "main term" entries. The "main term" entry gives "the fullest spectrum of terms in the subject of a researcher's inquiry. Main terms have been chosen for their usefulness, currency, and pertinence to a wide area of research" (p. vii). A main term entry includes scope notes to define the limits of the subject matter, and it then lists the eight sources showing the headings that each one uses.

It is important to note that not all cross-references are indicated. The editor states that "for reasons of space, no attempt was made to duplicate the most obvious s.a. references

among the sources." It should also be pointed out that there is no distinction made between LC's use of "s.a." (*see also*) and "xx" (*see also from*). Since these are distinct concepts, some indication of these differences in the *Cross-Reference Index* would have been helpful. *Cross-Reference Index* will nevertheless be useful for those doing research on subject headings as well as for those researching a particular subject.

659.   **Subject Cross Reference Guide.** Princeton, N.J., National Library Service, 1976. 602p. o.p. LC 76-3371.

First, a quotation: "From the seventy-year plus indexes of *The Readers' Guide* have been selected the most universally used subject headings for *The Subject Cross Reference Guide.* Under the individual subject headings may be found variants or related subjects. *The Subject Cross Reference Guide* is designed to serve a variety of people in a variety of ways. It can be used to determine subject headings for a new verticle [sic] file or for a subject index to audio-visual materials such as slides, photographs, film-strips, films, etc. It can be used as a tool by catalogers to assign or verify subjects that the Library of Congress treats too elaborately or that Sears treats too skimpily or not at all. And finally, it can be consulted by the library user to find his or her way through the labyrinthine paths of subject headings" (introduction). It is further claimed that "the subject headings listed here were selected and edited by professional librarians" (no names provided), and the accompanying press release indicates that this work contains "over 135,000 cross reference terms including geographical regions and political subdivisions in an easy-to-use format."

From these statements we expect that most of the subject headings were "taken" from *Readers' Guide;* but we hope that H. W. Wilson will not claim any credit for this publication. A few examples may properly illustrate the sophistication of this work. Under "Architecture" (listed in boldface) we find some 200 "subject cross-references"; among them are concrete, doors, doorways, plastering, sound, theological schools, tiles, wood. Now a few shorter entries: under "Arizona Indians" we find "Indians of North America"; under "Blond hair," "Hair"; under "Chicago—Art" is "Chicago-monuments" and "Painters, American." Finally, under "Ugliness" are "Aesthetics" and "Esthetics."

We think that all professional librarians who advised this probably unsuspecting publisher should stand up and be counted. Among other things, there is a heading for "American students," with cross-references to college students, high school students, and students. There is no similar entry for "American librarians—compilers of this volume." We suggest inserting such a heading as the 135,001st entry in the next edition. Most librarians, including this reviewer, will be eager to discover who they really are.

Bohdan S. Wynar

Introductory Texts and Manuals

660. Elrod, J. McRee. **Choice of Subject Headings.** 3rd ed. Metuchen, N.J., Scarecrow, 1980. 49p. illus. (Modern Library Practices Series, No. 5). o.p. LC 80-23719. ISBN 0-8108-1340-0.

As with the other programmed teaching units in this series (see *ARBA* 81, entries 227, 229-30, and 285), *Choice of Subject Headings* is intended for nonprofessional library workers. The student must have access to the *Sears List of Subject Headings* and the Library of Congress *Subject Headings*. Elrod suggests that the student should not begin this unit until completing *Construction and Adaptation of the Unit Card* (Scarecrow, 1980) and *Choice of Main and Added Entries* (Scarecrow, 1980). The program consists of an alphabetically arranged series of learning sequences, from authority file and autobiography to tracing and time subdivision. The student need not complete the entire program, but can review individual topics as required. Both the nonprofessional and the library student can benefit from this self-teaching workbook.

Janet H. Littlefield

661. Harris, Jessica Lee. **Subject Analysis: Computer Implications of Rigorous Definition.** Metuchen, N.J., Scarecrow, 1970. 279p. bibliog. index. o.p. LC 70-16406. ISBN 0-8108-0313-5.

This volume is an outgrowth of the author's 1969 Columbia University doctoral dissertation which embodies suggestions for the development of a subject heading list in machine-manipulable form which, if generated, could stimulate investigation into the theory basic to the construction of the headings. A book that is moderate, thorough, and very user-oriented. [R: C&RL, Mar 72, p. 151; LJ, 15 Feb 71, p. 611]

Charles D. Patterson

LC Subject Headings and Related Works

662. Berman, Sanford. **Prejudices and Antipathies: A Tract on the LC Subject Heads Concerning People.** Metuchen, N.J., Scarecrow, 1971. 249p. bibliog. index. o.p. LC 73-149419. ISBN 0-8108-0431-X.

A very personal, passionate, and thought-provoking attack on the Library of Congress list of subject headings and its "s.a." references which, according to the author, are derogatory and prejudicial to ethnic and religious groups as well as in areas of politics, sex and morality, and the recognition of the Women's Liberation Movement. Documented with illustrative examples, there is much that calls for immediate attention. [R: LJ, 15 Feb 72, p. 658]

Charles D. Patterson

663. Chan, Lois Mai. **Library of Congress Subject Headings: Principles and Application.** Littleton, Colo., Libraries Unlimited, 1978. 347p. bibliog. index. (Research Studies in Library Science, No. 15). $30.00. LC 78-9497. ISBN 0-87287-187-8.

Since the 1951 publication of David Haykin's *Subject Headings: A Practical Guide* (repr., Gregg Press, 1972), many changes in the formation, structure, and application of subject headings have taken place. Chan's text re-examines the underlying principles of LC subject headings in light of recent developments and describes current subject cataloging practices of the Library of Congress. Advances in both the theory and techniques of information retrieval through subject analysis, not previously brought together in one text, are presented along with practical suggestions for their implementation. The approach is descriptive rather than prescriptive; no attempt is made to formulate any rules. Rather, the book is an analysis of principles and a description of current practice. Part 1, "Principles, Form and Structure," covers topics such as forms of headings, subdivisions, cross-references, and proper names in subject headings. Part 2, "Application," provides guidelines for cataloging special types of materials and for items in subject areas requiring special treatment (e.g., music, art, and legal materials). Numerous card samples and examples occur throughout the text. Appended are current information on free-floating subdivisions, abbreviations, capitalization, punctuation, and filing; a bibliography; and a subject index. The second edition (1986) of this work is available. [R: LJ, 1 Dec 78, p. 2395]

664. Cochrane, Pauline A., with Monika Kirtland. **An ERIC Information Analysis Product in Two Parts: I. Critical Views of *LCSH*—The Library of Congress Subject Headings; a Bibliographic and Bibliometric Essay; II. An Analysis of Vocabulary Control in the Library of Congress *List of Subject Headings* (LCSH).** Syracuse, N.Y., ERIC, Syracuse University, 1981. 107p. $10.00pa.

Authorities Pauline A. Cochrane and Monika Kirtland present under this unwieldy title a historical perspective of subject heading use and control by the Library of Congress. *Part I, Critical Views of LCSH—The Library of Congress Subject Headings; A Bibliographic and Bibliometric Essay* notes critiques of LCSH published over a 35-year period. Among the 15 bibliographic sections are general reviews and revisions, language, syndetic structure, subdivisions, forms and spareness of headings, currency and prejudices, and ease of use. The authors' mastery of the subject becomes readily apparent in their lucid, concise summaries accompanying each bibliographic division. Of special interest is table 1, which succinctly summarizes 20 LC weaknesses or defects, lists suggested improvements, and names the critic or suggestor and the date of the critique. This tabular review of critical literature covers 1898-1979.

Part II, An Analysis of Vocabulary Control in the Library of Congress List of Subject Headings (LCSH) reprints and researches the introductions to *ALA List of Subject Headings* (second and third editions) and *LCSH* (first through eighth editions). The ninth edition introduction is reprinted but not analyzed. Fourteen variables were studied for changes in policy and practice. Again the results are effectively presented in tabular form. Cochrane and Kirtland conclude that the time has come to redesign LCSH and to state clearly the vocabulary control principles in effect. The topic is timely. Technical services librarians will welcome this *ERIC Information Analysis Product* for its historical overview. All librarians concerned with the design and use of online catalog systems for user efficiency will benefit from its contribution to an understanding of subject access. [R: JAL, Mar 82, p. 52]

Eleanor Ferrall

665. Immroth, John Phillip. **An Analysis of Vocabulary Control in Library of Congress Classification and Subject Headings.** Littleton, Colo., Libraries Unlimited, 1971. 172p. index. (Research Studies in Library Science, No. 3). o.p. LC 70-165065. SBN 87287-017-0.

This study is a descriptive investigation of the relationship between the classification schedules and their indexes, and of the relationship between the subject headings and the classification headings. An experimental model of chain indexing is developed, which may serve as both an index to the classification and a list of subject headings. In addition, 26 rules for chain indexing of Library of Congress Classification are formulated and demonstrated. [R: CLW, May 72, p. 527; LJ, 15 Jan 72, p. 172; LRTS, Summer 72, p. 405]

666. Marshall, Joan K., comp. **On Equal Terms: A Thesaurus for Nonsexist Indexing and Cataloging.** New York, Neal-Schuman; distr., Santa Barbara, Calif., ABC-Clio, 1977. 152p. $25.00. LC 77-8987. ISBN 0-918212-02-2.

This work presents a well-reasoned, constructive step toward the correction of some of the biases in the *Library of Congress Subject Headings* (*LCSH*). Although the use of the term "thesaurus" to describe its contents may be somewhat misleading, Marshall's list does attempt to provide more explicit syndetic relationships by the introduction of UF ("use for") to replace "x," BT ("broader term") for "xx," NT ("narrower term") for *see also*, RT ("related term") for the headings that LC lists under both "xx" and *see also*, and USE for *see*. Each person examining the list will probably find a number of terms and relationships that might have been improved. Why, for example, has "child abuse," a term appearing in popular literature, been divided into "child battering" and "cruelty to children"? Further, given the fact that "cruelty to children" is listed as a broader term than "child battering," a more precise thesaurus would equate "child abuse" with one term or the other, not both. Most such criticisms become minor, however, when the total value of the effort is considered.

Perhaps more important even than the term list is the section "Principles." Although the sixth precept is a general one not concerned with subject headings relating to people and places, the first five are well stated and particularly worthy of study. Marshall's volume is more than a "nonsexist" work, since it deals with racial and ethnic terms as well. One hopes that the significant effort begun here will be expanded and supplemented in the future. Though there is question whether LCSH will adopt all of Marshall's suggestions, her contribution should certainly give subject catalogers some viable alternatives to the perpetuation of prejudicial and stereotypical terminology in libraries. [R:

JAL, Jan 78, p. 364; LJ, 15 Feb 78, p. 443; RQ, Spring 78, p. 265]   Doralyn J. Hickey

667. Sinkankas, George M. **A Study in the Syndetic Structure of the Library of Congress List of Subject Headings.** Pittsburgh, Pa., Graduate School of Library and Information Sciences, University of Pittsburgh, 1972. 116p. illus. (The Pittsburgh Studies in Library and Information Sciences, No. 2). o.p.

A discussion of *see also* referencing of the Library of Congress subject headings, with some numerical analysis of the data gathered. It is concluded that the syndetic structure performs no guiding function at all.

668. U.S. Library of Congress. Subject Cataloging Division. **Library of Congress Subject Headings.** 9th ed. Washington, D.C., Library of Congress, 1980. 2v. $75.00/set. LC 79-22742. ISBN 0-8444-0299-0.

The publication of the ninth edition of *Library of Congress Subject Headings* (*LCSH*) did not elicit the discussions that greeted the publication of the eighth edition in 1975, perhaps because LC has been fairly conscientious in its publication of the microform edition, which virtually constitutes a new edition appearing every three months. Also, *LCSH* seems to have been overshadowed by the appearance of the *Anglo-American Cataloguing Rules*, second edition. Time and monetary constraints forced LC to limit the coverage of the ninth edition to headings existing through December 1978 and to omit the list of subdivisions that had been printed in the introduction to the eighth edition. (The subdivisions, however, are available in a reprint of the eighth edition introduction, sold by the Cataloging Distribution Service.) The Library of Congress, in addition to publishing the microform editions, continues to issue quarterly additions and changes to *LCSH* that are cumulated annually.

The ninth edition of *LCSH* has used computer-assisted procedures to a greater extent than previous editions. The new policy of using indirect local subdivisions (substitution of the instruction *Indirect* for *Direct* in the lists) was accomplished by computer. Also, many free-floating subdivisions (those that catalogers may use as appropriate without being specifically authorized in the list) have been removed from subjects if no cross-references to the subdivisions were involved. Unfortunately, the computer introduced some problems in this process that will be corrected in the next edition. So-called "nonprint" headings (a group of headings that include proper names, sacred books,

legendary and fictitious characters, geographic regions, buildings, works of art, biological names, and chemicals) had been omitted in the eighth edition of *LCSH*. However, it was decided that a standard list of "nonprint" headings would be valuable, so *LCSH*, ninth edition, has included those headings established for works cataloged since 1976. (No attempt is being made to compile a retroactive list.)

In many ways, the ninth edition of *Library of Congress Subject Headings* is an interim edition. Being limited by time and finances, recognized problems were allowed to exist, with the promise to correct the situation in the tenth edition. Many libraries would do better to invest in the microform edition, which is a year behind in its appearance, but still more up-to-date than the hardcopy ninth edition. The tenth edition is in preparation and scheduled for release in 1986. [R: LRTS, July 81, p. 306]

Janet H. Littlefield

669. Williams, James G., Martha L. Manheimer, and Jay E. Daily, eds. **Classified Library of Congress Subject Headings.** 2nd ed. New York, Marcel Dekker, 1982. 2v. (Books in Library and Information Science, Vol. 39). $125.00/set. LC 81-22158. ISBN 0-8247-6959-7 (v. 1); 0-8247-6958-9 (v. 2).

The random access technique of subject retrieval embodied in the traditional dictionary or divided catalog is sharply criticized by many of today's subject analysts. Various alternatives have been suggested, but the Library of Congress is reluctant to abandon or supplement *Library of Congress Subject Headings*. The work at hand undertakes to enhance the usefulness of *LCSH* by two correlative metamorphoses. "Part A: Classified List" puts into alphanumeric order those LC Classification numbers identified in *LCSH*, with some of its subject headings. "Part B: Alphabetic List" (the bulkier portion) starts from subject terms and *see* references, identifying their associated LC numbers. It thus provides not only a classified survey of *LCSH* but a fairly comprehensive classified index to the LC Classification schedules. Those subject headings not accompanied by LC class numbers, however, do not appear. Supplementary materials include a preface, an introduction, explanatory notes, and an essay reproduced from the original (1972) edition on subject indexing idiosyncracies that have surfaced in *LCSH* over its 80-year lifespan. The essay is informative, but its bibliography could well have been updated. Omitted are two further first-edition articles on the relationship of this work to the LC Classification scheme and the LC subject heading file as reproduced on magnetic tape.

This second edition, when compared with the first, is interesting for its omissions as well as for its new material. Changes range from 5 to 15 items per 80-item column, chiefly reflecting modifications of *LCSH9* materials over the *LCSH8* tapes on which the first edition was based. Jeanne Osborn

Sears List

670. Haycock, Ken, and Lynne Isberg Lighthall, comps. **Sears List of Subject Headings: Canadian Companion.** 2nd ed. New York, H. W. Wilson, 1983. 52p. $10.00. LC 83-1343. ISBN 0-8242-0691-6.

The first edition of this work was reviewed in *ARBA* 80 (entry 214). The revised edition has been prepared to tie in with the twelfth edition of *Sears List of Subject Headings* (see *ARBA* 83, entry 191) and to make available updated terminology for Canadian subjects. Revisions in the assignment of classification numbers reflect usage in the *Abridged Dewey Decimal Classification and Relative Index*, eleventh edition. The compilers stress that their list is strictly a companion to *Sears*. It is not a comprehensive list of subject headings or a Canadian substitute for *Sears*.

Although this Canadian companion is designed to be compatible with *Sears*, some anomalies do occur, and these are acknowledged by the compilers. For example, some Canadian headings that appear in *Sears* have been deleted from the Canadian companion, such as "French Canadians" and "French Canadian literature" regarded as part of the inclusive headings "Canadians" and "Canadian literature." The heading "Hockey" is preferred over *Sears*'s "Ice hockey"; "Totem poles" replaces "Totems and totemism."

Both U.S. and Canadian librarians will find this volume a very useful tool in cataloging Canadian materials.

671. **Sears List of Subject Headings.** 12th ed. Barbara M. Westby, ed. New York, H. W. Wilson, 1982. 624p. bibliog. $28.00. LC 82-7102. ISBN 0-8242-0676-2.

This work first appeared in 1923 with the title *List of Subject Headings for Small Libraries, Compiled from Lists Used in Nine Representative and Small Libraries*. Barbara M. Westby has continued to update *Sears List of Subject Headings* with this twelfth edition. (For a review of the eleventh edition, see *ARBA* 78,

entry 230.) Although computerized cataloging and resources networking have become available to larger libraries, smaller libraries continue to have a need for this reference work. The Dewey Decimal Classification numbers, reinstated in the eleventh edition, have elicited criticism in the past, but now as many as four different classification numbers may be shown (e.g., Christmas—Drama 394.2; 791; 808.82; 812.08, etc.) so this should eliminate the possibility of being misled in classification and cataloging. Users are cautioned in the preface to make use of *Abridged Dewey Classification and Relative Index*, eleventh edition, for expansion and reduction of numbers.

Though the LC Classification schedule is generally followed, there have been modifications in spelling and terminology. Some simplification of subject headings has taken place (e.g., "Bacteriology" for "Bacteria and Bacteriology"). An exasperating problem in using *Sears* is the assignment of children's literature. *Sears* follows the adult form used by LC, occasionally creating problems for those classifying and cataloging children's literature. *Sears* suggests, in this case, to consult LC's publication *Subject Headings for Children's Literature* (2nd ed., 1975).

Subject headings have been added and expanded to reflect interest in current events, ideas, and new technology (e.g., subject headings for hostages held in Iran, theories of creation and evolution, and home computers). *Sears* continues to be an outstanding and useful tool for those preparing books for use in small to medium-sized libraries. [R: CLW, May 83, p. 426; Emerg Lib, Nov 82, p. 24; LR, Autumn 83, p. 228] Anna Grace Patterson

Other Types of Subject Headings

672. Aman, Mohammad M., comp. **Arab States Author Headings.** New York, Department of Library Science, Graduate School of Arts and Sciences, St. John's University, 1973. 134p. (Occasional Papers, Library Science Series, 1). o.p. ISBN 0-87075-070-4.

This is a list of corporate entries, based on LC usage and AACR, for government agencies of the Arab states of the Near East and North Africa: Algeria, Egypt, Iraq, Jordan, Kuwait, Lebanon, Libya, Morocco, Saudi Arabia, Sudan, Syria, Tunisia; it excludes Yemen, South Yemen, the other shaykhdoms of Arabia, and the League of Arab States. The list consists of the names of government agencies entered under the name of the country in their *Arabic* form, with *see* references in the alphabetical listing from the English forms (and French in the case of the North African countries), including main agencies and distinctive autonomous bodies not entered under the name of an intermediate unit in the hierarchy. Under each main agency listed are provided the names of bodies that will be entered as subordinate units under that agency. In the alphabetical list are included *see* references in English (and French where appropriate) and Arabic to bodies that are not entered under the name of the country (e.g., some agencies entered under Cairo, etc.) but that users might expect to find so listed. Unfortunately, the English-French forms for the bodies listed as subordinate bodies under intermediate units are *not* provided, nor are there *see* references in the alphabetical list from the names of those subordinated bodies directly under the country. The result is that the user seeking the subordinated (indirectly entered) unit must wade through several possible agencies if he does not know the hierarchical structure, and he must know the Arabic name of that unit. Librarians using the list as a cataloging aid should make these additional *see* references. Despite the incomplete cross-referencing, which renders the list more time-consuming to use, it is a very worthwhile addition to processing sections and reference collections for librarians and readers dealing with Arab government materials: librarians are provided with a consistent list of headings and suggestions for cross-references; readers have a guide that can help them in their searching. [R: Unesco, Sept/Oct 74, p. 278]   David W. Littlefield

673. **Canadian Subject Headings.** 2nd ed. Ottawa, Ont., National Library of Canada, 1985. 477p. index. $22.20pa. ISBN 0-660-11786-X.

The first edition of this work (see *ARBA* 80, entry 207), published in 1978 but with a 1976 cutoff date, is out-of-print. Intervening changes in subject analysis make a significant impact on this second edition, but in no way affect its stated goal of compatibility with the ninth edition of *Library of Congress Subject Headings* (see *ARBA* 82, entry 258) and its supplements. The new Canadian list is designed, as before, to complement that work as needed to express concepts either uniquely Canadian, or of major interest to Canadians. Its approximately 20 percent increase in bulk permits it to expand the number of "representative" headings for use as examples of subject retrieval in their special fields.

Related to this aim is the greater application of pattern headings, free-floating subdivisions, numerous instructions on the intrepretation, use, and construction of headings, and similar LCSH devices. Forty-five pages of introductory material include extended comments on divergencies from LCSH, cross-references, Canadian acts, treaties, geographic names and chronological subdivisions, the relation to the *Répertoire de vedettes-materière* (9th ed., RVM, 1983), and similar aids. An index to specific points discussed, and a glossary of terms employed in *CSH2* complete the English portion, which is followed by a parallel French introduction and an English-French three-page bibliography. Regular supplements are planned. The first will list all *CSH1* headings which have been changed or cancelled in *CSH2*. American as well as Canadian libraries will find this a useful addition to the growing arsenal of subject analysis tools.   Jeanne Osborn

674. **Catholic Subject Headings: A Modification of the 5th ed. of** *Catholic Subject Headings.* Oliver L. Kapsner, ed. Haverford, Pa., Catholic Library Association, 1981. 240p. $25.00pa. ISBN 0-87507-009-4.

This modification of the fifth edition of *Catholic Subject Headings* was prepared under the general editorship of Catherine M. Pilley and Matthew Wilt of the Catholic Library Association. Using *The Catholic Periodical Index*, the ninth edition of the *Library of Congress Subject Headings*, and Catholic reference books such as the *New Catholic Encyclopedia*, it incorporates changes in Catholic terminology since Vatican II. The subject headings are accompanied by copious cross-references and when necessary, by helpful scope notes. This will be useful not only to catalogers of Catholic collections, but for reference, especially because of its scope notes and LC/DC Classification numbers.   Frances Neel Cheney

675. Dunlap, Alice, ed. **Hospital Literature Subject Headings.** 2nd ed. Chicago, American Hospital Association, 1977. 189p. (AHA Catalog No. 1371). $31.25pa. LC 77-519. ISBN 0-87258-202-7.

An excellent compilation of the subject headings developed for the cataloging activities of the American Hospital Association Library, and for use in its publication, *Hospital Literature Index.* Headings cover the economic and social aspects of health care and health care facilities, with emphasis on administration.

In view of the wide acceptance by librarians of this internal thesaurus as a definitive professional tool for the health sciences, it is regrettable that this second edition does not list the acronyms so commonly used in the press, such as PSRO. There are hundreds of cross-references, but more are needed. The general patterning of headings follows hospital department organization. Unless the user knows that "cat scanners" have to do with the radiology department, "consortia" with the purchasing department or library service, etc., difficulties can arise in using the list as a library authority file and in mastering the use of the various forms of the *Hospital Literature Index* based upon it. Familiarity with the extensive list of subheadings appearing under the departmental headings is essential for efficient use. General topics of interest to hospitals, such as insurance and health care planning and delivery, are also included. Harriette M. Cluxton

676. Muench, Eugene V. **Biomedical Subject Headings**. 2nd ed. Hamden, Conn., Shoe String Press, 1979. 774p. $60.00. LC 78-27206. ISBN 0-208-01747-X.

Although an earlier edition of this work appeared in 1971 (see *ARBA* 72, entry 126) standardization of subject headings has long been a controversial topic as far as specialized collections are concerned. However, in this era of machine-readable databases, it might appear as if several problems had been resolved through the production of authorized sources such as MARC. Unfortunately, in the field of medicine, the National Library of Medicine pioneered early in its own cataloging database and the two systems are based on different subject heading lists. As the introduction to Muench's volume notes, "the purpose of this comparative listing of these two controlled vocabularies is to state precisely where they are alike and where they are different and to enable librarians to convert this information from one system to the other to suit the objectives of the local library."

The work, in its second edition (the first was issued in 1971), is arranged in three parts: (1) the main section of the tool, an alphabetical list of MeSH headings followed by LC equivalents or cross-references to other MeSH terms; (2) a 10-page list of "Subheadings," i.e., MeSH terms with LC equivalents, and (3) a list of LC subject headings, with MeSH equivalents when those headings do not fall into the alphabetical sequence. Five caveats are also noted: (1) the major source for this volume was the alphabetic list of the *Index Medicus* MeSH, i.e., the large type headings (certain small type terms which occur as *see under* cross-references have been included but the "user is advised to consult the

introduction to MeSH"); (2) alpha-numeric symbols (A1-B4) refer to the categorized list (trees) materials, which are not found in this volume although there is a list of "Categories and Subcategories"; (3) since MeSH was produced for a specialized field, it usually excludes the word "medical" while the LC list often uses it to provide specificity; (4) certain concepts are obviously handled differently in the two sources; and (5) MeSH makes heavier use of inverted subject headings.

It is hard to question the value of this work for a cataloger who must make appropriate and consistent selections in terminology. Moreover, the editor notes, "with the increasing sophistication of computer software and hardware, technical processing in libraries will become fully automated. The ultimate value of this work lies in a computer interface between these two controlled vocabularies." In addition, of course, the reference librarian will invariably find the tool useful in effectively searching either a computer or manual database. Laurel Grotzinger

CATALOG MAINTENANCE

General Works

677. Bradshaw, Charles I. **Using the Library: The Card Catalog.** Provo, Utah, Brigham Young University Press, 1972. 104p. illus. o.p. LC 71-175298. ISBN 0-8425-0817-1.

Covers filing rules; call numbers; cross-referencing; author, title, and subject cards; tracings; and the LC subject headings. It is designed as a self-study manual to help students in their use of the card catalog. One of the strongest features of this little manual is its clear illustrations.

678. Freedman, Maurice J., and S. Michael Malinconico, eds. **The Nature and Future of the Catalog: Proceedings of the ALA's Information Science and Automation Division's 1975 and 1977 Institutes on the Catalog.** Phoenix, Ariz., Oryx Press, 1979. 317p. index. (A Neal-Schuman Professional Book). $32.50. LC 79-21629. ISBN 0-912700-08-4.

This interesting book presents the papers given at two institutes sponsored by ISAD. The first, "The Catalog: Its Nature and Prospects," was given in New York City in late 1975. The other, "The Catalog in the Age of Technological Change," was given in New York City and then repeated in Los Angeles in 1977. While some of the papers given might appear dated, they offer both the historical perspective and, more important, the views on cataloging and technology of some of the major figures in the profession.

The editors have done an excellent job with this book. The speeches at the conferences ranged from the traditional views of Seymour Lubetzky to those of the technological "seer" Fred Kilgour. The perspective of cataloging needs of research libraries was well presented by Joe Howard and Bill Welch, while the nontraditional approach was argued by Joan Marshall and Sanford Berman. While each talk stands by itself, they complement each other and give a focus to the book. Two themes predominate: inadequacies of LC's subject headings, and conflicts between the integrity of the card catalog and technology. The reproduction of the discussions following each paper makes fascinating reading and adds to the understanding of the problems involved. The second institute has more specific information on AACR2 (since it was closer to implementation) and has two good articles on government documents and nonbook materials. This is a very enjoyable and informative book; the only drawback is the index, which has been artifically expanded by inclusion of every suggested LC subject heading change. [R: C&RL, July 80, pp. 374-76; JAL, Nov 80, p. 293]   William Z. Schenck

679.   Hyman, Richard Joseph. **Shelf Access in Libraries.** Chicago, American Library Association, 1982. 178p. bibliog. index. $12.50pa. LC 81-22764. ISBN 0-8389-0357-6.

Economic constraints and the advent of electronic access to information (e.g., computer catalogs) provoke reevaluations of the topic of access to library collections (i.e., who is permitted to use the collection and how should the collection and the catalog be arranged to facilitate identification and retrieval of its contents?). At the core of these considerations is the question of direct access. In *Shelf Access in Libraries*, Richard Joseph Hyman discusses the conditions under which direct access is justified, methods of implementing direct access in various kinds of libraries in the United States, and the future of direct access. Endemic to a discussion of direct access is an evaluation of various shelf classification schemes, especially in relation to different types of public catalog arrangements. Hyman examines the usefulness of the LCC and DDC shelf schemes. Are they in fact merely "mark and park" operations, or do they satisfy the user's needs for browsing? What is the role of a classified catalog in today's libraries? Is it a better browsing tool and should it be tied to shelf location? These are timeless questions for

librarians in all types of libraries, but a publication focusing on such questions is very timely in the context of the technological possibilities and changes of the 1980s.

Hyman's basic theme is that traditional shelf classification has lost much of its value. He advocates broader classification schemes suited to the clientele of different types of libraries. He divides his discussion into six chapters, beginning with a historical account of shelf access and a chapter on the ambiguities of shelf classification and ending with a look into the future of direct shelf access. In between, there are separate chapters concerning the shelf arrangements in public libraries, school libraries and media centers, and research libraries. The book also includes a reprint of the Detroit Public Library's "Reader Interest Book Arrangement"; a bibliography of relevant books and articles; and an index.

Hyman's intent appears to be to generate interest in a new approach to shelf classification. His lucid writing style and comprehensive coverage of the subject will certainly inspire a resurgence of concern over the issues involved with shelf access in libraries. Librarians in public, school, academic, and library school libraries should add this book to their collections. [R: JAL, Sept 82, p. 242; LJ, 1 Dec 82, p. 2238]   Ann E. Hagedorn

680.   Malinconico, S. Michael, and Paul J. Fasana. **The Future of the Catalog: The Library's Choices.** White Plains, N.Y., Knowledge Industry Publications, 1979. 134p. bibliog. index. $24.50pa. LC 79-16619. ISBN 0-914236-32-6.

The authors of this volume have provided a useful compilation of retrospective, current, and future-oriented information related to types of library catalogs, advantages and disadvantages of various catalog formats, strategy for changing the format, and costs. The first chapter is somewhat repetitive of material found in a variety of works on cataloging history, although it is useful to review the information to set the catalog in perspective. Each chapter is accompanied by a summary and footnotes (placed at the end), although in such a work it is unlikely that the summaries will be needed. The format of the work itself is such that the text can easily be followed; the typeface is relatively large and considerable white space is provided. Considering the price in comparison with the total number of pages, the publishers might have been encouraged to sacrifice design for compactness and reduced cost.

The heart of the volume is the group of chapters describing alternatives to the card catalog, along with appropriate cost comparisons. Although no cost data can be treated as anything except loosely indicative of relationships among various catalog systems, since these data go out of date too quickly, the methodology used offers a valuable example of matters to be considered when a catalog change is in the offing. The generally objective treatment of the alternatives is unfortunately marred at points by the interjection of opinions which occasionally are rather biased. On page 21, for example, the Library of Congress is described as having "avoided computerization as long as possible." Such a generalization is in no way adequate to characterize the problems faced by LC in this field. Assuming that the reader will be able to separate opinion from fact, this work should be a useful addition to any library collection. [R: C&RL, July 80, pp. 374-76; LJ, 1 May 80, p. 1052]   Doralyn J. Hickey

681. Ryans, Cynthia C., ed. **The Card Catalog, Current Issues: Readings and Selected Bibliography.** Metuchen, N.J., Scarecrow, 1981. 334p. index. $17.50. LC 81-720. ISBN 0-8108-1417-X.

The issue of what to do about the card catalog has been renewed with a vengeance in the wake of the publication of the second edition of *Anglo-American Cataloguing Rules.* Because of computer capabilities, however, the ramifications of adopting a new cataloging code have taken on new possibilities. Computer output microform (COM) and online catalogs are no longer the catalogs of the future. Should they be the goal of all libraries?

This anthology of 40 articles attempts to provide a sequential look at the processes of analysis necessary for determining what type of catalog is most advantageous for a particular library. The articles, reprinted from journals in the library field dating from 1975 to 1980, are arranged within four topics: (1) the future of the card catalog, (2) alternatives to the card catalog, (3) preparing for an alternative form of bibliographic access, and (4) case studies. A selected bibliography is included with each section.

This collection of essays is a good one, bringing together many aspects of related issues on alternatives to the card catalog. My only wish was that the authors of the articles and their libraries had been clearly identified. This would have been extremely helpful to me when I tried to decide if a described situation could be relevant to my library. This is a small criticism, and one that should not detract from the tight

organization of the book and the excellence of the articles therein. Recommended for all libraries with a library science collection of any size. The issue of the card catalog is far from being closed. [R: JAL, Jan 82, p. 370; LJ, 1 Mar 72, p. 527; LR, Spring 82, p. 61]
                    Marjorie E. Bloss

682. Tauber, Maurice F., and Hilda Feinberg. **Book Catalogs.** Metuchen, N.J., Scarecrow, 1971. 572p. index. o.p. LC 72-149994. SBN 8108-0372-0.

This collection of articles will complement and supplement an earlier anthology by Tauber and Robert Kingery — *Book Catalogs* (Scarecrow, 1963). Although there are some articles written specially for this volume, most of them are reprints. Material is arranged under 14 broad subject categories (e.g., computerized book catalog, book catalog costs, the National Union Catalog), plus "Applications and Techniques" subdivided by types of library. Such well-known authors as Phyllis Richmond, John Cronin, and Jessica Harris are represented by some of their best writings. This handy volume will serve well library school students and also some catalogers who may not have subscriptions to many professional periodicals. [R: WLB, Nov 71, p. 276]   Bohdan S. Wynar

Filing

683. American Library Association. Resources and Technical Services Division. Filing Committee. **ALA Filing Rules.** Chicago, American Library Association, 1980. 50p. illus. index. $5.00pa. LC 80-22186. ISBN 0-8389-3255-X.

In 1981, both the American Library Association and the Library of Congress issued new filing rules for library catalogs in response to the demands of AACR2. The ALA rules are divided into two sections, general rules and special rules, with the special rules generally extensions of, rather than exceptions to, the general rules. The ALA rules are more straightforward than the LC rules, embracing, with very few exceptions, the "file-as-is" principle — character strings (words) are to be filed "in exactly the form and order in which they appear." Unlike the LC rules, ALA uses a nonhierarchical structure; in other words, the type of heading (person, place, thing, or title) is not a consideration in filing. Filing is word-by-word, ignoring punctuation as a filing consideration. Optional rules have been avoided. Special rules are provided for abbreviations; initial articles; initials, initialisms, and acronyms; names and prefixes; non-Roman alphabets; numerals; relators (designators of function) used in headings; and terms of honor and address. Two appendices cover modified letters and special characters, and articles in the nominative case in various foreign languages. Also provided are a glossary and an index. Throughout the rules are figures and tables that amplify and explain specific situations.

ALA Filing Rules is neatly typeset (the LC rules are reproduced from typewritten copy), and stresses arrangement that will be logical not only to librarians but also to filing clerks who must execute the rules. The rules are designed to be equally applicable to card catalogs and to other bibliographic displays — book, microform, and online catalogs. The introduction explains "aids in using bibliographic files" — categorical references, specific filing references, and arrangement guides — and suggests uses for these aids in the catalog. Both the ALA and LC filing rules, while differing in certain areas, are intended to create catalogs using language and entries most likely to be sought by users, rather than files accessible mainly to librarians. [R: C&RL, July 81, pp. 389-91]

Janet H. Littlefield

684. Carothers, Diane Foxhill. **Self-Instruction Manual for Filing Catalog Cards.** Chicago, American Library Association, 1981. 120p. illus. $9.00pa. LC 81-3606. ISBN 0-8389-0326-6.

This loosely programmed text, designed to accompany the *ALA Filing Rules* (American Library Association, 1980), covers the 10 basic precepts contained therein, plus many of their subsections. Some regrouping and rewording occurs, particularly for subfiling situations under rule 2 — "Access Points." The examples for rule 4 — "Initial Articles," illustrate specific usages from major European languages which are relegated to an appendix in the original work. There is also a special page on sequencing U.S./United States entries. The glossary omits a few terms found in the *Rules* glossary, but adds other pertinent ones gleaned from the *AACR2* glossary (see *ARBA* 80, entry 204). Although the *Rules* stress applicability to all forms of bibliographic display, the examples in this text appear in exclusively traditional card format, ranged from the bottom toward the top of each page. They come from the catalog of the University of Illinois at Urbana-Champaign. Translation to other formats and catalogs should not pose grave difficulties, however. Many libraries may find the emphasis on pictorial, over expository, communication helpful for training purposes. There is no index, but one is available in the *Rules*. Reference would be easier if running

titles in the *Manual* named the particular rule subsections under consideration, especially for the "general" rules 1-2, and for rule 8 — "Numerals." But such quibbles are minor. This exercise book will no doubt prove a useful supplement to the format code. [R: LJ, 15 Oct 81, p. 2001]

Jeanne Osborn

685. Elrod, J. McRee. **Filing in the Public Catalog and Shelf List.** 3rd ed. Metuchen, N.J., Scarecrow, 1980. 81p., plus 164 practice filing cards. illus. (Modern Library Practices Series, No. 2). o.p. LC 80-23723. ISBN 0-8108-1337-8.

Number 2 of the Modern Library Practices series (see *ARBA* 81, entries 227-30), this programmed training unit should enable inexperienced nonprofessional technical services workers to teach themselves to file catalog cards in the public catalog and the shelf list. This unit comprises a workbook and a set of 164 practice filing cards. The worker completes the exercises in the workbook, thus learning the rules of filing, and practices by arranging the cards in the correct sequence. The program may take a full day or more to complete, but can be completed in a few hours by an experienced worker using it for review. The unit is designed to require a minimum of professional supervision. The third edition incorporates suggestions made by users of previous editions and corrects errors found in the second edition. The filing unit can be equally useful for library students. The workbook, however, is bound in a flimsy paper cover.

Janet H. Littlefield

686. **Filing Rules for Author and Title Catalogs.** 1st ed. Kalamazoo, Mich., Western Michigan University Libraries, 1979. 135p. bibliog. index. o.p.

The complexity of the card catalog has become intimidating to users and library staff alike, even though librarians have adopted a variety of measures to make it easier to use. *Filing Rules for Author and Title Catalogs*, compiled by the Filing Rules Committee of Western Michigan University Libraries (WMUL), is a manual based on their experiences and needs. These experiences began in 1967 when the dictionary catalog of WMU's main library was divided into three sections: author, title, and subject. Series added entries were removed from the catalogs in 1968, and no new ones were added. The filing rules presented here can be applied to series as well as to author and title.

The filers continued to use the *ALA Rules for Filing Catalog Cards*, first the 1942 and then the 1968 edition. They found them somewhat irrelevant for a divided catalog. In addition, the nonprofessional staff found them difficult to use. After some attempts to modify the *ALA Rules* it was decided to try to draft new ones. The aim was to obtain a straightforward, filed-as-printed arrangement in the author and title catalogs. The result is this manual.

The manual offers 20 rules for the author and title sections (subject is not included), along with extensive examples and some procedural statements. These rules cover such topics (after the basic rule) as: alpha characters, punctuation, signs (symbols), numerals, articles, abbreviated forms and variant forms, uniform titles, and order of entries in the author and title catalog. Following the rules are a glossary of terms and a bibliography. The rules were developed for manual filing but were designed with computer filing in mind (e.g., all numbers are to be filed in numerical order at the beginning of the file). They were tested and are in use at a library with more than a million volumes.

Filing Rules for Author and Title Catalogs contains rules that are well thought out and reassuring to use due to the many examples and detailed explanations. The fact that these rules are successfully in use is a tribute to their authors. Marjorie E. Bloss

687. Hoffman, Herbert H. **What Happens in Library Filing?** Hamden, Conn., Linnet Books, 1976. 176p. illus. index. $15.00. LC 75-28187. ISBN 0-208-01557-4.

This examination of the second edition of the *ALA Rules for Filing Catalog Cards* is "an attempt to trace and record the principles behind the ALA Rules, and to provide a step-by-step guideline to the decisions a competent filer must make, and in what order" (p. 7).

Part 1 investigates principles of the rules and points out inconsistency and lack of logic. It ends with a chapter called "Prospects for Automation," whose premise is neatly stated on page 109: "If we seriously want to consider automation, we must begin with a thorough analysis of our entire system of cataloging and filing rules. We must lay our rules out in a well-defined, unambiguous, logical flow pattern that leads to a catalog arrangement that fulfills the objectives set for it."

Part 2, a "first aid guide" for filing, offers sample problems and a "permutation section" which outlines all possible combinations of 21 card patterns paired with themselves and with each other. Instructions and the applicable ALA rule number are given for each "pattern pair." A glossary and an index complete the book.

Hoffman's intentions are good, but his attempts to remedy discrepancies in the ALA rules do not always result in greater clarity. [R: LJ, 1 June 76, p. 1268]

Bohdan S. Wynar

688. **Library of Congress Filing Rules.** Prepared by John C. Rather and Susan C. Biebel. Washington, D.C., Cataloging Distribution Service, Library of Congress, 1980. 111p. index. $5.00pa.

The 1980 edition of the *Library of Congress Filing Rules* supersedes the 1956 edition of *Filing Rules for the Dictionary Catalog of the Library of Congress* and revises the 1971 provisional version, *Filing Arrangement in the Library of Congress*. The Library of Congress adopted these rules for use in its Add-on-Catalog beginning in 1981. AACR2 has been accommodated in the new rules. The LC filing rules still favor hierarchical filing (ALA does not), but LC leans more towards the "file-as-is" principle than it did in the earlier rules. In other words, "Mc" is filed *as is*, rather than *as if* it were "Mac." "Mac" is filed before "Mc." The LC rules still maintain the "person, place, thing, title" hierarchical arrangement that proves useful in large card catalogs, and this is the main distinction between the LC and ALA rules. The LC filing rules have been simplified to be more user-oriented, but contain more rules for specific situations than do the ALA rules. [R: C&RL, July 81, pp. 389-91; LJ, 15 Mar 81, p. 627] Janet H. Littlefield

689. Morse, Grant W. **Filing Rules: A Three-Way Divided Catalog.** Hamden, Conn., Linnet Books, 1971. 121p. illus. index. o.p. LC 70-146702. SBN 208-01150-1.

This set of rules is presented to meet the needs of a three-way divided card catalog (author, title, subject). In general the rules supplement *ALA Rules for Filing Catalog Cards*, but numerous adaptations are made. Word-by-word arrangement is used, all punctuation is ignored, initials and acronyms are filed in their alphabetical places. Eight rules are given and examples for filing by author, by title, and by subject are shown for subsections of each rule. The first appendix is a 49-page three-way alphabetical list to use as a guide. Appendix 2 explains how to change over to a three-way catalog, and the last appendix is a self-test. There is a short index. [R: CLW, Apr 72, p. 474; LJ, 1 Mar 72, p. 848]

ONLINE CATALOGING AND AUTOMATION

General Works

690.   Fayen, Emily Gallup. **The Online Catalog: Improving Public Access to Library Materials.** White Plains, N.Y., Knowledge Industry Publications, 1983. 148p. bibliog. index. (Professional Librarian Series). $34.50; $27.50pa. LC 83-12009. ISBN 0-86729-054-4; 0-86729-053-6pa.

Inevitably, this must be compared with two other books on online catalogs: Charles Hildreth's *Online Public Access: User Interface* (OCLC, 1982) and Joseph Matthews's *Public Access to Online Catalogs: A Planning Guide for Managers* (see *ARBA* 84, entry 244). Fayen attempts to cover installation of such a system, costs, contracts, funding, evaluation of the system, and integration with other library functions. Matthews has done a better job on all counts except evaluation, and Hildreth preempted that area with his excellent treatise on standards, definitions, and considerations that will affect the value of such systems. The five appendices in Fayen's book repeat what is found elsewhere—if not in Hildreth's or Matthews's books, then in the reports that cover the Council on Library Resources Online Catalogs User and Non-user Surveys. The directory of vendors and four short case studies are not very informative, and they are out-of-date already. All in all, the earlier publications are still the best buys, and this title does not add sufficient details or exposition to warrant its expense. [R: LJ, 15 Oct 83, p. 1936]   Pauline Atherton Cochrane

691.   **Freezing Card Catalogs: A Program Sponsored by the Association of Research Libraries, May 5, 1978, Nashville, Tennessee.** Washington, D.C., Association of Research Libraries, 1979. 83p. o.p.

H. William Axford argues in this little book that "successfully leading the campus community toward effective utilization of a fully automated cataloging data base, transcending the holdings of an individual campus, will require a commitment as intense as the one which led us to build the monumental research collections that are the great legacy of the three decades following World War II" (p. 74). All four of the papers included in the volume preach a similar gospel. Three were presented at the ninety-second ARL membership meeting "to bring the directors of large research libraries up to date on the nationwide movement toward computer-based alternatives to our present card catalogs" (preface). They update similar presentations in

The Future of Card Catalogs from the eighty-fifth ARL meeting in Chicago (see *ARBA* 76, entry 189).

Richard Dougherty's paper, while not a part of the 1978 program, reports an informal survey of ARL library directors. The 60 replies show some apprehension over adopting AACR2 ("the new rules may not be better, only different"—p. 10), and over the impact of LC's decision to close its own card catalog. Yet most agree that the days of the traditional catalog are numbered. Joseph Rosenthal describes the plan as of December 1977 for freezing the card catalogs of the general library at the University of California in Berkeley. Robert Blackburn tells of two different closings (in 1959 and again in 1975) at the University of Toronto. Axford exhorts ARL directors to meet the inevitable as an opportunity fraught with problems and dangers, but nonetheless promising. [R: LQ, Oct 80, p. 507]   Jeanne Osborn

692.   **The Future of Card Catalogs: Report of a Program Sponsored by the Association of Research Libraries, January 18, 1975.** Washington, D.C., Association of Research Libraries, 1975. 67p. illus. $3.00pa.

This publication consists of the transcript of a special program on the future of the card catalog given as a part of the January 1975 Membership Meeting of the Association of Research Libraries. Topics discussed include the rapid growth of catalogs and the spiralling costs of catalog maintenance, the Anglo-American Cataloging Rules, LC's policy of superimposition, and alternative forms of bibliographic records such as machine-readable files and microforms. Included are short papers by William J. Welsh and John C. Rather of the Library of Congress, as well as papers given from the point of view of large academic research libraries, by Judith Corin and Joseph A. Rosenthal. A reactor and discussion panel consisting of Paul Fasana, Hugh Atkinson, Rutherford D. Rogers, and Basil Stuart-Stubbs provides many brief, pithy comments. Three additional papers, by Richard S. Angell, John C. Rather, and Joseph Rosenthal, are included in the appendices.

Although the papers and discussion in this proceeding are out-of-date as a result of LC's decision to close its card catalog, this publication still deserves careful reading by library administrators, catalogers, and library school students. The majority of the text has the freshness of the oral approach, which is often so lacking in more formal papers in library science. Further, the discerning comments in the discussion provide much food for thought. Atkinson particularly makes some excellent and meaningful remarks. Rather's papers are also most helpful to the reader, and particularly to the student of the card catalog. [R: LRTS, Fall 76, p. 389]

John Phillip Immroth

693. Gapen, D. Kaye, and Bonnie Juergens, eds. **Closing the Catalog: Proceedings of the 1978 and 1979 Library and Information Technology Association Institutes.** Phoenix, Ariz., Oryx Press, 1980. 194p. index. $32.50. LC 80-23976. ISBN 0-912700-56-4.

Closing the Catalog is neither a directive to LC on whether or not to close, nor a "how to" manual on closing for other institutions; rather it is a philosophical and practical overview of reasons and probable consequences of both replacing retrospective card systems with prospective automated systems and adopting AACR2 or modifications thereof. Among the impact issues addressed by librarians (among them Pauline Atherton, Paul Fasana, Fred Kilgour, Seymour Lubetzky) are: staffing and services; user capabilities and needs; cost; networking (OCLC); MARC dislocations; mechanical and professional unreadiness; etc. Histories of closings are presented by Peter Paulson, Allen Hogden, Valentina DeBruin, and Susan Miller. Lucia Rather represents LC. And, although orientation is mainly toward administrators of large academic institutions which are definitely going to close their catalogs, the issue of the small library is addressed by Sanford Berman and Maurice Freedman. Bibliographies accompany many of the papers, and Berman has compiled a most thorough index to the volume.

Purchase should in no way be limited to libraries with closed or closing catalogs. (Obviously, implementers of the change, from highest to lowest levels, need to understand the whys and wherefores.) This volume should be part of the current professional literature in all libraries. Whether or not their institutions are moving with LC 100 percent, partially, or not at all, librarians need to be able to participate in the terminology and, at least, the introductory theory of what is probably the most enormous innovation in librarianship in this century. [R: C&RL, May 81, p. 262]　　Linda S. Batty

694. Gore, Daniel, Joseph Kimbrough, and Peter Spyers-Duran, eds. **Requiem for the Card Catalog: Management Issues in Automated Cataloging.** Westport, Conn., Greenwood Press, 1979. 200p. index. (New Directions in

Librarianship, No. 2). $29.95. LC 78-7129. ISBN 0-313-20608-2. ISSN 0147-1090.

Ten papers from a 1977 conference on management issues in automated cataloging, sponsored by the Associated Colleges of the Middle West, present a review of the rationale for library catalogs and analyze the conversion experiences undergone by a number of different types of libraries. The volume is well organized and covers a variety of issues without redundance. Regrettably, the accompanying figures and graphs lack adequate explanation.

Brett Butler distinguishes between collection and resource databases, making clear the need to understand their separate functions when planning network participation. Michael Malinconico indicates how online and COM catalogs can eliminate the rigidity which 3x5-inch cards have imposed on library practice. Given the flexibility of automation, Sanford Berman renews his arguments for locally relevant alternative files. Peter Spyers-Duran and William Axford discuss some of the planning and personnel issues that management confronts as a result of the reorganization of catalog departments for automation.

Henriette Avram states national needs, while Glynn Evans analyzes the network-library-utility problems in relation to OCLC's accomplishments. Neither of them confronts the problems of access between networks or how to meet data needs of local libraries.

Mary Fischer's account of COM catalog development at Los Angeles County Public Library and Robert Blackburn's summary of the University of Toronto's experience are detailed practical case studies. John Kountz's paper contains a helpful checklist of decisions to make before converting to an online shelf list. [R: C&RL, Sept 79, pp. 474-75; LJ, Aug 79, p. 1543]　　Valmai Fenster

695. Matthews, Joseph R. **Public Access to Online Catalogs: A Planning Guide for Managers.** Weston, Conn., Online, 1982. 345p. illus. bibliog. index. $28.50pa. LC 82-18777. ISBN 0-910965-00-5.

This is a clearly written, well-designed, and excellently illustrated basic primer on online public access catalogs. Coverage includes the obligatory chapter on the objective of the catalog and its alternative forms, choices for online catalog design, components of online catalogs, online catalog operations, the effects of online catalogs, planning and implementation, and the future of online public access catalogs. Over two-thirds of the text consists of profiles of 34 systems that are, or claim to be, online public access catalogs; profiles consist of a checklist of system features and samples of screen formats and system messages. A bibliography and glossary are also included.

This volume's principal use is as an introduction to online catalogs for library managers. The profile or checklist approach to comparing systems should be used with caution as the information will be quickly dated, and issues of design and performance quality are ignored. For its intended use, however, this is a temporarily valuable book. [R: LJ, 15 Dec 83, p. 2314; RQ, Summer 83, pp. 436-37]   Joe A. Hewitt

696. Matthews, Joseph R., Gary S. Lawrence, and Douglas K. Ferguson, eds. **Using Online Catalogs: A Nationwide Survey.** New York, Neal-Schuman, 1983. 255p. illus. index. $27.95. LC 83-8061. ISBN 0-918212-76-6.

This report on a survey of users and non-users of 16 online catalogs in 29 libraries, conducted in April-May 1982, describes how users responded to this bibliographic tool and provides data to enable designers to improve the human-computer interaction. The text is supported by a subject index, 33 tables, 16 figures, and 5 appendices, including the two questionnaires (one for users, one for nonusers) administered in all the libraries, respondent characteristics, and statistical analyses of responses by type of library.

Each participating library and its online catalog receive a brief review, illustrated with sample screens. Libraries are grouped into Association of Research Libraries members, academic libraries, community college libraries, public libraries, and state and federal libraries so that results can be compared by type of library. The summary report shows patrons' very positive attitude toward the online catalog and high level of satisfaction (80 percent are satisfied with results, over 90 percent like it), but closer examinations of the results are less exuberant and more questioning.

The final chapter interprets the survey findings to succinctly present their implications for library managers, reference staffs, system designers, and the library profession. This convenient summary reminds librarians of the more mundane factors, such as number and location of terminals, and suggests that the online catalog can enhance service; for example, having a terminal at the information desk can expedite teaching users while assisting them. Implications for systems designers and the library profession as a whole center on the need to improve and simplify subject searching. [R: JAL, Nov 83, p. 305; WLB, Oct 83, p. 143]

Joyce Duncan Falk

697. McCarn, David B., comp. and ed. **Online Catalogs: Requirements, Characteristics and Costs.** Washington, D.C., Council on Library Resources, 1983. 132p. bibliog. $10.00pa. LC 83-5246.

This is a report of a two-day meeting held in December 1982, sponsored by the Council on Library Resources and including 27 library administrators and library computer system experts brought together to discuss online catalogs. Along with the report are appendices that summarize a survey of online catalogs in 29 libraries sponsored by the council during 1982. There are also specific survey results from OCLC, the University of California, and the Library of Congress. The conference report identifies important issues on which a consensus was reached and areas in which the council, library administrators, and library system designers can contribute to the rational development of online catalogs. Participants were asked to address six issues in connection with costs, the ideal online catalog system, standards or guidelines for online catalogs, needed research, and strategies for implementing an online catalog in research libraries.

Among the areas of agreement are that existing cost studies are inadequate and that online catalogs should enhance the research process and improve access to information nationally and internationally. Very specific concluding comments range from designating the need for a good cost model for the development and installation of online catalog systems to the concept that libraries must move and keep up with the new technology for information delivery, or else become intellectual backwaters. The conferees recommended that library administrators attempt to develop costs for existing operations and recognize that online catalogs will require more terminals than they anticipate, resulting in higher usage of other library services. Library system designers are given several requirements (e.g., that online access should provide thesaurus and keyword searching and that inexperienced users should be provided with online tutorials). The Council on Library Resources is urged to initiate an effort to standardize the display of bibliographic information and also to undertake and publish a survey of available online cataloging systems currently in use by several organizations. [R: JAL, Sept 83, pp. 242-43]   Ann Allan

698. Ohio College Library Center. **On-Line Cataloging.** Columbus, Ohio, Office of Educational Services, The Ohio State University Libraries, 1973. 226p. illus. index. $2.00. LC 73-620122. ISBN 0-88215-035-9.

The guide is directed especially to "libraries employing the on-line cataloging system of the Ohio College Library Center," providing instruction to staff on the "steps required in the data collection process to prepare bibliographic data for conversion into machine readable form." The guide also describes the cathode ray tube terminal, gives instructions for its operation, and explains the tagging and coding of bibliographic data to conform with the Library of Congress MARC II Communications Format.

Although the guide is a very specialized publication that is limited to a specific audience, it makes excellent reading and is recommended for all librarians. Its easy style defines much of the computer jargon and explains how the computer can be exploited by libraries for purposes of bibliographical control.   Nabil Hamdy

699. Palmer, Richard P., with an introduction by Kenneth R. Shaffer. **Computerizing the Card Catalog in the University Library: A Survey of User Requirements.** Littleton, Colo., Libraries Unlimited, 1972. 141p. index. (Research Studies in Library Science, No. 6). o.p. LC 70-182405. ISBN 0-87287-041-3.

Although the number of computer installations in the United States has increased significantly in the past decade, this remarkable growth has not been reflected in widespread use of computer catalogs to replace the traditional library card catalog. Palmer is not attempting in this study to provide all the answers to this vital problem. Nevertheless, his study, based on a rewritten doctoral dissertation (University of Michigan), does provide an additional dimension to already numerous catalog use studies by explaining the feasibility of reproducing the card catalog on computer tape. Findings based on a survey of 5,067 users of University of Michigan public catalog are incorporated in this study. The *Library Journal* review indicated that "this study has succeeded in raising several important questions that cry out for further investigation. Because of the extensive use made by undergraduates of the catalog under study when a large undergraduate library was immediately adjacent, the question of the adequacy of undergraduate libraries was raised. The study also indicates a need for more in-depth research on the items of data that are included on catalog cards. In addition, the need was revealed for a

greater understanding of the subtleties of catalog use that should complement the simple author, title, subject approach.

Perhaps one of the more significant findings of this study is that the percentage of users seeking a specific work rather than information on a subject increases as the education level of the patron rises.... It should be of great importance to those concerned with development of computer catalogs." [R: LJ, 1 Oct 72, p. 3126]

700. Wassom, Earl E., Patricia W. Custead, and Simon P. J. Chen. **On-Line Cataloging and Circulation at Western Kentucky University: An Approach to Automated Instructional Resources Management.** Bowling Green, Ky., Division of Library Services, Western Kentucky University, 1973. 110p. illus. (Academic Services Library Bulletin 5). o.p.

Reclassification and computer application in this library operation at Western Kentucky University are the main theme of this publication. Also discussed is the online circulation system of Western Kentucky University, which was planned and implemented as a by-product of the reclassification project.

The publication contains a wealth of illustrations and flowcharts. However, some presentation of time and cost involved in the project would have added strength to the discussion. Generally, the study makes interesting reading for librarians wishing to reclassify from Dewey to LC Classification, and especially for those wanting to use the computer in this operation.

Nabil Hamdy

MARC

701. **The Exchange of Bibliographic Data and the MARC Format: Proceedings of the International Seminar on the MARC Format and the Exchange of Bibliographic Data in Machine Readable Form, Sponsored by the Volkswagen Foundation, Berlin, 1971.** Münich-Pullach and West Berlin, Verlag Dokumentation; distr., New York, R. R. Bowker, 1972. 196p. illus. bibliog. o.p. ISBN 3-7940-4006-6.

Based upon the 16 papers, and subsequent discussions, presented at the first formal international meeting of those concerned with exchange of bibliographic data in machine-readable form held in Berlin in June 1971. Ten papers are in English, six in German with English summaries. Specific problems are raised with possible, positive solutions given. [R: LJ, 1 Oct 72, p. 3127]   Charles D. Patterson

702.   U.S. Library of Congress. Information Systems Office. **Format Recognition Process for MARC Records: A Logical Design.** Chicago, American Library Association, Information Science and Automation Division, 1970. 150p. o.p. LC 70-139250. ISBN 0-8389-3122-7. (Available from Books on Demand, $78.50, ISBN 0-317-26828-7.

A technical manual issued by LC (under the ALA imprint) describing its process for automatic "format recognition" and intended for use by those working directly with MARC tapes and those interested in bibliographic data management. Appendices, flow charts, tables, and statistics enhance the volume. [R: LJ, 15 Oct 71, p. 3301; RQ, Fall 71, p. 79]

Charles D. Patterson

703.   U.S. Library of Congress. MARC Development Office. **Composite MARC Format: A Tabular Listing of Content Designators Used in the MARC Formats.** Washington, D.C., GPO, 1976. 179p. o.p. LC 76-49061. ISBN 0-8444-0218-4. S/N 030-000-00089-7.

"Intended to be used for comparative purposes and in the design of generalized computer programs for systems using the MARC formats for bibliographic records, this publication contains a listing in tabular form of the content designators used in various MARC formats." Every content designator now in use in the MARC program, and those defined for future use, are listed in sequence, and compared side-by-side for the following types of materials: books, films, manuscripts, maps, music, serials, and in-process materials. Designers of computerized bibliographic systems can use these tables to achieve a greater degree of conformity to MARC records. [R: BL, 15 Apr 77, p. 1247]

OCLC

704.   Allison, Anne Marie, and Ann Allan. **OCLC: A National Library Network.** Short Hills, N.J., Ridley Enslow Publishers, 1979. 248p. $18.95pa. LC 78-11948. ISBN 0-89490-019-6.

Unlike Manheimer's *OCLC: An Introduction to Searching and Input* (see *ARBA* 81, entry 258), which is a practical manual, *OCLC: A National Library Network* is a historical study of OCLC and its impact. Eight essays plus an extensive annotated bibliography comprise the book. The brief introduction outlines the origins of OCLC and lists its services. Although the introduction appears to assume no knowledge of the workings of the OCLC

system, the other seven essays are more suited to the practitioner. The essays discuss the following topics: "On-line Cataloging and the Library School Curriculum," "OCLC: The View from Regional Networks," "Staff Training and Development within the Network," "OCLC and Management in a Medium-sized University Library," "Cataloging Workflow and Productivity," "Acceptance of Cataloging Contributed by OCLC Members," and "Serials Control and OCLC."

The bibliography may prove to be the most useful portion of the book. It comprises the final third of the text, and its 244 annotated citations make it an excellent historical study. Included are citations to unpublished reports. The text, unfortunately, is reproduced from typewritten copy, and the book is paperbound. However, the essays bring together information previously scattered in journals, annual reports, and newsletters, and the bibliography is excellent. [R: C&RL, Jan 80, pp. 78-80]

Janet H. Littlefield

705.   Cope, Gabriele E. **Coping with the OCLC Cataloging Subsystem.** 2nd ed. Lincoln, Nebr., Ego Books, 1979. 81p. illus. index. o.p. LC 78-108748. ISBN 0-933540-01-9.

This is a short, practical text aimed at providing a basic competency in the operation of the OCLC online cataloging subsystem. It is not intended to be a self-instructional manual but must be used in conjunction with classroom instruction or supervised on-the-job training. The text assembles in convenient form the main points contained in the OCLC manual *Online Cataloging* and the many technical bulletins that update this manual. There is liberal use of well-chosen examples. The organization of the text appears to be more useful to the library school setting than to on-the-job training. *Coping with the OCLC Cataloging Subsystem* cannot be relied upon for the finer points of OCLC cataloging, but as a basic beginning text it is a competent and useful manual.

A third edition has been published under the title *Coping with the OCLC Subsystems* (1984).

706.   Manheimer, Martha L. **OCLC: An Introduction to Searching and Input.** rev. ed. New York, Neal-Schuman, 1981. 72p. $14.95; $9.00 (5 or more copies). LC 81-81986. ISBN 0-918212-48-0.

For self- or library school instruction, the manual-textbook is part explanation and part exercises for learning the capabilities and operation of an OCLC terminal for cataloging and bibliographic searching. This edition "has been revised to conform to the second edition of the *Anglo-American Cataloguing Rules*, to adjust to the changes in the OCLC system that affect searching, and to provide an introduction to new features," according to the author in her introduction.

The level assumes some knowledge of the vocabulary and procedures of library bibliography. The work probably could not be used as a training manual for beginning off-the-street clerical assistants without an explicator standing by. It could, however, function as a reference and review tool for those already practiced in using the system.

The manual opens with general material explaining OCLC and the terminal keyboard and listing supplementary reference texts. It continues with searching and interpretation of records; entering data for cataloging purposes; and using the main-entry authorization file, the records for serials and audiovisual materials, and the name-address directory. The work concludes with "Answers to Selected Exercises."

A flaw is the use of computer jargon (*input* and *format* used as verbs substituting for *enter* and *compose*) which leads to unacceptable extensions; for example, "I inputted it," and also "I keyboarded it." OCLC is used also as a reference tool by those who work with the public. Teaching the use of nonstandard forms ultimately results in an irritant to the lay library user because the terms are not generally understood and because they take liberties with the English language. Otherwise, the presentation is clear and informative. [R: CLW, May 82, p. 449; CLW, Apr 82, p. 404; IRLA, Nov 81, p. 2]
Kathleen McCullough

707. Maruskin, Albert F. **OCLC: Its Governance, Function, Financing, and Technology.** New York, Marcel Dekker, 1980. 145p. index. (Books in Library and Information Science, Vol. 32). $27.50. LC 80-23417. ISBN 0-8247-1179-3.

The author states that he attempted to organize "a mixture of material," "fragmented" and "abundant" (p. vi), including OCLC primary sources, reports, studies, papers, articles; and the Bible: "They that weave networks shall be confounded" (p. 122). The first three chapters are a straightforward historical account. Details of organization, incorporation, management, fees, and other administrative matters; the succession of computers; and technical problems (e.g., terminal response time) are examined.

It is in the last chapter, "OCLC Critique," that the author presents his personal insight.

Present and future problems plus the considerable accomplishments of OCLC are analyzed. Attempts by member networks beyond Ohio to participate in OCLC governance and the resulting reorganization are treated at length. Other areas are finances, whether OCLC is economical to use, one fully operational subsystem instead of the promised six, the variable quality of cataloging submitted by individualistic user-libraries, competitive networks, the lack of definitive research, and the future of OCLC. [R: JAL, Nov 81, p. 300]
Kathleen McCullough

708. **A New Governance Structure for OCLC: Principles and Recommendations.** By Arthur D. Little, Inc. Metuchen, N.J., Scarecrow, 1978. 96p. illus. o.p. LC 78-2099. ISBN 0-8108-1146-4.

This important study by Arthur D. Little, Inc. focuses both on the OCLC governance structure and the appropriate role for OCLC in the emerging national library network. The state of library networking is reviewed; the study assesses the shape of the national library network, OCLC's possible roles in it, and systems network architectures, in relation to OCLC's governance. The governance structure proposed here is a compromise between a tightly-held nonprofit corporation and a network cooperative. Library members of all organizations contracting with OCLC for services would be its members, and, significantly, a user's council would provide a formal institutional means for networks and other direct contractors of OCLC services to participate in policy decisions.

The study also identifies seven forces as being critical to the future of a national library network and also OCLC's role in the network: the economic plight of libraries and their parent institutions; central planning initiatives; availability of subsidies; incentives of private for-profit firms; new technological developments; library cooperation; and the incentives and drives of OCLC itself. The study is written in nontechnical language and is amply illustrated with tables and figures. Present OCLC users and all librarians concerned about the future developments of a national library network will need to review this important document. [R: JAL, May 79, p. 98]
Deborah Jane Brewer

Other Systems

709. Gilreath, Charles L. **CAIN Online User's Guide.** Washington, D.C., U.S. National Agricultural Library, 1976. 1v. (various paging). illus. bibliog. o.p.

"The goal of this manual is to introduce the National Agricultural Library's Cataloging and Indexing System (CAIN) to those who wish to use it for retrieving published literature on agriculture and its many related fields" (foreword). Its step-by-step approach will aid the librarian or information specialist who is beginning with online systems or the user with little experience. The introduction discusses the fundamentals of online retrieval, such as Boolean logic and online communication. Other sections cover CAIN indexing and cataloging, DIALOG searching and ORBIT III searching (the systems developed by CAIN's two commercial designers, Lockheed Information Systems and Systems Development Corporation). Appendices include a bibliography, ORBIT/DIALOG code glossaries, and the NAL subject code listing. [R: BL, 15 Sept 76, p. 128]

710.   Settel, Barbara, ed. **Subject Description of Books: A Manual of Procedures for Augmenting Subject Descriptions in Library Catalogs.** Syracuse, N.Y., Subject Access Project, School of Information Studies, Syracuse University, 1977. 1v. (various paging). (Research Studies, No. 3). o.p.

This work describes how the SDC database BOOKS was formulated by a CLR grant to the Subject Access Project in 1976-1977. The basic purpose was to augment approach to an online catalog through words and phrases from the tables of contents and indexes of selected books. Rules were established for the selection of the words and for the structure of the phrases. The techniques described are straightforward and, after a little study, seem to be fairly simple. The text contains some grammatical problems and some cases where the flow of words could be smoother; but as a start, the manual is a good one. The capacity to use this approach exists with some systems such as BALLOTS and UTLAS, but it does not exist with some others. Nonetheless, here is a system for the control of information that can develop into the online, multiple-index approach to collections that many librarians see as a basic need in the computer age.

The text is unpaged, which makes it difficult to use. The covers are heavy paper, and it has a plastic comb binding, which is anathema for library-related publication. Interestingly enough, the techniques suggested for the Subject Access Project and its formula will not work well in its own manual, since there is no index and the table of contents does not really meet the handbook's own criteria of "usability." But the handbook does provide a useful approach for a good start on in-depth subject analysis of books through computer-controlled systems. [R: LJ, July 78, p. 1363]

Neal L. Edgar

29 Censorship and Intellectual Freedom

711. Anderson, A. J. **Problems in Intellectual Freedom and Censorship.** New York, R. R. Bowker, 1974. 194p. (Bowker Series in Problem-Centered Approaches to Librarianship). o.p. LC 74-4107. ISBN 0-8352-0677-7. (Available from Books on Demand, $54.80pa., ISBN 0-317-19834-4).

Not every aspect of librarianship can be taught by the problem-solving method, but the technique is obviously appropriate to the teaching of intellectual freedom, where the aim is not to impart a body of knowledge but to develop the student's decision-making skill. On the job there is rarely a single easy and obvious solution when censorship problems arise — and the probability that they will arise is increasing steadily, so that no librarian can be considered fully trained without having been given some opportunity to analyze and evaluate intellectual freedom issues in a nonthreatening context. Anderson has assembled a collection of 28 typical problems, set in libraries of all types and involving librarians of varying age and experience, male and female, black and white; two of the problems are presented twice, with all the circumstances identical except the sex or race of the librarian involved. Few, if any, of the situations are theoretical; most are clearly rooted in actual events reported in the literature (this reviewer was involved some years ago in a close parallel to Case 16, a request by a home economics professor to remove Adelle Davis's works from an academic library). Many of the cases are not rigorously limited to intellectual freedom but require exploration of related aspects of civil liberties or professional ethics. Two impressive sample analyses by Anderson's students are appended. Anyone who teaches a unit on intellectual freedom will find this work worth considering a text or collateral reading. [R: AL, Dec 74, pp. 613-14; LJ, July 74, p. 1782]   Paul B. Cors

712. Bosmajian, Haig, comp. **Censorship, Libraries, and the Law.** New York, Neal-Schuman, 1983. 217p. index. $29.95. LC 83-2162. ISBN 0-918212-54-5.

The right (or freedom) to read is not specifically mentioned in the U.S. Constitution and does not appear anywhere in the Bill of Rights. Until 1982, moreover, the Supreme Court had sidestepped responsibility for interpreting whether the language of those documents actually implied that freedom, and for whom.

Bosmajian and Nat Hentoff, who supplied this book's foreword, contribute spirited essays toward an understanding of the legal verbiage handed down in the now-famous *Island Trees* case, which attempted to delineate the powers of a school board in removing controversial books from a library's shelves. The remainder of the book is a reprinting of the full text of legal opinions, recent and otherwise, that deal with school library censorship. Despite the title, the work treats only cases in schools, a fact that ought to have been more clearly specified. For its analysis and presentation of what the Court has, and hasn't, said, about the ability of authority to curtail students' reading, the book is of considerable value. We glean, from all the legalese and interpretation, the general sense that school boards will continue, when confronted by what they perceive as danger to their charges, to do as they please, and that the courts will be obliged to muddle through decisions dealing with the legality and fairness of such actions as those boards might take. Handsomely produced and sturdy, this book should be read by school librarians, principals, and board members. [R: BL, 15 Oct 83, p. 325; LJ, 1 May 83, p. 890; SLJ, Oct 83, pp. 126-27]
                                        Bruce A. Shuman

713. Busha, Charles H., ed. **Censorship in the Eighties.** Philadelphia, School of Library and

Information Science, Drexel University, 1982. 108p. (*Drexel Library Quarterly*, Vol. 18, No. 1). $6.00pa. LC 65-9911. ISSN 0012-6160.

This issue defends intellectual freedom and discusses recent censorship issues. Among the contributors are persons with doctoral work or books in the general area of censorship and selection. C. H. Busha, the guest editor, supplies a bibliography of 94 items, 1970-1981. In his introduction, he remarks on the increase in censorship incidents and predicts that "certain repressive forces ... if permitted ... would place numerous new restrictions on what is allowed to flow through our communication and information channels." C. W. Murray and L. B. Woods summarize the agenda and methods of the "New Christian Right" and are critical of where reactionary "pro-family, anti-secularism movements" can ultimately lead. B. A. Shuman continues the warning note in "The Moral Majority and Popular Political Issues." E. H. Richardson sees restraint arising from contemporary anxieties, with "textbook censorship and intolerance in the classroom" as an almost inevitable result. D. K. Berninghausen writes cogently "Toward an Intellectual Freedom Theory for Users of Libraries," while E. M. Oboler covers some "International Aspects of Intellectual Freedom." J. Serebnick's article is less of a piece with the other submissions. She takes a methodology, the checklist-based research, and analyzes it in relation to "Self-Censorship by Librarians." This article is definitely worth reading in research methodology classes; the other articles are useful, up-to-date reading. Overall, this theme issue is a standard but good offering. The subject is always worthy; reading new or déjà vu content on censorship in the 1980s is important for librarians. [R: SL, July 83, p. 314]   Claire England

714. Busha, Charles H. **Freedom versus Suppression and Censorship: With a Study of the Attitudes of Midwestern Public Librarians and a Bibliography of Censorship.** Littleton, Colo., Libraries Unlimited, 1972. 240p. index. (Research Studies in Library Science, No. 8). o.p. LC 72-91672. ISBN 0-87287-057-X.

Marjorie Fiske's *Book Selection and Censorship* (University of California Press, 1960) is already a classic of library literature. Her study indicated that librarians bear much of the responsibility for "censorship" of public and school library materials. Fiske found that some librarians avoided purchasing books they believed to be of controversial nature and that others restricted circulation of such books if purchased. The studies by Fiske and Busha,

using different methodology and examining geographic areas with vast cultural differences, support strikingly similar conclusions. Busha's study finds a "marked disparity between attitudes of many public librarians toward intellectual freedom as a concept and toward censorship as an activity" in the Midwest. We can no longer escape the evidence that librarians practice censorship. The study consists of eight chapters, and chapters five through eight present a revised version of a dissertation written in 1971 (Indiana University). A comprehensive bibliography of censorship, 1950-1971, concludes this study, which should be of interest to the library profession at large. [R: BL, 15 May 73, p. 872; LJ, 1 June 73, p. 1791; LQ, July 73, p. 256; RSR, Apr 73, p. 16]

715. Busha, Charles H., ed. **An Intellectual Freedom Primer.** Littleton, Colo., Libraries Unlimited, 1977. 221p. o.p. LC 77-7887. ISBN 0-87287-172-X.

An Intellectual Freedom Primer presents the essays of seven librarians and scholars, resolute in their commitment to principles of intellectual freedom. The purpose of the essays is to discuss twentieth-century developments as they have contributed to erosions of First Amendment rights and to focus on the protection of those rights. Covering numerous subareas of freedom of expression, the contributors offer many suggestions for strengthening particular freedoms.

The seven essays included are: "Freedom in the United States in the Twentieth Century," by Charles H. Busha; "Privacy and Security in Automated Personal Data Systems," by Stephen P. Harter; "Freedom of the Visual Arts: The Role of Governments," by Yvonne Linsert Morse; "Bibliographical Control of Erotica," by Rebecca Dixon; "Censorship and the Performing Arts: A Review of the Issues," by Barbara Connally Kaplan; "Censorship and the Contemporary Cinema," by Gail Linda Robinson; and "Censorship Research: Its Strengths, Weaknesses, Uses and Misuses," by Richard E. McKee. [R: BL, 15 Feb 78, p. 979; C&RL, Mar 78, p. 154; Choice, Mar 78, p. 52; JAL, Mar 78, p. 34; LJ, 1 Jan 78, p. 80; SLMQ, Summer 78, p. 268]

716. **Censorship Litigation and the Schools: Proceedings of a Colloquium Held January 1981.** Chicago, Office for Intellectual Freedom, American Library Association, 1983. 161p. $17.50pa. LC 82-24458. ISBN 0-8389-3279-7.

How can school libraries (and others) remain or become comparatively free from interference and censorship in their selection of materials in support of their curricula? This little book should help. In late January 1981 (at a location curiously left unnamed), about 60 attorneys, educators, publishers, and librarians met for the purpose of mapping strategy and tactics in school library censorship cases.

Present and speaking their minds at the colloquium were outstanding constitutional scholars, practicing attorneys (First Amendment types), and other interested parties, including John Culver, a former U.S. senator, all united in opposition to pressure-group attacks on libraries in schools for the purpose of removing materials deemed offensive or dangerous to segments of the school communities.

The upshot of this conference was a wealth of valuable material that can assist a beleaguered school library in resisting attacks by censorship-minded parents, clergy, or the general public. The unifying theme of all papers presented is that the other side will be well financed, persuasive, and persistent, and that any school, even one lucky enough to have escaped censorship attempts thus far, had best be prepared for problems in the future.

The thrust of the book is practical, and the strategies include ways to make the state work for the library, instead of against it, in keeping its collection free from those who would purge it, for whatever reasons. Most libraries of any size get ALA publications on standing order. The rest might well consider this important and timely book. [R: BL, 15 Oct 83, p. 325; JAL, Sept 83, p. 237; SLJ, Oct 83, p. 127]

Bruce A. Shuman

717. Children in Libraries: Patterns of Access to Materials and Services in School and Public Libraries; Proceedings of the Forty-first Conference of the Graduate Library School, May 16-17, 1980. Zena Sutherland, ed. Chicago, University of Chicago Press, 1981. 121p. $10.00. LC 80-53135. ISBN 0-226-78063-5.

For better or worse, this little volume is likely to be read only by students of library science who are in need of one more footnote or one more addition to a bibliography for a paper on children's librarianship and/or censorship. Most of the problems addressed by the various sections of this book are apparent to children's librarians: censorship through acquisitions or book removal, which books to make available to children (where shelved, library hours, etc.), accessibility of interlibrary loans for children, lack of non-English-language materials (including reviewing media for purchasing decisions), how much to rely on reviewers, etc. Thus few

librarians would be interested in purchasing a book that belabors what for them is the obvious.

The one section of the book that might make a reader sit up and take notice is Elaine Konigsburg's "Excerpts from My Bouboulina File," in which she details some examples of censorship from an author's viewpoint, humorously likening the practice of censorship to the world's oldest profession.

Yes, the book belongs in the libraries of colleges and universities that train librarians. No, please do not let students be told that it is a required personal purchase.

Judith E. H. Odiorne

718. Daily, Jay E. The Anatomy of Censorship. New York, Marcel Dekker, 1973. 403p. index. (Books in Library and Information Science, Vol. 6). $45.00. LC 72-95841. ISBN 0-8247-6065-4.

A rather interesting narrative, adequately documented, on various aspects of censorship. The emphasis (as the cover shows) is on sex. The text provided for the book cover does not do justice to the book; it indicates, among other things, that the author "watched through 75 pornographic movies; walked through 500 pornographic bookstores; waded through 1000 pornographic orgies; [and] was accompanied by his loyal and faithful wife through all of the above." [R: Choice, Mar 74, p. 70; LJ, 1 May 74, p. 1278; LQ, July 74, p. 285]

719. Haight, Anne Lyon. Banned Books, 387 B.C. to 1978 A.D. 4th ed. Updated and enlarged by Chandler B. Grannis. New York, R. R. Bowker, 1978. 196p. bibliog. index. o.p. LC 78-9720. ISBN 0-8352-1078-2.

This work was first issued in 1935, with a second edition in 1955 and a third edition in 1970 (see *ARBA* 71, entry 109). The heart of this edition is a 100-page chronology of events in censorship from Plato's time to 1977. The chronology itself is presented in short-form entries, some more detailed than others, and many following an item through more than one persecution; none are stunning revelations, but they do disturb nonetheless. Trial lawyer Charles Rembar's discussion of the legal status of censorship is perceptive, but sensibly makes no broad prescriptions other than vigilance on the part of anti-censors. Appendices discuss: (1) trends in censorship of various materials and in various institutions (government, schools, libraries), (2) various statements on freedom of the press, (3) excerpts from important U.S. court decisions, (4) excerpts from the report of the presidential Commission on Obscenity and Pornography, (5) a list of selected U.S. laws and regulations, and (6) a three-page bibliography on censorship. A useful index rounds out the volume. In this edition, some 60 entries have been added, and many more were revised. The volume will be useful for its new information if a library already has an older edition and would make for a good reference if none is at hand. [R: BL, 1 May 79, p. 1385; BL, 1 Jan 79, p. 734; C&RL, Jan 79, p. 79; JLH, Spring 79, p. 219; LJ, 1 Dec 78, p. 2407; LQ, Apr 79, p. 244; LR, Autumn 79, p. 168]	Koert C. Loomis, Jr.

720. Harvey, James A., and Patricia R. Harris. **Librarians, Censorship, and Intellectual Freedom: An Annual Annotated Bibliography, 1970.** Chicago, American Library Association, 1972. 52p. index. o.p. LC 72-7737. ISBN 0-8389-3139-1.

This second annual bibliography now has an index, a fact that should be appreciated. It briefly annotates all significant articles published in library periodicals in 1970, plus a few that were published in 1968 and 1969 but that were not included in the earlier volume. It is unfortunate that this annual manifests such a time lag—the use of "Chicago 1970" on the title page and the cover is perhaps symptomatic. One might suggest that coverage be expanded (on a selective basis) to nonlibrary periodicals, which would certainly provide librarians with more insight into this vitally important problem.

Bohdan S. Wynar

721. **Intellectual Freedom Manual.** 2nd ed. Compiled by the Office for Intellectual Freedom of the American Library Association. Chicago, American Library Association, 1983. 210p. bibliog. $15.00pa. LC 83-9958. ISBN 0-8389-3283-5.

In 1974, the American Library Association brought forth its long-awaited *Intellectual Freedom Manual* (see *ARBA* 75, entry 154), a looseleaf work that assembled all the positions, policies, interpretations, strategies, and tactics agreed to by the ALA membership. It was designed to be consulted both before and during confrontations with censors, whatever their reasons for demanding suppression of information or literature. Sections on the Library Bill of Rights, the freedom to read, intellectual freedom and the law, what to do before the censor comes, and assistance available from ALA were useful in dealing with opponents of free inquiry, and the format permitted replacement of pages or whole sections as policies shifted to meet new challenges or changing conditions.

This edition has come far from its predecessor. Gone is the looseleaf format; presumably ALA either is content with its formulas or will publish new editions from time to time. Added is a valuable chapter on the ways and means of state coalitions and local lobbying for intellectual freedom. All sections have been revised and updated, and they reflect conditions as of 1983. An annotated reading list is included, but one might wish for an index. The completeness of the table of contents somewhat blunts this criticism, however, as one should be able to find what one is looking for with a minimum of trouble. [R: BL, 15 Oct 83, p. 326]

Bruce A. Shuman

722. Jones, Frances M. **Defusing Censorship: The Librarian's Guide to Handling Censorship Conflicts.** Phoenix, Ariz., Oryx Press, 1983. 229p. bibliog. index. $29.50. LC 82-73734. ISBN 0-89774-027-0.

The first difficulty to meet us in this book is that of placement. Is this book a monograph? Is it a ready-reference work? The answers are "no" and "not exactly." Although the book is divided into several sections, among them chapters dealing with censorship in school and public libraries and a chapter on coping with the censorship problem, neither the index nor the arrangement of the text lends itself well to the solution of reference questions. This is primarily due to the fact that although the index is detailed, one has to know exactly what one wants before searching it or the text. On the other hand, the text, because it is mostly a recapitulation of censorship court cases, makes for very dull reading. Yet, to discard the book as useless might be a case of throwing the baby out with the bath water. Though the information they provide is readily available in other sources, the appendices could prove useful, with sample censorship policies and guidelines, intellectual freedom statements, a list of banned books, places to go for help in fighting a censorship case, and even an in-service training program designed to enlighten employees on the censorship issue.

But it is the philosophy Jones espouses that is most disturbing. Much of what is presented is a rebaking of the philosophy generated through ALA's Office of Intellectual Freedom. Anyone who has read that office's *Intellectual Freedom Manual* (American Library Association, 1974) will recognize the ideas expressed in Jones's work. For example, the preface to the *Manual* states, "The freedom to express one's beliefs or ideas, through any mode of communication, becomes virtually meaningless ... when accessibility to such expressions is denied other persons"; Jones states, "censors exercise power over the freedom of others to choose among intellectual options." Other expressions that bring to mind the philosophy expressed in the *Manual* are, "censorship restricts intellectual choices" and "censorship is not an issue that can be graded; there is no such thing as acceptable or 'good' censorship and unacceptable or 'bad' censorship." In Jones's mind the issue is, in other words, black and white. Other such statements are presented as fact when they are actually opinion, as when Jones states that "questioning" a selection is not a form of censorship, but "complaining" or "objecting" to a selection is.

Jones can be charged with opposing an intelligent use of judgment by implying that librarians must choose everything for fear of censoring anything. If that premise is true, what is the point of having an acquisition librarian?

Also not addressed anywhere in these pages is the question of whether, for example, in a public library setting, the members in a community must accept the decisions of the librarian as, for the most part, final. These members are generally, of course, the people who support the library with taxes. Have they no say?

Furthermore, words change meanings with a change in societal attitudes, but no one dealing with this issue of censorship, including Jones, has ever explained how, after some 2,000 years, the idea of censorship suddenly changed in the early 1900s to a totally negative concept. Jones never questions this premise but accepts it as correct.

Finally, no substantial and very little helpful information is provided the reader on what to do *after* a censorship case. Whatever the outcome, feelings are bound to be hurt, suspicions aroused, factions created, and ink spilled across miles of newsprint. How do librarians deal with the problem of rebuilding bridges? Jones states the position of the anticensorship camp strongly enough, but she seems to overlook the fact that her opponents are no less sincere and no less eager to help the community. The implication that all those who bring charges against libraries regarding "objectionable" materials are wrong leaves much to be desired. In emotional issues such as this one, both sides must be given equal time. The reader is provided with no information that would help explain why such issues are brought before librarians. Surely not all such individuals are merely enemies of freedom of speech.

What reference librarians need are not books that stroke unthinking sensibilities but full-bodies debates on intellectual freedom that present both sides as sympathetically as possible and assess the costs involved in such cases, both before and after the dust has settled. That no less a mind than Plato could have argued so convincingly for censorship should cause us to raise our eyebrows rather than shut our eyes. [R: BL, 15 Oct 83, p. 326; JAL, Sept 83, p. 249; LJ, 1 Sept 83, p. 1867; SLJ, Sept 83, p. 47; WLB, Oct 83, p. 142]   Mark Y. Herring

723. MacCafferty, Maxine, comp. **The Right to Know.** London, Aslib, 1976. 81p. (Aslib Bibliography, No. 1). £4.00pa. ISBN 0-85142-082-6.

This bibliography consists of 669 selected references culled from the monograph, newspaper, periodical, and report literature for the period January 1971 to February 1976. Issues concerning both the freedom of expression (the right to hear as well as to speak) and the right of access to information are explored in the writings cited.

The entries are classified under broad categories: censorship, privacy, computer privacy and security, secrecy, and freedom of the press. Since there is no index, the only approach to individual citations is through these categories and their subdivisions, which are identified in the classification scheme at the beginning. Some entries have very short annotations.

Although some reference is made to other countries, the main emphasis is on publications in and about the United Kingdom and the United States.

This first volume in the Aslib Bibliography series will be of value to the student, librarian, journalist, etc., who needs ready access to current literature on the "right to know."
                Sara R. Mack

724. McShean, Gordon. **Running a Message Parlor: A Librarian's Medium-Rare Memoir about Censorship.** Palo Alto, Calif., Ramparts Press, 1977. 237p. (Multinational Media Book). $11.95. LC 77-72737. ISBN 0-87867-068-8.

In the mid-1960s, McShean was involved in a number of battles against library censors, and this personal narrative describes these encounters, principally at the Roswell (New Mexico) Public Library, where McShean was head librarian. The all-too-familiar issues — book selection, equal access to materials, and library participation in controversial cultural programs — are treated in a rather lighthearted manner, while at the same time underscoring the serious nature of these attacks by censors. McShean also discusses reactions from other librarians as well as his own professional activities in library associations. This interesting, though tedious, autobiography, written in a folksy style, is not an essential item for those concerned with censorship. [R: BL, 15 Feb 78, p. 962; JAL, March 78, p. 37; LJ, 1 May 78, p. 947]   Alan Edward Schorr

725. Merritt, LeRoy Charles. Book Selection and Intellectual Freedom. New York, H. W. Wilson, 1970. 100p. index. $10.00. LC 79-116998. SBN 8242-0420-4.

This volume, written by the late LeRoy Merritt, dean of the School of Librarianship, University of Oregon, reflects the author's rich experience in this subject and is probably one of the more readable presentations. A number of basic documents are appended to the narrative, including the Library Bill of Rights, Intellectual Freedom in Libraries, and Resolution on Loyalty Programs, among others. [R: DLQ, Jan 71, p. 70]

726. Oboler, Eli M. Defending Intellectual Freedom: The Library and the Censor. Westport, Conn., Greenwood Press, 1980. 246p. index. (Contributions in Librarianship and Information Science, No. 32). $27.50. LC 79-8585. ISBN 0-313-21472-7.

Throughout a major portion of his professional life, Eli Oboler has been a courageous and outspoken champion of intellectual freedom, and the right of all persons to have access to whatever writings have meaning for them. In the pages of library literature and on the floor of the Council of the American Library Association he was constantly on the alert for any official action that might jeopardize such rights. Also, he has long been actively suspicious of computers or other mechanisms that might impose a barrier between the reader and the book.

In this volume, as in others that have preceded it, we have the fruit of his thinking on these vital problems. In this collection of essays he has dealt forthrightly and incisively with such topics as: "The Free Mind: Intellectual Freedom's Perils and Prospects," "The Politics and Censorship," "The Fear of Science," "The Young Adult and Intellectual Freedom," "The Etiology of Censorship," "Public Relations and Fighting Censorship," "The Censorship Battle in a Conservative State." There are also editorials and letters on intellectual freedom, reviews of recent literature on intellectual freedom, notes and maxims, and an Intellectual Freedom Creed. These last items had not been previously published. The collective essays cover the two decades between 1959 and 1979.

This is a very important book which should be read by every librarian and which should be in the collections of all academic, public, and school libraries. [R: BL, 15 Oct 81, p. 284; JAL, Sept 81, pp. 240-41]   Jesse H. Shera

727. Oboler, Eli M. The Fear of the Word: Censorship and Sex. Metuchen, N.J., Scarecrow, 1974. 362p. index. $15.00. LC 74-6492. ISBN 0-8108-0724-6.

Every now and again, one comes across an author so dedicated to his subject and so impressive a wordsmith that he almost overwhelms with both his erudition and his intensity. Eli Oboler is such an author.

His task in this volume is twofold: to chronicle the historical and philosophical origins of sexual censorship (as opposed to, say, political or religious censorship, which are related, if only tangentially) and to provide a strongly ringing defense of intellectual freedom in America.

His work is liberally spiced with challenging statements from a variety of well-known literary and political figures; some of these quotes are used as chapter leads, while others are incorporated into the body of the text. Oboler makes an attempt at objectivity early on, but seemingly abandons such even-handedness as he warms to his argument. In fact, his first appendix (of six) is entitled "An Anti-Censorship Chrestomathy" and includes a glittering array of apt quotations, ranging from the writings of Bowdler and Comstock, through D. H. Lawrence and G. B. Shaw to Dr. Alex Comfort (*Joy of Sex*) and Richard Ben-Veniste (more recently Leon Jaworski's right-hand man).

A few picayune problems are in evidence, which may attest either to Oboler's passionate neglect of detail or to one further manifestation of Scarecrow's midnight proofreading. For example, page 40, concerned with the repressive censorship of Girolamo Savonarola, firebrand monk of the Reformation, gives his dates as 1492-1534. The six other sources consulted by this curious reviewer agreed that Fra Girolamo was born in 1452 and died in 1498. Also, a reference is made to "the *climactic* severity" of the winters undergone by the Puritans in the new world (p. 66). Well ... Oboler's topic *is* sex, after all, and he is to be forgiven, perhaps, for a seemingly natural Freudian slip.

These quibbles aside, Oboler writes in lucid, elegant, and mordant prose; his conversational style is brimful of thoughtful observations on the inherent contradictions of the censor's moralistic stance. One of them just won't leave me alone: "If truth and beauty *are* identical, in Keats' famous dictum, then the 'facts of life' — writings about sexual conduct — must be beautiful, no matter how 'obscene'."

This book should be read and re-read by librarians, attorneys, educators, and all concerned with (or troubled by) intellectual freedom. It constitutes an important and valuable (if unabashedly partisan) appraisal of the nature of humankind and the forces driving us to attempt the suppression and/or concealment of the human body and the humanistic arts.

An epilog, entitled "Portrait of the Censor" is, alone, worth the price of admission. In two and a half pages, Oboler presents a telling paraphrase of Pogo's identification of the customary "real" enemy. He is us.

Highest recommendation. [R: AL, Dec 74, pp. 612-13]   Bruce A. Shuman

728.   Oboler, Eli M. **To Free the Mind: Libraries, Technology, and Intellectual Freedom.** Littleton, Colo., Libraries Unlimited, 1983. 124p. bibliog. index. $15.00. LC 83-19889. ISBN 0-87287-325-0.

Throughout his distinguished career, Oboler was dedicated to the cause of intellectual freedom. In his final work, Oboler explains his concerns about modern information technology and suggests that librarians must recognize the dangers as well as the benefits of adopting new technology. In interpreting the impact of high technology on librarianship, Oboler pays particular attention to the vulnerability of intellectual freedom and argues deftly for the extension into our computer age of the humanistic philosophies innate to librarianship. In the course of his text, Oboler examines the civil liberties implications of current phenomena ranging from micrographics to communications satellites. He urges librarians to consider such critical issues as the lack of privacy inherent in the information revolution, the question of copyright protection, the implications of government information policy, and the wide, free dissemination of ideas enabled by the combination of miniaturization, computerization, and networking. [R: AL, Apr 84, p. 246; BL, July 84, p. 1517; JAL, May 84, p. 104; LJ, 1 June 84, p. 1106; LQ, Oct 84, p. 430; RQ, Summer 84, p. 488; WLB, May 84, p. 670]

729.   Pope, Michael. **Sex and the Undecided Librarian: A Study of Librarians' Opinions on Sexually Oriented Literature.** Metuchen, N.J., Scarecrow, 1974. 209p. index. o.p. LC 73-14707. ISBN 0-8108-0678-9.

Unlike most dissertations, expanded or otherwise, the title of this one is a grabber! So

is the subject. Pope set out to gather, analyze, and describe the attitudes of several types of librarians in the United States to sexually oriented literature. In this, he went beyond previously conducted research by examining a wide spectrum of types of library practitioners and by confining his subject strictly to books concerned with, or containing, sexually oriented topics. He succeeds in confirming what most of us have known for some time — that no topic is so universally condemned by librarians, yet so widely practiced, as censorship.

One thing that becomes immediately evident is the meticulous planning that went into Pope's research. He seems to have spent hundreds of hours (and dollars) amassing a collection of sexually oriented materials of his own, so that his list of typologies of material might be quite comprehensive, if not exhaustive. His sources vary from federal documents to under-the-counter periodicals, pamphlets, and catalogs from darkest Times Square. His aim was to discover the attitudes of those engaged in the practice of book selection toward the materials that can (and do) offend a segment of the public for whom selection is performed.

Through the use of questionnaires designed to elicit (1) personal familiarity with various types of literature, (2) attitudes toward such materials, and (3) professional, institutional, and personal data on respondents, Pope has developed some interesting, if not altogether surprising, findings. In the potpourri of his results we learn that: generally, male respondents are less restrictive than are female respondents; school librarians tend to restrict more than public librarians; librarians in publicly controlled institutions respond in much the same way as those in privately controlled institutions. You get the idea. Little is astonishing, but the book makes interesting and even important reading. Many of Pope's conclusions approach the level of Berelson's celebrated "some do and some don't" in their practical value, but then most research in the social sciences looks that way. One important shortcoming worthy of note is that the questionnaire is introduced with a list of assumptions the respondent is asked to make, which might invalidate all the study's conclusions. The first assumption reads, "You have enough money to purchase anything you want and enough staff and room to handle the materials." With assumptions like that, conclusions must be viewed as hypothetical at best, possibly visionary.

Despite such problems, the book is highly recommended as a telling indictment of us all. In the words of Walt Kelly's Pogo, "We have met the enemy and he is us!" And besides, who can resist that title? [R: LJ, 15 June 74, p. 1681]

Bruce A. Shuman

730. Robotham, John, and Gerald Shields. **Freedom of Access to Library Materials.** New York, Neal-Schuman, 1982. 221p. bibliog. index. $27.95. LC 82-14309. ISBN 0-918212-31-6.

Useful both as a library school text and as a handbook for the practicing librarian, this is a well-organized, readable review of the present state of the ongoing struggle between freedom and censorship in U.S. libraries. (Though the title might suggest otherwise, censorship is the only impediment to access discussed.) If the authors have no really original insights to offer, they do provide an objective analysis of the issues, agreeably free from dogmatism and prescriptiveness, that will challenge readers to review their own attitudes. The first chapter is a somewhat abstruse examination of the concept of freedom; the balance of the book deals with the practical application of this concept in libraries (the examples are drawn from public libraries and public school libraries, but the principles apply to all publicly funded libraries). The authors do not shrink from considering such sensitive topics as the rights of children and young people, the place in libraries of materials potentially offensive to ethnic or other minorities, and the apparent special vulnerability of films. A detailed case study of an actual censorship controversy in a high school library, presented anonymously and without editorial comment, is both fascinating and terrifying. The book offers sensible advice on handling complaints; examples of complaint forms are provided, but the authors warn against seeing these as a panacea, suggesting that in some cases being required to fill out a form may only antagonize an already angry individual. A well-selected annotated bibliography complements the text. [R: BL, 15 Apr 83, p. 1074; JAL, May 83, p. 113; LJ, 15 Mar 83, p. 564; RQ, Summer 83, p. 436; SLQ, Oct 83, pp. 126-27; WLB, May 83, p. 783]

Paul B. Cors

731. Tucker, Nicholas, ed. **Suitable for Children? Controversies in Children's Literature.** Berkeley, Calif., University of California Press, 1976. 224p. $28.50. LC 76-6016. ISBN 0-520-03236-5.

Nicholas Tucker offers in this anthology a well-selected collection of British essays on con-troversial subjects in children's literature. Five topics receive special attention: fairy tales, comics, the impact of children's books on the arousal of fear, classics, and the value of children's literature. Areas of concern in the United States, such as racism, sexism, and vulgarities in children's books, are not treated in much detail here. The anthology does emphasize the permanent effects of literature on children. [R: BL, 15 Nov 76, p. 434]

732. Woods, L. B. **A Decade of Censorship in America: The Threat to Classrooms and Libraries, 1966-1975.** Metuchen, N.J., Scarecrow, 1979. 183p. bibliog. index. $15.00. LC 79-20960. ISBN 0-8108-1260-6.

This reworked dissertation is a when, where, what, why, and by whom of censorship attempts in public libraries, schools, colleges, and universities. Based on reports from the *Newsletter on Intellectual Freedom* (American Library Association), 1966-1975, it analyzes and arranges the reports in tables and descriptions to illustrate different points. For example, a graph shows the number of attempts over the decade in schools; a list shows 10 states where most noneducational censorship attempts occurred; and a table shows initiators (organizations like the PTA, NAACP, or groups like librarians, students, administrators) of attempts.

The publisher calls this book both a "comprehensive attempt to explore (censorship attempts) on a national scale — 900 cases" and "a primary reference tool." Both phrases are hyperbole. The study behind this book, while interesting and full, is meant to fulfill requirements of a doctorate. Hence, comprehensiveness is contained. In addition to describing the data, a section summarizes the decade's literature on censorship, noting the familiar pattern of articles on censured titles, court cases, freedom to read, and book selection, areas better covered by such titles as *Freedom of the Press: A Bibliocyclopedia 1967-1977* (see *ARBA* 80, entry 37) or De Grazia's *Censorship Landmarks* (R. R. Bowker, 1969). Beside these examples of more substantial standard reference works, *A Decade of Censorship* clarifies its contribution. It is a circulating item of potential use to someone wanting items about recent censorship attempts. [R: C&RL, May 80, pp. 261-62; JAL, May 80, p. 99; LJ, 1 Feb 80, p. 362; SLJ, Sept 80, p. 45]

Claire England

30 Collection Development

GENERAL WORKS

733. Osburn, Charles B. **Academic Research and Library Resources: Changing Patterns in America.** Westport, Conn., Greenwood Press, 1979. 187p. bibliog. index. (New Directions in Librarianship, No. 3). $27.50. LC 78-20017. ISBN 0-313-20722-4; ISSN 0147-1090.

Osburn presents what he considers to be "a realistic description of the historical evolution of the relationship between academic research and the development of large academic library resources." He points out that the post-World War II years have witnessed a shift from university-centered research to problem-solving research, supported in large measure by federal funds. This shift, with a strong emphasis on the needs of society, may be observed in the research being undertaken by scholars in the sciences, the social sciences, and the humanities.

In spite of this changing emphasis in the research activities of the academicians, academic libraries have by and large continued to build their collections in the traditional manner. Scholars in all areas have come to identify with the national research network in their respective fields; libraries somehow have been included in these networks in an ad hoc manner. Osburn emphasizes the need for planning at the national level and calls for the adoption of new concepts in collection building as well as the establishment of "standards of quality, rather than simply of quantity, for the evaluation of collections." A thoughtful and thought-provoking work. Included are a select bibliography, arranged by subject, containing 332 items, and an index. [R: BL, 15 Oct 79, p. 329]   John David Marshall

734. Schad, Jasper G., and Norman E. Tanis. **Problems in Developing Academic Library Collections.** New York, R. R. Bowker, 1974. 183p.

(Bowker Series in Problem-Centered Approaches to Librarianship). $10.95. LC 72-1944. ISBN 0-8352-0551-7. (Available from Books on Demand, $51.80, ISBN 0-317-19841-6).

As a teacher of selection and acquisition courses I was very disappointed by this book. I suppose I should not have been fooled by such words as "wholly new" or "radical alternative" used in the preface and in Bowker's advertisements. The high hopes these words generated were quickly dispelled after reading one or two cases.

To have some cases to use as supplementary material in a course is always very nice. Unfortunately, this book does not provide cases I could use in any acquisition course I teach. All of the cases require a background that most beginning library school students do not have. A person working on the cases must not only know the basics of selection and acquisition but must also have work experience in the field. In addition, the amount of time one would need to give to the projects, in order to do even a reasonable job, is much too great for class use. Almost any one case would represent a good term project for an experienced student, yet each case covers only a few of the issues of collection development. Finally, the type cases represented are too limited in coverage for use in most library school collection development courses.

Even if the book had a broader appeal, there are several other important problems. One problem is the general tone of the cases. My feeling after reading all the cases was that research library collection development personnel are "super beings" who are always right and whose collections must contain everything. Cases dealing with cooperative activities give the impression that cooperation is a great idea for everyone but "me." Faculty members and institutional administrators usually appear in the role of the problem persons and often as incompetents. Somewhere there must be one competent faculty member or administrator. Finally, although small four-year colleges and community college problems are represented, most of the cases concern research libraries, thus giving the impression that the only important libraries are research oriented.

Most of the cases seem to be more concerned with management problems than with collection development; collection development seems almost to be a side issue. I agree with the authors—collection development problems have broad implications and touch on problems not related to selection work. Nevertheless, we do have already a number of management case study books. Placing a personnel problem in a collection development situation does not change the nature of the problem; it is still a personnel matter.

There are a few cases that would make excellent problems for a seven-day management training workshop for experienced academic library collection development personnel. I see little use for this book in most library school courses. [R: LJ, 1 Dec 74, p. 3114]

G. Edward Evans

735. Spyers-Duran, Peter, and Thomas Mann, Jr., eds. **Shaping Library Collections for the 1980s.** Phoenix, Ariz., Oryx Press, 1980. 235p. index. $32.50. LC 80-21195. ISBN 0-912700-58-0.

Only a tenuous relationship exists between the conference theme (which is also the title of the book) and the papers presented at the three-day meeting (29-31 October 1979). Almost all of the papers review past practice (Vosper's "historical footnotes" is one of the few interesting historical pieces), and none focus on the future. Axford, Bank and LaCroix, Miller, Dewey, Schnaars, Leonhardt, Posey, Perrault, and Alldredge all review past practices in one or more libraries. Cenzer, Biblarz, Holleman, Buzzell and Cullen, and Putnam all describe some form of limited approval program, "retrospective," "special emphasis," and "distinguished press," for example, but none address the question of library collections for the 1980s. Kaiser, Walsdorf, Stave, Berkner, and Mosher discuss some special existing aspect of vendor performance or service. Wolf and Emery look at economic and management aspects of approval plans. There is nothing wrong with the papers, but then neither is there anything new.

The papers that are most interesting and that do contribute new information are William McGrath's "The Circulation Uncertainty Principle and the Cosmology of Collection Use" (unfortunately, the paper does not directly relate to approval plans) and Glyn T. Evans's paper, "Taxonomy of Instruction Progress (Hegis and Library Collection Approval Plans)." The latter is an excellent piece outlining a possible management information system based on *ABPR* tapes, OCLC distribution tapes, HEGIS/LC tables, circulation data, and institutional data on courses and enrollment. Combined, these "databases" would provide a good approval plan management system.

Robert Miller stated in his paper, "I had a fleeting fear ... that we might well spend two days belaboring the obvious or trying to square the circle" (p. 52). He concluded that the 25 papers presented at the conference, and reprinted in this volume, were a valuable contribution to the literature on approval plans. After reading all the papers it would seem his fleeting fear was well justified. What little new material is presented should have been published as journal articles. [R: JAL, Sept 82, p. 233]

G. Edward Evans

736. Stueart, Robert D., and George B. Miller, Jr., eds. **Collection Development in Libraries: A Treatise.** Greenwich, Conn., JAI Press, 1980. 2v. index. (Foundations in Library and Information Science, Volume 10, Parts A-B). $40.00/vol.; $60.00/set. LC 79-93165. ISBN 0-89232-106-7 (part A); 0-89232-162-8 (part B).

This two-volume addition to the Foundations in Library and Information Science series provides a timely discussion on issues which are central to the profession. This treatise on collection development edited by Stueart and Miller is a collection of 24 articles written by recognized practicing authorities in each particular area.

As stated in the preface, the purpose of this work is "to present theories, techniques and state-of-the-art analysis which have wide application to academic, research, public, school and special libraries" (p. xiii). Through the combined expertise of the contributors, this work provides an overview of the theory and practice of collection development.

The work is organized into six sections covering the topics of management, the process of collection development, the use of materials, formats, and the future of collection development. In part 1, Stueart offers an overview of collection development in the United States, highlighting the historical development and making a case for the need for well-planned, systematic collection development. Part 2, "Collection Management," provides a context for understanding remaining parts of this work. Articles on organization models relating to various types of libraries, budgeting, policy formation, a survey of attitudes toward collection development, resource sharing, and managing library collections comprise this important section. It is worthwhile noting that this separate treatment on the management of collection development differentiates it from the approach taken in recent texts on this topic, such as Katz, Gardner, and Broadus, which integrate the management component with specific aspects of collection building without discussing it separately in much depth. The arrangement of this work further substantiates the editor's position that systematic collection development is the result of the management process.

Part 3 discusses the collection development process, covering topics such as selection, mass buying programs, collecting foreign materials, retrospective materials, and preservation. Citation and use studies, as they relate to collection building, are addressed in part 4. The remaining two parts deal with formats (e.g., microforms, government publications, media, and serials), and the future of collection development. The article entitled "Toward a Theory of Collection Development," contained in the last section of readings, is particularly useful in drawing together the theories and practices exhibited in this treatise. In this article, the author states that four parts of collection development work together scientifically to produce a whole — selection, de-selection or weeding, evaluation, and funding. An author/subject index provides easy access to the information contained throughout the two volumes.

The authors have been successful in providing a philosophical (theoretical) framework and highlighting practical applications for collection development. This collection of articles should not only be read by students in order to stimulate discussion and interest in further study of specific aspects of collection development, but also by practitioners in order to facilitate decision making and planning. [R: JAL, Sept 81, pp. 238-39]   Ann Hartman

737. Van Orden, Phyllis, and Edith B. Phillips, eds. **Background Readings in Building Library Collections.** 2nd ed. Metuchen, N.J., Scarecrow, 1979. 417p. index. o.p. LC 78-31263. ISBN 0-8108-1200-2.

Many reprint collections seem to be a miscellaneous selection of articles in search of a reason for being published; that is not the case with this volume. Van Orden and Phillips have done a superb job of reviewing and selecting articles from the literature on collection development published between 1969 and 1978. They selected 57 excellent articles and arranged them in eight broad categories — "Theory of Collection Development"; "Development of Selection Policy"; "Selection Environment"; "The Community and the Collection"; "The Selection Process"; "The Evolution Process"; "The Role of Publishers, Producers and Distributors"; and "Recent Developments Creating Change in Collection Development."

Each of the sections concludes with a list of recommended readings, which is more than a straight bibliographic listing; the authors have developed "mini" bibliographic essays that provide some descriptive information about each of the recommended readings. The authors say that "the following citations were chosen to develop those themes" (p. 61), those themes being the ones developed by the reprinted articles. The list of authors included is very impressive and diverse; only three persons have more than one article included — LeRoy Merritt, Edward Holley, and Diana Spirt each have two articles in the collection. Although the articles are reprinted from readily available sources, the "packaging" makes the volume useful for teaching purposes as a supplement to a required textbook. [R: BL, 15 Oct 79, p. 327; C&RL, Nov 79, pp. 578-79; LJ, 15 Oct 79, p. 2177]
G. Edward Evans

REFERENCE WORKS

738. Godden, Irene P., Karen W. Fachan, and Patricia A. Smith, with the assistance of Sandra Brug, comps. **Collection Development and Acquisitions, 1970-80: An Annotated, Critical Bibliography.** Metuchen, N.J., Scarecrow, 1982. 138p. index. $15.00. LC 81-18530. ISBN 0-8108-1499-4.

Collection Development and Acquisitions, 1970-80 is intended to bring together the "best" or most "useful" articles reflecting trends in acquisitions and collection development during the seventies, as well as current and best texts and monographs. In order to select the most notable articles, the compilers solicited input from 300 collection development specialists listed in the *American Library Directory*, and reviewed the 10 years of *Library Lit. — The Best of ...* and the 1979 and 1980 volumes of *Library Resources and Technical Services.* A final selection was made by the compilers.

The bibliography is organized into three main sections. The first, which is only four pages long, lists "current and best texts and monographs." An unfortunate omission is Stueart and Miller's critically acclaimed *Collection Development in Libraries: A Treatise* (Greenwich, Conn., JAI Press, 1980; see *ARBA* 82, entry 268). Part 2, entitled "The Collection," has sections on allocation, evaluation, the selection process, maintenance, and new horizons (including resource sharing and networks). Part 3 is on acquisitions. In all, there are 345 entries, with descriptive rather than critical annotations. There are author, title, and subject indexes.

On the whole, this bibliography provides an interesting overview of trends in the collection development and acquisitions areas in the seventies as recorded in the journal literature. One wonders, though, how enduring the usefulness of a work which treats the literature so narrowly will be. [R: JAL, Nov 82, p. 304]

Heather Cameron

INTRODUCTORY TEXTS AND MANUALS

739. Broadus, Robert N. **Selecting Materials for Libraries.** 2nd ed. New York, H. W. Wilson, 1981. 469p. index. $20.00. LC 81-650. ISBN 0-8242-0659-2.

The second edition of Broadus's *Selecting Materials for Libraries* is one of several recent additions to the literature of collection development. Unlike either Stueart and Miller's *Collection Development in Libraries: A Treatise* (JAI Press, 1980) or Gardner's *Library Collections: Their Origin, Selection, and Development* (McGraw-Hill, 1981), which provide a broad overview of the total collection development function in libraries, Broadus's work focuses on the selection function. Like the first edition (see *ARBA* 74, entry 191), it is primarily concerned with selection as it relates to small and medium-sized libraries and is intended for use as a text in schools of library science. Certain topics such as materials for children, library organization for selection, acquisitions procedures, discarding, and censorship have been intentionally omitted or only lightly touched upon.

The book has five parts. The first two discuss problems and approaches to selection, including chapters on the library and its environment and fundamental principles of selection, as well as offering information on the publishing industry and book trade and aids for evaluating material. Parts 3 and 4 describe different types of materials found in libraries, both print and nonprint, such as reference works, periodicals, government documents, films, sound recordings, etc., and suggest guides to assist in their selection. The last and largest part discusses selection by subject field. For each subject area, the author provides an overview of the discipline, discusses the characteristics of its literature, and suggests aids for selection. Specific references cited have been updated throughout.

Broadus's style is down to earth, and his approach is practical. For those requiring a more detailed treatment of selection than is provided in other recent textbooks on collection development, Broadus would be a good choice. However, as a basic text on collection building in library schools today, it would be somewhat limited.

Heather Cameron

740. Curley, Arthur, and Dorothy Broderick. **Building Library Collections.** 6th ed. Metuchen, N.J., Scarecrow, 1985. 339p. index. $18.75. LC 84-23665. ISBN 0-8108-1776-4.

The author entry for this book may tend to obscure the fact that it is simply another edition of the familiar textbook originally prepared by Mary Carter and Wallace Bonk and later revised by Rose Mary Magrill. The organization, contents, wording, and bibliographies of this edition are much as they have been before. Considering the wide popularity of "Carter and Bonk" in library schools, this is probably for the good; one wishes, however, that the basic contributions of Carter, Bonk, and Magrill had been acknowledged on the title page.

There are five main changes in the sixth edition, apart from rephrasing of the wording. First, new chapters, "Why Libraries Exist" and "Philosophy and Framework of Collection Development," have been added. These stress the importance of basing effective collection development on a precise definition of the library's goals and a close study of the community's needs. The chapter "Studying the Library's Community" is accordingly expanded. Second, most of the appendices have been deleted, on the not wholly acceptable argument that this material is available elsewhere. Third, bibliographies and factual information have been brought up to date, though not, it would appear, later than 1983. Fourth, more emphasis is placed on nonbook materials. Finally, the material on selection by subject, formerly a separate chapter, has been integrated into the basic selection chapters.

The new editors are well known and well qualified. Their reinterpretations and revisions will give *Building Library Collections* the vitality and currency for continued usefulness. [R: JAL, Sept 85, p. 256; RQ, Fall 85, p. 151]

Samuel Rothstein

741. Evans, G. Edward. **Developing Library Collections.** Littleton, Colo., Libraries Unlimited, 1979. 340p. index. (Library Science Text Series). $20.00. LC 78-27303. ISBN 0-87287-145-2.

Evans's text provides an integrated approach to the process of building a library collection for a specific community of users. He identifies and examines six basic elements of the process—community survey, development/selection policies, selection of books and audiovisuals, acquisitions, weeding, and evaluating the collection—and the interrelated nature of these components.

The first part of the text introduces concepts of collection development and discusses sources of materials—publishers, producers, and distributors. The second section gives practical guidance in community survey techniques, collection development policies, selection of materials, weeding, and collection evaluation. The third section focuses on copyright, cooperative systems, and censorship in the context of their influence on collection development. The text is amply supported by illustrations, checklists, bibliographies, and an appendix which reprints portions of the Copyright Law of 1978. [R: C&RL, July 79, pp. 389-90; JAL, Nov 79, pp. 288-89]

742. Gardner, Richard K. **Library Collections: Their Origin, Selection, and Development.** New York, McGraw-Hill, 1981. 354p. index. (McGraw-Hill Series in Library Education). $31.95. LC 80-23831. ISBN 0-07-022850-7.

Richard Gardner, in *Library Collections: Their Origin, Selection, and Development*, has taken a somewhat different approach to teaching collection development than have Katz (see *ARBA* 81, entry 211), Evans (see *ARBA* 80, entry 189), or Broadus (see *ARBA* 82, entry 261). Also intended as a library school text, Gardner's book takes "the content of library collections—books, periodicals, microforms, A-V materials and so on—and ... [traces] them from their origin through the various phases of marketing and distribution to their final resting place in a library" (preface, pp. xi-xii). The book is divided into three main parts. Part 1 presents a lengthy discussion of the publishing industry and book trade (e.g., how library materials are produced and marketed). Part 2 describes how one finds out about library materials through

trade bibliographies, reviewing media, and retrospective tools. Part 3 discusses the theory and principles of selection, selection procedures, weeding and storage, collection development policies, collection evaluation and standards, resource sharing, and censorship. Short lists of suggested readings follow each section. Three appendices reprint documents on collection development policies, standards for library collections, and censorship. There is a short glossary.

What differentiates Gardner's book from the other recent additions to the literature is the author's emphasis (one-third of the text) on the publishing industry and book trade. While others have included information on this subject as part of the acquisition process, it is Gardner's *point de départ*. To use his own words, "If good materials are to be selected, the librarian must have some idea of how the product came into being" (preface, p. xi). Therefore, the reader is taken step-by-step through the publishing process from manuscript acquisition, editing, and production to distribution and marketing before learning about selection tools or collection development techniques and principles.

Gardner writes well. His material is presented clearly and logically. Overall he provides a good overview of the entire process of building library collections. While it could serve as an introductory text for library school students, other standard works which offer more in-depth coverage of specific areas like selection, for example, Broadus's *Selecting Materials for Libraries*, second edition (H. W. Wilson, 1981), should also be used to ensure that students are fully exposed to this important professional responsibility. [R: BL, 15 Oct 81, p. 283; LJ, July 81, p. 1394]

Heather Cameron

743. Katz, William A. **Collection Development: The Selection of Materials for Libraries.** New York, Holt, Rinehart and Winston, 1980. 352p. index. $26.95. LC 79-19861. ISBN 0-03-050266-7.

Katz has divided his text into three almost equal parts: an introduction, the selection of print, and the selection of nonprint materials. There is a fourth, much shorter section on censorship.

The introduction is further divided into five sections: the philosophy of selection, including objectives, goals, and policies; the public and selection, which covers the basic considerations of community analysis with a nod to information and referral services; collection development, including formulas, budgeting, etc.;

collection analysis; and the selection process. Part 2 covers book selection aids with an overview of acquisitions work, periodical selection, and the selection of other print materials such as microforms, pamphlets, and local history. Part 3 discusses the selection of nonprint materials in a similar fashion. It includes a discussion of media by type of library and separate chapters on recordings and film. Other types of media are grouped together in a short chapter.

This is essentially a textbook for library school classes. The information provided is too general to be used as a handbook to follow in improving a collection, and anyone with a few years' experience in several different libraries already knows what is here. Its value outside the classroom is as a bibliographical guide to the literature. For this purpose it is excellent and will assist any type of library in planning to improve its selection techniques and its usefulness to its public.

No emphasis is given to one type of library over another, nor is selection for particular subject fields considered. There is an adequate index, which includes authors and titles of works cited in the text but not those referred to only in footnotes. [R: JAL, Mar 80, p. 52; LJ, July 80, p. 1493]   David W. Brunton

ACQUISITIONS

General Works

744. Futas, Elizabeth, ed. **Library Acquisition Policies and Procedures.** 2nd ed. Phoenix, Ariz., Oryx Press, 1984. 579p. index. (A Neal-Schuman Professional Book). $38.50. LC 82-42925. ISBN 0-89774-024-6.

Presumably, this book's principal function is to serve as model or guideline for library authorities seeking either to devise collection development policies for their agencies or to overhaul existing ones which don't quite fit the climate of the eighties. The first edition of this title was published by Oryx in 1977; Futas is back in print with two dozen public and academic library policies reprinted in their entirety and selections and excerpts from over 60 more, chosen to illustrate specific points.

Futas provides analysis of the policies she includes, perceiving several significant trends in the past seven years. Among these are changes in terminology from selection or acquisitions policies to collection development policies, an emphasis on confidentiality in records as respects borrowers, and an even greater stress on money and the lack of it in the face of each

year's output of worthwhile materials. She perceives an even greater emphasis on selectivity and evaluation, as a result of ongoing financial crises in most public and academic libraries, and counsels library planners to look carefully at their collections and to be willing to part with anything which is inappropriate or which has outlived its perceived usefulness.

As a point of departure for those libraries still out there without collection development policies, this book is highly recommended. Other libraries might want to look it over, as well, to examine what the good policy contains and avoids. [R: BL, 15 Oct 84, p. 280; JAL, Sept 84, pp. 225, 244]   Bruce A. Shuman

745. Grieder, Ted. **Acquisitions: Where, What, and How: A Guide to the Orientation and Procedure for Students in Librarianship, Librarians, and Academic Faculty.** Westport, Conn., Greenwood Press, 1978. 277p. (Contributions in Librarianship and Information Science, No. 22). $35.00. LC 77-84762. ISBN 0-8371-9890-9; ISSN 0084-9243.

Grieder has written what he considers to be "a general view of acquisitions interrelationships in and out of the library" and provides a "*survey* of acquisitions concerns and activities" (p. ix). As the subtitle indicates, the book is intended for students, librarians, and academic faculty; after reading the book, one might change the subtitle to "for anyone who has not been an acquisitions librarian for at least fifteen years." The "where, what, and how" is handled in two very unequal parts; part 1 (48 pages) covers the "where" (interrelationships) and the "what" (activities), while part 2 (215 pages) covers the "how-to-do-it." The imbalance is not so bad as it might appear, as the "how to" is actually a detailed discussion of acquisition activities. Some of the topics covered include preparing a checking manual (84 pages), the order manual, gifts and exchange, approval plans, "useful" forms, statistics, accounts, bibliographic departments, clerical positions, and "explanations and defenses of operations."

Despite its coverage of all the basic activities of acquisitions and Grieder's statement that acquisition work is the same in all types of libraries, this is a book about large research library acquisitions. A serious problem is the tone of the book. I believe everyone should have a certain amount of cynicism; certainly library school students need to know about the "real world." Unfortunately, Grieder, in expressing his opinion about life in the acquisitions department, presents a very bleak picture. In part 1, he complains about everyone except acquisition librarians and never bothers to support his statements: "university administrators tend not to understand the concerns of their faculties" (p. 3); "university administrators will not usually be concerned about the library unless the student and faculty opinion seems to indicate that the library is not functioning properly" (p. 4); "the faculty is at least somewhat engaged in distributing some kind of learning" (p. 4); "acquisition librarians who have to deal with faculty unpredictabilities sometimes feel as if they were dealing with perverse and malevolent children. But they must remember that patience can educate almost anyone" (p. 4); and, finally, "if used as selectors, reference librarians have a propensity for ordering the same title over and over again and for presenting requests in illegible formats lacking correct (or even worse, containing incorrect) and essential bibliographic details" (p. 10). With what appears to be a negative attitude underlying his approach to acquisition work, Grieder's ideas on the subject must be used with great care. Also, the author provides no bibliography or footnotes, although the index is adequate.

If you wish to learn the gospel of acquisition work according to Grieder, this is the definitive work. If you wish to learn about acquisition work, use the dated but still valuable *Acquisition Work*, by G. Wulfekoetter (University of Washington Press, 1961), and S. Ford's *The Acquisition of Library Materials* (American Library Association, 1973). [R: C&RL, Sept 78, p. 418; LJ, 1 Oct 78, p. 1929]

G. Edward Evans

746. Guidelines for Handling Library Orders for In-Print Monographic Publications. By the Bookdealer-Library Relations Committee, Resources and Technical Services Division. Chicago, American Library Association, 1984. 21p. (Acquisition Guidelines, No. 4). $3.00pa. LC 83-22307. ISBN 0-8389-3299-1.

In two sections, for libraries and bookdealers, the basic requirements for maintaining effective working relationships in business transactions are presented. An appendix discusses the prepayment problem, including precautionary measures for libraries considering this option. Recommendations are limited to those for U.S. publications supplied by U.S. bookdealers. Novices and experienced acquisitions librarians should review these sensible guidelines periodically. The committee's plea for mutual understanding and effective communication between bookdealers and librarians is worth noting. [R: JAL, Nov 84, p. 304]

Margaret McKinley

747. Hensel, Evelyn, and Peter D. Veillette. Purchasing Library Materials in Public and School Libraries: A Study of Purchasing Procedures and the Relationship Between Libraries and Purchasing Agencies and Dealers. Edited by Doralyn J. Hickey. Chicago, American Library Association, 1969. 148p. o.p. LC 70-88860. SBN 8389-3103-0.

This study, undertaken for the American Library Association in cooperation with the National League of Cities, under a grant from the Council on Library Resources, attempts to describe some of the library-vendor relations by examining the book purchasing routines of publicly supported state, public, and school libraries. In December 1966 a questionnaire was sent to a selected number of libraries and the findings were supplemented by visits and interviews. The bulk of this little book summarizes the data provided by initial questionnaires, followed by six case studies of public and school library systems. In addition, authors provide some general information on bidding for library books, relations with jobbers and publishers, etc. Studying a copy of this questionnaire (provided in an appendix), one has to come to a sad conclusion that its wording and range of topics covered were rather disappointing, and this may explain the fact that only 47 percent of those surveyed replied. The recommendations and general principles that conclude this study are arranged under four headings: bidding, order procedures, invoicing and payments, and determining qualifications of wholesalers. Unfortunately, they, too, add little to the value of this study, and order librarians with two or three years' practice will be already familiar with most of the problems discussed. In short, this is a rather disappointing volume on an important topic that deserves a more thorough treatment. [R: AL, Jan 70, p. 90; CLW, Feb 70, p. 372; DLQ, July 70, p. 350]

Bohdan S. Wynar

748. Melcher, Daniel, and Margaret Saul. Melcher on Acquisition. Chicago, American Library Association, 1971. 169p. index. $10.00. LC 77-158719. ISBN 0-8389-0108-5.

This is probably one of the most readable (and interesting) presentations of this subject, written by a prominent publisher who knows the library market well. Melcher hardly needs an introduction. In this book he offers a number of good suggestions for the novice as well as for the experienced acquisition librarian. An impressive range of subjects is covered, starting with such topics as "how long it should take to get a book" or "the cost of placing an order" and ending with more complicated problems (e.g., "how to buy serials to best advantage" or "the art of valuing old and rare books"). One quotation will sufficiently illustrate some of the insights Melcher incorporates in his narrative: "A university press once learned that its titles were being routinely billed at short discount by one wholesaler even though the wholesaler was buying them at long discounts, i.e., at upwards of 40 percent, depending on quantity. When questioned, the wholesaler argued that 'everybody knew' that university press books were textbooks, and that textbooks carried short discounts. He added that, in any case, he considered any book to be in the short-discount category if he couldn't buy it in sufficient quantitites to give him his 46 percent.

"The library's problem is to know where it stands. It could be better to work at a basic 35 percent with a supplier who actually supplied most university press books at 35 off than at 36 percent with another supplier who actually supplied all university press books at 10 off.

"Just how tricky this gets can be illustrated by the following story. I was once visiting a wholesaler of photographic books...."

Well, the reader will have to read this for himself. For many years the acquisition librarian was blessed with works à la Wulfekoetter's *Acquisition Work Processes Involved in Building Library Collections* (University of Washington Press, 1961) serving as "standard texts" or guidebooks to this subject. Most of them were attempts to describe certain acquisition procedures, usually of the "how we do it in our library" type. This is not a textbook, although the author more than anybody else would be qualified to write one. It is a book of common sense based on the author's rich experience, with many strong views and even some biases. And, what is more important, it is a competent work—one of few in library literature on this subject. [R: LJ, 15 Sept 71, p. 2747]
Bohdan S. Wynar

749.   Simkin, Faye. **Cooperative Resource Development: A Report on a Shared Acquisitions and Retention System for METRO Libraries.** New York, New York Metropolitan Reference and Research Library Agency, 1970. 64p. bibliog. index. (METRO Miscellaneous Publications Series, No. 5). o.p. LC 74-21665.

This report draws upon and uses recommendations from an earlier work on cooperation by Edelman and Boice. An ad hoc committee on SHARES (Shared Acquisition and Retention System) studied manageable projects that could be tested for shared acquisition. These

include: college catalogs, U.S. government documents, American doctoral dissertations on microfilm, serials in H. W. Wilson indexes, and monographs analyzed in *Essay and General Literature Index.* Inherent problems are stated, conclusions drawn, and recommendations made. [R: C&RL, Nov 71, p. 483; LJ, 1 Sept 70, p. 2775]
Charles D. Patterson

Reference Works

750.   Kim, Ung Chon. **Policies of Publishers: A Handbook for Order Librarians, 1978 Edition.** Metuchen, N.J., Scarecrow, 1978. 146p. $8.50pa. LC 77-25063. ISBN 0-8108-1098-0.

Well received in its 1976 edition (see *ARBA* 77, entry 177) this edition is much larger and now lists 500 publishers. However, only a very small percentage of all American publishers is covered, despite the increased size. Most major publishers are listed, but the smaller publishers and specialty houses, for whom information is often difficult to obtain, are generally absent. This is a guide for acquisition rather than selection personnel. Although no indication of publisher's specialties is given, Kim does provide the address of the publisher, the address to which orders should be sent if different from the company address, prepayment information, discounts, return policy, shipping and billing policy, back order policy, and standing order plans, if any. If this guide provided information on a publisher's promptness and quality of service, and if a more comprehensive list of publishers were supplied, this would be the essential acquisition tool for those ordering directly from the publisher. Another edition (1982) has been published.   G. Edward Evans

751.   Wynar, Bohdan S. **Library Acquisitions: A Classified Guide to the Literature and Reference Tools.** 2nd ed. Littleton, Colo., Libraries Unlimited, 1971. 239p. o.p. LC 77-165064. ISBN 0-87287-035-9.

This bibliography provides order librarians, researchers, library school students, and teachers with a comprehensive view of the most usable and important articles, monographs, textbooks, and reference books necessary for the organization and administration of acquisition departments and networks. The five chapters, subdivided by topic, cover the role of technical services; organization and administration of acquisitions; publishing; purchases; cooperative acquisitions, gifts, and exchanges. An extensive list of reference tools is to be found at the end of each major section. [R: LJ, 1 Jan 72, p. 45]

Introductory Texts and Manuals

752. Ford, Stephen. **The Acquisition of Library Materials**. Chicago, American Library Association, 1973. 237p. index. o.p. LC 73-9896. ISBN 0-8389-0145-X.

There are good and bad books on this subject. A good one was *Melcher on Acquisition* (American Library Association, 1971); Wulfekoetter's *Acquisition Work Processes Involved in Building Library Collections* (University of Washington Press, 1961) may serve as an example of the second category. There are also books that are, so to say, in between. They are more than just simple how-to-do-it manuals (or rather, "how-we-do-it-in-our-library" manuals), yet they are not substantial enough to serve as a point of departure for the initiated. The 16 chapters of *Acquisition of Library Materials* provide a great deal of information about purchasing out-of-print materials, micropublishing, acquiring government publications, gifts and exchanges, and the like. There are chapters on acquisitions, searching, and bibliographies used in searching. What is lacking, however, is the conceptual framework for all these operations. Some of them are presented out of focus, a fact that most readers will discover in the first chapter, "Planning for Acquisitions." [R: AB, 1 July 74, p. 30; C&RL, Sept 74, p. 376; Choice, Jan 74, p. 1704; RSR, Oct 73, p. 20; SL, Nov 73, p. 540]   Bohdan S. Wynar

Approval Plans

753. Cargill, Jennifer S., and Brian Alley. **Practical Approval Plan Management**. Phoenix, Ariz., Oryx Press, 1979. 95p. bibliog. index. $29.95. LC 79-23389. ISBN 0-912700-52-1.

This is the first book published on approval plans that is not a theoretical or polemical view of their successes or failures, their prospects or their past. It is a manual for their administration. Chapters 1-3 echo the earlier literature on the relation of approval plans to traditional acquisition methods. The rest of the book has requisite information on choice of vendors, bids and contracts, profiling, processing of books, and fiscal management. Particularly helpful is the section on problem solving, which includes a listing of the types of problems that may occur so that the administrator of the plan will be aware of tell-tale signs and correct the situation

before it becomes extreme. The book is essential for any library that is considering the use of approval plans, and as a checklist for those wishing to reexamine their local procedures. A selective bibliography is included. [R: C&RL, Sept 80, p. 469]   Sharon C. Bonk

754. McCullough, Kathleen, Edwin D. Posey, and Doyle C. Pickett. **Approval Plans and Academic Libraries**. Phoenix, Ariz., Oryx Press, 1977. 154p. illus. bibliog. (A Neal-Schuman Professional Book). $32.50. LC 77-8514. ISBN 0-912700-05-X.

The state of approval plan acquisition in academic libraries was here explored by means of a questionnaire sent to 144 academic libraries, of whom 101 replied. A large number of questions were asked in the areas of institutional setting, funding and internal accounting, organization of book collections, book selection, personnel, book selection processes, coverage and reliance, and general satisfaction. The research was conducted by a university book selector, an approval plan manager for a large book jobber, and an academic subject specialist.

A large amount of testimony and data was gathered, with many examples of variant practice and experiences. General conclusions as to the worth of approval plan acquisition are not forthcoming; the senior author states that the principal conclusion to be drawn from the survey is that the answer to this question may never be generalized. Data gathered, however, will be useful in assisting those going into approval buying in avoiding, insofar as possible, the many pitfalls. [R: C&RL, Nov 77, pp. 548-49]   George Piternick

755. Spyers-Duran, Peter, and Daniel Gore, eds. **Advances in Understanding Approval and Gathering Plans in Academic Libraries: International Seminar on Approval and Gathering Plans in Large and Medium Sized Academic Libraries, 2d, Western Michigan University, 1969**. Kalamazoo, Mich., Western Michigan University, 1970. 220p. o.p. LC 78-631886. ISBN 0-912244-08-9.

Papers presented at the Second International Seminar on Approval Plans in Large and Medium Sized Academic Libraries held at Western Michigan University on 31 October 1969. Includes experiences of seven libraries using approval plans, role of the faculty in book selection, 13 dealers describing their services, and a report on a dealers' panel and ensuing question period. The seminar took place when book budgets were not only healthy but generously augmented by federal support. The volume contains useful information but leaves unanswered fundamental questions and concerns which should be addressed both critically and statistically. [R: C&RL, July 72, p. 334; LJ, 15 May 71, p. 1688]   Charles D. Patterson

756. Spyers-Duran, Peter, and Daniel Gore, eds. **Economics of Approval Plans.** Westport, Conn., Greenwood Press, 1972. 134p. bibliog. (Proceedings of the Third International Seminar on Approval and Gathering Plans in Large and Medium Sized Academic Libraries, Held in the Ramada Inn, West Palm Beach, Florida, February 17-19, 1971). $29.95. LC 72-836. ISBN 0-8371-6405-2.

Papers presented at a conference reflecting a state-of-the-art on approval plans in academic libraries. Although uneven in both quality and style, the several chapters provide useful information on choosing, establishing, and saving money with an approval plan. No new insights given for the persistent problems surrounding approval plans. [R: C&RL, Sept 73, p. 284; LJ, 1 Mar 73, p. 718]   Charles D. Patterson

Foreign Materials

757. **Acquisition of Foreign Materials for U.S. Libraries.** 2nd ed. Theodore Samore, comp. and ed. Metuchen, N.J., Scarecrow, 1982. 218p. index. $16.00. LC 82-5963. ISBN 0-8108-1560-5.

This work is arranged in four major sections: cooperative and federal U.S. acquisition programs, sources of foreign materials (gifts, exchanges, bookdealers, auctions), acquisition programs in specific areas, and acquisition of special materials. Contributors are bibliographers, acquisitions or technical services librarians, or booksellers. Acquisition of foreign materials from both industrialized and developing areas of the world is discussed. Essays are largely practical and informative, with worthwhile suggestions for maintaining good relations with bookdealers or agents and for acquiring many types of foreign materials. The book is replete with sources of information about foreign publishing and is a worthwhile reference tool for that reason.

The first edition was a collection of papers presented at a conference on acquisition of foreign materials in 1971 (see *ARBA* 74, entry 186). Some contributors revised their essays for the second edition, others did not, and some authors are new to the second edition. There are frequent references in the second edition to material in the earlier work. The two editions

are, therefore, complementary. The first edition has not been superseded.

The essays on special materials, ephemera, and microforms are only incidentally related to foreign acquisitions. A few essays will have diminished utility because the librarian-authors devote most of their space to personal opinions and experiences likely to be of limited value to other librarians. Errors in the text resulting from the lack of careful editing will jar the sensitive reader. The flaws in this work should, however, be overlooked. Assistance is sparse for librarians who cannot specialize but must acquire materials worldwide. A primary means of mastering their craft is through obtaining the advice of experts who share their knowledge and experience, as contributors to this work have generously done. [R: JAL, May 83, p. 95; LJ, 15 June 83, p. 1238]   Margaret McKinley

758. Bloomfield, B. C., comp. **Acquisition and Provision of Foreign Books by National and University Libraries in the United Kingdom.** London, Mansell, 1972. 217p. (Papers of the Morecambe Conference, 16 April 1972). o.p. LC 72-89234. ISBN 0-7201-0299-5.

This volume relates the experience of 22 British librarians meeting to discuss mutual problems encountered in developing adequate and representative book collections from all over the world. Similarities are drawn between the British and American endeavors and also the difficulty Britain has with the United States as a foreign dealer and as a foreign "problem." The key is cooperation. [R: LJ, 1 May 73, p. 1455]
     Charles D. Patterson

759. Clarke, D. A., ed. **Acquisitions from the Third World: Papers of the Ligue des Bibliothèques Européennes de Recherche Seminar 17-19 September 1973.** London, Mansell; distr., Portland, Oreg., International Scholarly Book Services, 1975. 276p. o.p. ISBN 0-7201-0453-X.

Proceedings of a seminar of 35 invited participants from 12 countries, at the University of Sussex, England, in 1973. The seminar was held by LIBER, an international nongovernmental organization, founded in 1971 to promote cooperation among Western European research libraries. D. A. Clarke provides a brief introduction on the purpose of the meeting. The 16 papers deal with broad areas such as Asia, the Middle East, Africa, Latin America, cooperative programs in the United States, Scandinavia, and West Germany, and acquisition methods at some British and Australian libraries. The papers range from brief surveys and factual, statistical reports to scholarly, well-documented presentations; the authors are well known (three of them are Americans). The term "Third World" is not defined, and there is no connecting commentary. A one-page "Recommendations of the Seminar" gives a clue as to why American plans such as the Farmington Plan (now defunct), Public Law 480, and NPAC were discussed—apparently to serve as possible models for similar programs, which would insure that one copy of every serious publication from the Third World is acquired by a library in Europe and available on interlibrary loan. One of the participants, B. C. Bloomfield, compiled *Acquisition and Provision of Foreign Books by National and University Libraries in the United Kingdom* (Mansell, 1972), with some unavoidable overlapping. Compared with the proceedings of a 1971 institute, *Acquisition of Foreign Materials for U.S. Libraries*, edited by T. Samore (Scarecrow, 1973), this book gives more in-depth treatment; it is a welcome addition to research libraries, though the lack of an index diminishes its usefulness. [R: C&RL, Jan 76, p. 80; JAL, Jan 76, p. 25; LJ, 1 Feb 76, p. 488; LQ, Apr 76, p. 191; LRTS, Fall 76, p. 390; SL, Dec 75, p. 609] Josephine Riss Fang

760. Clouston, John Samuel. **CILA: A New Approach to Problems in the Acquisition of Latin American Library Materials.** Urbana-Champaign, Ill., Graduate School of Library Science, University of Illinois, 1974. 53p. (Occasional Papers, No. 112). $2.00pa.

More than one-half of this issue of the Occasional Papers is devoted to an excellent presentation of the problems involved in acquiring publications from Latin America. The acronym in the title comes from Centro Interamericano de Libros Académicos (Inter-American Center for Academic Books). CILA was founded in 1964 with funds from the Rockefeller and Ford Foundations, and its purpose is to promote and distribute university and scholarly press publications throughout the Americas. Books from all cooperating presses in the Americas are received at the center's headquarters in Mexico City and are later distributed to libraries that request them. Anyone involved in the acquisition of Latin American materials will find this well-written paper to be full of valuable information.

Donald J. Lehnus

Gifts and Exchanges

761. Lane, Alfred H. **Gifts and Exchange Manual.** Westport, Conn., Greenwood Press, 1980. 121p. illus. index. $22.50. LC 79-7590. ISBN 0-313-21389-5.

Alfred Lane has drawn from his long experience in the area of gifts and exchange for this handbook of recommended procedures. He provides background on the philosophy and economics of exchange as a means of collection building, and organizational and personnel considerations. Topics covered include materials available on exchange, writing exchange agreements, record keeping, and cooperative exchange programs.

Gifts are viewed broadly to include more than processing unsolicited materials. They are viewed as sources of valuable material for the library and for use in exchanges. Gifts should be solicited with "boldness tempered with respectful courtesy." Suggestions on procedures, gift policies, acceptability of gifts, estimates and appraisals, and record keeping are given. A separate chapter is devoted to rare books and manuscripts.

Another valuable chapter is on the disposal of unwanted material in ways most advantageous to the particular library. Appendices include IRS deduction guidelines, a geographic listing of appraisers, sample gift policy statements, and sample record forms. The book is recommended for any library considering this method of acquisitions and as a practical guide and standard for those already engaged in this activity. [R: BL, 15 July 80, p. 1655; C&RL, Sept 80, pp. 466-68; LJ, 15 Apr 80, p. 933]

Sharon C. Bonk

762. **Studies in the International Exchange of Publications.** Peter Genzel, ed. Munich, New York, K. G. Saur; distr., Hamden, Conn., Shoe String Press, 1981. 125p. illus. (IFLA Publications, No. 18). o.p. ISBN 3-598-20379-9; ISSN 0344-6891.

Eleven papers presented at meetings of the Section on the Exchange of Publications (now the Section on Exchange and Acquisition) of the International Federation of Library Associations and Institutions from 1977 to 1979 are brought together in this volume. Of these, three are especially noteworthy. In the opening essay the editor, Peter Genzel, provides a summary of the activities of the Section on the Exchange of Publications during the years 1970 to 1979, citing projects, publications, and papers completed during this period. Historical perspective on the principle of international exchange is provided by Vladimir Popov in his "The Multi-lateral Unesco Exchange Conventions (1958) and Their International Significance." This paper outlines the basic tenets of the two conventions regulating the international exchange of publications and discusses the advantages a country derives from ratifying and adhering to these conventions. Perhaps the most timely paper is "Exchange of Publications with Developing Countries," which discusses the problems faced by librarians in developing countries and suggests ways in which industrialized nations can improve the exchange of publications with these countries.

Among the other papers, two provide cost analyses of exchange procedures in the Gift and Exchange Section of the British Library Lending Division and in the Universal Serials and Book Exchange (USBE), while a third reports on time studies involving exchange of duplicate monographs at the Institut danois des Echanges internationaux de Publications scientifiques et littéraires (IDE). Findings from questionnaires are analyzed in another three papers: "International Book Exchange of National Libraries in the Late 70s," "The Use of Photoreproductions in International Exchange," and "Rising Book Prices and the Exchange of Publications." The remaining papers consist of a procedure for "batch cataloging" donated monographs at the British Library Lending Division and a recommended format for international exchange lists.

Most of the essays in this volume would be of interest only to a highly specialized audience. Moreover, those papers based on economic data or statistical information may no longer be as relevant as when they were originally presented. [R: JLH, Summer 83, p. 359; LQ, Oc t 82, p. 416; LR, Winter 82, p. 268; LRTS, July 83, p. 325]   Marie Ellis

763. Vanwijngaerden, Frans, ed. **Handbook on the International Exchange of Publications.** 4th ed. Paris, UNESCO; distr., New York, UNIPUB, 1978. 165p. (Documentation, Libraries and Archives: Bibliographies and Reference Works, No. 4). $14.50. ISBN 92-3-101466-8.

The fourth edition of the handbook, if one can judge from the date of the preface, took about three years to complete. It not only attempts to update information contained in the previous edition, but traces developments since 1964 in areas such as international standardization, and the role of international organizations in promoting the exchange of documents. Also included are a directory of national exchange centers, examples of standardized forms which are to be used in the publications exchange process, and the texts of relevant international conventions and their signatories.

Being a compendium of a considerable amount of information, the handbook does not lend itself to easy reading. The writing style is sometimes stiff and pretentious, but this weakness may be overlooked in view of the mass of information that is conveyed. No fewer than eight different types of exchange programs are described (including nonbook media). An entire chapter is devoted to practical organization of and procedures concerning exchange, for, as the editor notes, "[it] cannot ... be looked upon as a friendly correspondence between public-spirited librarians. It requires an administrative organization, even on a small scale, in order to ensure smooth operation" (p. 39). The roles of IFLA and UNESCO in the exchange program are then discussed, and the handbook concludes with a section on exchange centers with a national responsibility (in the United States these would include the Smithsonian Institution, the Library of Congress, and the Universal Serials and Book Exchange). In summary, this is an invaluable tool and source of information for all who are interested in the international aspects of librarianship and scholarly communication. [R: A Arch, Oct 79, p. 478]

Thomas W. Shaughnessy

Nonbook Materials

764. Emmens, Carol A., comp. and ed. **Non-Theatrical Film Distributors: Sales Service Policies.** rev. ed. New York, Educational Film Library Association, 1974. 72p. $5.00; $2.50 (members). ISBN 0-317-34120-0; 0-317-34121-9 (members).

In order to facilitate selection and replacement of films and footage, Educational Film Librarians Association has compiled this booklet. Some 137 distributors are included here along with indications of their address and phone number; the chief executive's name; type of films handled (16mm, filmstrips, etc.); extent of distribution; information or publicity sources (catalogs, newsletters, etc.); types of distribution (sales, rental, or leasing); preview policy (length of time and fee); cost of replacement footage (including limitations on what can be supplied); print replacement policy (discount for return of old copy or purchase of same title); category of films handled; subject area specialties; and types of films they are looking for (for the benefit of filmmakers).

This compilation should prove of value for all those involved in film ordering and replacement; it indicates whom to contact, company policies, and the organizations that carry appropriate materials. [R: BL, 1 Jan 75, p. 454]

Judith K. Rosenberg

SELECTION PROCESS

General Works

765. Boyer, Calvin J., and Nancy L. Eaton, eds. **Book Selection Policies in American Libraries.** Austin, Tex., Armadillo Press, 1971. 222p. bibliog. (Applications of Library Science, Vol. 3). $6.45pa. LC 77-161921. ISBN 0-912556-00-5.

An interesting anthology of 31 book selection policies in use in college, public, and school libraries. [R: LJ, 15 Mar 72, p. 992]

766. Lunati, Rinaldo. **Book Selection: Principles and Procedures.** Translated by Luciana Marulli. Metuchen, N.J., Scarecrow, 1975. 167p. $15.00. LC 75-23498. ISBN 0-8108-0846-3.

The text of this book comprises translations of chapters 2, 3, and 4 of the author's *La scelta del libro per la formazione e lo sviluppo delle biblioteche* (Florence, Olschki Editóre, 1972). Lunati's book is addressed to the need for a theory of book selection that can speak to current Italian requirements. The longest and most substantial of the three chapters is the second, "Some Important Contributions to the Literature of Book Selection." The contributors are for the most part those who are well known to Anglo-American librarians — James Duff Brown, Lionel R. McColvin, Frances K. W. Drury, Ranganathan, Helen Haines. As an indication of the extent to which Italian bibliothecal theory is dependent on Anglo-Americans, this book is significant. It provides an interesting footnote to the annals of comparative librarianship. However, it offers Anglo-Americans little if anything that is new or substantive.

The quality of the translation is quite uneven. In most passages, it is reasonably lucid, though far from sparkling; in other passages it falls victim to the stylistic infelicities that characterize American library prose at its worst. [R: C&RL, July 76, p. 379; LJ, 1 Mar 76, p. 675; LQ, Apr 76, p. 219] Richard A. Gray

767. Perkins, David L., ed. **Guidelines for Collection Development.** Chicago, American Library Association, 1979. 78p. bibliog. $5.00pa. LC 79-16971. ISBN 0-8389-3231-2.

This volume is a long-awaited establishment of guidelines for collection development. It is the result of many hours of committee deliberations, open meetings, and program meeting discussions on this topic which have spanned a six-year period. It originated with the establishment of the Collection Development Committee of the Resources Section, Resources and Technical Services Division, American Library Association.

The guidelines are grouped into four major divisions: (1) "Formulation of Collection Development Policies"; (2) "Evaluation of the Effectiveness of Library Collections"; (3) "Review of Library Collections"; and (4) "Allocation of Library Materials Budgets." There is a bibliography attached for each of those major topics.

This handy volume offers the needed framework for the consideration of collection management in all types of libraries and is a must for any library. [R: C&RL, Mar 80, pp. 169-70; JAL, Jan 80, p. 362; LJ, 15 Jan 80, p. 182; SLJ, Nov 80, p. 48]

Robert D. Stueart

768. **Proceedings of a Workshop on Collection Development and Rationalization, May 15-16, 1980.** Ottawa, Ont., Collection Rationalization Committee, Canadian Government Publishing Centre, 1982. 1v. (various paging). (Council of Federal Libraries Publication Series). $21.00pa. ISBN 0-660-51023-5.

Collection development in Canada is at the same stage as it is in the United States, if these nine essays are a true reflection of the Canadian situation. Eight of the nine articles take a totally Canadian point of view — Helen Booth, "Collection Development in a Federal Library Setting"; Kristine Pieuk, "Collection Development ... at the Finance/Treasury Board Library"; Irene Lackner, "Financial Management and Budgetary Control"; Serge Campion, "Financial Planning ... in Federal Libraries"; Frances Groen, "Evaluation of Collections ..."; Ann MacNab, "Collection Rationalization ..."; Guy Sylvestre, "Resource Collections Sharing in the 80's"; and Valarie Monkhouse, "National Resource Collection." All of the papers are well written; however, they do not have much value to persons outside the Canadian Federal Library environment. There is some value for persons interested in international librarianship but only if the individual already has a general understanding of the Federal Libraries in Canada. Groen's essay about a specific technique employed to evaluate collections in the fields of psychology and social work in Ontario academic libraries is worthwhile reading for anyone planning to evaluate an academic library collection.

The one general essay which should be read by everyone involved in collection management is by L. Houser. This article should stir up some thoughts and reactions from professionals, as it tends to make strong statements—for example, "a great disservice to librarians in this matter is the publication of Guidelines for the Formulation of Collection Development Policies by the American Library Association (ALA) in 1977. This document embodies a number of assumptions, that is, statements taken as given, about which we know a) nothing of their truth or falsity, or b) that they are demonstrably false" (p. 4).

The Groen and Houser essays make the volume worth considering for most comprehensive library collections. Without these two essays, it would not be worth the purchase price for American libraries.   G. Edward Evans

769. Spiller, David. **Book Selection: An Introduction to Principles and Practice.** 3rd ed. London, Clive Bingley; distr., Hamden, Conn., Shoe String Press, 1980. 206p. index. $15.00. ISBN 0-85157-305-3.

First appearing in 1971 (see *ARBA* 72, entry 110) with a second edition in 1974 (see *ARBA* 75, entry 220), this third edition, with "coverage much expanded," is a simplified manual for librarians, particularly public librarians and primarily for those in Britain. Its emphasis is more on book selection than on collection development, and it is so oriented to the British scene, using terms and citing reports which are familiar almost exclusively to the British, that it is difficult to imagine its usefulness to a wider audience. The physical characteristics are also lacking; several pages are badly smudged to the point of illegibility. [R: LJ, 1 Sept 81, p. 1607]   Robert D. Stueart

College and University Libraries

770. Cline, Hugh F., and Loraine T. Sinnot. **Building Library Collections: Policies and Practices in Academic Libraries.** Lexington, Mass., Lexington Books, a division of D. C. Heath, 1981. 170p. bibliog. index. $21.50. LC 80-8602. ISBN 0-669-04321-4.

Commissioned by the National Endowment for the Humanities as one of several data collection activities for its *National Enquiry into Scholarly Communication*, this book represents a very slightly modified version of the final report on academic library collection policies and practices. The authors used a "comparative case study" approach to their research. They selected seven academic libraries—Earlham College; Stockton State College; Brown University; Pennsylvania State University; University of North Carolina-Chapel Hill; University of Wisconsin-Madison; and the University of California-Los Angeles—in a nonrandom manner. "Profiles" of the seven institutions and their libraries are presented (all in less than 35 pages); this is followed by a discussion of how book funds are allocated and expended at each institution (39 pages), and how "items" are selected (38 pages). The book concludes with a 30-page chapter on organizational theory and social change.

Details are lacking in all the sections, raw data are not provided, and insights and implications for academic collection management are totally lacking. With more work and effort, the authors could have their data with information from the existing literature, and the book would have been a fine addition to the literature of the field. Nonlibrarians will learn less about the process of academic library collection development from this book than they would from any of the several good introductory collection development textbooks currently in print. At best, this book would serve as a supplemental reading item in an academic library course or a special collection development seminar. Even then it would need to be used with caution, as the cases lack the detail needed for accurate comparative analysis. A disappointing work, which fails to live up to the great potential that existed for the project to create a basis for national planning for academic library collection building. [R: JAL, Sept 81, p. 241; LJ, July 81, p. 1394]   G. Edward Evans

771. Cline, Hugh F., and Loraine T. Sinnott. **Collection Development Policies and Practices in Academic Libraries.** Princeton, N.J., Educational Testing Service, 1979. 1v. (various paging). o.p.

This is a report of collection development policies and practices in seven academic libraries, providing short profiles of participating institutions, plus a description of procedures used. Of special interest are chapters 4 and 5, presenting a description of how the librarians allocate their resources to obtain materials for the support of instructional and research programs, and some insights into the selection procedures for a number of interdisciplinary and cross-disciplinary programs. A good supplement to such texts as Futas's *Library Acquisition Policies and Procedures* (Oryx Press, 1977).   Bohdan S. Wynar

772. The Libraries of Stanford University Collection Development Policy Statement, 1980. 1st complete ed. Paul H. Mosher, ed. Stanford, Calif., Collection Development Office, Stanford University Libraries, 1981. 1v. (various paging). index. $10.00.

As an example of narrative collection development policies among U.S. research libraries, this volume may well become a classic in the tradition of its predecessor—*Book Selection Policies of the Libraries of Stanford University* (1970). It is a successful attempt to communicate conceptually and coherently the programmatic needs of Stanford's faculty and students as regards the selection and collection of all formats of materials for library use.

Forty-seven individual collection development policy statements comprise the first section of this work, arranged under six broad categories including humanities, history, and area studies; social sciences; sciences; special collections; government documents; and the J. Henry Meyer Memorial Library (Undergraduate Collection). These are followed by a section of statements from coordinate libraries, including eight individual statements for the various collecting needs of the Hoover Institution on War, Revolution, and Peace, and one statement each for the Food Research Institute Library; J. Hugh Jackson Library, Graduate School of Business; Lane Medical Library; Law Library; and Stanford Linear Accelerator Center Library.

Each statement includes information regarding the name of the subject and program, the name of the principal bibliographer, the date, and information about the program. Also included is coordinative and cooperative information; the geographical, chronological, or language descriptors used to define the nature of the collecting effort for that specific field; a description of materials collected by type, format, and publication date; special considerations which may affect the building of the collection; and the actual guide to the collection effort itself, which includes a detailed conspectus of subject or field, with selection intensity levels indicated for each subsection of a discipline or field.

Although the work is a document of the working relationship between curriculum, faculty, and collection development officers at Stanford University, academic libraries may well make use of this document for comparative purposes in the evaluation of their own collections. More important, this volume may serve as a model for collection development policy statements of other academic libraries, and should

aid administrators in creating a format for institutional self-studies which include analysis and evaluation of library programs and their relationship to curricular needs.

Indexes by subject and by Library of Congress classification number are included, as well as a listing of principal bibliographers and a statement on the acquisition pattern of the Green Library Central Newspaper Collection. The editors have also provided valuable introductory remarks regarding formats; duplication of materials; conservation, preservation, storage, and discard; reliance upon cooperative efforts with other libraries; primary curatorial and vendor areas; and selection intensity levels.

Flawed in places with lack of coordinated language and style, as well as with occasional typographical errors, this work will nonetheless serve as a valuable document and model to many academic librarians and administrators.

Edmund F. SantaVicca

School Libraries and Media Centers

773. Issues in Children's Book Selection: A School Library Journal/Library Journal Anthology. New York, R. R. Bowker, 1973. 216p. index. o.p. LC 73-13553. ISBN 0-8352-0688-2.

Readers (anthologies) in library science and other areas are an accepted phenomenon these days, even though only too frequently they offer dreary selections of articles that elicit about as much excitement as last month's newspaper headlines. The thought of reading 29 articles reprinted from just one journal is in itself reason enough to pause and take a hard look at such a collection. The articles are carefully grouped under five topics: perspectives on selection; intellectual freedom or censorship?; images; themes and genres; and past, present and future. As a reflection of the *School Library Journal* editors' efforts to publish several viewpoints on major issues, we find in a few cases separate articles supporting opposite positions. In her introduction, Lillian Gerhardt points out several questions concerning children's book selection which remain virtually untouched, awaiting the time and talent of thoughtful, research-minded librarians. [R: Choice, Nov 74, p. 1273; RSR, Jan 74, p. 16]

Christine Gehrt Wynar

774. Taylor, Mary M., ed. School Library and Media Center Acquisitions Policies and Procedures. Phoenix, Ariz., Oryx Press, 1981. 272p. index. $32.50. LC 80-23115. ISBN 0-912700-70-X.

Based on 233 selection policies and 157 questionnaires received by the author, this report of policies and procedures provides much useful information for schools and school systems which need to develop and adopt policies for the first time and for others which have policies in need of revision or expansion. Fifteen full policies varying in length from several to 15 pages of text are included, and parts of an additional 33 policies are presented. Topics covered in both sections include introductions, philosophy, objectives, responsibility for selection, recommendations, selection criteria, interlibrary loan, weeding, and challenged materials. An appendix reprints statements on library policies such as the AASL Statement on the Library Bill of Rights, which should be available to every school and used in the formulation of policies.

Emphasis is on policies for collection development. The information about acquisition or ordering procedures is limited to approximately 40 pages, and consists mainly of sample forms. The need and uses for a selection policy in each school and district are discussed in the introduction. It also includes a wise admonition not to adopt a policy from another district but to use the information in the volume to determine guidelines for the formulation of a policy that is based on local needs. This is a valuable tool for systems forming a first policy and for systems with policies that should be reviewed on a regular basis. It also gives library science students information about policies that are in use and some insight into the formulation of a policy that will be their professional responsibility. It is highly recommended for these purposes. [R: BL, 1 Sept 81, p. 53; SLJ, Oct 81, p. 106]   JoAnn V. Rogers

775. Van Orden, Phyllis J. **The Collection Program in Elementary and Middle Schools: Concepts, Practices, and Information Sources.** Littleton, Colo., Libraries Unlimited, 1982. 301p. illus. bibliog. index. (Library Science Text Series). $18.50. LC 82-15325. ISBN 0-87287-335-8.

As an in-depth look at the processes involved in the media center collection program at the building level, this work focuses on the internal and external relationships influencing the media program and their implications for the collection program in elementary and middle schools. The work is divided into three parts: part 1 examines the collection of the media center and its relationship to the educational environment; part 2 deals with the selection of materials, examining both general selection criteria and specific criteria based on format and

special needs of users; part 3 pertains to administrative concerns, such as acquisition and maintenance, and the evaluation of the collection. The appendix provides lists of associations, agencies, and selection tools to aid in these processes. [R: BL, 15 Oct 82, p. 319; JAL, Sept 82, p. 239]

Other Topics

776. **Alternative Materials in Libraries.** James P. Danky and Elliott Shore, eds. Metuchen, N.J., Scarecrow, 1982. 245p. bibliog. index. $16.00. LC 81-21353. ISBN 0-8108-1508-7.

Culminating a study funded by grants from the Library Research and Demonstration Program of the United States Office of Education, this book presents 12 essays, a project report, and a list of sources identifying alternative-press materials. The study, the Alternative Acquisitions Project, 1979-80, sought to clarify the relationship of college libraries' acquisitions and alternative presses' publications. Various explanations are offered for the slight level of acquisitions of materials from noncommercial, independent presses whose products are not listed in traditional bibliographies or reviews, nor carried by traditional distributors.

Essays compare the alternative presses to the pamphlet presses of colonial America and find the contemporary publishing vanguard more timely and accurate than commercial publishers of books or periodicals. Other essays explain that broad bases of information sources are necessary for library collections. Lists of alternative-press distributors are included in some essays, in addition to the list of sources at the end of the book.

Much of the expository material in this book includes banner waving as well as explanatory rhetoric. The essays aim at motivating libraries to rectify the shortage of alternative-press materials in their collections. For librarians whose ideals include broad-based, current, and culturally representative collection development, this book is particularly valuable. However, any library will find this book a useful addition to its reference collection. [R: JAL, July 82, p. 182]   George V. Hodowanec

777. Atkinson, Frank. **Fiction Librarianship.** London, Clive Bingley; distr., Hamden, Conn., Shoe String Press, 1981. 107p. illus. bibliog. index. (Outlines of Modern Librarianship). $12.00. ISBN 0-85157-293-6.

This brief work (99 pages, excluding the final bibliography and index) treats a topic which is generally a part of collection development/materials selection texts. Although there is a one-page preface, the book lacks an introduction to explain its aims, objectives, and intended audiences. It appears most appropriate as a quick review for British "student librarians." The author is a recognized contributor to the British library scene. He has published a book on public libraries, as well as an introduction to the profession and two dictionaries.

The book's scope is broad, including the history of the "fiction problem"; selection, acquisition, and processing; binding, preservation, and reprints; promoting fiction; fiction for children and young people—in public libraries. There is a chapter on fiction in other types of libraries, and one on "future trends." A short list of references/further reading consisting of predominantly British citations follows each chapter.

The book's value and usefulness as a text or as supplementary reading for library school students or public librarians in the United States are limited by its British perspective and emphasis. For example, such terms as "country librarian" or "area librarian" (pp. 36, 37) and cost/money figures quoted in pounds (pp. 91, 92) are puzzling to a non-British reader. Because of the difference in the growth of British versus American librarianship, as well as differences between the British and American publishing and literary scenes, it is difficult to understand fully many aspects of the book. In addition, the book's scanty treatment of difficult and complex topics, such as censorship and sexism/racism in children's books, raises more questions than it answers. In sum, the work is of limited practical value to librarians in this country. Its importance for American librarians, library educators, and library school students is in the area of comparative librarianship. For example, cooperative ventures in Great Britain related to fiction is a topic of potential interest in this context. The book can be a useful addition to large, well-established library science collections, providing support for courses which use a comparative approach.

Susan J. Freiband

778. Hoffmann, Frank W. **The Development of Library Collections of Sound Recordings.** New York, Marcel Dekker, 1979. 169p. bibliog. index. (Books in Library and Information Science, Vol. 28). $39.75. LC 79-23064. ISBN 0-8247-6858-2.

While the scholar views recordings as primary documents of performance practice, the lay public sees them in an entertainment role,

and the library profession has made a valiant attempt to ignore them altogether. The need for a book on this subject is evident. Written two years after Hoffmann's dissertation on a related subject, the work devotes proper attention to selection of recordings and equipment, care, and cataloging, projecting throughout a philosophy in favor of the entertainment role. For the less musically trained librarian, Hoffmann offers more than 30 pages of acquisition recommendations wherein he displays that same weakness, mingling obscure pieces with major works, all evidently selected without any assistance. The book is handsomely produced from typescript, riddled with typos and split infinitives. An annotated bibliography of discographical journals could be of some help, were the details current, but it ignores such basic periodicals as the Schwann publications, *Ethnomusicology, Gramophone*, and the *Bielefelder Katalog*. Despite promises to the contrary, no consideration is given to classification. Specific figures related to budget matters are, of course, already part of the history. Had this work been developed with some formal guidance from the Music Library Association or the Association for Recorded Sound Collections, it might have been able to serve its purpose. [R: C&RL, July 80, p. 379]   Dominique-René de Lerma

779. Pascarelli, Anne M., with the assistance of the Committee on Library of the New York Academy of Medicine. **The New York Academy of Medicine Library Collection Development Policy.** New York, New York Academy of Medicine, 1982. 65p. index. o.p.

One of the popular activities in medical librarianship is compiling written policy statements describing how particular functions are carried out in individual institutions. The New York Academy of Medicine, one of the outstanding medical research library facilities in the United States, has expanded this trend by marketing its collection development policy. This very brief text follows the format established in the *Scope and Coverage Manual of the National Library of Medicine*. Medical libraries that are interested in seeing how such reports are created would be better advised to borrow NLM's report.

This extremely small work describes the main facets of this institution's various collections, such as historical materials, dictionaries, government documents, and directories. Unfortunately, not enough information is presented on these categories to guide other libraries in establishing their own collection development policies. Also, because of the unusual size and scope of, and financial support for, the New York Academy of Medicine, most medical libraries affiliated with a single school will find this document difficult to emulate in their own institutional setting. Twenty pages of this report present an unnecessarily detailed breakdown of the New York Academy of Medicine's subject headings by LC and NLM call numbers, thus leaving merely 34 pages of text describing the collection policy. No effort is made to explain how this collection development policy evolved.

The only substantial use of this publication is to describe the library holdings in the New York Academy of Medicine. Medical libraries interested in writing their own collection development statements will profit more from borrowing similar reports from NLM or more traditional medical school libraries, such as the one available from the University of Texas Health Science Center, Dallas. [R: LJ, 15 Mar 83, p. 564]   Jonathon Erlen

780. Wertheimer, Leonard. **Books in Other Languages, 1979: A Guide to Selection Aids and Suppliers.** Ottawa, Ont., Canadian Library Association; distr., New York, K. G. Saur, 1979. 144p. $15.00pa. ISBN 0-88802-125-9.

The fourth edition of this selection/acquisition guide includes five introductory sections on library service in other languages, children's books, languages in general, records and tapes, and large print books. Immediately following are 58 sections arranged alphabetically by language. These sections have a maximum of two subdivisions each for selection aids (reviewing sources) and suppliers. Some sections do not include selection aids, although each language does list at least one supplier. Listings in either the selection aids or suppliers sections may include a numerical code(s) given in brackets. A five-language key to these 38 potential codes, which indicate additional information concerning a source or supplier, is provided in the front of the book.

Libraries' continuing need for book trade information is addressed by this work, although most of these addresses may be found in the annual *International Literary Market Place* published by Bowker. The main value of *Books in Other Languages* is that it is arranged by language rather than country. The editor acknowledges that errors may crop up in entries, but that caveat does not detract to any degree from its usefulness. [R: BL, 15 May 80, p. 1381]
Ronald Rayman

SELECTION AIDS

College and Research Libraries

781. Bertalan, Frank J., ed. **The Junior College Library Collection.** 1970 ed. Newark, N.J., Bro-Dart Foundation, 1970. 503p. o.p. LC 76-122455. SBN 87272-012-8.

An expansion of the first (1968) edition of this work, the present volume lists "basic, dependable, and useful titles for the libraries of two-year colleges," recommended by subject specialists. Approximately 21,000 titles appear in classified arrangement by the Library of Congress class numbers, textbooks being omitted. There is an author index. The work appeared the year after *Books for Junior College Libraries* (American Library Association, 1969). [R: WLB, Feb 71, p. 597]

782. **Books for College Libraries: A Core Collection of 40,000 Titles.** 2nd ed. Chicago, American Library Association, 1975. 6v. index. $80.00pa./set. LC 74-13743. ISBN 0-8389-0178-6.

This work, affectionately known as *BCL II*, is, of course, the successor to *BCL I* (American Library Association, 1967). The number of 40,000 titles (the actual count is 38,651) was chosen because it represents four-fifths of the 50,000 minimum that the 1959 ALA Standards require for even the smallest four-year academic library. The remaining one-fifth, or 10,000 titles, each individual college is expected to choose in accordance with its own particular curricular needs.

The compilation was under the jurisdiction of the Association of College and Research Libraries, which was aided by a subvention of funds from the Council on Library Resources. The authority for the selections rested in a group of teaching scholars, specialist librarians, and staff members of professional associations, many of whom were *Choice* reviewers. Working from *BCL I* as a base, the *BCL II* team expanded, pruned, and modified the list as necessary. In most cases, final selections represented a consensus of contributor opinion.

The editors admit to a liberal arts bias, a concession that was absolutely necessary, given the extreme thinness of the offerings in science and technology. Part of the reason for this comparative neglect of science is the stress that *BCL II* places on monographs. There are no periodicals and only a few serials. Since science, even at the undergraduate level, places its prime reliance on serials, the science sections are inevitably meager.

The arrangement is by modified LC Classification. A modification was used to effect a coherent structure of the bibliography in five paperbound parts: 1, "Humanities"; 2, "Language and Literature"; 3, "History"; 4, "Social Sciences"; 5, "Psychology, Science, Technology. Bibliography" (LC's "Z" class). Volume 6 is an author/title index. The entries are LC catalog cards in *run-on* style, hence the elements or fields are identical to those of LC cards.

The root questions, of course, are: how good is selection? And has ACRL really identified four-fifths of the 50,000 titles that every four-year academic library worthy of the name must have?

On prima facie grounds, the effort itself seems presumptuous. Therefore, one is justified in viewing the results with skepticism. It was noted above that the editors concede the thinness of their science offerings; however, the situation is worse even than they imagine it to be. There are serious gaps in basic science monographs, particularly in reference works. Under QH (natural history, biology) only three dictionaries and encyclopedias are cited. Because of the decision against including serials, no abstracting and indexing services are cited, an omission which for science reference is almost fatal.

Serials aside, the number of monographs cited in the various "Z" categories are suspiciously few. Under Z5351-5360 (botany) two titles are listed. Under Z5521-5526 (chemistry) likewise there are two titles, both of which are out-of-date.

The books cited under the several subheadings of library science are both insufficient in number and unbalanced. Under Z678-686 (library administration), there are precisely four titles, two of which deal with library architecture. Other library science sections, Z675 and Z710-715 (reference circulation), not only contain citations to books that are inappropriate to the small college library (e.g., Wilson and Tauber's *The University Library*) but neglect titles of high relevance. Section Z710-715 lists only one book on reference, Gates's *Guide to the Use of Books and Libraries*. The selection of professional literature is definitely not appropriate to the needs of the managers and staff members of libraries with collections in the 50,000-volume range. [R: BL, 1 May 76, p. 1284; C&RL, Jan 76, p. 71; LJ, 1 Mar 76, p. 672; LQ, Apr 76, p. 219; RQ, Fall 76, p. 77]

Richard A. Gray

783. Pirie, James W., comp. **Books for Junior College Libraries.** Chicago, American Library Association, 1969. 468p. index. o.p. LC 76-82133. SBN 8389-0074-7. (Available from Books on Demand, $116.00pa., ISBN 0-317-26556-3).

A recommended buying guide of some 20,000 books for junior and community colleges, based primarily on a working list from three junior colleges submitted for evaluation to a team of subject specialists. Entries are arranged in broad subject categories; each title entry includes author and title, subtitle, publisher (in abbreviated form), date of publication, price in the currency of the country of publication, pagination, and LC card number if available. The list is indexed by author and subject. Entries are not annotated and there are no references to published reviews in this well-balanced, recommended list for opening a collection for junior colleges or undergraduate programs. [R: BL, 1 May 70, p. 1061; C&RL, Sept 70, p. 355; CLW, Apr 70, p. 494; LQ, Oct 70, p. 453; RQ, Fall 70, p. 67; WLB, Apr 70, p. 871]

784. **Vocational-Technical Periodicals for Community College Libraries.** rev. ed. Prepared by the Bibliography Committee, Community and Junior College Libraries Section, Association of College and Research Libraries. Middletown, Conn., Choice, 1976. 44p. index. (Choice Bibliographical Essay Series, No. 4). o.p. LC 75-38838. ISBN 0-914492-03-9.

A project of the Bibliography Committee of the Community and Junior College Libraries Section of ACRL, designed to assist in the selection of periodical titles for vocational-technical programs. Rather than an evaluative or inclusive tool, the titles represent the combined holdings of community colleges selected to take part in the project. The work is divided by seven major subject areas (agricultural and natural resources programs; allied health and related programs; applied arts programs; apprentice trades programs; business, office, and related programs; engineering technology and related programs; public services and related programs) and contains bibliographies for 98 programs. Titles were verified in the 15th edition of *Ulrich's International Periodicals Directory*, the 107th edition of Ayer's *Directory of Publications*, or directly with the publisher. Citations include the title, frequency, publisher and address, and where indexed or abstracted. High priority items (those held by a significant number of colleges) are designated by an asterisk. Prices are not included, since they are subject to frequent change. Contains a subject index. An invaluable monograph, as the location of elusive periodicals and publishers on these subjects is often difficult.

Rosemary Henderson Keller

Public Libraries

785. **Books for Public Libraries.** 3rd ed. Constance E. Koehn, ed. Chicago, American Library Association, 1981. 374p. index. $20.00. LC 81-14874. ISBN 0-8389-0328-2.

This volume was first issued in 1970 (see *ARBA* 71, entry 94) with a second edition in 1975 (see *ARBA* 76, entry 147).

ALA's Public Library Association appointed a committee of 15 public librarians representing both urban and suburban libraries and assigned them the task of developing "an alternative professional book selection tool." Three task forces were organized, and working papers were prepared describing the needs of particular age groups of public library users and new trends in selection and collection development. Each committee member was assigned specific subject areas and was to develop representative public library collections in those areas. Items in the second edition of *Books for Public Libraries* were reviewed to determine their current availability, and appropriate new titles were suggested. The scope of each subject area was determined by measures of publishing activity and by surveys of consumer use of nonfiction conducted at the Cleveland Public Library. Each of these measures was for the period 1979-1980.

The result is a good basic list with an emphasis on titles that have proved themselves useful. The arrangement of titles follows the nineteenth edition of Dewey (1979). Full bibliographic data are included, and there are subject and author/title indexes. The 1979-1980 completion date for entries requires that those responsible for collection development add new titles as they appear. If used as a base for collection development, adding new titles and expanding in some areas to meet specific community needs, this will be a most useful tool. [R: BL, Aug 82, p. 1505; JAL, May 82, p. 108]

Ann E. Prentice

786. Wilson, Pauline. **A Community Elite and the Public Library: The Uses of Information in Leadership.** Westport, Conn., Greenwood Press, 1977. 172p. bibliog. index. (Contributions in Librarianship and Information Science, No. 18). $27.50. LC 76-15336. ISBN 0-8371-9031-2.

This is not an especially important title. The first third of the book is devoted to assessing current library literature on public library clientele and service. Wilson cites Berelson, Shera, and a wealth of others and concludes that libraries are a bibliographic system, they serve primarily a select percentage of the public, and they play a nonmotivating role. The remainder of the book is devoted to Wilson's study of four social activist groups. She attempts to define what these groups' information sources and needs are and to provide guidance for collection building in public libraries. Wilson's research cannot be faulted, nor can her conclusions: that there is little need for libraries to acquire specialized tools for activist groups, but that libraries should concentrate on building a stronger reference collection and buying current books on social problems. However, this will not be news to most public librarians. [R: JAL, Nov 77, p. 290; JAL, July 77, p. 170; LJ, Aug 77, pp. 1584-85]

Saul J. Amdursky

School Libraries and Media Centers

787. American Library Association. Association for Library Services to Children, and Young Adult Services Division. **Selecting Materials for Children and Young Adults: A Bibliography of Bibliographies and Review Sources.** Chicago, American Library Association, 1980. 74p. index. $7.00pa. LC 80-12374. ISBN 0-8389-3241-X.

Prepared jointly by the Association for Library Services to Children and the Young Adult Services Division of ALA, this bibliography of bibliographies and review sources is a revision of a list issued in 1967. This edition is comprehensive in subject coverage, briefly describing nearly 300 titles. Included are selective lists, review sources, reference guides, and bibliographies by subject: literature, science and mathematics, social studies, special needs, and other topics such as biographies. A directory of publishers and a title index are included. The cutoff date is 1979, and the listings checked seem to be quite up-to-date and inclusive. The list includes sources for print and nonprint materials that are important to school and public libraries. Recommended for all collections serving youth and professionals working with young people. [R: BL, 15 July 80, p. 1679]

Christine Gehrt Wynar

788. **Books for Secondary School Libraries.** 6th ed. Compiled by the Ad Hoc Library Committee of the National Association of

Independent Schools. New York, R. R. Bowker, 1981. 844p. index. $34.95. LC 80-26369. ISBN 0-8352-1111-8.

This work first appeared in 1968. For a review of the fifth edition, see *ARBA* 77 (entry 231. This edition of *Books for Secondary School Libraries* was prepared by Pauline Anderson, coordinating editor, Rita Adams, and Mary Lou Treat. The volume lists more than 9,000 titles, an increase of about 3,000 entries from the previous (1976) edition. It is intended as "a comprehensive bibliographic guide and selection aid for librarians, teachers, administrators and others involved in developing book collections to meet the needs of college-bound students" (preface). Fiction is omitted. A seven-page section at the beginning of the book is devoted to professional tools, and a separate section lists more than 500 reference works. Entries include author, title, publisher, date of publication, price, and paperback publisher and price. In addition, there are subject tracings for most entries. The arrangement of the volume is in shelflist order by Dewey Decimal Classification number. Entry numbers are assigned consecutively through the volume, and references in the author and title indexes are to these numbers. There are no annotations. New to this edition is a subject guide, an alphabetical listing of the subject tracings. Each subject in the subject guide is followed by one or more Dewey numbers indicating location in the book. A directory of publishers with their addresses is appended.

Books for Secondary School Libraries in this edition has expanded coverage in practically all subject areas including religion and philosophy, which together include 756 titles, and fine and decorative arts and recreation, which now include more than 1,000 titles. But the basic emphases in the list continue to be on the standard precollege curriculum and the presumed interests of the college-bound. The social sciences, geography, travel, and history, literature, and the pure sciences account for more than 6,000 entries.

This selection guide will continue to be useful for all senior high school libraries. There is minimal overlap with H. W. Wilson's *Senior High School Library Catalog*, and it will serve as a complement to that guide for books that in general are on a somewhat more advanced level than is usual in the typical high school library. [R: BL, 15 Apr 81, p. 1148]   John Farley

789. Brown, Lucy Gregor, with the assistance of Betty McDavid. **Core Media Collection for Elementary Schools.** New York, R. R. Bowker,

1979. 263p. index. $18.95. LC 79-6969. ISBN 0-8352-1162-2.

The core media collection gathered for this guide encompasses some 16mm films, 35mm filmstrips, and other assorted nonprint formats recommended by a wide range of review journals and media specialists as suitable for instructional use in grades 7-12. Organization of the guide is essentially the same as the 1975 edition (see *ARBA* 76, entry 156). It features arrangement by *Sears* subject headings, with ample cross-references; DDC numbers and cataloging data; contents and brief annotations; and citations to recommending sources. A directory of producers/distributors is a helpful appendix. The stated 3,000 nonprint titles in the collection include all separate parts within a series or set; the number of actual title entries is much less — an estimated 1,400 items. Releases prior to 1973 are excluded in this edition.

Criticism of the guide rests more on the underdeveloped state of audiovisual reviewing and bibliographic access than on what is included in the collection itself. Brown accomplished a great deal in searching out this list of hard-to-find items. While the coverage is far from complete in scope or in depth, media specialists have in this one volume a valuable aid for developing existing media libraries or for initiating a new audiovisual collection. [R: WLB, Apr 80, p. 525]   Christine Gehrt Wynar

790. National Council of Teachers of English. Committee on the Elementary School Booklist. **Adventuring with Books: A Booklist for Pre-K —Grade 6.** new ed. Mary Lou White, ed. Urbana, Ill., National Council of Teachers of English, 1981. 472p. index. $9.75pa.; $7.50pa. (NCTE members). LC 81-11179. ISBN 0-8141-0075-9.

The 1981 edition of *Adventuring with Books* is an annotated list of 2,500 books chosen for high potential interest to children and for literary quality. Two other emphases are added in this new edition: treatment of minorities and the recognition of quality books of the past.

This version of the popular source covers the years 1977 through 1980. The range of the list is kindergarten through grade 6, and age level is indicated for each book. The typical annotation includes full bibliographic information, a two- or three-sentence plot summary, and an evaluative comment. Picture books are identified as such in the annotation, and Newbery and Caldecott Award and Honor Books are noted. The editor, Mary Lou White, says that the purpose of the book is "to inform teachers of recently published good books to share with children." It is also valuable for librarians, media specialists, and students of children's literature.

The book is organized into the following categories: wordless picture books, traditional literature, modern fantasy, science fiction, historical fiction, contemporary realistic fiction, poetry, holidays, concepts, social studies, biography, sciences, sports and games, the arts, language, crafts, hobbies, amusements, and professional. There is no subject index, and these 19 categories are separated into nearly 200 subject subdivisions, making the table of contents difficult to use. The subject specificity, however, makes locating related books easy. A well-planned subject index would have provided more effectively for subject entry while providing for the inclusion of secondary subjects where needed.

At the end of each major category is a list of noteworthy books of the past. These older books are not annotated. A publisher directory and separate indexes of authors and titles are included. A particularly noteworthy feature is a section on professional materials in children's literature. This annotated list of 68 sources published between 1976 and 1980 is helpful to librarians searching for reference sources and to persons attempting to stay abreast of developments in the field. It is encouraging to see so many quality professional materials being published in the field of children's literature.

NCTE's list remains one of the best sources of information on books of high quality and interest. For a review of the 1977 edition, see *ARBA* 78 (entry 189). [R: BL, 1 Feb 82, p. 710; Choice, Mar 82, p. 893; Emerg Lib, Jan 82, p. 27]   Patricia Tipton Sharp

791.   Peterson, Carolyn Sue, and Ann D. Fenton. **Reference Books for Children.** Metuchen, N.J., Scarecrow, 1981. 265p. index. $16.00. LC 81-5660. ISBN 0-8108-1441-2.

This revision of *Reference Books for Elementary and Junior High School Libraries* by Carolyn Sue Peterson (see *ARBA* 71, entry 156 and *ARBA* 76, entry 162) offers evaluative annotations for nearly 900 titles of interest to children and adults working with them. The introductory sections include an informative discussion about reference services to children, general criteria for evaluating reference sources, and criteria for specific types of reference works. Titles are arranged by type (almanacs, review sources, etc.) or subject covered (humanities, recreation, social science, etc.), subdivided by specific topics. Within these groupings titles

are arranged alphabetically. Cross-references are provided. The entries provide full bibliographic information, a description of the work, possible audience, and comparison with other works, and point out aspects which the librarian should consider before deciding to purchase the item.

Both this guide and Wynar's *Guide to Reference Books for School Media Centers* (3rd ed., Libraries Unlimited, 1986) cover selection tools and reference sources. [R: BL, 1 Dec 81, p. 506]   Phyllis J. Van Orden

792.   Richardson, Selma K. **Periodicals for School Media Programs.** Chicago, American Library Association, 1978. 397p. index. o.p. LC 77-25069. ISBN 0-8389-0243-X. (Available from Books on Demand, $104.80, ISBN 0-317-26568-7).

Continuing and building upon earlier works by Marian H. Scott (see *ARBA* 70, vol. 1, p. 22 and *ARBA* 74, entry 171), Selma Richardson has re-evaluated more than 500 periodicals for school youngsters in grades K-12. She supplies entirely new annotations about periodicals listed in the 1973 edition and identifies others that will be useful in school libraries. This selection tool provides a guide to periodicals (including foreign and ethnic) in a wide range of subjects, giving title; publisher; address for subscription; grade levels; frequency of issue; 1976 price for schools; a precise, honest, evaluative annotation; the source in which the periodical is indexed; and cross-references to other magazines and newspapers covering the same topic. Richardson also gives her criteria for selection and ideas for the use of the periodicals recommended. *Periodicals for School Media Programs* belongs on all school librarians' reference shelves as a useful selection tool. [R: BL, 15 May 78, p. 1499]   Ruth I. Gordon

793.   Winkel, Lois, ed. **The Elementary School Library Collection: A Guide to Books and Other Media, Phases 1-2-3.** 15th ed. Newark, N.J., Bro-Dart Foundation, 1984. 1070p. index. $79.95. LC 83-14383. ISBN 0-87272-090-X.

The Elementary School Library Collection is designed to be used as a tool in the evaluation, maintenance, and development of existing collections, and in the establishment of new library media centers. Because of its format, it can also be used as a cataloging aid.

This fifteenth edition contains 11,335 titles of recommended books, periodicals, filmstrips, recordings, kits, art and study prints, videocassettes, microcomputer programs, and games. Titles are chosen for their ability to implement the elementary school curricula as well as their interest and appeal to children in preschool through grade 6. Grade level and interest level are provided for each title, and acquisition priorities are indicated.

According to the introduction, this book describes "a minimum collection of quality print and audiovisual materials recommended as essential for a school library media center serving 250 or more students," based on the guidelines given in *Media Programs: District and School* (American Library Association, 1975). Excluded are items such as textbooks, 16mm films, and maps which "do not have a range of applied use or are generally not housed in the building level library media center."

Every two years, this book is completely revised in an effort to include only those titles which are in-print, up-to-date, and of use and interest in the elementary school library. Each title is evaluated individually, and only the best are included. For this fifteenth edition, 6,680 new items were considered, but only one-third of them were used.

As in the past five editions of this book, the introduction includes a statement of the problem facing collection developers. Though all titles included were in-print at the time this book was published, this may change quickly since "in print, out of print, out of stock, and availability of books and audiovisual materials fluctuate from day to day." Collection developers have been encouraged to buy retrospectively, possibly turning to used bookstores and remainders houses for these materials.

The fifteenth edition of this book continues a tradition as a reliable source for up-to-date materials for children. It is recommended for use by elementary school libraries, public libraries, and academic libraries serving programs in library science or teacher education.

Annette Pekarek

794. Wynar, Christine Gehrt. **Guide to Reference Books for School Media Centers.** 2nd ed. Littleton, Colo., Libraries Unlimited, 1981. 377p. index. $28.50. LC 81-2523. ISBN 0-87287-256-4.

This guide first appeared in 1973 (see *ARBA* 74, entry 173) with a supplement in 1976 (see *ARBA* 77, entry 234). The second edition of *Guide to Reference Books for School Media Centers* is a thorough revision and updating of the annotated list of selection aids and reference materials presented in the first edition and the supplement. The 1,936 entries in this edition reflect the wide range of subject areas represented in elementary and secondary school curricula as well as those topics of special interest to young people, media specialists, and school staff members. The purpose has been to provide a selective guide to media sources and reference tools designed specifically to fit this range of subject and reading-level requirements in school media centers. The scope of this volume, as well as earlier volumes, makes the guide valuable also for classes in children's materials.

Organization of the guide follows the same plan as the first edition. The first two chapters cover general bibliographic and review sources: media sources—bibliographies and catalogs of audiovisual media, including videotapes and microcomputer programs; books; government publications; periodicals and serials; and directories of publishers and producers; and media selection—review journals and indexes covering a variety of media and subjects, and sources which treat certain media formats (audiovisual, periodicals, and talking books) or grade levels (elementary, secondary, vocational). The titles selected for this chapter are general in subject coverage; selection aids and review sources in specific subject areas are listed in the subject-oriented chapters. The third chapter covers basic general reference works, including almanacs, encyclopedias, biographical sources, and quotations. The main part of the guide contains 48 subject chapters arranged alphabetically from agricultural sciences to zoology. Subdivisions by form or topic are used throughout the volume.

Each of the entries provides full bibliographic data, including LC card number. Prices quoted are those shown in *Books in Print 1980-1981* or in publishers' announcements. The code letter "E" flags entries that are suitable for elementary school students or for professional use in the elementary school. The annotations describe the content and level of presentation, and indicate strengths or weaknesses of the titles. Citations to reviews in major review sources are appended.

Selection of titles to be included was based on the appropriateness of the subject to the K-12 curriculum; the treatment of the subject in relation to students, teachers, and librarians; the accuracy, coverage, and reliability of the information; and ease of access. A determined effort was made on the part of the author to eliminate books of lesser quality and retain outstanding reference books of lasting value. The second edition contains a smaller number of entries than the 1973 guide and its supplement for this reason and because many highly specialized works, especially indexes and other references aimed at college-level users, were dropped to make room for expanded coverage of curriculum-oriented topics and for the addition of new areas of interest.

From this guide the school media specialist can select those materials for purchase which are best suited to the particular media center's needs. It is also a source for locating infrequent-ly used books which can be requested through interlibrary loan. Thus, it is both a selection and a reference tool to be consulted frequently by school media specialists, teachers, principals, and public librarians. A third edition (1986) is available. [R: BL, 1 Sept 81, p. 53; Choice, Dec 81, p. 494; WLB, Sept 81, pp. 60-61]

31 Comparative and International Librarianship

GENERAL WORKS

795. Danton, J. Periam. **The Dimensions of Comparative Librarianship.** Chicago, American Library Association, 1973. 184p. index. o.p. LC 73-7935. ISBN 0-8389-0154-9.

Written by a well-known library educator who is one of our pioneers in the field of comparative librarianship, this is a well-balanced study. It offers sound advice about the nature of international librarianship, and it tells how to design a meaningful curriculum in library school. The reader (if he is convinced that we do need to know something about library developments in foreign countries) will find here a number of convincing arguments about the educational benefits of such a program. The author also examines the deficiencies in the literature on this subject, and we feel that his observations are sufficiently documented. There are some typographical errors (see the title of Shamurin's work on page 109), but it is very difficult to avoid such errors in a work that cites so many foreign titles.

Although it is admittedly a minor point, we do not agree with Danton's assessment of the profile of the *Unesco Bulletin for Libraries*. It seems to us that quite a few of the articles in this otherwise useful journal are "pure propaganda"—and most of these are authored by East European librarians. On the other hand, since East European librarianship is still *terra incognita* for the majority of us, this is a question that does not seem to be of great concern to most people. [R: LJ, 15 Dec 73, p. 3614]
Bohdan S. Wynar

796. Foskett, D. J., ed. **Reader in Comparative Librarianship.** Englewood, Colo., Information Handling Services, 1976. 333p. index. (Readers in Librarianship and Information Science, Vol. 23). $28.50. LC 76-10124. ISBN 0-910972-61-3.

Most of the volumes in this series have been generally unsatisfactory in achieving the stated goal of drawing on material from outside the field of librarianship and/or from sources not commonly found in a professional collection. This volume is an outstanding exception.

Foskett selected 41 essays reflecting a truly international survey. He divided the essays into four categories: (1) "Comparative Librarianship as a Field Study: Definitions and Dimensions"; (2) "The Comparative Method in Practice: Examples and Lessons"; (3) "Case Studies in Comparative Librarianship"; (4) "Comparative Studies in Technical Problems of Library and Information Science."

Part 2 draws heavily on anthropology and education (9 of 15 essays). All of the authors are persons of world status in their respective fields (L. H. Morgan, E. E. Evans-Pritchard, Brian Holmes, Pedro Rosello, etc.). The librarians included are equally well known and represent almost every major region of the world (L. Asheim, D. Collings, S. Simsova, M. A. Kwakwa, N. Sharify, etc.). If there is any real fault with the selection, it is the somewhat heavy reliance placed on *International Library Review* as a source of material (9 essays). However, this small fault is more than offset by one original paper (S. I. A. Kotei) and the publication of three "unpublished" papers presented at IFLA and FID. As with other successful volumes in the series, this one has an excellent index, but then would you expect less from D. J. Foskett?

A real possibility as a textbook in courses on comparative librarianship and well worth reading for anyone interested in the world of librarianship.   G. Edward Evans

797.   Garde, P. K. **The United Nations Family of Libraries.** New York, Asia Publishing House, 1970. 252p. index. $5.50. SBN 210-22282-4.

Describes the origin and development of the libraries of the United Nations and its specialized agencies. Of special interest are the chapters on the UN libraries in Geneva and The Hague. The Dag Hammarskjöld Library receives a rather sketchy treatment, but of course there is much material on this subject in other sources. There is a rather comprehensive bibliography appended to this handy volume. [R: JLH, Oct 72, p. 378]

798.   Harvey, John F., ed. **Comparative & International Library Science.** Metuchen, N.J., Scarecrow, 1977. 286p. index. o.p. LC 77-8923. ISBN 0-8108-1060-3.

The title of this collection of writings brings into focus a distinction between *comparative studies* and *international involvement* in librarianship, or, as the editor prefers, in library science. The book is divided into two parts, the first of which reviews definitions and research; the second, recent progress. In part 1, J. Periam Danton reaffirms his acceptance of his own definition of comparative librarianship as advanced in 1973 (see his *Dimensions of Comparative Librarianship*, American Library Association, 1973), and he endorses J. Stephen Parker's 1974 definition of international librarianship (*Journal of Librarianship* VI [October 1974]: 219-32). D. J. Foskett surveys methodologies and studies in other fields, primarily in the social sciences, and urges the continuing use of systematic analysis and comparison in librarianship. Frank L. Schick warns of the problems encountered in research, notably those relating to standardization. Part 2 consists of 14 appraisals of nearly all of the major fields *except*, as the editor regretfully acknowledges, in library literature, special library science, archives studies, law library science, university library science, and the international dispersal of library science ideas. While such omissions weaken the volume as a whole, they in no way lessen the import of the contributions included.

Internationalism permeates the writings of David Kaser, Norman Horrocks, John G. Lorenz, Anthony Thompson, and Mohammed M. Aman. Kaser ("International Organizations") assesses the work of nine international organizations, noting their weaknesses but also the movement toward library cooperation and standardization. Horrocks ("National Organizations"), after viewing international activities of national library associations (in North America and Great Britain only, however), concludes that international involvement is at "something of a crossroads." Lorenz ("National Library Services") enumerates the international programs and activities of national libraries and of international agencies such as UNESCO, anticipates the creation of a National Library Association, and predicts increased sharing of bibliographic resources and information at both the national and multinational levels. Thompson ("Multi-Culturism, Libraries and International Terminology") relates the increase and interest in terminological works, which in librarianship are being more slowly coordinated than in other disciplines, to the development of multiculturism. Aman ("Comparative and International Bibliography") attempts, all too briefly, to survey world bibliographic activities both national and international. Aman, like Schick, recognizes the need for, and urges the adoption of, international standards.

The remaining contributors address progress in (1) types of libraries, (2) information science, and (3) library education. In addition to "Public Libraries" (H. C. Campbell), "Children's Library Science" (Anne Pellowski), and "School Librarianship" (Frances L. Carroll, with assistance from the IFLA Section for School Libraries), there are two brief contributions, "Health Library Science" (Joan Campbell) and "Art Library Science" (Judith A. Hoffberg). The latter two, plus "The Changing Role of Audiovisual Media" (Donald P. Ely) and "Information Science" (B. C. Vickery and A. G. Brown), extend the parameters for comparative and international studies far beyond the traditional. In "Library Education," Carroll notes the diversity in national and regional programs and in programs and opportunities offered by international short courses and international activity. Carroll concludes that an international approach is evident in the future planning of library education. Martha Boaz supplements Carroll's international review with a summary of her inquiry concerning courses in comparative and international studies in 56 schools that responded to her questionnaire.

Most of the contributors are known for their international or transnational activities. Since they all are primarily American (United States), British, or Canadian, an Anglo-American/European perspective is apparent. Some of the writing is descriptive rather than comparative; some is repetitive of information found elsewhere; all is informative and, in general, optimistic. A selective bibliography, largely of citations in English, accompanies each contribution. The editor, through his selection of contributors (and they, through their research) has added a book of distinction to the growing body of knowledge essential to an awareness of the international scene. [R: C&RL, Jan 78, p. 71; JAL, May 78, p. 96]

Sarah K. Vann

799. Koops, Willem R. H., and Joachim Wieder, eds. **IFLA's First Fifty Years: Achievement and Challenge in International Librarianship.** Munich, Verlag Dokumentation; distr., New York, K. G. Saur, 1977. 158p. (IFLA Publications, 10). $65.00. ISBN 3-7940-4430-4.

Koops and Wieder have selected 15 essays about the International Federation of Library Associations and Institutions (IFLA) to commemorate IFLA's fiftieth anniversary. The editors selected essays to reflect the range of IFLA's history and goals, from "An Outline of IFLA's History" to "A Prospective View on IFLA's Future." The essays are arranged in a logical order, beginning with the historical examination, proceeding to discussions of various aspects of IFLA and its relations with member nations, and concluding with essays on the future of the organization. Included are personal reminiscences of two past presidents of IFLA, Sir Frank Francis and Herman Liebaers. *IFLA's First Fifty Years* serves as a valuable overview of international librarianship. [R: JLH, Spring 79, p. 242]

800. Krzys, Richard, and Gaston Litton, with the assistance of Ann Hewitt. **World Librarianship: A Comparative Study.** New York, Marcel Dekker, 1983. 239p. bibliog. index. (Books in Library and Information Science, Vol. 42). $38.50. LC 82-22213. ISBN 0-8247-1731-7.

Assisted by eight "area research associates," authors Krzys and Litton have very carefully and precisely developed a comparative study of librarianship on five continents, the purpose of which is to "expand the readers' perception of librarianship from an activity practiced within the confines of a library to a profession serving people throughout the world."

This introductory textbook is arranged in two major sections – "Philosophy and Theory" and "The Study" – followed by several visionary conclusions. The three chapters in the first section, by Krzys and Litton, deal with the concepts of world study in librarianship and the underlying research methodology. In half of the four chapters in section 2, the authors have collaborated with the area research associates in presenting an outstanding historical survey and analysis of world librarianship: the Middle East, Asia, Africa, Western Europe, Eastern Europe, the Soviet Union, Latin America, the United States and Canada, and Australia/New Zealand/Oceania.

World Librarianship is a good text with a good index. Its primary audience will probably be advanced library science students and faculty researchers. Despite the stiff price, most library school libraries will want to add it to their collections. [R: LQ, Apr 84, p. 202]

Charles R. Andrews

801. Line, Maurice B., and Joyce Line, eds. **National Libraries.** London, Aslib, 1979. 328p. bibliog. index. (Aslib Reader Series, Vol. 1). $27.00pa.; $22.50pa. (Aslib members). ISBN 0-85142-116-4.

This work contains 30 papers in English and one in French that previously appeared in 7 monographs and 10 serials published between 1955 and 1977 in Denmark, France, Great Britain, India, the United States, and West Germany. Divided into three subject groups, each preceded by a brief introduction, the readings deal with (1) the nature and aims of national libraries, (2) special functions and aspects of national libraries, and (3) national libraries in individual countries and areas of the world. The authors of the papers – such distinguished authorities as Hedwig Anuar, K. W. Humphreys, K. Kalaidzieva, L. Quincy Mumford, and S. R. Ranganathan – discuss national libraries on every continent. As might be expected, the British viewpoint is represented more fully than others.

Following all the readings, the editors have supplied a pithy concluding commentary, an annotated bibliography of 53 references to further sources (arranged topically in the same manner as the readings), and an author index to all papers that are either reprinted in this volume or listed in the bibliography. The inclusion of a geographical index to every national library cited would have been useful. Nevertheless, Maurice and Joyce Line have done a first-class job of selecting and organizing the material in this book. It should be of value to all librarians and library school students interested in comparative and international librarianship. [R: LJ, 1 Oct 79, p. 2048]   Leonard Grundt

802. Lowrie, Jean E., ed. **School Libraries: International Developments.** Metuchen, N.J., Scarecrow, 1972. 247p. o.p. LC 72-3440. ISBN 0-8108-0526-X.

The formal establishment of the International Association of School Librarianship in 1971 was preceded by a number of meetings held from 1968 to 1971 by an ad hoc committee of the World Confederation of Organizations of the Teaching Profession (WCOTP). This volume is a collection of papers prepared for the WCOTP meetings, at which 18 countries were represented. A few of the papers were written especially for this volume. [R: CLW, Apr 73, p. 556; SLMQ, Winter 73, p. 150]

803. Price, Paxton P., ed. **International Book and Library Activities: The History of a U.S. Foreign Policy.** Metuchen, N.J., Scarecrow, 1982. 248p. bibliog. index. $16.00. LC 82-3297. ISBN 0-8108-1545-1.

Of interest primarily to students of comparative international librarianship and book activity, this small volume provides a terse documentary account of U.S. efforts between 1965 and 1969 to develop international policy in the areas of book and library activity. The word *documentary* must be stressed here, for the book is composed primarily of reprinted State Department directives and surveys inventorying regional activities and recommending future U.S. book and library policy in these areas.

Since the editor, as a member of the Interagency Committee on Books of the Council on International Educational and Cultural Affairs, was intimately involved in many of the conferences and activities surrounding establishment of the new State Department policy during this time, it is disappointing that he limits his interpretive narrative so severely. Omitted are references to any influences outside of government, influences such as professional library organizations or publisher organizations, and any personal or anecdotal observations which might have provided a more readable and interesting account of this laudable foreign policy initiative. [R: LJ, 1 Jan 83, p. 30; LR, Summer 83, p. 150]   Mary K. Fetzer

804. Sable, Martin H. **International and Area Studies Librarianship: Case Studies.** Metuchen,

N.J., Scarecrow, 1973. 166p. $15.00. LC 73-5547. ISBN 0-8108-0622-3.

International librarianship is a nebulous term that has been used and interpreted in many ways; this small volume doesn't clarify the situation. Rather—perhaps because of the misleading title—it contributes to the confusion. Although it is true that all of the cases deal with international resources, the problems presented are not unique to internationalism. Instead, they present situations that can and do occur in library organizations of all types.

The author attempts to apply the techniques implicit in case-method teaching to the subject matter of area studies and international librarianship. He has assembled 29 cases dealing with several phases of library activity—including acquisitions, reference service, cataloging, and circulation—as they relate to the international scene.

Questions following each case are designed to guide students toward case solutions and to direct their attention toward pertinent data and reference tools. The volume is reference-service-oriented, but most cases involve personnel, which makes the cases applicable to management classes as well.

Those educators who seek to use the case study technique in class will find this a very useful volume. The cases are well developed and succinctly presented. The questions at the end of each case are thought provoking.
          Robert D. Stueart

805. Simsova, S., and M. MacKee. **A Handbook of Comparative Librarianship.** 2nd ed. rev. and enl. London, Clive Bingley; distr., Hamden, Conn., Linnet Books, 1975. 548p. index. $25.00. LC 74-14856. ISBN 0-208-01355-5.

The second edition of this work follows the pattern and method of the first edition, which established comparative librarianship as a discipline and provided a bibliographic guide to the resources of study. There is nothing in the second edition that indicates a change of principle or purpose, although considerable effort has been made to amplify the introductory theoretical first part as well as the bibliographic second part. Unfortunately, this leaves considerable theoretical and bibliographical accuracy and thoroughness to be desired. While perfection in such works is beyond human achievement, in all likelihood, the reader is justified in asking for more than is presented here.

Unlike a treatise, in which the orientation of the authors would be expected and appreciated, this book attempts to summarize the method of comparative librarianship and its value as a discipline. The authors do not distinguish between comparative studies and international studies in a way that would demonstrate the most recent thinking on the subject. The treatment of comparative method is ample, but the value of the sources that follow in part 2 is not clearly delineated.

Above all else, bibliographies must be accurate. It is especially sad to see the *Encyclopedia of Library and Information Science* stubbornly cited as the *Encyclopaedia of Librarianship and Information Science* in the text, in the bibliography of references, as a source book, and in the index. So obvious an error should have caught someone's eye. That the reviewer's name was misspelled is perhaps just bad luck, but it casts doubt on all the other citations.

Nevertheless, this is an essential book for any library and for all students of comparative and international librarianship. A third edition was published in 1983. [R: LJ, 15 Sept 75, p. 1610]   Jay E. Daily

REFERENCE WORKS

806. **Collection Development Policy.** 2nd ed. Austin, Tex., The General Libraries, The University of Texas at Austin, 1981. 1v. (unpaged). index. (Contributions to Librarianship, No. 2). $15.00pa. ISBN 0-930214-10-2.

The *Collection Development Policy* is the result of a four-year project by librarians and faculty of the University of Texas at Austin. It relates the library's collecting policy to specific university teaching and research needs, as revealed in the curricula and in faculty and student interests. It is intended to coordinate collection development throughout the general libraries of the university. For each of the 59 subject policy statements, there is a detailed statement of purpose for the collection. General collection guidelines include languages, chronological and geographical guidelines, treatment of the subject, types of materials to be included, date of publication, and other general considerations. A section called "Observations and Qualifications by Subject Subdivision" provides definitions of the areas of interest and suggests the collecting level for each: minimal, undergraduate, research, comprehensive, or exhaustive.

Though the specific guidelines for this university will probably not be directly useful in other libraries, the format and content of the policy statements may provide models for other libraries preparing collection development policies. As financial resources dwindle, academic and research libraries are becoming increasingly aware of the value of such statements to avoid both duplicating purchases among library units and purchasing outside the stated limits in some subject areas.   Malcolm C. Hamilton

807. **Directory of Chinese Libraries.** Wang Enguang, Wu Renyong, and Xie Wanruo, eds. Beijing, China Academic Publishers; distr., Detroit, Gale, 1982. 500p. illus. (part col.). index. (World Books Reference Guide, No. 3). $84.00. ISBN 0-8103-4354-1.

Claimed by the distributor, Gale Research, to be the first such compilation ever published in China, this bilingual directory covers nearly 3,000 libraries in the People's Republic of China. After a brief (one and one-half pages) description of library services in China and 24 pages of photographs (8 in color) of selected libraries, the first 162 pages offer brief descriptions of 658 selected libraries with foreign holdings. This is followed by 182 pages listing Chinese libraries with addresses. As addenda, descriptions of an additional 73 libraries received too late for inclusion among the libraries with foreign holdings complete the volume.

Both the select descriptive section and the lengthier (2,887 entries) list of libraries with addresses are organized as public libraries, academic and special libraries, or college and university libraries, with group designator and an institutional number assigned each. Locating a specific library is possible through an index. Each of the entries in the address list and most of the descriptions of the libraries with foreign holdings are in both Chinese characters and English. The index, however, is only in English with Chinese names in pinyin in the roman alphabet. Rounding out the volume is an appendix listing 126 libraries with holdings greater than 500,000 volumes, arranged in order of size.

While the remainder of the volume may be of some limited use, the most useful section is the descriptions of libraries with foreign holdings, supplemented by the 73 additional institutions in the addenda. The descriptions provide detailed if succinct information on each library, including the year of its founding, overall holdings and special foci of collections, user services, publications, staffing, and address and telephone number. The directory should be of interest and value to anyone wishing to do research in China as well as to publishers, libraries, suppliers, and others seeking to contact Chinese libraries. [R: Choice, Jan 83, p. 689; LJ, 1 Jan 83, p. 42]

Hwa-Wei Lee

808.   Jovanović, Slobodan, and Matko Rojnić, comps. **A Guide to Yugoslav Libraries and Archives.** Columbus, Ohio, American Association for the Advancement of Slavic Studies, 1975. 113p. index. (The Joint Committee on Eastern Europe Publication Series, No. 2). o.p.

The rapid growth and development of libraries and specialized collections in Yugoslavia since World War II necessitated a guide to the function and purpose of these libraries, their history, organization, and future development. The present work represents such a guide. It also represents another sequel of a survey project which, initiated and sponsored by the Joint Committee on Eastern Europe of the American Council of Learned Societies (ACLS) and the Social Science Research Council (SSRC), aims at generating a series of handbooks on library and archival resources in the humanities and social sciences relative to East Central and Southeast Europe.

The data in this guide were originally prepared in the Croatian and Serbian languages by two distinguished bookmen and librarians in Yugoslavia: Matko Rojnić, Director of the National and University Library in Zagreb, and Slobodan Jovanović, formerly Assistant Director of the Narodna Biblioteka in Belgrade; the manuscripts were then translated and amalgamated into an English-language version. The arrangement is geographical, covering the six republics and the two autonomous provinces of present-day Yugoslavia. In each of the seven sections (Bosnia and Hercegovina, Croatia, Macedonia, Montenegro, Servia, The Autonomous Provinces, and Slovenia) the following information is provided for the major libraries and important archives: address, director, hours, and basic information regarding the founding and historical development. The guide also includes for each library and archive a description of the specialized materials and a listing of sources for further reference. In addition to information on libraries and archives, each section includes a brief introduction to the historical development of librarianship in the respective republic and a bibliography. The detailed and broad index and the inclusion of a glossary of special Turkish, Arabic, and Slavic terms will definitely facilitate the use of this publication. The work will be found useful by scholars, students, librarians, and researchers seeking information on the major area collections held by the leading libraries, archives, and similar repositories and on corresponding facilities and services offered by such institutions. It is recommended for all libraries. [R: C&RL, Jan 77, p. 66]   Katherine Cveljo

809.   Larouche, Irma, comp. **National Library of Canada: A Bibliography; Bibliothéque Nationale du Canada: Une bibliographie.** Ottawa, Ont., National Library of Canada, 1979. 179p. index. $11.95pa.; $9.95pa. (Canada). ISBN 0-660-50210-0.

In this bibliography celebrating the twenty-fifth anniversary of Canada's National Library, English and French works about the library are interfiled in three chronological sections. One span, 1822-1952, has citations from the first parliamentary sum voted for books to the act establishing the library. Another span, 1953-1967, records initial growth, while the final era, mid-1967-1978, coincides with new premises and recent endeavors.

In these sections, items appear alphabetically under headings of miscellaneous (monographs, briefs, papers, interviews), official publications, and periodical and newspaper articles. Familiarization suggests that the organization is suitable and the bibliographical work competent. Clear entries, some with notes, are full as to source, but exclude titles from periodicals or newspapers. Significant items may be traced through the index to the numbered documents. This comprehensive paperbound book supersedes other scattered bibliographies, and notes its sources, among them, F. D. Donnelly's *The National Library of Canada* (Canadian Library Association, 1973), a history which, together with this commendable bibliography as companion, creates satisfactory embonpoint on a subject of important, though quite limited, interest.

Claire England

810.   Nunn, G. Raymond. **Asian Libraries and Librarianship: An Annotated Bibliography of Selected Books and Periodicals, and a Draft Syllabus.** Metuchen, N.J., Scarecrow, 1973. 137p. index. o.p. LC 73-6629. ISBN 0-8108-0633-9.

Contains 353 annotated entries for books and periodical articles on this subject, plus a syllabus for a course on Asian libraries and librarianship. The book was developed from seminars in comparative librarianship (emphasis on Asia) offered at the University of Hawaii's Graduate School of Library Studies. [R: LJ, 1 Mar 74, p. 633]

811.   Pantelidis, Veronica S. **The Arab World: Libraries and Librarianship, 1960-1976: A**

Bibliography. London, Mansell; distr., Salem, N.H., Mansell, 1979. 100p. index. $18.00pa. ISBN 0-7201-0821-7.

Intended to provide coverage of the Arab world, the book includes all the member states of the Arab League and Chad. The last is included because of its high percentage of Arab population, but Nigeria, with substantial collections of Arabic library materials in its northern centers, is excluded.

The bulk of the listings, taken from books, journals, and worldwide and regional directories, are in English; only a few UNESCO French-language items are included, and an even smaller number of Arabic titles. Most of this last group were accessible to the compiler through an English-language summary. Many of the articles cited are therefore written by non-Arabs on the basis of libraries or training systems they had worked in or visited. This is not in itself a bad thing, but the absence of nearly all the Arabic-language articles makes for an unfortunate imbalance. These sources show a picture of Arabic librarianship through Western eyes, and, because of the time span covered, some of the more important or lengthier articles may describe situations more than 15 years old. A companion publication providing a listing of Arabic-language materials, perhaps with English summaries, would be most useful.

Because of the genuine dearth of materials on librarianship in the Arab world, the list has been comprehensive rather than selective, and titles covering several countries have been multi-listed under a general heading and under each country covered in their contents. This ensures maximum available information on each Arab country. [R: JAL, Nov 79, p. 293]

Margaret Anderson

812. Prasher, Ram Gopal. **Indian Library Literature: An Annotated Bibliography.** New Delhi, Today and Tomorrow's Printers and Publishers, 1971; distr., Houston, Tex., Scholarly Publications, 1973. 544p. index. $8.00. ISBN 0-88065-176-8.

This bibliography covers the period 1955 to 1970, providing listings of some 3,550 articles and books pertaining to Indian library science. Most entries are not annotated. The material is arranged according to Dewey Decimal Classification, with some modifications. In addition to books and articles directly related to library science, the author has decided to include Indian bibliographical sources. His criteria for inclusion in this area are not always clear; we find here a listing for a descriptive bibliography on Einstein's theory of relativity (entry 696). What

has this to do with India? The section on indexing services seems to have many important gaps, at least compared to the listings found in *Indian Reference Sources* (Indian Bibliographic Centre, 1972). Nevertheless, it is a useful book, and it is a good introduction to Indian library science.   Bohdan S. Wynar

INFORMATION SYSTEMS AND NETWORKS

813. Adams, Scott. **Information for Science and Technology: The International Scene.** Urbana-Champaign, Ill., Graduate School of Library Science, University of Illinois, 1973. 46p. (Occasional Papers, No. 109). $2.00pa.

Few titles published in the Occasional Papers series rate any detailed consideration as reference sources if one defines a reference source as any book "designed by its arrangement and treatment to be consulted for definite items of information rather than to be read consecutively" (*ALA Glossary*). The Adams paper is no exception to this trend; it is not, in any traditional sense, a reference tool. It is, however, a useful commentary on the "bases of American national policies relating to the international exchange of scientific and technical information." Adams, certainly one of the individuals best prepared to summarize this field, first presented these remarks for the 1972 Windsor Lectures in Librarianship at the University of Illinois. His discussion centers around three aspects of library and information science development: (1) information for postwar research and development, including efforts relating to freedom of information; (2) dimensions of international cooperation; and (3) information transfer to developing countries. Each section is approximately 15 pages long and is heavily documented to support Adams's conclusions. The report is replete with details on organizations (there is even a list of acronyms for the organizations cited), activities, and trends not easily located in other sources. Since it is unfortunately not indexed, it must be read from cover to cover for any effective use. Every librarian should read it and then place it in the circulating collection.   Laurel Grotzinger

814. Dewe, A., and J. Deunette, eds. **EURIM 3: A European Conference on the Contribution of Users to Planning and Policy Making for Information Systems and Networks.** Presented by Aslib in association with Association Nationale de la Recherche Technique, Bibliothèque Royale de Belgique, Consiglio Nazionale delle

Ricerche, Deutsche Gesellschaft für Dokumentation, NOBIN, NORDFORSK, 25-27 April 1978, Künstlerhaus, Munich, Germany. London, Aslib, 1980. 100p. illus. price not reported. pa. ISBN 0-85142-133-4.

The first EURIM on research into the management of information services and libraries was held in Paris in 1973; EURIM 2 on the application of research in information services and libraries was held in Amsterdam in 1976 (see *ARBA* 78, entry 267); and EURIM 3, with an emphasis on the users and their effects on information systems and networks, was held in Munich in 1978.

Unlike its predecessors, EURIM 3 had fewer papers but devoted more time to discusions. Of the 12 papers presented there were 2 each on networks and users; operations; compatibility and standards; finance, pricing and cost effectiveness; education and training; and international cooperation. Except for one in German and one in French, a majority of the papers are in English. The only non-European speaker was Martha E. Williams of the United States. The papers as a whole, together with the transcription of the discussions, provide an overview of developments in information systems and networks in Europe. These 100 pages contain much useful information.

Hwa-Wei Lee

815. Kraus, David H., Pranas Zunde, and Vladimir Slamecka. **National Science Information Systems: A Guide to Science Information Systems in Bulgaria, Czechoslovakia, Hungary, Poland, Romania, and Yugoslavia.** Cambridge, Mass., MIT Press, 1972. 325p. illus. index. o.p. LC 79-39164. ISBN 0-262-11046-6.

This book intends to serve as a directory of scientific, technical, and economic information centers located in the countries of the title. The first three sections discuss the common characteristics of the six national systems, while the remaining sections cover each country in more depth. The authors discuss the development, the organization, and the research programs in each country, also providing directory-type information about the existing centers (name, address, affiliation, brief description of services). A selected bibliography of pertinent publications is appended to each chapter. A well-executed book that should be of interest to all larger libraries.

SPECIFIC REGIONS AND COUNTRIES

Africa

816. Amadi, Adolphe O. **African Libraries: Western Tradition and Colonial Brainwashing.** Metuchen, N.J., Scarecrow, 1981. 265p. bibliog. index. $16.00. LC 80-29593. ISBN 0-8108-1409-9.

African Libraries is a well-written volume that approaches the subject from both psychological and sociological points of view, coupled with various theories borrowed from communication and library science. This is not a descriptive study of libraries in Africa. It is a contribution to developmental studies and cross-cultural studies in an African context. Education and communication institutions as well as libraries come under very careful scrutiny, as these are considered to be white institutions imported from the white man's world. The written word and its culture are weighed against the oral tradition and a culture that emphasizes rote-learning and socializing.

In his attempt to place the African library in the social context, Amadi raises questions about the role and significance of libraries and information in development. The questions are posed in an articulate manner, but are not necessarily being answered. Inquiries into the place and implications of graphic records in oral culture in transition to a print culture are either lacking or skimpy. The author attempts to fill this gap by elucidating deep-seated socio-psychological realities that influence the nature of library and education services in Africa.

Amadi's valuation of leisure and use of time, the magical power of the word, and the codification of reality can be applied to many of the Third World countries. The episodes and anecdotes make the scholarly presentation more enjoyable. At times, one feels that the author comes down hard on Nigeria and Nigerians, but this is perhaps due more to his own familiarity with the Nigerian scene than any personal feeling against the country or its people.

The book is well written, and the author is complimented for his scholarly approach to the subject, using his background in communication, management, and library science. [R: LJ, 1 Dec 81, p. 2293]   Mohammed M. Aman

817. Maack, Mary Niles. **Libraries in Senegal: Continuity and Change in an Emerging Nation.**

Chicago, American Library Association, 1981. 280p. bibliog. index. $20.00pa. LC 81-1600. ISBN 0-8389-0321-5.

The purpose of this work is to emphasize the continuity and change within the inherited structure of one African country, Senegal, whose library history the author has traced from the nineteenth-century through the first 15 years of national independence. The author examines the priorities and the patterns for library development that emerged during the colonial period and attempts to relate these findings to the subsequent development of libraries since independence. The impact that the French political and cultural legacy has had on librarianship is carefully analyzed. After independence, library development in Senegal continued to follow patterns of responding to the demands of research, a pattern which was established during the colonial period.

In describing library development and Senegalese cultural goals, the author links the neglect of public library development to other social and cultural efforts in Senegal such as the high rate of illiteracy, the preference for communal activities, the lack of vernacular publishing, and the limited number of books in French relevant to African interests. These factors are similar to those which have been articulated in another book, *African Libraries: Western Tradition and Colonial Brainwashing*, by Adolphe O. Amadi (Scarecrow, 1981). These two volumes complement each other and could provide the reader with an interesting comparison between the former French (West) and British (East) colonies in Africa, before and after independence. [R: LJ, 1 May 82, p. 865; LQ, Apr 82, p. 175]   Mohammed M. Aman

818. Wallenius, Anna-Britta, ed. **Libraries in East Africa.** Uppsala, Sweden, The Scandinavian Institute of African Studies; distr., New York, Africana Publishing Corp., 1971. 219p. $25.00. LC 70-163924. ISBN 0-8419-0091-4.

The 13 papers in this work discuss several aspects of the subject, but they hardly provide a complete picture. Two papers on the library and adult education in Tanzania are probably the best, and S. W. Hockey's article on the development of library services in East Africa is probably the worst. Papers from an institute or conference should be carefully edited before they are published in book form. The necessary editorial attention is sadly lacking in this volume. [R: LQ, Apr 72, p. 276]

Asia

819. Buckman, Thomas R., Yukihisa Suzuki, and Warren M. Tsuneishi, eds. **University and Research Libraries in Japan and the United States: Proceedings of the First Japan-United States Conference on Libraries and Information Science in Higher Education, Tokyo, 15-19 May 1969.** Chicago, American Library Association, 1972. 299p. o.p. LC 76-178155. ISBN 0-8389-3111-1.

The 47 papers in this collection cover a variety of topics (e.g., role of university libraries in both countries, library resources, acquisition and exchange of publications, national bibliographic control, applications of computers). This volume of proceedings is very welcome. Perhaps it will assist us in understanding basic differences in the administrative structure of university libraries in the two countries. [R: LJ, 15 Feb 73, p. 516; LQ, Apr 73, p. 174]

820. Kaula, P. N. **The National Library of India: A Critical Study.** Bombay, India, Somaiya Publications; distr., Mystic, Conn., Lawrence Verry, 1970. 175p. bibliog. index. o.p. LC 79-917760. ISBN 0-8426-0234-8.

A detailed and professional examination of the Indian National Library located in Calcutta, which houses resources that are the largest and most culturally diverse in the nation. This library also serves as a local public library with an attached children's division. Several appendices are included: a table of the world's national libraries, India's Delivery of Books and Newspapers Act of 1954, and charts of the National Library organization. [R: LJ, Aug 71, p. 2471]   Charles D. Patterson

821. Stevens, Robert D., Raynard C. Swank, and Theodore F. Welch, eds. **Japanese and U.S. Research Libraries at the Turning Point: Proceedings of the Third Japan-U.S. Conference on Libraries and Information Science in Higher Education, Kyoto, Japan, October 28-31, 1975.** Metuchen, N.J., Scarecrow, 1977. 240p. $16.00. LC 77-2535. ISBN 0-8108-1028-X.

"Interlibrary Networks: Pre-requisites for Sharing Resources" was the theme of a third United States-Japan Conference on Libraries and Information Science, held in Kyoto, Japan, in October 1975. This was a follow-up to two earlier conferences sponsored by the two countries, one in 1969 and the second in 1972. In preparing for the conference, the planners realized that Japanese and American libraries must prepare to meet rapidly increasing demands for service with limited resources and that a study of the underlying prerequisites for sharing resources, through interlibrary networks, was essential for both countries. The two countries had had sharply different approaches to networking systems.

Eighteen papers were given by recognized authorities representing Japanese and American directors of libraries, government officials, and planners. The program covered four major topics: "Library Networks: National Planning"; "Pre-requisites for Library Cooperative Activities: Standards and Compatability"; "Development to Meet Information Needs"; and "Managing Change: Library Facilities and Change." In addition to the papers, the book includes progress reports, information about university library cooperation, government support, and the recommendations of the conference working groups.

Containing valuable information for librarians, information scientists, and planners, the book is a splendid example of what two countries and two cultures can learn from each other. It represents an enlightened step towards more interlibrary cooperation and information transfer on an international scale. Recommended reading for all persons interested in library services.   Martha Boaz

822. Welch, Theodore F. **Toshokan: Libraries in Japanese Society.** London, Clive Bingley; distr., Chicago, American Library Association, 1976. 306p. illus. bibliog. index. $15.00. ISBN 0-85157-220-0(Bingley); 0-8389-0172-7(ALA). (Available from Books on Demand, $79.00pa., ISBN 0-317-26358-7).

Consists of 12 chapters covering several types of libraries and a number of selected topics, such as library education and associations, the role of the National Diet Library, technical processing of library materials, and the library employee. The appendices contain, among other things, a chronology of Japanese librarianship (1868-1968) and a glossary of selected library terms. This well-rounded survey is a real contribution to our growing literature on international librarianship. [R: JAL, July 77, p. 160; LJ, 15 May 77, p. 1161; LR, Spring 77, p. 54]

823. Wijasuriya, D. E. K., Lim Huck-Tee, and Radha Nadarajah. **The Barefoot Librarian: Library Developments in Southeast Asia with Special Reference to Malaysia.** London, Clive Bingley; distr., Hamden, Conn., Linnet Books,

1975. 120p. bibliog. index. $15.00. LC 74-30140. ISBN 0-208-01366-0.

The authors of the *Barefoot Librarian* claim that theirs is the first book on Southeast Asian libraries by Southeast Asian librarians. Whether this statement is strictly true or not, it does epitomize the underlying theme of the book: that Southeast Asian library problems will be solved only by librarians who are part of the regional culture.

The book contains nine chapters, the first of which is "The Southeast Asian Environment." Subsequent chapters deal with the several subfields of library development in the region, in schools, public libraries, universities, special libraries. Other chapters are on professional associations, library education, and library cooperation. An extensive bibliography concludes the work. [R: C&RL, Nov 75, pp. 516-17; LJ, 15 Oct 75, p. 1899]

Australia, New Zealand, and Related Areas

824. Baker, Leigh R. **Development of University Libraries in Papua New Guinea.** Metuchen, N.J., Scarecrow, 1981. 399p. illus. maps. bibliog. index. $22.00. LC 80-26936. ISBN 0-8108-1393-9.

University libraries in developing countries faced many problems in the building up of their collections and services. Those in Papua New Guinea were no exception. This book is a detailed survey of two Papua New Guinea university libraries, as well as a comprehensive survey of university libraries in English-speaking, former British colonial countries. Problems in the areas of resources, staffing, organization, funding, services, and buildings are highlighted. The work concludes with a list of 107 recommendations for the improvement of the university libraries, some of which are solutions used in libraries in other developing countries.

The survey of university libraries in several developing countries is of international interest, and the many intriguing little facts that emerge from the comparison whet the reader's appetite for more details. Fortunately, the author has provided bibliographical notes at the end of each chapter to lead to further reading.

The survey covers the period between 1955 and 1975, that period being considered the time when much progress was seen in the university libraries in developing countries. However, significant and rapid developments have occurred since then, especially in the field of library automation. One project that springs to mind is the Malaysian MARC Project (Malmarc), a cooperative computerized cataloging project among the university libraries and the National Library of Malaysia. What is needed now is another work to bring this one up-to-date.

This book should be a useful source for students of comparative librarianship and those interested in libraries and librarianship in developing countries. [R: LQ, Apr 82, p. 177]

Hwa-Wei Lee

825. Biskup, Peter, and Doreen M. Goodman. **Australian Libraries.** 3rd ed. London, Clive Bingley; distr., Hamden, Conn., Shoe String Press, 1982. 221p. bibliog. index. o.p. ISBN 0-85157-326-6.

The first edition of *Australian Libraries* was published in 1966 and written by John Belnaves and Peter Biskup. The authors revised and rewrote the book in 1975 (see *ARBA* 76, entry 212) and this third edition, revised in 1982 by Peter Biskup and Doreen Goodman, encompasses features of the first two editions and includes information since 1975. The dedication in the third edition indicates the retirement of John Belnaves, a probable explanation as to the change in authors in this third edition.

Australian Libraries attempts to draw a detailed overview of the library in Australia today. Various chapters deal with the history of Australia, the history and structure of library services, state, public, school, and special libraries and the national library, archival and manuscript repositories, associations of librarians, education for librarianship, and coordination, automation, and networking in libraries. Bibliographies for further reading are included at the end of each chapter, and appendices include a statement of state information policy and a statement of national information policy, added to this third edition. The book concludes with a detailed index.

The value of this reference tool lies in the depth of its coverage and the breadth of its perspective. Any attempt to profile Australia and its libraries would necessarily be defined by certain parameters due to the broad nature of the subject. In *Australian Libraries*, facts are presented to profile library organization on the local, regional, national, and international levels. Statistics are drawn from other library systems in order to place Australian libraries within an overall picture, both within their own boundaries and on an international level. [R: JAL, Mar 83, p. 38]

Barbara Sproat

826. Downs, Robert B. **Australian and New Zealand Library Resources.** London, Mansell; distr., Salem, N.H., Mansell, 1979. 164p. bibliog. index. $43.00. ISBN 0-7201-0913-2.

Robert B. Downs is well known both as a surveyor of individual libraries and as an investigator of library resources of large political units. Two of his large-scale surveys are: *American Library Resources: A Bibliographical Guide* (Gregg Press, 1972) and *British Library Resources: A Bibliographical Guide* (American Library Association, 1973). The methodology used in assembling, analyzing, and reporting the data for his *Australian and New Zealand Library Resources* follows in several respects the procedures applied to his earlier investigations. In the report on the Australian and New Zealand libraries Downs includes, in addition, general background material – his impressions, gathered during a two-month tour, of the land, the people, and the social conditions.

The author gives credit to several of the earlier investigators of the whole Australian and New Zealand library scene as well as to outstanding surveyors of notable collections of individual libraries. "A landmark study, now of historical interest," was conducted by Ralph Munn, who with co-authors surveyed both the Australian and New Zealand libraries as early as 1935 and 1934, respectively. Among others he singles out Lionel R. McColvin, Andrew D. Osborn, C. A. Burmester, and W. J. McEldowney. Downs acknowledges in particular the work of his fellow American, Maurice F. Tauber, who completed his survey of Australian library resources in 1961. Downs notes that in goals and objectives the "Tauber Report" is most closely related to his own inquiry, and he frequently quotes from it.

Downs's principal aim has been to gather from a wide variety of libraries data on resources for study and research, giving emphasis to special collections and specialized holdings.

The entries under which the descriptions and evaluations of the resources appear are assigned to two sections: "General Subjects and Types of Material" (section 1: 122 entries) and "Individual Biography, Bibliography, and Criticism" (section 2: 25 entries). The entries, of quite varying lengths, are arranged in alphabetical sequence. The descriptions are often accompanied by bibliographic references which lead to more comprehensive or more detailed information than could be included in the Downs volume.

Section 3 consists of a bibliography based on checklists, union lists, dealers' catalogs, articles, pamphlets, and any other materials which can lead to Australian and New Zealand library resources. The bibliography section includes 565 items, some of which are briefly annotated. The fourth and final section is a complete index of subjects, libraries, individual names, etc.

Downs has created an excellent tool for study and research. His work is distinguished by its discovery of strengths and weaknesses in the various subject fields, by its attention to the provenance of collections and to other historical facts, by its care for details without being overwhelmed by them, and by its clarity of presentation. [R: JAL, Mar 80, p. 45]   Fritz Veit

Canada

827.   Campbell, H. C. **Canadian Libraries.** 2nd ed. fully rev. and expanded. Hamden, Conn., Linnet Books, 1971. 144p. index. (Comparative Library Studies). o.p. SBN 208-01064-5.

The first edition of this work was published in 1969. This revision was made with the assistance of comments received from users of the first edition, and one has to admit that it shows a more balanced presentation. There are four parts in this book: "Canadian Libraries 1900-1960"; "Reference and Research Library Resources"; "Provincial and Regional Library Systems"; and "Library Planning and Co-operation in Canada." Appended are a list of directories and guides and a rather brief bibliography. In general, this introductory text covers the subject well and should be found in all library schools offering courses in comparative librarianship. [R: RQ, Fall 71, p. 78]

828.   **The Future of the National Library of Canada.** Ottawa, Ont., National Library of Canada, 1979. 1v. (various paging). bibliog. free. ISBN 0-662-50628-6pa.

To mark its quarter century in 1978, Canada's National Library invited briefs on its role and undertook an in-house review of role, services, and objectives. The review is summarized in this short final report, English/French text inverted. Past gains in building networks, maintaining national bibliography, initiating projects, and creating collections are logged. Current budgetary restraints for the National Library, as well as for other libraries, are underscored by deploring that library collections in Canada are declining relative to the world's publishing output.

This report proposes no curtailment of growth, but, on the contrary, argues for sustained continuation of present commitments, advocates extension of services, and aims at expansion of library and archive mandates, including integration of other facilities in the Canada Institute for Scientific and Technical Information or in the Public Archives. Information and Recommendations in this report may be of some general interest to all Canadian librarians. The recommendations will be of particular interest to those few persons who follow closely the histories and politics of large libraries and national institutions. [R: C&RL, July 80, pp. 390-91; LJ, 15 May 80, p. 1145]

Claire England

829.   Garry, Loraine Spencer, and Carl Garry, eds. **Canadian Libraries in Their Changing Environment.** Downsview, Ont., Centre for Continuing Education, York University, 1977. 593p. index. o.p.

These twenty-two papers were presented by Canadian library leaders at a conference of the same name on 24-26 February 1977, offered through York University's Centre for Continuing Education in Toronto. The history section has six offerings, covering all of the provinces and territories. The institute section has five papers detailing Canadian public, university (by Bruce Peel), school, and special libraries (by Beryl Anderson), plus the National Library. Six papers cover the profession, dealing with Canadian issues in library science education, library technicians, the elements of professionalism in library science, and library associations. The last section presents current issues papers on organizational problems, administrative difficulties, unionization, technical change, and the book trade. Each paper has footnotes, and there is a bibliography after each chapter. Surprisingly, there is also a general index, albeit comprising mainly proper names. The papers as a whole are interesting and informative. This is state-of-the-art writing: nothing really new, but adequate summaries. The intent of the conference was to present these papers to participants *beforehand* and to have the authors available for workshops. It might have been interesting to read transcripts of the discussions. As such, though, this is an excellent book that describes Canadian libraries. It should also be suitable as a textbook in Canadian schools of library education. [R: LQ, July 78, p. 359]

Dean Tudor

830.   **Project Progress: A Study of Canadian Public Libraries.** Ottawa, Ont., Canadian

Library Association, 1981. 120p. bibliog. $10.00 pa. ISBN 0-88802-154-2.

This is a report of a research project on the study of Canadian public libraries; it is intended to provide data for planning for the 1980s and beyond (the last major study of Canadian libraries was the Ridington survey of 1933, which was mainly a "survey"). *Project Progress* was designed to provide tools for public libraries (a) to measure their current effectiveness, and (b) to plan for the future. The idea sprang from the Canadian Association of Public Libraries in 1973. It was felt that despite strong grassroots support in public libraries and practical "hands-on know how," there should be access to (and the ability to use) the same management tools as used by governments. There was a seven-year effort to secure a funding of $150,000 (yet this was less than one-quarter of the funds needed for the project as originally visualized, not allowing for inflation); the study itself was one-and-a-half years in the making, and completed in January 1981 (released at the CLA Conference in June 1981).

The study's universe comprised 1,178 libraries, 90 library workers from 51 libraries, 200 users (polled by telephone), 18 "key" (but unidentified) decision makers, and 7 libraries involved in a task analysis study. Yet, this is a strange "naval gazing" report, introspective in that much of the data related to the physical collection of "things" rather than the aspect of "people" or "users."

The 12 recommendations can be summarized thus: (a) there should be use of data and tools for valid performance measures useful to governing agencies ("become more effective in the gathering and utilization of statistical materials designed to support their performance claims and budgetary requests," no. 11, p. 103); (b) there should be increasing staff development and effectiveness, especially through continuing education, with an eye to a delineation of "professional" and "technical" duties (there is too much overlap in tasks); and (c) there should be better marketing strategies, for the Canadian public library service should be aware of changing society (merging professional goals with societal goals), changing technologies, and competing information services (especially "user friendly," but mostly unidentified, services) — in short, to monitor client groups.

There are many deficiencies in this study. There is a vast lack of input from the governing bodies of public libraries themselves. Canada is too big and diversified for many regions to have and maintain "national" standards (the library survey data are for national averages that were not broken down; hence, small libraries, branch libraries, and large libraries were all lumped together). There was no consideration of community services, such as for the shut-in, adult education, or special programming. "Circulation" appears to be the only community-related outreach indicator. Some types of questions were not asked of the public librarians at interviews, such as, What is the purpose of the public library? What about performance measures? Or the use of information services competitors? And most of the recommendations appear to lack substantive supporting evidence. All of this concerns me, as there is some measure of discontent with the survey amongst Canadian libraries: that it was too superficial, too vague, with too little statistically reputable verifiable data to support its contentions. Much, much more needs to be done. [R: Emerg Lib, Jan 82, p. 29]   Dean Tudor

Developing Countries

831. Chandler, George, ed. **International Librarianship: Surveys of Recent Developments in Developing Countries and in Advanced Librarianship Submitted to the 1971 IFLA Pre-Session Seminar for Developing Countries Sponsored by Unesco.** London, Library Association, 1972. 208p. index. o.p. LC 72-195970. ISBN 0-85365-305-4.

The first part of this volume relates what representatives from 20 national library associations from developing countries say about library development in their respective countries. The second half of the book is devoted to surveys of recent developments in advanced librarianship in which Western experts treat subjects such as public libraries, university libraries, national libraries, library education, international cooperation, and international library technology. [R: LJ, 1 Oct 72, p. 3127]
Charles D. Patterson

832. Huq, A. M. Abdul, and Mohammed M. Aman. **Librarianship and the Third World: An Annotated Bibliography of Selected Literature on Developing Nations, 1960-1975.** New York, Garland, 1977. 372p. index. $55.00. LC 76-30916. ISBN 0-8240-9897-8.

The authors of this volume have provided us with a handy reference work in the area of comparative librarianship. They both have much knowledge about and experience in Third World countries, which adds to the authoritative treatment. The arrangement of this volume and its concentration on Third World countries make it more useful than previous works that have tried to be comprehensive and global and have been weakened in the process. The authors state in their introduction that the main reason they have conceived this volume is that "there is no systematic record of what has been published in the area" of library literature by and about the Third World.

One of the greatest limitations, as the authors admit, is that the "selection" of materials for inclusion was guided by the literature and by what was available in leading collections in the eastern United States. Consequently, over 90 percent of the citations are to articles written in English. Unfortunately, certain countries such as Nicaragua, Honduras, and several of the other Latin American countries have been omitted, as have China and Japan; all probably were omitted with reason, but the reason is not stated.

Of the almost 1,500 entries, several works are referenced more than once, and in a couple of cases the annotations vary—in one instance a work is cited as a "comprehensive critical analysis," while in another section the same article becomes a "brief introduction to current problems."

Despite some minor flaws, then, this is a useful work, well indexed and annotated. A good addition to any international collection. [R: JAL, July 77, p. 166; LJ, 1 Oct 77, p. 2017]

Robert D. Stueart

833.   Ingram, K. E., and Albertina A. Jefferson, eds. **Libraries and the Challenge of Change: Papers of the International Library Conference Held in Kingston, Jamaica, 24-29 April 1972.** Published for the Jamaica Library Association and the Jamaica Library Service. London, Mansell; distr., Portland, Oreg., International Scholarly Book Services, 1975. 266p. o.p. ISBN 0-7201-0523-4.

This is not a reference book but a series of 20 papers and summary reports dealing with public, national, academic, special, and youth libraries, library education, the role of UNESCO, international library cooperation, the role of professional associations, and national plans for library development in Latin America and Jamaica. Visiting speakers included such luminaries as D. J. Foskett, Dorothy Collings, Kenneth Roberts, Margreet Wijnstroom, William V. Jackson, and Edwin Castagna. "It was hoped that the free exchange of ideas and information generated by the conference would focus the attention of the public, of government and of other agencies upon the role and value of libraries and upon the nature of the

profession of librarianship, thereby promoting a wider understanding of the part which libraries can and ought to play in community as well as individual development." From the resolutions introduced at the closing session, the conference appears to have achieved its objectives.

Frances Neel Cheney

834.   Kumar, Krishan. **Research Libraries in Developing Countries.** New Delhi, Vikas Publishing House; distr., Portland, Oreg., International Scholarly Book Services, 1973. 464p. index. $15.00. ISBN 0-7069-0256-4.

This work is in two parts; the first deals with research libraries in social sciences in South and Southeast Asia (India, Pakistan, Indonesia, Malaysia, Singapore, Thailand, and Taiwan); the second and larger part is a detailed account of one social science research library, the Sapru House Library, which has served as a joint library of the School of International Studies (Jawaharlal Nehru University) and the Indian Council of World Affairs.

In the first nine chapters, the author summarizes details about each country's libraries under such topics as: selection and acquisition of material, organization of materials and provision of services, library education, administration. The author discusses the parent organizations that these libraries serve and provides suggestions for improvement.

The Sapru House Library study provides an interesting, detailed case study of an institution in transition, whose fate was yet to be determined when this study was published. Although the research on the users of the Sapru House Library is valuable, this reviewer found the most interesting part of this book to be the case study in public opinion, when it appeared that the library's collection would be divided and its diverse clientele of teachers, research scholars, and journalists would be served by a disjointed library. All the data on the library's organization, procedures for selection and acquisition of materials, and its classification, cataloging, documentation, and circulation work may be out-of-date because of a decision in 1971 to reorganize the library. As a model for a user study, this book provides adequate detail on methodology, analysis, and conclusions. When it is placed in the real situation of change and chance, such a study does appear quite academic. Nevertheless, one should not fault the author for providing an historical report of such a library on the brink of another period in its existence. [R: LQ, Apr 74, p. 181; SL, Feb 74, p. 95]

Pauline Atherton Cochrane

835. Lemos, Antonio A. Briquet de. **A Portrait of Librarianship in Developing Societies.** Urbana-Champaign, Ill., Graduate School of Library and Information Science, University of Illinois, 1981. 46p. bibliog. o.p. ISSN 0276-1769.

For most of us, comparative and international librarianship is a subject touched upon in library school and forgotten. As Lemos rightly suggests, much of that literature is of a descriptive or critical nature dealing with a particular country and doesn't deserve our attention. His work is an exception.

This short polemic by a noted Brazilian library educator deserves the careful attention of librarians throughout the world, but especially those of us in the developed nations. While not intended as an exhaustive review of the literature, Lemos has missed very little of significance, including appropriate general background material on developing societies, and is right on the mark in his analysis of that literature. His basic theme is that too much of the literature is descriptive, and that there is a serious lack of the kind of reliable research needed to counteract the impressionistic accounts that have dominated. He also concludes that foreign librarians, notably those from developed nations, have too often sought to impose "slavish imitations of the models that they know" to the detriment of appropriate library growth and development. Lemos's final conclusion, and one that deserves thought, is that the development of library service in Third World countries is the exclusive responsibility of librarians from those countries.

While a polemic, Lemos's reasoned approach is convincing. It should make all of us think how we might best contribute to assisting those librarians in that formidable task. It should give pause to those who are asked to serve as library consultants in a developing society. Take heed of what Lemos has to say!

Norman D. Stevens

836. Parker, Dorothy, and Angelina Carabelli. **Guide for an Agricultural Library Survey for Developing Countries.** Metuchen, N.J., Scarecrow, 1970. 241p. o.p. LC 76-13321. ISBN 0-8108-0322-4.

This work is divided into two parts, the first dealing with what is stated in the title. With adjustments, it could be used as a guide for any coordinated development of a national library system. It outlines specific steps for organization and identifies essential requirements as well as pitfalls. Part 2 is a reprint of the report of the libraries of the Indian Council of Agricultural institutes and universities, with recommendations. Both parts have appendices. [R: LJ, 15 Oct 70, p. 3453]   Charles D. Patterson

837. Parker, J. Stephen, ed. **Aspects of Library Development Planning.** London, Mansell; distr., New York, H. W. Wilson, 1983. 289p. index. $43.00. ISBN 0-7201-1661-9.

This collection of papers provides an introduction to national library and information service planning, particularly for developing nations. Certain of its papers are adapted from ones presented at a 1979 British Council course on this subject, held in Bristol, England, under Parker's direction. Four introductory papers treat general principles and four treat technical aspects, then two discuss sector planning, and the final seven discuss specific case studies. Eight Britons, two Brazilians, one Nigerian, and one Tanzanian compose the author group. Parker and several other contributors are well-respected international library consultants. The book does not pretend to comprehensiveness but concentrates on public libraries, with occasional attention to school and university and almost none to special libraries.

This guide should be widely used among national library planners and can be called a valiant attempt to provide a useful book. It supplements several well-known publications by UNESCO authors, including Carlos Penna, on this essential subject. Much useful advice is presented, particularly in the chapters by M. B. Line on access, P. H. Sewell on standards, E. Max Broome on costing, A. Wilson on public libraries, V. Berkeley on school libraries, and Parker on Bangladesh and Thailand. The book is a suggestive, not a definitive, volume.

The book makes clear, however, that the field is still in its infancy. Three of its chapters do not relate closely to planning—those on Belize, Brazil (Tarapanoff), and computer use; certain chapters are more historical than contemporary—those on Brazil (Tarapanoff) and Belize; and certain chapters are somewhat dated—those on Thailand, Belize, and Brazil. The book has many other weaknesses: It is superficial and vague, and its initial definitions and bibliographies are inadequate. Planning's principles and advice seem often to be followed by disappointing results. [R: LQ, July 84, p. 295]

John F. Harvey

838. Penna, C. V. **The Planning of Library and Documentation Services.** 2nd ed. rev. and enl. by P. H. Sewell and Herman Liebaers. Paris, UNESCO; distr., New York, UNIPUB,

1970. 158p. (UNESCO Manuals for Libraries, No. 17). $7.25pa. ISBN 92-3-100814-5.

This is a revised and somewhat enlarged edition of the booklet *Planning Library Services*, published in 1967. It is primarily designed for developing countries, and in this respect it provides all essential data on the subject. Among topics covered the reader will find a 30-page discussion on "Library Services—Their Contribution to National Development and the Need for Planning," an outline of basic principles of planning technique, a discussion of various tools and technical considerations, and a selective bibliography. Appended to this volume are articles dealing with aspects of planning library services in several countries, e.g., Malaysia, Central America, Ghana, Ceylon, the Soviet Union, India, Belgium, etc. A useful introductory text on the subject. [R: AL, Dec 71, p. 1224; LJ, 15 May 71, p. 1689]

839. Williamson, William L., ed. **Assistance to Libraries in Developing Nations: Papers on Comparative Studies; Proceedings of a Conference Held at the Wisconsin Center, Madison, Wisconsin, May 14, 1971.** Madison, Wis., University of Wisconsin, Library School, 1971. 68p. bibliog. $3.00pa. LC 72-610537. ISBN 0-936442-03-4.

Four of the six papers are concerned with comparative librarianship and include: the general historical development of comparative studies in scientific terms; a technical discussion of the scalogram as a tool for describing library development; library development as affected by social change from the traditional to the modern industrial society; and a comparison of librarianship in France and the United States. The remaining two papers deal with basic anthropological insights and "Patterns of Librarianship in West Africa." Although the results of only one conference, the papers provide insights useful for further exploration. [R: LJ, July 72, p. 2360]   Charles D. Patterson

Europe and the USSR

840. Burkett, Jack. **Library and Information Networks in Western Europe.** London, Aslib, 1983. 139p. index. £13.00; £11.00 (Aslib members). ISBN 0-85142-168-7.

This volume constitutes a detailed study of information sharing in Western Europe. Although "Western Europe" is mentioned in the title, the use of networking is extended throughout the world due to the nature of the "European community," whose existence is defined and detailed in the first portion of the book. The form and structure of the community are portrayed in detail, with its system of information networking explained and pursued on a parallel level. Following the complete pictures of both systems, items of information are dovetailed to accord the reader a concise picture of communication in Western Europe and other parts of the world linked to the European community.

Attention is also given to other organizations, such as the Council of Europe, the European Free Trade Association, and the United Nations in Europe, which have been formed to realize political and economic cooperation. As is evident in the European community, these organizations have their own systems of information management, and a portion of the book is devoted to outlining data banks and databases that service them. As implied in the title, both library and networking services are at play. The library plays an important role in information storage and retrieval and supplying documents to members of the European community and the general public. The information available through these traditional library resources and through computerized networking varies from technical reports written by committee members to journal articles outlining current affairs.

The remainder of the book is devoted to outlining specialized international organizations in the fields of science and technology, business and industry, and education and culture. An appendix lists the addresses of the various organizations included in the volume, and it is followed by an index. One excellent feature of the book is the inclusion of additional references at the end of each section for further reading. Due to the nature of the book, it is not a reference source that will be used every day; but as a sourcebook of networking and communication systems in Western Europe, it is invaluable, due to the amount of detail, its organization, and the fact that there is little other information available on the subject. For research and academic libraries and organiza-tions and schools involved with networking and communication systems. [R: JAL, Sept 83, p. 244]

Barbara Sproat

841. Chandler, George. **Libraries, Documentation and Bibliography in the USSR, 1917-1971: Survey and Critical Analysis of Soviet Studies 1967-1971.** New York, Seminar Press, 1972. 183p. index. (International Bibliographical and Library Series [Interbiblis], Vol. 2). $36.50. LC 72-84273. ISBN 0-12-785105-4.

Some readers may recall *Libraries in the USSR*, edited by Simon Francis and published in 1971 by Clive Bingley. This work, which was simply the translation of a special issue of the Soviet journal *Biblioteki SSSR*, was reviewed in *ARBA* 72 (entry 60). It was pointed out in the review that much of the information in this volume was distorted and that it would hardly enlighten the library profession as to what goes on in the Soviet Union. Later developments, especially the treatment of Soviet intellectuals, only proved our point; it is not widely known in the West, however, that some librarians lost their jobs simply because they quietly supported the intellectuals.

George Chandler's study is a critical survey of major trends in Soviet librarianship. Frankly, although it is brief, it seems to be the best treatment of this subject since Paul Horecky's *Libraries and Bibliographic Centers in the Soviet Union* (Indiana University, 1959). Probably one of the best parts of this book is the author's discussion of the Soviet "recommendatory bibliography." Even here, though, Chandler fails to point out the important role that Soviet censorship plays in the development of recommended lists prepared for specific audiences. We do agree that the aim of the "recommendatory bibliography" concept was to encourage "ethical and aesthetic education" — but perhaps not in our sense of the term. There are highly "selective" bibliographies on individual writers (published even in the 1960s) that meet such official Soviet criteria; they simply ignore (under the guise of not being comprehensive) any of the author's works that are unacceptable to the current regime. But this is a topic for another book. [R: BSA-P, July 74, p. 352; RSR, Oct 73, p. 25]   Bohdan S. Wynar

842.   Ferguson, John. **Libraries in France.** Hamden, Conn., Archon, 1971. 120p. index. (Comparative Library Studies). o.p. SBN 208-01058-0.

Another volume in this series. Previous volumes include *Australian Libraries, Canadian Libraries, Handbook of Comparative Librarianship, Lenin, Krupskaia and Libraries, Nicholas Rubakin and Bibliopsychology,* and *South African Libraries.* The volumes on Canadian and Soviet libraries are reviewed in *ARBA* 72; *Handbook of Comparative Librarianship* was reviewed in *ARBA* 71 (entry 102). Not all the volumes offer a similar structure of material. As the reader may have noted, the volume on Canadian libaries provided sufficient historical background plus information on current trends in Canadian librarianship. This volume concentrates almost exclusively on the modern library situation in France, and this is where its weakness lies. It is rather difficult to understand the structure of two national libraries "with a note on copyright deposit" (chapter 2) without the proper historical setting. Nevertheless, the material on different types of libraries, university, public, nonmunicipal, etc., offers all the essential information. There are also chapters on library education, archives and documentation, major libraries in Paris, interlibrary cooperation, etc. What can be said in 120 pages? Very little. The objective of this series is apparently to provide a rather brief introduction to libraries and library systems in different countries, and if the editors will stay away from more complex problems (e.g., *Lenin, Krupskaia and Libraries*) or will refrain from promising more than they deliver (e.g., *Handbook of Comparative Librarianship*), this series should be a useful acquisition for all library schools as a general orientation guide in international librarianship. [R: LR, Spring 72, p. 198]

Bohdan S. Wynar

843.   Francis, Simon. **Libraries in the USSR.** Hamden, Conn., Linnet Books, 1971. 182p. (Comparative Library Studies). o.p. SBN 208-01059-9.

This book is a translation of a collection of papers published in commemoration of the fiftieth anniversary of the Revolution, late in 1967, as a special issue of the Soviet journal *Biblioteki SSSR*. In his preface, Simon Francis points out that the purpose in editing this translation has been two-fold. "The first is to make available a body of information about Soviet librarianship.... The second is closely related to the first. If we find some of the writing in this collection exaggerated, it is still of importance to examine it and attempt to understand the reasons and climate which produce it. We may not agree with some of the implications that the authors draw from the factual material presented, but we cannot dismiss it as external propaganda. This is how they see themselves and how they wish to be seen by their colleagues and compatriots." Well, the author offers a simple translation, and there is nothing in terms of "examining certain facts" in order to understand "the reasons." There are hundreds of titles published every year on many aspects of Soviet affairs. Not a single subject specialist would attempt to write, say, a history of Soviet agriculture simply by translating certain Soviet official publications without any commentaries. We wonder whether the author knows what happened in the early 1930s in library science — why so many scholarly publications ceased to exist (together with some of their editors). Some other comments about contemporary library science in the Soviet Union are needed. Generally speaking (although this is obviously an oversimplification) there are two types of publication. The first category, for example, *Bibliotekar* and *Biblioteki SSSR*, have as their chief purpose to propagandize "achievements" of Soviet library science and offer very little in terms of substance. The second category, *Trudy* of several leading institutions and libraries, and partly even *Sovetskaia Bibliografiia* or *Kniga*, will usually quote Lenin in one of their editorial articles (usually something to the effect that library science should serve as an instrument for the Party, etc.), and later go about their business.

Most of the information in this volume, because of the lack of commentary, is simply distorted (look, for example, at the article on the library network of the Academy of Sciences) and will hardly enlighten the library profession as to what goes on in the Soviet Union. In conclusion, let us emphasize again one point. There are no different standards in scholarship, one for library science and another for all other disciplines. To examine Soviet developments is not an easy task. Numerous institutes created for this very purpose at our universities and in Great Britain know rather well how to do it. It won't hurt librarians interested in Soviet librarianship to make some attempt to learn more about it. [R: LJ, 1 Nov 71, p. 3580]

Bohdan S. Wynar

844. Lewanski, Richard C., comp. **Guide to Polish Libraries and Archives.** Boulder, Colo., East European Quarterly; distr., New York, Columbia University Press, 1974. 209p. bibliog. index. (East European Monographs, No. VI). $20.00. LC 73-91484. ISBN 0-231-03896-8.

Lewanski, a well-known bibliographer, is the author of a standard volume on Slavic literatures in English translation (published by Ungar and the New York Public Library in 1967) as well as many other works. This volume is the only English-language guide to Polish libraries and archives; it should be of substantial assistance to all scholars interested in this subject. Institutions are arranged by location and their resources are described in considerable detail. Thus, subject collections are not only listed under the institution concerned but are also brought together in the entry for the leading library in the field, so that the reader is guided to related collections in the given subject field. In addition to a questionnaire, the author

made use of numerous secondary publications in compiling the guide, including many works in Polish. The only important omission is his otherwise well-prepared bibliography (pages 190-5) is a guide to libraries of the Polish Academy of Arts and Sciences (L. Loś, *Biblioteki Polskiej Akademii Nauk*, 1973), which provides well-organized information about this network of very important Polish libraries. [R: C&RL, July 75, p. 309]   Bohdan S. Wynar

845. Patrinostro, Frank S., comp. **A Survey of Automated Activities in the Libraries of the Soviet Union.** Tempe, Ariz., LARC Association, 1972. 95p. illus. (World Survey Series, Volume 7). o.p. ISBN 0-88257-064-1.

A useful series that started with the 1971 publication of *A Survey of Automated Activities in the Libraries of the United States.* Because of structural peculiarities of library organization in the Soviet Union, this particular volume departs from the format of previous volumes (which provided a library-by-library survey of activities) and concentrates primarily on the functions of central agencies (e.g., the role of the Academy of Sciences in planning automated library activities, VINITI, etc.). There are separate chapters on the Lenin Library and the State Public Scientific and Technological Library of the USSR.

846. Roxas, Savina A. **Library Education in Italy: An Historical Survey 1870-1969.** Metuchen, N.J., Scarecrow, 1971. 260p. index. bibliog. o.p. LC 70-167643. ISBN 0-8108-0419-0.

The title of this historical survey is somewhat misleading, since the year 1870 (the unification of Italy) has little to do with the history of library education. The author offers here brief information on "land and people," an historical sketch of Italian education and library development, a separate chapter on library schools (pp. 59-116), and one chapter on independent course offerings. The study is well documented and contains a selected bibliography in a separate appendix. [R: LJ, 15 Apr 72, p. 1406]

847. Saunders, W. L., ed. **British Librarianship Today.** paperback ed. Syracuse, N.Y., Gaylord Professional Publications, 1977. 378p. index. o.p. ISBN 0-85365-620-7.

This anthology, published on the threshold of the centennial of the founding of the British Library Association, supersedes a similar collection of essays published some 10 years earlier, also edited by Saunders under the title *Librarianship in Britain Today.* Those 10 years brought many changes and innovations to librarianship in the United Kingdom—the formation of the British Library, local government reorganization, the emergence of the polytechnic libraries, the growth of the Libraries Division of the Department of Education and Science, a substantial increase in research and development programs and activities, and the rise in importance of the computer in librarianship. These and other aspects of modern British librarianship are here described and evaluated in 18 chapters by Saunders and 23 other contributors, all of whom are intimately associated with and can speak with authority about their respective subjects. Thus, the volume is an important statement of the state of librarianship among our English cousins.

The achievements of the British Library are treated in five chapters and in an introductory essay by H. T. Hookway, with one chapter each on the Library's four divisions, written by their respective directors. There is one chapter each on the three British library associations: the Library Association, Aslib, and the Institute of Information Scientists. Other chapters survey the main types of libraries currently operating in Britain: public, university, polytechnic and college, special, and school. The volume concludes with chapters on the great potential of the computer in library operations and services, international library activities, and library education and research. This excellent volume, which is authoritative, informative, and well written, is of substantial value to librarians on this side of the Atlantic, and in the opinion of this reviewer is superior to the two comparable anthologies that memorialized our own ALA Centennial. [R: LQ, July 78, p. 310]   Jesse H. Shera

848.   Von Busse, Gisela, and Horst Ernestus. **Libraries in the Federal Republic of Germany.** rev. and enl. English ed. Wiesbaden, W. Germany, Otto Harrassowitz; distr., Chicago, American Library Association, 1972. 308p. illus. index. $25.00. ISBN 0-8389-0135-2.

This is a revised and enlarged version of the original German edition—*Das Bibliothekswesen der Bundesrepublik Deutschland* (Harrassowitz, 1968), translated by John S. Andrews and Gregory Walker. It describes different types of libraries, their organization and cooperative activities, bibliographic centers, etc. As is indicated in the preface, the original German edition was intended primarily as an introduction for the visitor from abroad—an intent that is even better served by this English translation, which offers in a handy volume a popular

presentation of all important aspects of German library development. [R: LJ, July 73, p. 2056]

849.   Watson, Peter G. **Great Britain's National Lending Library.** Los Angeles, Calif., School of Library Service, University of California, 1970. 93p. illus. bibliog. o.p. LC 73-633442.

A lively, detailed, and highly personal description of the way the National Lending Library (NLL) functions, written by a visiting staff member in 1967-1968. Well documented, the volume draws heavily upon the substantial professional library and information as well as scientific literature, but effectively presents the NLL and its role in the British intellectual system. [R: LJ, 15 Oct 70, p. 3453]
                                        Charles D. Patterson

850.   Welsch, Erwin K. **Libraries and Archives in France: A Handbook.** rev. ed. New York, Council for European Studies, Columbia University, 1979. 146p. bibliog. o.p.

This guide is considerably enlarged from the first edition and is divided into three sections: libraries in Paris, archives in Paris, and libraries and archives elsewhere in France. The entries, arranged by broad subject, include the address, hours, holdings, procedures to be followed in obtaining a user's card, catalogs, publications, photocopying rules, and the like. No indexes or cross-references are provided. Most of the entries, especially those for libraries in Paris, are very detailed, covering a page or more. The Bibliothèque Nationale is described in detail, covering seven pages, and the Archives Nationales takes up 10 pages. Archives and libraries outside Paris have much shorter descriptions. Many of the libraries were visited, and their descriptions are obviously first-hand accounts; others were taken from brochures and correspondence (the author does not say which are which).

There are three bibliographies on archives and library holdings plus appendices on classification schemes and how to locate manuscripts. In addition, the preface gives useful information about the problems and prospects of obtaining information from French libraries and archives, and the steps to take to gain access. The guide should be valuable to students and scholars planning research trips to France. Typographical errors throughout are disconcerting. [R: C&RL, Nov 79, p. 561]
                                        A. Neil Yerkey

851.   Whatley, H. A., ed. **British Librarianship and Information Science, 1966-1970.** London, Library Association; distr., Detroit,

Gale, 1972. 712p. illus. index. $26.00. ISBN 0-85365-175-2.

A very comprehensive review of British librarianship from 1966 to 1970. The primary aim of the editor was that this volume should "present a *picture* of what had happened during the five-year period and that it should not be a comprehensive review of the *literature* on each subject." The book, therefore, is not literature oriented, but activity oriented. Some of the specific areas included are cataloging, classification, indexing and abstracting services, library cooperation, information science, buildings, management, activities in specific types of libraries, and associations.

This book is organized like and reads like any annual review. It is literally packed with information about British librarianship, and it thoroughly covers almost all aspects of the subject. It should certainly be the first approach in any search for information on the subject; since each chapter provides additional references, the reader can further his interests in an organized way. Most of the chapters are well written and range in difficulty from typical narrative discussions to technical treatises incorporating mathematical expressions. Overall, the book must be considered an excellent source for information on its subject areas. [R: RSR, July 73, p. 30]

Donald P. Hammer

Latin America

852. Jordan, Alma Theodora, ed. **Research Library Cooperation in the Caribbean: Papers of the Association of Caribbean University and Research Libraries.** Chicago, American Library Association, 1973. 157p. o.p. LC 73-4218. ISBN 0-8389-0148-4. (Available from Books on Demand, $39.30pa., ISBN 0-317-27849-5).

Fourteen papers of the First and Second Conferences of the Association (ACURIL) were presented (and are published in English in this volume) by archivists and librarians of the Caribbean region in response to the need for access to research materials produced in the region. Papers cover cooperative acquisition; bibliographic, indexing, and microfilming proj-

ects; communication in the region; results and experience in bibliographical control of Commonwealth government publications; acquisition of official publications; role of regional libraries; and suggestions for preservation of publications in the tropics. Cooperative national acquisitions and bibliography in the Caribbean are described in the appendix. The papers generally describe history, needs, problems, plans, and proposals for the region. There is a table of contents but no index. [R: LJ, 15 Dec 73, p. 3615]

Charles L. Bernier

853. McCarthy, Cavan. **Developing Libraries in Brazil: With a Chapter on Paraguay.** Metuchen, N.J., Scarecrow, 1975. 207p. index. $15.00. LC 74-23681. ISBN 0-8108-0750-5.

This book will have a familiar ring for specialists in international and comparative librarianship. The author—a young British librarian who spent 1971-1972 in the area—describes the poor funding, low prestige, and uneven distribution of library service, common to most Third World countries. Instead of the traditional approach by types of libraries, however, McCarthy attempts to look through the libraries at the society itself. He has organized his informal, first-person narrative around such themes as "reaching out," "cataloging and other forms of bureaucracy," and "lock 'em up and count 'em." Two general themes stand out: the overwhelming predominance of women in the profession, and the enormous (but frustrated) potential of Brazilian library services. For the study of national planning, McCarthy could have given more direct attention to the working relationships between librarians and the holders of purse and power. Readers must either infer or piece together the answers to this central question to library development. Still, this is an outspoken, objective, and readable contribution to the literature, and a worthy complement to more traditional works, such as W. V. Jackson's articles in the *Encyclopedia of Library and Information Science*.

The chapter on Paraguay is both depressing and optimistic. [R: C&RL, Sept 75, p. 422]

John Robert Wheat

32 Conservation and Preservation

GENERAL WORKS

854. Baker, John P., and Marguerite C. Soroka, eds. **Library Conservation: Preservation in Perspective.** Stroudsberg, Pa., Dowden, Hutchinson & Ross; distr., New York, Academic Press, 1978. 459p. illus. index. (Publications in the Information Sciences). o.p. LC 78-16133. ISBN 0-87933-332-4.

The 34 papers presented in this anthology were selected because of their philosophical and epistemological orientation. Essays dealing with methods and techniques of preservation were excluded from the collection to avoid any sense of the prescriptive in dealing with conservation treatment. The anthology is divided into 10 sections: "Why Preservation?"; "The Nature of Library Materials"; "Causes of Deterioration"; "The Role of the Librarian"; "The Roles of the Conservator and the Scientist"; "Binding"; "Manuscripts and Documents"; "Preservation Microrecording and Other Copying Methods"; "Disaster and Salvage"; and "National Planning."

Each section begins with a commentary by the editors that provides a historical perspective and sets the tone for the papers that follow. At the conclusion of each commentary, there is a brief list of further readings pertinent to the subject of the section. The papers are reproduced in the forms in which they first appeared, so the reader is confronted with a variety of styles and methods of presentation. A footnote provides the place and date of the original publication of each paper, and any omissions in the text are clearly marked by the editors.

This anthology, besides its very useful function of providing the reference librarian with a convenient source of information on this important topic, makes available to the librarian, curator, and administrator a full array of principles, practices, and arguments for the establishment of a conservation program. The book is recommended for all those concerned about the preservation of library material and should be available in most library collections. [R: C&RL, Mar 79, pp. 190-91]   Dean H. Keller

855. Brown, Margaret R., comp., with the assistance of Don Etherington and Linda K. Ogden. **Boxes for the Protection of Rare Books: Their Design & Construction.** Washington, D.C., Preservation Office, Library of Congress; distr., Washington, D.C., GPO, 1982. 289p. illus. (A National Preservation Program Publication). $18.00 looseleaf. LC 81-607965. ISBN 0-8444-0365-2. S/N 030-000-00124-9.

With millions of nineteenth- and twentieth-century books deteriorating in library book stacks, librarians and conservators are fighting a holding action against time, acidic paper, and environmental pollutants. One effective way to retard deterioration is to box rare and fragile items. In this work the Library of Congress Preservation Office provides step-by-step illustrated directions for making sturdy protective boxes and portfolios designed to hold fragile books and manuscripts. Both the nonpermanent "phase box" and a variety of standard boxes are included. For each type of box instructions are followed by diagrams, but the looseleaf format permits rearrangement of pages. There is no index, but a detailed table of contents suffices. The book includes a list of materials suppliers that the Library of Congress uses.

The Library of Congress deserves praise for publishing such a complete instruction book for box making. Although other sources, notably

Cunha and Cunha's *Library and Archives Conservation: 1980s and Beyond* (see *ARBA* 84, entry 160), contain directions for phase boxes and pamphlet folders, none is as detailed as this work. Libraries with large rare book collections and in-house conservation labs will find this book useful for teaching box-making techniques to new employees. The instructions are clear and complete, and the well-drawn diagrams include enough detail to explain operations without confusing the reader.

Linda S. Keir

856. Cunha, George Martin, and Dorothy Grant Cunha. **Conservation of Library Materials, Volume I.** 2nd ed. Metuchen, N.J., Scarecrow, 1971. 406p. $25.00. LC 77-163871. SBN 8108-0427-1.

In 1967 Cunha published an introduction to the various facets of conservation. It included a vast bibliography with a critical description of the literature on the subject. It was a brave attempt (so many experts had been in the field for years, and yet in spite of the books little heed had been taken, by librarians in particular, of their warnings of the need for restoration and conservation). Cunha, who was trained as a chemist but returned to chemistry only after retiring from the Navy, was completely successful in producing a manual of practical guidance for librarians, curators, archivists and others. With one or two exceptions, the book was received with acclaim, and with Plenderleith's approbation its success was assured. In the next three years, the author took note of criticisms, added to the bibliography, and generally updated his first edition. This work is meticulous, with every conceivable aspect of preservation and conservation explored and explained, and with remedies suggested. There are chapters on the historical background, the nature and enemies of library materials, preventive care, repair and restoration. The final chapter, "When Disaster Strikes," prescribes action to deal with emergencies. The appendices contain sketches on the action of light, acid deterioration, adhesives, and many other causes of damage to materials. Illustrations are excellent—and cautionary. The authors remark that a dramatic change has taken place since the publication of the first edition—libraries, librarians, and library science have become increasingly aware of conservation—and this is all to the good. (For a review of volume 2, see entry 857.) Both volumes are essential to everyone who has library materials in their care. [R: A Arch, July 72, p. 421; CLW, May 72, p. 525; LJ, 1 June 72, p. 2056; RQ, Spring 72, p. 272]

P. William Filby

857. Cunha, George Martin, and Dorothy Grant Cunha. **Conservation of Library Materials: A Manual and Bibliography on the Care, Repair and Restoration of Library Materials. Vol. II: Bibliography.** 2nd ed. Metuchen, N.J., Scarecrow, 1972. 414p. $25.00. LC 77-163871. ISBN 0-8108-0525-1.

In 1967 Cunha published the first edition of a work on conservation of library materials. It met with instant success, but techniques discovered and works written in the years after that made a completely updated study necessary. The Cunhas worked diligently for four years and produced volume 1 of the second edition late in 1971. In it they note that a dramatic change had taken place: libraries, librarians, and library science are increasingly aware of conservation. It is strange how disasters such as Florence, tropical storm Agnes, Temple University, and others have affected the thinking of those who for long should have known of the possibilities of water damage. Volume 1 discussed all that was known about conservation of library materials. But a bibliography is essential if the reader is to derive the full benefit of the instruction, and the bibliography, exhaustive as it was in the first edition, received criticism, chiefly on its arrangement. But the second edition is better organized (by subjects) to correspond with the arrangement of text in volume 1. There is an author index arranged alphabetically, so with these two volumes the student, librarian, conservator, and amateur can now proceed with complete confidence when the normal problem develops. It is also clear from these two volumes when or whether an expert must be called in to the trouble. Meanwhile there is much to be done by staffs to prevent damage and deterioration. The astounding number of 4,882 references to books and articles is given. This is an exhaustive work which should satisfy every expert and should be in any library of consequence.

P. William Filby

858. Cunha, George Martin, and Dorothy Grant Cunha, assisted by Suzanne Elizabeth Henderson. **Library and Archives Conservation: 1980s and Beyond.** Metuchen, N.Y., Scarecrow, 1983. 2v. illus. bibliog. index. $16.00/vol. 1; $28.50/vol. 2; $39.50/set. LC 82-10806. ISBN 0-8108-1587-7 (vol. 1); 0-8108-1604-1 (vol. 2).

The authors state that their intention is "first, to provide an overview of some of the developments in the last fifteen years that are influencing conservation now; second, to provide broad general guidance on conservation management, preventative and restorative conservation, training and education, and disaster control; and third, to cautiously predict the future of this important aspect of librarianship." The second volume may be used in conjunction with *Conservation of Library Materials* (see *ARBA* 73, entry 72); it continues the numbering begun in that work, bringing the total listing up to 10,871 items, mostly published in English.

Appended to volume 1 are the "Principles of Conservation and Restauration [sic] in Libraries" issued by the IFLA Standing Committee on Conservation; a set of guidelines for library binders; instruction on devising an organization plan for conservation; a list of research centers and professional associations concerned with the matter; information on paper treatment, protective boxes, and wrappers; and a list of suppliers of materials. Although it is not a manual aimed at specific types of libraries in the same sense that S. G. Swartzburg's *Preserving Library Materials* (Scarecrow, 1980) is, this work does what its authors claim, providing an overview of the past and making suggestions for the future. Interestingly, however, despite the fact that the Cunhas predict sufficiently rapid changes in the field to outdate their work in the reasonably near future, the two volumes are printed on paper with a life expectancy of 100 years, something that other manuals recently published on the same topic have not been.

These two volumes maintain the level of excellence for which the Cunhas are renowned in the library and archival worlds. [R: BL, 1 Dec 83, p. 556; C&RL, July 83, pp. 302-3; LJ, 1 May 83, p. 890; WLB, May 83, p. 782]

Margaret Anderson

859. Cunha, George M., Howard P. Lowell, and Robert E. Schnare, Jr. **Conservation Survey Manual.** Ballston Lake, N.Y., Section on the Management of Information Resources and Technology of the New York Library Association (SMART), 1982. 64p. illus. bibliog. $7.95pa. ISBN 0-931658-05-5.

This manual is a convenient collection of basic information for librarians on how to assess the conservation needs of their buildings and collections. Cunha's and Schnare's articles provide the rationale and background data for a conservation program, while Lowell's "Needs Assessment Manual," prepared as a result of the Colorado Conservation Study of 1980, sets down specific guidelines for reviewing the conservation needs of the institution and provides some specific instructions for some basic conservation activities. The reference librarian will find especially useful two bibliographics of books and articles on conservation and preservation matters and two lists of sources of supply and information for the conservation of library material. Both bibliographies and lists of suppliers have been edited so that the entries are not repeated. Sample forms for recording data about storage conditions and the condition of collections, and specific instructions on surface cleaning, repairing paper, and polyester film encapsulation are also convenient for reference. [R: LRTS, July 83, p. 311]   Dean H. Keller

860. Gandert, Slade Richard. **Protecting Your Collection: A Handbook, Survey, & Guide for the Security of Rare Books, Manuscripts, Archives, & Works of Art.** New York, Haworth Press, 1982. 144p. bibliog. (Library & Archival Security, Vol. 4, Nos. 1/2). $19.95. LC 81-7004. ISBN 0-917724-78-X.

Gandert assembled 29 essays, a few less than two pages long, touching on ideas, history, and occasionally gossip, which relate to book and art theft. The essays are informal, although most are supported by impressive bibliographic notes. The book reads at times as if it were spoken; it is eclectic and anecdotal. Most of the book retells stories of thefts from libraries and archives, making interesting case-history material and valuable material as background for librarians concerned with the shining of their collections. One article is a good literature survey, and the bibliography is quite good for both historical and contemporary sources.

The book's subtitle is somewhat misleading, since this collection is neither a handbook nor a survey. Check into Alice Bahr's *Book Theft and Library Security Systems* (Knowledge Industry Publications, 1981) for that. The foreword says that the work is "not a theoretical or a 'how to prevent' treatise," and that is so. It also says that the book "is a practical text," and that is not so. The book contains a few misstatements, for example, "Paper was, prior to the twentieth century, made carefully and in small quantities" (p. 82). Gandert is right, however, in that many collections may need expert advice about collection security. This book does not inform librarians about how to prevent theft or how to establish security for valuable materials, but it is a supplement to technical guides and provides well-informed advice on library, archival, and museum security. [R: JAL, Sept 82, p. 256]

Neal L. Edgar

861. Middleton, Bernard C. **The Restoration of Leather Bindings.** rev. ed. Chicago, American Library Association, 1984. 266p. illus. bibliog. index. (LTP Publication, No. 20). $25.00pa. LC 83-15371. ISBN 0-8389-0391-6.

As the author notes in his preface, the field of binding restoration has experienced a number of changes during the years since the first edition of this work was published, not the least of which is an increased awareness of preservation problems and solutions. Middleton has taken that awareness into account, particularly in his expanded bibliography, but he is more concerned with advances in techniques and materials which have affected the craft of fine bookbinding. A comparison of the first and second editions shows many small but important changes where the author has updated the information in accordance with new research, particularly in the treatment of leather.

The major addition to the new book is the chapter on antiquarian books which discusses the practical, aesthetic, and moral issues involved in rebinding rare books and describes the construction and binding of old books. People interested in antiquarian books who will never be bookbinders will find this chapter informative and thought provoking. Illustrations in this chapter and throughout the book help clarify textual explanations.

This well-written but technical book will be useful to the practicing book binder and conservator. Because of its additions and revisions it should be preferred over the first edition. [R: C&RL, Nov 85, p. 531; JAL, Mar 85, p. 43]

Linda S. Keir

862. Morrow, Carolyn Clark. **Conservation Treatment Procedures: A Manual of Step-by-Step Procedures for the Maintenance and Repair of Library Materials.** Littleton, Colo., Libraries Unlimited, 1982. 191p. illus. bibliog. $19.50pa. LC 82-181. ISBN 0-87287-294-7.

Illustrated with detailed photographs, this step-by-step manual demonstrates the procedures for basic book repair, maintenance, and protective encasement. All procedures include a discussion of the treatment options; a list of specific equipment, tools, and supplies needed; the actual procedures to be followed; and, finally, any special instructions.

The text is intended for the librarian who manages the book repair and maintenance activities and for the paraprofessional or technician who actually does the work. Understanding treatment options and organizing and supervising the conservation workshop are discussed in the introductory chapter. The procedural chap-

ters are followed by an appendix, offering a decision-making checklist for book repair; profiles of four hypothetical libraries; a directory of equipment, tools, supplies, and suppliers; a dexterity test; a glossary; and a selected bibliography. A second edition is now available. [R: JLH, Summer 83, p. 362; LQ, Apr 83, p. 187; SL, Jan 83, p. 101]

863. Morrow, Carolyn Clark, with Gay Walker. **The Preservation Challenge: A Guide to Conserving Library Materials.** White Plains, N.Y., Knowledge Industry Publications, 1983. 231p. illus. bibliog. index. (Professional Librarian Series). $34.50; $27.50pa. LC 82-18726. ISBN 0-86729-028-5; 0-86729-027-7pa.

Designed and organized as an overview of the problems and techniques of conservation/preservation, this excellent introductory study is indeed a guide to an area far too often overlooked and avoided by many librarians because of the special knowledge and training it requires. Initial chapters point out the problems of collection deterioration and the pressing need to accept the challenge for action. Following chapters introduce some of the activities available to nearly all librarians for basic collection preservation, such as: environment control, proper handling, materials and techniques for repair and binding, developments in conservation, and the salvage of disintegrating materials. A chapter and an appendix briefly name some professional resources and educational opportunities available to librarians. Footnotes and a bibliography suggest some further sources, although some omissions occur. The chapter of case studies is of particular value. Each discusses a different problem in restoration, describing a conservation challenge by pointing to the steps taken with some details about tools and materials used but without many points of technique. This kind of detail is better presented in sources such as Laura Young's *Bookbinding & Conservation by Hand* (see *ARBA* 82, entry 273), which is not in Morrow's bibliography although it is in a footnote at the beginning of her own case study. Other parts of the book are written by recognized figures, such as Jean Gunner, Jane Greenfield, and Gay Walker; and Pamela Darling's excellent introduction lends additional authority. The language and discussions are detailed enough to be an intelligent survey of primary topics but not so overloaded with artificial erudition as to be pedantic or dull. Far from it. This text flows freely and easily, teasing the reader to find more details elsewhere. Materials covered also go beyond print, including film, sound recordings, and various tape formats. This is a first-rate overview of the problems covered. [R: C&RL, Sept 83, pp. 392-94; JAL, Sept 83, p. 229; WLB, Apr 83, p. 702] Neal L. Edgar

864. Planning for Library Conservation: A Needs Assessment Manual. Howard P. Lowell, project director. Denver, Colo., Colorado State Library, 1981. 1v. (unpaged). o.p.

This manual, a product of the Colorado Conservation Study (commissioned by the Colorado State Library), is intended to assist those concerned with the physical deterioration of documentary resources in libraries, archives, and manuscript collections. Aimed at librarians, archivists, and curators, it is a "self-assessment guide, offering a series of questions on program operations and building and storage conditions" (preface), most particularly with respect to materials in paper and book format.

Beginning with a general discussion of why and how library materials deteriorate, the manual moves on to a discussion of how to determine what one's specific conservation needs are and how to plan a program which addresses them. A set of questions concerning various points to be considered is provided, covering building environment, security, and lighting and storage facilities; provisions of properly trained staff is discussed as well. Sample survey forms for noting both general and specific conditions within the building and the collections are supplied.

The final section of the manual contains valuable information for the beginner wanting to mount a conservation program: there are a list of suppliers of conservation materials, together with the types of supplies they stock and complete with addresses and phone numbers; guidelines for the library's binder; instructions for surface cleaning of items and for the repairing of paper (a recipe for wheat starch paste is included); instructions for polyester film encapsulation of documents; and, finally, a basic bibliography for conservation administration. Certainly this manual would be of considerable use to any library administrator anxious about the preservation of the collection, most especially as costs of both new and replacement materials escalate in direct contrast to the declining library budget. [R: LJ, 1 Apr 82, p. 695]

Margaret Anderson

865. Swartzburg, Susan G. **Preserving Library Materials: A Manual.** Metuchen, N.J., Scarecrow, 1980. 282p. bibliog. index. $16.00. LC 80-11742. ISBN 0-8108-1302-5.

Very little has been written on this topic, not to mention, of course, the standard work prepared by George M. and Dorothy G. Cunha, *Conservation of Library Materials* (Scarecrow, 1971-1972). This work is based not only on rich personal experiences of the author (Swartzburg established the Preservation Office at Yale University Library), but also on a thorough knowledge of pertinent library literature. This manual, written primarily for smaller libraries, covers all important aspects of collection maintenance, including such topics as environmental factors, bookbinding, as well as preservation of various nonbook media (e.g., microforms, records, tapes and film, prints, etc.). The author also discusses long-range planning to preserve library materials through cooperative efforts among libraries and regional centers. This useful and highly recommended work concludes with a number of appendices (e.g., a well-selected and annotated bibliography, a glossary of terms, a fire safety self-inspection form, the standards of the Library Binding Institute, etc.). [R: LJ, 1 Sept 80, p. 1713] Bohdan S. Wynar

866. Young, Laura S. **Bookbinding & Conservation by Hand: A Working Guide.** New York, R. R. Bowker, 1981. 273p. illus. bibliog. index. $39.95. LC 81-7669. ISBN 0-8352-1375-7.

Using her many years of direct practice, Laura Young provides one of the best available primers on hand bookbinding in an attractive format which is easily read, well illustrated, and organized by a master of the art. She begins with an elementary description of a book's makeup, a chapter on types of binding and book design, another on basic equipment, and another on materials. Three chapters on techniques (basic, general, and specific) plus a chapter on finishing are together about 60 percent of the book. Two chapters cover other binding styles and protective cases. Only the eleventh chapter (16p.) deals directly with conservation, although many other points on repair, preservation, restoration, and related binding techniques are made throughout the book. Conservation is discussed as an extension of fine binding, and the conservation of nonbook materials, except by inference, is beyond Young's scope and purpose. The history of bookbinding, decorated papers, and other esoteric matters are deliberately omitted. These are considered beyond this beginning guide's general topics. References are found to some of this information in the bibliography.

The directions are clear, crisp, and functional. If a book were worked on as a test, following these paragraphs an amateur should have few troubles. Some instructions will be more beneficial if directed by an experienced binder. Some procedures are more difficult than others, but the narrative tends to treat them all equally. Problems frequently arise at all steps in hand binding, and many of the more common ones are brought up at the point when they might occur. Each is carefully solved, and at least one suggestion, sometimes two or more, is discussed. A valuable feature is that, where appropriate, a list of tools and supplies is given at the beginning of each process.

The illustrations, either line drawings or photographs, are used to demonstrate a process or to display tools. They are well placed; and, if anything, more of them, especially the drawings, could have been added. Having the drawings follow the text so well leads to one, probably unimportant, muddle: the definitions of tools and equipment are not in any real order except that they follow the photographs. Once or twice the captions to the illustrations are confusing or sometimes inconsistent (e.g., on page 19 "spoke shave" in the caption, but "spokeshave" in the text); and the caption of the frontispiece is a puzzle.

The index is fairly detailed and an adjunct to the table of contents. The brief, subject-arranged bibliography is a good beginning for additional information, although some well-known sources are not included. In at least one case, the work of James Faraday on leather decay, while cited in the text, is not detailed in the bibliography. There are no footnotes.

This book cannot, by itself, substitute for hands-on work. However, practice will be made more nearly perfect when this book is on the bench with other tools. Binders with years of experience will gain new insights and ideas from these pages. Highly recommended to anyone with any interest in hand binding. [R: WLB, Dec 81, p. 314]   Neal L. Edgar

REFERENCE WORKS

867. Harrison, Alice W., Edward A. Collister, and R. Ellen Willis. **The Conservation of Archival and Library Materials: A Resource Guide to Audiovisual Aids.** Metuchen, N.J., Scarecrow, 1982. 190p. index. $15.00. LC 82-652. ISBN 0-8108-1523-0.

Conservation and restoration of archival, library, and museum collections are topics of increasing importance, and this new volume fills some general and some specific needs. First, this is a selective and annotated listing of items appearing mostly between 1955 and 1980 which are intended to assist librarians, archivists, cura-

tors, teachers, bookbinders, and others concerned with the preservation and restoration of collections. Second, and of considerable importance, this book lists audiovisual materials: kits, sound recordings, motion pictures, slides, filmstrips, video recordings, and some other media such as charts and models. As such, the bibliography is an excellent supplement to the Cunhas' *Conservation of Library Materials* (Scarecrow, 1971-1972) and Paul N. Banks's *A Selective Bibliography on the Conservation of Research Library Materials* (Newberry Library, 1981).

The selection lists, for example, the two slide/tape programs issued in the Yale University Library conservation program. However, no way exists to locate these materials directly by their source; it is necessary to know the titles and to have them reasonably correct. But if the title is known, the main body of the book is the place to start, since it is alphabetical by title. Entries usually include the type of media, descriptive details, an annotation, sometimes one or two standard numbers, a producer/distributor, and sometimes a library source. A list of LC subject headings is followed by those headings for which materials were found, with titles arranged alphabetically under each heading (most titles are under more than one heading). Next come the list of the Consortium of University Film Centers and a solid list of producers'/distributors' addresses. Finally, a brief list of reference sources is provided. Most of the 500 items are from the United States, but a few Canadian, European, and Japanese items are found. A small number of important titles predating 1955 also appear. The editors have a broad definition to follow, since topics unrelated to specific conservation activities are included, for example: items on disasters, heat, insects, pollution, security, and television.

The content is reproduced from typed, camera-ready copy and sewn into a serviceable case binding. The production is typical of Scarecrow's style, quirks, and expected qualities. This positive addition to guides in the conservation field should have a wide audience. [R: LJ, 15 Dec 82, p. 2321]   Neal L. Edgar

868. Rath, Frederick L., and Merrilyn Rogers O'Connell, eds. **Care and Conservation of Collections: A Bibliography on Historical Organization Practices.** Compiled by Rosemary S. Reese. Nashville, Tenn., American Association for State and Local History, 1977. 107p. index. o.p. LC 75-26770.

This slim bibliography aims at serving two publics, and at providing them with the most current information in the area of collection conservation. The compilers note that the more general first sections (general reference and conservation organizations; philosophy, history, and principles of conservation; conservation laboratories and instrumentation; training of conservators) will be of most interest to trustees, administrators, curators, and the like. Professional conservators will possibly have use for the whole volume, but they also will find technical material listed in the section on environmental factors and those on the conservation of library materials, paintings, works of art on paper, and objects.

A basic reference list precedes the actual sections, and they are followed by an appendix listing periodicals cited (addresses, prices, etc.). The index is primarily title and author, but the fine subject division precludes the absolute necessity for a subject index; such an index might have helped to locate material in the general works cited, however. Chapters have introductory notes, and entries whose titles are not self-explanatory are annotated as to their contents. Material (primarily post-1945) has been selected to emphasize the most contemporary methods, and the bibliography does not attempt to present a historical perspective on conservation matters. Likewise, obscure or unattainable items were not included. Nicely organized, this work has a companion volume, *Historic Preservation*, reviewed in *ARBA* 77 (entry 381).

869. Roberts, Matt T., and Don Etherington. **Bookbinding and the Conservation of Books: A Dictionary of Descriptive Terminology.** Washington, D.C., Library of Congress; distr., Washington, D.C., GPO, 1982. 296p. illus. (part col.). bibliog. (A National Preservation Program Publication). $27.00. LC 81-607974. ISBN 0-8444-0366-0. S/N 030-000-00126-5.

Once again the Library of Congress has contributed to the growing number of publications on book conservation. Based on an extensive list of sources and on the authors' experience, this dictionary covers all aspects of the book as a physical object: paper making, printing, binding, and conservation. The book also includes entries for famous practitioners of the book arts through the ages. The definitions are well written in lay language, but with enough detail to make them useful to the specialist. Extensive cross-references guide the reader to appropriate entries. Line drawings illustrate some definitions but are rather sparse for a volume defining physical characteristics of the book. The long bibliography lists only works in English.

The most complete dictionary of its type, this work overlaps with but does not replace entirely Geoffrey Glaister's *Glossary of the Book* (Allen and Unwin, 1960). Printed on high-quality, acid-free paper with a sturdy binding, it will be useful to conservators, librarians, and students of bibliography. [R: Choice, Jan 83, p. 692; C&RL, Nov 83, pp. 500-504; LJ, Aug 83, p. 1458]   Linda S. Keir

870. **A Selective Bibliography on the Conservation of Research Library Materials.** By Paul N. Banks. Chicago, Newberry Library, 1981. 1v. (various paging). index. $10.00pa. ISBN 0-911028-26-9.

Numerous fiscal pressures, bibliographic requirements, and the intellectual desire to gather and organize cultural heritage are among the reasons for an increased emphasis on conservation and preservation in libraries, archives, and museums. Banks, who is conservator of the Newberry Library, revised an earlier bibliography to answer a part of the need for a simple approach to selected information on conservation.

No cutoff dates are announced, but very few items from the 1950s or before are included, with the majority from the 1960s and 1970s. A quick scan of approximately 1,200 entries found about 30 from both 1978 and 1979, with only 1 from 1980. Banks does not mention, for example, the start of the Yale University Library Preservation Pamphlets, two of which were published in 1980, nor Laura Young's *Bookbinding & Conservation by Hand* (R. R. Bowker, 1981). Although few, if any, references are used more than once, Banks does have a selection of periodicals, some of which are partially analyzed. Some of these periodicals do carry conservation articles on occasion but are not conservation journals (e.g., *American Libraries* and *Library Journal*).

The previous major work in this field is the Cunhas' *Conservation of Library Materials* (Scarecrow, 1971-1972), whose second volume includes 4,882 numbered entries. Some of these are used more than once, but even if half are, the Cunhas' book is much larger than Banks. The "decimal" classification scheme, which looks like an ISO standard but isn't one, has admitted weaknesses but serves as the subject approach. The items selected are limited to those in English. And several sections of the bibliography contain only two or three items with white space left to fill the pages. The editing is somewhat inconsistent, with citation practice not always being the same. Nevertheless, the Banks list is a good starting place, with its advantages of considerable selectivity and tight organization. This list does answer a part of the need for a simple approach to conservation and preservation. The list also reminds users that current literature must be studied for those materials published in the 1980s. [R: JLH, Spring 83, p. 222]   Neal L. Edgar

PROCEEDINGS AND SEMINARS

871. Cunha, George Martin, and Norman Paul Tucker, eds. **Library and Archives Conservation: The Boston Athenaeum's 1971 Seminar on the Application of Chemical and Physical Methods to the Conservation of Library and Archival Materials, May 17-21, 1971.** Boston, Library of the Boston Athenaeum, 1972. 255p. illus. o.p. LC 72-1894.

Contains over 30 papers by 15 participants on various aspects of this subject, including such factors as acid deterioration, environment control, air conditioning, pest control, etc. [R: LJ, 15 Feb 73, p. 515]

872. **Disasters: Prevention and Coping; Proceedings of the Conference, May 21-22, 1980.** James N. Myers and Denise D. Bedford, eds. Stanford, Calif., Stanford University Libraries, 1981. 177p. index. $10.00.

With advances in available library technology has come a large increase in interest about prevention of and planning for a wide range of potential library disasters. This edited volume, which contains nine papers originally presented at a major conference at Stanford University, provides a very general, limited overview of how to avoid or deal with these large-scale problems which threaten all library collections, and is intended for the beginning rather than the expert conservationist.

These nine papers, which vary greatly in length and quality, discuss the hazards library collections face from fire, water, people and pests, the chemical contents of the library material, and the library environment. The lack of references, bibliographies, and illustrations in these reports seriously diminishes their value. The five sections in the appendix which describe the difficulties created by and the actions taken to remedy these situations following the severe flooding of Stanford's library in November 1978 are the most worthwhile part of this book. Useful illustrations and photographs add to the value of the appendix, which comprises more than half of the volume.

The growing concern about conservation of library collections has created a sizeable litera-ture in this important specialty area. Unfortunately, this collected work offers little or no new information for library conservationists. Librarians looking for useful studies on protecting and preserving library materials should examine the outstanding publications by Carolyn Horton, Paul N. Banks, and other acknowledged leaders in this field.

Jonathon Erlen

873. Russell, Joyce R., ed. **Preservation of Library Materials: Proceedings of a Seminar Sponsored by the Library Binding Institute and the Princeton-Trenton Chapter of Special Libraries Association Held at Rutgers University, July 20-21, 1979.** New York, Special Libraries Association, 1980. 96p. illus. $10.50pa. LC 80-20706. ISBN 0-87111-270-1.

An aggregation of experts discuss the state of the art in the field of conservation and preservation of library materials. Aimed at a general audience of practicing librarians, the proceedings avoid the extremely technical, with papers more on the nuts and bolts level than on the theoretical or philosophical level. The typography is rather indifferent and utilitarian—probably done on an IBM composer. Proofreading might have been improved (e.g., the table of contents lists Susan Thompson as Sarah Thompson). The continuity is lost between pages 40 and 41; a page must have been left out.

Joyce Russell was the conference chairperson; she edited the papers and also provides an introduction. Susan G. Swartzberg presented a paper on "Preservation: An Overview." Others include: "Housekeeping," by Pamela W. Darling; "Education and Training," by Paul N. Banks; "Disasters," by Willman [sic] Spawn; "Changing World of Library Binding," by Stephen H. Roberts; "Book Making and Book Binding," by Werner Rebsamen; "Book as Object," by Gaylord Brynolfson; "Third and Fourth World Materials," by Peter T. Johnson; "Lamination and Encapsulation of Archival Materials," by Robert I. Boak; "Mass Deacidification," by George B. Kelly, Jr.; "Microforms," by Helga Borck; and "Regional Conservation Center," by Ann Russell.

The papers were followed by a panel discussion and Susan Thompson's list of "Audio Visual Aids for the Teaching of Preservation of Library Materials." Each paper is followed by a record of the ensuing discussion, and several of the papers have brief bibliographies appended to them. The contributors are identified on the last page, along with their position titles and institutional affiliations.

Like most conference proceedings, the papers are uneven in quality. The time lapse between conference, publication, and review inevitably means that the information is dated. This will probably be useful supplementary reading for library school students, or as a quick study for practicing librarians. [R: JAL, May 81, p. 127; LJ, 1 Dec 81, p. 2293]

Frank J. Anderson

874. Winger, Howard W., and Richard Daniel Smith, eds. **Deterioration and Preservation of Library Materials: The 34th Annual Conference of the Graduate Library School, August 4-6, 1969.** Chicago, University of Chicago Press, 1970. 200p. illus. bibliog. $14.00. LC 78-115971. ISBN 0-226-90201-3.

Sixteen specialist contributions examine all aspects of printed materials in libraries including storage and use environments, nature and characteristics of printing papers, and binding and preservation problems. Although some materials must be preserved for their own sake, alternatives to preservation, such as film and ensuing problems, are discussed. Highly technical in some sections, the volume should be read by all librarians responsible for collection preservation. [R: BL, 1 Jan 71, p. 345; LJ, 1 Oct 70, p. 3251]

Charles D. Patterson

33 Copyright and Reprography

GENERAL WORKS

875. King Research, Inc. **Library Photocopying in the United States: With Implications for the Development of a Copyright Royalty Payment Mechanism.** Washington, D.C., National Commission on Libraries and Information Science, 1977. 251p. bibliog. o.p. LC 77-91033. S/N 052-003-00443-7.

Two unresolved questions concerning the copyright law, as far as libraries are concerned, are: what is the level of allowable library photocopying? and how many items photocopied would be kept to royalty payments? With librarians (and other users of copyrighted works) on one side and publishers and producers on the other, who could be trusted to undertake an objective study to answer these questions? After some debate, it was decided the National Commission on Libraries and Information Science should fund a study by an independent research group.

King Research Incorporated of Rockville, Maryland, was selected, and in all likelihood, its study will satisfy neither the users nor the producers of copyrighted works. Dissatisfaction on both sides may mean that the study is reasonably accurate. Certainly, the data the firm collected and the statistical techniques they employed were impressive. Librarians will be unhappy with the report because of the data on the volume of copying of copyrighted works. In 1976, an estimated 114 million *items* were copied just by library staff members, and of that number, 54 million were copyrighted. Producers of copyrighted materials, however, will also be dissatisfied because of the findings regarding how many of the 54 million items copied would be subject to royalty payments. Using the CONTU (Commission on New Technological

Uses of Copyrighted Works) guidelines for reasonable copying of serials for interlibrary loan purposes (3.1 million copyrighted items were photocopied for ILL), only 500,000 would have been subject to royalty payments. Thus the report indicates a high volume of photocopying of copyrighted material, but under the CONTU guidelines, only a very small percentage of the total is actually subject to royalty payments.

In terms of identifying one mechanism for collecting and distributing royalty payments due from photocopy activities, the report is a failure. What it does do is to explore the nine most "acceptable" methods as far as libraries are concerned — acceptable in the sense that if there must be *something*, these nine are the least objectionable. As with every other publication discussing the copyright law, this report concludes with the statement, "there are still uncertainties concerning the circumstances in which royalty payments would be legally required.... Until these uncertainties are resolved, it will continue to be difficult to assess the impacts of alternative royalty payment mechanisms" (p. 199).

The report does raise one such important "uncertainty" that has seldom been discussed — intrasystem photocopying. P.L. 94-553 specifically mentions individual users, fair use, and a limited amount of photocopying for interlibrary loan. One major finding of the King study is that intrasystem copying of protected works for "internal use only" is twice that of ILL photocopying (over 7 million items copied). No one is certain in which category intrasystem photocopying falls — subject to or not subject to royalty payments. If all of these items are subject to royalty payments, libraries will have a major problem to solve. Not everyone needs to read the entire report, but every librarian should read the first and last chapters, which provide the overview and conclusions of the study. [R: BL, 15 Apr 78, p. 1335; LJ, 15 June 78, p. 1238]

G. Edward Evans

876. LaHood, Charles G., Jr., and Robert C. Sullivan. **Reprographic Services in Libraries: Organization and Administration.** Chicago, American Library Association, 1975. 74p. illus. index. (Library Technology Program Publication, No. 19). o.p. LC 75-25585. ISBN 0-8389-8166-9. (Available from Books on Demand, $20.00, ISBN 0-317-26573-3).

This manual provides guidelines for the establishment and operation of reprographic services in small, medium-sized, and large libraries. Primary emphasis is on planning and administration rather than technical considerations. Individual chapters deal with the history of reprographic services in libraries, types of services appropriate to libraries of various sizes, order processing procedures, establishment of pricing policies and fees, and bibliographic considerations in reprography. The discussion in all chapters is brief and general. The several appendices provide a list of selected national reprographic standards, a list of documents that it is illegal to reproduce photographically, and a sample fair use copyright pledge. The glossary consists of selections from the National Microfilm Association's *Glossary of Micrographics*.

Although the book is well written and reasonably priced, readers should be alerted to a few shortcomings. The section on photocopier technology uses the term "electrostatic" incorrectly to denote a type of reprographic process that differs from "Electrofax." In fact, as the book's glossary indicates, the Electrofax process is a variant of the electrostatic process. The authors ignore the potential of Small Office Microform (SOM) products for many smaller scientific and technical libraries. Finally, since the manuscript was completed in late 1973, the bibliography fails to reflect recent work in this fast-growing field. [R: C&RL, Nov 76, pp. 569-70; LJ, 1 Sept 76, p. 1717; RQ, Summer 76, pp. 367-68]   William Saffady

877. McDonald, Dennis D., Colleen G. Bush, with others. **Libraries, Publishers and Photocopying: Final Report of Surveys Conducted for the United States Copyright Office.** Rockville, Md., King Research, Inc., 1982. 1v. (various paging). illus. $25.00.

The five-year review of library photocopying conducted by King Research was intended to supply hard data to assess how well the new copyright law was working. Their study did supply data, but an examination of the comments about the data in the open literature leads one to realize how difficult it will be to assess the effectiveness of the law. The study also could be used as a classic example of how the same data can be interpreted by interest groups as supporting opposite points of view.

This document is a straightforward report of six surveys King Research conducted for the U.S. Copyright Office during 1981 (five years after the law went into effect). The authors do not attempt to interpret the data; they simply report what was done, when and where, and what the results were. Three of the surveys examined various aspects of library photocopying; one was concerned with publishers, and two were related to library patrons. The first survey was a long questionnaire about materials, budgets, photocopy operations, photocopy permission requisition, interlibrary loan activities, and reserve book operations (790 public, academic, federal and special libraries were contacted, and 554 responded). Of the responding libraries, 150 participated in the two follow-up surveys, one of which was on interlibrary loan requests (a log of requests made during three time periods in 1981) and the other was a transaction log survey of photocopying done by the library staff for patrons. The publisher survey went to 450 U.S. book and serial publishers, of whom 231 responded. Data collected covered such items as number of titles published between 1976 and 1980, price changes for publications, number of serial subscribers, photocopy permission requests received, licenses issued to document delivery services, and photocopy royalty income. User surveys were conducted in 21 public, academic, federal, and special libraries. One survey related to individuals' past photocopying of library material and their use of interlibrary loan services (1,157 interviews were conducted); the other survey was of persons who were actually using a photocopy machine in the library to determine what they were copying (823 interviews were conducted).

A copy of this report should be in every library system to help staff members with the highly debated issue of fair use and copyright.

G. Edward Evans

878. New, Peter G. **Reprography for Librarians.** London, Clive Bingley; distr., Hamden, Conn., Linnet Books, 1975. 109p. illus. index. $12.50. LC 75-11631. ISBN 0-208-01373-3.

This book is introductory in character and directed toward librarians and students of librarianship. Thus, it covers the subject reprography in general. It discusses the factors to be taken into consideration in choosing one reprographic method over another, the various microcopy methods and uses, and photocopy and multiple reproduction techniques. The last chapter of the book, entitled "Information Sources," includes advanced readings on the subject, a list of independent organizations that can give expert advice, and a list of international manufacturers and suppliers. The book is invaluable for its emphasis on principles rather than technical detail, and for its simplified approach to the subject. It makes very good reading for the uninitiated. [R: LJ, 15 May 76, p. 1188]   M. Nabil Hamdy

879. **Report of the Register of Copyrights: Library Reproduction of Copyrighted Works. (17 U.S.C. 108).** Washington, D.C., National Technical Information Service/U.S. Department of Commerce, 1983. 363p. $17.50pa. LC 82-600662. ISBN 0-8444-0419-5.

This report provides an essential piece in the puzzle of whether library and information center reproduction of copyrighted works under the current copyright law is within the limits intended. The report presents the copyright office's position on the question: Does section 108 of the Copyright Act of 1976 provide "a workable structural framework for obtaining a balance between creators' rights and users' needs"? Chapter 9 of the report contains several recommendations from the copyright office for statutory changes for improvements in and clarifications of section 108 and a number of recommendations for nonstatutory modifications. The entire document is worth reading, and chapter 2 ("Background and Legislative History") should be required reading for all library school students, as it provides an excellent overview of how we arrived at this situation. Anyone who reads the "Executive Summary" (chapter 1) will probably be intrigued enough to read one or more of the remaining eight chapters to get the details and specifics so briefly touched upon in the opening chapter. "Balance," the central issue of the report, is the topic of chapters 3 and 4. King Research's five-year review of library photocopying is detailed and commented upon in chapter 5. Implications of new technologies, in terms of both needed and existing coverage, under the existing law, are outlined in chapter 6. Problems of international copyright and library photocopying are examined in chapter 7. Chapter 8 provides a summary and analysis of various legislative proposals the copyright office placed on record

during the preparation of the report. Does the copyright office feel balance has been achieved? The answer is a qualified yes, if the recommended statutory changes are implemented. Unfortunately, none of the seven appendices listed in the table of contents accompanied the review copy. The appendix material listed was the King Report and transcripts of the hearings on the question of balance in Chicago, Houston, Washington, Anaheim, and New York. Well worth the price for anyone interested in copyright.   G. Edward Evans

880. Whitestone, Patricia. **Photocopying in Libraries: The Librarians Speak.** White Plains, N.Y., Knowledge Industry Publications, 1977. 112p. bibliog. index. o.p. LC 77-8924. ISBN 0-914236-08-3.

This report presents the results of a questionnaire and interview survey designed to elicit an accurate picture of the current extent and significance of photocopying in libraries. The methodology employed is similar to that featured in other offerings of this publisher. A questionnaire was mailed to 280 libraries, of which 138 responded. Personal interviews were conducted at an unstated number of large and small libraries. Additional libraries were the subject of telephone interviews. The conclusions will surprise no one: photocopying machines were found to be readily available in libraries; the bulk of copies made on those machines were created from library materials; periodicals are more heavily copied than other library materials; and most libraries make some charge for photocopies. The report does, however, contain some information on the percentages and types of reprographic equipment used by librarians that is not readily available in any other source. These data, presented in tables interspersed throughout the text, will be of interest to librarians responsible for the design of reprographic systems and for the analysis of reprographic trends. [R: JAL, July 78, p. 162; RQ, Spring 78, p. 268]   William Saffady

REFERENCE WORKS

881. Nitecki, Joseph Z. **Directory of Library Reprographic Services.** 8th ed. Westport, Conn., Meckler Publishing, 1982. 540p. bibliog. index. $29.95pa. LC 82-2137. ISBN 0-930466-47-0.

This publication first appeared in 1959 with the title *Directory of Library Photoduplication Services in the United States, Canada, and Mexico.* Now issued as the *Directory of Library*

Reprographic Services and in existence for 23 years, it is sponsored by a section of the American Library Association. This eighth edition supersedes the seventh edition, published in 1978. (For a review of the fifth edition, 1973, see *ARBA* 75, entry 161; for the sixth edition, 1976, see *ARBA* 77, entry 181.) The objective of the directory is to provide information about copying and duplicating facilities which are available at major foreign and domestic libraries. Represented here are 428 domestic and 92 foreign institutions.

The directory is divided into two sections, the first section listing the domestic libraries and their services by state and then by name, followed by a listing of the foreign libraries and their services by country and then by name. Entries include addresses of departments accepting orders. Section 2 includes additional ordering information; an index to states, Canadian provinces, and countries included in the directory; a bibliography of related sourcebooks; and a list of previous editions of the directory.

The use of the same form for each entry and the printing of one entry per page add to the overall usefulness of the directory. In addition, the extensive information about services rendered by each institution (price of copying services, type of printing process used, type of film used, etc.) makes the directory a valuable reference tool. However, use and purchase of the tool will depend a great deal upon the needs of the interlibrary loan or acquisitions department.

Many libraries exchange policy statements which outline the information included in the directory. The directory is not an annual publication, and thus will not remain as current as necessary.   Barbara Sproat

ESSAYS

882. Heilprin, Laurence B., ed. **Copyright and Photocopying: Papers on Problems and Solutions, Design for a Clearinghouse, and a Bibliography.** College Park, Md., College of Library and Information Services, University of Maryland, 1977. 158p. (Student Contribution Series, No. 10). $6.00pa. LC 77-620028. ISBN 0-911808-14-0.

This consists of two reports and a bibliography on the copyright photocopying problem. The reports were written as class projects in library operations research at the University of Maryland during 1975 and 1976. The bibliography was carried out as an independent study in 1976. The first report sifts through proposed solutions to the problem of photocopying copy-

righted works and presents objective pros and cons to each solution. The second report is an in-depth study of one of the solutions, a copyright clearinghouse, including its organization, economic considerations, and requirements for implementation.

From the standpoint of reference value, the bibliography is the most important part of the book. It consists of 275 citations, about one-half of which are annotated. It is divided into two parts: the first covers citations on photocopying and copyright law from 1970 through 1976, arranged alphabetically by author. The works cited represent the conjunction of the topics of photocopying and copyright, and of course, do not include hundreds of articles on the separate aspects of each subject. Some articles are indicated as being news items and some as covering international copyright. The second part is a list of references to the important *Williams and Wilkins vs. U.S.* case; it consists of 55 citations.

The title indicates that this is a selective bibliography, but it is not clear on what criteria the selection is based. It is also not clear why citations go back no further than 1970, except that 1970-1976 is the "period immediately prior to passage of the Copyright Revision Act of 1976." The annotations are well written and informative. All in all, this bibliography is a worthwhile pulling together of resources with helpful annotations. [R: RQ, Spring 78, p. 262]
                                A. Neil Yerkey

COPYRIGHT

883. Bush, George P., and Robert H. Dreyfuss, eds. **Technology and Copyright: Sources and Materials.** 2nd rev. ed. Mt. Airy, Md., Lomond Books, 1979. 552p. index. $22.50; $15.50 microfiche. LC 79-65635. ISBN 0-912338-17-2; 0-912338-18-0 microfiche.

The first edition of *Technology and Copyright* was published in 1972 (see *ARBA* 74, entry 53). Since that time, the enactment of the 1978 Copyright Law has clarified some points on the legal protection of technology; but this area remains ambiguous, and will be subject to much debate and conflicting judicial opinion. The timely second edition of *Technology and Copyright* does, as its preface states, "present the reader with reference and resource materials which will not only inform and educate, but will also provide a sense of the debate centering on the provisions of the Copyright Law relating to technology and copyright" (p. v).

Part 1 is an annotated bibliography, divided into subjects ranging from specific technologies (computer systems, reprography, video communications, microforms) to technological applications (education, libraries, networks and information systems, permissions and payments). The scope of each section and references to other applicable sections are given in headnotes. The bibliography is representative rather than exhaustive, but presents a balance of views expressed on the law in the context of the technological environment.

Part 2 is a superlative selection of reprinted articles and documents drawn from legal, technological, and information science literature. The deicision of the *Williams & Wilkins* case is also reprinted. These are key papers which should be read by everyone involved in the information transfer process.

The back matter includes a list of the 101 periodicals cited, and separate name, subject, and case indexes. The work is, appropriately, issued in dual media. This is an excellent presentation, and is highly recommended for all but the smallest general collections.

Theresa Maylone

884.   Chickering, Robert B., and Susan Hartman. **How to Register a Copyright and Protect Your Creative Work: A Basic Guide to the New Copyright Law and How It Affects Anyone Who Wants to Protect Creative Work.** New York, Scribner's, 1980. 216p. index. $12.95. LC 80-23203. ISBN 0-684-16705-0.

As the title indicates, this book is designed to help readers understand the nature of copyright protection and to take the steps necessary to protect their rights under the copyright law. Written in the second person, the book is directed to the nonexpert, and is practical in orientation. It is more than a mere "how to" guide, however; a considerable amount of general information is provided in concise form.

The first four chapters focus on such topics as the requirements for and the benefits of copyright, obtaining and completing the appropriate forms, and the notice requirement. Reproductions of various forms and instructions are included. (It should be noted that some 68 of the book's 216 pages consist of reproduced forms.) The remaining three chapters discuss other aspects of copyright law, including transfer of ownership, design patents, public domain, fair use, infringement, and royalties. Other subjects discussed are the reproduction and distribution of copyrighted works by libraries and archives, and copyright exemptions. Appendices provide brief treatment of the following topics: major

changes brought about by the Copyright Act of 1976, forms of legal protection for intellectual property other than copyright, and the resources and services of the United States Patent Office. There is an index, but no bibliography.

The book is roughly comparable to Warren L. Patton's *An Author's Guide to the Copyright Law* (Lexington, 1980). The latter, however, is directed to the creator of written work, whereas the present book is addressed to the creator of any form of copyrightable material. The Patton book is more discursive and provides fuller treatment of such areas as infringement and permissions. This book may also be compared with William E. Strong's *The Copyright Book: A Practical Guide* (MIT Press, 1981). The Strong book furnishes more general information and includes legal citations, but does not provide detailed, step-by-step treatment of the actual copyright registration procedure, as do Chickering and Hartman.

Clearly and carefully written, the book renders accessible a difficult area of law. The authors are to be commended for this achievement. [R: BL, 1 Jan 81, p. 602; RQ, Summer 81, p. 433]

Irene Berkey

885.   **The Complete Guide to the New Copyright Law.** By the New York Law School Law Review. Dayton, Ohio, Lorenz Press; distr., Port Washington, N.Y., Independent Publishers Group, 1977. 448p. $25.00. ISBN 0-89328-013-5.

The book contains a series of expert commentaries on each major section of the copyright law that was revised by PL 94-553. Each contributor has a national reputation as an attorney and is an expert in copyright issues.

The text is divided into two sections: part 1 covers aspects of the proposed legislation that did not change as a result of the final Senate debates, and part 2 provides commentaries on the law as passed. The discussions are as detailed and as authoritative as possible, especially when the topics are fine points of law. Topics include works made for hire; duration of copyright; notice, deposit, and registration; analysis of infringement sections; fair use; CATV copyright; sound recordings; termination of transfers and licensing; and international copyright. Of the dozens of books and articles that have appeared, this work and the *Copyright Handbook*, compiled by Donald Johnston (R. R. Bowker, 1978), are the two most useful items for answering a librarian's questions about copyright.

G. Edward Evans

886. **Copyright Law Symposium: Nathan Burkan Memorial Competition, Number Twenty-Seven.** New York, Columbia University Press, 1982. 331p. bibliog. index. $20.00. LC 40-8341. ISBN 0-231-05296-0; ISSN 0069-9950.

Since its inception in 1953, the Nathan Burkan Memorial Competition, sponsored by the American Society of Composers, Authors, and Publishers, has attracted the efforts of the best and brightest of third-year law school students. The prize-winning essays published in this series over the years deal with every aspect of copyright and reflect the major issues of current interest. The six essays in this volume, written in 1977, the year following passage of the Copyright Act and preceding its implementation, explore some of the areas of most interest at present. The topics covered include: the impact of the federal preemption clause on the role of state courts in trying cases of misappropriation of literary property, fair use, performance rights in sound recordings, record piracy, originality in art reproductions, and the provisions for notice of copyright. The volume includes an extensive list of cases and articles referred to, an excellent index, and a listing of past prize-winning essays.

Robert D. Stevens

887. Johnston, Donald F. **Copyright Handbook.** 2nd ed. New York, R. R. Bowker, 1982. 381p. $29.95. LC 77-27449. ISBN 0-8352-1488-5.

This handbook is essentially the publisher's book-length version of how the 1976 Copyright Law should be interpreted. The second edition includes all the significant developments since its 1978 edition was published. As before, the book provides a narrative explanation of most of the major issues of the new law: user rights; copyrightable material; copyright notice; deposit copies; registration; ownership, transfer, and licenses; exclusive rights; infringement remedies; duration; international considerations; fair use; library reproduction; limits on exclusive performance and display rights; and compulsory licenses. New areas covered include computer programs, databases, and home video recording and cable television. Hypothetical case studies help clarify complex concepts. The over 150 pages of appendices include, among other items, the full text of both the 1909 and the 1976 laws, the CONTU guidelines, and examples of many of the copyright forms. Since Johnston is legal counsel for R. R. Bowker, he presents more of the publisher's point of view. However, the handbook provides the best rendition of both legal text and possible interpretations of all available sources.

G. Edward Evans

888. McCormick, Marilyn G., comp. **The Williams & Wilkins Case: The Williams & Wilkins Company v. The United States, Volume One.** New York, Science Associates/International, 1974. 275p. o.p. LC 74-12461.

The *Williams and Wilkins* case has done more than any other legal action to signal the obsolescence of our copyright laws. Hence, the documents of the case deserve careful study. Part 1 of this volume consists of the papers and briefs filed before the U.S. Court of Claims, from the Report of the Commissioner and the Defendant's Brief (the government's defense of the right of the National Library of Medicine to photocopy articles from the plaintiff's journals), the Plaintiff's Brief, and no fewer than 19 *Amicus Curiae* ("friends of the Court") briefs, including, of course, that of the American Library Association.

Part 2 consists of the papers filed before the Supreme Court. The papers and briefs are the full texts; they are not excerpts or condensations.

A necessary purchase for law libraries as well as for the personal collections of librarians with a strong professional interest in problems of copyright litigation and legislation. [R: LJ, 15 Mar 75, pp. 597-98]

889. Miller, Jerome K. **Applying the New Copyright Law: A Guide for Educators and Librarians.** Chicago, American Library Association, 1979. 144p. index. o.p. LC 79-4694. ISBN 0-8389-0287-1.

The new copyright law and its numerous new provisions have brought teachers and librarians face to face with questions of copyright compliance. The limits of this work are clearly stated by the author. This book does not attempt to offer final solutions or legal opinions; instead, it focuses on the major copyright issues that face librarians and teachers, discusses the pertinent provisions of the law, and presents typical copyright situations that may occur in schools and libraries. Positions taken on these questions are not intended as the minimum rights, nor the outermost limits of the law, but tend toward a safe middle passage. The positions stated were reviewed by several competent authorities on copyright. The first part of the book discusses a brief history of copyright; the concept of fair use; library photocopying; ways of obtaining permission; and procedures for securing copyright protection. The text is clearly written and direct.

This is in no way a reference manual to be tersely consulted and set aside. Care must be taken to study the entire text and the documents, which are presented in the appendices. Miller has rendered an admirable service by preparing an understandable introduction to the new copyright law, with some reasonable guidelines for teachers and librarians to follow in resolving certain questions of fair use and rights. [R: JAL, Nov 79, p. 291; LJ, 15 Oct 79, p. 2176] Christine Gehrt Wynar

890. Miller, Jerome K. **U.S. Copyright Documents: An Annotated Collection for Use by Educators and Librarians.** Littleton, Colo., Libraries Unlimited, 1981. 292p. bibliog. index. o.p. LC 80-24768. ISBN 0-87287-239-4.

The enactment of the Copyright Revision Act of 1976 brought teachers and librarians face to face with copyright issues and problems of determining their particular rights and limitations regarding the duplication of copyrighted works. Jerome K. Miller, author of *Applying the New Copyright Law* (see entry 881), provides clear, concise discussions of those sections of the law that pertain to educators and librarians.

Seven essays in part 1 elucidate the ambiguous concept of "fair use," and the complex regulations regarding the duplication of journal articles for reserve reading collections; the duplication of musical, pictorial, graphic, and audiovisual works by libraries and archives; interlibrary loan; registration and deposit; the reproduction of unpublished materials; and copyright warning notices.

The Copyright Revision Act of 1976 is reprinted in its entirety in part 2, interspersed with the corresponding sections of the three congressional reports (the Senate report, the House report, and the Conference Committee report), providing a convenient parallel reading of the law and its supporting documents. A few additional documents have been included to supplement the four major documents. These include: (1) passages in older congressional reports cited in the three key congressional reports, (2) selected Copyright Office regulations, and (3) copyright documents issued by the American Library Association and other recognized groups, such as CONTU. The editor's notes, interspersed among the passages, clarify key points of the law and refer the reader to related sections of the law. Also included in part 2 are the Transitional and Supplementary Provisions. A selected bibliography and a detailed index complete the volume. [R: LJ, 1 Oct 81, p. 1889; RQ, Summer 81, p. 433]

891. Patton, Warren L. **An Author's Guide to the Copyright Law.** Lexington, Mass., Lexington Books, a division of D. C. Heath, 1980. 192p. index. $27.00. LC 76-16329. ISBN 0-669-00740-4.

This handbook explains the basics of copyright protection in easy-to-understand language aimed primarily at the inexperienced author. Even for the experienced author, the changes in copyright law since PL 94-553, effective 1 January 1978, are a whole different set of rules to understand. Patton covers such potentially gray areas as derivative works and works for hire. He also discusses permissions to copy copyrighted works, the author's option to refuse copyright, fair use, and penalties for infringement. For the author dealing with a publisher or other authors it is important to understand ownership and transfer of copyright, assignments, and licenses. These, too, are explained in lay terms. For authors publishing their own work, the form of the notice of copyright on individual and collective works is discussed. Appendix C reprints the "Interim Rules: Methods of Affixation and Position of the Copyright Notice." Other appendices are: "The Agreement on Guidelines for Classroom Copying in Not-for-Profit Educational Institutions"; "Copyright Bulletin No. 38(a): International Copyright Relations of the United States"; a reduced reproduction of the "Application for Copyright Registration for a Nondramatic Literary Work, Form TX"; a sample permission request form; and the "United States Copyright Act of 1976, PL 94-553," reprinted in full.

Patton has done an excellent job of explaining this potentially confusing subject. Although he does not go into detail on the problems which may arise when filling out form TX, very often this is done by the publisher, and answers to specific questions can be sought from the Copyright Office; they are very good about returning a questionable application with suggested alternatives for resolving the problem. The explanations in this book will cover most copyright situations. For unusual cases or where there is a real question of copyright infringement, the author wisely advises consultation with a copyright lawyer. *An Author's Guide to the Copyright Law* is certainly recommended for college, public, and corporation libraries, as well as publishers faced with explaining the law to their authors. [R: C&RL, Sept 80, p. 255; JAL, Sept 80, p. 245]

Louise Stwalley

892. Strong, William S. **The Copyright Book: A Practical Guide.** 2nd ed. Cambridge, Mass., MIT Press, 1984. 224p. index. $13.95. LC 81-742. ISBN 0-262-19234-9.

This excellent introduction to copyright law will be welcomed by people who use copyrighted works—teachers, librarians, performers, business people—and the artists and authors who create them. Written in nontechnical language for laypersons by a lawyer specializing in copyright law, the book takes the reader through the intricacies of the 1976 copyright law, which came into effect in January 1978.

The 11 chapters, all clearly subdivided for easy access, cover topics such as the subject matter of copyright ownership, transfers of copyright, registering a copyright claim, subsidiary rights, compulsory licenses, and infringement and "fair" use. A detailed subject index allows ready access to the text.

Heather Cameron

893. Tseng, Henry P. **New Copyright U.S.A.: A Guide for Teachers and Librarians.** New York, AMCO International, 1979. 434p. bibliog. index. $23.00pa. LC 78-75114. ISBN 0-9602406-0-8.

While Jerome Miller's *Applying the New Copyright Law* (see *ARBA* 80, entry 54) is a practical handbook on the everyday application of the Copyright Law of 1976, Tseng's *New Copyright U.S.A.* is an explanation of the provisions of the law which apply to teachers and librarians. Part 1 discusses the main provisions of the copyright law, such as the single system of copyright protection, duration of copyright, works for hire, fair use, reproduction by libraries and archives, jukebox royalty, cable television, and divisibility of copyright. Part 2, "More about Copyright," goes into more detail on the topics of subject matter and scope of copyright; exclusive rights in copyrighted works; duration of copyright; copyright notice, deposit, and registration; and copyright infringement and remedies, citing specific sections and subsections of the law. Part 3 discusses the concept of fair use, its historical development, definitions, and determination, illustrated with 23 selected cases of how the courts have ruled from 1841 to 1978. It also covers photocopying for classroom use and library photocopying under this law and such proposed solutions and recommendations for photocopying problems as various types of fees and licensing, including CONTU's (National Commission on New Technological Uses of Copyrighted Works) proposed statutory amendment. The text is supplemented by reprints of relevant documents, including the full text of the "Revised Copyright Act of 1976," the "Agreement on Guidelines for Classroom Copying in Not-for-Profit Educational Institutions," guidelines for the proviso of subsection 108(g) regarding interlibrary arrangements on photocopying, an exchange of letters regarding the 1976 act, and the "Recommended Record Maintenance and Retention Procedure for Interlibrary Loan Departments."

One-fourth of this book is the reprinted documents, which, while handy for quick reference, do add to the size and price of the book. The large, pica typewriter-sized type, double spaced, also expands the apparent size. In spite of this, Tseng's detailed explanation of the law and its implications, together with its historical development, lends to its understanding. *New Copyright U.S.A.* should definitely be in any large or professional library's growing collection of copyright books. [R: JAL, Jan 80, p. 364]

Louise Stwalley

894. White, Herbert S., ed. **The Copyright Dilemma: Proceedings of a Conference Held at Indiana University April 14-15, 1977.** Chicago, American Library Association, 1978. 199p. $10.00pa. LC 78-5929. ISBN 0-8389-0262-6.

Public law 94-533 (copyright) has generated a number of books and a veritable flood of journal articles. During the 10 years preceding passage of the law, everyone had their say as to how the bill should be written. Needless to say, the act that passed has not completely satisfied anyone. Critics now feel they must expound upon what is wrong with the law and how it should be interpreted. This volume consists of the papers presented at a copyright conference held at Indiana University as well as an edited version of the discussions that followed each paper. Certainly, the list of speakers reads like a who's who of copyright—Thomas Brennan (chief counsel, Subcommittee on Patents, Trademarks, and Copyright, U.S. Senate), Jon Baumgarten (general counsel, Copyright Office, Library of Congress), Robert W. Frase (assistant executive director, National Commission, New Technological Uses of Copyrighted Works), Lee Curchinal (director, Division of Science Information, National Science Foundation), Irwin Karp (general counsel, Authors League of America), Robert Wedgeworth (executive director, American Library Association), etc. Each paper was carefully prepared, and Herbert White did a fine job of editing the papers and discussion material.

Unfortunately, if you are looking for an answer on how to handle "the problem," this is not your sourcebook. It merely rehashes old views and problems and provides no resolution. However, it does provide a very readable review of all of the old positions on copyright. [R: C&RL, Jan 79, p. 80; Choice, July 79; p. 633; JAL, May 79, p. 95; JLH, Spring 79, p. 240; LJ, 1 Jan 79, p. 86]   G. Edward Evans

34 Education

GENERAL WORKS

895. Boaz, Martha, ed. **Toward the Improvement of Library Education.** Littleton, Colo., Libraries Unlimited, 1973. 171p. index. o.p. LC 73-82167. ISBN 0-87287-057-8.

The eight position papers in this book are aimed at establishing a framework for planning and for improvement of library education. The papers, commissioned through a grant from the U.S. Office of Education, were prepared by leading librarians and library educators. They discuss general educational and social trends as well as types of libraries and services for the future. [R: LJ, July 74, p. 1783]

896. Borko, Harold, ed. **Targets for Research in Library Education.** Chicago, American Library Association, 1973. 239p. index. o.p. LC 72-9923. ISBN 0-8389-0098-4. (Available from Books on Demand, $20.00, ISBN 0-317-26362-5).

The articles in this collection were written by some of the most prominent educators in the field—Frank L. Schick, Jesse Shera, Gerald Jahoda, Irving Lieberman, Robert Downs, and Leon Carnovsky, to mention only a few. The study was administered through the Institute of Library Research at the University of California at Los Angeles. [R: LJ, 15 Oct 73, p. 2982]

897. Bramley, Gerald. **World Trends in Library Education.** London, Clive Bingley; distr., Hamden, Conn., Linnet Books, 1975. 234p. index. $19.50. LC 74-34355. ISBN 0-208-01368-7.

This book focuses on the education of librarians and discusses the development of library schools as an important influence on attitudes and philosophy in the library profession.

The content of the book emphasizes Anglo-American sources but discusses and compares other major patterns of professional library education in the world. The four major parts of the book cover: (1) the English-speaking countries, (2) Europe, (3) the developing countries, (4) the practice of library education.

This is a concise, valuable, well-written summary of trends in library education and the teaching of librarianship. It should be in use in every library school and by all people who are interested in library education. [R: LJ, 15 Nov 75, p. 2119]   Martha Boaz

898. Conant, Ralph W. **The Conant Report: A Study of the Education of Librarians.** Cambridge, Mass., MIT Press, 1980. 210p. bibliog. index. $25.00. LC 79-28675. ISBN 0-262-03072-1.

The final report of a study begun in 1972 under the auspices of the American Library Association, but officially "not endorsed by that body," this is based almost totally on interviews with faculty, students, librarians, and trustees. The author attempts to analyze the role of library schools, discuss success of existing programs, and propose improvements. The most salient of the latter are a reduction in number of schools and total enrollments, and expansion of the MLS program to two years, with a one-semester internship.

Considering the effort that went into this report, it is very disappointing. Although discussion of method is vague, there seems to have been little effort at historical review, and no attempt to compare library education with disciplines with similar problems, such as journalism or education. Selection criteria for the interviews include such imprecise terms as "available" faculty and alumni "in proximity to" schools visited; they are marred by such inconsistencies as a change in the total number of students interviewed from 218 on page 4 to 197 by page 57.

Potentially significant information discovered during the research, such as an almost perfect correspondence between students' goals and schools enrolled in, is ignored, as are job potentials in nonlibrary fields such as the information industry. Doctoral programs are barely mentioned, even in the context of demanding higher quality faculty and better research in the schools.

Given the controversy resulting, all librarians should read the report. Just as much useful information, however, could be gained from a year's worth of the *Journal of Education for Librarianship*, especially the spring 1978 reports of the Association of American Library Schools Conference (vol. 18, pp. 268-345). [R: BL, 15 Oct 80, p. 304]   James H. Sweetland

899. Cronin, Blaise. **The Education of Library-Information Professionals: A Conflict of Objectives?** London, Aslib, 1982. 58p. (Aslib Occasional Publication, No. 28). £9.50pa.; £8.00pa. (Aslib members). ISBN 0-85142-164-4.

Cronin's report affords some discussion on a recurrent topic, the question of relevancy of library school education to actual entry-level employment requirements.

Cronin offers his report as a "short-term investigation" on the extent to which discrepancies exist between employers' expectations and the goals and objectives of library/information science education. To achieve his objective the author peruses prospectuses of 17 library schools in Great Britain. In a sense his analysis may tend to substantiate or conform claims of some critics, and it does offer the reader some thoughts for possible resolution, for example, that more field work placement might be desirable in library schools. Cronin concludes that a lack of articulation appears to exist in the relationship between professional education and actual practice. However, the report really does not offer any perceptive insights concerning discrepancies between expectations of employers and education of students.

Cronin then discusses entry-level requirements of employers in the special libraries sector of commercial and industrial organizations as expressed in 66 job advertisements. He generalizes that subject discipline seems to be most important and that an information science back-

ground is also desirable. His statement that most ads seek a mixture of experience, specific skills, knowledge, and positive personal attributes is hardly revealing.

The report certainly does not entail the in-depth analyses evident in Ralph Conant's *The Conant Report: A Study of the Education of Librarians* (see *ARBA* 81, entry 302), which examines the objectives, scope, and content of 15 U.S. graduate library schools and 1 undergraduate library program and surveys libraries employing graduates of these schools. Cronin's monograph may be viewed as a small segment of numerous analyses assessing the effectiveness of the education of library students, so that despite its limitations it does attempt to focus upon some expectations of the private sector in Great Britain. It is perhaps of some academic interest to information professionals, particularly to any person critical of current teaching in library schools. [R: AL, Apr 83, p. 225]

Ray Gerke

900. Houser, L., and Alvin M. Schrader. **The Search for a Scientific Profession: Library Science Education in the U.S. and Canada.** Metuchen, N.J., Scarecrow, 1978. 180p. bibliog. index. o.p. LC 77-17563. ISBN 0-8108-1062-X.

The authors say that this study concerns "scientific research in library science education" and "relies almost exclusively on the published record." In doing the research for this book, they found that very little of the literature on library science education has been written from an intellectual perspective, and that it suffers from the lack of a firm philosophical foundation or theoretical framework. It is strongly suggested that the entrenchment of library schools militates against a serious effort by library science educators to change their research and teaching behavior. Therefore, the greatest possibility of change rests with the influence practicing librarians might have.

The book consists of eight chapters: (1) periods in the development of library science education, (2) a theoretical framework for the study of library science education, (3) "1887-1928 – Dewey to Works," (4) "Works to Wilson at Graduate Library School," (5) "1932-1942 – Wilson at the Graduate Library School," (6) post 1942 – quantitative growth to intellectual confusion, (7) findings, and (8) towards education for a scientific profession. No doubt this book will be of special interest to all who teach in graduate library schools. [R: BL, 15 May 78, p. 1479; C&RL, Sept 78, p. 416; LJ, 1 Nov 78, p. 2176]   George H. Fadenrecht

901. Morehead, Joe. **Theory and Practice in Library Education: The Teaching-Learning Process.** Littleton, Colo., Libraries Unlimited, 1980. 139p. bibliog. index. (Research Studies in Library Science, No. 16). $25.00. LC 80-17431. ISBN 0-87287-215-7.

This study is a philosophical and analytical examination of the perennial problem of reconciling theory and practice in professional education, with emphasis upon graduate library education. Morehead begins with an analysis of this issue in professional education in general, using selected professions as examples. He then turns to library education specifically, discussing early theoreticians, modes of instruction, library-centered library education, participant observation, and John Dewey's inquiry model in the quest for the resolution of theory and practice. The final chapter assays the resolution of theory and practice within the context of information studies and current technologies. The study as a whole comprises a philosophical essay about a critical issue relatively neglected in the literature. [R: JAL, Mar 81, p. 37; LJ, 15 Jan 81, p. 128; SL, Jan 81, p. 86]

902. Shera, Jesse H. **The Foundations of Education for Librarianship.** New York, Becker and Hayes, 1972. 511p. index. (Information Sciences Series). o.p. LC 72-3851. ISBN 0-471-78520-2.

Here we have a competent study on this subject written by one of the most prominent library educators in this country. In this study Shera not only discusses major aspects of the subject (see his chapters "The Professional Program," "The Doctoral Program and Research," "The Faculty," "Administration," etc.) but also, as is typical for this author, examines library science in its intellectual context. Thus, first, the book examines the psychological makeup of the individual's communication system, then the communication system within society and the librarian's specific role in the communication process. In his introduction, the author wrote: "I have devoted considerable attention to the origins of libraries and to the history of library education. I believe that a knowledge of the historical development of any human activity is prerequisite to an understanding of it. It is essential that the librarian and the library educator have an awareness of the historical origins of the profession if library education is to be improved." We can only agree with this. [R: CLW, Apr 73, p. 555; LJ, 15 Apr 73, p. 1259; LQ, July 73, p. 247; SL, Apr 73, p. 215]

903. Shores, Louis. **Library Education.** Littleton, Colo., Libraries Unlimited, 1972. 187p. index. o.p. LC 74-187784. ISBN 0-87287-043-X.

This is a collection of some of the best essays, speeches, and articles prepared by Louis Shores during his long and productive career in library education. The anthology is arranged in four main parts: "Foundations," "The Next Generation," "Professional," and "Paraprofessional." Of the 25 essays presented, one is an article written especially for this anthology — "Toward a Philosophy of Library Education." Others discuss such topics as "Practice versus Education in Librarianship"; "Accreditation versus Certification"; "Library School Students"; "Library Education and the Junior College"; and "Prologue to a National Plan."

All libraries concerned with the professional aspects of librarianship might be interested in acquiring this publication, which provides much-needed insight into the present status and the future developments of library education and the impact of library education on library practice. [R: LJ, 15 Jan 73, p. 141; RQ, Spring 73, p. 321; RSR, Jan 73, p. 17]

REFERENCE WORKS

904. **Association of American Library Schools Library Education Statistical Report, 1982.** 3rd ed. State College, Pa., Association of American Library Schools, 1982. 1v. (various paging). $15.00 spiralbound.

The third edition of this annually published AALS statistical guide covers primarily the 1981-1982 year for 69 accredited programs and many of the associate members. The data presented are divided into five sections: faculty; students; curriculum; income and expenditures; and continuing education. There is no question that this is a comprehensive statistical report on the AALS, and as such provides an excellent survey of its development. The amount of data is overwhelming, with representative examples including: a list of library schools which offer joint programs with other disciplines and the degree(s) requirements in hours; the dollar amount from the parent institution, the federal government, and "other" funding sources for each AALS member school; the average salary of an associate professor for the academic year 1981-1982 ($27,058); and the most costly ($10,300) and least costly ($431) tuition and fees reported as being necessary to obtain a master's degree.

Written explanation, selected retrospective data, and analysis of important trends make this statistical compilation quite intelligible. No index is provided, but this problem is somewhat alleviated by having a detailed table of contents. A useful work that is recommended for those schools offering a library education program at any level as well as for larger academic libraries.

Frank Wm. Goudy

905. Association of British Library Schools. **Directory of UK Library School Teachers.** 3rd rev. ed. By John J. Eyre. London, Clive Bingley; distr., Hamden, Conn., Shoe String Press, 1973. 79p. o.p. LC 73-162876. ISBN 0-85157-145-X.

This brief directory is divided into three alphabetically arranged sections: (1) "Schools and Their Staff"; (2) "Teachers"; and (3) "Subjects." [R: LJ, 1 Mar 73, p. 718]

Charles D. Patterson

906. **Directory of Institutions Offering Programs for the Training of Library-Media Technical Assistants.** 5th ed. Edited by Raymond G. Roney and Audrey V. Jones. University, Miss., Council on Library/Media Technical-Assistants, 1981. 129p. index. $5.00pa.

This work first appeared in 1968 as a publication of the University of Baltimore with the title *Directory of Institutions in the United States and Canada Offering or Developing Courses in Library Technology.* The COLT directory contains information received from respondents from 115 educational institutions in the United States and Canada. This is a decline from the 157 programs described in the fourth edition, 1976 (see *ARBA* 77, entry 175). These institutions offer programs which are creditable towards an associate degree or a certificate. Each entry includes the name, address, and telephone number of the institution; the name of the person in charge of the program; the name of the program; enrollment and faculty statistics; a statement of purpose; and a listing of courses offered. All institutions are listed again by state in a five-page appendix, which seems somewhat unnecessary. The index provides needed access by name of institution. This latest directory will be useful for high school counselors and libraries employing clerks interested in library training.

Louise Stwalley

907. Lieberman, Irving, with the assistance of Corinne McMullan and Bruce McMullan. **A Working Bibliography of Commercially Available Audiovisual Materials for the Teaching of Library Science.** 2nd ed., rev. and expanded. Syracuse, N.Y., Syracuse University, ERIC Clearinghouse on Information Resources, 1979. 115p. index. (IR-36). o.p.

Designed to support the instruction of library science, this bibliography is a selective, nonevaluative listing of audiovisual resources available for purchase. It is arranged alphabetically in seven major categories including "Introduction to Librarianship," "Reference," "Teaching the Use of Books and the Library," "Classification and Cataloging," "Selection of Library Materials (Including User Guidance)," "Printing and the History of Books and Libraries," and "Automation in Libraries, Including Special Libraries." The introduction lists materials under philosophy of modern librarianship, citizenship leadership, children's services, adult services, state libraries, school libraries, intellectual freedom, and hospital and institutional services. Entries for films, filmstrips, slides, video- and audiotapes, overhead transparencies, and charts include annotations and bibliographical information. The introduction provides abbreviations. There is an alphabetical list of producers/distributors as well as a title index.

The compiler has done an excellent job in identifying titles which would be of benefit under given subject areas. The titles will be of primary use to instructors at the college and university level in various library science courses. Schools of library science will find this a must for collections. [R: JAL, Nov 80, pp. 305-6; LJ, 1 Oct 80, p. 2042]

Paula Montgomery

908. **North American Library Education: Directory and Statistics 1969-1971.** Edited by Frank L. Schick and D. Kathryn Weintraub. Chicago, American Library Association, 1972. 87p. o.p. LC 68-8967. ISBN 0-8389-3109-X.

This work presents statistical data gathered from a survey of departments or schools of library and information science in 447 academic institutions in the United States and Canada. The study includes data from 1969-1970 graduate, undergraduate, and technician programs; projects the findings to 1970-1971; and compares the results with the previous study, *North American Library Education Directory and Statistics 1966-1968* (American Library Association, 1968).

The survey was cosponsored by the University of Wisconsin—Milwaukee School of Library and Information Science and the Library Administration and Library Education Divisions of the American Library Association.

It was funded by the U.S. Office of Education, Bureau of Research.

The survey reports on enrollments, degrees, placements, financial support, and related aspects of library education programs. The new publication provides additional data about the support of programs by federal resources by identifying amounts of funds granted under various federal acts and specific benefits realized through federal funds. [R: LQ, Apr 73, p. 162]

909. **World Guide to Library Schools and Training Courses in Documentation.** 2nd ed. London, Clive Bingley; distr., Hamden, Conn., Shoe String Press, 1981. 549p. index. $50.00. ISBN 0-85157-309-6.

Like the earlier 1972 edition (see *ARBA* 74, entry 237), this revised volume presents library programs offered, admission requirements, teaching staffs, diplomas offered, length of course, plus comments on various library programs and training programs in documentation throughout the world. The survey, conducted through the use of questionnaires, is primarily in English or French.

Although an attempt is made at completeness, the editors realize that the directory is not as complete as it could be. The objectives are to update the earlier edition, provide information for students wishing to become librarians, documentalists, or archivists in their own country or elsewhere, and be an advocate of the programs offered in each school. The last objective results in an unevenness in the reports. If some training program seems particularly interesting or unusual, more emphasis may be given it. Some 87 countries are represented in comparison with 60 in 1972. The material gives one an overview of different programs throughout the world. [R: JAL, May 82, p. 105; LJ, 1 Mar 82, p. 527]

Anna Grace Patterson

PROCEEDINGS AND SYMPOSIA

910. Cassata, Mary B., and Herman L. Totten, eds. **The Administrative Aspects of Education for Librarianship: A Symposium.** Metuchen, N.J., Scarecrow, 1975. 407p. index. $21.00. LC 75-15726. ISBN 0-8108-0829-3.

Using the 1972 Standards for Accreditation as the basis for this book, 26 contributors provided original essays on the administrative aspects of library education. The authors, all knowledgeable about library education, using both primary and secondary sources as well as their own expertise, have presented interesting essays. As Russell Bidlack said about the authors in the introduction, "Neither a uniformity in point of view nor style was sought; the personality and, in several instances, the bias of the writer was evident." Both the writers and the editors, Mary B. Cassata and Herman L. Totten, are to be commended on producing a book that gives valuable information to library schools preparing for accreditation for their programs.

Among the topics covered are: the standards; program goals and objectives; curriculum; faculty; students; governance, administration, and financial support; physical resources and facilities; and the accreditation visit.

These essays will serve as a source of information about library education and about the standards for the accreditation of library education programs. All persons interested in library education and libraries should read this book. [R: LJ, 15 Nov 75, p. 2119]   Martha Boaz

911. **Library and Information Science Education in the Americas: Present and Future: Papers from a Conference Held in Austin, Texas, 14 February 1980.** William Vernon Jackson, ed. State College, Pa., Association of American Library Schools, 1981. 85p. $5.00pa. LC 81-66342.

This paperbound publication contains four papers and five "reactions" to these papers presented at a one-day conference sponsored by the Association of American Library Schools (AALS), the Organization of American States (OAS), and the Seminar on the Acquisition of Latin American Library Materials (SALALM). The purpose of the conference was to bring library school educators together from throughout the Americas and Caribbean to exchange ideas on curriculum requirements and developments in library education.

The four papers deal with curriculum changes in library and information science in Mexico, library education in the United States, and the continuing education of teachers of library and information science in Latin America and in the United States. Also included in this volume are the conference program, short bibliographies following each paper, some recommendations from the participants, and a list of those participating. Although this may be a volume of some interest to many librarians, actual reference application would be limited to schools of library and information science.

Patrick J. Kenrick

CONTINUING EDUCATION

912.   Conroy, Barbara. **Library Staff Development and Continuing Education: Principles and Practices.** Littleton, Colo., Libraries Unlimited, 1978. 296p. bibliog. index. $30.00. LC 78-18887. ISBN 0-87287-177-0.

A practical guide to well-planned and coordinated learning programs for library personnel, this book is arranged in three major sections: planning, implementing, and evaluating the learning program. These are divided into guidelines, each covering the step-by-step procedures necessary for establishing a successful program. Checklists in questionnaire and chart form are included in many of the guidelines. The appendix describes three models of learning programs in staff development and continuing education, and a bibliography and glossary are also included. The tools presented here can be used by conference planners, proposal writers, program developers, individual learners, educators, and institute and workshop planners. They are useful to develop new learning programs, to upgrade existing ones, and to coordinate existing and future programs with one another. [R: LJ, 15 Dec 78, p. 2494]

913.   **Directory of Continuing Education Opportunities for Library/Information/Media Personnel, 1977.** 2nd ed. Washington, D.C., Continuing Library Education Network and Exchange, 1977. 265p. index. o.p.

The title very fittingly describes the book, since it is indeed a directory of programs of continuing education for library, information, and media personnel. According to the statement in the introduction, regular courses that are offered for degrees—A.A., B.S., Ph.D.—are not included. However, some programs listed do give graduate credit.

The first edition of this directory was published under the title *Continuing Education Courses and Programs for Library, Information and Media.* Entries for all data that were issued in that hard copy edition were placed online for immediate entry of material and immediate retrieval by CLENE. The online entry has been continued for the second edition.

Information on each program includes, among other things, the level of the program, method of instruction, name of instructor, objectives, cost, and type of person the program is for. The length of programs varies, but they are usually of short duration. In the total listing are 239 programs offered by 53 institutions from 28 states, the District of Columbia, and one

Canadian province, covering the calendar year 1977. The table of contents and the index are quite adequate and must be used, since the main body of the directory is arranged by subject.

No doubt this directory can indeed be a great help for anyone looking for a specific type of program. [R: JAL, July 77, p. 166]

George H. Fadenrecht

914.   Edwards, Ronald J. **In-Service Training in British Libraries: Its Development and Present Practice.** Syracuse, N.Y., Gaylord Professional Publications, 1978, c1976. 232p. bibliog. index. o.p. ISBN 0-85365-219-8.

Ronald J. Edwards has had varied experience as a county librarian in Great Britain. His book is an expansion of his thesis for the master's degree in librarianship at the University of Strathclyde. He defines in-service training as "training carried out in the library or under the direct control of the library, and for members of the staff of that library. This includes training courses run by the library at outside centers but excludes the sending of members of staff on courses run by outside bodies." Preliminary chapters provide a history of in-service training in British libraries from the midnineteenth century to the mid-1970s, and there is a chapter on library school field work. The core of Edwards's book, however, is his study of British practice regarding in-service training in libraries. His data are from published and unpublished studies and reports and from questionnaires returned by 67 libraries (with municipal, county, academic, national, and special libraries represented). He presents a wide-ranging and thorough survey of the types of in-service training that are provided, analyzes the role of the training officer, and assesses trends and the probable future directions of in-service training. A definitive bibliography of more than 300 items is appended. While analogies with North American practice are minimal, the book is valuable as a concise and readable state-of-the-art report on a significant aspect of British librarianship.

John Farley

915.   **Evaluation of Alternative Curricula: Approaches to School Library Media Education.** Prepared by the School Library Manpower Project. Chicago, American Library Association, 1975. 183p. o.p. LC 74-34592. ISBN 0-8389-3165-0.

The publication of this final report brings to a close the work of the School Library Manpower Project, initiated in 1968; this report represents the evaluation study conducted during phase 3. Phase 1 identified tasks performed by school library media personnel and developed job descriptions. Phase 2 was concerned with launching six experimental program models in school library media education. Phase 3 was developed to evaluate the phase 2 programs by a follow-up survey of the graduates after six months on a job. The findings of the study are based on comments of graduates and supervisors in relation to the students' degree of preparation to perform tasks required by their jobs and also tasks covered in the experimental programs. Summaries of responses from the data collecting instrument, Behavioral Requirements Analysis Checklist (BRAC), are included. The program results and evaluation findings offer little that is new and certainly do not point to any strong program that can be recommended as a national model. If anything, the results indicate a possible resurgence in undergraduate library science programs. [R: LQ, Oct 76, p. 451]   Christine Gehrt Wynar

916. Michael, Mary Ellen. **Continuing Professional Education in Librarianship and Other Fields: A Classified and Annotated Bibliography, 1965-1974.** New York, Garland, 1975. 211p. index. (Garland Reference Library of the Humanities, Vol. 16). $31.00. LC 75-8998. ISBN 0-8240-1085-X.

This 10-year survey of the literature in the area of continuing professional education for librarianship provides a compact and useful guide. It is divided into three sections: (1) "Continuing Professional Education in Librarianship in the U.S."; (2) "Continuing Professional Education in Librarianship in Other Countries" (37 citations); and (3) "Continuing Professional Education in Other Fields" (117 citations). Each section is arranged alphabetically by primary author. The annotations give a good synopsis of content and deliberately stay away from evaluations of the quality of the work. The author index provides access across sections, and to secondary authors. The compiler has also distinguished between *theory and philosophy* and *examples* of in-service programs, and has so divided parts 1 and 2. Such division may provide some difficulties in finding items dealing with both areas.

The comment is made in the introduction that there is little theoretical work concerning how adults learn. While this may be very true of the library literature, the interested reader should also consult a similar bibliography appearing in Elizabeth Stone's *Continuing Education as Viewed in Relation to Other Continuing*

Professional Education Movements (American Society for Information Science, 1974), which contains a section on this particular topic as well as another lengthy annotated bibliography. [R: LQ, Jan 76, p. 109]

Pauline V. Angione

917. Sage, Mary. **Continuing Library Education: An Interdisciplinary Approach.** Washington, D.C., Metropolitan Washington Council of Governments, 1976. 190p. o.p.

This book provides a detailed look at a series of six workshops sponsored by the Washington, D.C., Council of Governments from November 1975 to May 1976. Funded by the U.S. Office of Education, the project was designed to develop a "model interdisciplinary continuing education program for librarians." The immediate goal was to "encourage cooperation and communications among libraries and between librarians and those in other disciplines." Toward that end, workshops were held on the following topics: communications techniques, advertising and public relations, personnel administration, consumer protection information, planning and budgeting, and supervisory skills. Evaluation of the series revealed that skills from other disciplines were brought to bear in some degree in the library; also, the hoped-for increase in communication among libraries and between them and other agencies did materialize.

Background information on the study is provided first. The various workshops are then described, and evaluations and recommendations for improvement round out the main portion of the text. Appendices reproduce much of the printed material used at the workshops, as well as the evaluation forms used at the end of the project. The author notes that academic and special libraries were not represented on the project's Advisory Committee, but this should not detract from the usefulness of this book for any library, agency, or association contemplating a similar enterprise.

Koert C. Loomis, Jr.

918. Stone, Elizabeth W., ed. **Continuing Education Resource Book: Compilation of Selected Continuing Education Resources and Products Developed by the Participants and Staff in the 1976-1977 CLENE/USOE Institute for State Library Agency Personnel Involved in Continuing Education.** Washington, D.C., Continuing Library Education Network and Exchange, 1977. 1v. (various paging). illus. bibliog. $3.00pa.; $2.55pa. (members). ISBN 0-686-39873-4.

This publication, supported by HEW, is "designed to assist those who are developing, implementing, and/or evaluating a plan for coordinating area-wide continuing education for library/information/media personnel ... its primary purpose is for use by those involved with multi-organization planning." However, single libraries might also find it worthwhile.

The papers in this collection are essentially those that were presented at the 1976-1977 CLENE/USOE Institute and that addressed themselves to the following six criteria: needs assessment; goals and objectives; resources; roles; dissemination; and evaluation. This compilation of papers, many of them mimeographed, is divided into three main sections: (1) printed tools and products from CLENE/USOE Institute for State Library Agency Personnel Involved in Continuing Education; (2) examples from the real world; (3) bibliographies. The annotated bibliographies (59 and 9 pages long, respectively) would be helpful for anyone beginning continuing education endeavors. Since there is no index, one is entirely dependent upon the table of contents, which refers not to pages but to the color of the paper upon which each section is produced.

George H. Fadenrecht

919. Stone, Elizabeth, Eiieen Sheahan, and Katherine J. Harig. **Model Continuing Education Recognition System in Library and Information Science.** New York, K. G. Saur, 1979. 313p. bibliog. o.p. LC 79-11538. ISBN 0-89664-145-7.

The timeliness of this work reflects the growing interest in participation in and production of continuing education for library and information science practitioners, as well as the increase of library literature on the topic. Parallel to these trends is an increase in interest in recognition for individuals who participate in continuing education. The volume's comprehensive coverage brings together research from other professional fields, field research of practitioner opinions on recognition, and project staff's synthesis. It well deserves a place as librarianship's contribution to the continuing professional education literature such as that from other fields cited in Stone's *Continuing Library Education as Viewed in Relation to Other Continuing Professional Education Movements* (American Society for Information Science, 1974). The authors justify the need for a recognition system on the basis of similar efforts of other professional fields. In addition, they cite recognition as a motivator, a demonstration of public accountability, and a means

to establish and maintain quality standards for programs.

Originally issued in October 1977 as the final report of this U.S. Office of Education funded project, the work describes the project's methods and procedures, makes recommendations on the basis of findings, and proposes plans for a recognition system in librarianship. It also suggests a strategy for implementation of these plans and includes important issues that must be addressed, such as financing, record keeping, and criteria for continuing education programs. Strong recommendations are made for a voluntary rather than a mandatory system, for inclusion of nontraditional learning formats, for a continued leadership role for the Continuing Library Education Network and Exchange (CLENE), and for quality control and record keeping functions. Because of its depth and comprehensiveness, this volume will probably be frequently used in present and future efforts to consolidate continuing education efforts for library and information science personnel. [R: JAL, Nov 79, p. 294]

Barbara Conroy

920. Virgo, Julie A., Patricia McConaghey Dunkel, and Pauline V. Angione. **Continuing Library Education: Needs Assessment and Model Programs.** Washington, D.C., Continuing Library Education Network and Exchange (CLENE), 1977. 237p. illus. (CLENE Concept Paper, No. 5). o.p.

Despite the generality of the title, the primary audience for this volume would be medical/health sciences librarians. It details efforts within the Medical Library Association to assess the needs of those librarians and to meet those needs through continuing education efforts. The book would also have value for anyone interested in continuing education in general, since it statistically documents an actual case study.

The authors first study continuing education needs in medical librarianship by examining changes in librarians' concerns, as reflected in the professional literature. The next chapters detail their surveys of librarians themselves to determine needs and their survey of library agencies and associations, library schools, and libraries to determine what was available to answer those needs. They then investigate organizational support for continuing education and the extent of such programs in other associations and professions. Their model program for health sciences library personnel is followed by an examination of MLA's own program for 1973-1975. Their conclusions then describe which of their expectations were confirmed as well as the surprises revealed by their data.

The book illustrates the advantages and disadvantages of approaching a highly theoretical topic by means of a very specialized model. Anyone seriously interested in continuing education, especially for specialized aspects of librarianship, would want to examine this work. At the same time, they should be prepared to abstract from it those concepts that might apply to their own situation. The graphs and figures clutter the book a bit, but they are also useful enough to overcome any confusion they might cause. [R: JAL, Nov 77, p. 297]

Koert C. Loomis, Jr.

921. Warncke, Ruth. **Planning Library Workshops and Institutes.** Chicago, American Library Association, 1976. 178p. bibliog. index. (The Public Library Reporter, No. 17). $6.50. LC 75-43835. ISBN 0-8389-3178-2.

The author has called upon her long experience in planning and conducting continuing education activities of all kinds in compiling this useful aid to the promoter of such enterprises. All aspects are covered—from selection of the appropriate sponsors to the smallest detail of necessary physical and social arrangements. All directions, suggestions, and recommendations made are sensible, practical, and clearly put forward. [R: LJ, 15 Jan 77, p. 182]

George Piternick

CURRICULUM STUDIES

922. Danton, J. Periam. **Between M.L.S. and Ph.D.: A Study of Sixth-Year Specialist Programs in Accredited Library Schools.** Chicago, American Library Association, 1970. 103p. illus. bibliog. $5.00pa. LC 74-133380. ISBN 0-8389-0089-5.

The author examines 20 Sixth-Year Specialists Programs offered in ALA-accredited library schools. Following a brief historical account of the program, the study is based largely upon 153 questionnaire responses from those graduates through 1967-1968. Findings are presented clearly and these are illustrated with numerous textually integrated tables. Conclusions and recommendations will be of interest to library educators, especially those planning similar programs. [R: LJ, 15 June 71, p. 2063]

Charles D. Patterson

923. **Education and Training for Information Services in Business and Industry in Developing and Developed Countries: The Needs, the Experience, the Newer Trends.** The Hague, International Federation for Documentation, 1980. 122p. (FID Publication, No. 584). Fl.55 (Dutch). ISBN 92-66-00584-3.

The papers here were presented at a meeting of FID's Education and Training Committee, held in Minneapolis in October 1979. The volume editor and committee's chair, Paul Wasserman, presents a dozen papers, with summaries from session reporters, whose theme is an "exchange of perspectives" between educators working in world areas with considerable development and those working in areas just awakening to the possibilities of applying information services to business and industry as a means of increased productivity and efficiency.

Some of the papers are only three or four pages, but still manage to promote questions in an area which has little formal or structured literature or tradition. Some papers discuss basics of training and provide good guidelines for a first line of printed information or consultation advice on the organization and content of programs. A few papers, in discussing training techniques, focus on modern technology such as online databases or video equipment, until now nearly unknown in large parts, if not the larger part, of the underdeveloped world. Such papers must be read as proposing ideas which need time for implementation. Wasserman's own essay is a description, syllabus, and bibliography for a course in business information services. As a whole, three issues are discussed: organized technical assistance, training of personnel, and machine vs. human resources. Both sides are presented, and solid positions are taken for the structured and formal as contrasted with less-demanding situations. Many questions are raised, but few dogmatic or absolute answers are given. The implication, however, is clear: information science is needed as a framework for providing business and industry in developing countries with the intellectual tools needed for growth. This brief compilation, while by no means definitive, is a start. [R: LR, Winter 80, p. 289]

Neal L. Edgar

924. Goldhor, Herbert, ed. **Education for Librarianship: The Design of the Curriculum of Library Schools.** Urbana-Champaign, Ill., Graduate School of Library Science, University of Illinois; distr., Urbana-Champaign, Ill., Illini Union Bookstore, 1971. 195p. index. $5.00. LC 78-633332. SBN 87845-033-5.

Ten papers presented at a Conference on the Design of the Curriculum of Library Schools

(6-9 September 1970) are reproduced in this volume. Among the authors one will find here Sarah Reed (a historical overview), Lester Asheim (new trends), Margaret Monroe (public libraries), and Andrew Osborn. The volume is well documented and indexed. [R: AL, Nov 71, p. 1113]

SCHOOL MEDIA PERSONNEL

925. **Certification Model for Professional School Media Personnel.** By the Certification of School Media Specialists Committee, American Association of School Librarians. Chicago, American Library Association, 1976. 32p. bibliog. $4.00pa. ISBN 0-8389-3179-0.

The AASL Committee on Certification of School Media Specialists has performed a valuable service in preparing this certification model. The model contains criteria for assessment procedures and a set of definitions of seven areas of competencies necessary for all media personnel. These areas are: relation of media to instructional systems; administration of media programs; selection, utilization, and production of media, research, and evaluation; and leadership and professionalism. Levels of competency within each area may vary depending on job assignment, and additional areas may be added as desired. While competencies are set forth as the basis for certification, this report does not suggest that all states adopt a strictly competency-based system. When an educational program has been evaluated in terms of the proficiencies it develops, the traditional method of earned credit hours can be used as a basis for certification.

Designing the candidate assessment process, based on the criteria set forth by the committee, will pose problems of definition as well as implementation. One aspect of the candidate's behavior to be assessed, for example, is the "psycho-motor domain," yet this does not appear to be related to any competency listed. Arguments over the means of assessment will no doubt continue, but this report gives a sensible basis for discussion. Library educators, school media personnel, and administrators at all levels will find it useful in setting up and evaluating programs.   Adele M. Fasick

926. Chisholm, Margaret E., and Donald P. Ely. **Media Personnel in Education: A Competency Approach.** Englewood Cliffs, N.J., Prentice-Hall, 1976. 378p. illus. index. o.p. LC 75-33054. ISBN 0-13-572461-9.

Reacting to educators' interest in a competency approach to validating the ability of prospective teachers (and media staff), *Media Personnel in Education* expands on the philosophy of *Media Programs: District and School* (ALA and AECT) and *Behavioral Requirements Analysis Checklist* (AASL). The authors, following a too-familiar technique, present the competencies that are needed in the form of a four-layer circular figure, like a cake, representing "aide," "technician," "media professional-specialist," and "media professional-generalist." The figure is divided into 10 sections, labeled "Organization Management," "Personnel Management," "Design," "Information Retrieval," "Logistics," "Utilization," "Production," "Instruction," "Evaluation," and "Research." Each of these functions is treated at length in a separate chapter that discusses the competencies subsumed under each and suggests resources, mastery items, and typical responses. References are also listed.

The title, intended as a textbook for prospective school media staff, suffers from the same faults that mark most educational texts— that is, emphasis on formulae which are rather divorced from the realism of the actual school day and its human problems. An additional caveat in using this text is its obvious bias in favor of the audiovisual and production aspects of school library media programs. For example, under directories useful for ordering materials the *Audiovisual Market Place* is listed, but not the *Literary Market Place*. In general, the bibliographies show that the authors have greater knowledge of audiovisual materials, titles, and activities than of resources in print format. [R: Choice, Dec 76, p. 1338]

Lillian L. Shapiro

927. Daniel, Evelyn H., and Donald P. Ely. **A Process for Developing a Competency Based Educational Program for Media Professionals.** With a selected, annotated bibliography by Faith Stein. Syracuse, N.Y., ERIC Clearinghouse on Information Resources, Syracuse University, 1977. 1v. (various paging). bibliog. o.p.

This compact monograph records the response to the "goal agreed to" during 1977 by Syracuse University's Schools of Education and Information Studies in the area of instructional technology for "an integrated, unified, rigorous, competency-based educational program for media students" (introduction). Part 1 concerns the program design and methodology and describes the process of involvement represented in the initial planning and structuring of the "collaborative process." This part also contains a description of the selection of consortium members, the working schedules of meetings (with agenda items), and the timetable for submission of the completed program to the New York State Education Department. Part 2 lists the competencies for the school media specialist agreed to on 5 May 1977 by the consortium members. Part 3 presents a selected, annotated bibliography on competency-based education [CBE] that comprises five sections: theoretical overviews, competencies, specific issues in CBE, issues in assessment, and existing CBE programs. Part 4 contains the appendices:

the text of the teacher education program proposal of the New York Education Department; a conceptualization of the media professional; details of CBE programs' various admission requirements and procedures; a list of student guidance and assessment procedures; a course-by-course competency matrix; an explanation of the program evaluation process; and a list of members of the consortium. This very clear, tightly knit work, quite in harmony with the subject it covers, can serve as a prototype or comparative model for practitioners in the field.

Clara O. Jackson

35 Employment

928. ALA Survey of Librarian Salaries. Mary Jo Lynch, project director. Chicago, Office for Research and Office for Library Personnel Resources, American Library Association, 1984. 1112p. $40.00pa. LC 82-11537. ISBN 0-8389-3301-7.

ALA's Office for Research (OFR) and Office of Library Personnel Resources (OLPR) conducted this survey, assisted by the University of Illinois Library Research Center. The published report consists of many tables, with interpretive sections and several appendices.

The table show salary ranges (low, mean, and high average) actually *paid* in 1984, as well as starting and maximum *scheduled* salaries. The selected positions are those about which ALA has most often received requests for information, including directors; assistant directors; department or branch heads; reference, cataloging, documents, and serials librarians; subject specialists or bibliographers; and coordinators for children's, young adult, or adult services. Salaries for each position are further broken down within the tables according to five selected library categories (small public, large public, two-year college, four-year college, and university) and four designated regions (North Atlantic, Great Lakes and Plains, Southeast, and West and Southwest).

The report might be improved if all of its designated geographical areas represented traditional regions and if the categories for academic libraries included a place for five-year colleges. For example, does one look under colleges or under universities for data on schools that confer a master's but not a doctorate? And how does one evaluate regional salaries in such large and diverse areas as "Great Lakes and Plains" or "West and Southwest"?

These objections aside, the report goes a long way toward filling an information gap. Mary Jo Lynch, whom many still remember for her columns in *RQ*, directed the survey and wrote the report with the assistance of Jeniece Guy and Margaret Myers of OLPR. It should prove useful to administrators setting salaries, librarians seeking employment, and others interested in equitable pay for librarians. A first edition of this survey was published in 1982.

Mary Jo Walker

929. Dwoskin, Robert P. **Rights of the Public Employee.** Chicago, American Library Association, 1978. 269p. bibliog. index. $15.00. LC 78-1658. ISBN 0-8389-0257-X.

Public employees are often viewed by the general public as individuals with ensured lifetime employment. Nothing could be further from the truth. True, it is difficult to dismiss a public employee, but it can be and is done. The how and when of dismissal and public employee rights are complex issues made more complex because, ultimately, every public employee action may be viewed as an act of government and every act can thus be subject to political interpretation. There is nothing similar in the private sector.

Robert Dwoskin, who has represented a number of dismissed public employees, including Ellis Hodgin (public librarian from Martinsville, Virginia), was asked by ALA to prepare a text on public employee rights. His background as legal counsel on a number of cases in which public employees attempted to retain positions by court action gives him a special perspective on the subject. He divided his topic into seven chapters under three parts: (1) basic issues in public employment, (2) public employees and the First Amendment, and (3) nonjudicial recourses for public employees. In the seven chapters, he covers historical background, exclusion and dismissal from public service, freedom of expression, political activities, loyalty oaths and association membership, procedural due process, and public employee unions.

This book deals with public employee rights, not just librarian employee rights. The author uses a variety of job classes as examples, and only a few are drawn from library situations or problems. A major purpose of the book is "to provide the public employee with an idea of the legal framework of his employment" (p. x). One pleasant surprise is that the book does not read like a legal treatise, despite the numerous legal footnotes. However, the bibliography for further reading is disappointing – only fifteen books and four law review articles. In summary, the book is well worth reading, preferably before there is a problem of rights. [R: CLW, Oct 79, p. 140]　　　　G. Edward Evans

930. Heim, Kathleen M., and Leigh S. Estabrook. **Career Profiles and Sex Discrimination in the Library Profession.** Chicago, American Library Association, 1983. 82p. bibliog. index. $15.00. LC 83-3838. ISBN 0-8389-3282-7.

Heim and Estabrook undertook this study for the Committee on the Status of Women in Librarianship of the American Library Association "to provide data for evaluating the status of women in librarianship." A seven-page questionnaire was distributed to a random sample of 3,000 ALA members. Some 2,000 usable responses were received; women made up 78.3 percent of this final sample. The questionnaire sought information in four major areas: overall career pattern, current or most recent job situation, educational background and professional involvement, and personal and family matters. The analysis focused primarily on the 86.6 percent of the sample that was employed at the time of the survey.

The study did find significant variations in men's and women's personal and professional backgrounds. For example, women were found to be less likely to be married or in a long-term relationship than men, less likely to have children, but more likely to report limitations to their potential mobility. Men held a higher proportion of advanced degrees, were more prolific in publishing, and were more active in professional associations. Men were represented in greater numbers in academic libraries, women in public libraries, and men were found significantly more often in positions of administrative

responsibility. As for salary, the investigators found women "lag far behind men in both base salary and total family income."

Multivariate analysis revealed, as one might expect, that much of the variance in salaries can be attributed to age and date of receiving the MLS degree. Nonetheless, the authors found that "evidence suggests that salary discrimination for women exists even when one allows for the personal, career, and professional variations that contribute to salary differences."

The authors are careful to point out the limitations of their investigation as a onetime, cross-sectional study of members of one professional association. Yet in their careful review of the literature, they made an effort to pull together approaches and concepts from a wide range of other related studies. Their study is likely to set the standard for further investigations into the status of women in librarianship. [R: BL, 15 Oct 83, p. 326; JAL, Sept 83, p. 253]
　　　　　　　　　Catherine R. Loeb

931. Josey, E. J., and Kenneth E. Peeples, Jr., eds. **Opportunities for Minorities in Librarianship.** Metuchen, N.J., Scarecrow, 1977. 201p. index. $13.00. LC 77-375. ISBN 0-8108-1022-0.

The editors of this volume, E. J. Josey and K. E. Peeples, Jr., state in their introduction that "while this book is primarily intended for minority students considering careers in librarianship, the editors believe that it contains invaluable information for anyone investigating the possibility of deciding on a career in librarianship" (introduction). They are correct in this assumption. This publication is very timely in regard to recruitment of minority candidates for the library profession.

The essays, arranged in six major parts, were contributed by 20 specialists with various ethnic and professional backgrounds. Essays cover: (1) native Americans and librarianship; (2) Chicanos and librarianship; (3) Afro-Americans and librarianship; (4) Puerto Ricans and librarianship; (5) Asian-Americans and librarianship; and (6) minority library specialists. Articles within each section pertain to various types of libraries (academic, public, special, media center, etc.) and expose the information-seeking student to the various concepts and services in different types of library institutions. The reviewer agrees with the editors that there is a need for a dynamic recruitment program to enroll future librarians from various minority groups, who are underrepresented in our profession. Furthermore, this critical problem is directly related not only to financial support for these candidates but first of all to the necessary and ethnic-oriented curricula in American graduate library schools. It is unfortunate that this volume does not contain a separate analysis of ethnic curricula in our library schools, a field that continues to be ignored in many instances by library educators. The irregular programs geared to grants from the federal government do not replace a permanent curriculum. Probably the best illustration of this phenomenon is described by Daniel Davids in regard to Columbia University's School. The author writes that for "four years the Columbia University School of Library Science had a program for minorities funded by the federal government. However, in 1975-76 it had no candidates for the program because of a shortage of funds" (p. 119). Regardless of funding, it seems clear that schools of library science should include on a permanent basis courses pertaining to ethnic librarianship. In general, it should be pointed out that students representing various American ethnic groups cannot afford to limit their professional interest to one or two ethnic groups. They have to comprehend minority or ethnic librarianship on a comparative basis in terms of cultural heritage of various ethnic communities. They must master the major professional skills in order to serve ethnic communities as well as society at large. In this respect, the articles by M. M. Aman on library computerization and J. C. Welbourne on information specialists are very useful. It is hoped that this valuable volume will be instrumental in creating a positive image of librarianship to potential minority/ethnic candidates for the library profession. It should also remind our library educators about the need to expand the library science curriculum in order to reflect the pluralistic nature of American society and its needs. [R: LJ, 1 Oct 77, p. 2017]

Lubomyr R. Wynar

932. Kortendick, James J., and Elizabeth W. Stone. **Job Dimensions and Educational Needs in Librarianship.** Chicago, American Library Association, 1971. 503p. bibliog. $14.00. LC 70-157141. ISBN 0-8389-3126-X. (Available from Books on Demand, $127.30, ISBN 0-317-29359-1).

A well-documented survey of the educational needs of middle- and upper-level library personnel. Of special interest is the chapter about building a post-master's program in library science. [R: LJ, 15 May 72, p. 1786]

933. Sellen, Betty-Carol, ed. **What Else You Can Do with a Library Degree.** New York, Gaylord Professional Publications in association with Neal-Schuman Publishers, 1980. 350p. index. o.p. LC 79-14852. ISBN 0-915794-46-2.

What with the deplorable employment market for traditional librarians, it's nice to know that we have at least some transferable skills. The idea for this book originated with publisher-librarian Patricia Schuman during an American Library Association conversation on jobs for librarians in a time of scarcity. Most of the book is devoted to brief chapters (from 3 to 10 pages) of the real-life experiences of some 50 librarians who have branched out to sometimes related careers—as library entrepreneurs, information specialists, researchers and indexers, and careerists in the book industry, or in art, government, communication, or education. (No one, unfortunately, covered my alternative career of reference book author.) The accounts of "how and why I did it" are individual and vary widely; most authors discuss the virtues and defects of their new fields; a few philosophize, and a few concentrate on the nuts and bolts of getting started. Though their chosen fields vary considerably, most of these metamorphosed librarians appear to rank high on individuality, determination, and the ability to seize or make opportunities. The book succeeds well in conveying the personal attributes that coincide with this kind of enterprise; it does not tell how to do it.

The accounts are preceded by a survey—a compilation rather than a scientific study—of librarians working outside libraries. A thoughtful appendix A, by Susan Klement, proposes a 13-week course in alternatives for librarianship. Overall, an excellent resource for any librarian contemplating a move to greener pastures. [R: BL, 15 July 80, p. 1655; LJ, 15 Nov 80, p. 2392]

Marda Woodbury

934. Sullivan, Peggy, and Kathleen M. Heim. **Opportunities in Library and Information Science.** Skokie, Ill., VGM Career Horizons/National Textbook, 1982. 147p. illus. bibliog. $7.95; $5.95pa. LC 81-85799.

This book is one of the "Opportunities in ..." guides produced as part of the VGM Career Horizons series. It focuses on "career information for persons who may potentially be interested in librarianship or information science as a career." Written by two experienced librarians and library educators, the book presents a concise and accurate overview of library careers. All types of library and information settings are described, and potential positions, ranging from library technicians to information scientists, are summarized. Approximately one-third of the book outlines the type of work librarians perform. Examples of specialization by library type and professional function are given, as are opportunities for librarians in other settings (e.g., freelance librarians). The strongest third of the book is the two chapters that deal with the placement and employment process of librarians and information personnel. The information included here would be particularly valuable for graduates of library schools who are seeking their first professional position. The remainder of the book deals with library education and future trends in librarianship.

This book offers a very realistic appraisal of all aspects of library employment. The "uneven" quality of the original 1977 edition (see *ARBA* 78, entry 259) has generally been eliminated. Career opportunities in information science are frequently and appropriately discussed. It is, however, surprising that the impact of microcomputers on all library operations is slighted. The appendices, which include recommended readings and lists of major journals and publishers, library and information science organizations, and educational programs, should prove helpful. Although no career guide

can answer all questions regarding a particular occupation, this book should enable students and guidance counselors easily to discover the various opportunities available in library work. [R: LJ, 15 Jan 83, p. 114]   Greg Byerly

935. Wallington, C. James, et al. **Jobs in Instructional Media.** Washington, D.C., Department of Audiovisual Instruction, 1970. 304p. o.p.

This elaborate and multi-faceted study is a carefully planned interior report that sought to produce "1) an analysis of jobs currently performed at all levels of the instructional media field; 2) a systematic clustering of tasks with an emphasis on the paraprofessional level, which could become an articulated career ladder; and 3) guidelines for training programs which will provide the competencies needed to perform the tasks as they have been analyzed." The report is technical and tedious in this form but will have appeal for those who have a methodological interest and also those needing ideas regarding structuring of paraprofessional positions. [R: LJ, 15 Oct 70, p. 3606; SL, Winter 71, p. 45]

Charles D. Patterson

36 Government Publications

GENERAL WORKS

936. Fry, Bernard M. **Government Publications: Their Role in the National Program for Library and Information Services.** Washington, D.C., National Commission on Libraries and Information Science; distr., Washington, D.C., GPO, 1979. 128p. o.p. S/N 052-003-00648-1.

The author is one of the most knowledgeable persons in the field of government publications, and his insightful study merits the attention of all members of the information community. The report covers documents at all levels of government, raises crucial questions of coordination and cooperation among governments to further access and availability, and proposes a national center for government publications, which would provide a unified repository and bibliographic center for national information service.

In developing this rationale for this entity, Fry reviews the inadequacies of multiple distribution systems where the federal, state, and local units and the private sector all fail to cooperate to serve their own best interests and those of the public. What emerges clearly from Fry's keen analysis is the need for a national information policy for government materials. One benefit of such a policy would be an end to the adverse and duplicative relationship between the private sector and government. Another would be the improvement of access services—including indexing, abstracting, document delivery, and computer-assisted retrieval systems—that cut across jurisdictional lines and embrace all publications of the several governmental entities.

Some may argue that a national center will create yet another cumbersome bureaucracy, subject to the well-ascribed potential for ineptness and indifference. But the lack of system is so appalling that the idea, cogently and effectively presented by the author, has great merit. Fry strikes a responsive chord when he avers that the "right to know" (exemplified by Freedom of Information legislation) must be accompanied by the "right to be informed," which, if not realized, places in jeopardy the democratic dialectic. This study is indispensable reading for all interested in the role of government information in a democratic society.

Joe Morehead

937. Harleston, Rebekah M., and Carla J. Stoffle. **Administration of Government Documents Collections.** Littleton, Colo., Libraries Unlimited, 1974. 178p. illus. index. o.p. LC 74-81960. ISBN 0-87287-086-3.

This work was the first comprehensive handbook for the administration and the organization of documents collections since Ellen P. Jackson's *A Manual for the Administration of the Federal Document Collection in Libraries* (American Library Association, 1955). It is an essential basic manual for beginning documents librarians and is an invaluable reference aid for documents specialists. Detailed information is provided for all aspects of administration of depository or nondepository libraries, with chapters on the nature of a federal documents collection, the Superintendent of Documents classification system, bibliographic control, types and forms of records, acquisitions sources and procedures, and all the day-to-day processes and routines important for the efficient operation of a documents collection. This handbook will be especially important in depository collections, where federal laws govern certain procedures in the handling of documents. [R: AL, Mar 75, p. 170; C&RL, Mar 75, p. 158; RQ, Fall 75, p. 85]

938. Hernon, Peter, and Gary R. Purcell. **Developing Collections of U.S. Government Publications.** Greenwich, Conn., JAI Press, 1982. 289p. illus. bibliog. index. (Foundations in Library and Information Science, Vol. 12). $45.00. LC 82-21226. ISBN 0-89232-135-0.

This research monograph is intended as a guide for librarians who are responsible for depository collections of U.S. government publications. It will also be of interest to library directors and supervisors who, in a period of reduced resources and rising costs for library materials, are responsible for developing collection development policies.

Introductory chapters discuss the evolution of the theory of collection development in general. The operational elements of collection development for government publications are reviewed, with emphasis on the depository item number as the prime selection tool. The authors report on their research in several areas. An analysis was made of the 200 depository items most frequently selected and the 200 items least frequently selected against a number of variables. Data from the 1979 Biennial Survey of Depository Libraries related to percentage of items selected were analyzed against several variables, including organization and use of Superintendent of Documents classification system, resource sharing, and discarding.

Research results are reported of a survey of economics faculties at 17 academic institutions in the Midwest on their use of U.S. government publications. This is a follow-up to Hernon's earlier survey at the same institutions, which was reported in his *Use of Government Publications by Social Scientists* (Ablex, 1979). The authors present a model government publications development policy at an imaginary university library and include in the appendices reprints of approved collection development policies at seven academic institutions. These provide an excellent guide and starting point for any depository library to develop and tailor a policy for its specific needs. Appendices also include a list of the 200 depository items most frequently selected and the faculty questionnaire used by Hernon. [R: JAL, July 83, p. 167; LJ, 1 Sept 83, p. 1667; WLB, Apr 83, p. 703]

LeRoy C. Schwarzkopf

939. Jones, H. G. **Local Government Records: An Introduction to Their Management, Preservation, and Use.** Nashville, Tenn., American Association for State and Local History, 1980. 208p. index. $9.95pa. LC 79-24743. ISBN 0-910050-42-2.

The author's intent is to "provide an introduction to the management, preservation, and use of local public records" (preface), and in this purpose he succeeds admirably. Jones divides his account into two parts. Part 1, "Management and Preservation," consists of chapters about the history of records management, establishing a local records management program, the benefits of microfilm and the computer in coping with the evils of quantity, examples of local governments with innovative programs, and a glimpse into the future of local records management. Part 2, "Use of Local Government Records," was more interesting from this reviewer's perspective. Here the chapters deal with the marvelous diversity of local government patterns, and thus the ways in which records are formed and used. Records are assayed from a topical approach, with birth, death, marriage, divorce, election, tax, school, wills, and other records discussed. The concluding chapter is an excellent introduction to the sources and strategies for researching local government records. A couple of useful appendices and a detailed index round out the book.

The author presents a cogent argument for better management and more extensive research use of local records. Sadly, despite the advent of computer-microfilm technology which can dramatically reduce bulk and improve access, Jones finds that progress in records management at the local level has been minimal in the United States. This situation is in large part due to the low priority given to the task by archivists, records managers, state and local officials, and the communities themselves. Nevertheless, the wealth of materials to be found in local records will reward the patient researcher. Jones's book inspires one to become the town historian, or at least to appreciate the value of local documentation. Highly recommended for all libraries that have government records or local history collections. [R: LJ, 15 Sept 80, p. 1798]

Joe Morehead

940. Marulli, Luciana. **Documentation of the United Nations System: Co-ordination in Its Bibliographic Control.** Metuchen, N.J., Scarecrow, 1979. 225p. bibliog. index. $18.00. LC 79-17510. ISBN 0-8108-1233-9.

The author assays the problem of bibliographic control and its coordination within the UN system. The growth of specialized agencies, UN subsidiary bodies, agency programs and activities, and languages in which official business is transacted is reflected in the growth of documents published—number of titles, languages employed, subjects covered. Hence the importance of coordinated bibliographic control is palpable.

Marulli's study includes a historical overview of the search for bibliographic coordination, the structural documentation of the specialized agencies, types of bibliographic tools, elements of bibliographic information, and compliance with bibliographic standards. A final chapter is devoted to conclusions and recommendations, followed by a brief, unannotated bibliography, appendices, and an index. Appendix A is an organization chart of the UN system; appendix B is a glossary of terms defining bibliographic elements. The index is attenuated but appears to be adequate. Moreover, there are tables and figures that serve as readers' aids to the analysis.

The author's conclusions suggest a compatibility of bibliographic policy and practice among the organizations in the UN system. She believes that this commonality of approach "amounts to a substantial *de facto* coordination," despite the "great diversity of bibliographic outputs" (p. 191). Many librarians working with these forward materials would be reluctant to agree with those findings. Nevertheless, with the growth of and interest in international documentation, the study is apposite and useful. Recommended for libraries with holdings of IGOs and for library science libraries. [R: C&RL, July 80, pp. 359-60; JAL, Mar 80, p. 55]　　　　　　　　　　　　Joe Morehead

941. McClure, Charles R., and Peter Hernon. **Improving the Quality of Reference Service for Government Publications.** Chicago, American Library Association, 1983. 270p. bibliog. index. (ALA Studies in Librarianship, No. 10). $35.00. LC 83-3754. ISBN 0-8389-0388-6.

This study, conducted by 2 library educators with the assistance of 18 library school students, seeks to assay the quality of reference service provided by staff members of documents collections in selected academic depository libraries. The methodology, based on unobtrusive testing, included the tabulation of responses to "documents-related" questions, "staff willingness to engage in referral, and the characteristics of the reference interview." The findings indicate that "staff members frequently are unsuccessful in (1) meeting user requests for factual data and bibliographic citations, (2) providing referral services, and (3) utilizing innovative interview and search strategies." Although document librarians work assiduously through

national or local organizations to improve the *Monthly Catalog*, bibliographic control, microforms, relations with the Government Printing Office, and a host of other worthy projects, all these efforts are ultimately vitiated, the authors argue, if these professionals do not provide competent and accurate service to users.

The writers present the conceptual and methodological bases of the study, assess the findings, and offer a number of suggestions for improving the quality of government documents reference service. Although these recommendations are basically sound, not enough attention is directed to specific teaching-learning strategies used in library school courses in government documents or reference and to the basic intellectual equipment of students who choose to enter a graduate library school program and eventually find themselves in responsible positions in documents reference work. The importance of these factors is made palpable when one examines the sources used to answer the reference questions employed in the study. One is struck by the simplicity of the question and familiarity of the source; again and again the *Monthlyh Catalog* and *Publications Reference File* are given as the sources wherein the citation leading to the answer may be found. As the authors suggest, this study is based on "exploratory" research, and a great deal remains to be done. One of their better recommendations is for more research in this area of inquiry, a task particularly suitable for library/information science programs with a doctoral component.

The book contains numerous figures and tables, and appendices that include the notoriously easy reference questions used in the study. A bibliography and index round out the work. [R: BL, 15 Oct 83, p. 326; JAL, Nov 83, pp. 311-12; LJ, 1 Oct 83, p. 1858]
　　　　　　　　　　　　Joe Morehead

942. Morehead, Joe. **Introduction to United States Public Documents.** 3rd ed. Littleton, Colo., Libraries Unlimited, 1983. 309p. illus. index. (Library Science Text Series). $28.50; $19.50pa. LC 82-22866. ISBN 0-87287-359-5; 0-87287-362-5pa.

The third edition of this text on U.S. government publications has been extensively revised and updated to include many of the changes that have occurred in the production and distribution of government information. Like previous editions, this work offers an introduction to the basic sources of information that compose the bibliographic structure of federal government publications. New or expanded material includes that on the continual growth and evolution of the *Monthly Catalog of United States Government Publications*; the significant changes in the format and distribution of the Congressional Serial Set; the legislative process (recounted in detail), including private legislation; the 1980 census; and the proliferation of online databases and microform collections covering federal documentation. Beginning with an introductory review of issues, problems, and themes associated with public policy and the process of information transfer, the author continues by describing the administration and general bibliographic systems by which both government and libraries carry out the delivery and sharing of public information. Chapters 5 and 6 present an account of the financial support activities of agencies like the National Technical Information Service and discuss some of the prominent guides, indexes, and checklists that provide access to government publications. The remaining four chapters examine the types of products and services generated by or in support of the activities of the legislative, executive, and judicial branches; the independent agencies with regulatory powers; and the advisory committees and commissions. A listing of selected online databases for federal government information is offered in the appendix. [R: JAL, Sept 83, p. 250]

943. Nakata, Yuri. **From Press to People: Collecting and Using U.S. Government Publications.** Chicago, American Library Association, 1979. 212p. illus. index. $15.00. LC 78-26306. ISBN 0-8389-0264-2.

This is one of the best overviews of federal government publications to date, with the emphasis on reference service and delivery to the user. Topics covered include a history of government printing and the depository library program; selection, organization, and arrangement of materials; technical services; and the *Monthly Catalog* and other bibliographical sources. There are five appendices, comprising one-quarter of the book, which are primarily reprints of readily available GPO forms, statements, etc. This title can be compared to three books: Laurence Schmeckebier's *Government Publications and Their Use* (Brookings Institution, 1969); Rebekah Harleston and Carla Stoffle's *Administration of Government Documents Collections* (Libraries Unlimited, 1974; see *ARBA 75*, entry 214); and Joe Morehead's *Introduction to United States Public Documents* (Libraries Unlimited, 1983; see *ARBA 84*, entry 50).

Schmeckebier, though hopelessly outdated, still contains superb information on the history

of government publishing and certain types of publications, though it provides little useful information on modern practices. Harleston and Stoffle prepared a good practical guide to the technical services aspects of a documents collection; however, much has changed in the last five years, and this book is currently undergoing revision. Morehead has written a solid textbook that covers some of the same areas as Nakata, though his emphasis is on specific publications. However, there is overlap, including areas such as the depository system, organization of collections, and bibliographical resources. Both are very good books, though Morehead's is primarily designed as a library school text. *From Press to People* is strongly recommended for the library school student, the beginning documents librarian, and the more experienced practitioner, as well as all concerned with government documents librarianship. [R: C&RL, Nov 79, pp. 571-72; SLJ, Dec 79, p. 2532] Alan Edward Schorr

944. Nakata, Yuri, Susan J. Smith, and William B. Ernst, Jr., comps. **Organizing a Local Government Documents Collection.** Chicago, American Library Association, 1979. 61p. bibliog. $6.00pa. LC 79-21297. ISBN 0-8389-0284-7.

The virtue of this manual is its practical brevity in presenting the various problems and suggested procedures in acquiring, organizing, cataloging and classifying, and providing reference service for that most frustrating and elusive category—local documents. The authors begin auspiciously by distinguishing among local documents, local records, local history, and local information, and noting that these categories will consist of nongovernment materials as well as official materials. A core collection of types of materials is suggested. The authors point out wisely that a written policy statement for local materials is necessary not only as a guide for current operations but also for future reference as the collection develops. The importance of having a mandatory distribution ordinance is emphasized, plus a vigilant "selling" campaign to educate the various municipal departments and agencies in their distribution requirements.

The section on internal organization covers the merits and shortcomings of a vertical file, an integrated versus segregated collection, a newspaper clipping file, and the value of newspaper indexing. Various cataloging and classification suggestions are given for serial and monographic documents. The section on reference services emphasizes the importance of a community

organizations file for ready-reference local information and an authority file for recurring
local questions. Desirable search strategies are
developed, with several useful sample reference
questions and their accompanying strategy. The
final chapter is a brief account of publicizing
one's local documents collection to stimulate
and guide user interest. Eight appendices include useful specimens, such as a sample distribution ordinance, a checklist of local documents, and an example of a newspaper clipping.

The guide concludes with a selected bibliography of articles and other materials about local
documents. There is no index, but the organization of the guide does not make this a fault. I
am very impressed with the amount of first-rate
advice and practical wisdom packed into these
pages. It seems to me that all libraries large and
small that have any kind of local documents collection would be remiss if they did not purchase
a copy of this most useful source and be advised
by its suggestions for the organization and
development of local materials. [R: BL, 15 Oct
79, p. 329; C&RL, Nov 79, pp. 571-72; JAL,
Nov 79, p. 301]   Joe Morehead

945. O'Hara, Frederic J., ed. **Reader in
Government Documents.** Washington, D.C.,
NCR/Microcard Editions, 1973. 420p. (Reader
Series in Library and Information Science). o.p.
LC 72-86633. ISBN 0-910972-24-9.

Fred O'Hara has compiled here a selection
of 25 articles; some of them are still available
from GPO, and several of them are frequently
revised. United States documents are emphasized, with only one article on UN documents. It
would be helpful if there were more information
on state documents, or more articles describing
procedures in handling government documents
(e.g., Documents Expediting Project). [R: LJ, 1
Oct 73, p. 2828; RSR, July/Sept 73, p. 12]
                          Bohdan S. Wynar

946. Pemberton, John E., ed. **The Bibliographic Control of Official Publications.** New
York, Pergamon Press, 1982. 172p. illus.
$25.00. LC 82-12358. ISBN 0-08-027419-6.

This volume, the eleventh in the Guides to
Official Publications series, is intended to
stimulate progress toward the establishment of a
comprehensive system for the bibliographic control of official publications and to identify the
principles upon which a new and definitive
coding could be based. To this end, 13 specialists—librarians in Australia, Canada, England,
Ireland, and the United States—address the
topic in 11 chapters, replete with illustrative
cataloging/classification entries. (Bibliographic

notes are appended to most chapters.) Identifi-
cation of the writers, their institutions, and
chapter titles will make clear the diversity of
library situations represented: "Notation for the
Arrangement of Official Publications in the
Library of La Trobe University, Australia," by
Ann E. Miller; "Official Publications at the
Library Board of Western Australia," by W. H.
Lamble; "The Treatment of Official Publica-
tions in the Library of Parliament, Ottawa," by
Pamela Hardisty; "The CODOC (Co-operative
Documents) Scheme, Canada," by Ellen Pear-
son and Virginia Gillham and F. Anne Cannon;
"The Documents Shelving Notation of the Leg-
islative Library, British Columbia, Canada," by
J. H. MacEachern; "The Development of Bib-
liographic Control of Official Publications in
Trinity College Library, Dublin," by John
Goodwillie; "The University of Colorado Classi-
fication System for Documents of International
Intergovernmental Organizations," by Cath-
arine J. Reynolds; "The University of Virginia's
Documents Classification System," by Walter
L. Newsome; "Bibliographic Control of Official
Publications at the Institute of Development
Studies, England," by G. E. Gorman and J. A.
Downey; and "Official Publications in a New
Bibliothecal Context," by John E. Pemberton.
These contributors, by sharing their varied experiences, have candidly reminded documents
librarians once more of both the complexity and
the necessity of bringing systematic biblio-
graphic control to official publications, an important information source. [R: LJ, 15 Mar 83,
p. 564]   Wiley J. Williams

947. Sachse, Gladys. **U.S. Government Publi-
cations for Small and Medium-sized Public
Libraries: A Study Guide.** Chicago, American
Library Association, 1981. 195p. bibliog. index.
(Public Library Reporter, No. 20). $7.50pa. LC
81-14998. ISBN 0-8389-3268-1.

The author has designed a series of "instructional modules" to help "library assistants"
learn about federal documents so that they can
better select, acquire, control, and provide
reference service. To this end she has written 15
modules, or lessons, with questions for self-
study purposes. Included are lessons covering
basic selection aids (both commercial and
governmental), purchasing government publications, housing the materials in a vertical file or
integrating them into the library's main collection, several lessons on the reference use of
federal documents, generally and by selected
subjects, a module on bills, laws, and regulations, government periodicals, the Superintendent of Documents classification system,

depository libraries, and publicity. Appendices cover sources to write to for free publications, a list of GPO bookstores, and a list of regional branches of the national archives. Before the index and a brief bibliography of other sources, there are answers to the test questions provided in the modules. There are numerous specimens of entries, forms, etc.

As the title suggests, the work is intended for small and medium-sized libraries, where integration or pamphlet use of government documents is assumed. Moreover, in both the preface and introduction the author states that the self-study guide is for library assistants. This accounts for the very simple style and narrative, deliberately basic. What disturbs me is the presumption that nonprofessionals should be permitted to acquire documents, answer questions on tracing legislation, use the *Code of Federal Regulations* and *Federal Register*, etc. These are professional tasks, and although library assistants can add to the resources of staff by knowing more rather than less about government publications, I find it appalling that the professionalization of librarianship should so casually be breeched in one of the more difficult areas of library science.

If indeed there are so few professionals available to manage documents acquisitions and reference, then this book serves a useful purpose. The sources given as exemplary are adequate, and the technical aspects cover the basic information. But the problem here is that the impression is given that government publications are basically easy. Nothing of the complexity of nondepository materials is given, and a number of things are by definition omitted. As a patron I would not want to rely too much on a library assistant for my documents needs. With this caveat I would recommend that this guide by purchased by small and medium-sized libraries. [R: BL, 15 Apr 82, p. 1066; JAL, Mar 82, p. 53]   Joe Morehead

REFERENCE WORKS

948. **Directory of Government Document Collections & Librarians.** 3rd ed. By the Government Documents Round Table, American Library Association. Jane M. Mackay and Barbara L. Turman, eds. Washington, D. C., Congressional Information Service, 1981. 672p. index. $32.50pa. ISSN 0276-959X.

This directory was first issued in 1974 and is a product of the Government Documents Round Table (GODORT). As a result of a systematic effort to contact new special libraries for possible inclusion, this edition contains information on some 2,700 libraries in the United States with federal, state, local, foreign, or international documents holdings, 400 more than the second edition (see *ARBA* 80, entry 124). The format remains the same, with section 1, "Guide to Libraries, Collections, and Staff," providing collection descriptions (federal, state, local, or international; subject specialties; depository status), staff, and special features for each library collection. Each collection is identified with an accession number for reference from sections 2, 3, 4, and 7.

Section 2, "Library Index," is an alphabetical listing of all libraries by name of institution and/or library name. Section 3, "Documents Collection Index," indexes state, local, international, and foreign collections. Section 4 indexes special subject collections, with subject terms, agency names, and acronyms found in this section identified in the appendix. Section 7, "Library Staff Index," indexes all individuals included in sections 1, 5, and 6. Section 5, "Library School Instructors, Government Documents," is a geo-alphabetical listing of library schools and faculty offering instruction in government documents. Section 6, "State Document Authorities," revived from the first edition, is an alphabetical listing, by state, of agencies and individuals responsible for administering their respective state document programs. Section 8, "Names to Know," provides information about key people and organizations (such as GODORT) involved in government document activities. This directory improves with each edition; expanded and updated, it is a must for documents, reference, and interlibrary loan librarians. [R: BL, July 82, p. 1465; Choice, Dec 81, p. 483; Gov Pub R, Mar 82, p. 154; IRLA, Dec 81, p. 8]   Louise Stwalley

949. Lane, Margaret T. **State Publications and Depository Libraries: A Reference Handbook.** Westport, Conn., Greenwood Press, 1981. 573p. bibliog. index. $55.00. LC 80-24688. ISBN 0-313-22118-9.

Nineteen eighty-one was a sterling year for the literature on state government publications. We had David Parish's second edition of *State Government Reference Publications: An Annotated Bibliography* (Libraries Unlimited) and Margaret Lane's outstanding compendium. Her work is divided into three parts. Part 1 is an extended essay entitled "Characteristics of Depository Library Legislation," but its seven chapters go beyond depository considerations and discuss state documents collections that encompass nondepository libraries as well.

Throughout, Lane emphasizes the crucial importance of defining key terms such as "state publication," "state agency," "printed material," and the like, for without precise definitions legislation affecting state depository systems is diminished.

Part 2, "State Publications—The Literature," is a thorough account of ways to keep abreast of state documents activities, such as state documents newsletters, checklists and manuals, authority lists, etc., and a bibliography of articles, monographs, proceedings, directories, and other forms, with emphasis on the period following World War II. Part 3, "The States," consists of the text of current depository legislation, appropriate citations to opinions of the state's attorney general, and a bibliography, with annotations, of articles that are apposite to that state's depository arrangements. At the end of this part, the text of a model law developed by the Library of Congress is reprinted from the December 1969 issue of the *Monthly Checklist of State Publications*. A number of tables and lists illuminates the text and permit comparative analysis of state depository policy matters and other important arrangements. An index rounds out the book.

This effort is the best study of state publications as they relate to depository libraries that has ever been compiled. As the author warns, the legislative information given in part 3 is subject to change and the current statute or code must be consulted. Nevertheless, its reproduction here in one place is useful. Parts 1 and 2 are classic and timeless contributions to the literature. Lane says that her tome is targeted for "administrators of state document distribution programs and librarians attempting to establish depository library programs" (preface), but it should be of interest to all librarians working with any level of government materials. That Margaret Lane took the time and effort to compose this nonpareil book is a happy circumstance which commands our gratitude. [R: LJ, 15 Oct 81, p. 2001]   Joe Morehead

950.   Lester, Marilyn A. **Federal and State Government Publications of Professional Interest to the School Librarian: A Bibliographic Essay.** Urbana-Champaign, Ill., Graduate School of Library Science, University of Illinois, 1971. 31p. (Occasional Papers, No. 100). $1.00pa.

The author of this bibliographic essay is no newcomer to the government documents field: she and her husband are the compilers of the fourth edition of the *Checklist of United States Government Publications, 1789-1970*, a major work released in 1971 (see *ARBA* 73, entry 219). This bibliographic essay is a well-written guide to federal and state publications of interest to school librarians, children's librarians in public libraries, or anyone who works with children and their books. [R: AL, Apr 72, p. 432]
Sally Wynkoop

951.   Schorr, Alan Edward, comp. **Government Documents in the Library Literature 1909-1974.** Ann Arbor, Mich., Pierian Press, 1976. 110p. index. $16.50pa. LC 77-70340. ISBN 0-87650-071-8.

The introduction to this comprehensive bibliographic guide to the literature on U.S. federal, state, and municipal documents and UN and League of Nations documents points out that the 1,206 entries cover the whole range of documents librarianship, from acquisition policies to reference services to instruction in library schools. And so they do, particularly for the literature on U.S. federal documents, which accounts for two-thirds of the citations. Arrangement of the guide is by section—U.S. government, state government, UN, and League of Nations publications—further subdivided by topics, which for federal publications include: general; acquisition and distribution; bibliographies, guides, and indexes; cataloging and classification; depository library program; microform; and teaching. Municipal documents are treated as a topic in the state government section. A listing of serial abbreviations used and two alphabetical indexes (one by state and one for personal names) complete the volume. While one might be inclined to quibble with the compiler's assignment of topics for some of the articles, this bibliography does indeed meet Schorr's objective—to provide a handy, access tool to the literature available in the complex field of documents librarianship.
Barbara E. Smith

952.   Vandercook, Sharon. **A Guide to British Documents and Records in the University of Virginia Library.** Charlottesville, Va., Reference Department, University of Virginia Library, 1972. 104p. index. $3.00pa.

Composed of a list of the library's holdings, this guide describes the more important British documents, primarily of the nineteenth and twentieth centuries. The library's holdings are quite extensive; where some volumes of a set are lacking, the author has indicated what constitutes a complete set. Therefore, the guide has utility for other libraries with British official publications.

Included in this list are the classic Sessional papers of the Commons and Lords, Command Papers, "Blue Books" (a term designating certain important Sessional papers, often reports of Royal Commissions and departmental committees), the "Green Papers" of the foreign office, and the records of Parliament (including the debates, diaries, and proceedings). Appendix 4 lists some of the more significant records before the nineteenth century, including those of the Chancery and Curia Regis. An adequate index completes the guide.

Organized logically and with brief but adequate explanatory notes, the guide is a useful addition to libraries with extensive holdings in this area. Joe Morehead

953. Van Zant, Nancy Patton. **Selected U.S. Government Series: A Guide for Public and Academic Libraries.** Chicago, American Library Association, 1978. 172p. index. $15.00. LC 77-10337. ISBN 0-8389-0252-9.

This convenient acquisitions and reference tool is intended for librarians in academic libraries with collections of up to 300,000 volumes and medium-sized public libraries serving a population of 50,000 users. The 600 annotated items constitute a basic collection for depository libraries and a purchasing guide for nondepository libraries; they were selected from the March 1977 *List of Classes of United States Government Publications Available for Selection by Depository Libraries.* The items are arranged by 28 broad subject categories; subject/title and item number indexes follow. Each entry identifies the depository item number and SuDocs number for that item. The format for the entry follows that of LC and the *Monthly Catalog of United States Government Publications* as much as possible. The annotations are generally quite good, as most state the range of topics covered by the series, the subject and level of treatment, examples of titles issued in the last five years, and a recommendation for purchase by type of library. Important individual series titles are also identified. *Selected U.S. Government Series* fills a need in the library literature on government publications, and it should be used in conjunction with other important tools listed at the end of the introduction.

Deborah Jane Brewer

954. Wittig, Alice J. **U.S. Government Publications for the School Media Center.** Littleton, Colo., Libraries Unlimited, 1979. 121p. illus. index. $12.50. LC 79-24798. ISBN 0-87287-214-9.

Designed as a guide to using and displaying government publications in schools and media

centers, this book lists and annotates 348 such documents in 41 subject groups. Each entry includes, in addition to the annotation, the date of publication, pagination, SuDocs number, GPO stock number, and price. For non-GPO materials, the agency publisher is given, and a complete address for each is supplied in an appendix.

The initial section gives a brief introduction to the history of government printing, the Superintendent of Documents Classification System, and the depository library system. Also in part 1 are a list of suggested basic reference tools — including indexes and selection aids — and a bibliography of helpful professional books on government documents. Complete instructions on how to order government publications are also included. An outstanding feature of this section is the group of illustrated ideas of ways that documents may be effectively displayed. In addition, the author's cartoon illustrations throughout the book serve as starter ideas for other ways that documents may be used on bulletin boards and in display areas. [R: BL, 15 Apr 80, p. 1997; SLJ, Oct 80, p. 120; SLMQ, Summer 80, p. 272]

PROCEEDINGS

955. Hernon, Peter, ed. **Collection Development and Public Access of Government Documents: Proceedings of the First Annual Library Government Documents and Information Conference.** Westport, Conn., Meckler Publishing, 1982. 160p. bibliog. $35.00. LC 82-3435. ISBN 0-930466-49-7.

Collection Development and Public Access of Government Documents is a compilation of nine papers presented at the first annual Library Government Documents and Information Conference held in Boston 3-4 March 1981, sponsored by Microform Review, Inc. From the table of contents, it is difficult to see the focus of the conference. However, two themes struggle to emerge from the widely diverse topics of the conference papers. Public access to government documents is discussed in five papers by Bernard Fry, LeRoy Schwarzkopf, Charles McClure, Joe Morehead, and William Barrett in several areas, including establishing effective access to government publications by setting a theoretical foundation based on standards, in order to meet the needs of a growing field; the legislative history of the depository library system; the GPO depository program; patrons' uses and misuses of statistics in government publications and librarians' roles in relation to them; and trends of the Government Printing Office in the 1980s. The second theme, collection development of the United Nations, UNESCO, or U.S. government publications, is covered in four papers by Luciana Marulli-Koenig, Peter Hajnal, Peter Hernon and Gary Purcell, and Peter Hernon and Clayton Shepherd. Each article has its own footnotes at the end of the paper, which are reorganized into a bibliography by publication type at the end of the book. There is no index. Although expensive for its size, the book is attractive and is in an easy-to-read format. Purchase is suggested for those libraries involved with government publications or for library school libraries.

Barbara L. Bell

956. Hernon, Peter, ed. **Communicating Public Access to Government Information: Proceedings of the Second Annual Library Government Documents and Information Conference.** Westport, Conn., Meckler Publishing, 1983. 153p. illus. bibliog. $35.00. LC 82-14334. ISBN 0-930466-59-4.

This volume continues the excellent work Meckler Publishing began with the publication of the proceedings of the first annual Library Government Documents and Information Conference (*Collection Development and Public Access of Government Documents*; see *ARBA* 84, entry 181). This is an admirably prompt report of the second annual conference held at Arlington, Virginia, in March 1982. The volume reports on a number of topics of immediate relevance to government documents librarians.

Bernardine Hoduski opens the volume with a consideration of the kinds of political activities that documents librarians could become involved with in order to have direct impact on the governmental processes that directly affect their work. In doing this Hoduski also gives some of the background behind recent changes in GPO/SuDocs activities. Joseph Caponio then provides a brief explanation of his agency's work and gives a glimpse of future activities. Brian Land follows this with an excellent explanation of Freedom of Information legislation in Canada and how it parallels FOIA laws in the United States.

Several disparate, but important, topics are presented in the remaining papers. Kathleen Heim discusses in some depth the problems of accessing government-produced machine-readable statistical data files, an important but often neglected component of the social sciences information system. She makes a carefully reasoned argument for placing these resources squarely in the information system handled by

librarians and provides some suggestions as to how documents librarians can be involved in the process. Charles Seavey follows with a brief examination of another neglected library resource, government-produced maps, and urges librarians to avoid this "cartographic illiteracy." Michael Tate is also concerned with the issue of neglect, but of a very different type. He reviews a few of the problems that face researchers who deal with government reports, census data, and archival records on American Indians. Peter Hernon and Charles McClure report on the results of a pilot study of the quality of reference work in academic depository libraries and compare these results with more general studies of reference service. Their results are not encouraging, since they report a 37 percent rate of correct answers. Specific suggestions are made to the GPO and to depository libraries to deal with these findings. John Richardson gives a brief resume of his *Graduate Research in Government Publications* (Oryx Press), and Gary Purcell provides a summary of the conference from the perspective of its theme, public access to government information.

Overall, the volume is a good compilation and summary of the issues and problems that confront librarians who attempt to provide access to government information. This strength, however, is also somewhat of a weakness since the topics of the contributors do not form a unified treatment of the public access theme. [R: C&RL, May 83, p. 272]

Robert V. Williams

957. Hernon, Peter, ed. **New Technology and Documents Librarianship: Proceedings of the Third Annual Library Government Documents and Information Conference.** Westport, Conn., Meckler Publishing, 1983. 107p. bibliog. (Government Documents and Information Conference). $35.00. LC 83-896. ISBN 0-930466-64-0.

The articles in this compilation are edited versions of papers presented at the 1982 conference, the emphasis of which was to assay the role and impact of "new technology ... on the bibliographic control and availability of government information to library clientele." Discussed in these pages are by now relatively "old" systems—OCLC, online databases, microforms, Canada's CODOC, and several automated systems in use by a number of state legislatures. One paper does report on the cutting edge of technology: teletext and videotext systems "which have been around less than fifteen years." Moreover, the authors largely cite one another's earlier research to stress the inescapable and melancholy fact that a majority of documents librarians are neither psychologically prepared nor financially able to harness these technologies in the service of greater access to users.

Charles R. McClure, in a wide-ranging survey, focuses upon bibliographic accessibility, physical availability, professional service and status, criteria that should be applied to technology and government information in libraries. Judy E. Myers examines the problems associated with the cataloging, distribution, and access of government information appearing in nonprint formats. Bruce Morton discusses some of the negative attitudes of librarians toward information technologies within the context of automated systems he developed for his documents collection. Susanna Schweizer explores the exciting technologies of teletext and videotext and their advantages and drawbacks in the dissemination of federal government information. Terry L. Weech addresses the several uses to which state governments have employed technologies. And Virginia Gillham summarizes the renowned CODOC system originally developed at the University of Guelph in Ontario, Canada, showing examples of its comprehensive features.

Because information technologies exist in a state of constant change, proceedings like this are important vehicles for continuing education and training. [R: LJ, 15 Oct 83, p. 1936]

Joe Morehead

37 History

GENERAL WORKS

958. Dunlap, Leslie Whittaker, comp. **Readings in Library History.** New York, R. R. Bowker, 1972. 137p. illus. o.p. LC 71-38429. ISBN 0-8352-0518-5.

Some 24 writers are represented in this anthology. The success of an anthology usually depends on the criteria used for selection and on the actual objectives. Apparently the editor thinks that this book "was compiled primarily to help students in library schools who encounter difficulty in comprehending the development of libraries in early Western civilization." We think that graduate students in our library schools are more sophisticated and that this will simply not do. Dunlap really should have known better. [R: LJ, 15 Oct 72, p. 3295]

Bohdan S. Wynar

959. Ellsworth, Dianne J., and Norman D. Stevens, eds. **Landmarks of Library Literature, 1876-1976.** Metuchen, N.J., Scarecrow, 1976. 520p. index. o.p. LC 75-45139. ISBN 0-8108-0899-4.

Forty-one items have been selected as "landmarks" for the first century of American librarianship: articles, editorials, and "notable documents or reports." Twenty-two were written before 1940, and eleven before 1900. The topical division of the contents ties the articles to the major components of our professional development which have occupied the minds of librarians and library educators in the past 100 years. Such topics as the "social responsibility of libraries," the "National Library Concept," "library management," and "cataloging and classification" are documented, as are the various types of libraries and also library automation. The articles chosen all appear to have

lasting value, and their authors represent some of the giants of our history—Louis Round Wilson, Melvil Dewey, C. C. Williamson, Ralph Shaw, and Pierce Butler, to mention only a few of those chosen.

The anthology could well be at least twice as large, but the editors have delineated their selection criteria well and, on the whole, have chosen well to serve these criteria. All of us have favorite items that do not appear here, but there seems to be little to quarrel with in what is included. We find, though, no landmark literature concerning documentation and information science as they relate to libraries, and these topics most decidedly mark our first 100 years. There is a further puzzling omission: Ralph Beals is cited twice in the introduction, on the characteristics of library literature. None of his writings has been included in the text.

While it is normal to view as "landmarks" older articles that have proved their viability over time—and thus we find the bulk of the items chosen from the years before 1965—in the section on "The Management of Libraries and Their Resources" only one article, by Meier, is of recent vintage, and it was published in 1961. As management principles are being more steadily applied to library operations, one hopes that some "landmark literature" is now being prepared in this area. [R: C&RL, Nov 76, pp. 568-69; LJ, 15 Nov 76, p. 2352]

Margaret Anderson

960. Harris, Michael H. **A Guide to Research in American Library History.** 2nd ed. Metuchen, N.J., Scarecrow, 1974. 283p. index. $15.00. LC 74-17113. ISBN 0-8108-0744-0.

The aim of this second edition of the guide (first edition, 1968) is to provide for the field of American library history a concise assessment of the extent and materials of its research; a brief discussion of its theoretical framework, methods, and tools; an annotated listing of works dealing with it; and a list of doctoral dissertations and master's theses (through 1973) represented in it. This edition also corrects previous errors and includes previously omitted materials.

The guide is divided into two parts. The first comprises three relatively brief essays on the state of the art, the philosophy and methods of research, and a guide to resources.

The second, and by far the larger, section is divided into 12 parts: predecessors of the public library, the public library, academic libraries, special libraries, school libraries, state libraries, types of service, library education, library associations, biographies of librarians and library benefactors, the literature of American librarianship, and miscellaneous studies. The work concludes with author and subject indexes. This revision of a very useful book will be welcomed not only by students of American library history but also by scholars working in American social history. [R: C&RL, July 75, pp. 330-31]

Jesse H. Shera

961. Harris, Michael H., ed. **Reader in American Library History.** Washington, D.C., NCR Microcard Editions, 1971. 242p. (Reader Series in Library and Information Service). $10.95. LC 71-165293. SBN 910972-10-9. (Available from Greenwood Press, $28.50, ISBN 0-313-24040-X).

The fourth volume in this series groups articles under six major subject headings: "The study of American Library History"; "Books and Reading in Colonial America"; "Libraries in the New Nation"; "Public Libraries in the United States"; "Dewey, the American Library Association, and Education for Librarianship"; and "Growth of Specialization—Into the Twentieth Century." Several of Shera's articles are reprinted here, including "The Value of Library History," published in 1952 in *Library Quarterly*. The same journal also published "The Literature of American Library History" (January 1945) by the same author. This article is not included, although it is one of the best written by Jesse Shera on this subject. [R: C&RL, Sept 72, p. 417; LJ, 15 Mar 72, p. 992]

962. Hobson, Anthony. **Great Libraries.** New York, Putnam, 1970. 320p. illus. (part col.). bibliog. index. o.p. LC 79-115032.

An anthology of the author's very personal sketches about great libraries, primarily from the Middle Ages but also some more recent ones, all of which are considered because of their respective collections of rare books. Many illustrations enhance the text, making the volume of interest to librarians and bibliophiles. [R: LJ, 15 Jan 71, p. 174]

Charles D. Patterson

963. Jackson, Sidney Louis. **Libraries and Librarianship in the West: A Brief History.** New York, McGraw-Hill, 1974. 489p. illus. bibliog. index. (McGraw-Hill Series in Library Education). o.p. LC 73-13619. ISBN 0-07-032118-3.

Approximately two-thirds of this work is devoted to the history of Western libraries and librarianship from the seventeenth century to the present; such history through the period including the Renaissance and Reformation is disposed of in fewer than 145 pages. While the time division seems fair, one might question the geographical inclusion of the library developments of the Soviet Union in a work specifically referring to "the West" when there is no more than incidental reference to the Western world nations in Latin America or librarianship in Canada.

The various aspects of librarianship are discussed as the author moves forward in time and from country to country—book collecting, organization of materials, storage, bibliographic problems, and personnel assigned to take care of the library collections. Some of the boldface headings that indicate the contents of the succeeding sections, however, demonstrate an application to the past of the historical terminology of the present: "Call numbers in the catalog" used to describe methodology in the late Middle Ages, and "Book trade advances in bibliographic control" used to describe the seventeenth century. And what is one to make of such headings as "French nourishment" (p. 101), "The white nonscholar in the United States" (p. 407), "Women and children" (p. 272)?

The text is not made easier to read by the inclusion of what would normally be footnote references in parentheses within the body of the text. And the use of such unanswered questions as "What does this reveal?" or "What would so and so have done?" does no more than break up the reader's flow of thought. If such questions have value for student reflection when this is used as a textbook—and they may well have—the author would have done better to place them at the end of chapters or, at least, at the end of the major chapter divisions.

If this study had been presented as a two-volume work, perhaps all major aspects of library history could have been allowed their proper degree of expansion.

The study as written lays an emphasis on one aspect of economics and economic history only. While one would not choose to quibble about the importance of libraries receiving enough money, and while it may be true that there are bourgeois and capitalist nations on the one hand (every nation but the Soviet Union), and socialist nations on the other, seeing library history mainly in terms of the proletariat, revolution, and the bourgeoisie is an insult to both sides of the European frontier, not least to Soviet bibliographers of international stature. It is perhaps as well that there *are* only passing references to the Canadian scene, since some of these are erroneous. On page 434 there is a reference to "private liberal arts colleges for whites in the United States and Canada"; a minimal amount of research on the author's part would have turned up the information that Canadian universities have never proclaimed themselves exclusively for whites (nor been so in fact), and that they have not been "private institutions" in the same sense as U.S. institutions.

The final major division in the last chapter is "Librarianship almost a profession." Even though the author seems to have effectively stopped discussing librarianship and its history in the general vicinity of 1950, this is still sufficiently late in time to make one wonder what such giants in library education and "professional librarianship" as Louis Round Wilson, Pierce Butler, Ralph Shaw, Ralph Beals, and Verner Clapp would have made of it all. As for those of us who are concerned about the welfare of American publishing as well as of librarianship, we cannot help wondering what happened to the high editorial standards of McGraw-Hill. [R: Choice, Sept 74, p. 922; LJ, 15 June 74, p. 1681]   Jesse H. Shera
and Margaret Anderson

964.   Jackson, Sidney L., Eleanor B. Herling, and E. J. Josey, eds. **A Century of Service: Librarianship in the United States and Canada.** Chicago, American Library Association, 1976. 354p. $30.00. LC 76-41815. ISBN 0-8389-0220-0.

This ably edited collection of 18 essays, by far the most significant contribution to the centennial, was commissioned by an ad hoc committee of library historians. As the editors indicate, "it honors a profession and those who practice it, by reviewing broadly, facet by facet, the advances, failures, and present prospects of

libraries and librarianship" (p. vii). The first group of essays, focusing on service to specific constituencies, features such authors as Hardy Franklin ("Service to the Urban Rank and File"), Clara Jackson ("Service to Urban Children"), an exceptionally well-documented article by Haynes McMullen ("Service to Ethnic Minorities Other than Afro-Americans and American Indians"), A. P. Marshall ("Service to Afro-Americans"), Samuel Rothstein ("Service to Academia"), and Angelina Martinez ("Service to Special Clienteles"). The second group, with an article by David Kaser and Ruth Jackson and one by Dee Garrison, addresses the major questions of professional personnel. The third part, "Facilities," consists of four articles covering reference services, technical services (two articles), and library buildings. The broader organizational environment is examined in part four, "Environment," with articles by John Cole ("The National Libraries of the United States and Canada"), Peter Conmy and Caroline M. Coughlin ("The Principal Library Associations"), Grant T. Skelley ("The Library World and the Book Trade"), Neal L. Edgar ("Image of Librarianship in the Media"), Vivian D. Hewitt ("Services to Library Life Abroad"), and Sidney L. Jackson ("Research"). A well-executed volume. [R: C&RL, July 77, p. 347; JAL, Sept 77, p. 217; LJ, 1 Oct 77, p. 2016; RQ, Fall 77, p. 77]

Bohdan S. Wynar

965.   Johnson, Elmer D., and Michael H. Harris. **History of Libraries in the Western World.** 3rd ed., completely rev. Metuchen, N.J., Scarecrow, 1976. 354p. index. o.p. LC 76-25422. ISBN 0-8108-0949-4.

The third edition of this well-known work retains the basic structure of previous editions. Substantial additions have been made in several chapters, especially in part 3, "Modern Library Development in the West" and the concluding part 4, "The Library in History." In addition to the much-improved narrative, one finds at the end of each chapter additional reading, with selective listings of books and some articles that pertain to the topic under discussion. All in all, this is a well-balanced introductory text that should be of interest to library school students. [R: C&RL, July 77, p. 354; LJ, 15 Feb 77, p. 464]

966.   Karetzky, Stephen. **Reading Research and Librarianship: A History and Analysis.** Westport, Conn., Greenwood Press, 1982. 385p. bibliog. index. (Contributions in Librarianship and Information Science, No. 36).

$37.50. LC 80-1715. ISBN 0-313-22226-6; ISSN 0084-9243.

Language is the most complex and necessary of human creations; and reading, while not the most widespread of humanity's arts, implies the printed, or at least the written, word. Without that, no repositories of information are possible, and the transmission of culture ceases. Reading is but one of the language arts on which communication depends. For many, reading is an almost natural activity, often done automatically. But for librarians, educators, sociologists, psychologists, and others, questions about reading need to be answered so that improvements can be made in curricular structure and in library collection development decisions. What do people read? Why? How? What effect does reading have on other activities? And so on. Karetzky does not directly answer these questions, but he summarizes research on these and other areas performed in the United States and elsewhere during the first 40 or so years of this century. Some concentration is also found on the work of Douglas Waples, the force behind the movement to scientifically study reading, and Louis Round Wilson, dean at Chicago, the center for most of the reading research in the 1930s. What research was done? What did it show? How was this work made known? What have the effects of this research been on schools and libraries of all sizes, publishing, journalism, mass communication, and in other communities?

Karetzky's careful research in his 1978 dissertation is made available here for the experts and scholars who need this background and summary. The bibliography and footnotes are excellent, and the index is a detailed guide to the content of this research contribution. New technologies will mean new investigations, and Karetzky's work is essential for those who want an understanding of the past or those who intend to break new ground in the dynamic trends reading will provide tomorrow. [R: JAL, Sept 82, p. 237] Neal L. Edgar

967. McCrimmon, Barbara. **Power, Politics, and Print: The Publication of the British Museum Catalogue, 1881-1900.** London, Clive Bingley; distr., Hamden, Conn., Linnet Books, 1981. 186p. index. $17.50. LC 80-28124. ISBN 0-85157-342-8(Bingley); 0-208-01874-3(Linnet).

The massive 95-volume *BM Catalogue* "was the first national library catalogue to be printed and so to become available in other libraries, and its importance in the bibliographic world has been enormous. To discover why and how such a historic event came about was the purpose of this study" (p. 7).

This work was based on the author's 1973 Florida State dissertation under Martha Jane K. Zachert. McCrimmon's principals include three successive head librarians: Antonio Panizzi, John Winter Jones, and Edward Bond. Only the latter and a young assistant keeper, Richard Garnett, strongly favored getting the existing manuscript catalog into print. Their project was fraught with internal struggles, especially with the unenthusiastic keeper of printed books, George Bullen, and the lower civil service staff, as well as extenal political struggles with Gladstone, Disraeli, and their chancellors of the exchequer.

Indeed McCrimmon's story is one of politics and personalities. Her research (220 notes for 13 chapters) makes strong use of primary sources, especially the British Parliamentary Papers and the Letter Books of the BM's Department of Printed Books. Some of the more provocative professional issues are raised, but not fully addressed: the idealistic idea of universal catalog versus more realistic subject bibliographies, the concepts of economy and efficiency in late nineteenth-century librarianship, and the elemental role of librarians in providing access to the physical record versus access to the intellectual contents. As for the latter issue, there is no doubt the BM librarians settled for preserving the physical record; the BMC contains two to four million items. [R: C&RL, May 82, p. 258; LJ, 15 Mar 82, p. 616] John V. Richardson, Jr.

968. Ollé, James G. **Library History.** London, Clive Bingley; distr., Munich, New York, K. G. Saur, 1979. 114p. bibliog. index. (Outlines of Modern Librarianship). $12.00. ISBN 0-85157-271-5.

James G. Ollé did not intend for his book to be a reference book, nor should it be treated as one. Instead, he tried to define the state of library history in 1979. In doing so, he focused on developments in both British and American library history. Thus his book has an international flavor, which is rather unusual for such a publication.

The growth of libraries in the two countries was curiously parallel, since their national professional associations were founded only one year apart. Likewise, library history in both countries had its beginnings in the latter part of the nineteenth century. However, only after World War II did library history emerge fully as an accepted field for research and writing in Great Britain and the United States.

While Ollé's book should be classified in the circulating collection, reference librarians may find it useful as a secondary source because of the bibliography of American and British publications on library history in chapter 6. Two publications Ollé considers especially valuable are *American Library History: A Bibliography* (see *ARBA* 79, entry 328) and the *Dictionary of American Library Biography* (see *ARBA* 79, entry 185). He describes the latter as "the most thorough, authoritative and readable reference work on library history yet published."

Ollé performs a service by broadening the international library horizon for his readers, but he also raises a question. Are there not other countries whose developments should be better known to American librarians? J. Periam Danton made a beginning with his studies of libraries in Norway, Germany, and Jamaica, but much more needs to be done. [R: C&RL, May 80, p. 267; JLH, Fall 80, p. 478; LR, Winter 80, p. 298]　　　　Thomas S. Harding

969.　Ollé, James G. **Library History: An Examination Guidebook.** 2nd ed., rev. London, Clive Bingley; distr., Hamden, Conn., Archon, 1971. 131p. bibliog. index. o.p. LC 70-598679.

A revised and expanded version of the 1967 handbook designed for use primarily by those preparing to sit for the examinations given by the Library Association. Chapters deal with special libraries, legal deposit, private libraries, the Library Association and, new with this edition, American library history. The work is really a guide and is best used as a point of departure and in conjunction with other works. [R: LJ, 15 May 71, p. 1688]
　　　　　　　　　　　Charles D. Patterson

970.　Pearson, Edmund Lester. **The Librarian: Selections from the Column of That Name.** Edited by Jane B. Durnell and Norman O. Stevens. Metuchen, N.J., Scarecrow, 1976. 634p. bibliog. index. o.p. LC 75-35725. ISBN 0-8108-0851-X.

Edmund Lester Pearson was an iconoclastic and acerbic critic of librarianship. He is known to a few library historians as the author of the widely read and controversial column "The Librarian," which appeared in the *Boston Evening Transcript* from 1906 to 1920. During that time Pearson contributed over 700 installments of his "Librarian" to the conservative and influential paper. He was one of those rare librarian-bookmen who knew the library world in all of its aspects, and he had the nerve and energy to comment critically on developments in the field for some 15 years. In this book,

Durnell and Stevens have collected the best of Pearson's work, and they argue (rightly, we think) that "The Librarian" is an extremely valuable commentary on American librarianship during the early decades of the twentieth century. As such this book represents a major contribution to library literature and a fitting monument to the man who might well rank as the profession's most consistent and entertaining critic. [R: LJ, 15 Sept 76, p. 1838]
　　　　　　　　　　　Michael H. Harris

971.　Rider, Alice Damon. **A Story of Books and Libraries.** Metuchen, N.J., Scarecrow, 1976. 173p. index. o.p. LC 76-7596. ISBN 0-8108-0930-3.

This historical handbook is designed for use in the "Arts, Social Sciences and Humanities courses in high schools" (preface). It is arranged in nine chapters, which cover the earliest records and writing materials; ancient Babylonian, Assyrian, Egyptian, and Greek libraries; libraries and books in the medieval period; and early printing in Asia, Europe, and America. A separate chapter is devoted to book collecting. Its clear form of presentation will prove to be beneficial to high school students. The author also provides helpful suggestions for teachers who may integrate the presented material into school curricula. [R: JLH, Winter 78, p. 68]
　　　　　　　　　　　Lubomyr R. Wynar

972.　Stone, Elizabeth W. **American Library Development 1600-1899.** New York, H. W. Wilson, 1977. 367p. bibliog. index. $50.00. LC 77-7881. ISBN 0-8242-0418-2.

With this volume, Stone presents a sometimes fascinating chronological approach to events in American library history up to the end of the nineteenth century. She has, moreover, arranged the material in such a manner as to make it accessible both by year and by topic. The actual summaries of events are provided in the main body of the book, which is divided into eight categories: private, special, and government libraries; academic and school libraries; public libraries; technical services; legislation; publications; professional activities; and buildings and miscellaneous. Each of these sections is arranged chronologically, with boldface headings on each entry to facilitate fast searching. Preceding these sections, and providing the common thread among them, is the chronological chart, which is divided into eight columns for each year, those columns duplicating the text's section headings. Thus, the reader has the choice of starting with a particular year and seeing what happened in various areas, or starting within one of the specialized sections and using the chronological chart as a reminder of developments in other areas not directly under study. The thorough index (author/title/subject) provides yet another means of entry. The bibliography is only of works cited in the text, and short-form citations to it for quotations and opinions in the text are convenient without being distracting.

The cut-off date of 1899 is explained as being convenient both for the size of the book and for the fact that it includes the 50 years of American librarianship following 1850, vital years in the development of our present library information resources. Too, the relatively early cut-off ensures that the achievements in the 250 years prior to 1850 are not obscured by later, more easily charted accomplishments. This is a look at roots, not the whole tree, and should be commended as such. Stone's entries are compressed, yet they don't sacrifice clarity or information, and the references quickly lead to more extended accounts of various incidents. Students of library history and of social history will be interested in this easily-read, well-designed publication, which provides its information (a wealth of it) in such a clear and useful fashion. [R: AL, Mar 78, p. 172; BL, 15 May 78, p. 1513; BL, 1 Jan 78, p. 738; C&RL, Jan 78, p. 64; CLW, Feb 78, p. 311; JLH, Winter 78, p. 62; LJ, 15 Mar 78, p. 624]

Koert C. Loomis, Jr.

973. Thomison, Dennis, **A History of the American Library Association, 1876-1972.** Chicago, American Library Association, 1978. 301p. bibliog. index. $15.00pa. LC 77-27966. ISBN 0-8389-0312-6.

Most rewritten doctoral dissertations are not pleasant reading; however, this work *is* an exception. Thomison has done an excellent job of describing the ALA's development from its founding through the retirement of David Cliff in 1972. He acknowledges that most of the book is based on secondary sources, but the primary source (ALA archives) was still not open for general research. Although published by ALA, the work is critical of many of its policies and actions. The select bibliography provides the interested reader with some suggested readings; however, Thomison's "notes" from the main text will provide more assistance for those interested in further research. This work will be very useful as supplemental reading in any introduction to librarianship course. [R: C&RL, Jan 79, p. 65; JAL, Jan 79, p. 455; JLH, Spring 79, p. 191; LJ, 1 Mar 79, p. 569; LQ, Oct 79, p. 487; RQ, Spring 79, p. 302]   G. Edward Evans

974. Wright, H. Curtis. **The Oral Antecedents of Greek Librarianship.** Provo, Utah, Brigham Young University Press, 1977. 237p. illus. bibliog. index. o.p. LC 77-73645. ISBN 0-8425-0623-3.

Wright's four essays treat Greek communication from the estimated beginnings to the Alexandrian Library. Stressed are the gradual overwhelming of the oral tradition by the rise of the temple, the city-state, and writing; and the pioneer work in bibliographic control in the ancient Near East. His method is to draw very generously from scholarly treatises and often to comment thereon; his own views are usually firm. Much of the message is not new, but introducing some luminaries of classical scholarship may be salubrious for librarians. Wright rarely quotes anything from the primary sources himself. Checking his references to Pfeiffer's *History of Classical Scholarship* against the original revealed only one misrepresentation (probably inadvertent).

Bearing more directly on libraries is the afterword, reprinting Vleeschauwer's paper on the origins of the Mouseion, edited by Wright. It includes the statement (p. 190) that "library methods" are at least as old as the Hittites (second Millenium B.C.), not to speak of Assurbanipal's library (seventh century B.C.), a tribute repeated in Shera's foreword. No evidence is adduced in either place. There is also a remark (p. 191) about the great scope of what the Nineveh collection "was to include." A reading of Oppenheim's analysis of the extant tablets in *Current Anthropology* (volume 1 [1960]: 412-13) or his *Ancient Mesopotamia* (1964, pp. 15-16, 241, 244) will throw heavy doubt on that notion.

It is necessary to call attention to the most important work of all, issued too late for Wright, Rudolf Blum's masterpiece on Callimachus and Greek literature (*Archiv für Geschichte des Buchwesens*, volume 18 [February 1977]: 1). [R: C&RL, Nov 77, p. 540; LJ, 1 Oct 77, p. 2016]   Sidney L. Jackson

975. Young, Arthur P. **Books for Sammies: The American Library Association and World War I.** Lexington, Ky., College of Library Science, University of Kentucky, Beta Phi Mu Chapbooks, c1981 [1982]. 149p. illus. bibliog. index. (Beta Phi Mu Chapbook, No. 15). $12.50. LC 81-17085. ISBN 0-910230-15-3.

Young has produced an admirable study of library history. The Library War Service was created upon the entrance of the United States into World War I and continued until 1920 as U.S. troops served in occupied Europe.

Coordinated by the American Library Association, library service to these troops took three main directions: technical reading material, recreational reading in the form of fiction, and materials to support the educational ambitions of servicemen who saw a need for a career after the war. ALA established reading programs for stateside camps and posts in Europe, as well as in hospitals and, later, on naval and shipping vessels. Both male and female librarians wore military-type uniforms, and, after considerable difficulty, the women served both at home and abroad. In the organization's last years, even blinded victims of war were supplied with reading materials.

Young believes the Library War Service helped to redirect ALA and to promote its post-war accomplishments. Inspired by prominent leaders like Herbert Putnam and Carl Milam, ALA overcame bureaucratic obstacles and provided a service respected by most military officials.

Two useful appendices identify the 49 libraries established at camps in the United States as well as camp librarians and a list of the books and pamphlets banned by the War Department. Young's work represents solid research and should stand as the definitive study on the subject. [R: C&RL, July 83, p. 300]

Boyd Childress

REFERENCE WORKS

976. Harris, Michael H., and Donald G. Davis, Jr. **American Library History: A Bibliography.** Austin, Tex., University of Texas Press, 1978. 260p. index. $22.50. LC 77-25499. ISBN 0-292-70332-5.

This publication fills the need for a bibliography in the field of American library history. *American Library History* lists a total of 3,260 entries under 13 major categories. Several of the categories are subdivided; for example, "Special Aspects of American Librarianship" has three subdivisions: international relations; cataloging and classification; and reference work. The individual entries are not annotated, but each major division has an introduction, with an overview and commentary on the literature of each respective area. The coverage is comprehensive, consisting of monographs, periodical articles, and both doctoral dissertations and master's theses. A total of 384 journal titles was mined, including not only the library periodicals, but also a great many in related fields.

Some duplication of entries was inevitable, although the editors kept it at a minimum. Jesse

H. Shera's *Foundations of the Public Library* appears three times: twice under "Predecessors of the Public Library," and once under "Public Libraries." Evidence of meticulous editing appears throughout the work. The only noticeable error is the listing of H. O. Severance's article on "The Columbia Library, 1866-1892" (no. 1845) under "New York," when it refers to a subscription library at Columbia, Missouri.

American Library History is a valuable addition to library school collections, and to personal collections of librarians. The final section on biographies is especially valuable when used in conjunction with the *Dictionary of American Library Biography*. One value of any good bibliography lies in making provision for keeping it up-to-date by means of supplements. This should be possible by means of "The Year's Work in American Library History," which is a feature of the *Journal of Library History*. [R: C&RL, Nov 78, p. 512]   Thomas S. Harding

977. Keeling, Denis F., ed. **British Library History: Bibliography 1973-1976.** Mrs. A. H. Brodie and others, comps. London, Library Association; distr., New York, Nichols Publishing, 1979. 200p. index. o.p. ISBN 0-85365-781-5.

This second supplement to *British Library History: Bibliography 1962-1968*, also edited by Keeling (Library Association, 1972), follows the format, systematic arrangement, pattern of descriptive annotations, and style of the main volume. Its 776 entries, 20 more than in the first supplement (see *ARBA* 76, entry 225), reflect a sustained interest in British libraries and related topics. While the scope remains essentially the same, the plan of using 1960 as the cut-off date for the content of the studies and of limiting citations to those in English, Welsh, and Gaelic has been relaxed. The author index continues to exclude corporate authors and writers of obituaries, but does include reviewers of books.

Sources consulted include publications of individual libraries, specialized publications such as *Leeds Art Calendar*, *Private Library*, and *Proceedings of the Huguenot Society of London*, and theses. Among the sources published in the United States are *Encyclopedia of Library and Information Science*, *Journal of Library History*, and *Library Quarterly*. Though some of the less important British library catalogs are omitted, neither the value nor the *integrity*, as the editor states, has been impaired.

The number of writings varies according to interest; for example, there are 100 entries for academic libraries, but fewer entries for ecclesiastical and mechanics' institute libraries. Inquiry, however, on libraries for the working classes has resulted in studies on workers' institutes other than those for mechanics. These, together with studies of personal collections and libraries of titled and untitled persons and analyses of reading in different eras, suggest a deepening awareness of the total range of library history.

The editor demonstrates with the variety of authors represented that "the study of library history would certainly be the poorer (and duller) if it were monopolised by librarians." It is equally true that bibliohistorians would be poorer indeed, if not duller, had not the Library History Group of the Library Association undertaken and pursued faithfully their rewarding search for appropriate references. This volume is indispensable for those interested in the study of and research in British library history or in undertaking similar studies about library development in other countries. A third supplement, expanding coverage through 1980, appeared in 1983. Sarah K. Vann

PROCEEDINGS

978. Goldstein, Harold, ed. **Milestones to the Present: Papers from Library History Seminar V.** Syracuse, N.Y., Gaylord Professional Publications, 1978. 306p. index. o.p. LC 77-18992. ISBN 0-915794-21-7.

The contents include "Liberty and Knowledge, Then and Now: 1776-1876-1976," by Dan Lacy; "Temples of Knowledge: A Study of H. H. Richardson and His Times and Small Public Library Architecture in Massachusetts, 1865-1890," by S. C. Bonk; "American Library Architecture and the World's Columbian Exposition," by D. E. Oehlerts; "Scholars, Gentle Ladies and Entrepreneurs: American Library Leaders, 1876-1976," by E. G. Holley; "Herbert Putnam and the National Library," by J. Y. Cole; "Dewey's 'Splendid Women' and Their Impact on Library Education," by L. Grotzinger; "Public Libraries in California: 1850-1920," by R. F. Wood; "The Rise of the Public Library in Texas: 1876-1920," by D. G. Davis, Jr.; "The Rise of the Public Library in Wisconsin 1850-1920," by J. C. Colson; "Libraries in the German-American Community and the Rise of the Public Library Movement," by R. E. Cazden; "The Contemplation of the Library in America," by R. Michener; "The Intellectual History of American Public Librarianship," by M. H. Harris; "Coffee House to Stock Exchange: A Natural History of the Reading

Room," by D. Kaser; "Outreach Programs in Public Libraries—How New? With Specific Reference to the N.Y. Public Library," by P. Dain.

Also provided are D. C. Dale's essay on ALA's first century (supposed to be accompanied by slides) and a number of brief "commentaries" on some of the papers. It is a pleasure to have an index in a composite work with considerable overlap. The papers are mainly of the high quality one expects of their authors. It is disappointing that all use "American" when they mean "United States." [R: C&RL, Nov 78, p. 510] Sidney L. Jackson

979. **Libraries & Culture: Proceedings of Library History Seminar VI, 19-22 March, 1980, Austin, Texas.** Austin, Tex., University of Texas Press, 1981. 478p. index. $25.00. LC 81-13015. ISBN 0-292-74632-6.

The 34 papers contained in this volume (31 selected on the basis of the "call for papers" and the 3 presented at the plenary session) focus, as the title implies, on the place of the library in the cultural milieu of various societies. The tone of the seminar is set by the plenary session papers, which examine the place of the library in overall national political strategy, its relationship to the culture of the people as a whole, and the changes in the historiography of our cultural institutions. The other papers are classified as follows—libraries and antiquity; early modern European libraries; establishment of unique collections; biographical studies of noted librarians and bibliographers; reading interests and information needs; public libraries and society; and British, American, French, and twentieth-century trends in international librarianship in such countries as China, Peru, and Russia.

Since the 31 papers were selected from the 109 prospectuses submitted, it is not surprising that they are of uniformly high quality. In addition to the philosophical themes developed in the plenary session, two further items deal with philosophical, theoretical frameworks for librarianship—the paper titled "An Idea of Librarianship: An Outline for a Root-Metaphor Theory in Library Science," by J. S. Nitecki, and Victor H. Yngve's "Stoic Influences in Librarianship: A Critique," which looks to the future as well as the past of librarianship and information science through an examination of the "theory of sign," the theory connecting words, thoughts, and things, a theory we know from Plato, Aristotle, and the Stoics.

The worth of this book, a reprint of the papers published in *Journal of Library History* (volume 16), can be found in its comprehensiveness, both in time and geography. By moving away from the purely Anglo-American concept of the cultural nature of the library, based on the philosophies of the Society for the Diffusion of Useful Knowledge, and the personal convictions of Andrew Carnegie and others, we are able, from the depth and scholarship of the studies, to develop one of the generalizations sought for in comparative, international studies, a genuine reaffirmation of the fact that the library has truly universal claim to being ranked as a cultural institution. [R: AB, 5 July 82, p. 89; JAL, Sept 82, p. 231; JAL, May 82, p. 102]

Margaret Anderson

BIOGRAPHY

980. Bruntjen, Scott, and Melissa L. Young, comps. **Douglas C. McMurtrie: Bibliographer and Historian of Printing.** Metuchen, N.J., Scarecrow, 1979. 206p. bibliog. index. (The Great Bibliographers Series, No. 4). $16.00. LC 78-25682. ISBN 0-8108-1188-X.

This volume, following ones on McKerrow, Pollard, and Dibdin (reviewed in *ARBA* 75, entry 266; *ARBA* 77, entry 283; and *ARBA* 79, entry 187, respectively), attempts to portray, through selections of the subject's published writings, a cross-section of his thought and activity. McMurtrie is an especially apt person for this kind of treatment because of the quantity of short, pithy, and very readable material he produced. The volume begins with two biographical sketches by friends of McMurtrie, and follows with 14 selections from McMurtrie's large canon, ranging from identification of difficult references in Evans's *American Bibliography*, to the vagaries of geographic place names, to the sexual role of the corset. The result is an impression of dynamic energy and intellect, an impression only reinforced by the concluding comprehensive bibliography of his writings, both separate and periodical, listing 789 items.

Yet there is a frustrating lack of editorial rigor throughout. Why is there only a distant snapshot (p. 27) of McMurtrie, when an appropriate frontispiece portrait is available? Why is a part of a passage showing McMurtrie's typography, apparently intended to be deleted, merely lined through rather than excised entirely? Why are three titles in the bibliography in the Hebrew, Greek, and Cyrillic alphabets (items 24, 239, and 672) not even transliterated? There is, however, an even more serious criticism of the bibliography. This bibliography is arranged

in a single alphabetical list of titles, unindexed. Given McMurtrie's quantity and range of output, that is little better than a random arrangement. A classified system, perhaps, based on Charles F. Heartman's bibliography, *McMurtrie Imprints* (The Book Farm, 1942), would have had obvious advantages. A chronological arrangement, however, might have been the most suitable for this volume in allowing the reader to trace the development of McMurtrie's thought and activity. [R: C&RL, Sept 79, pp. 467-68; Choice, Sept 79, p. 808; JAL, July 79, p. 165; LJ, 15 Apr 79, p. 898]

Philip A. Metzger

981. **Charles Ammi Cutter: Library Systematizer.** Francis L. Miksa, ed. Littleton, Colo., Libraries Unlimited, 1977. 344p. bibliog. index. (Heritage of Librarianship Series, No. 3). o.p. LC 76-58870. ISBN 0-87287-112-6.

In Francis Miksa's publication, *Charles Ammi Cutter: Library Systematizer*, Cutter emerges as one of the most articulate and thorough theorists ever to have focused his attention on library affairs. In his writing on Cutter, Miksa's goal is threefold: (1) to provide a critical introduction that indicates the sources of his thought and work, (2) to include a selection of writings (46 in all) which show both the breadth and forcefulness of Cutter's views, and (3) to provide a basic bibliography of his writings. Those writings most representative of Cutter's interests were selected, as were items that are essential for understanding his key ideas, especially in cataloging and classification. A few items previously available only in manuscript have been included, as have some materials that give a fuller personal picture of Cutter. [R: JAL, Nov 77, p. 295]

982. Cole, John Y., ed. **Ainsworth Rand Spofford: Bookman and Librarian.** Littleton, Colo., Libraries Unlimited, 1975. 203p. bibliog. index. (Heritage of Librarianship Series, No. 2). o.p. LC 75-31517. ISBN 0-87287-117-7.

To most librarians, Ainsworth Rand Spofford, if he is known at all, is recognized only vaguely as "an early Librarian of Congress." Actually, he was the first real bookman to be appointed to that position. He was nominated as head of our National Library by Abraham Lincoln in 1865 and held that position until 1897; from that year until 1908, he was the Chief Assistant Librarian. Thus, his career carried him well into the Putnam years. David C. Mearns treats him sympathetically in his brief history of the Library, and a few assiduous readers know his collection of essays, *A Book for All Readers*; but other than that the record is meager.

In the first four chapters of this book, Cole has written an excellent biography of the man. But the bulk of the volume is devoted to selections from his writings, which add substantially to the value of the volume. The third part of the book provides information on manuscripts and archival collections, and writings by and about Spofford. The entire work is scholarly and well documented. This, the second volume in the Heritage of Librarianship series, edited by Michael Harris, fills an important gap in the literature of American library history; it will be welcomed by all who are seriously interested in that growing field. [R: C&RL, July 76, p. 375]

Jesse H. Shera

983. Cutler, Wayne, and Michael H. Harris, eds. **Justin Winsor: Scholar-Librarian.** Littleton, Colo., Libraries Unlimited, 1980. 196p. bibliog. index. (Heritage of Librarianship Series, No. 5). $25.00. LC 80-19310. ISBN 0-87287-200-9.

Justin Winsor, chosen founding president of the American Library Association in 1876, was one of the farsighted greats of the profession and contributed significantly to bringing librarianship successfully into the information age. *Justin Winsor: Scholar-Librarian*, the fifth volume in the Heritage of Librarianship series, is a brief, appreciative biography and a compilation of the most significant of Winsor's many publications. Also included are a comprehensive bibliography of Winsor's published and unpublished writings, and secondary source materials about Winsor. [R: C&RL, May 81, p. 258; JAL, Mar 81, p. 42; LJ, 1 June 81, p. 1193; LQ, July 81, p. 331; SL, July 81, p. 306]

984. Dosa, Marta L. **Libraries in the Political Scene.** Westport, Conn., Greenwood Press, 1974. 226p. index. (Contributions in Librarianship and Information Science, No. 7). $29.95. LC 72-5218. ISBN 0-8371-6443-5.

The author's doctoral dissertation, rewritten, uses full documentation, and authoritative and original sources, in this presentation of the fascinating life of Germany's leading librarian, Georg Leyh. He brought a sense of professionalism that went beyond the political harrassment of his times, whether from the right or the left. He resisted the efforts of the Nazi bureaucracy to turn the large research libraries of Germany into further elements of the propaganda machine, and yet, as a good German, he supported the Nazis where he could without sacrificing professional principles. (An evocative

passage recounts the trials of his daughter as a member of the Hitler Jugend.)

Beginning in the period of Germany's fullest reach toward scientific excellence, through the disaster of World War I and its equally disastrous consequences, and concluding with the Nazi regime, the worship of warfare, and the destruction of those libraries he had directly or indirectly assisted toward full development, Leyh at last fell victim to the opinions of his professional critics by accepting an award from the East German government. If there is a moral to be found in the life of anyone, Leyh's life conveys the idea that professionalism reaches beyond political considerations and can be guided only by the evidence of experimentation. The evidence of things unseen is limited to the belief that no government can survive independent of the cultural accumulation that libraries represent.

Strangely, librarianship has never developed a broad range of biographies and few doctoral candidates have turned to biography as a way of satisfying academic requirements. If nothing else, this excellent book establishes biography as a valid approach to librarianship and as an excellent form for historical investigations. Beyond that, the book is worth reading just for the story alone, and equally for the compilation of original sources for the study of German library history. [R: C&RL, Nov 74, pp. 460-61; LJ, 1 June 74, p. 1524]

Jay E. Daily

985. DuBois, Paul Z. **Paul Leicester Ford: An American Man of Letters, 1865-1902.** New York, Burt Franklin, 1977. 212p. illus. bibliog. index. o.p. LC 76-55804. ISBN 0-89102-033-0.

Paul Leicester Ford accomplished an incredible amount of work in his short life of 37 years. A fall suffered in infancy stunted his growth and deprived him of the advantages of a formal education. Nevertheless, Ford published his first book at the age of 11, became a best selling author at 29, and continued to add to his reputation as an editor, bibliographer, historian, and novelist until his tragic death.

Yet Ford has been largely ignored by later generations. His contributions as a bibliographer, a historian, and a researcher in libraries have been almost forgotten. DuBois has done an excellent job in redressing this neglect.

For three years Ford was an editor of the *Library Journal*. He was an early advocate of union catalogs, interlibrary loans, open book stacks, cooperative buying among libraries, and agreements among libraries in the specialization of their collections. His printings of little-known manuscripts and pamphlets, and his editions of the writings of historical figures are important research materials.

As a bibliographer and editor, Ford made three notable contributions. His *Franklin Bibliography* is the standard work in its field. His edition of *The Federalist* was for many years the most useful version.

Although this publication is not precisely a reference book, it will be of value to reference librarians for its many citations to research materials in bibliography and American history. [R: Choice, Feb 78, p. 1643]

Thomas S. Harding

986.   Harris, Michael H., ed. **The Age of Jewett: Charles Coffin Jewett and American Librarianship, 1841-1868.** Littleton, Colo., Libraries Unlimited, 1975. 166p. bibliog. index. (Heritage of Librarianship Series, No. 1). o.p. LC 75-14205. ISBN 0-87287-113-4.

For an enthusiast of library history to review the first volume of a new series in library history is to introduce a high degree of bias in the review. Regardless, the Heritage of Librarianship series, edited by Michael H. Harris, must be received with loud huzzahs and an "at long last" by even the least appreciative admirer of library history. The first of the Harris titles, edited by Harris himself, provides a significant analysis of one key figure. As Harris notes in his foreword, "Jewett was the first among his colleagues in an age that witnessed the first faint glimmerings of professional librarianship in America." That alone would justify Jewett's selection and treatment.

In the first part of the volume Harris provides some 40 pages of biographical data, which include comments on Jewett's early life and education, his movement into librarianship and success as a librarian, the librarians' conference of 1853, and his final years at the Boston Public Library. The second, major portion of the volume includes a selection of Jewett's writings on "books, libraries, and librarianship," which emphasizes Jewett's consuming interest in a national organization and national bibliographical control of materials. The third and final bibliographical section includes a list of his published works, as well as selected items related to his life and contributions. There is a brief subject index.

Although the volume does not constitute a definitive biography of Jewett, it does fill an obvious gap in the literature of the historical foundations of contemporary librarianship by placing one significant leader in perspective

through an overview of his work and his writings.

Laurel Grotzinger

987.   Healey, James Stewart. **John E. Fogarty: Political Leadership for Library Development.** Metuchen, N.J., Scarecrow, 1974. 132p. index. $13.00. LC 73-19661. ISBN 0-8108-0689-4.

The author has based this biographical study (originally a doctoral dissertation in library science at Columbia University) on the Fogarty papers in the Library of Providence College and on personal interviews and correspondence.

Healey's goal is to find out why and how John Fogarty, Democratic congressman from Shade Island, became "Mr. Library" in legislative circles. Fogarty had been a bricklayer and did not have a college education. He had not been a library user as a child and did not have an inordinate love of books. And yet, in the "golden age" of federal library legislation from 1960 to 1967, he was the key figure in the passage of library bills that had a great impact in providing funds for all types of libraries. There has never been anyone like him.

The author discovered that Fogarty was a liberal Democrat who felt that the federal government had a responsibility for the health, education, and well-being of citizens. After the passage of the Library Services Act of 1956 he was shown the value of libraries by Elizabeth Myer, of the Rhode Island State Library. ALA followed up with further information and justification. His death in 1967 was a tragic loss for librarianship.

This important work should be read widely by librarians. It shows the value of library involvement in the political process. It is a fascinating, well-written, and well-documented biography, which also includes an excellent historical survey of attempts at federal library legislation from 1920 to 1956. [R: JLH, July 75, p. 281; LJ, 1 Jan 75, p. 34; LQ, July 75, p. 324; RSR, July 74, p. 33]   George S. Bobinski

988.   Immroth, John Phillip. **Ronald Brunlees McKerrow: A Selection of His Essays.** Metuchen, N.J., Scarecrow, 1974. 240p. index. (The Great Bibliographers Series, No. 1). $16.00. LC 73-19882. ISBN 0-8108-0690-8.

Ronald B. McKerrow is remembered as the father of twentieth-century descriptive bibliography and the author of numerous bibliographical studies, essays on printing, printers, booksellers, and Shakespeare studies. Most of his material was previously available, but in various articles, reviews, etc., that were more or less difficult to locate. Immroth has collected, in one place, some of the "more fugitive writings from among the great number of articles and reviews McKerrow produced." These include articles dealing with techniques of sixteenth-century printing, material on the Elizabethan printer, bibliographical terminology, and others. The introduction presents a brief study of the life and contributions of McKerrow (1872-1940); written by W. W. Greg, this introduction first appeared in 1940 in the *Proceedings of the British Academy*. There is also a most useful chronological listing of the writings of McKerrow, compiled by F. C. Francis, which appeared in the fourth series of *The Library* in 1940. This useful volume is the first in a series that examines the long-neglected activities of famous bibliographers, including Pollard, Sadleir, and Blades.   Paul A. Winckler

989. Johnston, Mary Tabb, with Elizabeth Johnston Lipscomb. **Amelia Gayle Gorgas: A Biography.** University, Ala., University of Alabama Press, 1978. 168p. illus. bibliog. index. $12.95. LC 77-18889. ISBN 0-8173-5235-X.

Mary Tabb Johnston and Elizabeth Johnston Lipscomb have written an engaging and carefully researched biography of Amelia Gayle Gorgas. In doing so, they pictured the antebellum South, the Civil War years, the readjustments of the Reconstruction period, and finally the New South, which has emerged since the 1880s. As the daughter of a governor of Alabama in the 1830s, the wife of the head of the Confederate Ordnance Department, and the mother of General William Gorgas, the conqueror of yellow fever in Cuba and the Panama Canal Zone, Amelia Gayle Gorgas lived through these periods during a lifetime of 86 years. However, Amelia is of interest also for her own achievements, especially for her services as the first full-time librarian of the University of Alabama during almost a quarter of a century. Apparently she was not active in the emerging library profession, and the authors do not refer to any annual reports that she may have made. Nevertheless, she was an efficient librarian and wielded an incalculable influence on University of Alabama students. Today, the Amelia Gayle Gorgas Library stands on the Alabama campus as her memorial. This is a fascinating biography, but it cannot be considered a reference book. It properly belongs in the circulating collection.   Thomas S. Harding

990. **Librarians of Congress, 1802-1974.** Washington, D.C., Library of Congress; distr., Washington, D.C., GPO, 1977. 273p. illus.

index. $7.75. LC 77-608073. ISBN 0-8444-0238-9. S/N 030-001-00080-0.

This attractive volume, unusually so for a government publication, is composed of 11 biographical essays, each dealing with one of the Librarians of Congress, from John Beckley, the first to hold that position, to L. Quincy Mumford. Each essay is by a different author, and, wisely, their selection has not been restricted to either members of the Library staff or to librarians. In a few instances (e.g., Edward N. Waters on Herbert Putnam and Ben Powell on Mumford), the authors knew their subjects intimately. In a book such as this, the portraits tend, of course, to emphasize the positive aspects of their subjects' contributions to the Library, but they are not uncritical, and a substantial amount of research has gone into their preparation. The compilation has an informative preface by Daniel Boorstin, who sets forth some of his thoughts on the role of the Library in both the federal government and the library profession at large. There is no indication of the individual who planned and edited the volume, but one may properly hypothesize that Boorstin had a major responsibility for it. Throughout the work there are many illustrations of considerable historical interest.

In reading these pages, however, one cannot but regret the necessity for the omission of the name of Verner Clapp. Probably no one since Putnam himself has been more responsible for the growth in resources and for the expansion of programs than has Clapp, who served as Deputy Librarian of Congress under Putnam, Archibald MacLeish, and Luther Evans. In the world of scholarship, as well as in the library world, both within and without the boundaries of the United States, no Librarian of Congress was as well known. This is a book that every library, and many librarians, will want to own. [R: BL, 15 Jan 78, p. 803; C&RL, July 78, p. 321; JAL, Sept 78, p. 228]   Jesse H. Shera

991. Liebaers, Herman. **Mostly in the Line of Duty: Thirty Years with Books.** The Hague, Martinus Nijhoff Publishers; distr., Hingham, Mass., Kluwer Boston, 1980. 240p. index. $29.00. LC 79-23942. ISBN 90-247-2228-4.

A Belgian librarian with a cosmopolitan point of view, Herman Liebaers has produced a book that is midway between autobiography and memoir. He describes himself as "a librarian by accident." After the liberation of Belgium in 1944, he accepted a minor position in the Royal Library in Brussels. Liebaers stayed on for 30 years, ultimately becoming the director. In this capacity he presided over the transformation of the Royal Library into a genuine national library, despite numerous problems with the government bureaucracy. As his library horizons broadened, Liebaers served as a consultant in the building of a number of foreign libraries, including one at Tehran. He became president of the International Federation of Librarians, presiding at six meetings between 1967 and 1974. His comments on the relations between IFLA and UNESCO are not entirely flattering to the latter.

Although Liebaers devotes several chapters to his achievements in acquiring valuable books for the Royal Library, this publication is of interest primarily for its international flavor. The author's opinion of American librarians is high, and he mentions several by name. In an address at the Centennial Meeting of the American Library Association, Liebaers urged its members to participate actively in international cooperation, since nongovernmental organizations will guarantee the eminence of the profession over politics. While one chapter describes the promotion of an international art seminar in Brussels, this book will be of value primarily to library school collections, where it will illustrate comparative librarianship and international library cooperation. Liebaers gives American librarians a somewhat different and refreshing perspective. [R: JAL, Mar 81, p. 38; LJ, 15 Jan 81, p. 128]   Thomas S. Harding

992. Lyle, Guy. **Beyond My Expectation: A Personal Chronicle.** Metuchen, N.J., Scarecrow, 1981. 219p. illus. $15.00. LC 81-5071. ISBN 0-8108-1426-9.

Guy Lyle began his library career at age 13 as a page in the Strathcona Branch of the Edmonton Public Library, which "housed the largest collection of third-rate adventitious rubbish that it has ever been my pleasure to find brought together in one place." He ended his career some 50 years later as librarian of one of this country's most distinguished institutions of higher education. Lyle has written a straightforward account of his childhood and youth in Canada, his college years at the University of Alberta where the 1927 student yearbook described him as "a librarian of much fame," his graduate study at Columbia University's School of Library Service, and his work at the New York Public Library, Antioch College in Ohio, the Woman's College of the University of North Carolina at Greensboro, Louisiana State University in Baton Rouge, and Emory University in Atlanta, Georgia. Along the way he taught and lectured at various library schools in this country and abroad, wrote for the professional journals, produced eight books (among them *A Bibliography of Christopher Morley*), and was active in various professional associations.

While the bookman-librarian may well be (as some claim) on the way to extinction, Guy Lyle's *Beyond My Expectation* will provide ample proof to future generations of librarians (information scientists or whatever) that the bookman-librarian was/is alive and well in the last half of the twentieth century. A first-rate autobiography this is. [R: LJ, 15 Nov 81, p. 2219]   John David Marshall

993. Metcalf, Keyes DeWitt. **Random Recollections of an Anachronism, or Seventy-five Years of Library Work.** New York, Readex Books, a division of Readex Microprint, 1980. 401p. illus. index. $19.95. LC 79-67213. ISBN 0-918414-02-4.

There's an unmistakable twinkle in his eye when he talks to people. He immediately gives the impression of someone who thoroughly enjoys his work, his profession, and his life in general. That's the same intangible which emerges from the pages of the first volume of the autobiography of this giant in the library world. It surfaces when Metcalf describes his response to the Oberlin faculty's decision in 1913 not to allow students to whisper or talk in the library. It surfaces when Metcalf notes how the New York Public Library (NYPL) treated "flashers" in the 1920s (the head of security punched them in the nose). It surfaces when Metcalf discusses positions he "was not offered" and positions he "did not take." Metcalf admits he doesn't write very well, and he certainly can be criticized for too much repetition of facts already mentioned in previous sections of his text. But calling himself an "anachronism" is hardly accurate, especially in view of the variety of important positions he held at the Oberlin College Library and the NYPL between 1905 and 1937. The library profession needs more autobiographies like it. [R: BL, 15 July 80, p. 1655; C&RL, Sept 80, pp. 454-57; LJ, Aug 80, p. 1613]   Wayne A. Wiegand

994. Neuburg, Victor E., comp. **Thomas Frognall Dibdin: Selections.** Metuchen, N.J., Scarecrow, 1978. 245p. bibliog. (The Great Bibliographers Series, No. 3). $16.00. LC 77-18012. ISBN 0-8108-1077-8.

This is the third volume in the Great Bibliographers series edited for Scarecrow Press by Norman Horrocks, and it is a welcome addition to the literature. In his introduction, Victor E. Neuburg presents a general characterization of Dibdin's writings on bibliography, outlines the main events of his life, and describes the state of bibliography and book collecting in England during Dibdin's lifetime. All of that is essential as one reads the selections from Dibdin's works that follow.

It is not an easy task to make selections from Dibdin's work, but Neuburg has done his work well. First, is a section from the second edition of Dibdin's first bibliographical work, *An Introduction to the Knowledge of Rare and Valuable Editions of the Greek and Roman Classics* (1804); then follows the entire text of the first edition of *The Bibliomania* (1809); two excerpts from volume three of *The Bibliographical Decameron* (1817); two extracts from *The Library Companion* (1824); the preface to the second edition of *A Bibliogrpahical Antiquarian and Picturesque Tour in France and Germany* (1829); the first reprinting of the entire text of *Bibliophobia* (1832); and finally two short pieces from *Reminiscences of a Literary Life* (1836). The book concludes with a selected bibliography, a list of pseudonyms used by Dibdin for himself and his contemporaries, and the text of an extended contemporary account of Dibdin by William Jerdan. [R: C&RL, Sept 78, p. 407]   Dean H. Keller

995. Raymond, Boris. **Krupskaia and Soviet Russian Librarianship, 1917-1939.** Metuchen, N.J., Scarecrow, 1979. 222p. bibliog. index. o.p. LC 79-1041. ISBN 0-8108-1209-6.

With the exception of S. Simsova's *Lenin, Krupskaia, and Libraries* (Archon, 1968), little has been written in the United States about Lenin's wife, who, as Raymond indicates, "provided Soviet librarianship with a new theoretical foundation, based upon the theories of Marx and on the Leninist principle of *partiinost'*— the notion that the interests of the Communist Party should have decisive priority in the formulation of policies" (p. 2). Indeed, it is an interesting study, and apparently Raymond consulted most of the dozen or so books written on this subject in the Soviet Union. Obviously, not everyone agreed with Krupskaia, but who would quarrel with Lenin's widow? There were some interesting discussions during the 1920s involving many noted individuals, a few of which include: J. Mezhenko, probably the most prominent Ukrainian librarian, who was arrested in Kiev and later deported to Leningrad; E. Shamurin, the foremost Russian theoretician and author of many books on the history and theory of literary classification; P. Berkov; and many more. All of them at one time or another opposed Krupskaia.

George Chandler, in his critical analysis of Soviet studies, indicated that "Lenin's conception that libraries shall be used for party political ends is shared by totalitarian government of all kinds, whether Fascist or communist. One of the first acts of Nazi Germany was to burn books" (*Libraries, Documentation and Bibliography in the USSR 1917-1971*, p. 15). One of Krupskaia's first acts was to make sure that all librarians opposing her views were silenced. Indeed, she herself was later removed by Stalin, as were all other persons not directly subservient to him. And, as correctly stated by the author, "Soviet libraries, without even stating so publically [sic], were to become primarily practical, propaganda and work-oriented institutions, designed to aid the party's general line" (ibid., p. 103). This process, however, was not actually started by Stalin but by Krupskaia. There are even some indirect hints about this made by O. Chubarian in his third edition of *Obshchie bibliotekovedenie*, published during the early 1970s, which unfortunately was not utilized by Raymond in the present work. [R: BL, 15 Oct 79, p. 329; C&RL, Nov 79, pp. 562-64; JAL, Nov 79, p. 293; LJ, 15 Nov 79, p. 2422]   Bohdan S. Wynar

996. Rayward, W. Boyd. **The Universe of Information: The Work of Paul Otlet for Documentation and International Organization.** Moscow, All-Union Institute for Scientific and Technical Information for International Federation of Documentation, 1975. 340p. illus. bibliog. index. (FID, 520). o.p.

A vexing void concerning Otlet, the "Brussels Institute," UDC, etc., has been very largely filled. Rayward's offering is based on thorough exploration of numerous sources, published and unpublished, especially in Brussels. The documentation is peruasive, the index rich. Some may regret that there is no unifed bibliography except for Otlet's own writings.

Like Sandburg's *Lincoln: The War Years*, this is virtually a blow-by-blow account. Since very few will want to read such detail, the work is probably destined to become a valued reference resource. It is indispensable regarding Otlet, his numerous bibliographic undertakings, DC and UDC, international organizations, and the history of Belgian bibliography—interesting facets of the age of trusts and cartels.

Rayward has taken due note of the influence of positivism, but apparently much less of the long history of attempts at universal bibliography—at least since Gesner, and including wistful remarks at the 1877 international conference in London.

The prose is good though seldom stylish. The occasional typographical errors are not likely to impede reader comprehension. We are much indebted to Rayward, the sponsoring FID, and the publisher, Moscow's All-Union Institute for Scientific and Technical Information. [R: C&RL, Mar 77, p. 165]

Sidney L. Jackson

997. Ready, William B. **Files on Parade: A Memoir.** Metuchen, N.J., Scarecrow, 1982. 268p. $16.00. LC 81-23310. ISBN 0-8108-1516-8.

A short summary and a dismissal are sufficient for these autobiographical reminiscences. Will Ready, 1914-1981, recalls his youth in Wales, his war experiences with the British Army, and his library experiences in the United Kingdom, the United States, and in Canada, where he retired from his self-styled "librarianating" as university librarian of McMaster University in Ontario. The acquisition of the Bertrand Russell papers by McMaster is the "file" of most general or enduring interest to librarians. Like many another retired gentleman's memoirs, the book is a somewhat egotistical rummage through memory's records. Ready died before his readable style was well polished or his composition tightened, but the anecdotes may yet be enjoyed by those who knew Ready or who know the libraries, the locale, and the people to whom he refers. *Files on Parade* is not likely to have or to deserve much wider recognition. [R: LJ, 15 Dec 82, p. 2321]

Claire England

998. Rhodehamel, Josephine DeWitt, and Raymund Francis Wood. **Ina Coolbrith: Librarian and Laureate of California.** Provo, Utah, Brigham Young University Press, 1973. 531p. illus. index. o.p. LC 78-84093. ISBN 0-8425-1445-7.

This exhaustively researched biography is engagingly written by authors who know their subject well. The result is a harmonious blend of sympathetic treatment and penetrating analysis of Coolbrith (1841-1928), whose life and its contemporary significance fall into five major chronological divisions. Following her prime as a poet, she was the first librarian of the Oakland Free Library from 1878 to 1892. As literary biographers, the authors have studied the corpus of Coolbrith's work and skillfully mention more than 300 pieces in the narrative, quoting nearly 60 in part or in whole. It is imaginatively based on primary sources, manuscript and printed, and contemporary materials. Outstanding bibliographical appendices, complete documentation, careful indexing, and 36 illustrations enhance the usefulness of the work. [R: LJ, 15 Jan 74, p. 118]

Donald G. Davis, Jr.

999. Roper, Fred W., comp. **Alfred William Pollard: A Selection of His Essays.** Metuchen, N.J., Scarecrow, 1976. 244p. bibliog. index. (The Great Bibliographers Series, No. 2). $15.00. LC 76-25547. ISBN 0-8108-0958-3.

Edited by Norman Horrocks, the Great Bibliographers series started in 1974 with the publication of the volume on McKerrow, prepared by John Phillip Immroth. This second volume provides some insight into the work and life of Alfred William Pollard, the great British bibliographer, editor of *Library* and creator of *Short Title Catalogue*. It consists of a selection of his writings, with two articles on early printed works and seven articles representing Pollard's philosophy and thought on the theory of bibliographic description. The biographical sketch on Pollard is reprinted from *Proceedings of the British Academy* and was originally published in 1945. The volume also includes Roger Leachman's paper on Pollard's influence on bibliography (apparently an abridgment of his master's thesis) as well as a checklist of Pollard's published writings, somewhat expanded from the original checklist, published in 1938.

1000. Shores, Louis, **Quiet World: A Librarian's Crusade for Destiny; The Professional Autobiography of Louis Shores.** Hamden, Conn., Linnet Books, 1975. 309p. index. $21.00. LC 75-2220. ISBN 0-208-01477-2.

Louis Shores has led a rich and varied professional life. In his autobiography he gives us a picture of his experiences as a library educator and as senior editor of a major encyclopedia (*Collier's*), and in such areas of librarianship as continuing education, the training of library technicians, the "library college," and developing tools for the teaching of reference services. His account of his experiences throws much light on American librarianship from the 1930s to the present. Because he has been active in the profession during a period when librarianship was experiencing important changes, his narrative will be of interest to those concerned with the librarian's professional heritage. [R: C&RL, Nov 75, p. 517; LJ, 15 Dec 75, p. 2308]

Jesse H. Shera

1001. Stevenson, Gordon, and Judith Kramer-Greene, eds. **Melvil Dewey: The Man and the Classification.** Albany, N.Y., Forest Press Division, Lake Placid Education Foundation, 1983.

210p. index. $11.00. LC 83-1607. ISBN 0-910608-34-2.

The mention of Melvil Dewey conjures thoughts of the Dewey Decimal Classification (DDC) and its enormous impact on the library world. Yet Dewey brought much more than the DDC to librarianship; he was the originator of library education, an early publisher in the field (as editor of *Library Journal*), and an instrumental figure in the founding of the American Library Association. These and other contributions Dewey made to the library profession are significant but often unrecognized. This publication will help clarify Dewey's invaluable influence.

The volume is a collection of papers from a seminar held at Albany, New York, in December 1981. A total of eight papers is included that range from Keyes Metcalf's recollection of Dewey to Fran Miksa's excellent analysis of Dewey and the corporate ideal as applied to the library world. Wayne Wiegand presents an overview of Dewey's role at four ALA conventions from 1876 to 1907, and Dee Garrison views Dewey as the apostle. She aptly remarks that Dewey's "streamroller qualities allowed him to almost single-handedly organize and nurture a new profession." Three other papers treat the DDC, John Comaromi compares the first two editions of the DDC, and Boyd Rayward examines the early impact of the DDC abroad.

The seminar papers present a view of Dewey that is critical where necessary yet praises his obvious accomplishments. They supplement Sarah K. Vann's sympathetic Dewey biography (see *ARBA* 79, entry 188). [R: LJ, 15 Mar 84, p. 556; WLB, Mar 84, p. 513]   Boyd Childress

1002. Stokes, Roy. **Michael Sadleir 1888-1957.** Metuchen, N.J., Scarecrow, 1980. 154p. index. (The Great Bibliographers Series, No. 5). $16.00. LC 80-11419. ISBN 0-8108-1292-4.

This study of Michael Sadleir is the fifth volume in the Great Bibliographers series. Unlike earlier British subjects of this series who terminated their bibliographical work before 1800, Sadleir elected to concentrate on the nineteenth century. Himself a publisher and novelist, Sadleir focused attention on a number of mid-nineteenth-century English novelists, including Bulwer-Lytton, Disraeli, Marryat, Charles Reade, and especially Anthony Trollope. More than anyone else, Sadleir restored Trollope to a position as one of the major English novelists of this period. He contributed also to the revival of interest in Herman Melville.

Sadleir's bibliographical studies covered the full spectrum of Victorian life, including its less respectable aspects. He was also the first bibliographer to document the evolution of publishers' binding styles, beginning about 1770 and continuing throughout the nineteenth century. Aside from concentrating on the nineteenth century, Sadleir's greatest contribution was to show that books are inextricably entwined with the social, cultural, economic, literary, technological, and political life of their times.

Because of its specialized scope, this bibliography will be of value primarily for libraries with strong collections of nineteenth-century English fiction. [R: C&RL, Sept 80, pp. 474-76; JAL, Sept 80, p. 233]   Thomas S. Harding

1003. Sullivan, Peggy. **Carl H. Milam and the American Library Association.** New York, H. W. Wilson, 1976. 390p. illus. bibliog. index. $20.00. LC 76-3686. ISBN 0-8242-0592-8.

Peggy Sullivan's work (a revised doctoral dissertation) is a substantial contribution. The narrative is readable and well documented, making a well-balanced study of the former executive secretary of ALA, who was responsible for many innovations.

The eight chapters cover American librarianship and the ALA from 1876 to 1920, Milam's career before 1920, the ALA from 1920 to 1948, relations with foundations and government, ALA's programs for international development, Milam as the profession's spokesman, Milam and man, and Milam's last years. The defeat of Milam's stand for the ALA presidency is one of the most interesting portions of the book. Sullivan writes well and is able to document even some of the more controversial statements. Not many biographies of prominent library leaders can meet the standards of this well-executed book. [R: LJ, 15 Dec 76, p. 2553]   Bohdan S. Wynar

1004. Vann, Sarah K. **Melvil Dewey: His Enduring Presence in Librarianship.** Littleton, Colo., Libraries Unlimited, 1978. 278p. bibliog. index. (Heritage of Librarianship Series, No. 4). o.p. LC 77-21852. ISBN 0-87287-134-7.

Sarah Vann, who has written on the history of library education during the Dewey era and who has studied Dewey for many years, presents a concise interpretation of Dewey's career. Part 1 is a 30-page biographical sketch of Dewey's formative years, his formal education, and his subsequent library employment, which led to his interest and involvement in early American librarianship. Vann describes Dewey as a futurist among his peers, for he constantly surveyed the horizon for new trends and further extentions of services. This is further evidenced in part 2, the main body of the book, which presents Dewey's most significant and representative writings, in which he discusses librarianship as a profession; the American Library Association; women in librarianship; education for librarianship; the future of library schools; cooperative library cataloging; classification; and the future of librarianship. These writings have much to say to the librarians today. Parts 1 and 2 are indexed at the end of the book. Part 3 is a detailed 40-page bibliography of works by and about Dewey.

COLLEGE AND UNIVERSITY LIBRARIES

1005. Bentinck-Smith, William. **Building a Great Library: The Coolidge Years at Harvard.** Cambridge, Mass., Harvard University Library, 1976. 218p. illus. index. $18.50. LC 75-27901. ISBN 0-674-08578-7.

In addition to revised articles from the *Harvard Library Bulletin*, one finds here a biographical sketch of Archibald Cary Coolidge (1866-1928) and a historical outline of the growth of Harvard University Library under his administration. Beautifully produced, this volume should be of interest to all students of library history. [R: LJ, 15 Nov 76, p. 2353]

1006. Brough, Kenneth J. **Scholar's Workshop: Evolving Conceptions of Library Service.** Urbana-Champaign, University of Illinois Press, 1953; repr., Boston, Gregg Press, 1972. 197p. index. (The Library Reference Series). o.p. LC 72-8744. ISBN 0-8398-0193-9.

Brough examines the relationship of the university faculty to the library, the status of the chief librarian, accessibility of materials, aids to readers, general characteristics of the clientele, etc. Library practices at Chicago, Columbia, Harvard, and Yale universities from 1876 to 1946 were studied to determine the basic concepts of library service. Although this study was first published in 1953, some of the author's observations remain valid.

1007. Hamlin, Arthur T. **The University Library in the United States: Its Origins and Development.** Philadelphia, University of Pennsylvania Press, 1981. 271p. bibliog. index. $30.00. LC 80-54049. ISBN 0-8122-7795-3.

This is an engaging and enlightening history of the American academic library. The author has had a long and varied career in university libraries, beginning as a student assistant at the Harvard College Library in 1931. Intended primarily for "the academician outside the library profession who is a user of libraries," this work should also appeal strongly to practicing librarians.

The first 80 pages of the book are devoted to the chronological growth of university libraries from colonial times to the present. The early period has already been well chronicled in the late Louis Shores's *Origins of the American College Library, 1638-1800* (Barnes and Noble, 1934; repr., Shoe String Press, 1966). Hamlin compresses Shores's work and presents newer research, chiefly in an anecdotal format. This approach works well, since the history of eighteenth- and nineteenth-century American libraries is rich with astounding and bizarre regulations and practices. For example, "in its early days, Dartmouth adopted the questionable practice of supporting the library by charging students according to their use of it." Until the mid-1800s, most libraries were only accessible a few hours a week and were supervised by a faculty member. This situation improved considerably after 1876, a year that Hamlin rightly considers a turning point for the library profession (ALA was formed, *Library Journal* began publication, the Dewey Decimal System emerged, etc.). The gradual development of research libraries and post-World War II expansion receive a concise and informative treatment, and Hamlin is generous in citing the contributions of prominent twentieth-century academic librarians (e.g., Louis Round Wilson, Keyes D. Metcalf, Robert B. Downs, Ralph Ellsworth, Herman Fussler, Julian Boyd, William Dix, William Warner Bishop, Margaret Stillwell).

The central section of the book contains a historical examination of how various aspects of librarianship have developed. In these chapters (which cover such topics as collection building, governance, patterns of service, classification systems, and cooperation among libraries), Hamlin expands considerably on some information presented in the previous section. The essays by Robert Downs and Fritz Veit in the July 1976 issue of *Library Trends* also address some of these developments. The final chapter, on the technological revolution in libraries, surveys the introduction of microforms, photocopiers, and security systems, and provides a fine sketch on the growth of the computerization of library services. There are five statistical appendices, four pages of notes, an essay on sources, an extensive bibliography, and an index. Hamlin's book is well researched, lucidly written, and a joy to read. It belongs in all academic libraries. [R: ABC, Mar 82, p. 65;

JAL, Jan 82, p. 373; LQ, Apr 82, p. 159; LR, Winter 81, p. 250]   Thomas A. Karel

1008. Johnson, Richard D., ed. **Libraries for Teaching, Libraries for Research: Essays for a Century.** Chicago, American Library Association, 1977 (c1976). 259p. illus. index. (ACRL Publications in Librarianship, No. 39). $15.00. LC 77-9097. ISBN 0-8389-0247-2.

This is a reprint of 13 articles originally published in *College and Research Libraries* in 1976 by such well-known authors as Ed Holley ("Academic Libraries in 1876"), Connie Dunlap ("Organizational Patterns in Academic Libraries, 1976-1976"), Keyes D. Metcalf ("Six Influential Academic and Research Librarians"), and others. Unfortunately, historical research has been sadly neglected by the library profession; this volume sufficiently illustrates the historical development of our research libraries over the past century. This is one of the most appropriate tributes to our centennial and a must for all library school students interested in academic librarianship. [R: JAL, May 78, p. 96; JLH, Spring 78, p. 226; LJ, 15 Feb 78, p. 442]

1009. Shiflett, Orvin Lee. **Origins of American Academic Librarianship.** Norwood, N.J., Ablex Publishing, 1981. 308p. bibliog. index. (Libraries and Librarianship). $35.00. LC 81-14969. ISBN 0-89391-082-1.

This thorough treatment of academic librarianship's place in and contribution to higher education in the United States documents many developments—or lack thereof—which have become major concerns for the professional. Beginning with the "librarians" status as scholars who, in fact, were professors who undertook the chore because of their "love of books," the discussion brings us to the point where library schools were preparing "workers in the newly expanded fields" of Dewey's day, to the point where librarianship "was a minor position in the academic hierarchy," indeed a disturbing confirmation.

The volume accomplishes what the author set out to do: "evaluate the role of the academic library and librarianship in a context broader than that of the immediate institutional setting," a feat which had heretofore not been successfully accomplished. In the process it raises important issues which are still facing the profession. Must reading for anyone interested in academic librarianship, including presidents and chancellors. [R: C&RL, Sept 82, pp. 406-8; JAL, May 82, p. 108; LJ, 15 Sept 82, p. 1735]
                                        Robert D. Stueart

1010. Thompson, James, ed. **University Library History: An International Review.** London, Clive Bingley; distr., Hamden, Conn., Shoe String Press, 1980. 330p. illus. index. $35.00. ISBN 0-85157-304-5.

This work is a collection of 15 essays by a distinguished list of contributors on a variety of aspects of university library history. The themes covered include growth of collections, staffing, library organization, finance, buildings, cataloging and classification, and cooperation. For the most part, the essays display a strong, if not exclusive, British focus, with an occasional "cursory glance at the other side of the Atlantic," as it was put by one of the contributors. Only three contributions deal specifically with American university library history: David Kaser's on collection building, Jerrold Orne's on the evolution of library staffs, and John Y. Cole's on the Library of Congress and American research libraries. There are also contributions treating the general history of university libraries in Italy, Canada, Australia, and New Zealand.

The contributions are of generally high quality in terms of both content and readability. However, *University Library History* is neither organized nor presented as a reference tool, and is most suitable for reading collections on the history of university libraries. [R: LJ, 15 Dec 81, p. 2372]   Joe A. Hewitt

1011. Wright, Louis B. **Of Books and Men.** Columbia, S.C., University of South Carolina Press, 1976. 179p. index. $12.95. LC 76-26493. ISBN 0-87249-344-X.

"It has been my aim to relate in some detail the evolution of the Huntington and the Folger libraries from ducal collections of wealthy men into active research institutions." With these opening words Louis B. Wright described his long experience in building research library collections, first at the Huntington Library (1932-1948), and later in the more responsible position of director of the Folger Shakespeare Library (1948-1968).

If any evidence were needed that huge endowments alone are not enough to build great research libraries, Wright provides it in this book. Despite the endowments of Henry E. Huntington and Henry Clay Folger, both libraries would have remained literary museums if a few dedicated scholars and librarians had not collaborated in determining in what areas the two libraries would specialize, and in building up strong research collections in those areas.

As a graduate student at the University of North Carolina, Wright saw Louis Round

Wilson make the university library adequate for graduate research. When he visited Oxford he was impressed with the achievements of Thomas Bodley in securing donations of books and money for the Bodleian Library. From his visits to the Bodleian and the British Museum, Wright concluded that "research libraries must grow by accretion, by accumulating rarities preserved by the care and diligence of many collectors over the years."

Wright's account will fascinate librarians, especially his admonition that "during the Dark Ages a few monasteries kept alive the desire for learning. In a similar way today institutions like the Folger must join with the universities in combating forces of darkness almost as overwhelming as those that nearly wiped out classical culture in the eighth century."

Aside from a misplaced line on page 16, no flaws were noticed in the printing or format. [R: C&RL, Nov 77, pp. 531-32; JAL, Sept 77, p. 222; JAL, July 77, p. 171]

Thomas S. Harding

PUBLIC LIBRARIES

1012.   Braverman, Miriam. **Youth, Society, and the Public Library.** Chicago, American Library Association, 1979. 289p. bibliog. index. $20.00. LC 78-17267. ISBN 0-8389-0260-X.

Mainly material culled from an impressively large number of in-house reports of young adult librarians and coordinators, other library documents, and personal interviews done by the author, this volume discusses the history of young adult work in three library systems for the following years: New York Public Library, 1920-1966; the Cleveland Public Library, 1926-1959; and the Enoch Pratt Free Library, 1932-1962. The years studied coincide with the tenure in each institution of the individual mainly responsible for the philosophy of young adult work and its expression in library activities. They include Mabel Williams, Jean Roos, and Margaret Edwards.

Two major hypotheses described in the author's dissertation abstract for the study are the disjunction between the humanistic orientation of young people's work in a materialist-oriented industrial society and the inconsistency between the humanism expressed by the librarians and their lack of ability to relate to minorities and those not in school.

Lacking more objective measures of library service and effectiveness during the periods studied, the primary source material presented does give us a great deal of informa-

tion about young adult work in three large urban systems with active young adult programs. It helps to fill a void in library history. The strength of the study is in its description of personnel and programs rather than in its interpretation of the material, which suffers from an imprecise or shifting definition of humanism and attempts to prove that materialism and humanism are "mutually contradictory" and yet co-existed as foundations for public library young adult service. Another problem is the implication that these programs can be considered models for young adult services nationally. The convincing evidence that each program was affected significantly by the personality of its leader and the community in which the library is located belies this assumption, although certainly the three librarians, their publications, and library programs did and continue to influence young adult work. The effect of that influence is another story. Looking at young adult work from these periods is intriguing for the young adult specialist; distilling the essence of young adult work for a 50-year period from three systems and viewing it as "flawed humanism" seems to distort its shape nationally and to impose a value system on the material studied rather than draw from a more complete picture the essence of the time. [R: BL, 15 Jan 80, p. 698; SLJ, Apr 80, p. 38]

JoAnn V. Rogers

1013.   Cramer, C. H. **Open Shelves and Open Minds: A History of the Cleveland Public Library.** Cleveland, Ohio, Press of Case Western Reserve University, 1972. 289p. o.p. LC 70-170150. ISBN 0-8295-0219-X.

A well-documented account covering the first 100 years of this outstanding public library. [R: AL, Sept 72, p. 925]

1014.   Dain, Phyllis. **The New York Public Library: A History of Its Founding and Early Years.** New York, New York Public Library, 1972. 466p. illus. bibliog. $21.00. LC 70-163359. ISBN 0-87104-136-6.

As stated in the introduction, the purpose of this work is twofold: "to complement and to some extent supersede Dr. Harry Miller Lydenberg's *History of the New York Public Library*" (1923) and to present the historical development of the NYPL "against the history of New York City and its library conditions." Dain describes the merger of previously independent libraries (Lydenberg's quite different objective was to describe individual collections), providing a good account of the existing climate for this undertaking. A valuable study. [R: LJ, 15 Oct 72, p. 3294]

1015. Davies, D. W. **Public Libraries as Culture and Social Centers: The Origin of the Concept.** Metuchen, N.J., Scarecrow, 1974. 167p. index. o.p. LC 74-8420. ISBN 0-8108-0738-6.

The author, formerly librarian at the Claremont Colleges, has done a scholarly job in historically tracing the view held by many that public libraries must be more than repositories for books—that they should also attempt to serve as social, educational, cultural, and even entertainment centers. Davies tries to show that these nonbook activities of modern public libraries are a continuation of the voluntary uplift and cultural societies of the nineteenth century.

His major recommendation is that librarians should stop attempting to make public libraries something for everyone and stop competing with social, educational, and cultural agencies. Public librarians should instead become book specialists and experts and should cater only to serious readers and users of books.

This is an elitist view and one that does not take into account the societal changes engulfing public libraries. Davies himself admits that the book-reading segment of the population has never been large. He does not take into account the massive growth of nonprint media. Finally, public libraries could not survive with such a narrow goal of service. Since they are supported by the community at large, they must attempt to serve everyone in the community.

Nevertheless, this is an important work of library history. It provides much new historical information, and it is well organized and well written. Both Great Britain and the United States are covered. It is the most comprehensive work available presenting this particular point of view. [R: C&RL, Mar 76, p. 175; JLH, Apr 76, p. 179; LJ, 1 Mar 75, p. 458]
George S. Bobinski

1016. Du Mont, Rosemary Ruhig. **Reform and Reaction: The Big City Public Library in American Life.** Westport, Conn., Greenwood Press, 1977. 153p. bibliog. index. (Contributions in Librarianship and Information Science, No. 21). $27.50. LC 77-71864. ISBN 0-8371-9540-3; ISSN 0084-9243.

The period from 1890 to 1915 was critical for the public library in the United States. Rosemary Du Mont comments on those years in this book, linking the techniques developed then to reach and to socialize the immigrants and poor with the more recent outreach efforts of the American public library. A brief history, then reviews of philosophy and of changes in operational and service policies, and a chapter on book selection practices make up most of the book. Strangely enough, for a text that began as a Ph.D. dissertation, the volume lacks a well-stated thesis, a point of view, and integration of and/or response to some of the views reported. Most of the sources cited are published articles and books, along with some libraries' annual reports. Often, the author has been content with citing a reference second-hand rather than checking it herself. Footnotes are plentiful, but the constantly improving format of Greenwood Press books still presents the text well, with the print being only a bit too small for tired eyes. Du Mont seems, however, to have taken almost all her sources at face value and to have drawn few inferences, conclusions, or even connections of her own. [R: LJ, Aug 78, p. 1489]
Peggy A. Sullivan

1017. Garrison, Dee. **Apostles of Culture: The Public Librarian and American Society, 1876-1920.** New York, Free Press/Macmillan, 1979. 319p. bibliog. index. $14.50. LC 78-66979. ISBN 0-02-693850-2.

This is a historical analysis of the formation and growth of public libraries in America from 1876 to 1920. Part 1 discusses selected library personalities; part 2 considers the developing function of public libraries as social institutions; part 3 examines Melvil Dewey's influence on the profession; part 4 discusses the role of women in the public library. Garrison's work is documented with references to professional journals of the period, library reports, and library-related statements, both published and unpublished. Appended are 36 brief biographies of public library leaders, and a bibliography. [R: JAL, July 80, pp. 163-64; JAL, Mar 80, p. 49]
Mary Alice Deveny

1018. Green, Samuel Swett. **The Public Library Movement in the United States 1853-1893: From 1876, Reminiscences of the Writer.** Boston, The Boston Book Co., 1913; repr., Boston, Gregg Press, 1972. 336p. illus. index. (The Useful Reference Series No. 8). o.p. LC 72-8825. ISBN 0-8398-0671-X.

A reprint of a well-known work first published in 1913. Shows the progress of the public library from year to year, gives the history of ALA up to 1893, and provides sketches of several early leaders of the library profession.

1019. Held, Ray E. **The Rise of the Public Library in California.** Chicago, American

Library Association, 1973. 203p. bibliog. index. $54.30pa. LC 73-12719. ISBN 0-8389-0124-7. (Available from Books on Demand, $54.30pa., ISBN 0-317-27845-2).

This volume continues the story begun in Held's *Public Libraries in California, 1849-1878* (University of California Press, 1963). This volume covers the years between the enactment of the state's first public library law and the entry of the United States into World War I.

Like the first book, this one provides a detailed consideration of the establishment of libraries and the reasons why they either flourished or failed to flourish. Quite properly, emphasis is placed on the role of the strong state library under James L. Gillis and the development of the famous county library system; however, other forces and movements are given due attention. The contributions of various library leaders are noted, but little attempt is made to bring these people to life. The nature of the library collections is barely mentioned; we learn almost nothing about what Californians found when they went to their libraries. Appendices give data about individual libraries; there are full bibliographical notes.

This is a straightforward, scholarly work, essential for an understanding of the way in which American libraries developed during a significant period. [R: LJ, 15 Apr 74, p. 1107]

Haynes McMullen

1020.   Hendry, Joseph D. **A Social History of Branch Library Development with Special Reference to the City of Glasgow.** Glasgow, Scottish Library Association, 1974. 359p. illus. bibliog. index. (Scottish Library Studies—2). $45.00. ISBN 0-900649-04-6.

Anticipation ... disappointment—these two words summarize Hendry's effort from cover to cover. The book, originally written and accepted as a thesis by the Scottish Library Association in 1972, deals with a subject ripe for historical analysis. The City of Glasgow did not begin developing its branch library system until the turn of the century, long after other major British cities had their systems well under way. Glasgow's turn finally came when city fathers passed the Glasgow Corporation Act of 1899 and Andrew Carnegie donated substantial sums of money for library construction. Within six years (1901-1907) Glasgow had 13 new branch libraries. Because growth and money came so quickly, planners were able to benefit from the experiences of other systems before establishing their own. Therein lay this reader's anticipation; since the book is entitled *A Social History of Branch Library Development*, he happily

anticipated an answer to the unavoidable question: "To what social needs was the branch library system responding?" Unfortunately, the author's reply is "public demand"; and therein lies the disappointment.

Society is a microcosm of smaller publics, each of which seeks to exert its influence on the whole. The term "public demand," if left undefined, is autocentric. One must further ask "which publics?" and "what were the ends that these publics were attempting to attain?" Answering these questions requires a social history. Failure to answer them threatens to result in chronology. Hendry's real accomplishment is a chronology of branch library development in Glasgow from 1860 to 1964. Even exhaustive research does not serve to strengthen a shallow thesis. [R: LR, Winter 74/75, p. 356]

Wayne A. Wiegand

1021.   Kaser, David. **A Book for a Sixpence: The Circulating Library in America.** Pittsburgh, Pa., Beta Phi Mu; distr., Lexington, Ky., Beta Phi Mu Publications Office, College of Library Science, University of Kentucky, 1980. 194p. illus. bibliog. index. (Beta Phi Mu Chapbook, No. 14). $20.00. LC 79-4298. ISBN 0-317-33842-0.

The circulating library has been too long ignored in appraisals of the American cultural scene, both colonial and later, and in its relation to the public library. With this study, the author clarifies that relationship and removes any questionable taint that may have been superimposed on the concept of profit-oriented library services as the tax-supported library movement triumphed. He traces the origin of the circulating library to England, and views, in a cultural and social perspective, the growth, zenith, and decline of such libraries in America. Skillfully interwoven with the development of the circulating library, which attempted to attract both men and women as readers, are the reading interests of an emerging middle class and the growing appeal of the novel, following the appearance in 1740 of *Pamela, or Virtue Rewarded*, by Samuel Richardson.

The motive, other than commercial, for creating circulating libraries, from William Rind, who proposed one in 1762, to those who followed him, was similar to that of later proponents of tax-supported libraries: "To open and extend the Fountains of Knowledge, which are at present shut against all but Men of affluent Fortunes." That the "Fountains of Knowledge" quenched thirst through fiction is evident from the "Subject Analysis of Circulating Catalogues" (appendix 1), despite the increasing apprehension concerning fiction reading and the ambivalent attitude taken by public libraries toward the inclusion of fiction in their collections. More than 200 years later, the idea of the circulating library persists, and vestiges of it may be found in rental collections in public libraries, a popular example being that of the McNaughton Plan.

This study complements *Foundations of the Public Library: The Origins of the Public Library Movement in New England, 1626-1855,* by Jesse H. Shera (University of Chicago Press, 1949). Even more significantly, it serves as a belated supplement to the 1876 report on *Public Libraries in the United States of America: Their History, Condition, and Management* (GPO, 1876), which failed to include either a chapter on or an index entry or entries on circulating libraries. Despite these omissions, however, Kaser extracted data on 80 circulating libraries included in the 1876 report and found that three-fourths of them had been in existence for less than a decade. In addition, Kaser located 48 more circulating libraries through consulting sources cited in his bibliography and through examining extant library catalogs (appendix 1). A major reference value, therefore, lies in the "Checklist of American Commercial Library Enterprises, 1762-1890," in which all the known libraries are listed. This checklist is acknowledged as being a contribution toward a census of such institutions yet to be completed.

The excellent bibliography reflects the author's long-sustained interest in libraries, reading interests, and publishing in the cultural and literary scene. Two titles that would illuminate reading tastes further but which are not included in the bibliography are *Golden Multitudes: The Story of Best Sellers in the United States*, by Frank Luther Mott (Macmillan, 1946), and *The Popular Book: A History of America's Literary Taste*, by James D. Hart (Oxford University Press, 1959).

The author's research for this study and his appealing literary style enhance his reputation as an outstanding historian on printing, books, and libraries in American society. The book, in its design and content, adds prestige to the increasingly important series of Beta Phi Mu Chapbooks, of which this is the fourteenth. Indispensable to students and scholars interested in the heritage of American librarianship. [R: C&RL, Sept 80, p. 472; JLH, Fall 80, p. 489; LQ, Jan 81, p. 104]   Sarah K. Vann

1022. Laugher, Charles T. **Thomas Bray's Grand Design: Libraries of the Church of England in America, 1695-1785.** Chicago, American

Library Association, 1973. 115p. index. (ACRL Publications in Librarianship, No. 35). $31.30. LC 73-16332. ISBN 0-8389-0151-4. (Available from Books on Demand, $31.30, ISBN 0-317-29444-X).

This book details the projects of Thomas Bray, an Anglican clergyman who held the living of Sheldon, near London, and who acted as commissary to the colony of Maryland from 1695 on. His concern for the education of the ministers in the colony, as well as in the other British colonies in North America, led to his sending the Maryland Assembly a series of proposals from 1695 to 1700; in 1700 he visited the colony to urge, among other things, that parish libraries be established so that each minister could "better inform himself and instruct others." The book also points out that Bray was the moving force behind the establishment, in the years 1698 to 1704, of one library in each of the following colonies: New Jersey, New York, Rhode Island, Massachusetts, Virginia, and North Carolina. The extension of this work was carried out by Bray's organization, the Society for the Propagation of the Gospel in Foreign Parts.

Small and short-lived as some of these libraries were, they are historically important. But they have been neglected by historians of the American public library movement. Laugher's study, begun as a doctoral dissertation at Case Western Reserve University, is the first full-dress inquiry into the subject. Prior to his work, the only other major treatment of any worth was a long article (1896-1897) by Bernard C. Steiner in the *American Historical Review.* The article, although excellent, limits itself to a discussion of the libraries in colonial Maryland.

Laugher's work begins with an essay on the colonial cultural setting and then moves on to provide a biographical narrative of Bray's early work, his basic design for the work of the Church, and the work done by the two societies he founded, the Society for the Promotion of Christian Knowledge and the Society for the Propagation of the Gospel in Foreign Parts (later the Bray Associates). The useful appendices list the various Bray libraries (with dates and locations of establishment) and give the contents of surviving library catalogs. The work is carefully documented, and Laugher has had access to the financial records of Bray's benefactions. The work fills an important need in the annals of American librarianship; it will be welcomed by all students of library history. [R: Choice, May 74, p. 419]

Jesse H. Shera

1023. Lord, Caroline M. **Diary of a Village Library.** Somersworth, N.H., New Hampshire Publishing, 1971. 269p. o.p. LC 78-151177. ISBN 0-912274-09-3.

A highly personal and very readable account by the librarian (1943-1960) of the small village library in Francestown, New Hampshire, that is written in a warm and witty manner which reflects the force of her philosophy of devotion, dedication, and service. [R: LJ, 1 Jan 72, p. 46]   Charles D. Patterson

1024. McDonough, Irene Roberts. **History of the Public Library in Vigo County 1816-1975.** Terre Haute, Ind., Vigo County Public Library, 1977. 203p. illus. bibliog. index. o.p. LC 77-18403. ISBN 0-9601522-1-0.

The public library of Vigo County, Indiana was founded in 1816 under the terms of the state constitution, which permitted 10 percent of the funds received from the sale of "public lots" to be used for such a purpose. Thus, it ranks as one of the very earliest of public libraries in the Middle West. After a series of vicissitudes, it emerged in 1882 as the municipal public library for the city of Terre Haute. Because of the library's history, this book has more than local interest.

The author divides her treatment into three periods: 1816-1927, from the library's beginning as a county library to its emergence as a public library supported from tax revenues; 1928-1952, the years of the depression, followed by new directions and new library directors; and 1953-1975, during which time the role of the library was redefined and the present library building was erected.

Because books such as this are localized in their treatment and general appeal, they tend to be given a relatively low valuation in the writing of library history, yet they cannot be neglected since they are the building blocks of which the larger historical reconstruction is made, and in many instances, they are the only resource that the historian has. In the writing of library history, they are of the genre of Josiah Quincy's *History of the Boston Athenaeum* (Metcalf and Co., n.d.) and Lydenberg's *History of the New York Public Library* (New York Public Library, 1923).   Jesse H. Shera

1025. Morris, R. J. B. **Parliament and the Public Libraries: A Survey of Legislative Activity Promoting the Municipal Library Service in England and Wales 1850-1976.** London, Mansell; distr., Lawrence, Mass., Merrimack Book Service, 1977. 477p. bibliog. index. $34.00. ISBN 0-7201-0554-4.

This book proposes to describe the activities of the British Parliament with regard to the expansion of municipal library service in England and Wales from 1850 to 1976. There is also a short first chapter which gives an overview of public library development before 1850. The text, contained in only 202 pages, is devoted to some 66 bills and acts, particularly those of 1850, 1855, 1892, 1919, the landmark bill "Public Libraries and Museums Bill of 1964," and the "Public Lending Right Bill of 1976."

The significance of this work, however, is not in the text, but in the six appendices. The most important of these are the "Procedural Stages and Texts of Promoted Bills" (each has a concise synopsis) and a chronology of "Parliamentary Questions" regarding libraries from 1865 to 1976 (there are references to *Hansard*). There is a select bibliography of books, articles, government reports, white papers, circulars, etc.

The book is based on Morris's dissertation, and he says that this type of material had never been brought together in this form. It must have required years to complete.

The index requires some study before using. For instance, there are 2½ columns under the heading "public libraries, admission to or borrowings from to be free or not." This book is printed by photolithography, and the right margin is unjustified, which is disturbing to this reviewer. My copy also is poorly and unattractively bound.

Several histories of British libraries were published during the centennial year of the Library Association. Another on the same subject is *Politics and Public Libraries in England and Wales, 1850-1970*, by John E. Pemberton. [R: LR, Spring 78, p. 53]   Gil McNamee

1026. Ring, Daniel F., ed. **Studies in Creative Partnership: Federal Aid to Public Libraries during the New Deal.** Metuchen, N.J., Scarecrow, 1980. 145p. illus. index. $15.00. LC 80-15762. ISBN 0-8108-1319-X.

This publication examines the accomplishments of the much maligned Work Projects Administration (WPA) as they affected public libraries during the 1930s and early 1940s. It consists of case studies in seven public libraries: New York, Baltimore, Cleveland, Chicago, Milwaukee, Minneapolis, and San Francisco.

The WPA activities showed considerable variation among these libraries. Chicago, Cleveland, and Milwaukee used WPA funds for bibliographic projects that preserved local records. On the other hand, New York concentrated on broad cultural projects. The attitudes of the chief librarians did much to determine the effectiveness of the WPA performance in their respective libraries. Librarians like Harry Lydenberg and Joseph L. Wheeler encouraged maximum use of WPA projects. By contrast, Robert Rea felt little sympathy with WPA programs at the San Francisco Public Library.

Use of WPA funds and manpower was not altogether smooth sailing for these public libraries. The professional library staff tended to look upon the WPA workers as intruders, and friction developed. This was especially true at Baltimore and New York. Nevertheless, most of the achievements of the WPA in public libraries were of high quality and permanent value.

This study highlights one of the few bright spots in the depression years of the 1930s. It should be of interest to public librarians, political scientists, and economic historians. [R: LJ, 15 Dec 80, p. 2554]   Thomas S. Harding

1027. Rogers, Frances. **The Story of a Small Town Library: The Development of the Woodstock, N.Y., Library.** Woodstock, N.Y., Overlook Press, 1974. 236p. index. o.p. LC 73-87135. ISBN 0-87951-019-6.

The Woodstock library was founded in 1913, but the author logically begins her story in 1902, with the social and cultural developments of the community. This is a volume somewhat unusual in library history—an account of the founding and progress of a social library, a voluntary association to provide books for the town without municipal support from the public treasury. Frances Rogers, a member and a trustee of the society for many years and who, as an experienced author, is in an excellent position to view the library and the many struggles to maintain it, carries her story forward to a time when the library had become a thriving institution providing library service to a growing community. Her writing is simple, direct, unencumbered by the machinery of scholarship, and touched with sympathy and obvious affection for the institution. Her book will be welcomed by all those concerned with the origins and growth of the American public library, for she has woven a brightly shining thread into the tapestry that is the history of the American public library. [R: AL, July/Aug 74, p. 367; LJ, 1 Sept 74, p. 2045]   Jesse H. Shera

1028. Shera, Jesse H. **Foundations of the Public Library: The Origins of the Public Library Movement in New England, 1629-1855.** Chicago, University of Chicago Press, 1949; repr., Hamden, Conn., Shoe String Press, 1974. 308p. bibliog. index. $19.50. LC 65-17979.

This is an "unaltered and unabridged" reprinting of Shera's classic history of the public library movement in New England, first published in 1949. The book has long been recognized as one of the most brilliant studies of library history ever published. Shera's *Foundations of the Public Library*, first completed as a doctoral dissertation at Chicago, represents a remarkably successful attempt to view the history of public libraries within the context of what Arnold Borden referred to as its "coeval culture." As such it marks a distinct break with the older and less interpretive histories of libraries, and it is frequently cited as a benchmark denoting the rise of the "new" library historiography.

It is the brilliance of Shera's interpretive framework that makes his work the locus of historical research on the American public library. His first, and still controversial, breakthrough came when he announced that his study defined the public library as a "social agency," one that is controlled by society's "institutions" and through which institutions maintain their "social control." This insight allowed Shera to proceed to investigate the development of the public library in the light of such societal needs as security, health, education, and social stability. The second major contribution was embodied in the last chapter of his book, entitled "Causal Factors in Public Library Development"; this chapter set out the factors which Shera argued were central to the rise of the American public library, and which focused all subsequent research on public library history. Shera's book, along with a parallel and equally impressive study by Sidney Ditzion entitled *Arsenals of a Democratic Culture* (American Library Association, 1947), has proven a particularly hardy and persuasive interpretation of the origins of the public library movement in this country. It remains, along with Ditzion's work, the foundation upon which all students of the public library must build, and the extremely formidable opponent that any revisionist must better.   Michael H. Harris

PRIVATE AND SPECIAL LIBRARIES

1029. Carroll, Frances Laverne, and Mary Meacham. **The Library at Mount Vernon.** Pittsburgh, Pa., Beta Phi Mu, 1977. 184p. illus. bibliog. index. (Beta Phi Mu Chapbook, No. 12). o.p. LC 77-22482. ISBN 0-910230-12-9.

The Library at Mount Vernon continues the pattern of previously published additions to the Beta Phi Mu Chapbook series. The effort is a handsome product in format — attractively bound and printed, extremely well designed, and richly adorned with twelve eye-pleasing color plates. In terms of quality, however, the Chapbook merits mixed reactions. Chapter 4, "Washington's Books," and appendices 2 through 6 deal with the printed contents of Washington's library as well as with the books he inherited and passed on to others. Historians will agree that knowing what significant individuals read will aid contemporary society's understanding of how they developed certain ideas. The historical and library worlds need more of this, and it would have been appropriate for the authors to add depth to their effort by attempting a more serious analysis of the impact of Washington's reading on his behavior and actions. Chapters 1 through 3 have limited utility and value. The first chapter, "Colonial Libraries and the Young Washington," is a weak narrative profuse with speculative statements. Chapters 2 and 3, "The Architecture and Interior Decoration of the Library" and "Furniture in the Library at Mount Vernon," are interesting, but hardly substantive. [R: LJ, 15 June 78, p. 1239]   Wayne A. Wiegand

1030.   Cole, John Y. **For Congress and the Nation: A Chronological History of the Library of Congress.** Washington, D.C., Library of Congress; distr., Washington, D.C., GPO, 1979. 196p. illus. index. o.p. LC 76-608365. ISBN 0-8444-0225-7. S/N 030-003-00018-7.

A brief chronological listing of events from 1774 through 1975, with the emphasis on the origins of the library's principal collections, services, and administrative units. In comparison to the more recent period, the early development of the collections is described in more detail, providing references to sources used in this well-edited chronological narrative, accompanied by numerous illustrations. The volume concludes with an analytical index that will help its users to locate the desired information. [R: A Arch, Oct 79, p. 469; CLW, Nov 79, p. 184; JLH, Spring 80, p. 257; LR, Winter 79, p. 269]   Bohdan S. Wynar

1031.   Dale, Doris Cruger, ed. **Carl H. Milam and the United Nations Library.** Metuchen, N.J., Scarecrow, 1976. 132p. illus. bibliog. index. $13.00. LC 76-14866. ISBN 0-8108-0941-9.

The volume is a follow-up to the editor's previous work, *The United Nations Library: Its Origins and Development* (ALA, 1970). In that volume the author noted, "It was Carl Milam's administration, although lasting only two years, that set the library on a firm course. He was

responsible for internal administrative reorganization and the recruitment of an excellent staff which he used to good advantage" (p. 150). This volume is an amplification of Milam's role in the development of the UN library. A brief diary kept by Milam during his two years as the library's initial director comprises the bulk of the volume. Dale has edited the diary to clarify Milam's references and has added a personal names index. In addition, she has supplied a short biographical introduction, a bibliography of Milam's published works, and six appendices consisting of articles by Milam and testimonials by others concerning his work.

While providing some insight into the beginnings of the UN library and the people behind it, the diary is not particularly interesting on its own. A good diarist must be capable of unmitigated gossip, penetrating insight, or keen observation (if not all three). Milam, unfortunately, does not especially distinguish himself in any of these qualities. Consequently, the volume would be of limited interest to those who are not either building a complete collection on the historical development of the United Nations, or entertaining library school students with reading material on the administrative difficulties of beginning a new library. [R: LJ, 15 Dec 76, p. 2553]   Walter L. Newsome

1032.   Dale, Doris Cruger. **The United Nations Library: Its Origins and Development.** Chicago, American Library Association, 1970. 236p. illus. bibliog. index. o.p. LC 74-132060. ISBN 0-8389-0090-9.

Based upon the author's 1968 Columbia University doctoral dissertation, this well-documented work draws upon access to UN archives and files, personal files, and interviews with those intimately involved with the beginning and early development of this important international library. Very readable, although at times very tedious because of its ponderous academic style, it is an important and useful work of interest to all librarians. [R: C&RL, July 71, p. 321; LJ, 1 Jan 71, p. 50; RQ, Spring 71, p. 266]   Charles D. Patterson

1033.   Donnelly, F. Dolores. **The National Library of Canada: A Historical Analysis of the Forces Which Contributed to Its Establishment and to the Identification of Its Role and Responsibilities.** Ottawa, Ont., Canadian Library Association, 1973. 281p. index. o.p. ISBN 0-88802-096-1.

In 1971 H. C. Campbell published a rather condensed treatment of the history and growth of the Canadian library movement. This study,

Canadian Libraries, is part of the Clive Bingley series Comparative Library Studies, which probably explains why the book emphasizes library planning and regional library systems at the expense of a proper historical perspective. This study is quite different in its approach. As we know, Canada's National Library was established only in 1953, and the objective of this historical study is to describe the forces that operated—both positively and negatively—in the emergence of the National Library. There are eight chapters in this study. One of the most interesting of them is "The Twentieth Century: First Four Decades—Struggle for a National Purpose," which includes a number of good comments on Canadian regionalism and the role of Lawrence J. Burpee. Also interesting is chapter 3, which discusses the organized effort of the Canadian Library Association (established in 1946) toward the enactment of national library legislation. All in all, it is an interesting study presented in a readable form. [R: LJ, 1 May 74, p. 1279]

1034. Gurney, Gene, and Nick Apple. **The Library of Congress: A Picture Story of the World's Largest Library.** rev. ed. New York, Crown Publishers, 1981. 180p. illus. o.p. LC 81-9751. ISBN 0-517-54517-9.

This revision of the original 1966 picture text on the history of the Library of Congress and its activities is, ostensibly, expanded from 200 to 440 photographs (all black-and-white) and by some additional text. It still suffers from some earlier problems: poor quality photography and simplified text. Also, the updating of the text is minimal considering all the changes and advances in techniques of information storage and retrieval made in the 15-year period since the first edition was published. However, brief mention is made of LC's development of MARC tapes and of "networking" and of the "new" Audio-Visual Division.

While the original text and photographs formed an interesting juvenile introduction to the Library of Congress, this revision and expansion is poorly done: many "contemporary" photographs of the daily processes of the Library of Congress are dated, and the text is, at best, only partially updated. Even with the addition of an index this work is a minimal improvement over the older one, which should be retained as a useful introduction for school and public libraries. The emphasis the book places on the services provided by the Library of Congress (five of the nine chapters are concerned with research and reference services and with some of the national programs that the Library of Con-

gress sponsors) provides the reader with an idea of the scope of its services, but as the color photograph on the dust jacket suggests, the Library of Congress is remarkable in many ways, not the least of which is its own architecture and its art holdings. This national institution deserves better treatment than the changing of the introduction from one Librarian of Congress to another, the addition of a few photographs, and a fill-in-the-blanks updating of a fairly well done original text.

John Sigwald

1035. Houghton, Bernard. **Out of the Dinosaurs: The Evolution of the National Lending Library for Science and Technology.** Hamden, Conn., Linnet Books, 1972. 127p. illus. index. (The Management of Change; Studies in the Evolution of Library Systems, No. 1). $14.50. ISBN 0-208-01183-8.

Using the historical development of the National Lending Library as the matrix, the author discusses the rise of interest in scientific literature in Britain after World War II and the attempts to provide a central repository and distribution system for that literature. Starting in 1956, with the somewhat limited resources of the Science Museum Library in South Kensington as nucleus, the NLL had a stock of 35,500 science serials by 1970. In that same year, out of 1,080,400 requests, it had the fantastic success rate of 88.4 percent from its own stock alone. For the decade of the 1970s, NLL moved towards becoming a lending library for the humanities. Although this book is primarily a history, it is also intended to be a guide to others who wish to make their libraries relevant and useful. Accordingly, the various management ideas, activities, and services of NLL and especially of its director, D. J. Urquhart, are detailed. Any librarian, not only information specialists, would profit from reading this book and considering whether and how the experiences of NLL could be used to make a library more effective. [R: C&RL, Sept 73, p. 285; CLW, Apr 73, p. 556; LJ, 1 May 73, p. 1454]

John E. Kephart

1036. Keep, Austin Baxter. **History of the New York Society Library: With an Introductory Chapter on Libraries in Colonial New York, 1698-1776.** New York, New York Society Library, 1908; repr., Boston, Gregg Press, 1972. 607p. illus. index. (The Library Reference Series). o.p. LC 72-11505. ISBN 0-8398-1086-5.

A detailed history of the oldest library in New York State and one of the earliest literary organizations in the United States. Large academic libraries that do not have the original edition might be interested in this reprint of a classic work.

1037. Miles, Wyndham D. **A History of The National Library of Medicine: The Nation's Treasury of Medical Knowledge.** Bethesda, Md., National Library of Medicine, U.S. Department of Health and Human Services; distr., Washington, D.C., GPO, 1982. 531p. illus. index. (NIH Publication, No. 82-1904). $14.00. S/N 017-052-00224-4.

During the nineteenth and twentieth centuries no library has had a greater influence on the evolution of medical librarianship than the Army Medical Library, now called the National Library of Medicine (NLM). Miles's very readable account of this institution's origins and growth, from Surgeon General Joseph Levell in 1818-1819 up to circa 1980, provides a fascinating, in-depth examination of the development of this major library and the various services it has provided and continues to render to the nation.

The author details in chronological format the development of this library's various collections and divisions during its first 160 years. Through the use of biographical sketches of the head librarians and other prominent individuals in NLM's history, Miles adds a human dimension to the story of this institution's growth. Particular attention is given to the techniques used by John Shaw Billings in building the library's monographic, journal, manuscript, and portrait collections. This study is an excellent source for the history of *Index Medicus* and the major library departments dealing with the history of medicine and MEDLARS. The last several chapters cover the progress made by the National Medical Audiovisual Center, the Lister Hill National Center for Biomedical Communications, and the various NLM grants programs.

Throughout the text the inclusion of lengthy quotes from primary sources, numerous illustrations of individuals and facilities, and facsimiles of major items in NLM's various collections greatly enhances the value of this study. The explanatory footnotes following each chapter show the depth of the author's research. Miles's work, although not a standard reference book, will be a useful addition to all medical library and library science collections. [R: IRLA, Dec 83, p. 11]   Jonathon Erlen

1038. Mount, Ellis. **Ahead of Its Time: The Engineering Societies Library, 1913-80.** Hamden, Conn., Linnet Books/Shoe String

Press, 1982. 213p. illus. index. $25.00. LC 81-17155. ISBN 0-208-01913-8.

The publication of this work is so important to the history of engineering libraries that it caused this reviewer to recast the knowledge on that topic before doing a long review elsewhere.

It is perhaps sufficient here to mention that the Engineering Societies Library (ESL) in New York City is based on the collections of the five major professional societies of the engineering profession and that it is the largest public engineering library in the free world. This work originated in 1979 as a doctoral dissertation for Columbia University and was rearranged and amplified for the present purposes.

The outstanding personalities connected with ESL included H. W. Craver, R. H. Phelps, and Margaret Mann. Mann's classified catalog based on Universal Decimal Classification numbers is so important that G. K. Hall has published it in two editions.

The symbiotic relationship between ESL and Engineering Information, Inc. (the publisher of *Engineering Index* and of the database COMPENDIX), is well covered and in part accounts for the title Mount has selected for the volume.

No major engineering library, academic, industrial, public, or governmental, should be without this work. Users will be only marginally interested in such an addition to the collection, but engineering librarians have an obligation to know the heritage of this branch of special librarianship. [R: JLH, Winter 83, p. 68; LQ, Jan 83, p. 85; SL, Apr 83, p. 203]

E. B. Jackson

1039. Skallerup, Harry R. **Books Afloat & Ashore: A History of Books, Libraries, and Reading among Seamen during the Age of Sail.** Hamden, Conn., Archon Books, 1974. 277p. illus. bibliog. index. $22.50. LC 73-15879. ISBN 0-208-01408-X.

This book represents a significant new contribution to the literature dealing with American library history. Skallerup has written a remarkably readable and informed study of "shipboard and shoreside libraries for seamen." He treats the period from the invention of printing to the outbreak of the Civil War.

Drawing on what is obviously a thorough knowledge of his subject, Skallerup traces the history of libraries and reading for seamen, with all but the early chapters being devoted to American developments. Perhaps the most impressive aspect of this book is the degree to which the author succeeds in interpreting the development of libraries for seamen within the context of American social, political, and military history. Skallerup is particularly successful in his analysis of the motives of those who founded libraries for seamen, and his work might well provide a useful model for those examining other aspects of eighteenth- and nineteenth-century American library history.

This is a handsomely printed work containing well-chosen illustrations throughout. Extensive documentation, and five appendices describing the contents of a number of antebellum American seamen's libraries, will prove of real value to the serious historian. [R: BSA-P, Apr 75, p. 288; RSR, July 74, p. 34]

Michael H. Harris

1040. Smith, Murphy D. **Oak from an Acorn: A History of the American Philosophical Society Library 1770-1803.** Wilmington, Del., Scholarly Resources, 1976. 291p. illus. bibliog. index. o.p. LC 75-29736. ISBN 0-8420-2076-4.

This is not so much a "history" of the APS Library as a catalog of its early acquisitions. The first two chapters do cover such matters as the housing, arrangement, and administration of the collection at various stages, and the compilation of catalogs. The bulk of the text, however, although it is in narrative form, is essentially a chronological list of acquisitions, filled out with some details concerning the nature of the work, the author, donor, or the circumstances of the gift or purchase. It is really not for "reading through." This section provides references, by number, to the complete alphabetical listing (by author, with full citations) which follows and takes up a third of the volume. A very thorough index is at the back. Only printed materials are included (no manuscripts). For the most part, these reflect the early interests of the APS, which were scientific and practical—*not* "philosophical" in the modern sense. The period covered is from the founding of the society to the appointment of its first true librarian. Intellectual and social historians of the eighteenth century may find this work useful, and perhaps it will have some appeal for bibliophiles as well. Otherwise, it is of very limited interest. [R: RQ, Fall 77, p. 84]

Hans E. Bynagle

LIBRARY EDUCATION

1041. Bassam, Bertha: **The Faculty of Library Science, University of Toronto and Its Predecessors 1911-1972.** Toronto, University of Toronto, Faculty of Library Science in association with The Library Science Alumni Associa-

tion, 1978. 141p. illus. index. o.p.

This historical study, written by the second director of the University of Toronto Library School (who was associated with its operation since its inception in 1928), provides comprehensive, factual, historical coverage of the training programs offered for librarians in Ontario from their beginnings to the period ending 30 June 1972. Library training in Ontario began with a four-week summer course offered by the Ontario Department of Education in June/July 1911, was transferred to the University of Toronto as a one-year diploma course in 1928, and eventually turned into a professional degree program in 1936-1937. By 1972, it had been transformed at the University of Toronto into a two-year degree program for the MLS, and had seen the beginnings of Ph.D.-level training for research-oriented Canadian librarians.

Bassam discusses the various changes that occurred during this period from nearly every aspect a historian should cover. She describes changes in curriculum, with the rationale for such changes very carefully spelled out, particularly when the change from the diploma to the degree program was planned, and again when the school changed from offering the one-year BLS to the two-year MLS as the initial professional degree. We are given a sound, reliable set of portraits of the major supporters of the library school, those from among its faculty and from the outside world (first the superintendents of education for the province, and later, librarians from the university and elsewhere), many of whom were Bassam's personal friends. There is a good discussion of the relationship of the library school and its parent university, particularly during the years of the Bissell administration when expanded library and training facilities were being planned, a relationship which perhaps reached its zenith when the facilities for the newly designated Faculty of Library Science were officially opened in 1972. This is a well-documented narrative of development, written by someone who took part in most of it and remembers it very clearly. [R: JLH, Winter 80, p. 112; LW, Jan 80, p. 175]

Margaret Anderson

1042. **The Book Mark 51 & 52: Fiftieth Anniversary School of Library Science.** Chapel Hill, N.C., University Library and the Friends of the Library, University of North Carolina, 1982. 173p. illus. o.p. ISSN 0006-7393.

The 11 essays in this nicely balanced collection were delivered at the four-day fiftieth anniversary celebration of the University of North Carolina's School of Library Science in March

1981. These essays address thorny matters that doubtless will continue to be with us (interinstitutional collaboration, continuing education for librarians, the changing curricula in library education) or review in historical perspective issues that were prominent during the last decade (personnel matters, library research and library history, collection management). Also treated are information science and libraries, bibliographic control, and medical librarianship.

If any one quality marks almost all of these essays, it is good writing—clarity, tight organization, and felicity of phrasing. Ed Holley deserves praise for opening and closing the book with the thoughtful essays of master wordsmiths David Kaser and Lester Asheim. [R: LJ, 15 May 83, p. 984]　　　　Charles R. Andrews

1043. Brewster, Beverly J. **American Overseas Library Technical Assistance, 1940-1970.** Metuchen, N.J., Scarecrow, 1976. 434p. bibliog. index. o.p. LC 75-23006. ISBN 0-8108-0827-7.

This book is a history of United States technical assistance to libraries in other countries between 1940 and 1970. It is particularly concerned with the transfer of manpower through visits by experts and technicians from one country to another. It describes the overseas work of several hundred library advisors and consultants. The study is divided into three parts: the public sector, the private voluntary agencies, and the American Library Association. The technical assistance of each sponsoring agency is examined and comparisons are made in order to reveal patterns of development taken by American international library technical assistance. Each project is discussed and documented, although very little information is given on costs, grants, gifts, etc. Among the appendices is a list of all American Library Association international committees from 1907 to 1969, and a 52-page bibliography. Also includes an excellent index. [R: LJ, 15 Dec 76, p. 2553]
　　　　Donald P. Hammer

1044. Davis, Donald G., Jr. **The Association of American Library Schools, 1915-1968: An Analytical History.** Metuchen, N.J., Scarecrow, 1974. 385p. bibliog. index. o.p. LC 73-16014. ISBN 0-8108-0642-8.

Davis has written a detailed narrative of the history of the association from its beginnings to 1968, including a description of the groundwork for the 1915 meeting, which had been prepared by the meetings of the Round Table of Library School Instructors of the American Library Association.

This is an "analytic historical case study" that has made considerable use of archival and statistical materials to answer such questions as: "What has been the actual role of the AALS in education for librarianship?"; "In what ways has it fulfilled or not fulfilled its potential?"; and "How can the influence of the AALS on library education be evaluated?"

It is a detailed and thoroughly documented account of the association's history, but it fails to explain fully the reasons for the association's lack of effectiveness in library education. Perhaps an in-depth sociological study of the reasons behind the "proliferation of autonomous subgroups of practitioners" (which, Davis points out, do not characterize other professions as they do librarianship) should be prepared as a companion volume to this text.

The author has interviewed a wide variety of persons active in the association over a span of time, and has quoted their varying reactions to its objectives and activities.

This work will be an important source of information concerning the association and its development, and Davis offers some valid suggestions for those areas that need considerable future work. His statistics and tables present an interesting and useful picture of the association's structure over a period of time.

This deserves our consideration as a chronology, a sourcebook, and an attempt at explanation. Other studies have a respectable basis on which to build. [R: AL, June 74, pp. 298-99; LJ, 1 Sept 74, p. 2045]　　　Jesse H. Shera

1045. Davis, Donald G., Jr. **Comparative Historical Analysis of Three Associations of Professional Schools.** Urbana-Champaign, Ill., Graduate School of Library Science, University of Illinois, 1974. 39p. (Occasional Papers, No. 115). o.p.

In 1974 Scarecrow Press published Donald G. Davis's impressive and thorough analytical history of the Association of American Library Schools, 1915-1968. That work, which was critical of the association's leadership, argued convincingly that AALS's failure to develop a sense of identity had contributed to its lackluster performance. When the publisher was considering Davis's manuscript for publication, he decided to publish it without the lengthy section devoted to a comparative analysis of the AALS, the Association of American Law Schools, and the Council on Social Work Education. Such a decision seemed justified, but many looked forward to seeing the very interesting analysis of the three organizations in print. The University of Illinois has now provided us with Davis's comparative historical analysis, and every professional library educator will find it of considerable interest. This paper further documents Davis's interpretation of the failure of AALS and concludes that, when compared with the other professional associations, the AALS always comes in a poor third. Supporters of AALS as a viable professional group will find little solace in this work. [R: C&RL, Mar 75, p. 157]   Michael H. Harris

1046.   Richardson, John, Jr. **The Spirit of Inquiry: The Graduate Library School at Chicago, 1921-51.** Chicago, American Library Association, 1982. 238p. bibliog. index. (ACRL Publications in Librarianship, No. 42). $35.00. LC 82-11582. ISBN 0-8389-3273-8.

Richardson has written a superlative history of the Graduate Library School of the University of Chicago during its formative and early productive years. There is an appreciative foreword by the late Jesse H. Shera, whose plea for "a well-documented and evaluative history of the Graduate Library School at Chicago" in 1972 motivated Richardson to undertake this project. Richardson himself is not an alumnus of the university, and he was able to maintain the objectivity needed for writing this history.

Richardson has made judicious use of a wide range of sources at Chicago and elsewhere. He traces the origins of the school from the recommendation of the Chicago Library Club in 1923 for an advanced library school in Chicago. He follows with painstaking care the evolution of the school from the appointment of a professional educator, George A. Works, as the first dean. Although Works left after only two years, he had gathered a small but dedicated and talented faculty and a group of promising students. During an interim of three years, the faculty kept the school in operation, until the appointment of Louis Round Wilson as the second dean in 1932.

A professional librarian and a successful administrator, Wilson shifted the emphasis of the school from teacher training to administration and to researching library problems. When Wilson retired after ten years, he left the school firmly established and serving as a model for other library schools. Richardson concludes his history with a survey of the years from 1942 to 1951, which saw the dispersal of the original faculty and their replacement by many of the school's graduates.

This is a significant book in library education and an example of painstaking historical

research. [R: JAL, July 83, p. 166; LJ, 15 Apr 83, p. 803]   Thomas S. Harding

1047.   Vann, Sarah K. **The Williamson Reports of 1921 and 1923: Including Training for Library Work (1921) and Training for Library Service (1923).** Metuchen, N.J., Scarecrow, 1971. index. 441p. o.p. SBN 8108-0417-4.

This is a rewritten version of Vann's dissertation, discussing major historical events dealing with library education. In her study, the author concentrates on the famous Williamson reports of 1921 and 1923 that were instrumental in reconstructing library education in this country. [R: AL, Mar 73, p. 326; LJ, 15 Jan 72, p. 171; LQ, July 72, p. 352]

1048.   White, Carl M. **A Historical Introduction to Library Education: Problems and Progress to 1951.** Metuchen, N.J., Scarecrow, 1976. 296p. index. $17.00. LC 75-28086. ISBN 0-8108-0874-9.

This is a revision and expansion (the text has been increased by one-third) of the author's *The Origins of the American Library School*, first published in 1961. The chapters have been retitled and their number increased from six to nine. Also, the narrative has been brought to 1951, a natural watershed, as it was in that year that new standards were adopted for accreditation by the Board of Education for Librarianship, later the Committee on Accreditation.

The author, who has a long and distinguished service in library education at the University of Illinois and later at Columbia, has here given us a study that is not so much a description of the library schools and their work, as a search for perspective in which major problems, as well as the course pursued in solving them, can be more fully understood. Throughout, it has been the author's objective to throw light on how library education came to be what it was at mid-century. As White says in his introduction, the roots of the present lie deep in the past, and he has attempted to uncover those roots. For this thoughtful study, by one who has devoted much of his professional life to library education and has directed two major library schools, the profession must be grateful. [R: LJ, 15 Sept 76, p. 1838]

Jesse H. Shera

OTHER TOPICS

1049.   Johnson, Elmer D. **Communication: An Introduction to the History of Writing,**

Printing, Books and Libraries. 4th ed. Metuchen, N.J., Scarecrow, 1973. 322p. index. o.p. LC 73-83. ISBN 0-8108-0588-X.

Johnson's purpose is to provide a concise introduction to the history of libraries. The emphasis is definitely on libraries, with only token mention of writing, printing, and books. Chapter titles include: "Communication and the Library," "Early Writing," "Ancient Libraries," "Books and Libraries in the Middle Ages," "Early Printing," "European Books and Libraries, 1500-1900," "English Books and Libraries, 1500-1900," "Printing in Colonial America," "Libraries in Colonial America," "American Libraries, 1775-1850," "A Period of Library Progress, 1850-1900," "Books and Printing Since 1775," "Modern Foreign Libraries," "Modern American Libraries," "The Growth of the Profession of Librarianship," and "Current Trends in Books and Libraries." Each unit has a bibliography of books and periodical articles.

This work attempts to show the relationship of libraries to society and to delineate the evolution of the library by revealing the impact of various social, cultural, intellectual, economic, and political influences that have helped to form the library as it developed through the various historical periods.

Like the previous editions, this work is not particularly attractive in format. The typescript used throughout results in an uninviting product. In the fourth edition the spacing is closer than in the third edition, but the type is larger. There are no illustrations. It is a shame that this useful and most readable account on communication cannot be more aesthetically pleasing. However, Johnson's work is still a basic text of "the librarian's role in human communication." [R: LJ, 1 Nov 73, p. 3237]   Paul A. Winckler

1050.   Miksa, Francis. **The Subject in the Dictionary Catalog from Cutter to the Present.**

Chicago, American Library Association, 1983. 482p. bibliog. index. $55.00. LC 83-2556. ISBN 0-8389-0367-3.

Not since Samuel Rothstein documented the beginning of reference service in U.S. libraries (in "Measurement and Evaluation of Reference Service," in a 1964 *Library Trends*) have we had such a thorough review of the nineteenth-century foundations of modern professional practices. A critical review of the past and present of *LCSH* is needed before we transform it into an online subject-access tool. Miksa helps us understand why we should not blame Charles Ammi Cutter for the apparent inconsistencies in form and structure, cross-references, and the like. He carefully documents the fact that J. C. M. Hanson, David Haykin, and others at the Library of Congress never really followed or understood Cutter's rules and concepts. The pragmatic approach and the pressure to adopt LC practices over local procedures is a result of 40 or more years of ad hoc-ism and misunderstanding about the criticisms raised by such theorists as Eric Coates in England and S. Ranganathan in India.

As to the coverage of the subject of the book, this reviewer must comment on the sparsity of references for the near past. The coverage is not up "to the present," as is stated in the title, but only up to 1965 or so. The impact of computer-based retrieval systems, online catalogs, free-text searching, and so on is given no real review in this book. Another historian will have to tackle that period; but this author has given us a very valuable review, with authoritative insights, into a very important period of our professional development. The notes and bibliography add up to more than 70 pages, and the index is adequate. [R: LQ, Jan 84, p. 109; RQ, Winter 83, p. 245; WLB, Sept 83, p. 62]

Pauline Atherton Cochrane

38 Humor

1051. Armour, Richard. **The Happy Bookers: A Playful History of Librarians and Their World from the Stone Age to the Distant Future**. New York, McGraw-Hill, 1976. 133p. illus. o.p. LC 75-28313. ISBN 0-07-002303-4.

The author means no harm. It is all a matter of taste and good humor. This reviewer was never fond of puns because they remind him of giggly teenage girls. Apparently the girls are over 25 now, and, as librarians, their giggles are being solicited for this punning approach to libraries and their history. Gags are fine, and Armour is not malicious. But he certainly is corny. [R: LJ, 15 June 76, p. 1397]

Bohdan S. Wynar

1052. Stevens, Norman D., ed. **Library Humor: A Bibliothecal Miscellany to 1970**. Metuchen, N.J., Scarecrow, 1971. 427p. index. o.p. LC 76-149995. SBN 8108-0379-8.

This anthology presents, we think, a well-balanced selection of humorous and not-so-humorous writings by, about, and for librarians. Contributors include bibliographers, reference librarians, information "specialists," a few poets, and even catalogers and indexers. Stevens is right in his introduction: this is not a contents analysis and should not be construed as the librarian's self-image or other such nonsense. We certainly agree with *Wilson Library Bulletin*: "This anthology fills a much needed gap, to quote an earlier but uncited source." Hopefully our quotes are not out of context. [R: WLB, Sept 71, p. 86]

1053. Wiegand, Wayne A. **The History of a Hoax: Edmund Lester Pearson, John Cotton Dana, and the *Old Librarian's Almanack***. Pittsburgh, Pa., Beta Phi Mu, 1979. 75p. index. (Beta Phi Mu Chapbook, No. 13). o.p. LC 78-23377. ISBN 0-910230-13-7.

By no stretch of the imagination can this book be considered a reference book. Rather, it is a reprint of a delightful literary hoax—one of the very few associated with library literature. Concocted by the fertile minds of Edmund Lester Pearson, who was both a professional librarian and a newspaper columnist, and John Cotton Dana of the Newark Public Library, the *Old Librarian's Almanack* was intended as a caricature of the traditional librarian, whose creed was summarized in the admonition: "Guard well your books—this is always your foremost duty." Yet so authentic was the appearance of the *Almanack* that it was thought to be genuine when published in 1909, and resulted in a number of critical reviews. When the hoax was exposed a few months later, largely by Helen E. Haines in two reviews, it was accepted with good-natured indulgence and then quietly forgotten by most librarians.

Two earlier accounts of Pearson's hoax have been published—one in 1963 and another in 1971. However, this edition by Wayne A. Wiegand is the first to make use of the primary source materials in the John Cotton Dana papers at the Newark Public Library, and the scrapbook kept by Pearson. The *Old Librarian's Almanack* deserves a place on library shelves, along with such literary hoaxes as the Donation of Constantine, George Psalmanazar's history of Formosa, and the forgeries of John Payne Collier and Thomas J. Wise. [R: JAL, Nov 79, p. 295]

Thomas S. Harding

39 Indexing and Abstracting

GENERAL WORKS

1054. Anderson, M. D. **Book Indexing.** New York, Cambridge University Press, 1971. 36p. index. (Cambridge Authors' and Printers' Guides). o.p. SBN 521-08202-1.

This little booklet provides essentials for a beginner, discussing such topics as planning the index, standard procedures in compilation, and other useful details. The text has a number of helpful examples, especially in such areas as method of alphabetization, how to handle names with prefixes, etc. All issues in this series have a practical, how-to-do-it approach. Previous volumes covered such topics as punctuation, notes and references, and preparation of manuscripts.

1055. Borko, Harold, and Charles L. Bernier. **Indexing Concepts and Methods.** New York, Academic Press, 1978. 261p. bibliog. index. $20.00. LC 77-77229. ISBN 0-12-118660-1.

Perhaps the most complete treatment of indexing available in the English language, this work is intended to be used as a textbook for indexing courses and is based upon the classroom experiences of the two authors. Although they state that this is "a welcome alternative to learning indexing by trial and error," the authors emphasize that much practice is necessary. Both manual and computer indexing methods are included. The text is divided into five broad topics: part 1 provides an overview of indexing (both past and present systems); part 2 is concerned with the structure of indexes (entries, syndetic systems, formats, standards, and alphabetization); part 3 explores indexing and editing procedures (common methods, indexing monographs and serials, typesetting and proofreading, thesauri, computer-aided indexing); part 4 covers various types of indexes (subject/author, citation, word indexes and concordances, and special forms); and part 5 deals with the issues of evaluation and professionalism. The book should be helpful to anyone interested in indexing and can be used either in the classroom or for independent study. [R: C&RL, May 79, p. 284; LJ, 15 Apr 79, p. 898]

1056. Cadwallader, Laura H., and S. Ada Rice. **Principles of Indexing and Filing.** 4th ed., rev. Baltimore, Md., H. M. Rowe, 1971. 160p. illus. index. o.p.

This little book, intended primarily for small businesses, covers all aspects of this subject on a rather elementary level. Nevertheless, the information is presented in clear language, and there are a number of helpful illustrations throughout the narrative. Some small libraries might be interested in acquiring this publication.

1057. Cleveland, Donald B., and Ana D. Cleveland. **Introduction to Indexing and Abstracting.** Littleton, Colo., Libraries Unlimited, 1983. 209p. bibliog. index. $19.50. LC 82-17297. ISBN 0-87287-346-3.

The authors have designed a text that provides guidance for both the student and the practitioner on the fundamentals of indexing and abstracting. After discussing the basic concepts of information and its bibliographic control, they describe the nature and types of indexes and abstracts. Included are topics on the levels of indexing, author indexes, alphabetic subject indexes, permuted title indexes, PRECIS, vocabulary control, methods and procedures of indexing and abstracting, and index evaluation. There is also information on indexing and abstracting services, online services, and careers in indexing and abstracting. The book focuses on what indexers and abstractors do and how they go about doing it, by presenting the principles and practices in an illustrative manner. Step-by-step instructions for indexing books and documents and suggested readings that follow most chapters make this a useful text for students as well as for others interested in learning the art of indexing and abstracting. [R: JAL, Sept 83, p. 230; LJ, 15 Oct 83, p. 1936]

1058.   Cleverdon, Cyril, and others. **Studies in Indexing and Cataloging.** Detroit, Management Information Services, 1970. 507p. illus. o.p. LC 72-120543.

Includes factors determining the performance of indexing systems, by C. Cleverdon, J. Mills, and M. Keen; a comparison of some machine-produced indexes, by W. M. Adams; and simultaneous production of catalog cards and computer input, by R. W. Butler and P. Z. Schofield.

1059.   Collison, Robert. **Abstracts and Abstracting Services.** Santa Barbara, Calif., ABC-Clio, 1971. 122p. index. o.p. LC 78-149635. SBN 87436-078-1.

This is a condensed presentation of an introductory nature, covering such areas as general principles and standards, types of abstracts, editing, indexing, definitions, costs, etc. In addition, the reader will find here a brief historical sketch on twentieth-century abstracting services, some comments on mechanization (regrettably lacking in sufficient documentation or even description of some important projects), and a rather interesting narrative on the future of abstracting services. The chapter "Abstracting Services" lists the more important publications, most of them in English, and there is also a list of selected readings. In general, this is a useful introductory text and, like most of Collison's other publications, it is quite readable. This book should be recommended to library school students as supplementary reading. [R: WLB, Dec 71, p. 367]

Bohdan S. Wynar

1060.   Collison, Robert L. **Indexes and Indexing: Guide to the Indexing of Books, and Collections of Books, Periodicals, Music, Recordings, Films, and Other Material, with a Reference Section and Suggestions for Further Reading.** 4th rev. ed. London, E. Benn; distr., New York, DeGraff, 1972. 232p. illus. bibliog. index. o.p. ISBN 0-510-45722-3.

Indexes and Indexing is a clearly written introduction to indexing theory; it is also a comprehensive guide to the practical task of index-

ing. The discussion of the theory of chain, co-ordinate, or catch word indexing, for instance, is grounded in the practical application of the theory to the construction of an index. Collison, an experienced indexer and one of the founders of The Society of Indexers, also offers advice on such practical matters as how to read a book one is going to index, how to select subject headings and references, and how best to shuffle the numerous slips of paper an indexer must shuffle. Twenty rules for indexers and a dozen rules for arranging index entries, included in the reference section, are particularly useful summaries of the advice presented in the text; these basic and concise guides to the construction of an index would also be useful in index evaluation. The greater portion of the work is devoted specifically to the indexing of books, but the chapters on the indexing of other materials are sufficiently detailed to provide assistance in the construction and evaluation of indexes to nonmonographic materials. *Indexes and Indexing* well deserves its reputation as a standard work in the field; it is a model of clarity in technical writing, and a delight, therefore, to read. Unfortunately, the addition of one brief chapter on research is the extent of revision for the fourth edition. The addition does not add significantly to the text and hardly warrants purchase if one owns the third edition. [R: CLW, May 73, p. 602]

Joan K. Marshall

1061.   Feinberg, Hilda, ed. **Indexing Specialized Formats and Subjects.** Metuchen, N.J., Scarecrow, 1983. 288p. illus. index. $37.50. LC 82-23155. ISBN 0-8108-1608-3.

This volume consists of 14 chapters that emphasize "indexing systems design and new indexing techniques for indexers, information centers, database managers, and librarians," to quote from the publisher's announcement. In content it should be compared to *Indexers on Indexing*, edited by Leonard Harrod (see *ARBA* 79, entry 331).

The level of writing is clearly superior in Harrod's book, but the acceptance of technology is superior in Feinberg's. Feinberg often echoes principles stated by Harrod, but the "glitter" provided by the chapter on videotext plus the importance of the only chapter this reviewer has seen on law book indexing (with its usual five to six levels of indexing depth) means that Feinberg's book would be more attractive to library school students as supplementary reading in their courses in indexing and abstracting than would Harrod's. This is, perhaps, its prime use.

The widely perceived stagnation in machine-aided indexing seems about to be broken by the increasing volume of text upon which free-text searches may be made. Three authors in this book point out, however, the greater possibility of unskilled searchers' being "buried" under such free-text search results. They see the emergence of hybrid searching systems whereby the search would appear to be free text but would actually be under the control of a loose thesaurus. This would slow down the response time but result in better searches.

One of the better-written chapters is that on the masterful indexes to *Chemical Abstracts*. By contrast, the ERIC chapter rambles.

The page size is more than twice that of earlier Scarecrow readers. This results in larger type size, about 20 percent more text, and the possibility of using larger illustrations. Only one typo was noted.

Reference librarians would be well advised to suggest this book to scholars facing the necessity to index their own books, along with the texts of Harold Borko and Charles Bernier's *Indexing Concepts and Methods* (see *ARBA* 79, entry 330) and G. Norman Knight's *Indexing, the Art of* (see *ARBA* 81, entry 315). [R: LJ, 1 Dec 83, p. 2228]	E. B. Jackson

1062.	Harrod, Leonard Montague, ed. **Indexers on Indexing: A Selection of Articles Published in** *The Indexer*. New York, R. R. Bowker, 1978. 430p. index. o.p. LC 78-56880. ISBN 0-8352-1099-5.

The British Society of Indexers was formed in 1957. *Indexers on Indexing* is a selection of 51 articles from issues of *The Indexer* on seven pertinent topics: the history of indexing; book indexing; index typography; indexing periodical and multivolume publications; indexing scientific and technical literature; variations in indexing systems and methods; and the application of modern technology to indexing. In these short, very focused articles, *Indexers on Indexing* presents an overview of indexing issues and areas of concern as viewed by practicing professional indexers. The approach taken is generally practical, yet the level of concern is thoroughly professional. This is not a how-to-do-it book, although valuable information is imparted on the principles and techniques of book indexing, case histories, indexer-author-publisher relations, and the ownership of indexes. Other works on indexing have covered how-to-do-it problems, a particular subject area, or, like *A Glossary of Indexing Terms*, served as support documents. As a review-of-the-art with a strong pragmatic emphasis, *Indexers on Indexing* fills

a need in indexing literature. As can be surmised, the context of the articles is British, and the total omission of any mention of the American Society of Indexers is unfortunate. [R: C&RL, Nov 78, p. 515]	Deborah Jane Brewer

1063.	Knight, G. Norman. **Indexing, the Art of: A Guide to the Indexing of Books and Periodicals.** Winchester, Mass., Allen & Unwin, 1979. 218p. index. o.p. LC 79-40882. ISBN 0-04-029002-6.

In comparison to Borko and Bernier's *Indexing Concepts and Methods* (Academic Press, 1978), which is intended to be used as a textbook for indexing courses in this country, Knight's volume is less comprehensive and presents the British point of view. Nevertheless, both volumes will supplement and complement each other. After an introductory chapter, Knight describes in some detail the mechanics of compiling an index, following with specific instructions on how to prepare headings and subheadings, proper-name headings, subject headings, and classified entries, references, and cross-references. Specialized aspects of indexing are discussed next (e.g., indexing of periodicals, newspapers, cumulative indexing, editing procedures, correction of proofs, etc.). Six appendices conclude this volume, incorporating information about British, American, Australian, and Canadian societies of indexers, the Wheatley Medal, and the Carey Award. The author, late president of the Society of Indexers (Great Britain), died in 1978, shortly after the text of this book was sent to the printer. A highly recommended book to all interested parties. [R: BL, 15 Apr 80, p. 1177; C&RL, Nov 80, pp. 551-52]	Bohdan S. Wynar

1064.	Neufeld, M. Lynne, Martha Cornog, and Inez L. Sperr, eds. **Abstracting and Indexing Services in Perspective: Miles Conrad Memorial Lectures, 1969-1983, Commemorating the Twenty-fifth Anniversary of the National Federation of Abstracting and Information Services.** Arlington, Va., Information Resources Press, 1983. 300p. bibliog. index. $27.50. LC 82-084484. ISBN 0-87815-043-9. [Editor's note: index inside pocket on back cover.]

Acting on a strong conviction that reference librarians know too little about the practicalities of producing the tools they use daily, this reviewer can only urge each significant reference department to get a copy of this volume for staff members to read about their favorite "a&i" service and/or personality. (This recommendation goes double for reference departments in special libraries where the journal collection forms the heart of the information resource.)

These librarians, however, need not read the volume from cover to cover; there is far too much repetition and overlap. Some of this could have easily been edited out of the Conrad Lectures, which needed some oral bridging from year to year; but the main offenders are the one-and-one-half-page statements labeled "Perspectives" that occupy pages 31-82.

Phyllis V. Parkins's 1973 talk still reads well. Four others that merit special mention for relevance and writing are those of William O. Baker (1977), Donald W. King (1979), Carlos A. Caudra (1980), and Russell J. Rowlett, Jr. (1981). There is a good bibliography. The index is a good example of compliance with ANSI standards. [R: LJ, 1 Oct 83, p. 1858]

E. B. Jackson

1065. Rowley, Jennifer E. **Abstracting and Indexing**. London, Clive Bingley; distr., Hamden, Conn., Shoe String Press, 1982. 155p. illus. bibliog. index. (Outlines of Modern Librarianship). $15.00. ISBN 0-85157-336-3.

The series title characterizes this book accurately and completely: it is in fact a narrated outline. It could also be called a "plain vanilla" treatment of indexing and abstracting. It is the British equivalent of Donald Cleveland and Ana Cleveland's *Introduction to Indexing and Abstracting* (see *ARBA* 84, entry 136), and U.S. libraries would prefer the latter. On the other hand, Canadian librarians might prefer Rowley's version because of the examples chosen.

This is not to say that U.S. samples and citations are wholly ignored: this reviewer particularly liked the recognition of the late Mortimer Taube's Science and Technology Project in the 1950s as the ancestor of postcoordinate indexing systems.

The chapter arrangement is straightforward: abstracts, abstracting, bibliographical references, indexing, indexing languages, postcoordinate indexing systems, precoordinate indexing systems, title indexes, and the use of abstracting and indexing data. The usual appendices in such works on editing, proofreading, and further readings were included. [R: Indexer, Oct 82, p. 133; LRTS, July 83, p. 277]

E. B. Jackson

REFERENCE WORKS

1066. Buchanan, Brian. **A Glossary of Indexing Terms**. London, Clive Bingley; distr., Hamden, Conn., Linnet Books, 1976. 144p. o.p. LC 75-20312. ISBN 0-85157-208-1(Bingley); 0-208-01377-6(Linnet).

One *sought label* for this *monograph* does not appear in the *CIP* data and the *characterisation* is incomplete. One *false drop* may occur because the *thesauri* or *subject heading list* used for the *subject analysis* exhibits *subjective intention*. The *tracings* show "Cataloging—Dictionaries" and "Indexing—Dictionaries" but not "Classification—Dictionaries," which is what the book is mainly about. Although *notes, centralized cataloguing, authority file,* and *author* are defined (as are the words italicized above), terms like imprint, Festschrift, media, compiler, compound name, surname, signature, publisher, and date of publication are not.

About 1,000 terms chosen for inclusion are those Buchanan thought to be necessary when discussing indexing at basic levels. The glossary is an enlarged version of a word list he provided students at Loughborough School of Librarianship in England. It has a pronounced British bias, with many, many definitions of esoteric classification terms (e.g., *leap in division, retroactive notation, predicables*). Such acronyms as SLIC and BTI are included, but there is no mention of MARC, ISBD, NFAIS, or OCLC. Books by Coates, Foskett, Lancaster, Gilchrist, Langridge, Mills, Ranganathan, and Sharp were checked, but Bourne, Collison, Becker and Hayes, Wynar, and Immroth were not. The style of entry is commendable: basic definition with examples, amplification, and related terms. Nevertheless, although this may be a helpful aid for the intended audience in Great Britain, it does not do justice to the entire field of indexing, classification, and cataloging for students at large. A comprehensive glossary for this core subject of librarianship and information science is still lacking and is sorely needed. This slender volume will not suffice. [R: LJ, Aug 76, p. 1606]

Pauline Atherton Cochrane

1067. Neufeld, M. Lynne, and Martha Cornog. **Abstracting and Indexing Career Guide**. Philadelphia, Pa., National Federation of Abstracting and Information Services, 1983. 54p. bibliog. o.p.

This slight pamphlet contains answers to two questions frequently raised by current library school students: "Why should I register for a course on indexing and abstracting? Will it lead to a valid alternative career for me?" On the other hand, it lacks sufficient detail on what an abstractor or indexer really does to enable graduates to determine if they should enter that specialty at their current career stage. These graduates would need also to consult a self-help text, such as Edward T. Cremmins's *The Art of Abstracting* (ISI Press, 1982).

Neufeld and Cornog feel it will be some time before computers take over. A useful appendix has an "A&I Services Comparison Chart" showing titles of some positions, duties, salaries, required training, and turnover. Some college placement offices may need to have this pamphlet in their career files.

E. B. Jackson

1068. NFAIS Membership Directory, 1981. Philadelphia, Pa., National Federation of Abstracting and Indexing Services, 1981. 71p. o.p.

The 1981 *NFAIS Membership Directory* is a brief but welcome reference book which should be appreciated by most reference librarians in major research libraries. The information included in this 71-page booklet is not easily securable elsewhere. Consequently, this item fills a prominent gap within many reference collections.

The directory contains the names, addresses, areas of concern and concentration, products, and services for the 43 organizations included, all of which are engaged in the documentation process. The directory provides a listing of the organizational memberships. A major portion, although not all, of the indexing and abstracting services and database producers is included.

The information contained in the directory is quite straightforward. There is a list of the organizations by alphabetical order in the table of contents at the beginning of the book, with the page number for the full listing of the organization or group. The groups are arranged in alphabetical order and contain full address and telephone number, as well as additional valuable information: contact person or persons, general objectives of the organization, principal products and services, and coverage. Where available, the directory also provides the logo for the organization. An important part of the information provided is the name of the representative to the National Federation of Abstracting and Indexing Services. Membership in this association is the key to the inclusion of organizations in the directory. The listing for

each group or organization also provides the names of others to be contacted.

There are some recommendations which should be considered by potential users and the producers of this directory. First, a name index that would list persons who are NFAIS assembly representatives, as well as contact people, would be desirable. (Very often organizations are not recognized directly, but indirectly because of a person's reputation or prominence in a particular field.) In this day of computer-produced lists, it would be possible to prepare such an index, and update or purge the name file on an annual basis. Next, it would be very valuable to have a broad subject index, enabling users to identify those organizations and groups which are concerned with particular disciplines, areas, or fields (i.e., aerospace research which overlaps with physics [AIP], engineering, and NASA). Finally, the National Federation of Abstracting and Indexing Services, while providing all of us with important information about abstracting and indexing services and database producers, has forgotten to say something about themselves, who represents them, and what their role is.   Roberto P. Haro

1069. Wellisch, Hans H. Indexing and Abstracting 1977-1981; An International Bibliography. Santa Barbara, Calif., ABC-Clio, 1984. 276p. index. $45.00. LC 84-3064. ISBN 0-87436-398-5.

The first edition of this book was printed in 1980. The reviewer must apply the term definitive sparingly, yet it is deserved by the present listing of 1,426 items appearing in the "open" literature in the half-decade shown plus an additional 220 items from earlier years missing from the predecessor *Indexing and Abstracting: An International Bibliography* (see *ARBA* 81, entry 317). (One hopes the compiler is able to monitor the inevitable body of research reports with security or proprietary classifications for future candidate entries.)

The introduction deserves careful reading before the 19 categories of entries under "Indexing" and the 3 under "Abstracting" are consulted. Scope, sources, and selection policy are all spelled out. From the tabulation of languages, English drops to 64.5 percent of the entries as compared to 85 percent in the basic volume, but many of the 220 items mentioned earlier appear to be non-English. As one Russian service was a basic source, the number of entries in that language grew 9.7 percent. As before, careful separation of entries was made among "Automatic Indexing," "Computer-aided Indexing," and "Computer-produced Indexes."

The fine author, title, and subject indexes illustrate Wellisch's concerns with the past sloppiness of the library/information profession with romanization and obsolete filing rules. (For example, additional author entries appear in the Arabic, Chinese, Hebrew, Japanese, and Russian characters).

The inclusion of nonbook materials (such as video aids from publishers of indexing and abstracting services) is a welcome addition.

E. B. Jackson

OTHER TOPICS

1070. Coates, Eric, Geoffrey Lloyd, and Dusan Simandl. **BSO, Broad System of Ordering: Schedule and Index.** The Hague, International Federation for Documentation; Paris, UNESCO, 1978. 1v. (various paging). index. (FID Publication, 564). o.p. ISBN 92-66-00564-9.

Broad system ordering (BSO) was designed for use in UNESCO's UNISIST program to perform as a "switching mechanism" between various information systems using diverse indexing/retrieval languages. BSO is a subject code using assigned numerical designations for particular subject materials. It is a *broad* ordering system since subjects could be more finely discriminated than they are. But because BSO is designed to apply to a variety of information systems that are not necessarily compatible, the system must remain flexible. This document results from a field test with 26 organizations. [R: LQ, Oct 79, p. 444; LR, Summer 79, p. 109]

1071. Feinberg, Hilda. **Title Derivative Indexing Techniques: A Comparative Study.** Metuchen, N.J., Scarecrow, 1973. 297p. bibliog. index. $27.50. LC 73-2671. ISBN 0-8108-0602-9.

An investigation of the permuted title index, the study presupposes the existence of a vast and growing amount of literature and the inability of conventional (manual) indexing to keep pace, among other problems. Objectives of the study are to describe available types of title-derivative-automatic-indexes, noting comparative features, examples, advantages, recommendations, etc.

The complications of effective indexing are dramatized by the sheer quantity of material (and this study is not going beyond the title!). Principal sections deal with index evaluation (thankfully *not* suggesting some kind of mechanical formula), advantages and disadvantages of KWIC and KWOC, the effectiveness

of indexing from titles, stoplists, innovations, recommendations, glossary, etc.

This work is a compact survey of the state of this indexing technique; it will be of value to those engaged in this activity, or in its study. It should also have a cautionary effect on those entering this field with inadequate preparation or simplistic delusions. Bibliographies are extensive, but the book's own index is too sparse. [R: LJ, 1 Dec 73, p. 3532]   Joseph W. Sprug

1072. Foskett, A. C. **A Guide to Personal Indexes Using Edge-Notched, Uniterm and Peek-A-Boo Cards.** 2nd ed. rev. and enl. Hamden, Conn., Archon, 1970. 91p. index. illus. o.p. SBN 208-01063-7.

The first edition of this little book was published in 1967. In a rather popular style it provides essential information on such topics as indexing techniques, the use of edge-notched cards, and a more detailed section on "feature card indexes." It will be useful for the establishment and maintenance of small index files, and it also may serve as a simple introduction to this subject for library school students. [R: WLB, Apr 71, p. 788]

1073. Garfield, Eugene. **Citation Indexing; Its Theory and Application in Science, Technology, and Humanities.** New York, John Wiley, 1983. 274p. $24.95; $18.95pa. ISBN 0-89495-024-X; 0-89495-025-8pa.

The first edition of this book was printed in 1979. This book is a synthesis of the author's writings on his "personal obsession," citation indexing (CI), since 1955. It details the history, method, and implications of CI, with special reference to the *Science Citation Index* (*SCI*) (see *ARBA* 76, entry 1327). Garfield has developed the method of Shepard's *Citations* (the law guide that has been in existence since 1873) and extended its application to the sciences, the social sciences, and — more recently — arts and humanities.

In a citation index, primary access to material is by way of cited sources rather than through subject analysis. CI can be used to measure a researcher's recognition by his peers, and this in turn becomes a kind of barometer to the impact a particular author has in his field.

The various chapters describe the historical background of CI: how it is made; application to patent literature; CI as a research tool; a thorough description of *SCI*; the use of *SCI* (to evaluate the research role of journals, scientists, and organizations; to define relations between journals and fields of study; to measure the impact of research; to define developments in scientific advances); etc. The cumulative effect of CI is to provide a comprehensive bibliography. Journals to be indexed are selected by a process of citation analysis. Garfield is satisfied with the hypothesis that a relatively small percentage of science journals publish the bulk of significant articles in any field; by citing every reference contained in these journals, comprehensive coverage is achieved.

When the approach to bibliographical searching of a subject is through the writings of researchers active in the field (i.e., searching by author's name), there is no doubt that CI — with the help of computer processing — does provide exhaustive coverage. Most of this book deals informatively with that type of entry. Garfield's disparagment of conventional subject indexing could well be modified; at least for incipient scholars, there is no doubt about their preference for an entry form as found in Wilson's *Social Sciences Index* over the *Permuterm Subject* volume of *SSCI*. But there we are comparing different models, which is not the proper task of this review. Any library subscribing to the various citation indexes should acquire Garfield's book.   Joseph W. Sprug

1074.   Gilchrist, Alan. **The Thesaurus in Retrieval.** London, Aslib, 1972. 184p. illus. bibliog. index. £13.00. LC 77-127210.

This volume centers on the general problem of constructing thesauri with emphasis upon those for coordinate retrieval systems. Defines basic terms, discusses techniques (relational indexing, concept coordination, links, roles), and has sections which aid the indexer and searcher in using a thesaurus. Explanation of Boolean algebra and Venn diagrams are provided. Contains much useful information. [R: LJ, Aug 72, p. 2551]   Charles D. Patterson

1075.   Jones, Karen Sparck. **Automatic Keyword Classification for Information Retrieval.** Hamden, Conn., Archon, 1971. 253p. index. o.p. SBN 208-01201-X.

This book is the product of the author's research into the problems encountered in assessing the purpose and character of keyword classification for information retrieval from the point of view of automatic grouping and search techniques. Includes descriptions of a number of experiments conducted to assess the effects of assigning different values to variables characterizing the classification and the class-using retrieval processes.

1076.   Lancaster, F. W. **Vocabulary Control for Information Retrieval.** 2nd ed. Washington,

D.C., Information Resources Press, 1985. 250p. index. $27.50. LC 78-186529. ISBN 0-87815-053-6.

This book deals with the construction, organization, display, maintenance, and properties of index vocabularies for indexing and searching document collections. Vocabularies for postcoordinate retrieval systems are emphasized. The author has had extensive experience with information retrieval systems. He prepared this book as a text for a course in vocabulary control. The book should also be of interest to those concerned with the design, operation, and evaluation of indexing systems. Reference librarians, as users and instructors in the use of indexing systems, might benefit from reading this book, since vocabulary control (or the absence thereof) plays an important role in the performance of such systems. The book contains pages of indexes and thesauri as well as other indexing records. There are a subject index and a list of controlled vocabularies arranged by subject.   Gerald Jahoda

1077.   Perica, Esther. **Newspaper Indexing for Historical Societies, Colleges and High Schools.** Monroe, N.Y., Library Research Associates, 1975. 55p. bibliog. index. $3.45pa. LC 74-20822. ISBN 0-912526-15-7.

Contains an introductory statement giving an appreciation and general philosophy of indexing; a listing of bibliographical tools and supplies; a table of the categories of indexible matter found in newspapers; the mechanics of making the index; rules, with examples, of various kinds of index entries; filing rules; a list of abbreviations; and an index. This brief booklet is characterized by commendable common sense; a beginning indexer could well benefit from this guide, with one major caveat: the author apparently assumes that in addition to author and subject entries there will be an entry for each headline! The indexing of a single issue will suffice to convince the novice of the uselessness of such a practice. A few minor flaws are noted: the typography is satisfactory, but the paper is cockled; rule B-17 prescribes the use of brackets, but the illustration uses parentheses; at least one entry ("Headlines") in the booklet's own index does not give the right page reference; rule A-8 should be explicitly restricted to Oriental-type names and not to "foreign" names generally; and, if there is a chronological arrangement for "continuation of entries" (A-7), why not make it easy to file by using a year, month-number, day format rather than the month-word, day, year format that is suggested? Perica's work is recommended, especially for those beginners who have not yet been schooled in the manual authored by Harry Friedman; his 1942 work of some 250 pages is still not outdated or superseded; nor will you find Friedman espousing a file of entries for sterile headlines. Joseph W. Sprug

1078. The PRECIS Index System: Principles, Applications, and Prospects. Proceedings of the International PRECIS Workshop, sponsored by the College of Library and Information Services of the University of Maryland, October 15-17, 1976. Hans H. Wellisch, ed. New York, H. W. Wilson, 1977. 211p. index. $15.00. LC 77-1932. ISBN 0-8242-0611-8.

PRECIS (PREserved Context Index System) "approaches the task of subject indexing and the construction of subject headings for books and other documents from a completely new direction. PRECIS is based on the fundamentals of natural language and an ingenious conjunction of human indexing skills and computer capabilities. It is also a practical system that has been applied by the British National Bibliography (BNB) to more than 30,000 titles annually since 1971" (preface). This volume is the result of the first workshop on PRECIS in the United States. The papers included fall into three groups: part 1 explains the principles of the system; those in part 1 discuss research projects and comparative studies involving PRECIS; and part 3 outlines the system's practical applications.

Derek Austin, one of the developers of PRECIS, wrote three of the four papers in part 1, and they explain the development, syntax, semantics, and management aspects of the indexing system. The multilingual aspects, and the potential for PRECIS to be applied to any language, are explored by Jutta Sørensen in the final paper. The section on research projects contains three papers: "PRECIS Compared with Other Indexing Systems," "PRECIS in a University Library," and "Machine Searching of UK MARC on Title, Library of Congress Subject Headings, and PRECIS for Selective Dissemination of Information." The second paper, by Valentina de Bruin, discusses the growing need of large academic libraries for machine-readable subject authority files, and the advantages of computer-based PRECIS system over the manual system of Library of Congress Subject Headings (LCSH). The other papers in this section compared various indexing systems, PRECIS and LCSH included, and found that PRECIS provides more access points and more precise subject definition. The third section on practical applications contains

reports of a manual PRECIS system in a Canadian high school, of nonbook indexing at the Ontario College Bibliocentre, and of film indexing at the National Film Board of Canada. C. Donald Cook proposes that the Library of Congress study the possible replacement of LCSH with PRECIS in the last paper. The result of this volume is to establish PRECIS as the opponent of, and perhaps successor to, LCSH.

It is true that LCSH was not designed as a machine-manipulative system, and this will prove to be a growing problem in the future. PRECIS has the distinct advantages of being computer-based, in use in Great Britain, and gaining acceptance elsewhere. Combine these facts with its apparent superiority of subject definition, and it will become obvious that PRECIS is an important development in librarianship and information science. Librarians in the United States should familiarize themselves with this system. [R: C&RL, Nov 77, pp. 549-50; JAL, Sept 77, p. 244]

Janet H. Littlefield

1079. Ramsden, Michael J. An Introduction to Index Language Construction. Hamden, Conn., Linnet Books, 1974. 206p. (Programmed Texts in Library and Information Science). o.p. LC 73-19843. ISBN 0-208-01187-0.

This book is a practical manual on how to construct a structured index language such as a classification scheme, an alphabetical list of subjects, or a thesaurus. Prepared in the form of a programmed text, it is part of a series of learning texts that have emanated from the College of Librarianship Wales.

In assessing this particular text, one must distinguish between the faults of what is presented and the virtues of the presentation itself. What is presented is a series of steps—a technique—by which a structured index language can be constructed. Little rationale is given for the technique presented, although the suggestion is made that the technique is simply assumed to be a good one because it is part of an accepted and exciting tradition. The learning of this technique, moreover, does not always seem to be well served by the programmed instruction format. For instance, certain steps in the technique—such as determining the order of categories in a classification schedule—require complex and at times even arbitrary decisions; a programmed text's method of "right guesses" seems somewhat inappropriate to such decisions.

Drill in the "this is the way it is done" approach may be offensive to those who want to pause and ask why, but most assuredly it is a quick means of training nondoubting builders of index languages. The drill in this book is impressive because of the speed with which it entrenches concepts, its economy of style, and its avoidance of jargon. And there are nice touches, like the introduction, a concept index, a self-test at the end, and the inclusion of encouraging comments like "we are at this stage approximately 40 per cent of the way through."

Elaine Svenonius

1080. Ramsden, Michael J. **PRECIS: A Workbook for Students of Librarianship.** London, Clive Bingley; distr., Hamden, Conn., Shoe String Press, 1981. 152p. (Outlines of Modern Librarianship). $12.00. ISBN 0-85157-334-7.

PRECIS is an acronym for Preserved Context Index System, a technique for information control in which an individual selects terms to create logical sequences of words and in which a computer then creates the actual entries. Derek Austin designed this system as a part of the UK MARC Project, and the system is a part of the operational software of several British and Canadian systems. PRECIS has had little support in the United States, especially since LC has decided against its use. An early description of the system is Austin's *PRECIS: A Manual of Concept Analysis and Subject Indexing* (London, Council of the British National Bibliography, 1974). Periodical literature contains several dozen articles describing PRECIS, but few say much about actual system use. Some assistance is given by Hans Wellisch in *The PRECIS Index System* (H. W. Wilson, 1977), and Phyllis A. Richmond helps even more with *Introduction to PRECIS for North American Usage* (see *ARBA* 82, entry 251).

The system is simple in some ways, and in some applications is rather complex. Even after study, a workbook is a useful tool for a full understanding and the ability to apply the system's concepts of information manipulation. The Ramsden book, which needed and well designed at least in its major contents, is a mixed blessing. (Part of the text design problem is the lack of an index and any bibliography, both nearly essential for books in this field.) This is a self-instruction manual for learning the basic elements of this alphabetical subject indexing technique. Ramsden begins with brief and succinct definitions and outlines. The book develops the syntax, semantics, and manipulation of PRECIS with increasingly complex and integrated units of work application. Answers are provided for all exercises. The brief book is not overwhelming in content, and presents lessons which can be grasped and mastered. At the same time, the language and idiomatic usage are British and will present some difficulties for U.S. users. The book is also perhaps too compact and even cryptic on some points. Explanations are needed, and Ramsden should be used with a fuller text such as that by Richmond, the best single item on PRECIS to appear through 1981. Nonetheless, Ramsden is a good start, especially for the potential users who do not have access to formal training. [R: LQ, Apr 82, p. 193; LR, Autumn 81, p. 184]

Neal L. Edgar

1081. Richmond, Phyllis A. **Introduction to PRECIS for North American Usage.** Littleton, Colo., Libraries Unlimited, 1981. 321p. index. $30.00. LC 80-25977. ISBN 0-87287-240-8.

Originally designed for use as a subject index to the *British National Bibliography*, the Preserved Context Index System has been made part of the MARC records generated in Australia and is accessible for North American use. In her precise introduction Phyllis Richmond provides a complete course in this system of subject analysis for those involved in processing book and nonbook materials either with or without access to a computer.

After presenting the background of the system — its predecessors and its development — Richmond explains its format, terms, and operations. She begins with the process of assigning an item a "title-like phrase" and proceeds through the techniques of providing subject access to that phrase. The text covers compound terms and their management, operations for sequence and coordination, inverted format, the concept of the agent, agents and roles, multiple themes, interactive situations, manipulative coding, and the building of a cross-reference system. Every step, every code, every symbol is clearly explained, and scores of examples move the user from the simplest of cases to the most complex. Attention is paid to the relationships between strings and entries, as needed for accurate indexing, and the final chapter on analysis for string writing is intended as a summary of the decision-making process in indexing. The PRECIS indexing method is especially useful for libraries with special collections that cannot be indexed in a satisfactory manner using standard systems of thesauri. [R: WLB, June 81, p. 794]

1082. Soergel, Dagobert. **Indexing Languages and Thesauri: Construction and Maintenance.** Los Angeles, Calif., Melville, 1974. 632p. illus. bibliog. index. (Information Science Series). o.p. LC 73-20301. ISBN 0-471-81047-9.

(Available from Books on Demand, $16.00pa., ISBN 0-317-10279-6).

Comprehensive and highly technical, yet organized so that the beginning indexing student or the reader interested only in a general orientation to indexing languages and thesauri is directed to those portions of the text that are on his or her level or that suit his or her particular needs or interests. The author analyzes and compares the function, structure, and construction of existing manual and computer-related indexing languages and thesauri, criticizes and evaluates these and proposed alternatives, and offers much original thought toward solutions. The final section of the text, "Thesauri as a Basis for Cooperation in Information Services," provides much food for thought. Recommended for library schools, research libraries, and special libraries, but it is definitely more of a circulating book than a reference book. [R: LQ, Oct 75, p. 435; LR, Autumn 75, p. 127; SL, Mar 76, p. 175]   Joan K. Marshall

1083.   Vickery, B. C. **Classification and Indexing in Science.** 3rd ed. Boston, Butterworths, 1975. 228p. illus. index. o.p. ISBN 0-408-70662-7.

The first edition of this book was published in 1958. In this edition five of the six main chapters have been rewritten. The first chapter (only slightly revised) provides the historical background for the value of classification in the retrieval process and discusses major applications of documentation. The second chapter, which discusses the classification of a subject field, has been considerably expanded and includes new examples. The same is true of the remaining chapters (e.g., classification for arrangement, notation for the classified catalog, classification in indexing, and classification in postcoordinate systems). Most of the bibliographical apparatus has been updated. Most library schools will be interested in acquiring this substantially revised edition. [R: C&RL, Mar 76, p. 179; LQ, July 76, p. 340]

1084.   Wilson, T. D. **An Introduction to Chain Indexing.** London, Clive Bingley, 1971. 85p. bibliog. index. (Programmed Texts in Library and Information Science). o.p. LC 70-22688. ISBN 0-208-01069-6.

This is the sixth title in a series of programmed textbooks in which the authors, using Dewey, seventeenth edition, as an example, explain the basics of chain indexing. Included are discussions of false links and unsought links and missing links, and unsought hidden links, as well as the problems of compound headings and redundant digits and the use of verbal extension of classes. The several appendices include worked examples, a self-tester, and examples in UDC, LC, and Bliss. Although there is no glossary, there is a short bibliography. [R: LJ, Aug 71, p. 2471]   Charles D. Patterson

40 Information Management

GENERAL WORKS

1085. Arnold, Denis V. **The Management of the Information Department.** Boulder, Colo., Westview Press, in association with The Institute of Information Scientists, 1977, c1976. 143p. bibliog. index. (Institute of Information Scientists—Monograph Series; A Grafton Book). $20.00. LC 76-43375. ISBN 0-233-96652-8.

Although slanted specifically toward industrial information departments, the text provides a broadly applicable review of issues involved in the management of an information department. It is part of the Monograph series organized by the Institute of Information Scientists, which aims to meet the needs of people teaching, of people learning on the job, and of information scientists brushing up their knowledge in a particular field.

The contents are divided into seven chapters reflecting major concerns facing managers in any organization. These are communication patterns, management, planning and design, organization, coordination, control, and analysis. Theories of communication patterns are reviewed in the first chapter, but are also repeatedly noted in practical terms in other sections; the author emphasizes information flow between users and staff, among staff, and within organizational structures. Management is defined as "getting things done through people" and the text suggests methods by which to accomplish this. Contemporary management principles are emphasized, including planning through the establishment and continual processing of objectives, motivation through staff participation in decision making and design of

procedures, coordination of operations in terms of users (publicity) and of management (organizational hierarchy), and control through establishment of standards and their use in evaluation. Definite guidelines emerge from the text, particularly on organization, staffing, finances, and evaluation. References accompany each chapter, and a bibliography of additional relevant literature follows the text; a useful index is included. The text is written in easily readable English with an unobtrusive balance of quotations and footnoted references. The book's format is more that of a textbook than a reference tool. However, its straightforward presentation, supplemented by relevant citations, makes it a useful source for general, introductory information on management, albeit written specifically for the information industry. [R: C&RL, Sept 78, p. 415]   Danuta A. Nitecki

1086. Boaz, Martha. **Strategies for Meeting the Information Needs of Society in the Year 2000.** Littleton, Colo., Libraries Unlimited, 1981. 197p. index. $25.00. LC 81-11751. ISBN 0-87287-249-1.

Practical plans for meeting the information needs of tomorrow's society are the focus of this collection of 15 essays by specialists and authorities in their fields. "The Third Revolution: The Information Explosion—Information Access in the Year 2000," by Boaz, opens the volume. Other essays discuss societal problems and issues requiring information service; telecommunications and value systems; user needs; information needs of business; productivity; expected advances in computer and communications technology during the next 20 years; PRESTEL and the trend toward personal computers; information networks; the place of authors in the coming information society; privacy and security issues in information systems; copyright ownership, reproduction, and use conditions; and financing and governance of information networks of the future. Boaz concludes with her own recommendations for developing information technologies that can be controlled and used constructively and efficiently. [R: JAL, July 82, p. 166; JAL, Mar 82, p. 55]

1087. Debons, Anthony, ed. **Information Science: Search for Identity.** New York, Marcel Dekker, 1974. 491p. illus. index. (Books in Library and Information Science, Vol. 7). o.p. LC 73-85383. ISBN 0-8247-6096-4.

Twenty-four papers and nine working group reports record the deliberations of a group gathered to examine our present understanding of information. Anthony Debons, in a 20-page epilog, attempts a summary of the 10-day meeting and the "movement toward understanding." He identifies a framework of four major areas in which the basic concepts of information can be clearly defined: the nature of information, technology and its ability to meet human needs, the impact of information technology on humanity and its institutions, and the professional needs of institutions that deal with information. His attempt at a synthesis is admirable, but the papers by such well-known authors as Yovits, Samuelson, Otten, Belzer, Heilprin, Neelameghan, and Kochen still defy codification. In his own words, "the concepts underlying information generation are often confused [at the Institute] with the problems of information transfer." A number of authors (Robert Landau, Hammer, Auerbach, Turoff, Donahue) presented their views on information technology. These papers and the subsequent discussion helped the group arrive at the general consensus that there is abundant technology to meet human needs.

J. C. Licklider's overview is perhaps the most accurate summary of the Institute's proceedings: "The most conspicuous thing is that it is not clear what the information science field is ... [It] is a large complex field with ongoing activities ... information scientists ought to concentrate on two objectives: One is to get squared away on the fundamental concepts of the field. The other is to establish a leading motif that would be motivating and capable of putting dynamism into the whole field." [R: LJ, 15 Jan 75, p. 105]   Pauline Atherton Cochrane

1088. Kunz, Werner, Horst W. J. Rittel, and Werner Schwuchow. **Methods of Analysis and Evaluation of Information Needs: A Critical Review.** Munich, Verlag Dokumentation; distr., New York, K. G. Saur, 1977 (c1976). 84p. bibliog. index. o.p. ISBN 3-7940-3450-3.

This summary derives from a study, "Methods of Analysis and Evaluation of Information Needs to Be Satisfied by National Documentation, Library and Archive Infrastructures," conducted for the Federation Internationale de Documentation (FID) in connection with the information projects of UNESCO. It is an overview of trends and approaches of user studies in the information sciences suggesting a reorientation of research policy. In the words of Martyn (note 112, page 20), "system design must be based on understanding rather than detailed specific knowledge." A system approach is required that begins with understanding the user's information needs and behavior in the face of problems. After a review of different theoretical concepts and approaches, there follows a discussion of conventional methods of user research, and a presentation of advantages and disadvantages of each in practical use. Novel kinds of systems approaches for the analysis and evaluation of information needs follow. A tentative conclusion reached is that formal and informal information systems must be joined so that the user really becomes an integral part of the process. Prospects for the future, not all bright, conclude this report.

Included is a 13-page list of references, many in German, but most in English. An index of authors cited, which refers to the preceding list of references, ends the book. Perhaps one could go to numerous use studies listed in *Library Literature* for more specific, pertinent material and not acquire this slender volume. [R: C&RL, Nov 77, p. 537; LJ, 1 Mar 78, p. 525]   Edward A. Richter

1089. McClure, Charles R. **Information for Academic Library Decision Making: The Case for Organizational Information Management.** Westport, Conn., Greenwood Press, 1980. 227p. bibliog. index. (Contributions in Librarianship and Information Science, No. 31). $29.95. LC 79-8412. ISBN 0-313-21398-4; ISSN 0084-9243.

The investigation is based on two research projects which complement each other: the Information Contact Study and the Information Evaluation Study. The Information Contact Study was undertaken by the author at four medium-sized academic libraries located in the northeastern part of the United States, and the

Information Evaluation Study at four medium-sized academic libraries in the southwestern part of the United States. The analysis of the data obtained by means of these projects is preceded by a summary of "recent thought, on an interdisciplinary basis, regarding information for decision making" (p. xv). A number of the writings included in this summary have supplied elements for McClure's research procedure. His interdisciplinary approach is evident also from an examination of the bibliography and the notes, which accompany each chapter of the book.

The author observes that with the increasing competition for funds, academic libraries must make decisions that lead to efficient administrative measures. Decision making should be based, he stresses, on pertinent, accurate, and timely information. McClure differentiates between kinds of information sources. He lists decision situations which require information input for their resolution. He further establishes categories of organizational members and the kinds of contacts they may have with information sources.

The author finds it especially useful to characterize organizational members as either information-rich or information-poor, the characterization depending on the number of contacts individuals have with information sources. Organizational information-rich persons have been found to publish more, to read more, and to have more interpersonal contacts. They usually also have higher status in the organization and are involved in decision making. McClure pleads for accessibility of information sources to all staff members in order that everyone may be able to contact information sources and participate effectively in decision making. To assure that information sources receive due attention, McClure advocates that the position of information manager be established at each institution.

To obtain a higher degree of certainly as to whether McClure's findings can be applied to other than medium-sized academic libraries, it would seem desirable to conduct similar studies at representative groups of institutions both smaller and larger in size than those investigated by McClure. His methodology of research, supported by data from information science and several other social science disciplines, is well reasoned and clearly described. It could well serve as a model for future investigations. Librarians, as well as practitioners and researchers outside of the library field who wish to explore the potential of information sources for

decision making, could profit from reading McClure's study. [R: LJ, July 80, p. 1492]

Fritz Veit

1090. Meadow, Charles T. **The Analysis of Information Systems.** 2nd ed. Los Angeles, Calif., Melville, 1973. 420p. illus. index. (Information Sciences Series/A Wiley-Becker & Hayes Series Book). $49.95. LC 72-11518. ISBN 0-471-59002-9.

This is a major revision of the popular and well-received 1967 text. More than 100 pages have been added to cover such topics as data access systems, interactive information retrieval, programming languages (BASIC, FORTRAN, COBOL, JCL, List Processing languages), and generalized data management systems. The other chapters have been only slightly revised, with some illustrations added or updated, the exercises sections removed, and a list of recommended readings added to each chapter. The glossary was deleted. This feature will be missed by the novice. Reference to two glossaries in the preface does not suffice.

Originally intended for programmers, this edition's purpose is to be used as a textbook for information science graduate students and users. The emphasis is still on the design of languages for entering data into a computer, asking questions of the data, and evaluating the results of retrieval.

The author has achieved his purpose of providing an *introduction* to the software technology of information systems. The reader will have to look elsewhere for an in-depth treatment of the topics covered. But this is probably one of the best sources to start reading in the field. [R: Unesco, Mar/Apr 74, p. 107]

Pauline Atherton Cochrane

1091. Reynolds, Michael M., and Evelyn H. Daniel, eds. **Reader in Library and Information Services.** Englewood, Colo., Microcard Editions Books, 1974 (c 1973). 618p. illus. (Reader Series in Library and Information Science). o.p. LC 73-94310. ISBN 0-910972-25-7.

This reader assembles 39 previously published writings, chiefly articles on information sciences, under seven part headings: "Systems Approach to Librarianship"; "The Environment and the Library"; "The Management Subsystem"; "Boundary Activities"; "The Production Subsystem"; "The Maintenance Subsystem"; "The Adaptive Subsystem."

Produced by photoreproduction of the original writings, the book exhibits a wide variety of typefaces and sizes. The names of most contributors are well known to those who have followed the progress of information science in library operations over the last 20 years. [R: C&RL, Nov 75, pp. 523-24; LJ, 1 Nov 75, p. 1988]

1092. Saracevic, Tefko, ed. **Introduction to Information Science.** New York, R. R. Bowker, 1970. 751p. o.p. LC 77-108783. SBN 8352-0313-1. (Available from Books on Demand, $120.00, ISBN 0-8357-90442-8).

A compilation of readings from a number of sources (e.g., *American Documentation, Nature, Journal of the Association for Computing Machinery*, and others) arranged by broad subject categories. It is a well-selected compilation. [R: RQ, Spring 71, p. 279]

REFERENCE WORKS

1093. Basova, I. M., A. I. Chernyi, and F. A. Sviridov, comps. **Publications on Theoretical Foundations of Information Science: Abstracts of Selected Publications.** Moscow, All-Union Institute for Scientific and Technical Information; distr., The Hague, International Federation for Documentation, 1974. 105p. index. (FID Publication 513). o.p.

The stated purpose of the bibliography is to make an inventory of the "most well known," "major" publications on information science since 1960. The primary audience is "scientists and other specialists dealing with the elaboration of theoretical fundamentals of information science."

Some 311 papers in more than 15 languages are listed alphabetically by author. *Not* all references were available to the compilers, but English abstracts or annotations are given for many of the works in Russian, Czech, Polish, etc. Unfortunately, books rarely, if ever, are abstracted, and nondescript titles like "Letter to Editor" are not amplified. There are some notable omissions, such as the series Annual Review of Information Science and Technology, Lancaster's books, the work of Needham and Sparck Jones, Katter, Dahlberg, Ranganathan, Neelameghan, Tell, and many others. The index, a so-called subject index, is both a topical and a geographic index, with entries under Bulgaria, France, Great Britain, Poland, Rumania, United States, USSR, and Venezuela, but none for Sweden, Italy, or Canada. Although the index appears to be of the PRECIS type, the strings of words linked by semicolons are not always permuted. Somewhat difficult to use, with minor errors in printing.

The page size and typeface used for the publication are unsuitable. The single-column page is too small and the typeface too large and too heavily leaded for easy scanning. The bibliographic citations use abbreviations that are not explained. All in all, a most unsatisfactory bibliography. [R: LQ, Apr 76, p. 176]

Pauline Atherton Cochrane

1094. Kesner, Richard M., comp. and ed. **Information Management, Machine-Readable Records, and Administration: An Annotated Bibliography.** Chicago, Society of American Archivists, 1983. 153p. index. $11.00pa.; $8.00pa. (members). LC 83-60318. ISBN 0-931828-57-0.

This 843-item bibliography is a revision of Kesner's *Automation, Machine-Readable Records, and Archival Administration: An Annotated Bibliography* (see *ARBA* 82, entry 381). It is intended to expand the coverage of the earlier work and to address some of the criticisms cited by reviewers. Among these were the lack of a structured subject approach and the need to eliminate many dated items. In response to the first area of concern, the author has created eight chapter divisions: periodicals and reference tools, bibliographies, electronic data-processing applications in archives, machine-readable records and archives, records management and automation, library automation, information theory and systems, and future directions for archival automation. Each division is preceded by a brief description and rationale for selection. The annotations that follow are short (at times too brief to be helpful), descriptive, and noncritical.

The separate author, subject, and journal indexes of the earlier work have been combined into a single index, which is more usable and comprehensive. In addition to expanding the number of items annotated (from 293), Kesner broadened the scope and purpose of this work to include even more citations dealing with automation in general—a thrust indicated by the modified title.

Although the earlier work was limited in its appeal to the archivist, this expanded version is a broad-based reference tool for professionals in all areas of information management. [R: A Arch, Fall 83, p. 465]   Bill J. Corbin

PROCEEDINGS, SYMPOSIA, AND ESSAYS

1095. **The Design of Information Systems for Human Beings: Informatics 6; Proceedings of a Conference Held by the Aslib Informatics**

Group Oxford, 24 September 1981. Kevin P. Jones and Heather Taylor, eds. London, Aslib, 1981. 96p. £15.00pa. ISBN 0-85142-156-3.

The sixth proceedings of the Aslib Informatics Group Conference, this collection of six papers addresses the "human aspects of the exploitation of computer technology." Boden's opening paper stresses the importance of reducing the mystification surrounding computers through education and creating more user-friendly systems. Development of this theme of the "meeting of man and machine" begins with the paper by Jones, "Man versus Computer: A Pragmatic Approach to the Problems Associated with Online Retrieval Systems." Line offers an illustrated proposal for "redesigning information packages for electronic transmission" based on speculations of how people read journal articles. With the aid of a communication system model, Duckitt examines the "human factor in designing a public online databank," with special attention to marketing, ease of operation, structural design, and retrieval aids. Crawford discusses "the hardware approach to information retrieval systems," specifically describing a concept where data are selected by content rather than file position. The closing paper, by Blake, proposes a machine-aided management of machine-retrieved output.

Typical of many Aslib proceeding papers, these are written by British information scientists and practitioners, and assume from the reader a basic inclination toward technical reports of informatics research. These do not require technical knowledge of the topic, but draw on background data from such fields as linguistics, computer science, librarianship, and artificial intelligence.

The collection is not a reference tool. There are no collected data for specific questions and no index. Rather, the volume is a thought-provoking summary of a few projects aiming to diminish the awkward gap between man and information-processing machines.

Danuta A. Nitecki

1096. **EURIM II: A European Conference on the Application of Research in Information Services and Libraries.** Presented by Aslib in association with Association Nationale de la Recherche Technique, Bibliothèque Royale de Belgique, Consiglio Nazionale delle Richerche, Deutsche Gesellschaft für Dokumentation, NOBIN, NORDFORSK. London, Aslib, 1977. 226p. illus. o.p. ISBN 0-85142-091-5.

Following up on the first conference held in France, this three-day conference in Holland on 23-25 March 1976, gathered researchers and experts from France, Belgium, Italy, West Germany, the Netherlands, the United Kingdom, and Scandinavia. Forty-two papers were presented, all in English except for three in French and one in German.

Five papers described the application of research carried out by "permanent" research units: Aslib, INSPEC, SCANNET, SIS, and BNIST. The other brief papers (five pages or less) were grouped for discussion, and the reports of these discussion groups are included so that nonattendees reading these proceedings have the benefit of recorded criticism and comments on both papers and topics. The research topics discussed included: bibliometrics, economic problems, cooperative systems and networks, indexing languages, machine systems, interlingual problems, user/system interface, user studies, and barriers to information use.

In content and style, this volume is similar to an ASIS conference proceedings volume, with two or three notable exceptions: no author index, but with reports of discussion, and a conference attendee questionnaire report. This latter report included an interesting summary of attendees' opinions of under-researched and over-researched areas as compared to current research projects. The highest number of respondents considered user studies to be one of the under-researched areas, and classification and indexing one of the over-researched areas.

This proceedings volume, and its predecessor and successors, would be valuable additions to any information professional's library, as this series will serve as a good bellwether for the kind of work going on in Europe. [R: JAL, Sept 77, p. 225]

Pauline Atherton Cochrane

1097. Griffith, Belver C., ed. **Key Papers in Information Science.** White Plains, N.Y., published for the American Society for Information Science by Knowledge Industry Publications, 1980. 439p. illus. $25.00. LC 79-24288. ISBN 0-914236-50-4.

Key papers in five areas of information science (structure and dynamics of science information flow, innovation: required flows of knowledge, the structure of literature and documents, information retrieval and analysis, and tools and ideas) are presented in this new volume of the ASIS Key Papers series. Through a detailed selection process, the editor of this volume has assembled 30 reprints from a variety of interdisciplinary academic and professional journals and publications, such as *Science, American Psychologist, Journal of the American Society for Information Science,*

Journal of Documentation, Information Processing and Management, and others.

The selection process for inclusion in this Key Papers series was based on the examination of citations received by all articles appearing in the "several" research-oriented information and library science journals. The editor then examined the citations of articles written by authors who had been frequently mentioned in the first seven volumes of the *Annual Review of Information Science and Technology (ARIST).* These were complementary "starting points," and persons who were discovered as publishing well-cited articles in specialized journals were also searched in the author listing. This process of selection identified about 60 percent of the final selections and all the principal topics. The "Appendix" development (supported by a PHS grant from the National Library of Medicine, #RO1-LM00911-07) uses a variety of citation retrieval strategies to identify recent publications based upon the papers (reprints) in the present volume. Lists numbering 15 for both document and author searches are included in the appendix.

The volume has the appearance of a "cut-and-paste" job in format. The introduction and the five parts were apparently typeset for this book, but the reprints have various type sizes and different page orientation (i.e., double-column pages for some articles, while others run in lines across the full page, but in both cases, right and left margins are corrected). The paper has a gray appearance, and the binding does not seem to be substantial. Noted library authorities in the field of information science, such as Don Swanson and Gerald Salton, are included in this volume, but I don't believe the overall content and quality of printing warrant purchase. [R: JAL, May 81, p. 125]   Donald D. Foos

1098. **Information Management and Organisational Change: Proceedings of an Aslib Conference Held at the London Tara Hotel on 6-8 April 1981.** Heather Taylor, ed. London, Aslib, 1981. 113p. £15.00. ISBN 0-85142-148-2.

This volume comprises the complete proceedings of the Aslib conference named in the title. The complete texts of 10 papers are included under four major session headings: organisational factors; the technology; people and professional aspects; information management and the outside world. While many of the papers are interesting individually, when taken as a whole they present a very uneven treatment of the topic which the conference intended to address. Some, such as a report on a user study in special libraries, and a paper on new technology and

communications, barely mention information management at all, much less address the issues of this emerging field which is seeking to define its role. Rather, these papers are presentations of the more traditional issues and concerns facing the library and information science fields generally. Other papers, particularly those on training and qualifications of information managers, and the opening paper on coordination of information activities in large organizations, are fine treatments on information management issues and concerns. While these proceedings add little to information management literature, the publication will be of interest to those already knowledgeable about and interested in the information management field, although they will want to read it selectively. [R: SL, Apr 83, p. 207]   Richard G. Akeroyd, Jr.

1099. **International Federation for Documentation. Committee on Terminology on Information and Documentation (FID/DT). Essential Problems in Terminology for Informatics and Documentation.** Moscow, All-Union Institute of Scientific and Technical Information; distr., The Hague, International Federation for Documentation, 1979. 114p. (FID 569). £25.00. ISSN 0203-6444.

This slim collection of papers is devoted to six specific studies in informatics terminology. Koblitz (German Democratic Republic) identifies problems in terminological work in the fields of information and documentation. Leski and Leska (Poland) analyze typical mistakes in terminology, encourage greater rigor in use of terminology, and consider methods of terminological banks. Cleverdon (Great Britain) reviews the factors governing the appearance of new terms and the problems of standardization, particularly in fields such as the social sciences. Gorkova and Shishova (USSR) propose structural methods to link terms in informatics texts and thereby offer unambiguous criteria for evaluating structural terminological links. Kaplun and Azgaldov (USSR) recommend procedures to qualitatively assess terms and terminological systems. Rondeau (Canada) describes results of implementing a terminological bank, including an analysis of the philosophy of the structure of banks, concepts of data organization, and methods of servicing information users.

Although "international" in authorship, the collection noticeably omits any contributions from American writers and makes no reference to any research conducted in the United States in areas such as cross-file thesauri, invisible term translation, and automatic indexing, which seem to parallel many of the concerns expressed in this volume. The few references cited are all to Russian-language works.

This is not a reference book as commonly used in the United States. There is no index, no central glossary of the terms defined, and no easily identified linkage to sources available in U.S. libraries. The papers are each reports of research; most are written in technical language; several require a good understanding of mathematical notation. It may be an interesting (though expensive) sample of work being done abroad for inclusion in a specialized collection in information science or linguistics. [R: LQ, Oct 80, p. 509; LR, Summer 80, p. 90]

Danuta A. Nitecki

1100. International Federation for Documentation. Committee "Research on the Theoretical Basis of Information" (FID/RI), and Committee "Terminology of Information and Documentation" (FID/DT). **Theoretical Problems of Informatics: New Trends in Informatics ånd Its Terminology (Collection of Papers).** The Hague, International Federation for Documentation, 1979. 143p. (FID 568). £25.00. ISSN 0203-6495.

This volume contains all 13 papers presented at a joint meeting of two committees of the International Federation for Documentation (FID) held in Moscow on 16-18 May 1978. The impressive list of contributors from seven different countries (Czechoslovakia, Germany, Great Britain, Hungary, Japan, Romania, USSR) includes names such as Brookes, Kitagawa, Mikhailov, and Shreider. Topics cover scientific, technical, and social considerations pertaining to the nature of information and its role in modern society. Some of the papers contain a brief review of informatics and examine research problems under current investigation. With two exceptions the papers are nonmathematical and fairly conceptual in nature, which will be appreciated by the less technically inclined reader.

All papers appear in English although seven of them were presented in Russian. Nine of the papers contain references, but most foreign-language references are not translated into English. Shortcomings of the volume are primarily technical in nature and do not detract from the contents significantly. The absence of an index is not particularly disturbing for a volume of this size. The typography varies and the quality of print is poor. An errata list pasted on the last page corrects some of the printing errors, although others are scattered throughout the volume.

Despite these minor flaws, the volume will be welcomed by the library and information science community. Educators, practitioners, and students have the rare opportunity of tasting the international flavor of thoughts on the role of informatics in society. [R: LR, Summer 82, p. 128]

Andrew G. Torok

1101. Jackson, Eugene B., and Ruth L. Jackson. **Industrial Information Systems: A Manual for Higher Managements and Their Information Officer/Librarian Associates.** Stroudsburg, Pa., Dowden, Hutchinson & Ross; distr., New York, Academic Press, 1978. 314p. bibliog. index. (Publications in the Information Sciences). o.p. LC 78-15890. ISBN 0-87933-328-6.

Providing new perspectives in the area of industrial information systems, this volume is a rewarding experience. It is an in-depth presentation of guidelines and recommendations, based upon the experiences of two well-known authorities, for the establishment and operation of an industrial information service. No other source on this subject exists in such a comprehensive and easy-to-use format. The book focuses on guidelines for the optimum use of information to achieve corporate objectives. Beginning with the characteristics of information and their implication for management, the authors move on to the practical aspects of industrial information systems, their functions, administration, personnel, users, budgeting, and other topics of interest to management and special librarians.

The volume outlines the functions and activities of an information service, and advises management and information workers on the topic of information, its production, and organization. It includes a useful discussion on the merchanizing of IIS functions. The other areas covered include centralization/decentralization of services, training for information service managers, use of consultants, word processing, and records management. Distinctions and relationships between the functions and activities of an IIS have been clearly elucidated, and fresh insights into these activities emerge. Of special note are the case studies: "Bell Telephone Laboratories," by Robert A. Kennedy, and "The General Motor Research Laboratories Library: A Case Study," by Eugene B. Jackson. The authors also provide, in convenient outline form, information on the resources of some 300 of the Fortune 500 companies, which provides these companies with a means of comparing their own resources with those of competing companies. The bibliography and detailed index (with extensive references) will be helpful to all users of this volume.

There is no doubt that this book contains a wealth of valuable, sometimes hard-to-come-by, information in one compact volume and that it will remain up-to-date in its content for a long time. It is an important work directed at the management and the information officer, and will be found just as useful by the novice to the profession and the library science student as by the experienced special librarian. This landmark work is highly recommended for its illumination of the basic structure and operation of an industrial information service. [R: C&RL, July 79, pp. 371-72; JAL, Nov 79, p. 297]

Katherine Cveljo

1102. Jones, Kevin P., and Verina Horsnell, eds. **Informatics 3: Proceedings of a Conference Held by the Aslib Co-ordinate Indexing Group on 2-4 April 1975 at Emmanuel College, Cambridge.** London, Aslib, 1978. 137p. $22.00pa. ISBN 0-85143-112-1.

Informatics is a discipline that investigates meaning in words and structure in extensive natural language texts for the purpose of information retrieval. As the introduction states, "the informaticist is concerned with structure in large units of text. The syntax of sentence is on too small a scale to be of much interest." Although the Informatics Group has previously attempted to produce standardized terminology for coordinate indexing, the 11 articles in this collection deal with topics that are more theoretical than practical, for example, "Artificial Intelligence: What Can It Offer Information Retrieval?"; "Chasing the Enthymene, Part III"; "Beyond the Sentence: Clause Relations and Textual Analysis"; and "Informatics: Conceptual Analysis and Epistomology."

Deborah Jane Brewer

1103. Kent, Allen, and Thomas J. Galvin, eds. **The On-Line Revolution in Libraries: Proceedings of the 1977 Conference in Pittsburgh, Pennsylvania.** New York, Marcel Dekker, 1978. 303p. index. (Books in Library and Information Science, Vol. 23). o.p. LC 78-15800. ISBN 0-8247-6754-3.

Whether online technology in libraries constitutes a revolution or is a result of an evolutionary process is one theme among the papers published here from a 1977 Pittsburgh conference. Other key topics include costs, fee versus free services, training, quality control, standards, relative user benefits, user's direct interaction with the technology, and access through resource sharing and networks.

The volume consists of three major parts; each includes a position paper, reaction papers, and excerpts from discussions. Led by Kent's paper, part 1, "The Potential of On-Line Information Systems," explores the potential for new opportunities to access knowledge, customized output, the social impact and new roles for librarians, nonbibliographic databases, and the price spiral's impact on the "library ecology." Three position papers in part 2, "Impact of On-Line Systems," examine the impact in terms of the national informational policy and local, state, and regional library planning (Buchanal), of library operations (Day), and of the user (Peters and Detlefsen). Among the reactions is the stressed importance of creating a "full service network" as a means to insure full access through all types of libraries. In part 3, Caruso's lead paper, "Training and Retraining of Librarians and Users," stresses the need for a new approach to training to reflect new uses of search tools and to reduce the expense of inefficient and ineffective searches by improving the understanding of the content and organization of data files. The editors provide an introduction (Kent) and final summary (Galvin). A conference evaluation is appended. The wealth of authoritative opinions and bibliographic footnotes can be easily retrieved through a detailed index.

The volume gives both a general overview and a good starting point for further study of online activities in libraries. Online reference services are emphasized rather than ones used primarily for cataloging or circulation. The conference attendance of nearly 750 persons from the United States and abroad confirms the importance and widespread interest in this important topic. [R: C&RL, July 79, pp. 375-77; LJ, 1 Feb 79, p. 360]

Danuta A. Nitecki

1104. King, Donald W., Nancy K. Roderer, and Harold A. Olsen, eds. **Key Papers in the Economics of Information.** White Plains, N.Y., published for the American Society for Information Science by Knowledge Industry Publications, 1983. 372p. $29.95; $23.96 (ASIS members). LC 82-21222. ISBN 0-86729-040-4.

This collection of reprints of 23 journal articles, most of which were published in the 1970s, includes 7 on the cost and 8 on the pricing of information products and services, and 8 on the value of information. Several authors discuss the difficulty of applying traditional economic theories and methodologies to information, or the knowledge content, in various media. They suggest that this difficulty has caused most research to be directed to the economics of information products and services.

The collection contains much substantive material, such as Jacob Marshak's discussion

"Economics of Inquiring, Communicating, Deciding," Fritz Machlup's treatise "Uses, Value, and Benefits of Knowledge," Marilyn K. Gell's two-part article "User Fees," T. P. Barwise's "The Cost of Literature Search in 1985," Michael D. Cooper's "A Cost Model for Evaluating Information Retrieval Systems," and D. M. Lambertson's stimulating review of factors to be considered in a "National Policy for Economic Information." However, the editors have contributed only very brief introductions to the three sections and have failed to highlight, summarize, or index. The collection will, in consequence, serve primarily as a background reader for students in economics or information science or for information professionals who are new to economic considerations. The cost figures given in the abstract of one article are the exact reverse of the findings reported in the article's summary. [R: JAL, Sept 83, p. 247]

Richard Palmer

1105. MacCafferty, Maxine, and Kathleen Gray, eds. **The Analysis of Meaning; Informatics 5: Proceedings of a Conference Held by the Aslib Informatics Group and the BCS Information Retrieval Specialist Group, 26-28 March 1979, The Queen's College, Oxford.** London, Aslib, 1979. 302p. o.p. ISBN 0-85142-125-3.

This work is a paperbound collection of 27 papers, in varying typescript formats, presented at a conference sponsored by Aslib's Informatics Group (formerly known as the Co-Ordinate Indexing Group). The title of the work— *The Analysis of Meaning*—reflects the theme of the conference, whereas the underlying question addressed was: "Can any development in the use of computing devices and procedures to handle meaning, deepen our insights into the nature of meaning?" The writer of the introduction admitted that "though the standard of the individual papers presented was consistently high, their degree of relevance to the central theme was often less so." The presentation of papers follows the structure of the conference, four "sessions" of 5 to 10 papers each: (1) "Semiotics and General Semantics"; (2) "Linguistic Semantics"; (3) "Applied Semantics: Artificial Intelligence Systems"; and (4) "Applied Semantics: Information Retrieval Systems." There is no index. [R: LR, Autumn 80, p. 209]

Glenn R. Wittig

1106. Mason, Robert M., and John E. Creps, Jr., eds. **Information Services: Economics, Management, and Technology.** Boulder, Colo., Westview Press, 1981. 211p. index. (Westview

Special Studies in Information Management). $31.50. LC 80-16214. ISBN 0-89158-938-4.

This book is an outgrowth of a discussion at the 1975 annual meeting of the American Society for Information Science (ASIS) concerning rapid developments in economics and management issues associated with access and delivery of information. Several of the papers are based on subsequent presentations and research projects supported by the Division of Information Science and Technology of the National Science Foundation (NSF).

Fourteen papers explore three information-related policy and decision-making areas associated with information service management. These are: (1) economics and government policy, (2) management and marketing of services, and (3) innovations and impacts of technology. The concept of information as a commodity is neatly fit into the framework of management and marketing theory. The design and use of scientific and technical information systems are balanced by technological and behavioral constraints. Bibliographies and a brief index support the development of a coherent theme that information managers need to cope with an increasingly complex society. Although not all issues are fully developed, and contributions from the library sector are in short supply, information scientists, special librarians, and library science students will find this and other titles in the series of great interest.

Andrew G. Torok

1107. **The Nationwide Provision and Use of Information; Aslib, IS, LA Joint Conference, 15-19 September 1980, Sheffield: Proceedings.** London, Library Association; distr., Phoenix, Ariz., Oryx Press, 1981. 414p. illus. index. $31.25pa. ISBN 0-85365-563-4.

Fifty-three mostly British librarians and information scientists presented papers on a wide variety of topics relating to "the nationwide provision and use of information" at this 1980 Joint Conference of Britain's Library Association, Aslib (its special library association), and Institute of Information Scientists. The description of conditions, practices, and issues predominates, with relatively little reporting of actual research. The environment is necessarily British, but most of the issues, if not the details, relate to all highly developed societies.

Papers on information provision consider the role of libraries, industry and research associations, learned societies, commercial suppliers, the mass media, and the academic community in providing information to various segments of society. One of the best theoretical papers focuses on how and why information needs are generated in various types of users. Current issues receiving separate attention include freedom of information, information ownership and control, the impact of technology, and the ethics of information supply. Several papers focus on community information services, the "new technology," information policies, information service for young people, indexing, information service for business, and education for information professionals.

A 13-page index is designed to provide access to "the main and subordinate themes of each paper." Persons quoted are also indexed. Many entries are necessarily compound or complex, but alternative access to such entries is not always provided (e.g., the entry "assessment methods, library school courses" cannot be found under library education or library schools). These proceedings are recommended as a good overview of information provision and use in an emerging "post-industrial," information-dependent society. [R: Indexer, Oct 81, p. 225; LQ, July 82, p. 227; LR, Winter 81, p. 245]   James D. Anderson

1108. Swanson, Don R., and Abraham Bookstein. **Operations Research: Implications for Libraries; The Thirty-Fifth Annual Conference of the Graduate Library School August 2-4, 1971.** Chicago, University of Chicago Press, 1972. 160p. illus. (The University of Chicago Studies in Library Science). $10.00. LC 73-185760. ISBN 0-226-78466-5.

The papers of this conference, originally published in *Library Quarterly* (January 1972), cover such topics as measures of library effectiveness, graph models for library information networks, mathematical programming models, catalog use in large research libraries, etc. A selective bibliography on library operations research, prepared by V. Slamecka, is appended. [R: LJ, 1 Oct 72, p. 3126]

1109. Taylor, Peter J., ed. **New Trends in Documentation and Information: Proceedings of the 39th FID Congress, University of Edinburgh, 25-28 September 1978.** London, published on behalf of FID by Aslib, 1980. 519p. index. (FID Publication, 566). price not reported. ISBN 0-85142-128-8.

These proceedings comprise 60 speeches and contributed papers that range from a keynote address on information pollution, through the theoretical bases, if any, of information/ documentation, to new trends in electronic publishing, telecommunications, computer-output-microform (COM), reprographics, and computer-aided translations; to new classification and information retrieval systems, including the Broad System of Ordering, which appeared of interest to several speakers; to new patterns in the organization and management of information, including measures of effectiveness and cost analyses; to the education of information professionals in both developed and developing countries; to, finally, an outline of a Fédération Internationale de Documentation (FID) Mid-Term Program of action, which would give particular attention to user needs.

Because technological capabilities are well advanced beyond present information applications, and because some international agreements must precede early transferability of data across systems and national borders, the topics discussed in these proceedings must be better understood by more library and information professionals. This collection is important not only to librarians and library school students, but also to members of governments who need to improve their national information systems and their links with other nations' information activities. Included are a list of 291 delegates and a one-page author index. [R: C&RL, Mar 81, p. 167; LQ, Apr 81, p. 214; LR, Winter 80, p. 280]   Richard Palmer

1110. UNESCO and International Council of Scientific Unions. **Unisist: Study Report on the Feasibility of a World Science Information System.** Paris, UNESCO; distr., New York, UNIPUB, 1971. 161p. index. o.p. ISBN 92-3-100881-1.

The result of a joint committee formed in 1967 to investigate areas of cooperation on an international scale. Twenty-two recommendations to implement a worldwide network of scientific information services are presented for consideration by governments, professional organizations, and information service specialists. Although a beginning has been made, "more remains to be done in the 'politicalities' than in the technicalities of information transfer." [R: C&RL, May 72, p. 243; LJ, 1 Jan 72, p. 45]   Charles D. Patterson

1111. Weiss, Edward C., ed. **The Many Faces of Information Science.** Boulder, Colo., published by Westview Press for the American Association for the Advancement of Science, 1977. 128p. bibliog. (AAAS Selected Symposium, 3). o.p. LC 77-12103. ISBN 0-89158-430-7.

Five papers examine various interrelated research issues that reflect different facets of information science as an emerging discipline. The paper by Goffman, "On the Dynamics of Communication," develops a general theory of information transfer by synthesizing the epidemic, genetic, and diffusion models, which were adapted from the disciplines of epidemiology, biology, and physics, respectively. "Development of a Theory of Information Flow and Analysis," by Yovits and Abilock, deals with the development of a general theory of information flow designed to permit the analysis and quantification of information. The theory is concerned with information use in decision-making environments. Sager's paper, "Information Structures in the Language of Science," presents results and computer applications of research into the relation between language structure and information, particularly as it appears in the language of science. "Knowledge Transfer Systems," by Hillman, explores and evaluates the underlying technology for the retrieval of fac-

tual information. It produces a model of a knowledge transfer system designed to enable a scientific user to obtain specific answers concerning an area of research. The final paper, by Pearson and Slamecka, "The Portent of Signs and Symbols," is concerned with semiotics, and the study determines the structure of various types of signs, and the relationship between sign structure and information properties.

It is a pleasure to find a text that successfully consolidates research contributing toward a theoretic foundation for information science. The papers are for the most part nontechnical and provide informative reading for the information scientist and the librarian. The lack of an index does not hinder the use or value of this volume. However, the title is somewhat misleading in that only a few of the many faces of information science are presented. [R: C&RL, Nov 78, p. 499; LJ, 15 Oct 78, p. 2057]

Andrew G. Torok

41 Legislation, Public Policy, and Funding

LEGISLATION AND PUBLIC POLICY

1112. Gardner, Frank M. **Public Library Legislation: A Comparative Study.** Paris, UNESCO; distr., New York, UNIPUB, 1971. 285p. bibliog. (Documentation Libraries and Archives: Studies and Research, No. 2). o.p. LC 72-189344.

This study, commissioned by UNESCO and originally intended to produce a Model Library Act for guidance of developing countries, is the first serious attempt to deal with public library legislation at the international level. Library legislation of 14 countries is surveyed (10 are considered developed and 4 are in the developing stage) and a chapter is devoted to each of these. One conclusion of the study is that problems of an adequate and effective public library law are just as great in the more advanced countries as in the developing ones. [R: LJ, 15 Nov 72, p. 3691]

Charles D. Patterson

1113. **Improving State Aid to Public Libraries.** Prepared for The Urban Libraries Council by the Government Studies and Systems, Inc. Washington, D.C., National Commission on Libraries and Information Science; distr., Washington, D.C., GPO, 1977. 1v. (various paging). bibliog. o.p. S/N 052-003-00325-2.

This report is intended for state legislators and officials as well as library administrators to show the need and value of increased state aid to public libraries. Along with historical background to support this hypothesis, it provides comparative information on various state aid programs, documenting their inadequacies and suggesting strategy for improvements that could be applied in all states. The divergence between aid from state to state, while not surprising, is nonetheless quite interesting. In this era of budgetary problems, librarians could find this information quite valuable for implementing better library aid programs in their own states.

1114. **Into the Information Age: A Perspective for Federal Action on Information.** Vincent Giuliano, project director. Chicago, American Library Association, 1978. 134p. bibliog. $9.00. LC 78-26851. ISBN 0-8389-0283-9.

Written for policymakers and agency managers, this is a report of an NSF grant to study the federal role in the process of facilitating scientific and technical information (STI) flow in the national interest. To establish how information relates to society today, it offers a framework that describes three modes of STI transfer: era I involves discipline-based information systems (e.g., libraries) typical of pure science, academia, and basic research; era II involves mission-based information systems typical of big government-sponsored missions (e.g., NASA); and era III involves problem-based information systems (still being determined) needed to solve societal problems.

The country's existing STI structure (journals, data banks, indexing and abstracting services, and libraries) is superb, but inadequate to meet the requirements of the problem-solving and decision-making processes accompanying many issues today. The federal government has poorly coordinated use of era II models of organization to handle contemporary information needs of era III. Improvement requires an interplay of two change dynamics — a market economy and federally centered resource planning.

The well-organized report gives both a skeletal synopsis of the study and its underlying logic, and a more detailed discussion presented from four viewpoints: that of diagnosis, of issues and problems, of stake holders, and of action. An appendix on information flow and libraries describes the reality of libraries within the publishing and information market, and suggests the era III role these traditional era I institutions need to assume. A short annotated bibliography and a list of resource organizations of interest close the report. Not a reference tool useful for answering specific questions, this is, however, a reference for anyone interested in the broader question of how information can be used to assist in the process of solving social issues problems. [R: C&RL, Sept 79, pp. 465-66; LJ, 1 Sept 79, p. 1634]

Danuta A. Nitecki

1115. Josey, E. J., ed. **Libraries in the Political Process.** Phoenix, Ariz., Oryx Press, 1980. 322p. bibliog. index. (A Neal-Schuman Professional Book). $32.50. LC 80-16996. ISBN 0-912700-25-4.

This thought-provoking and important collection of essays has as its unifying theme that a correct understanding of the political process is essential if librarians are to be able to effectively compete for increasingly scarce governmental resources. Although the book concentrates on public libraries, the techniques discussed may be applied, in some instances, to school and academic libraries. As Cecil Beach points out in "Legislative Support of Library Services in Florida," an understanding of effective lobbying techniques is a necessity for the director of any college library.

There are 27 essays divided into seven sections. The first section, which is concerned with providing a national perspective of legislative support of libraries, contains an essay by Gerald Shields that provides a general overview of the history of federal legislation and American public libraries. The following five sections correspond to the different geographic areas of the United States, and contain essays that provide a workable and functional guide to conducting a successful campaign to develop state-level legislative support programs for libraries. The essay

by Patricia Mautino examines the program in New York, a state that has a history of favorable support to libraries. "Legislative Support of Library Services in North Carolina," by Kenneth Shearer, examines a state in which, prior to 1973, "the public library was viewed in law as an unnecessary social institution and lacked official legislative endorsement." The final section contains such essays as "Harnessing the Mass Media," by Bruce Pomerantz, and "How to Develop a Legislative Workshop," by Atauar Faruquee, which focus on the inauguration of special programs and the development of special skills to overcome problems connected with launching drives for library legislative support. There is a comprehensive index with adequate cross-referencing.

This is a useful reference for library administrators at all levels as well as all those who are concerned with maintaining public support of libraries. [R: BL, 15 Jan 81, p. 669; LJ, 1 Feb 81, p. 315]

Norman Frankel

1116. Ladenson, Alex. **Library Law and Legislation in the United States.** Metuchen, N.J., Scarecrow, 1982. 191p. bibliog. index. (Scarecrow Library Administration Series, No. 1). $14.50. LC 81-23176. ISBN 0-8108-1513-3.

The legal structure of librarianship is certainly of vital significance to library administrators and librarians as well as supporters and users of libraries. Yet, the topic has received limited attention in the professional literature. Under these circumstances alone, *Library Law and Legislation in the United States* would be a welcomed addition to the literature. The publication is especially gratifying, however, because it is so well done.

Beginning with a brief introduction to constitutional, statutory, and administrative law, the book proceeds to outline details of law, legislation, and case history by type of library. For each type, the author presents the historical basis for the law or legislation, the functions of the law, and a comprehensive description of the legal structure in which the library operates.

Other topics which are addressed include federal library legislation, library systems, multitype library cooperation, and special legal problems of concern to libraries. Copyright, library security, and right to privacy are some of these special issues. An appendix contains three model library laws: one for a metropolitan area library authority, one related to library theft, and one on state aid in support of public libraries.

While the book is quite broad and generally thorough in its coverage, there are some omissions. For example, OCLC and CLASS are discussed at length; yet no mention is made of other networks such as RLIN, WLN, SOLI-NET, AMIGOS, PALINET, or INCOLSA. Also, collective bargaining is raised as an issue in the academic library section but not fully discussed here or elsewhere.

Library Law and Legislation in the United States is a very well written and well organized publication. The language is straightforward and clear. Numerous examples of explicit laws and cases are presented throughout the text. In addition, Ladenson, an authority in the field, does not hesitate to recommend policy, suggest trends, and project future developments. The book should be included in all libraries. [R: JAL, Nov 82, pp. 304-5; LJ, 15 Nov 82, p. 2152]
P. Grady Morein

1117. Mason, Marilyn Gell. **The Federal Role in Library and Information Services.** White Plains, N.Y., Knowledge Industry Publications, 1983. 177p. bibliog. index. (Professional Librarian Series). $34.50; $27.50pa. LC 83-11970. ISBN 0-86729-010-2; 0-86729-009-9pa.

The author, well qualified to speak on the subject from previous positions as director of the 1979 White House Conference on Library and Information Services and as a library planner with the Metropolitan Washington, D.C., Council of Governments, has prepared a brief but thorough introduction to the role of the federal government in library and information services. Chapters in the book highlight federal involvement in directly providing library and information services (Library of Congress, National Library of Medicine, National Agricultural Library, National Technical Information Service, etc.), grants-in-aid (Library Services Act, Library Services and Construction Act, Elementary and Secondary Education Act, etc.), and support of library and information service research, and an overview of federal "information policy" (including the Freedom of Information Act and the Privacy Act). There are two short chapters on the 1979 White House Conference and the future of federal involvement with libraries and information services. A short appendix chronicles recent federal information policy activities as reported in the *ALA Washington Newsletter* from 1981 to 1983. In addition to the index there is a selected bibliography.

There is a degree of interpretation in this narrative (certainly in the final chapter on the future of the federal role), but, in all, it is a reasonable, though brief, presentation. It will be useful as an introduction to the subject for beginning students in library education programs (perhaps as a reserve item due to its cost), but it should be supplemented with more thorough treatments of specific subtopics such as Kathleen Molz's *Federal Policy and Library Support* (MIT Press, 1976). [R: BL, 15 Apr 84, p. 1148; WLB, Feb 84, p. 448]
Christopher Albertson

1118. **National Library and Information Services: A Handbook for Planners.** C. V. Penna, D. J. Foskett, and P. H. Sewell, eds. Boston, Butterworths, 1977. 231p. bibliog. index. o.p. LC 76-54296. ISBN 0-408-70818-2.

There is an obvious need for a one-step source on planning library and information services at the national level. This book is not designed for librarians but for laypersons, officials, etc., who are responsible for national policy and program development, including libraries. The material is arranged under six chapters and discusses organizational structure and legislative basis, planning procedures, implementation, etc. The authors are not always familiar with existing American books on certain topics of this subject, as shown in their brief bibliography of sources consulted. Nevertheless, it is an interesting book, and students taking courses in comparative librarianship should be familiar with this title. [R: LJ, Aug 77, p. 1585]

1119. St. Angelo, Douglas, Annie Mary Hartsfield, and Harold Goldstein. **State Library Policy: Its Legislative and Environmental Contexts.** Chicago, American Library Association, 1971. 118p. o.p. LC 71-171256. ISBN 0-8389-0112-3.

Covers the expanded role of the state library agency; the agency in the systems context; patterns of state library activity; agencies and the policy process; and state library development, summary, and challenge. Six appendices and a three-page bibliography are at the end. [R: C&RL, July 72, p. 335; LJ, 15 June 72, p. 2163]

1120. **State Aid: A Survey Report.** Compiled and edited by the ASCLA State Aid Study Committee. Chicago, Association of Specialized and Cooperative Library Agencies/American Library Association, 1982. 123p. bibliog. $20.00 spiralbound. ISBN 0-8389-6526-1.

State aid to public libraries is a high-priority topic for all state librarians. With rising costs there is not enough money from local taxes to carry out the programs that local libraries have initiated. This situation necessitates additional funding from the state. This report by the

State Aid Study Committee of the Association of Specialized and Cooperative Library Agencies surveyed all 50 states in the spring of 1979, with 36 states reporting on their state aid programs. The survey collected information about existing programs, including changes or developments. As a result, a clearinghouse for information about state aid programs was established, and this special report was produced. The report discusses state aid legislation, funded programs, administrative practices, goals, formulas for allocating state aid grants, elibility requirements, and recommended changes. There is a selected three-page bibliography covering state aid to public libraries. The questionnaire that was used in the survey is also included. This report should be useful to all state librarians and should be of interest to public librarians, as well as being an informational document for state legislators who are on state library committees and for governors.

H. Robert Malinowsky

1121. Wellisch, Jean B., and others. **The Public Library and Federal Policy.** Westport, Conn., Greenwood Press, 1974. 349p. illus. bibliog. index. $29.95. LC 73-20302. ISBN 0-8371-7334-5.

This is a foreboding book to pick up for the first time; it feels and looks like a "marriage" (as President Ford would say) between a photocopied Ph.D. thesis and one of those abominable illustration-less books from library school. Once you get past the paper curtain and into the splendid content and organization of it, the format isn't quite so tasteless.

Most impressive about the book is its synthesis of crucial information, which is in three parts: (1) history and status of the public library, (2) synthesis and recommendations, and (3) the appendices. A bewildering array of citations is used to analyze the basis for past public library support; the role of private, local, state, and federal economic help; and the possible projections into the future.

Especially valuable is the analysis (through 1972) of federal and state funding (e.g., revenue sharing and LSCA projects), user studies and evaluation criteria, and the focus on the many factors that may influence the picture in the future (NCLIS, social trends, mass communications, etc.).

I was fascinated by the DELPHI exercise in an appendix. Five panels made up of educators, information and communications technology people, librarians, managers, and social scientists (and others) ranked "potential events" in terms of "probability," "desirability," and

"impact on public libraries." Responses went into columns: "consensus" ("unlikely," "as likely as not," "likely"); "no consensus." And "consensus" was ranked according to "no impact" or "impact." The quixotic thing was that so many responses fell into the "no consensus" columns! Which, I think, recommends the concerns and findings of this volume to the reader, especially to library administrators, library board members, library schools, and interested public officials. [R: AL, June 74, pp. 300-301; LJ, 1 Oct 74, p. 2454]			Donald L. Roberts

FUNDING

1122. Boss, Richard W. **Grant Money and How to Get It: A Handbook for Librarians.** New York, R. R. Bowker, 1980. 138p. bibliog. index. $19.95. LC 80-17880. ISBN 0-8352-1274-2.

Boss, former director of libraries at the University of Tennessee, has put together a guide to the technique of obtaining grant money for libraries. Following a brief introduction are nine chapters: "Sources of Funds"; "Assessing Fund Raising Chances"; "Organizing the Library Resources" (which includes legal and tax aspects); "Where to Look for Potential Fund Sources," a guide to information about foundations and other grantors; "Requesting a Proposal"; "Contacting Funding Sources"; "Developing the Proposal"; "Proposal Submission and Followup"; and "Grants Administration." Each chapter is followed by a section of questions and answers.

Five appendices provide a list of regional collections of reference books provided by The Foundation Center; a list of foundations which have made grants to libraries or have stated interest in so doing; a bibliography of directories of foundations by state; federal sources of grants; and addresses of federal regional centers. There are a glossary and an index.

With only 85 pages of actual text, it seems unnecessary to list on page 38 foundations with a stated interest in libraries and a similar list on page 92 in an appendix. The lists are not identical, which also raises some questions. The sections on organizing the library resources and on the development, submission, and following up of proposals should be particularly helpful. Much of the information in the appendices and in other lists throughout the book should be readily available to most libraries. Nevertheless, the 60 or 70 pages which are the meat of the book may well be worth much more than the price of the book to a successful grantee. [R:

BL, 15 Jan 81, p. 669; JAL, Jan 81, p. 358; LJ, 15 Feb 81, p. 434; RQ, Spring 81, p. 313; SLJ, Oct 81, p. 107] David W. Brunton

1123. Breivik, Patricia Senn, and E. Burr Gibson. **Funding Alternatives for Libraries.** Chicago, American Library Association, 1979. 174p. bibliog. $10.00pa. LC 78-27865. ISBN 0-8389-0273-1.

The fiscal crunch that has descended on libraries in the 1970s has alerted the entire field to the need for special attention in obtaining new sources of revenue. This work, an outgrowth of a 1976 workshop held at the Pratt Institute GSLIS, focuses on methods for libraries to secure financial support from nontraditional sources. Specifically, the emphasis is on procuring private and corporate gifts, with only brief attention paid to governmental funding.

The articles are divided into two areas. One area addresses methods for organizing a fundraising campaign, with factors such as promotional activities, staffing, and record keeping receiving special emphasis. A second area identifies specific categories where potential support is available and suggests alternative methods for securing that support. An especially valuable section concentrates on foundation funding and provides background material on The Foundation Center, source directories, types of foundations and their characteristics, and ideas on developing a proposal.

Funding Alternatives for Libraries certainly fills a void in the library literature on this important topic. The articles are practical and informative, although this effort is not a definitive source for all the phases involved in such a complex endeavor. Useful for any public or academic library administrator seeking to explore new sources of financial assistance. [R: C&RL, Sept 79, p. 484] Frank Wm. Goudy

1124. Corry, Emmett. **Grants for Libraries: A Guide to Public and Private Funding Programs and Proposal Writing Techniques.** Littleton, Colo., Libraries Unlimited, 1982. 240p. illus. index. $22.50. LC 82-20886. ISBN 0-87287-262-9.

Federal library grant programs and foundation grants for school library media programs; college, university, and public libraries; and library and information science programs are described and analyzed in this guide. Contact persons, addresses, and telephone numbers are provided for each program and grant. In addition, step-by-step guidelines for developing and writing a successful proposal are outlined. The

chapter on foundation philanthropy for libraries describes the reference tools and services available from the foundation centers and cooperating collections of foundation information located throughout the country.

Eight appendices provide source material for the grant applicant. A complete listing of 113 federal programs as of FY 1981, with abstracts, application sources, and closing dates, is given for school, college and university, and public libraries. Other appendices include information on the use of the *Catalog of Federal Domestic Assistance*; a list of state coordinators of ESEA programs, together with four sample projects; abstracts of actual grants awarded; and a complete proposal for faculty development in information science. A second edition is available. [R: BL, 15 Oct 82, p. 292; JAL, Nov 82, p. 302]

1125. Frase, Robert William. **Library Funding and Public Support.** Chicago, American Library Association, 1973. 80p. illus. maps. o.p. LC 73-17396. ISBN 0-8389-3150-2.

This publication provides a statement regarding the scope and severity of the problems confronting U.S. libraries because of the withdrawal of federal support. The potential of revenue sharing is evaluated as a possible substitute and found to be ineffective.

It is brought to our attention that books and journals lead other media in conveying intellectual and practical knowledge to the public. Also, that the United States is one of the chief exporters of printed materials abroad. Skyrocketing postal rates will have devastating effects on the acquisition and dissemination of these materials unless some relief is provided.

Tables, charts, and supporting documents are included throughout to illustrate and verify statements made regarding the status of libraries. Four important source documents are: Eileen D. Cooke's testimony before a subcommittee of the House of Representatives; a statement to the president and U.S. Senate by a group of concerned citizens experienced in the field of communications; the ALA Resolution to the U.S. Congress on 30 January 1973; and the Memorandum of the Association of American University Presses.

The information presented would be of interest to anyone concerned with library funding. The book's clearcut case for public support of libraries and its demonstration of the results of cutbacks remains valid. [R: LJ, 1 May 74, p. 1279] Marilyn Strong Noronha

42   Library Instruction

GENERAL WORKS

1126.   Beaubien, Anne K., Sharon A. Hogan, and Mary W. George. **Learning the Library: Concepts and Methods for Effective Bibliographic Instruction.** New York, R. R. Bowker, 1982. 269p. bibliog. index. $39.95. LC 82-4262. ISBN 0-8352-1505-9.

A how-to book on bibliographic instruction, *Learning the Library* is aimed at a broad audience: library school students, librarians contemplating developing a BI program, and librarians already involved in BI work. It was published as a companion to the more theoretical *Theories of Bibliographic Education* (see *ARBA* 83, entry 256), but stands on its own.

The book's four-part structure opens with a survey of the environment in which a BI program must develop. Lists of questions that front-line librarians and administrators must answer before planning a program cover the institution, the potential audience, the program objectives, and selecting a mode or modes of instruction. Despite the authors' claim that their advice can be applied to various types of libraries, little of it has applicability outside four-year colleges and universities. The second part attempts to establish a theoretical base for BI, taking as its starting point Michael Keresztesi's model of a discipline's development as an indicator of the extent and depth of development of its bibliographic tools. One doubts the claim that this can be used as an instrument in instruction with any but very advanced undergraduate and graduate students since it assumes an appreciation on the student's part of the discipline's development and its internal information transfer dynamics. Such an approach surely requires considerable watering down and explanation by

the BI librarian, especially if used in a single lecture. The "one-shot" lecture and practical approaches to planning it form the bulk of the third part, along with similar discussion of separate BI courses. The fourth part, on how to implement a BI program, its costs, and the role of the library administration in BI, resembles the first in its thorough litanies of practical questions which must be answered.

Learning the Library can help reference and BI librarians analyze activities they perform and assumptions they make instinctively when advising users on search strategy. By studying its applications of Keresztesi's model to the humanities and the social sciences, librarians can sharpen their understanding of why they do what they do the way they do. Such analysis of the research process is, of course, essential in planning effective BI programs. To this extent the book can and does have value to public service librarians outside academe. [R: BL, 15 Oct 82, p. 292; LJ, 15 Oct 82, p. 1954]

James Rettig

1127.   Freedman, Janet L., and Harold A. Bantly. **Information Searching: A Handbook for Designing & Creating Instructional Programs.** rev. ed. Metuchen, N.J., Scarecrow, 1982. 198p. index. $16.00. LC 81-21417. ISBN 0-8108-1509-5.

The first edition of this book was published in 1979 by the Board of Commissions. This revised edition by two academic-oriented authors provides a simple approach for developing instructional programs in library skills. The authors state that the process is useful for all types of libraries. However, most examples and activities would be more helpful for academic settings or more mature public library patrons. This guide reviews needs assessment, program development, approaches and methods, and program evaluation for introducing and teaching library skills. In the section "Program Potpourri," there are 11 pathfinder guide examples. These may be used as models for developing search strategies in a number of subjects. There are seven complete scripts which librarians or library media specialists might adapt. Most useful for instruction are the subject-related units and the complete course syllabus for information searching. A final section includes references to other guides useful in teaching. Educational libraries and library schools will want to purchase this for workshop use. [R: JAL, Sept 82, p. 243]

Paula Montgomery

1128. Lubans, John, Jr. **Educating the Library User.** New York, R. R. Bowker, 1974. 445p. bibliog. o.p. LC 74-11794. ISBN 0-8352-0674-2.

The 39 original essays, case studies, and reports in this collection cover three topics: the rationale for educating library users, the problems of faculty involvement in library-use instruction, and the implementation and evaluation of library-use instruction programs. The authors represent a wide range of library specialties and the essays are concerned with educational libraries at every level, including graduate school. Subjects vary from developing programs for two-year colleges to the usefulness of library-use tests to problems of faculty involvement. Just as various are the authors' attitudes — from whole-hearted support of library-use programs to veiled pessimism about their possible success. Most articles include bibliographies, and the book concludes with an exhaustive list of reports on library-use instruction. While the collection is not a text, its authoritative reports should interest every librarian. [R: AL, Mar 75, p. 170; C&RL, May 75, p. 233; CLW, May 75, p. 450; JAL, May 75, p. 46; LJ, 1 Mar 75, p. 458; RQ, Fall 75, p. 88; RSR, Jan 75, pp. 30 and 118; SLJ, Apr 75, p. 37]

Nancy P. Schneider

1129. Lubans, John, Jr., ed. **Progress in Educating the Library User.** New York, R. R. Bowker, 1978. 230p. bibliog. index. $15.95. LC 78-12758. ISBN 0-8352-1102-9.

Interest in providing library instruction to users of the library has been great during the past years, as this book's 11-page bibliography illustrates. Almost all of the more than 200 entries were published between 1974 and 1978.

This volume updates *Educating the Library User* (see *ARBA* 75, entry 237), published in 1974. Of the fifteen original papers included, eight review events in all types of libraries, from elementary schools through adult education programs. Other articles review research in the field; the library school's role; developments in British, Canadian, and Scandinavian libraries; and the use of traveling workshops. The introductory essay, written by the editor, provides an overview and discusses how to establish a "partnership" between teachers and librarians. The volume provides an interesting and adequate review of progress and developments in this field. [R: C&RL, July 79, p. 362; JAL, May 79, p. 97; LJ, 1 Mar 79, p. 569]

G. Edward Evans

1130. Rader, Hannelore B., ed. **Library Instruction in the Seventies: State of the Art.** Ann Arbor, Mich., published for the Center of Educational Resources, Eastern Michigan University by Pierian Press, 1977. 130p. illus. (Library Orientation Series, No. 7). $19.50. LC 77-75678. ISBN 0-87650-078-5.

This volume collects the papers presented at the sixth annual Conference on Library Orientation for Academic Libraries, held at Eastern Michigan University, 13-14 May 1976. The papers vary in quality and informational content. Luckily, the longer papers are the best. Sheila M. Laidlaw opens the collection with an excellent survey of the various approaches used in academic libraries to teach library use skills to students. Thomas Kirk concentrates on one of the more promising approaches, course-related instruction, discussing historical as well as current ideas and practices. Richard H. Dewey focuses on the use of self-teaching guides or workbooks and describes their use in Montreal and in Cairo, Egypt. He includes a copy of the guide he used at the American University in Cairo. Shorter papers report experiences and problems in specific institutions and the difficulties of testing and surveying participants and evaluating results of library use instruction. Unfortunately, these latter papers are too brief to do more than indicate problems. Carolyn Kirkendall describes the activities of Project LOEX, a clearing house for information and sample instructional materials. The volume concludes with Hannelore B. Rader's useful annotated list of books and articles on library use instruction through 1975, reprinted from *Reference Services Review* (vol. 4, no. 4, October/December 1976, pp. 91-93).

Parts of this volume will be useful for library school students and faculty and for all librarians concerned with this vital aspect of reference/information service. [R: C&RL, Jan 78, p. 65; CLW, Feb 78, p. 311; JAL, July 78, p. 163; LQ, Apr 78, p. 218]

James D. Anderson

1131. Renford, Beverly, and Linnea Hendrickson. **Bibliographic Instruction: A Handbook.** New York, Neal-Schuman, 1980. 192p. illus. bibliog. index. $24.95. LC 80-12300. ISBN 0-918212-24-3.

Bibliographic instruction in libraries is a service of major importance, but the activity often lacks formal organization and sometimes haas weak results. The Renford/Hendrickson "handbook" is designed to provide the basics of organized library-user education programs and to improve existing programs. Library instruction areas include orientation, printed guides, materials for courses, workbooks, computer-assisted instruction, and audiovisual equipment. Basic and complex materials are included and discussed, and each chapter has a list of additional readings which add a rich source of both general and specific materials. The clearly written and developmental text addresses questions and concerns involved in training programs, such as analyzing user needs, establishing goals and objectives, designing steps to meet these ends, gaining staff support, and convincing administration of the program's value.

The book is designed for academic libraries, but many points can eaily be transferred to other situations. The intended audience is the librarian rather than the library user, and this is not a how-to-use-the-library approach. The printing is clear and the paper is firm and strong, but the "perfect" binding and the paperback cover may be drawbacks, especially when the text is heavily used. This is an excellent small volume which provides a strong framework for a library's program of training users to use collections with intelligence and effective results. [R: C&RL, May 81, p. 270; CLW, Feb 81, p. 313; JAL, July 81, p. 177; RSR, Apr 81, p. 70]

Neal L. Edgar

1132. Rice, James, Jr. **Teaching Library Use: A Guide for Library Instruction.** Westport, Conn., Greenwood Press, 1981. 169p. bibliog. index. (Contributions in Librarianship and Information Science, No. 37). $27.50. LC 80-21337. ISBN 0-313-21485-9.

The stated intent of the author is "to help librarians, media specialists, and teachers design library instruction programs at any educational level." Even though most of the examples given in the text and nearly half the bibliographic

citations relate to college and universities, transference to other types of libraries should not be difficult.

The book provides an overview and general discussion of the areas to be considered and dealt with in developing a formal library instruction program. It does not provide a detailed instructional program or plan. The user will have to employ resources such as those listed by the author in the text and appendices to develop these. Areas addressed by the author are getting people involved, planning an instructional program, testing and evaluation, instruction through library design, and strategies for library orientation, library instruction, and bibliographic instruction.

The chapters dealing with planning an instructional program (chapter 3) and testing and evaluation (chapter 7) are well done. The first deals with the instructional cycle, which begins with identifying goals and objectives and ends with testing, evaluation, and feedback. The second deals with developing tests, questionnaires, and evaluation of the instructional program. The final chapter, "Library Instruction through the Library's Design," fails to clearly define the connection between library design and instruction. [R: JAL, Sept 82, p. 230; LJ, 1 Mar 82, p. 527]

Donald C. Adcock

1133. Roberts, Anne F. **Library Instruction for Librarians.** Littleton, Colo., Libraries Unlimited, 1982. 159p. bibliog. (Library Science Text Series). $26.00; $18.50pa. LC 82-13997. ISBN 0-87287-298-X; 0-87287-331-5pa.

The purpose of this text is to introduce and familiarize both library school students and practitioners with the subject of library instruction and to offer techniques on how to set up, organize, implement, manage, and evaluate a library instruction program. Background information includes a review of the literature and a description of the state of the art. Orientation, teaching, and concepts and structures are covered in discussing the implementation of library instruction programs. Methods and modes are thoroughly explored, presenting the advantages and disadvantages for each method, such as tours, formal courses, course-integrated structure, seminars, mini-courses in library instruction, and computer-assisted instruction, as well as samples used in actual library instruction programs. Most chapters end with lists of suggested assignments and readings designed to reinforce the concepts presented. [R: BL, 15 Jan 83, p. 657; JAL, May 83, p. 93; JAL, Jan 83, p. 373; LJ, 15 Mar 83, p. 564; RQ, Spring 83, p. 321; WLB, Dec 82, p. 344]

1134. Schuster, Marie. **The Library-Centered Approach to Learning.** Palm Springs, Calif., ETC Publications, 1977. 112p. bibliog. index. $9.95. LC 76-54328. ISBN 0-88280-047-7.

The library-centered concept of learning is independent study at the individual's pace in the library rather than group teaching at an average rate in the classroom. Promoters of this concept feel that no matter what people learn, they do it on their own and in a manner that has meaning to them; therefore, the library-centered concept is needed because it is capable of challenging a student as far as he or she wants to go. Marie Schuster does not point out, however, that some students cannot cope with the freedom of independent study but need the traditional structured classroom.

In a philosophical narrative, Schuster shows the importance of the learning facilitator, the learning environment, and the library-centered approach to learning in primary school, junior high school, and college. She explains how the library-centered approach to learning provides wholeness in the learning process, how reading is an experience of wholeness, how writing is a personal response, how one learns through insight, and the learner's transcendental nature. She fails to point out that faculty must make the library an integral part of the educational process to make this concept work. The library will then be thought of as a center for learning rather than a place where students can study their textbooks.

Kathleen J. Voigt

REFERENCE WORKS

1135. Lockwood, Deborah L., comp. **Library Instruction: A Bibliography.** Westport, Conn., Greenwood Press, 1979. 166p. index. $27.50. LC 78-20011. ISBN 0-313-20720-8.

An important part of a librarian's job is to instruct patrons in the use of library materials. To assist librarians in this function, Deborah Lockwood has prepared a bibliography that provides sources of information about library instruction. The book lists hundreds of titles of books, articles, and other publications that should be of value to librarians and students of library science who are developing instruction programs.

The material is arranged in three major sections: general philosophy, types of libraries, and teaching methods and formats. Each item is annotated, and frequent cross-references are furnished. There is an author index. Inclusion of material was selective, according to the compiler, with the following criteria observed: (1) only items in English are included; (2) coverage of items published before 1970 is selective; and (3) the material must be published or available in the ERIC system and be written for the librarian developing a program, not for the patron who is learning to use the library. The ultimate objective here is to develop extensive use of libraries by educating patrons in the use of library materials and services. Deborah Lockwood's experience as a reference librarian at Indiana University and at George Washington University has given her the background to produce this book, which will be invaluable to librarians. [R: C&RL, July 79, pp. 387-88; JAL, July 79, p. 172; LJ, 15 May 79, p. 1121; RQ, Fall 79, pp. 87-88]

Martha Boaz

PROCEEDINGS, SYMPOSIA, AND ESSAYS

1136. Atkinson, Ross, ed. **Back to the Books: Bibliographic Instruction and the Theory of Information Sources: Papers Presented at the 101st Annual Conference of the American Library Association, ACRL—Bibliographic Instruction Section.** Chicago, Association of College and Research Libraries, American Library Association, 1983. 76p. $15.00 spiralbound; $12.00 spiralbound (ACRL members). ISBN 0-8389-6587-3.

The volume contains four papers and a summary delivered 11 July 1982, at the annual program meeting of the Bibliographic Instruction Section of the Association of College and Research Libraries. The primary purpose of the papers was to relate bibliographic theory to bibliographic instruction. The papers are: "Pragmatic Bibliography," by Patrick Wilson; "Bibliographic Instruction as a Liberal Art: An Application of Patrick Wilson's Theory of Pragmatic Bibliography," by Frances Hopkins; "On the Nature of Literatures: A Synergetic Attempt," by Conrad Rawski; and "Shaping a Bibliographic Instruction Program for Undergraduate Science Students: Application of a Model of the Structure of the Scientific Literature," by Thomas Kirk. The papers contain references, and for the most part they provide interesting reading.

Although one might question the price for such a flimsily constructed and reproduced volume, it should be a part of library school collections. [R: JAL, Sept 83, p. 228; RQ, Fall 83, p. 115]

Andrew G. Torok

1137. Beeler, Richard J., ed. **Evaluating Library Use Instruction: Papers Presented at the University of Denver Conference on the Evaluation of Library Instruction, December 13-14, 1973.** Ann Arbor, Mich., Pierian Press, 1975. 97p. (Library Orientation Series, No. 6). o.p. LC 75-677. ISBN 0-87650-062-9.

This is an anthology of papers of varying quality pertaining to library use instruction. It contains summaries of instructional programs at various institutions (the panelists included Patricia Culkin, Betty Hacker, Richard Stevens, and others). The first two papers, by Thomas Kirk and Richard Johnson, are probably the most interesting — this is particularly true of Johnson's, which investigates the methodology of data collecting. Rowena Swanson's piece on questionnaire design is rather disappointing; this author can do much better. As we all know, meditation is good for the body as well as for the soul; the topic of this conference is indeed interesting. [R: C&RL, May 76, pp. 280-81; RQ, Summer 76, p. 367]   Bohdan S. Wynar

1138. Kirkendall, Carolyn A., ed. **Reform and Renewal in Higher Education: Implications for Library Instruction: Papers Presented at the Ninth Annual Conference on Library Orientation for Academic Libraries Held at Eastern Michigan University, May 3-4, 1979.** Ann Arbor, Mich., published for the Center of Educational Resources, Eastern Michigan University by Pierian Press, 1980. 126p. (Library Orientation Series). $19.50. LC 80-81485. ISBN 0-87650-124-2.

As libraries grew in size, they also became more complicated and difficult to use. During the 1970s, the necessity for an effective program of instruction in the use of the library at all levels became apparent to librarians. One result has been the annual Conference on Library Orientation held at Eastern Michigan University since 1971. The volume under review is the ninth in the series of papers presented at these conferences.

The Ninth Annual Conference began with the assumption that library instruction will be conditioned by changes and reforms in higher education itself, including the back-to-basics movement. The speakers represented the major types of academic libraries: university, liberal arts college, and community college. The majority of those attending the conference were reference librarians and "instructional services" librarians. They were a "grass roots" audience, and the speakers pitched their remarks accordingly. Richard M. Dougherty sounded a warning that with the prospect of tighter budgets,

librarians may have to cut back on some services in order to give top priority to bibliographic instruction and database searching. Ruth Foley went to the heart of the subject, saying that library instruction programs will succeed only with faculty commitment and involvement. Current professional interest in library instruction was reflected in an appended bibliography with 133 entries published during 1977 and 1978.

Because of its broad coverage and subject content, this volume is recommended for libraries of every type. [R: JAL, Sept 80, p. 240]

Thomas S. Harding

1139. MacCafferty, Maxine, ed. **User Education: Towards a Better Use of Information Resources; Proceedings of the Eusidic Conference, Graz, 1st-3rd December, 1976.** London, Aslib, 1977. 139p. illus. $18.00pa. ISBN 0-85142-096-6.

These proceedings offer a collection of papers on problems of education in the use of machine-readable databases. Organized into five sessions, the 15 papers contributed from 10 countries include descriptive reports and research summaries.

M. E. Williams's keynote address, "Education & Training for Online Use of Data Bases," reviews both training and marketing issues. Session 1, "Education of Future Users," includes summaries of university-level user training for information retrieval in both France (Rozensztroch) and Denmark (Sabsay). Session 2 papers discuss "User Aids" from the perspectives of a large industrial user (Schulkes), a commercial producer (Collier), and an academic user (Haarala). Session 3, "Education in the Use of Specific Data Bases," reflects commercial marketing interests (Elias), a future-oriented perception of potential nonusers (Lea), and an information center's workshop experiences (Thiriet). Session 4 presents two papers (Roraas and Leirnes) on "Education in the Use of Specific Systems in Scandinavia." Session 5, "Review of Current Information Education Activities in Selected Countries," highlights Hungary (Schiff), Spain (Alverez-Ossorio), Austria (Fischer), and the worldwide efforts of UNESCO/UNISIST (Tocatlian). Additional information sources include several citation lists and an address list of the 109 international participants.

These proceedings sample observations and suggestions for training and marketing in a field where rapid change, widespread impact, and required skills demand that attention be given to user education.

Danuta A. Nitecki

1140. Oberman-Soroka, Cerise, ed. **Proceedings from the 2nd Southeastern Conference on Approaches to Bibliographic Instruction, March 22-23, 1979.** Charleston, S.C., College of Charleston Library Associates, 1980. 71p. o.p.

Experts on bibliographic instruction met to discuss the methodology and implementation of bibliographic instruction. The purpose of their presentation was to clarify some of the issues facing the practice of this art. Ann Roberts described the politics of library instruction within the profession, within the institution, and within the library itself. Hazards such as rocking the boat, drinking coffee with the wrong person, or the difficulties caused by not including the right people in planning the program are identified. Articles on designing a credit-bearing course combining instruction with specific research, on class-related bibliographic instruction, the benefits of integrating bibliographic instructions into the academic curriculum, and the self-paced workbook method are viewed with both benefits and drawbacks pointed out.

Dare, in his article "Integrated Library Instruction: Abdicating Responsibility," serves as a devil's advocate and asks, "Is being a librarian not enough? Why should one give up being a skilled librarian to become a semi-skilled teacher?" The final article is a plea for a clear view of what bibliographic instruction is and what it is not.

The proceedings are organized as a whole, beginning with a description of political environments, going on to types of instructional modes, and concluding with articles demanding a justification for bibliographic instruction, which brings us back full circle to the political environment. Not an introduction to bibliographic instruction, this is of considerable worth to the more experienced practitioner who needs to know what the program options are and how to implement them. This was the stated purpose of the conference planners, and it has been accomplished. [R: C&RL, Sept 80, pp. 482-83; JAL, Sept 80, p. 242; LJ, Aug 80, p. 1613]

Ann E. Prentice

1141. **Theories of Bibliographic Education: Designs for Teaching.** Cerise Oberman and Katina Strauch, eds. New York, R. R. Bowker, 1982. bibliog. index. $39.95. LC 82-4270. ISBN 0-8352-1506-7.

Most of the essays in this carefully crafted compilation take a cue, in one way or another, from Michael Keresztesi's opening argument for a science of bibliography which examines and explains the vehicles by which scholars in the various disciplines communicate among themselves. He facilely develops its implications for bibliographic instruction and library science in general. Others posit theoretical considerations and relate them to existing and possible bibliographic instruction practice. Especially exciting among these is Jon Lindgren's proposal that bibliographic inquiry approach the records retrieved as pieces of evidence in argument rather than as just so many citations. It offers an excellent basis for fuller integration of academic library instruction into freshman research paper English courses.

Keresztesi, Lindgren, and Raymond McInnis's discussions of bibliographic records as metaphors for bibliographic entities are the highlights. Development of implications for practice in the others is not as thorough or is obscured by too much description of particular implementation programs. For example, Constance Mellon's essay does not do enough with the implications of her explanation of the developmental stages of the audience to be taught. Only one of the essays—Williams and Davis's survey of computer-assisted instruction—does not fit with the rest, being more a history than an exposition of theoretical concerns. The topic is apt, however.

The selective bibliography is too selective. Putting aside this shortcoming and the inevitable unevenness of such collections, *Theories of Bibliographic Education* is essential reading for anyone who wants to plan any sort of bibliographic instruction program on a sound theoretical foundation. Its companion, *Learning the Library* (see *ARBA* 83, entry 248), will help them in their practical planning. [R: JAL, Sept 82, p. 244; LJ, 15 Oct 82, p. 1954]

James Rettig

1142. Trinkner, Charles L., ed. **Teaching for Better Use of Libraries.** Hamden, Conn., Archon, 1969. 344p. index. o.p. LC 73-99445.

This collection is a good starting point for those librarians and teachers interested in the teaching function of the library. There are 57 articles covering the period in the literature from 1949 to 1958 and primarily concerned with programs of instruction in school libraries but at least one-third of the articles pertain to working with college and university students. The points of view represented come from the pages of most of the significant professional library and educational journals in the United States. As one would expect in a collection of this sort much of the writing is trite and even bland. However, this need not take away from the effectiveness of the volume as a source of readings for library school students, both graduate and undergraduate, and as an addition to the professional collections in school and academic libraries. [R: LJ, 1 Sept 70, p. 2775; WLB, Sept 70, p. 89]   M. M. Jackson

COLLEGE AND UNIVERSITY

1143. Breivik, Patricia Senn. **Planning the Library Instruction Program.** Chicago, American Library Association, 1982. 146p. illus. bibliog. index. $10.00pa. LC 82-8827. ISBN 0-8389-0358-4.

In this concise and well-organized document, the author presents the specifics for providing library instruction to students through an academic library. Breivik begins with a rationale for library instruction based on six elements of high-quality learning. The politics of obtaining support for an instructional program from library staff, the library director, faculty, administrators, and students are carefully delineated. Eight chapters follow that deal with setting program goals and objectives, group needs, priorities, methodologies, content, time, grouping, and characteristics of good library instruction. There are charts that are useful in working with each of these topics and many suggestions for successful student and program evaluations. The book is geared toward adult education and is "traditional" in its approach to library skills instruction. The library coursework is considered as a subject in itself. It does present a sound, rational structure for this type of approach. Notes are extensive. This publication will be of use primarily to college and university librarians involved in bibliographic or library instruction programs. [R: BL, 15 Jan 83, pp. 656-57; C&RL, Nov 83, pp. 493-94; JAL, Jan 83, p. 372; JAL, May 83, p. 94; LJ, 15 Mar 83, p. 564; RQ, Spring 83, p. 321]
Paula Montgomery

1144. Cammack, Floyd M., Marri DeCosin, and Norman Roberts. **Community College Library Instruction: Training for Self-Reliance in Basic Library Use.** Hamden, Conn., Linnet Books, 1979. 283p. illus. bibliog. index. $22.50. LC 79-17531. ISBN 0-208-01825-5.

The scope and usefulness of this book are much broader than the title indicates. Part 1, in three chapters, describes the procedures used at Leeward Community College, Pearl City, Hawaii, to organize and implement a library instruction unit in a basic English course required of all students. These chapters review the establishment of guidelines, goals, and objectives, as well as program development and evaluation. Part 2, also composed of three chapters, includes actual samples of teaching and testing materials for four sections of instruction: the library tour, the card catalog, library subject headings, and periodicals and periodical indexes. The appendices include flow charts, sample memoranda, and other useful items.

Of special significance is the fact that the "copyright is ... waived for all sample materials included in part 2 and the appendixes to this volume" (p. 15). This fact alone makes the book worth purchasing; however, the major advantage of the work is that the program described has been developed, implemented, tested, repeatedly revised, and proven successful. The authors state that "from next-to-no knowledge about library use, the average student completing the library unit reached the 80 percent level prescribed as the satisfactory performance objective" (p. 79).

This book is recommended for all academic librarians, whether in two-year or four-year colleges, who are currently teaching library instruction units or who are contemplating doing so. As an aside to administrators who wish to see such programs implemented in their libraries, they should be made aware of the fact that the authors recommend a 30 percent allocation of staff time in order to implement an effective teaching program in the library. [R: C&RL, July 80, pp. 378-79; LJ, 1 Jan 80, p. 80]
Doris Cruger Dale

1145. **A Comprehensive Program of User Education for the General Libraries, the University of Texas at Austin.** Austin, Tex., University of Texas, General Libraries, 1977. 1v. (various paging). (Contributions to Librarianship, No. 1). $5.00pa.

To lay "a foundation for improved user services including the development of a more comprehensive user education program" was the goal of this pilot project developed at the University of Texas at Austin during 1975-1976. Although largely untested and not to be fully implemented until 1979, the user education program was published to help other libraries develop similar programs. As an initial step, the User Education Committee designed and implemented two questionnaires to learn the requirements of students for library instruction and the opinions of students and faculty as to the types of instruction needed. Results of this study are included. Effectiveness of existing user education activities was analyzed in preparation for planning the expanded program. Finally, a three-part, three-year implementation was

designed: establishment of an educational resource center in the new library building; development of pilot programs for bibliographic instruction and orientation and for support among faculty and students for an expanded program; and, in the third year, full implementation of the user education program. Appendices comprise half the book, including student and faculty questionnaires, report forms for evaluating user education sessions, and a list of the program's objectives and goals. The full documentation of this ambitious project will help other libraries plan similar programs. [R: JAL, July 77, p. 172; LJ, 1 Sept 77, p. 1737]
Janet H. Littlefield

1146. Evaluating Bibliographic Instruction: A Handbook. Chicago, Bibliographic Instruction Section, Association of College and Research Libraries, American Library Association, 1983. 122p. bibliog. index. $17.00pa.; $13.00pa. (members). ISBN 0-8389-6608-X.

The handbook is intended to help people inexperienced in research methods to devise a formal approach to evaluating programs in bibliographic instruction so that objective, reliable, and useful information will result. The authors make the point that the handbook is only an introduction to the topic and that further reading is advisable, but that the evaluation process need not be complex.

Initial chapters supply an overview of the process and the reasons for evaluation. Subsequent chapters cover goals and objectives, choice and design of an appropriate procedure, ways to gather data, and methods of analyzing the resulting statistics. Finally, there are a review of previous evaluative studies, a glossary of research terms, a bibliography, and an index. Each of these is done by a different person, some of them members of the sponsoring committee. All apply educational research methods specifically to bibliographic instruction. [R: JAL, Nov 83, p. 304]   Kathleen McCullough

1147. Hardesty, Larry L. **Use of Slide/Tape Presentations in Academic Libraries.** New York, Jeffrey Norton Publishers, 1978. 222p. illus. bibliog. index. $8.95pa. LC 77-9215. ISBN 0-88432-006-5.

Many academic libraries have been experimenting with slide/tape as a possible solution to the problem of teaching large numbers of students how to use the library. Based on two surveys (129 libraries in the first, 193 in the second), this book presents a review of the use of slide/tape for library instruction and orientation in academic libraries.

Following a description of the surveys and their results, two sections ("Instruction" and "Orientation") provide information on specific slide/tape programs used in 136 individual academic libraries. Included for each library is a list of their slide/tape productions (including their length, number of viewers in the last year, and where and how used; how the programs were produced—by audiovisual specialists, librarians, etc.; the cost in money and time; whether and how they have been evaluated; their usefulness and availability to other libraries; the equipment used; and usually some additional comments from the producing library). Included with the instruction programs are some presentations consisting of audio tapes and sample pages, as well as some slide/tapes designed to train student library workers. Another chapter, written by John Murphy, presents six common faults of sound/slide presentations. A selected bibliography, a description of the British SCONUL group for slide/tape guides, and a directory of information sources for library instruction complete this work. Since slide/tapes are not always inexpensive to make, the author feels that academic librarians' efforts in this area should be shared. This reference book greatly aids, and hopefully will encourage, such cooperation among academic libraries. [R: C&RL, Nov 78, p. 513; LJ, 1 Oct 78, p. 1930]
Judith M. Pask

1148. Kirk, Thomas, comp. **Course-Related Library and Literature-Use Instruction: Working Models for Programs in Undergraduate Science Education.** New York, Jeffrey Norton Publishers, 1978. 31p. 11 microfiche. illus. index. $14.95. LC 79-64352. ISBN 0-88432-013-8.

Earlham College, long known for its commitment to course-integrated library instruction, conducted a series of workshops during 1976-1977 for librarians and faculty engaged in undergraduate science education. Twelve colleges and universities sent librarian-faculty teams to Earlham, where they were exposed to the precepts of integrated library instruction and planned a course of instruction for their institutions. Workshop goals and brief descriptions of the projects are provided in 27 typeset pages. Full reports of the projects, including objectives, instructional materials, and student work, are found in 11 microfiche cards jacketed at the end of the volume. The microfiche are of excellent technical quality, and the information contained in these reports should find an appreciative audience among library instruction practitioners. [R: C&RL, Nov 79, p. 576; LQ, Jan 80, p. 178]   Arthur P. Young

1149.   Kirkendall, Carolyn A., ed. **Directions for the Decade: Library Instruction in the 1980s: Papers Presented at the Tenth Annual Conference on Library Orientation for Academic Libraries Held at Eastern Michigan University, May 8-9, 1980.** Ann Arbor, Mich., published for the Center of Educational Resources, Eastern Michigan University by Pierian Press, 1981. 160p. (Library Orientation Series, No. 12). $19.50. LC 81-80191. ISBN 0-87650-131-5.

Directions for the Decade is a collection of papers that were presented at the Tenth Annual Conference on Library Orientation for Academic Libraries, which was held at East Michigan University in May 1980. The contributing participants considered both the accomplishments and the goals for the future of academic library instruction.

Included in the formal presentations are such topics as assessing library instruction, bibliographic instruction as an emerging professional discipline, and politics and personalities. The special section entitled "Post-Prandial Reactions" includes helpful discussions on the library administrator's role in library instruction, instruction librarians as a possible barrier to information, the necessity of the details of conducting research for today's college students, the eventual acceptance of library instruction, and whether or not students really need to know how to use the library.

In addition to the papers themselves, the notes and bibliographical materials at the ends of the chapters will be most useful to those who are involved in library instruction; and in the appendix, Hannelore B. Rader has contributed a 32-page annotated bibliography entitled "Library Orientation and Instruction – 1979," which includes source material for community college libraries, college and university libraries, public libraries, school libraries, special libraries and groups, and for all levels.

Jefferson D. Caskey

1150.   Kirkendall, Carolyn A., ed. **Improving Library Instruction: How to Teach and How to Evaluate; Papers Presented at the Eighth Annual Conference on Library Orientation for Academic Libraries Held at Eastern Michigan University, May 4-5, 1978.** Ann Arbor, Mich., published for the Center of Educational Resources, Eastern Michigan University, by Pierian Press, 1979. 142p. (Library Orientation Series, No. 9). $19.50. LC 79-87707. ISBN 0-87650-109-9.

Library instruction continues to be a vital concern of many academic librarians, so it is good to see the publication of another volume in Pierian Press's Library Orientation series. The focus this time is on the basic methods of teaching library usage and testing the effectiveness of those methods. A panel of three librarians presents brief reports on instruction used at different types of academic libraries, while a second panel describes three methods of evaluation. These are all useful examples and can serve as preliminary models for libraries establishing such programs; however, none of them provide enough detail to be truly effective models. One would hope that the library orientation conferences would elicit a few fully documented papers, comparable to the fine article by Shelley Phipps and Ruth Dickstein published in the *Journal of Academic Librarianship* ("The Library Skills Program at the University of Arizona: Testing, Evaluation, and Critique," *JAL* 5 [September 1979]: 205-14).

The most substantial speeches collected in this volume are concerned with the broad area of library instruction. Larry Hardesty deals, in considerable detail, with the nature of bibliographic instruction and the historic development of instructional programs in libraries. Hardesty contends that faculty acceptance of library use as "a viable instructional method" is the key factor in the success of bibliographic instruction. This paper is the heart of the collection (19 pages long, with ample footnotes) and deserves to be widely read. Other highly recommended pieces are Israel Woronoff's "Perceptives on Learning and Motivation" (a general survey of learning theories, which features an amusing comparison of library orientation with military boot camp), and Edward G. Holley's perceptive overview of library instruction and its crucial importance to the small liberal arts college.

As with previous volumes in the series, *Improving Library Instruction* contains a brief report on Project LOEX by Carolyn Kirkendall, and Hannelore Rader's annotated bibliography of relevant items published in 1977. Most academic libraries should purchase this volume as a supplement to the invaluable works by John Lubans (*Educating the Library User*, see *ARBA* 75, entry 237; and *Progress in Educating the Library User*, see *ARBA* 79, entry 291). Faculty members especially need to be aware of this series, so its use must not be restricted to the reference or professional collections. [R: CLW, Feb 80, p. 307; JAL, May 80, p. 98; LQ, Apr 80, p. 279]

Thomas A. Karel

1151.   Kirkendall, Carolyn A., ed. **Putting Library Instruction in Its Place: In the Library and in the Library School; Papers Presented at** the Seventh Annual Conference on Library Orientation for Academic Libraries Held at Eastern Michigan University, May 12-13, 1977. Ann Arbor, Mich., Pierian Press, 1978. 108p. (Library Orientation Series, No. 8). $19.50. LC 78-53996. ISBN 0-87650-092-0.

This seventh conference has given birth to an unusually strong collection that has practical value for librarians planning programs of instruction. Joseph A. Boisé offers an enlightening look at the fragile link between the academic administrative structure and bibliographic instruction programs. Joyce A. Bennett's account of the program at Sangamon State University (Illinois) details an innovative style of library management that is helpful in promoting such instruction. The matter of training librarians to provide better bibliographic instruction is admirably addressed by Charles A. Bunge, who recommends several methods of influencing library school curricula, and urges a stronger commitment to continuing education programs. In "Things We Weren't Taught in Library School," the inadequacy of existing curricula is further examined by three University of Michigan librarians, who propose a stimulating range of remedies. A narrower focus is found in a short paper by Richard Werking, which documents approaches used to provide bibliographic instruction for history majors (he neatly distinguishes the different levels of research and cites titles of major reference works). The other papers on course-related instruction tend to be more prescriptive and suggest broad guidelines rather than specific strategies.

Thomas A. Karel

1152. Lee, Sul H., ed. **A Challenge for Academic Libraries: How to Motivate Students to Use the Library.** Ann Arbor, Mich., published for Eastern Michigan University Library by Pierian Press, 1973. 98p. illus. (Library Orientation Series, No. 2). $19.50. LC 73-78295. ISBN 0-87650-039-4.

Four short chapters discuss contemporary efforts to make college and university libraries really part of the academic scene through orientation programs. The opening chapter, by Mary Jo Lynch, covers the field in general. Each of the following sections is concerned with a specific orientation program at one college or university. M. E. Wiggins discusses "A Scientific Model for the Development of Library Use Instructional Programs" as implemented at Brigham Young. It is management-centered, based on setting goals and objectives; analyzing the participants and their needs; establishing norms and tests; and, finally, evaluating results.

Computer-assisted library instruction for individuals is reported by Alice S. Clark. She covers primarily the OSU approach, which is somewhat limited in scope but which has good growth potential. Charlotte Millis relates the use of trained student assistants as reference aides and motivators of other students. Millis appends a number of examples of teaching instruments used with her aides. Academic librarians should familiarize themselves with the contents of this book even though it does not live up to its subtitle. [R: C&RL, May 74, p. 217; LJ, 1 Feb 74, p. 344]   John E. Kephart

1153. Lee, Sul H., ed. **Library Orientation: Papers Presented at the First Annual Conference on Library Orientation Held at Eastern Michigan University, May 7, 1971.** Ann Arbor, Mich., published for the Eastern Michigan University by Pierian Press, 1972. 45p. (Library Orientation Series, No. 1). o.p. LC 76-172770. SBN 87650-028-9.

Contains four papers—"Why Academic Library Instruction?"; "A Separate Course in Bibliography or Course Related Library Instruction?"; "Motivating Students and Faculty"; and "Library Orientation Is Reaching Out to People." The concept of library orientation is not new and, unfortunately, there is nothing new in this small pamphlet. It is an "Ich Erzählung" about Eastern Michigan University and how it "has enjoyed a growing distinction among institutions of higher education for its demonstrated drive to achieve a high degree of educational quality" (p. ix). [R: LJ, 15 Oct 72, p. 3295]

1154. Morris, Jacquelyn M. **Bibliographic Instruction in Academic Libraries: A Review of the Literature and Selected Bibliography.** Syracuse, N.Y., Syracuse University, ERIC Clearinghouse on Information Resources, 1979. 49p. index. bibliog. (IR-43). o.p.

Following a brief discussion on the difficulty of locating literature on the various aspects of "bibliographic instruction" in *Library Literature* and the ERIC database, the author provides an index with 386 citations to 174 representative articles on bibliographic instruction in academic libraries under 102 subject headings. The articles indexed represent six categories of literature on bibliographic instruction: general, planning and implementation of a program, methods of instruction, samples of materials, descriptions of specific programs, and foreign-language articles. Each category has a number of specific subject headings in the index. For example, subject headings for "methods of instruction" include: audiovisual, course-related library instruction, courses (credit or noncredit), team teaching, workbook method, etc. Index terms for which the meanings are not readily apparent are defined in appendix A. The bibliography of articles indexed includes a brief abstract when document titles are not descriptive. Not as comprehensive a list as Deborah L. Lockwood's *Library Instruction: A Bibliography* (see *ARBA* 80, entry 231), but the alphabetical organization of the subject headings is easier to use.   Robert D. Little

1155.   Rader, Hannelore B., ed. **Faculty Involvement in Library Instruction: Their Views on Participation in and Support of Academic Library Use Instruction.** Ann Arbor, Mich., published for the Center of Educational Resources, Eastern Michigan University by Pierian Press, 1976. 119p. index. (Library Orientation Series, No. 6). $19.50. LC 76-21914. ISBN 0-87650-070-X.

As the library instruction movement coalesces into a solid organizational pattern with leaders, guidelines, and recognized activities, there is a natural tendency to expect improvement with each effort. The fifth annual Eastern Michigan library orientation conference reported in this collection both excites and disappoints the reader expecting solid information. Most of the speakers, in particular the quartet from the University of Michigan who developed the topic "Reaching Graduate Students: Techniqes and Administration," offered a few thoughtful remarks based on their experience in introducing change through library instruction. Jacquelyn Morris's case study is a candid appraisal of one library's initial naiveté in course planning and campus politics. It has an honesty rare in library literature. The overall stress on reaching students through faculty and on the need for a variety of approaches when dealing with faculty shows a healthy development. Library instruction is moving away from an emphasis on the techniques of tours and slide tape productions into the area of integrated curriculum development. While none of the speeches begin to approach the caliber of the Knapp Monteith College experiments of the 1960s, I would judge this collection to be a good complement to the ARL SPEC Kit on library instruction and useful in academic libraries and library schools concerned with developing active programs of public service. [R: C&RL, July 77, pp. 356-58]   Caroline M. Coughlin

1156.   Williams, Nyal Z., and Jack T. Tsukamoto, eds. **Library Instruction and Faculty Development: Growth Opportunities in the Academic Community: Papers Presented at the Twenty-Third Midwest Academic Librarians' Conference Held at Ball State University, May 1978.** Ann Arbor, Mich., Pierian Press, 1980. 86p. $19.50. (Library Orientation Series, No. 11). LC 80-82263. ISBN 0-87650-125-0.

Another volume in the Library Orientation Series, this time on faculty development and library instruction. There is a total of five essays and a panel discussion. The essays of each author address the need for greater understanding or even establishing a dialog between librarians and professors, and the necessary rapprochement between the two. Patricia Breivik, one of the contributors, expresses the general theme of this volume: "within this changing environment, there comes a better opportunity than ever before to expand library instruction—all programs and for us, as librarians, to become involved in the educational mainstream of our institutions" (pp. 29-30). Indeed, librarians occupy an enviable position in higher education, because they are an integral part of one of the most rapidly developing components of the educational process. [R: C&RL, May 81, p. 269; JAL, Jan 81, p. 364; LJ, 1 Apr 81, p. 718]
                Bohdan S. Wynar

SCHOOL LIBRARIES AND MEDIA CENTERS

1157.   Bantly, Harold A., and Janet L. Freedman, comps. **Information Searching: A Handbook for Designing & Creating Instructional Programs.** Boston, Massachusetts Board of Library Commissioners, 1979. 144p. bibliog. o.p.

"Information Searching presents a guide for the practicing librarian who would like to create successful programs to teach students how to locate and utilize the invaluable learning aids in our library/media centers" (p. 2). Developed as a result of a Library Services and Construction Act, Title III grant, the workbook was compiled in meetings with Massachusetts academic and school librarians. The text is double-spaced, easy to read, and well organized, being divided into four major areas: needs assessment, program development, approaches and methods, and program evaluation. Needs assessment includes several pretests to determine a student's knowledge base in information searching. Program development includes a discussion of goals, program ideas, and public relations. The methods chapter is the longest and perhaps most valuable, offering suggestions for examples of pathfinders, slide tape programs, workshops, and a course syllabus

(three credit hours) on information searching from Salem State College. An annotated bibliography is appended. This looseleaf, three-holed paperback is a practical sourcebook/workbook that should fulfill its intended function. [R: JAL, Sept 80, p. 234]

Mary Alice Deveny

1158. Hart, Thomas L. **Instruction in School Library Media Center Use (K-12).** 2nd ed. Chicago, American Library Association, 1985. 431p. bibliog. $12.50pa. LC 84-18405. ISBN 0-8389-0418-1.

The first edition of this text was published in 1978. This resource updates the 1978 title and serves as an index to instructional materials and activities for library/media skills programs. The author has prepared an overview of the current attitudes and practices in library/media instruction including the presentation of a sample scope and sequence chart (from the Leon District Schools in Tallahassee, Florida). Following this are brief articles from a variety of individuals examining many different instructional approaches: individualized, tutorial, programmed, computer-assisted, and others. These brief articles provide a variety of perspectives on library/media skills instruction.

The majority of the book is devoted to an index of materials for library/media skills instruction. Areas covered include library orientation, citizenship, parts of a book, location and arrangement of materials, classification, card catalog, methods of research, reference tools, and equipment operation. Within each section, the author lists sources which contain activities for instruction. For example, when presenting information about the card catalog to first graders, Hart includes a brief "success story" article and a reference to a library skills manual with spirit duplicating masters. Another area might include filmstrips, pamphlets, and cassette tapes. The sources that Hart cites are usually annotated, with a more general annotation included in the bibliography.

Librarians who are interested in updating their materials for library/media skills instruction will find this a very useful compilation. Hart includes a variety of types of materials and gives enough information about each one to allow for readers to decide about its usefulness. The bibliography is especially helpful since it divides the materials into types (i.e., books, microcomputer software, motion pictures, etc.). [R: BR, Sept/Oct 85, p. 54]

Rebecca L. Thomas

1159. Peterson, Violet E. **Library Instruction Guide: Suggested Courses for Use by Librarians and Teachers in Junior and Senior High Schools.** 4th ed. Hamden, Conn., Shoe String Press, 1974. 70p. illus. bibliog. index. $12.50. LC 73-17168. ISBN 0-208-01418-7.

This brief guide illustrates how librarians and teachers in junior and senior high schools can establish and organize instruction periods to introduce students to the use of various library resources. It is carefully organized, suggesting instructional content, projects, and assignments appropriate to each age group, and it has a useful bibliography. Restricting discussion to conventional resources, Peterson fails to mention the use of programmed texts, slides, and other multi-media materials. Her emphasis on continual quizzes and memorization of minutiae might repel students and discourage library use. Her annoying, though apparently unconscious, condescension toward both students and teachers further flaws the book. This guide is more an historical curiosity than an effective handbook for the school librarian. [R: RSR, July 74, p. 34]

Nancy P. Schneider

OTHER TOPICS

1160. Evans, A. J., R. G. Rhodes, and S. Keenan. **Education and Training of Users of Scientific and Technical Information: UNISIST Guide for Teachers.** Paris, UNESCO; distr., New York, UNIPUB, 1977. 143p. bibliog. $10.50pa. ISBN 92-3-101452-8.

The introduction states that "this *Guide* has been written for people who have the task of teaching information retrieval to users of scientific and technical information." The users are defined as graduate or undergraduate students, or working scientists and technologists who want to improve their information retrieval skills. While the *Guide* is "intended to have particular application in developing countries," it is certainly appropriate for use in similar teaching situations anywhere. The book is structured as one might present such a course. There are several appendices which cover bibliographic tools (the majority are United States publications), literature search techniques, examples of completed exercises, and a suggested bibliography of further reading. The authors recommend that the book not be used as a programmed learning guide by individuals, since it was written specifically for those involved in training users in retrieval of scientific and technical

information. An intention stated in the preface
is that "this is only the first edition of what must
be regarded as an initial effort."

Jennie B. Cross

43 Library Orientation Guides

GENERAL WORKS

1161. Baker, Robert K. **Doing Library Research: An Introduction for Community College Students.** Boulder, Colo., Westview Press, 1981. 283p. illus. bibliog. index. $33.00. LC 80-22943. ISBN 0-89158-778-0.

Guides and handbooks for using the library are many. Is still another needed? The apologia for this one is that it meets the needs of students coming from various backgrounds and following diverse study programs offered in community colleges. This goal is met amply. The guide is divided into three parts. The first is a general explanation of the library and its catalog. The second part, "General Tools," lists and describes the use of the basic dictionaries, encyclopedias, and other reference tools found in most libraries. Titles are not annotated, but their differences and their use are discussed in a general note for each type of source. Part 3, "Specialized Tools," lists more than 1,000 reference books and textbooks for some 90 separate fields of study. Included are many of the careers, such as secretarial science, dental assistance, cosmetology, and mortuary science, for which community colleges prepare students. These titles are unannotated, and only a brief note introduces each field.

This is an excellent guide. Explanations are clear and thorough. The style is informal but not condescending. There is a complete and accurate index of authors, titles, and subjects. Despite the intent to answer diverse community college needs, perhaps too much is attempted here. Ninety subject fields are too many to cover, even succinctly. In part 1, it is questionable whether a student's attention should be burdened with details like the interpretation of data in *Library of Congress Subject Headings* or the breakdown of sample LC and Dewey Classification numbers and author numbers. The introduction to the catalog and the explanation of basic sources are so adequate that this guide is recommended. [R: BL, 1 Apr 82, p. 988; LJ, 15 Jan 82, p. 164; RQ, Summer 82, pp. 416-17]　　　　Rolland E. Stevens

1162. Bloomfield, Masse. **How to Use a Library: A Guide for Literature Searching.** Reseda, Calif., Mojave Books, 1970. 33p. $4.00pa.

It is stated in the introduction that "this manual will inform the university student or research worker how to perform a literature search." All this on 33 pages. The author thinks that *How to Locate Educational Information and Data*, by Alexander and Burke (4th ed., 1958), is the most recent edition of this well-known guide, and that Wynar's *Guide to Reference Materials in Political Science* was published in 1966, just to use two examples. Not recommended.

1163. Bradshaw, Charles I. **Using the Library: The Card Catalog.** Provo, Utah, Brigham Young University Press, 1972. 104p. illus. o.p. LC 71-175298. ISBN 0 8425 0817-1.

Covers filing rules; call numbers; cross-referencing; author, title, and subject cards; tracings; and the LC subject headings. It is designed as a self-study manual to help students in their use of the card catalog. One of the strongest features of this little manual is its clear illustrations. [R: SLMQ, Winter 73, p. 144]

1164. Byrd, Patricia, Carol A. Drum, and Barbara J. Wittkopf. **Guide to Academic**

Libraries in the United States for Students of English as a Second Language. Englewood Cliffs, N.J., Prentice-Hall, 1981. 184p. illus. index. $13.95pa. LC 80-16030. ISBN 0-13-367979-9.

Designed to be used in an "intermediate or advanced ESL class with a teacher who can serve as a guide" (preface), this guide to library use contains explanations of library services, the card catalog, and all types of reference sources including online searching, sample searches, and notetaking. An additional chapter on research in science and technology is welcome, as these are the fields of study for a great number of foreign students in U.S. universities. Each chapter concludes with exercises and questions designed to get students to use the materials explained and to test their understanding of the chapter.

The coverage of library use is very thorough, but the book has some problems and errors. The section on call numbers explains that call numbers are "at least two lines in length. The top line refers to the classification, and the second line refers to the author's name and the book title"—true of Dewey, but not Library of Congress. The index, while it includes specific titles, is incomplete; a page and a half of the text is given to explaining how to use the *Science Citation Index*, but the title is not included in the index.

The preface indicates that the book can also be used as "a self-teaching tool by students with advanced proficiency in English." Although the book begins with simple and easy-to-read sections on types of library services (reference, reserve, interlibrary loan, etc.), arrangement of materials, and use of the card catalog, it continues with details on filing and attempts to explain how to use such tools as Sheehy and the *Monthly Catalog*. A mini-reference course in itself, the book has value as a textbook with a teacher to direct its study, but it would be an exceptional student who could use it on his or her own.

Susan Dedmond Casbon

1165. Cleary, Florence Damon. **Discovering Books and Libraries: A Handbook for Students in the Middle and Upper Grades.** 2nd ed. New York, H. W. Wilson, 1977. 196p. illus. index. $8.00pa. LC 76-55368. ISBN 0-8242-0594-4.

Following the same format as its earlier edition, this handbook contains eleven chapters, each designed as a specific lesson in reading, library, or study skills. It is designed for use by students in grades 6-9 (individually or as a classroom project). A review section, quiz, and/or suggestions for special projects conclude each chapter. Although the emphasis is still definitely on print materials, Cleary does recognize the role of multimedia in the school library and includes information on the arrangement, cataloging, and indexing of such materials. Generally, however, the lessons provide guidelines for the study of library basics: the parts of a book, shelf arrangement, the card catalog, reference tools, research skills, and special interest reading.

The clear type, wide margins, and distinct topic headings are particularly suitable for a student handbook. A detailed table of contents and index assist in finding specific information. Clearly treats her audience with respect and occasionally even speaks in their language (e.g., "don't get uptight"). The handbook will be welcomed both by librarians familiar with the earlier edition and by others needing basic lesson material in library instruction. The paper format and inexpensive price encourage purchase of multiple copies for individual study. [R: JAL, July 77, p. 167]

Roberta J. Depp

1166. Collison, Robert. **30,000 Libraries: A Practical Guide.** Encino, Calif., Dickenson, 1973. 214p. illus. index. o.p. LC 72-90244. ISBN 0-8221-0084-3.

If Robert Collison is correct in his assessment of the impact of a huge university library on students unfamiliar with the ways of such institutions, then perhaps all those gorgeous new libraries were designed around the wrong principle. A "supermarket-style" undergraduate library just may be the best plan. Realizing the total inability of many university students to cope with large library collections, Collison put together this brief guide hoping to demonstrate how to understand the library. The main idea is to assure the student, stunned by the size of the library, that he or she is capable of extracting some information from it. To keep the whole thing simple, the text is made up of 39 thumbnail sketches of various library resources, methods, and tools—arranging books, abstracts, encyclopedias, news, people, history, periodicals, note-taking, making a bibliography, etc. Part 2 is a section of photos showing areas of a library. Part 3 is a section that lists basic reference materials. An index is, of course, included. This new guide is not outstanding and will not offer much competition to other instructional aids already on the market. [R: LJ, 15 May 73, p. 1561]

1167. Cook, Margaret G. **The New Library Key.** 3rd ed. New York, H. W. Wilson, 1975.

264p. index. $8.00pa. LC 75-11754. ISBN 0-8242-0541-3.

The third edition, like the two previous editions (1956 and 1963), is addressed primarily to freshman college students and to individual adults who need guidance in the use of libraries. In fulfillment of her purpose, the author has organized her book into 18 chapters, the first six of which are concerned with such technical aspects of orienting oneself in a library as the organization of a college library, the book itself and its formal components, library catalogs and classification systems, and the technique of writing term papers.

The body of the book consists of 12 chapters, which treat separate categories of reference books either by form (e.g., encyclopedias, dictionaries, bibliographies) or by subject (e.g., the arts, the social sciences, literature).

The author's treatment of relevant topics in the first six chapters is fairly standard for guides of this kind in that there is marked variation in the relative thoroughness of coverage of included topics. The discussion of the parts of a book is excellent. The author's treatment of filing rules in card catalogs, on the other hand, generates more confusion than enlightenment. She correctly points out the fact of varied practice (i.e., the 1968 ALA filing rules versus the older rules), but she does not explicate these differences nor does she advise students to do the obvious: investigate and master the *local* filing practice.

In her annotations for reference books in 12 categories, the author is frequently guilty of excessive simplification. Admittedly the book is not addressed to librarians or library school students, hence some details that professionals need to know can be legitimately omitted. On the other hand, the reference tools she discusses are those that will be put to immediate use by college freshmen who do need minimal understanding. The deficiencies of her approach to descriptive and explicative annotation of reference books become clear when she does deal with complex tools like the OED. Of the latter she says that it is "frequently referred to as the N.E.D.," that it is "massive," and that "the compilers examined every work available in English from 1150." I seriously question whether what she says of this dictionary is sufficient to allow a college freshman to proceed to use it immediately.

Her discussion of book reviews suffers from a similar superficiality. Here she cites the *Book Review Digest*, *Book Review Index*, *Books Abroad*, and Eichelberger and comments briefly on *Choice* and the *Library Journal*. The author does not, however, point out that the Wilson subject indexes, all of which she has cited in other chapters, also can be used to retrieve book review citations.

In evaluating this book, the root question has to be: does it effectively meet the needs of the intended audience? In my judgment, the author's annotations of complex tools frequently fail to provide college freshmen with minimal practical understanding. [R: LJ, 15 Dec 75, p. 2308; WLB, Nov 75, p. 263]

Richard A. Gray

1168. Downs, Robert B., and Clara D. Keller. **How to Do Library Research.** 2nd ed. Urbana, Champaign, Ill., University of Illinois Press, 1975. 298p. bibliog. index. $3.45pa. LC 74-28301. ISBN 0-252-00535-X. (Available from Books on Demand, $76.50pa., ISBN 0-317-10545-0).

When a book title starts off "How to ...," a reader expects practical guidance in acquiring a skill. Unfortunately, Downs's book does not fulfill this expectation. The book begins with a chapter on libraries; this is of little value to the scholar, who almost invariably must start by using the library at hand, no matter what great research library may exist in some other part of the country. Even the chapter entitled "The Practical Use of Reference Books" does not provide guidance in selecting or using these books. In fact, the author intimidates the reader by listing a sample of the multitude of reference books that contain information on Japan without suggesting any appropriate plan for choosing among them.

The structure of this book is unchanged from that of the 1966 edition. One new chapter, "The Nonbook World," has been included and new titles and editions have been added throughout. Most of the book consists of annotated lists of reference works. There are odd omissions: juvenile literature is listed under "The Literary World," but Virginia Haviland's indispensable *Children's Literature: A Guide to Reference Sources* is not included, while outdated song and poetry indexes are given. Annotations are often so brief as to be useless. There is no indication, for example, of the difference in coverage between *Book Review Index* and the *Book Review Digest*. The topics under which specialized reference books are listed seem idiosyncratic: Australia is a topic, but not Asia or China; moving pictures, but not television; libraries, but not library science.

As a relatively inexpensive listing of reference books, this may serve some purpose, but serious scholars will still turn to Winchell for bibliographies of reference books and will need other guides to learn how to use them. [R: C&RL, May 76, p. 278]   Adele M. Fasick

1169.   Fjalbrant, Nancy, and Ian Malley. **User Education in Libraries.** 2nd ed. London, Clive Bingley; distr., Hamden, Conn., Shoe String Press, 1984. 1v. bibliog. index. $19.50. LC 77-19192. ISBN 0-85157-361-4.

This book should be valuable to academic librarians in the United States for its case studies of user education practices—and the thinking behind them—in Scandinavia and the United Kingdom. It is something of a practically oriented historical review and overview with helpful charts, case studies, concise histories, with a good chapter on the pros and cons of various methods of education of library users, and another on evaluating success. The interesting chapter on the cooperative SCONUL (Standing Conference of National and University Libraries) scheme for cooperative production of tape/slide programs includes a list of finished programs and their sources. The three case studies (two in Great Britain, one in Scandinavia) similarly, are admirably concise and informative, including background information, the perceived problem in educating library users, and how it was solved. The background overviews of the situation in Scandinavia, the United Kingdom, and the United States are interesting and backed by a separate chapter of current references. [R: C&RL, Mar 79, p. 186; LQ, Apr 79, p. 219]   Marda Woodbury

1170.   Gates, Jean Key. **Guide to the Use of Libraries and Information Sources.** 5th ed. New York, McGraw-Hill, 1983. 338p. index. $21.95; $16.95pa. LC 82-14961. ISBN 0-07-022990-2; 0-07-022989-9pa.

This work has become a standard introductory guide to academic libraries since it was first published in 1962. The fifth edition's revised title reflects the changing nature of library collections over the last two decades due to the rapid expansion of nonprint materials and the availability of computerized information sources. In her preface, the author indicates that her work is intended primarily "to serve as a textbook for college freshmen and other students who want or need instruction in the use of libraries and library materials" but that it can also be useful in basic library science courses.

The general arrangement follows that of earlier editions. The work is divided into five parts. Part 1 briefly traces the history of books and libraries, discusses the parts of a book, and

provides a concise overview of academic libraries. Part 2 covers the organization and arrangement of library materials, including an explanation of the Dewey Decimal and Library of Congress Classification systems and a description of library catalogs. Each chapter in part 3 is devoted to a specific type of general information source (e.g., encyclopedias, indexes, dictionaries). Following introductory information about each category are suggestions on how to select and use such sources and an annotated bibliography of representative titles. In part 4, specialized information sources in eight broad subject fields are listed and annotated. The bibliographies in parts 3 and 4 have been brought up-to-date to include 1982 imprints. Part 5 outlines the steps involved in writing an undergraduate research paper. The guide concludes with a useful index by subject and by titles cited.

The brief treatment given to automated information sources is somewhat disappointing. Additional explanation about the advantages of a computer search, such as the ability to combine multiple concepts and to limit by date, language, type of material, or other parameter, could have been provided. In addition, some mention of nonbibliographic databases would have been appropriate.

In spite of this shortcoming, the guide continues to be an accurate and reliable introduction to the use of academic libraries and their resources. For reviews of previous editions, see *ARBA* 70 (vol. 1, p. 18), *ARBA* 75 (entry 138), and *ARBA* 80 (entry 227).   Marie Ellis

1171.   Gorden, Charlotte. **How to Find What You Want in the Library.** Woodbury, N.Y., Barron's Educational Series, 1978. 123p. illus. index. o.p. LC 77-12534. ISBN 0-8120-0696-8.

Barron's new library instruction manual for middle school and high school students covers traditional topics and skills (part 1—card catalog, arrangement of materials, indexes; part 2—reference books; and part 3—the reference paper) in clear and concise form. What raises this text above the average is the definitive selection of important concepts and essential facts that students need to master. Also, the text avoids nonessential library history and background filler. Concentration is on explanation of the purpose, organization, and use of tools, with emphasis on specific search questions.

Mastery of part 1 is expected of all students; self-checking quizzes help students evaluate the need for additional study. Search problems offer practice in the application of each skill or use of each tool. Part 2 explains selected general and specialized reference books. Not all disciplines are represented here; for example, ethnology, economics, and law are omitted. Here the text is illustrated with sample pages from the reference tools, most of which are keyed to search questions. No particular order of study is demanded by this part. Reference books and their search problems are treated as separate segments, allowing students or instructors to plan individual sequences of study. Part 3 emphasizes notetaking and bibliography, but provides an overview of the mechanics of preparing a reference paper.

The author, a former teacher and reference center coordinator, obviously knows her audience well and keeps the text tuned to student interests and needs. A handy format feature is the list of problems and annotations at the front. A negative aspect is the extreme miniaturization of some catalog card and index samples. In summation, this is a concise and well-planned manual that can be very useful for self or group instruction in library skills for middle and secondary grade school students.

Christine Gehrt Wynar

1172. Gore, Daniel. **Bibliography for Beginners.** 2nd ed. New York, Appleton-Century-Crofts; distr., Englewood Cliffs, N.J., Prentice-Hall, 1973. 248p. o.p. LC 73-3860. ISBN 0-390-37660-4.

The previous edition of this text, published in 1968, was entitled *Bibliography for Beginners: Form A*. Two new chapters are included here: one on government documents, and one called "What Is a Library?" In fact, those seem to be the only textual changes. There are corresponding additions to the section of student exercises as well. The section on government documents does not include many of the important works such as *Checklist '70, CIS/Index* or *American Statistics Index*. "What Is a Library?" seems to present Gore's philosophy of librarianship and will not assist students in completing the corresponding exercise on library censorship.

As a text for courses in how to do library research and prepare bibliographies, *Bibliography for Beginners* falls short of what is needed. [R: LJ, 1 Apr 74, p. 969]

1173. Gover, Harvey R. **Keys to Library Research on the Graduate Level: A Guide to Guides.** Washington, D.C., University Press of America, 1981. 65p. illus. bibliog. $7.00pa. LC 80-5841. ISBN 0-8191-1370-0.

Another in a long and undistinguished line of nuts-and-bolts guides to coping in an aca-

demic library, Gover's title belies its content since *all* college and high school students require this same basic information. Gover treats the usual topics—card catalog, classification (LC rather than Dewey), indexes and abstracts, bibliographies, guides to the literature, and specialized periodicals and indexes (by which he means *Ulrich's*)—succinctly and accurately, although with considerable oversimplification. He unaccountably omits *Library of Congress Subject Headings* but does demonstrate the utility of subject tracings and frequently discusses the changes in libraries wrought by technology. The typewritten text, separation of explanations from corresponding examples, and absence of an index are all disappointments. Nothing is wrong in this little book, and its tone is friendly enough—it just does not convey the intellectual process that should govern the mechanics of library research. Gover's guide has no place in a reference collection, but would be appropriate for a bibliographic instruction or educational media collection or to suggest to a faculty member as an adjunct reading in any course requiring a research project.

Mary W. George

1174. Hauer, Mary G., and others. **Books, Libraries, and Research.** Dubuque, Iowa, Kendall/Hunt Publishing, 1979. 125p. index. o.p. LC 78-70655. ISBN 0-8403-1953-3.

Another entry into the field of library use instruction for college students. The topics and their sequence, as well as the style of presentation, are so familiar that this could be any manual developed by any college library. It opens with a brief statement on the purpose of libraries and special arrangements to accommodate student research needs. Then follows the litany of: the book, the research paper, classification, card catalog, reference books, indexes, and government publications. Sample cards and extracts from key reference tools illustrate the text. A brief glossary and an index conclude the work. *Books, Libraries, and Research* offers nothing new in the way of motivating the reader or in devising a sound teaching method of library instruction. Jean Gates's *Guide to the Use of Books and Libraries*, 4th ed. (see *ARBA* 80, entry 227) is a better choice as a comprehensive student library orientation guide. The 1983 edition of this work is still available.

Christine Gehrt Wynar

1175. Johnson, H. Webster, Anthony J. Faria, and Ernest L. Maier. **How to Use the Business Library: With Sources of Business Information.** Cincinnati, Ohio, South-Western

Publishing, 1984. 267p. illus. $7.45pa. LC 83-60484. ISBN 0-538-05750-5.

This unique and inexpensive volume does a credible job of accomplishing two goals simultaneously. While the authors tout its "textbook" insights into library research methods, they also manage to list a surprising breadth of useful business publications. After a concise first chapter on how to use the library, a number of vital research concepts are highlighted throughout the book. Oft-overlooked topics such as interlibrary loan and the "volume indexes" found in periodicals are described, as well as database searching, federal depository libraries, and even computer output microfilm.

While such explanations are indeed useful to business students and researchers, the numerous annotations of business information sources will interest librarians and instructors as well. Unfortunately, many annotations do not include publication date or frequency, and both redundancies and overlooked titles can be spotted. In addition, this volume's format consists of run-together source lists which lack precise subject arrangement. On the plus side, however, a number of associations and databases are described, although frequent revisions will be required to keep entries up-to-date. Particularly interesting chapters feature aids to small business, business report writing, audiovisual materials, and international information sources.

Although inconsistencies in organization and the lack of an index limit this volume's usefulness as a reference work, it remains a unique instructional and collection development tool. Overall, the sheer number of important information sources described makes this inexpensive compendium a worthwhile investment.

Mary Ardeth Gaylord

1176. Katz, William. **Your Library: A Reference Guide.** 2nd ed. New York, Holt, Rinehart and Winston, 1984. 242p. index. $19.95; $11.95pa. LC 83-12713. ISBN 0-03-063011-8; 0-03-060312-6pa.

The first edition of this text was published in 1979 (see *ARBA* 80, entry 229). In this edition, Katz has responded to comments about his earlier edition by updating and condensing much of the material. The book has been reorganized, and includes notable material on computers and new material on preparing a research paper. There are numerous illustrations and boxed inserts that enhance understanding of the text. In this heavily revised version, this tool is now more useful for the beginning student.

1177. Katzel, Randall. **Guide to Libraries and Reference Books: An Introduction to the Organization of Libraries and an Annotated Guide to 463 Reference Books with Questions Designed to Reveal Their Content.** Pittsburgh, Pa., Kansas, Norkan, 1970. 60p. o.p.

"This book has been designed to be inclusive enough to serve as an initial text for beginning students in reference courses; yet simplified enough to be used by the student unfamiliar with libraries" (introduction). We don't think so. Some annotations might be helpful for instruction of freshman classes, but there is nothing on the use of the library, the catalog, etc. The introductory comments in "Departments and Divisions of the Library" are more misleading than helpful. Beginning students have many other texts at their disposal and hardly need this one.

Bohdan S. Wynar

1178. Lindberg, John. **Routines for Research: A Handbook of Basic Library Skills.** Washington, D.C., University Press of America, 1982. 163p. $23.50; $11.25pa. LC 82-15962. ISBN 0-8191-2750-7; 0-8191-2751-5pa.

The purpose of this handbook is to instruct undergraduate college students in how to write papers using periodical indexes. The author's step-by-step instructions would be difficult for freshmen and sophomores to follow unless they have had previous writing experience.

Chapter 1 gives advice on how to work in the library. Skills needed for understanding how to use each index appropriate for a subject, skills needed for selecting appropriate "selector-items" (i.e., subject headings), and skills needed for determining the appropriate information to record on note cards are discussed. Chapter 2 gives careful instructions on how to avoid paraphrase. Chapter 3 is an explanation of how to use the major periodical indexes for searching topics in the humanities, social sciences, and sciences. How to search for information in a government documents collection is also included. The student is led through a series of cases, with each case grouping related sources appropriate for a particular paper. Students must realize that every library does not have the exact information on the spine labels that the author implies it does. The description of the ERIC indexing system is not accurate and will cause confusion for any student not familiar with the system's use. Chapter 4 bridges the gap from periodical indexes to book sources necessary for upper-class and graduate work.

The text was computer printed, which has led to several words being hyphenated inaccurately. The book is easy enough to read, but a few typographical errors occur.

M. Kathy Cook

1179. Lolley, John, in consultation with Samuel J. Marino. **Your Library: What's in It for You?** New York, Wiley, 1974. illus. index. (Self-Teaching Guides). $5.95pa. LC 73-18293. ISBN 0-471-54365-9.

Library skills booklets abound, but here is a new one with some merit. Brief and presented with a light, humorous touch, it attempts to be self-pacing. Each section has two parts: (1) the presentation of information, with examples; and (2) practical exercises (fill-in). The four chapters cover the card catalog, periodicals, reference books, and library services. It is intended for college students and adults who return to the classroom. An appendix gives suggestions on writing a research paper; however, this is too brief to be of much help for anything but the simplest paper [R: RSR, Jan 75, p. 30]

Christine Gehrt Wynar

1180. Morse, Grant W. **Concise Guide to Library Research.** New York, Fleet Academic Editions, 1975. 262p. illus. index. $15.50; $8.50pa. LC 74-21358. ISBN 0-8303-0143-7; 0-8303-0148-8pa.

Apparently believing that Robert Downs's *How to Do Library Research* (2nd ed., University of Illinois Press, 1975) and many similar books fail of their purpose, Morse has prepared his own work. It purports to guide beginning college students and even bright high school students in the mysteries of doing "research" (read "preparation of term papers") in an academic library. He is correct in his assumption that Downs et al. fail to meet the existing need, but he has not remedied their deficiencies. He has only perpetuated the inadequacies of their formula, and in an attenuated form.

The body of the book is given over to a classified list of reference books. There are either no annotations at all or telegraphic phrasal notes that are so perfunctory as to be useless. For example, *Macmillan Book of Proverbs, Maxims and Familiar Phrases* is characterized as "very useful." No other book in the quotations section receives a similar accolade except Bartlett's, which is called "most famous." Incidentally, Morse has a bibliographic style all his own. Usually authors, editors, and compilers are completely ignored — usually, but not always. We are told that *Familiar Quotations* had something to do with a "J. Bartlett."

As far as imprint data are concerned, Morse's citations are inexcusable. For example, *Modern English Biography*, by Frederic Boase, has the following imprint: "1965, Frank Cass & Co." Apparently Morse does not acknowledge the distinction between copyright dates and reprint dates, or he thinks it trivial. This reviewer cannot agree.

The above eccentricities are mere annoyances. The fundamental defect of the book lies in the misleading superficiality of its organizational scheme. In the main section, dictionaries, Morse has a subheading "Origins of Words and Phrases," under which he subsumes the *Oxford English Dictionary* and the *Dictionary of Word and Phrase Origins* (no author given; "1962, Harper"). The *OED*, which requires a minor essay just to explicate its organization and scope, sits cheek-by-jowl with fluff, and the author makes no effort to call to the student's attention the fact that the imcomparable *OED* is *sui generis*. This kind of organizational triviality, which is endemic in the book, can't be expected to guide anyone's "research." Frankly, the audience to which it is directed is better off with nothing than with this. [R: BL, 1 May 76, p. 1289; LJ, 1 Apr 76, p. 872; WLB, Feb 76, p. 489]

Richard A. Gray

1181. Whittaker, Kenneth. **Using Libraries: An Informative Guide for Students and General Users.** 3rd rev. ed. London, Andre Deutsch; distr., New York, Seminar Press, 1972. 140p. illus. bibliog. index. (A Grafton Book). $7.50. ISBN 0-233-96358-8. (Available from Philosophical Library, $6.00, ISBN 0-8022-1879-2).

Introductions to library use aimed at grade and high school students, to library use and services aimed at the general library user, and to libraries and librarianship aimed at the prospective librarian would all be welcome. *Using Libraries*, unfortunately, since it attempts to meet all these needs, meets none of them fully. Whittaker's style is suited to the younger reader; it is jarring to an adult. The levels of advice range from the simplistic (use a bookmark so that you can find your place again immediately) to the sophisticated (a research bibliography should be given a classified arrangement); the levels of discussion range from the basic (a definition of fiction) to the general (why large libraries are difficult to use) to the technical (the physical make-up of a book). The chapter "How Libraries Are Arranged" presents a good, brief introduction to the card catalog, to filing practices, and to the interpretation of catalog cards; the introduction to Dewey Decimal Classification in the same chapter, however, is unnecessarily complete and is aimed, as is the appended subject guide to Dewey, at providing the user with enough information about the scheme to enable him to circumvent use of the card catalog. *Using Libraries* has good points, but its rough spots, coupled with its reference to specific British practices which would be confusing or irrelevant to the publics it is supposed to serve, makes its popular use highly unlikely. The work could, however, be helpful to librarians who are responsible for formal instruction in library use. [R: RSR, July 73, p. 28]

Joan K. Marshall

1182.   Wolf, Carolyn E., and Richard Wolf. **Basic Library Skills: A Short Course.** Jefferson, N.C., McFarland, 1981. 127p. illus. index. $9.95pa. LC 81-4865. ISBN 0-89950-018-8.

Boiling the skills needed for effective library use down to a key selection of topics is difficult. This book is a well-designed and useful example. The organization is logical and helpful. It starts with a tour of the library, the catalog, and an introduction to bibliography. Then chapters cover book reviews, general information sources, periodicals and newspapers, literature and criticism, government information and documents, biography, business and consumer information, and nonprint and special materials. The final chapter includes some hints on term paper preparation.

Each chapter opens with objectives, and continues with brief and cogent narrative paragraphs on the basics of the chapter's content. Each chapter has several exercises, a list of terms, and a list of sample reference sources for the chapter's subject. The book concludes with answers to the exercises and an index. A few minor errors can be found. Examples are: COM is called "catalogs on microfiche," and the sample catalog cards are all pre-*AACR2*. However, these records are in catalogs also.

The writing is simple, easy to read, and even superficial. But these are among the aims of the book, and thus are desired qualities. The book is designed to enable a student to master basic library skills, and careful use should accomplish this quite well. A mastery of the titles here will be an excellent start for anyone. Users will then be ready to graduate to other sources such as Katz and even *ARBA* itself. Other similar books are by Renford (see *ARBA* 81, entry 254), Gorden (see *ARBA* 80, entry 170), and Gates (see *ARBA* 80, entry 227). This book is designed to be a self-contained short course in the use of the library. It does this quite well, and is recommended for introductory library

training. [R: CLW, Sept 83, p. 92; RSR, Spring 83, p. 53]

Neal L. Edgar

PRECOLLEGE LEVEL

1183.   Barnes, Donald L., and Arlene B. Burgdorf. **Study Skills for Information Retrieval.** Boston, Allyn and Bacon, 1979. 1v. illus. $6.16pa., $7.44 teacher's ed. LC 75-84947. ISBN 0-205-06436-1pa.; 0-205-06440-X teacher's ed.

This collection of exercises on three levels of difficulty, presumably for grades 4, 5, and 6, attempts to provide the classroom teacher with a balanced resource for teaching library skills. The authors' concept of such skills extends to alphabetizing, use of the dictionary, parts of a book, arrangements of encyclopedias, types of indexes, using the card catalog, Dewey decimal system, main divisions of the library, skills in reading maps and charts, report writing, outlining, choosing keywords, differentiating between fact and opinion, and order in report writing.

Unlike Beck and Pace's *Library Skills* (Denison, 1965), this set does not provide lesson plans and includes nothing for the primary level. It intends to be an exercise resource rather than a curriculum outline. Brief background information and adequate instruction accompany the exercises but are not intended to do more than introduce the worksheet. In scope, *Study Skills for Information Retrieval* goes far beyond the Beck and Pace set by including map skills, keyword exercises, outlining, differentiating between fact and opinion, and use of reference books. The areas just mentioned are rarely included in library skills workbooks for intermediate grades. Many exercises in level 3 are useful in junior high school.

Because the scope of these study skills goes beyond most library skills books and relates to skills usually treated in social studies and language arts, this set will provide a useful resource. *Study Skills* and Palovic's *The Elementary School Library in Action* (Parker, 1968) complement each other.

Shirley A. Hibbeln

1184.   Blazek, Ron. **Influencing Students toward Media Center Use: An Experimental Investigation in Mathematics.** Chicago, American Library Association, 1976. 238p. illus. bibliog. (ALA Studies in Librarianship, No. 5). $9.00pa. LC 75-26769. ISBN 0-8389-0201-4.

Much of what has been written previously concerning the factors influencing student use of the media center has been based on assumptions made by a particular author. Few persons have designed proper research studies on the subject. Therefore, this report of a carefully organized and scientifically executed study is a welcome addition to the professional literature.

The research, conducted in partial fulfillment of the requirements for the Ph.D. in library science, is described in interesting detail in this volume, which was adapted from the author's dissertation. Working under the assumption that it is the teacher who is most influential in facilitating the use of the media center, he chose a teacher of mathematics (a subject neglected by student users of the media center) and his students (subfreshmen at University High School, the laboratory school of the University of Illinois) for his study. Although his sample was small (two sections of only 17 pupils each), he not only proved his basic assumption valid but also reached other important conclusions that have significance for all school personnel.

Not limited to mathematics or any one teaching mode, Blazek's findings have value in that they identify the responsibilities of teachers, media specialists, and administrators in influencing pupils to use media center materials and services effectively in the total educational process. Sara R. Mack

1185. Bowers, Melvyn K. **Library Instruction in the Elementary School.** Metuchen, N.J., Scarecrow, 1971. 170p. illus. index. $15.00. LC 72-155283. SBN 8108-0391-7.

The subject matter is restricted to an outline of library instruction K-8 within a very traditional framework of weekly scheduled classes. The content and methods of instruction are based on the author's program at the East Lake School in Clear Oaks, California. A chapter is devoted to a description of the program on each grade level and mentions, for example, the importance of storytelling, rules of the library, reports, parts of the book, discipline, and shelf arrangements. An appendix reproduces a programmed booklet on call numbers and another on footnotes. There is a small index. The author does provide sensible suggestions for presenting some topics to children and preparing homemade teaching aids. However, no lists of commercially prepared instructional aids are suggested. While such introductory outlines are interesting to look at, the narrow interpretation of "library instruction" that is employed may limit the aspirations and cool the creative enthusiasm of some beginning librarians. The idea that library instruction

begins and ends with shelf arrangement, use of an index, book reports, and story hour is probably widely accepted in many schools. Nevertheless, we can hope for a broader approach, one that will place the planned sequence of skills within the total curriculum and find ways to relate library instruction to what's happening in the classroom. The reluctance to show how classroom and library can function together rather than operate as separate entities is one of the major weaknesses of the book. For example, no attempt is made to illustrate how library instruction can be related to a class or group study unit. Certainly even one chapter describing the planning and strategies required for such typical instructional needs would demonstrate that library instruction has more than one dimension. If, as the author says in chapter 1, one of the greatest values of the plan is its use "as a comparison for evaluation of a program already in existence" (p. 15), then one must admit to using a very short yardstick. [R: WLB, Nov 71, p. 276]

Christine Gehrt Wynar

1186. California Association of School Librarians. **Library Skills: A Handbook for Teachers and Librarians.** rev. ed. Belmont, Calif., Fearon Publishers, 1973. 88p. illus. o.p. LC 73-78275. ISBN 0-8224-4300-7.

The California Association of School Librarians published the first edition of this skills handbook in 1958. The purpose of this second edition is to present a variety of games and projects that can be adapted for use at various grade levels. Most of the learning experiences are best suited for elementary and junior high school. The 85 projects are grouped under eight categories: library orientation; alphabetizing; Dewey Decimal Classification; card catalog; parts of a book; finding information; appreciation; and miscellaneous. A selected bibliography is included. Each project lists the suggested grade range, behavioral objective, materials needed, directions, sample questions, cards, worksheets, etc. The handbook is designed to help the teacher or librarian prepare meaningful learning experiences for children. It is planned as a resource book and not as a self-teaching device. The presentation of each problem and the educational setting in which the games and worksheets are used will determine, in the end, the value of such instructional aids. Teacher training programs and school libraries will certainly need to add the handbook to their collections. [R: RSR, Apr 74, p. 19]

Christine Gehrt Wynar

1187. Gillespie, John, and Diana Lembo. **Introducing Books: A Guide for the Middle Grades.** New York, R. R. Bowker, 1970. 318p. o.p. LC 74-94512. ISBN 0-8352-0215-1.

Over 80 titles suitable for readers from about 9 to 14 receive detailed treatment in this book for teachers and librarians, a companion volume to the authors' *Juniorplots* (R. R. Bowker, 1967). The titles have been classified according to generally accepted developmental goals which are expressed by 11 headings such as "Making Friends," "Developing Values," "Understanding Physical Problems," and "Identifying Adult Roles." The material for each title is arranged in four parts: (1) plot analysis, (2) thematic material, (3) booktalk material and (4) additional suggestions (including related books). There is an author/title index, and the subject index rearranges the titles under topics rather than themes.

The titles are well selected, representing new and old works with an emphasis on children's choices, not just award winners. Anyone responsible for presenting books to young readers will appreciate the plot and character summaries, and the page references to suggested passages for reading aloud are most welcome. [R: LJ, 15 Nov 70, p. 3976; RQ, Fall 70; WLB, June 70]   Christine Gehrt Wynar

1188. Hostrop, Richard W., comp. **Education Inside the Library-Media Center.** Hamden, Conn., Linnet Books, 1973. 178p. illus. bibliog. index. o.p. LC 72-13425. ISBN 0-208-01324-5.

This volume deals with the library media center and its effectiveness as an educational force in learning settings from kindergarten through the university. It strongly emphasizes use of technology and the philosophy and practice of the library college idea. Useful to the practitioner and those studying to be media specialists. The index, however, is inadequate. [R: Choice, Sept 73, p. 955; JAL, Mar 75, p. 30; LJ, 1 Sept 73, p. 2409; LQ, Oct 74, p. 356]   Charles D. Patterson

1189. Jay, Hilda L. **Stimulating Student Search: Library Media/Classroom Teacher Techniques.** Hamden, Conn., Library Professional Publications/Shoe String Press, 1983. 176p. index. $18.50; $14.50pa. LC 82-22916. ISBN 0-208-01936-7; 0-208-01926-Xpa.

Manuals can be very useful, or they can anger purchasers who think that they were duped into purchasing an undistinguished amalgamation of library procedures. Happily for all, Jay's text is in the first category. It offers librarians interested in library instruction by librarians and teachers an excellent combination of general organizing principles to consider and various subject-oriented examples to recycle. The stated focus is the library instruction program opportunities of a high school with a good academic program, but the manual will also benefit academic librarians offering instructional sessions to college freshmen and sophomores.

One of the pleasures of using this manual is that readers are able vicariously to experience the author's caring, commonsense approach to stimulating and nurturing teachers and students into becoming good independent library users. Her library instruction exercises are based on sound educational principles and are both creative and practical. [R: Emerg Lib, Jan 84, p. 27; SLMQ, Spring 84, p. 238]
            Caroline M. Coughlin

1190. Karpisek, Marian E. **Making Self-Teaching Kits for Library Skills.** Chicago, American Library Association, 1983. 97p. illus. $12.00pa. LC 82-18488. ISBN 0-8389-0374-6.

This manual was created to help the elementary school library media specialist prepare multimedia library skills kits for individualized instruction. These teaching kits were developed to be used with children in grades 3-6, and each kit is independent of the others. Kits are provided for the following topics: parts of a book, card catalog, encyclopedias, *Children's Magazine Guide*, *Abridged Readers' Guide to Periodical Literature*, almanacs, atlases, and the vertical file.

Each self-teaching kit includes a "visual book," audiotape, and "hands-on" component. The "visual book" contains examples, copies of pages from a book, and a book itself or other appropriate print and illustrative material. The audiotape teaches the lesson and provides continuity between the visual book and the "hands-on" experience. Reinforcement of the lesson comes from the follow-up "hands-on" activity.

Individual chapters in the manual contain complete detailed instructions for making a specific kit. An overview of the skill and behavioral objectives is followed by a list of the software materials needed to create the kit. Step-by-step directions are given for the visual book, and a complete audio script is included. Options are provided for the individual school library media specialist to adapt the material to a specific school, thus overcoming the major problems with most commercially prepared materials.

Both new and experienced elementary school library media specialists will find this a useful skills manual. The time involved in the preparation of each kit would be well spent, and the materials costs are minimal. Additional kits could be created as needed using the format developed by Karpisek. [R: Indexer, Oct 83, p. 283; SLJ, May 84, p. 40]   Carol J. Veitch

1191. Knight, Hattie M. **The 1-2-3 Guide to Libraries.** 5th ed. Dubuque, Iowa, William C. Brown, 1976. 80p. illus. index. write for price. LC 72-11551. ISBN 0-697-06301-1.

This work is intended as an introductory text for orientation classes in library science at the college or university level. It introduces the student to the organization and services of a library, to classification systems and the card catalog, and to types of reference tools. The writing style is clear and straightforward, the material is well organized, and the reference tools covered are those basic sources any beginning student should learn. There is an appendix of assignments, in workbook fashion, at the end of the book.

This is the fifth edition of a work first published in 1964. The format is essentially the same as that of the fourth edition (1970) but the content has been revised to include new basic reference tools and to delete obsolete entries.

Kathleen Phillips

1192. Kuhlthau, Carol Collier. **School Librarian's Grade-by-Grade Activities Program: A Complete Sequential Skills Plan for Grades K-8.** West Nyack, N.Y., Center for Applied Research in Education, 1981. 204p. $23.50. LC 81-10121. ISBN 0-87628-744-5.

This work provides the outline for a complete sequential learning program designed to teach library skills to students from kindergarten to eighth grade. The progression of skills is based upon the developmental stages of the child. The author, who has been both an elementary teacher and a library media specialist, stresses the importance of integrating the teaching activities outlined into various content areas.

The book is divided into grade-level sections. Within these sections are an overall description of the program for that age; helpful hints for teaching the activities; a listing and explanation of the skills to be developed; a checklist to be used for monitoring individual progress; and a myriad of learning activities to reinforce the skills. The kindergarten section contains useful suggestions for storytelling and gaining the attention of this age student. The activities range from a location game called "Where Does It Live?" to a means of teaching keywords through literature. At least one audio-visual activity is presented in each section. Research skills are made interesting, and one activity introduces the idea of using a computer as a card catalog.

Library media specialists will find the wide variety of activities provided useful and student-oriented. The progression of skills is natural and well suited to students. Students learning with this method will progress to active library media center users who are capable of researching a topic and selecting, evaluating, and interpreting materials. [R: JAL, July 82, p. 174]

Joanne Troutner

1193. Nordling, Jo Anne. **Dear Faculty: A Discovery Method Guidebook to the High-School Library.** Westwood, Mass., F. W. Faxon, 1976. 163p. illus. $10.00pa. LC 76-8667. ISBN 0-87305-114-9.

This book is not a lesson plan guide for high school librarians but a guide to library resources and research, directed to the classroom teacher. The librarian is not neglected, however, as the author (a high school librarian and former teacher) stresses that the two professionals must work together to create productive student learning situations. Eleven sample research units—ranging from basic research skills to career guidance, history, ethnic studies, literature and public library use, etc.—are presented as structural units that can be adapted by the teacher to fit in with the resources available in a particular high school library or the specific needs of individual curriculum units. The basic premise is that students will learn library/research skills more effectively if those skills are directly tied in with the classroom work they are doing. Objectives, resource lists, and well-organized student worksheets are given for each sample research unit. The first chapter provides suggestions for adapting the units. Accompanying each chapter is a clever little memo from the librarian to the faculty. Some of these border on the condescending or take the attitude that the librarian "knows all"; they probably serve better as humorous expressions of some of the frustrations and brighter moments of librarian/faculty relations than as guides for actual practice. Memos to individual teachers might be more effective than these blanket notes; certainly communication should be encouraged.

Since there seems to be a dearth of materials available for library instructional use at the high school level, this book will also be of value to librarians for both its philosophy and its practical suggestions. [R: SLMQ, Summer 77, p. 294]   Roberta J. Depp

1194.   Shapiro, Lillian L. **Teaching Yourself in Libraries: A Guide to the High School Media Center and Other Libraries.** New York, H. W. Wilson, 1978. 180p. illus. index. $8.00. LC 78-16616. ISBN 0-8242-0628-2.

This guide to using libraries is set up as a series of curriculum-oriented units suitable for independent study—apparently intended to help high school students learn more about ways to use libraries for both personal goals and academic purposes. An introductory chapter on the library media center is followed by seven chapters on different fields: citizenship, health and science, vocational and college information, war and peace, poetry, values, and "getting it together." It is a difficult book for me to review, as I empathise completely with the author's goal and, like her, believe in the importance of libraries. Still, it is hard for me to picture circumstances in which high school students would voluntarily choose to read this book, even though it contains a great deal of well-chosen and well-organized information. The goals are diffuse, and the vocabulary is difficult (particularly for students who do not know how to use libraries). In the San Francisco area, most public libraries would not have her media items, and many high school libraries would not have many of the suggested reference books.

The book does present a useful overview of what students ought to know about libraries by the time they leave high school. Still, guides to libraries such as Robert Collison's *30,000 Libraries: A Practical Guide* (Dickenson Publishing, 1973) seem to me more interesting and more inspiring. Guides to writing term papers seem to provide better motivation, while guides to reference materials seem clearer. [R: BL, 15 Nov 78, p. 540]   Marda Woodbury

1195.   Spirt, Diana L. **Library/Media Manual.** New York, H. W. Wilson, 1979. 160p. illus. bibliog. index. $8.00. LC 79-4839. ISBN 0-8242-0615-0.

Diana L. Spirt has prepared a successor to the much used *Library Manual* prepared by Marie A. Toser. The aim of the *Manual* is to help high school students learn how to locate and analyze information and how to conduct library research. Both print and nonprint materials are treated in this edition. The four chapters cover the library media center (resources, organization); guides to media resources (catalog, indexes, guides); reference books (almanacs, dictionaries, encyclopedias,

special sources); and the research process (search strategy, taking notes, forming a mediagraphy). Quizzes are presented with each chapter, and there is a brief mediagraphy at the end of the book. Preceding the text are instructions to teachers, including a teaching guide with learning objectives, projects, and a comprehensive examination.

The text is planned to engage students in three modes: self-instruction; instructor directed; and student performed (projects, puzzles, activities). Numerous sample pages are reproduced from indexes and other reference books, perhaps more than are necessary. It is disappointing to find no real innovations here; the efforts to vary mode of instruction are laudable, but the text itself seems drab and uninspired. In the hands of a highly motivated librarian, it can be of help in planning learning activities for students with specific needs. It is more difficult to see this as a text the student will follow through unit by unit. [R: JAL, Nov 79, p. 300; LJ, 15 Nov 79, p. 2422; WLB, Nov 79, pp. 196-97]   Christine Gehrt Wynar

1196.   Walker, H. Thomas, and Paula Kay Montgomery. **Teaching Library Media Skills: An Instructional Program for Elementary and Middle School Students.** 2nd ed. Littleton, Colo., Libraries Unlimited, 1983. 207p. illus. index. $19.50. LC 82-23977. ISBN 0-87287-365-X.

Instruction in library media skills, those student skills required to locate and use information in both print and nonprint formats, has become increasingly important in the total school library media program. This work suggests a complete program of library media instruction and includes substantially revised and updated content, activities, and resources. Part 1 covers the objectives for library media skills; library media skills instruction, including methods, instructional variables, and planning; evaluation of student performance; and implementation of a skills program. Sample library media skills activities are offered in part 2, covering subject areas such as art, career education, math, reading and language arts, music, science, and social studies. A bibliography of instructional materials for use in developing library media skills, including both print and nonprint resources, and a list of vendors are provided in the final section of this edition. The program suggested here looks toward the future and provides a guide for teaching lifelong information skills that students will require. For an evaluation of the first edition (1977), see *ARBA* 78 (entry 188). [R: JAL, Sept 83, p. 238]

1197. Wehmeyer, Lillian Biermann. **The School Librarian as Educator.** 2nd ed. Littleton, Colo., Libraries Unlimited, 1984. 455p. illus. index. (Library Science Text Series). $22.50. LC 84-19367. ISBN 0-87287-372-2.

This second, revised edition of a text which first appeared in 1976 has much to recommend it in terms of its application and documentation of educational theory as it relates to learning in the school library and in terms of the soundness of the practical suggestions it offers to school librarians. Very broad in scope, the volume begins with a chapter on learning theory and moves to several excellent chapters concerned with library skills instruction and teaching search strategies. Several of the appendices also relate to library and study skills and library instruction.

Four of the 13 chapters and several of the appendices are new to this edition. They cover learners with special needs; puzzles, games, and so forth; nonprint media; and teaming with teachers. Each of the chapters includes numerous references and limited suggestions for further reading, both of which have been somewhat updated in this edition. Emphasizing the educational role of the school library media specialist, this volume serves a purpose much different from that served by the many texts on management of the school media program. It can be used as a companion volume to texts such as Ruth Ann Davies's *The School Library Media Program: Instructional Force for Excellence*, third edition (R. R. Bowker, 1979) and Emanuel T. Prostano and Joyce S. Prostano's *The School Library Media Center*, third edition (Libraries Unlimited, 1982). [R: SLJ, Dec 84, p. 42]   JoAnn V. Rogers

COLLEGE LEVEL

1198. Mews, Hazel. **Reader Instruction in Colleges and Universities: Teaching the Use of the Library.** Hampden, Conn., Linnet Books, 1972. 111p. index. o.p. ISBN 0-208-01174-9.

The need to educate the library user is quite obvious not only in this country but also in Great Britain. In this little book Mews relates some of her experiences with respect to such topics as formal courses in library instruction, their subject content, methodology, etc. Several chapters use the so-called case history approach, in which Mews describes seminars "covering several different subjects, conducted for students at several different levels" (p. 53). Her descriptions of the step-by-step methodology of the seminars may be somewhat simplistic, but

they will be useful for neophytes. [R: WLB, May 72, p. 847]   Bohdan S. Wynar

1199. Schwartz, Barbara A., and Susan Burton. **Teaching Library Skills in Freshman English: An Undergraduate Library's Experience.** Austin, Tex., The General Libraries, University of Texas at Austin, 1981. 1v. (various paging). illus. (Contributions to Librarianship, No. 6).

The instructional staff of the University of Texas developed over a five-year period a joint program for teaching library skills to students in freshman English composition which will serve as a model of cooperation. Clearly stated goals, development of course-integrated instruction, questionnaires used in testing the program's impact on the library, and needed resources are followed by six sections which include 1980 and 1975 instructional materials, a questionnaire, and the UGL organizational chart. A self-guided tour, a list of topics for research, and instructions for finding pertinent information are well developed and will be useful to any librarian involved in library instruction. [R: JAL, Jan 82, p. 384]   Frances Neel Cheney

1200. Strawn, Richard R. **Topics, Terms, and Research Techniques: Self-Instruction in Using Library Catalogs.** Metuchen, N.J., Scarecrow, 1980. 90p. $15.00. LC 80-12569. ISBN 0-8108-1308-4.

This programmed text is designed primarily for college freshmen preparing, or about to prepare, their first term papers. It emphasizes techniques for subject access to library collections which have been arranged by the Library of Congress Classification, and subject-indexed from *LC Subject Headings*, eighth edition. Its six sections comprise: (1) how to read an LC catalog card, (2) words to use as possible search tools, (3) translation of search topic terms into controlled subject-heading language, (4) relief from the dead-end frustration of searching for topics too specific for the subject-heading structure, (5) the nature and function of subject subdivisions, and (6) basic alphabetic and categorical concepts used to file the LC subject heading list. Pre-tests introduce each section, encouraging the user to diagnose his or her needs in order to fill them most effectively from the ensuing exercises. The examples cover well-chosen, practical topics tested by actual student searches in the Wabash College Library. The workbook is structured to serve as either a self-instruction guide or a class text. It is clearly written and attractively formatted. [R: JAL, Nov 80, p. 299]   Jeanne Osborn

1201. Teaching Library Use Competence: Bridging the Gap from High School to College; Papers Presented at the Eleventh Annual Library Instruction Conference Held at Eastern Michigan University, May 7-8, 1981. Carolyn A. Kirkendall, ed. Ann Arbor, Mich., published for the Center of Educational Resources, Eastern Michigan University, by Pierian Press, 1982. 228p. (Library Orientation Series, No. 13). $19.50. LC 82-62645. ISBN 0-87650-145-5.

The conference from which papers are collected in this volume is an event that used to be billed as the Annual Conference on Library Orientation for Academic Libraries. This meeting was called simply the Library Instruction Conference. This volume's rather awkward title, and particularly its subtitle, seem to indicate that the scope of the conferences and the series has been broadened. "Bridging the Gap from High School to College" might suggest high school and college librarians exploring together ways of bringing young people to an appropriate level of competence in library use. In fact, however, as the preface to the volume states, the 13 conference papers that are presented were intended only to "establish a link in the library instruction chain" and to establish "communication between teaching librarians from different school levels" to deal with the question, "Why aren't we talking to each other?" Practically all of the papers are by college or university librarians; only three are by school people. The conference papers are uneven, and the translation of the informality of the occasion to the printed page is often inappropriate and sometimes irritating. Some papers are offhand accounts of instruction programs rather than formal, systematic presentations. One is simply a lecture that a college reference librarian gives to freshman classes. Some library skills tests that were distributed at the conference are reprinted in the volume. A final chapter, "Library Orientation and Instruction— 1980: An Annotated Review of the Literature," a 109-item bibliography, provides the only reference value that the volume has. [R: JAL, Sept 83, pp. 229-30; JAL, May 83, p. 110]

John Farley

44 Management

GENERAL WORKS

1202. Anderson, A. J. **Problems in Library Management.** Littleton, Colo., Libraries Unlimited, 1981. 282p. (Library Science Text Series). $27.00; $20.00pa. LC 81-8153. ISBN 0-87287-261-0; 0-87287-264-5pa.

Problems in Library Management comprises 22 case studies that illustrate important concepts of library management in the areas of planning, organizing, staffing, directing, and controlling. The emphasis is on the kinds of problems library school graduates are likely to encounter in the early years of their careers, rather than on high-level administrative decisions. Each case is drawn from the experiences of practicing librarians, media specialists, and information scientists in academic, school, public, or special libraries. In his introduction, Anderson suggests ways in which the case studies may be most effectively used, offering tips for step-by-step analysis of the cases.

Since the cases are arranged according to the five basic principles of management as discussed by Robert D. Stueart and John Taylor Eastlick in their text, *Library Management*, second edition (Libraries Unlimited, 1981), *Problems in Library Management* may be used as a companion volume in management courses in schools of library and information science, or independently in workshops, conferences, in-service training programs, etc. [R: JAL, Mar 82, pp. 38 and 58; LJ, 1 Feb 82, p. 237]

1203. Bommer, Michael R. W., and Ronald W. Chorba. **Decision Making for Library Management.** White Plains, N.Y., Knowledge Industry Publications, 1981. 178p. bibliog. index.

(Professional Librarian Series). $27.50pa. LC 81-17160. ISBN 0-86729-000-5.

Decision Making for Library Management is not a treatise on theories of decision-making processes in libraries, as one could easily infer from the book's name, nor is it a treatise, as one could also infer, on how library directors and supervisors do, can, or should arrive at policy and operating judgments. Indeed, today's library manager does face an increasing need for timely, objective data for decision making, and the authors do get at how to define these needs and how to collect, organize, and use the quantitative information thus derived. It appears that their interviews with managers of numerous academic and special libraries helped them put together a taxonomy of decision tasks for the major functional areas—collection development, technical services, reference and bibliographic services, collection access, and access to interlibrary loan and physical facilities—but weaknesses are apparent in the authors' exposition, or lack of it, of implementing a database management information system.

Can a system be constructed that will allow for the variety of decisions required and for the unique personal styles of the managers responsible for making them? Yes, with the services of a staff database management person, augmented by outside consultants to help design the system, and, if the authors' advice is to be followed, substantial outlays for a stand-alone micro or mini mainframe, or hardware to interface directly with the institution's central computer—lots of money up front and not inconsiderable problems over several years getting an efficient and effective system running. But for strategic planning and control, library managers can ill afford to do without it. The book's proposed framework is a good starting point. [R: BL, Aug 82, p. 1505; LJ, 15 Sept 82, p. 1735]

Charles L. Hinkle

1204. Dougherty, Richard M., and Fred J. Heinritz, with the assistance of Neal K. Kaske. **Scientific Management of Library Operations.** 2nd ed. Metuchen, N.J., Scarecrow, 1982. 274p. illus. index. $15.00. LC 81-18200. ISBN 0-8108-1485-4.

In an era of declining library budgets and increased demand for services, the most effective use of staff has become increasingly important. As did its predecessor, this second edition focuses upon the tools necessary for the analysis and management of library systems as they relate to the worker and the work environment. Among the many specific tools and procedures detailed are flowcharting, operations analysis, forms, time study, sampling, and monitoring methods. The revised edition is not, however, a mere repetition of the original.

Despite the usefulness of this work, it should be noted that the implementation of the concepts discussed would probably be most effective for positions requiring technical knowledge rather than public contact. Also, such techniques are more adaptable to and appropriate for clerical than for professional employees. Each chapter contains a section of selected problems relevant to the subject covered and a list of additional readings that combine to make it especially useful for library science students. [R: C&RL, July 83, pp. 298-99; JAL, Sept 83, p. 226; WLB, Feb 83, p. 518]

Frank Wm. Goudy

1205. Evans, G. Edward. **Management Techniques for Librarians.** 2nd ed. New York, Academic Press, 1983. 330p. index. (Library and Information Science). $21.00. LC 82-6875. ISBN 0-12-243856-6.

This second edition of *Management Techniques for Librarians* has essentially the same objective as the first edition — "it emphasizes the basic issues and concepts of management that are especially important for persons starting out in the field." As in the first edition the author presents descriptions and practical examples that provide readers with a general overview of many of the important concerns faced by today's library and information center managers regardless of type of library or specific position.

Several changes, however, have been introduced in this edition. The revision contains 16 chapters—two more than the original. Three chapters have been added; the first is entitled "Management Training and Background," the second, "Leadership in Management," and the third, "Personnel: The System Side." Two chapters dealing with history and styles of management were combined and one chapter on delegation of authority was revised and retitled "Power, Authority, and Accountability." In addition, the number of examples has been expanded and much of the text has been rephrased using a more informal writing style.

The changes improve as well as refine the book, but the text remains regrettably rudimentary. While this may be necessary in a beginning text, management is more than technique, and libraries and information centers are not simple institutions; they are extremely complex organizations operating in increasingly complicated environments. These organizations require considerable management knowledge and skill.

Managers of these organizations need more than an elementary introduction to the issues. Though management is admittedly still more art than science, a considerable amount of research relevant to administration has been developed over the years. Library and information center managers will not be effective unless they are provided with an adequate foundation in the science as well as in the art of management. Evans offers an introduction, but greater depth would have added substantially to this edition. [R: SLMQ, Fall 84, p. 433]

P. Grady Morein

1206. Lowell, Mildred Hawksworth. **Library Management Cases.** Metuchen, N.J., Scarecrow, 1975. 260p. index. $16.00. LC 75-23077. ISBN 0-8108-0845-5.

This volume is organized in four sections, each corresponding to a major category of library management cases. The first is "Organizing Cases"; the second, "Planning and Decision Cases"; the third, "Controlling Cases"; and the fourth, "In-Basket Cases."

In this book a typical case states a library management problem and concludes with one or more questions to the students (e.g., did the librarian handle this challenge effectively, tactfully?). The author herself does not answer any of her questions, this part of the assignment being left to the instructor and students. [R: C&RL, July 76, p. 380; LJ, 1 Apr 76, p. 872]

1207. Lowell, Mildred Hawksworth. **The Management of Libraries and Information Centers.** Metuchen, N.J., Scarecrow, 1968-1971. 4v. index. o.p. LC 68-12642.

Volume 1: **The Case Method in Teaching Library Management.** 1968. 167p. ISBN 0-8108-0089-6.

Volume 2: **The Process of Managing: Syllabus and Cases.** 1968. 359p. ISBN 0-8108-0090-X.

Volume 3: **Personnel Management: Syllabus and Cases.** 1968. 1v.

Volume 4: **Role Playing and Other Management Cases.** 1971. 420p. ISBN 0-8108-0424-7.

Volume 4, published several years after the initial volumes of this set, covers 94 cases, ranging from "an uncertified school librarian" or "the immature reference librarian" to "busy, busy, busy." [R: BL, 15 Apr 72, p. 692; C&RL, May 72, p. 246; LJ, 15 May 72, p. 1787]

1208. Person, Ruth J., ed. **The Management Process: A Selection of Readings for Librarians.** Chicago, American Library Association, 1983. 423p. $20.00pa. LC 83-3788. ISBN 0-8389-0381-9.

This collection of 24 readings, articles from journals, and excerpts from monographs in the management literature approaches the discussion of the topic from a "process" viewpoint. The chapters, each containing three or four well-chosen articles, divide the book into seven topics, beginning with "Management in the Library Setting"—thereby placing the discussions in a not-for-profit setting—and continuing through decision making, control, organizing, communicating, staffing, and directing. About 70 percent of the articles were written between 1977 and 1980, with some earlier ones by Peter Drucker and Richard Huseman that are considered classic introductions to the topics being discussed.

The volume is enhanced by a succinct introduction to each chapter and a fine, though limited, "Additional Readings" section at the end of the unit. One could argue about why one article has been included and another equally relevant and dynamic one ignored, but that is always the case with a book of selected readings. The articles that have been chosen are relevant, are provocative, and fit well within the general theme. The volume is a desirable addition to any professional library and should prove helpful both to students who would want to use it with a management text and to practi-

tioners who want to do some serious thinking about a process that affects all of our working lives. [R: LJ, 15 Nov 83, p. 2144]

Robert D. Stueart

1209. Rizzo, John R. **Management for Librarians: Fundamentals and Issues.** Westport, Conn., Greenwood Press, 1980. 339p. index. (Contributions in Librarianship and Information Science, No. 33). $37.50. LC 79-8950. ISBN 0-313-21990-7.

Management for Librarians is a welcome addition to the increasing volume of library management literature, bringing fresh air from the management field to the librarian. Although the author claims no formal education in librarianship, he is certainly not a stranger to the library field. In simple, concise, and clear style, the book is a good introduction to management and its applications for libraries, specifically in the areas of organizational effectiveness and efficiency, structural design and dynamics, and the components of work life related to behavioral and/or organizational psychology. Management is a very broad term, and managerial techniques undoubtedly involve many interdisciplinary fields. The author is fair to state that his book steers away from quantitative techniques in management, operations research techniques, and computer applications. It covers only briefly budgeting and financial matters, personnel selection, labor management contracts and law, marketing, and so forth. Thus this is not the book for these managerial topics. For what the author intends to cover, this is a good book. [R: C&RL, July 81, pp. 387-88; JAL, July 81, p. 176]

Ching-chih Chen

1210. Shaffer, Kenneth R. **The Experience of Management: Case Studies in Public and Academic Library Administration.** Metuchen, N.J., Scarecrow, 1972. 167p. o.p. LC 72-6323. ISBN 0-8108-0536-7.

This work presents 30 "classic" cases selected from Shaffer's three earlier casebooks, revised for inclusion here. The casebooks are now out-of-print, but they have been widely used in library schools both in this country and in Europe, in workshops, in-service training programs, and by individual library administrators. The cases chosen for this volume are those with enduring value for both the practicing library administrator and the library school student. [R: LJ, 15 Mar 73, p. 849; LR, Summer 73, p. 74; RQ, Summer 73, p. 408; RSR, July 73, p. 28; SLMQ, Spring 73, p. 226]

1211. Shimmon, Ross, ed. **A Reader in Library Management.** With linking commentaries by John Allred, K. H. Jones, and Peter Jordon. London, Clive Bingley; distr., Hamden, Conn., Linnet Books, 1976. 213p. illus. bibliog. $16.00. LC 76-10382. ISBN 0-208-01378-4.

An even dozen journal articles have been reprinted, with linking commentaries of two to four pages. The reader's aim is to introduce a beginning student of library management to such topics as purpose and planning, style of management, personnel, and evaluation of a library's effectiveness. Compiled first for a British readership, the selection, with as many North American as British articles, is explained by a comment on the international character of "the problems confronted and in the solutions attempted" and by reference to a few excellent readers that this selection would complement (e.g., Wasserman and Bundy, *Reader in Library Administration*, 1968), since its selections are from journal issues from 1969 to 1972.

Neither the selections nor the commentaries and appended bibliography are worth the price. Distribution of the reading list to a class of students would serve the purpose of this book at one hundredth the price. [R: C&RL, Mar 77, p. 171; JAL, Mar 77, p. 39; LJ, 15 Mar 77, p. 692; LR, Winter 76/77, p. 329]

Pauline Atherton Cochrane

1212. **Strategies for Library Administration: Concepts and Approaches.** By Charles R. McClure and Alan R. Samuels. Littleton, Colo., Libraries Unlimited, 1982. 451p. bibliog. $28.50; $19.50pa. LC 81-12408. ISBN 0-87287-265-3; 0-87287-390-0pa.

This work is a collection of 34 original articles and reprinted writings which have been drawn from a broad spectrum of the social and behavioral sciences, as well as library literature, to assist the reader in dealing with basic administrative problems affecting today's libraries. Arranged into 13 categories, such as financial basis of the library, administrative theory, unionization, and organizational change, the writings deal with nontraditional approaches to administrative problem solving. The original introduction to each category assists the reader in understanding the topic's significance in today's administrative thought. The articles cover topics such as zero-base budgeting, developing human resources, and applying theory to library management. [R: LJ, July 82, p. 1304; RQ, Fall 82, p. 107; SBF, Nov/Dec 82, p. 60]

1213. **Studies in Library Management.** London, Clive Bingley; distr., Hamden, Conn.,

Shoe String Press, 1972-1982. price varies. Volume 1 edited by Brian Redfern; volumes 2-4 edited by Gileon Holroyd; volumes 5-7 edited by Anthony Vaughen. $16.00/vol. 1; $17.00/vols. 2-4; $14.00/vol. 5; $19.00/vol. 7.

This series is no longer published. The stated purpose of this series was "to bring to librarians and others of recent developments in librarianship, and surveys and analyses of current practices and issues." *ARBA* reviews of earlier volumes are as follows: Volume 2, see *ARBA* 76 (entry 178), volume 3, see *ARBA* 77 (entry 247), volume 4, see *ARBA* 78 (entry 209), volume 5, see *ARBA* 80 (entry 199), volume 6, see *ARBA* 82 (entry 288), volume 7, see *ARBA* 83 (entry 270). The following review of volume 7 (237p.), published in 1982, serves as an example.

This volume comprises an examination of the role of women in libraries; a survey of education and training for nonprofessional library staff; a discussion of the work ethic and its implications for management; a review of the administrative aspects of automated cataloging; an analysis of the ultimate value of a library; a consideration of the new technology in academic libraries; a study of the British Library Reference Division; an examination of projects in collective management in Denmark; and a historical survey of the French library system. Only the latter two are focused outside Great Britain; the others, written by authors whose primary affiliations are with British institutions, primarily examine problems, issues, and situations in their nation's library systems. Part 2 of the book includes two studies—one on the value of libraries, and the other on attitudes toward automation and technological change—that present ideas of more general significance to librarians and library administrators. Excellent bibliographies follow the papers. [R: C&RL, Jan 84, p. 80; JAL, Jan 83, p. 384; LR, Summer 83, p. 153; WLB, Nov 82, p. 247]

Charles L. Hinkle

1214. Stueart, Robert D., and John Taylor Eastlick. **Library Management.** 2nd ed. Littleton, Colo., Libraries Unlimited, 1981. 292p. bibliog. index. (Library Science Text Series). $30.00; $21.00pa. LC 80-22895. ISBN 0-87287-241-6; 0-87287-243-2pa.

The first edition of this basic management text (see *ARBA* 78, entry 212) appeared in 1977. This edition of *Library Management* has 23 sample library objectives and planning documents, organization charts, job descriptions, employee performance evaluations, labor contracts, and budget and justification forms. These have been collected from public, university, and state library systems and reprinted in their entirety for maximum usefulness in a classroom or library situation. Also in this edition is the chapter on the impact of change on library management development. The authors discuss the effects of such factors as increased staff participation in the decision-making process, unionization and collective bargaining, the historical background and development of library management, networking, and women and minorities as managers.

The text is arranged according to the five basic principles of management: planning, organizing, staffing, directing, and controlling. It examines the dynamics of the library as an organization—the behavior of individuals and groups within the library, the policies and programs of the library, and the relationship of the library to its staff and its clientele. The concepts and principles presented in the text are discussed not only individually but also in the larger context of the library—its immediate environment and its extended environment.

The purpose of this edition, as with the previous one, is to present the principles of management for libraries and information centers in a conceptual framework, both as a text for formal classroom situations and as a guide for self-instructed or group-related continuing education. [R: JAL, Nov 81, pp. 295-96; LJ, 15 Mar 81, p. 627]

1215. Zachert, Martha Jane K. **Simulation Teaching of Library Administration.** New York, R. R. Bowker, 1975. 297p. index. (Problem-Centered Approaches to Librarianship). $18.95. LC 74-32041. ISBN 0-8352-0612-2. (Available from Books on Demand, $78.80pa., ISBN 0-317-10402-0).

Ardent advocacy of simulation techniques for the teaching of library administration characterizes this case book in the Bowker series of Problem-Centered Approaches to Librarianship. The book begins with expository material on simulation; teaching materials; the teacher's role in orientation, coordination, and evaluation; experiential techniques (such as role playing, regular, multimedia, and sequential in-basket exercises, action maze, and games); and research efforts in simulation instruction and the design of simulation materials. This material is followed by two major simulation exercises. One simulation involves an industrial library, wherein planning of services, personnel, library materials, physical facilities, financial arrangements, and communicating of library services are treated. The other simulation concerns a federal government library, in which planning,

adjusting of space, an intern program, revision of budget, adjudication of personnel problems, quality control, coordination of division plans, handling of complaints, and allocation of new equipment are presented. Both cases include organization charts, documents, and specific problems.

Designed for the library school market, this volume includes a six-page bibliography, figures, exhibits, and an index. It should prove a useful supplementary text for those desiring to explore the virtues of experiential instruction. [R: C&RL, Sept 75, p. 421; LJ, 1 Oct 75, p. 1778]   Richard P. Palmer

REFERENCE WORKS

1216. Schumacher, August. **Development Plans and Planning: Bibliographic and Computer Aids to Research.** New York, Seminar Press, 1973. 195p. illus. index. (International Bibliographical and Library Series [Interbiblis], Vol. 3). o.p. LC 76-189942. ISBN 0-12-909150-2.

Contains three bibliographical essays: "Bibliographies Relevant to Development Plans and Planning," which mentions about 100 bibliographies on such widely diversified topics as agriculture, education, industry and management, etc.; "Documentation Centers and the Computer"; and "Technology and Modern Library Usage." There are 19 appendices, plus author, subject, and country indexes. [R: LQ, July 74, p. 263; RSR, Apr 74, p. 22; RSR, Oct 73, p. 26]

1217. Shonyo, Carolyn. **Library Management: A Bibliography with Abstracts.** Springfield, Va., National Technical Information Service, 1977. 188p. (NTIS/PS-76/1037/RC). o.p.

Covering the period 1964-1976, the cited references include reports on management of library operations and personnel. A total of 188 abstracts are included, covering such topics as management of acquisitions, processing of library holdings, management planning of programs and activities, operations analysis, community library services and needs, library personnel management, etc. There is no index.

PROCEEDINGS, SYMPOSIA, AND ESSAYS

1218. Boaz, Martha, ed. **Current Concepts in Library Management.** Littleton, Colo., Libraries Unlimited, 1979. 292p. index. $27.50. LC 79-20734. ISBN 0-87287-204-1.

This collection of 11 original essays authoritatively addresses the practical application of management principles and administrative policies in various types of library and information contexts. Invited contributors Neely Gardner, Peggy Sullivan, Duane E. Webster, Chase Dane, and Jerry Cao offer essays on management concepts, and on the management of public, academic, school media, and technical libraries. Also included are Ellsworth Mason's "Managing the Planning of Library Buildings" and Hillis L. Griffin on management considerations in library automation. Editor Boaz discusses the library administrator's role in individual and staff development, the management of library schools and facilities, and extra-institutional funding. In four concluding appendices, Boaz focuses on the management of the library profession itself.

This collection is intended as a primer in the field, and will be valuable to both the library school student and the practicing administrator. [R: BL, 15 July 80, p. 1654; JAL, Sept 80, p. 228; LJ, 15 June 80, p. 1371]

1219. Chen, Ching-chih, ed. **Library Management without Bias.** Greenwich, Conn., JAI Press, 1980. 225p. illus. index. (Foundations in Library and Information Science, Vol. 13). $37.50. LC 80-82482. ISBN 0-89232-163-6.

What is bias in library management? For purposes of this book, it was defined as "the discrimination of minorities and women in library management" (p. xxi). The book is the proceedings of the Institute on Library Management without Bias held at MIT and organized by the library school at Simmons College during 1979. Each of the 15 major papers and the question and answer sessions are reproduced in the first 177 pages. Topics covered are: the status of bias in libraries, the psychology of bias, decision making, productivity, organizational structure, racism and sexism, communication (3 papers), affirmative action, employee selection practices, performance appraisal, staff development, public relations, and "new objectives for library management." All of the papers are high quality, but the ones by A. J. Anderson, Estelle Jussim, Mary A. Hall, and Margaret Chisholm are particularly interesting. Seven appendices round out the volume's text and are followed by an author/subject index.

The book will have some value as a source of supplemental readings in management courses in library schools. [R: JAL, Jan 82, p. 371; SL, Jan 82, p. 91]

G. Edward Evans

1220. **Library Management in Review.** Alice Bruemmer, Janet Reed, and Karen Takle Quinn, eds. New York, Special Libraries Association, 1981. 104p. $13.75pa. LC 81-13562. ISBN 0-87111-294-9.

This thin volume of 20 papers, 16 of which are reprinted from the *Library Management Bulletin* (1978-1980), is loosely arranged under seven broad headings: "Management Styles"; "Financial Management"; "Time Management"; "Communications"; "Vendor Services"; "Interviewing"; and "Career Planning." With about 80 pages of actual text, the average paper is four pages in length, an indication that no in-depth analysis is presented.

Whether this volume brings "together the best of the Library Management Divisions' publications" is questionable. Certainly some articles are interesting and might prove helpful for some managers. However, it is doubtful that the depth of papers or the wide range of topics makes this useful for anything other than a collection of writings on management. One could better spend the money by subscribing to the *Library Management Bulletin.* [R: JAL, Sept 82, p. 256]

Robert D. Stueart

1221. **Library Management, Volume I: Papers from the Management Workshops Sponsored by the Special Libraries Association Library Management Division and Cosponsored by the Business and Finance, Insurance, and Military Librarians Divisions.** Janette S. Caputo Closurdo, ed. New York, Special Libraries Association, 1980. 91p. o.p. ISBN 0-87111-266-1. (Available from Books on Demand, $25.30pa., ISBN 0-317-01347-4).

Papers are presented from four of five workshops held during the seventieth Annual Conference of the Special Libraries Association, 7-14 June 1979. The main topics are: "Job Descriptions and Performance Standards"; "Management Communication Problems"; "Cost Recovery as a Source of Library Funding"; "Career Paths for Special Librarians"; and "Cost/Benefit Analysis in the Special Library." Papers from workshop V. are not included. The papers are often only summaries rather than the entire text, since they were intended primarily to stimulate discussion during the workshops. Some charts and figures are included, and lists of suggested readings draw heavily on the management literature. Library science students and entry-level special librarians will find the book of particular interest. The volume is a welcome addition to the rather scanty literature on special library management. [R: LJ, 1 Sept 81, p. 1607]

Andrew G. Torok

1222. **Management by Design.** Shirley Loo, ed. New York, Special Libraries Association, 1982. 66p. (Library Management, Vol. 2). o.p. ISBN 0-87111-301-3.

Disappointments come in all shapes and sizes; and this second volume in the Library Management series is consistently disappointing. The work opens with a paper on decision making and problem solving which appears to be more of a compilation of definitions which the author has tried to weave into a viable fabric of understanding, yet which leaves the reader with little more than an increased vocabulary and a confused mind. This is followed by a paper on staff productivity which, while touching on some important points, cannot replace discussions of the topic which appear in basic management textbooks. A brief and chit-chatty "paper" on staff coaching and counseling appears as the third entry, while a last minute substitute paper on long-range planning (note the irony) concludes the cacophonous quartet.

Taken as a whole, this wee volume is a disaster. Although the bibliographies for each paper will prove useful to researchers, one would do better to invest in a basic management textbook, supplemented by readings in the current periodical literature. [R: JAL, Sept 82, p. 240] Edmund F. SantaVicca

1223. Tsuneishi, Warren M., Thomas R. Buckman, and Yukihisa Suzuki. **Issues in Library Administration: Papers Presented at the Second United States-Japan Conference on Libraries and Information Science in Higher Education; Racine, Wisconsin; October 17-20, 1972.** New York, Columbia University Press, 1974. 181p. illus. index. $32.00. LC 74-3002. ISBN 0-231-03818-6.

The 12 papers comprising this volume serve to contrast developments in Japanese and American university libraries in the areas of administrative reform, the changing role and status of the library director, the organization, administration, and management of libraries, library personnel and staffing, and interlibrary cooperation. The Japanese papers are largely descriptive of past and present patterns in university libraries in Japan. The American papers, more theoretical and forward-looking, discuss findings from recent management studies.

The papers cover the impact on libraries of substantial changes in financial support, the process of learning and teaching, the dynamics of decision making, the rising expectations for library service, advancing computer and photo-graphic technology, and modifications in publishing. An increasing emphasis on reader's services and a stabilizing of technical services are anticipated, along with a more rapid turnover of library directors and more participatory management. Improvisation in planning will be requisite. Uneven international cooperation is predicted.

Of modest use to those interested in library management, this volume includes an index, but no bibliographies. [R: AL, Mar 75, p. 171; C&RL, 1 Feb 75, p. 271; RSR, Oct 74, p. 136] Richard P. Palmer

FUNCTIONS

Budgeting and Finance

1224. Alley, Brian, and Jennifer Cargill. **Keeping Track of What You Spend: The Librarian's Guide to Simple Bookkeeping.** Phoenix, Ariz., Oryx Press, 1982. 96p. illus. bibliog. index. $25.00pa. LC 81-11289. ISBN 0-912700-79-3.

This book should prove to be extremely valuable to a large number of small libraries and to clerical staff in larger libraries. As the authors make clear, it is conceived as an overview of practical methods of fund accounting. It presents in a very clear manner the basics of financial management. Although it is presented as a guide to simple bookkeeping, the book would be stronger if the treatment of some topics were either expanded upon or included (e.g., claiming, compensatory time, forms design, handling state and local funds), and the number of "filler" pages reduced. Does anyone really need a full-page picture of a cart for housing ledgers, or two full-page examples of ledger pages? In fact, at least 40 pages of the 96 which comprise this book are full-page pictures or illustrations of various business forms.

One of the stronger sections of the book is on auditing and conducting one's own audit. The process of encumbering funds is also very well explained. The brief treatment of filing rules, however, seems to be both out of place and superfluous. A short bibliography (eight titles) of books on recordkeeping and simple accounting methods is included, along with a glossary of 33 items. Finally, there is a brief listing of vendors of various types of equipment and supplies. Despite some reservations, this should prove to be a very useful book. [R: JAL, May 82, p. 121]

Thomas W. Shaughnessy

1225. Brown, Eleanor Frances. **Cutting Library Costs: Increasing Productivity and Raising Revenues.** Metuchen, N.J., Scarecrow, 1979. 264p. illus. bibliog. index. $16.00. LC 79-19448. ISBN 0-8108-1250-9.

The best one can say for this work is that it is probably well intentioned and is mistitled. A more apt title would be *Eleanor's Helpful Hints for Running a Better Library*. It is a potpourri of suggestions and recommendations which in the aggregate, alleges their author, will, if adopted, enable the library manager to effect considerable cost savings. A library manager will find little help here. Most of the advice and discussion is superficial or puerile or both. Possibly, nonprofessional heads of all-volunteer libraries might glean some help from the contents, but it would be at the cost of considerable insult to their intelligence.

Any librarian seriously concerned about costs and their control could do no better than to master *Cost Analysis of Library Functions: A Total System Approach* (see *ARBA* 79, entry 256). Effective cost-cutting begins with an accurate and thorough knowledge of costs coupled with responsible goals and priorities. [R: BL, 15 Apr 80, p. 1176; C&RL, July 80, pp. 365-66; JAL, Mar 80, p. 58; LJ, 15 Feb 80, p. 488]   Joseph McDonald

1226. Chen, Ching-chih. **Zero-Base Budgeting in Library Management: A Manual for Librarians.** Phoenix, Ariz., Oryx Press, 1980. 293p. illus. bibliog. index. (A Neal-Schuman Professional Book). $35.00. LC 80-12055. ISBN 0-912700-18-1.

The use of a strict zero-based budgeting procedure as a permanent fixture in public sector financial management does not appear to be gaining momentum. However, advocates of the system believe that in this era of decreasing public resources ZBB is essential in forcing a prioritization of difficult economic decisions. Opponents of ZBB argue that it is too complex and too time-consuming as well as often running counter to political factors that public agency managers must take into consideration. Regardless of these concerns, it appears that the general idea behind ZBB will be increasingly used to enforce greater fiscal accountability. This reality underscores the importance of this book, which is the first that relates ZBB specifically to libraries. A previous work by Sul H. Lee, titled *Library Budgeting: Critical Challenges for the Future* (see *ARBA* 78, entry 211), did include one chapter on ZBB.

The limitation of Chen's work is the brevity with which it treats the historical, philosophical, and practical aspects of ZBB. Only 68 pages of text are provided to include both background information and specific applications of ZBB. The material presented is well written and logically organized, but significantly more detail is essential before one could use this as an effective guide for executing ZBB. A redeeming feature of this effort is the case studies provided. Examples, including special forms and submitted budgets, are documented from public, academic, and special libraries where ZBB has actually been used. Such information can be valuable in generating ideas and programs for those contemplating either partial or total implementation of this system. A glossary of terms, relevant bibliography, and subject index are provided. [R: JAL, July 81, p. 174; JAL, Jan 81, p. 378; LR, Summer 81, p. 102]
Frank Wm. Goudy

1227. Kent, Allen, and others. **Use of Library Materials: The University of Pittsburgh Study.** New York, Marcel Dekker, 1979. 272p. index. (Books in Library and Information Science, Vol. 26). o.p. LC 79-11513. ISBN 0-8247-6807-8.

This study, funded by the National Science Foundation and previously issued in report form under the title "A Cost Benefit Model of Some Critical Library Operations in Terms of Use of Materials," was conducted to measure the extent to which library materials are used and the full cost of such use. The landmark report, commonly referred to as the "Pittsburgh Study," has been widely discussed in library literature and at conferences. This volume provides additional data that will be useful to those interested in replicating the study. However, much of the information has already been published in other sources. For instance, large portions of the chapter "Cost Benefit Model of Library Operations" and the one "Alternatives to Local Acquisitions" are included in the proceedings of a Pittsburgh conference, which were published under the title *Library Resource Sharing* (Marcel Dekker, 1977). Kent, Cohen, and Montgomery have edited the summer 1979 issue of *Library Trends* on "The Economics of Academic Libraries," which should provide supportive information for this volume.

Several technical points in the book are distracting to the reader: the offset form of printing leaves some charts and graphs less than attractive and difficult to read (pp. 59 and 149, for example); blind footnotes (p. 48, for example); and a very superficial index. [R: BL, 15 Oct 79, p. 330; C&RL, Nov 79, pp. 557-58; JAL, Nov 79, p. 288]   Danuta A. Nitecki

1228. Koenig, Michael E. D. **Budgeting Techniques for Libraries and Information Centers.** New York, Special Libraries Association, 1980. 71p. bibliog. (Professional Development Series, Vol. 1). $7.50pa. LC 80-27698. ISBN 0-87111-278-7. (Available from Books on Demand, $20.00pa., ISBN 0-317-09538-2).

This is a primer on budgetary techniques and financial planning that would be most applicable for beginning librarians who are responsible for the administration of their first library. A cursory outline of budgetary approaches such as line item, ZBB, PPBS, and performance is provided, along with a brief overview of the foundations of cost analysis. The various intricacies of budget justification are presented in readily understandable language with workaday advice that allows one to have at least a superficial understanding of this difficult and complex process. A selected passage revealing of the approach of this title is the comment: "If padding is the norm, however, any move toward a more straightforward budget presentation should be done carefully and with preparation." As an elementary handbook, this does not have the depth of such works as Martin's *Budgetary Control in Academic Libraries* (see *ARBA* 79, entry 199) or Prentice's *Public Library Finance* (see *ARBA* 78, entry 176). As a result, the value of this effort is limited to those with virtually no scholarly or practical knowledge of library administration. A selective bibliography and glossary of costing terms are provided. [R: JAL, Nov 81, pp. 298-99]   Frank Wm. Goudy

1229. Lee, Sul H., ed. **Library Budgeting: Critical Challenges for the Future.** Ann Arbor, Mich., Pierian Press, 1977. 111p. illus. bibliog. (Library Management Series). $24.50. LC 77-85231. ISBN 0-87650-083-1.

Everyone has had some experience with budgeting and fiscal problems. This small collection of seven essays addresses a variety of library budgeting difficulties. Four of the essays (authored by Robin Downes, Jerome Yavarkovsky, Duane Webster, and Beverly Lynch) explore the numerous problems associated with "no growth"/"steady state" budgets. Richard Denman discusses zero-base budgets; Kenneth Allen describes the revisions in the Washington State Library formula; and Michael Bommer examines problems of performance measures, decision models, and budget making. Perhaps the most useful part of the book is the 15-page bibliography; most of the items are post-1970 and are among the best on the subject. One significant drawback is that, although the title

and introduction do not indicate it, the book is directed toward academic libraries. The authors are all involved in an academic environment and their papers reflect that fact. Nonacademic librarians will have to dig for any practical applications for their own libraries.

All of the essays make interesting reading for anyone with library budgeting experience; however, none can be considered essential reading. [R: C&RL, Mar 78, p. 151; LR, Autumn 78, p. 138; SL, July 78, p. 279]
                    G. Edward Evans

1230. Lee, Sul H., ed. **Planning-Programming-Budgeting System (PPBS): Implications for Library Management.** Published for the Eastern Michigan University Library. Ann Arbor, Mich., Pierian Press, 1973. 112p. illus. bibliog. (Library Management Series, No. 1). $24.50. LC 73-78314. ISBN 0-87650-040-8.

This volume represents the proceedings of an institute on library management that convened at Eastern Michigan University on 21 April 1971. The institute was an attempt to find the answers to basic questions concerning the Planning, Programming and Budgeting System prior to the adoption of the system at Eastern Michigan.

PPBS is well explained by the speakers, but it is really necessary to read only the Jenkins paper to understand the use of the technique. That paper provides a step-by-step procedure for the implementation of PPBS, and the explanation is clear, concise, and well illustrated. The final section of the book consists of an extensive bibliography on the subject.

Not a reference book in the usual sense of the term, but an excellent source for instruction on how to implement a program budget system. [R: C&RL, May 74, p. 216]
                    Donald P. Hammer

1231. Martin, Murray S., ed. **Financial Planning for Libraries.** New York, Haworth Press, 1983. 131p. (*Journal of Library Administration*, Vol. 3, Nos. 3 and 4). $22.95. LC 82-23346. ISBN 0-86656-118-8.

The title of this work is broader than the content. It could more appropriately have been called "Financial Planning for Academic Libraries," with an article on the public library included. Eight of the nine contributors are associated with or have written about academic libraries. Within this more limited universe, there is relatively good coverage of an important and timely aspect of the managerial process. Each of the contributors is knowledgeable about his or her particular topic and writes about it in an informative if often elementary fashion. There is a fair amount of exhortation to do better and some complaint that the university environment lacks sensitivity to library needs. One author discusses the academic environment within which we plan; another reports on a questionnaire to librarians in publicly supported universities and their views of planning needs in the 1980s. The implementation of a planning model at Columbia University is discussed by Jerome Yavarkovsky, assistant university librarian for planning, and the purpose, design, and use of decision support systems are presented in another chapter. The section titled "Specific Issues" provides good general information on salary planning, costs of interlibrary loan, and collection management. This book would be useful as a supplement to management texts and as a source of information on the financial implications of certain academic library activities. [R: BL, 15 Oct 83, p. 326; WLB, Oct 83, pp. 142-43]   Ann E. Prentice

1232.   Mitchell, Betty Jo. **ALMS: A Budget Based Library Management System.** Greenwich, Conn., JAI Press, 1983. 235p. 12 microfiche. bibliog. index. (Foundations in Library and Information Science, Vol. 16). $42.50. LC 82-81208. ISBN 0-89232-246-2.

ALMS is a system that is based on a budget that satisfies stated needs. It analyzes the use and quality of personnel hours provided in the present budget and then applies the results to personnel justification and goals establishment. This book "describes a system of data collection, and how that quantitative data, coupled with professional judgment, may be utilized in the various facets of library management— budget, personnel, and goal setting." Mitchell has drawn upon her personal experiences at the California State University Library in Northridge in preparing this well-written guide for library management. She discusses the strategies for developing a management system, justification and defense of a budget, allocation of personnel, and goal setting. The text is straightforward, with numerous examples and references for additional reading. A large part of the book is devoted to over 140 pages of appendices that pertain to reports, mission statements, programs, bibliographies, and labor analyses used at California State University in Northridge. As budgets are critical in most libraries, this book should prove to be useful for library management in helping to make budget decisions. [R: JAL, Sept 83, p. 252]

H. Robert Malinowsky

1233.   Prentice, Ann E. **Financial Planning for Libraries.** Metuchen, N.J., Scarecrow, 1983. 222p. bibliog. index. (Scarecrow Library Administration Series, No. 8). $14.50. LC 82-7330. ISBN 0-8108-1565-6.

Prentice covers a variety of topics relevant to financial planning for libraries. Most interesting is her extensive treatment of environmental factors that influence the availability of financial resources. In addition, she presents budgeting as an integral part of the planning process. The author also discusses data-gathering methods, budget design, financial control, and capital budgets. Certainly, the most relevant topics for budgeting are discussed in this work.

The book is, however, quite difficult to read, even for those whose primary interest is finance. A careful examination of the book suggests that more generous use of subheads, outline form, and boldface type would have made it more readable. In addition, certain important topics are not covered in depth. One example is the treatment of unit costs. Prentice appears to be aware that most librarians are unfamiliar with the computation of unit costs. But after going through her section on the subject, most readers will know in general what should be considered but will still be unable to compute unit costs. The use of a few actual computations would have greatly increased the value of the book. [R: BL, 15 Oct 83, p. 327; JAL, May 83, p. 123; SBF, Sept/Oct 83, p. 1777]

Jo Ann H. Bell

1234.   Quirk, Dantia, and Patricia Whitestone. **The Shrinking Library Dollar.** rev. ed. White Plains, N.Y., Knowledge Industry Publications, 1982. 170p. bibliog. index. (Communications Library). $24.95. LC 81-12319. ISBN 0-914236-74-1.

As noted on the recto of the title page, this volume is a revision of a 1978 industry study, *The Library Market for Publications and Systems.* The first edition, as well as this volume, was based heavily on data and statistics provided by the Book Industry Study Group, which is a "not-for-profit corporation funded by organizations concerned with the future of the book industry," the Association of American Publishers, and the Association of Media Producers.

The work comprises eight chapters including an introduction, "Overview of Libraries in the United States," "The Library Market for General Books," "The Library Market for Professional and Reference Books," "The Library

Market for Periodicals," "The Library Market for Systems," "The Library Market for Audiovisual and Other Materials," and summary and conclusions. A special section of "Profiles" of selected (22) major library suppliers, publishers, etc., is followed by a two-page list of references, and an index. The work is heavily illustrated by tables, 54 in all, which graphically project a wealth of information not easily located in any other source, e.g., "Estimated Academic Library Materials Expenditures, Even Years, 1976-1984"; "Book Publishing Costs at Alternative Levels of Production"; "Periodical Publishing Revenue and Percentage from Advertising and Circulation, 1975-1981"; "Leading Micropublishers in the Market"; "Estimates of Total Library Market, 1980 and 1984"; etc. The data supplied by the associations are from 1979 and 1980, but many of the references are to 1981 activities and statistics. Each chapter is carefully organized, as, for example, the introductory one, which notes current economic trends in libraries, defines the objectives of the study, and points out its limitations. The remaining chapters all have summary sections as well as footnotes where appropriate.

The publisher has described the volume as a "unique study [which] analyzes budget and spending trends ... with the emphasis on what libraries spend for publications and related materials — and its impact on libraries, publishers and others. Existing figures and estimates are carefully compiled for academic, public, school and special libraries, and such trends as the declining acquisition budget and the shift from books to periodicals are carefully assessed." That description is accurate, and it should be noted that the "related materials," notably in chapters 6 and 7, deal with library networks, online bibliographic services and other databases, automated circulation systems, theft prevention/electronic security systems, cataloging and processing services (not-for-profit and commercial), audiovisual equipment, furniture, supplies, and microforms. All in all, this is a work which every library manager needs to own for his or her personal understanding of the industry trends. Certainly, every library school will want this as a resource for a number of classes. It is to be hoped that Knowledge Industry Publications will issue new editions on a regular basis. [R: JAL, Sept 82, p. 233; LJ, July 82, p. 1304]   Laurel Grotzinger

Evaluating and Measurement

1235. Blagden, John. **Do We Really Need Libraries?: An Assessment of Approaches to the**

Evaluation of the Performance of Libraries. London, Clive Bingley; distr., Hamden, Conn., Shoe String Press, 1980. 162p. bibliog. index. $18.50. ISBN 0-85157-308-8.

The question "Do We Really Need Libraries?" cannot be answered by a simple yes or no. There are many factors that may determine the answer. Among them: clientele to be served; expectations of the clientele; character of the funding agency (public or private); cost of the service (whether it is to be cost effective); competing, perhaps less costly, nonlibrary channels of document delivery; accessibility of library service.

In his book, based on a thesis prepared at University College, Blagden considers these and various other factors that may answer the question he poses. Blagden reviews the attempts made toward developing a "methodology by which a library's (and by inference the librarians's) contribution to the goals laid down by the funding body can be more easily assessed" (p. 7). About half of the book consists of a comprehensive, thorough, critical evaluation of largely British and American literature, dating mainly from the middle sixties through the late seventies. Special attention is given to some of the major studies, particularly with regard to the techniques and criteria they applied. Blagden then focuses on two investigations — the pilot study conducted at the Construction Design Library of the Greater London Council (GLC), and the more broadly conceived, yet similar, exploration at the British Institute of Management (BIM). At the GLC and at the BIM, "penetration" and "impact" were chosen as the criteria for performance assessment. The purpose of "penetration" is to ascertain whether the message reaches the audience for which it is intended, and the purpose of "impact" is to discover the extent to which the message is used and produces the outcome desired by the client. Some investigators maintain that the library must achieve "impact"; others say the library's responsibility ends when the message reaches the intended clientele.

At the GLC and at the BIM, library use was very low. But the small percentage of the intended clientele which did use the library found this provider of information very helpful. Since in these and other instances investigated by Blagden library service has proven beneficial to clients taking advantage of it, he feels justified in giving a positive answer to the question posed by the book's title. However, he urges the profession to engage in further research and to further develop and refine the methodology for library performance assessment.

Blagden has probed performance assessment for special libraries. With some modifications, the methods can be applied to public and academic libraries. Modifications might, for instance, be indicated in the cost-benefit area.

The author uses quotations frequently and appropriately. They are skillfully woven into the text. He supplies author, title, and date of the source but not the page from which the quoted material is taken.

The book is highly readable. It should be an especially helpful guide to those librarians who have to justify to funding agencies the financial investments required for maintaining library service. However, it may also be recommended to any practitioner or student who wishes to get a clearer view of the complex problem of library performance assessment. [R: JAL, Sept 81, p. 260; LR, Summer 81, p. 96]

Fritz Veit

1236. Chen, Ching-chih, ed. **Quantitative Measurement and Dynamic Library Service.** Phoenix, Ariz., Oryx Press, 1978. 290p. bibliog. index. (A Neal-Schuman Professional Book). o.p. ISBN 0-912700-17-3.

The title and promotional material do not indicate just what this book is and is not, although it is apparently another of the institute/workshop instant publications that have been appearing all too frequently. Judging by the nature of the content (15 of the 19 articles are from participants), it apparently is the result of a two-part seminar. This assumption is corroborated by the fact that a number of the participants were students in the Simmons doctoral program supervised by Chen. The stated purpose of the book is to help and encourage those individuals with little statistical background to use analytical and quantitative methods in library decision-making processes.

The first part of the book presents four papers that were read at the institute (those by Chen, F. W. Lancaster and Deanne McCutcheon, Morris Hamburg, and F. F. Leimkuhler). These papers are the most worthwhile reading and cover statistical methods and systems approaches to problems in library management and decision making. However, they are so brief and general in content that they do little to help a practitioner understand quantitative methods for library management; without further study, one would not be able to put the techniques to work.

Part 2 is a collection of reports on the "application" of quantitative techniques prepared by the participants in the institute. The

reader must realize that the participants applied the techniques *after* attending the institute, and that they were, in effect, in the same position as students who are required to write a paper after attending a short course on statistical research techniques. Certainly, the editor is correct in stating that "the results of the studies [the participants' reports] demonstrate that statistical and analytical tools can be picked by any librarian and used in the manner and to the extent s/he desires" (p. xv). The main message the papers convey is that it takes more than one short course and a "research" paper to enable an inexperienced person to make effective use of quantitative research methods in the management of a library. [R: C&RL, Nov 79, pp. 575-76; LJ, 1 Nov 79, p. 2290]

G. Edward Evans

1237. Daiute, Robert J., and Kenneth A. Gorman. **Library Operations Research.** Dobbs Ferry, N.Y., Oceana, 1974. 368p. index. $28.50. LC 73-20303. ISBN 0-913338-01-X.

Library Operations Research reports the results of a research project funded by the U.S. Office of Education on in-library book use at Rider College library in Trenton, New Jersey. It includes sections on sampling theory and study methodology, an explanation of the computer methods employed in the analytical process, suggested applications of sampling methods to library problems, and the computer programs that were used in the study of in-library book use. As such, a more descriptive title for the book would have been "Generalized Statistical Methods for the Analysis of In-Library Book Use."

The basic conclusion reached by the study was that "most library use, which includes in-library use along with books used in circulation, is directly related to course work by students"—a conclusion that will surprise few college librarians. The major contribution that this work makes to the library profession lies in its generalized statistical methodology, which should be of some interest to research personnel studying in-library book use and to others interested in the application of statistical methods to the analysis of library operations and services. It is unlikely that the average professional librarian will possess sufficient statistical expertise to apply the study methodology in a local library environment.

The major shortcomings of the book relate first to its structure—it reads like a technical report and much of the substantive content of the study is obscured by excessive statistical detail—and second to the characteristics of the study sample, which severely limit the extent to which the research results can be generalized to a larger population. [R: C&RL, July 75, p. 329; JAL, July 75, p. 24]   Michael H. Harris

1238. Goldberg, Robert L. **A Systems Approach to Library Program Development.** Metuchen, N.J., Scarecrow, 1976. 172p. illus. bibliog. index. $15.00. LC 76-18157. ISBN 0-8108-0944-3.

This volume, the result of a Ph.D. dissertation at Rutgers University, presents the need for planning library services and develops a conceptual model for libraries, drawing on other institutional models that have been developed. The model, called PIES (Planning, Implementation and Evaluation System) is built on such previously developed concepts as CIPP (Context, Input, Process, Product), PPB (Program, Planning, Budgeting), and MBO (Management by Objectives).

Proof of the workability of the model will come through its adaptation and use. The required commitment to the model, just as for adoption of PBO or MBO or any other model, is one of time and money. Perhaps its greatest drawback is that it came at a time when many libraries were curtailing rather than expanding services. This volume should be of interest to librarians concerned with a systems approach. [R: C&RL, Sept 77, pp. 436-38; LJ, 1 June 77, p. 1257; RQ, Summer 77, pp. 344-45]
          Robert D. Stueart

1239. Goodell, John S. **Libraries and Work Sampling.** Littleton, Colo., Libraries Unlimited, 1975. 60p. index. (Challenge to Change: Library Applications of New Concepts, No. 1). o.p. LC 74-79026. ISBN 0-87287-087-1.

Work sampling is a management technique that has proved highly effective as a device for testing the efficient use of employees and of material objects. Goodell demonstrates how to apply the technique to the library scene. In five chapters, he explicates all the steps of a work sampling study, from an initial felt need through the intervening processes to the conclusions which a valid study makes possible. Key operations of a work sampling study include definition of the problem, identification of the pertinent categories, determination of appropriate observation times, mathematical processing of the raw data, and interpretation. A valid study can lead to important organizational changes such as consolidation of tasks and restructuring of job descriptions. The work contains two appendices: additional mathematical

refinements and a review of library literature on work sampling. It concludes with a bibliography of the leading work sampling books and articles. [R: C&RL, Mar 76, p. 175; JAL, May 76, p. 91; LJ, 1 June 76, p. 1268]

1240. Gough, Chet, and Taverekere Srikantaiah. **Systems Analysis in Libraries: A Question and Answer Approach.** London, Clive Bingley; distr., Hamden, Conn., Linnet Books, 1978. 158p. bibliog. index. $16.00. LC 78-7539. ISBN 0-85157-278-2(Bingley); 0-208-01753-4(Linnet).

The majority of textbooks on systems analysis tend to be filled with charts, graphs, and statistics. For many beginning students in library school, such books are uninteresting and, to some extent, incomprehensible. This brief introduction to systems analysis is the exception; it is written in a clear, direct style with almost no use of charts, graphs, or statistics. In 10 short chapters, the authors distill the essence of systems analysis for the beginning student ("Understanding Systems"; "The Library System"; "Stating Goals and Objectives"; "Methods of Description"; "Systems Engineering"; "Evolution of Computers"; "Programming Languages"; "Library Automation"; "Cost Studies"; and "Evaluation"). Naturally, a price must be paid—the treatment of topics is superficial. Thus, the book must be used in conjunction with a more detailed treatment of the topics.

Both authors are former library school faculty members, and the text is based upon the systems courses they taught. Included are 25 pages of exercises, which provide some depth to the book but not enough for it to be used as the sole textbook in a systems course. Their bibliography provides an excellent sampling of pre-1974 books and articles; post-1974 material is not so well represented nor as well chosen. This is a good book for the beginning library school student who has doubts concerning systems analysis, computers, and libraries. [R: C&RL, May 79, p. 280; LJ, 15 Jan 79, p. 174]
          G. Edward Evans

1241. Howard, Edward N. **Local Power and the Community Library.** Chicago, American Library Association, 1978. 56p. bibliog. (The Public Library Reporter, No. 18). $5.00. LC 78-13493. ISBN 0-8389-0274-X.

"You librarians have some big guns, but you use awfully soggy ammunition." Unfortunately, this quote is buried in the preface instead of appearing as the opening sentence of this powerful little booklet. Describing how to identify "library guns," this booklet not only explains how to keep the powder dry but how to aim and fire more effectively. In eight brief chapters ("The Community"; "A Community of Organizations"; "Sectors of the Community"; "Competitive Interdependence"; "The Power of Sanction"; "The Power Structure"; "Sanctional Relationship"; and "Who Speaks for the Library?"), the author provides solid guidance on how to assess the local power structure. Used in conjunction with Aaron Wildavsky's *The Politics of the Budgetary Process*, second edition (Little, Brown, 1974), the booklet could be of great help in strengthening the library's position in the community. Although written in terms of local power, it can be applied to the analysis of power at the state, regional, or national level. Undoubtedly, some librarians will consider this book too political, too oriented toward playing "games," or even too Machiavellian. However, because so many librarians feel that "politicking" and "playing the power game" are inappropriate activities for librarians, libraries fail to gain the financial and community support needed to be effective service organizations. This book will not change attitudes, but it is an important tool for those willing to fight for more support.   G. Edward Evans

1242. Hu, Teh-wei, Bernard H. Booms, and Lynne Warfield Kaltreider. **A Benefit-Cost Analysis of Alternative Library Delivery Systems.** Westport, Conn., Greenwood Press, 1975. 286p. bibliog. index. (Contributions in Librarianship and Information Science, No. 13). o.p. LC 74-5989. ISBN 0-8371-7528-3.

The Hu-Booms-Kaltreider work is a welcome addition to the literature of library management, which is in dire need of contributions dealing with the evaluation of publicly supported activities by the use of the techniques of benefit/cost analysis. Alternative library delivery systems (bookmobiles and books-by-mail) have been surveyed, data on users and nonusers have been collected, statistical cost analysis has been performed for each system, and user-perceived benefits have been compared. The resulting quantitative juxtaposition of benefits is based on cost alternatives. Finally, benefit/cost ratios calculated for both MOD and bookmobile delivery allow the authors to offer carefully drawn conclusions and make recommendations for further research concerning some more elusive but highly relevant aspects of the problem. There are copies of the questionnaires and cover letters, a rather extensive bibliography of the subject, and a good index to names and subjects. The work may serve as a handy reference source or guide, with a model for organizing and conducting library research as well as for evaluating the data through the use of well-tried methods of economics, industrial management and, to some extent, psychology. [R: JAL, Jan 76, p. 25; LQ, Apr 76, p. 182]   Ivan L. Kaldor

1243. King, Donald W., and Edward C. Bryant. **The Evaluation of Information Services and Products.** Washington, D.C., Information Resources Press, 1971. 306p. index. $27.50. LC 76-141595. SBN 87815-003-X.

A useful compendium of the essential elements and procedures involved in the evaluation of document transfer systems. Evaluation objectives, methodology, and measures are considered in relation to the functions, processes, organizational structure, and components of such systems. The text covers the evaluation and control aspects of indexing processes and languages, document screening processes, composition, reproduction, acquisition, storage and presentation systems, and user-system interfaces. Useful information is provided on user surveys and marketing research. Fundamental statistical ideas and concepts are explained in the final three chapters, "Statistics Primer," "Sampling Methods," and "Experimental Design." A number of basic concepts such as reliability and confidence limits are defined. The work would have been improved by a more substantial index in that the three-page one provided is skimpy and meager. [R: LJ, 1 Apr 72, p. 1250]   Alan M. Rees

1244. Lancaster, F. W., with the assistance of M. J. Joncich. **The Measurement and Evaluation of Library Services.** Washington, D.C., Information Resources Press, 1977. 395p. illus. index. $37.50. LC 77-72081. ISBN 0-87815-017-X.

F. W. Lancaster has a record of producing award-winning books and articles (1969 — Best American Documentation Paper; 1970 and 1975 — ASIS Best Book Awards). Because his awards were in the information science field, some librarians consider him a "computer person," but this book should make it clear he is a librarian who understands all aspects of librarianship/information science.

Performance evaluation of people or institutions is one of the most difficult tasks confronting a manager, since the differences between theory and practice are very great. Evaluation of institutional performance is perhaps most difficult in the not-for-profit government sector. Such agencies can operate with very vague statements about goals and objectives and very limited performance guidelines. Lancaster has written a very readable, comprehensive, nonmathematical review of both the theory and practice of library evaluation. In 14 chapters, he covers all aspects of library work—public catalogs, reference, technical services, collections, retrieval systems, and physical accessibility. He does *not* provide a quick, easy answer to the problem of evaluation; what he does provide is the background data so that each library can develop its own system. This is essential reading for anyone concerned with improving library services. [R: C&RL, Jan 78, p. 57; JAL, May 78, p. 90; LJ, 15 Jan 78, p. 146; RQ, Spring 78, p. 264; SL, Apr 78, p. 186]

G. Edward Evans

1245. Mitchell, Betty Jo, Norman E. Tanis, and Jack Jaffe. **Cost Analysis of Library Functions: A Total System Approach.** Greenwich, Conn., JAI Press, 1978. 192p. index. (Foundations in Library and Information Science, Vol. 6). $37.50. LC 77-2110. ISBN 0-89232-072-9.

The implications of the subtitle of this book—"*A* Total System Approach," (emphasis added)—should be understood before the reader purchases the volume. The book describes the system that was used at California State University, Northridge (CSUN) Library to measure the cost of its services. Aside from the foreword and introduction, the text is solely concerned with the method used by CSUN. Certainly, there is merit in making this method available to the library profession. However, since there are only 56 pages of text, and the remaining 136 pages are appendices (primarily reproductions of computer print—67 pages), perhaps a journal article and an ERIC microfiche would have been more appropriate—especially since a five-fiche set (in a pocket part) represents appendix 9 of the book. The methods described are worth considering for anyone undertaking a library cost study. The authors provide a step-by-step guide to duplicating their study. Although the authors make repeated references to controlling costs in the library, their publisher did not get the message, and the buyer is expected to pay for what is, in essence, the final report of the CSUN library cost study. Final research reports, like most doctoral dissertations, require rewriting and often need to be expanded before they are worth publishing in book form; this report is no exception. [R: C&RL, July 79, p. 369; JAL, July 79, p. 163]

G. Edward Evans

1246. Rowley, Jenny E., and Peter J. Rowley. **Operations Research: A Tool for Library Man-**
agement. Chicago, American Library Association, 1981. 144p. bibliog. index. $10.00. LC 81-12899. ISBN 0-8389-0337-1.

The authors make several claims in their preface—that this is an introductory account for library managers, using the simplest manner of presentation, that it serves as an appetizer on the subject to the readers, etc. Unfortunately, they failed to achieve their intended purposes.

Perhaps the main reason for the failure is the authors' outdatedness in OR applications in libraries. I am amazed that, given the developments in library OR, no reference in the book (including bibliography and footnotes) was made to any work later than 1978. Throughout the text, there is much evidence to show that the authors are equally outdated on the development of other management techniques—for example, the mention of "planning programming budgeting" but not "zero-base budgeting," etc.

Many of the examples are quoted almost directly from the referred author's work, and are placed in the wrong places. For example, Morse used "a simple mathematical model" for his Markov circulation model, but his renewal and duplicate model is certainly not "simple" to most librarians. If the readers do not yet understand probability (presented in the following chapter), how do the authors expect them to understand Morse's duplication model, though labeled as "simple"?

The few texts (all published prior to 1979) listed in the bibliography are all general introductory texts and are not specifically library-oriented. This one, though meant for library managers, fails to make the subject attractive to its intended readers. [R: JAL, Mar 82, pp. 59-60; LJ, 15 June 82, p. 1198]

Ching-chih Chen

Planning and Decision-making Systems

1247. Brown, Eleanor Frances. **Modern Branch Libraries and Libraries in Systems.** Metuchen, N.J., Scarecrow, 1970. 747p. illus. bibliog. index. $22.50. LC 77-12808. ISBN 0-8108-0276-7.

This is a compendium of information on all aspects (establishing, building, operating) of branch libraries along with information about floor plans, basic reference collections, and special services. Marred only by poor organization and editing and based largely upon only opinion, the book is a useful source for information on a subject needing solid research. [R: LJ, 1 Nov 70, p. 3749; RQ, Winter 70, p. 178]

Charles D. Patterson

1248.   Chapman, Edward A. **Library Systems Analysis Guidelines.** New York, Wiley-Interscience, 1970. illus. bibliog. index. 226p. $12.00. LC 75-109391. ISBN 0-471-14610-2. (Available from Books on Demand, $46.00pa., ISBN 0-317-10516-7).

This volume aims to provide guidelines for administrators and systems analysts in evaluating existing operating systems and aids in designing new ones. It is based on a mid-1960s Rensselaer institute, an ASIS preconference tutorial, portions of a LARC report, and some data drawn from *Library Automation: A State of the Art Review* (American Library Association, 1969). It is uneven in treatment in some portions and lacks clarity. Great emphasis is placed on the use of forms and their completion with little consideration given to forms analysis and design. Systems analysis usually means automation, which can aid many larger libraries in providing better service to growing numbers of users. The volume can aid in this endeavor. [R: C&RL, July 71, p. 318; LJ, 15 Dec 70, p. 4234]   Charles D. Patterson

1249.   Hamburg, Morris, and others. **Library Planning and Decision-Making Systems.** Cambridge, Mass., MIT Press, 1974. 274p. index. o.p. LC 73-16422. ISBN 0-262-08065-6.

This work was written primarily for managers of university and large public library systems. It reports on a major research project conducted at the Wharton School of Finance. The research team conducted intensive studies at the University of Pennsylvania Libraries and the Free Public Library of Philadelphia in an effort to develop a flexible statistical information system that would provide quantitative information for the effective management of libraries.

The result of this work is reported in six chapters entitled "Introduction and Summary," "Library Objectives and Overall Performance Measures," "A Framework for Library Decision Making," "Library Models and Empirical Findings," "Development of a Management Information System for Libraries," and "Higher-Level Decision Making."

The volume contains a detailed table of contents, an extensive bibliography, and an index; these, combined with the useful summary in chapter 1, help to make the work a useful reference source. It should be read by library managers and educators. [R: AL, Dec 73, pp. 669-70]   Emanuel T. Prostano

1250.   Lubans, John, Jr., and Edward A. Chapman. **Reader in Library Systems Analysis.** Englewood, Colo., Microcard Editions Books,

a division of Information Handling Services, 1975. 471p. illus. charts. bibliog. (Reader Series in Library and Information Science). o.p. LC 75-6253. ISBN 0-910972-45-1.

This book contains 34 photographic reprints of previously published articles and chapters from books on such aspects of library systems analysis as sampling techniques, costs and costing, flow-charting, computers and libraries. The publication dates of the articles range from Fremont Rider's "Library Cost Accounting" published in *The Library Quarterly* in 1936 to the mid-1970s.

Because the pieces are straight photographic reprints (no resetting of type), there is a visually disturbing variety of typefaces and sizes, a kind of typographic kaleidoscope.

There is little point in commenting on the content of a book like this, which merely assembles in a convenient manner materials that are well known to librarians; but it is pertinent to ask what the editors have done with them. Judging from the extremely meager sectional introductions, it is apparent that the editors' contributions have been minimal. They interject their own commentary in exactly six places: a one-page general introduction and five sectional notes. What they have to say in their interjected commentaries is not critical. In essence, all they do is recapitulate the arguments of the selections to follow, which would seem to be totally unnecessary, since presumably students are to be asked to read the selection for themselves.

With few exceptions, the articles in this anthology could be bibliographically identified and located through an intelligent use of *Library Literature* and other related indexing tools. Why is it not preferable to ask library school students to do their own bibliographic digging to find the materials they need? If they were to search for a citation to Rider's 1936 article on library cost accounting, they would find it in *The Library Quarterly*; moreover, the typography of the original would be identical to that available in this reader. [R: JAL, May 76, p. 109; LJ, July 76, p. 1501; LQ, Oct 76, p. 465]   Richard A. Gray

1251.   Lynch, Mary Jo, and H. M. Eckard, eds. **Library Data Collection Handbook.** Chicago, American Library Association, 1982. 227p. price not reported. pa. ISBN 0-8389-5600-9. (Available from Books on Demand, $57.00, ISBN 0-317-26561-X).

Designed to outline a system for data collection in all types of libraries and to define the essential terms of the system, this book is aimed at managers of libraries as well as persons involved with library resources in other areas. It also identifies data useful in communicating with others in the field and completing information requests. Such subjects as the classification scheme, suggestions for recording and reporting, and problems in the numeric and semantic areas are covered. A glossary of terms important in standardizing the language for library communication concludes the book. [R: JAL, Mar 83, p. 61]

Staffing and Personnel

1252. Bailey, Martha J. **Supervisory and Middle Managers in Libraries.** Metuchen, N.J., Scarecrow, 1981. 210p. bibliog. index. $15.00. LC 80-23049. ISBN 0-8108-1400-5.

A considerable portion of this book is based on work of the author previously published or at least previously written. The book defines several categories of managers, giving special attention to the middle manager and the supervisory manager. In Bailey's view, which is shared by many writers in the field, the middle manager stands between the top manager and the supervisory manager. The sphere of the middle manager does not have any exact limits. It typically includes division and department heads and, in Bailey's opinion, also staff specialists. Supervisory managers have the responsibility for planning and controlling the activities of nonsupervisory personnel, usually on a face-to-face basis. They are "in charge of a generally cohesive or specialized function while middle managers are charged with directing and coordinating dissimilar functions" (p. 3).

Bailey describes the middle manager's profile for academic, public, and company libraries. She outlines the middle manager's usual academic background and professional experience. We learn of the often sporadic and meager training given to middle managers. We find that in training and selecting suitable persons, company libraries are usually superior to academic and public libraries.

The principal sources for discovering the characteristics of the middle and supervisory managers were job advertisements in selected professional journals and interviews with a group of middle managers and some of their superiors. For comparison the author has also analyzed pertinent literature. For company libraries the method of investigation had to be changed in several respects. A questionnaire was used instead of advertisements to obtain data. Further, in the case of company libraries — which are usually small and do not have a multi-faceted organization — only the director's position was considered, and only his or her role in the parent organization was determined.

Bailey emphasizes that a library does not exist in a vacuum but within the framework of its parent organization. She provides brief descriptions relating to the background and the setting of academic, public, and company libraries. Some of the characterizations seem rather subjective, and some stress negative extremes and do not reveal the wide range of professional attitudes observable in practice.

The book contains over 60 tables, helpful notes at the end of each chapter, and in the appendix a list of selected references. In the text there is some repetitiveness, caused probably by including in the book several self-contained previously prepared articles.

The title under review is a valuable contribution in spite of a few shortcomings. Bailey has studied many aspects of management deeply and broadly and has succeeded in presenting a comprehensive view of supervisory and middle managers in the library. [R: LJ, 15 June 81, p. 1287] Fritz Veit

1253. Cowley, John. **Personnel Management in Libraries.** London, Clive Bingley; distr., Hamden, Conn., Shoe String Press, 1982. 109p. index. (Outlines of Modern Librarianship). $13.00. ISBN 0-85157-324-X.

This British handbook on library personnel management includes chapters on the theory behind personnel management, leadership and decision making, selection of personnel, staff development, new employee training, review and promotion, communication within an organization, merger management, labor relations, and future developments in personnel management.

In this book, "induction training" is the terminology used for training a new employee. "Labour relations" is not a discussion of labor unions as we know them, though British labor unions are discussed. Theory X and Theory Y are mentioned several times, though Maslow is not. Position terms and other terminology differ from those familiar to U.S. librarians. Affirmative action, an important facet of U.S. personnel management, is not mentioned. In general, the book has lost some relevance in traveling to this country. It can provide some background reading, but it will not meet most personnel management needs in U.S. libraries. [R: JAL, Jan 83, p. 384] Jennifer Cargill

1254. Creth, Sheila, and Frederick Duda, eds. **Personnel Administration in Libraries.** New

York, Neal-Schuman, 1981. 333p. bibliog. index. $29.95. LC 81-11348. ISBN 0-918212-25-1.

It is unusual for a collection of essays to function as a good textbook for a course; however, this book appears to be an exception. All the essays were planned to create an integrated work, and Creth and Duda seem to have exercised good editorial control. The result is a focused collection of essays that could serve as a supplement textbook in library personnel administration courses. Six people contributed to the effort — Arthur Curley, "Legal Framework of Personnel Administration"; Margaret Myers, "Staffing Patterns in Libraries"; Sheila Creth, "Personnel Planning and Utilization" and "Staff Development and Continuing Education"; Billy Wilkinson, "Recruitment and Selection"; Frederick Duda, "Labor Relations"; and Maxine Reneker, "Performance Appraisal in Libraries: Prupose and Techniques." As can be seen from the list of chapter titles, the book is not comprehensive in coverage. It lacks coverage of motivation, communication, turnover, and internal mobility, and includes almost nothing about clerical-professional staff relations, or employee conduct, discipline, and ethics.

At best, this is an overview of some of the major issues in personnel administration. While it lacks the depth to be the sole textbook in a course, used in conjunction with a current basic personnel administration textbook it will be a valuable addition to a library school teacher's and student's library. The comment in the introduction (p. xi) about "implied and direct criticisms of library education" suggests that the editors have not spent much time reviewing library school curriculums and that they are unaware of the fact that many library schools recommend their students take personnel administration courses from a school of management. This brings up the major flaw in the work, which is the references; to some extent the text reflects the late 1960s and early 1970s picture. For example, Reneker's essay does not discuss any of the 1970s research that identifies major problems in the area of performance appraisal. Thus, the book must be used to supplement a 1980 or later edition of a general personnel administration textbook. [R: C&RL, July 82, pp. 360-61; JAL, Sept 82, p. 260]

G. Edward Evans

1255. DeHart, Florence. **The Librarian's Psychological Commitments: Human Relations in Librarianship.** Westport, Conn., Greenwood Press, 1979. 208p. bibliog. index. (Contributions in Librarianship and Information Science, No. 27). $27.50. LC 79-7059. ISBN 0-313-21329-1; ISSN 0084-9243.

Librarians study materials and are knowledgeable about content; they spend less time studying people, their reactions and needs, and techniques for service to patrons who do not articulate or who come to libraries for nonlibrary purposes. DeHart provides some principles and many suggestions for interaction in a wide variety of patron and staff situations. Additional sources for guidance and technique development widen the value of this brief but useful text on the human dimension of librarianship.

The book's three sections define the basics for a librarian's commitment; the structuring of attitudes toward self, other staff, and patrons; and several types of skills needed in both positive and negative situations. The section and chapter headings use vague and pseudotechnical terminology, resulting in a somewhat muddy outline rather than a crisp summary. The text would communicate more forcefully if fewer ambiguous terms and less sociological jargon were used.

The discussions of verbal and nonverbal communication, both deliberate and unintentional, focus on contacts librarians have, the effects of these contacts, and suggestions for improvements which will shape image-making activity. Other topics include the librarian's role in specific environments, group dynamics, the rights of patrons, the sources and meanings of "operational power" in librarianship, change, and aspects of behavior. The chapters are sprinkled with case studies and examples of positive and negative situations, but solutions are too seldom offered.

Each of the chapters has extensive footnotes using a wide variety of materials, many selected from outside librarianship. The list of 56 suggested readings is in good bibliographic form, is annotated, and points to supportive and useful sources, most of which are readily available. Thus, the text is a bibliographic essay on each topic. The total is an impressive list of readings on the psychological background of interpersonal relationships. The index, largely of names in the text, is an aid to locating known information, but is not a subject approach to the book's contents.

This is a needed book, even though it sometimes expresses itself in sweeping terms. The author manages to summarize and highlight major communications and psychological aspects of librarianship. An understanding in these areas will improve a librarian's approach to patrons and staff, and most librarians would benefit from study in these areas. [R: C&RL, July 80, pp. 366-67; LJ, 1 Jan 80, p. 79]

Neal L. Edgar

1256. Emery, Richard, **Staff Communication in Libraries.** London, Clive Bingley; distr., Hamden, Conn., Linnet Books, 1975. 213p. illus. bibliog. index. o.p. LC 74-23795. ISBN 0-208-01364-4.

This handy volume explores the attitudes and phenomena that form the relationship between staff members and the organization; it examines the functions and characteristics of staff communication in public and academic libraries in the United States, the United Kingdom, Ireland, and Australia. Originally written as a FLA (Fellow of the Library Association — Britain) thesis in 1973, the study is based on information obtained from 70 libraries in those countries, plus other printed sources.

Exchange of ideas and information is the lifeblood of any organization, and Emery does an admirable job of presenting a detailed analysis of this process. He examines the directions in which formal and informal communication flows; the means (as McLuhan maintains, "medium is the message") chosen to communicate, with all of the nuisances of when, where, and how; and the things that either aid or hinder communication.

The final chapter is an outline of a proposed communications program for a library. The program is one that the author feels is necessary in the administrative process of ensuring that service requirements can be met and that the most effective use is made of all available resources. This outline, applicable to all types and sizes of libraries, is succinct yet thorough.

Truly, this is a communications handbook. It should be required reading not only for "senior executives" but also for personnel officers and middle management personnel and for students in library school management courses. [R: LJ, 15 May 75, p. 928]

Robert D. Stueart

1257. Guyton, Theodore Lewis. **Unionization: The Viewpoint of Librarians.** Chicago, American Library Association, 1975. 204p. bibliog. index. o.p. LC 74-19164. ISBN 0-8389-0187-5.

This monograph on unionization was originally written as a dissertation in the Graduate School of Management at UCLA. The author bases his study on a quantitative survey of 460 public librarians in Southern California. The questionnaire elicited personal and background data and measured degrees of satisfaction with respect to three factors: material rewards, the library's organization and administration, and the intrinsic satisfaction provided by the job.

Even if one can ignore dissertationese, which is sometimes distracting, the definition of terms is somewhat naive. For example, it is both questionable and arbitrary that "a professional librarian is normally defined as one who has completed a course of study in a graduate library school" (the author modifies this statement for the purposes of his study) and then to group libraries into three main types ("public, college and university and those maintained by industrial and special agencies") ignoring the whole area of school library media centers. The title is also a bit misleading, for, although the author identifies "types" of libraries, he discusses only public libraries, beginning with the historical overview of unionization in public libraries and the Professional and Employee Association. The second portion of the study deals with the occupational characteristics; the economic position; and the employment environment.

The final portion of the survey, "A Theory of Library Unionism," presents a descriptive model which indicates that library unionization is essentially a function of the degree of opportunity consciousness and certain exogenous factors that promote or hinder unionization. The one is influenced by degree of bureaucracy and degree of aggregate professional training, the other includes legislative climate, proximity to organized employees, and availability of unions.

The study attempts to make theoretical statements concerning the origins of library unionism and to improve the research on professional unionization by using professional librarians as a case study. [R: AL, Mar 75, p. 171; C&RL, Sept 75, pp. 428-29; LJ, 15 Sept 75, p. 1610]

Robert D. Stueart

1258. Harvey, John H., and Elizabeth M. Dickinson, eds. **Librarians' Affirmative Action Handbook.** Metuchen, N.J., Scarecrow, 1983. 305p. index. $18.50. LC 82-10644. ISBN 0-8108-1581-8.

The editors of this work have assembled an impressive selection of original chapters to define, describe, and recommend library practices with regard to equal employment opportunity and affirmative action. Extensive bibliographies provide a broad overview of the literature on the subject that is particularly of interest to library situations.

After a thorough introduction, chapters are divided by type of library — public, academic, or special—and by specific area of interest: women librarians, black librarians, the handicapped. Further chapters are devoted to how to develop an affirmative action program as well as an agenda for future research. The concluding chapter chronicles ALA's record in support of affirmative action. Three appendices include the California "Day-one" entry-level librarian skills list and two checklists for evaluating an agency's affirmative action posture.

This well-prepared book, when used in concert with the more general texts devoted to affirmative action and discrimination, will be of use in libraries of all types and sizes as well as to library science students. [R: BL, 15 Oct 83, p. 326; JAL, July 83, pp. 166-67; JAL, May 83, pp. 124-25; WLB, May 83, p. 782]

Christopher Albertson

1259. Kemper, Robert E. **Library Management; Behavior-Based Personnel Systems (BBPS): A Framework for Analysis.** Littleton, Colo., Libraries Unlimited, 1971. 104p. (Research Studies in Library Science, No. 5). o.p. LC 73-165063. SBN 87287-036-7.

The six chapters of this work detail the nature of personnel administration, the process of skill level development, and the functional relationship between behavior-based personnel planning and strategic long-range library planning. [R: AL, Dec 71, p. 1223; WLB, Oct 71]

1260. Kemper, Robert E., and Richard E. Ostrander. **Directorship by Objectives.** Littleton, Colo., Libraries Unlimited, 1977. 80p. illus. bibliog. index. (Challenge to Change: Library Applications of New Concepts, No. 2). o.p. LC 76-56238. ISBN 0-87287-138-X.

The authors, experienced library managers, attempt to explain the central reality of library directorship training in a modern library organization. The purpose of the book is to provide a perspective on what the authors define as an upwardly mobile library manager. Four focal points are: (1) the nature of the library manager position; (2) the nature of necessary skill requirements; (3) the forces contributing to the uncertainty of the environment; and (4) the process of directorship by objectives.

Peter Hiatt in his foreword to the book sums up the impact and value of this small text: "The authors convey a terrifying sense of reality. They were there. I hurt reading some passages: I was there.... The chapters build one on the other with a sense of momentum resulting from both the content and the psychological approach. They ask—and tell—why someone might want to be a library manager, what the world of the library manager is really like, and how the job looks from below, from above, and from the middle." [R: C&RL, Sept 77, p. 435; JAL, Nov 77, p. 290; LJ, 15 Dec 77, p. 2487]

1261. Maloney, R. Kay, ed. **Personnel Development in Libraries: Proceedings of the Thirteenth Annual Symposium Sponsored by the Alumni and the Faculty of the Rutgers University Graduate School of Library Service.** New Brunswick, N.J., Bureau of Library and Information Science Research, Graduate School of Library Service, Rutgers University; distr., New Brunswick, N.J., Rutgers University Press, 1977. 115p. index. $6.00pa. LC 77-5025. ISBN 0-8135-0843-6.

This thin volume, as the title suggests, incorporates the proceedings of an "Alumni Day Symposium" held at the Rutgers library school in 1975. Three speakers covered topics of performance evaluation, task analysis, and job enrichment. There were small discussion groups that addressed those issues from each type of library's perspective—school, academic, public, and special. Those discussions have been summarized by the editor. Many of the comments made by major speakers have already been recorded in other published sources, so there is little "new" information here. Probably the most useful part of the volume is a 100-item-plus annotated bibliography of works published on the subject between 1970 and 1975. This bibliography also includes a helpful grid, which both relates items in the bibliography to 14 topics and indicates whether they are case studies, general surveys, literature reviews, etc. The volume is useful if for nothing else but the bibliography. [R: LJ, 1 July 78, p. 1362]

Robert D. Stueart

1262. Mathews, Anne J. **Communicate! A Librarian's Guide to Interpersonal Relations.** Chicago, American Library Association, 1983. 79p. bibliog. index. $8.00pa. LC 83-2557. ISBN 0-8389-0379-7.

Communicate! functions nicely as an introductory handbook and guide for practicing librarians and for students about to become practicing professionals. The culmination of 20 years of experience with libraries, librarians, users, and others, the work presents some interesting and thought-provoking points.

The first part of *Communicate!*, "Communicate with the Public," discusses some of the dynamics of communication, as well as the obstacles, that are likely to be encountered in the library setting. Included are discussions of the physical environment, the psychological context of communication, and the sociological context. Mathews makes a clear delineation between positive and negative communication, carrying this over to an analysis of the reference interview, including a review of listening skills.

Succinct and valuable, much of the information nevertheless suffers from being introductory in nature, with necessary development lacking in certain areas. Exercises are included to test one's thoughts and reactions in varying situations — except in a subsection labeled "The Problem Patron," where the author seems more concerned with delivering life-saving advice than with developing professional reactions to a particular situation.

The second part of *Communicate!*, "Communicate with Each Other," focuses upon the obstacles to communication among professionals. Presenting an overview of communication concerns in libraries, Mathews reviews a number of points that are part of the communications problems of any organization, putting these in the context of the library environment. Problems with supervisors, professional/paraprofessional problems, difficulties of written and verbal communications, and motivation, orientation, and performance evaluation problems are examined, accompanied by pertinent exercises to test the professional's philosophies and behavior.

Included as supplementary material are a sample policy regarding problem patrons, a library code of conduct, rules of thumb (which have the ring of common sense), a bibliography for further reading, and a perfunctory index.

As an introductory work on the dynamics and value of communication within varied library settings, Mathews's work succinctly reviews major issues that need to be studied in greater depth in other contexts — in the classroom, through formal work experience, or through continuing education. Much of the information is commonsensical in nature, yet vital to the successful operation of a library.

It is to be hoped that library educators and administrators alike will recognize the value of this work. A small additional step in the cross-pollination of the behavioral sciences with the information sciences, *Communicate!* deserves the undivided attention of all those who have been "too busy to talk about it now" for the past few centuries of librarianship. [R: BL, 15 Oct 83, pp. 326-27; JAL, July 83, p. 187; LJ, Aug 83, p. 1458; RQ, Fall 83, pp. 116-17]
Edmund F. SantaVicca

1263. O'Reilly, Robert C., and Marjorie I. O'Reilly. **Librarians and Labor Relations:**

Employment under Union Contracts. Westport, Conn., Greenwood Press, 1981. 191p. bibliog. index. (Contributions in Librarianship and Information Science, No. 35). $27.50. LC 80-1049. ISBN 0-313-22485-4; ISSN 0084-9243.

This work attempts to be a comprehensive consideration of the economic, political, and historical background of librarian's increasing involvement in unionization. Public, school, and university libraries are covered with a rather successful attempt to discuss organization, bargaining, contract disputes, and arbitration in an objective manner. Each chapter includes numerous, relevant charts that provide important data necessary to the explanation of the text. Especially useful sections focus on contract item analysis, affirmative action and unions, and the unionization of library support personnel.

While this title does provide a good primer on the collective bargaining process in libraries in general, more attention is needed on the details of how unionization specifically affects both the librarian and the administrator. In addition, recent years have witnessed the rapid organization of academic librarians. However, only four pages of text and one page of charts were included in a discussion of this important trend. Weatherford's *Collective Bargaining and the Academic Librarian* (see *ARBA* 77, entry 207) could be consulted except for the fact that it has become increasingly dated and was based upon personal experiences rather than upon a systematic study. Despite these limitations, this work should be considered by larger academic libraries as well as library schools. A selective reading list and an excellent glossary of collective bargaining terms add value to this effort. [R: BL, 15 Oct 81, p. 284; LJ, July 81, p. 1395]
Frank Wm. Goudy

1264. **Professional and Non-Professional Duties in Libraries.** 2nd ed. Compiled by a Working Party of the Research and Development Committee of the Library Association. London, Library Association, 1974. 86p. index. o.p. ISBN 0-85365-307-0.

The Library Association has published the second edition (first in 1962) of job analyses of professional and nonprofessional duties in libraries. These job descriptions provide a great deal of useful detail on the activities in all types of libraries. The chapters are devoted to functions in libraries: administration, personnel management, public relations, selection, acquisitions, cataloging, processing of materials, information and reference work, and circulation work. In each chapter, professional duties precede nonprofessional duties. No attempt is made to distinguish different levels of professional duties.

Naturally, the book has a British bias, but it should be useful for American libraries. The bias is especially noticeable in the index: there is no entry or referral for "circulation work." Those looking for examples of job descriptions will find that this useful work compares favorably with the U.S. Department of Labor's *Occupations in Library Science* (GPO, 1973). [R: LJ, 1 Jan 75, p. 35; LR, Spring 75, p. 28]

Casper L. Jordan

1265. Rawles, Beverly A. **Human Resource Management in Small Libraries.** Hamden, Conn., Library Professional Publications/Shoe String Press, 1982. 136p. illus. bibliog. index. $16.50; $12.50pa. LC 81-20834. ISBN 0-208-01966-9; 0-208-01950-2pa.

Once appointed, the new library administrator is immediately faced with managing the library's major resource, its staff. This handbook for the new and inexperienced manager of a small library (public, school, or special) offers guidance, support, and clarity.

Chapters deal with the specifics of communications, performance appraisal, salary administration, equal employment opportunity and affirmative action, and labor relations. Throughout each chapter, planning, budgeting, and programming are selectively introduced as they relate to the topic. Clear and direct explanations of basic management principles are nontechnical. That, together with sound coverage of the basics, good organization of material, and application to library situations, is the book's strength. In addition, the work is indexed.

Brevity has its price, however, and though this is an excellent introduction, it leaves a need for further study through more extensive works—some in management and some from library literature. Annotated references to help such pursuit accompany each chapter, but the citations are to sources from the 1970s although excellent later works are available. Thus, they are misleading and suggest that more in-depth works applying management principles to the small library are not available or important.

Barbara Conroy

1266. Ricking, Myrl, and Robert E. Booth. **Personnel Utilization in Libraries: A Systems Approach.** Prepared for the Illinois Library Task Analysis Project. Chicago, published in cooperation with the Illinois State Library by American Library Association, 1974. 158p.

illus. bibliog. $8.50pa. LC 74-8688. ISBN 0-8389-3155-3. (Available from Books on Demand, $42.00pa., ISBN 0-317-26570-9).

Five appendices ("Scales Used in SERD Report," "Excerpt from *Handbook for Analyzing Jobs*," "Evaluation System: U.S. Civil Service Commission," "Library Education and Manpower Policy Statement," and "ILTAP Phase II") follow a five-chapter (36-page) essay packed with footnotes and illustrative charts and diagrams and a one-chapter (35-page) description of the Task List used.

The essay chapters might well serve as an introduction or as a summary of a course in personnel use for a knowledgeable group. As a complete document to be studied in and of itself, however, the work is much too terse to be really useful. Follow-up study would have to be done, particularly by those new to some of the various management concepts involved.

As a report to the Illinois Library Task Analysis Project, the essay and appendices form a useful summary. As a guide to an outsider wishing to apply the material to his own situation, it is at best a starting point toward the increasingly essential study of the various areas of personnel use on the way to better understanding. [R: LJ, 15 Feb 75, p. 275; Unesco, July/Aug 75, p. 224]   William L. Cohn

1267. Rosenberg, Jane A., and Maureen Sullivan. **Resource Notebook on Staff Development.** Washington, D.C., Office of Management Studies, Association of Research Libraries, 1983. 309p. $25.00pa.

This compilation offers valuable tools—significant for their practicality and specificity—for the academic library's staff development officer or administrator. It revises and expands ARL's earlier *Staff Development Resource Notebook* (1978).

Opening with a succinct description of the importance of staff development and the elements in such an effort, the work is a well-organized collection of assorted documents. Many of the documents include management techniques developed by ARL's Office of Management Studies, long active and highly credible for the depth of its experience in working with academic libraries. Other documents are from various academic libraries that have active, in some cases innovative, staff development programs.

A broadly defined staff development concept is reflected in all four sections of the notebook: data-gathering techniques, descriptions and evaluations of recent staff development programs, program improvement efforts, and bibliographies. Some of the documents are from the noted ARL Spec Kits; others are reprinted from library reports, correspondence, memos, and policy statements.

Particularly valuable for academic libraries considering expanding or improving their staff development programs, the documents mainly resulted from self-study efforts from which other libraries can learn. All are keyed to the premise that staff development programs encourage and guide personnel in acquiring skills and knowledge.   Barbara Conroy

1268. Sager, Donald J. **Participatory Management in Libraries.** Metuchen, N.J., Scarecrow, 1982. 196p. bibliog. index. (Scarecrow Library Administration Series, No. 3). $14.50. LC 82-783. ISBN 0-8108-1530-3.

Participatory management, still the catch phrase for democratic style, may be less panacea than Pandora's box. Donald Sager sees its pitfalls and advantages, and he states them unequivocally. He comes down solidly in favor of selective applications in libraries. His definition is carefully arrived at and clear. He also provides admirably succinct summaries of management theory's advances since Frederick W. Taylor's scientific management and Elton Mayo's Hawthorne experiment in the first chapters. One of the results of the movement toward democracy: "There are probably more committees than families in existence in the world today" (page 94).

Most of Sager's experience has been in public libraries, and he gives some attention to differences between private and public sectors. The major part of this writing is devoted to how, why, and when participatory management might be advantageous, with a generous selection of case studies. The author provides a masterly coverage of situations appropriate for participation and those where there are high chances for benefits both to the institution and to employees, and he carefully points out instances inappropriate for democratization. On page 160: "Participatory management is not the most rapid means of making a decision ... [although] in the long run time may be saved."

Theory Z is not mentioned. Mayo's book is listed without the superior description of the experiment by Roethlisberger in *Management and the Worker* (Harvard, 1939). And it is hard to imagine that the best work on Swedish management is the account in the *Wall Street Journal*. Personal preferences aside, the book, with its excellent bibliography, is a good candidate for *must* reading for library managers in the coming decade. [R: JAL, May 83, p. 96; LJ,

15 Feb 83, p. 359; RQ, Spring 83, p. 320; SL, Apr 83, p. 208; WLB, Nov 82, p. 247]
                                        Doris H. Banks

1269. Schlipf, Frederick A., ed. **Collective Bargaining in Libraries.** Urbana-Champaign, Ill., Graduate School of Library Science, University of Illinois, 1975. 179p. bibliog. index. (Allerton Park Institute Number 20). o.p. LC 75-25240. ISBN 0-87845-042-4.

This volume in the Allerton Park series contains original papers, the editor's introduction, a bibliography on collective bargaining in libraries, a glossary of labor terms, and an index. The approach of all the papers is factual, not polemical, the purpose of the conference having been to provide "a thorough overview of the way in which collective bargaining actually functions in libraries" (editor's introduction).

The papers easily divide into three sections: two on general problems and current extent of unionization, by Archie Kleingartner and Jean R. Kennelly and by Don Wasserman. A second group of six papers deals with a number of technical issues, such as the duty to bargain, grievances, recognition, and bargaining units. The authors of papers in the first two groups are academics in industrial relations or professional and governmental workers in arbitration. The last two papers deal with the implications for public libraries (Milton S. Byam) and for academic libraries (Margaret A. Chaplan). [R: LR, Winter 77, p. 310]   Richard A. Gray

1270. Slater, Margaret. **Ratios of Staff to Users: Implications for Library-Information Work and the Potential for Automation.** London, Aslib, 1981. 123p. bibliog. (Aslib Occasional Publication, No. 24; British Library Research and Development Report, No. 5627). £17.00pa.; £14.00pa. (members). ISBN 0-85142-144-X.

The author details findings of an Aslib project involving results of a questionnaire distributed in 1979 to 2,100 special library and/or information units in England. In the study, 655 units actually responded; three specified categories in this special sector of the library-information field are industry/commerce, government, and societies/associations. Slater provides a succinct summary of the study's purposes and findings in the first two chapters.

This reader had an expectation of gaining some enlightenment regarding implications of staff-user ratios, especially related to automation. Although Slater does indicate the report's intent to provide guidelines for practitioners attempting to plan and forecast, she in fact does not venture into any substantive discussion pertinent to application of ratios to impending automation. Reported are ratios of staff to actual user populations, as well as to potential user and theoretically possible user populations (i.e., those beyond an existing organization); ratios also concern perceived acceptable levels for both adequate services and extensions of existing services. Indicated are size and composition of staff, levels of qualifications, users in qualitative terms, types of nonroutine services available in the information units, access and/or usage of computers, and other details on the prevalency of automation. Slater cautions that more qualitative information regarding potential outside users is necessary for reasonable assessments and reliable ratios for staffing needs applicable to a larger user population.

The book serves as a useful primary source of information. Slater's analyses of available data contribute to an understanding of England's special libraries. A reader also may gain some basis for comparisons with other special libraries and information services, and develop some insights concerning methods to assess staff requirements. [R: C&RL, Sept 82, p. 408]

Ray Gerke

1271. Stevens, Norman D. **Communication Throughout Libraries.** Metuchen, N.J., Scarecrow, 1983. 177p. index. (Scarecrow Library Administration Series, No. 6). $14.50. LC 82-10502. ISBN 0-8108-1577-X.

One of several books on communication in the library to appear in 1983, this small volume provides a highly readable overview of the major issues in organizational communication. Stevens writes with a sense of humor, and, although he states that the book represents his view of communication, he does discuss many of the classic works in the field. He does not attempt to review all the literature, but the items he does cover are major works with only one or two exceptions. The exceptions are from the field of librarianship, and Stevens's interpretation of the value or importance of these items is highly personal; some readers will agree with his views, and others will not. His approach is to treat communication as a process without too much concern about the type or size of the library. A basic assumption of the book "is simply that in smaller and less complex libraries the communication process can be generally less formal and less organized"; not everyone will agree with that assumption. He expects readers to modify the process to fit the environmental context they are interested in.

Overall, the book is very worthwhile reading. It is not a how-to book, nor does it present a "communication package" for every library to consider. It does provide an overview of the process and a great deal of food for thought in ten short chapters. It is rounded out with an appendix suggesting ways of improving communication in an academic library, and an index. The book would be useful to most students in a library administration class. [R: BL, 15 Oct 83, p. 327; C&RL, Sept 83, pp. 390-92; JAL, Nov 83, p. 292; LJ, 1 May 83, p. 890; RQ, Fall 83, pp. 116-17]

G. Edward Evans

1272. Stevens, Rolland E., ed. **Supervision of Employees in Libraries.** Urbana-Champaign, Ill., University of Illinois, Graduate School of Library Science, 1979. 113p. index. (Allerton Park Institute, No. 24). $9.00. LC 79-10860. ISBN 0-87845-051-3.

The proceedings of the 24th annual Allerton Park Institute discuss various management theories and principles and their applications to library situations. The objective of the Institute was to provide first-line supervisors in libraries with practical assistance in learning how to perform their supervisory responsibilities. The contributors include both practicing librarians and experts in other disciplines.

Among the areas covered are: evaluation of employee performance; skill areas, such as the management of time, timing of meetings, and methods of running meetings, that supervisors should master; job-centered and employee-centered supervision styles; limitations of library management, and problems facing the library supervisor; changing attitudes toward work and their impact on the methods used to motivate employees; the role of the supervisor in training and staff development; principles of communication and effective techniques for communicating with employees; dealing with employee problems; and the effect of equal employment opportunity rules and regulations on library supervision. Unfortunately, the link between the "theory" underlying supervision and the practical application of the theory to libraries is often weak and in some cases nonexistent.

Robert D. Little

1273. Van Zant, Nancy Patton, ed. **Personnel Policies in Libraries.** New York, Neal-Schuman, 1980. 334p. index. $29.95. LC 80-11734. ISBN 0-918212-26-X.

Edited as a collection of excerpts from actual written policies of 52 academic and public libraries, *Personnel Policies in Libraries* covers a range of topics as follows: affirmative action and equal opportunity; staff selection; evaluation; tenure and grievance procedures; professional conduct and standards; staff development; personnel classification; working conditions; employee relations; employee benefits; and absences and terminations. The full texts of four policies (three public and one academic) are also included. Readers of the volume will find the responses to a questionnaire survey conducted by the author very interesting reading (survey, pages xv-xxxvii). Questionnaires were sent to over 1,300 public libraries and to over 1,000 academic libraries. Public librarians returned 510 useable questionnaires, and academic librarians, 416. Designed to "go a step further" than the *Library Personnel Manual: An Outline for Libraries* (American Library Association, 1977), policies for this book were selected from a letter mailed to 560 public and 550 academic libraries in the United States. Over 600 replies and 325 personnel policies or parts of policies were received. The author waives endorsement of any policy in particular. This volume should provide policy information for those libraries without personnel policies. [R: BL, 15 Oct 81, p. 285; C&RL, May 81, p. 257; JAL, July 81, p. 174; LJ, 15 June 81, p. 1287; LR, Summer 81, p. 100]

Donald D. Foos

TYPES OF LIBRARIES

College and Research Libraries

1274. Abell, Millicent D., ed. **Collective Bargaining in Higher Education: Its Implications for Governance and Faculty Status for Librarians.** Chicago, American Library Association, 1976. 161p. bibliog. (ACRL Publications in Librarianship, No. 38). o.p. LC 76-51403. ISBN 0-8389-3189-8.

This ACRL Publication in Librarianship deals effectively with the highly controversial subject of collective bargaining in higher education, with special emphasis on librarianship. The document grew out of a conference organized by the Academic Status Committee of the Association of College and Research Libraries. It successfully attempts to help libraries understand and evaluate the collective bargaining issue by providing readers with information on the nature of collective bargaining and its impact on governance in higher education. The successive articles deal with the objectives of various collective bargaining agents, a history of bargaining, alternative approaches, current status of academic libraries, and issues and

strategies. These proceedings are deftly and gracefully edited by Millicent Abel.

Throughout the book, the question of whether a faculty senate and a collective bargaining unit can coexist is treated, as well as the benefits to be expected from a shift to collective bargaining.

The framework developed by NLRB for private sector institutions and by various states for their own universities is given, then the representatives of the principal faculty associations present the approaches to negotiation that the associations favor. The appendices of these proceedings contain exceedingly useful information on labor terms, legal principles of public sector bargaining, and a useful bibliography.

A useful compilation on the status of this "art form," the book illuminates many dark shadows in this process. It is very helpful to libraries, academic administrators, and legislators. [R: C&RL, July 77, pp. 361-62; JAL, July 77, p. 182]

Norman E. Tanis

1275. Allen, Kenneth W., and Loren Allen. **Organization and Administration of the Learning Resources Center in the Community College.** Hamden, Conn., Shoe String Press, 1973. 187p. illus. index. o.p. LC 73-7539. ISBN 0-208-01306-7.

This work presents a model for incorporating a community college's learning resources into one unified administrative unit—or learning resources center. Using relevant data and studies, the book provides information on the nature of the community college, job descriptions for director, media and library personnel, finance, selection, instructional and technical services, library technical assistants, building programs, and new trends.

All chapters contain ideas worthwhile for the uninitiated in the community college situation. In the chapter "Building Program for New Facilities," for example, spatial relations are discussed for both the library and the media departments. Also, the need for planning for the future is delineated. However, like all the chapters, it is incomplete and should be considered just a starting point, rather than the final word on the subject.

The writing is not always clear, but perhaps the greatest weakness of the volume is its insistence that this is the *only* way a community college learning resources center may be organized, which is simply not so. It may be the most practical for the most people, but it is not the only way; others have been successfully organized under different administrative units. The book would perhaps have been more valuable had different organizational patterns been explored and had fewer topics been treated in greater depth. Because there is so little literature on the subject, and because it does contain useful ideas, this book would be considered necessary for most community college learning resources centers. [R: Choice, Mar 74, p. 68; LJ, 15 Mar 74, p. 739; RSR, Apr 74, p. 26]

Rosemary Henderson

1276. Branscomb, Lewis C., ed. **The Case for Faculty Status for Academic Librarians.** Chicago, American Library Association, 1970. 122p. index. (ACRL Monograph, No. 33). o.p. LC 75-118198. ISBN 0-8389-3114-6.

A collection of 14 previously published papers written by mostly upper-level library administrators, 11 of whom were members of the ad hoc Committee on Academic Status of the University Libraries Section, Association of College and Research Libraries. The papers cover the most important aspects of the subject and include an historical review from 1876. Although speaking in favor of faculty status for academic librarians, arguments are not always effective or entirely convincing. [R: C&RL, May 71, p. 234; LJ, 1 Jan 71, p. 50]

Charles D. Patterson

1277. Durey, Peter. **Staff Management in University and College Libraries.** Elmsford, N.Y., Pergamon Press, 1976. 170p. index. (International Series in Library and Information Science, Vol. 16). $19.00. LC 75-31515. ISBN 0-08-019718-3.

"The Organizational Framework" and "The Human Aspects" are two parts of this rather pedestrian book. Even the bibliography was dated at the time of publication; apparently the author found little to consult after 1973. It is a kind of chatty discussion of "happenings" in some universities and colleges in the United States as well as some foreign universities and colleges (Great Britain, Australia, Canada). It adds little to our knowledge. We can, however, give thanks to Durey for his frequent citing of Rogers and Weber's *University Library Administration* (H. W. Wilson, 1971); at least he knows that much. [R: LJ, 1 Dec 76, p. 2461]

Bohdan S. Wynar

1278. **Faculty Status for Academic Librarians: A History and Policy Statements.** Compiled by the Committee on Academic Status of the Association of College and Research Libraries. Chicago, American Library Association, 1975. 55p. bibliog. o.p. LC 75-29403. ISBN 0-8389-5455-8.

This pamphlet reprints official ALA/ ACRL statements on faculty status for academic librarians. The longest one is Arthur M. McAnally's paper "Status of the University in the Academic Community," first published in 1971. Following this are three briefer reprinted statements: ACRL's "Standards for Faculty Status" adopted in 1971; ACRL's "Statement on Faculty Status"; and ACRL's "Model Statement of Criteria." Appendices and a selective bibliography conclude the work. [R: C&RL, Mar 76, p. 176; LJ, 15 Apr 76, p. 988]

Richard A. Gray

1279. Gore, Daniel, ed. **Farewell to Alexandria: Solutions to Space, Growth, and Performance Problems of Libraries.** Westport, Conn., Greenwood Press, 1976. 180p. illus. $27.50. LC 75-35345. ISBN 0-8371-8587-4.

This collection of papers—presented on 17-18 April 1975, at the Conference on "Touching Bottom in the Bottomless Pit," sponsored by the Associated Colleges of the Midwest—treats the issue of growth problems in academic libraries from almost every angle. Some papers (Richard Dougherty's "Regionalization of University Library Services," Carl Spaulding's "Microtechnology and the Space Problem," and Joanne Harrer's "Cooperative Storage Facilities and the Space Problem") are not included in this published version. Daniel Gore, editor of the collection, has added his paper on "The Theory of the No-Growth, Higher Performance Library," which was not delivered at the conference.

That the topic is an important one is evident from the amount of attention it is receiving in the library literature. The papers raise a number of important questions and reveal some basic applied research that is being conducted in the area. Although some "how we done it" articles are practically useless and distract from the overall quality of the series, several outstanding articles are present, among them Mike Buckland and Anthony Hindle's discussion of a systems approach to related problems of acquisition, growth, and library size; Richard Trueswell's continued studies on circulation statistics; Blair Stewart's observations on periodical collections; and Gore's wrap-up article, which continues the Performance Rate emphasis which he previously espoused in "Zero Growth for the College Library" in *College Management*.

This series of 10 papers plus a panel discussion, a definite beginning, only touches the top of the bottomless pit of problems relating to growth problems in academic libraries. Highly recommended for all those who are facing or should be facing this issue. [R: C&RL, Nov 76, pp. 556-58]   Robert D. Stueart

1280. Johnson, Edward R., and Stuart H. Mann. **Organization Development for Academic Libraries: An Evaluation of the Management Review and Analysis Program.** Westport, Conn., Greenwood Press, 1980. 199p. bibliog. index. (Contributions in Librarianship and Information Science, No. 28). $27.50. LC 79-8289. ISBN 0-313-21373-9; ISSN 0084-9243.

This is a very interesting and sometimes provocative book. Of its seven chapters, only three focus specifically on the evaluation of the Management Review and Analysis Program. Two are devoted to organizational development, the first of these being a very superficial review of the OD literature, and the second being a very useful summary of OD activities in libraries. A middle chapter, written by Duane Webster, describes the MRAP program and provides information on its applications.

The chapters on the evaluation of MRAP are clearly the basis of this book. The evaluation, however, focused on the *process* of self-study, rather than discrete organizational outcomes or *products*. Although the research indicated that "overall, MRAP was successful in achieving most of the goals for self-review as established by the Office of Management Studies" (p. 130), the study is, from a methodological viewpoint, quite weak. For example, the 10 MRAP libraries which participated in the study were self-selected; the library directors of these institutions selected the staff members to participate in the questionnaire phase of the evaluation. Consequently, the entire process of sample selection is significantly flawed. Then, as a measure of MRAP's influence on staff development, the 91 participants (plus a control group) were tested on their respective abilities in writing a clear goal statement. To suggest a significant relationship between what amounts to a technical writing ability and MRAP participation would seem to be extremely questionable. Although the book raises far more questions than it answers, it is recommended reading for all library administrators. [R: LJ, 1 June 80, p. 1282]   Thomas W. Shaughnessy

1281. Lyle, Guy R. **The Administration of the College Library.** 4th ed. New York, H. W. Wilson, 1974. 320p. index. $14.00. LC 74-18427. ISBN 0-8242-0552-9.

This is the fourth edition of a work which appeared for the first time in 1944; its third edition appeared in 1961.

As in the three preceding editions, Lyle's book is primarily addressed to the administration of the four-year private college. He explicitly excludes university libraries, for which he refers readers to books by Wilson and Tauber and Rogers and Weber. Although in chapter 2, "Institutional Backgrounds," Lyle carefully distinguishes four-year private colleges from public community colleges and teacher's colleges and then states that administrative problems of all types exhibit underlying uniformities, in general the remaining chapters make clear that he gives a preponderant emphasis to the four-year private college.

This edition contains 17 chapters ranging from the first historical chapter through a final one on the evaluation of a college library. Intervening chapters cover such topics as the governance of the library, administrative organization, cataloging, curriculum, reference, personnel, business and financial affairs, etc.

Each chapter has its own notes as well as additional references. The notes and references as well as the text, of course, indicate that there has been substantial revision and updating since the third edition was published in 1961. Most of the cited sources relating to such topics as computer use, cooperative library programs, and microforms bear post-1961 publication dates.

Although many relatively new topics of intense current interest are well treated in the fourth edition, others are surprisingly not. For example, while he devotes substantial space to the use of the computer as a technical service tool (acquisitions and cataloging), he neglects it as an instrument of student instruction (CAI). Some other topics either omitted or given short shrift are copyright, photoreproduction problems, audiovisual resources, and unionization of library staffs.

The topics that Lyle either does not cover or covers inadequately indicate that, as in previous editions, the author takes a conservative approach to his subject. Its deficiencies notwithstanding, however, the book does deal with the vast majority of topics relevant to college library administration, and it deals with them in a clearly organized and clarifying manner. [R: C&RL, July 75, pp. 327-28]   Richard A. Gray

1282. Marchant, Maurice P. **Participative Management in Academic Libraries.** Westport, Conn., Greenwood Press, 1977 (c1976). 260p. illus. bibliog. index. (Contributions in Librarianship and Information Science, No. 16). $29.95. LC 76-8740. ISBN 0-8371-8935-7.

Based on Marchant's doctoral dissertation, the work is basically a report of empirical research carried out to determine the relationships between management style and library performance measurements in academic libraries. Marchant begins by discussing participative management and its development, the open system theory of organization, and the development of library administration. The bulk of the book is concerned with the research model of the effect of participative management. The measures of performance that were used in collecting data from 22 universities are: staff job satisfaction; extent of long-range planning; uniformity in library evaluation; circulation of materials for home use; and faculty evaluation of library services, facilities, and resources.

Marchant concluded that involvement of university library staff in the library's administration results in greater staff job satisfaction, and, ultimately, better libraries. To complement his call for evaluation of systems behavior and managerial style, the author proposes improved administrative skills in these areas. At the end of each chapter, references are provided together with a brief summary of each chapter's contents. Appendices include supplementary statistical tables, profile of organizational characteristics, and statistical values of major variables. A bibliography at the end of the book provides 77 references. Unfortunately, fewer than 20 of them bear dates of publication later than 1970.

Participative management is a very interesting and "hot" managerial topic. Regrettably this book is written in such a way, with extensive statistical manipulation, that it will be difficult for a great majority of library managers either to understand or to appreciate. [R: C&RL, Sept 77, pp. 432-34; JAL, Nov 77, p. 292; LJ, 15 June 77, pp. 1356-57]　　Ching-chih Chen

1283.　Martell, Charles R., Jr. **The Client-Centered Academic Library: An Organizational Model.** Westport, Conn., Greenwood Press, 1983. 136p. bibliog. index. (Contributions in Librarianship and Information Science, No. 42). $29.95. LC 82-9378. ISBN 0-313-23213-X.

Incorporating systems theory and organizational design theory, the author focuses on the formidable task of restructuring academic libraries from traditional organization by function (e.g., reference, cataloging, circulation) or by subject to an organization with small, "client-centered" work groups performing a number of functions as units depending on the needs of the client group. Pointing out the basic need for academic libraries to be sensitive and responsive to changing client needs for information ser-

vices, Martell suggests that this new client-centered approach would accomplish this goal as well as increasing the job satisfaction of academic librarians by infusing intellectually stimulating challenges.

As academic libraries are caught up in the rapidly changing university environment, a client-focused, grassroots-level approach to information services, as Martell envisions it, is certainly a thought-provoking idea. Although Martell has adequately reviewed the appropriate literature, this book will be of most value to those who have a working knowledge of management theory. [R: JAL, Nov 83, p. 292; LQ, Jan 84, p. 113; RQ, Fall 83, p. 115]

Sherrilynne Shirley Fuller

1284.　Martin, Murray S. **Budgetary Control in Academic Libraries.** Greenwich, Conn., JAI Press, 1978. 219p. bibliog. index. (Foundations in Library and Information Science, Vol. 5). $37.50. LC 76-5648. ISBN 0-89232-010-9.

"When budgets were growing rapidly in the late sixties, good management seemed less necessary than the expansion of programs. Since that time the availability of funds has been reduced and management has become indispensable." Following that introduction is a succinct discussion of a broad range of matters relating to the library budget including its preliminary analysis, presentation, and justification, determination of priorities, and monitoring of funds.

One of the real values of this work is that for such exceptions as Sul Lee's *Library Budgeting: Critical Challenges for the Future* (see *ARBA* 78, entry 211), there is a dearth of textual material on budgeting in academic libraries. Martin's effort is even more important in that he deals with the subject on a more applied, less theoretical level than do most other works on this topic. Practical advice on such concerns as the use of reserve funds, the potential pitfalls of federal funding, and the reallocation of dollars during budget cutbacks are discussed in a manner readily understood by those with even a rudimentary knowledge of academic library functions and procedures. To further relate the concepts of this effort, copious charts and diagrams in both the text and appendix provide specific, quantitative examples of the matters discussed. In addition, a brief but useful glossary of commonly used budgetary terms is provided. This work is not a definitive study of budgetary practices, nor does it claim to serve that purpose. Thus, it is not intended for the experienced library administrator who would be seeking the tools of the analyst or accountant applied in a library context. However, this is an important title for the library management student and the librarian who seeks an elementary but solid insight into the complexities of the budget process. [R: LJ, 15 Oct 78, p. 2057]

Frank W. Goudy

1285. Martin, Murray S. **Issues in Personnel Management in Academic Libraries.** Greenwich, Conn., JAI Press, 1981. 266p. bibliog. index. (Foundations in Library and Information Science, Vol. 14). $40.00. LC 81-81649. ISBN 0-89232-136-9.

In this carefully thought through, precisely written, and narrowly focused study, Murray Martin has taken a hard look at what is probably the most rewarding yet most frustrating aspect of academic library management. The 14 heavily footnoted chapters are not intended as a comprehensive guide to personnel practices, but rather as a "consideration of major issues which are likely to persist over the next decade." Among the issues are leadership, professionalism, communication, staff development, salaries and other rewards, goal-setting, accountability and authority, management styles, and the organization of libraries.

As he develops his narrative, Martin continually evidences his concern about the impact that shrinking library budgets are going to have on personnel management, and stresses the need to think now about how best to deal with the "reduction, reallocation, and retrenchment" of the near future. Experienced academic librarians, particularly administrators, from department heads to directors/deans, will find that Martin's excellent analyses may well lead them into new ways of thinking about old issues. This is a sound, well-organized book that deserves to be unhurriedly read and reflected on. Library school, university, research, and management libraries should find a way to add this fine work to their collections. [R: C&RL, July 82, p. 357; JAL, July 82, p. 164; LQ, July 82, p. 276]

Charles R. Andrews

1286. Massman, Virgil F. **Faculty Status for Librarians.** Metuchen, N.J., Scarecrow, 1972. 240p. index. o.p. LC 76-181317. ISBN 0-8108-0446-8.

A Michigan doctoral dissertation presenting an extensive review of previous studies and related materials on faculty or academic status for librarians. This study provides important background material for further investigation on the role of women in librarianship-obtained as an adjunct to the main purpose of the collected research data. Massman does not totally answer the question of faculty status for librarians, but his study does provide an important base for further investigation in this area. Recommended for all library science collections, as well as for academic librarians confronted with this problem. [R: C&RL, Nov 72, p. 491; RQ, Spring 73, p. 320]

Donald D. Foos

1287. Merrill, Irving R., and Harold A. Drob. **Criteria for Planning the College and University Learning Resources Center.** Washington, D.C., Association for Educational Communications and Technology, 1977. 117p. illus. bibliog. $6.95pa. LC 77-2612. ISBN 0-89240-003-X.

This work sets out space and staff criteria for the development of a "learning resources" program in colleges and universities. The term "learning resources center" is used in this work to mean "the facilities for the origination, distribution, and display of audio, television, and graphic materials for group and individual presentation; the instructional materials thus created and recorded; and the persons employed to participate with the teacher in their creation, presentation, and evaluation" (p. 3). Needless to say, periodicals and books are excluded. The problem of terminology is appropriately noted by the authors, and readers need to be aware of the limitation of coverage.

The authors do a good job in covering the area specified. The history of the development of the "learning resources" concept is traced briefly in chapter 1. The relationship to the library is covered in chapters 2 and 3, along with the advantages of a separate LRC (learning resources center). The authors do not close the door on a combined library and media program and appropriately note that "the crucial question, it would seem, is whether or not the campus instructional program, including the extension and alternative programs, is best served by a merged print and nonprint media facility or by separate facilities" (p. 39). Chapter 4 provides helpful criteria for staff and space, which can be used in the context of one's unique local situation. Chapter 5 concludes the work with a sketchy overview of budgeting. Overall, this work proves to be useful for all educators concerned with the "print and multi-media" world. [R: LJ, 1 Dec 77, p. 2413]

Dwight F. Burlingame

1288. **Organization and Staffing of the Libraries of Columbia University: A Case Study.** Westport, Conn., Redgrave Information Resources, 1973. 210p. index. o.p. LC 72-13447. ISBN 0-88276-002-5.

Sponsored by the Association of Research Libraries in cooperation with the American Council on Education, and financed by the Council of Library Resources, this is a comprehensive report on the administrative structure of the Columbia University libraries. It contains a number of specific suggestions applicable not only to Columbia but to other institutions of similar size. Some of the study's interesting comments and generalizations could be quoted here, but this has already been done in other reviews. Since Columbia has a rather traditional administrative structure (see the chapter on staffing, administrative responsibilities, etc.), it might be interesting to prepare a similar study for Cornell. We personally think that staff involvement in decision making is a good idea, provided, of course, that there is a sufficient mechanism and someone of authority to implement the decisions. Using a rotating base for an administrator is also a fine idea, and no one will quarrel with the study's recommendation that the library director should be made a vice president of the university. But what about realities? The appended bibliography lists a number of works that deal with corporate structure. As we know, corporations are seldom run by committees, and their decision-making process is somewhat different. Nevertheless, a few important lessons can be learned even from corporations, since most of them are quite efficient. [R: AL, Oct 73, p. 552; LJ, 15 Sept 74, p. 2135]

Bohdan S. Wynar

1289. **Problems in University Library Management. (A Study Conducted by Booz, Allen & Hamilton, Inc., for The Association of Research Libraries and The American Council of Education).** Washington, D.C., Association of Research Libraries, 1970. 63p. o.p. LC 78-139752.

A study funded by the Council on Library Resources that included site visits to six university libraries: Connecticut, Cornell, Duke, Iowa, Pennsylvania, and UCLA. Chapters deal with place of the library in development of higher education; management problems in planning, budgeting, operations, organization, staffing, facilities, and interinstitutional cooperation; detailed recommendations for improvement and areas of further research. Accurately identifies and diagnoses many real problems faced by numerous university libraries. [R: C&RL, May 71, p. 229; LJ, 1 Jan 71, p. 53]

Charles D. Patterson

1290. Rogers, Rutherford D., and David C. Weber. **University Library Administration.** New

York, H. W. Wilson, 1971. 454p. illus. index. $23.00. LC 75-116997. SBN 8242-0417-4.

Continuous changes in demands on the university library necessitate corresponding changes in the administration of the services, resources, and staff. Rogers and Weber's book on library administration represents a much-needed effort in this area. This work is rather comprehensive and, to a certain extent, its content bears resemblance to its two predecessors. *University Library Administration* is divided into 11 units followed by some 75 pages of appendices which include sample personnel evaluation forms, acquisition policies, purchase agreements, floor plans, and the like. Topics included under each unit are: "The Library Program"; "Personnel Policies"; "Library Organization and Communication"; "Budgeting and Fiscal Management"; "Book Collections"; "The Technical Processing Function"; "The Reader's Services Function"; "Special Types of Materials"; "Measurement and Evaluation"; and "Automation." A bibliography is included at the end of each unit. *University Library Administration* is illustrated and includes a number of diagrams, charts, and sample forms. It is an attractive volume, aesthetically appealing, written in a readable and pleasant style. The authors discuss administrative operations in terms of staff, resources, and facilities. They raise various issues related to a particular aspect of the administrative operation. Examples as well as sample forms often illustrate a case in point and help the reader to acquire a better understanding of the particular operation being discussed. The usefulness of this work is not exclusively limited to one particular group, although it seems that library school students will be the ones to gain most from its use. Seasoned library administrators might find the appendices useful for comparative and reference purposes. Units included in this work which were not covered extensively in the earlier works on university library administration—such as automation, measurement and evaluation, to mention a few—are brief and require the use of supplementary materials by anyone with special interest in these aspects of the administrative operation. [R: LQ, July 72, p. 347]

George V. Hodowanec

1291. Steele, Colin, ed. **Steady-State, Zero Growth and the Academic Library: A Collection of Essays.** London, Clive Bingley; distr., Hamden, Conn., Linnet Books, 1978. 148p. o.p. LC 78-7030. ISBN 0-208-01680-5.

This work consists of the reactions of eight academic librarians to the recommendations of the Atkinson Report of 1976, which states that as funds for academic libraries become scarcer, library growth must be stablized (i.e., steady-state situation). The situation described by the title of this work, *Steady-State, Zero Growth and the Academic Library*, is in actuality a euphemism for the decline of academic libraries. All eight essays take issue with the report in varying degrees, but the strongest opposition is voiced in "The State of the Argument: Australia," wherein John Horacek contends that the Atkinson Report could have a stultifying effect if it were codified into official doctrine. If it becomes an accepted fact that academic libraries must be kept at the "no-growth" level, then any possibility for future growth will be eliminated. This could have disastrous consequences for the developing countries of the Third World, as well as for the developed countries.

This collection of short essays is well written and united by a common thread of opinion that the Atkinson Report was perhaps the result of political expediency and had minimal informed input from academic librarians. Such questions as delayed access to materials, weeding, and the effect of new university programs on library usage have been neglected. Proposed quantitative cuts do not take sufficiently into consideration the qualitative changes that would almost certainly result.

As John Dean says in "Growth Control in the Research Library," administrators and politicians will tend to use the simplistic method of balancing the number of incoming books exactly against the number of those retired. This practice would have completely different results when applied to a humanities library as opposed to a health sciences library. The message of this well-written book is that academic librarians will have to come to terms with decreased budgets and decreased enrollments by formulating a coherent strategy. The "zero-growth" library philosophy does not seem to offer such a strategy. However, it remains an urgent problem, because if librarians do not act, the politicians will. [R: C&RL, Mar 79, p. 172; LR, Spring 79, p. 31]   Norman Frankel

1292. Thompson, James. **An Introduction to University Library Administration.** 3rd ed. London, Clive Bingley; distr., New York, K. G. Saur, 1979. 160p. illus. bibliog. index. $18.75. ISBN 0-85157-288-X.

This is the third edition of an introductory text on university library administration. As in the first two editions (1970; 1974, see *ARBA* 75, entry 182), the subject matter is arranged under eight headings: the context of the university

library; the role of the university librarian; university library staff; university library stock; processes and routines; reader services; university library buildings; and cooperation. Changes in the text regarding such concerns as the financial exigencies of the 1970s, academic recognition for librarians, and the development of computerized techniques have been included to update the effort and make it more relevant to today's library world.

The difficulties with this book are twofold. First, its 143 pages of actual text provide only a cursory examination of the eight areas outlined. For this to be of solid use to "student librarians and practitioners within the world of librarianship," greater detail and more practical examples from a work context are needed to explore and explain the environment of academic libraries. Second, the value of this book rests primarily with those involved in British librarianship, as the practices and writings mentioned make only secondary use of North American situations and research. For instance, the use of OCLC is not mentioned, and there is no analysis of the impact that collective bargaining exerted in the 1970s. While this work is logically organized and clearly written, these limitations lessen its appropriateness to U.S. academic librarians.

American readers desiring a text on this subject would still find it more useful to consult *University Library Administration* (see *ARBA* 72, entry 94) by Rogers and Weber, and Lyle's *The Administration of the College Library* (see *ARBA* 76, entry 139). [R: C&RL, Sept 80, p. 462; LJ, 1 May 80, p. 1052]

Frank Wm. Goudy

1293. Thomson, Sarah Katharine. **Learning Resource Centers in Community Colleges: A Survey of Budgets and Services.** Chicago, American Library Association, 1975. 146p. illus. o.p. LC 75-16150. ISBN 0-8389-0206-5.

This work is a product of a CLR grant awarded to the author in 1973-1974. The community college campuses visited provided the basic database for the study. The work's central focus is comparing expenditures with user results. The reader is provided with a comparison survey of budgets, staff, reader services, student use, selection procedures, attitudes, and so forth, that the author distilled from the institutions studied. A bibliography or a summary chapter would have been helpful. Used with Veit's *The Community College Library* (Greenwood Press, 1975) and Allen and Allen's *Organization and Administration of the Learning Resources Center in the Community College*

(Linnet Books, 1973), this work serves as a useful supplement for the community college administrator. [R: C&RL, Jan 76, p. 79; CLW, Feb 76, p. 306; JAL, Sept 76, p. 191; LQ, Oct 76, p. 450]   Dwight F. Burlingame

1294. Weatherford, John W. **Collective Bargaining and the Academic Librarian**. Metuchen, N.J., Scarecrow, 1976. 147p. illus. bibliog. index. $16.00. LC 76-45424. ISBN 0-8108-0983-4.

John Weatherford has been director of libraries at Central Michigan University, the second university in the United States to have experienced faculty collective bargaining. Most of the material presented here is based on the author's personal experience, his visits to several campuses during 1973, and his correspondence on the subject. The seven chapters of this interesting book (plus a bibliography) cover several aspects of this topic (e.g., compensation, the bargaining unit, terms and conditions of employment, etc.). The selective bibliography, covering 1971 to 1975, includes a separate subsection on librarians. The author does not necessarily advocate any specific courses of action but simply presents the material from both points of view. It seems to us that this summary of seven years of activities in this field will be of interest to many librarians. It should be noted that the October 1976 issue of *Library Trends*, "Employee Organizations and Collective Bargaining in Libraries," covers more or less the same ground. [R: C&RL, July 77, p. 358; JAL, July 77, p. 161; RQ, Summer 77, p. 366]

1295. Whitbeck, George W. **The Influence of Librarians in Liberal Arts Colleges in Selected Decision Making Areas**. Metuchen, N.J., Scarecrow, 1972. 147p. bibliog. index. o.p. LC 71-183945. ISBN 0-8108-0445-X.

This is a study based on the author's doctoral thesis. The book contains some empirical evidence to confirm what many librarians have subjectively felt to be true: that librarians operate only on the periphery of some of the most important areas of decision making on a college campus. This study, conducted on ten small college campuses, covered three specific areas of decision making: (1) development of the curriculum, (2) budget allocations, and (3) key appointments on the campus.

The most conclusive evidence in the study pertains to the librarian's role in curriculum development. Some 84 percent of the faculty and administrators surveyed did not see any significant role for the librarians in decision

making with respect to curriculum development. The librarians themselves expressed a lack of interest in and knowledge about curricular issues. Such an admission on the part of the librarians surveyed is a significant factor to consider when the argument is made—as it is so often—that librarians should be given full faculty status, because they are equally involved in the academic life of the campus.

Some other interesting conclusions of this study are: (1) few librarians serve on college committees, and even fewer serve on what are considered "important" committees; (2) the faculty have little contact with librarians, seeing them once a month or less and then usually to discuss collection development; (3) the librarians viewed their position more as administrators than as faculty; (4) at the departmental level of budget decisions faculty are much more involved than librarians; (5) there was little involvement by either faculty or librarians in the area of key appointments on campus; and (6) faculty are more likely to be involved in decisions on staffing their departments than librarians are in staffing the library.

Whitbeck concludes that "librarians do appear overall to have a very minimal role in the mainstream of events at the college; but, in certain areas they are apparently no more involved than the bulk of the faculty."

The conclusions of this work were based on data gathered at ten small private colleges (the largest with about 2,000 students) in a limited geographic area. The narrow scope of this study does not warrant any generalizations about all librarians, but it would be interesting to see the results of similar studies at larger institutions. Despite its limitations, the study would be of interest to most college and university librarians. [R: LJ, 1 Nov 72, p. 3555]

Marty Bloomberg

1296. Young, Harold Chester. **Planning, Programming, Budgeting Systems in Academic Libraries: An Exploratory Study of PPBS in University Libraries Having Membership in the Association of Research Libraries**. Detroit, Gale, 1976. 227p. bibliog. index. $58.00. LC 76-10667. ISBN 0-8103-0264-0.

This volume, the culmination of a 1974 Ph.D. dissertation, is based on a questionnaire submitted to the 78 academic libraries that were members of the Association of Research Librarians in 1971, and on 21 interviews and many internal documents from five of those libraries chosen for more intensive investigation. The extraordinarily high return of the questionnaire

(94 percent responded) confirms the interest and timeliness of the survey.

The first four chapters introduce the concept of planning, programming, budgeting systems (PPBS), including its development and use in business and government in the United States and its belated introduction into libraries — the topic first appeared in *Library Literature* in 1969. Chapter 4 is an interesting but somewhat digressive account of the development of academic libraries in the United States. One can only assume that the author's intent for this chapter is to prove the point that the time is ripe for the introduction of PPBS into academic libraries. This can be accomplished by libraries "reassessing and reestablishing control measures to provide a more viable library service for users."

Chapter 5, full of dissertationese, recapitulates in narrative and graphic form the introtory chapter.

The second part of the monograph is devoted to the five "case studies," with accounts of the interviews. Essentially, this part accomplishes the objective of summarizing "the experience to date of selected libraries which have PPBS and [of describing] their methodologies in introducing PPBS."

Some conclusions are couched in vague terms: "as of Winter 1973, no one academic library had implemented an integrated PPB System"; and "cost of developing a total PPBS library program is an unknown factor." Other conclusions, such as the one relating to organizational structure in which "the library budget officer's position is not equivalent to that of an assistant or associate director, and problems were encountered by the budget officer," seem irrelevant to PPBS, since that position is usually a "staff" rather than a "line" one anyway.

The author has a very good writing style, but he unfortunately suggests tentative conclusions based on limited, loosely structured data. Opinions are often stated as facts and the overall impact is less than one would hope for or, indeed, expect. [R: C&RL, Jan 77, p. 81; JAL, Jan 77, p. 307]   Robert D. Stueart

Public Libraries

1297. Altman, Ellen, ed. **Local Public Library Administration.** 2nd ed. Chicago, American Library Association, 1980. 251p. bibliog. index. $20.00. LC 80-20168. ISBN 0-8389-0307-X.

This book constitutes a thorough revision of the popular handbook on public library administration which first appeared in 1964.

Under the able editorship of Ellen Altman, 18 separate topics are covered by 22 authors. The aspects covered range from such quickly dated issues as "contemporary society" to less rapidly changing issues such as "collection development" and "budgeting." All of the papers are quite short, and as one would expect, the papers vary in quality and usefulness. Nevertheless, several papers are both innovative and provocative, with those by Altman, "The Administrator" and Douglas Zweizig, "Community Analysis" representing seminal assessments of the two areas. Unfortunately, this book as a whole is neither fish nor fowl. Too basic for most practicing administrators, and too uneven for most students, it should be read selectively by those interested in developments in public library administration. [R: LJ, 15 Sept 81, p. 1705]   Michael H. Harris

1298. Altman, Ellen, and others. **A Data Gathering and Instructional Manual for Performance Measures in Public Libraries.** Chicago, Celadon Press, 1976. 1v. (various paging). illus. o.p.

As the companion volume to the 1973 *Performance Measures for Public Libraries* (American Library Association), this manual reveals the details behind the Beasley, DeProspo, Altman, and Clark innovative and exploratory approach to the challenge of public library measurement. The authors are to be commended for continuing their clear dialog about the research process with an audience composed largely of librarians unskilled in doing or interpreting research. The desire of the authors to involve others in the learning process of research is illustrated by the carte blanche they give people using the manual to photocopy or duplicate as many forms as might be required for their own in-library studies.

However, in the introduction to this manual, library staffs are cautioned that the techniques reported are not measures of individual performance but rather indicators of patterns of usage and availability in the entire library. With this caveat in mind, it might have been more appropriate to call this volume a study of activity measurement techniques.

The July 1974 *Library Quarterly* review of the 1973 base work raises points about particular techniques, but it also recognizes the study as important for indicating the need and providing direction for the further development of performance measures in a decision-making and planning context. Obviously, this companion volume is in the same tradition. Although the total study does not achieve perfection and the manual has some unnecessary duplication of forms, given the authors' blanket permission to photocopy, it belongs in the collections of those libraries interested in analyzing themselves and in all library schools and state library agency collections. It is not a magic wand; it is a record of our continuing attempt to become a self-monitoring service-oriented profession. [R: LJ, 15 May 77, p. 1161]   Caroline M. Coughlin

1299. Brown, Robert E. **Joetta Community Library: A Simulation Exercise in Library Administration.** Urbana-Champaign, Ill., Graduate School of Library Science, University of Illinois, 1975. 78p. illus. (Occasional Papers, No. 118). o.p.

This work represents a collection of documents, memoranda, and other materials related to the daily administrative procedures and practices of a small public library. It is essentially a reference manual to be used as a supplementary text for a public library administration course. Some portions of this work have been compressed or altered in form to reduce the size of the book. In the introduction, however, the author states that the user can secure the original version of compressed portions of the book simply by writing to him.

The opening section of this book includes an announcement of a vacancy for library director. It is followed by a description of his or her responsibilities, a statement on the minimum qualifications, and general information about the library, the city, and the community. All of this information is intended to be used as an example for formulating such memos and, of course, to be used for class discussion in an administration course. In the subsequent portions of this work an example of personnel policies includes a statement on fair employment practices, staff structure, job descriptions, performance evaluations, and working conditions. In general, the author has tried to give the user a variety of examples of information necessary for the director to make various administrative decisions. On the other hand, a group of charts, diagrams, minutes of board of trustees meetings, annual budgets, and floor plans included in this book may be helpful to its user in planning and developing appropriate library programs. An inexperienced library director or a person just about to assume such responsibilities will find this work helpful. It also has potential value as supplementary classroom material in a library administration course. [R: LQ, July 76, p. 330]
George V. Hodowanec

1300. Brown, Royston. **Public Library Administration.** London, Clive Bingley; distr., New York, K. G. Saur, 1979. 95p. index. (Outlines of Modern Librarianship, Vol. 9). $12.00. ISBN 0-85157-276-6.

This monograph, one in a series of Outlines of Modern Librarianship, is intended for use primarily as an introduction to the subject in support of academic courses. As such, the thin 95 pages serve simply that purpose. The outline addresses purpose, governance, structure, finance, staffing, materials, services, physical facilities, and cooperation, in broad sweeping generalizations. Since the volume is intended primarily for a British audience, examples, when given, are of British laws, funding, governance, structure, etc. This combination of brevity and orientation limits its usefulness. For classroom discussion, one must consult other sources for a fuller analysis of public library administration. [R: JAL, Mar 80, p. 49; LJ, 1 Nov 80, p. 2280]   Robert D. Stueart

1301. Bundy, Mary Lee, and Paul Wasserman. **The Public Library Administrator and His Situation.** College Park, Md., Urban Information Interpreters, 1972. 1v. (various paging). (Urban Information Series Publication, No. 6). o.p.

This study was designed to "analyze the characteristics of administrators and of the organizations and the environments in which they function," with the aim of increasing the understanding of "the human and organizational variables which tend to spawn or to inhibit change" (summary). [R: LJ, Aug 73, p. 2250]

1302. Coughlin, Robert E., Françoise Taieb, and Benjamin H. Stevens. **Urban Analysis for Branch Library System Planning.** Westport, Conn., Greenwood Press, 1972. 167p. illus. index. (Contributions in Librarianship and Information Science, No. 1). o.p. LC 71-133496. ISBN 0-8371-5161-9.

Much of the analysis of statistics for Public Library System Planning is based, as might be expected (considering the involvement of Emerson Greenaway), on the Philadelphia Free Library System. For many of the questions raised there are no definitive answers, but some conclusions have been reached. For example, the use of a branch library is determined for the most part by the socio-economic level of the population. Book stock is extremely important, and the selection of books for libraries in lower income areas may not, in some cases, be suited to the tastes, interests, and reading ability of the public. There is a higher rate of use by juveniles and young adults than by adults. This is probably true throughout large segments of the United States. Other conclusions are drawn which might be of interest for administrators in preliminary planning, but the value of locations of branch libraries (near shopping centers, schools, etc.) is not proven. Items for future research, in connection with broader community objectives, are delineated (the effect of library use on school performance and earnings, and the effect of a good library upon residential location decisions). How significant the statistical tables are in comparison with what has already been published is a moot question, but library administrators may wish to add this book to their shelves of professional material. [R: AL, Jan 73, p. 30; C&RL, May 73, p. 230; LJ, 15 Feb 73, p. 516]   Marjorie P. Holt

1303. De Prospo, Ernest R., Ellen Altman, and Kenneth E. Beasley. **Performance Measures for Public Libraries.** Chicago, Public Library Association, American Library Association, 1973. 71p. bibliog. o.p. LC 73-16427. ISBN 0-8389-3149-9.

The data collected show, by use of sampling techniques, the character of the collection, the use of the facility, and the characteristics of the users. Additional information on outreach services is also provided. [R: LQ, July 74, p. 273; RQ, Fall 74, p. 75; RSR, Apr 74, p. 19]

1304. Jenkins, Harold R. **Management of a Public Library.** Greenwich, Conn., JAI Press, 1980. 258p. bibliog. index. (Foundations in Library and Information Science, Vol. 8). $37.50. LC 76-13957. ISBN 0-89232-038-9.

Within the brief period of a few months, three books dealing with public library administration appeared. Each treats the subject in a different way. Wheeler and Goldhor's *Practical Administration of Public Libraries* (Harper & Row, 1981), updated by Carlton Rochell, is direct, practical, and expansive. The reader is told what to do now, and then is led to additional information for further study. *Local Public Library Administration*, second edition (see entry 1297), by Ellen Altman, provides an excellent base and overview of the subject rather than immediate, specific answers to problems. Jenkins's approach is closer to autobiography than management guide. It is a personal statement based on long-term experience as the director of a major public library.

Content is organized by topics of varying length and importance, which have a tendency to overlap. Chapters begin with general opinions concerning a topic. The topic under consideration is interspersed with lists of things to do in certain situations, abstracts of favorite articles, and question-and-answer sections that highlight specific points. If one reads this as an anecdotal account of one man's life in public libraryland with detours for personal views ("I would advise library boards to consider women as very good prospects. There are more of them in the library field." "Coming home to a crying family to a wife who feels that she has been unjustly uprooted, can weaken the position of the most important administrator"), the raconteur's style and the evidence of lessons learned and wisdom gained make this an informative, sometimes frustrating, sometimes charming book. [R: JAL, May 81, p. 114; LJ, Aug 81, p. 1511]
                              Ann E. Prentice

1305. Lushington, Nolan, and Willis N. Mills, Jr. **Libraries Designed for Users: A Planning Handbook.** Syracuse, N.Y., Gaylord Professional Publications, 1979. 289p. illus. bibliog. index. $27.50. LC 78-27114. ISBN 0-915794-29-2.

A librarian and an architect have produced a useful overview of the process and particulars of planning a public library building for communities of up to 100,000 population. The guiding principle is user convenience in a library building that makes possible personalized service and efficient self-service, and enables a complex service organization to function on an intimate personal level.

The book is as valuable for its approach to the planning process as it is in offering checklists of service areas and processing requirements. Knowledge of the community, a library self-study of its physical needs and its function for the community, use of consultants on planning and selecting, and working with an architect are discussed. Sample cases for critiquing are offered to illustrate more technical points in the text.

Information is provided on lighting choice, energy conservation, graphics, facilities for handicapped users, parking, and site location. This information is not technical, but provides a framework for intelligent discussion of specific plans to be developed by the architect. Included are chapters on overall library organization for services, designing children's and adult service areas, and school library media center design.

Weaknesses include a lack of specific documentation to take the reader further into the technical aspects. Some informal citations are included in the text, but are not repeated in an appendix or in the bibliography. The bibliography reflects the book's more social, user-centered approach to design. The handbook will be useful to librarians and trustees who were introduced to planning in *Design of the Small Public Library* (R. R. Bowker, 1966) and who received more specific planning information not focused on the public library in *Planning and Design of Library Buildings* (see *ARBA* 79, entry 260). [R: LJ, 1 Nov 79, p. 2290]

Sharon C. Bonk

1306.   Newhouse, Joseph P., and Arthur J. Alexander. **An Economic Analysis of Public Library Services.** Lexington, Mass., Lexington Books/D. C. Heath, 1972. 138p. illus. bibliog. index. o.p. LC 72-6727. ISBN 0-669-85027-6.

This study addresses itself to a number of questions—budget allocation, the cost of typical services provided by the library, the steps needed to improve these services, etc. The authors studied these questions in the context of one public library—the Beverly Hills (California) Public Library—and offer a number of interesting generalizations based on their studies. [R: LJ, 1 Apr 73, p. 1096]

1307.   Palmour, Vernon E., Marcia C. Bellassai, and Nancy V. DeWath. **A Planning Process for Public Libraries.** Prepared for the Public Library Association, a division of the American Library Association. Chicago, American Library Association, 1980. 304p. bibliog. $15.00pa. LC 80-13107. ISBN 0-8389-3246-0.

This planning manual is the result of a two year effort by ALA's Public Library Association and the authors, of King Research, Inc. Before publication, libraries at three sites used the draft as a guide through the planning process. Criticisms and comments generated from these libraries were eventually incorporated as changes in this final publication.

The purpose of this work is to assist public libraries in developing standards which reflect local conditions and needs, create plans to reach these standards, and implement a continuing planning process which will insure the ongoing evaluation of methods, objectives, and community needs. All of this is done in an effort to create a library which is in touch with the many changes occurring in each community, and to reflect these changes in a service program which is responsive to citizens' needs.

The manual is intended for use by a library planning committee composed not only of representatives from the library, but also individuals from the board, city government, and the community in general. The role of the committee, as outlined in this guide, is to assess community library needs; evaluate service; determine the role of the library; set goals, objectives, and priorities; and design strategies for change based on the collected data. Each step in the planning process is clearly outlined here, with activities divided into three sections: preparing to plan, the planning process, and collecting and using data. Sample forms, maps for the community profile, sample tables, surveys, and a bibliography add useful information to this volume.

The focus of this guide is on change—changing goals, objectives, roles, and processes to more realistically reflect the library's community. However, the planning process recommended here involves a great expenditure of time, not only the time of library personnel, but also time committed by local citizens. Another problem with this manual is its failure to relate planning to other management components, such as the budgeting function. Nevertheless, the result of this effort and expenditure involved in the planning process is a long-range plan designed to meet the needs of a specific community.

Prior to this publication, the only tool that libraries had to use in developing plans for future services was *Minimum Standards for Public Libraries, 1966* (American Library Association, 1967). This work did not assist in planning for growth after a certain point, once minimum standards were reached, nor did it allow for as much involvement by local citizens in the planning process.

This is a major work in the area of planning for public libraries, reflecting sound principles of management and marketing research techniques. Although a great deal of time is required in following this planning process, the results should produce important changes in public library service. [R: LJ, 15 Jan 81, p. 128]

Ann Hartman

1308.   Perkins, John W. **Branch Library Service.** Inglewood, Calif., Inglewood Public Library, 1977. 67p. o.p. (spiralbound). LC 77-17557. ISBN 0-913578-17-7.

This comprehensive manual on branch library service was designed both for training new branch librarians and for familiarizing the staff with the functions of a branch library. It includes position descriptions, a branch librarian work evaluation form, and a detailed checklist of items to be inspected or reviewed by the branch librarian or that librarian's supervisor to insure that the branch library operation is effective. It can serve as an aid for administrators and officials in understanding the function of branch libraries and can enable library administrators to make comparative evaluations of their own operations. Also providing material for case studies in library school courses, it will be a useful addition to college and university libraries that serve library school students and faculty. Theodore Manheim

1309. Prentice, Ann E. **Public Library Finance.** Chicago, American Library Association, 1977. 150p. bibliog. index. $8.00pa. LC 77-9096. ISBN 0-8389-0240-5.

This book is designed "to assist the library manager and student of library management to become knowledgeable about the current political realities of public library finance and to provide guidelines and direction in obtaining and utilizing funds for the public library in responsible and responsive fashion" (preface). This is not a "how-to" book, so a knowledge of management principles and budgeting practices would be helpful. The political nature of public library funding is of growing concern, and the author stresses budgeting with this fact in mind. Sources of funds—federal, state, local, and private—are examined, as well as the mutual responsibilities involved in the relationship of public libraries and government. Three types of budgets—line item, performance, and program—are evaluated and compared, and a model budget is developed. Finally, control of expenditures and continuing evaluative programs are outlined, with accompanying financial statements and potential applications to the annual report demonstrated. This is not a text for use in a beginning library management course, but will be of value to both the advanced library management student and the public library administrator. [R: LJ, 1 May 78, p. 947] Janet H. Littlefield

1310. Prentice, Ann E. **The Public Library Trustee: Image and Performance on Funding.** Metuchen, N.J., Scarecrow, 1973. 176p. charts. index. o.p. LC 73-1648. ISBN 0-8108-0597-9.

A straightforward presentation of the basic characteristics of trustees, with a discussion of their relationships to library administration and to the political structure of the community. Among the author's conclusions one finds that "the library trustee of 1970 had much in common with the trustee of 1935. Today's trustee is white, male, with an average age of 53 years, and has served as a trustee for five years or less.... Politically, today's trustees are not particularly active, but more than half do participate in non-partisan activities such as

conservation and education" (p. 140). As the reader can guess by now, this is a doctoral dissertation (Columbia University). There is another dissertation on this subject, by Jane Robbins—"Policy Formation in American Public Libraries: Effects of Citizen Participation" (University of Maryland). It is quite different in approach and, although it is based on a case study, it provides a broader framework for the topic. [R: CLW, Dec 73, p. 240; RSR, Apr 74, p. 22] Bohdan S. Wynar

1311. Shaffer, Kenneth R. **Decision Making: A Seminar in Public Library Management.** Hamden, Conn., Linnet Books, 1971. 191p. o.p. LC 70-150395. ISBN 0-208-01207-9.

Despite the author's claim that this book is not a case book, his "situations" are not unlike those found in his earlier works expounding the case method. A succinct and readable book that presents each "situation" in two parts: "The Problem" and "Recommendation." A useful teaching tool that presents Shaffer's humane approach to library administration and management. [R: BL, 1 Nov 71, p. 214; LJ, 1 Oct 71, p. 3100] Charles D. Patterson

1312. Sinclair, Dorothy. **Administration of the Small Public Library.** 2nd ed. Chicago, American Library Association, 1979. 156p. index. $15.00. LC 79-12338. ISBN 0-8389-0291-X.

Although intended for the "new and unexperienced administrator of the small public library," this overview would be better suited to the nonprofessional who, perhaps by default, is in charge of a small public library. The content is much too simplified in content and approach for the recent graduate of an MLS program. The presentation is uneven. The chapters on policy, finance, and personnel are quite good, while those on library objectives, community study, and library governance omit much of the research that has been done in the past decade. There is a tendency to overgeneralize on the basis of insufficient information. The role of the system, rather than being integrated into each chapter so that implications to each aspect of library operations could be explored, is relegated to a brief chapter. Resource sharing at the local level gets less than two pages. In its approach to the administration of the small public library and in its response to basic issues—networking, resource sharing, attitudes toward professional education—the second edition has, with the exception of the chapters on policy, finance, and personnel, brought the reader to 1970. [R: AL, Dec 79, p. 673; BL, 15 Jan 80, p. 699; LJ, 15 Feb 80, p. 489]

Ann E. Prentice

1313. Sullivan, Peggy, and William Ptacek. **Public Libraries: Smart Practices in Personnel.** Littleton, Colo., Libraries Unlimited, 1982. 95p. index. $13.50. LC 82-15334. ISBN 0-87287-278-5.

The authors have written a handbook for public library administrators that offers techniques, methods of conduct, and strategies related to personnel administration in public libraries. This book explains the essentials of personnel administration from the perspective that any public library, regardless of size or its degree of autonomy from affiliated governments, can develop an effective personnel program.

Divided into three major sections—"Personnel Form and Structure," "Personnel Management and Evaluation," and "Communication"—this book covers topics such as staffing, salary, position, benefits, budgets, laws, employee organizations, recruitment, retirement, collective bargaining, interviews, and personnel forms. [R: WLB, Oct 82, pp. 168-69]

1314. Totterdell, Barry, and Jean Bird. **The Effective Library: Report of the Hillingdon Project on Public Library Effectiveness.** Edited by Margaret Redfern. London, Library Association; distr., New York, Nichols, 1976. 207p. illus. index. (Research Publication No. 16). o.p. ISBN 0-85365-248-1.

Not as comprehensive as *Performance Measures for Public Libraries* (American Library Association, 1973), since this report is based on only one public library system. Nevertheless, it provides sufficient documentation of the effectiveness of British public library programs. The American study and its British counterpart both fail to give sufficient attention to the use of nonprint materials. [R: LJ, 1 Dec 76, p. 2461]

1315. Vignone, Joseph A. **Collective Bargaining Procedures for Public Library Employees. An Inquiry into the Opinions and Attitudes of Public Librarians, Directors and Board Members.** Metuchen, N.J., Scarecrow, 1971. 179p. index. o.p. LC 79-160579. SBN 8108-0412-3.

This book is on a timely subject, examining two central problems in collective bargaining. First, it provides a descriptive sample of the opinions and attitudes of library directors, librarians, and library board members in Pennsylvania; second, it summarizes the opinions of these three groups as they relate to the provisions of a model of collective bargaining procedures for public library employees. A selected bibliography, a sample questionnaire, and a subject index conclude this study. [R: BL, 1 May 72, p. 740; DLQ, Apr 72, p. 212]

1316. Wheeler, Joseph Lewis, and Herbert Goldhor. **Wheeler and Goldhor's Practical Administration of Public Libraries.** Completely rev. by Carlton Rochell. New York, Harper & Row, 1981. 464p. bibliog. index. $28.80. LC 79-3401. ISBN 0-06-13601-4.

This edition of the 1962 classic text on public library administration has been completely revised to reflect many of the changes in public library service. Rochell has organized this edition into three parts: part 1 addresses the administrative perspective on planning, management, personnel, finance, and organization, which includes discussion of budgeting techniques, collective bargaining, and the planning process; part 2 explores the administration of public services, which includes services to particular groups as well as coverage of branch work, community relations, nonprint materials, and systems and networks; and part 3 offers discussions on support services, which the author defines as technical services, office procedures, building maintenance, and evaluation.

Although this revision has retained the basic purpose of the original work, it has been reorganized and incorporates a number of the changes in theory and practice of administering public libraries, such as systems and networks and automation's impact in technical services. One wonders, however, why certain other important issues were not included, for example, user's fees, certainly a timely and controversial topic within the profession. The author does, however, provide an extensive bibliography of additional sources of information at the end of the text.

Most of the text is in narrative form, with important and relevant sentences and paragraphs from the original work interspersed, but the extensive use of direct quotations, especially in the chapters on systems and networking, and nonprint, tends to break up the flow of the material.

Two other works on this topic are Dorothy Sinclair's *Administration of the Small Public Library*, second edition (American Library Association, 1979), and Royston Brown's *Public Library Administration* (K. G. Saur, 1979). Sinclair's book is much more limited in its coverage and simplified in its approach—better suited for a nonprofessional audience (see

ARBA 80, entry 197). Brown's is aimed at a primarily British audience (see *ARBA* 81, entry 175).

Because the author has attempted to offer an overview or guide to this multifaceted operation, this text is best used by students who are being introduced to the administration of public libraries. It will be less useful for the seasoned practitioner who seeks more in-depth coverage and practical techniques related to specific administration problems. Regardless of its limitations, this revision is a welcome addition to the literature and should provide as much guidance as did its predecessor. [R: BL, 15 Jan 81, p. 673; LJ, 15 Mar 81, p. 627]   Ann Hartman

1317. Young, Virginia G. **The Library Trustee: A Practical Guidebook.** 3rd ed. New York, R. R. Bowker, 1978. 192p. bibliog. index. $15.95. LC 78-13065. ISBN 0-8352-1068-5.

Since the only requirement for becoming a library trustee is an interest in libraries, a guide to librarianship for trustees is invaluable. For many years, various editions of this small book have provided trustees with such information. This collection of 24 essays (prepared by experienced trustees and librarians) covers all of the basic issues of the trustee/library relationship. The list of contributors reads like a who's who of librarianship and trustees (e.g., John Frantz, Alex Ladenson, Dorothy Corrigan, and Keith Doms). Some of the topics covered include duties and responsibilities of trustees; trustee relationships with librarians and staff; trustee and labor management relations; gifts, grants, and bequests; library systems; and the trustee in tomorrow's world. The nine appendices following the essays illustrate such basic documents as the Freedom to Read Statement, the Library Bill of Rights, and sample bylaws. This volume exhibits the same fine quality as the first two editions. [R: AB, 18 June 79, p. 4674; JAL, Nov 79, p. 288]   G. Edward Evans

1318. Zweizig, Douglas, and Eleanor Jo Rodger. **Output Measures for Public Libraries: A Manual of Standardized Procedures.** Chicago, American Library Association, 1982. 100p. $8.00pa. LC 82-1720. ISBN 0-8389-3272-X.

This work is the result of an effort by the Goals, Guidelines, and Standards Committee of the Public Library Association to provide a means of consistent measurement for the output of library activities. These measures are ones which are community based and therefore reflect local library needs rather than some arbitrary national measure of excellence, mediocrity, etc.

The resulting 12 output measures relate to goals that are common to most public libraries and are intended to support and expand upon chapter 13 of the *Planning Process for Public Libraries* (American Library Association, 1980). Included are measures relating to circulation, reference, programming, browsing, registration, document delivery, and the turnover rate for the collection. Each of these measures receives individual treatment explaining the function of the measure, how it is to be computed, a clear example of its application, useful measurement instruments, and some indication of the interpretation of the outcome and possible strategies for change. Also included are examples of additional refinements of each measure. These Level II measures are intended to provide additional insights into a library's performance. A detailed data elements summary sheet is in an appendix. A very brief glossary is included as well, but these terms find better definition in the text itself.

A useful volume for anyone concerned with performance measures for any type of library. A bibliography of library evaluations would have added to the value of this work. [R: LQ, Apr 83, p. 180]   Robert A. Berk

School Library Media Centers

1319. **Achieving Accountability: Readings on the Evaluation of Media Centers.** Ron Blazek, ed. Chicago, American Library Association, 1981. 266p. $14.50pa. LC 81-19085. ISBN 0-8389-0349-5.

This document contains several of the best journal articles written since 1970 on the subject of accountability. The editor has arranged these articles in five major sections: "Understanding Accountability," "Preparing for Accountability," "Selecting a Course of Action," "Measuring Service," and "Evaluating Impact." An epilog deals with "Measurement and Evaluation of School Media Centers." The value of this paperback is that it provides an overview for building- and system-level library media personnel of various evaluation and planning methods. For those unfamiliar with the field, it will be a good beginning document. For those more familiar, it will serve as a reference. Major experts in this field, such as James W. Liesener, Jane Anne Hannigan, Elizabeth Fast, Mary Gaver, and Shirley Aaron, to name a few, are represented. This will be a useful reference to all types of personnel in the school library media field. [R: SLJ, Oct 82, p. 116]

Paula Montgomery

1320. Bennie, Frances. **Learning Centers: Development and Operation.** Englewood Cliffs, N.J., Educational Technology Publications, 1977. 346p. illus. bibliog. index. $27.95. LC 76-58528. ISBN 0-87778-097-8.

Based upon the author's doctoral dissertation, her book is designed to present the origins of the learning center concept, its present "manifestations," and if properly implemented, its potential for the achievement of "true individualization of instruction." Unfortunately, although evidencing sincere, total commitment to the learning center concept, Bennie makes no attempt to include alternative approaches. Instead, the reader is given a detailed account of just one model. Added to an extensive exposition are 100 pages of appendices, with forms for needs assessment profiles, prescriptions, contracts, conference records, and even an observation guide for visitations to learning centers.

The model described is unrealistic for the average community, demanding staffing far beyond that possible in most schools suffering from declining enrollments, inflated costs, and reduced budgets. The library media specialist is labeled as an instructional communications specialist, but the assumption is made that librarians will require retraining and "much exposure to some of the premises of open education and the learning center approach." This view indicates lack of research in the literature, evidenced by Bennie's references to the AASL/DAVI 1969 *Standards for School Media Programs* instead of to the 1975 guidelines *Media Programs: District and School*, which outline the wide range of competencies demanded of today's media specialist. The entire text exhibits a patronizing tone, implying that the reader lacks an introduction to audiovisual equipment and the wide range of audiovisual "media materials." The need for Bennie's book in today's professional library is doubtful. Most educators have been exposed to less prescriptive writing that presents the learning center concept in broader terms and recognizes that no *one* avenue can be replicated throughout the United States and thus meet the needs of all students.
Mildred Knight Laughlin

1321. Billings, Rolland G., and Errol Goldman. **Professional Negotiations for Media/Library Professionals: District and School.** Washington, D.C., Association for Educational Communications and Technology, 1980. 90p. bibliog. $8.50pa.; $6.50 (AECT members). LC 80-67724. ISBN 0-89240-037-4.

This slender paperback is directed essentially toward school librarians who have no previous experience with union negotiations and need a simple manual to guide them through the complex process. The book is as simple as possible, as objective as possible, and as factual as possible. There are a very brief glossary of terms and a small bibliography in which the section on master agreements will likely be most useful. Chapter 4 is probably the most helpful one. It analyzes specific excerpts from actual bargaining agreements which apply to library and media personnel. A good source if you're actually involved in any way in union negotiations; otherwise, it is probably too specific. [R: SLJ, Apr 81, p. 39]
Fay M. Blake

1322. Bomar, Cora Paul, M. Ann Heidbreder, and Carol A. Nemeyer. **Guide to the Development of Educational Media Selection Centers.** Chicago, American Library Association, 1973. 102p. (ALA Studies in Librarianship, No. 4). o.p. LC 73-3362. ISBN 0-8389-0123-9.

In 1968 the National Book Committee started a comprehensive study of educational media selection centers. Findings of phase 1 were reported in *Educational Media Selection Centers: Identification and Analysis of Current Practices* (American Library Association, 1971), which was reviewed in *ARBA* 72 (entry 153). This report, covering phase 2, presents ideas and data on how EMSCs can be organized, staffed, administered, and evaluated; it also discusses their role in in-service education. The authors of the report emphasize that the guide is not a set of standards but that it should assist those who wish to establish and improve EMSCs. Phase 3, will provide for demonstration centers to be set up to test the policies and procedures advocated in this report. The report presents neither a broadly based plan for model EMSCs nor a detailed view of an ideal center. It does offer ideas on functions of EMSCs, list of points to consider when preparing a plan for an EMSC, and some other helpful comments on programs, facilities, and budgets. [R: LQ, Oct 73, p. 431; RSR, Oct 73, p. 18]

Christine Gehrt Wynar

1323. Brewer, Margaret L., and Sharon O. Willis. **The Elementary School Library.** Hamden, Conn., Shoe String Press, 1970. 113p. illus. index. o.p. LC 77-127793. SBN 208-01092-0.

Brewer and Willis designed this text for a broad audience (librarian, school administrator, and volunteer parent) to introduce all elements of administration and organization of the elementary school library. The opening chapters deal with the history and philosophy of the elementary school library. Subsequent chapters discuss functions, staffing, organization, technical processes, facilities, multimedia resources, and evaluation of the library. Compressing this number of topics within 113 pages results in superficial coverage. In addition, the need to explain procedures (such as assigning subject headings) to an audience of nonprofessionals as well as librarians produces results that are at best inadequate. The lack of in-depth discussions of such important topics as library instruction or censorship tends to give the impression that library operation is a simple routine job. Selection tools are not described.

Christine Gehrt Wynar

1324. Coburn, Louis. **Library Media Center Problems: Case Studies.** Dobbs Ferry, N.Y., Oceana, 1973. 144p. index. $13.00. LC 73-2587. ISBN 0-379-00019-9.

Coburn has prepared an interesting collection of 30 case studies relating to typical problem areas encountered in school media centers. The cases are generally well developed, although occasionally the questions suggested for discussion miss the target. The situation describing administrative functions of the head librarian (No. 12), for example, reveals an undercurrent of personnel problems that may end up being more serious than administrative decisions on accession records. The volume concludes with an appendix containing standards, guidelines, sample selection policies, and other materials; a list of readings; and a subject index. [R: C&RL, Mar 74, p. 136; LQ, July 74, p. 278; RSR, Jan 74, p. 26]   Christine Gehrt Wynar

1325. Delaney, Jack J. **The Media Program in the Elementary and Middle Schools: Its Organization and Administration.** Hamden, Conn., Linnet Books, 1976. 222p. illus. bibliog. index. $17.50. LC 75-29434. ISBN 0-208-01344-X.

As Jack Delaney's title indicates, his book is intended for the elementary and middle school librarian/media specialist. Most of the material is derived from his own 14 years of experience as an elementary school librarian and the sharing of experiences with other librarians. He laces his discussions with program and management examples from operating school media centers across the country, and he uses photographs of actual students and staff to illustrate his points attractively. In 11 chapters, he covers such areas as staffing, circulation, cataloging and processing, reference services, and teaching; he includes a short but instructive chapter on media production, which defines the

basic processes employed. References are made throughout each chapter to further sources for more specific information on a given topic, and "study questions" at the end of each chapter present realistic management situations. These may be more useful to the library school student or a workshop situation than to the practicing school librarian, but they can serve to stimulate thought. A good bibliography on school library management is included. His discussions maintain a balanced mix of theory and practical application, although he occasionally assumes acceptance of certain library practices, such as maintaining an accession record. [R: CLW, Dec 76, p. 232; LQ, July 77, p. 398]

Roberta J. Depp

1326. **Evaluating Media Programs: District & School.** Washington, D.C., Association for Educational Communications and Technology, 1980. 77p. $8.95. looseleaf. ISBN 0-89240-039-0.

With overall content essentially the same as the 1976 draft edition (see *ARBA* 78, entry 183), this work has been reorganized into eight sections: (1) school district profile, (2) media program goals and policies, (3) budget, (4) personnel, (5) operation and services, (6) collections, (7) facilities, and (8) opinionnaires. It was designed to evaluate programs on the basis of standards established in *Media Programs: District and School* (Association for Educational Communications and Technology and American Library Association, 1975).

Critics of the earlier edition cited lack of attention to programs at the district level as a major flaw of the work. Unfortunately, this weakness has not been corrected. The looseleaf format is undeniably useful, allowing for easier compilation of data from different evaluators. Introductory explanations for each section are clear, although some user familiarity with evaluation processes is assumed. Even though the paper is durable and of good quality, typography is substandard. This, coupled with smeared cover graphics on the review copy, lends a sloppy appearance that tends to damage the credibility of the work.

This is an adequate and relatively inexpensive source, but James W. Liesener's *Instruments for Planning and Evaluating Library Media Programs*, revised edition (University of Maryland Press, 1980) is a more comprehensive choice.   Judith Ann Copler

1327. Freeman, Patricia. **Pathfinder: An Operational Guide for the School Librarian.** New York, Harper & Row, 1975. 325p. illus.

bibliog. index. o.p. LC 75-287. ISBN 0-06-042184-3.

In *Pathfinder* Patricia Freeman attempts to present various alternatives available in library management practice, indicating possible advantages or disadvantages of each but leaving the choice of practice to the librarian responsible for the operation of a particular school library. Not directed at any particular grade level, the book serves as a general guide to a "philosophy of work," providing practical information needed to carry out the role of school librarian effectively and stressing throughout the primary goal of service to the whole school community. Freeman organizes 13 specific chapters under three broad headings: (1) "Planning and Administering the Library" — covering staff, budgeting, physical facilities, and philosophical objectives of both the library and the librarian; (2) "Planning and Building the Collection" — including selection, ordering, cataloging, and processing; and (3) "Planning and Giving Service" — circulation, public relations, reference, instruction, and other examples of service to patrons. Nearly one-third of the book comprises appendices that correspond to the three broad headings. These include flowcharts, a list of procedures, relevant quotes from other sources (e.g., the PTA statements on school libraries), filing rules, sample catalog cards, list of suggested bulletin board displays, supply and furniture suggestions, etc. An extensive bibliography organized by subject (although she missed some titles, such as Shirley Miller's *The Vertical File and Its Satellites*, Libraries Unlimited, 1971, under the heading "Information Files"), a directory of publishers and distributors, and indexes (to the bibliography and the book) contribute to making this work a practical handbook as well as a general introduction to school library management. [R: SLMQ, Spring 76, p. 246]　　　　　　　　　　Roberta J. Depp

1328. Gaver, Mary Virginia. **Services of Secondary School Media Centers: Evaluation and Development.** Chicago, American Library Association, 1971. 131p. illus. (ALA Studies in Librarianship, No. 2). $7.00pa. LC 77-165675. SBN 8389-0095-X.

The purpose of this study by Mary V. Gaver is "to provide a means of evaluating the media center program of secondary schools, specifically the variety and balance of services" (p. xi). Presented is a picture of the status of secondary school media centers in New Jersey and a checklist for evaluation of several aspects of programs. The checklist contains 274 items and records the variety of services offered but does not probe the depth of services. Only a subjective evaluation of the checklist was carried out through interviews with 19 media center directors. The study is hardly a model of research methodology, but it may serve to stimulate the study of media center evaluation. [R: AL, Jan 72, p. 86]

Christine Gehrt Wynar

1329. Gillespie, John T. **A Model School District Media Program: Montgomery County as a Case Study.** Chicago, American Library Association, 1977. 207p. illus. bibliog. index. (ALA Studies in Librarianship, No. 6). $12.00pa. LC 77-5022. ISBN 0-8389-3192-8.

What is the secret of Montgomery County's success? Gillespie credits the county superintendent and his administrative team who, in 1961, achieved school board adoption of a policy of districtwide media center development. As a result of this early start, the district had a well-entrenched program at a time when others, still groping for a way, got caught in the budget squeeze.

Interestingly, luminaries from both the audiovisual and the library communities (James W. Brown and Frances Henne) served as consultants in the early stages of Montgomery County's move to implement media centers. The two components are said to be smoothly integrated in the district's operation — evidently not by accident. Since Gillespie so unequivocally credits the school superintendent, it is strange that he does not mention the gentleman's name.

Administratively, media centers in Montgomery County schools are a part of instructional services, not of supporting services. Chapter by chapter, this thorough yet readable study details the county's character, its school organization, the evolution of the Department of Educational Media and Technology, and the operation of each of its divisions. Data appear to be as of 1975, and problems in the operation are pointed out. (These generally involve delays in communications and transactions between teachers and central office.)

Though descriptive rather than analytical, this slim volume should prove a valuable reference to school media professionals in practice and in training. [R: JAL, Nov 77, p. 299]

Mary R. Sive

1330. Gillespie, John T., and Diana L. Spirt. **Administering the School Library Media Center.** New York, R. R. Bowker, 1983. 381p. index. $34.95. LC 83-2807. ISBN 0-8352-1514-8.

Creating a School Media Program (1975) has been expanded and revised into this book, but the approach and content of the earlier work have been retained. The book opens with the development of school libraries into media centers, then moves to practical chapters on the administrative responsibilities (functions, program development, budget, staff, facilities, selection, acquisition, managerial concerns), retained from the previous work. New chapters are: "Computers and the School Library Media Center" (operations, use, information utilities, periodicals); "Networks and Networking" (benefits, existing networks, evaluating, implementing); and "Beyond the Single School Library Media Center" (associations, agencies, recommended professional titles). A new section on book fairs is based on the authors' earlier writing. The appendices include directories of state school library media center agencies, other associations and agencies, selected library furniture and supply houses, and key documents (e.g., the Library Bill of Rights). Suggestions for further reading are provided at the end of many chapters, a change from the earlier central bibliography. One distraction in some of the tables is their placement within the text; notes do assist the reader.

Readers familiar with the previous edition will recognize much of the text and many graphs and lists, which have retained their appropriateness. Two appendix sections have been moved to the text: criteria on selecting educational media and criteria for equipment. Reference is made to the 1973 work for descriptions of the actual programs on which the lists in chapter 2 are based.

This edition provides practical information and considers the needs of media specialists in small or large school systems. [R: BL, 1 Oct 83, p. 304]   Phyllis J. Van Orden

1331. Guide for the Conversion of School Libraries into Media Centres. Paris, UNESCO; distr., New York, UNIPUB, 1977. 62p. illus. bibliog. (Educational Studies and Documents, No. 22). $3.25. ISBN 92-3-101389-0.

Drawing from five case studies (which were presented at the UNESCO/International Bureau of Education meeting in Geneva, 10-13 June 1975), Jean Pierre Delannoy has attempted to synthesize the information into a guide that addresses the following questions apparent in the conversion of secondary school libraries into media centers: for whom? why? with whom? with what? when (distribution of school time)? where (premises)? how? The second half of the volume contains extracts from the case studies

presented by representatives from the United Kingdom, Switzerland, United States (M. V. Gaver), Sweden, and France. These are followed by a "guide to the fitting up and equipping of a multi-media self-instructional centre in an existing school" by Robert Quinot, intended for use in developing countries.

This is not the practical how-to-do-it guide one might expect. Rather, the author lists and analyzes the problems that arise and indicates strategies that have been used successfully. He therefore permits the reader the latitude in which to choose appropriate procedures for local needs. This volume will have value for persons from countries other than the United States, where much has already been written on this subject in greater detail and with more practicality. [R: LQ, July 79, p. 350]

Sara R. Mack

1332. Liesener, James W. A Systematic Process for Planning Media Programs. Chicago, American Library Association, 1976. 166p. illus. bibliog. $9.00pa. LC 76-3507. ISBN 0-8389-0176-X.

Using the basic principles of PPBS, Liesener has detailed a nine-step process for the systematic planning and development of media programs that effectively communicate and document "what is done, why it is done, and what resources are required to do it." The procedure requires a survey of client perceptions of current services in order to set priorities, a determination of resource requirements for specific levels of current or preferred services, a reallocation of resources and implementation of operational changes as needed, and periodic evaluation to assess achievements and changing needs. The emphasis on accountability demands accurate data, and the process outlined is comprehensive and detailed. The suggested plan has merit, but it is a complicated, time-consuming one that should not be adopted as a whole without prior commitment from the staff and without a full understanding of the time allocation needed for implementation. It seems unlikely that the data collection devices could be used effectively unless a consultant is available to conduct an in-service workshop for initial staff training and to advise during implementation. Since the planning instrument was published in 1974, it is unfortunate that no written documentation is readily available from districts that have completed the initial process to convince administrators and reluctant media specialists that the results will justify the efforts. All school media specialists should find the thorough examination of the Liesener work a valuable experience. If the entire process does not seem appropriate because of local restrictions, aspects of an individual program may be measured using suggested adaptations. Even though a district is satisfied with the local evaluation process, ideas gleaned from the instruments may improve effectiveness. [R: LQ, Oct 77, p. 496; LR, Summer 77, p. 119; SLMQ, Winter 77, p. 134]   Mildred Knight Laughlin

1333. Mancall, Jacqueline C., and M. Carl Drott. **Measuring Student Information Use: A Guide for School Library Media Specialists.** Littleton, Colo., Libraries Unlimited, 1983. 145p. illus. index. $19.50. LC 82-24965. ISBN 0-87287-376-5.

Understanding students' information-seeking behavior is essential in building collections and designing services and instructional programs that address real student needs. The authors studied almost 2,000 students who were required to go beyond classroom texts to locate information for school assignments. The sample included students from a broad spectrum of ability levels and social and economic backgrounds. This study developed and tested a straightforward, replicable methodology to measure students' information use patterns. Each of the six chapters offers the reader an understanding of the data collected in the study and of the implications for practice and provides enough how-to information to enable school library media specialists to collect their own data. Chapter 1 explains the development of a use- and user-centered approach and the techniques used to gather data. Remaining chapters cover student use of community facilities; materials students use; magazines as information resources; user-centered applications; and a summary and implications for school library media specialists. Included along with the step-by-step instructions are questionnaires and forms that can be easily adapted by practitioners to study local use. [R: BL, 1 June 83, p. 1270; JAL, July 83, p. 173]

1334. Marshall, Faye Dix. **Managing the Modern School Library.** West Nyack, N.Y., Parker, 1976. 214p. illus. index. o.p. LC 75-41307. ISBN 0-13-550467-8.

If *Managing the Modern School Library* had been published 20 years ago, it would probably have become a classic. Its prescriptive, needlessly detailed approach to library organization might have been welcome then. But with the tremendous increase in the demand for service brought on by the school library media center concept, a librarian's time should be used

as productively and efficiently as possible. An example of the circuitous methods suggested by Marshall is found in the chapter on cataloging, where record-keeping devices from the chapter on ordering are continued. By the time all the suggested red marks and penciled symbols are added to the accession book indicating status of catalog card orders, it would be barely legible and valuable time would have been wasted. Discussion of the Wilson cataloging cards is dated, as these are no longer available. The section on cataloging books is hardly relevant. Here two and one-half pages are taken up by such questions as the height of fiction versus nonfiction books, attractiveness of the cover, readability (paper and print quality), and reference potential of the book. Only one paragraph is devoted to identifying the descriptive elements needed for actually cataloging a book. And while several pages are also devoted to the various methods of typing a catalog card and preparing the Cutter number, only brief mention is made of the *Dewey Decimal Classification and Relative Index* (although there is a short bibliography of titles that are helpful in cataloging procedures). Despite the author's claim that the reader "will find this book to be an invaluable, practical guide for the experienced librarian," it appears more useful as a handbook for the library clerical staff or as a cursory introduction for library school students to some of the everyday aspects of school library management. The glossary of terms and the short list of basic professional references are useful, but it is disappointing that full bibliographic information was not provided. Either the Freeman (entry 1327) or the Delaney (entry 1325) book should be preferred over this misnamed title. [R: LQ, Oct 77, p. 498; SLMQ, Spring 77, p. 214]
Roberta J. Depp

1335. **Media Programs: District and School.** Prepared by American Association of School Librarians, ALA, and Association for Educational Communications and Technology. Chicago, American Library Association; distr., Washington, D.C., Association for Educational Communications and Technology, 1975. 128p. index. $4.00pa. LC 74-32316. ISBN 0-8389-3159-6.

Media Programs, which replaces the *Standards for School Media Programs* (American Library Association/National Education Association, 1969), is the joint effort of the American Association of School Librarians and the Association for Educational Communications and Technology. *Media Programs* sets down guidelines and recommendations for media programs and resources essential for quality education. Emphasis is on qualitative goals, offering criteria for both districtwide and school-level media programs. The guidelines demonstrate the interrelationships between system and building operations. Quantitative measures are provided, but there is recognition of the need for alternative choices in program, staffing, etc., to fit a variety of administrative and educational patterns. [R: LQ, Apr 76, p. 198]

1336. Nickel, Mildred L. **Steps to Service: A Handbook of Procedures for the School Library Media Center.** rev. ed. Chicago, American Library Association, 1984. 129p. illus. index. $9.95. LC 84-9368. ISBN 0-8389-0387-8.

The first edition of this book was published in 1975. *Steps to Service* is the second edition of a very basic guide to school media services. Its preface states that the work is "designed to give practical help and guidance to inexperienced and beginning professionals." The text is divided into sections on function, activities, and facilities.

As a review, the source is useful, though it presents one way to do most tasks, ignoring the many approaches possible. As a guide for beginning and inexperienced librarians, its primary drawback is that one cannot teach school media center management in 129 pages, and to try to teach catalog and classification in 20 pages is ludicrous. However, the concepts are generally sound, the explanations are concise, and the information is easy to locate.

References are not provided for much of the data included. For example, cost comparisons of various kinds of bindings and rebindings are given in a handy chart, but no citation is provided for the source of the information. The same is true for the whole chapter on facilities planning. Since this handbook is a basic one, one expects that major works on each topic will be cited to give the user sources of more extensive information on the subject. *Steps to Service* has sound advice for school media specialists, but it needs more documentation to support its assertations and to enable the user to locate further information.   Patricia Tipton Sharp

1337. Prostano, Emanuel T., and Joyce S. Prostano. **Case Studies in Library/Media Management.** Littleton, Colo., Libraries Unlimited, 1982. 106p. bibliog. index. (Library Science Text Series). $13.50pa. LC 82-13051. ISBN 0-87287-344-7.

A companion volume to the authors' text, *The School Library Media Center*, third edition,

this collection of 38 case studies addresses problems and issues of the 1980s related to school library media center management. The cases presented here are drawn from actual problems and situations at both the individual school and district levels. Building upon earlier editions of this work, the authors have included 11 new cases, selected to introduce additional concerns and managerial problems facing heads of school library media programs and district library media directors and focusing on activities such as planning, organizing, staffing, directing, and controlling. Cases and chapters in *Case Studies in Library/Media Management* and *The School Library Media Center* have been cross-referenced. [R: AL, Dec 82, p. 734; Emerg Lib, Nov 82, p. 29]

1338. Prostano, Emanuel T., and Joyce S. Prostano. **The School Library Media Center.** 3rd ed. Littleton, Colo., Libraries Unlimited, 1982. 199p. illus. bibliog. index. (Library Science Text Series). $28.00; $20.00pa. LC 82-7193. ISBN 0-87287-286-6; 0-87287-334-Xpa.

The first edition of this textbook appeared in 1971 (see *ARBA* 72, entry 151); the second was reviewed in *ARBA* 78 (entry 187). The third edition of this work focuses on the purpose, structure, and function of the school library media center. It continues to present the library media center as a unified system of elements existing within and for the educational program of the school. Emphasis is placed on the application of basic management functions—planning, organizing, staffing, directing, and controlling—to the library media program in the individual school. This management focus and the concepts of foundation, support, and primary elements of the system have been expanded in this edition. Consideration is also given to district-level media affairs and developing activities in the field, including resource sharing and technological networking. At the end of each chapter is a list of suggested activities to be used to reinforce the concepts presented. [R: BL, 15 Oct 82, p. 305; IRLA, Dec 82, p. 11; SLMQ, Winter 83, p. 144]

1339. School Library Manpower Project. **Occupational Definitions for School Library Media Personnel.** Chicago, American Library Association, 1971. 24p. o.p. LC 72-151111. SBN 8389-3125-1.

The four occupational definitions contained in this small report are the direct result of the work of the Task Analysis Committee's study of the results of its Task Analysis Survey. The four positions defined are school library media specialist, head of the school library media center, district school library media director, and school library media technician. A 14-item bibliography is appended to the report. The statement of occupational definitions is a much needed step which should help to clarify terminology confusion. [R: AL, Apr 71, p. 424]

1340. School Library Manpower Project. **School Library Personnel Task Analysis Survey.** Prepared by the Research Division of the National Education Association. Chicago, American Library Association, 1969. 91p. o.p.

A report prepared in phase 1 of the School Library Manpower Project in a national study to identify the tasks performed by school library personnel in unified service programs at the building level. The report is in three parts: (1) background for the survey including methodology, (2) profile of staff characteristics, (3) task and duty analysis. Data were gathered from 953 schools judged by state and local school library supervisors as outstanding library media center programs. [R: AL, Feb 70, p. 190]

1341. Sullivan, Peggy. **Problems in School Media Management.** New York, R. R. Bowker, 1971. 245p. (Bowker Series in Problem-Centered Approaches to Librarianship). o.p. LC 78-126032.

This second volume in a series contains 30 cases, covering a wide range of topics involving the organization, administration, and utilization of a media program. [R: LJ, 15 Dec 71, p. 4169; RQ, Winter 71, p. 174; WLB, Nov 71]

1342. Toor, Ruth, and Hilda K. Weisburg. **The Complete Book of Forms for Managing the School Library Media Center.** West Nyack, N.Y., Center for Applied Research in Education, 1982. 256p. illus. index. $34.50 spiral-bound. LC 82-9674. ISBN 0-87628-229-X.

Toor and Weisburg have compiled this book of 170 forms in an effort to provide "a one-step source for all forms needed to manage today's media center." The book is divided into ten sections: (1) "Analyzing Your Facilities and Collection," 15 forms; (2) "Developing Personnel Relationships and Organizing Clerical/Volunteer Staff," 16 forms; (3) "Circulation Control," 41 forms; (4) "Technical Services," 10 forms; (5) "Managing Library Programs," 24 forms; (6) "Working with Teachers," 14 forms; (7) "Working with the Administration," 12 forms; (8) "Correspondence," 18 forms; (9) "End-of-Year Activities," 22 forms; and (10) "Professional Growth and Development," 7 forms. Each section contains a brief discussion

of the necessity of accurate record keeping in the designated area, filled-in sample forms, and, in most cases, a blank, ready-to-use form. Two additional features are an index and an appendix listing the names and addresses of commercial suppliers of library forms.

Since record keeping methods in individual school media centers are usually controlled and directed by local school districts, this book is of little value to building-level media specialists. Although the authors state that the forms in this book should be altered to meet individual needs, the book's content alone could frustrate a media specialist in "today's media center," where the trend is toward more direct contact with students and less time spent on clerical duties. [R: SLJ, May 83, p. 37]   Pat R. Scales

1343. Woolls, Blanche, David Loertscher, and Donald Shirey. **Evaluation Techniques for School Library/Media Programs: A Work Shop Outline.** Pittsburgh, Pa., Graduate School of Library and Information Sciences, University of Pittsburgh, 1977. 85p. o.p.

The subtitle identifies the intended purpose and use of this booklet. Collected here are reprints of checklists, various "handouts," and outlines for the workshop (held July 1976 at the Graduate School of Library and Information Sciences, University of Pittsburgh). In this raw, uninterpreted form, the material may be of interest to some school library supervisors who are involved in developing evaluation instruments and who need to collect a complete file of information.   Christine Gehrt Wynar

Special Libraries

1344. **The Administration of a Public Affairs Library: A Report on the JRL Collection; with Bibliographies of Reference Books and Periodicals in Public Affairs Areas.** Chicago, Public Administration Service, 1971. 65p. bibliog. o.p. LC 77-146046.

This little publication provides some background information for beginners interested in establishing a public administration library. One will find here a description of the routine operations used by the Joint Reference Library in Chicago. Appendix A contains a list of reference books in the JRL, and appendix B, holdings of periodicals. Entries provide complete bibliographical description plus price, but there are no annotations.

1345. Aufdenkamp, Jo Ann, and others. **Special Libraries: A Guide for Management**

with Revisions through 1974. Edward G. Stra-ble, ed. New York, Special Libraries Association, 1975. 74p. illus. bibliog. o.p. LC 74-19252. ISBN 0-87111-228-0.

The subtitle of this informative little book means exactly what it says. The book is addressed to corporate management officials who must answer such questions as: what is a special library and what is it good for?; should company X have one and if so, how should it be established?; and what resources in manpower, equipment, and space does it require? Thus, the book contains little that librarians, even non-special librarians, don't know.

Since its primary audience consists of management officers of companies where special libraries do not yet exist, it will be most useful in such companies. Richard A. Gray

1346. Bailey, Martha J. **The Special Librarian as a Supervisor or Middle Manager.** New York, Special Libraries Association, 1977. 42p. (SLA State-of-the-Art Review, No. 6). $6.00pa. LC 77-5021. ISBN 0-87111-249-3.

This brief but concise volume reviews selected library and information science literature concerning the role of the special librarian as a supervisor or middle manager. When library-oriented information is unavailable, it draws on the literature of business management. References include general literature as well as reports on relevant research.

After defining the terms "supervisor" and "middle manager," the author describes various library environments. These environments include industrial and business organizations; academic institutions; public libraries; professional, trade, and research organizations; government agencies; networks and consortia; and other public and private institutions. This is followed by an examination of position responsibilities and the education and work experience desired. The report concludes with recommendations for further research.

Although it is by no means comprehensive, it is refreshing to find a well-structured approach to an area where research material is limited and difficult to identify. It will be of value to special librarians, to librarians with managerial responsibilities, and to library educators. [R: LJ, 1 Mar 78, p. 526]
Andrew G. Torok

1347. Bolté, Charles G. **Libraries and the Arts & Humanities.** Syracuse, N.Y., Gaylord, 1977. 239p. bibliog. index. $14.50pa. LC 77-12926. ISBN 0-915794-13-6.

This paperback volume is a manual in "grantsmanship," aimed at helping librarians "to become more fully a part of the national movement designed to bring the arts and humanities more closely into the lives of more people." The work emphasizes government support for the arts and humanities at the federal and state levels, and the author's purpose is to demonstrate the role that some librarians are now playing, and more might play, in the increasing activity in these areas. By way of highlighting this role, a case study of the Lewiston (Maine) Public Library's "Cultural Outreach" — LPL + — is presented.

The work opens with a brief survey of American cultural history, followed by a discussion of the activities of both the National Endowment for the Arts and the National Endowment for the Humanities. Subsequent chapters discuss the activities of state councils and commissions in both arts and humanities. The concluding chapter sets out possible avenues for librarians to explore in the future. Among the appendices are three essays, entitled respectively: "The Arts in Europe," by Clark Mitze; "Some Reflections on Libraries and Culture," by Lester Asheim; and "Museums and Libraries: Some Random Thoughts," by T. L. Freudenheim. There is also a series of tables giving the memberships of the state and federal councils discussed above, and a survey of fiscal spending of both NEA and NEH. This is a useful book that should be welcomed by both librarians and museum personnel interested in developing their own cultural outreach programs. [R: C&RL, July 78, p. 327; LJ, 1 Oct 78, p. 1931]
Jesse H. Shera

1348. Chen, Ching-chih. **Applications of Operations Research Models to Libraries: A Case Study of the Use of Monographs in the Francis A. Countway Library of Medicine, Harvard University.** Cambridge, Mass., MIT Press, 1976. 212p. illus. bibliog. index. $32.50. LC 75-28210. ISBN 0-262-03056-X.

In recent years there has been a great deal of interest in the possible application of operations research procedures in libraries. Several volumes in this area have already been published by MIT (e.g., *Library Effectiveness: A Systems Approach*, by Philip M. Morse, or *Library Planning and Decision-Making Systems*, by Morris Hamburg and others). Ching-chih Chen discusses in this book Morse's theoretical models (book use and circulation). Part 2 of the book deals with the testing of these theoretical models at Countway Library of Medicine. The final part analyzes the experimental results in some detail and discusses how these analyzed data have tested the validity of the theoretical probabilistic models developed by Morse. [R: C&RL, Jan 77, p. 65; JAL, Mar 77, p. 38; LQ, Oct 77, p. 505; SL, Mar 77, p. 138]

1349. Christianson, Elin. **Paraprofessional and Nonprofessional Staff in Special Libraries.** New York, Special Libraries Association, 1973. 70p. (SLA State-of-the-Art Review, No. 2). o.p. LC 73-6868. ISBN 0-87111-218-3.

It has long been recognized that a library's performance is entirely dependent upon the quality of its personnel. There are a number of studies on professional employees (Anita Schiller's *Characteristics of Professional Personnel in College and University Libraries* [U.S. Department of Health, Education and Welfare, 1968] is an excellent example), but few prominent works on the nonprofessional staff. Elin Christianson, a special library consultant, reviews the library research literature on the two categories of nonprofessional staff and paraprofessionals (the American Library Association's Library Technical Assistant category) attempting to develop and identify the state-of-the-art. A comparison is made with the research findings in other fields, notably the health sciences and education. The work concludes with a short section on recommended directions for future library research in the manpower area. As in most areas of library research, two general conclusions are evident: there is a definite lack of basic research, and, even more important, there is a lack of *good* research. The author feels that the most pressing research need is an adequate collection of special library statistics; most pressing would be a simple "census of special library manpower." [R: BL, 15 Dec 73, p. 406; LJ, 15 Jan 74, p. 119]   Jerry E. Stephens

1350. Harvey, Joan M. **Specialised Information Centres.** London, Clive Bingley; distr., Hamden, Conn., Linnet Books, 1976. 112p. bibliog. index. o.p. LC 75-22152. ISBN 0-208-01521-3(Linnet); 0-85157-202-2(Clive Bingley).

This small (112-page) British book is a very elementary treatise on the administration of a specialized information center. Briefly and superficially covered are such subjects as administration, acquisition, document analysis, dissemination, and the economics of a center. A cursory list of information centers in the United Kingdom and the United States is included, along with an even more limited list of information dissemination services. Attempts are made to compare information centers in the United

Kingdom with those in the United States. There is nothing in the book that cannot be found in many better sources. It certainly cannot be considered a substantial book since the information provided is much too limited. [R: C&RL, Sept 76, pp. 473-74; LJ, 15 June 76, p. 1397]

Donald P. Hammer

1351. MacDonald, Arley Ripin. **Managers View Information.** New York, Special Libraries Association, 1983. 90p. bibliog. $24.50. LC 82-19570. ISBN 0-87111-283-3.

MacDonald's study, originally a doctoral dissertation for Columbia University, presents an exploratory, descriptive analysis of attitudinal relationships between special library managers and the corporate managers to whom they report. The research design is carefully explained: the library heads of 486 for-profit business and industrial organizations supporting special libraries and information centers in the Northeast corridor (Connecticut to Virginia) were sent letters explaining the study and requesting that they agree to participate in the study and that they identify the corporate manager to whom each reported. In the end, 98 librarians and 85 corporate managers returned usable instruments (not reproduced in the volume).

Two basic hypotheses were tested and accepted in this study: (1) that librarians' (i.e., library managers') and managers' responses to the attitude measures would not differ to a statistically significant degree, and (2) that within this close correspondence of attitudes, those of librarians would be measurably more positive than those of managers. MacDonald recognizes, however, that "within the convergence, significant differences of attitudes and areas of potential conflict are present," and she declares that the study's significance "lies in its concurrent exploration of the attitudes of the two groups toward the same group of concepts and the ways in which those attitudes converge or diverge." From the variety of findings that MacDonald summarizes in the concluding chapter the following is the most dramatic: "Corporate managers perceive information as neither of value nor of no value to the firm's ability to make a profit. Library managers perceive that information has a positive value as a contributor to profitability. The special library's existence ... presupposes that some positive concept of the value of its primary product—information—prevails. The fact that this belief is not demonstrated by the corporate managers ... is the single most important finding of the study."

MacDonald's research into attitudes in a special libraries context deserves careful study by librarians and information scientists — practitioners, teachers, students — everywhere. [R: JAL, July 83, p. 174]   Wiley J. Williams

1352. Rees, Alan, ed. **Contemporary Problems in Technical Library and Information Center Management: A State-of-the-Art.** Washington, D.C., American Society for Information Science, 1974. 211p. index. o.p. LC 74-14289. ISBN 0-87715-107-5.

In 1972, the Technical Information Support Activities (TISA) Project of the U.S. Army Scientific and Technical Information Program of the Army Corps of Engineers supported and directed a series of draft papers; the objective was to improve the efficiency and effectiveness of Department of Defense (DOD) technical libraries, information centers, and information analysis centers. The establishment of the priorities to be covered was undertaken by the Indiana Long Range Research Project of the Graduate Library School of the University of Indiana under the direction of Bernard M. Fry. The topics fell into the following categories: management, performance measures, and costing techniques; user studies; networking, library cooperation, and functional integration of technical and information analysis centers; and innovative library and information services. The charge to the authors was to present a clear description of the present state-of-the-art and to identify a number of problems amenable to short-range, applied research efforts that might lead to maximum impact on library and information center operations. The final papers appear in this volume. Many of the papers were written by well-known authorities such as Cloyd Dake Gull, F. W. Lancaster, Claire K. Schultz, Barbara Evans Markuson, and Henry Voos. Although most of the papers are oriented toward DOD and other federal libraries, other special libraries will find some of the papers directly applicable to their daily problems. The four most applicable in a general sense are: "The Effects of Reduced Support for Technical Libraries and Information Services," by F. Raymond Long; "Performance Measures for Libraries and Information Centers," by Claire K. Schultz; "Design of a Management Instrument for Technical Library Information," by Henry Voos; and "Improved Costing Techniques and Cost-Effective Operators for Technical Libraries and Information Centers," by John H. Wilson, Jr. Since the reviews were based on existing knowledge rather than a basic-type research, the bibliographies are of value to libraries of all sizes and types. The index is also very helpful as a guide to the cited references and conclusions drawn by their review. [R: LQ, Jan 77, p. 94; SL, Feb 77, p. 101]

Robert J. Havlik

1353. Strauss, Lucille J., Irene M. Shreve, and Alberta L. Brown. **Scientific and Technical Libraries: Their Organization and Administration.** 2nd ed. New York, Becker and Hayes, 1972. 450p. illus. index. (A Wiley-Becker-Hayes Publication). $49.50. LC 71-173679. ISBN 0-471-83312-6.

This is really the third edition (published in 1951 as *Technical Libraries: Their Organization and Management*; second edition, 1964). Strauss and her coauthors have maintained their aim of providing a textbook for library school students and beginning special librarians. Twelve chapters discuss scientific and technical libraries, budgets, staffs, buildings, materials, services, processes, and acquisitions. References and the many bibliographies are through 1970.

Actually, this book is a curious cross between an introduction for library technicians and a handbook for graduate students. The writing is pedestrian and often says the obvious (when searching information monographically, "try the card catalog"; hardly a scientific/technical distinction). The illustrations (punch cards, circulation cards, a reference librarian referencing) fail to increase the book's value. Yet the authors make extensive reference to further reading, thus taking the book beyond a technician's manual. At times, the footnoting is so heavy that one senses the authors qualifying their own opinions.

A 105-page appendix "Basic Reference Sources" for scientific/technical materials in print as of 1 May 1970, does not evaluate but merely lists titles by subject groupings. Citations usually include author, title, edition, publisher, place, and publication date. Strangely, periodicals and many abstracting services lack place and periodicity. Knowledgeable people would use this list with care; library technicians and beginners should be guided more by annotations and reviews. That one needs to be wary becomes evident when the authors say that *Choice* reviews "some science book" but that *Science Books* has a "good coverage." As a matter of fact, *Choice* reviews more adult science books than any other similar broad medium.

Libraries which have good combinations like Jenkins's *Science Reference Sources*, fifth edition (MIT Press, 1970) and Whitford's *Physics Literature*, second edition (Scarecrow, 1968) or Bottle's *The Use of Biological Literature* do not need *Scientific and Technical Libraries*. [R: LJ, 15 Sept 72, p. 2819]

Peter Doiron

45 Marketing and Promotion

1354. Angoff, Allan, ed. **Public Relations for Libraries: Essays in Communications Techniques.** Westport, Conn., Greenwood Press, 1973. 246p. illus. index. (Contributions in Librarianship and Information Science, No. 5). $29.95. LC 72-776. ISBN 0-8371-6060-X.

As a contribution to librarianship, this collection of essays is restricted to examples of public relation activities carried on in a variety of types of libraries. The inexperienced librarian who suddenly finds himself or herself in charge of public relations may discover some project ideas or be alerted to some common pitfalls. Suggestions like those contained in E. J. Montana's article, which provides guidelines for writing publicity releases, are useful to inexperienced publicity directors. Those with experience or training in communications techniques may consider the collection somewhat tiresome, especially Edward L. Bernay's underdeveloped essay. [R: LJ, 15 Nov 73, p. 3357]

Christine Gehrt Wynar

1355. Baeckler, Virginia Van Wynen. **PR for Pennies: Low-Cost Library Public Relations.** Hopewell, N.J., Sources, 1978. 89p. illus. $4.00pa. LC 77-90578.

The author's goal is to "demystify a number of practical public relations techniques for those who wish to start producing materials on their own with a minimum of time and money," and she does exactly that. Ideas and examples of how to use the resources around us abound, from an adaptation of Burger King's "have it your way" slogan to scrounging junk to make an "eco horse" (an animal figure made from recycled materials—used to display the potential of recycling) that can serve as the central focus of an exhibit. Rules of good public relations are

emphasized—brevity, clarity, and appeal—and techniques of preparing brochures, exhibits, and speeches are described, with examples and suggestions given for each. Writing in a clear, journalistic style, the author follows her own advice, and the result is a useful guide to creative public relations at a price that any library can afford. It can be used as a how-to-do-it guide or as an idea bank by librarians, trustees, and volunteers. [R: LJ, 15 Sept 78, p. 1709]

Ann E. Prentice

1356. Baeckler, Virginia Van Wynen. **Sparkle! PR for Library Staff.** Hopewell, N.J., Sources, 1980. 73p. illus. o.p. LC 80-50566. ISBN 0-9603232-1-X.

This book on library public relations written for library staff is, as its title indicates, full of "Sparkle!" Although designed primarily for school and public libraries, it has merit for others as well. The major theme of the small paperbound opus is, in the words of the author: "Place responsibility and challenge into the realm of a library employee. Give him a feel for the goals of the institution. Ensure his technical skills are commensurate with his job needs. Give him the independence to use all these and there will be a by-product of inestimable worth—in-house PR."

The contents include: service policy, telephone diplomacy, desk appeal, the perfect answer (library information service), creative idea flow for programs and exhibits, hiring, developmental training, and other topics. Numerous humorous illustrations and examples, along with lists of skills, exercises, equipment, and services, are given. The direct practical advice should be of assistance to the entire staff of a library in its public relations efforts and services. [R: JAL, Nov 80, p. 302]

Martha Boaz

1357. Baeckler, Virginia, and Linda Larson. **GO, PEP, and POP!: 250 Tested Ideas for Lively Libraries.** New York, U*N*A*B*A*S*H*E*D Librarian, 1976. 72p. illus. $4.50pa. LC 75-20328. ISBN 0-916444-01-5.

GO is Getting Outside of the public library to new people in new ways. PEP is Programs, Exhibits, Projects that will result in broader services beyond traditional approaches. POP is Positive Operating Procedures to support a live information and learning center. Designed to stimulate your own creative ability, it may just do it! [R: LJ, 15 Oct 76, p. 2115]

Arthur W. Swarthout

1358. Carey, R. J. P. **Library Guiding: A Program for Exploiting Library Resources.** Hamden, Conn., Linnet Books, 1974. 186p. illus. bibliog. index. o.p. LC 73-18477. ISBN 0-208-01350-4.

In these reports on research, surveys, and experiments in library instruction from 1969 to 1973, the author provides a useful manual in library marketing, in the sense of making the library's contents easy to locate. The "exploiting" of the title is not concerned here with outreach or advertising but with enabling users to find materials once they've entered the library.

This book provides a systematic study of a neglected area of librarianship. It deals with the obvious permanent visuals, library publications, audiovisual materials, and orientation, with clear descriptions and illustrations. It promotes self-service programs, which may be the salvation of librarians in this era of tightened budgets. After specifying the necessary elements of a program, it then proposes an organizational siting of the exploitation activities, to provide for interaction with all library sections. The British terminology creates an aura of objectivity, or in instances of materials and equipment, of frustration. It's a very good beginning for a concern that cries for attention. [R: LJ, Aug 74, p. 1915]

Doris H. Banks

1359. Cassata, Mary B., and Roger Cain Palmer, eds. **Reader in Library Communication.** Englewood, Colo., Library and Education Division of Information Handling Services, 1976. 278p. illus. index. (Readers in Librarianship and Information Science). o.p. LC 76-10123. ISBN 0-910972-68-0.

This stimulating collection of classic essays aims "to reveal to librarians what their precise role in the communication process is or might be." The editors' own experiences illustrate the book's commitment to the "natural convergence of library science with communication." The other expert authors of this anthology's nineteen essays have diverse backgrounds, such as journalism, mathematics, industrial psychology, government services, and librarianship.

Between an "Introduction to the Study of Communication," and a future-oriented "Epilogue," five groups of essays reflect major areas of communication study—personal, small group, organizational, mass, and intracultural communications. Most of the essays are not explicitly related to librarianship; however, they offer a librarian discussions of numerous highly relevant issues. Among the implications proposed are (1) that librarians need to be aware of people's individual perceptions, needs, and frame of reference; (2) that librarians need to be conscious of small group dynamics and their effects on power manipulation; (3) that a library is a complex organization having both formal and informal interactive communication systems; (4) that as agencies of mass communications, libraries have a vital role as gatekeepers of information; and (5) that since cultural differences may affect communications, a library needs to incorporate in its services and collections the implications presented by its community's different cultural groups.

References following most of the essays, abstracts, short sectional introductions, and a brief index help the reader locate specific information.

The book challenges the profession to look beyond its own methodology and traditional attitudes and to consider more consciously librarianship as an important part of the social communication process.   Danuta A. Nitecki

1360. Coplan, Kate. **Poster Ideas and Bulletin Board Techniques: For Libraries and Schools.** 2nd ed. Dobbs Ferry, N.Y., Oceana, 1981. 248p. illus. (part col.). bibliog. index. $25.00. LC 80-24971. ISBN 0-379-20333-2.

Reproductions of posters and bulletin boards, most of which are in black-and-white (approximately 30 pages in color), are included in this volume. Each visual is followed by a materials list and a brief description of methods used in construction. Display ideas are organized in several categories such as creative posters, attention-getting bulletin boards, seasons and special events, and communicating through visual display. Other chapters include "Color Notes," "Classroom Practices," "How-to Helps," and "Care and Preservation of Display

Materials." One chapter, "Classroom Practices," is the only chapter devoted exclusively to classroom teachers. The "how to" chapter briefly lists and describes inexpensive materials and art techniques such as ink resist, cardboard printing, papier-maché, "sculpture," and a paper flower process. An appendix lists sources of supplies and equipment, related readings, and three calendars for reference. Experienced librarians and teachers responsible for displays may find the art techniques familiar; however, ideas and inspiration can be gleaned from the many reproductions. [R: BL, 1 Dec 81, p. 504]   Jeanne Wieckert

1361. Dolnick, Sandy, comp. **A Directory of Friends of Libraries Groups in the United States.** Chicago, Friends of Libraries Committee, Public Relations Section, Library Administration Division, American Library Association, 1978. 297p. o.p.

A cooperative endeavor of many people, this directory is arranged in two sections. In the first part, seven statewide friends groups are identified (there are two in Florida). In the second part, local friends groups are arranged by state, and public library and academic library friends groups by city. The name of the library and the address are given, but names of officers are not included. In the introduction, a statement is made that a form has been included on the back page of the directory to be sent to ALA when a new group is formed or an inactive group disbanded; this form was missing from the copy reviewed. Although the arrangement of the directory is obvious, a brief table of contents would have been helpful. [R: LJ, 15 Mar 79, p. 688]   Doris Cruger Dale

1362. Edsall, Marian S. **Library Promotion Handbook.** Phoenix, Ariz., Oryx Press, 1980. 244p. illus. bibliog. index. (A Neal-Schuman Professional Book). $35.00; $27.50pa. LC 79-26984. ISBN 0-912700-15-7; 0-912700-12-2pa.

Public relations is an integral part of the program planning process that relates library activity to the needs and interests of the community served. As this community changes, so should the library program. PR is the continuing activity necessary to assure that the library and its staff are meeting community needs. The author provides a wealth of information concerning planning for informing the community of library services and programs. The roles of staff attitude and library environment in the public relations effort are stressed, as everything done in a library and the library environment

itself are part of public relations. Good media relations, the relative value of different PR approaches, how to control a potential blizzard of printed information, the role of staff newsletters, coverage of special events, and crises are discussed, and checklists of things to consider in each instance are included.

Presented in a format that is a good example of how to communicate effectively in print, the *Library Promotion Handbook* is an overall comprehensive plan for putting library service forward to its many publics in as many formats. It should be used in the planning stages for service, through implementation, and as a guide to evaluation of programs. A good, current annotated bibliography further expands its usefulness. [R: BL, 15 Oct 80, p. 304]

Ann E. Prentice

1363. Franklin, Linda Campbell. **Display and Publicity Ideas for Libraries.** Jefferson, N.C., McFarland, 1985. 264p. illus. bibliog. index. $14.95pa. LC 84-43229. ISBN 0-89950-168-0.

The first edition of this book was published in 1980 under the title, *Library Display Ideas.* *Display and Publicity Ideas for Libraries* provides both practical and creative ideas on how to merchandise library services and materials. Most of the suggestions are organized around themes, such as library services and book care, reading and learning, social issues, and sports and games. Each display idea lists the materials needed and describes the technique for assembling the display. One section suggests "Versatile Display Elements" that would involve some woodworking skills but which could be eye-catching ideas for ongoing displays.

As a school librarian, I do not feel this book is particularly essential. Caroline Feller Bauer's programming books, *Celebrations* (H. W. Wilson, 1985) and *This Way to Books* (H. W. Wilson, 1983), meet my needs more effectively by incorporating display ideas into programs using specific titles. The suggestions in *Display and Publicity Ideas for Libraries* are much more general and might better serve the needs of public librarians. In all, however, this is a useful overview of suggestions for planning and producing library displays. One feature worth noting is the brief "Display and Promotion Calendar" which lists some possible events for potential displays. Another useful feature is the annotated bibliography of selected resources.

Rebecca L. Thomas

1364. Garvey, Mona. **Library Displays: Their Purpose, Construction and Use.** New York,

H. W. Wilson, 1969. 88p. index. $14.00. LC 79-86918. SBN 8242-0395-X.

Unlike the usual book on displays or bulletin boards that provide page after page of photos of "outstanding" displays in libraries, this little book gets to the heart of the matter. The author discusses why displays should be done, what services they perform for the public, and how they should convey ideas. There are informative discussions on function and types of displays, sources of display ideas, design principles and how they work in practice. Numerous illustrations of display techniques are provided but this is not a "pattern" book of samples. A selected list of additional references would have been useful in this otherwise well-organized and edited book. [R: BL, 1 Jan 70, p. 532; DLQ, Apr 70, p. 194; LJ, 1 Jan 70, p. 47; LR, Fall 70, p. 381; WLB, Jan 70, p. 563]

1365. Garvey, Mona. **Library Public Relations: A Practical Handbook.** New York, H. W. Wilson, 1980. 160p. illus. index. $18.00. LC 80-17669. ISBN 0-8242-0651-7.

As a primer for library PR, Garvey's book is among the best. It offers some promotional ideas for school, academic, and special libraries, but will appeal mostly to public librarians. Garvey defines PR as "an integral component ... and extension ... of the best kind of library operation and service." It should combine effective internal communication among staff, trustees, and administrators with external communication with the public, both users and non-users. According to the author, a PR campaign should begin with a survey of the library's philosophy, policies, regulations, and access. Then a marketing survey, even a partial one, is needed to define the library's general audience and special interest groups. Programming should relate to the library's activities and materials, provide needed services to special audiences, and contribute to the education and well-being of the community. Many program ideas are offered.

Garvey describes how to use press, radio, and TV, but cautions against too much reliance on mass media. Print publicity is extensively covered, including over 30 pages of sample graphics, how to's for the do-it-yourselfer, and tips on designing signs, posters, bulletin boards, exhibits, displays, floor plans, flyers, and brochures. The book assures librarians that they can do their own PR. Experts are helpful, but not essential.

Library Public Relations offers creative, practical, economical, and explicit advice. It is readable, attractively printed, and well bound.

A good value. [R: BL, 15 Oct 81, p. 283; JAL, Jan 81, p. 364; LJ, 15 Apr 81, p. 863]
									Mary Anne Heaphy

1366. Harrison, K. C. **Public Relations for Librarians.** 2nd, rev. ed. Aldershot, England, Gower Publishing; distr., Lexington, Mass., Lexington Books/D. C. Heath, 1982. 144p. bibliog. index. (A Grafton Book). $19.00. ISBN 0-566-03454-9.

A wise, engaging, and commonsense introduction to the subject by a distinguished British librarian. Harrison was city librarian of Westminster for 19 years and served for 11 years as editor of *The Library World.* An earlier book, *The Library and the Community,* now in its third edition, established him as an authority on the relationships between libraries and their publics. The present volume is a revised, updated, and rewritten version of the first edition of *Public Relations for Librarians,* published in 1973. The tone of the book continues to be British, but the point of view is consistently international. Many of the examples that are cited of public relations (PR) activities in libraries refer to U.S. practice.

The coverage is thorough. The eight chapters treat all aspects of library public relations, including library publications, relations with the media, cooperative PR ventures among libraries, talks, lectures, guided tours, audiovisual presentations, exhibits, and displays. A recurring theme is the preeminent place that excellent service to clientele holds in a PR program. There are a well-selected 20-item bibliography and a useful index. A clear, practical, and readable survey that will benefit any library anywhere. [R: Indexer, Oct 83, p. 284; LR, Winter 83, p. 291]							John Farley

1367. Kies, Cosette. **Problems in Library Public Relations.** New York, R. R. Bowker, 1974. 179p. (Bowker Series in Problem-Centered Approaches to Librarianship). o.p. LC 74-4062. ISBN 0-8352-0678-5.

Because good public relations are of vital concern to contemporary library staffs, intelligent discussions of problems in this area are always welcome. *Problems in Library Public Relations* presents just such an intelligent discussion of 22 typical situations that have occurred in public, academic, and special libraries. The case studies cover an interesting range of subjects—"The Making of a Nonuser," "The Talented Volunteer," "the Reorganization," "Attacked in the Stacks." Following each case the author provides an analysis of the situation, suggests preventions and possible cures, and in the process emphasizes that good public relations policy is more than a facade, that it must be intrinsic to every library operation. Although the case study approach makes the book particularly suited for library school use, it should also be required reading for every professional. [R: LJ, 15 Oct 74, p. 2587]

Nancy P. Schneider

1368. Kies, Cosette. **Projecting a Positive Image through Public Relations: Including a Communication Audit for School Media Centers.** Chicago, American Association of School Librarians, American Library Association, 1978. 88p. bibliog. (School Media Centers: Focus on Trends and Issues, No. 2). $6.00pa. LC 78-21250. ISBN 0-8389-3219-3.

School media centers, like other service organizations, depend upon the informed support of their clientele for their effectiveness. Cosette Kies has written a short book aimed at helping school media specialists maintain the kind of public relations programs that will keep students, teachers, and the community aware of media center activities. Drawing on communication and marketing theory, she discusses such aspects of public relations as identifying and establishing objective standards, assessing existing situations, identifying strong and weak points, overcoming problems, establishing evaluative procedures, and providing for a continuing and constantly improving program. An appendix includes a "Communication Audit," which can be used to assess what the clientele know about the media program.

Unfortunately, the book includes very few examples that would explain the concepts mentioned. Kies exhorts school media specialists to use guidelines that are never made clear, as in the following: "Sometimes in the spirit of enthusiasm and a desire to do a thorough job the media specialist can overdo to the point of overkill, and turn people off by too much information too often. Obviously a delicate balance is required—just one more factor to keep in mind in the implementation of the program. This caution, however, should be kept in perspective; if in doubt, the media specialist would probably do better to err on the side of a little too much." How is a media specialist to maintain a "delicate balance" with only this as a guide? This book may well be useful in helping media specialists consider the bases of their public relations efforts, but many will be left unsatisfied because of the lack of concrete detail and relevant examples that would help them in developing programs. [R: JAL, July 79, p. 168]

Adele M. Fasick

1369. Kohn, Rita. **Experiencing Displays.** Metuchen, N.J., Scarecrow, 1982. 237p. illus. index. $16.00pa. LC 82-3187. ISBN 0-8108-1534-6.

Kohn presents display ideas in a creative manner rather than a step-by-step approach. The book is organized by sections dealing with type of idea or shape (e.g., "Seesaw," "Hourglass," and "Cylinders"). Each section presents a display objective, related actions which can be done in connection with the display, and an overall discussion of the display idea with suggestions made toward preparing it. Some color would have enhanced the presentation, but the numerous black-and-white illustrations and photographs adequately demonstrate the author's ideas. Appendices provide information on display philosophy and technique, planning forms, a glossary of terms, and photographs of displays in libraries. An index allows quick access to the contents.

The author uses her background in public relations and business to effectively assist her with display ideas and promotion philosophy. In addition to displays, she recognizes that marketing a library requires other essential elements. She has written other books on public relations, presented PR programs, and held a position dealing with promotion and publicity at a university.

Linda Campbell Franklin's *Library Display Ideas* (see *ARBA* 82, entry 293) is a similar book which emphasizes the calendar and has a less complex form of organization. Kohn's book serves as a catalyst to spark the imagination of school and public librarians as well as anyone who prepares displays. [R: JAL, Sept 82, p. 242]

O. Gene Norman

1370. Kohn, Rita, and Krysta Tepper. **You Can Do It: A PR Manual for Librarians.** Metuchen, N.J., Scarecrow, 1981. 232p. illus. bibliog. index. $16.00pa. LC 80-24217. ISBN 0-8108-1401-3.

This is a fairly comprehensive source book for ideas and considerations in planning for an ongoing library public relations program. The work's strength is its highly organized approach and the consideration of nearly all aspects of library public relations. The format is principally outline form, and this makes it highly unreadable, but for use as a reference source it should prove useful. It can be used to alert the librarian to items that might have been overlooked in a PR effort, provide sample forms and procedures for various types of PR, and identify key individuals who should be involved in the library's PR program either as recipients or participants. In addition to the usual topics one might expect to find, such as displays, signing, audiovisual presentations, ink print advertising, etc., one also finds such interesting and unusual approaches to PR as "eliminate hazards before they become negative PR factors," and with regard to the library's personnel, "staff self-inventory for 'smile level.' " Annual reports as a form of PR are given only cursory treatment.

A very few vignettes are used to emphasize the need for PR. Unfortunately this style was not employed to a greater extent to make the text more readable. In addition to the ample illustrations (primarily sample forms), the text is presented in a series of steps (1-74). The user is occasionally directed from one step to another, thus bringing related concepts together or at least to one's attention. There are an adequate index and two appendices—one on giving a speech and the other on writing a book feature for local publication.

Because tedious checklists and guidelines are probably necessary for well-organized and carefully controlled PR work, this reference source should be of use to public librarians, for whom it is intended, and also for other librarians who must address these issues. [R: BL, 15 Oct 81, p. 284; LJ, 1 June 81, p. 1193; SMQ, Fall 81, pp. 68-69]   Robert A. Berk

1371.   Krummel, D. W., ed. **Organizing the Library's Support: Donors, Volunteers, Friends.** Urbana-Champaign, Ill., Graduate School of Library Science, University of Illinois, 1980. 119p. index. (Allerton Park Institute, No. 25). $10.00. LC 80-14772. ISBN 0-87845-054-8.

At the Allerton Park Institute on Library Friends, 12 papers were delivered by members and friends of the profession, divided into "The Library Context" (3 papers) and "Special Topics" (9 papers). Topics included history, state of library friends, networks, academic libraries, development functions, governing board, volunteers, perquisites, publications, and foundations. Anne Mathews's paper, "Library Friends and Regional Library Networks," provides a wealth of information for friends groups. Edward Holley's "The Library and Its Friends" was most descriptive of how-we-did-it at the University of Houston library, and Elaine Seaton's "With Friends Like These" presented the "negative" side of friends groups. All papers were general in nature and in some cases were how-we-did-it-at-my-library presentations. After reading all the papers, one complete article may appear.

Donald D. Foos

1372.   Leerburger, Benedict A. **Marketing the Library.** White Plains, N.Y., Knowledge Industry Publications, 1982. 124p. illus. bibliog. index. $24.50pa. LC 81-18132. ISBN 0-914236-89-X.

Written by a freelance writer, editor, and public library trustee, this well-organized book emphasizes the promotional aspect of marketing. Leerburger identifies the "three major means of marketing available to the library: the published word, personal contact and ... 'atmospherics.' " He stresses the effective use of the local newspaper, radio and television, the newsletter, the annual report, and exhibits and displays. In addition, the author explores a variety of library products such as musical events, movies, lectures, kite flying, discussion groups, trips, plays, reading lists, and bibliographies. He notes the importance of maintaining good community relations with local government officials, clubs and organizations, the friends of the library, and state and federal legislators. The critical problem of fund raising is covered in detail, and a separate chapter is devoted to the needs of promoting academic and special libraries. A 41-item bibliography and a three-page index complete the book.

A similar work, Marian S. Edsall's *Library Promotion Handbook* (see *ARBA* 81, entry 264) contains almost twice as many pages. It also has more illustrations, a 141-item annotated bibliography, and an 11-page index. As a result, Edsall may be considered the better buy, but Leerburger should be recognized as an effective guide for public and other librarians to use in promoting library materials and services. [R: BL, Aug 82, p. 1506; JAL, July 82, p. 177; LJ, Aug 82, p. 1391]   O. Gene Norman

1373.   **The Library Connection: Essays Written in Praise of Public Libraries.** Compiled by the Public Library Association, a division of the American Library Association. Chicago, American Library Association, 1977. 86p. $5.00pa. LC 77-24687. ISBN 0-8389-0245-6.

With the financial assistance of the Council on Library Resources, the Public Library Association has commissioned a number of "known" people, such as Nat Hentoff, Norman Cousins, Marchette Chute, Dorothy Rodgers, etc., to write essays that show "how public libraries have been and can be used by individuals." The essays are directed to specific audiences—among others, the consumer, homeowner, the aged, women, Hispanic Americans, blacks.

They are rather uneven in quality; some good, some not. And they read as one might expect commissioned articles to read, and I paraphrase—"How the library helped me to restore a home"; "learn investing"; "find recipes"; "trace ancestors." I discover that librarians love what they're doing and take no end of trouble finding what you're looking for. One essay also told me that the library is the place to take children when they're driving one to distraction and, oh yes, while you're there with them, "take home some books from the adult shelves."

To the librarian, there is nothing new here. But then, this collection wasn't written for librarians. Nor will the librarian be able to use this as a "reference" work. It is not designed to be referred to, but to be read—not by librarians but by the 70 percent (?) of the population who do not now use the public library. The basic problem with this collection, it seems to me, is how can it be used? Not by cataloging it in a library science classification—reference or circulating—and shelving it. For on that shelf it will stay.

In some locales, it is probable that a good librarian with publicity "pizzazz" could get the local newspaper to print these as a series, once a week—or maybe even get one or two read on the radio. Unfortunately, the verso of the title page puts a damper on this use as well—"No part of this publication may be reproduced in any form...." Perhaps copies could be purchased and given to neighborhood groups, playgrounds, schools, etc., for their use, but at $5.00 for an 86-page paperback, this seems unlikely.

Allie Beth Martin's first plan of action in *A Strategy for Public Library Change* (American Library Association, 1972), is "first, a publication should be commissioned which will be an eloquent statement to direct widespread attention to the American public library as an active community agent capable of meeting the real needs of real people today and in the future."

I don't think that is that publication. [R: CLW, Apr 78, p. 405; JLH, Fall 78, p. 487]

Gil McNamee

1374. **The Marketing of Library and Information Services.** Blaise Cronin, ed. London, Aslib, 1981. 360p. illus. index. (Aslib Reader Series, Vol. 4). £20.50; £12.00pa. ISBN 0-85142-153-9; 0-85142-154-7pa.

This volume contains 38 reprints from 30 different English-language monographs, serials, and government reports published on three continents between 1951 and 1980. The majority appeared after 1975. Selections from business publications as well as library literature are included.

The papers are organized into six main sections: (1) principles and practice of marketing, (2) the application of marketing principles to the management of library and information services, (3) marketing practice, (4) marketing research, (5) marketing as communication, and (6) cooperation and coordination. Each section consists of a group of reprints preceded by Blaise Cronin's introductory notes and suggestions for further reading. An author index to papers reprinted in this book, as well as those cited by the editor in his comments, is provided.

Cronin has compiled a well-balanced, up-to-date collection of previously published materials on the marketing of library and information services. Writings by well-known proponents and critics of "selling the library" are included. Unfortunately, the contributions are not all of uniformly high quality, and frequent changes in the size of type and typeface are often annoying to the reader. This book, nevertheless, will be very useful to library students and practitioners who do not have the time to gather together and peruse more than two dozen sources. [R: LR, Winter 82, p. 280]

Leonard Grundt

1375. Pennell, H. Barrett, Jr., ed. **Find Out Who Your Friends Are: A Practical Manual for the Formation of Library Support Groups.** Philadelphia, Friends of the Free Library of Philadelphia, 1978. 66p. illus. o.p.

Although written "to help foster the library support movement underway in the neighborhoods of Philadelphia and across the Commonwealth of Pennsylvania," this manual's message is applicable nationwide. It outlines the purposes of friends groups and tells how to start a steering committee, elect a board, set objectives and action plans, cope with legal necessities (such as articles of incorporation), how to recruit members, handle finances, hire a staff, cooperate with library employees, promote and publicize friends activities, and participate on the library's behalf in the political scene without jeopardizing the friends' tax-exempt status. The book is full of ideas for programs, fund raisers, and service projects. The phenomenal successes of the Friends of the Free Library of Philadelphia (their 1976-1977 annual report showed a net worth of nearly $38,000, a membership of 1,100 individuals and 12 organizations, volunteers numbering 116, and an impressive array of programs for children, the handicapped, consumers, and governmental officials) should give confidence to other burgeoning library support groups. At the same time, the manual acknowledges the budget limitations that beset friends groups in both small and large libraries.

The book has some weaknesses. The review copy's binding was coming apart when I received it. There are several typos, and a duplicate page appeared at the end.

Mary Anne Heaphy

1376. Powell, Judith W., and Robert B. LeLieuvre. **Peoplework: Communications Dynamics for Librarians.** Chicago, American Library Association, 1979. 190p. index. $8.00pa. LC 79-18018. ISBN 0-8389-0290-1.

This is not a reference book; it is a what-would-you-do-about-this-situation-or-that-situation book. Together the authors have worked to produce a book for librarians that will "demythologize the psychology and communication requirements and dynamics that are important both in human relationships and in library service." The branch of psychology known as humanistic psychology is examined, and the reader is told the importance of human feelings, attitudes, and needs. This discussion is intended to help librarians communicate better by making them more aware of human behavior. Transactional analysis, Gordon's theories of effectiveness training, and Glasser's reality therapy are explained. The authors give examples of communication problems librarians encounter, and provide criteria from the literature for evaluating possible modes of communication. The book is based entirely on the writings of others, and there has been no attempt to apply this research in a library setting. Indeed, the book contains no detailed discussion focusing on the experiences of people using a library and the meaning of this experience to them as library users, as individuals, as human beings, etc.

Librarians would be better advised to read the work of Frederick Perls, Carl Rogers, Gordon Allport, and Abraham Maslow instead of this explanation of their important work with a few made-up examples of communication problems involving a library setting thrown in. References to articles and books are listed at the end of each chapter. There is an index, a table of contents, and a short introduction. Only libraries with large library science collections will need to add this book to their collection. [R: BL, 15 Apr 80, p. 1177; C&RL, May 80, p. 277; JAL, Sept 80, p. 229; LJ, 1 June 80, p. 1282]

Milton H. Crouch

1377. Rice, Betty. **Public Relations for Public Libraries: Creative Problem Solving.** New York, H. W. Wilson, 1972. 133p. illus. index. $10.00. LC 72-2421. ISBN 0-8242-0476-X.

Using a pragmatic approach to this complex problem, the author seems to cover all its major aspects. Of special interest are chapters on displays and exhibits as public relations tools and on how to work on bond and budget issues. The volume is well illustrated and indexed. [R: LJ, 1 Jan 73, p. 52]

1378. Roberts, Don, with Deidre Boyle, eds. **Mediamobiles: Views from the Road.** Chicago, American Library Association, 1979. 116p. bibliog. index. (The Public Library Reporter, No. 19). $7.00pa. LC 79-18488. ISBN 0-8389-3232-0.

Designers and librarians of mediamobiles discuss, in a series of interviews, five different types of vehicles. These conversations, conducted in 1972 and 1973, are casual and follow no predetermined format. However, specific features of the vehicles are examined: efficiency, design, special features, and utilization. This is not a buying guide, but it does discuss strengths and weaknesses of various vehicles with the designers and librarians who use them. It is useful as an introduction and as an outline of points to consider before purchasing a mediamobile. The bibliography notes books and articles published between 1961 and 1974. The index provides access to both the text and the bibliography. [R: BL, 15 Apr 80, p. 1177; JAL, Mar 80, p. 49]

1379. Robotham, John S., and Lydia LaFleur. **Library Programs: How to Select, Plan and Produce Them.** 2nd ed. Metuchen, N.J., Scarecrow, 1981. 352p. illus. bibliog. index. $19.00. LC 81-2149. ISBN 0-8108-1422-6.

Written by two experienced librarians in library programming, this second edition contains an updating and reorganizing of material found in the first edition (see *ARBA* 77, entry 163). Important additions include programs for the handicapped, senior citizens, and prisoners. A new chapter on miscellaneous programs contains ideas and suggestions for contests, tournaments, collector's fairs, carnivals, happenings, open houses, and bus trips.

The format of the book is similar to the first edition. Part 1 presents a variety of types of programs, whereas part 2 assists the reader with identifying programs which fit the needs of a particular library. The details involved in planning and producing the program are described in part 3. The six appendices, the annotated bibliography, and the detailed index have also been expanded and updated.

This new edition is an improved source for locating, designing, and implementing a wide variety of free and inexpensive programs for libraries. It can be used effectively alone or in conjunction with such books as Virginia Van Wynen Baeckler's *PR for Pennies* (Sources, 1978) and Steve Sherman's *ABC's of Library Promotion* (2nd ed., Scarecrow, 1980). It is aimed at public libraries, but academic, school, and special libraries can profit from it when in need of ideas for and assistance with a program. [R: BL, 15 Jan 82, p. 634; Emerg Lib, Mar 82, p. 26; JAL, Jan 82, p. 383; LJ, 1 Jan 82, p. 45; SLJ, Apr 82, p. 35]   O. Gene Norman

1380. Sherman, Steve. **ABC's of Library Promotion.** 2nd ed. Metuchen, N.J., Scarecrow, 1980. 242p. index. $15.00. LC 79-24232. ISBN 0-8108-1274-6.

A concise, clearly written, practical, and upbeat PR primer especially useful for small and medium-sized public libraries with limited PR staff and budgets. Short on theory, and long on examples, it tells how to cultivate local print and electronic media to bring the library's positive image and news to the public. It shows how to write press releases, feature stories, radio and television public service announcements and programs, and explains how to prepare video, film, and slide/tape presentations with actual scripts and techniques for using camera and audio equipment. It suggests simple, inexpensive ways to make the library more convenient for users. Librarians are reminded that they should know and nurture local VIPs who can, in turn, support the library, and *ABC's of Library Promotion* tells how to develop a continuous PR program and how to evaluate its effectiveness. A case study of one library's successful campaign to get a new building, specific PR ideas for public, school, and academic libraries, and appendices of quotable quotes and interesting, factual tidbits about libraries conclude the book.

This second, revised edition differs little from the earlier, 1971 version. The typeface is larger and clearer, the table of contents is more detailed, and statistical and price information is updated, but the content is nearly identical. Experienced, creative librarians will probably already know or have used the PR ideas in the book. It is valuable mostly as a compendium of "how-to's" for preparing newspaper, radio, television, film, and slide/tape promotional

material. [R: LJ, 15 June 80, p. 1371]
                                    Mary Anne Heaphy

1381. **68 Great Ideas: The Library Awareness Handbook.** Peggy Barber, ed. Chicago, American Library Association, 1982. 68p. illus. index. $7.50pa. LC 82-11518. ISBN 0-8389-0376-2.

This unique publication contains the most promising ideas and activities selected by a review committee from hundreds of ideas submitted by a variety of librarians from throughout the United States. A sampling of ideas described includes: consumer information program on electronic games; "stump the librarian" road show; direct mail campaigns; health awareness day; promotion to introduce a new microfiche (catfiche) catalog; and the unbelievable pig day celebration.

Each idea has a standard format of identifying the target audience, describing the idea, and noting the group or institution which originated the idea. A discussion of the idea follows, and the person to contact for further information is listed at the end with an address and telephone number. Descriptions of ideas range from one-half to two pages. Ideas are arranged into 12 categories—from special markets to new library services.

Librarians looking for new promotional ideas should find this work a thought-provoking supplement to such books as Benedict A. Leerburger's *Marketing the Library* (see *ARBA 83*, entry 273) and Marian S. Edsall's *Library Promotion Handbook* (see *ARBA 81*, entry 264). Persons benefiting from ideas in the book should thank Elizabeth W. Stone, 1981-1982 ALA president, who had the insight to solicit ideas from among ALA membership and to publish them for the benefit of all. Readers are invited to send in their ideas for a sequel entitled *Great Ideas II*. [R: Emerg Lib, Nov 82, p. 27]
                                    O. Gene Norman

1382. Stoakley, Roger. **Presenting the Library Service.** London, Clive Bingley; distr., Hamden, Conn., Shoe String Press, 1982. 109p. index. (Outlines of Modern Librarianship). $12.50. ISBN 0-85157-320-7.

As the eighth title in the Outlines of Modern Librarianship series, this book has been written primarily for students interested in public library service. The author's British point of view does not limit the text's broad applicability. Presenting library service is more than public relations, according to Stoakley. For public relations is only as effective as certain fundamentals. The first two chapters are devoted to the qualities needed by a librarian, both as an individual and as a member of an organization. The next basic elements concern accessibility of library services, the library building, library maintenance, service qualities, extension activities, publicity, and local government relations. The directness and simplicity of the statements are suitable to students but also serve as reminders to experienced librarians of management principles. Each short chapter is followed by a brief bibliography, and there is an index. [R: LR, Autumn 82, p. 210]

Mary Kay Donahue

1383. Usherwood, Bob. **The Visible Library: Practical Public Relations for Public Librarians.** London, Library Association; distr., Phoenix, Ariz., Oryx Press, 1981. 207p. illus. bibliog. index. o.p. ISBN 0-85365-522-6.

The Visible Library is useful for reminding public library managers to think about the "why" as well as the "how to" of public relations. Usherwood emphasizes that PR is "a management tool for obtaining, retaining, and maximizing resources." He discusses the uses of press releases, radio and television publicity and promotion, displays, audiovisual, and miscellaneous PR tools such as buttons, bookbags, memorials, and library tours. There is hardly any reference to library programming because British libraries, the book's intended audience, make little use of it. Usherwood reiterates the need to know your community and to cultivate good relations with the library's public, including staff, patrons, nonusers, and government officials. The chapter on public speaking is especially good. The bibliography of PR books published within the last 10 years is a well-selected list covering general works, ideas and methods, and management implications.

For an American audience, this British publication is a superfluous purchase. While readable, practical, and attractively laid out, *The Visible Library* contributes little to the literature of library PR that can't be found elsewhere. [R: LJ, 1 Feb 82, p. 237]

Mary Anne Heaphy

1384. Williams, James G., with the assistance of Elspeth Pope. **Simulation Activities in Library, Communication and Information Science.** New York, Marcel Dekker, 1976. 246p. illus. index. (Communication Science and Technology, Vol. 6). $55.00. LC 75-32390. ISBN 0-8247-6376-9.

The "Communication Science and Technology" series is "designed for communication leaders in the media, libraries and information specialization." Patrick R. Penland is general editor as well as principal author of the first four titles in the series. This work is the sixth to appear.

The book, although not specifically labeled accordingly, is organized into two parts. The first part, composed of chapters 1 through 3, covers the traditional background and introductory materials but offers as well a thorough— and valuable—discussion of "The Analysis and Design of Simulation Activities." The remainder of the work (chapters 4 through 8) comprises a collection of selected examples of simulation activities deemed appropriate for use in library education environments. From five to nine "exercises" (not "games") are outlined for five areas: communications, information science, administration, technical services, and reference work; and up to six "Other Suggested Simulation Activities" are briefly mentioned for every area except reference work.

The book has a number of serious deficiencies. It lacks a stated purpose. While the authors make no claim for originality, neither do they acknowledge (let alone cite) the growing body of literature available on the subject. They also present little more than a lifeless catalog of exercises for use (presented according to the following uniform format: audience, goals of the exercise, time required, group size, setting, goals of the participants, resources, roles, process and rules, evaluation; followed by various instructions and game elements). The potential communication dynamics accruing from actual use, however, are not discussed, and the book ends without a conclusion or wrap-up of any kind. [R: C&RL, Mar 77, pp. 174-75; LJ, 15 Jan 77, p. 182]

Glenn R. Wittig

1385. **Winning the Money Game: A Guide to Community-Based Library Fundraising.** New York, Baker and Taylor, 1979. 136p. bibliog. o.p. LC 79-90713. ISBN 0-8480-2000-6.

After a brief preface by Robert Wedgeworth, *Winning the Money Game* follows a course of "Managing Special Events for Fun and Profit," which includes a basketball marathon, a musical revue, a community barbecue, a theater gala, and a book fair. Chapters 1-3 provide information on people as power, planning money game strategies, and going to the voters. Chapter 5, "Building Group Support," and chapter 6, "Creating Support for Special Programs," provide designs for friends groups, PTA, book fairs, etc. Chapter 8, "More

Winning Ideas ... in Brief," provides details on bank promotions, book showers, book fairs, used book sales, wheelbarrow campaigns, thrift shops, etc. This paperback book's appendices provide a checklist (A), selected resources (B), and friends and funds (C). The Baker and Taylor Company must be complimented on the publication of this helpful guide to "community-based library fund raising"; and with the effects on libraries of Proposition 13 and similar legislation throughout the nation, it must be time for libraries to consider playing to win "the Money Game." [R: BL, 15 July 80, p. 1654]

Donald D. Foos

46 Microforms

1386. American Association of Community and Junior Colleges. **A Microform Handbook.** By Dale Gaddy. Silver Spring, Md., National Microfilm Association, 1975. 1v. (various paging). illus. bibliog. o.p. LC 73-92621.

The primary purpose of this short book is to give a basic introduction to microforms. Librarians and administrators of junior and community colleges are the audience, especially those that have or are planning learning resource centers (LRC). In addition to six chapters written by Gaddy, there are six appendices: a bibliography, NMA Buyer's Guide (National Microform Association), a list of NMA chapters, micrographic standards, names and addresses of micropublishers, and periodicals relating to micrographics. All six of these appendices are publications of the NMA, and they are also available separately.

Because this is an NMA-sponsored publication, the usefulness of microforms is exaggerated and their problems downgraded. Still, the book gives information about applications of machines and techniques that are available. Specific products and brands are not evaluated. A major failing is the lack of information about how to store microforms so as to lengthen their life span. A directory of terminology and definitions would have been an asset. This handbook serves as a basic guide to microforms and related machinery for those in community and junior colleges.   William Z. Schenck

1387. Bahr, Alice Harrison. **Microforms: The Librarians' View, 1978-79.** White Plains, N.Y., Knowledge Industry Publications, 1978. 118p. illus. bibliog. index. $24.50pa. LC 78-10645. ISBN 0-914236-25-3.

With so many libraries studying the benefits of computer-output-microform (COM) catalogs, the role of microforms in libraries is receiving renewed attention. *Microforms: The Librarians' View, 1978-79* provides an overview of current issues in microform selection and acquisition; traditional and innovative uses of microforms; space and financial implications; maintenance and processing; and equipment. Appended is a helpful list of illustrations of various kinds of microform equipment. While more *librarians* have come to accept microforms, *user* resistance is a continuing problem, particularly with respect to the COM catalog. This problem involves the availability and condition of microform equipment, and related aspects of microform use, such as proper room lighting (it should be dimmer than normal). Thus, before committing library funds to microforms, librarians must make an effort to ensure that the user's environment promotes microform acceptance.

This work gives a fairly good state-of-the-art picture of the issues involved with microform use in libraries, but does not give an in-depth look at micropublishing, the microform industry, or the historical development of microformats. For better coverage of these topics, William Saffady's *Micrographics* (Libraries Unlimited, 1978) should be consulted. [R: C&RL, Mar 79, p. 181; CLW, Oct 79, p. 140; JAL, Mar 79, p. 34]

Deborah Jane Brewer

1388. Boss, Richard W., with Deborah Raikes. **Developing Microform Reading Facilities.** Westport, Conn., Microform Review, 1981. 198p. illus. index. (Microform Review

514

Series in Library Micrographics Management, 7). $38.95. LC 81-3963. ISBN 0-913672-09-2.

The authors rightly maintain that poor planning of microform facilities contributes to microform underuse in libraries. To help, they provide brief chapters on microformats, space selection and use, equipment, and training and orientation of staff and users. Since the authors are a microforms consultant and a microforms librarian who have interviewed the librarians of about 50 microform collections in recent years, the book abounds in practical hints they have gathered from experience or from other practitioners. The training chapter, much of it adapted from the Princeton University student assistants' manual, is especially useful.

For the most part, however, the various topics are treated very sketchily. Most of the technical information provided is easily available elsewhere in more detailed and authoritative versions—especially in issues of *Library Technology Reports*. This lack of detail would be more acceptable if the text were heavily footnoted so the reader could quickly locate further information on a particular topic. This is not the case, and the bibliography at the end of the book is very general. An extreme example of the book's shortcomings is the section "Selecting Good Quality Microforms," which provides the reader with virtually no useful information. The authors merely avow that several journal articles (none cited) have been published which give guidelines for evaluating microforms (none listed), but that they feel anyone can identify good quality microforms with experience and most publishers produce excellent products anyway. The book suffers throughout from incomplete information and undocumented statements. A glaring example of careless preparation and inadequate editorial review is the full-page diagram, captioned "The Michigan State University microform area is an integral part of the 3d floor service areas," in which *no microform facilities are labeled or otherwise identified.*

This slim volume—reproduced from wide-margined, double-spaced typescript and loaded with oversized illustrations—is outrageously overpriced. While the book has value as a general introduction to the subject and a source of practical hints, it fails to meet standards of scholarly publication and does not give the purchaser his (or her) money's worth. [R: JAL, Jan 82, p. 384]   Joseph W. Palmer

1389. Diaz, Albert James, ed. **Microforms in Libraries: A Reader.** Weston, Conn., Micro-form Review, 1975. 428p. illus. bibliog. $9.95pa. LC 75-6666. ISBN 0-913672-03-3.

The difficulty with readers, no matter how well edited they be, is that inevitably they present a confused or distorted temporal picture. In the Diaz work, there are 42 reprinted articles ranging in publication dates from 1964 through 1973 or 1974. These differences introduce a disjointedness because the offerings reflect their authors' views as of critically different times. For example, the first section of Diaz contains an article on "Planning for Scholarly Photocopying" written in 1964. In 1964 no one anticipated the Williams and Wilkins case or the Pandora's box of legal, judicial, and financial problems that legal action has opened up. And yet everything relating to Williams and Wilkins is highly relevant to planning for scholarly photocopying.

Readers, of course, are not textbooks, and one category cannot be judged by the standards appropriate to the other. Textbooks written by a single author over a brief period of time can achieve coherence and avoid the disjointedness that always afflicts readers.

Readers always run the risk of presenting a picture containing numerous unconnected threads of argument and exposition. Sometimes, however, the results are more unsatisfactory than is generally the case. It is possible that in rapidly changing fields, the reader simply is not an appropriate instructional instrument to use.

The editor does try, in his introductions to sections, to integrate the readings that follow. However, I seriously question whether his efforts are successful. Finally, it should be noted that every one of the readings could have been located by a judicious use of the major bibliographic tools in our field, *Library Literature*, et al. [R: C&RL, Jan 76, p. 81; Choice, Mar 76, p. 52; JAL, Sept 76, p. 193; RQ, Winter 75, p. 183]   Richard A. Gray

1390. Fair, Judy H., ed. **Microforms Management in Special Libraries: A Reader.** Westport, Conn., Microform Review, 1979. 272p. illus. index. (Microform Review Series in Library Micrographics Management, No. 5). $21.95. LC 78-13494. ISBN 0-913672-15-7.

Divided into five sections, general and administrative information for microform management, management of microform resources, management of equipment, management of the user—microform interface, and management of COM, this reader includes 30 articles previously published in *Journal of Documentation,*

American Society for Information Science Journal, Special Libraries, Microform Review, and other periodicals and monographs, and the thirty-first article excerpted from *Law Library Journal,* which includes an annotated bibliography listing "major publications and other sources presently available for microform information" (pp. 77-87). Each section has an introduction, briefly summarizing the articles in that section and providing the reader with "Additional Readings" references. The author has gathered a comprehensive selection of articles about microforms, which provide an extensive overview of the literature in the profession and also from other related fields. Represented in this reader are microform experts such as William Saffady. An index is included. [R: JAL, July 80, p. 164]　　　　Donald D. Foos

1391. Folcarelli, Ralph J., Arthur C. Tannenbaum, and Ralph C. Ferragamo. **The Microform Connection: A Basic Guide for Libraries.** New York, R. R. Bowker, 1982. 210p. illus. bibliog. index. $39.95. LC 81-21702. ISBN 0-8352-1475-3.

Aiming to provide "basic, practical, nontechnical information on micrographic services in libraries," *The Microform Connection* is directed primarily toward librarians in small and medium-sized libraries, but also to library and information science students. As its subtitle suggests, it is a guide for the librarian who is faced with administering a microform collection, or it may serve as a textbook to support class coursework.

The book is organized into four parts. Part 1, "The Impact of Microform in the Library," provides a history of this fast-developing format, evaluates the advantages and disadvantages of establishing such collections, and discusses the basics of software and hardware. Part 2, "Building and Developing Microform Collections," summarizes what is available in microform (including serials, government documents, and special collections), and describes technical service factors such as selection, acquisition, bibliographic controls (cataloging and classification), and storage of microform materials. Part 3, "Managing and Administering Micrographic Services," considers issues such as the physical setting, staffing, financing, promoting the materials, and the COM (Computer Output Microfilm) catalogs. Part 4, "Recommendations and the Future," highlights expectations for future developments for the micropublishers, the library profession, and library managers. The guide also includes a glossary, an extensive, up-to-date bibliography, and appendixed lists of both micropublishers and micrographic associations and organizations. A concise index concludes the volume.

Use of different font size and of outline summaries throughout the book enhances its quick reference and textbook functions. This is a good, recommendable basic source of background information on all aspects of microform services. In this one volume, the authors use findings of various technical studies and report literature as appropriate, but present the topic in an easy-to-understand manner. [R: BL, Aug 82, p. 1506; JAL, May 82, pp. 111-12; SLJ, May 82, p. 32]　　　　Danuta A. Nitecki

1392. Gabriel, Michael R. **Micrographics 1900-1977: A Bibliography.** Mankato, Minn., Minnesota Scholarly Press, 1978. 266p. index. $19.00.

As the name implies, this book provides a retrospective bibliography dealing with micrographics, from the earliest literature through 1977. The work emphasizes literature dealing with the application of micrographics in libraries, but many of the citations will prove useful to persons interested in more general applications as well. Coverage is limited to English-language works and, within that scope, is not comprehensive, although the number of citations included is substantial. An author index is provided, and citations are grouped under major subject headings. This bibliography should prove useful to those researchers who are interested in the history of reprographic applications in libraries as well as to practicing librarians who are seeking case studies or state-of-the-art reports dealing with micrographics.

　　　　William Saffady

1393. Gabriel, Michael R., and Dorothy P. Ladd. **The Microform Revolution in Libraries.** Greenwich, Conn., JAI Press, 1980. 176p. illus. bibliog. index. (Foundations in Library and Information Science, Vol. 3). $47.50. LC 76-5646. ISBN 0-89232-008-7.

This volume begins with a short history of microphotography and an overview of the many types and uses of microforms and their associated materials. It does not go into the technical details of the physics and chemistry of the field. A chapter discusses computer output microfilm and the history of its library applications. This is followed by chapters on serials and monographs in microform. The serials chapter discusses why they are used, gives a list of journals published only in microform, and includes a brief discussion of the implications of copyright law and good coverage of interlibrary loan networks.

The monographs chapter includes a useful list of the major collections that are available. A chapter on microform and government publications describes the great range of materials available from NASA, ERIC, NTIS, and other agencies, and serves as a good preliminary guide to accessing this wealth of materials.

This overview fills about half of the book. The remainder includes a chapter on acquisitions, including selection and a thorough guide to the bibliographic control of microforms. There is a four-page list of publishers with addresses and a consumer's guide to purchasing reading equipment. Another chapter surveys studies which have been conducted to compare the use of microforms with hard copy. A final chapter concerns setting up a micro-facility with references to what libraries have done respecting furniture, lighting, and management.

A good glossary and an index complete the volume, which is much more than a "state-of-the-art survey." It is a good textbook and handbook for a microfilm librarian. [R: C&RL, July 80, p. 387]   David W. Brunton

1394. Hernon, Peter. **Microforms and Government Information.** Westport, Conn., Microform Review, 1981. 287p. bibliog. index. (Microform Review Series in Library Micrographics Management, 6). $29.95. LC 81-4393. ISBN 0-913672-12-2.

While this book emphasizes the increasing and significant role of microforms in government publishing, it also deals on a broader level with bibliographic control, collection development, and user patterns of government publications regardless of format, and with the U.S. government depository library system. There are separate chapters on the Government Printing Office micropublishing program; the National Technical Information Service micropublishing program; state government publications in microform; and local documents in microform. These surveys provide historical background, status, issues and problems, and future trends. The last three of these chapters were contributed by experts in those areas: Gary R. Purcell, Terry L. Weech, and Michael Owen Shannon. The treatment is uniformly excellent. A chapter is also provided by Charles R. McClure on administrative basics for the effective organization and operation of the documents service in general, and the microform collection in particular.

The book is significant since the author, in his broad discussion of bibliographic control, collection development, and user patterns, adopts a philosophical viewpoint and presents controversial doctrine not found in the existing literature of documents librarianship. He criticizes the "vacuum cleaner" philosophy, which is standard doctrine for not only comprehensive bibliographic control of, but also comprehensive collecting of, government documents. He advocates a more critical selectivity not only in collection development but in bibliographic control as well. The author also offers an alternative organizational structure for the U.S. government depository library system based on four levels of service. The value of the book is enhanced by the excellent selection of references which follow each of the 11 chapters. [R: LJ, Aug 82, p. 1390]   LeRoy C. Schwarzkopf

1395. Reichmann, Felix, and Josephine M. Tharpe. **Bibliographic Control of Microforms.** Sponsored by the Association of Research Libraries under contract with the Office of Education. Westport, Conn., Greenwood Press, 1972. 256p. bibliog. index. $27.50. LC 72-2463. ISBN 0-8371-6423-9.

In 1971 Allen Veaner published a handbook, *The Evaluation of Micropublications*, which was originally conceived solely as a manual for the reviewers of *Choice* (see *ARBA* 72, entry 83). This work, much larger in scope and detail, covers the whole spectrum of bibliographical control of micropublications, with a well-selected bibliography in the appendix. The book consists of four chapters that report the findings of a survey based on existing literature on this subject, the results of a questionnaire, and personal experience of the authors. The remainder (actually a major portion) of the book is made up of four appendices that cover government publishing, machine-readable indexes, American university presses that plan to publish microforms, and a microform bibliography. [R: C&RL, July 73, p. 321; LJ, 1 June 73, p. 1790]

1396. Saffady, William. **Computer-Output Microfilm: Its Library Applications.** Chicago, American Library Association, 1978. 190p. illus. bibliog. $12.00pa. LC 78-18416. ISBN 0-8389-3217-7.

Well organized, readable, and library-oriented, this compact report provides useful and up-to-date information on existing and potential library uses of computer-output microfilm (COM). Its logical, factual format makes it a valuable resource for administrator, system designer, or student—anyone with an interest in and need to know more about COM. From the six-page glossary to the appended bibliographies, it provides data, comparative figures, formulae for determining COM costs, relevant standards, equipment specifications, suppliers' and manufacturers' addresses, along with many pages of thoughtful commentary on library applications of this technology. Anyone considering adopting a COM system, or more important, anyone who has not considered COM as an alternative to online or line printer output cannot afford to be without it. [R: LJ, 15 Dec 78, p. 2495]   Pauline V. Angione

1397. Saffady, William. **Micrographics.** Littleton, Colo., Libraries Unlimited, 1978. 238p. bibliog. index. (Library Science Text Series). $28.00. LC 78-1309. ISBN 0-87287-175-4.

This introductory textbook is designed for practicing librarians and library school students who want a systematic presentation of the basic facets of micrographics as applied to library work. The first chapter introduces the topic of microforms and libraries, presenting an overview of major areas of application. The subsequent eight chapters discuss types of microforms and their uses; microfilm production and duplication; computer-output microfilm (COM); micropublishing; the use of microforms in the library, including types of readers and reader/printers; bibliographic control of microforms; microform storage and retrieval systems; and a look at the future of micrographics in the library. Numerous illustrations and photographs accompany the text, and extensive references conclude each chapter. A six-page glossary defines essential terms used throughout the book. A 10-page selected bibliography on library applications of micrographics and a detailed index round out the work. The second edition of this work was published in 1985. [R: C&RL, Nov 78, p. 497; LJ, 15 Nov 78, p. 2318]

1398. Smith, Charles. **Micrographics Handbook.** Dedham, Mass., Artech House, 1978. 297p. illus. index. $20.00. LC 78-2561. ISBN 0-89006-061-4.

Providing a useful guide to the application and production of microforms, the *Micrographics Handbook* begins with a brief history of micrographics and proceeds with a discussion of the various available microforms, their production, and utility in various applications. The book contains much useful information on production equipment and methodologies and is illustrated with well-selected photographs and line drawings. An appendix provides information about typical microfilm supply costs, reduction ratios, microform storage capacities,

and forms used in the microfilm production activity. [R: Choice, Feb 79, p. 1696]
William Saffady

1399. Teague, S. J. **Microform Librarianship.** 2nd ed. Woburn, Mass., Butterworths, 1979. 125p. illus. index. $29.95. LC 78-41090. ISBN 0-408-70930-8.

This second edition of Teague's brief introduction to microfilm librarianship updates a number of sources of equipment and microforms. The information on copyright is also updated, although the hearings of CONTU are not noted. Information on development in Great Britain, and British sources of microform and microform research will be of interest to American readers. This book is useful as an introduction to the various aspects of using microforms in libraries, covering content areas similar to those found in the first edition (see *ARBA* 79, entry 335). The bibliographic references will guide readers to more detailed reports and research on the various topics discussed. [R: SL, May 80, p. 288]   Kieth C. Wright

1400. Veaner, Allen B. **The Evaluation of Micropublications: A Handbook for Librarians.** Chicago, American Library Association, Library Technology Program, 1971. 72p. illus. index. (LTP Publication, No. 17). $5.00pa. LC 73-138700. SBN 8389-3128-6.

As indicated in the preface, this handbook was originally conceived solely as a manual for the reviewers for *Choice*; it has been somewhat modified in order to make it suitable for distribution to the library profession at large. The handbook covers all important aspects of micropublications, except their subject content. The material is arranged under two major sections: micropublishing and micropublications, and evaluation procedures. The first section offers general background about the industry, including such topics as the registration and preservation of master films, locating original material, production of hard copies, etc. In the second part Veaner offers a number of specific guidelines to evaluate micropublications, discussing among other things such topics as physical inspection of microforms, laboratory inspection, viewer inspection, etc. A selective bibliography and a subject index are appended to this handy and well-balanced little handbook. One comment might be in order: as any librarian working with micropublications well knows, one of the most important problems is the problem of bibliographical control. Unfortunately, the reader will find practically nothing here on this topic; it seems to us that even brief information on this subject might be helpful. For example, we have a number of selection tools, reliable and not so reliable, catalogs or *Microform Review*. Some of these are produced simply for the promotion of certain products and should be used with caution. It would be helpful, especially for an inexperienced librarian, to have some assistance in this matter. [R: AL, Nov 71, p. 1114; LJ, 1 Dec 71, p. 3990; WLB, Oct 71, p. 194]   Bohdan S. Wynar

1401. Williams, Bernard J. S. **Miniaturised Communications: A Review of Microforms.** London, Library Association; distr., Portland, Oreg., International Scholarly Book Services, 1970. index. o.p. SBN 85365-112-4.

This outstanding volume is truly international in coverage. The author deals with troublesome issues such as copyright, standardization (country by country), use studies, surveys of products and systems, performance characteristics, and customer service. Original and retrospective publication are covered in depth. Chapter titles are (1) "The Terminology of Microreproduction," (2) "Some Historical Sources," (3) "Microform Formats and Materials," (4) "Library Microtext Systems," (5) "Original Publication on Microform," (6) "Information Retrieval," (7) "Evaluation of Library Microform Hardware," (8) "Standardisation." Appendix 1 is a glossary of terms used in the text. Appendix 2 is a list of sources. The indexes are by author, name and trade name, and subject. [R: LRTS, Winter 72, p. 116]

Don Roberts

47 Networking and Resource Sharing

GENERAL WORKS

1402. **The ASLA Report on Interlibrary Co-operation, 1978.** 2nd ed. Compiled and edited by the ASLA Interlibrary Cooperation Committee. Chicago, Association of State Library Agencies, a division of the American Library Association, 1978. 446p. index. $12.50pa. LC 77-94411. ISBN 0-8389-5539-8.

The first edition of this work, reviewed in *ARBA* 77 (entry 173) was well received, and this edition is even better. The material on each state and territory averages 4½ pages and describes their cooperative activities. Listings of multistate networks (numbers of libraries by state and city), the unit in each state responsible for interlibrary cooperation, the number and sources of funding of cooperative programs in each state, and a detailed index add to the utility of this book. Improvements in this edition include a section providing an overview of the state's cooperative activities, the name and address of each person administering a cooperative program, and more complete information on multistate activities. This is the most comprehensive single source of information on library cooperation. [R: LJ, 1 Feb 79, p. 360]

G. Edward Evans

1403. Association of Research Libraries. **Access to Periodical Resources: A National Plan.** By Vernon E. Palmour, Marcia C. Bellassai, and Lucy M. Gray. Washington, D.C., Westat, Inc., for ARL, 1974. 171p. o.p.

The objective of this study was to outline specific requirements for the long-range improvement of the interlibrary loan system. The authors recommend the establishment of a single new national center for acquiring, storing, and lending periodical materials. Three alternatives were compared before this conclusion was reached: a single facility; a multilocation system, with a number of satellite resource centers and a new national center to serve as the major resource; and a regional network based on existing library collections. Demand and cost estimates were projected for each of these alternatives. [R: AL, Sept 74, p. 414; LJ, 1 Oct 74, p. 2455]

1404. Association of Research Libraries. **A System for Inter-Library Communication (SILC).** By Robert M. Hayes. Washington, D.C., Becker and Hayes, Inc., for ARL, 1974. 311p. o.p.

The purpose of this study was to develop data for evaluating the feasibility of using commercial time-sharing computer systems for communicating, accounting, message switching, and referral for interlibrary loan requests. The results are reported in terms of technical feasibility, operational feasibility, management feasibility, and economic feasibility. SILC, it was projected, can handle six million requests during the first five-year period, at a cost package of $1.5 million. [R: AL, Sept 74, p. 414; LJ, 1 Oct 74, p. 2455]

1405. Buchinski, Edwin J. **Initial Considerations for a Nationwide Data Base.** Edited and revised by Henriette D. Avram, and Sally H. McCallum. Washington, D.C., Library of Congress, 1978. 56p. (Network Planning Paper, No. 3). o.p. ISSN 0160-9742.

This report summarizes the results of Phase I of a broader study to determine the role of authority files in the creation of a national library database. Phase I, funded by NCLIS in

1976, concentrated on the library aspects of bibliographic control. It identified problems needing investigation and recommended 19 tasks required to perform the investigations. The tasks are divided into the following three categories: (1) background data, (2) network configuration, (3) authority system design. Phase II, the carrying out of the tasks identified in Phase I, was designed to address the configuration of the national database to include authority, bibliographic, and location files. The report also includes a summary of the tasks, a glossary of terms, a list of abbreviations, and a bibliography. It will be of use to both library school educators and practitioners.

Readers may wish to examine other reports in the series. These are: No. 1, *A Nationwide Location Data Base and Service* (Brett Butler, 1978); No. 2, *A Glossary for Library Networking* (Dataflow Systems, 1978); No. 4, *Message Delivery System for the National Library and Information Service Network, General Requirements* (Network Technical Architecture Group, 1978); No. 5, *Study of Message Text Formats: Bibliographic Search Queries* (Philip L. Long, 1979). Andrew G. Torok

1406. **Cooperative Services: A Guide to Policies and Procedures in Library Systems.** Helen A. Knievel, ed. New York, Neal-Schuman, 1982. 300p. index. $34.95. LC 81-22406. ISBN 0-918212-56-1.

This volume, containing a 14-page summary of a one-page survey of 84 library systems plus selected policy statements on administration and services, is a grim reminder that not all cooperative library ventures are networks characterized by what Brett Butler termed in 1975 a "dependent organization or system providing duplex digital distribution." Without an explanation of how the 100 systems asked to participate in the survey were selected, the summary data on population of service area, budget, per capita support, and so on are relatively meaningless. Populations range from 18,000 to 4.5 million, with 14 over 1 million and 58 under 500,000. All 84 systems provide services to public libraries, 39 to academic, 38 to school, and 31 to special libraries. Only about 12 systems use computer technology, mainly OCLC, and that on a limited basis.

Policies dealing with system administration occupy about 175 pages, and statements of services under 100. The service statements are reminiscent of cooperative activities found in inventories of library cooperation and resource sharing in the 1960s and early 1970s. They hardly serve as examples to follow. Some of the

administrative policy statements, such as that from the Nassau Library System in Uniondale, New York, occupying more than 30 pages, might be more relevant for those looking for guidance in system operations. The volume contains little useful information for those hoping to find guidelines for development of library systems. The reports on cooperative library systems published by the Association of Specialized and Cooperative Library Agencies (American Library Association) provide more information and suggest which systems are worthy of study. [R: JAL, Mar 83, p. 48; RQ, Spring 83, pp. 318-19]

JoAnn V. Rogers

1407. Gregory, Ruth W., and Lester L. Stoffel. **Public Libraries in Cooperative Systems: Administrative Patterns for Service.** Chicago, American Library Association, 1971. 315p. index. o.p. LC 78-172295. ISBN 0-8389-0110-7.

According to the preface, "this book was written as an introduction to the administrative relationships between small and medium-sized public libraries and the cooperative library system." The eight chapters cover, among other things, such topics as patterns of responsibility and interrelations, capital improvements, administrative responsibilities, collection building and maintenance, and continuing education for librarianship. The authors emphasize the basic principles which preserve the autonomy of the member library and ensure its involvement in the productive evaluation and effective use of system services. The appendices contain several examples of documents, such as bylaws of a system, illustrative workshop material, and a sample system reference request form. There is a selected bibliography covering 1960 to 1970. This work should be of interest to all library administrators and consultants. [R: LJ, 15 May 72, p. 1787]

1408. Hamilton, Beth A., and William B. Ernst, Jr., eds. **Multitype Library Cooperation.** New York, R. R. Bowker, 1977. 216p. bibliog. index. o.p. LC 77-24092. ISBN 0-8352-0980-6.

The possibility for library cooperation has been discussed since the beginning of this century. The advantages of a union catalog of periodicals and of collective book acquisition and cataloging make the formation of cooperative library networks urgent in the face of inflation and budgetary restrictions. Existing networks that are geographically bound often embrace various types of libraries. This multitype library network has been given greater impetus by federal financial encouragement through

LSCA Title III, and by state governments and private foundations.

This volume, mainly based on papers first presented at the ALA Centennial Conference in 1976, explores both philosophically and in particular cases the various aspects of these multitype networks, some libraries of which are run by public or private funds, and serving public schools, the general public, colleges and universities or, in the case of many special libraries, serving the needs of profit-oriented organizations.

This book is composed of four sections. Section 1 describes and examines the multitype network. Section 2 addresses itself to the various units of organization: federal, multistate, state or nodal. Section 3 deals with individual networks as case studies. Section 4 covers the potential for future growth. Section 3 is of particular value, for the problems and limitations of cooperation are faced squarely and ways in which these are either mitigated or balanced by advantages are discussed for the school library, the large and small academic libraries, and the special library.

There are two minor flaws: the index does not indicate that two METRO cooperatives are discussed, one in Colorado and the other in New York; also there is no key to acronyms. The generally excellent index, however, does cite the full name of those acronyms referred to in the text, and the useful annotated bibliography at the end includes an inexpensive network acronym dictionary, with instructions for ordering. This book will make a fine contribution to the important subject it covers. [R: AL, Jan 78, p. 49; BL, 15 Feb 78, p. 979; C&RL, Mar 78, p. 150; JAL, May 78, p. 96; LJ, 1 Mar 78, p. 526]
Dorothy E. Litt

1409. Markuson, Barbara Evans, and Blanche Woolls, eds. **Networks for Networkers: Critical Issues in Cooperative Library Development.** New York, Neal-Schuman, 1980. 444p. index. $27.95. LC 79-24054. ISBN 0-918212-22-7.

With an impressive array of practical and very useful information on library networks, Barbara Evans Markuson and Blanche Woolls, as editors of an invaluable compendium, have provided the library and information science community with basic information on networks as a mechanism for connecting libraries to foster and expedite information sharing. The 19 papers in this collection were delivered at a national conference of library users, librarians, and administrators from all types of libraries assembled in Indianapolis, Indiana in 1979. The authors of the papers are considered leaders in

this field and were described by Markuson in her introduction as representing "the professional stakeholders in network development."

The volume is divided into five parts: "The Network Revolution," "National Policy and Network Development," "Network Technology and Standards," "Network Governance and Funding," and "Network Users and Services." Of special reference value are the appendices, which include critical issues submitted by conference participants; a summary of a debate between Roderick G. Swartz and Glyn T. Evans on whether or not state-level networking should evolve principally from the state library agency rather than the cooperatively governed member library network information on federal information agencies and networks; a compilation of official resolutions related to network issues adopted by delegates at the Pre-White House Conference on Libraries and Information Services; and a glossary and list of acronyms for library networking.

While there are inherent dangers in networking, Markuson admonishes that "many people suppose that the greatest threat to networking will come from new technologies such as minicomputers with extraordinary memory capabilities, from videodiscs on which whole libraries of information can be stored ..., but it is difficult to see how they would be competitive with two major network benefits: access to millions and millions of holdings in other libraries and sharing of human labor through input to a common data base."

This volume should be read not only by directors of library systems, consortia, and the library utilities, but should also be carefully studied by librarians in public, school, college and university, research, and special libraries that are involved in networks. Speaking optimistically about networking and its benefits for the future, R. Kathleen Molz suggested at the conference that "networking and the wiring of our society may indeed eradicate these rivalries and enable the nation to govern itself in its third century with greater cohesion and less separatism." This volume is highly recommended and should be in all types of libraries. [R: BL, 15 Oct 80, p. 304; LJ, 1 Nov 80, p. 2044]
E. J. Josey

1410. Martin, Susan K. **Library Networks, 1981-82.** White Plains, N.Y., Knowledge Industry Publications, 1981. 159p. bibliog. index. (The Professional Librarian Series). $29.50; $24.50pa. LC 80-26710. ISBN 0-914236-55-5; 0-914236-66-0pa.

The first edition, *Library Networks, 1974-75*, was reviewed in *ARBA* 75 (entry 139); the volume for 1976-77 was reviewed in *ARBA* 77 (entry 161). There is also a volume for 1978-1979. To contribute to librarians' understanding of the jigsaw puzzle of evolving library networks at local, regional, and national levels is the mission of this volume. The author not only provides an extensive directory of 22 networks and their member libraries, but discusses the role and scope of networks in enlarging information services to the nation; the implications of machine-readable data for improved access to information; the services of computer utilities such as OCLC, RLIN, UTLAS, and WLN; the nature of network organizations; the variety of suppliers of network data; the range of issues and problems confronting library administrators who are considering involvement with networks, and the specific steps that need to be taken for successful implementation of network affiliations.

The merger of traditional library functions with advanced technological procedures—many of which continue to change at a rapid rate—requires more expertise than is possessed by most library managers. This volume, therefore, which includes a useful glossary, bibliography, and index, will help managers, librarians, and library school students understand the multiplicity of networks that exist and prepare for the increasing interaction with networks that will characterize library practice in the coming decade. A valuable reference work. [R: C&RL, July 81, pp. 384-86]   Richard Palmer

1411. Patrick, Ruth J. **Guidelines for Library Cooperation: Development of Academic Library Consortia.** Santa Monica, Calif., System Development Corp., 1972. 220p. illus. bibliog. o.p.

The basic purpose of the study, conducted by System Development Corporation, was to develop a fund of descriptive and prescriptive information about activities of academic library consortia in the United States. The study was carried out in two phases. Phase 1 consisted of two questionnaire surveys, whose results were published under the title *Directory of Academic Library Consortia* (1972). Phase 2 involved a case study analysis of 15 selected library consortia, using field interviews. [R: C&RL, Mar 73, p. 164]

1412. Patrick, Ruth J., Joseph Casey, and Carol M. Novalis. **A Study of Library Cooperatives, Networks, and Demonstration Projects.**

Munich, New York, K. G. Saur, 1980. 2v. bibliog. $42.50/set. LC 79-20231. ISBN 0-89664-313-1.

A 1978 evaluation of the impact and effectiveness of two federally funded programs—Library Research & Demonstration (HEA Title II-B) and Interlibrary Cooperation (LSCA Title III)—is summarized in these two volumes. This study was the first comprehensive evaluation of either program. Its purpose is to provide a "body of evaluation information of immediate value to policymakers and program managers at all levels" by addressing three objectives: (1) to determine the extent to which each program accomplished its objectives; (2) to identify the factors contributing to the success or failure of each program; and (3) to recommend possible postures in federal policy affecting each program. Although a separate methodology was designed to evaluate each program, both incorporated an extensive review of legislation and literature, interviews, telephone and mail surveys of persons involved with specific funded projects, and detailed case studies.

Volume 1 summarizes the findings and recommendations of the study, treating each program separately and concluding with a section on the future direction for federal policy in library cooperation and networks, and in library research and demonstration. Volume 2 reports the findings of the 22 case studies examined; 12 projects sponsored by the HEA II-B program and 10 states using LSCA III funds are reviewed.

The well-written, detailed findings are effectively presented using varied typography to identify background information, descriptions, and specific recommendations. A useful glossary and list of selected references contribute to the reference use of the study. This is an excellent source of material for any student of library development and especially library cooperation and networking occurring during a 15-year period. It also is a good example of much-needed evaluative methodology to review development programs and to provide substantiated arguments for continuing, while also improving, federal support of library activities. [R: JAL, Nov 80, pp. 293-95; LJ, July 80, p. 1492]
                              Danuta A. Nitecki

1413. Reynolds, Michael M., ed. **Reader in Library Cooperation.** Washington, D.C., NCR/Microcard Editions, 1972. 398p. (Reader Series in Library and Information Science). o.p. LC 72-86635. ISBN 0-910972-22-2.

Similar in structure to other volumes in this series, it offers 39 articles on various aspects of library cooperation. The four main parts cover theory, state of the art (24 articles), future directions, and "the nature of systems." [R: LJ, 15 Oct 73, p. 2982]

1414. The Role of the School Library Media Program in Networking. Washington, D.C., Task Force on the Role of the School Library Media Program in the National Program, National Commission on Libraries and Information Science; distr., Washington, D.C., GPO, 1978. 91p. bibliog. o.p. S/N 052-003-00622-7.

This document was produced by a task force of eight district-level coordinators, four state school library supervisors, a building-level professional, and two professors of library science, with several NCLIS members and the executive secretary of AASL acting as resource staff. It attempts to define the potential role of the school library media specialists and school media program in a national resource sharing network. The well-organized paper covers rationale for inclusion of schools, potential contributions of school libraries, benefits, problems, and recommendations. Based on two position papers, the report, omitting state-of-the-art information, concentrates on immediate (within two years), intermediate (three to five years), and long-range recommendations. With each recommendation suggested, action agencies are included. The single long-range goal is to have "library networks in which school library media programs are full participating members ... in every region, state and area in the nation."

Contributions and benefits are outlined in clear, simple language, with good concrete examples. Introducing the recommendations are some very basic principles, such as "networking is not free," which could have been expanded for the benefit of school media people who have not been immersed in the literature of networking and have not participated in any great numbers in the many professional meetings about networks. Also missing is a bibliography for further reading.

Recommendations are grouped in a problem-solving pattern and begin with those designed to overcome psychological factors that inhibit cooperation. They include items such as the establishment of an information clearinghouse by AASL and the identification of materials and services that school libraries could contribute to network activities by media specialists. Political and legal factors, funding, communication, and planning are then con-

sidered in the same way. The structure of the document itself aids in an understanding of networking, and many of the recommendations are well expressed and important. Unfortunately, there seems to be an overemphasis on the role of some national agencies, especially AASL. Why, for example, should AASL establish an information clearinghouse when ERIC is already functioning and funded for these efforts?

A very short list of state, regional, and districtwide, full-service networks and specialized networks doing acquisitions, cataloging, film evaluation, etc., is appended. In general, this is a clear, uncluttered statement of the possible role for school libraries and should be available to all people involved with schools and libraries. With the exception of a few problems mentioned, this document is an important overview for school media people and others who should aid in the integration of schools in existing and developing networks.

JoAnn V. Rogers

1415. Rouse, William B., and Sandra H. Rouse. Management of Library Networks: Policy Analysis, Implementation, and Control. New York, Wiley Interscience, 1980. 288p. bibliog. index. (Information Science Series). $45.95. LC 80-12644. ISBN 0-471-05534-4.

The Rouses (or perhaps Wiley) have mistitled this treatise on the use of mathematical modeling in the analysis of interlibrary loan. Using their combined backgrounds of systems engineering and information science, William and Sandra Rouse have used the mathematical modeling approach to study the flow of ILL requests to ILLINET (Illinois Library and Information Network), used graph theory to compare routing policies for ILL with respect to probability of fulfillment, cost, and turnaround time, presented three case studies, and talked generally about library networks and management issues and the role mathematical modeling plays in relation to them.

The authors make several convincing arguments for the help of mathematical modeling in examining a library network's performance. First, it facilitates the study of the situation and forces those examining the system to think more logically and question certain aspects that may otherwise have been glossed over. Second, it helps to evaluate the system and even predict "average" results. The third, more nebulous, advantage is the strong political use of "hard" data. Facts and figures can always help to support an otherwise controversial system. In this regard, the political and legal aspects of library networks can be affected and their implications examined.

Mathematical analysis is not a new idea in library science, but its use in the type of cases and examples the Rouses have looked at may finally lead to such ideas being implemented in actual management situations. [R: JAL, July 81, p. 176; LJ, 15 Apr 81, p. 863]

Daniel F. Phelan

1416. Wareham, Nancy L., comp. and ed. **The Report on Library Cooperation 1982.** 4th ed. Chicago, Association of Specialized and Cooperative Library Agencies/American Library Association, 1982. 466p. index. o.p. LC 80-67287. ISBN 0-8389-6540-7.

A unique source of broad coverage for information pertaining to library cooperative activities in the United States, this edition of *The Report on Library Cooperation* profiles cooperative activities of libraries in 46 states, the District of Columbia, and the Virgin Islands. States that did not respond to a request for information were Alaska, North Dakota, Arkansas, and Oregon.

Arranged alphabetically by state, the profiles of cooperative activities include the following information: a brief directory/identification section on the reporting agency, an overview of the status and scope of library cooperation for the state, and, included in this latter section, a description of the level of participation of various types of libraries and any major developments.

If the reporting agency has a specific unit whose sole responsibility is the coordination of library cooperation, this is indicated. In addition, other governmental agencies or units, as well as nongovernmental organizations involved in cooperative activities, are identified. Sections profiling single-type library cooperatives and multitype library cooperatives provide the following facts for each activity: name, address, telephone number, name of administrator, type and number of libraries served, and source and amount of federal, state, local, and/or other support for the activity.

Also included are a matrix regarding library cooperative support and funding and a profile of statewide communication devices and statewide service networks. Profiles of multistate networks (indicating name of network, financial support, level of participation, and services) follow, concluding with a matrix of local, regional, state, and multistate cooperative programs and services. Ten appendices present summary data in tabular format.

A valuable compendium of information on cooperative ventures, this report should serve as a handy directory, guide, and inspiration for library administrators and planners throughout the country. For those who can read between the lines, it will also serve as an indicator of future needs and directions of library services. The fifth edition was published in 1984 (474p.; $25.00; $22.50 members; ISBN 0-318-12142-5).

Edmund F. SantaVicca

REFERENCE WORKS

1417. **Directory of Library Networks and Cooperative Library Organizations, 1980.** By Helen M. Eckard. Washington, D.C., National Center for Education Statistics; distr., Washington, D.C., GPO, 1980. 181p. index. (NCES 80-226). $6.00pa. S/N 065-000-00039-3.

Although listed as the 1980 edition, this directory reports results of a survey conducted by the National Center for Education Statistics between 1976 and 1979. Claimed to be the first national survey of cooperative library organizations, it gathered information on organization name (acronym), address, name and title of director, telephone and teletype numbers, operational year, whether computerized, frequency of operation, number of paid staff, and annual operating cost. Criteria for entry in the directory are that each organization (1) is composed primarily of library participants, (2) has cooperative activities beyond the scope of traditional ILL, (3) extends its activities beyond reciprocal borrowing, (4) operates for mutual benefits of its participants, and (5) has an interinstitutional scope.

The directory is composed of a main listing of the general profiles of the 608 organizations qualified for inclusion, and three indexes, one each arranged by state, by acronym, and by activity. The headings in the main body are not easy to locate because they are not typographically distinguished and are located on the inside rather than on the outer edge of each page. Since no organizational requirements were among the criteria for inclusion, the directory includes organizations with staff and budgets as well as those without much administrative structure. The reliance on participants' responses and the lack of preselected subject headings for the activities index may explain the exclusion of known examples under key terms such as "resource sharing," "delivery service," or "book mobile." Without being able to verify each entry, one can only sense the inconsistent level of completion among the entries listed.

Despite some of its technical limitations, the directory serves the purpose of uniquely listing a group of cooperative organizations. No other directory could be found with the same specific focus, yet broad coverage. Networks, consortia, and other cooperative library organizations are listed in a small section of the *American Library Directory*, in Martin's *Library Networks 1978-79* (Knowledge Industry Publications, 1978), in Delanoy and Cuadra's *Directory of Academic Library Consortia*, and in Kruzas and Sullivan's *Encyclopedia of Information Systems and Services* (3rd ed., Gale, 1978). Recommended for those who need information about this specialized category of organization, although it may not be essential for those needing access to the major institutions found listed in other more widely available tools. [R: BL, 15 Feb 81, p. 800]

Danuta A. Nitecki

1418.   Stenstrom, Ralph H. **Cooperation between Types of Libraries, 1940-1968: An Annotated Bibliography.** Chicago, American Library Association, 1970. 157p. index. o.p. LC 71-140212. SBN 8389-0094-1.

The entries are arranged chronologically, first by year, then by season or month, "to enable users interested in most recent developments to turn directly to such entries." A total of 383 entries is included, covering conventional library sources. Annotations are long and well done, and they describe in concise terms the contents of the material. Some attempt was made to include foreign materials, such as British, but obviously, since the author was limited primarily to *Library Literature*, his results are not very impressive in this area. In general, however, this is a useful compilation, with a good index and interesting information about interlibrary cooperation in individual states, gathered through correspondence. [R: RQ, Summer 71, p. 364; WLB, May 71, p. 885]

PROCEEDINGS, SYMPOSIA, AND ESSAYS

1419.   **Conference on Interlibrary Communications and Information Networks, Warrenton, Va., 1970. Proceedings.** Joseph Becker, ed. Sponsored by the American Library Association and the U.S. Office of Education, Bureau of Libraries and Educational Technology, held at Airlie House, Warrenton, Virginia, September 28, 1970 – October 2, 1970. Chicago, American

Library Association, 1971. 347p. illus. bibliog. o.p. LC 70-185963. ISBN 0-8389-3123-5.

A study conference of 125 invited participants whose "aim was to explore and study the implications that would follow if a network of libraries and information centers were established in the United States." Thirty-one special papers were commissioned as source material and were then used as the jump-off point to explore the potential and the implications of information networks. The conference was organized into five working groups: network needs and development, network services, network technology, network organization, and network planning. The proceedings have also been organized according to those aspects and cover the subject of networking from many different approaches. Some of the areas covered include interlibrary cooperation, bibliographic and reference services, telecommunications technology, legal and financial considerations, network structure, copyright, and social implications. A very extensive bibliography has been given. Unfortunately, no index has been included, nor has a list of participants been provided. [R: C&RL, Sept 72, p. 418; LJ, 1 Sept 72, p. 2703]

Donald P. Hammer

1420.   Gibson, Robert W., Jr., ed. **The Special Library Role in Networks: A Conference Held at the General Motors Research Laboratories, Warren, Michigan, May 5-6, 1980.** New York, Special Libraries Association, 1980. 296p. $10.50 spiralbound. ISBN 0-87111-279-5. (Available from Books on Demand, $76.50pa., ISBN 0-317-30408-9).

Contained in this volume are the proceedings of a conference held in 1980 to describe and analyze the participation of special libraries in formal networks. Seventeen papers by distinguished librarians, along with transcripts of the taped discussions that followed the presentation of papers, are included. The two-day meeting was divided into four parts: session 1, moderated by Lorraine Kulpa, General Motors legal staff; session 2, moderated by Mark H. Baer, Hewlett-Packard Co.; session 3, moderated by Aphrodite Mamoulides, Shell Development Co.; and session 4, moderated by George H. Ginader, Morgan Stanley & Co. Shirley Echelman of the Medical Library Association presented the conference wrap-up. A listing of the 112 librarians who attended the meeting is appended.

This book presents a good look at how special libraries use and contribute to cooperative networks of various types. While most of the discussions were limited to networks in the United States, speakers also dealt with Exxon's international network of information centers, the Textile Information Users Council, the International Road Research Documentation System, and the gamut of networking activities in Canadian special libraries.

As is true of practically any conference, the contributed papers are not of uniformly high quality. Some are far more informative than others. Also, the editing could have been much tighter, since there are too many typographical errors. On the whole, however, this publication is very worthwhile and deserves to be widely read. [R: JAL, May 81, p. 111]

Leonard Grundt

1421. Kent, Allen, ed. **Resource Sharing in Libraries.** New York, Marcel Dekker, 1974. 393p. bibliog. index. (Books in Library and Information Science, Vol. 8). o.p. LC 73-90724. ISBN 0-8247-6130-8. (Available from Books on Demand, $101.30pa., ISBN 0-317-07889-5).

With the publication of this book, Allen Kent strikes a significant blow for cooperative acquisitions; considering its cost, its purchase should appropriately be limited. Basically this book consists of papers presented at a conference held at the University of Pittsburgh on 11-12 April 1973. It presents the rationale behind resource sharing, the mechanics involved, a section stressing the need for immediate action, and some individual perspectives. Unfortunately, it suffers from the usual deficiencies to be found in published proceedings. Papers overlap (with a resulting redundancy of information), presentations are uneven, and the thrust is not clearly defined. This is not to say that the book is without merit. It does bring together a significant amount of information, particularly in the area of technology. But its overall usefulness is limited both by its narrow geographic emphasis on libraries in Pennsylvania, and its preoccupation with problems concerning academic and research libraries at a time when many cooperative efforts are concerned with the development of intertype programs. [R: LJ, 1 Nov 74, p. 2823]

Marilyn Gell

1422. Kent, Allen, and Thomas J. Galvin. **Library Resource Sharing: Proceedings of the 1976 Conference on Resource Sharing in Libraries, Pittsburgh, Pennsylvania.** New York, Marcel Dekker, 1977. 356p. index. (Books in Library and Information Science, Vol. 21). o.p. LC 77-5399. ISBN 0-8247-6605-9.

This compilation of papers and transcriptions of discussions records an important conference on the development of library networks. Approximately 350 librarians, students, information scientists, and others from all over the United States, Canada, England, and Switzerland participated in what has become a significant sharing of viewpoints and problems by nationally known library leaders.

The basic papers, which address the long-range goals of resource sharing, progress toward these goals, problems needing attention, the economics of libraries and networks, and performance criteria for the design and evaluation of networks, are excellent background reading for anyone interested in networking. Also included are papers on policy issues relating to the communications required for resource sharing and on areas needing research attention. *Library Resource Sharing* should be required reading for library administrators, trustees, and directors and should be available to all persons who have a stake in the future of library resource sharing. [R: LQ, Apr 79, p. 201]

Sara R. Mack

1423. Kent, Allen, and Thomas J. Galvin. **The Structure and Governance of Library Networks: Proceedings of the 1978 Conference in Pittsburgh, Pennsylvania, Co-sponsored by National Commission on Libraries and Information Science and University of Pittsburgh.** New York, Marcel Dekker, 1979. 352p. index. (Books in Library and Information Science, Vol. 27). o.p. LC 79-12704. ISBN 0-8247-6866-3.

The National Commission on Libraries and Information Science co-sponsored this 1978 Pittsburgh conference as a forum for identifying and clarifying one of the central concerns of the White House conference scheduled for the fall of 1979. The Pittsburgh pre-White House conference was attended by about 500 persons from many branches of the library and information community, from the public and the private sectors. The agenda included network anatomy and network objectives; functions of existing networks; impact of technology; and the governance of library networks—purposes and expectations, and alternatives for the future.

There were position papers prepared in advance, papers presented at the conference, and discussion sessions. Many of the contributors are authorities in their respective fields; it is therefore not surprising that most of the contributions were of very high caliber. The result of this interplay of ideas between people of various backgrounds and perspectives was a comprehensive picture showing a variety of channels that may lead to a national library network. Of the items discussed, we shall single out a few that elicited particularly strong interest:

definition and scope of "network"; symmetrical versus asymmetrical relationships; inclusion of children's and popular libraries in the network structure; technological advances (e.g., new information relationships may eliminate libraries as intermediaries between publisher and user); the human factor in technology; barriers to networking; standards; use of methods developed for the governance of already existing networks, such as OCLC, in shaping the governance for a broad-based national network; and—probably the most controversial issue—the character and legal form of the agency which would govern (or coordinate) the nationwide library network.

These proceedings can be consulted with profit by anyone who seeks an understanding of the concept of networking, of networking as it functions in our country, and of networking as it may emerge on a nationwide scale. [R: BL, 15 Oct 79, pp. 329-30]   Fritz Veit

1424.   Matzek, Richard A., ed. **Network Concepts: Four Points of View.** (Proceedings of the April 1, 1970, Meeting of the College and University Libraries Section, Catholic Library Association, Boston). Haverford, Pa., Catholic Library Association, 1971. o.p.

Views expressed by well-known authorities at the meeting of the College and University Section of the Catholic Library Association in Boston in April 1970. Presented in layperson's language are remarks concerning networking by Carlos Cuadra, Henriette Avram, Sam Goldstein, Donald E. Vincent, and Robert S. Taylor. [R: LJ, July 71, p. 2280]

Charles D. Patterson

INTERLIBRARY LOAN

1425.   Association of Research Libraries. **Methods of Financing Interlibrary Loan Services.** By Vernon E. Palmour, Edwin E. Olson, and Nancy K. Roderer. Washington, D.C., Westat, Inc., for ARL, 1974. 77p. o.p.

Presents statistical and cost data to support the position that interlibrary lending involves significant costs to net lending libraries. This is particularly discouraging for larger research libraries, which lend much more than they borrow. The study recommends that libraries be recompensed for such loans by fees charged to the borrowing institutions until such time as special subsidies are available from public agencies. The existing imbalance, which may result in a loss to the net lending institution of as much as $50,000 to $100,000, cannot be tolerated in the long run. The study suggests the amount of

fee to be charged ($3.50), which is actually only 50 percent of the total cost ($7.00) for one transaction. This is, indeed, one of the best studies on this subject. [R: AL, Sept 74, p. 414; LJ, 1 Oct 74, p. 2455]

1426.   **Interlibrary Loan Procedures Manual.** Ottawa, Ont., Canadian Library Association, 1971. 25p. o.p. LC 72-194598. ISBN 0-88802-075-9.

This brief manual is intended for use by libraries following the Inter-library Loan Code and Library Telecommunications Code both issued by the Canadian Library Association. Outlines procedures for borrowing and lending within Canada and directions for interaction with the Library of Congress, foreign libraries, and the International Federation of Library Associations and Institutions. [R: LJ, 1 Sept 71, p. 2606]   Charles D. Patterson

1427.   Morris, Leslie R., and Patsy Brautigam. **Interlibrary Loan Policies Directory.** 2nd ed. Chicago, American Library Association, 1984. 448p. $27.50pa. LC 83-11897. ISBN 0-8389-0393-2.

The first edition of this book was published in 1975 under the direction of Sarah K. Thomson. It contained 276 interlibrary loan and photocopy policies of major lending libraries in the United States. The second edition, edited by Leslie R. Morris and Patsy Brautigam, shows a substantial increase in context. With 830 interlibrary loan policies, this text exemplifies a change in format and coverage. The libraries included in this new text were chosen by their collection size and number of interlibrary loan transactions. The entries are arranged alphabetically and with the help of a key-term geographic index they are easily located. The entries include: NUC and OCLC codes; ILL address and telephone number; interlibrary loan policies for books, periodicals, microfilms, government document publications, dissertations and theses, audiovisual materials, and computer software; availability of photoduplication and microfilming services; and charges. This directory is highly recommended for those libraries involved with extensive interlibrary loan transactions.

Larissa Kolody

1428.   Palmour, Vernon E., and others, comps. **Interlibrary Loans in Academic Libraries.** Prepared for the Association of Research Libraries by Westat, Inc., and others. Westport, Conn., Greenwood Press, 1972. 127p. bibliog. o.p. LC 70-39344. ISBN 0-8371-6340-4.

Results of a study proposed by the Interlibrary Loan Study Committee of ARL and the actual project done by Westat Research, Inc. Examines five important areas: (1) value of an interlibrary loan, (2) National Interlibrary Loan System, (3) amortized collection costs, (4) cooperative study of state systems, and (5) National Lending Concept. Provides excellent material on costs, characteristics of materials, and existing and future systems. [R: LJ, 1 Dec 72, p. 3878; RQ, Spring 74, p. 277; RQ, Fall 73, p. 83]   Charles D. Patterson

1429. Thomson, Sarah Katherine. **Interlibrary Loan Involving Academic Libraries.** Chicago, American Library Association, 1970. 127p. (ACRL Monograph, No. 32). bibliog. o.p. LC 70-124575. ISBN 0-8389-3010-7.

Based upon and summarizes the author's 1967 Columbia University doctoral dissertation. The investigation uses data drawn from statistics of items borrowed, analysis of interlibrary loan requests, two questionnaires, and analysis of unverified requests, all of which the author has thoroughly sifted, combed, realigned, and searched. The text consists of short essays which identify specific problem areas. Provides a realistic picture of interlibrary loan practice. [R: BL, 15 Dec 70, p. 317; C&RL, Jan 71, p. 54; LJ, 1 Feb 71, p. 453; RQ, Winter 70, p. 180]   Charles D. Patterson

1430. Thomson, Sarah Katherine. **Interlibrary Loan Procedures Manual.** Chicago, American Library Association, 1970. 116p. $5.00pa. LC 71-125942. ISBN 0-8389-3113-8.

Issued by the Interlibrary Loan Committee, Reference Services Division of ALA, this volume contains the 1968 revisions of the "Interlibrary Loan Code" and a new "Model Interlibrary Loan Code for Regional, State, Local and Other Special Groups of Libraries." Reflects change of emphasis and clear instructions (many examples and illustrations of forms) for efficient handling of interlibrary loans. [R: BL, 15 Dec 70, p. 317; LJ, 1 Feb 70, p. 453]   Charles D. Patterson

INTERNATIONAL DEVELOPMENTS

1431. Burkett, Jack. **Library and Information Networks in the United Kingdom.** London, Aslib, 1979. 261p. index. $36.00. ISBN 0-85142-117-2.

This work is a comprehensive and authoritative survey of the development, organization, and exploitation of nationally important library and information networks in the United Kingdom. It presents descriptions of library holdings and databases, relationships between units, and services offered through such organizations as the British Library divisions; networks of the Department of Trade and Industry, Ministry of Defence, Central Electricity Generating Board, UK Atomic Energy Authority, INSPEC, Department of Health and Social Security, and Department of the Environment; and the information services of the National Coal Board, Chemical Abstracts Service, Ministry of Agriculture, Fisheries, and Food, the Agricultural Research Council, and the University of London Library Resources Coordinating Committee and Central Library Services.

Included are references, charts of most British networks, information systems, and bibliographic services, and an index that explains acronyms. For reference libraries, library schools, and for all interested in understanding the vast range and complexity of modern information networks and systems, most of them computer based, this Aslib-produced volume is essential. [R: LR, Spring 80, p. 43]
Richard Palmer

1432. Campbell, H. C. **Developing Public Library Systems and Services: A Guide to the Organization of National and Regional Public Library Systems as a Part of Overall National Information Service Planning.** Paris, UNESCO; distr., New York, UNIPUB, c1982, 1983. 186p. (Documentation, Libraries and Archives: Studies and Research, No. 11). $18.75pa. ISBN 92-3-101995-3.

It has often been said that one of the best ways of understanding one's own situation is to stand outside it and look at it from a different direction. Campbell's objective is to provide a summary of the main issues of public library development and guidelines on how a public library can be promoted and developed. In providing an international approach to many of the aspects of public library development and service, he has given us a platform a bit to one side of our daily activities from which we can also reexamine our own services.

Public library development is placed within the context of worldwide problems: literacy, the lack of sufficient information materials in many countries, and the lack of financial support. Initial steps in constructing a framework for library service are described including the development of plans, policies, and guidelines at the national level. The roles of government, library associations, and the community are outlined. A guide to setting up the library is provided with information on the organization of public services and technical services. Collection development, bibliographic control, and cooperation among libraries are described. Considerable attention is given to staffing requirements and to evaluation of services.

This is intended as an outline of general requirements for public library service in developing countries. Not only does it meet that objective well, it also gives those of us who are involved with more advanced libraries an opportunity to look at our own development in relation to politics, policies, and programs. Each chapter includes a brief bibliography, largely in English, of an international range of materials.

Ann E. Prentice

1433. Jefferson, George. **Library Co-operation.** 2nd ed. London, Andre Deutsch; distr., Boulder, Colo., Westview Press, 1977. 189p. bibliog. index. (A Grafton Book). $20.00. ISBN 0-233-96851-2.

George Jefferson, the distinguished British librarian, has updated and rewritten his 1966 monograph on cooperation between libraries of various types and sizes. Although the emphasis is on developments in the United Kingdom, there are many references to cooperative efforts in the United States and continental Europe, along with a sizable chapter devoted to international cooperation. The author has succeeded in producing a well-organized overview of cooperative library activities, including interlibrary lending and exchanges, cooperative and centralized acquisition and storage schemes, union catalogs and bibliographies, and computerized networks. However, while OCLC is described, all of its American competitors have been omitted, possibly because they were not as well established when this publication was being prepared.

Jefferson's approach to library cooperation is historical as well as evaluative, and he makes the reader aware of the need for thorough planning. His comprehensive review of regional library systems, specialized library cooperatives, and the national network in Great Britain— replete with a plethora of strange acronyms— should be of particular interest to American librarians as they formulate their own plans for cooperation in the 1980s. The author's comments on the future of library cooperation, which are found in the final chapter, are well worth reading, too. The extensive bibliography (arranged chronologically, not in alphabetical order) and the index contribute to the value of this readable volume. Every librarian can

benefit from perusing it. [R: LJ, 15 Feb 78, p. 442]

Leonard Grundt

1434. **National and International Library Planning: Key Papers Presented at the 40th Session of the IFLA General Council, Washington, DC, 1974.** Edited by Robert Vosper and Leone I. Newkirk. Munich, Verlag Dokumentation; distr., New York, UNIPUB, 1976. 162p. (IFLA Publications 4). o.p. ISBN 3-7940-4424-X.

This book contains reports on national library planning activities in the United States, the Soviet Union, Great Britain, the Federal Republic of Germany, Jamaica, Southeast and Western Asia, Africa, and Scandinavia. There is an introductory paper on national and international library planning by Robert Vosper, then an article on UNESCO's proposal for a National Information System (NATIS), covering its requirements, planning, financing, promotion, relationship to universal bibliographic control, and objectives. [R: C&RL, May 77, p. 255; LJ, 15 Sept 77, p. 1827; LQ, Oct 77, p. 522]

1435. Vervliet, H. D. L., ed. **Resource Sharing of Libraries in Developing Countries: Proceedings of the 1977 IFLA/UNESCO Pre-Session Seminar for Librarians from Developing Countries, Antwerp University, August 30-September 4, 1977.** Munich, New York, K. G. Saur, 1979. 286p. index. (IFLA Publications, 14). $15.00. LC 79-17272. ISBN 0-89664-114-7. ISSN 0344-6891.

This book, which is based on the proceedings of the 1977 IFLA/UNESCO Pre-Session Seminar for librarians from developing countries, examines problems these librarians face in making optimum use of the resources available to them. Library resource sharing is becoming increasingly important everywhere, since the volume of information grows in geometric proportions while the resources available to cope with the information explosion expand at a much slower rate, if at all. However, the problem is most acute in developing countries, where resources are usually in short supply and the library infrastructure is in its infancy.

The book consists of four chapters and a closing essay entitled "Library Resource Sharing in the United States," by A. Eaton. Each chapter contains both specific case studies and essays on a given theme. Chapter 1, "Cooperative Acquisition," includes case studies such as J. M. Newa's "Cooperative Acquisition in Tanzania: The Role of the University of Dar es Salaam Library" and A. Rydings's "Cooperative Acquisition for Libraries of Developing Countries: Panacea or Placebo?," which approaches the subject from a broader perspective. Chapter 2, "Processing Centers," contains an essay by A. A. Briquet de Lomos, "On the Feasibility of Processing Centers in Brazil," which describes the role of processing centers in Brazilian library development. "Do Developing Countries Need Processing Centers?," by E. M. Broome, weighs the advantages and disadvantages of processing centers for developing countries. Chapter 3, "Cooperative Storage and Delivery," and chapter 4, "The Impact of Computerized Systems and Networks in Resource Sharing of Libraries," follow a similar format.

This book serves a useful purpose by focusing on the problems faced by librarians in developing countries, and showing them to be of a different type and magnitude than those faced by librarians in developed countries.

Norman Frankel

48 Online Searching

GENERAL WORKS

1436. Atherton, Pauline, and Roger W. Christian. **Librarians and Online Services.** White Plains, N.Y., Knowledge Industry Publications, 1977. 124p. bibliog. index. o.p. LC 77-25275. ISBN 0-914236-13-X.

Librarians and Online Services is a valuable report that provides discussions, guidelines, and answers to many practical problems and questions related to library online services. As stated by the authors, it deals with how and why libraries provide online reference services to their patrons. It addresses many practical topics related to this type of service, including start-up considerations, financial and charging considerations, operational procedures, training of service personnel, marketing and promotion, management and control, future trends, etc. The authors not only present their own views on these topics, but also share many of the ideas and views of people in the field, who were interviewed by the authors (either personally or by phone), and the results of various studies. Thus, it becomes a useful document for experience sharing.

Two checklists related to the presearch interview are helpful. So are several sample forms related to online services from actual libraries. The writing is simple, straightforward, and very easy. The 124-page report, in paperback format, should be a handy tool for all librarians and library school students who want to learn more about online services. [R: LJ, 1 Oct 78, p. 1930]
Ching-chih Chen

1437. Chen, Ching-chih, and Susanna Schweizer. **Online Bibliographic Searching: A Learning Manual.** New York, Neal-Schuman, 1981. 244p. illus. bibliog. index. (Applications in Informa-

tion Management and Technology Series). $24.95pa.; $19.50pa. (5 or more copies). LC 81-83497. ISBN 0-918212-59-6.

The eight chapters in this text present an overview of online bibliographic retrieval vendor systems, the fundamentals of online database searching, question negotiation, use of database indexes, multidatabase searching, comparisons of vendor systems (BRS, Lockheed DIALOG, and SDC ORBIT), search service management considerations, and a concluding segment on the future of online searching. The book includes numerous illustrations (photographs and line drawings), samples of forms, extensive lists of suggested readings, and reproductions of interactions with systems as well as reprinted material supplied by database vendors and producers. The primary orientation is to DIALOG, although additional coverage is included for the BRS and ORBIT systems. A glossary, answer sets to exercises in the *DIALOG Lab Workbook*, and an index complete the text.

Beginners will find a great deal of information packed into the eight chapters. The material will be of maximum benefit to the new user when presented under the watchful eye of an experienced searcher. [R: BL, 15 Jan 82, p. 633; JAL, July 82, p. 164; LJ, 15 June 82, p. 1198]
Roger Palmer

1438. Deunette, J. B., comp. **UK Online Search Services.** London, published on behalf of the Online Information Centre by Aslib, 1982. 106p. index. £14.00pa. ISBN 0-85142-141-5.

A useful directory, current through November 1980, of UK sources that offer online searches. Arranged alphabetically by institution, the directory contains 60 sources willing to provide online searches to the public, and an additional 28 with some sort of user restrictions. The table of contents presents a list of participating institutions, while indexes provide sources for SDI services, institutions that allow individual searchers access to a terminal, and a list of 24 vendors and the institutions that use their databases, including UK sources for both Lockheed and SDC. A discipline index identifies institutions offering online capabilities for broad subject areas.

The directory is easy to use, with information presented in a clear format and consistency in main headings to provide essential information at a glance. Entries are limited to one page per institution and include: availability, coverage, charges, speed of service, participation by enquirers, when the service began, the number of searches performed per year, staffing, and backup services. This last category includes such things as reference, photocopy, and advisory services to visiting enquirers. A valuable tool for someone who has an occasional need for an online search or the need to refer others to sources for such searches in the United Kingdom. [R: LJ, 1 Nov 81, p. 2095]

Robert A. Berk

1439. Fenichel, Carol H., and Thomas H. Hogan. **Online Searching: A Primer.** 2nd ed. Marlton, N.J., Learned Information, 1984. 184p. bibliog. index. $14.95. ISBN 0-938734-01-6.

Carol Fenichel and Thomas Hogan's *Online Searching: A Primer* succeeds very well in doing what it intends: to provide a "basic introduction to all facets of online searching." It joins the ranks of several other publications in the same area, including Chen and Schweizer's *Online Bibliographic Searching: A Learning Manual* (see *ARBA* 83, entry 276) and Hartner's *An Introduction to Automated Literature Searching* (see *ARBA* 83, entry 278).

Separate chapters cover databases, vendors, online users, searching, equipment, the reference process, costs and changing policies, setting up and managing an online reference service, education and training, nonbibliographic databases — all in 151 pages, including index! A helpful, if dated, bibliography covers each topic treated in the text. While this primer will no doubt be useful in assisting the beginning searcher to get a sense of the online world, it is unlikely to prove very effective as a library school text or training resource because of its general treatment. [R: IRLA, Nov 81, p. 2; WLB, Nov 81, p. 235] Heather Cameron

1440. Hartner, Elizabeth P. **An Introduction to Automated Literature Searching.** New York, Marcel Dekker, 1981. 145p. bibliog. index. (Books in Library and Information Science, Vol. 36). $27.50. LC 81-7831. ISBN 0-8247-1293-5.

The stated purpose of this book is to provide "an introduction to the practical side of performing computer searches of scientific and technical literature." The book is divided into six chapters that provide a logical overview of online searching, ranging from how to find information to how computerized information retrieval works. However, the book has serious faults that limit its usefulness.

While any book in the constantly changing field of information retrieval will necessarily be dated at the time of its publication, one assumes that the information used in its compilation was as current as practically possible. However, in this 1981 publication the most recent journal articles cited are from 1978, and, of those, 9 out of 15 were from the May issue of one journal. In addition, when references are made to standard works, the author typically cites earlier editions without noting their later revisions or updates. While it is noted that the references are not "the result of exhaustive literature searches," it is also stated that the purpose of the references is to "start the reader along a path which will take him as far into the technology and theory as he wants to go." Clearly, such dated references defeat the author's purpose. Also, it is never clear whether the book is intended to be used as a general guide to computer searching (as stated on the cover) or as a specialized handbook for searching scientific and technological literature (as stated in the preface). Finally, the decision not to include actual examples from any of the major search services is very questionable. [R: LJ, 15 Mar 82, p. 616; SBF, Mar/Apr 82, p. 185] Greg Byerly

1441. Hoover, Ryan E., ed. **Online Search Strategies.** White Plains, N.Y., Knowledge Industry Publications, 1982. 345p. bibliog. index. (Professional Librarian Series). $37.50; $29.50pa. LC 82-17179. ISBN 0-86729-005-6; 0-86729-004-8pa.

This book is intended for librarians who are already familiar with online searching and who have used at least one of the four major U.S. services: BRS, DIALOG, NLM, and SDC. Its chapters deal with search strategies in the areas of government information, chemistry, biosciences, energy and the environment, social and behavioral sciences, newsbanks and news databases, patents, legal research, health sciences, and business and economics. Each chapter is written by an experienced searcher or team of searchers in one of the above subject areas. The book suggests ways to improve and develop one's own strategies, as well as describing tried and true existing ones, and encourages the librarian/searcher to continue to improve by going on to other works listed in the bibliography. [R: C&RL, July 83, pp. 301-2; JAL, Sept 83, pp. 226-27]

1442.   Hoover, Ryan E., with Alice H. Bahr and others. **The Library and Information Manager's Guide to Online Services.** White Plains, N.Y., Knowledge Industry Publications, 1980. 270p. illus. bibliog. index. $34.50. LC 80-21602. ISBN 0-914236-60-1.

A survey of online information retrieval services contained in 10 chapters provides the reader with types of databases available, research on the supplies and vendors of online services (including detailed descriptions of the key systems), three chapters on the management of online services in the library, planning for the introduction of online services to operational and budgetary consideration, measurement and evaluation of online services, the promotion of online services (with samples of effective promotions materials), mechanics of searching, searcher training, the growth of online user groups, and the future of online services. The "Glossary of Online Terms" in this volume should be useful to those with limited experience in this field. A "Selected Bibliography" will be helpful to readers seeking additional information. The book is extensively illustrated with tables, figures, and photographs. Prospective users and those purchasing online services will find this volume helpful in the search to understand the complexities of online services. [R: BL, 15 Oct 81, p. 284; C&RL, May 81, p. 272; JAL, Mar 81, p. 50; SL, Oct 81, p. 411]

Donald D. Foos

1443.   Markey, Karen, and Pauline A. Cochrane. **Ontap: Online Training and Practice Manual for ERIC Data Base Searchers.** 2nd ed. Syracuse, N.Y., ERIC, Syracuse University, 1981. 177p. o.p.

This self-improvement manual for experienced online searchers first appeared in 1978 (see *ARBA* 79, entry 264). It successfully parried complaints of searchers that aids were unavailable to help them improve search techniques after intensive initial training and mastery of the mechanics. A revision proved necessary, as the database producer and vendor

improved subject access. ERIC completed its Identifier Clean-Up, Vocabulary Improvement Project, and published the eighth edition of *Thesaurus of ERIC Descriptors.* DIALOG updated and reloaded online the ERIC database. Fortunately for searchers, Markey and Cochrane undertook a revision of the manual to encompass these changes.

As with the first edition, section 1 outlines, abstracts, and then details the functions performed during eight steps identified for effective online searching. Section 2 introduces ERIC ONTAP (DIALOG File 201), then presents online training exercises designed to sharpen searching skills. Searchers, using the ONTAP ERIC EVAL capability, may then evaluate their online exercise search results with "answer sets" loaded into the database. Appendices include search save concepts and the DIALOG *Guide to ERIC* and ONTAP ERIC. An index follows. Although *Ontap* deals specifically with ERIC, a study of the manual's techniques and procedures produces rollover value for searching other databases.   Eleanor Ferrall

1444.   Meadow, Charles T., and Pauline Atherton Cochrane. **Basics of Online Searching.** New York, John Wiley, 1981. 245p. index. (Information Science Series; A Wiley-Interscience Publication). $25.50. LC 80-23050. ISBN 0-471-05283-3.

This textbook, which presents the principles of interactive bibliographic searching, may be used as a self-instruction manual if studied in conjunction with more detailed users' manuals provided by such search services as DIALOG, ORBIT, or Bibliographic Retrieval Services. It presents basic definitions and search vocabulary, elements of interactive searching, the presearch interview, steps in conceptualizing the search, terminals and networks, search languages and commands, database characteristics, text searching, combinatorial logic, and search strategies.

Included are sample searches, procedures for beginning and ending a search, for storing searches, and for providing selective dissemination of information services. Found in the appendices are a useful summary of online functions and commands, a sample listing of databases, with references to the Landau, Wanger, Berger, *Directory of Online Databases* (Cuadra) and Martha E. Williams's, *Computer-Readable Data Bases: A Directory and Data Source Book* (KIP), and examples of database descriptions and search aids, including sources of more detailed publications.

This work reflects the experience and skill of the educators who have prepared it; it is a sound and well-balanced introduction to the complex topic of online bibliographic database searching. However, as the authors clearly state, it cannot be used alone. Effective searching requires search services users' manuals, database directories, and search aids—as well as hands-on experience under experienced tutelage. Those interested in online searching may also wish to consult Chen and Schweizer's *Online Bibliographic Searching: A Learning Manual* (Neal-Schuman, 1981), which includes the fundamentals of searching as well as management considerations, multidatabase and multivendor searches, system-to-system comparisons, a quick reference index guide, answers to the Lockheed workbook searches, reading lists, and a glossary. Many learners will find both works helpful. Richard Palmer

1445. Palmer, Roger C. **Online Reference and Information Retrieval.** Littleton, Colo., Libraries Unlimited, 1983. 149p. illus. index. (Library Science Text Series). $18.50pa. LC 82-21648. ISBN 0-87287-347-1.

This basic text is designed to introduce students to information retrieval services offered by three commercial computer-based systems: Bibliographic Retrieval Services, Inc. (BRS), DIALOG Information Retrieval Services of the Lockheed Missile and Space Company, Inc. (DIALOG), and the SDC Search Service ORBIT® of the System Development Corp. (ORBIT). It has three parts. The first offers an overview of the role of database producers, vendor systems, and searchers, while the second provides a practical orientation to searching on ORBIT, DIALOG, and BRS. An analysis of the interview process, a term project, and a discussion of trends and issues related to online searching are contained in the final section. The student is led in a systematic way to an understanding of how online systems are organized, how search statements are processed by online systems, and how the command language of an actual online system operates. Search strategy formulation and the transferability of techniques and strategies from system to system are discussed in detail. The author also includes in-depth coverage of the client interview, including the personal attributes a searcher needs to insure successful performance, a sample interview, interview analysis, and a discussion of the searcher/client interview. Individual and class assignments, illustrations taken from interactions with the systems, and reading lists supplement the text. Although primarily designed as a text, this practical, hands-on guide to major online bibliographic/information retrieval systems will also be useful to those who own personal microcomputers. [R: JAL, May 83, p. 109; LJ, 1 June 83, p. 1114; RQ, Fall 83, p. 120]

REFERENCE WORKS

1446. Byerly, Greg. **Online Searching: A Dictionary and Bibliographic Guide.** Littleton, Colo., Libraries Unlimited, 1983. 288p. index. $27.50. LC 83-853. ISBN 0-87287-381-1.

This dictionary and bibliographic guide provides easy access to concise, understandable definitions of more than 1,200 terms related to online searching and presents a selective, annotated bibliography of pertinent journal articles published between 1970 and June 1982. In addition, representative books and other reference tools are given as further sources of information. In the definitions, certain terms appear in boldface to indicate that they are defined elsewhere in the dictionary section of the book. System-specific terms for BRS, DIALOG, and SDC are also defined. The 722 annotated journal articles in the bibliography section are divided into two major parts: "General Overview of Online Searching" and "Specialized Subject Areas and Databases of Online Searching." Entries within each are arranged by specific topics, such as "Academic Libraries and Online Searching," "Reference Uses of Online Searching," and "Setting Up and Managing an Online Search Service." Part 2 includes articles for the experienced searcher, detailing how to perform searches in specific subject areas with their representative databases. Among the 10 general subject areas are agriculture, business, law, political science, and medicine. The dictionary and bibliography sections are designed to complement each other. Online terminology or databases mentioned in the descriptive annotations of articles are defined in the dictionary section. Readers using the dictionary to identify an unfamiliar database may consult the thorough subject index to locate related journal articles. In addition to the subject index, indexes to periodicals cited and authors are also provided. [R: BL, 1 June 84, p. 1385; Choice, Nov 83, p. 399; WLB, Oct 83, p. 147]

1447. Dewe, Ainslie, with Mary Ann Colyer, comps. **British Information Services Not Available Online: A Select List.** London, Aslib, 1980. 105p. index. o.p. ISBN 0-85142-137-7.

In 1972, Aslib published *A Guide to Selected Computer-Based Information Services.*

As a complement to this guide, Aslib published *A Guide to Selected British Non-Computer-based Commercially-Available Information Services* in 1975. The compilation under review is essentially an update of this 1975 guide.

The information services included in this compilation are all commercial and available on an unrestricted basis, although in some cases it is required for an enquirer to subscribe to a specific publication, or provide information on a reciprocal basais. Research and trade associations offering information services have been included only when there is no restriction on the use of the services. Publishers of abstracting and indexing sources have been excluded, unless they also provide some form of back-up service, such as responding to specific queries or supplying copies of indexed articles. Costs, prices, and fees are, of course, subject to change; however, they have been included as an indication of the level of the service.

A compilation of information services as useful as this one should be made available online through some database vendor, and then it can be updated more frequently. [R: LR, Summer 81, p. 106]   Anindya Bose

1448. Directory of Online Information Resources. Kensington, Md., CSG Press, a division of Capital Systems Group, 1978- . 2/yr. o.p. ISSN 0197-1646.

Published in March and September, the directory was generally limited to databases publicly accessible from a user's own terminal. Information on the databases includes database name (with cross-references), relationship to printed indexes, subject coverage, responsible organization, file size, vendors offering the file, type of records (abstracts, citations, etc.), and price. In addition to the alphabetical descriptions, there is an expanded (but still inadequate) subject index containing 179 subject headings and cross-references. A vendor index and a vendor and producer address list complete the volume.

When compared with such similar works as the *Directory of Online Databases* (1979-) and Williams's *Computer-Readable Bibliographic Data Bases: A Directory and Data Sourcebook* (American Society for Information Sciences, 1976-), this directory was less comprehensive in its coverage. However, since very few of the omitted databases are accessible to the average online searcher, their inclusion would be of little, if any, assistance.

Various volumes have been reviewed in *ARBA*; see *ARBA* 80 (entry 127) and *ARBA* 82, entry 138. [R: IRLA, May 83, p. 18]
Bill J. Corbin

1449. Guide to Online Databases. Boca Raton, Fla., Newsletter Management, 1983. 152p. index. o.p. ISBN 0-942180-39-9.

This guide comprises a subject index to online databases, an alphabetical directory of databases, and a directory of distributors. Brief entries for the databases (approximately 1,020, including duplicates) give the name, topics, scope, update frequency, distributor, and producer. The "user-friendly" feature of the guide, the subject index, is conveniently placed at the front of the book, but it is inadequate and misleading. The entry "History" references a federal case law file and an agricultural sciences database but not the more relevant *Religion Index* or *Social Scisearch*. Other entries are equally illogical. "Spain" has the *Wine Library* but not *Historical Abstracts* or *PAIS*; "Latin America" lists the *MLA Bibliography* (primarily on literature) but not the history or current affairs files; and "Tennis" includes the *Dow Jones Sports Report* but not the *Sport* file from SDC. Inconsistencies abound: "Justice System" refers to both *Criminal Justice Periodicals* and *National Criminal Justice Reference*, but "Criminal Justice" lists only the former, even though criminal justice is listed as a topic in the NCJRS database directory entry. There is no subject index entry for art or fine arts despite those subjects' being the main subject of *ArtBibliographies Modern*, listed in the database directory.

Database entries, brief as they are, are also problematical. An erroneous title is used for *America: History and Life*. There are three different, unrelated entries for ERIC. Duplicate entries for other databases have different details and no cross-references. The entry for the *Eighteenth-Century Short Title Catalog* gives little idea of what it is, and the directory of distributors omits the address for its U.S. distributor, RLIN.

The excuses given in the introductory pages do not justify the errors and inconsistencies of this compilation. Users cannot afford to rely on this guide. [R: LJ, 15 Nov 83, p. 2141]
Joyce Duncan Falk

1450. Hall, James L., and Marjorie J. Brown. Online Bibliographic Databases: A Directory

and Sourcebook. 3rd ed. London, Aslib; distr., Detroit, Gale, 1983. 383p. bibliog. index. $95.00. ISBN 0-8103-0530-5.

The unusual features that make this more than a directory are the addition of typical record printouts so that the style of indexing, data elements, and related features can be compared. These printouts are available for almost all of the 179 databases listed. The section on relevant published literature about the database is another desirable and useful feature that many other directories do not include. The 30-page commentary in the beginning gives a fine overview of online databases and retrieval, along with some statistical information about the database repertory over the last few years. The 215-item general bibliography is not by any means exhaustive, but it certainly gives a fine overview. The general index and two subject guides to the databases and the references round out the book.

Although it is not a U.S. publication, the book does appear to be comprehensive in coverage of English-language content databases. It does not purport to cover numeric databases (or databanks, in the authors' terminology) so that its coverage is not the same as that of the three-volume *Directory of Online Databases*, edited by Ruth Cuadra, David Abels, and Judith Wanger (Cuadra Associates, 1979-1981; see *ARBA* 83, entry 114). A valuable addition to the reference shelf for any library doing online searching or for any library school in which students must acquaint themselves with the myriad databases and services available. For evaluations of the first (1979) and second (1981) editions, see *ARBA* 80 (entry 131) and *ARBA* 82 (entry 139). [R: JAL, Sept 83, p. 242]

Pauline Atherton Cochrane

1451. Hall, J. L., and A. Dewe. **Online Information Retrieval, 1976-1979: An International Bibliography.** London, Aslib, 1980. 230p. index. (Aslib Bibliography, 10). £20.00; £17.00 (Aslib members). ISBN 0-85142-127-X.

Aiming to present a compilation of the literature about online bibliographic files appearing from mid-1976 through 1979, this bibliography does not attempt to cover either numerical data retrieval or automated catalog access. To produce it, approximately 14,000 titles were scanned and original articles were examined whenever possible. With an obvious international scope, no language restrictions seem to exist.

Citations for 890 references are arranged in alphabetical order by a unique "document identifier" consisting of author or title keyword.

Annotations are provided except for a few self-evident titles. An additional 168 unannotated references are cited in a supplement, and reflect citations appearing under the compilation's June 1979 cut-off date. Entries appear in standard bibliographic format, with titles in boldface type to facilitate browsing. Three indexes are provided for personal author, report number, and subject access. References in the supplement are not included in these indexes, but are separately arranged and also indexed by a brief "guide" page.

Eleven other bibliographies of online information retrieval are cited in the index, though none duplicates this one's time span, international coverage, or broad subject approach. It is more useful than its closest comparison, the annual bibliographies produced since 1977 by D. T. Hawkins in *Online Review*, which collectively cover citations from 1965; Hawkins's four bibliographies provide no annotations and have subject access limited to KWIC indexing.

This is a handy reference tool, and with the earlier Aslib Bibliography No. 8, covering 1965-1976 literature, should be readily available for anyone interested in the technology, products, services, or impact of online retrieval. Its short introduction also provides a state-of-the-art literature review and a brief comment on the cost factors contributing to the production of such a tool. [R: C&RL, Mar 81, p. 166; LR, Winter 80, p. 284]   Danuta A. Nitecki

1452. Kambayashi, Yahiko. **Database: A Bibliography, Volume 1.** Rockville, Md., Computer Science Press, 1981. 499p. index. $45.00. LC 80-26672. ISBN 0-914894-64-1.

Covering books and journal articles regarding database systems from 1970 to 1980, this computer-produced bibliography includes a master list of 3,912 items under 160 different topics; a subject table of publications arranged according to date of publication; a KWIC index with a secondary listing of index terms; an author index; and a list of 39 journals and 50 conferences dealing with database systems. Each of the items in the bibliography is assigned a unique identification code. Since the indexes list only the identification code, users must locate the numerically keyed topic and search for desired items in the alphabetic author array under each topic. A careful study of the instructions permits reasonably effective access to specific titles.

Among the topics covered in this work are general references, database models, languages, management systems, maintenance, hardware architecture, and applications, as well as design and analysis of database systems, query processing, integrity, security, distributed systems, data organization, information retrieval, algorithms, and information theory.

Since the publisher has already produced four volumes of bibliographies on computer-aided design of digital systems, covering the years 1960-1979, it may be expected that this first volume on database systems will be succeeded by additional bibliographies.

This work, produced in Japan, will require some slight ingenuity on the part of U.S. users in selecting appropriate search terms and strategies. However, the KWIC index, which keeps index terms in context, will aid users in identifying relevant articles. The volume will be helpful to serious researchers in the computer field. [R: LJ, 15 Dec 81, p. 2381]

Richard Palmer

1453.   MacLean, Ian A. **An Inventory of Bibliographic Data Bases in Canadian Degree-Granting Institutions.** Ottawa, Ont., National Library of Canada, 1981. 1v. (various paging). index. o.p. ISBN 0-662-51478-5.

This is the first of the two documents generated from the Data Base Inventory Project (DBIP) commissioned by the National Library of Canada (NLC) in 1980-1981. The DBIP attempted to provide comprehensive coverage, through a questionnaire survey, of the machine-readable files created by the Bibliothèque Nationale du Quebec, the NLC, the Canada Institute for Scientific and Technical Information (CISTI), and all Canadian degree-granting educational institutions. In total, 63 institutions (of the 70 addressed) responded to the questionnaire.

In addition to general type databases, "library-processing oriented data bases," supporting one or more library processing functions, such as circulation, cataloging, acquisition, etc., are also included. These databases are grouped alphabetically under the institutions, which are also alphabetically arranged. As is standard in all Canadian government publications, both English and French are used to provide all information in two sequences.

For each database included, concise but most helpful information is provided. This includes file type, file size, growth rate, time span, search mode, access points, format standards, data standards, character set, data source, related files, scope/coverage, data areas, subject terms, classification, holdings, products, machine, storage, software, consortia, plans, contact, etc. Several indexes to the databases— by province (geographical), by function, by file

type, and by availability—are provided in the beginning of the publication.

This is a useful tool. It should be a very welcome addition to network planners and users. The only difficulty is the physical size of the publication—a huge, bulky three-ring loose-leaf binder. Many pages are already torn even before the book is used.   Ching-chih Chen

PROCEEDINGS

1454.   Hickerson, H. Thomas, ed. **SPINDEX Users Conference: Proceedings of a Meeting Held at Cornell University, Ithaca, New York, March 31 and April 1, 1978.** Ithaca, N.Y., Cornell University Libraries, Department of Manuscripts and University Archives, 1979. 125p. o.p. LC 79-53690.

Selective Permutation Indexing (SPINDEX) is a computerized system for accessing archival holdings. This book contains the proceedings of a conference held at Cornell University in the spring of 1978 on the SPINDEX system. The 40 members participating were representatives of 21 institutions that use the system. Sessions dealt with the role of automation in the various repositories, database design, database entries, finding aid production, technical aspects of system use, system maintenance, and development. Papers, discussion, and forms are included in this volume. Member institutions are widely diversified: state, church, municipal, corporate, etc. Archivists interested in automated access to records would do well to examine this volume. [R: C&RL, Mar 80, pp. 151-52]   Joseph W. Sprug

1455.   Pratt, Gordon, and Susan Harvey, eds. **The On-Line Age: Plans and Needs for On-Line Information Retrieval; Proceedings of the EUSIDIC Conference, Oslo, 4th-5th December 1975.** London, Aslib, 1976. 127p. illus. index. (European User Series 3). £13.00; £11.00pa. ISBN 0-85142-080-X.

This volume covers a four-session conference (15 papers) on the relationships between information users, mediators and politicians, planning of scientific and technical information systems in the online age, pricing and service policies, and the relationships between U.S. and European suppliers and users. The viewpoints of government agencies, Lockheed Retrieval Service, System Development Corporation Service, SCANNET (the Nordic network), EURONET (the European network) and EUSIDIC (the European Association of Scientific Information Dissemination Centres) are ably represented. Discussions following each of the four sessions are summarized.

Many valuable insights are provided into the level of development of online services in Great Britain and on the European continent. A list of about 120 delegates and a list of authors and their affiliations are included. There are some very useful charts and diagrams on satellite-linked systems. Richard Palmer

1456. Watson, Peter G., ed. **On-Line Bibliographic Services—Where We Are, Where We're Going.** Chicago, Reference and Adult Services Division, 1977. 91p. o.p. ISBN 0-8389-6342-0.

Twelve presentations at a one-day meeting in Chicago in 1976 (organized by the Information Retrieval Committee of the Reference and Adult Services Division of the American Library Association) compose this unindexed and un-footnoted (except for two papers) volume. Included are (1) surveys of the impact of, attitudes toward, and observations on online bibliographic services; (2) comments on operational considerations in buying, leasing, planning, integrating, training, costing, promoting, and evaluating online services; and (3) management implications of introducing innovative reference services, such as book delivery systems. Since some prominent names in the world of library and information science are represented, the proceedings are not totally lacking in substance, but the work is hardly essential for any reference collection. [R: C&RL, Mar 78, p. 142; JAL, May 78, p. 91] Richard Palmer

49 Professional Status

GENERAL WORKS

1457. Chaplin, A. H., ed. **The Organization of the Library Profession: A Symposium Based on Contributions to the 37th Session of the IFLA General Council, Liverpool, 1971.** Munich, Verlag Dokumentation; distr., Totowa, N.J., Rowman & Littlefield, 1973. 132p. o.p. ISBN 3-7940-4309-X.

The subtitle of this work is somewhat misleading; some papers presented at that conference are not included, while papers not presented at the conference—on library education in Great Britain and on cooperation between IFLA and FID—are included.

The coverage is by no means comprehensive, which is perhaps one of the book's greatest weaknesses. It is an excellent concise source of information on the library profession in a number of countries, and it gives the type of information that is not readily available for those countries. In this regard the papers on Malaysia and Southeast Asia, East Africa, West Africa, and Latin America are the most informative. Unfortunately, almost half of the volume deals with those countries in Europe and the United States about which a great deal is already known and has already been said, with extensive documentation. The remaining portions of the monograph deal with Asia, Africa, and Latin America (about one-third) and international organizations. The Middle East and the Far East are not represented.

Most articles, particularly those on topics like "The Organization of Our Profession: Public Libraries," which is covered in three and one-half pages, and "The Professional Organization of Academic Libraries," based on a questionnaire sent to "a large number of countries" of which 29 responded, are too vague and general to be of much interest or value. In some instances charts showing the characteristics being described would have been much more useful than the repetitive enumeration found in the text.

The articles on international cooperation, although brief, give a good view of the type of cooperative efforts that are taking place at the international level.

This small volume might be useful for those interested in international librarianship, but it is too broad, too superficial, and too limiting to be of much general interest. It is of little research value. [R: AL, Dec 73, p. 669; LJ, 1 June 74, p. 1524]

Robert D. Stueart

1458. Debons, Anthony, and others. **The Information Professional: Survey of an Emerging Field.** New York, Marcel Dekker, 1981. 171p. bibliog. (Books in Library and Information Science, Vol. 38). o.p. LC 81-15093. ISBN 0-8247-1872-0.

The Information Professional reports the first phase of a heroic research project, presided over by investigators from the University of Pittsburgh's School of Library and Information Science, whose ultimate purpose is to "ascertain what gaps exist in the education and training of information professionals and how these might be filled; and to determine what changes (if any) in job classifications for information work should be made" (p. 3). The first phase of this investigation, called the Occupational Survey of Information Professionals, sought to identify and to estimate the number and distribution of information professionals employed by organizations in the United States.

Among other things, the investigators report that approximately 1,640,000 persons work in information-related positions, about 70 percent of them in industry. Detailed data are provided concerning the kinds of work done by information professionals, their job titles, and the institutions in which they are employed.

This book will be useful to those concerned with the education of information workers, as well as to economic planners, institutions which make use of information services, and, not least, to librarians, themselves among the information professionals surveyed. In libraries, it will be placed in the general collections, since it is a research monograph and has little value in reference work. [R: LJ, 1 June 82, p. 1076]
Robert Balay

1459. Edwards, Ralph M. **The Role of the Beginning Librarian in University Libraries.** Chicago, American Library Association, 1975. 120p. bibliog. (ACRL Publications in Librarianship, No. 37). illus. o.p. LC 75-30693. ISBN 0-8389-3167-7.

A dissertation based on the California system universities was the origin of this monograph, which has attempted to make the specialized study applicable to more generalized users. In this, it has succeeded, but the work remains more interesting than really useful. Its main use will be in raising questions about library education and beginning library positions, and about the relationships that should exist between them.

The data suffer from the fuzziness of the term "professional" in library thinking. Both in the gathering and in the interpretation, Edwards had difficulty because of the lack of agreement about what was meant. Whether a task was professional, or whether it was seen as one properly done by a beginner, depended on the view of what is professional in the eyes of the person questioned. Agreement on task assignment and appropriateness was minimal—a fact that is important to know but hard to use.

This work is important as a start toward studying the issues of professional tasks and the beginning librarian; because of this, it should be read by those in the field and in library schools. It is not the final statement and does not pretend to be. It does clearly point out the need for more study of what is professional, what should be professional, and of how the two can be reconciled. It underlines the need for accurate communication of what is expected and why, particularly for the beginning librarian. If the bibliography is fully indicative of the works studied, there are some strange gaps (almost

everything published by ERIC, works by Carroll and by sociologists), but for the points made, it is sufficient. [R: C&RL, Sept 76, pp. 477-78; LJ, 1 Nov 76, p. 2237] William L. Cohn

1460. **Library Leadership: Visualizing the Future.** Donald E. Riggs, ed. Phoenix, Ariz., Oryx Press, 1982. 153p. index. $32.50. LC 82-2174. ISBN 0-912700-64-5.

This book consists of a dozen essays on leadership in libraries and library organizations solicited by the editor, Donald E. Riggs, from leaders and persons who have substantial experience in the areas covered by each essay. Riggs himself contributed one of the essays.

Riggs's interest in this area was aroused by the scarcity of books and journal articles on leadership in librarianship. For example, over a span of five years (1975-1981) *Library Literature* had fewer than five entries on leadership and leaders. Of the 12 contributors to *Library Leadership*, there are a few familiar names, like Thomas J. Galvin and Elizabeth W. Stone. However, the majority may be considered to represent the views of the younger generation who came forward in the 1970s.

Several definitions of leadership are offered. The one with the most general application was suggested by Donald J. Sager: "the leader as a person who clarifies goals and removes barriers." The contributors are in agreement that the last two decades of the twentieth century will be a difficult and challenging time for all libraries, and that wise leadership will be needed. Special mention should be made of the excellent essays on the large public library; technical services; collection development; library education; state libraries and library associations; and the role of the American Library Association at the national level.

While this publication has material of interest to all librarians, it will be primarily of value to library school students and deserves a place on the shelves of their libraries. [R: BL, 15 Oct 82, pp. 292-93] Thomas S. Harding

1461. Marshall, John David. **Of, By and For Librarians: Second Series.** Hamden, Conn., Shoe String Press, 1974. 242p. index. (Contributions to Library Literature). o.p. LC 73-16428. ISBN 0-208-01333-4.

This is a very compassionate and thought-provoking book—a broad relief from technical data. It is at the same time inward-looking, defining who we are, how others see us, and where we are going. Marshall has selected 24 general interest pieces from the writings of about 20 contributors. Not all the contributors are librarians, but they are certainly all book-oriented. The main criteria for selection were a lively style of writing and a bookish-scholarly attitude; and, for a welcome change, there are very few footnotes.

The diverse topics center around two general themes, plus one ringer (Matthew Gant's oft-reprinted story "The Crate at Outpost 1," from a 1954 *EQMM*). The first theme, books and libraries, is carried out with Barbara Home Stewart's short plea for the book's endurance, G. D. Lillibridge's thoughts on reading books, Jennifer Savary's paper on why people read, Peter Rosenwald's discussion of the high sales of books, Bill Ready's comments on books in the computer age, and Louis Shores's belief in his profession, among others. The second theme is libraries and librarianship. It includes Catherine Drinker Bowen's salute to librarians; for many years she kept a large notebook itemizing the librarians and archivists she met, with brief characterizations and their special quotes, such as "I wish I had never laid *eyes* on you" or "You don't want *printed* material, do you?" Other articles on the theme are Larry Powell's personal elements of a good librarian, the important reprint of Lester Asheim's "2 Library Lectures" given at Kansas State Teachers College in 1959, which deal with the professional importance of librarianship, and, of course, Ortega y Gasset's "The Mission of the Librarian" (even in 1934 there were too many books).

I'm not going to comment on agreements, issues, or differences. This is a "think" book of timeless articles; though they are not current in publication date, they are right on in stimulation of the little gray cells. Surely there is a need for an oasis in library literature, if only for therapy. It is something to hand onto in the tumult of new and changing ideas and goals in the field of librarianship. [R: AL, June 74, p. 298]

Dean Tudor

1462. Raffin, Margaret R., and Rona Passmore, eds. **The Information Worker: Identity, Image and Potential.** London, Aslib, 1977. 58p. illus. $9.75pa. ISBN 0-85142-099-0.

This work consists of six papers presented at a one-day joint Aslib/Institute of Information Scientists conference held at the Geological Society of London on 22 November 1976. The topics include: (1) "The Information Worker: The Present Situation"; (2) "The Image of the Library Information Worker"; (3) "Image and Reward"; (4) "Tomorrow's Information Worker: New Man or Chip Off the Old Block"; (5) "There Won't Be an Information Profession in

2000 AD"; (6) "Expanding with the Service: Challenge of a New Role."

The papers explore the need for information workers today and in the future, and they discuss the purposes and functions of information work. Emphasis is on the impact of technology on information work.

Ultimately, more questions are raised than answered, although the preliminary results of some research in the area are presented. Of major concern for future activity is the need for a clearer definition of the functions of information workers. References are provided. [R: JAL, Nov 77, p. 311]   Andrew G. Torok

1463. Reeves, William Joseph. **Librarians as Professionals: The Occupation's Impact on Library Work Arrangements.** Lexington, Mass., Lexington Books, a division of D. C. Heath, 1980. 167p. bibliog. index. $24.50. LC 79-2389. ISBN 0-669-03163-1.

Fortunately, this is not a typical book (one of many) centering on the perennial issue of whether or not library science is a profession. It is based on the author's study of Alberta libraries conducted in 1974 and presents in 12 chapters a rather well-balanced investigation of library service and work patterns, with major emphasis on reference and selection functions. As indicated in the introduction, the major purpose of this study was to identify circumstances and conditions that fostered occupational control over work in organizational settings. This was accomplished by the author by surveying the policies advocated by library associations versus realities of actual library work settings. Indeed, a refreshing study that should be required reading in all library schools. [R: LJ, 1 Oct 80, p. 2042]   Bohdan S. Wynar

1464. Stueart, Robert D. **The Area Specialist Bibliographer: An Inquiry into His Role.** Metuchen, N.J., Scarecrow, 1972. 152p. index. o.p. LC 72-1300. ISBN 0-8108-0487-5.

This study is actually a doctoral dissertation from the University of Pittsburgh, with some minor changes. It consists of six chapters: area study programs in universities, research on the role of the librarian, the area specialist bibliographer's profile development and its influence on expectations, role perceptions and expectations, conclusions and recommendations, and selected bibliography. The study is limited to the role of the area specialist bibliographer in connection with the emergence of the variously organized area study programs at our universities. The problems are adequately discussed by the author, and some of his conclusions might be of interest.

First, as supported by the data, the area specialist bibliographer is a generalist par excellence. Second, and this is rather interesting, "there is no significant relationship between the education, experience, and language knowledge of area specialist bibliographers and the expectations of faculty and library administrators toward those variables—at least in the population studies" (p. 113).

It should be noted that these conclusions are primarily based on 362 questionnaires (75 percent of which were returned) sent to bibliographers, faculty, and library administrators. It is probably unfortunate that Stueart decided not to separate these three groups of respondents for tabulation, since the results would probably be even more revealing. The author of this review recalls his participation in one of the early conferences sponsored by Columbia University that dealt with the Soviet area programs. During long and often heated sessions, the difference in opinion between faculty and librarians was quite apparent. Most of the faculty quite frankly do not understand why in our library schools we do not prepare more subject-oriented bibliographers (as is done, for example, in the Soviet Union). I had quite a job trying to defend our concept of the "generalist training." It is hoped this interesting study will contribute to a better understanding of the problem. [R: LJ, 15 Oct 72, p. 3295]   Bohdan S. Wynar

1465. Warren, G. Garry. **The Handicapped Librarian: A Study in Barriers.** Metuchen, N.J., Scarecrow, 1979. 147p. bibliog. index. $15.00. LC 79-21811. ISBN 0-8108-1259-2.

During the early decades of the present century there was a strong insistence among professional librarians that recruits to librarianship should be completely normal people. In large measure this attitude was due to a widespread popular belief that librarians were different from other people, mentally if not physically. Even after World War II, army vocational advisers were disposed to think that any man who could not be absorbed into the work force, for whatever reason, would be an excellent candidate for a career in librarianship. Every library school dean could give testimony to this assumption.

Barriers, both physical and mental, have been removed in many institutions, including the library, due to a growing belief in equal opportunities for employment, and to the need to implement federal legislation which mandated that requirement for all institutions receiving federal grants. This study is an attempt to reveal the extent to which handicapped librarians can find employment in libraries. The method used was interrogation of handicapped employees, employers, and library administrators, and those working along with the handicapped in libraries.

The picture is still not an attractive one. As this study shows, the barriers were not entirely removed and there remains prejudice in many places. This book, therefore, is a welcome addition to the literature of library administration and career guidance. It should be in every library, and library administrators should be thoroughly familiar with it. [R: BL, 15 Apr 80, p. 1178; C&RL, July 80, pp. 383-84; JAL, July 80, pp. 164-65; LJ, Aug 80, p. 1613]

Jesse H. Shera

1466. Wilson, Pauline. **Stereotype and Status: Librarians in the United States.** Westport, Conn., Greenwood Press, 1982. 225p. bibliog. index. (Contributions in Librarianship and Information Science, No. 41). $29.95. LC 82-6119. ISBN 0-313-23516-3.

The purpose of this book is to help librarians decide upon and implement actions necessary "to help overcome the unfortunate stereotype that has plagued the library profession throughout this century." The author begins with the assumption that although the stereotype can't be completely eradicated, its potency and harmful effects can be reduced. The responsibility, Wilson argues, lies squarely with librarians themselves to improve the stereotype. The book provides a thorough, clear, straightforward analysis of the stereotype problem, its pervasiveness in librarianship, its numerous manifestations, and the ways it affects librarians and their behavior. By bringing the whole stereotype issue into the open, Wilson aids in thereby dealing with it effectively. She suggests ways in which the stereotype may be defeated and offers steps toward getting rid of "the habit that librarians have fallen into of negative criticism of their profession and its members."

Wilson begins by defining the problem, discussing stereotyping and stereotypes. Through content analysis she examines librarians' response to the stereotype. Publications that perpetuate the stereotype are discussed, as well as personality and the stereotype, and occupational choice and the stereotype. The chapter on library education and the stereotype is especially interesting and controversial. The concluding chapter pulls ideas together and suggests ways in which librarians can take the stereotype in stride, improve it, and control their response to it. The author draws upon research in minority group behavior to reach conclusions about how librarians handle their occupational identity. The book is heavily annotated. There are an extensive bibliography, an appendix on methodology, and an appendix of documents used. The author is a library educator and frequent contributor to the literature. The book is the result of years of systematic study and collection of material. It expands on earlier research, completed in 1979, on the reaction of librarians to their stereotype. This is a perceptive and scholarly book that should interest all types of librarians, even if they disagree with some statements made. [R: C&RL, Nov 83, pp. 498-500; JAL, Nov 83, p. 293; LJ, July 83, p. 1345; RQ, Summer 83, p. 439]   Susan J. Freiband

PARAPROFESSIONALS

1467. Borkowski, Mildred V. **Library Technical Assistant's Handbook.** Philadelphia, Dorrance, 1975. 400p. illus. bibliog. o.p. LC 74-84484. ISBN 0-8059-2071-4.

The author's intention is to provide a brief but comprehensive handbook of technical services and library functions for students enrolled in library technical assistant programs. The scope of library areas and duties presented is comprehensive, but the brevity of discussion is a serious weakness of the work. The text is composed of 63 cursory chapters which include repetitive review questions and varied enrichment activities. The depth of coverage is such that mending of library materials is covered in two pages while periodicals and serials are presented in four pages.

Important library developments that affect the work of LTA's are neglected, and no references are made either to revisions in the *Anglo-American Cataloging Rules* or to later editions of the *Library of Congress Subject Headings*. Databases such as OCLC are not mentioned, and the area of library computerization is sketchily outlined. Library cooperation, an important trend of the 1970s, is ignored.

The author has presented a work that at best provides a superficial overview of the work to be done by library technical assistants and certainly cannot be recommended.

Johnnie Ann Ralph

1468. Campbell, Alan, and Irene Dawson, eds. **The Library Technician at Work: Theory and Practice; Proceedings of the Workshop Held at Lakehead University, Thunder Bay,** **Ontario, May 8-9, 1970.** Ottawa, Ont., Canadian Library Association, 1970. 232p. o.p. LC 78-572081.

Proceedings of a workshop at Lakewood University, Thunder Bay, Ontario, 8-9 May 1970. Enumerates list of professional, technical, and clerical duties; job descriptions from school, public, and special libraries; and testimonial reports from four practicing library technicians concerning their respective training as it relates to actual work situations. Of greatest interest to library technician programs and to those libraries in which these people work. [R: LJ, 15 May 71, p. 1689]

Charles D. Patterson

1469. Chernik, Barbara E. **Introduction to Library Services for Library Technicians.** Littleton, Colo., Libraries Unlimited, 1982. 187p. bibliog. index. (Library Science Text Series). $28.00; $20.00pa. LC 81-15663. ISBN 0-87287-275-0; 0-87287-282-3pa.

Designed to be used in an introductory course in a library/media/technical assistant program or for the beginning untrained library assistant, this text provides a survey of the development of libraries, their personnel structure, materials and resources, organization and services of the major types of library (public, school, academic, and special), administration, and automation and networking. The author also discusses library functions such as circulation, acquisitions, and reference in order to identify the role of the library technician within these areas. Charts, samples, and photographs help to clarify library organization and personnel functions. Review questions and a selected list of readings conclude each chapter. Information on job availability, application procedures, and how to get the job you want comprises the final chapter. [R: LJ, 15 May 82, p. 972; SBF, Nov/Dec 82, p. 59]

1470. Chirgwin, F. John, and Phyllis Oldfield. **The Library Assistant's Manual.** 2nd, rev. ed. London, Clive Bingley; distr., Hamden, Conn., Shoe String Press, 1982. 137p. bibliog. index. (Outlines of Modern Librarianship). $14.00. ISBN 0-85157-350-9.

The first edition of this British textbook appeared in 1978, and there appears to be little reason to have a second edition. Basically, the book is a general overview of just about everything in British library science: library users, types of libraries, organization, record keeping, technical services, reference services, office practice, and so forth. The book is comparable to an introductory text for library technicians, but the material is so elementary that most North American students would have no use for the book. On the other hand, it is perfectly adequate for library clerks or other personnel without formal training to peruse as a primer, for, as the preface states, "it is intended to be an introduction to elementary principles of librarianship for non-professional staff in libraries, and it attempts to describe simple library routines in a non-technical manner." The old-fashioned pedagoguery probably accounts for there being only six illustrations of forms and a main bibliography that lists only six dictionaries and one-volume encyclopedias. Each of the 10 chapters, though, does contain a short list of reading references and some assignment questions. The book may be of value for British library education programs, but it is not for those in North America. For an evaluation of the first edition (1978) see *ARBA* 79 (entry 321). [R: LJ, May 83, p. 103]   Dean Tudor

1471. Mugnier, Charlotte. **The Paraprofessional and the Professional Job Structure.** Chicago, American Library Associaiton, 1980. 157p. bibliog. index. o.p. LC 80-12543. ISBN 0-8389-0303-7. (Available from Books on Demand, $40.80pa., ISBN 0-317-26564-4).

Based on data collected in 1972(?), this paperback provides information on the library associate within the library personnel community. Using the library associate as defined in "Library Education and Personnel Utilization (LEPU): A Statement of Policy Adopted by the Council of the American Library Association, June 30, 1970," the author delivers an interesting discussion of the associate's role in the function of the library. The average number of associates per library in January 1972 was 21.1 (p. 20). The information was gathered via a questionnaire sent to 136 public libraries serving populations of 225,000 or more. Of the 113 respondents (83 percent), 100 (88.5 percent) indicated the existence of a category of library worker that met the LEPU policy definition of associate. The author, through her investigation, provides a justification of the associate in the library, especially in chapter 5, "A Comparison of Tasks Assigned to Library Associates and First-Level Librarians." The appendices provide further information on the survey, questionnaire, and tables. The bibliography is current.

This study warrants serious consideration for replication in the 1980s. Recommended reading for library administrators. [R: JAL, Nov 80, p. 316]

Donald D. Foos

1472. Wright, Alice E. **Library Clerical Workers and Pages (Including Student Assistants).** Hamden, Conn., Linnet Books, 1973. 86p. illus. index. o.p. LC 73-937. ISBN 0-208-01130-X.

This slim pamphlet will be of little assistance in our small libraries. It has amusing cartoon illustrations, but the presentation is so simplistic that one wonders just who the intended audience is. Presumably, to judge from the examples used, the book is for an American audience. According to the introduction, the material "is presented with the hope that librarians of the many small and medium-sized libraries will have an outline to follow and materials to use in the selection, training, and supervision of clerical assistants and pages" (p. v). All this and more in 86 pages! [R: LJ, 15 Oct 73, p. 2983]

Bohdan S. Wynar

SCHOOL LIBRARY MEDIA PERSONNEL

1473. Cleaver, Betty P., and William D. Taylor. **Involving the School Library Media Specialist in Curriculum Development.** Chicago, American Association of School Librarians, American Library Association, 1983. 69p. (School Media Centers: Focus on Trends and Issues, No. 8). $7.00pa. LC 82-22759. ISBN 0-8389-3280-0.

This series was developed to generate innovative concepts that would lead to the change and improvement of service in school media centers. The philosophy of this title is that the media specialist should be involved with the school's instructional program at its inception rather than after the planning is completed. In order for the media specialist to initiate change, a strong working relationship must be established between the media specialist and the faculty. To facilitate this partnership in curriculum development, the authors present the TIE (Teaching, Involving, Evaluating) model for practical, systematic cooperation. The book concludes by presenting a method for analyzing the decision-making process and then presents "simulated" situations in which readers can evaluate their role as decision makers. Again, cooperation is the key to working with anyone who might object to the media specialist's recommendations.

Although the stated goal of this book is to direct the media specialist toward taking a strong role in curriculum development, the focus of the book is on working with faculty to provide a full array of media for the implementation of the curriculum. Since curricula are usually designed by the administration, more emphasis should have been given to working with the administration in curriculum development. Nevertheless, advocating this strong role for the media specialist in curriculum development should lead to a thoughtful reevaluation of one's role in the school curriculum. The TIE model is practical, and its presentation is clear and logical. It should enhance the media specialist's importance within the school. [R: BL, 1 June 83, p. 1270]   Hannah Pickworth

1474. Wisdom, Aline C. **Introduction to Library Services for Library Media Technical Assistants.** New York, McGraw-Hill, 1974. 364p. illus. bibliog. index. o.p. LC 73-21957. ISBN 0-07-071140-2.

This book tries to cover all major aspects of the library services that might involve library technical assistants. The material is arranged in five major chapters: "Introduction to Libraries and Library Services," "Organization and Arrangement of Materials," "Introduction to Public Services of a Library," "Introduction to Technical Services Routines," and "A Closeup of Libraries and the Role of the LMTA in Making Them Work." Appended are the "Code of Ethics for Librarians," organizational charts, a glossary, a bibliography, and an index.

In view of the voluminous literature on this subject, our examination of the bibliography proved rather disappointing. The two-page bibliography is limited to textbooks and monographs (plus one article), and even within these limitations, some of the omissions were rather striking. One of the pioneers in this area, of course, is Louis Shores, the author of numerous articles and a rather comprehensive syllabus that was published in book form. He is not even mentioned. Nor is Jay E. Daily, who wrote several books on this subject, notably *Cataloging for Library Technical Assistants* (1969 and 1972), .with a workbook published in 1972. Bloomberg and Evans's *Introduction to Technical Services for Library Technicians* is listed (Libraries Unlimited, now in its 5th ed., 1985), but not Bloomberg's *Introduction to Public Services for Library Technicians* (Libraries Unlimited, now in its 4th ed., 1985). The author is also not familiar with later editions of many standard books (e.g., Eaton, Gates, Katz, and Piercy, to name only a few). Certain of the titles listed, such as Fargo, Hutchins, and even Tauber's *Technical Services in Libraries*, were published so long ago that they are of only marginal value.

Equally disappointing is the content of this book. The author tries to cover practically everything, from ordering and receiving material and revising shelves of books [sic] to a brief history of libraries and library services and a discussion of the equipment involved in use of library materials.

In the chapter on public services activities, the author devotes 17 pages to a discussion of the circulation of library materials. Examining this presentation, however, reveals that the approach is so simplistic as to be almost painful. A number of circulation control systems exist (e.g., the Newark system, the Gaylord system, a variety of IBM card systems, photographic charging, etc.). Wisdom mentions the well-known 1961 Library Technology Project Report; this is followed by very brief paragraphs on "the three basic types" (p. 138) of circulation systems: book-card file systems, charge-card file systems, and transaction systems. And this is the extent of the discussion of circulation control systems. Other topics are afforded the same sort of cursory treatment.   Bohdan S. Wynar

WOMEN

1475. Heim, Kathleen M., ed. **The Status of Women in Librarianship: Historical, Sociological, and Economic Issues.** New York, Neal-Schuman, 1983. 483p. bibliog. index. $35.00. LC 82-7887. ISBN 0-918212-62-6.

Heim's collection of essays about the status of women in librarianship is an important contribution to the growing body of scholarship on women and work. Heim, whose work on status issues regarding women in the library profession is well known, has included essays that address the ideological reasons behind the status issues. Heim takes as a given that intraoccupational segregation exists within librarianship. "The power, the prestige, and the largest salaries within the field go to the minority of practitioners"—to men. The other essayists lucidly explore the historical, sociological, and psychological aspects of why women are not given an equal break. They are an impressive group of librarians, historians, and social scientists, all of whom have either written previously about women in the profession or have made their mark in librarianship, or both: Barbara Brand, Katherine Dickson, Janice Fennell, Marianne Ferber, Elizabeth Futas, Laurel Grotzinger, Betty Jo Irvine, Jean Martin, Nancy O'Brien, Patricia Reeling, Leila Rhodes, Judith Robinson, Adelaide Sukiennik, and Marion Taylor.

Also impressive is the range of the material in this collection, which includes studies on Canadians, black women, the Class of 1955,

academic and public librarians, reentry librarians, and library students. There are also several studies dealing with males in the field. Heim herself notes that gaps exist in the volume and suggests that the book is "a beginning step." [R: BL, 15 Oct 83, p. 327; JAL, Sept 83, pp. 231-32; RQ, Fall 83, p. 119; WLB, June 83, pp. 878-79]
　　　　　　　　　　　　Esther F. Stineman

1476.　Lundy, Kathryn Renfro. **Women View Librarianship: Nine Perspectives.** Chicago, American Library Association, 1980. 99p. bibliog. (ACRL Publications in Librarianship, No. 41). $8.00pa. LC 80-23611. ISBN 0-8389-3251-7.

This small paperback records interviews with nine women who have achieved eminent positions in librarianship. Five were heads of library schools at the time of the interview, and four held positions, three as directors, in large academic research libraries. Brief biographical information and a small pencil sketch set the stage for each interview. The opinions of these capable women on various library issues, such as discrimination against women in library promotions, restructuring ALA, and directions for library education in the future, are fairly interesting. There is some advice to young (or newly entering) librarians; for instance: change your position if you want to go up the ladder, even if you enjoy what you are doing on your present rung. Somehow the book as a whole was disappointing; the interviews failed to allow the dynamic personalities of these successful women to come through to the reader. It would be most useful in academic libraries, in special library science collections, and for career advising. [R: LJ, 15 Dec 81, p. 2372]　　　Laura H. McGuire

1477.　Myers, Margaret, and Mayra Scarborough, eds. **Women in Librarianship: Melvil's Rib Symposium.** Proceedings of the Eleventh Annual Symposium sponsored by the Alumni and the Faculty of the Rutgers University Graduate School of Library Service. New Brunswick, N.J., published for the Bureau of Library and Information Science Research, Graduate School of Library Service, by Rutgers University Press, 1975. 112p. bibliog. (Issues in the Library and Information Sciences, No. 2). $4.95pa. ISBN 0-8135-0807-X.

Various aspects of sex discrimination in the professional world, particularly librarianship, are discussed in this symposium from essentially the same point of view—such discrimination exists and is unfair. Three of the panelists are librarians, who present an introductory spoof on the invention of the library (amusing but

irrelevant) and statistical and experiential material on status levels, types of jobs, and pay differentials. The fourth, a psychologist, discusses the problems and frustrations of professional women in general. Each paper is followed by a brief discussion and a list of references. The two extensive and useful appendices provide a bibliography of English-language works between 1920 and 1973 and a review of federal laws and executive orders through 1972. Despite American Library Association conferences, the proliferation of concerned interest groups, the intrusion of governmental regulations, and an abundance of journal material on the status of women in librarianship, there is a tendency to ignore the problem of sex discrimination. This symposium helps to focus serious attention on a matter of concern to the largely feminized profession. [R: C&RL, Jan 76, p. 74; SLJ, Mar 76, p. 84]　　　　　　　　Margaret Norden

1478.　Weibel, Kathleen, and Kathleen M. Heim, with assistance from Dianne J. Ellsworth. **The Role of Women in Librarianship 1876-1976: The Entry, Advancement, and Struggle for Equalization in One Profession.** Phoenix, Ariz., Oryx Press, 1979. 510p. bibliog. index. (A Neal-Schuman Professional Book). $32.50. LC 78-27302. ISBN 0-912700-01-7.

Librarianship (a female-dominated profession, in case anyone doesn't know this fact by now or the grim economic implications of this truth) has traditionally associated the male librarian's role with management, innovation, and technology, and the female role with service, routine, and transmission, of societal values. Only with the second wave of feminism in the 1970s did librarianship begin to stand back and critically scrutinize the status and role of women in the field with an eye toward regrouping.

Heim and Weibel bring together 50 significant articles and reviews on women's changing role in librarianship, carefully placing these writings in the context of their times, and enhance their superb anthology by compiling the most substantial bibliography ever annotated on the subject, drawing from the literature of Great Britain and the United States. Opinion pieces, descriptions of women's status, exhortations, reports of activities, and sociological/historical analyses—all related to women in the library profession—span the period from 1876, which saw the emergence of librarianship as an organized profession, to the second feminist movement, which the authors follow up to 1976. "Women's status in librarianship, as in nursing, social work, and teaching reflects the societal pattern of women's place in the work force," the authors point out in the introduction. Articles and speeches by the likes of Robert Alvarez (1938), Melvil Dewey (1886), Salome Cutler Fairchild (1904), George Putnam (1912), Anita Schiller (1973), Jesse Shera (1934), and Kathleen Weibel (1976) document the truth of this assessment during the last century. There is no doubt that this is the authoritative historical and sociological work on women in librarianship. [R: JAL, Sept 79, p. 224]

Esther F. Stineman

1479. **Women and Library Management: Theories, Skills and Values.** Darlene E. Weingand, ed. Ann Arbor, Mich., Pierian Press, 1982. 124p. bibliog. (Current Issues in Librarianship, No. 1). $24.50. LC 82-60743. ISBN 0-87650-142-0.

These papers from a University of Wisconsin extension conference on women and library management address many of the problems confronting women librarians who are entering administration circles. Kathleen Heim discusses the status differentiation between male and female librarians, and Peter Hamon gives the male viewpoint of men and women in the workplace. Peggy Sullivan gives political advice to women participating in library associations. Of particular interest are the papers on conducting effective meetings by Marcia Koslov and on women publishing and editing library journal literature by Nancy Jean Melin.

Leadership, personal growth, and women in management are discussed in other presentations. A selected bibliography compiled by Linda Parker and a section identifying the presenters complete the book. Although the papers are uneven in quality and in information imparted, most do provide relevant advice for new women library managers. [R: JAL, May 83, p. 97]

Jennifer Cargill

50 Public Services

GENERAL WORKS

1480. Bloomberg, Marty. **Introduction to Public Services for Library Technicians.** 3rd ed. Littleton, Colo., Libraries Unlimited, 1981. 323p. illus. bibliog. index. (Library Science Text Series). $28.00; $20.00pa. LC 81-8210. ISBN 0-87287-257-2; 0-87287-263-7pa.

This text is an introduction to public services and basic reference materials for the library media technical assistant (LMTA) and other paraprofessional personnel. This edition contains significant revisions: (1) updated editions of reference materials; (2) addition of more recent reference works and deletion of older materials; (3) newer material on automated circulation systems; (4) revisions reflecting *AACR2, Library of Congress Subject Headings* (9th ed.), *Sears List of Subject Headings* (11th ed.), and *Dewey Decimal Classification* (19th ed.); (5) newer material on automation in interlibrary loan; (6) a new section on bibliographic databases; (7) numerous changes throughout the text reflecting advances in librarianship; and (8) revised bibliographies. Bloomberg explains for the paraprofessional the basic procedures and materials used in the public service functions of a library: circulation services, reference services, the card catalog, library classification systems, basic reference tools, library cooperation and interlibrary loan, and special services such as computerized databases. The text is generously illustrated with sample forms, cards, classification and filing systems, etc. The chapters on reference sources annotate the basic materials found in a general reference collection. A glossary, list of abbreviations, and index facilitate use of the text. Useful as a classroom text, in an in-service training program, and as an on-the-job handbook, the materials in

this text are meant to help paraprofessionals develop a foundation on which to build skills quickly through work experience. For a review of the first (1972) and second (1977) editions, see *ARBA* 72 (entry 115) and *ARBA* 78 (entry 231). A fourth edition (1985) is available. [R: LJ, 1 Nov 81, p. 2095]

1481. Brooks, Jean S., and David L. Reich. **The Public Library in Non-Traditional Education.** Homewood, Ill., ETC Publications, 1974. 244p. illus. index. $12.95. LC 73-21903. ISBN 0-88280-008-6.

The subtitle for this book should be "The Independent Study Project of the Dallas Public Library," for it is a detailed description of this exciting and innovative project by its director (Jean Brooks) and by the then deputy director for Public Services at the Dallas Public Library.

The project goal was to have the Dallas Public Library, through five specific branches and with the cooperation of Southern Methodist University, acquaint the public with the possibilities of obtaining college credit through CLEP (College-Level Examination Program). The Dallas Public Library acted as a learning resource center and provided independent study services and materials at no cost. The two-year project (1971-1973) was supported by a grant of $100,000 from three sources—the National Endowment for the Humanities ($50,000), the Council on Library Resources ($25,000), and the College Entrance Examination Board ($25,000).

This work includes a description of how the project was formulated, of the independent study students, the study tools used, relationships with SMU, the effects on the library, and a general overview of the entire project. An extensive addendum includes the original grant proposal and samples of publicity items and study guides – all of which would be very useful to other public libraries that should be stimulated into this kind of activity. Herein lies the value of this important publication. It shows that the public library can successfully play a leadership role as a center for independent study in its community. It should be required reading for all public librarians and should serve as a model for widespread adoption across the United States. [R: RQ, Fall 74, pp. 74-75]

George S. Bobinski

1482. Drake, Miriam A. **User Fees: A Practical Perspective.** Littleton, Colo., Libraries Unlimited, 1981. 142p. bibliog. index. $22.50. LC 81-6032. ISBN 0-87287-244-0.

The financing of library and information services is a major issue at all levels of government and for all institutions. Several methods have been and will continue to be explored in an effort to make library services available to the people who want and need them. This book contains 11 papers dealing with one method of funding those services: user fees. The papers represent a diversity of approaches by professionals working in a wide variety of situations. Both sides of this controversial issue are presented, in general and as applied to different types of libraries – public, academic, and special. This collection will serve as a stimulus to discussion of the issue, further reading (additional important readings are cited in the concluding bibliography), and informed decisions by those faced with the problem of finding alternative sources of library funding. [R: C&RL, July 82, p. 364; JAL, May 82, p. 99; LJ, 15 Feb 82, p. 414]

1483. Maurstad, Betty L., ed. **The Library and the Contemporary Arts.** Detroit, Wayne State University, Division of Library Science, 1977. 99p. o.p.

This small anthology contains papers and bibliographic surveys presented at two series of seminars sponsored by the Michigan Council for the Arts and administered by the Division of Library Science at Wayne State University. The sessions, held at Henry Ford Centennial Library in Dearborn and Grand Rapids Public Library, were designed to assist librarians in selecting materials and providing services in the contemporary arts.

Three of the five papers are by Wayne State University faculty: "Public Library Programs and the Contemporary Arts," by Genevieve M. Casey; "Trends in Contemporary Music: Surveying an Enigmatic Landscape," by Martin M. Herman; and "Modern Architecture," by Wayne Andrews. Also included are "Trends in the Movies in the 1970s (and Beyond)," by James L. Limbacher; and "Funding for the Arts," by Gertrude Pinkney. Excellent general bibliographic surveys on contemporary music, art, architecture, and film were prepared by Betty L. Maurstad and one on funding for the arts was prepared by Gertrude Pinkney.

This booklet will be of most value to small to medium-sized public libraries lacking extensive holdings in the arts. It provides a good introduction to current philosophies, practices, and social contributions of libraries to the arts. [R: LJ, 15 Oct 77, p. 2143]

Carole Franklin Vidali

1484. Robotham, John S., and Lydia LaFleur. **Library Programs: How to Select, Plan and Produce Them.** 2nd ed. Metuchen, N.J., Scarecrow, 1981. 352p. illus. bibliog. index. $19.00. LC 81-2149. ISBN 0-8108-1422-6.

Both Robotham and LaFleur have had many years of experience; thus, they bring to this book their knowledge, expertise, and a practical approach to library programming.

This book is planned as a guide for "librarians who want to produce successful programs – for those who want to do programs for the first time, for those who want to improve the quality of their programs and do more programming, and for those looking for fresh ideas." The purpose of the book is to "describe the techniques we have learned and the pitfalls we have encountered – and sometimes fallen into – on the way to successful programming." They define library programs as "any activity, in or out of the library, in which a librarian and two or more members of the public are involved."

The authors indicate that library programs have many purposes, but that the two most important are to "lure people into the library" and to serve as "extensions of material on library shelves." Programs are also a useful form of publicity, and if "well-presented, provide a valuable free public service."

The book is divided into three parts: "Kinds of Programs" examines discussion groups, film showings, the performing arts, talks, demonstrations, instruction, workshops, videotape, multimedia, automated programs, and children's programs; "Finding and Selecting Programs" lists sources of programs and tells how to choose the right program; and "Producing the Program" covers planning, scheduling, supervising, and publicity, concluding with an exemplary library program. In addition there are five appendices, which provide useful data on lists of books and films for discussion, film sources, sample film programs, and sample flyers and posters. There are a brief annotated bibliography and an index. The emphasis of the book is on public libraries, since they do the most programming, but other types of libraries would also find this book useful.

The physical format of the book is unattractive. This is unfortunate since the topic lends itself to a more imaginative and aesthetically pleasing production. However, this is still a useful contribution to an area that has not been covered in depth in library publications. The authors hope that librarians will use their book as a help in their library programming, but they state that "the kind of program one can have in a library is only limited by one's imagination— plus such mundane matters as money, staff, space, and equipment." They also hope librarians "will use these ideas as launching platforms for their own imaginations, and will develop programs that fit the needs of their own libraries." [R: LQ, Apr 78, p. 223; RQ, Spring 78, p. 278; SLMQ, Spring 77, p. 218]

Paul A. Winckler

1485. Van House, Nancy A. **Public Library User Fees: The Use and Finance of Public Libraries.** Westport, Conn., Greenwood Press, 1983. 140p. bibliog. index. (Contributions in Librarianship and Information Science, No. 43). $29.95. LC 82-11741. ISBN 0-313-22753-5; ISSN 0084-9243.

Van House was coauthor (under the name of DeWath) of *A Planning Process for Public Libraries*, for ALA. She here adapts some reasonable economic theories to the very timely problem of whether (and which) public library services ought to cost the patron and which services are part of the government's provision of service to the community. Beginning with the very definition of what a library is, she moves to arguments both for and against its justification as a tax-supported agency. Her clever economic analysis of services hinges on the way one views "public goods" and whether, say, an online literature search is of benefit to the individual or to a larger community of people.

In these times of increasingly austere government budgets, nearly everybody interested in library service will find something of interest in this book. In fact, its arguments could be used by those who wish to make a case for self-supporting, cost-recovery library provision as easily as by those who wish to keep the public library forever "free." It's all in what one finds and takes away from this expensive but valuable little work. For the application of scholarly theory to the commonsense problem of "fee or free," this book is especially recommended for governments and libraries, and it deserves the widest possible readership. [R: JAL, July 83, p. 176; RQ, Summer 83, pp. 437-38; WLB, May 83, p. 783]

Bruce A. Shuman

CIRCULATION SYSTEMS

1486. Bahr, Alice Harrison. **Automated Library Circulation Systems, 1979-80.** 2nd ed. White Plains, N.Y., Knowledge Industry Publications, 1979. 104p. illus. bibliog. index. $24.50pa. LC 79-16189. ISBN 0-914236-34-2.

The major part of this book includes excellent descriptions of one dozen automated library circulation systems. In addition, Bahr provides a good overview of this field, along with criteria for selection and implications of these systems for libraries. There has been increased competition from vendors over the last decade and the market remains in a state of flux, due in large part to hardware innovations (mini- and microcomputers). For all libraries concerned with automated circulation systems, this is the best book around; it is accurate, comprehensive, and comprehensible. Included are a directory of manufacturers offering and libraries using automated systems as of January 1979 and a useful bibliography. However, this reviewer is dismayed by the excessive prices of Knowledge Industry Publications paperbacks. [R: C&RL, Mar 80, p. 160]

Alan Edward Schorr

1487. Dranov, Paula. **Automated Library Circulation Systems, 1977-78.** White Plains, N.Y., Knowledge Industry Publications, 1977. 102p. illus. index. o.p. LC 77-7382. ISBN 0-914236-10-5.

The labor-intensive and time-consuming nature of library circulation activities makes them likely candidates for automation. A number of manufacturers offer minicomputer-based "turnkey" systems that include, for one price, all of the hardware and software required to automate circulation in a wide range of libraries. Since these systems often cost more than $100,000, it is important that librarians responsible for their evaluation have access to the latest available information about their features and limitations. This book by Paula Dranov provides a description of 11 systems, with a brief introductory analysis of automated circulation in general and reports of telephone interviews with librarians using the systems. The product descriptions, which include illustrations, appear to have been compiled largely from manufacturers' literature. There are a directory of manufacturers and a brief bibliography. [R: C&RL, Mar 78, p. 146; JAL, May 78, p. 94]   William Saffady

1488. Hubbard, William J. **Stack Management: A Practical Guide to Shelving and Maintaining Library Collections.** Chicago, American Library Association, 1981. 102p. index. $8.00. LC 80-28468. ISBN 0-8389-0319-3.

Hubbard refers to William H. Jesse's *Shelf Work in Libraries* as the work under revision. He follows Jesse's planning, updates ideas, adds illustrations, and uses current literature as support material. An example of the compact information presented by Hubbard is in his chapter 3, "Moving and Shifting Books." He summarizes basic moves and then refers in a footnote to a larger, more detailed source, in this case, Peter Spyers-Duran's *Moving Library Materials.* Hubbard uses the 1964 edition in his note but should have used the revised edition (American Library Association, 1965). Other chapters cover collection management; shelving books; stack management; care of books; missing books and inventory; and personnel management. An appendix discusses sampling as a statistical technique for libraries. The information here is nontechnical and useful for beginning purposes. One example is a small table of the numbers required for valid samples. The audience ranges from people new to libraries through experienced staff. Some of the information may seem obvious, but the gathering into one text of a wide range of materials in a clear, coherent, well-organized manner is the book's greatest value.

This volume would serve as a training manual for public service staff, even in small libraries. The shelving practice section of chapter 1, "Collection Management," is a compact review of format-related factors any librarian should read. Some routines are stated as universal truths rather than as ideas, but the book as a whole is suggestive and consequently an excellent planning tool. Numerous bibliographic footnotes provide access to support material, but an overall bibliography is lacking. The index does its job. The paperback binding is strong, and the heavy paper should stand considerable wear. Any librarian concerned with collection management in libraries should have this working tool close at hand. [R: A Arch, Fall

81, p. 368; C&RL, May 82, p. 260; JAL, Jan 82, p. 372]   Neal L. Edgar

1489. Hyman, Richard Joseph. **Access to Library Collections: An Inquiry into the Validity of the Direct Shelf Approach, with Special Reference to Browsing.** Metuchen, N.J., Scarecrow, 1972. 452p. bibliog. index. o.p. LC 77-169134. ISBN 0-8108-0434-4.

How useful is direct access to bookstacks in aiding the reader to locate the material he or she needs? American libraries almost universally have employed shelf classification with relative location to permit readers to browse for desired materials. This study of the validity of the direct shelf approach is divided into two distinct parts. The first, and most interesting, part is a review of the literature, beginning with a linguistic analysis of the browsing concept and reviewing the literature of some problems affecting access such as acquisitions policies, the role of classification, and the way library materials are used by patrons.

The second part of the study is based on a questionnaire soliciting responses from teachers and librarians to hypotheses derived from the literature. The study indicates that librarians have no convincing theoretical justification for direct access, although browsing was defended as one desirable approach to materials. The author reaches some conclusions and makes some suggestions for policy changes, but more questions are raised than answered by the study. The brief survey of the literature and the thought-provoking questions raised by the responses to the questionnaire make this study both interesting and worthwhile. [R: LJ, 15 Sept 72, p. 2818]   Paul H. Spence

COMMUNITY SERVICES AND INFORMATION

1490. **Community Information: What Libraries Can Do; A Consultative Document.** London, Library Association; distr., Phoenix, Ariz., Oryx Press, 1980. 135p. illus. o.p. ISBN 0-85365-872-2.

This publication of the British Library Association is a careful and thorough examination of the various roles a public library can play in providing community information and referral services. The title precisely describes the book's function—it is indeed a guide to what libraries can do and is a helpful document to consult. The authoring committee found the term "community information" confused and first establishes a clear definition. It next portrays the various types of information agencies in England, the major divisions being urban and rural, in meaningful detail but with an economy of words. These sections provide good instruction and insight into the complex and difficult functions such agencies perform and the skill and care required to establish and manage them effectively.

The chapters "What Libraries Can Do" and "What Libraries Do Now" are of value to any library considering providing information and referral services. They outline the scope of possible services, the types of materials and community networking that will be necessary, and give descriptions of existing library CI services in England and how they operate.

Important concepts discussed in the book include the role of advice, not a dirty word in England, and the fact that providing "information alone didn't solve many problems" (p. 9). People frequently require "advice to help them translate that information into effective action" (p. 7) because of a "lack of competence in pursuing their own problems" (p. 37). This is an attitude not usually seen as appropriate for library personnel and one that must be faced when considering involvement in I&R functions. The fact that the advocacy role can produce conflict with community organizations which provide services is also not dodged. The book itself gives advice in a helpful, practical, direct, and forthright manner. It does a good job of outlining the problems and obstacles as well as the tasks that must be done and methods for accomplishing them [R: LJ, 15 Jan 81, pp. 128-29]   Judith W. Devine

1491. Correy, Therese. **Library Community Services.** Inglewood, Calif., Inglewood Public Library, 1977. 98p. illus. bibliog. o.p. LC 77-28184. ISBN 0-913578-18-5.

This plastic-ring-bound, looseleaf manual gets down to the basics of library community services to those people unable to use the public library in the traditional way. Retirees, convalescents, the physically handicapped, exceptional children—even the city's parks, recreation, and fire departments—are special groups involved. Certain other persons more difficult to contact, such as illiterates, speakers of neither English nor Spanish, and juvenile delinquents, are excluded. The Inglewood (California) Public Library established extramural book collections at hospitals, retirement homes, and fire stations. Large print books, braille books, and talking books were provided for those patrons with sight difficulties. This manual shows how such services operate within a library's organizational framework, and it will point out ways for librarians at similar posts to meet the needs of like

groups. Some chapter headings, for example, are: "Organization" (including a job description for community services librarian), "Programs and Publicity," "Evaluation of Effectiveness," and "Suggested Community Services Resources." A proposed service for shut-ins, complete with forms, is highlighted. A chapter on plans and projects provides interesting ideas for future development. Examples of forms used are valuable. A bibliography, a list of periodicals, films, and a list of pertinent Inglewood Public Library publications conclude the volume. This library community services manual seems to be a more-than-adequate blueprint for action.   Edward A. Richter

1492. Evans, Charles. **Middle Class Attitudes and Public Library Use.** Littleton, Colo., Libraries Unlimited, 1970. 126p. (Research Studies in Library Science, No. 1). o.p. LC 70-131929. SBN 87287-015-4.

This survey focuses upon the relationship between library use and predetermined attitudes toward the library, revealing some reasons why people do not use public libraries. The work also offers a comprehensive analysis of previous studies, examining a number of critical factors and their relationships. The results of this survey provide timely research design and some solutions in this vital area. [R: WLB, Jan 71, p. 504]

1493. Garrison, Guy, ed. **Total Community Library Service: Report of a Conference Sponsored by the Joint Committee of the American Library Association and the National Education Association.** Chicago, American Library Association, 1973. 148p. o.p. LC 73-4310. ISBN 0-8389-0149-2.

The purpose of the conference was to clarify the concept of coordinating library and educational services in a community. One of the more interesting papers is the one given by Kathleen Molz ("Past and Present Efforts at Coordination of Library Services at the Community Level"), while one of the most cliché-ridden is by Gerald R. Brong ("Man and Media: The Library"). There are two additional papers, plus reactions from participants. In general, conference proceedings benefit from a little prepublication editing. As the editor bravely states in his preface, however, these papers are "basically unchanged from the preprints" (p. ix). Too bad. [R: RQ, Fall 73, p. 84]

Bohdan S. Wynar

1494. Hanna, Patricia Brennan. **People Make It Happen: The Possibilities of Outreach in**

Every Phase of Public Library Service. Metuchen, N.J., Scarecrow, 1978. 153p. bibliog. index. $15.00. LC 78-5923. ISBN 0-8108-1136-7.

People Make It Happen is the biography of a library breaking out from its paternalistic, patrician nineteenth-century mold to welcome the late twentieth-century community in all of its black, white, and Hispanic diversity. It is the story of how the librarian and the library's trustees took notice of the community and did something about it. Hanna's assumption "that outreach ... was the key both to the successful conduct of the public library's overall program and to full community support of that program," is to a large extent supported by her narrative.

Written as a master's thesis, the study includes a useful state-of-the-art review of the literature dealing with service to the Spanish-speaking. She also conducted a brief survey of public library service to the Spanish-speaking elsewhere in New York and reports her findings. They are descriptive only and are a brief part of the study. Thus the stage is set for her study of service to the Spanish-speaking in Beacon, New York. Although a small Hudson River city, Beacon has many of the characteristics of older and much larger cities—depressed inner city, middle class movement away from the center of the city, and an increasing black and Spanish-speaking population not yet a part of the mainstream of the community. Her account is a personal statement, supported by experience of what a library is and can be. It is an account of how the library board of trustees, the public library system and a dedicated staff identified needs, used resources, and made things happen. Much more than a "how we did it at Howland," this is an assertion that the library must respond to community needs, indeed it must to some extent anticipate them. It is a guide to how to begin, how to persevere, and how to conduct real outreach. What makes the difference is the social philosophy of the librarian who can translate idealism into practical terms. Once again it has been established that a necessary ingredient for success is leadership—the person who is actively concerned for the community in all of its images and who believes that indeed people make it happen, can make it happen. Pat Hanna writes well and believes in what she writes. [R: LJ, 1 Oct 78, p. 1929; SLJ, 15 Dec 78, p. 34]

Ann E. Prentice

1495. Holt, Raymond. **Focusing Library Services on the Economic Community: An Evaluation of an LSCA Demonstration Project in**

Pasadena and Pomona. Delmar, Calif., Raymond M. Holt and Associates; distr., Pasadena, Calif., Pasadena Public Library, 1971. o.p.

This volume is the final report of a one-year study funded by LSCA money and can serve as a blueprint for any library desiring to begin or expand its services to the business and industry population it serves. Charts, tables, graphs, and photographs enhance its usefulness as a point of departure. [R: LJ, Aug 72, p. 2550]

Charles D. Patterson

1496. Jordan, Robert T. **Tomorrow's Library: Direct Access and Delivery.** New York, R. R. Bowker, 1970. 200p. index. o.p. LC 75-102993. ISBN 0-8352-0292-3.

This is a compendium of information about direct access library programs and is useful to public, school, and academic librarians interested in making their holdings more accessible and convenient. Includes comments of librarians describing advantages and disadvantages, comparisons, costs, and promotional needs. Looks to the future in terms of proposed and projected plans, newer technology, and advances in librarianship. Overall arrangement and organization are haphazard but has a good index. [R: BL, 1 Oct 70, p. 116; C&RL, Sept 70, p. 356; LJ, July 70, p. 2432]

Charles D. Patterson

1497. Kronus, Carol L., and Linda Crowe, eds. **Libraries and Neighborhood Information Centers.** Urbana-Champaign, Ill., Graduate School of Library Science, University of Illinois, 1972. 142p. index. $6.00. LC 78-81002. ISBN 0-87845-034-3.

Contains papers presented at an institute conducted by the University of Illinois Graduate School of Library Science, 24-27 October 1971. The emphasis is on inner-city service of libraries as an informational and interpersonal link between community residents and social agencies. Among topics covered we find a number of case studies (e.g., Project Aurora in Elyria, Ohio, and the Model Cities Community Information Center in Philadelphia). There is also an informative article by James Welbourne on training urban information specialists. Well indexed. [R: CLW, Apr 73, p. 555; LR, Summer 73, p. 75]

USER STUDIES

1498. Dougherty, Richard M., and Laura L. Blomquist. **Improving Access to Library Resources: The Influence of Organization of**

Library Collections, and of User Attitudes toward Innovative Services. Metuchen, N.J., Scarecrow, 1974. 180p. illus. index. o.p. LC 73-20482. ISBN 0-8108-0637-1.

The central subjects of this study are two: how does the dispersion of literature relevant to the interests of a university faculty member affect his or her use of, and attitude toward, the library, and how do the faculties of two universities compare in their receptivity toward a document delivery service, in which a book or journal wanted by the individual is delivered to his or her office by the library? For an answer to the first question, several ingenious measures were used to determine the amount of scattering of relevant materials among campus libraries at Syracuse University for each of 100 randomly selected faculty members. Through interviews, the investigators determined which libraries they prefer to use and how much success they expect in obtaining needed materials. For the latter question, a comparison was made of data obtained from faculty at Ohio State University, where a document delivery service had been offered for the previous year, and at Syracuse University, where the service was not available. Both of these questions are matters of considerable interest to university library administrators, and reliable research on them is welcome.

In general, the research methodology was satisfactory and, in some respects, innovative. Separate interview guides for use on the two campuses were carefully made up and tested, and interviewers were rehearsed in order to ensure uniform practice. Preparation covered rules of procedure, definitions, and training of staff to carry out the several measures. The analysis of data was objective, and reporting of results was honest. For example, general conclusions were not drawn from the data obtained at OSU, since the sample of faculty members interviewed there was neither adequate nor random.

Major findings were (1) that a faculty member will prefer to use a nearby or pleasant branch library rather than a more distant or less pleasant one with a larger collection in his or her subject area; (2) instead of bringing relevant material closer to the faculty by creating branch libraries, the decentralization of the library may actually make materials less accessible through dispersion; (3) faculty members at OSU who are users of the document delivery service have a more positive attitude toward the library and

toward the delivery service than do those OSU faculty who do not use it or the SU faculty, who do not have the service. Several related aspects of faculty use of the library were explored more briefly and reported. Better writing would have made the study easier to understand, but the methodology and data are given in complete form, so that any interested reader can check the conclusions. [R: AL, July/Aug 74, p. 369; LJ, 1 Oct 74, p. 2454]   Walter C. Allen

1499. **Index to Users Studies.** Compiled by FID Study Committee Information for Industry (FID/II). The Hague, International Federation for Documentation, 1974. 103p. o.p. ISBN 92-66-00515-0.

The International Federation for Documentation, Study Committee Information for Industry (FID/II) has compiled an index of 200 user studies. The majority of the studies included were published in the 1960s and 1970s and come from 20 different countries. The committee was highly selective to include user studies judged most important.

The index is organized into three sections. The first section is basically a subject approach index. The subject headings were determined by members of the committee. While the subject heading index is very important and, in this case, useful, the level of inclusiveness of the individual terms tends to vary. These terms are not structured according to a definite plan but rather are based on the subject area of the individual user surveys chosen. In spite of this, they contribute considerably to the usefulness of this work.

The second section consists of an alphabetical list of authors, with identifying numbers indicating where the complete bibliographic data corresponding to the appropriate user survey are available. Finally, the third part includes full bibliographic data and a very brief description of each survey. Each study is assigned a chronological number. This same number appears under the appropriate author and subject indexes.

This work brings together many interesting user surveys. It organizes them by subject and author as well as briefly describing them. It has potential utility for anyone involved with public services or research work in general. [R: Unesco, May/June 75, p. 159]

George V. Hodowanec

51 Reference Services

GENERAL WORKS

1500. Brittain, J. M. **Information and Its Users: A Review with Special Reference to the Social Sciences.** New York, Wiley, 1971. 208p. index. o.p. LC 71-152735. SBN 900843-08-X.

In this survey of some 500 user studies, the material is arranged under five major headings: introductory chapter describing terminology and the interrelation between information science and user studies; methodology; studies in the social sciences; studies of communication artifacts; and a concluding chapter in which the author points out some neglected apects of users and their information requirements. This study is an offshoot of the Investigation into the Information Requirements of the Social Sciences (INFROSS) that was conducted in Great Britain. In general, the coverage is adequate, if one keeps in mind the facts. First, the author, as a psychologist, emphasizes the material he knows best. Obviously, APA's Scientific Information Exchange in Psychology series, with the preliminary works of Paisley, is very important; but equally important are other projects mentioned only briefly by the author or not mentioned at all. This reviewer found nothing in the appended bibliography of references on *The Universal Reference System* (reviewed in *ARBA* 71), which is rather disturbing. A few little things may even irritate an American reader. Why mention Walford and not Winchell, or, as a matter of fact, *American Reference Books Annual*? Nevertheless, these are minor items that need not detract from the overall usefulness of this compilation. [R: LJ, 1 Nov 71, pp. 3580-81]   Bohdan S. Wynar

1501. Chen, Ching-chih, and Peter Hernon. **Information Seeking: Assessing and Antici-pating User Needs.** New York, Neal-Schuman, 1982. 205p. illus. index. (Applications in Information Management and Technology Series). o.p. LC 82-6320. ISBN 0-918212-50-2.

This volume was prepared with the aid of a grant from the Office of Libraries and Learning Technology, U.S. Department of Education. It is, therefore, a government research report and is available from NTIS and ERIC. In its present form it may receive wider dissemination and thereby have a greater effect on the library community. What it reports is a telephone survey in New England of more than 2,000 households with the prime objective of determining the role of U.S. libraries in providing information to their communities and relating this role to information-seeking patterns. The survey's methodology differed slightly from that of earlier studies of this type performed in California, Washington, and Maryland. Unfortunately for library science researchers, this report does not fully compare all related studies adequately. Nevertheless, it does document, as well or better than a dissertation would, the methodology, the survey instrument, the findings, and the recommendation for further study.

The work may be of some value to public librarians who are attempting to react to the White House Conference report and to library science students who need an example of survey research in their field. [R: C&RL, July 83, pp. 292-93; LJ, 15 Jan 83, p. 114]
Pauline Atherton Cochrane

1502. Collison, Robert L. **Library Assistance to Readers.** New York, Philosophical Library, 1963; repr., Westport, Conn., Greenwood

Press, 1972. 139p. index. $15.00. LC 75-14126. ISBN 0-8371-5858-3.

This volume is a reprint of the fourth edition, which was published in 1963. In 1965 there was a fifth edition published with some updating and additional material. The reviewer does not know why the earlier edition was chosen for reprinting; it would seem more useful to have reprinted the later edition. In fact, what is needed is a new edition, not a reprint of a work over 10 years old.

The book is divided into four parts. Parts 1 and 2 discuss the use of the library by patrons, and public relations. Part 3 covers readers' advisory work and includes brief sections on reference methods, the vertical file, making an index, and other related topics. Part 4 discusses a select number of reference materials with some emphasis on titles most useful in British libraries. Many of the titles, however, are commonly found in libraries in the United States.

The author has written a readable book with some good ideas. It is limited, however, by its lack of discussion of basic library problems and its failure to differentiate between the problems faced by different types of libraries and their goals. The book should prove useful to the beginning student of library science if it is read as one of several introductory texts.

The format is acceptable, and the author's style is readable.   Marty Bloomberg

1503.   Covey, Alma A. **Reviewing of Reference Books: An Evaluation of the Effectiveness of Selected Announcement, Review and Index Media in Their Coverage of Reference Books.** Metuchen, N.J., Scarecrow, 1972. 142p. index. o.p. LC 70-182831. ISBN 0-8108-0456-5.

In this rather interesting study the author analyzed some 1,000 reference books in several reviewing media in an attempt to determine the effectiveness of major reviewing media with respect to reference books. Because librarians evaluate and select on the basis of reviews, it is important to know the relative strengths of such announcement media as *Library Journal* ("Books to Come"), *PW* ("Weekly Forecasts"), and *Forthcoming Books*; the quality and quantity of reviews in *Booklist, Choice, College and Research Libraries, LJ, School Library Journal,* and *WLB*; and finally, the coverage in "index media"—that is, *Book Review Digest, Book Review Index, Index to Book Reviews in the Humanities,* and *Technical Book Review Index.*

Here are some of the conclusions. The Winchell supplement for 1967-1968 (used as a basis for this study) is far from complete in its coverage of books published in 1967 or 1968 in

the United States and abroad. "Weekly Record" does not provide a complete record of reference books published in the United States; approximately one-fourth of the U.S. reference books under study were not listed in "WR." Review coverage of U.S. reference books is far from complete, since approximately one-third of U.S. reference books under study were not reviewed in any of the seven media studied. And finally, there is little duplication in coverage of reference books by the seven review media studied. It is probably unfortunate that this study was completed (apparently) in 1969—that is, before the first edition of *ARBA* was published.

Since we obviously are not able to retrace the author's methodology here, step by step, it might be rather difficult to argue with all of her findings. Nevertheless, from our experience (and referring to our statistical tabulations in *ARBA*), we do not think that *Choice* "provided the greatest coverage" (p. 128). To be specific, in 1969 *Choice* reviewed 124 reference books with 1969 imprints, as compared to 311 reviewed in *Library Journal.* Second, contrary to the author's conclusion, there is a great deal of duplication between the seven reviewing journals (approximately 70 percent). And her statement that "approximately one-third of the U.S. reference books under study were not reviewed in any of the seven media studied" (p. 128) is somewhat optimistic; our statistical records show closer to two-thirds that were not reviewed—which is the reason why the author of this review started *ARBA.* [R: LJ, 1 Sept 72, p. 2819]   Bohdan S. Wynar

1504.   Davinson, Donald. **Reference Service.** London, Clive Bingley; distr., Munich, New York, K. G. Saur, 1980. 235p. index. $17.50. ISBN 0-85157-291-X.

Refreshingly readable, Davinson's work is clearly the result of practical experience, astute observation, and the scope and perspective that library education often gives to an author. The book's 12 chapters deal with the traditions, the existing practice, and the future prospects of library reference service. Enriched with opinion as well as a clear view of the realities of reference, Davinson writes of the need for a balance between knowledge of sources of information and competence in dealing with the seekers of information. His style is usually good, and occasionally charming and elegant. A few errors of proofreading and diction mar the text.

Davinson shows an awareness of professional writing and views from the United States as well as from the United Kingdom, a characteristic unfortunately rarer on this side of the Atlantic. His references, listed at the end of each chapter, are excellent for his theses. The modest separate indexes for subjects and authors are scarcely worth including. Sample chapter headings show the scope of the book: "Reference Theory"; "Costing and Evaluation of Reference Service"; "Librarian-User Relationships: The Library Network"; "Instruction in Library Use" (especially provocative), and "Teaching Reference Service."

Probably not useful as a basic text, but welcome when such texts have dulled the senses, this book is one to stimulate practitioners and observers of the reference scene. [R: LJ, 1 Sept 80, p. 1713]   Peggy Sullivan

1505. Grogan, Denis. **Practical Reference Work.** London, Clive Bingley; distr., Munich, New York, K. G. Saur, 1979. 144p. bibliog. index. (Outlines of Modern Librarianship). $12.00. ISBN 0-85157-275-8.

Grogan alerts readers at the outset (p. 8) that this work treats reference work in the sense defined by Samuel Rothstein ("the personal assistance given by the librarian to individual readers in pursuit of information") and eschews discussing reference services in general, which William A. Katz defined as "whatever reference librarians are doing." On that basis, Grogan omits certain topics: the study and evaluation of reference works, bibliographical compilation, administration of reference/information dissemination (the subject of another volume in this series), and reader's advisory service.

Considering that this is admittedly a prescriptive (how-to-do-it) work to "advise young reference librarians of the best way to practise their art" (p. 9), it is dismaying that the author chose not to support the quotations he has used with precise citations. Instead we have his confession (p. 9): "I have drawn on most of my colleagues' work without acknowledgement." To Grogan's credit, however, the six chapters—reference work, the reference question, the reference process, the reference interview, the search, the response—offer much cogent advice. Each concludes with a brief list of suggested readings, cited precisely. The volume concludes with a 13-item (2 by Grogan) "Books on Reference Work," beginning with James I. Wyer's *Reference Work* (American Library Association, 1930) and ending with William Katz's *Introduction to Reference Work: Volume II, Reference Services and Reference Processes* (3rd ed., McGraw-Hill, 1978)—all bibliographically complete. The index locates subjects and

persons mentioned in the text. Keeping in mind that it is intended only as an overview, this title should come to the attention of library/information science students and teachers. [R: C&RL, July 80, pp. 389-90]   Wiley J. Williams

1506. Katz, Bill, and Anne Clifford, comps. **Reference and Information Services: A New Reader.** Metuchen, N.J., Scarecrow, 1982. 417p. $17.50. LC 81-16680. ISBN 0-8108-14830-8.

When anthologies are compiled with discriminating judgment and drawn from a wide range of journals, they make valuable time-savers for those interested in the subject covered. Such is the case with this reader, whose 30 articles, all new, except one, since the first edition in 1978 (published under the title *Reference and Information Services: A Reader* and edited by Bill Katz and Andrea Taril), were selected by the prolific and indefatigable Bill Katz and his co-compiler. Five sections cover: (1) reference process; (2) expanding reference service; (3) online reference services, television, and networks; (4) interview and search; and (5) reference forms. The latter include two British journal articles, Walford's on compiling his *Guide* and Bakewell's on inadequate indexes. Several articles are reprinted from *Scholarly Publishing*, one being Preece's "Notes toward a New Encyclopedia." Most are from American state and national library periodicals. Since selections were based on their relevance for students and working librarians, together with their style and balance of research, this is a good supplement to Katz's annual *Library Lit.*, whose contents are not reprinted in the reader. [R: BL, Aug 82, p. 1506; JAL, Sept 82, p. 232; LJ, 15 Mar 82, p. 616]   Frances Neel Cheney

1507. Katz, Bill, and Anne Clifford, eds. **Reference and Online Services Handbook: Guidelines, Policies, and Procedures for Libraries.** New York, Neal-Schuman, 1982. 581p. index. $37.50. LC 81-11290. ISBN 0-918212-49-9.

Bill Katz and Anne Clifford have compiled an extremely interesting and useful publication in *Reference and Online Services Handbook*, the substance of which is the reference and online reference policy manuals or excerpts from them of selected American and Canadian libraries.

During a 14-month period, from the first part of 1980 to March 1981, the editors requested policy statements from a group of academic, public school, and special libraries. Material was received from 53 academic libraries and 33 public libraries, and online statements from a combination of 40 academic, public, and special libraries. Responding libraries tended to be medium- to large-sized, leading the editors to surmise that as the number of patrons increases, larger libraries attempt to deal with the growing problems and procedures of reference work by clarifying and codifying the method of service. No pertinent material was received from school libraries: "Most [school librarians] who responded noted that they had no such policy or simply sent material about collections and acquisitions" (introduction).

The book is arranged into five main sections. The first consists of contributed articles, including one by Patricia Payne entitled "Why School Librarians Lack Reference Policy Statements—and What's to Be Done about It?" Also in this first section are RASD's policy guidelines, "A Commitment to Information Services: Developmental Guidelines, 1979." The second and third parts, on academic and public libraries, respectively, include excerpts from the various reference policy statements arranged according to RASD's outline. Section 4 excerpts the online policy statements from academic, public, and special libraries. The final section reprints in full model reference policies from one academic library, Rice University Library, and one public library, Los Angeles Public Library, and a model online reference policy from the University of Houston Library.

Any library going through the difficult process of creating a reference or online reference policy or interested in comparing aspects of an existing one with another library's will find *Reference and Online Services Handbook* a very valuable resource. [R: BL, Aug 82, p. 1506; JAL, Sept 82, p. 243; LJ, Aug 82, p. 1390]

Heather Cameron

1508. Kochen, Manfred, and Joseph C. Donohue, eds. **Information for the Community.** Chicago, American Library Association, 1976. 282p. illus. bibliog. index. o.p. LC 75-40168. ISBN 0-8389-0208-1.

As its preface clearly states, this book is primarily concerned "with an individual's need for everyday information ... [and with] the agencies that make it their primary business to provide that information." Specifically, the editors aim to provide background concepts and methods both to measure needs and to design appropriate "Information & Referral" ("I&R") services to meet them. In addition to their own experiences and insights into the topic, the editors present contributions of several authors

from fields of information sciences and social services.

Both theoretical and pragmatic information is offered throughout the book's four parts. Part 1 presents background concepts, vocabulary, historic perspective, and suggestions to identify community information needs and services. A few philosophical concerns are raised in part 2, which for the most part describes several functioning "I&R" services. Research techniques and results are presented in part 3, and the concluding part 4 offers comments and recommendations on the applications of such findings and on further needs for research in this area. An annotated bibliography, which lists both the literature and organizations concerned with "I&R" services, together with the lists of references concluding each chapter, provides the interested reader with additional sources of information.

The book is not a reference tool itself but is rather a discussion of the generic problems of reference within the specific area of community information services. Thus it is intended for a variety of audiences concerned with helping individuals and groups function within a growingly complex society. [R: Choice, Feb 77, p. 1578; LR, Winter 76/77, p. 327]   Danuta A. Nitecki

1509. Mathies, M. Lorraine, and Peter G. Watson. **Computer-Based Reference Service.** Chicago, American Library Association, 1973. 200p. bibliog. index. $15.00pa. LC 73-9967. ISBN 0-8389-0156-5.

This book is an outgrowth of a program that began at the 1968 Annual Conference of the American Library Association in Atlantic City. It offers a number of practical suggestions on computer searching and indexing. ERIC is presented as a prototype of a computerized database, from which broader generalizations are drawn. Other machine-readable databases are also discussed, such as MARC, the 1970 census apparatus, etc. The book is well indexed and should be of interest to all larger library systems. [R: C&RL, Sept 74, p. 379; Choice, May 74, p. 419; LR, Summer 74, p. 270; RSR, Apr 74, p. 21]

1510. McInnis, Raymond G. **New Perspectives for Reference Service in Academic Libraries.** Westport, Conn., Greenwood Press, 1978. 572p. bibliog. (Contributions in Librarianship and Information Science, No. 23). $29.95. LC 77-94742. ISBN 0-313-20311-3.

The literature of reference services is vast, as a glance at Murfin and Wynar's *Reference*

Services: An Annotated Bibliographic Guide attests (see *ARBA* 78, entry 240). McInnis has wisely concentrated on a specific variety of the reference function—service to the academic community, with the concentration on the needs of students. As his *Social Science Research Handbook*, co-authored with James W. Scott (see *ARBA* 76, entry 239), shows, McInnis is well grounded in his knowledge of the available sources, and his experience with the academic community shows as well. The book's five sections provide: (1) a review of the state of teaching in the social sciences and of the relationship of research and scholarly consensus, (2) a discussion of how published sources in social sciences are organized, (3) a classification (ranging along a spectrum from substantive works to pure bibliographies) of kinds of reference sources, (4) a demonstration of how library guides can be organized to assist students in learning research strategy, and (5) a discussion of preparing area studies research guides.

McInnis sees the crucial point in the student's learning the library's potential at the time when the student has a specific problem to solve and the librarian assists in the solution. (The "hands on" approach enhances both immediate learning and retention, thereby establishing a solid base for future learning of research skills.) McInnis's hope that librarians will be eventually invited into the classroom may be optimistic, given most academics' sense of territorial imperative, but it does not seem unreasonable. His chief contributions here are his thorough analysis of difficulties and the opportunities to overcome them and his flexible classification scheme for types of reference works. [R: LJ, 1 Nov 78, p. 2176]   Koert C. Loomis, Jr.

1511.   Shores, Louis. **Reference as the Promotion of Free Inquiry.** Littleton, Colo., Libraries Unlimited, 1976. 189p. index. o.p. LC 76-6150. ISBN 0-87287-156-8.

Shores's ideas on reference work as a positive and necessary support to a democratic society have had a remarkable consistency for many years and, as this collection bears out, they continue to hold a significant message for all librarians. Gathered together in this anthology are 22 essays, articles, and speeches on a single coherent theme, which dominated Shores's long career as an activist librarian. The section headings of this anthology demonstrate both the range and the coherence of his views on reference services: "Delineation of a Theory"; "The Promotion of Free Inquiry"; "The Two Cultures of Librarianship"; "Information Education"; "Reference Literary Criticism"; and

"Encyclopedics." This volume is a permanent embodiment of Shores's work as a reference theoretician and it is a significant contribution to the study and understanding of reference services. [R: C&RL, Nov 76, pp. 573-74; LJ, 15 Oct 76, p. 2151]

1512.   Turick, Dorothy. **Community Information Services in Libraries.** New York, Library Journal/R. R. Bowker, 1978. 80p. illus. index. o.p. ISBN 0-8352-1070-7; ISSN 0362-448X.

The fifth in the series of *LJ Special Reports* provides a description of the philosophical foundation, the educational opportunities, and planning procedures for community information services in libraries. Over a dozen community information service programs in public libraries are described. In most cases, names and addresses of persons to contact for further information are given. Nonlibrary organizations concerned with community information services are profiled, ranging from the Alliance of Information and Referral Services (AIRS) to the United Way of America. Samples of logos and other publicity illustrations relating to community information programs are interspersed in the text. This publication will undoubtedly be useful to those people planning such programs, but it does leave something to be desired as a comprehensive state-of-the-art report on the "CIS" concept. The serious sections of the publications are not well coordinated and do not flow as smoothly from one to another as one might expect. Some appear to be reprints from external sources, while others appear to be compilations of correspondence and conversations with the author. Citations to sources, quotations, and other references are not consistently given. An annotated bibliography on selected publications on the topic is included. Although not as well edited as some of the other *LJ Special Reports*, it does provide a convenient background to community information services in libraries.   Terry L. Weech

1513.   Vavrek, Bernard, ed. **Current Trends in Reference Services.** Urbana-Champaign, Ill., Graduate School of Library and Information Science, University of Illinois, 1983. 1v. (various paging). (*Library Trends*, Vol. 31, No. 3). o.p. ISSN 0024-2594.

The editor of this issue of *Library Trends* states in his introduction that the goal is to "identify current and future trends facing reference librarians and reference librarianship." This goal was implemented here with nine articles that address the trends and issues facing reference service in various types of libraries.

There are articles that cover trends in reference service in the four major types of libraries. Other articles are topical, such as "Research in Library Reference/Information Service," "Online Searching in the Reference Room," and "Standards for Reference Service." The articles present a current bibliographic review of the topics as well as a synthesis of views from the field. Although the articles are all of high quality, of particular note is the one by Samuel Rothstein titled "The Making of a Reference Librarian" that deals with education for reference librarianship.

Library Trends has a well-established reputation for publishing high-quality review articles on selected topics. This issue maintains that reputation with a collection of articles that collectively provide the reader with a good overview of the state of reference service in libraries. This should be read and assimilated by library educators and active reference librarians alike.   Gary R. Purcell

REFERENCE WORKS

1514. Murfin, Marjorie E., and Lubomyr R. Wynar. **Reference Service: An Annotated Bibliographic Guide. Supplement 1976-1982.** Littleton, Colo., Libraries Unlimited, 1984. 353p. index. $35.00. LC 84-16388. ISBN 0-87287-402-8.

This supplemental publication marks a continuing effort to provide complete access to the literature of librarianship. Like its predecessor (see *ARBA* 78, entry 240), the supplement records the sources of reference service and, in sheer numbers of citations and pages, surpasses the original *Reference Service* published in 1977. The supplemental volume includes 1,668 annotated entries, divided into nearly the same 14 subject chapters as the original. Entries include books, articles, book chapters, theses, dissertations, conference proceedings and papers, and other materials such as ERIC documents. The coverage is generally from 1976 to 1982, although some 1976 and 1983 publications are included. An author/title and a subject index conclude the book.

Topics treated correspond to the 14 chapters and include such subjects as the theory of reference service, reference service by the type of library, research in reference, and the application of the computer to reference service. The mention of 4 of the 14 topics hardly does justice to the scope of the volume, as it provides a comprehensive source for most of the essential

activities which merge to form reference service in any type of library.

While the compilers recognize the impossibility of including all aspects of the reference process (interlibrary loan and translation services are omitted, for example), it is unfortunate that more space could not be devoted to library instruction. The compilers do include some citations as they relate to reference service; however, the list is incomplete. Missing are significant articles by John Mark Tucker on user education in academic libraries (*Library Trends*, volume 29, 1980) and Peter Hernon's study of library instruction (*Journal of Library History*, volume 17, 1982). Instead there is increased emphasis on the computer and reference service. This section is expanded from 20 pages in the original edition to about 70 pages in the supplement. Recent technological innovations applied to the reference function warrant this expansion.

The few criticisms of the supplemental volume are negligible when compared to the thoroughness of the book. The original and supplement represent a significant addition to the literature of reference librarianship.

                    Boyd Childress

INTRODUCTORY TEXTS AND MANUALS

1515. Chandler, G. **How to Find Out: Printed and On-line Sources.** 5th ed. New York, Pergamon Press, 1982. 250p. index. $16.50. LC 80-42154. ISBN 0-08-027433-1.

This is the fifth edition of a work begun in 1963 by George Chandler. Continuing to follow the Dewey Decimal Classification System, it now contains 19 chapters. Few changes have been made in the first 15 chapters since the fourth edition was reviewed (see *ARBA* 75, entry 3). Titles of reference books are mentioned, with only brief information given for each one. Much of the information is dated (e.g., *Publishers Weekly*, instead of its now separate publication, *Weekly Record*, is used as a U.S. bibliographic source). Over 120 illustrations of sample pages of reference works are not included. The major change has occurred in the last four chapters, which include information on online sources of the United States, the United Kingdom, Canada, Australia, Europe, and Japan. Although some updated information is provided, this work still lacks completeness as a guide for information sources. [R: RSR, Spring 83, p. 53]

                    Anna Grace Patterson

1516.   Cheney, Frances Neel, and Wiley J. Williams. **Fundamental Reference Sources.** 2nd ed. Chicago, American Library Association, 1980. 351p. index. $15.00. LC 80-21617. ISBN 0-8389-0308-8.

The second edition of *Fundamental Reference Sources*, like the first (see *ARBA 72*, entry 104), is intended as "an introduction to selected sources of bibliographical, biographical, linguistical, statistical and geographical information." Unlike the first, which was addressed to the "beginning library school student," no specific audience is indicated. It adheres strictly to the first edition in format. The introductory chapter on the nature of reference/information service was updated to include some later developments in the field. Six additional chapters, each beginning with informative and well-written narratives, describe different types of information sources: bibliographies, sources of biographical information, dictionaries, encyclopedias, statistical sources, and sources of geographical information. Material published since 1971 has been added, and chapter 6, "Sources of Statistics," has been substantially enlarged. The appendix contains guidelines for evaluating particular types of reference books.

Both in the introductory chapter on reference service and in the chapters on different sources, the emphasis is on printed material. By 1981, the use of machine-readable databases for information retrieval/reference was commonplace in many libraries, and their impact on the nature of reference service is a subject of considerable professional discussion. Any beginning librarian today should be familiar with these sources as well as the traditional, fundamental reference sources that Cheney and Williams have so ably described.

Because many of the reference sources cited have been updated, and because of the informative narratives that introduce each type of information source, this work would likely prove useful along with William Katz's *Introduction to Reference Work*, third edition (see *ARBA 79*, entry 294) as a basic introduction to reference literature for the library school student. It might also serve as a useful tool in libraries offering library instruction programs. [R: JAL, Sept 81, pp. 239-40; LJ, July 81, p. 1395]

Heather Cameron

1517.   Doyle, James M., and George H. Grimes. **Reference Resources: A Systematic Approach.** Metuchen, N.J., Scarecrow, 1976. 293p. illus. bibliog. index. o.p. LC 76-7080. ISBN 0-8108-0928-1.

This text is arranged in three parts: "The Structure and Identification of Reference Resources," "Resource Use and User Behavior," and "An Operational Model of the Searching Process." The book is intended for two basic audiences—as a guide for librarians and as a searcher's manual for "the average intelligent adult who is pursuing an information need" (introduction). This interesting experiment will probably be tested by instructors in library schools. [R: C&RL, July 77, p. 342; JAL, Sept 77, p. 218; LJ, 1 Feb 77, p. 343; LQ, Oct 77, p. 500]

1518.   Galvin, Thomas J. **Current Problems in Reference Service.** New York, R. R. Bowker, 1971. 162p. bibliog. (Problem-Centered Approaches to Librarianship). o.p. LC 77-162527. SBN 8352-0425-1. (Available from Books on Demand, $34.20, ISBN 0-8357-9040-1).

This is the first volume in a series devoted to problem-centered approaches to librarianship. It contains 35 cases based on actual situations. A selected bibliography lists other collections of case studies. [R: LJ, 15 Oct 71, p. 3301; RQ, Winter 71, p. 174; WLB, Sept 71, p. 86]

1519.   Grogan, Denis Joseph. **More Case Studies in Reference Work.** Hamden, Conn., Linnet Books, 1972. 293p. bibliog. o.p. LC 72-185911. ISBN 0-208-01070-X.

In 1967 the author published *Case Studies in Reference Work*, which was favorably reviewed in library literature. This sequel offers 189 new case studies. While the older work chiefly concentrated on encyclopedias, bibliographies, and dictionaries, *More Case Studies* includes books of quotations, biographical directories, and gazetteers. It should be noted that contrary to some texts in this area (primarily those published by R. R. Bowker), Grogan's work offers "Resolved Cases," thus providing step-by-step guidance for answering specific questions. [R: AL, Oct 72, p. 1019; LJ, 1 Dec 72, p. 3879]

1520.   Hede, Agnes A. **Reference Readiness: A Manual for Librarians and Students.** 3rd ed. Hamden, Conn., Archon/Shoe String Press, 1984. 200p. $21.50; $15.00pa. ISBN 0-208-02001-2; 0-208-02002-0pa.

This third edition has revised most of the entries in the 1977 edition and added some new ones, now covering over 300 basic titles. Descriptive and analytical annotations are provided for dictionaries, bibliographies, atlases, etc. Subject sections include an introduction to each form, and each chapter has a bibliography of additional titles. A section on computers has now been added. For reviews of the first (1971) and second (1977) editions, see *ARBA* 72 (entry 111) and *ARBA* 78 (entry 152).

1521. Hillard, James M. **Where to Find What: A Handbook to Reference Service.** rev. and updated ed. Metuchen, N.J., Scarecrow, 1984. 357p. $22.50. LC 83-14272. ISBN 0-8108-1645-8.

Though the introduction does not say so, this is in effect the third edition of *Where to Find What.* As such, this guide to reference materials has already proven that it fills a need.

The need is that of inexperienced librarians to find quickly a book that will supply information on a very specific subject (e.g., astrology, dinosaurs). Hillard has arranged, under 595 subject headings, some 2,000 titles which provide help with the "more commonly asked questions." These titles (normally limited to in-print items) include not only reference books but also circulating materials suitable for the above purpose. For each title, Hillard supplies bibliographical information and, usually, a brief descriptive annotation.

Hillard states that the subjects were selected after wide consultation with reference librarians. Still, some features of his guide seem quite idiosyncratic. Thus, the subject headings were not taken from standard lists but are of Hillard's own devising, this resulting in some oddities and inconsistencies. Simiarly, the choice of subjects for inclusion is sometimes difficult to understand. For example, why have no separate entries for any countries other than the United States yet give "Dice," "Knives," and "Thermometers" sections of their own? The lack of an index is another severe drawback and the paucity of titles published after 1981 raises troubling doubts about up-to-dateness.

Still, these failings cannot negate the essential value of Hillard's guide. For the many times that reference librarians want "just the book" for a very specific reference question, *Where to Find What* may be just the thing. [R: JAL, July 84, pp. 161-62; LJ, 15 Feb 84, p. 336; RBB, 1 Dec 84, p. 512]   Samuel Rothstein

1522. Katz, William A. **Introduction to Reference Work.** 4th ed. New York, McGraw-Hill, 1982. 2v. index. (McGraw-Hill Series in Library Education). $19.95 (vol. 1); $21.00 (vol. 2). LC 81-12432. ISBN 0-07-033333-5 (vol. 1); 0-07-033334-3 (vol. 2).

Katz's two-volume *Introduction to Reference Work*, in its fourth edition, remains the standard basic text on reference work. Substantial revisions reflecting the growth in reference book publishing and in professional approaches to reference work have characterized each of the editions, and this one is no exception. As one might expect, the area of greatest revision is online services.

Volume 1, *Basic Information Sources*, follows the same organizational pattern as in the third edition. After a brief introduction to reference work, information sources, and the computer in the library, the text is divided into chapters on traditional forms, such as bibliographies, indexes, encyclopedias, and dictionaries. Only foundation or basic reference works are considered. While Katz's coverage within these self-imposed limits is adequate, Cheney's more sophisticated and thorough treatment in *Fundamental Reference Sources*, second edition (see *ARBA* 82, entry 300) should also be available to the library school student. A brief, nontechnical section on computer-assisted reference has also been added to volume 1, but Katz has reserved his in-depth consideration of this topic for volume 2.

Approximately half of the text of volume 2, *Reference Services and Reference Processes*, is given over to the subject of online reference service. Separate chapters cover the computer and reference service, the online search, bibliographic databases, and networks and interlibrary loan. Katz's agreeable writing style and systematic approach have resulted in a very clear *introduction* to the theoretical and practical aspects of computer-assisted reference. It should serve as an excellent overview for the uninitiated library school student and practitioner, even though it is unlikely to offer much that is new to the experienced searcher. In addition to his discussion of the process of online reference, Katz devotes an entire chapter to bibliographic databases, treating individual sources separately in the same fashion as printed works are treated in the first volume. It provides an excellent review of databases, with emphasis on general and ready-reference works as well as on those likely to be used in the social sciences and humanities. One does wonder, though, why this chapter was not placed in the first volume, along with the discussion of other reference sources.

As with previous editions, this edition of Katz's *Introduction to Reference Work* will be welcomed by library school educators and reference librarians as a very important contribution to the professional literature. For reviews of the first (1969), second (1974) and third (1978) editions, see *ARBA* 70 (volume 1, p. 19), *ARBA* 75 (entry 245), and *ARBA* 79 (entry 294). [R: BL, Aug 82, p. 1506]   Heather Cameron

1523. McCormick, Mona. **Who-What-When-Where-How-Why Made Easy. A Guide to the Practical Use of Reference Books.** Chicago, Quadrangle Books, 1971. 192p. o.p. LC 70-138903.

Joining the parade of guides to reference materials is this new publication described as a "clear and comprehensive guide to the staggering number and variety of reference materials spawned by today's 'information explosion.' " There are three basic sections in this guide: reference books by type (e.g., almanacs, biography, etc.); reference books in subject areas; and finding and using reference books — providing information on the library and its catalog, "a few words on writing a paper," and a sample term paper. The first paragraph in the introduction reads as follows: "Listen, a terrible thing is happening. Today there is such a flood of printed material that students and readers are easily confused about where to begin and how to conduct a search of information." The author also promises that "in addition to listing basic sources," this guide "is designed to indicate the wide range of material available. The bibliography on page 185 is included as a suggestion for further reading." Well, to start with, this "bibliography" of 14 titles is listed on page 183, and of the 14 titles at least half of them are listed in old editions or are out of print. Now let's examine one of the typical sections. "Biography" numbers six pages. There is a brief and rather misleading discussion of *DAB* and *DNB*, followed by a few comments on works about other "historical people" (to use the author's terminology), lengthy examples for *Current Biography* (there is no indication of scope for this work), plus again two random notes on "Information about People in Special Fields." Appended to this as well as to other sections is a bibliography that provides a more or less literate bibliographic description of works mentioned in the text. The book is copyrighted by the New York Times Company. Who is fooling whom? [R: WLB, Oct 71]   Bohdan S. Wynar

1524. Stevens, Rolland E., and Joan M. Walton. **Reference Work in the Public Library.** Littleton, Colo., Libraries Unlimited, 1983. 269p. index. $28.50. LC 82-17147. ISBN 0-87287-332-3.

This book introduces the library school student and the library staff member who have had no formal library training to the kinds of reference questions they will most often encounter in the average medium-sized or large public library, and to those major reference books and information sources of most use in answering these questions. It is divided into 27 subject areas, including business, consumer information, do-it-yourself information, genealogy and local history, travel, the occult, careers and occupations, and sports and recreation, and then organized generally according to the frequency of reference questions that arise about a particular subject in the average public library. Most of the encyclopedias and other general works and annual publications described in each chapter are available in most reference collections. The authors also suggest certain titles that reflect a type of reference source that should be represented in the collection. In some cases where a number of similar titles are presented, the authors have added a summary paragraph explaining the preference of one source over another for particular types of reference needs. The chapters also include typical questions and describe reference sources that best provide answers to these and other similar questions. [R: LJ, 15 May 83, p. 984]

1525. Taylor, Margaret T., and Ronald R. Powell. **Basic Reference Sources: A Self-Study Manual.** 3rd ed. Metuchen, N.J., Scarecrow, 1985. 335p. $16.50pa. LC 84-13880. ISBN 0-8108-1721-7.

This, the third edition of a self-paced manual for the study of reference titles, had a "preliminary edition" (1971) and a first edition (1973), both authored by Taylor. This third edition has two authors (from the University of Michigan's School of Library Science). One congratulates the authors for the minimal changes made to the volume. The major change is, again, to bring the sources and questions up-to-date (i.e., to December 1983), and to add new sources (e.g., *Biography and Genealogy Master Index*), dropping old ones.

The book consists of 1,757 questions, with answers, carefully relating to a given list of sources. The answers are sometimes factual (e.g., "Yes, there is an alphabetical index ..."), some require more judgment. It is a nice mix. The questions are arranged in twenty-three sections the titles of which have remained virtually unchanged since 1971. Most sections reflect a type of source (e.g., yearbooks and almanacs, bibliographic sources for government publications). One section looks at search strategy in

U.S. national bibliographic records. There are two sections of review questions. Within each section there is, first, a brief (longest is fifteen titles) list of sources followed by questions requiring use of those sources. The answers follow separately.

An augmented list of sources showing Sheehy numbers is at the beginning of the book. The list is noticeably heavy on U.S. sources. For example, five sections are devoted to U.S. national bibliography, while there is one section covering all of Britain, France, and Germany. There is no mention of Canada's national bibliographic sources, which hampers use of the manual in North America. The authors have found only an inadequate answer to the challenge of electronic reference sources: they have placed a distinguishing mark beside the sources having a corresponding database.

There are small aggravations in an otherwise useful and unpretentious work. The manual does not attempt to address the broader processes of reference (the reference interview, etc.). It deals with the problem of learning reference titles. It does that admirably. It is useful in library schools as a supplement to lectures and discussions. It would serve as an invaluable guide to independent students and practitioners seeking to update their knowledge of, to review, or to begin a study of, reference sources. [R: JAL, Nov 85, p. 321; RBB, 1 June 85, p. 1376]   Elizabeth Frick

PROCEEDINGS AND ESSAYS

1526. Butler, Pierce, ed. **The Reference Function of the Library: Papers Presented before the Library Institute at the University of Chicago June 29 to July 10, 1942.** Chicago, University of Chicago, 1943; repr., Boston, Gregg Press, 1972. 366p. index. (The Library Reference Series). o.p. LC 72-8800. ISBN 0-8398-0192-0.

Contains 17 essays on reference work as it relates to various library types (e.g., public, college, special, school) and also in relation to subject areas (e.g., science and technology, humanities, and social sciences). For a number of years this compendium was a very useful supplementary text in library schools, providing some of the best writing on the subject. Now, obviously, it is only of historical interest.

1527. Fine, Sara. **Developing Career Information Centers: A Guide to Collection Building and Counseling.** New York, Neal-Schuman, 1980. 157p. index. $22.95. LC 80-11634. ISBN 0-918212-19-7.

The library's role as a career information center is explored in this brief volume of conference papers. Eleven chapters, based upon presentations prepared for a United States Office of Education institute at the University of Pittsburgh in 1978, address such topics as theories of career development, counseling strategies, and selection/evaluation of materials. Participant reaction to the conference is discussed, and a 40-page, annotated bibliography of career information literature is appended. Individual chapters are generally well written and concise. The volume's arrangement, however, is illogical and distracting. Chapters on communication and counseling techniques appear before the goals and programs of career information centers are defined. Lest the reader (and the contributors) come away with the impression that career development is a new focus for the public library, consultation of the historical record will reveal many such efforts during the 1920s. [R: JAL, Jan 81, p. 364; LJ, 1 Apr 81, p. 718]   Arthur P. Young

1528. Lee, Sul H., ed. **Reference Service: A Perspective.** Ann Arbor, Mich., Pierian Press, 1983. 129p. bibliog. index. (Library Management Series, No. 6). $24.50. LC 83-60917. ISBN 0-87650-150-1.

This slender volume contains papers given at a conference at the University of Oklahoma in October 1982. The conference theme was "the dynamics of reference service in a changing environment," and conference participants were asked to critique the present provision of reference services in various types of libraries, from their respective points of view. Part indictment, and part hope for a brighter tomorrow, these papers contrast what is with what ought to be and find us all in need of improvement.

Curiously, Charles Bunge's keynote address, entitled "The Personal Touch: A Brief Overview of the Development of Reference Services in American Libraries," was not given at the conference, a fact that Lee passes along to us without explanation. It is, however, included in these proceedings, along with a half-dozen other papers that attack various aspects of reference provision in modern libraries.

Perhaps the best paper is the briefest: Mike Marchant's application of systems theory to evaluation and measurement of reference services. All of the papers are valuable in their way, although nothing new or startling comes out of a careful reading of this book.

For library school students, this is a worthwhile assignment. For those of us concerned, in one way or another, with improving reference service to the public, it will serve as a useful point of departure. [R: LJ, 15 Oct 83, p. 1936]

Bruce A. Shuman

REFERENCE STRATEGIES

1529. Finer, Ruth. **Referral Centres and Services: A Review.** London, Aslib, 1979. 59p. bibliog. index. (Aslib Occasional Publication, No. 22). £6.00. £5.00pa. ISBN 0-85142-120-2.

This brief but lively and well-written pamphlet seeks to identify the "state of the art" on mostly non-American literature concerning information and referral centers and the principle of referral ("that aspect of the reference process whereby an enquirer is directed to an appropriate organizational or personal source of information, and in which no substantive answer to the enquiry is supplied by the agent of referral"—p. 1).

Following a brief two-page introduction are five chapters identifying and summarizing the literature of "the referral centre concept," "research" in information and referral, "spontaneous referral" systems like OCLC, and "referral systems in an international context" (the United States merits seven pages of attention here). A 3-page final chapter identifies "topics for further thought," followed by a 13-page bibliography (including 10 pages of text references). The author concludes from her literature review that the concept of information and referral may be supported by the information community, but is seldom put into practice. A useful study, but not essential. [R: LR, Spring 80, p. 45]

Wayne A. Wiegand

1530. Morris, Jacquelyn M., and Elizabeth A. Elkins. **Library Searching: Resources and Strategies, with Examples from the Environmental Sciences.** New York, Jeffrey Norton, 1978. 129p. bibliog. index. $8.95; $5.95pa. LC 77-9214. ISBN 0-88432-004-9; 0-88432-005-7pa.

This handbook on the strategy of literature searching is the equivalent of a minireference course. Not only does it cover basic elements of any library, such as book and serial catalogs, indexes, filing rules, forms of literature, and levels of sources, but it provides flow charts of searches, a skillfully selected list of indexes and abstracts especially useful in the environmental sciences, and a brief glossary of library terms and abbreviations. It is an excellent, concise how-to-find-out handbook for all students and researchers, and, most particularly, for those working in interdisciplinary fields. [R: C&RL, Sept 78, p. 424]

Richard Palmer

1531. Slavens, Thomas P., ed. **Informational Interviews and Questions.** Metuchen, N.J., Scarecrow, 1978. 154p. o.p. LC 77-18502. ISBN 0-8108-1102-2.

Thomas P. Slavens provides lists of reference interviews and questions for 10 types of informational sources. There are chapters on encyclopedias, yearbooks, statistical sources, biographical sources, bibliography and library science, dictionaries, handbooks, serial publications, directories, and government publications. Each chapter lists interviews and questions. The interviews are records of actual reference interviews from all types of libraries and are included to give students a feel for real reference situations. The questions, specific and short answer, total more than 1,800. The number of questions for each type of source ranges from 63 for statistical sources to 337 for bibliography and library science. Slavens, with limitations based on security considerations, will send professors the list of sources where the answers can be found.

The book's purpose is to help students in beginning reference classes, library staff involved in development programs, and students in bibliographic instruction programs to learn about sources by actually using them. The interviews and questions will certainly assist these users. However, the book cannot be used on its own, since there is no explanation of the purposes and limitations of types of informational sources, no list of sources from which to start answering questions, and no information on developing search strategies. The usefulness of this book for library school professors and librarians involved in bibliographic instruction will depend on their philosophy of teaching, but every reference librarian will certainly enjoy browsing through this work. [R: LJ, 1 June 78, p. 1150]

Mary Reichel

RESEARCH STUDIES

1532. Crowley, Terence, and Thomas Childers. **Information Service in Public Libraries: Two Studies.** Metuchen, N.J., Scarecrow, 1971. 210p. bibliog. index. o.p. LC 77-154298. SBN 8108-0406-9.

This volume contains the reports of two separate attempts to study scientifically the quality and effectiveness of reference service. As "scientific" studies neither is entirely successful; they are academic exercises. The structure of the problems and the results of the statistical operations performed on the data are questionable, but the studies are valuable for their descriptive content. Crowley attempted to show that library expenditures are directly related to the effectiveness of library information services, but the study showed no significant relationship. Childers attempted to show a relationship between standard statistics reported by public libraries and the effectiveness of information services; he found a relationship between the total resources available to a library and the quality of reference service provided. Both studies present unflattering pictures of the performance of reference librarians. Personnel in reference departments in selected public libraries were asked a predetermined group of simple fact reference questions. In each study the number of satisfactory responses received was only slightly above 50 percent. While the investigators attempted to correlate the findings with other characteristics of the libraries studied to determine causes, the most significant cause may be the caliber of the individuals in library positions. Both of the investigators are aware of many weaknesses in their studies. In spite of the limits of the scientific investigation for the purposes of studying human behavior, they have presented two valuable reports which should cause all librarians to think carefully about requirements for satisfactory reference service. [R: LJ, 1 Dec 71, p. 3990]   Paul H. Spence

1533.   Metcalfe, John. **Information Retrieval, British & American, 1876-1976.** Metuchen, N.J., Scarecrow, 1976. 243p. index. o.p. LC 75-29154. ISBN 0-8108-0875-7.

This work on "information retrieval" is a valuable contribution to professional literature in that it furnishes us, for the first time, with a chronological treatment of what North Americans would usually designate "techniques of subject analysis" or "classification and verbal subject indexing." This is not to say that chronological treatment is the best approach to a still ill-defined and highly subjective area, characterized by periodic reinventions of the wheel, but it is another approach. The dates and nations stated in the title merely indicate concentration; Metcalfe takes us from 3000 B.C. to the present. Cutter and Dewey are here at length, as are UDC, LC, Colon, and Bliss. Haykin, Taube, and Austin are not neglected.

The book is discursive, even for a history. But its discursiveness furnishes us with many important products of the author's long career of study in these areas, and there is point in even the most esoteric digressions that fill the book. It will be welcomed by those already in the field as a distillation of earlier thought and evidence; by other librarians as an interesting "curate's

egg." The best parts are those on modern pre- and post-coordinate indexing — the last two chapters.

The index, which has an entry for "Procrustean bed" but none for "Facet analysis" is singularly dysfunctional in light of the subject matter of the book. [R: JLH, Summer 77, p. 297; LQ, Apr 77, p. 196; RQ, Winter 76, p. 179]
George Piternick

SUBJECT APPROACHES

1534.   Freides, Thelma K. **Literature and Bibliography of the Social Sciences.** Los Angeles, Calif., Melville, 1973. 284p. (A Wiley-Becker & Hayes Series Book). $42.50. LC 73-10111. ISBN 0-471-27790-8.

The author, who holds a master's degree in international relations and library science, has attempted to write a new library textbook in the literature of the social sciences. The work is divided into three major parts: (1) "Science, Scientific Literature, and Social Science"; (2) "Structure and Components of the Social Science Literature"; and (3) "Literature Retrieval and the System of Bibliographic Records."

At the outset Freides states that the aim "of this book is to describe the literature and bibliography of the social sciences, and the strategy of literature searching, against the background of some basic idea about communication in science" (preface). Consequently, she discusses the nature of science and the process of scientific communication.

Since this text is intended for the library student, the reviewer has to evaluate it in the context of the graduate library science curriculum. Students taking courses in the literature of the social sciences are expected to comprehend the subject and bibliographical structure of the social science disciplines, stressing their similarities, differences, and interrelationships. Unfortunately, this textbook is rather weak and superficial in this respect. The author discusses the nature of science and scientific method, which is covered in library research methodology courses, but fails to discuss in-depth the nature and subject structure of individual social sciences. Her discussion of science and the distinction between "literature" and "data" is rather artificial and does not apply to a number of social sciences covered in this publication (e.g., history, social anthropology, sociology).

The basic sections that discuss the literature of the social sciences are weak from the methodological point of view. The author arranges her material by type of published material (e.g., handbooks, encyclopedias, dictionaries, etc.), instead of using a subject reference approach. Thus, anyone interested in reference sources in sociology or history has to peruse all chapters, which is time-consuming and impractical. The "type of material" approach might be justified for undergraduate students. In most instances, the discussions of the titles included are descriptive instead of critical; their length varies from one sentence (e.g., pp. 48-49) to several sentences (e.g., pp. 84-85). A brief analysis of the subject index indicates omissions of such important subject entries as ethnology, ethnic studies, oral history, auxiliary historical sciences, urbanology, and others.

This textbook may expose library students to the author's interpretation of the structure of scientific communication and her understanding of science and the classification of scientific materials; but it will not provide in-depth analysis of the subject and bibliographical structure of the social sciences, or the role and responsibilities of social science librarians. The author states that the basis of the present work constituted her "hefty course syllabus" prepared for her own course on the literature of the social sciences at the Atlanta University School of Library Service. This limited basis may explain the structure and subject content of her publication. What is good for Atlanta is not necessarily good for other parts of the world. [R: Choice, Sept 74, p. 910; RQ, Summer 74, p. 372; WLB, Nov 74, pp. 248-49]   Lubomyr R. Wynar

1535. Hale, Barbara M. **The Subject Bibliography of the Social Sciences and Humanities.** New York, Pergamon Press, 1970. 147p. (International Series of Monographs in Library and Information Science, No. 12). o.p. LC 78-113358. SBN 08-015791-2.

This is not a conventional "guide" to reference materials on the subject but rather a narrative exposé of certain historical and theoretical problems. For example, there is a chapter on historical development of subject bibliography, and observations of modern trends, including such topics as scholarly communication, characteristics of different subject literatures, information storage and retrieval, etc. Probably the most disappointing section is on "characteristics of different subject literatures," to use the author's terminology. Hale fails to comprehend that the structure of a given discipline is directly related to its bibliographical control. To put it in simple terms, in such a field as history, monographic material still plays a rather important role as a vehicle for scientific communication,

due to the nature of this particular "traditional" discipline. This is reflected in existing tools of information retrieval, say, *Writings on American History*. Obviously, such a time lag cannot be tolerated in psychology, because in this particular discipline serial literature executes a much more important role and, for all practical purposes, "writings on American psychology" would be an unthinkable tool. So, we have *Psychological Abstracts*, different in their internal structure from *Historical Abstracts*. A survey of loan applications conducted in 1964 by the National Central Library in London has hardly anything to do with "characteristics" of subject literature, and in this respect numerous user studies produced in this country are much more relevant. Obviously, in speaking about the structure of literature we have to distinguish between the internal and the external structure of a particular discipline. But we may go too far. The author had good intentions and tried to summarize information available to her. On the other hand, this topic requires a little more depth of presentation. [R: WLB, Jan 71, p. 502]
     Bohdan S. Wynar

1536. Long, Maureen. **Musicians and Libraries in the United Kingdom.** London, Library Association, 1972. 152p. bibliog. (Library Association Research Publications). o.p. LC 72-187856. ISBN 0-85365-355-0.

This is an excellent study, carefully conceived, executed, and undertaken, the purpose of which was to determine to what extent musicians make use of library facilities, to determine resources, evaluate standards of collections and services, and to make recommendations. The author concludes that there is much to be desired but the study provides a solid basis for improving and extending services. The work is a model for what could be done with music collections in the United States. [R: LJ, 15 Nov 72, p. 3690]   Charles D. Patterson

1537. Malinowsky, H. Robert, and Jeanne M. Richardson. **Science and Engineering Literature: A Guide to Reference Sources.** 3rd ed. Littleton, Colo., Libraries Unlimited, 1980. 342p. index. (Library Science Text Series). $22.50; $14.50pa. LC 80-21290. ISBN 0-87287-230-0; 0-87287-245-9pa.

This edition includes publications and editions that appeared between 1976 and 1980, for a total of 1,273 annotated reference sources. Major bibliographies and abstracting services are given primary attention.

The text to this edition has been decreased, emphasizing the importance of the bibliographic citations. The introductory chapters are shorter, and references to individual titles are combined in a chapter called "Multidisciplinary Sources of Information." The book continues to present a progression of material from the general to the specific, using similar form divisions in each chapter for ease of instruction. The major subjects covered are history of science, mathematics, astronomy, physics, chemistry, biological sciences, geoscience, energy and environment, engineering, and biomedical sciences.

Each bibliographic chapter is subdivided by subdisciplines and by type of reference work: guides to the literature, abstracts, encyclopedias, handbooks, atlases, directories, etc. Chapters have been restructured to reflect extensive new materials appearing in such subjects as energy and environment. Annotations throughout the text are designed to call attention to the scope of the work, its intended audience, and special features. The annotations may be one sentence or several paragraphs in length, depending on the importance and the type of the sources. An updated bibliography has been added, as has a section on databases in chapter 1.

1538. Matarazzo, James M. **Library Problems in Science and Technology.** New York, R. R. Bowker, 1971. 167p. index. (Problem-Centered Approaches to Librarianship). $9.95. LC 70-164033. SBN 8352-0486-3. (Available from Books on Demand, $47.80, ISBN 0-8357-9043-6).

This third volume in the Bowker library science series Problem-Centered Approaches to Librarianship offers 35 cases designed to familiarize the reader with the typical situations in the fields of science and technology. In addition, information is provided in the appendix on the use of the Library Pathfinder as a teaching tool to complement the case method. Further information on Library Pathfinders is available from the Model Library Project of Project Intrex at Massachusetts Institute of Technology. [R: LJ, 15 Apr 72, p. 1406; WLB, May 72, p. 841]

1539. Rogers, A. Robert. **The Humanities: A Selective Guide to Information Sources.** 2nd ed. Littleton, Colo., Libraries Unlimited, 1979. 355p. index. (Library Science Text Series). $33.00; $21.00pa. LC 79-25335. ISBN 0-87287-206-8; 0-87287-222-Xpa.

The basic text and bibliographic guide to reference sources and selection aids in the humanities is now available in a second edition. It covers philosophy, religion and mythology, the visual arts, the performing arts, and lan-

guage and literature. All sections are revised, new sources have been added, and more detailed, comparative annotations are included.

A new introductory chapter annotates multidisciplinary reference and selection aids in the humanities. Thereafter, each discipline is treated separately with one chapter devoted to accessing information in that discipline and one chapter describing the principal information sources in that discipline. The "trends" chapters from the first edition (1974, see *ARBA* 75, entry 174) have been eliminated, and recommended general readings have been incorporated into the chapters on accessing information, which also discuss the major divisions of each discipline; information cataloging and classification practices specific to the humanities; and major professional organizations, information centers, and special collections for individual disciplines.

The bibliographical chapters concentrate on 1,200 works that serve either a selection or reference function. General introductions and histories are omitted unless of selection or reference value. Periodicals without major reviewing sections or features of major reference value have also been eliminated. Annotations are longer and more comparative than in the first edition, with many for older titles rewritten to provide more evaluative information. The chapter on the computer and the humanities, now at the end of the text, discusses applications to the various disciplines and bibliographic databases and reference service. The bibliographical chapters are indexed by author and title, and the textual chapters are indexed by broad subject categories. [R: C&RL, Sept 80, pp. 484-85]

1540. SantaVicca, Edmund F. **Reference Work in the Humanities.** Metuchen, N.J., Scarecrow, 1980. 173p. $15.00. LC 80-18783. ISBN 0-8108-1342-4.

Reference Work in the Humanities is a practical tool especially useful for library educators in developing search questions for courses using humanities reference works. Titles of individual reference works are not listed, but rather this publication lists questions to be researched in the subject areas of philosophy, religion and mythology, literature, music, fine arts, and theater arts. Traditional questions such as, "What are the basic tenets of pantheism?," "What is the vocal range of a basso profundo voice?," and "What is an aquatint?," are interspersed with such intriguing questions as, "What exactly does a deipnosophist believe in?," "Why are tubas so big?," and "Who was the greatest art forger of all times?"

Each section lists several questions followed by a group of search problems and case studies. The appendix gives examples of possible but not definitive solutions to three selected search problems. This book whets the appetite in seeking out answers to the questions included. [R: LJ, 1 Dec 80, p. 2480]

Marilyn T. Thompson

1541. Slavens, Thomas P., ed. **Library Problems in the Humanities: Case Studies in Reference Services, Collection Building, and Management.** Munich, New York, K. G. Saur; distr., Hamden, Conn., Shoe String Press, 1981. 113p. o.p. ISBN 3-598-40026-8.

Twenty-eight case studies, written by practitioners from a variety of libraries (academic, public, school) in various parts of the country, comprise this book. Each begins with a description of a library and its resources, proceeds to narrate an encounter with a patron whose information request may or may not be answerable in the type of library described, and concludes with a series of questions related to information sources, search strategies, and library policies. The first paragraph of the editor's preface states: "The purpose of this book is to assist students in learning to cope with library problems in the humanities, which include art, literature, mythology, music, philosophy and religion. The work is designed primarily for library science students...." In subsequent paragraphs, the editor goes on to indicate other possible uses: bibliographic instruction, in-service training, and workshops, as well as guidance for students in the humanities generally.

How well does the book fulfill its stated purposes? In preparation for this review, a few case studies were "field tested" with a graduate class in humanities information sources and services. The students were enthusiastic and found the cases useful in sharpening their reference skills. The primary purpose of the book is admirably carried out in relation to the needs of its target audience. Use with librarians in workshops or in-service training sessions would probably be successful as well. However, this reviewer has reservations about the book's usefulness in bibliographic instruction and for students in the humanities in general. The case studies and the questions are too obviously slanted toward librarians and library school students. With revamping and supplementary guidance from a librarian, some of them might be useful as part of a bibliographic instruction program.

The book, by itself, would appear to be less useful to most students in the humanities than

classified, annotated bibliographies or library pathfinders. [R: JAL, May 82, p. 105]

A. Robert Rogers

1542. Slavens, Thomas P., ed. **The Retrieval of Information in the Humanities and the Social Sciences: Problems as Aids to Learning.** New York, Marcel Dekker, 1981. 136p. (Books in Library and Information Science, Vol. 37). $29.75. LC 81-12477. ISBN 0-8247-1542-X.

This title is a practical, everyday tool for library educators that provides a ready-made list of over 4,000 search questions in some 13 different disciplines of the humanities and social sciences. It is intended primarily as an aid to bibliography and literature classes at both the undergraduate and graduate levels. Typical entries include such questions as: What is a "neologism"? What is a mutual fund? Who was Euryplus? Did Chopin ever compose a military march? For security reasons, an answer key can be obtained only by writing the publisher using official stationery.

Essentially, this effort is very similar to Slavens's *Information Interviews and Questions* (see *ARBA* 79, entry 298), which provides specific, short-answer questions focusing on encyclopedias, yearbooks, dictionaries, statistical sources, etc. The questions provided in this more recent book are certainly quite varied and representative, although at times they need to be more explicit in terms of the information requested. Also, it might have been a valuable addition if this work had presented search problems as well as short-answer questions, as did *Reference Work in the Humanities* (see *ARBA* 81, entry 276) by SantaVicca. Overall, however, this title is quite useful and should certainly be purchased by those who need such material in their library orientation and bibliographic instruction classes. [R: JAL, Mar 82, p. 43]

Frank Wm. Goudy

OTHER TOPICS

1543. Bundy, Mary Lee, ed. **Alternatives to Traditional Library Services: A Case Book.** College Park, Md., Urban Information Interpreters, 1977. 242p. o.p.

Mary Lee Bundy, a long-time advocate of organizational and ideological change in libraries, has edited this casebook of readings on various types of information centers. The volume consists of an extended introduction by the editor and a collection of 22 mission/activity statements provided by information centers. The volume is intended for those who are interested in the "utilization of information for social improvement" and the goal of "citizen participation in government." According to Bundy, alternative agencies of information dissemination are needed to counterbalance the established sources of information that promote the status quo and engage in secrecy, censorship, and surveillance. One may question the severity of her indictment of the government and the private sector, but there is little doubt that information deprivation is a serious detriment to social equity and political power. The key distinction between information centers and most libraries is the former's commitment to effect social change through aggressive programs of information acquisition and dissemination. These centers focus on such issues as child care, ecology, legislation, media, and women's rights. A bibliography of selected readings is appended. Implications for libraries abound. Read, digest, and react. [R: BL, 15 Apr 78, p. 1328; LJ, 15 Sept 78, p. 1710]   Arthur P. Young

1544. Myers, Marcia J., and Jassim M. Jirjees. **The Accuracy of Telephone Reference/ Information Services in Academic Libraries: Two Studies.** Metuchen, N.J., Scarecrow, 1983. 270p. bibliog. index. $17.50. LC 82-10785. ISBN 0-8108-1584-2.

This work, based on the dissertations of the two authors, has a methodical air throughout. Myers surveys reference services in a selected sample of 40 southeastern academic libraries; Jirjees measures the accuracy of reference services in selected four-year state colleges in the Northeast having graduate programs. Both studies are supported by questionnaires, tables, appendices, notes, and bibliographies. The index appears adequate and accurate.

The method of nonreactive unobtrusive measurement of reference service in academic libraries was used by both authors. This method was actively applied to reference work in public libraries by Terence Crowley and Thomas Childers in *Information Service in Public Libraries: Two Studies* (see *ARBA* 72, entry 112), but this is the first application of the method to academic libraries. Using a sample of typical reference questions received by academic libraries, proxies posing as students telephoned these questions to preselected academic libraries. Unaware that their performance was being evaluated, the reference staff members who were asked to answer the questions were evaluated on how they answered a question, how long it took them, and whether the answer was correct.

Although these studies were done systematically, objections have been raised about this method of measurement in earlier studies. Some feel it to be unethical. Also, there is no opportunity to follow up the results of the survey with an analysis of tools used and no opportunity for staff members to learn from their mistakes, as there is in some methods. However, these authors felt the most objective results could be gathered using the unobtrusive method. Another problem with the method is that by nature it cannot take into account a library's policy toward telephone questions. Some library staffs give preference to "in-house" patrons, postponing telephone queries until they are free.

The results of both studies were discouraging. Only about 50 percent of the questions were answered correctly. This fact points out the need for telephone and general reference standards. The question of accountability in answering a reference question is addressed and needs to be answered: "What is not clear is the extent to which librarians generally have set objectives ... concerning their role in giving reference service."

This book would have been much more helpful if the compatibility and comparability of the two studies had been discussed. Ralph Blasinggame's foreword is not intended to be and does not function as an introduction to the studies. Also, a joint conclusion including practical applications, implications, recommendations, and suggestions for applications that could be part of a library's course of action to improve reference service by telephone would have been most beneficial. Jirjees's six general, brief recommendations come the closest to giving some concrete suggestions for applicability. It would have been advantageous to expand on these points. [R: C&RL, Sept 83, pp. 394-95; JAL, Sept 83, p. 231; JAL, May 83, p. 109; LJ, 15 May 83, p. 984; RQ, Summer 83, pp. 434-35]   Barbara L. Bell

1545. Rees, Alan M., ed. **Developing Consumer Health Information Services.** New York, R. R. Bowker, 1982. 296p. index. (Consumer Information Series). $34.95. LC 81-18029. ISBN 0-8352-1473-7.

Prepared as a companion volume to *The Consumer Health Information Source Book* (R. R. Bowker, 1981), this guide is primarily intended for health information providers as well as those librarians involved in the development and management of consumer information services. It contains a collection of essays written by librarians and health professionals and is divided into four sections. Part 1, "The

New Medical Consumerism," contains chapters that address such topics as the consumer in society, decision-making, the role of the library, and legal and ethical considerations in providing health information. Part 2 contains chapters that examine programs, objectives, structure, function, training, and promotional activities of seven library-based consumer health information programs in this country and in Canada. This allows the user to examine the strengths and weaknesses of each of the model programs, especially if the groundwork is being laid for future implementation of a consumer health information program. Questions relating to management and administration are the focus of the third section. Here various authors examine collection development, reference tools and techniques, training library personnel, and public relations and funding. Part 4, "Networks and Networking," focuses on interlibrary cooperation, federal health clearinghouses, and modern technology and health promotion.

Because of the increase in the demand for consumer health information over the last decade, the library is increasingly becoming the focal point of information dissemination. This work will definitely assist the librarians involved in developing consumer health information programs within their communities. [R: JAL, May 82, pp. 118-19; LJ, 1 May 82, p. 878]

Anna Wynar

1546. Warnken, Kelly. **The Information Brokers: How to Start and Operate Your Own Fee-Based Service.** New York, R. R. Bowker, 1981. 154p. bibliog. index. (Information Management Series, 2). $24.95. LC 81-10170. ISBN 0-8352-1347-1.

Kelly Warnken's *Directory of Fee-Based Information Services* is reviewed in *ARBA* 82 (entry 145). This work is a rudimentary, but earnest, guide for those who are considering becoming information brokers. It deals with such matters as how to get started, how to get clients, and offers a long list of kinds of services that might be offered. It also covers some business considerations, such as money flow, time commitments, and the selection of a banker, an attorney, and an accountant. Some thoughts are given to the importance of establishing personal and organizational networks. Some works about what they would do differently if starting over are provided by individuals who are now working successfully in the information brokerage business. Some predictions about the future of fee-based services are made by a few librarians, library or information school deans, and information consultants.

In an era when more and more libraries are offering fee-based information services, and when major corporations are viewing the merger of computers and telecommunications systems as opportunities to offer a variety of information services, the future of individual information brokers will likely be determined by the sophistication, quality, and timeliness of their value-added services. This volume will be of modest assistance to individuals who are considering going the entrepreneurial route. The book includes some basic questions and answers at the end of each chapter, a briefly annotated bibliography, and an index. [R: JAL, Jan 82, p. 384; LJ, 1 Jan 82, p. 90]

Richard Palmer

52 Research

GENERAL WORKS

1547. Busha, Charles H., ed. **A Library Science Research Reader and Bibliographic Guide.** Littleton, Colo., Libraries Unlimited, 1981. 201p. bibliog. index. $25.00. LC 80-22507. ISBN 0-87287-237-8.

Six original essays were prepared especially for this project designed to stimulate further interest in the pursuit of systematic inquiry pertaining to library and information science, an area in which the literature remains meager. The first essay, "Library Science Research: Paths to Progress," prepared by the book's editor, provides background information about the development of library science research during the last four decades. The other five essays are: "Methodology of Library Science Inquiry—Past and Present," by Laurel Grotzinger; "Understanding the Research Process: An Analysis of Error," by Jeffrey Katzer; "Historical Research and Oral History in Librarianship," by Carol McCombs and Charles H. Busha; "Organizational Theory and Research: Implications for Libraries and Learning Resources Centers," by Stephen B. Walter; and "Obtaining Grants for Library and Information Science Research," by Carolyn Graddick Teal. In addition to the supplementary reading lists that follow several of the papers, the reader concludes with a 23-page bibliography of works published from 1931 to 1979 that deal with either the status or the methods of library science research. [R: JAL, Nov 81, p. 296]

1548. Busha, Charles H., and Stephen P. Harter. **Research Methods in Librarianship: Techniques and Interpretation.** New York, Academic Press, 1980. 417p. illus. bibliog. index. (Library and Information Science). $21.50. LC 79-8864. ISBN 0-12-147550-6.

This book guides both the student and the practitioner through research methods used in the field of librarianship, offering both theoretical and practical information. The authors have focused on the methods of inquiry used in librarianship, including design, measurement, and analysis.

In addition to an introductory chapter which covers the basic concepts of research, discussion of the scientific method, finding a research topic, ethical considerations in research, and evaluation of completed research, there are four other parts to this text. Part 2, "Methods of Research," is especially comprehensive and includes the following topics: experimental research; survey research which offers in-depth suggestions for designing questionnaires, as well as exploring the advantages and disadvantages of the questionnaire; historical research; operations research; and additional research methods in librarianship, such as the case-study method, library user studies, the Delphi method, and documentary research. Descriptive statistics and inferential statistics are the topics of parts 3 and 4. In their treatment of statistics, the authors assume no mathematical background on the part of the user; therefore, terms and concepts are clearly defined and the information can be readily understood by even the beginning library student. The final section of this work is devoted to aids to research, including the computer and calculator, and writing the research proposal and the research report. A list of references and a selected bibliography accompany each chapter. Since research in librarianship can involve many other disciplines (e.g., communications, psychology, etc.), the additional sources listed in the bibliographies will lead the user to materials in these related fields, and perhaps to more in-depth coverage of a particular topic. Each section contains not only a review of the method in question, but also descriptions of some completed research projects in librarianship which used a particular method. Appendices of random digits, statistical symbols, and normal frequency distribution are also included. An index provides ready access to information contained in this work.

In our review of *Library Research: An International Journal* (see *ARBA* 81, entry 166), the reviewer suggested that "more discussion and research are needed on the scope and nature of library and various research methodologies used in library science." This text begins to fill this gap in the literature. In addition, one of the authors of this text, Charles Busha, edited a selection of readings on library science research entitled *A Library Science Research Reader and Bibliographic Guide* (Libraries Unlimited, 1981; see *ARBA* 82, entry 304), which would be a good companion to this text since it offers an extensive bibliography of related works. Due to its thorough treatment and understandable style, this text will be useful to academic, public, school, and special librarians, as well as library students embarking on research projects. [R: C&RL, Jan 81, p. 66]   Ann Hartman

1549. Gustafson, Kent L., and Jane Bandy Smith. **Research for School Media Specialists.** Athens, Ga., Department of Educational Media & Librarianship, University of Georgia, 1982. 156p. bibliog. $10.00pa.

This volume may prove useful to the school media specialist who has the time and the initiative to do research applicable to the school media center. The main part of the text serves as a handbook for those who wish to review various research techniques. The appendix provides a time and cost data collection instrument, a pathfinder section which cites approaches to various reference sources including computers, a resource list of titles, and an evaluation form. [R: SLMQ, Fall 83, p. 66]

Peggy Clossey Boone

1550. Kochen, Manfred. **Integrative Mechanisms in Literature Growth.** Westport, Conn., Greenwood Press, 1974. 275p. illus. index. (Contributions in Librarianship and Information Science, No. 9). $29.95. LC 72-815. ISBN 0-8371-6384-6.

In his preface, the author states "we are finding that we need systems that help reintegrate the fragmented literature more than we need systems to help us gain access to the fragments." This quotation effectively summarizes his theme. The 11 chapters of the book are as follows: "Research on Research and Information Science," "Stability in the Growth of Knowledge," "Fact Accumulation and Intellectual Bridge-Building as Complementary Processes," "Information Processing with Contemporary Computers: An Assessment," "The Growth of Literature Cited by Review Papers," "Information Science and Computer Aids in Education," "An Experiment to Change Attitudes toward New College Mathematics," "Newer Techniques for Processing Bibliographic Information," "A Cost-Effectiveness Analysis of See-Reference Structure in Directories," "Information-Seeking Behavior of Catalog Users," and "Integration and Disintegration in the Knowledge Industry."

In all chapters of this conceptually complex book, the author is concerned with a number of interrelated questions. His initial query is whether there are laws that govern the growth of knowledge. The next question is: Under what conditions is the growth process stable? This leads directly into a still more complex inquiry, which can be indicated by the specific questions: Is it possible to intervene in the growth process in order to increase its efficiency and stability and can such intervention be successful?

His final question relates the entire problem directly to libraries: How can libraries be used to design and implement effective interventions?

Although most of the author's guiding questions are not answered to anyone's satisfaction, least of all to the author's, it is sufficient that he has asked them, forcefully and clearly. [R: RQ, Spring 75, p. 253]   Richard A. Gray

1551. Lathem, Edward Connery, ed. **American Libraries as Centers of Scholarship.** Hanover, N.H., Dartmouth College, 1978. 107p. o.p.

This beautifully designed and produced volume records "proceedings of a convocation held at Dartmouth College on June 30th, 1978, marking the fiftieth anniversary of Fisher Ames Baker Memorial Library" (subtitle). Included are the opening remarks by John Sloan Dickey, a retrospective view of the role of research libraries in American scholarship, future prospects, and a panel discussion involving eight librarians and scholars. The addresses and panel discussion provide pleasant reading, as well as a discussion of the accomplishments, failures, and goals of librarianship in aiding and promoting scholarship. Warren J. Haas's "Future Prospects" details six factors necessary for the model library of the future to adequately serve scholars. Haas's specifications for change can be seen as a theoretical basis for performance of the academic research library. Many examples used in the book apply directly to Dartmouth College, but this does not limit its applicability. *American Libraries as Centers of Scholarship* is a pleasant introduction to the theory and goals of research librarianship.   Janet H. Littlefield

1552. Lynam, Peter, Margaret Slater, and Rennie Walker. **Research and the Practitioner: Dissemination of Research Results within the Library-Information Profession.** London, Aslib, 1982. 83p. (Aslib Occasional Publication, No. 27). £16.50pa. ISBN 0-85142-163-6.

Compiled from data gathered from 854 library information professionals in the United Kingdom in 1980, this study explores the phenomenon of information dissemination of both published and nonpublished sources to this population. Specified categories of information professionals are industry/commerce, government, societies, local government, and education, with further delineation by educational qualifications and years in the profession. The study attempts to measure the extent of professionals' awareness of ongoing research, discern their attitudes toward research and its usefulness, and identify their view of desired research.

The authors explore organizational memberships of professionals; reader behavior, usage of periodicals in the field, and usage of secondary sources such as indexes; and preferences for medium under the categories of journals, newspapers, personal contacts, meetings, training courses, seminars, workshops, conferences, letters, telephone contacts, secondary sources, reports, and theses. The authors conclude that reports and theses are the least preferred sources among information professionals and that journal articles are the most heavily used medium. Different media are favored, however, by different sectors of the library/information field. The authors suggest the possibility that group activity (e.g., conventions and seminars) may need further exploitation as an important channel of communication.

The introduction notes that because extensive bibliographies are available in earlier reports, cited herein, no bibliography is needed in this monograph. This reviewer nevertheless found the omission frustrating, as several reports are not readily available in the United States.

The content of this monograph is indeed informative. It serves, in part, to identify an appropriate forum for reports and studies relative to particular groups of information professionals. It also illuminates the extent to which information professionals review research and identifies these professionals' preference for future research, which is ranked in 35 categories in order of preference. [R: C&RL, Sept 83, p. 392]

Ray Gerke

1553. Stevens, Rolland E., ed. **Research Methods in Librarianship: Historical and Bibliographical Methods in Library Research.** Urbana-Champaign, Ill., Graduate School of Library Science, University of Illinois; distr., Urbana-Champaign, Ill., Illini Union Bookstore, 1971. 140p. index. (Monograph No. 10). $5.00. LC 79-631732.

Beginning in 1963, the Graduate School of Library Science at Illinois attempted to cover general as well as specific aspects of research in library science, conducting conferences with invited subject specialists. The papers of the first conference, dealing with general problems of library research, were published in the July 1964 issue of *Library Trends*; papers of the second conference, "Research Methods in Librarianship: Measurement and Evaluation," were published in 1968 as number eight in the above series. This volume includes the papers for the third conference, concentrating on historical and bibliographical research. The 12 papers included cover such topics as the use of archives in historical research, primary sources in library research, biographical research, textual criticism in library history, etc. Most papers have numerous bibliographical references and some, such as Louis Gottschalk's "Problems of Textual Criticism," are good examples of a readable presentation of a rather complex topic. Probably some articles (e.g., "Needed Research in Library History") are slightly chatty, at least for this reviewer. Nevertheless, all in all, this is a valuable contribution to our professional literature. [R: AL, June 71, p. 652]

Bohdan S. Wynar

1554. Walker, Donald E., Hans Karlgren, and Martin Kay, eds. **Natural Language in Information Science: Perspectives and Directions for Research.** Stockholm, Sweden, Skriptor; distr., Fairfax, Va., Roberts Information Services, 1977. 194p. o.p. ISBN 91-7282-131-0.

With the predicted disappearance of print-on-paper in information science only 12 years away, the vocabularies used in the information process should be of fundamental concern to information scientists and to linguists. It appears from these papers that linguistics (the science attempting to explain how language works) and information science (the area of activity concerned with storage, retrieval, and transfer of information of all kinds) are not cooperative disciplines; indeed, each tends to go its own way. It was the function of a 1976 workshop to analyze the potential effectiveness of collaboration between the two fields. Using concepts and data from *Linguistics and Information Science* (Academic Press, 1973), an attempt was made to outline research areas and to give perspective to current trends. The papers from the workshop are informative, analytical, and clearly and well presented. Though not a listing of potential research topics, the consideration given to fundamental issues provides the practicing librarian with a state-of-the-art review and the doctoral student with areas of concern, both basically and practically.

The Workshop on Linguistics and Information Science was held at Biskops-Arno, Sweden, under the auspices of the Committee on Linguistics in Documentation and the KVAL Institute for Information Science. Participants included F. W. Lancaster, D. Austin, N. Sager, and, of course, the editors of these papers. The volume is not a reference work but a compilation of the papers presented at a worthwhile workshop. [R: LQ, Oct 79, p. 466]

William Brace

1555. Wynar, Bohdan S. **Research Methods in Library Science: A Bibliographical Guide with Topical Outlines.** Littleton, Colo., Libraries Unlimited, 1971. 153p. index. o.p. LC 79-168376. SBN 87287-018-9.

This bibliographical guide presents 782 monographs, Ph.D. dissertations, articles, and other research literature. It is designed to aid students and teachers in their selection of readings on the basic characteristics of research problem solving. Includes topical outlines for each chapter, and author and title indexes. [R: AL, Dec 71, p. 1225; WLB, Dec 71, p. 369]

STATISTICAL APPROACHES

1556. Carpenter, Ray L., with Ellen Storey Vasu. **Statistical Methods for Librarians.** Chicago, American Library Association, 1978.

119p. index. $15.00. LC 78-3476. ISBN 0-8389-0256-1.

Despite librarians' general dislike of mathematics and statistics, it is necessary that they have a sound knowledge of statistical concepts for those times when a local situation must be assessed or a report or article evaluated. As some statistical books are too "mathematical," and others, such as Huff's *How to Lie with Statistics* (W. W. Norton, 1954), too superficial, this small book has much to offer students, teachers, and practitioners of librarianship.

In five brief chapters ("Descriptive Statistics," "Sampling," "Inductive Statistics," "Correlation and Regression," and "Nonparametric Tests and Measures"), the authors provide sufficient coverage of the basic statistical concepts of interest to the majority of librarians. Although the book is not much more than an introduction to statistics, its style and library examples make it valuable to librarians. The text is clearly written, with examples drawn from library situations. An eight-page glossary adds to the value of the text. It would be inappropriate to close any review of this book without commenting on an inaccurate statement made by the authors: "The research process is a special and powerful mode of thinking. It yields an understanding of how related events behave, and will often provide ways of coping with the environment. It comprises *all the methods* of gathering numerical data [emphasis added] and drawing conclusions about their characteristics and their behavior" (p. ix). Is it possible that the authors have never heard of historical and other nonnumerical research? [R: C&RL, Jan 79, p. 78; JAL, May 79, p. 96; LJ, 1 Jan 79, p. 86; LQ, Oct 79, p. 498]

G. Edward Evans

1557. Hoadley, Irene Braden, and Alice S. Clark, eds. **Quantitative Methods in Librarianship: Standards, Research, Management.** Westport, Conn., Greenwood Press, 1972. 256p. index. (Contributions in Librarianship and Information Science, No. 4). $35.00. LC 73-149962. ISBN 0-8371-6061-8.

These are the proceedings of an institute held at Ohio State University from 3 August to 16 August 1969. The volume consists of four parts—quantitative management, standards, research, and management—with a total of 25 papers. [R: LJ, Aug 73, p. 2250]

1558. Simpson, I. S. **Basic Statistics for Librarians.** 2nd ed. London, Clive Bingley; distr., Hamden, Conn., Shoe String Press, 1983. 238p. bibliog. index. $19.50. ISBN 0-85157-352-5.

This book is intended as an introductory text for students in library schools and for practicing librarians who need to carry out statistical analyses. The greatly expanded second edition reflects topics and examples included in research methods and statistics courses taught by the author after the first edition appeared (see *ARBA* 76, entry 122). The most significant addition is probably the chapter titled "Computer Packages." This chapter presents coding and sample output for a release of SPSS (Statistical Package for the Social Sciences) but fails to name other popular packages. The other chapters are devoted to the more frequently used statistical measures applied to qualitative and quantitative data. The book also contains an adequate index; eight short but useful appendices of mathematical operators, symbols, and statistical tables; and a list of 20 references. The author specifically excludes techniques for data collection and interpretation, choosing to refer readers to texts with a broader scope, such as Charles Busha and Stephen Harter's *Research Methods in Librarianship* (see *ARBA* 82, entry 305).

The new edition is a significant improvement over the first edition but does not go far enough to serve the beginning U.S. library school student. For the most part, examples are carefully chosen; thus, the British terminology (e.g., pounds rather than dollars) should not confuse the reader. Statistical terminology is somewhat limited, however, making it more difficult for students to use supplementary texts such as Ray Carpenter and Ellen Vasu's *Statistical Methods for Librarians* (see *ARBA* 79, entry 336). Terms such as "inferential statistics" or "parametric and nonparametric statistics" are not used and some units (e.g., "degrees of freedom") need further explanation. The author's decision not to include a discussion of units of measurement might further confuse or mislead the reader as to the appropriate technique to apply to different types of data.

Clearly, the book is designed to supplement a course in statistics or research methods. Its primary value will be the numerous exercises and the graphic presentation of data using basic statistics. [R: JAL, May 83, p. 124]

Andrew G. Torok

1559. Srikantaiah, Taverekere, and Herbert H. Hoffman. **An Introduction to Quantitative Research Methods for Librarians.** 2nd ed. Santa Ana, Calif., Headway, a division of Rayline Press, 1977. 223p. illus. bibliog. o.p. ISBN 0-89537-002-6.

Following a brief discussion of research methods, this book deals exclusively with statistical techniques. Like most statistics texts for nonstatisticians, it is written and organized in cookbook style, without pretention of any mathematical rigor. Yet the mathematical recipes it provides are accurate and are generously illustrated with library examples. Of the examples chosen to introduce the normal distribution concept, however, some are clearly inappropriate, because they fail to approximate the normal distribution themselves (e.g., numbers of books borrowed by library users in a certain town, or collection sizes of all related libraries in a certain country). A cookbook statistics text must give careful attention to all the assumptions and limitations that accompany any statistical technique, and in most cases this book has done that very well. The section on sampling treats the major ideas satisfactorily, including the estimation of sampling error. But wrongly omitted from that section are the limitations inherent in the use of a formula that is given for estimating appropriate sample sizes for preselected confidence levels and limits. A parallel formula for estimating the same from a bivariate population is not even mentioned. The appendix contains a handy refresher on basic algebraic operations, as well as abbreviated statistical tables and a glossary of statistical terms. Lack of an index diminishes the book's reference value, but for those familiar with its organization, access to formulas and main concepts is not difficult. Library education for years has needed a basic text on statistical methods for library research. This book is not quite that standard work, but it easily surpasses the only other serious entry in the field, I. S. Simpson's *Basic Statistics for Librarians* (Linnet Books, 1975; see *ARBA* 76, entry 122). [R: C&RL, Mar 78, p. 153; LJ, 1 Mar 78, p. 525]

Bruce C. Bennion

53 Retrieval Systems

GENERAL WORKS
BEFORE 1976

1560. Jahoda, Gerald. **Information Storage and Retrieval Systems for Individual Researchers.** New York, Wiley, 1970. 135p. index. (Information Sciences Series). o.p. LC 74-101969. SBN 471-43715-8.

This book is addressed primarily to the researcher interested either in improving the index to his document collection or in starting one. It is an introductory text and does not require substantial background in this subject area, although reading of some basic texts (such as Collison) might be helpful. It covers all important aspects of indexing, including controlled index vocabularies, conventional indexes, coordinate indexes, keyword-from-title indexes, citation indexes, as well as other types. There is also a separate chapter on the planning, design, and evaluation of personal indexes. All the information is presented in a readable form and is well documented and well balanced. This text should be required as supplementary reading in library schools and will obviously be helpful to researchers interested in indexing their documents collection. [R: DLQ, Jan 71, p. 77]

1561. Kochen, Manfred. **Principles of Information Retrieval.** Los Angeles, Calif., Melville, 1974. 203p. illus. bibliog. index. (Information Sciences Series/A Wiley-Becker & Hayes Series Book). o.p. LC 74-1204. ISBN 0-471-49697-9.

Investigating the interrelationships between IR systems and the system of knowledge and communication in which they function, Kochen analyzes "the growing knowledge system for how well it helps people recognize, select, and cope with problems." The components of the system—people, documents, and topics—are examined by three approaches: behaviorally, in terms of input/output; by algorithms that could generate such behavior; and by analyzing relations and interactions among the three components. These analyses are used to formulate a model of an IR system, with constituent parts of a database, a communication system, and a system of representation, and to produce a set of design principles. Finally, key issues and problems are summarized. Numerous references to the literature are integrated within the text, and an outstanding feature is the excellent, thorough bibliography. Although it requires some mathematical sophistication on the part of the reader, the book appeals to a wide audience, from students to experienced users and designers of retrieval systems. [R: Choice, Dec 74, p. 1504]   Julie Bichteler

1562. Lancaster, F. W., and E. G. Fayen. **Information Retrieval On-Line.** Los Angeles, Calif., Melville, 1973. 597p. illus. index. (Information Science Series/A Wiley-Becker & Hayes Series Book). $18.50. LC 73-9697. ISBN 0-471-51235-4. (Available from Books on Demand, $116.50pa., ISBN 0-8357-9911-5).

Information retrieval is a rapidly changing field. Computers have brought about vast changes in the methods of handling information. This reference work covers the online systems for bibliographical search and retrieval, with emphasis on design, evaluation, and use. After discussing the characteristics of online retrieval systems, the authors proceed to a presentation of the latest advances in such areas as equipment, searching, performance, evaluation, vocabulary, indexing, instruction, and cost performance. A final chapter discusses the requirements for future systems; some of the trends suggested are an increase in remote access, more use of natural language, and increased instructional capabilities. The material is presented in such a way that the nonspecialist is able to follow the text and gain the needed knowledge of online terminology. An outstanding text—a must for anyone who is involved with any aspect of information retrieval. [R: LQ, Jan 76, p. 79]   H. Robert Malinowsky

1563.   Montgomery, K. Leon. **Document Retrieval Systems: Factors Affecting Search Time.** New York, Marcel Dekker, 1975. 114p. index. (Books in Library and Information Science, No. 14). o.p. LC 75-18692. ISBN 0-8247-6195-2.

The purpose of this experimental study in information science was to ascertain whether there are quantifiable measures of difference in the time it takes to search a linear file versus an inverted file in relation to two other variables: the number of questions searched and the number of documents in the file. A linear file contains documents one after another (e.g., 1, 2, 3 ... nth). An inverted file consists of index term records—that is, each index term is used to represent a document or documents. Both kinds of file organization are in current use by various operational computing systems and both can be used to search files containing a varying number of documents. The simple question becomes the purpose of this experiment: to find the time differential, if any, in searching files organized according to these two different structures. The book is organized along traditional lines of experiment reports. There is first the statement of the problem, then a literature review, a general description of the experimental design, a detailed statement of the bimodal search program, a survey of the data, and a chapter of "conclusions, extensions and generalizations."

Because they are obviously of far more than routine interest to all concerned with data searching problems, I quote the author's summary conclusions (pp. 108-9): "At least in this experiment it has been shown that the particular combination of linear file organization and search technique begins to become less efficient when more than 64 questions are asked. Specifically, the search time required per question begins to increase after 64 questions.

"Alternately, it has been shown that the inverted file organization and search technique

becomes more efficient from a search time point of view for situations having more than 32 questions and more than 512 documents." [R: C&RL, Mar 76, p. 181]

Richard A. Gray

1564.   van Rijsbergen, C. J. **Information Retrieval.** 2nd ed. Boston, Butterworths, 1979. 208p. bibliog. index. $39.95. LC 78-40725. ISBN 0-408-70929-4.

This work, which concerns only automatic information retrieval systems, serves as a state-of-the-art review of the experimental aspects of such systems. The seven chapters are as follows: "Introduction," "Automatic Text Analysis," "Automatic Classification," "File Structures," "Search Strategies," "Evaluation," "The Future." The bibliography lists some 200 items (including journal articles and monographs), but fewer than half a dozen of the entries have imprints later than 1973. There is a brief index.

For the coverage that this rather skimpy work provides, it is simply overpriced. A more substantial work reflecting British experiences in automatic information retrieval would be welcome. There are better sources on this subject. [R: Choice, Sept 76, p. 856]

Bohdan S. Wynar

1565.   Vickery, B. C. **Information Systems.** Hamden, Conn., Archon, 1973. 350p. illus. index. o.p. LC 72-14284. ISBN 0-208-01346-6.

Consists of 12 chapters that discuss the basic channels of information exchange, components of information systems, reference retrieval, conceptual and mathematical models, retrieval language models, and the design of the system. Most readers are familiar with Vickery's *On Retrieval System Theory*, second edition (Butterworths, 1965), and we are sure they will welcome this one, too. [R: Choice, Mar 74, p. 126; LR, Fall 73, p. 120; RSR, Oct 73, p. 48; SL, Nov 73, p. 537]

1566.   Vickery, B. C. **Techniques of Information Retrieval.** Hamden, Conn., Shoe String Press, 1970. 262p. bibliog. index. o.p. ISBN 0-208-00983-3.

Primarily a textbook which largely centers on procedures and practices of retrieving information within the context of computerized systems. Discussions of general questions about document analysis, bibliographic description, indexing terminology and its coordination, file organization search strategy, system design, and evaluation. A good introduction to the subject. [R: LJ, 1 Dec 70, p. 4149]

Charles D. Patterson

1567. Weisman, Herman M. **Information Systems, Services, and Centers.** New York, Becker and Hayes, 1972. 265p. bibliog. index. (Information Science Series). $10.50. LC 72-1156. ISBN 0-471-92645-0.

Designed and written as a teaching text at the university level, this volume presents the step-by-step process of planning and organizing an information retrieval operation. Its several chapters treat the basics including terms and definitions, the information process, design of information systems, documentation practices and techniques, management of information systems, and description of the Information Analysis Center. One hundred forty-three pages are taken up with appendices, index, bibliography, discussion problems/exercises, and tables/figures. [R: Choice, Apr 73, p. 319; LJ, 1 May 73, p. 1456; SBF, May 73, p. 1]

Charles D. Patterson

GENERAL WORKS SINCE 1976

1568. **Books Are for Use: Final Report of the Subject Access Project to The Council on Library Resources.** Syracuse, N.Y., Syracuse University, School of Information Studies, Subject Access Project, 1978. 172p. o.p.

The purpose of this project was to determine the feasibility and costs of constructing an online bibliographic database of monographs. Most existing databases contain surrogates of journal articles or reports; monographs do not readily lend themselves to the creation of surrogates of the richness required for online searching. The idea of this project was to create a useful search vocabulary by augmenting the subject description of books with index and table of contents extracts.

A sample of 1,979 books were selected from the University of Toronto Libraries and about 30 entries made for each book to create a BOOKS database. The cost of selecting and inputting these subject descriptions was about $5.00 per title. The file was maintained by Systems Development Corporation. A number of tests were conducted using BOOKS and an equivalent MARC (unaugmented) database. In comparison to MARC, BOOKS searches took about half as long, recalled more relevant items, and recalled different items, but the precision was not particularly impressive in either database. Although search costs of BOOKS were about half as much as MARC, no direct comparison was made of the input costs of the two systems; thus, we cannot compare total costs.

This report contains details of creating the database; some anecdotal reports from the user community, which had access to the database during 1977; and a more rigorous statistical evaluation of 90 searches conducted at Syracuse. The researchers conclude that their approach provides a better record for subject searching than does MARC, and their analysis would seem to support this conclusion. However, like most such evaluations, it depends on human relevancy judgments of recall and precision, with all the well-known pitfalls relating to it. Nevertheless, the augmentation of monographic records would seem to be a necessary approach to creating a useful database, *providing* recall and precision are high enough to justify the higher input costs. This report contains a wealth of information for others planning such projects. [R: LJ, 1 Jan 79, pp. 85-86]

A. Neil Yerkey

1569. Davis, Charles H., and James E. Rush. **Guide to Information Science.** Westport, Conn., Greenwood Press, 1979. 305p. index. $35.00. LC 78-75240. ISBN 0-313-20982-0.

Information science is an extraordinarily diverse interdisciplinary field with many faces; thus, it is impossible to write a one-volume, introductory book covering all aspects of information science. The *Guide to Information Science*, with its general title, covers the major aspects of the information storage and retrieval process, as pointed out clearly by the authors. Yet, one certainly agrees that information storage and retrieval is only one large aspect of "information science."

The book is really a revised and expanded version of the authors' earlier book, *Information Retrieval and Documentation in Chemistry* (Greenwood Press, 1974), with new chapters on "History and Fundamentals of Computing" (seventh chapter) and "Data Structures and File Organization" (eighth chapter). The authors should be congratulated for their inclusion of excellent discussions on basic research methods and statistics in the chapter on retrieval system evaluation. I only hope that they will not be neglected by most readers, since the table of contents, with its first five chapter headings as "The Human Factor," "Indexing and Classification," "Abstracts and Abstracting," "General Principles of Retrieval Systems," and "Retrieval Systems Evaluation," does not necessarily imply such an extensive coverage of statistical methods. On the whole, this is a much welcomed introduction to the information storage and retrieval process. [R: BL, 15 Jan 80, p. 698;

C&RL, July 80, p. 365; LJ, 1 Jan 80, p. 80]

Ching-chih Chen

1570. Gill, Suzanne L. **File Management and Information Retrieval Systems: A Manual for Managers and Technicians.** Littleton, Colo., Libraries Unlimited, 1981. 193p. illus. bibliog. index. $18.50. LC 80-22785. ISBN 0-87287-229-7.

Record making and record keeping, essential to the smooth and profitable running of any library, company, or other institution, are probably the costliest part of office practices in terms of space, salaries, and equipment. Whether large or small, these organizations must handle a large variety of information in the form of correspondence, invoices, reports, proposals, memos, payroll, personnel records, and many other types of records. To control this information effectively requires filing systems designed for effective retrieval, disposition, and retention of records. This manual introduces the library technical assistant, student, office manager, or secretary to a variety of practical filing methods, all of which are in actual use. While learning file organization theory, the student also develops a procedures manual tailored to the particular needs of his or her situation. While many other file manuals maintain that there is one set of rules that have to be bent to the particular organization's needs, Gill explains many filing systems and allows the "rules" to be developed to fit the organization's unique needs, insisting, however, that these rules should be followed consistently once established.

The text is illustrated with types of files, equipment, cards, labels, and other filing aids. Microforms and computerized records are treated briefly. The author suggests referring to a more specialized manual as a guide to handling these formats, reserving treatment in this book for the more traditional paper formats. Two case studies of the record management systems of actual companies illustrate the principles set forth. The text also includes a glossary of terms, a bibliography, and an index. [R: LJ, 15 Oct 81, p. 2001]

1571. Heaps, H. S. **Information Retrieval: Computational and Theoretical Aspects.** New York, Academic Press, 1978. 344p. illus. index. (Library and Information Science). $25.00. LC 78-3338. ISBN 0-12-335750-0.

This is a useful book for both computer and information scientists as well as students in these fields who are interested in the basic computational and theoretical concepts of information retrieval, and in the design and structure of

the relevant computer programs. "Topics covered in detail include general concepts, the organization of data for computer-accessible storage, query language for information retrieval, information structures, the structure of search programs, and the characteristics of the vocabularies of document data bases." Numerous examples, exercises, and illustrations included should be of particular benefit to those who are relatively new to the subject. Due to the emphases on the computational and theoretical aspects, the book will naturally appeal more to those with computer science and mathematical backgrounds. [R: C&RL, May 79, pp. 278-79]

Ching-chih Chen

1572. Lancaster, F. Wilfrid. **Information Retrieval Systems: Characteristics, Testing and Evaluation.** New York, Wiley, 1979. 381p. bibliog. index. (A Wiley-Interscience Publication). $42.95. LC 78-11078. ISBN 0-471-04673-6.

The first edition of this introductory work, published in 1968, received the "Best Book in Information Science" award from the American Society for Information Science. Completely rewritten, and greatly expanded (from 16 to 25 chapters), this edition has as its focus the "intellectual" aspects of information retrieval systems and services—in contradistinction to an equipment orientation. In it Lancaster examines such issues as the functions of IR systems, user-system interactions, the strengths and weaknesses of various indexing subsystems (precoordinate, postcoordinate), vocabulary control, search strategies, "pertinence" and relevance, and design and evaluation of systems and services. The closing chapter looks into the future, to the time of paperless information systems. Also included are three appendices (an interview guide and a questionnaire, used in different projects, as well as the conclusions and recommendations from one of them), a 15-page bibliography, and a 7-page index.

As enumerated above, Lancaster has covered a wide range of topics, but regrettably the sequence and organization of them lack coherence. Some topics introduced significantly in chapter 1 (e.g., the components of IR systems) are either thereafter dismissed or treated in a blurred, disjointed fashion. Some chapters are repetitious of previous ones, while other related ideas often appear in widely separated locations. The chapters are not connected to each other via progression of thought or any other literary device. Proportion is likewise askew; not all facets of bibliographic retrieval (e.g., prefix-code searching) are treated, and the emphasis on evaluation is overly strong. The book as a whole seems badly organized and will not, consequently, serve well as a text. [R: C&RL, Nov 80, p. 548; LQ, Jan 81, p. 134]

Glenn R. Wittig

1573. Lancaster, F. W. **Toward Paperless Information Systems.** New York, Academic Press, 1978. 179p. illus. bibliog. index. (Library and Information Science). $33.00. LC 78-51237. ISBN 0-12-436050-5.

Print-on-paper methods of disseminating scientific and technical information will be replaced soon by a global information system in which the composition, publication, dissemination, and use of information may be performed by electronic mode. Activities in the U.S. intelligence/defense community are explained to illustrate the growing need for implementation of paperless systems. Formal communication is becoming increasingly inefficient due to the growing volume of literature, the rising cost of print-on-paper production and distribution, and the long publication delays. A "scenario for an electronic information system for the year 2000" is described, in which scientists will have access from their own terminals to public data, to their personal files, and to electronically transmitted "mail." Routinely, they will use their terminals to create, to transmit, and to receive information.

The benefits of a paperless system include lower costs and increased speed for information dissemination, increased accessibility, and the ability to combine informal and formal exchange channels within the same system. Though nearly feasible today, there are still some technological, intellectual, and social problems in implementing such an electronic system (these are reviewed).

Although a strong argument is made for a greater user-operated information system, the author also perceives a continued role for libraries to include providing online access to resources free or at low cost for people who do not have their own terminals, making available printouts of information needed in paper form, collecting and organizing materials of local interest, improving selection procedures to increase relevance for users, and linking printed with electronically processed materials. Librarians are challenged to prepare themselves for servicing information needs in the future library, which will likely be one without walls.

The text covers a technical topic in an easily understood manner, and is thoroughly documented with reference to numerous sources cited in an extensive bibliography. Although this book is not primarily a reference tool, it does provide a provocative view of the ongoing transition to a paperless system that will profoundly affect the nature of reference services. [R: JAL, Nov 79, p. 306; LRTS, Summer 79, pp. 342-43]

Danuta A. Nitecki

1574. Lancaster, F. Wilfrid, ed. **The Use of Computers in Literature Searching and Related Reference Activities in Libraries.** Urbana-Champaign, Ill., Graduate School of Library Science, University of Illinois, 1976. 159p. index. (Papers Presented at the 1975 Clinic on Library Applications of Data Processing, April 27-30, 1975). o.p. LC 76-1790. ISBN 0-87845-043-2; ISSN 0069-4789.

The Twelfth Annual Clinic on Library Applications of Data Processing must have been, as is usual in this series, a useful conference. This report, lacking the demonstrations, is still a helpful book. Oriented to librarians interested in practical applications, it is neither too elementary nor too computer-technical.

The contributions represent both users and retailers of databases, and public, academic, and special libraries. A report from Australia presents an international view. One paper is on the possibility of developing machines to answer factual questions; one covers the public library as a community information center (including microfilming arrest records for the sheriff's office and license records); and one is on CAI (computer-assisted instruction) in the library. The other seven papers are about library aspects of searching bibliographic databases: advantages, availability, disadvantages, how to evaluate, how to use, where the terminal should be, who does the searching, problems of marketing, training, budgeting. A final summary paper emphasizes inadequacies of available services and makes suggestions for the future.

In general, these proceedings can be useful for anyone interested in the uses of a computer in the library reference department. The promptness of publication adds another advantage. [R: LJ, 15 Nov 76, p. 2353]

Shirley B. Hesslein

1575. Maranjian, Lorig, and Richard W. Boss. **Fee-Based Information Services: A Study of a Growing Industry.** New York, R. R. Bowker, 1980. 199p. illus. bibliog. index. (Information Management Series, 1). $24.95. LC 80-20176. ISBN 0-8352-1287-4.

Fee-Based Information Services is the inaugural volume in Bowker's Information Management series. Chapter 1, "Surveying a

Growing Field," is an outline of the results of a survey conducted by the authors in 1979 on a variety of information services. Topics such as marketing, information-gathering techniques, economics of the industry, FIND/SVP—a close-up, profiles of major fee-based information services, the freelancer, fee-based information services abroad, fee-based information services and the library, and what happens next? (an analysis of present concerns and future directions of the information industry) are included as chapters 2-11. The "Selected Bibliography" (pp. 169-86) provides additional information on fee-based services, etc. An important section of the book is appendix 3, "Directory of Fee-Based Information Services—United States, Canada, The UK." This volume may not be considered a serious contribution to the literature, but it will provide the reader with a current overview of the fee-based information industry. [R: JAL, Jan 81, p. 367; JAL, July 81, p. 174; LJ, 1 June 81, p. 1193; LQ, Oct 81, p. 461; SL, Apr 81, p. 185]   Donald D. Foos

1576. Pratt, Gordon, ed. **Information Economics: Costs and Prices of Machine-Readable Information in Europe.** Gordon Pratt and Susan Harvey, comps. London, Aslib, 1976. 115p. illus. (European User Series 2). £6.00; £5.00pa. ISBN 0-85142-078-8.

This slim volume deals concisely, perceptively, and expertly with the current status of British and Continental computerized information services. It deals with pricing by major information retrieval agencies, expected future costs of retrieval, usage of existing databases, and requisite education and marketing efforts necessary for economic viability of computer-based information retrieval services, such as Lockheed Retrieval Service, System Development Corporation Service, and Space Documentation Service.

There is an excellent synthesis of major economic considerations in using computers for retrieving information. Very useful tables, charts, and diagrams on databases, costs, and prices. No index or bibliography.
          Richard Palmer

1577. **Progress in Documentation: Some Themes and Topics: A Selection from the Progress in Documentation Articles Published in** *Journal of Documentation,* 1969-1979. London, Aslib, 1981. 245p. £13.00; £11.00 (Aslib members). ISBN 0-85142-140-7.

The eight articles appearing in this volume were selected by the *Journal of Documentation's* editorial board from a series of Progress

in Documentation articles which had appeared in that journal between 1969 and 1979. S. E. Robertson deals with theories and models in information retrieval; Robert A. Fairthorne with the Bradford-Zipf-Mandelbrot distributions; Maurice B. Line and A. Sandison with obsolescence and changes in the use of literature with time; R. H. Orr with quantitative measures for measuring library services; Elizabeth D. Barraclough with online searching; Karen Sparck Jones with automatic indexing; Herbert Coblans with the bibliographic control of periodical literature in librarianship and documentation; and W. J. Hutchins with machine and machine-aided translation.

The articles, though a mixed bag, serve as helpful introductions to a variety of topics of importance to Aslib members and documentalists throughout the world. The volume includes a list of the authors and titles of all of the Progress in Documentation articles that have appeared in the *Journal of Documentation* between 1969 and 1980, including such distinguished names as C. W. Cleverdon, J. Mills, J. Farradane, D. J. Foskett, Manfred Kochen, Derek Austin, Tefko Saracevic, C. D. Batty, and C. J. Van Rijsbergen.

While the eight selected articles include references, some quite extensive, there is no index or comprehensive bibliography. This work will be of primary interest to devout documentalists. [R: LR, Winter 81, p. 249]
          Richard Palmer

1578. Stibic, V. **Personal Documentation for Professionals: Means and Methods.** Amsterdam, North-Holland Publishing; distr., New York, Elsevier North-Holland, 1980. 214p. illus. bibliog. index. $35.00. LC 80-11906. ISBN 0-444-85480-0.

Written by a research professional with extensive experience with both manual and computer personal file control and retrieval systems, this book covers explicitly the organization of personal records; the structure, classification, and indexing of information materials; the techniques for information retrieval, such as peek-a-boo and card files; and automatic indexing; and four case histories of personal documentation systems.

Managers and professionals are increasingly recognizing their need to have a variety of information documents, including books, periodicals, reports, clipping, photocopies, slides, microfiche, drawings, correspondence, etc., arranged for rapid and, if possible, easy retrieval. The author, having developed several systems for his own changing and expanding information needs, writes with great conviction and penetration. The manual moves from basics of information sources, document description, classification and indexing, and technical means and devices for control systems to the use of computerized indexes, personal computers, and remote mainframe computers, and concludes with some predictions about future technologies and information-manipulating work stations.

Included are much useful illustrative material, a good index, and a thematic bibliography. A valuable aid to individuals and small organizations in designing their own custom information systems. [R: Indexer, Oct 82, p. 133]
Richard Palmer

1579. Strizich, Martha D., and Kathryn S. Lawhun, eds. **Document Retrieval: Sources & Services.** San Francisco, Information Store, 1981. 171p. index. o.p. ISBN 0-940004-00-3.

The term "document" is used by the directory's compilers "to describe any sort of non-book items." The intent is to list suppliers of "document retrieval services," yet nearly a third of the entries claim "retrieval of any and all kinds of publications" or access to books in specific collections. Suppliers include 171 libraries, information centers of nonprofit organizations, and commercial enterprises located in 16 countries, though most are in the United States. Suppliers were identified from computerized search service documentation, brochures, and other sources; details were gathered by mail and by phone.

The major portion of the directory is an alphabetic listing of suppliers, arranged by name; each entry includes supplier's name, address, telephone number, and other communication points (e.g., electronic maildrop, telex, dialorder), name of service representative, materials supplied, fulfillment time, ordering procedures, rates/prices, and copyright compliance. Cross-references from variant name forms are included in a listing of suppliers. Additional access is provided by two indexes: one by subject, the other by geographic location, specific to state and to country. A variety of subjects is covered, with the exception of topics in high demand by genealogists, and sources in the humanities such as films, recordings, and sheet music. Technical, legal, and government documentation are well represented.

The directory's format is conducive to quick referral. The looseleaf ring-notebook is organized with one entry per page; entries and indexes have distinctive headings. However, numerous sources are listed in other contexts

such as the more extensive, yet compact, *Information Industry Market Place 1981* (R. R. Bowker, 1980). The price of the directory seems high for its coverage and overlap with more commonly available tools. The directory may be helpful for information-seekers not familiar or not satisfied with interlibrary services provided by most libraries. Danuta A. Nitecki

1580. van Rijsbergen, C. J. **Information Retrieval.** 2nd ed. Boston, Butterworths, 1979. 208p. bibliog. index. $39.95. LC 78-40725. ISBN 0-408-70929-4.

In this volume, information retrieval (IR) is examined in terms of automatic as opposed to manual systems, and within experimental, laboratory situations, rather than operational settings as provided by commercial vendors. The results of IR inform the user of the existence and whereabouts of documents relating to the inquiry, as opposed to data retrieval, which informs the user of the subject of the inquiry.

Following an introduction of basic background information, the text is organized into six chapters reflecting the components necessary for the design of an experimental IR system: automatic text analysis, automatic classification, file structures, search strategies, probabilistic retrieval, and evaluation. The author's intent is "to give a complete coverage of the more important ideas current in various special areas of information retrieval." The text emphasizes the use of automatic classification techniques and rigorous methods of measurement of effectiveness. Automatic content analysis is only superficially covered, in part due to extensive treatment of the topic elsewhere. A final chapter contains speculations on the future of IR and identifies areas desperately needing further research. An extensive bibliography and a detailed index conclude the volume.

This second edition expands on the first by addition of a chapter on "probabilistic retrieval." It describes a formal model where the frequency of occurrence and co-occurrence of index terms in relevant and nonrelevant documents is sampled and used to enhance retrieval effectiveness.

The intended audience for this book includes advanced undergraduates in information and computer science, postgraduate library science students, and IR researchers. A basic mathematical background is needed to understand many sections of the text. This is a well-organized, adequately referenced, descriptive textbook concerned with the research aspects of designing IR systems. It is not a simplified reference for the average librarian concerned with practical system use. [R: C&RL, Nov 80, p. 548; LQ, Jan 81, p. 134]   Danuta A. Nitecki

REFERENCE WORKS

1581. Christian, Roger. **The Electronic Library: Bibliographic Data Bases, 1978-79.** White Plains, N.Y., Knowledge Industry Publications, 1978. 105p. illus. bibliog. index. o.p. LC 78-18408. ISBN 0-914236-15-6.

This tightly-written, but superbly readable, condensation of the state-of-the-art in online database production, distribution, and use is an excellent introduction to an increasingly important area of library service. Problems are identified, alternatives are explored, and the future is projected in footnoted chapters. The volume's effectiveness is enhanced by its perceptiveness and brevity. Helpful index and up-to-date selective bibliography. [R: C&RL, May 79, p. 285; JAL, Mar 79, p. 33; LJ, 1 Oct 79, p. 2048]

Richard Palmer

1582. Cibbarelli, Pamela, Carol Tenopir, and Edward John Kazlauskas, comps. and eds. **Directory of Information Management Software for Libraries, Information Centers, Record Centers.** 1985-1986 ed. Studio City, Calif., Cibbarelli, 1985. 239p. index. $49.00pa. ISBN 0-913203-14-9.

Derived from handouts and other materials used in workshops given by the publisher, this slim paperback directory describes or lists roughly 100 diverse software "packages," from stand-alone turnkey cataloging systems, such as Mini Marc, to such database utilities as The Source. The main body of this publication consists of an alphabetical compilation of 55 entries analyzed by approximately two dozen descriptive characteristics, such as system hardware requirements, programming languages used, and typical costs (described for three situations: time-share access for a small collection, time-share access for a medium-sized collection, and outright purchase or lease). Fifty-four other "packages" (including bibliographic utilities, records management systems, and others) are more briefly listed. Indexing is by vendor, hardware manufacturer, and system application (cataloging, acquisitions, etc.), and there is also a general index.

Because of the book's high price, the advisability of purchasing it must be questioned by all but the largest libraries or library system headquarters; and in those collections, much of the information provided in this title would probably already be available through periodicals or such titles as the *Encyclopedia of Information Systems and Services*, edited by John Schmittroth (7th ed., Gale, 1986), or R. R. Bowker's *Information Industry Market Place* (annual). [R: A Arch, Winter 84, p. 65; AL, July 83, p. 500; CLW, Oct 83, p. 108]

Christopher Albertson

1583. Hall, J. L., comp. **On-Line Information Retrieval 1965-1976: A Bibliography with a Guide to On-Line Data Bases and Systems.** London, Aslib, 1977. 125p. index. (Aslib Bibliography, No. 8). £13.00pa.; £11.00pa. (Aslib members). ISBN 0-85142-094-X.

The body of this work lists by author over 900 references to publications on online information retrieval from 1964 to mid-1976. There are no annotations, although notes in the entries indicate the system(s) or database(s) covered when this is not clear from the title. The purpose is to provide an introduction to the literature of online retrieval, supplemented by guides to available databases and to both past and present systems. The scope is limited to retrieval of subject-oriented information from bibliographic files; numerical databases and computer-based catalog access have been excluded. There is some coverage of networking and telecommunications. A broad range of types of literature is included – not just journal articles, but conferences, reports, and monographs.

There are also tabular notes on available online databases, giving information on coverage, scope, installations, and access costs. Online systems, developments, and installations (107 of them) which were operational or experimental during the period 1965-1976 are described. A useful feature of this section is the references to citations in the bibliography, which cover such factors as dialog, search time and costs, and documentation for each system listed.

During the course of preparing the work, the author acknowledges that it went out-of-date; hence, what appears to be the coverage for 1976 is listed in a separate "Supplementary References" at the end of the work; these references are neither indexed nor included in the tabulation of systems.

The special use of this work is as a bibliography; other publications will serve the directory function. [R: JAL, July 77, p. 177]

Jessica L. Harris

1584. Herner, Saul, and Matthew J. Velucci, eds. **Selected Federal Computer-Based Information Systems.** Washington, D.C., Information

Resources Press, 1972. 215p. illus. $15.00. LC 72-85016. ISBN 0-87815-007-2.

Thirty-five federal computer-based information systems are described in this compilation, which is essentially a revised and enlarged edition of *Selected Mechanized Scientific and Technical Information Systems* (1968). This edition was prepared in cooperation with the Panel of Operational Techniques and Systems of COSATI—a partnership which must have been instrumental in the broadening of the scope of the resulting publication. United States governmental agencies whose information systems are described include the Departments of Agriculture, Commerce, Defense, Health, Education and Welfare, the Department of Interior, the Department of Transportation, the AEC, LC, NASA, and the Smithsonian Institution. The description of each information system consists of a verbal and a graphic section. The verbal section lists the name, address, and telephone number of the agency, identifies the system manager, and offers a detailed description of the system proper. Standard items in this narrative are: objectives, major components and services, scope, user/audience, staff, equipment, relationship with other systems, present operations, and future plans. Brief bibliographies are added. The graphic part of each section consists of several flow charts illustrating and clarifying the description. [R: SL, Jan 73, p. 60]   Ivan L. Kaldor

1585.   Schneider, John H., Marvin Gechman, and Stephen E. Furth, eds. **Survey of Commercially Available Computer-Readable Bibliographic Data Bases.** Washington, D.C., American Society for Information Science, 1973. 181p. o.p. LC 72-97793. ISBN 0-87715-102-4.

For this survey, 130 organizations were queried about whether they prepared commercially available computer-readable bibliographic databases. Of this number, 55 organizations (40 of which are in the United States and 15 in other countries) responded with camera-ready copy describing 81 of their databases as of November 1972. Each organization's response lists such information as frequency of issue, time span, scope of data, sources of information (reports, journal articles, patents, monographs, etc.), indexing and subject analysis methods, tape specifications, availability of programs to conduct retrospective searches or provide selective dissemination of information, names of organizations and individuals who can provide further information about the databases, type and cost of search services

offered, and availability and charges for the databases.

The responses to this survey by the American Society for Information Science should help librarians and information centers locate available bibliographic databases, forestall duplication of effort in the preparation of such arrays, and establish better bibliographic control of constantly expanding literatures. Until such surveys are themselves included in machine-readable networks, information about databases that is less than a year or so old will be difficult to obtain. Individuals who find this survey of interest are also likely to find value in Saul Herner and Matthew Velucci's *Selected Federal Computer-Based Information Systems* (Information Resources Press, 1972). [R: C&RL, Jan 74, p. 68]   Richard Palmer

1586.   Schultz, Claire K. **Thesaurus of Information Science Terminology.** Completely rev. and expanded ed. Metuchen, N.J., Scarecrow, 1978. 288p. o.p. LC 78-16878. ISBN 0-8108-1156-1.

This thesaurus was developed as a tool for indexing and searching the author's personal collection of reports and articles on information storage and retrieval. This edition revises and expands previous editions, keeping up with the growth of the collection on which it is based. The thesaurus itself consists of an alphabetic list of terms, a hierarchical arrangement, and an index to multiword terms. In addition, the book contains seven interesting and helpful tutorial chapters on thesaurus building and use. Its taxonomy is based on the cybernetic system model, in which the field of information science is divided into environment, input, processing output, and feedback. Each of these aspects is a node under information science, and every legal term has a unique place in this hierarchy.

Partly because it was developed for a private collection and partly because of the particular taxonomy underlying the thesaurus, there seem to have been some unusual choices made as to legal, related, and referred terms (e.g., DATA BASES use INDEXES; RETROSPECTIVE SEARCHING use DATA GATHERING; AUTOMATED CIRCULATION use DELIVERY OF DOCUMENTS), and some inconsistencies (e.g., most information centers, such as ERIC, are referred to INFORMATION SCIENCE SERVICE ORGANIZATIONS, but DEFENSE DOCUMENTATION CENTER is a legal term). There are no entries for some information science concepts (e.g., bibliometrics, PRECIS).

The thesaurus makes no attempt to be exhaustive, nor are the terms very specific—many specific terms are referred to broader terms, some of which are unusual (e.g., BRADFORD'S LAW use STATISTICS; AUTOMATED INDEXING use INDEXING; NTIS use INFORMATION SCIENCE SERVICE ORGANIZATIONS). In fact, the *use* references seem to outnumber legal terms, suggesting that many specific concepts are subsumed under fewer broader ones. The thesaurus should be useful for indexing a relatively small collection of documents on information science, if the indexer keeps these caveats in mind. Additionally, the tutorial chapters make it useful for students of indexing, thesaurus building, and information retrieval. [R: LJ, 1 Mar 79, p. 619]

A. Neil Yerkey

1587. Townley, Helen M., and Ralph D. Gee. **Thesaurus-Making: Grow Your Own Word-Stock.** London, Andre Deutsch; distr., Boulder, Colo., Westview Press, 1980. 206p. bibliog. index. (A Grafton Book). $30.50. ISBN 0-233-97225-0.

This guide covers the basic principles of thesaurus construction and maintenance. Section 1 introduces the theory and context; section 2 works through a specific example, using the development of a legal thesaurus to illustrate various concepts and problems. Remaining sections deal with evaluation, revision, and the storage and display capabilities of machine-readable thesauri. There are a glossary, primarily of linguistic terminology; three useful appendices (extracts from the international standard for monolingual thesauri, a list of software packages for thesaurus construction, and sample pages from various vocabularies); a decent bibliography; and an unsatisfactory index. The prose is occasionally somewhat florid.

The authors make it very clear that the book is aimed at the small information center, and this has resulted in some limitations. Important and interesting topics, such as multilingual thesauri, intermediate lexica, and facet analysis as a basis for thesaurus construction, are all too briefly mentioned. A curious hostility towards anything resembling automatic indexing can be detected at several points throughout the text.

The practical information found in this book is covered as well or better by Jean Aitchison and Alan Gilchrist's *Thesaurus Construction: A Practical Manual* (Aslib, 1972), and the theory is treated in more depth by A. C. Foskett's *The Subject Approach to Information*, 3rd ed. (Linnet Books, 1977). However, the former is hard to obtain in America, and

this work does have many useful examples and helpful appendices. [R: Indexer, Oct 81, p. 228; LQ, Apr 82, p. 201]

Candy Schwartz

1588. Williams, Martha E., and others, comps. and eds. **Computer-Readable Data Bases: A Directory and Data Sourcebook.** Washington, D.C., American Society for Information Science; distr., White Plains, N.Y., Knowledge Industry Publications, 1979. 1367p. index. o.p. LC 76-46249. ISBN 0-914236-45-8.

In 1976, *Computer-Readable Bibliographic Data Bases—A Directory and Sourcebook*, compiled and edited by Martha E. Williams and Sandra H. Rouse, was published by the American Society for Information Science (ASIS). It was published in looseleaf form as a subscription service, and between April 1977 and 1978 three sets of updated pages were published. The subscription service was discontinued in 1978.

This directory, *Computer-Readable Data Bases: A Directory and Data Sourcebook*, was computer-produced and printed on a Sander (Model 12/7) printer in bound form. "Subsequent issues will also be published in bound form at two-year intervals so long as the growth in data bases—both in size and number—and changes within them warrant." The 1976 directory contained 301 databases, and this one (1979) includes 528 databases. Many databases found in the 1976 issue have been deleted "for a variety of reasons: they are non-terminated totally, they no longer are updated, they have been subsumed into other data bases, etc." Nearly 300 databases not included in the 1976 publication are in the 1979 directory. Both directories were compiled from the database on databases maintained at the University of Illinois Information Retrieval Research Laboratory (IRRL). Listings contain the name and producer of the database, its coverage (subject matter and scope), year of origin, number of items in the database, availability in either batch or online mode, frequency of update, pricing, and other information (e.g., "Time Span Covered by Data Base," "Anticipated Growth Rate," "Current and Back Files, etc."). Databases are listed by either acronym/short name or full name (e.g., "ALLOY is listed as NBS Alloy Data Base" in the "Data Base Contents"). Producer, processor, name, and subject indexes are provided, with *see* and *see also* references. Databases included in this directory fulfill three criteria: computer readability, public availability, and information retrieval (used for information retrieval purposes or are available through the major online vendors). Items included, "Subject Matter and Scope," "Subject

Categories," "Target User Community," "Language(s)," etc., provide the directory user with a wealth of database information. This directory should prove to be an essential reference tool, providing information on current databases as well as information on "quasi-data bases," consisting of bases that are outmoded, those replaced by later bases, or ones whose existence cannot be verified. In 1985 a two-volume edition was published by the American Library Association ($157.50pa./set, ISBN 0-8387-0415-7). [R: RSR, October 80, p. 21]   Donald D. Foos

PROCEEDINGS AND SYMPOSIA

1589. The Management of Information Analysis Centers. (Proceedings of a Forum sponsored by the COSATI Panel on Information Analysis Centers). Springfield, Va., U.S. Dept. of Commerce, 1972. 192p. $3.25pa. LC 72-602733.

Proceedings of this forum represent a wide range of descriptions concerning the nature and activity of information centers. Problems of copyright, relation of automatic data processing to information analysis centers, problems with abstracting and indexing services, effective marketing, etc., are all discussed. An interesting and valuable collection which, unfortunately, lacks an index. [R: LJ, 1 May 73, p. 1456]

Charles D. Patterson

1590. Sherrod, John, ed. **Information Systems and Networks: Eleventh Annual Symposium, March 27-29, 1974.** Co-sponsored by Informatics, Inc., and the University of California at Los Angeles. Westport, Conn., Greenwood Press, 1975. 200p. $29.95. LC 74-11941. ISBN 0-8371-7717-0.

Twenty papers were delivered at this three-day 1974 conference on *bibliographic* information systems and networks; ten of the papers are under eight pages in length. Many of the authors are well known to readers of library and information science literature: Joseph Becker, Arthur W. Elias, Thomas H. Martin, Roger K. Summit, Harold Borko, and Paul G. Zurkowski. Most of the papers describe existing database suppliers and retrieval systems (Wiginton on Chemical Abstracts, Schultz on Biological Abstracts, Caponio on CAIN at the National Agricultural Library, Kissman on TOX-LINE at the National Library of Medicine, Pryor on NASA/RECON), or review the state-of-the-art of automated information systems in libraries (Kissman from USC), information networks in universities (Borko), database genera-

tion (Elias). Four papers are personal expressions of future prospects (Hersey, Penisten, Rector, and Speer). Three highly technical papers, comprising a quarter of the text pages, appear peripheral to the themes of the above papers: King and Brown on economic model of interactive information systems, Lientz on computer network usage-cost-benefit analysis, and Siler on GDBMS (Generalized Data Base Management Systems).

Except for the last three mentioned, the papers are easy to read and informative. Much of the content can be found elsewhere, since several authors hit a recurring theme in most of their writings. Some of the factual data about trends, existing conditions, and the comments about the future make the book of some value. Unfortunately, there is no record of the discussion of conference participants and no index to the contents, so it would be difficult to locate either disagreements with the papers' contents or specific information on some topic. [R: C&RL, Jan 76, p. 82; LQ, Jan 76, p. 81; SL, July 76, p. 349]

Pauline Atherton Cochrane

1591. Tou, Julius T., ed. **Information Systems, COINS IV.** New York, Plenum, 1974. 506p. bibliog. index. $69.50. LC 74-4403. ISBN 0-306-35134-X.

The theme of these proceedings of the Fourth International Symposium on Computer and Information Science is information systems. This is fitting since research in information science has increasingly turned toward the development of information systems in education, government, industry, and science. The 24 papers in this volume range from general papers such as "The Objective of Database Management," by Gordon C. Everest, through theoretical papers such as M. Shimura's "Nonparametric Learning Using Contextual Information." Also included are papers dealing with existing information systems, programs, and languages such as LEADERMART, BOLTS, SPIRAL, SEFIRE, EMISARI, and APL Programs. Although these papers were presented in December 1972, persons involved in environmental information systems will find three papers to be of particular interest and value: "Information Systems for Urban Problem Solvers" (by Manfred Kochen), "An Experiment with a Rational Data Base System in Environmental Research," and "Representing Geographical Information for Efficient Computer Search."

Robert J. Havlik

OTHER TOPICS

1592. Davis, Charles H., and James E. Rush. **Information Retrieval and Documentation in Chemistry.** Westport, Conn., Greenwood Press, 1974. 284p. index. (Contributions in Librarianship and Information Science, No. 8). $25.00. LC 72-791. ISBN 0-8371-6364-1.

The first part of the book provides a concise introduction to information storage and retrieval systems (I S&R) through six chapters dealing with human factors of I S&R, types of indexes and major index variables, abstracts and abstracting, general principles and evaluation of I S&R. The chapters are brief but well written and extensively illustrated with flowcharts, extracts of indexes and other visual aids. Each chapter includes references to additional materials on the subject. Experimental studies on automatic abstracting, though perhaps not basic to the subject under discussion, are covered particularly well. This is not surprising since one of the authors is an active participant in research in this field.

Perhaps more might have been said by Davis and Rush about online computer searched indexes. This mode of index searching is used more and more as portions of *Chemical Abstracts* and other abstracting and index journals become available for online searching through commercial services. The second part of the book, which deals with chemical structure representation, consists of three longer chapters subtitled nomenclature, linear notation, and topological systems. These chapters are as well written, illustrated, and referenced as those of part one, but they are directed to a more specialized audience. There is a combined author and subject index. The book is highly recommended for chemical libraries; it should also be useful in other libraries that need an introduction to I S&R and chemical nomenclature. [R: LQ, Apr 75, p. 221; SL, Sept 75, p. 497]   Gerald Jahoda

1593. Coates, Eric, Geoffrey Lloyd, and Dusan Simandl. **The BSO Manual: The Development, Rationale and Use of the Broad System of Ordering.** The Hague, International Federation for Documentation, 1979. 157p. index. (FID 580). £55.00pa. ISBN 92-66-00580-0.

The *Schedule and Index* of a new general classification scheme was published in 1978 by the International Federation for Documentation (FID) and UNESCO (see *ARBA* 79, entry 300). Known as the Broad System of Ordering (BSO) and designed to handle relatively coarse blocks of information, it was a third revised

draft of a scheme scientifically constructed to serve a proposed worldwide information network covering the whole field of knowledge.

The present manual traces the development through the field test of an earlier version, using 28 respondents from 11 countries. Modifications based on the feedback from that test resulted in the draft *Schedule* cited above. It contains just over 4,000 terms. Since certain failures in the field test were traced to inadequacies of the test instructions, chapters 6 and 7 of the manual contain explanations and suggestions on how to interpret and apply different features or techniques of the system. They supplement the tabulated "procedures for combining notation" and the explanatory notes found in the *Schedule* proper. Anyone wishing to understand and use BSO should read them carefully. Further refinements are projected. The designers envision an eventual scheme structured to ensure up to a 70 percent mean matching consistency when applying BSO as a "transformer" between different local indexing languages. This success, if and when achieved, will compare favorably to the 70 percent recall commonly accepted as satisfactory for typical indexing systems. [R: LR, Autumn 80, p. 199]   Jeanne Osborn

1594. Gillespie, Paul D., Paul Katzenberger, and John Page. **Problems of Document Delivery for the EURONET User Technical Report.** New York, Munich, K. G. Saur, 1979. 228p. bibliog. index. o.p. ISBN 3-598-10069-8.

"This report was commissioned to investigate an important user problem with on-line search services for scientific and technical information—how, having identified promising references in the literature, to obtain the actual documents in a speedy, comprehensive and economic way." The purpose of the study is to highlight the requirements, problems, and possible solutions for document ordering and delivery for EURONET, the telecommunications network of the Commission of the European Communities. The present and potential demand for scientific and technical documents, the existing delivery mechanisms, and copyright problems were examined through surveying document delivery systems in European Community member countries—Canada, Sweden, and the United States. The approach to the study, the results, and the analysis of the results are presented in a detailed and thorough manner and include statistics and specific comments on the operation of various existing services. Specific attention is given to copyright problems, and copyright laws in the different countries are carefully examined.

                                          Gail M. Nichols

1595. Kiewitt, Eva L. **Evaluating Information Retrieval Systems: The PROBE Program.** Westport, Conn., Greenwood Press, 1979. 168p. bibliog. index. $29.95. LC 78-55322. ISBN 0-313-20521-3.

This work, written by a former director of the Educational Resources Information Center (ERIC)/PROBE (a computer retrieval search service) Project at Indiana University, covers briefly a variety of evaluative techniques appropriate for the comparison of bibliographic information retrieval systems and reports on a cost-effectiveness study of the ERIC/PROBE project. The major components of this volume are: guidelines for evaluation; a brief history of retrieval system user studies; a summary of some major user studies; a description of evaluation measures, such as recall and precision tests; a description of the steps in the PROBE study; a report on user evaluation of retrieval effectiveness; and a cost-and-delivery comparison of the batch-processed searches provided by PROBE and online searches available from Lockheed Information System.

The differences between retrieval results gained from online interactive searches and PROBE batch-processed searches were not explored. The cost comparison covered an apples and oranges situation because the online fees for Lockheed searches included overhead costs, while the batch PROBE searches did not. The work demonstrates that significant research in the library/information science field remains to be done. Footnotes, a 19-term glossary, a 130-item bibliography covering 1956 to 1977, and an index are provided. [R: C&RL, July 79, pp. 388-89; JAL, Nov 79, p. 306; LJ, 1 June 79, p. 1231]

                                          Richard Palmer

1596. Rossmassler, Stephen A., and David G. Watson, eds. **Data Handling for Science and Technology: An Overview and Sourcebook.** Amsterdam, North-Holland Publishing, for Committee on Data for Science and Technology (CODATA), and United Nations Educational, Scientific and Cultural Organization (UNESCO); distr., New York, Elsevier North-Holland, 1980. 184p. index. $35.00. LC 80-16219. ISBN 0-444-86012-6.

Data Handling for Science and Technology is designed to "introduce the reader to the literature on the various aspects of numerical data handling" where data are "numerical representations of the magnitude of various quanti-

ties" and data handling covers all aspects of generation, publication, evaluation, and dissemination of the numeric scientific and technical data. The sourcebook consists of 11 chapters written by 14 contributors. These chapters deal with generation, analysis, interpretation, and presentation of data, retrieval of data from primary literature, and their compilation, evaluation, and dissemination. Three appendices are included which list national and international data programs as well as individual papers presented at the four most recent international conferences held by the Committee on Data for Science and Technology (CODATA).

The sourcebook is a flawed but important work for science librarians. Flawed because many of its articles are rather superficial; important because it presents succinctly a facet of scientific communication which is treated all too briefly in the literature oriented to science librarians. Although the sourcebook is not an essential reference book for many collections, it should be read by all those involved in scientific information work.   Rao Aluri

1597. Tessier, Judith A., Jennifer Kuehn, and Terry Noreault. **Feasibility of Maintaining and Providing Access to Data Archives through ERIC.** Syracuse, N.Y., ERIC Clearinghouse on Information Resources, Syracuse University, 1977. 71p. bibliog. o.p.

Although not a reference tool itself, this report should be of interest to librarians concerned with providing access to numerical descriptions of research data. The report summarizes a study that "explored the feasibility of establishing an archive for machine-readable data within the scope of the ERIC Clearinghouse on Information Resources" and of making available such survey data for new studies or secondary analysis. The authors refer to a separate ERIC document containing a display of survey instruments and data used. The benefits of access were identified as economy through full exploitation of already collected data and consolidation of knowledge through critical reanalysis and cross-study comparison.

The study consisted of three parts: (1) estimate of data availability, (2) estimate of demand for data, and (3) system design consideration. Availability of data and demand for a data sharing service were investigated through a survey mailed to potential users and contributers, including educators and researchers in library science, information science, and instructional technology. Results showed that data sets on diverse topics are generated and have been informally shared. Although a system of personal contact is perceived to provide adequate access to data, it is criticized for its unevenness; some seekers fail to find wanted data. Eight alternative services, ranging from no new service to creation of an archive with development of instructional data sets, were identified and evaluated in terms of cost.

The recommendations made by the feasibility study group included implementation of a formal data sharing system to be organized within ERIC/IR. The appropriate level of service identified after analysis of costs and need would be inclusion in the ERIC indexes and publication of an annual directory; an archive was not recommended at this time. The report itself reads easily, being organized around well-identified questions of inquiry, methodology, results, and cost evaluative analysis. A brief list of references concludes the volume. A lack of an index and the research reporting format of the document do not make this an easy reference tool; however, this is not its intention.

Danuta A. Nitecki

1598. Yska, Gerda, and John Martyn. **Final Report on 'Databases Suitable for Users of Environmental Information.'** London, Aslib, 1978. 58p. o.p. ISBN 0-85142-113-X.

This slim volume constitutes a technical report prepared by Aslib's R&D Department for the Commission of the European Communities. Its purpose is first to identify, then to evaluate, secondary information services having significant environmental content and, finally, to recommend certain of these as to their "suitability" for European users. The report discusses the difficulties in compiling a workable definition of "environment" and the consequences of translating the concept into a multiterm subject reference profile. It also reviews the five different approaches normally employed for database evaluation and relates them to the commission's task. The method selected for the study is a modified "question array" procedure, which tests for a database's coverage (number of items retrievable) by matching the reference profile against the base's indexing or authority list. Individual relevance judgments were not undertaken because of the lack of time and the bulk (1.75 million) of "hits" to be considered.

Of the 97 international databases identified, 45 were evaluated. These fall into three categories: (1) those searched interactively via remote telecommunications links, (2) those searched off-line via a computer batch operation, and (3) those "not automated but whose indexes lend themselves" to computerized searching. Only one non-English database was examined, and Aslib has recommended further study to resolve the language questions. Suitability for access through the developing EURONET was established by two criteria: (1) size of yearly input, and (2) "relevance factor" (number of hits divided by total input, each on an annual basis). These criteria were used to recommend the 10 largest and 10 most relevant databases. Most important among the tabulated data presented is a comprehensive database-profile term matrix of hits achieved. The tables also give the distribution of environmental content (percent of air, water, noise, etc.) and principal database parameters (name, address, input rate).

Published as a typewritten manuscript, the report lacks editorial polish. Despite this, Martyn's previous experience with database evaluation should make it useful to a special library in the environmental sector which is contemplating an online bibliographic connection. [R: LR, Summer 79, p. 131]

Philip H. Kitchens

54 Serials

GENERAL WORKS

1599. Brown, Clara D., and Lynn S. Smith. **Serials: Past, Present and Future.** 2nd rev. ed. Birmingham, Ala., EBSCO Industries, 1980. 390p. illus. index. $19.50. LC 80-81267. ISBN 0-913956-05-8.

Intended as a guide for new serials librarians, *Serials: Past, Present and Future* is a handbook on dealing with serials, and contains a wealth of basic "nuts and bolts" information. Specific sections deal with serial kardexes, binding records, handling mail, claiming missing issues, and all of the other functions of a serials department. There are many sample forms, too many really, and too few are presented with an explanation of their use. A revision and enlargement of a much smaller paper title, *Serials: Acquisition and Maintenance*, this edition is broader in scope and includes chapters by Lynn Smith on serials cataloging and serials processing at LC. It does reflect the authors' collective experience with all sorts of serial problems. Even though the book is packed with solid nuggets of information, it lacks a clear focus and, hence, at points seems jumbled. The text also relies heavily on lists and step-by-step procedures to make its points. While the end result could be better and the editing job more polished, *Serials* is, nonetheless, a worthwhile purchase for serials staffs. [R: C&RL, Jan 81, pp. 77-78; LJ, 15 Mar 81, p. 627]
Jean W. Farrington

1600. Davinson, Donald. **The Periodicals Collection.** rev. and enl. ed. Boulder, Colo., Westview Press, 1978. 243p. index. (Grafton Books on Library and Information Science). $26.50. LC 78-17873. ISBN 0-89158-833-7.

First published in 1960, and improved in two later editions in 1964 and 1969, Davinson again appears with a slightly revised title and largely revised contents to provide a generally valuable and accurate handbook covering some of the aspects of the technical side of identifying, acquiring, processing, and controlling periodicals in libraries. The British origin and background provide an emphasis on periodical history which, while not American, does highlight important points. The discussions of the "nature" of periodicals, and what are called "primary" and "nonprimary" periodicals, suggest numerous philosophical and practical concepts about serials in general that will inform even an experienced librarian. These four chapters of the first part are a firm support for the two other parts: bibliographic control, and organization and management.

Unfortunately, bibliographic control does not mean cataloging. This is the one major omission in this book—nothing on cataloging. Material on UNISIST, ISSN, CODEN, and the ISBD(S) points toward cataloging, but doesn't quite reach. In addition, Davinson discusses the incorrect edition of the ISBD(S), and is inaccurate in doing that. He cites the 1974 edition, which was superseded in 1977, in time to be included in this book. He also says that the first element is the "key title," when it is "distinctive title" in the 1974 edition; "key title" is a part of the ISDS, not the ISBD(S). And further, in the 1977 ISBD(S), the first element is "title proper." This may be confusing, but should be right in a book like this. The chapters on bibliographies, abstracts, indexes, and other accesses to periodicals include a number of helpful publications, some unfamiliar to Americans.

The ideas on management presented in the book's last part provide some of the best reading. The many thought-provoking ideas are well written and logically presented. Non-British librarians may disagree with some of the practices and techniques, but Davinson also draws widely from American library sources to present as balanced a mix as possible.

Each of the 17 sections has a list of references, and these are wide ranging but likely to be readily available in most large collections. The indexes are adequate but should be more detailed in a handbook of this type. This is an improvement on earlier editions, and Davinson, in most respects, will be of assistance in the practice of serials librarianship. The many strong points and the store of information outweigh the drawbacks and inaccuracies, which, in the large picture, are relatively minor. [R: C&RL, July 79, pp. 370-71; JAL, Nov 79, p. 294] Neal L. Edgar

1601. Osborn, Andrew D. **Serial Publications: Their Place and Treatment in Libraries.** 3rd ed. Chicago, American Library Association, 1980. 486p. illus. bibliog. index. $20.00. LC 80-11686. ISBN 0-8389-0299-5.

The first edition of this work (1955) earned the reputation as a "classic" in its subject. The second edition (1973) was praised for treating such emerging topics as computer technology, AACR, the use of Coden, the emergence of the book catalog for serials, and cataloging and classification in larger libraries. Yet it proved somewhat disappointing in other aspects, for example, the reference use of serial publications and the distinctions between various kinds of indexes. In short, it seemed a bit unfinished.

Following seven years after the publication of the second edition in 1973 (see *ARBA* 74, entry 217), Osborn's third edition is a somewhat updated and more completed version of his second edition. Chapter 9, "Computer Methods of Check-In," briefly mentions "Minicomputers" in a short paragraph (and again briefly throughout the book) but does not provide any pertinent information about this valuable electronic aid. The second edition of *Anglo-American Cataloguing Rules* (*AACR2*) is covered throughout the book, but the author does not always advise the use of these rules in the control of serial records. OCLC is included in this edition, but little is actually stated except for casual references and illustrations of "OCLC check-in record" (p. 203), "CRT screen OCLC entry" (p. 195), and the "OCLC number" on a visible index (p. 183). The author gives OCLC full credit for computer control of serials. CONSER is extensively mentioned throughout the book. Abstracting and indexing information is expanded.

This third edition is a needed version, but libraries involved in computer control of serials

and information on user fees related to online databases will need to seek additional information elsewhere. [R: AB, 22 June 81, p. 4942; BL, 15 Jan 81, p. 671; C&RL, Mar 81, p. 158; LJ, 1 Feb 81, p. 315; LQ, July 81, p. 342; Ser R, Apr 81, p. 62] Bohdan S. Wynar and Donald D. Foos

1602. **The Serials Collection: Organization and Administration.** Nancy Jean Melin, ed. Ann Arbor, Mich., Pierian Press, 1982. 160p. (Current Issues in Serials Management, No. 1). $24.50. LC 82-81133. ISBN 0-87650-140-4.

This is the first volume in a series of which two others, entitled *Union Lists: Issues and Answers* and *Serials Collection Development: Choices and Strategies*, have been published. Fourteen essays address such issues as "Serials Organization in Academic Libraries," "Technical and Public Aspects of Serials," "Serials: Separate or Merged?," "The Rate of the Central Serials Unit in an Automated Library," "Serials Staffing Guidelines for the 80's," "AACR2 and Serials Record," "The Central Serial Record at New York Public Library: An Analysis and Survey," "Serials Automation: Four Years Later," "Popular Serials," "Managing and Building a Newspaper Collection," "Computerized Management of Microforms," "Government Publications of Serials," "Little Magazines in Special Collections and Rare Book Departments," and "The Exchange of Publications: An Alternative to Acquisitions."

The average length of each essay is 13 pages. In general, the essays are easy reading. With the exception of a few of the more narrowly focused topics, much of the information is a replicate of Benita Weber's "The Year's Work in Serials: 1981," *Library Resources and Technical Services* (July/September 1982). Although the essays are interesting and some quite good, they probably would have received wider readership as journal articles. Except for the collected format advantage, one must ask, Why this book? [R: JAL, Sept 82, p. 256] Jackson H. Carter

1603. Tuttle, Marcia. **Introduction to Serials Management.** With chapters by Luke Swindler and Nancy I. White. Greenwich, Conn., JAI Press, 1983. 324p. bibliog. index. (Foundation in Library and Information Science, Vol. 11). $42.50. LC 81-81658. ISBN 0-89232-107-5.

The temptation to compare any book on serials with Andrew D. Osborn's classic *Serial Publications* is great indeed. Some works don't hold up terribly well; others do. Tuttle's volume falls into the second category. Even more than that, her work can stand on its own without being viewed as merely a supplement to Osborn's.

The book can be viewed from two different perspectives. According to the author, "the purpose of the book ... [is] to provide a textbook for library school courses on library management...." Does the book achieve this goal? As can be expected, chapters describe the technical aspects of serials: acquisitions, cataloging, and preservation (binding and microforms). Public service concerns are given equal time, with chapters on collection development and serials reference and circulation work. The final chapter deals with serials resource sharing and automation, including descriptions of the North American bibliographic utilities. Even though the information contained in it is, naturally, a bit out-of-date, it still is especially strong where Osborn's work is weak. An excellent and lengthy annotated bibliography concludes the work.

A few criticisms can be made from the standpoint of the student user. The numerous quotes sometimes obscure the point being made. Different perspectives are important, but they frequently cloud the issue for the novice. Second, the cost of the volume is rather prohibitive for a library school student.

On the other hand, the quotes and the occasional acerbic comments regarding the nature of serials, which can be fully appreciated only by those who have worked with them, are enjoyable and are stimulating to the serials professional. This book works much better as a source for individuals with some serials experience than as a primer for the beginner. [R: C&RL, Nov 83, pp. 496-98; JAL, July 83, pp. 167-68; LJ, Aug 83, p. 1458; WLB, Apr 83, p. 703]

Marjorie E. Bloss

1604.   Walsh, Patricia M., ed. **Serials Management and Microforms: A Reader.** Westport, Conn., Microform Review, 1979. 302p. index. (Microform Review Series in Library Micrographics Management, 3). $21.50. LC 78-13179. ISBN 0-913672-11-4.

The *Reader* is a collection of articles, chapters, proceedings, and technical reports published between 1948 and 1977, the majority of which were written in the late 1960s and early 1970s. Appended are an excerpt from the development plan of the National Periodicals Center and a very brief description of the CONSER/COM project. Although they are dated, these selections offer a comprehensive overview of the issues in microforms in serials management, offering a basic exposition of the

subject, and, in many instances, have not been superseded by more recent articles on the same subjects. They document the fact that some of the unresolved problems of today have been with us for a generation. Earlier books, including others in this series, have only secondarily treated or alluded to the myriad problems of serials in microformat.

These readings cover five general areas: use reactions; economics of conversion to microforms; case studies of specific university, college, junior college, school, and medical library experiences with serials in microformat; consideration of the implications for future journal publication; and case studies of other applications of microforms in serials management. The index is primarily a proper name index.

By no means is this a state-of-the-art review. For that literature, the reader should turn to issues of *Microform Review* and *Serials Librarian*. This work is an introduction to the basic questions and as such will serve the student and the professional considering the issues for the first time. [R: C&RL, Jan 80, p. 75; JAL, Jan 80, p. 349; LJ, 15 Mar 80, p. 686; LR, Summer 80, p. 137]

Sharon C. Bonk

PROCEEDINGS, SYMPOSIA, AND ESSAYS

1605.   Allen, Walter C., ed. **Serials Publications in Large Libraries.** Urbana-Champaign, Ill., Graduate School of Library Science, University of Illinois, 1970. 194p. illus. bibliog. index. $6.00. LC 74-629637. ISBN 0-87845-011-4.

A collection of 11 lectures about various general aspects of serials (publishing, selection, acquisition, cataloging, binding, machine application) in libraries given at an institute at the University of Illinois in November 1969. The treatment is uneven as each author elaborates upon a favorite issue. Not intended as a textbook or guide, the volume is a timely, lively, and well documented source book for serials librarians and others concerned with control of serial publications. [R: LJ, July 71, p. 2280]

Charles D. Patterson

1606.   Mayes, Paul, ed. **Periodicals Administration in Libraries: A Collection of Essays.** London, Clive Bingley; distr., Hamden, Conn., Linnet Books, 1978. 158p. index. o.p. LC 78-8456. ISBN 0-208-01675-9.

Periodicals Administration in Libraries represents an attempt by nine British librarians to describe the characteristics and bibliographic control of periodicals and the ways they are selected, acquired, recorded, preserved, stored, weeded, promoted, and used in libraries. The results are mixed. Allan Foster and Lynn Parker's extensive discussion of traditional and newer formats (synoptic, microform, on-demand, and electronic on-line journals) and their impact on library operations is excellent and makes the entire volume worthwhile. Their treatment of alternative approaches to binding surpasses any I've seen. On the other hand, the chapter on bibliographical control is best skipped. The few bibliographic tools discussed are given inadequate citations and some of the information provided is erroneous: the *Union List of Serials* has not been renamed *New Serial Titles*, and it is not published by R. R. Bowker! There is no mention of online serial databases, such as CONSER, and the important topic of cataloging (description, access points) is discussed neither here nor elsewhere in the volume. Other chapters on "Types of Periodical," "Selection, Acquisition and Recording," "Relegation" (weeding and remote storage to Americans), "Use" and "Promotion" are thorough, covering most, if not all, relevant aspects of their respective topics. Chapter bibliographies are up-to-date, including references to 1977 literature. The editor's index provides an average of 1.7 entries per page, but some important topics (such as usage studies, discussed in several of the chapters) are missed. Because of its good chapters, *Periodicals Administration in Libraries* can be selectively recommended to librarians, administrators, and library school students. [R: C&RL, Mar 79, p. 171; JAL, Mar 79, p. 33; LR, Spring 79, p. 33; Ser R, Apr 79, p. 76]

James D. Anderson

1607. Spyers-Duran, Peter, and Daniel Gore, eds. **Management Problems in Serials Work: Proceedings of the Conference Held at Florida Atlantic University, Boca Raton, Florida, March 26-27, 1973.** Westport, Conn., Greenwood Press, 1974. 145p. $27.50. LC 73-10775. ISBN 0-8371-7050-8.

In an economic crisis, maintaining a serials collection and providing access to serials not available locally cause major budgetary problems for libraries. Although some of the papers presented at the 1973 conference on Management Problems in Serials Work deal specifically with the library's budgetary crisis, the majority of the papers are concerned, and rightly so, with efficient and basic library serials work. It seems to take a crisis to make libraries aware of the importance of efficiency and basic business procedures. The papers in this collection speak to this issue; many of the timely and valuable

statements made here have been previously iterated but not heeded or followed.

Susan Brynteson's paper, "Serial Acquisitions," is a basic distillation of serials management in a large library, while the National Serials Data Program and its international implications are cogently discussed by Paul Vassallo. Library cooperation on the regional and national level and especially the development and use of periodical banks are dealt with both generally and specifically in papers by Leslie W. Dunlap, Daniel Gore, Irma Lucht, and Blair Stewart. Two periodical jobbers, Frank F. Clasquin and Philip E. Greene, III, explain the situation clearly from their vantage point; both of their papers are honest about vendor services and critical of inefficient library practices. Hugh C. Atkinson explores the possibility that scholarly journals of the future might exist only as regionally deposited microforms of editorially compiled manuscript articles. Gore brings us back to the immediate and practical with a brief article against the use of oversewn binding for periodicals.

Mark M. Gormley concludes his summary statement with a note that "this has been a challenging and pithy conference." The publication of these papers justifies his assertion. The editors of these conference papers have provided the profession with a challenging and pithy collection of articles on serials management. These papers are all more readable and useful than comparable material in professional journal articles.

There are a few criticisms. The boldface sans serif type is somewhat tiring to read. Individual authors are not identified by their professional positions at the beginning of their papers and are so identified only in the conference program in the appendix. There are misspellings ("original" is spelled "orginal" on pages 69 and 71). Finally, there is no index.

Obviously, these criticisms do not reduce the worth of the individual papers. This interesting and valuable collection of papers should be useful to both libraries and library schools; some of the papers will certainly become required reading for library school students as well as for librarians. [R: AL, May 74, pp. 248-49; LJ, 1 May 74, pp. 1278-79]

John Phillip Immroth

ACQUISITIONS

1608. Brown, Clara D. **Serials: Acquisition and Maintenance.** Birmingham, Ala., EBSCO

Industries, 1972. 201p. illus. bibliog. index. o.p. LC 76-189654.

This clearly written manual on standard procedures covers fundamentals, checking-in procedures, ordering, gifts and exchanges, claims, etc. There are also chapters on computer problems (a rather simplistic presentation), binding, and library tools. It is too bad that Brown provided only two- or three-line notes for the major reference books in this area—not to mention the fact that her criteria for selection could well be challenged. Nevertheless, as a simple manual this book will do. A much better text on this subject is Osborn's new edition of *Serial Publications*, also reviewed in *ARBA* 74 (entry 217). [R: LJ, 1 May 73, p. 1455]

1609.   Katz, Bill. **Magazine Selection. How to Build a Community-Oriented Collection.** New York, R. R. Bowker, 1971. 158p. index. o.p. LC 72-171066. SBN 8352-0506-1. (Available from Books on Demand, $42.00pa., ISBN 0-317-10360-1).

It is almost embarrassing to admit that serial publications receive so little attention in our professional literature, not counting hundreds of articles of the how-we-do-it type. There are, of course, Osborn's *Serial Publications* (American Library Association, 1955) and its British counterpart, Davinson's *The Periodical Collection* (1969), several issues of *Library Trends*, and good annual summaries in *Library Resources and Technical Services*. Bill Katz offers us his second book on this subject; his first, *Magazines for Libraries* (R. R. Bowker, 1969), had good reception in library circles. All important aspects of this subject are discussed (e.g., types of magazines, their audiences, the art of selection and standard procedures, major selection aids, indexes and abstracts, as well as such related topics as "aspects of censorship," "the littles and the underground," etc.). As a matter of fact, not counting the three introductory chapters ("The Magazine," "Audiences," and "Art of Selection"), Katz is at his best discussing little magazines, the underground press, satire and comics, and other topics found in the last two chapters. The presentation is well balanced and sufficiently documented; the book is well written and, taking into consideration the author's points of view, long overdue. The reader who is looking for an updated version of Osborn will obviously be disappointed. For example, certain aspects of acquisitions are not sufficiently detailed, and occasionally the author is somewhat helpless discussing the relationship between the jobber and the library (pp. 50-52) or such purely technical aspects as bind-

ing and discarding. Just one hint. In discussing the pros and cons of how to select a jobber, the author did not mention a well-known and painful fact of today—namely, the numerous bankruptcies of many even leading and well-known jobbers. How should the librarian protect his investment, since obviously the subscriptions have to be paid in advance? Well, this is a different "ball game," as most order librarians know. To use an oversimplification, Bill Katz knows magazine selection from the point of view of the reference librarian. As a matter of fact, he knows the field well and, as the author himself admits in the preface, "this is one man's view of magazines." The reader who knows Bill Katz's writings will not be disappointed. [R: BL, 1 Apr 72, p. 636; Choice, May 72, p. 354; CLW, Apr 72, p. 476; LJ, 1 June 72, p. 2057; WLB, Mar 72, p. 651]   Bohdan S. Wynar

1610.   Lee, Sul H., ed. **Serials Collection Development: Choices and Strategies.** Ann Arbor, Mich., Pierian Press, 1981. 89p. bibliog. index. (Library Management Series, No. 5). $24.50. LC 81-84645. ISBN 0-87650-136-6.

Providing an excellent overview of the problems confronting university libraries in developing and managing serials collections, this book represents a compilation of the papers presented by a group of leading library administrators at the Conference on the Impact of Serials on Collection Development in Oklahoma City on May 21-22, 1981. The speakers and their papers were the following: (1) Robin N. Downes, "Journal Use Studies and the Management of Journal Collections in Research Libraries"; (2) Charles B. Osborn, "Marketing the Collection Development Aspects of Serials Control"; (3) Lester J. Pourciau, Jr., "Development and Management of Microform Serial Collections"; (4) Herbert S. White, "Strategies and Alternatives in Dealing with the Serials Management Budget"; (5) Roger K. Hanson, "Serials Deselection: A Dreadful Dilemma"; and (6) Donald B. Simpson, "The Expanded Journals Access Service at the Center for Research Libraries: Its Impact on North American Libraries." An introduction was written by the editor, Sul H. Lee.

The broad knowledge and experience of the contributors are manifested in their insights and solutions to the crisis being endured by libraries as a result of the proliferation and escalating costs of serials. Their solutions emphasize more cooperation among libraries, the use of advanced technology in document storage and delivery, as well as a more positive role for libraries both within universities and with respect to publishers. If this book has a fault, it is insufficient attention to the significance of recent developments in bibliometric research for serials control in libraries. The text is supplemented by an index and by a bibliography that is designed to serve as a starting point for further reading and research on the topics covered at the conference. Acquisition of this book is highly recommended so that librarians, scholars, university administrators, and others may become acquainted with the provocative ideas it presents on this important and controversial subject. [R: JAL, Sept 82, p. 230; LJ, 1 Nov 82, p. 2055]

Stephen J. Bensman

1611. Woodward, A. M. **Factors Affecting the Renewal of Periodical Subscriptions: A Study of Decision-Making in Libraries with Special Reference to Economics and Inter-Library Lending.** London, Aslib, 1978. 114p. bibliog. $25.20pa. ISBN 0-85142-108-3.

This work presents the results of a 1977 Aslib study of periodical subscriptions in a representative sample of 250 libraries in the United Kingdom. The Aslib study group reviewed the factors affecting the cancellation of periodical subscriptions and took a special look at the effect of the availability of interlibrary lending on the decision to purchase a journal. The survey revealed that, for the first time "in a long time," in 1976, the rate of journal cancellations exceeded the rate of additions for the Aslib library sample. The study measured the impact of user interest, financial pressures, and alternative access on the decision to cancel a specific journal. The results indicate that financial pressures are more a general determining factor than either alternative access or user interest. As one would expect, however, alternative sources, photocopying, and interlibrary lending play important roles in the decision to cancel any specific journal.

The stated objective of the Aslib study was to determine whether a relationship existed between interlibrary lending and periodical subscription cancellation. The survey shows that there is no direct causal relationship between the two. Not surprisingly, the study revealed that libraries that were well off financially cancelled the lowest number of periodical subscriptions. Finances, then, according to this study, play the major role in the ability of a library to meet the periodical needs of its patrons. The Aslib study has many useful insights into periodical acquisition, and most librarians will want to review the findings. [R: C&RL, Sept 78, p. 413]

Ralph L. Scott

AUTOMATION

1612. Johnson, Donald W. **Toward a National Serials Data Program: Final Report of the National Serials Pilot Project.** Washington, D.C., Association of Research Libraries, 1972. 92p. illus. bibliog. $5.00pa. LC 73-154468.

The project was designed to test the feasibility of creating a central serials record in machine-readable form. This report contains original intentions for the program and records progress toward these goals and participation of the three sponsoring national libraries: Library of Congress, Agriculture, and Medicine. The overall prognosis for a National Serials Data Program is positive—there is no record of difficulties and nonsuccesses encountered during the project. Contains 38 pages of flow charts. [R: LJ, 1 Jan 73, p. 52]

Charles D. Patterson

1613. **Library Systems Evaluation Guide. Volume 1: Serials Control.** Powell, Ohio, James E. Rush Associates, 1983. 1v. (various paging). bibliog. index. o.p. LC 83-9584. ISBN 0-912803-00-2.

One of eight volumes (the others cover automation of circulation, public services, acquisitions, management services, interlibrary loan, cataloging, and system integration), this book tackles one of the most difficult areas in the library to automate. Although no evaluation of specific automated serials systems is given, a thorough method for the evaluation of and the techniques for comparing automated systems are clearly presented. The work is comprehensive, beginning with the purposes of the guide, a brief introduction, and an in-depth discussion of the fundamental requirements for automated serials control systems. In addition, there are sections concerning a methodology for system evaluation, various types of lists defining data elements, functions of various automated techniques, an inventory of available serials control systems, and a bibliography.

This type of work is invaluable if for no other reason than the amount of time it saves an individual who is trying to get a grasp of the whole serials automation problem. Because the guide is thorough, the librarian is presented with opportunities for new ways of doing things, automated claiming or report generation, for example, and confronted with completely new situations, such as a complete accounting system with the possibility for the cost of each magazine's being assigned to a specific subject area. Whether or not a library uses all of the information and possibilities for automation it presents, the guide enables the library staff to investigate a wide range of topics and choose those features that are most relevant to the situation. The cost of the guide is modest when compared with the effort needed to create a similar report or the overall cost of the automated system being considered. The guide is a worthwhile investment. [R: LJ, 15 Feb 84, p. 336]   Jackson H. Carter

1614. The Management of Serials Automation: Current Technology & Strategies for Future Planning. Peter Gellatly, ed. New York, Haworth Press, 1982. 293p. index. (A Monographic Supplement to *The Serials Librarian*, Volume 6, 1981/1982). $45.00; $24.95pa. LC 82-6166. ISBN 0-917724-37-2; 0-86656-310-5pa.

Representing a valuable summary of the state-of-the-art in respect to serials automation in libraries, this book consists of 25 essays written by contributors with a broad range of experience in library and information science. These essays are introduced by Peter Gellatly, who is noted for his work with serials (see *ARBA* 77, entry 199, and *ARBA* 78, entry 160).

The essays in this book can be divided into six basic groups. Of these, the first comprises an analytical survey of the literature published on automated serials control during the 1970s with special emphasis on the latter half of the decade. As part of this survey, there is presented a selected bibliography which is arranged in chronological order and stresses items on automation activities in the United States. The second group of essays is dedicated to the description of a number of automated serials systems, including the pioneer system at the University of California-San Diego as well as those at Brigham Young University, Northwestern University, Ohio State University, and the University of Illinois-Urbana-Champaign. Attention in these essays is given to the problems and techniques involved in the transition from manual to machine mode, and the group concludes with a discussion of the cooperative serials data conversion project implemented by Stanford, UCLA, and the University of California-Berkeley.

The third group of essays focuses on the changes occurring in serials cataloging as a result of the growth of automated systems and the introduction of AACR2. Among the subjects analyzed in this group are the availability and acceptability of serial records in the OCLC database, the copy cataloging of serials with OCLC according to AACR2, the assignment of ISSNs by the National Serials Data Program

(NSDP), and the use of ISSNs for the retrieval of OCLC records. The next two groups of essays are devoted to an investigation of the interrelated topics of union lists and library networking. Here are reviewed not only the development of the capability for online union lists of serials, the work of the ALA Ad Hoc Committee on Union Lists of Serials, and the California Union List of Periodicals (CULP), but also the serials systems of OCLC, the Research Libraries Group (RLG), and the Washington Library Network (WLN), as well as the progress made under the guidance of the Library of Congress Network Advisory Committee toward the establishment of a nationwide library network. The final group of essays treats such supplemental but important matters as the use of computers by a serials subscription agency and the potential of the new technologies to transform the traditional journal.

In general, the essays in this book are of a high quality, and an index at the end provides access to specific topics in them. [R: BL, 15 Oct 82, p. 293]   Stephen J. Bensman

1615. Pitkin, Gary M. **Serials Automation in the United States: A Bibliographic History.** Metuchen, N.J., Scarecrow, 1976. 148p. index. $15.00. LC 76-18116. ISBN 0-8108-0955-9.

Intended as a source "to all information published on the automation of serials control functions in the United States and cited in *Library Literature*," this work lists 101 articles published between 1951 and 1974. Excluded from the list, for no given reason, are "articles on union lists or other cooperative projects such as the Ohio College Library Center or the National Serials Data Program."

Generally, the articles are arranged in chronological order by publication date. Each article is followed by three categories of information to identify its content. The first is "Applications" or serials control functions, including binding information, check-in, claiming, holdings information, language information, ordering, renewal, routing, statistics, subject information, and title lists. The second is the "Type of Library" and the third is the "Institution." Most of the articles are annotated. The annotations, however, "rely heavily on quoted matter." An important feature of this work is the appendix following the bibliography. It is an index of the articles by serials control function, showing type of library and name of institution. This index can assist the user of the bibliography to trace historically the automation of a particular serials control function. The appendix is followed by an "Author Index with Titles," which could help the user seeking a particular article.

This work is a very specialized bibliographical source on the subject of automation of serials control functions. It should be of value to serials librarians and to others interested in the subject, such as students and researchers. [R: C&RL, May 77, p. 262; JAL, May 77, p. 99; LJ, 1 Apr 77, p. 778; RQ, Summer 77, p. 358]

M. Nabil Hamdy

1616. Potter, William Gray, and Arlene Farber Sirkin, eds. **Serials Automation for Acquisition and Inventory Control: Papers from the Institute, Milwaukee, September 4-5, 1980, Library and Information Technology Association, American Library Association.** Chicago, American Library Association, 1981. 181p. bibliog. index. $15.00pa. LC 81-10798. ISBN 0-8389-3267-3.

This institute continues the work of two similar institutes held over five years ago. While the previous institutes dealt with serial bibliographic control, this institute focused on acquisition and inventory control. Six papers were selected for publication from those given, plus the dialog of a panel discussion on available automated check-in systems. The beginning article, by Dan Toubery, provides an overview of the evolution of automated serials control.

Michael Gorman's concluding article raises provocative questions as to the worth of serials, while the four intervening articles deal with the nuts and bolts aspects of acquisition and inventory control. A question and answer section follows each paper. An appendix contains short papers describing automated systems in five libraries, and is followed by a selected, annotated bibliography which is included to round out the information published from the institute. Entry to topics in both papers and discussions is provided by an index.

The editors should be complemented for publishing papers so relatively soon after the institute was complete. The work overall is an important state-of-the-art summary of serials automation for acquisition and inventory control. [R: JAL, July 82, p. 164; LJ, 1 June 82, p. 1076]

Jackson H. Carter

1617. **Serials Management in an Automated Age: Proceedings of the First Annual Serials Conference, October 30-31, 1981, Arlington, VA.** Nancy Jean Melin, ed. Westport, Conn., Meckler Publishing, 1982. 93p. $35.00. LC 82-2302. ISBN 0-930466-48-9.

Presented here are the eight papers delivered at the first annual Serials Conference,

held in Arlington, Virginia on 30-31 October 1981. Several aspects of serials and computers are dealt with, including the impact of AACR2, the online retrieval of full texts of journal articles, online abstracts and indexes, automated indexing, and online serials control. The articles go into some depth concerning the problems which occur and the decisions which must be made: for example, filing order in the cardex, revision of the catalog entries, whether entries for current periodicals should be filed into the old or new catalog.

The papers present a thought-provoking glimpse of the serials library of the future. Among the innovations discussed is the publication of journals solely in online form. Bills for royalties would be generated automatically for any printouts requested from the system.

Technical presentation is good, and the typeface is easy to read. Each paper is accompanied by its own bibliography. [R: JAL, Sept 82, p. 255; LJ, 15 Dec 82, p. 2351]

Barbara E. Brown

OTHER TOPICS

1618. International Business Machines Corporation. **Library Automation: Computerized Serials Control.** White Plains, N.Y., IBM Data Processing Application; distr., IBM branch offices, 1971. 106p. bibliog. index. $1.50pa. NUC 73-69123.

This manual is part of an IBM series on library automation and covers all aspects of serial control and related areas including coding, data conversion, statistics, and data elements. Operational systems of many libraries are discussed including public, academic, and special libraries including that of the Argonne National Laboratory Library. The manual is well written and profusely illustrated, with excellent examples and clear explanations. [R: LJ, 15 Apr 72, p. 1407]

Charles D. Patterson

1619. Little, Arthur D. **A Comparative Evaluation of Alternative Systems for the Provision of Effective Access to Periodical Literature.** Washington, D.C., National Commission on Libraries and Information Science; distr., Washington, D.C., GPO, 1979. 1v. (various paging). o.p. LC 79-6278. S/N 052-003-00715-1.

This study examines whether earlier studies regarding a National Periodicals Center (NPC) were broad enough in scope and considered sufficiently cost-effectiveness, new technology, private market developments, and societal consequences. Three possible approaches to a system are examined: (a) nonintervention; (b) a single-collection NPC as a main component of NPS, as envisioned in the Council on Library Resources technical development plan (the "Burgundy Book"); and (c) a subsidized utility that offers access tools and switches requests to multiple market-oriented, fee-charging supplier sources.

Considerable statistical data are provided in comparing these approaches, with the usual cautionary statements regarding the shortness of the study (six weeks) and the many assumptions necessary to derive estimates. Several interesting observations highlight the narrative report. NCLIS's Research Committee, say the authors, considered the issue as seen by the commission and by the library community as not whether NPC should exist but rather how it would be organized. The authors, however, concluded that the time for a centralized NPC has come and gone because of expected technological changes in periodical access. They further concluded that cost economies by themselves do not provide a rationale for adopting either approach (b) or (c), as opposed to a nonintervention approach. [R: C&RL, May 80, p. 251]

Jerry Cao

1620. Meadows, A. J., ed. **The Scientific Journal.** London, Aslib, 1979. 300p. index. (Aslib Reader Series, Vol. 2). $45.00; $27.00pa. ISBN 0-85142-119-9.

As editor Meadows succinctly states in the first sentence of his introduction, "journals represent the most important single source of information for the scientific research community." The papers that comprise the second volume to the Aslib Reader series (volume 1 was *National Libraries*, by Maurice B. Line and Joyce Line, 1979) attempt to provide a useful and significant selection of writings on that theme. "They are," Meadows argues, "intended to suggest possible lines of development in terms of which past, present, and future changes in journal production and usage may be considered." The work has seven main sections: "The Development of the Scientific Journal"; "Economics of Journal Publication"; "Some Basic Problems of Journal Publication"; "The Refereeing of Scientific Journals"; "The Characteristics and Interrelationships of Journals"; "An Alternative Viewpoint" (comprising three articles that examine journals as communication channels, the optimization of the structure of publications, and the disposition of scientific works); and, finally, "The Future of the Scientific Journal." In total, there are 24 reprinted articles with references, some annotated. Each of the seven sections also has an introductory commentary that justifies its purpose and choice of articles.

The Aslib Reader series is akin to many of its British companions in that useful data are brought together expeditiously. It is akin to many of its American companions in that the method of publication is as inexpensive as possible. The articles are reproduced from their original typesets, and the variation in font and size of reproduction is considerable. Some of the print size borders on the unreadable unless the reader's eyes are keen and his or her interest unbounded. However, given the nature of the topic, the diversity of viewpoints, and the overall value of the papers, which touch on every important issue related to scientific journals, few professional librarians who work with the scientific community should ignore the content. Needless to say, its British origin is evident, but Great Britain is also one of the prime locations for basic analysis and research in this area. [R: LJ, 15 Dec 79, p. 2632; LR, Spring 80, p. 51]

Laurel Grotzinger

1621. **A National Periodicals Center: Technical Development Plan.** Washington, D.C., Council on Library Resources, 1978. 255p. bibliog. o.p. LC 78-14692.

This publication is a link in a chain that appears to be leading toward the creation of a National Periodicals Center. Since 1970, studies have indicated a need for a coordinated and accessible, yet archival, store of periodicals. The Library of Congress, mentioned frequently as the agency to operate such a center, requested that CLR prepare this Technical Development Plan. The plan has been left intentionally flexible in many details. What is presented here is in the main conceptual: a rationale for the center, a description of the parameters of its operations, collection, governance, costs and funding, as well as a procedure for implementation. As the NPC would be a new level in the information-delivery system—thereby affecting publishers, libraries, and library users—the plan discusses some possible functions, as its becoming an outlet for on-demand publishing, that could result from this unique position. Future discussion and development of our nation's periodical access system will be a function of this plan; thus, those concerned with that access system need to become conversant with it and its implications. [R: Ser R, Apr 79, p. 72]

Johanna W. Thompson

1622. Taylor, David C. **Managing the Serials Explosion: The Issues for Publishers and**

Libraries. White Plains, N.Y., Knowledge Industry Publications, 1982. 156p. bibliog. index. (Professional Librarian Series). $34.50; $27.50pa. LC 82-14062. ISBN 0-91436-94-6; 0-91436-54-7pa.

David C. Taylor is well qualified to write a book on the crisis confronting publishers and libraries as a result of the rising costs and numbers of serials. He was serials librarian at Michigan State University (1970-75), served on the ALA RTSD Serials Section Policy and Research Committee (1972-74), and was honorary president (1973-81) of LUTFCSUSTC (Librarians United to Fight Costly Silly Unnecessary Serials Title Changes). Taylor has also written an article entitled "The Serials Librarian as Activist" (*Drexel Library Quarterly*, July 1975) and edited the newsletter *Title Varies* (1973-81).

The book is divided into eight chapters, each centered around a given topic but which as a whole constitute a coherent synopsis of the present state of serials. In it Taylor defines serials, traces their historical development, and analyzes their role in scholarly communication and popular information. He then examines the financial pressures on publishers that cause them to cover their costs by raising subscription prices to libraries and thus create a revolutionary crisis in which the traditional journal system is being called into question. The fundamental principles of library serials operations are next discussed within the context of the problems which these operations not only solve but cause. Having thus posed the dilemma, Taylor considers the solutions being tried by libraries and publishers. Concerning libraries, he outlines the causes for the problems and inefficiencies involved in networks and interlibrary loan, whereas in respect to serials automation he warns that "no library has been able to demonstrate that its automation project has saved money" (p. 78). As for publishers, there are analyzed the potentialities of such new serials alternatives as on-demand publication, microforms, video, and the electronic journal. Taylor sums up his findings in two concluding chapters in which he not only predicts continuing economic hardship for libraries and the rapid growth of experimental forms of publications, but makes suggestions on how libraries and publishers should cope with the developing situation.

As a reflection of its author, this book is provocative and based on broad experience. Moreover, Taylor writes in a lively and often humorous manner. There are also a selected bibliography and an index. [R: BL, 15 Apr 83, p. 1074]   Stephen J. Bensman

55 Special User Groups

ADULT EDUCATION

1623. Birge, Lynn E. **Serving Adult Learners: A Public Library Tradition.** Chicago, American Library Association, 1981. 215p. bibliog. index. (ALA Studies in Librarianship, No. 8). $18.00pa. LC 81-14999. ISBN 0-8389-0346-0.

This useful book provides a needed resource in the literature of adult education through the public library. The author traces the progression of library adult education from its genesis in the late 1800s, through its periods of expansion and contraction, and concludes with the advisory service experiments of the last decade.

Arranged in a general chronological format, the book merges historical fact with analysis of adult education development, critique of gaps in service and absence of consistent philosophy/attitude in the profession, and an overall advocacy perspective. The author draws upon both the literature and research studies to create the basis for presenting a plan for providing library service to independent learners. Appendices include a sample adult education policy statement and a statement of purpose and objectives of a program for adult independent learners. Extensive notes and a selected bibliography are included.

This book will be useful to public librarians, persons in the wide variety of adult education agencies and programs who (can) interact with the public library, and students in preservice undergraduate and graduate programs. The coverage is well organized, and the chapters are clearly identified.

Since much of the literature on library adult education is now historical, this book offers a valuable longitudinal link between the evolutionary processes of this century and attempts at serving adult learners. The author's honest appraisal of relative success is refreshing and certainly presents a challenge to the library and information science profession. [R: BL, Aug 82, p. 1505; JAL, May 82, p. 108; LJ, July 82, p. 1304]   Darlene E. Weingand

1624. Burge, Elizabeth J., ed. **Adult Learners, Learning and Public Libraries.** Urbana-Champaign, Ill., Graduate School of Library and Information Science, University of Illinois, 1983. 1v. (various paging). (*Library Trends*, Vol. 31, No. 4). o.p. ISSN 0024-2594.

This issue of *Library Trends* purports to be an update of the topic of adult learning, with a heritage dating back to a 1959 issue, "Current Trends in Adult Education." The editor states that a deliberate selectivity has focused on three themes: the adult education context, the individual learner, and institutional responses. On the list of excluded approaches are: discussion of library-based work adult learners (however, two articles on specific libraries were allowed), historical reviews and earlier summaries of practice, contemporary general writing, and writing on library futures. These exclusions have perforce eliminated some of the most noteworthy scholars in the field (for example, Margaret E. Monroe) from the author list. While a narrowing of focus can often produce a compact body of knowledge—and, in fact, does so to some degree in this issue—the exclusions are so profound that unless it is supplemented by another issue carrying out the exploration of these uncharted areas, this issue must be regarded as a partial treatment of the topic. Beyond these stated limitations, this issue contains much valuable information on learning and adult education. In some articles, the connection with libraries is tenuous, but a creative and experienced reader should be able to form reasonable linkages. The issue is less than might be hoped for but is not without merit.

Darlene E. Weingand

1625. Foos, Donald Dale. **The Role of the State Library in Adult Education: A Critical Analysis of Nine Southeastern State Library Agencies.** Littleton, Colo., Libraries Unlimited, 1973. 139p. bibliog. index. (Research Studies in Library Science, No. 9). o.p. LC 72-89045. ISBN 0-87287-054-5.

The purpose of this study is to investigate the involvement of the state library in the development of adult education programs at the state, regional, and local levels. Nine states—Alabama, Florida, Georgia, Kentucky, Mississippi, North Carolina, South Carolina, Tennessee, and Virginia—served as a basis for this study. The author provides historical background for each state agency, including its administrative organization, its early involvement in adult education activities, a description of its most important workshops and institutes, and a discussion of the role of the agency in adult education. [R: LJ, 15 May 73, p. 1561]

1626. Reilly, Jane A. **The Public Librarian as Adult Learners' Advisor: An Innovation in Human Services.** Westport, Conn., Greenwood Press, 1981. 152p. bibliog. index. (Contributions in Librarianship and Information Science, No. 38). $27.50. LC 80-27307. ISBN 0-313-22134-0; ISSN 0084-9243.

The readers' advisor/learners' advisor is nearly as old as the public library. The author has discovered it anew, adding a dimension of nonprint resources and some emphasis on independent study for college credit. In rediscovering this aspect of service, the author has not built upon the strong foundations of her home library, the Chicago Public Library, or on the equally notable programs of the New York Public Library, Enoch Pratt, and others. The nonconnection with the literature and experience of these programs plus a partial connection with similar programs in England and variations on programs connected to independent study courses in the United States prevent the reader from focusing clearly on the information presented here.

The use of audiovisual materials as a starting point for the advisement process is a helpful idea, but despite the statement that "very few

persons are able to master a subject or a skill merely by reading books" (p. 48) it is not the entire idea. A more balanced approach to the whole range of learning materials would have been useful. When discussing the roles of collection development specialist, administrator, educators, or other information personnel, there appears to be a secondhand awareness of the roles, and criticism of these roles appears to be based on less than objective information.

There are numerous lists of things to do, approaches to take, and skills to acquire, as well as many helpful ideas about how to structure the advisor/learner interaction. This does not, however, make up for a general lack of overall organization of the text, repetition, and a style of writing that is not always easy to follow. The author has suggested a fresh approach to a tried and true service. Further efforts in the organizing and editing of the material would have made the reader's appreciation of this approach easier. [R: LJ, 15 Jan 82, p. 154]

Ann E. Prentice

CHILDREN

General Works

1627. Baker, D. Philip. **School and Public Library Media Programs for Children and Young Adults.** Syracuse, N.Y., Gaylord, 1977. 412p. index. o.p. LC 76-54919. ISBN 0-915794-09-8.

Concerned with media programs to serve the child from age 3 to 18, this volume brings together descriptions of approximately 30 school and 25 public library media programs in about 20 states. They are intended to serve as models for adoption or adaptation and are presented to stimulate thought about new programming. Included in the five-page descriptions of each program are numbers and type of program staff, one or two budget figures, and ages and numbers of the target population. Also included are program objectives and suggestions for improvement. Programs were selected from among 400 responses to a survey questionnaire. Site visitors (including academicians, state school library supervisors, and public library coordinators) provided the author with additional information. In an afterword, the author distills 15 factors most commonly found in programs reported by their administrators to be successful.

The descriptions of media programs suffer from oversimplification and a desire to applaud rather than analyze. Program objectives are usually general in nature, making the evaluation and measurement of program impact promised in the introduction difficult, if not impossible. The author's discussion of the existing and future framework for library planning and the collection of programs with varying focuses will stimulate thought and action, however. [R: LQ, July 79, p. 349]   JoAnn V. Rogers

1628. Broderick, Dorothy M. **Library Work with Children.** New York, H. W. Wilson, 1977. 197p. bibliog. index. $14.00. LC 77-14288. ISBN 0-8242-0620-7.

Dorothy Broderick set out to revise her earlier text, *An Introduction to Children's Work in Public Libraries* (1965), only to discover that changes in both the children's library field and her own attitudes and thinking demanded a "new beginning." The result is a completely different book, one that is very much a personal statement of the author's advocacy of children's rights and her views on sex, sexism, sexuality, and racism in children's books, and on the social responsibilities of librarians. She claims to offer "no answers" in her book but tried "to write a book that identifies issues and will force readers to make up their own minds about where they stand" (preface). In this, she haas succeeded to a large extent, and for this contribution, Broderick's book deserves reading by professional children's librarians and students. She has no illusion that all readers will agree with her opinions, and many will not. Nor will all readers appreciate the I/we style of presentation and the emphasis on her personal reactions to and experiences with specific library problems.

Part 2, "The Collection," examines building a collection, selection standards, controversial topics, and the selection process. Part 2, "Library Services," treats the child in the library, programs, the library and the community, areas related to work with children, and continuing education. At the end are four appendices containing official ALA and CSD policy statements, bibliography, audiovisual sources, list of children's books mentioned in the text, and an index. [R: BL, 15 Apr 78, p. 1359; SLJ, Apr 78, p. 56]   Christine Gehrt Wynar

1629. Burke, J. Gordon, and Gerald R. Shields, eds. **Children's Library Service: School or Public?** Metuchen, N.J., Scarecrow, 1974. 131p. bibliog. index. o.p. LC 73-18454. ISBN 0-8108-0688-6.

Although the title does not indicate its limited scope, this book deals almost exclusively with the New York State *Report of the Commissioner of Education's Committee on Library Development 1970*, which recommended that all library service to children be transferred to elementary school media centers. The main section of the book consists of four articles, three of which were published in *American Libraries* in 1971. J. Gordon Burke's "Where Will All the Children Go?" outlines the Regents's plan and represents a response to it by some Nassau County librarians. Helen R. Sattley's "Run Twice as Fast" looks at the CCLD proposals from a school librarian's point of view, while Anne Izard's "Children's Librarians" emphasizes the value of public library work with children. Dorothy Broderick's "Further Reflections on the CCLD Report," the only article written especially for this collection, analyzes changes in community attitudes between 1971 and 1973, which in her opinion make the CCLD proposals even less feasible than they seemed when they first appeared. Broderick mentions the growth of community information services, the increasing dissatisfaction with public schools, and the cutback of federal funds for libraries as trends that threaten both school and public library services.

The text of the Regents's recommendations for children's library services and the "Guidelines for Library Service" that were prepared for pilot projects offering different types of children's services are included as appendices. Both of these have also been published previously.

Edna Berg's annotated bibliography on public/school library cooperation lists 45 articles that appeared in major journals between January 1971 and May 1973. This listing is the only attempt to broaden the book's scope beyond the context of New York.

Having these materials collected in one convenient place will be useful for library school students faced with writing term papers and for historians concerned with the immediate impact of the CCLD proposals. Librarians in the field, however, have probably read these articles as they appeared and will be looking for new evaluations or further proposals. The question of the most effective way to provide library service to all children in the community is an important one for librarians and educators throughout North America. The issue involves complex political, economic, and educational decisions that can have far-reaching effects on generations of children. In his brief introduction to this book, Burke expresses the hope that this collection will provide the beginning of a re-evaluation of library work with children, but to do that would require a volume far less limited in time and scope. Both the library profession and the children deserve such a volume. [R: SLMQ, Spring 75, p. 242]   Adele M. Fasick

1630. Dyer, Esther R. **Cooperation in Library Service to Children.** Metuchen, N.J., Scarecrow, 1978. 152p. bibliog. index. $15.00. LC 77-28190. ISBN 0-8108-1111-1.

For her 1976 doctoral dissertation, Dyer approached a selected list of experts in the field of children's services about children's services and the possibilities of school and public library children's service cooperation in 1990. Results discussed were based on 1975 reactions, and this book is a synthesis of her dissertation. To insure expert integrity and honesty, a Delphi approach was used to elicit responses. Many of the confidential answers reveal insecurities, fears, distrust, and rhetoric about the issues. Clearly, virtually little work or attempts to work are at hand in school and library cooperation. Though the answers are not necessarily surprising to anyone who has been involved with children's services for a while, this book for the first time documents and organizes various sides of the issue for accessibility. Expert and panel reactions are summarized for each question, with statistics and narrative for clarification.

Dyer does not take sides. Her unbiased report neatly summarizes the issue and is carefully organized in a readable and usable fashion. She has done a laudable job in drawing out honest responses through logically developed questionnaires. Two successful experiments are mentioned only briefly; there should have been more discussion of these. The appended bibliography is one used in the development of the book; it is not a comprehensive bibliography of the subject. Dyer concludes that so long as administrators and coordinators continue their rhetoric, school and library cooperation will remain a figment of an undefined future. For any person or institution contemplating cooperative efforts, this book is revealing reading and a necessary introduction to the inherent problems of the issue. [R: BL, 1 Nov 78, p. 485; LJ, 15 Dec 78, p. 2494]

Jim Roginski

1631. Fasick, Adele M., and Claire England. **Children Using Media: Reading and Viewing Preferences among the Users and Non-Users of the Regina Public Library.** Regina, Sask., Regina Public Library, 1977. 79p. o.p.

A concise, scholarly research report on children's attitudes and receptivity toward library usage, as well as their media habits (television viewing, newspaper, magazine, and book reading), this was based upon a study commissioned by the Regina Public Library (Saskatchewan), to "investigate how well the collection and services of the public library meet the educational and recreational needs ... to indicate the steps the library might take to extend and enrich these services...." Two library science faculty members at the University of Toronto undertook the project, and data were collected for two groups of children: beginning readers, ages 6-9, and independent readers, ages 10-12. Results showed that children went to the library because 90 percent were interested in the book collection; others, because of programs or nonprint materials. All experienced a high level of satisfaction with services offered. Even though this study focuses upon one particular library, its implications are global in nature. With appendices indicating the methodology, instrumentation, statistical analysis, questionnaire, and checklists used, libraries can adapt these items to their own local needs. This item would be for library schools, public library children's departments, and researchers interested in the library needs of children. [R: LQ, Oct 78, p. 559]   Ilene F. Rockman

1632. Ray, Colin, ed. **Library Service to Children: An International Survey.** Munich, Verlag Dokumentation; distr., New York, K. G. Saur, 1983. 168p. (IFLA Publications, 12). $20.00. LC 78-8705. ISBN 3-598-20392-6.

Earlier editions of IFLA's survey of library service to children were first published in 1963, with a second edition appearing three years later. This third international survey was prepared as a wholly different work representing the position of children's library services in 21 countries. Each article (as much as possible) follows a broadly consistent pattern (e.g., background of public library service, buildings, collections, services, extension activities, staffing, and future plans). Countries represented are the major developed states of Asia and the West, a few African nations, and several communist countries. Self-surveys whereby the image of a nation goes on display to the world may often result in somewhat less than accurate reports; and some, as in the case of the Soviet survey, contain serious distortions in the presentation of facts. Two examples may suffice as illustrations. According to I. Ganitskaya's article, the 1970 census showed "142 million people indicated that their vernacular was Russian; apart from this, 42 million indicated that Russian was their second language and that they knew it well. Thus the census showed that 184 million used Russian" (p. 152). Ganitskaya obviously wants the reader to be assured that Russian is the only important language spoken in the Soviet Union; no others are mentioned here, not even Ukrainian, which is spoken by some 50 million people. The author neglects to mention that to obtain entrance to higher education or any good job opportunities, the Soviet citizen must know Russian well. Contrary to Soviet law, the actual policy of the government is to discourage and prohibit use of other languages in a determined effort to Russify all other nationalities. In another paragraph (p. 152), the article says that all citizens "have the right to choose the language in which they prefer to be taught." The author neglects, again, to tell the reader the consequences of choosing education in, for example, the Ukrainian language. Ganitskaya doesn't explain that such education is required to be carried on without a supply of new textbooks and with all possible forms of harrassment. The reader should be adequately prepared to evaluate these national surveys, to sift fact from myth, and to encounter occasional barrages of amazing accomplishments. [R: LQ, Jan 80, p. 162]　　　Christine Gehrt Wynar

1633.　Ray, Sheila G. **Children's Librarianship.** London, Clive Bingley; New York, K. G. Saur, 1979. 126p. bibliog. index. (Outlines of Modern Librarianship). $12.00. ISBN 0-85157-268-5.

Sheila G. Ray surveys the whole area of children's library service in 12 brief chapters ranging from accommodation for children's library services and routines in the children's library to staffing, materials, service to children through other agencies, and public relations. Each chapter opens with a quotation from authorities such as IFLA Standards, the Bullock Report, or UNESCO public library manifesto, thus setting what are often ideal goals for children's services.

Ray succinctly describes the status of children's services and library practice in the United Kingdom, with occasional comments on corresponding practices in other countries. In nearly every case where she perceives that common practice may run counter to good sense, she offers her own advice; thus the text reads much like a smoothly flowing lecture rather than a critical or scholarly monograph. When discussing the problem of lowering the age limit for children to obtain library tickets (cards), she remarks: "It is foolish to enrol children as members of the library until they have reached the stage when the library has a plentiful supply of books related to their interests and abilities" (p. 19). Librarians on this side of the Atlantic accustomed to demands by various groups for rights to access, demands to censor books, and

for service to groups now unserved, etc., may wonder at the very practical but arbitrary methods that are suggested for resolving common administrative problems. Senior staff possess much more discretion in determining and applying library rules. In fact, the emphasis on written policies so ingrained in American library practice is hardly mentioned in this text.

A considerable treasure of personal experience and good advice is presented here in a low-key, understated style. The reader does come away with a clear picture of children's libraries, but may be somewhat disturbed over the professional role of children's librarians when considering statements such as this one: "Producing booklists is one of the few really creative jobs done by a librarian...." (p. 105). Suggested as an introduction to British children's librarianship for those interested in comparative studies. [R: LR, Winter 79, p. 276]
　　　　　　　　　　Christine Gehrt Wynar

1634.　Richardson, Selma K., ed. **Children's Services of Public Libraries.** Urbana-Champaign, Ill., Graduate School of Library Science, University of Illinois, 1978. 178p. index. (Allerton Park Institute, No. 23). $9.00. LC 78-11503. ISBN 0-87845-049-1.

The 1977 Allerton Park Institute addressed the status of the field of children's services of public libraries. The approximately 20 papers presented do not discuss specific issues, but serve as a self-assessment to identify areas that needed to be improved to strengthen children's services. The papers fall into eight general categories: goals, the child, the children's librarian, services, facilities, materials, research, and evaluations of the institute's program. The papers are of variable quality and length, and most sections are preceded by panel moderators' comments. While not an in-depth study of children's services, the volume serves as a useful overview of goals and problems.
　　　　　　　　　　Janet H. Littlefield

1635.　Turow, Joseph. **Getting Books to Children: An Exploration of Publisher-Market Relations.** Chicago, American Library Association, 1978. 137p. bibliog. (ALA Studies in Librarianship, No. 7). $10.00pa. LC 78-24103. ISBN 0-8389-0276-6.

An expansion of the author's university thesis, this study about the production of quality and mass-market children's books and their distribution to institutions and bookstores attempts (but fails) to give a clear picture of the operations involved. Theoretical library systems and publishing companies have been created from real-life models. The author presents historical backgrounds for each of his sections and outlines the differences between the institutional-bookstore markets and the quality-mass-market publisher of children's books.

The writing is somewhat academic, relying on too many words and phrases to make a point, and the reading is slow and difficult when it need not be. Most of the information is generally correct, although there are instances of specific data and numbers which are not. The author clearly has a grasp of the subject, but his execution of it, especially for the reader new to the subject, is pedantic and unclearly presented. Since the book is geared to a layperson, there are a number of assumptions made of the reader's background and a noticeable lack of definitions for clarity. Seemingly, this volume will have some use in academic libraries, large libraries, and children's literature classes by virtue of the dearth of material on the subject. [R: BL, 1 July 79, p. 1585; C&RL, July 79, pp. 386-87; Choice, Oct 79, p. 1001; JAL, July 79, p. 168; SLJ, Sept 79, p. 47]

Jim Roginski

Reference Works

1636. American Library Association. Association for Library Service to Children. *Let's Read Together* Revision Committee. **Let's Read Together: Books for Family Enjoyment.** 4th ed. Chicago, American Library Association, 1981. 111p. index. $5.00pa. LC 80-39957. ISBN 0-8389-3253-3.

The fourth edition of *Let's Read Together* is a handy literary tool which cites many titles relevant to the interests of young people today. Age and grade interest levels range from preschool to ages 13 and up. All titles selected were in print as of early 1980, including timeless favorites as well as selections published during the past decade. A convenient table of contents quickly leads the user to a variety of topics, such as divorce, death, disabilities, human sexuality, mystery and suspense stories, picture story books, etc. Librarians, teachers, and parents should find this paperback book extremely practical and useful. It is well worth the price. [R: BL, 1 Oct 81, p. 241; SLJ, Sept 81, p. 45]

Peggy Clossey Boone

1637. **Children's Media Market Place.** 2nd ed. Carol A. Emmens, ed. New York, Neal-Schuman, 1982. 353p. index. $29.95pa. LC 82-82058. ISBN 0-918212-33-2.

Children's Media Market Place, second edition, is a compendium of information valuable to teachers, librarians, parents, those in the book trade, and others connected with children's literature and services for children. The major part of the directory is divided into 21 numbered areas of interest, such as publishers of children's materials, audiovisual producers, periodicals for children and professionals, review journals, and reviewers of children's media. The directory also lists wholesalers, juvenile bookstores and clubs, children's radio and television program sources, public library coordinators of children's and young adult services, a calendar of events and conferences, awards honoring excellence in children's media, and a bibliography of selection tools. The remainder of the directory is devoted to a name index of all sources mentioned in the body of the directory. Entries are arranged in alphabetical order with the number of the appropriate area of interest.

The value of this directory lies in its thoroughness, its inclusiveness, and the fact that the information is current. Although other sources list some of the information found in the directory, none include all of the information in such depth and in one volume. The directory serves as a ready-reference guide to current and up-to-date information. This second edition of the directory has been revised and expanded, with entries based on information culled from questionnaires, telephone calls, and research. An over-sized, paperback format, coupled with clear print and simple organization of subject matter, makes the directory easy to use. Due to the scope of the directory, the *Children's Media Market Place* serves as a professional tool for individuals and for members of organizations and information networks. For an evaluation of the first edition (1978), see *ARBA* 79 (entry 225). [R: BL, 15 Oct 82, p. 318; JAL, Sept 82, p. 239]

Barbara Sproat

Proceedings, Symposia, and Essays

1638. Dyer, Esther R. **Cultural Pluralism & Children's Media.** Chicago, American Association of School Librarians, American Library Association, 1978. 77p. (School Media Centers: Focus on Trends and Issues, No. 1). $6.00pa. LC 78-25845. ISBN 0-8389-3218-5.

This first in a series of papers on issues of concern to media specialists is addressed to the value of culturally pluralistic materials and service for library media programs. Esther Dyer's discussion of the potential role of the media center in smoothing the transition from a melting pot to a multicultural philosophy inspiringly sets the tone for the publication. Readers may not necessarily agree with the differing viewpoints of the individual authors of four of these chapters, but the principles may well form the basis for serious study and thought as the needs of students and the design of a total library media collection are examined.

Cheryl Metoyer discusses "American Indian People and Children's Resources." She places emphasis on social issues faced by contemporary American Indians and gives specific recommendations for the future development of children's library resources and services for and about American Indian people. Catherine Annelli, a specialist in reading and educational psychology, in her discussion of materials on Afro-American heritage, integrates the results of her analysis of the representation of blacks in children's fiction and gives examples that typify each of the four stages in black-identity development.

"Although a small ethnic minority in the United States today, Asian Americans can lay claim to a richness of heritage that includes the cultures of Japan, China, Korea, Vietnam, and the Philippines," writes Esther Dyer in her introduction. Florence Makita Yoshiwara and Vivian Kobayashi, in their chapter, stress the need to consider linguistic and cultural diversity in developing programs and materials for and about Asian Americans.

The United States vies with Venezuela for status as the fifth largest Spanish-speaking country in the world, and the ethnic group of Spanish speaking forms the largest and most widespread minority in the country. In view of these facts, Ruth Anne Thomas writes about the diversity of resources available and the myths surrounding selection of Spanish-language materials. Numerous informational notes, helpful references, and excellent bibliographies are found at the end of each chapter to encourage media professionals, teachers, and educators to read further.

M. Ruth Graham

1639. Johnson, Ferne, ed. **Start Early for an Early Start: You and the Young Child.** Chicago, American Library Association, 1976. 181p. illus. o.p. LC 76-44237. ISBN 0-8389-3185-5. (Available from Books on Demand, $47.80pa., ISBN 0-317-26575-X).

As more public and school libraries become involved in preschool programs, the need for guidance in planning library-related services becomes urgent. Under the editorship of Ferne Johnson, two committees on early childhood education, representing CSD and AASL, joined forces in compiling this collection of 16 articles, which together comprise a variety of methods, techniques, and resources that were used in successful programs in various libraries. The five parts are: "The Preschool Child"; "Parent/Child Interaction"; "Experiencing Literature"; "Parents in Search of Information"; and "Opening More Doors." In the section on literature is an extensive article written by Spencer G. Shaw, which carefully outlines the essential steps for planning and implementing a successful preschool storytelling program. Of special interest is the inclusion of a program evaluation report and an extensive bibliography of suggested books for children and resources for the storyteller. Charlotte Leonard's article, "Poetry to Please Preschoolers," helps to promote the sharing of rhymes and verse. A large selection of suggested poems and picture books accompanies the article. Among other brief but interesting articles is one by Mary Anne Corrier, which sketches the major problem areas and possible solutions that need to be carefully considered in planning a public library program series for parents. Her outline for an eight-session series will be helpful to librarians responsible for setting up such programs. The collection will be of interest to newly established preschool programs or to librarians who anticipate involvement in such projects. [R: AL, June 77, p. 348; SLJ, May 77, p. 40]

Christine Gehrt Wynar

Media Skills and Curriculum Enrichment

1640. Bell, Irene Wood, and Robert B. Brown. **Gaming in the Media Center Made Easy.** Littleton, Colo., Libraries Unlimited, 1982. 205p. illus. index. $22.50pa. LC 82-9913. ISBN 0-87287-336-6.

Gaming in the Media Center Made Easy presents 98 games for elementary school students designed to be used in numerous combinations to teach a variety of skills in the media center and in the classroom. Some of the target skills included in each of the nine sections are: introducing students to the LMC; alphabetizing; explaining the logic and use of the card catalog; teaching the structure and application of the Dewey Decimal Classification; understanding the use of dictionaries; identifying reference sources and their uses; understanding the use of maps, globes, and atlases; developing an appreciation of literature; and demonstrating the relevance of audiovisual hardware and software. The games are constructed from regular classroom supplies and require little preparation time on the part of the media specialist or classroom teacher. The purpose, grade level, time required, materials, and procedure are described for each game. [R: BL, 15 Jan 83, p. 682; Emerg Lib, May 83, p. 21; SLMQ, Winter 83, p. 144]

1641. Polette, Nancy. **Nancy Pollette's E Is for Everybody: A Manual for Bringing Fine Picture Books into the Hands and Hearts of Children.** 2nd ed. Metuchen, N.J., Scarecrow, 1982. 177p. illus. index. $15.00. LC 82-10508. ISBN 0-8108-1579-6.

This resource guide to picture books is designed to assist teachers, librarians, and parents in presenting and using books with students in grades K-8. The introduction by Marjorie Hamlin provides the rationale. In part 1 the author identifies 126 books to be introduced and used. The books cover a wide range of picturebook subject areas and have copyrights from 1975 through 1982. Suggestions for integrating these books through art and media are given in part 2. This section is most helpful because it includes specific instructions for such activities as book making, slide production, and puppet making. The activities described for each book in part 1 range from suggestions for discussion groups to puzzles and artwork. This is an excellent resource for education collections in academic libraries, for professional collections in school systems, and for parents using public libraries. The activities are a springboard for reading motivation in children. [R: BL, 1 Apr 83, p. 1041; JAL, Mar 83, p. 45]

Paula Montgomery

1642. Polette, Nancy, and Marjorie Hamlin. **Celebrating with Books.** Metuchen, N.J., Scarecrow, 1977. 175p. illus. index. $15.00. LC 77-3862. ISBN 0-8108-1032-8.

Following the chronology of the school year, the authors offer information on holidays in a set pattern: a brief, superficial description of the origin and meaning of the holiday, a list of children's books (author, title, and suggested grade level) related to the celebration, and the same titles repeated with full bibliographic note, annotation, and suggested activities. Illustrations are, for the most part, simple and clear, but the organization of the book allows considerable redundancy, and many of the suggestions are not especially imaginative. More useful might be some general notes (i.e., unrelated to

specific titles) on how to build activities around books and reading. The point of view sometimes shifts, with some directions addressed to children, most to adults.

Books suggested for activities range considerably in quality, and the activities are sometimes only tenuously connected. Jews who resent the disproportionate emphasis schools often place on Hanukkah because of that holiday's proximity to Christmas will note glumly that it is the only Jewish holiday mentioned here. To the extent that the book may stimulate teachers and librarians, it will be useful, but that stimulus is not likely to be strong nor especially creative. [R: Choice, Dec 77, p. 1408]

Peggy Sullivan

1643. Preslan, Kristina. **Group Crafts for Teachers and Librarians on Limited Budgets.** Littleton, Colo., Libraries Unlimited, 1980. 105p. illus. index. o.p. LC 80-13145. ISBN 0-87287-218-1.

Classroom teachers, children's librarians, and other children's groups leaders can supplement the curriculum by including one of the 45 crafts from this fully illustrated activity book. Each activity can be completed under the direction of one adult by a group of up to 30 children for a cost of under $5.00. Crafts included may be adapted to different age levels and to a variety of special events, holidays, and story book themes.

Each craft activity is arranged in recipe style — first listing the supplies needed, then indicating that portion of the craft which it is advisable to prepare ahead, and finally explaining how the children can complete the craft. A full-page illustration gives step-by-step guidance. Each activity is self-contained on one page, back and front. It can be torn out if desired for filing in special resource files for holidays, seasons, etc. The index locates the crafts not only by their titles, but by materials required. [R: BL, 1 Jan 81, p. 628]

1644. Silverman, Eleanor. **101 Media Center Ideas.** Metuchen, N.J., Scarecrow, 1980. 203p. illus. index. $16.00pa. LC 80-17034. ISBN 0-8108-1329-7.

Eleanor Silverman, an elementary school media specialist, has compiled a useful reference book of 101 media center ideas. Each idea/activity is outlined on one to two pages and includes information on participants, location, time span, frequency, purposes, materials needed, step-by-step procedures, and additional suggestions. The format makes the book especially useful for writing lesson plans and planning activities in an organized fashion. The ideas are adaptable to any elementary school media center; however, the outline format does not always give adequate procedural examples for an inexperienced person.

101 Media Center Ideas is divided into eight sections, each dealing with a specific type of activity. Ideas for optimal use of physical facilities are presented first. The section on media center symbols stresses the importance of a symbol (logo) and the uses one can make of the logo. Other sections discuss opportunities for personal growth (art, music, games, and poetry activities), puppetry, stimulating interest in reading, storytelling, theater-in-the-round, volunteers, and working with teachers. Black-and-white photographs illustrate media center activities. Examples of worksheets, media center forms, puppet patterns, and play scripts are also included. The book has a table of contents and an index for quick retrieval of ideas/activities. [R: BL, 1 Jan 81, p. 628; CLW, May 81, p. 454; JAL, Jan 81, p. 363]   Carol J. Veitch

1645. Silverman, Eleanor. **Trash into Treasure: Recycling Ideas for Library/Media Centers.** Metuchen, N.J., Scarecrow, 1982. 138p. illus. index. $16.00pa. LC 81-18198. ISBN 0-8108-1489-7.

Trash into Treasure presents 86 very simple and unimaginative ideas ostensibly for using recycled materials in the library media center. Several of the ideas, however, emphasize the recycling concept more than the library media center usefulness, such as making a planter (one idea) or making a vase for flowers (one idea). Many of the ideas are redundant: reuse cassette tapes (four ideas—one for music, one for special effects, one for interest centers, and one to loan), or recycle games (three ideas—one for checkers, one for chess, and one for Scrabble). Some of the suggestions are at cross-purposes; for example, some encourage students to cut up books for storyboards while others recommend having students trace pictures so that they learn proper book care. A number of the ideas are really art projects—make a candle stick (one idea) or make a candle (one idea)—while others involve simple common sense—use old ditto paper for bookmarks (one idea) or for scrap paper (one idea). Because of its simplistic scope and content, this book is not recommended for purchase. [R: BL, 1 Sept 82, p. 50; JAL, May 82, p. 107]   Rebecca L. Thomas

1646. Thomas, James L. **Turning Kids on to Print Using Nonprint.** Littleton, Colo., Libraries Unlimited, 1978. 168p. illus. bibliog.

index. $18.50. LC 78-9075. ISBN 0-87287-184-3.

This book provides a simple, practical approach to the key questions concerning student audiovisual media production: what project should be chosen? How should students be involved in the planning process? what skills and equipment are needed? With the step-by-step chapter on "storyboarding" as the key, Thomas demonstrates all of the procedures involved in planning and producing simple projects in various media—filmstrips, slide/tapes, 8mm films, single-camera television, transparency lifts and story laminations, and dioramas. All steps are fully illustrated with line drawings and photos. [R: Choice, Feb 79, p. 1706]

Storytelling

1647. Baker, Augusta, and Ellin Greene. **Storytelling: Art and Technique.** New York, R. R. Bowker, 1977. 142p. illus. bibliog. index. $15.95pa. LC 77-16481. ISBN 0-8352-0840-0.

The authors of this small volume on storytelling are noted specialists in children's literature and master storytellers. They present a concise guide to both the art and technique of storytelling. The art is covered in the first two chapters, which are devoted to a brief history of storytelling, a review of the work of five well-known storytellers (Marie Shedlock, Anna Cogswell Tyler, Mary Gould Davis, Ruth Sawyer, and Gudrun Thorne-Thomsen), and to a short statement on the purpose and values of storytelling. The remaining six chapters are devoted to the technique of storytelling and include information on the selection of stories to tell, preparation of the stories, presentation of the stories, storytelling in special settings or to children with special needs, program planning, and administrative procedures. Three appendices add to the value of this work. The first covers the planning of a storytelling workshop and festival, the second is a list of sources for the storyteller, and the third is a short glossary. Many of the subheadings in the last six chapters are in the form of questions, a few of them two or three lines long. This reader found them distracting. However, the guide is well written and could be used as a text for a course on storytelling or as a manual for the librarian or teaacher about to embark on a storytelling program. [R: BL, 15 Apr 78, p. 1358]

Doris Cruger Dale

1648. Bauer, Caroline Feller. **Handbook for Storytellers.** Chicago, American Library

Association, 1977. 381p. illus. index. $15.00. LC 76-56385. ISBN 0-8389-0225-1.

Bauer's handbook is a first-rate text that helps the reader present literature to children, young adults, and adults, through storytelling. It is practical without being dull and is chock-full of ideas. Personal anecdotes enliven the text. Excellent bibliographies are provided, as well as information concerning the storyteller's pack of equipment—mental, physical, audio-visual, new and old. Anyone who has ever seen Bauer conduct a workshop will know she writes from true life experience, not theory. She stresses program planning, promotion, and the art of narrative, as well as the nuts-and-bolts of the art of oral interpretation.

The book is best read in bits and pieces, since it is so full that the reader needs to spend time thinking about what the author has presented. *Handbook for Storytellers* belongs in the hands of any person seriously interested in storytelling or any person who wishes to use storytelling in any way. [R: BL, July 77, p. 1657; LJ, Aug 77, p. 1637; SLJ, Oct 77, p. 92]

Ruth I. Gordon

1649. Lawrence, Carol, Jennabeth Hutcherson, and James L. Thomas. **Storytelling for Teachers and School Library Media Specialists.** Minneapolis, Minn., T. S. Denison, 1981. 56p. bibliog. o.p. LC 81-65700. ISBN 0-513-01714-3.

This paperback book is a very fine and very affordable resource on this topic. Included are 10 essays dealing with "Why Tell Stories in Schools," "Using Storytelling to Promote School Objectives," and "Storytelling for Special School Children." All of the essays originally appeared in other publications, but it is convenient to have them in this compilation. Although some information is repeated in several of the articles, the overall presentation is excellent. One article, "Language Development through Storytelling Activities," by Elner C. Bellon, is especially useful as it cites research evidence of the effects of storytelling. The book has an excellent bibliography which includes sections on "Storytelling on Record," "Storytelling on Film and Video," and "Storytellers, Live," which gives names and addresses of some well-known storytellers. [R: Emerg Lib, Nov 81, p. 30]

Rebecca L. Thomas

1650. Moore, Vardine. **Pre-School Story Hour.** 2nd ed. Metuchen, N.J., Scarecrow, 1972. 174p. $13.00. LC 78-188549. ISBN 0-8108-0474-3.

The second edition adds material to update the discussion of preschool education, focusing mainly on topics such as Head Start and Sesame Street. Other chapters, with their bibliographies and reading lists, were also updated. The book is a brief overview of the purpose and requirements of public library story hours for preschool youngsters. The author presents her case in favor of the story hour and proceeds to offer practical suggestions for planning and presenting programs. Also includes chapters discussing characteristics of preschool children, physical arrangements for the program, the storyteller and the role of the parent, and selection of program material. A subject-arranged booklist for use in programs, a short list of recordings, and a few basic group games are also included. Useful as an introduction to practical aspects of the traditional story hour in public libraries and preschool groups. [R: SLJ, Dec 72, p. 50]

Christine Gehrt Wynar

1651. Pellowski, Anne. **The World of Storytelling.** New York, R. R. Bowker, 1977. 296p. illus. bibliog. index. $19.95. LC 77-16492. ISBN 0-8352-1024-3. (Available from the National Association for Preservation and Perpetuation of Storytelling, $19.95, ISBN 0-318-15104-9).

Heavily documented and well written, *World of Storytelling* contains fascinating details about storytelling and storytellers through the ages in various cultures. In addition to the historical information, the author—a noted children's librarian and an accomplished storyteller—discusses the methods of training storytellers and the techniques for improving storytelling skills. A unique feature of this book is the glossary of terms for storytellers, their stories, the places where stories are told, etc., from many languages. An extensive bibliography adds to the value of the work, and the index is more than adequate. Written primarily for the layperson rather than the scholar, this is the kind of reference book that also can be read cover to cover, so put a copy in the circulating collection. [R: BL, 15 Apr 78, p. 1359]

Melinda D. Davis

1652. Peterson, Carolyn Sue, and Brenny Hall. **Story Programs: A Source Book of Materials.** Metuchen, N.J., Scarecrow, 1980. 294p. illus. bibliog. index. $16.00pa. LC 80-15112. ISBN 0-8108-1317-3.

Attention all children's libraries who have been "meaning to" make a book of their story program materials: it has been done. Peterson and Hall have collaborated in this handbook for beginning librarians, teachers, and daycare workers. The book contains sample programs for three age groups: toddlers (2-3 years), pre-schoolers (4-5 years), and primary age children (6-8 years). The book is arranged in six sections. "The Story Program," totaling four pages, lists four sample programs for each age group. The lists include titles of books, fingerplays, songs, etc., centering on a particular subject (e.g., the farm). "Picture Books in the Story Program" is a selected, annotated list of 100 suggested books which probably can be found in all children's collections and will undoubtedly be familiar to the children's librarian. "Flannel Board Activities" is 60 pages of traceable, full-sized patterns for story characters, and the accompanying story or verse (e.g., "The Three Little Kittens," "The Little Red Hen," "The House That Jack Built"). "Physical Activities" includes finger-plays and participation songs (e.g., "Little Jack Horner," "Ten Little Fingers," "Where Is Thumbkin?"). "Creative Dramatics" gives movement suggestions for stories such as "The Three Bears" and rhymes such as "Little Jack Horner." "Puppetry" includes 125 pages of traceable characters and props, instructions for making these hand puppets, and accompanying rhymes or stories (e.g., "The Lion and the Mouse," "The Frog Prince," "The Shoemaker and the Elves"). Included is a bibliography of works that provide similar information for the story program leader. Those new to the area of storytelling who do not have access to the listed standard titles (such as Anderson's *Storytelling with the Flannel Board* and Grayson's *Let's Do Fingerplays*), or to a core collection of picture books and story books (or who do not have time to peruse them), should find this book useful in developing their own story program repertoire. An indexed, sturdily bound paperback. [R: SLJ, Nov 80, p. 48] Mary Alice Deveny

1653. Ziskind, Sylvia. **Telling Stories to Children.** New York, H. W. Wilson, 1976. 162p. bibliog. index. $14.00. LC 75-42003. ISBN 0-8242-0588-X.

A guide to many aspects of storytelling by an experienced storyteller-librarian with background in speech and drama. Gives practical suggestions for selecting the story, learning it, mastering presentation techniques, reading poetry, creative dramatics, and planning the story hour. There are also specifics on memorization, setting up a story file, and working with youngsters on choral speaking.

An important part of the book is the extensive bibliography section, which occupies over 40 pages (about one-fourth of the volume). This

lists background books; periodicals; booklists and indexes; commentaries by anthologists and their anthologies; where to look for stories to tell: collections, special stories, special poetry; what to read to improve your skill: voice and speech, oral interpretation, choral speaking, fingerplays, creative dramatics, puppetry; what to use for language differences: Danish, French, German, Italian, Japanese, Spanish, Swedish, multilingual; and stories for maturer children.

The lists are selective, based on the author's personal preferences, and are not annotated. No prices are given, and some items may be out-of-print. Book dates range from 1906 to 1974.

The text is indexed; the headings of the bibliographic portion are also indexed, but not the individual titles therein. [R: BL, 15 Sept 76, p. 183; LJ, July 76, p. 1524; SLJ, Dec 76, p. 41]
Eleanor Elving Schwartz

DISABLED USERS

General Works

1654. Bramley, Gerald. **Outreach: Library Services for the Institutionalised, the Elderly, and the Physically Handicapped.** London, Clive Bingley; distr., Hamden, Conn., Linnet Books, 1978. 232p. bibliog. index. $17.50. LC 78-7281. ISBN 0-208-01663-5.

For those librarians who think of outreach as extending services to nonusers by new and innovative means, this title is misleading but is clarified promptly by its full subtitle. Over one-third of the book deals with hospital libraries and prison libraries, with brief mention of public library services provided to people in those institutions. The next largest quantity of information concerns the blind and partially sighted. There are only a few pages for the deaf, and a few more for the elderly and the mentally retarded.

The book's purpose is not stated; probably its intent is to be an introductory text. International in coverage, its outlook and emphasis are clearly British, with a once-over-lightly touch on practices and experiments. The slow evolution of the philosophy that the public library has a duty to reach out to those people confined to homes or institutions is traced. The author does not overcome the handicap of negative labeling—"handicapped," "disabled," "subnormal." Bramley notes a growing acceptance by librarians of the notion that all members of society have a right to receive adequate library service, and that it is rare for action to accompany the "impassioned assertions of the pressing need." He finds that librarians do not exhibit leadership in meeting these needs. The United States Supreme Court decision that established the constitutional right of those in prison to have access to legal materials is praised. The question of whether hospital patients should have access to medical information is treated with vagueness, noting however a perceptible rise in hospital practice to provide for patient education. The information contained in this book might serve librarianship best if somehow it were to reach the voting public. [R: LJ, 15 Dec 78, p. 2495]   Doris H. Banks

1655. Davis, Emmett A., and Catherine M. Davis. **Mainstreaming Library Service for Disabled People.** Metuchen, N.J., Scarecrow, 1980. 200p. bibliog. index. $15.00. LC 80-12280. ISBN 0-8108-1305-X.

Focusing on providing library services through regular community information centers (school and public libraries), the authors discuss overcoming "handicapism" through effective staff training, an integrated system design, improved selection and service, nonstereotyped processing and display, and subject cataloging materials and services. A final chapter describes "prescriptive cataloging" as used in the Special Education Departments Material Center of the Minneapolis public schools.

As usual, sources listed may have different organizational structures and location such as NIMIH (pp. 67-68), and need careful updating by the local library. A "mediagraphy" contains an annotated list of print and film/video materials. Public libraries and school media specialists will find much useful information in the first four chapters and numerous valuable suggestions on staff training and developing a "mainstreamed" philosophy of library service. Chapter 4 and chapter 6 will be useful to those who do (or are able to do) their own subject and/or user-oriented cataloging or vertical file organization. [R: LJ, Sept 80, p. 1713]
          Kieth C. Wright

1656. Hébert, Françoise, and Wanda Noel. **Copyright and Library Materials for the Handicapped: A Study Prepared for the International Federation of Library Associations and Institutions.** Munich, New York, K. G. Saur; distr., Hamden, Conn., Shoe String Press, 1982. 111p. (IFLA Publications, No. 21). $20.00. ISBN 3-598-20381-0; ISSN 0344-6891.

Librarians have generally not had to concern themselves with copyright matters, except in the area of photocopying. But librarians attempting to provide services to the handi-

capped are becoming more directly involved with copyright, because of the production/publishing activities libraries have had to resort to in order to serve their patrons. This book looks at library services for the handicapped and recognizes copyright problems associated with the production and dissemination of materials in braille, audiotape, and large print. Possible legislative action concerning the copyright problems is considered. Recommendations for the International Federation of Library Associations and Institutions action, and for actions at other levels, conclude this study. Recommended for libraries that serve a large handicapped population. [R: C&RL, July 83, p. 300; LJ, 15 Nov 83, p. 2152; LR, Winter 82, p. 289]
          Janet R. Ivey

1657. **Hospital Libraries and Work with the Disabled in the Community.** 3rd ed. Compiled and edited by Mona E. Going in collaboration with Jean M. Clarke. London, Library Association; distr., Phoenix, Ariz., Oryx Press, 1981. 311p. bibliog. index. o.p. ISBN 0-85365-723-8.

There are many similarities in and differences between the physical, collection, and personnel components of hospital libraries in Great Britain and the United States. Anyone interested in comparing the typical American hospital library and hospital library services with their British counterparts should read Going's edited study.

This volume, after reviewing in the first quarter of the book the development of British hospital libraries and hospital library services, presents a series of chapters written by experts covering the status of these institutions and services, primarily in England and Wales. These chapters vary greatly in length, from 3 to 50 pages, resulting in tremendous differences in depth of coverage presented. The topics discussed include the appropriate types of reading materials for various kinds of patients (children, psychiatric, etc.), an annotated list of official British government publications that deal with many aspects of health care, and the space and equipment needs of a district general hospital (400-600 beds). Very brief descriptions are given for bibliotherapy and the value of literature to the hospitalized patient. Separate chapters examine the special problems encountered by libraries in providing services for disabled children, geriatric patients, the visually handicapped, and the hearing impaired.

The addition of useful illustrations, reading lists following most chapters and a general bibliography, and a subject index enhances the value of and the access to the information in the text. This volume provides a very competent survey for all readers interested in studying the basic scope and services of British hospital libraries. [R: CLW, Dec 82, p. 192; LR, Autumn 82, p. 213]   Jonathon Erlen

1658. The Mainstreamed Library: Issues, Ideas, Innovations. Barbara H. Baskin and Karen H. Harris, eds. Chicago, American Library Association, 1982. 293p. illus. bibliog. index. $35.00. LC 82-16463. ISBN 0-8389-0359-2.

Forty-seven articles, primarily reprints, are arranged under six headings—physical environment, materials selection, technology, software, program, and outreach—in this reader designed for use by librarians in all types of settings as a guide "to develop a full range of services for patrons with exceptional needs." Selections were made from state and national journals in the fields of library science, special education, rehabilitation, and architecture. The 36 pages of introductory material and the book's divisions by the editors are supplemented by inclusion of three of their articles. A three-page index is included.

The topical arrangement, high-quality selection of nonlibrary sources, and introductory material reflect the expertise and sensitivity of the editors. An excellent balance is maintained between theoretical and practical emphases, services and programs for children and adults, and a variety of exceptionalities, including physical, mental, and learning disabilities and giftedness.

This work will not replace such standard texts as Kieth C. Wright and Judith F. Davie's *Library and Information Services for Handicapped Individuals* (see *ARBA* 84, entry 173) or Ruth Velleman's *Serving Physically Disabled People* (see *ARBA* 81, entry 271), but it is an excellent and stimulating supplement to them. [R: BL, 15 Apr 83, p. 1074; JAL, May 83, p. 108; RQ, Fall 83, p. 118]   Kathryn McChesney

1659. Needham, William L., and Gerald Jahoda. **Improving Library Service to Physically Disabled Persons: A Self-Evaluation Checklist.** Littleton, Colo., Libraries Unlimited, 1983. 135p. bibliog. $18.50. LC 82-16200. ISBN 0-87287-348-X.

This work is designed as a checklist and reference source for self-evaluation of services and facilities for librarians and library administrators who need to assess their libraries' ability to serve physically disabled persons. The first chapter provides suggestions for evaluating general library services to disabled persons by focusing on such aspects as users, facilities,

services, resources, staffing, funding, and external relations. Subsequent chapters contain the checklists on these aspects for specific types of libraries. The final chapter contains lists of resources helpful to libraries that have pinpointed their weaknesses by using the evaluation checklist. Resources include lists of organizations, sources for print and nonprint materials (braille, recordings, etc.), and professional readings. Through extensive field study, academic research, and personal experience, the authors have created this book for libraries interested in identifying the barriers to their services, and thereby helping them to determine where and how to begin improving their services for disabled persons. [R: BL, 15 Oct 83, p. 327; JAL, May 83, p. 109; LJ, 1 Sept 83, p. 1667; RQ, Fall 83, p. 118; WLB, May 83, p. 782]

1660. Pearlman, Della. **No Choice: Library Services for the Mentally Handicapped.** London, Library Association; distr., Phoenix, Ariz., Oryx Press, 1982. 61p. bibliog. index. o.p. ISBN 0-85365-543-X.

The author wrote this book initially as a thesis for partial fulfillment of a B.A. in librarianship in England. By addressing the issue of providing library service to the mentally retarded child and adult, it introduces a subject that many librarians and library school students have still not considered. Traditionally, mentally retarded people are not supposed to be able to read. However, as in the "normal" population, they have different levels of ability and many do use printed materials. In the modern library, there is a whole range of nonprint items and accompanying services available that would be appropriate for this potential library user group. The author feels that this special library service could contribute significantly to the mainstreaming process.

The book offers suggestions for obtaining and presenting materials and educating the staff and library patrons to this relatively new user group. It would be a useful addition to a library school collection, primarily as a textbook and source of inforamtion for service to these users. This softcover book contains 46 pages of text with 53 references. Appendix 1 is a selected list of 21 bibliographies and booklists of items "suitable for use with and by the mentally handicapped." Appendix 2 has two selected reading lists, one dealing with the topic of "mental handicap" and the other with "appropriate library services." There are about 190 selected sources, although less than a third are from the United States. A brief subject index relating to the book's topic is included. [R: AL, Apr 83, p. 225; LR, Autumn 82, p. 211]   Jean Crosby Shearer

1661. Phinney, Eleanor, ed. **The Librarian and the Patient: An Introduction to Library Services for Patients in Health Care Institutions.** Chicago, American Library Association, 1977. 352p. illus. index. $25.00. LC 76-45178. ISBN 0-8389-0227-8.

Addressed to professional librarians and administrators interested in planning and developing library services for patients in long-term health care facilities, this long-awaited text represents the standards, philosophy, and expertise of a virtual honor roll of practitioners in the field.

Library service to patients must be based on their individual needs and capabilities and on the health care goals of the institutions in which they are residing. Background chapters describe the patient, the institution, and the library as a therapeutic environment. Planning, organizing, equipping, staffing, operating, and supplementing library services are discussed from the viewpoint of principles to be applied rather than required techniques. Examples are frequently presented.

Topical summaries precede most chapters. Bibliographies are extensive. The "Patient Bill of Rights," sample agreements with public libraries providing service to institutions, and hints on classification of materials and on relating to patients appear in appendices. This book will become a classic in health science librarianship. [R: JAL, July 77, p. 169; LJ, 1 Sept 77, p. 1737]   Harriette M. Cluxton

1662. Task Force on Library Access for the Handicapped. **Library Access for the Handicapped: A Guide to Materials, Services and Physical Accessibility of Public and Academic Libraries in the New York Metropolitan Area.** New York, METRO, New York Metropolitan Reference and Research Library Agency, 1979. 82p. (METRO Miscellaneous Publication, No. 20). o.p. ISSN 0076-7018.

This paperback provides information about access for the handicapped to libraries in the New York metropolitan area (New York and New Jersey). In two listings, public libraries and academic libraries, the directory lists name, address, telephone number, contact person, special equipment, special materials and services, and physical accessibility. Special equipment includes braille writers, ceiling projectors, electric typewriters, large-print typewriters, magnifying lenses, opticon, page turner, talking book machines, teletypewriters or MCM, and

tape recorders. Loan availability is noted. Special materials include captioned films, braille materials, music and spoken records and cassettes, and large-print books and periodicals. Special services include books by mail, homebound service, and listening rooms. A library with staff members who read to the blind or who know sign language is reported. Accessibility is described in detail.

Suggested use of this volume, besides the obvious one of helping handicapped information seekers, is as a guide for architects and library staff when designing or remodeling library buildings. The project was partially funded by a Library Services and Construction Act, Title III grant.   Mary Alice Deveny

1663. Thomas, James L., and Carol H. Thomas, eds. **Academic Library Facilities and Services for the Handicapped.** Phoenix, Ariz., Oryx Press, 1981. 568p. bibliog. index. $80.00. LC 81-14020. ISBN 0-912700-95-5.

Information in this directory is based on questionnaires received from colleges and universities throughout the United States and its outlying territories. As the title indicates, it lists and describes library facilities available to disabled students in alphabetical order by institution within each state. Included for each library are the name of the institution; name, address, and telephone number of the library; name of the person to contact for further information; the library's accessibility, special equipment, and special services for handicapped students. Accessibility is indicated by answers to some 18 specific questions dealing with such things as the width of doors and the height of telephones and drinking fountains. Information on 16 specific types of equipment, including large-print typewriters, the opticon, talking calculators, and teletypewriters, is also given.

The data for each library are clearly and concisely given. There is no index as such, but there is a listing of all the institutions in alphabetical order giving the states in which they are located, so it is fairly simple to find the information. Material in the appendices shows in graphic form some of the data generated by the survey and also includes a bibliography and a list of regional libraries serving the blind and physically handicapped. Considering the high cost of the volume, the 40-plus pages in this section, though interesting, might well have been omitted.

In that many more disabled young people will probably be entering college than ever have in the past, the work should be extremely valuable for those students planning their education, as well as their parents, teachers, and counselors. School, public, and academic libraries of any size should have the volume in their collections. [R: LJ, 15 June 82, p. 1198]

Lucille Whalen

1664. Thomas, James L., and Carol H. Thomas, eds. **Library Services for the Handicapped Adult.** Phoenix, Ariz., Oryx Press, 1982. 152p. index. $29.50. LC 82-2544. ISBN 0-89774-007-6.

This book is a collection of readings, most of which were already published, intended to upgrade both the services to the handicapped provided by libraries and the education offered to students in library schools. Part 1 provides background information and a brief history of this special kind of librarianship. In Part 2 is found a collection of descriptive articles detailing specific kinds of services to adult clientele with specific handicaps, including the blind and visually impaired, the physically handicapped, the deaf, the developmentally disabled, the emotionally disturbed, and the institutionalized.

Part 3, "Resources for Assisting the Handicapped," is a carefully selected (and annotated) list of resources, which includes articles, books, databases, equipment, nonprint sources, pamphlets, brochures, catalogs, periodicals, and newsletters. This list would be useful to both librarians and adult handicapped consumers, which was the main criterion Thomas and Thomas used in examining available resources.

Library Services for the Handicapped Adult is a valuable sourcebook, particularly for library school students who, as the article dealing with library education points out, are generally not provided with the necessary training and background to embark on a career of serving the library and information needs of handicapped people. [R: JAL, Sept 83, p. 241; LJ, 1 Sept 83, p. 1667; WLB, Apr 83, p. 703]

Lawrence Grieco

1665. Thomas, Carol H., and James L. Thomas, eds. **Meeting the Needs of the Handicapped: A Resource for Teachers and Librarians.** Phoenix, Ariz., Oryx Press, 1980. 479p. bibliog. index. o.p. LC 80-12504. ISBN 0-912700-54-8.

Providing free public education for the handicapped was empowered when the Education Amendments were passed in 1946. It was accelerated by passage of PL 94-142 in 1975 and PL 95-602 in 1978. The monumental task of implementation has spurred a spate of articles in educational journals. From those published between 1973 and 1979, the most impressive are reproduced here, especially those whose ideas for one or more groups of handicapped students are replicable. There are sections on general concepts and the law; students who are mentally retarded, learning disabled, hard of hearing, visually handicapped, and orthopedically impaired; and on vocational preparation, as well as three appendices—one devoted to materials selection, one a directory of producers of materials, and one listing organizations and publications related to the handicapped.

There is an entire shorthand terminology in the field. Among the terms clearly defined in these pages are: *LD*—the learning disabled, caused by other than physical, environmental, or cultural disadvantages; *IEP*—Individualized Education Programs; *TMR*—trainable mentally retarded; *Mainstreaming*—educating the handicapped in a program which is as close as possible to the regular educational program and best suited to meeting the particular needs of the person. This collection offers valuable information in an efficient form, a necessity for today's library services and school programs. [R: BL, 15 Jan 81, p. 671; SLJ, May 81, p. 28]

Doris H. Banks

1666. Velleman, Ruth A. **Serving Physically Disabled People: An Information Handbook for All Libraries.** New York, R. R. Bowker, 1979. 392p. bibliog. index. $21.95. LC 79-17082. ISBN 0-8352-1167-3.

Serving Physically Disabled People is arranged in four parts. Part 1 introduces physically disabled people, including social attitudes and definition of specific disabilities. Part 2 describes the civil rights enacted into law on behalf of disabled persons. This part lists sources of inexpensive materials available to libraries, as well as basic illustrated barrier-free design criteria for library facilities. Specific needs of the blind and deaf are discussed by Hanan C. Selvin and Alice Hagemeyer, respectively. Part 3 gives an overview of rehabilitation history and philosophy, as well as a list of materials for a model rehabilitation library. Part 4 discusses school and university libraries in the context of the development of special education and library services to students with special needs. A suggested core special education collection is included. Appendices provide information on professional and volunteer agencies, independent living centers, national rehabilitation associations, research and training centers, and other related centers. Since many rehabilitation and information facilities are federally funded, the reader is advised to check listings against the latest changes in the federal system.

The book is based on Velleman's experience at the Human Resources School, her national workshop and consultant experience in this field, and her teaching experience at the Palmer Graduate Library School of Long Island University. The book is a benchwork of library services for the physically disabled as of 1979. [R: BL, 15 Apr 80, p. 1178; C&RL, May 80, pp. 250-51; Choice, July/Aug 80, pp. 658-59; JAL, Sept 80, p. 228; SLJ, Apr 80, p. 38]

Kieth C. Wright

1667. Wright, Kieth C., and Judith F. Davie. **Library and Information Services for Handicapped Individuals.** 2nd ed. Littleton, Colo., Libraries Unlimited, 1983. 184p. index. $20.00. LC 83-13560. ISBN 0-87287-391-9.

Handicapped individuals' legal rights, once thought to be established, have been reinterpreted by the courts, placing the future of library laws and regulations (including the Library Services and Construction Act) in question. This updated and expanded second edition addresses these changes and the library's critical role in informing handicapped persons and their families. Because of their active participation in state and national programs related to service for handicapped individuals, the authors have become increasingly aware of the need for librarians to examine their own attitudes and confront their own prejudices in order to effectively serve handicapped persons. To address these needs, a new chapter, "Library Staff Development: Self-Assessment and Attitude Change," has been added to this edition. Topics that are discussed include services for the speech-impaired individual; definition of major handicapped groups; reviews of legal decisions and implications; presentation of ideas for library programs and services; identification of sources of information; outline of problems facing handicapped populations, solutions, and the library community's resources and programs; and enumeration of programs and services that librarians can modify to meet needs in their particular settings. For an evaluation of the first edition (1979), see *ARBA* 80 (entry 232). [R: BL, 15 Apr 84, p. 1149; LJ, 15 Feb 84, p. 336; RQ, Fall 83, p. 118; RQ, Summer 84, p. 490]

Reference Works

1668. **Directory of Outreach Services in Public Libraries.** Chicago, Office for Library Service to the Disadvantaged, American Library Association, 1980. 632p. index. $25.00 spiral-bound. ISBN 0-8389-3243-8. (Available from Books on Demand, $160.00pa., ISBN 0-317-26558-X).

This directory is a tool prepared for librarians by librarians. Jean Coleman, responsible for compiling it, hopes that the information provided "will be a guide and stimulant to those librarians who may wish to establish outreach programs in their libraries." The directory is the result of a mail survey of outreach services offered by public libraries in the United States. Information is included on 410 different outreach programs from public libraries in 34 states. The data were collected and assembled prior to the Proposition 13 vote in California (June 1978). This time limitation is important when considering the usefulness of the directory. Another limitation is the directory's representativeness. It is impossible to know how many outreach services are not included because the librarians involved failed to complete and return the questionnaire as requested. A description of the survey methodology used would have been helpful to include as part of the introduction. For example, the number of questionnaires mailed, the response rate, the time allowed to complete, the type of follow-up used are important considerations in this respect. The *total* picture of public library outreach services in this country remains to be uncovered.

The directory is organized alphabetically by state, then by name of individual library. Entries are assigned a program number which is used as a reference point in the topical index (the only index). The information in each entry includes: program title and description, location, contact person, clientele, purpose, staff, beginning and sources of funding, results/follow-up, citations in library literature. Some of the resulting profiles are extensive (several pages), while others are much shorter.

The programs themselves cover a broad spectrum of activities. The OLSD guidelines requested information on programs serving "the economically disadvantaged and minority groups of all ages, including senior citizens." Definitions are included for "outreach," "disadvantaged," and "minority." The interpretation of these guidelines appears to be quite broad, since programs are included which address clientele, such as the elderly and the physically handicapped, who are not necessarily either economically disadvantaged or members of a minority group. There is also a broad or loose interpretation of the term "program" or "service." Having a collection of Spanish or bilingual materials does not necessarily constitute a program. The distinction between materials on the one hand, and programs or services on the other, appears (in some instances) to be ignored.

Nevertheless, as a convenient, useful handle for librarians and library school students to learn about kinds of outreach programs happening in this country, the directory is invaluable. It is recommended for library science or professional collections in library schools, as well as in medium- and large-sized public libraries. [R: BL, 15 Jan 81, p. 669; RQ, Spring 81, pp. 310-11] Susan J. Freiband

1669. Keys, Carol, comp. **Reference Books in Special Media.** Washington, D.C., National Library Service for the Blind and Physically Handicapped, Library of Congress, 1982. 74p. index. o.p.

What does a librarian do when a blind patron needs to write a thesis and must use the *MLA Handbook* as a source? If the library is fortunate enough to have ordered through the U.S. Government Printing Office *Reference Books in Special Media*, the librarian can direct the patron to Recording for the Blind, a source that lends the *MLA Handbook* on two cassettes.

Reference Books in Special Media, issued by the National Library Service for the Blind and Physically Handicapped, is a must for public and college libraries. Reference books are grouped under broad subject categories (e.g., business management, English literature, and foreign languages), and then by medium (braille, cassette, disk, and large type). Each entry contains bibliographic information for the printed edition, followed by special-format edition information. If it is provided by the producer, the number of cassettes, volumes, or pages in the special-format edition is indicated.

Section 2 lists complete addresses of all sources cited. General purchase, loan, or exchange arrangements are also described in this section. If purchase, loan, or exchange arrangements are not indicated for a source, the titles from that source are available for purchase only at the prices listed in section 1.

Section 3 is an alphabetical index by title only. This book would be better if section 3 included an index by subject also.

Janet R. Ivey

Blind and Physically Handicapped

1670. Association of Specialized and Cooperative Library Agencies. Standards for Library Service to the Blind and Physically Handicapped Subcommittee. **Standards of Service for the**

Library of Congress Network of Libraries for the Blind and Physically Handicapped. Chicago, American Library Association, 1979. 72p. bibliog. index. o.p. LC 79-22963. ISBN 0-8389-0298-7.

This work updates and expands ALA's Library Administration Division's 1967 *Standards for Library Services for the Blind and Visually Handicapped*. It responds to multiple changes which have occurred: technologies relating to these services; broader recognition of special needs and the legislation which empowers library support agencies to meet them; and the development of Library of Congress/National Library Service Network.

Particularly valuable, of course, are the specific descriptions of special services: guides to physical facilities, especially space requirements, materials and formats specifications, network responsibilities and cooperative activities, the appendices, and the definitions. Much applies to all library services, and librarians generally can benefit from the basic philosophy; for instance, in Standard 4.4 on Public Education and Information, "All libraries in the network shall assume responsibility for interpreting their library services to the community and for promoting a climate of public opinion and awareness favorable to library development, expansion and improvement." Hear, hear! The guiding hand of Phyllis Dalton, who wrote the foreword, is evident. The committee, from its origins late in 1977, deserves commendation. [R: BL, 15 July 80, p. 1654]

Doris H. Banks

1671. Cylke, Frank Kurt, ed. **Library Service for the Blind and Physically Handicapped: An International Approach; Key Papers Presented at the IFLA Conference 1978, Štrbské Pleso, ČSSR.** Munich, New York, K. G. Saur, 1979. 106p. (IFLA Publications, 16). $19.80. LC 79-14646. ISBN 0-89664-013-2; ISSN 0344-6891.

Efforts to improve international cooperation for the flow of library materials, the transmission of bibliographic information, and the provision of library services have intensified in the last decade. Some issues in international library cooperation, notably standardized bibliographic description, have become quite controversial, especially when weighed against domestic concerns. When these efforts and concerns are placed under the microscope of materials and services for the blind and physically handicapped, they appear even larger.

These published conference papers dissect the major issues in this field: the need for standardization of talking book and braille technology and formats, copyright restrictions that limit blind readers' and special agencies' access to many books, postal regulations and custom laws that sometimes help and other times hinder international exchange of materials, the relationships among international organizations serving the blind and physically handicapped, and the difficulties in adapting ISBD formats to materials produced for the blind.

Each of these areas shares fundamental issues with more traditional international library cooperation; yet in each, the requirements of special users create additional complications, all clearly explained here. Taken together, the five papers make a fine introduction to the problems vexing professionals who are trying to provide quality library service to special users regardless of the origins of the materials they need. All of the authors go beyond their uniform hortatory tone to suggest solutions to the problems. Because the blind are the group least able to use traditional library materials, all emphasize efforts to satisfy their needs. The discussion of postal and custom problems includes several useful appendices on international postal agreements. A roster of IFLA's Working Group of Libraries for the Blind concludes the volume.

For library school libraries this is a must purchase. Any librarian interested in the complexity of international library cooperation will find it worthwhile. A second volume, edited by Bruce E. Massis, was published in 1982. [R: C&RL, May 80, pp. 250-51]   James Rettig

1672. Eldridge, Leslie, comp. and ed. **Speaking Out: Personal and Professional Views on Library Service for Blind and Physically Handicapped Individuals.** Washington, D.C., National Library Service for the Blind and Physically Handicapped, Library of Congress, 1982. 188p. free. pa. LC 82-600336. ISBN 0-8444-0414-4.

This book was written to provide an open forum in which librarians, students, educators, and users of library services for blind and physically handicapped individuals could freely express their thoughts and feelings, whether positive or negative, concerning attitudes, education, and experiences they have encountered.

Speaking Out does indeed have interviews from a variety of people; however, it is strictly regionalized. The compiler, a San Francisco librarian, unfortunately did not interview people from other areas of the United States. Librarians in many parts of the country will feel

frustrated that there is no representation from areas other than California.

This book should be of particular interest to librarians serving blind and physically handicapped individuals. The interviews of the users are most interesting. Unfortunately, the users are all but one visually handicapped. Nevertheless, their comments were enlightening and, in many cases, more perceptive than the librarians' comments.

This book fulfills the purpose intended; however, it does seem to be specialized to library services to the blind in California. [R: LJ, 15 June 83, p. 1238]   Janet R. Ivey

1673. **Planning Barrier Free Libraries: A Guide for Renovation and Construction of Libraries Serving Blind and Physically Handicapped Readers.** Washington, D.C., National Library Service for the Blind and Physically Handicapped, Library of Congress, 1981. 61p. illus. o.p. pa. LC 80-607821. ISBN 0-8444-0352-0.

This guide to making library buildings free from barriers for the handicapped was prepared by Charles A. Moss, Jr., of an Alabama architectural firm, in consultation with a regional librarian, Miriam M. Pace. It serves both architects who are unfamiliar with library programs and librarians who do not know architects' information needs. Emphasis is on new buildings, although there is a final chapter on renovations. There are many illustrations of the architect's way of thinking — functional relationship design drawings, schematic designs, elevations, and material movement flow diagrams. Every page is idea-laden; for instance, topics covered include the fragrance garden, the tactile map floor plan, a recess for blind guide sticks with a break at each stopping point, changes in floor surfacing to differentiate area changes, and restroom adaptations. Appropriate standards and codes, as well as sources for more information, are identified.

Any librarian who is contemplating major, or even minor, building or renovation will find this an important reference. Construction of functional space for both workers and patrons is difficult enough; adding barrier-free environment spices up the challenge, as the authors assert.   Doris H. Banks

1674. **Print for the Visually Handicapped Reader. Papers and Proceedings of a Conference Sponsored by the Library Association and the National Association for the Education of the Partially Sighted, 28 October 1970, at Commonwealth Hall, London.** London,

Library Association, 1971. 64p. (Library Association Research Publication, No. 6). o.p. LC 72-177827. ISBN 0-85365-394-1.

This volume consists of the verbatim transcript of five papers presented on three separate subjects: the design, the production, and the use of large print. These present facts and details but do not address the problems of making large-print books more readily available and more widely used. Libraries can encourage their use by making them more accessible in their libraries. [R: LJ, July 71, p. 2281]

Charles D. Patterson

1675. Schauder, Donald E., and Malcolm D. Cram. **Libraries for the Blind: An International Study of Policies and Practices.** Stevenage, England, Peter Peregrinus; distr., Forest Grove, Oreg., International Scholarly Book Services, 1977. 152p. bibliog. index. (Librarianship and Information Studies, Vol. 4). $36.00. ISBN 0-901223-91-3.

This book is based on research done by the senior author for his master's degree in 1972. Through literature search, re-evaluation of the original text, personal visits, and correspondence, the work was updated to 1976 and represents the first comprehensive "state of the art" review of this limited branch of librarianship on an international basis. Most library services for the blind began as private charitable ventures. That history and the attitudes of communities still influence its delivery today, although much responsibility has been assumed by governmental bodies. Social workers and volunteers continue to work with media specialists and professional librarians to provide modern library services for the blind and partially sighted.

Adult services are emphasized in this book, and chapters cover the regular library functions of management, selection, acquisition, bibliographic control, and use of facilities. Brief paragraphs describe what is known about these functions in other countries. Especially interesting are the later chapters on cooperation, new technologies (such as computer brailling), and the wider use of sound recordings. Through this book and its extensive bibliography, the individual librarian working in this field can compare his or her services with what has been accomplished elsewhere. Other librarians will certainly gain a new perspective on the services that their profession can render the handicapped. [R: LR, Spring 78, p. 48]

Harriette M. Cluxton

1676. Strom, Maryalls G., ed. **Library Services to the Blind and Physically Handicapped.** Metuchen, N.J., Scarecrow, 1977. 285p. index. $18.50. LC 77-24686. ISBN 0-8108-1068-9.

This book emphasizes the services of the Library of Congress Division for the Blind and Physically Handicapped (DBPH). The blind librarian editor, importuning all librarians to reach out to these special people, points out that the articles are merely a sampling of the literature written about this subject. They are primarily librarians talking to librarians, and *Catholic Library World* has provided most of them. One touching story by a blind reader lends sensitivity and awareness. The spread of topics is cursory; the appendices are the gold mine, with location information on special libraries, sources of information about library services for the handicapped, and sources of reading material for them. In spite of the strong emphasis on the blind, however, two outstanding sources for special materials are omitted: Howe Press, from Perkins School, and Twin Vision Publishing, whose books combine pages of print and braille so that blind and sighted readers can enjoy them together.

After the section on DBPH and its regional and related libraries, there is a section on the special needs of the handicapped. Here it is made clear that deaf and mentally retarded people are generally not served by DBPH, yet articles included show that librarians are coming to realize their special needs. Section 3 speaks of materials sources and selection aids, and of ways to deal with special problems such as physical barriers. The final section is concerned with library services for the homebound. It is a bit shocking that these service extensions are said to have come about, not because librarians are growing in their recognition of the responsibility to serve all of the public, but because libraries are in danger of losing financial support if they don't reach out to the underserved. [R: BL, 15 Apr 78, p. 1328; C&RL, May 78, p. 229; JAL, Sept 78, p. 225; LJ, 1 Apr 78, p. 725; SLJ, Apr 78, p. 56]

Doris H. Banks with Doris Sadoski

Children and Young Adults

1677. Baskin, Barbara Holland, and Karen H. Harris, eds. **The Special Child in the Library.** Chicago, American Library Association, 1976. 199p. illus. index. $9.00pa. LC 76-21268. ISBN 0-8389-0222-7. (Available from Books on Demand, $51.80pa., ISBN 0-317-26574-1).

The trend to integrate special education students as fully as possible within regular classrooms brings with it the imperative to modify the library to meet the needs of those children. The term special (exceptional) children is broadly defined to encompass those youngsters with physical, visual, or auditory impairments, learning disabilities, and emotional problems, and those who are intellectually gifted.

The 51 articles—selected from library literature, educational journals, and professional journals devoted to the deaf or blind or related to psychiatry—are grouped under six general categories: components of the physical environment of the library; selection criteria; materials utilization; programming; bibliotherapy and reading guidance; resources for serving the special child. A number of the articles date to the early and mid-sixties, but more recent literature is also represented; a small number of articles was prepared specifically for the collection, especially in the first section. A careful balance of articles relating to each type of special child designation is maintained in each group. Brief introductions offer adequate summaries of the key topics and themes set forth by the writers in each section.

The problem inherent in readers and especially noticeable in collections as broadly defined as this one is that no one topic can be systematically examined or thoroughly treated. For example, the literature on gifted children and accompanying curriculum development and teaching strategies is so large as to call for its own reader and bibliography. Including four articles, no matter how nicely balanced numerically this is to the whole collection, barely sets the stage for serious consideration of this important subject.

The editors intend this reader as "a handbook which will cogently present a philosophical base for procedures, a compendium of information on materials, examples of creative, unusual and effective programs, and guidelines for environmental modifications" for school and public libraries. Let us say that a reader is not a handbook. The collection does serve a useful orienting function by offering brief glimpses into the demanding professional tasks of adapting library skills and knowledge to the educational needs of special children; it is a hopeful beginning in an oft-neglected area of children's librarianship. A handbook and reference guide to materials and sources, however, remains as a future project for a taskforce or an interested author. [R: AL, May 77, p. 265; SLJ, Apr 77, p. 44]

Christine Gehrt Wynar

1678. Denquin, Henry C. **Librarians Serving Disabled Children and Young People.** Littleton, Colo., Libraries Unlimited, 1983. 303p. bibliog. index. $22.50. LC 83-5381. ISBN 0-87287-364-1.

Librarians need to broaden their knowledge of disabled persons and need to expand and update their professional expertise in serving the needs, interests, and abilities of disabled persons. This book is intended to help those librarians who serve disabled children and young people from kindergarten through high school. It emphasizes the services that librarians can provide. The book covers assessing the need for library services; the question of who is disabled; the right to library and educational services; attitudes; serving individual abilities, needs, and interests; general and special library services; library programs; locating, evaluating, and selecting materials; and equipment and devices. Appendix A contains the standard criteria for the selection and evaluation of instructional materials, and appendix B covers criteria for media selection. There is an extensive selected bibliography. [R: JAL, Sept 83, p. 241]

1679. Lucas, Linda, ed. **Library Services to Developmentally Disabled Children and Adults.** Chicago, Association of Specialized and Cooperative Library Agencies/American Library Association, 1982. 63p. bibliog. (ASCLA Occasional Paper, No. 1). $10.00. ISBN 0-8389-6538-5.

The developmentally disabled are people with mental or physical impairments. Prior to this 1978 definition, these disabled were thought to be mentally retarded. This category was broadened to include people with cerebral palsy, epilepsy, or other neurological condition, and those with autism or reading disabilities. From another standpoint, any disability that occurs in a person of less than 18 years is a developmental disability. The eight articles included have been collected to assist librarians in identifying adjustments needed to best serve disabled people, and "the greatest barrier to good library service for a disabled person can be the attitude of library staff." Insofar as knowledge is one agent for attitude change, distribution of these papers will serve to meet the purpose of their gathering. There are three institutional libraries represented, two public and one school. One paper deals with the physically, not mentally, disabled, and one advocates advocacy. If library administrators subscribe to the doctrine of the right to equal access for all people, the challenge of serving the handicapped cannot be ignored.

Doris H. Banks

1680. Lucas, Linda, and Marilyn H. Karrenbrock. **The Disabled Child in the Library: Moving into the Mainstream.** Littleton, Colo., Libraries Unlimited, 1983. 288p. bibliog. index. $22.50. LC 83-1035. ISBN 0-87287-355-2.

This book is designed to assist the reader in successfully designing and implementing services in mainstream libraries. Three kinds of barriers that are important to keep in mind when planning services are discussed: barriers created by the disabilities themselves, by societal attitudes, and by environmental conditions. Part 1, "The Disabled Child," explores attitudes toward and of disabled children and discusses some of the disabilities found among children who attend public schools and use public libraries, including mobility, dexterity, and chronic health problems; hearing, vision, and speech impairments; and mental disabilities. Part 2, "Serving the Disabled Child in the Library," includes basic information about currently available resources and offers practical approaches for beginning library service to disabled children. Needs assessment, materials and equipment, services, legislation, environmental design, and planning are discussed. A bibliography and list of standard criteria for the selection and evaluation of instructional materials are offered in the appendix. [R: BL, 15 Oct 83, p. 326; JAL, Sept 83, p. 241]

1681. Macon, Myra, ed. **School Library Media Services to the Handicapped.** Westport, Conn., Greenwood Press, 1982. 208p. bibliog. index. $27.50. LC 81-4262. ISBN 0-313-22684-9.

This collection of seven essays on various aspects of service, well conceived and executed, provides an excellent philosophical framework for the school media specialist with no background on the subject. Kieth C. Wright deals with federal legislation, characteristics of the handicapped, and funding services in his usual competent, readable style. The history of education of the handicapped, by Austin W. Bunch, is recapped admirably. The essay on selecting materials, by Barbara H. Baskin and Karen H. Harris, provides an overview with helpful concrete comments, and Jo-Ellen Ostendorf's information on the National Library Service for the Blind and Physically Handicapped details exactly that information which the media specialist needs to provide referral services for students and teachers. Less directly useful is the information on Individualized Education Programs (IEPs) by Ellen C. Fogan. This information is too detailed and becomes rather tedious. Some editing here would have helped.

Useful reference material includes four appendices—goals and activities; a directory of selection sources; a selected list of organizations; a list of collection sites of The Foundation Center—and a 12-page annotated bibliography of fiction and nonfiction about disabled individuals, ranked by broad grade level.

Media specialists unfamiliar with working with handicapped children may wish for more specific information, but the editor wisely has opted for a more philosophical approach in this ground-breaking work. The coverage is just the information needed to develop a sensitivity and desire to provide media services to this neglected group. The cost may be a little prohibitive, but the work is more useful to Americans than M. R. Marshall's *The Library and the Handicapped Child* (Westview Press, 1981), which has a British slant and is concerned with school and public library work. This work is recommended reading for both media specialists and teachers. [R: BL, 1 Mar 82, p. 108]

Kathryn McChesney

1682. Petrie, Joyce. **Mainstreaming in the Media Center.** Phoenix, Ariz., Oryx Press, 1982. 219p. bibliog. index. $27.50pa. LC 82-2182. ISBN 0-89774-006-8.

The basic assumption of *Mainstreaming in the Media Center* is that the media center is the school's focal point of learning. Given this thesis, it is logical that the media center would be in the forefront of compliance with PL 94-142, the Education for All Handicapped Children Act. The mandate of PL 94-142 is that disabled children be educated in the least restrictive environment, which is to say that they be integrated, or mainstreamed, into regular classrooms and other regular public school settings.

The book provides a background for understanding mainstreaming and defines the philosophy of the media center. It analyzes the media program in terms of its functions and goes on to address very specific types of disabling conditions. In the last part of the book there are materials to aid in assessing the value, potential, and degree of success of a media program. Then suggestions are provided for media center planning.

Throughout, sources of further information are cited, including books, periodicals, organizations, and so on, that will facilitate efforts to mainstream in the media center. This book is a necessary tool for school media specialists. [R: Emerg Lib, May 83, p. 21; SLMQ, Spring 83, p. 228]

DISADVANTAGED USERS

1683. Baker, D. Philip, and David R. Bender. **Library Media Programs and the Special Learner.** Hamden, Conn., Library Professional Publications/Shoe String Press, 1981. 384p. index. $19.50; $14.50pa. LC 80-24806. ISBN 0-208-01852-2; 0-208-01846-8pa.

A discursive, if intelligent and literate, monograph on factors, backgrounds, and requirements for superior media programs for special learners, with presentations (rather than reports) on 27 "exemplary programs": 14 for special learners, 8 for mentally and physically limited or disabled, and 5 for gifted and talented. These program descriptions are based on visits by 24 "site observors" during the year 1979-80, using a form of the authors.

While the authors seem to know what they are talking about, the book's style is so hortatory and generalized that it is difficult to understand the nuts and bolts, mechanisms, and purposes of the exemplary programs. The background chapters include many nuggets of wisdom and insight, often buried and surrounded by digressive mini-essays that are sometimes related or interesting in themselves. The philosophical approach dominates to the point that it is hard to isolate key points and recommendations. One longs at times for journalistic oversimplifications or for some of the charts and tables through which educators communicate. The first chapter and appendix 3 do present Public Law 94-142 and the legal basis of special education with reasonable clarity, while the background chapters present the needs of particular groups of children. Other appendices include the site visitation form, an unannotated list of associations and organizations, and descriptions of 22 special education projects, taken from Far West Laboratory's *Educational Programs That Work* (edition not specified). The reporting model in this work would have been a good model to adapt (not adopt) for the other descriptions in this book. [R: SMQ, Fall 81, pp. 65-66]   Marda Woodbury

1684. Brown, Eleanor Frances. **Library Service to the Disadvantaged.** Metuchen, N.J., Scarecrow, 1971. 500p. illus. index. o.p. LC 78-162668. SBN 8108-0437-9.

This compendium covers a wide range of topics (e.g., the economically disadvantaged, the physically disadvantaged, service to older citizens, service to illiterates, etc). Appended are a book-subject list for collections for the disadvantaged and a list of bibliographies. [R: BL, 1 Apr 72, p. 636; C&RL, Sept 72, p. 414; CLW, Nov 72, p. 242; WLB, Feb 72, p. 543]

1685. Childers, Thomas, assisted by Joyce A. Post. **The Information-Poor in America.** Metuchen, N.J., Scarecrow, 1975. 182p. bibliog. index. o.p. LC 74-19482. ISBN 0-8108-0775-0.

Under a USOE grant Childers studied the available literature on the information needs of the disadvantaged. He came up with a very brief description of the most insistent needs (health, consumer affairs, housing, employment, etc.) and a brief list of those who constitute the information-poor (if you're poor, you're likely to be information-poor, too). The most substantive result of the survey is an unannotated bibliography of more than 700 items, mostly post-1968, and a topical index to the items. There are no startling new insights (I wish Childers didn't repeat some hoary old ones so often like the alleged "fatalism" and "unwillingness to delay gratification" of the disadvantaged) and no new data, since the study did not attempt to generate any, but the bibliography gives ordered access to a wide and various literature about what the disadvantaged need to know. [R: LJ, 1 June 75, p. 1110]

Fay M. Blake

1686. Lipsman, Claire K. **The Disadvantaged and Library Effectiveness.** Chicago, American Library Association, 1972. 197p. illus. o.p. LC 72-1375. ISBN 0-8389-0129-8.

The U.S. Office of Education initiated this study "to examine the scope, nature, and effectiveness of [public] library services to the disadvantaged in urban areas." Using statistical counts, in-depth interviews, detailed program analyses, and comparative studies of programs, Lipsman determines that those libraries that successfully serve the disadvantaged have effective staff, community involvement, autonomy for the program director, quality materials, and effective publicity. The author recommends that all libraries implement surveys to determine what people want. She further suggests that they test the effectiveness of their services through systems analysis and, in turn, that they redefine the library's role in the community. The author severely criticizes most libraries for their poorly collected, inadequate statistics and calls for them to apply her techniques to measure their effectiveness. She suggests the kinds of information libraries should collect and indicates ways to use the data to improve or redirect library services. This research report has implications for all public libraries, whether or not they serve primarily the disadvantaged. Despite its turgid style, it should be read by all public library administrators. [R: LJ, 15 May 73, p. 1560]

Nancy P. Schneider

1687. Martin, William, ed. **Library Services to the Disadvantaged.** London, Clive Bingley; distr., Hamden, Conn., Linnet Books, 1975. 185p. $15.00. LC 75-12955. ISBN 0-208-01372-5.

According to the editor, "this collection of papers is an attempt to bring together in convenient form the diverse views and experiences of several groups and professions with an interest in the role of the library in society." The collection consists of articles on "Public Library and Community Development" (G. Finnegan), "Libraries and Literacy in Great Britain" (M. Redfern), "Library Services to Indian and Pakistani Immigrants in Great Britain" (S. V. Croker), "The United States: An Historical Critique" (J. C. Colson), "Two Prison Libraries in Sweden" (L. Enge), and other articles pertaining to the library services for so-called "disadvantaged groups." The editor does not provide the reader with a clear definition of the term "disadvantaged," which constitutes the central theme in this volume. For the purpose of this publication, he considers the terms "disadvantaged" and "deprived" as synonyms, and states that "they will both be taken as indications of the existence of want or of needs waiting to be served" (p. 10). This reviewer agrees with Joshua Smith, who introduced the concept of "special groups" (*Library and Information Service for Special Groups*, Science Associates/International, 1974; pp. v-vii), in regard to library services to immigrants, ethnic and minority communities, prisoners, and other special groups. This term is more flexible and comprehensive. Taking into consideration the present library "outreach" programs aimed at special groups in the United States and other countries, this publication is a valuable addition to the professional library literature. [R: LJ, 15 Apr 76, p. 988; LR, Autumn 75, p. 130]

Lubomyr R. Wynar

ETHNIC MINORITIES

1688. Clough, Eric, and Jacqueline Quarmby. **A Public Library Service for Ethnic Minorities in Great Britain.** Westport, Conn., Greenwood Press, 1978. 369p. bibliog. index. $35.00. LC 78-13622. ISBN 0-313-21201-5.

Library services for ethnic minorities is a significant worldwide library problem. This volume contains the results of a major research project on the use of six London borough public libraries by ethnic minority patrons, the joint effort of the Library Association and the Polytechnic of the North London School of Librarianship.

The first 100 pages of the book are devoted to in-depth analysis of the magnitude of the problem (i.e., how many persons are in the various ethnic groups, what groups are represented, the unique problems of the various groups, etc.). The next 130 pages describe the field work, with special emphasis on patron use of the library. Nonuser needs and views are almost completely ignored; however, as with almost any research project, one always wishes that more had been done. Use of nonpublic library resources is considered, but only regarding the use by minority groups of government agency libraries or information services. Nothing is mentioned about the type of information the groups secured through commercial sources, such as bookstores, newsstands, or newspapers.

In the final 100 pages of text, the authors draw their conclusions and make projections about the future. Three appendices conclude the volume: the first, on bookstores, emphasizes ethnic materials; the second, ethnic newspapers and periodicals; and the third is a select bibliography. The usefulness of the book is enhanced by an excellent index. This is a good source of ideas for conducting ethnic services surveys. [R: LJ, 15 Apr 79, p. 898]   G. Edward Evans

1689. Haro, Robert P. **Developing Library and Information Services for Americans of Hispanic Origin.** Metuchen, N.J., Scarecrow, 1981. 286p. bibliog. index. $19.00. LC 80-29168. ISBN 0-8108-1394-7.

The book is especially well documented, with data based on the author's own research. The approach is both theoretical and practical: important issues as well as concrete library experiences are discussed. It is important to remember that the discussion is colored by the author's Chicano perspective, and permeated by the ideological framework of the movement. In addition, the time lag between the 1981 publication date and surveys/studies (from the mid- and early seventies) affects the validity of statements made and conclusions drawn which are based on this research (for example, Mexican-American and Chicano attitudes toward libraries, pp. 93-94). Changes during the past few years have made a difference in staffing patterns, collection development, and provision of library services vis-à-vis Hispanics in this country. This time lag is a major weakness of the book.

Another weakness is the omission of a description about the activities of Reforma, a national organization (with local chapters) of Hispanic librarians and others interested in improving library services to the Spanish-speaking. *Amoxcalli*, the newsletter published by the active El Paso chapter, is an important communication link with much useful information, news, etc. The resolutions adopted by Reforma, "El Plan de Reforma," at the 1979 ALA Conference should be mentioned. Another omission is the status and activities of Proyecto Leer, located since 1979 at the School of Library Science, Texas Woman's University in Denton, Texas. The institutes and workshops on library services and materials for the Spanish-speaking organized by Proyecto Leer, as well as its expanded role in library education, testing, evaluation, and research, are important. Mention of the resources and publications of the Mexican American Library Program at the University of Texas at Austin is also missing, as is the work of an important Chicano librarian in Austin, Marta Cotera. The discussion of the 1979 White House Conference on Library and Information Services (p. 235) omits the fact that Hispanic delegates organized and formed a Hispanic caucus, bringing forth a resolution (calling for a Hispanic office within the proposed National Library Agency) which, although eventually failing for lack of support, did indicate a concern on the part of conference participants for the needs of the Hispanic population in the United States.

In spite of these weaknesses, the book is useful and helpful to those interested in learning about library and information services for and about Hispanics in the United States. It represents an important and needed step toward documenting the experience that ethnic and minority groups have had and are having with libraries and information services, so that recognized problems and difficulties can be overcome, and the quality of that experience be improved. [R: LJ, 15 Sept 81, p. 1705]

Susan J. Freiband

1690. Josey, E. J., ed. **What Black Librarians Are Saying.** Metuchen, N.J., Scarecrow, 1972. 324p. $15.00. LC 72-5372. ISBN 0-8108-0530-8.

Ably edited by E. J. Josey, this anthology presents 27 essays by black librarians on several subjects. Of special interest are the sections "Black Communities and Informational Needs" and "Toward Better Public Library Service for Black People." In his introduction, E. J. Josey raises a critical question by paraphrasing Albert Camus, "Is it possible for black people to love their country and still love justice?" He concludes that each of the essayists would respond, "Yes, I love my country, but not the injustice that I have had to suffer." [R: BL, 15 May 73, p. 872; C&RL, July 73, p. 315]

1691. Josey, E. J., and Marva L. DeLoach, eds. **Ethnic Collections in Libraries.** New York, Neal-Schuman, 1983. 361p. index. $32.95. LC 82-14361. ISBN 0-918212-63-4.

An increased interest in ethnicity and the revival of interest in ethnic roots have resulted in the establishment of a number of special ethnic heritage collections in U.S. public and academic libraries. *Ethnic Collections in Libraries* consists of 18 articles devoted to three major themes: (1) "Ethnic Collections: Challenges for Libraries"; (2) "Major Collections on Ethnic Minorities"; and (3) "Archives, Programming, Federal Policy and Linkages." Various authors stress the importance of a well-balanced ethnic collection in the context of library services to ethnic communities. Wendell Wray presents a major article, "Criteria for the Evaluation of Ethnic Materials," that provides very helpful guidelines for librarians and ethnic specialists engaged in building ethnic collections. The section on major collections on ethnic minorities is limited to four ethnic groups: native Americans, black Americans, Asian Americans, and Hispanic Americans. Alma Jordan's chapter "Library Resources on Caribbean Peoples" and Miles Jackson's "Library Resources on Pacific Island Peoples" add new and valuable information on collections pertaining to Caribbean and Pacific islanders—topics that are to a major degree neglected in library professional literature. The development of ethnic archival collections is skillfully discussed by Stanton F. Biddle and Verdia Jenkins. All other articles are highly informative and contribute to a better understanding of ethnic resources and library responsibilities to ethnic communities in the United States. This reviewer regrets only that the editors of this useful publication limited its scope to only four ethnic groups, excluding such major ethnic groups in the United States as Italians, Poles, Germans, French, and many other ethnic communities; that there is no separate chapter on the role of the ethnic press vis-à-vis library services to ethnic communities on building ethnic collections; and also that there is no article on courses in graduate library schools pertaining to ethnicity and librarianship, especially acquisition of ethnic resources and other related library services.

In general, the editors and authors of this interesting and valuable publication should be congratulated for their contributions. [R: JAL, Nov 83, p. 293; JAL, Sept 83, p. 249; LJ, July 83, p. 1345; WLB, Oct 83, p. 142]

Lubomyr R. Wynar

1692.   Library and Information Services for Special Groups. Joshua I. Smith, advisory ed. Published in cooperation with the American Society for Information Science. New York, Science Associates/International, 1974. 337p. o.p. LC 72-93999. ISBN 0-8737-003-X.

Published in cooperation with the ERIC Clearinghouse on Library and Information Sciences, this volume consists of six articles covering library services to American Indians, to Mexican Americans, in Appalachia, to blacks, and in correctional institutions. According to Joshua Smith, who wrote the introduction to this collection, "the purpose of this book is to provide a look at what has been done to attempt to meet the needs of each of these groups in the area of libraries and information services, and to evaluate these efforts in terms of effectiveness and, more specifically, in terms of these needs as perceived by the groups themselves" (p. v). There are notable discrepancies in the execution of individual articles. The article with the best documentation is probably the one by Casper Leroy Jordan, "Black Academic Libraries—State of Affairs and Selected Annotated Bibliography of Black Academe and Its Libraries." [R: LQ, Oct 75, p. 442; SL, Aug 76, p. 406]

1693.   Peterson, Anita R. Library Service to the Spanish Speaking. Inglewood, Calif., Inglewood Public Library, 1977. 50p. illus. o.p. LC 77-22847. ISBN 0-913578-16-9.

Library Service to the Spanish Speaking is an in-house manual written for the purpose of formalizing policies and programs as well as defining future goals of the Spanish Service at the Inglewood (California) Public Library. The manual describes the objectives, goals, and activities of the Spanish Service; its organization; its resources and programs; the means used to evaluate their effectiveness; and plans and projects for the future. It also includes samples of information in Spanish on the library and its use, its services, and its cultural events and recreational programs for Spanish-speaking patrons. It is regrettable, though, that the Spanish used in the samples is not idiomatic.

The manual is basically a procedural one: there is no elaborate exposition of policies, and the objectives of the Spanish Service are stated in broad, general terms. However, specific activities employed to achieve broadly defined goals are enumerated in detail. Through description of specific activities and their function, the reader gains a good understanding of the place of the spanish Service in the overall organization of library services, of its interdependence with other functions and programs, and of the interrelationship of the Spanish Service personnel with the rest of the staff. Written in simple, direct language, logically organized and effectively arranged, the manual well achieves the purpose of describing in a formally structured manner what the Spanish Service is and how it functions. It therefore can serve a variety of needs of librarians, not only at the Inglewood Public Library, but elsewhere too. The manual could be used as a model for planning a bilingual/bicultural program, as a checklist for evaluating an ongoing service or some of its aspects, as instructional material for library students interested in special services, and even as instructional material for training staff.

Lola Januskis

1694.   Report of the Task Force on Library and Information Services to Cultural Minorities. Washington, D.C., National Commission on Libraries and Information Science; distr., Washington, D.C., GPO, 1983. 106p. bibliog. price not reported.

The report prepared by the Task Force on Library and Information Services to Cultural Minorities is a very valuable one that belongs at the fingertips of every U.S. librarian. It is a useful source of information on minorities, attuned to the needs of librarians and information services professionals.

The report is divided into five major sections, with an appendix section that contains miscellaneous data, tables, added reports, and a list of the people on the Cultural Minorities Task Force. The executive summary is very readable and an important distillation of key issues included in the report. The major divisions of the report focus on library and information needs, library personnel, services and programs, materials and resources, and financing library programs for cultural minorities. The report contains provocative information about a major demographic change that is under way and that will eventually influence every U.S. library system. It could be used as an awareness document and as an entry level point to a topic of national importance.

Some areas of the report will be dated quickly (e.g., population counts and projects). Also, a few important recommendations are not made plainly, such as the need to reallocate funds from conventional services to those actually needed by the increasing minority clientele. Aside from these minor criticisms, the report remains a valuable resource.

Roberto P. Haro

OLDER ADULTS

1695. Jeffries, Stephen R. **A Model for Service to the Elderly by the Small/Medium Sized Public Library.** Denton, Tex., North Texas State University, Center for Studies in Aging, 1979. 79p. bibliog. o.p.

This report focuses on one of the fastest growing segments of the population, and for this reason alone merits some attention. But in addition, it summarizes a considerable body of library literature (through 1976 but including a few 1977 citations) on the topic. The literature survey is very well written and is even eloquent in places. From this review of both library and nonlibrary literature, the author develops a model for public library services to the elderly. The title of the report specifies only "the small/medium sized public library," but the report cites several examples of services produced by large libraries; the model appears to be applicable to public libraries of any size. The report includes an example of a needs assessment questionnaire, which is not very useful, and a listing of titles (books, periodicals, and newsletters) that are said to comprise a "core collection" of literature on the aging. The list appears to be fairly selective, but there is no indication as to the criteria used in selecting titles.

The chief accomplishments of this report are that it pulls together a widely scattered literature, extracts and describes some "tried and true" library programs, and offers some fairly helpful guidelines for establishing programs for the elderly. It is much less a source of innovative ideas than it is a summary of past programs that were relatively successful.

Thomas W. Shaughnessy

1696. Kramer, Mollie W. **A Selected Bibliography on the Aging, and the Role of the Library in Serving Them.** Urbana-Champaign, Ill., Graduate School of Library Science, University of Illinois, 1973. 39p. (Occasional Papers, No. 107). o.p.

This annotated bibliography is primarily limited to more recent works. Articles from newspapers are excluded, with the exception of a very few from *The New York Times, The New York Post,* and the news bulletin of the American Association of Retired People. As the reader may recall, in 1960 ALA published a monograph, *Library Service to an Aging Population,* where one may find older citations on this subject.

1697. Turock, Betty J. **Serving the Older Adult: A Guide to Library Programs and Information Sources.** New York, R. R. Bowker, 1982. 294p. bibliog. index. (Serving Special Populations Series). $29.95. LC 82-20772. ISBN 0-8352-1487-7.

Serving the Older Adult will be welcomed not only by librarians but by many professionals and paraprofessionals in the field of gerontology since it covers a wide range of topics, including background of the field, current theories of aging, and planning of services. The work is divided into four parts: "A Framework for Service," "Program Planning and Management," "Service Programs and Delivery Systems," and "Information Sources." Especially for those new to the field, the first part provides an excellent summary of the nature of the older population, the legislation upon which most of the services are based, and the relationship of the theories regarding aging to effective service. Although the second part contains much that is found in general management theory, there are specific applications for librarians planning programs. One of the most important of these is the concept of citizen participation (i.e., involving older persons in every level of decision making and planning for programs relating to them)—a concept some librarians have seemed not to understand in implementing programs for special groups in the past. Many different types of programs are included in the third part. Over one-third of the volume is devoted to the fourth part, on information sources. These include not only materials for older adults but books, organizations, and databases in the field of gerontology. A lengthy bibliography, based on those at the ends of the chapters, and an index add considerably to the value of the book. Although there is some overlapping with Prisca Bagnell's *Gerontology & Geriatric Collections* (see *ARBA* 84, entry 265), some material is not duplicated—integrating information technology in gerontology, for example—so the two together could be used as the basis for both public and academic or special library work in gerontology. Such works become out of date rather quickly, but Turock's should prove to be a valuable handbook for some time to come. [R: BL, 15 Oct 83, p. 327; LJ, 15 May 83, p. 984; RQ, Fall 83, pp. 118-19]

Lucille Whalen

PRISONERS

1698. Association of Specialized and Cooperative Library Agencies. Library Service to Prisoners Section. **Survey of Library Service in Local Correctional Facilities.** Chicago, American Library Association, 1980. 279p. o.p. ISBN 0-8389-6421-4.

The survey is an attempt to document, on a national scale, the existence, quantity, and quality of library service provided to inmates (both adult and juvenile) housed in city and county jails, detention centers, work farms, halfway houses, diagnostic treatment centers, or other local correctional institutions within their public libraries' jurisdictions. The survey includes all 50 states and the District of Columbia. Each state report includes a narrative summary providing a general overview of the types of materials and services provided, funding, problem areas, how services began, and hopes for the future; a directory giving names and addresses of libraries serving in any capacity, whether the service is past, present, or future, plus a notation of the type and size of facility served; and a chart giving details of services, staffing, and materials provided by those libraries with extensive or varied programs. A "Guide to the Use of the Survey Report" is provided along with "Abbreviations Used in Directories and Charts."

Donald D. Foos

1699. Englebarts, Rudolf. **Books in Stir: A Bibliographic Essay about Prison Libraries and about Books Written by Prisoners and Prison Employees.** Metuchen, N.J., Scarecrow, 1972. 168p. index. o.p. LC 70-180625. ISBN 0-8108-0450-6.

This work has two main parts. The first offers a survey of prison libraries in the United States, providing a well-balanced account of this subject, while the second annotates some 84 books written by prisoners or prison employees. Again, it is well done, although, as the author points out in his preface, the list is not complete. We think that this book, with its timely topic, will be of interest to all librarians. [R: AL, Sept 72, p. 923; LJ, 1 Apr 72, p. 1249]

Bohdan S. Wynar

1700. Gulker, Virgil. **Books Behind Bars.** Metuchen, N.J., Scarecrow, 1973. 120p. index. o.p. LC 73-305. ISBN 0-8108-0587-1.

This recounts an attempt to discover the reading interests and needs of prison inmates at the federal correctional institution at Milan, Michigan, and the subsequent effort to provide books that respond to their intellectual, emotional, and spiritual needs. A bibliography of about 650 titles the author considers essential makes this book of reference interest, but only because of the virtual nonexistence of material on the subject. Something is better than nothing.

Timothy W. Sineath

1701. Rubin, Rhea Joyce. **U.S. Prison Library Services and Their Theoretical Basis.** Urbana-Champaign, Ill., Graduate School of Library Science, University of Illinois, 1973. 21p. (Occasional Papers, No. 110). o.p.

A brief report on the development of prison library services, beginning with the first such library in Massachusetts in 1676. The author traces the changing philosophy of prison library service, itself reflecting the change in general penal philosophy from punishment to rehabilitation; he begins with collections consisting mainly of religious tracts and proceeds to the modern movement for well-stocked collections designed to provide both reading challenge and an educational opportunity. In general, the author finds the nationwide situation to be depressing: a lack of carefully selected library materials; rules and regulations that limit use of libraries by inmates; censorship of the types of materials made available; a very deficient professional staffing picture. The author concludes this report with a brief section on the value of bibliotherapy, pointing out that studies "demonstrate that bibliotherapy is one means to a truly rehabilitative phase of correctional library theory."

Jerry E. Stephens

1702. Werner, O. James. **Manual for Prison Law Libraries.** South Hackensack, N.J., published for the American Association of Law Libraries by Fred B. Rothman, 1976. 120p. illus. index. (American Association of Law Libraries Publications Series, No. 12). $12.50. LC 75-37331. ISBN 0-8377-0110-4.

A small manual packed with useful information written primarily for prison law library personnel who have no training in law or library science, or for personnel who have library science training but no legal training.

The idea for this manual grew out of the author's work on the American Association of

Law Libraries' Committee on Law Library Service to Prisoners, in response to suggestions from prisoners and others working in prison law libraries.

The needs and problems of prison law libraries are many. Werner explains that they have a long way to go, and he suggests that any law library worker who wants to do a proficient job should read one or more of the recommended texts after reading his manual.

Seven chapters cover the basics: the prison law library and its staff, library quarters and equipment, law books and their use, acquisitions and records, cataloging and shelving books, lending and borrowing books, and where to get more help (which gives information on law library consultants, prisoner aid organizations, *Law Library Journal*, funds for libraries, and books on prisoners' rights). Appendices list books recommended, legal publishers and dealers, national library supply companies, and the *Gilmore v. Lynch* case.

Notes and an index are included.

An excellent, simple manual designed to help prison library workers get started. [R: LQ, Oct 77, p. 499] Kathleen J. Voigt

READING

1703. Jennison, Peter S., and Robert N. Sheridan, eds. **The Future of General Adult Books and Readings in America (with an Introduction by Daniel Bell).** Chicago, American Library Association, 1970. 160p. $8.75. LC 79-122508. ISBN 0-8389-3105-7. (Available from Books on Demand, $44.00pa., ISBN 0-317-26829-4).

Papers and summarized discussions of the 1969 invitational conference sponsored, with funding by J. Morris-Jones World Book Encyclopedia-ALA Goals Award, by ALA's Adult Services Division and attended by some 85 authors, editors, critics, librarians, media specialists, and publishers. Background papers are thought provoking, with discussions presenting a generally optimistic outlook for the future of the book and predicting an increase of both quality and quantity of reading in America. Although expected differences of opinion are expressed, the volume is both interesting and informative and should be required reading by adult services librarians. [R: BL, 1 July 71, p. 879; LJ, July 71, p. 2281] Charles D. Patterson

1704. Lyman, Helen Huguenor. **Reading and the Adult New Reader.** Chicago, American Library Association, 1976. 259p. bibliog. index. o.p. LC 76-44431. ISBN 0-8389-0228-6.

"Adult new reader" in this title is somewhat of a misnomer, since the author includes in the term anyone "progressing from beginning literacy to an increasingly mature use of print." That seems to include everybody. *Reading and the Adult New Reader* is intended to stimulate and guide people involved with adult reading material, its evaluation, its use, and its creation. The author states that the book is founded on an earlier report of a study extending from 1967 through 1974, *Library Materials in Service to the Adult New Reader*, also published (perhaps prematurely?) by the American Library Association in 1973. Emphasis is on ethnic minorities, who are referred to as "disadvantaged adults" rather than, less abrasively, as "special groups" or "the underserved."

There are, it is claimed, various levels of literacy: "coping skills," "survival literacy," and "functional literacy." And literacy has now to be extended to all the nonbook media. The librarian has a responsibility for corrective action. That being so, the subject deserves a more attractive treatment in terms of an accurate title designation and some emphasis on what can be done about the problem of illiteracy. Correction takes a dynamic vitality, and this book lacks appeal both in its design and in its contents. [R: JAL, July 77, p. 172; LJ, 15 Oct 77, p. 2143] Doris H. Banks

1705. Martin, Lowell A. **Adults and the Pratt Library: A Question of the Quality of Life.** Baltimore, Md., Enoch Pratt Free Library, 1974. 85p. charts. (Deiches Fund Studies of Public Library Service, No. 4). o.p.

This study, the fourth and last in a series on the Enoch Pratt Free Library System, is concerned with the impact of the library on the general adult reader. Through information derived from questionnaires sent to a cross section of Baltimore's urban population over a period of years, Martin attempts to pinpoint problems and gaps in service at the Pratt Library. The survey first determines what part of the population reads and the nature of what they read. It next assesses the importance of the library to patrons and the group patterns of adult reader use. Finally, through in-library interviews, the study attempts to describe individual patterns of use. The results suggest "a planned shift from the supply function to an information and professional advisory function in service to nonspecialized adults." While this study and its companion reports on student use, space allocations, and service to the disadvantaged represent the self-examination of a single library system, the conclusions could very well be relevant to other urban systems.

Nancy P. Schneider

YOUNG ADULTS

General Works

1706. Bodart, Joni. **Booktalk!: Booktalking and School Visiting for Young Adult Audiences.** New York, H. W. Wilson, 1980. 249p. bibliog. index. $12.00. LC 80-16461. ISBN 0-8242-0650-9.

In *Booktalk!* Joni Bodart describes how she and other librarians visit young adults in junior and senior high school classrooms and libraries of Alameda County, California to present booktalks. A booktalk is "sharing your enjoyment of a book with other people and convincing them that they would enjoy it too." It "resembles an unfinished murder mystery—it doesn't say 'who dunnit,' but it makes you want to find out." The first 85 pages are divided into nine chapters that cover topics such as the rationale for talks, their writing, performance in schools, preparation, "hassles," and how to teach booktalk techniques through workshops. Included are samples of a class visit information card, a teacher's evaluation form, and a class visit summary sheet. Directed to "the novice," this work is packed with practical advice which attempts "to cover all the details." As a result, the reader is almost overwhelmed by its chatty and discursive style. Its breezy comments lead the author herself to warn that "maybe you can't be as flip as I am and get away with it." Had the writer's energy and ideas been systematically edited and the resulting structure clarified by judicious use of headings and variation in typography, a busy librarian could more easily refer to this work without the necessity of reading every word.

Having encouraged readers to establish their own repertoire of talks and not to rely on those prepared by others, Bodart includes 134 talks of five to seven minutes duration. Arranged alphabetically by title, the talks, though signed by the various authors, do not indicate their affiliations. Titles are well chosen for their interest to young adults, and sometimes more than one talk allows for varied approaches to the same title. It is not always clear whether the stories described are about real or fictional characters.

Following the talks, 18 bibliographies are presented in categories such as "Junior High School—General," "Science Fiction and Fantasy," and "Women's Studies." Grade levels are suggested, and citations include author, title, publisher, and date of publication, with full addresses of publishers separately listed. For some reason, a list of books considered easy for talks has only title and surname of the author. Because the bibliographies fail to indicate which of the titles are represented by talks, much time is wasted paging between talks and bibliographies. Furthermore, because there are no annotations, it is difficult for an unfamiliar reader to foresee the use of all titles. An index gives access by author and title to the booktalks and to the preceding discussion.

Bodart mentions "You Can Do It," an excellent article by Mary Kay Chelton in *School Library Journal* (April 1976, pp. 39-42) and *The Fair Garden and the Swarm of Beasts* (1974) by Margaret Edwards. For summaries of books she suggests *Book Bait* (3rd ed., 1979) by Elinor Walker, and ALA's *Doors to More Mature Reading* (1964). Perhaps these and other titles, such as *Juniorplots* (1967), *More Juniorplots* (1977), *Introducing Books* (1970), and *Introducing More Books* (1978), will already be available to librarians so that they can budget the $12.00 for young adult books and follow the author's advice by creating their own booktalks. [R: BL, 15 Oct 80, p. 314; SLJ, Dec 80, p. 34]

Valmai Fenster

1707. Edwards, Margaret A. **The Fair Garden and the Swarm of Beasts: The Library and the Young Adult.** rev. and expanded ed. New York, Hawthorn Books, 1974. 194p. index. o.p. LC 74-4166.

The literature about young adult librarianship is sparse, but Margaret Edwards's autobiographical book would stand as an inspiring work even in a flood of publications. Many parts of the book were originally published as articles from 1944 to 1967. The revised edition includes a tribute to Joseph L. Wheeler, which was presented at the American Library History Round Table in 1971. The author describes her experiences at Enoch Pratt library where, after establishing one of the first young adult departments in the country, she continually sought innovative ways to communicate with the young people of Baltimore. There is an appendix of booklists and discussion ideas. The memoirs reflect a distinguished record of achievement, ingenuity, and sensitivity to the needs of a community. It is remarkable, and somewhat sad, that so many of the controversial issues of young adult librarianship identified by Edwards are still unsolved. [R: BL, Nov 74, p. 283; SLJ, Jan 75, p. 32]   Christine Gehrt Wynar

1708. LiBretto, Ellen V., ed. **New Directions for Young Adult Services.** New York, R. R. Bowker, 1983. 225p. index. $29.95. LC 83-11752. ISBN 0-8352-1684-5.

Intended for library professionals concerned with public library programs for teenagers (e.g., young adult librarians, consultants, media specialists, library administrators, library school professionals, and library school students), this work offers 17 previously unpublished essays on materials, services, and management concerns unique to the young adult area.

It is divided into four sections. "New Directions" focuses on nonprint media, microcomputers, services, participation, and merchandising; "Young Adult Literature" includes literary analysis, censorship issues, and booktalking; "Information and Referral Services and Networking" covers resource sharing and coordination with other community services; and "Professional Development" centers on library education, professional organizations, and state policies and standards. The American Library Association Young Adult Services Division publications on youth participation in decision making and competencies for young adult librarians are included as appendices. An index provides quick reference to topics, book titles, authors, and organizations.

Although it does not break any really new ground, as promised by the title (the use of nonprint materials and youth participation, for example, are both continuing trends), the book fills a gap by bringing together practitioner-oriented information on young adult service. The authors—librarians, educators, and consultants—provide articles that might appear in popular professional journals (e.g., *Library Journal*). Books related to this one by their focuses on different aspects of the field are Philip D. Baker's *School and Public Library Media Programs for Children and Young Adults* (Gaylord, 1977; see *ARBA* 78, entry 178), which describes 55 model programs, and works on young adult literature, e.g., Kenneth L. Donelson's *Literature for Today's Young Adults* (Scott, Foresman, 1980; see *ARBA* 82, entry 1284).   Michael B. Eisenberg

1709. Shapiro, Lillian L. **Serving Youth: Communication and Commitment in the High School Library.** New York, R. R. Bowker,

1975. 268p. illus. index. o.p. LC 75-4712. ISBN 0-8352-0763-3.

Lillian Shapiro's *Serving Youth* represents a side of school librarianship that is widely acknowledged by the profession but that seldom appears in textbooks and is rarely expressed with the insight and style she offers. The human aspect of school librarianship is the focus of her book, emphasizing that the students and learning are paramount. The purpose is well stated by the author: "to describe the recent psychological and sociological findings which affect the library setting in the high school today; the kind of personnel who can best perform in this setting; the other influences, educational and human, which impinge on the library's relationship with its users; the standards which have been suggested as necessary or desirable; and the realities as evident in actual high school library programs existing in various schools" (pp. xiii-xiv). Organization and administration of libraries and the daily routines that maintain smoothly functioning libraries are wisely omitted from the book, since these topics have already been treated in more traditional textbooks and in a score of handbooks. The opening chapter is a comprehensive survey and analysis of the educational and sociological literature and the cultural milieu that nurtured the present generation of young people. This "sets the scene" for understanding the numerous pressures on schools and on school libraries to become more responsive to the needs of all students. The other six chapters cover personnel, programs, staff and school relationships, communicating with the community, standards and certification, and futurism. Appendices contain selected guides to materials and reprints of three policy statements. An author/title/subject index is appended.

The book is an important statement on high school librarians' responsibilities to their communities and on the qualities and characteristics most essential to school library candidates. It is unique in that the author successfully describes and interprets the complexities of communicating with young people in the high school library setting. Highly recommended for academic collections and high school libraries and for supplementary reading in courses for prospective high school librarians. [R: LQ, July 76, p. 332]

Christine Gehrt Wynar

Reference Works

1710.   **Books for You: A Booklist for Senior High Students.** new ed. Prepared by Kenneth L. Donelson and the Committee on the Senior High School Booklist of the National Council of Teachers of English. Urbana, Ill., National Council of Teachers of English, 1976. 482p. index. $2.95pa. LC 76-41688. ISBN 0-8141-0362-6.

The sixth edition of NCTE's booklist for senior high school readers, *Books for You*, aims to encourage reading for pleasure and to assist in finding enjoyable and pertinent books for school assignments. The editor stresses that the selections were made solely on the basis of pleasurable reading and the interests of students. The intention was not to prepare a list of classics or even best books. The 2,700 briefly annotated titles are grouped under 43 broad categories developed by the Booklist Committee as a "natural lure toward wider reading." Headings include "Mystery," "Adventure," "Love," "Problems and Young People," "Problems of Modern Humanity," "Reflections," "Careers," "I Am Woman," "American Indian Experiences," "Politics," "Popular Culture," and others. Fiction and nonfiction, appropriately marked, are arranged together in the lists. Titles published in the 1970s predominate, but there is an abundance of 1960s titles. A limited number of selections from the 1950s or earlier are in evidence; a few old standard titles are included, such as *The Red Badge of Courage, Dr. Jekyll and Mr. Hyde, Anna Karenina*. Books on specific topics are sometimes difficult to locate. The broad categories are not subdivided, and there is no subject index. Bernstein and Woodward's *All the President's Men*, for example, is not listed under "Politics, the Law, and Humanity" but is found in the section "U.S. since the Civil War." The criterion for selecting books ("pleasurable reading") leaves plenty of room for argument about what should or should not be included. In essence, the booklist represents the personal and professional judgments of the NCTE Committee and editorial chair. The list suggests a large number of selected recent titles, many available in paperback, and can be a useful antidote to the "What can I read that is good" syndrome. Recommended for high school and public libraries and for education collections. A seventh edition was published in 1982. [R: SLMQ, Summer 77, p. 297]

Christine Gehrt Wynar

1711.   Gillespie, John T. **Paperback Books for Young People: An Annotated Guide to Publish-** ers and Distributors. 2nd ed. Chicago, American Library Association, 1977. 223p. index. $12.00pa. LC 77-21627. ISBN 0-8389-0248-0.

The growing importance of juvenile paperbacks and the increase in series led John T. Gillespie to revise his 1972 edition (see *ARBA* 73, entry 184). Part 1, an alphabetical directory, lists twice as many publishers as in 1972, with over 200 U.S. houses and their series and a separate listing of 30 from Canada. Only publishers with a substantial listing of titles valuable for children or young adults are included. Each entry lists types of books published, general series, series for young people, special services such as catalogs or sales representation, prices, and ordering information. Cross-references lead from series names to their listing beneath publisher. Part 2 lists U.S. and Canadian distributors under city by state. Details include name and address of distributor, whether orders from school libraries are filled, number of suitable titles in stock, minimum order per out-of-stock title, types of paperback (whether mass market or quality), and promotional aids available. Included are a general note on sources of paperbacks and information on the Educational Paperback Association, founded in 1975. Part 3 is an alphabetical, annotated listing of 15 selection aids for in-print titles. A new feature is the subject index of 32 broad categories (such as "Hobbies" and "Mathematics") under which are listed publishers concentrating on such topics, usually in a separate series. Teachers, reading specialists, and librarians will find this a useful directory to aid in acquisition of quality paperbacks for children and young adults. [R: BL, 15 July 78, p. 1730; WLB, April 78, p. 646]

Valmai Fenster

1712.   **Media and the Young Adult: A Selected Bibliography, 1973-1977.** By the Media and Young Adult Subcommittee, Research Committee, Young Adult Services Division, American Library Association. Edited by W. Bernard Lukenbill and Elaine P. Adams. Chicago, American Library Association, 1981. 328p. index. $12.50pa. LC 81-7977. ISBN 0-8389-3264-9.

Research in several related fields (education, sociology, psychology, etc.) was surveyed to produce the earlier volume of this bibliography of studies concerned with adolescent attitudes, needs, and their use of various media (*Media and the Young Adult: A Selected Bibliography 1950-1972*; see *ARBA* 78, entry 190). The first volume contained 362 entries. The bibliography is limited to studies written in English, with an emphasis on American and Canadian materials. Generally, studies dealing with the problems of drop-outs, delinquents, or the disadvantaged are not included unless they specifically relate to library services.

With close to 600 annotated citations to research on the social, psychological, and developmental needs of youth aged 11-22, this second volume continues (but doesn't cumulate) the earlier volume. Arrangement is by subject, and annotations identify the research study, its purpose, methodology, and conclusions. Studies on such topics as family relations, adolescent personality development, sex role identity, reading interests, and the impact of the media on behavior are included. Citations were selected from the *Current Index to Journals in Education, Dissertation Abstracts International, Psychological Abstracts, Resources in Education, Sociological Abstracts,* and 19 individual journals. There is an author index keyed to entry numbers, but no subject access other than the table of contents keyed to page numbers. Those engaged in young adult services will find this work to be a welcome source.

Ilene F. Rockman

1713. Sarkissian, Adele, ed. **High Interest Books for Teens: A Guide to Book Reviews and Biographical Sources.** 1st ed. Detroit, Gale, 1981. 295p. bibliog. index. $72.00. LC 81-6889. ISBN 0-8103-0599-2.

Designed to aid teachers and librarians, the guide "lists both classic and contemporary books that have been identified as 'high interest/low-readability level' materials for young adults" (p. vii) in recommended reading lists or publishers' catalogs. The main portion of the book is a listing arranged by author with references to the biographical sources, then individual titles (no annotation or imprint information) with references to review sources. Pseudonyms and co-authors are identified and cross-referenced where appropriate. The editor's position that "there are no firm limits to the concept of a 'young adult'; and there is no single, universally-accepted measurement of reading difficulty" (p. viii) may explain the absence of recommended reading/interest levels usually found in tools of this type.

The title index identifies the author under whose name the work is listed. The end pages list the "Key to Book Review Sources" and "Key to Biographical Sources." The latter titles are more fully identified in the introduction. The review sources include standard library science and education journals, as well as titles such as *American Anthropologist, Guardian Weekly, Illustrated London News, Progressive, Punch,*

Yale Review, and *Yachting.* The biographical sources include *Celebrity Register; Foremost Women in Communication; Who's Who in ... Advertising, ... Football, ... Government, ... Public Relations; O'Dwyer's Directory of Public Relations Executives;* and *Yesterday's Authors of Books for Children.* Use of the guide requires familiarity with the authors, knowledge of the titles (information not provided in the guide), and access to the sources, which are more apt to be found in college and university libraries than in junior high, high school, or medium-sized public libraries. Phyllis J. Van Orden

Proceedings and Symposia

1714. Barnes, Melvyn, and Sheila Ray. **Youth Library Work: Exploratory Essays.** 2nd ed., rev. London, Clive Bingley; distr., Hamden, Conn., Linnet Books, 1976. 113p. bibliog. index. o.p. LC 75-32553. ISBN 0-85157-214-6 (Bingley); 0-208-01531-0(Linnet).

Library service to that "comparatively modern phenomenon—the teenager" (the 13 to 17 age group) is the subject of the six "exploratory" essays by two British librarians. The essays examine adolescence, the teenage "drift" away from library use, organization and staffing of youth libraries, cooperation between the library and other youth-oriented agencies, library activities and publications, and a new chapter on library resources (materials). The authors realize that if the teenage drift is allowed to continue indefinitely, then soon the library will have few adult members. Their goal is straightforward and clear: "We must persuade teenagers to read books" (p. 7). American young adult librarians, who will quickly recognize the major problems outlined, have long ago exhausted the ideas suggested for attracting teenagers as library users and moved ahead to more informal and imaginative promotion and programming. The essays touch on several ways to cooperate with teachers and staffs from outside agencies but rarely, if ever, do they suggest that youth librarians make contact with teenagers in order to develop new ideas and attract more readers. The American librarian will find the book useful only as a review of British youth libarianship. Margaret Edwards's *Fair Garden and the Swarm of Beasts* (Hawthorn, 1974) conveys a philosophy of young adult librarianship that is more in tune with American practice and is a better starting point than this volume for anyone interested in exploring youth librarianship.

Christine Gehrt Wynar

1715. Corrigan, John T., ed. and comp. **Today's Youth/Today's Librarian.** Haverford, Pa., Catholic Library Association, 1980. 64p. illus. bibliog. (Studies in Librarianship, No. 3). $5.00pa. ISBN 0-87507-007-8.

This booklet contains six addresses by librarians, editors, and educators delivered at a Catholic Library Association institute in 1979. Two deal with the characteristics of young adults, two are concerned with media and their selection, and two with the school library media center program, especially in the Catholic school. Librarians working with young adults will find the author's enthusiastic dedication both informative and stimulating. [R: JAL, Jan 81, p. 362]   Frances Neel Cheney

1716. Pillon, Nancy Bach. **Reaching Young People through Media.** Littleton, Colo., Libraries Unlimited, 1983. 279p. index. $23.50. LC 83-13543. ISBN 0-87287-369-2.

This book is a collection of 15 original articles on the role of the young adult librarian in our high-technology age, written by prominent young adult specialists. This collection, with its pertinent information on the topics of materials selection, organization, and services, is designed as a handbook for practicing librarians in public libraries or secondary schools or as a text for college courses in adolescent literature. Part 1 consists of eight articles that focus on different aspects of materials selection. Research on the reading interests of young adults is presented, including an analysis of personal determinants such as age, sex, intelligence, and socioeconomic, ethnic, and environmental factors. Materials selection is covered, as well as high interest/low reading level materials. Other chapters deal with literary genres: adolescent novels, science fiction works, and sex education books. Part 2 deals with the successful implementation and promotion of these various materials. The history of programming is presented along with concrete suggestions for selecting, planning, and producing library programs. The adjunct roles of the librarian as an advocate for youth and as an arbiter in the climate of censorship constitute the themes of two additional chapters. Other articles relate to technological advances in the media center, offering suggestions for the implementation of computers, videocassettes, films, and sound recordings. [R: BL, 15 Apr 84, p. 1162]

1717. Rogers, JoAnn V., ed. **Libraries and Young Adults: Media, Services, and Librarianship.** Littleton, Colo., Libraries Unlimited, 1979. 238p. bibliog. index. $18.50. LC 79-15. ISBN 0-87287-195-9.

This collection of 17 original essays is intended as a supplementary reader for courses in young adult literature and librarianship. It is also designed for use by librarians serving young adult clientele. Each of the three sections explores one of the facets of concern to both librarians and others interested in the part that the library plays in the total program of community services for young people. The selections are intended to provide an overview of some issues concerning print and nonprint media, library services, and young adult librarianship.

A short introduction by Rogers precedes each group of essays, among which are: "Roadblocks to YA Crisis Service in the Public Library," by Rosemarie E. Falanga; "Library Cooperation to Serve Youth," by Peggy Sullivan; "Young Adult Library Service: The International Scene," by Jean E. Lowrie; "Education of the Young Adult Librarian," by Susan Steinfirst; and "Research in Young Adult Literature and Services," by W. Bernard Lukenbill. Each essay has its own bibliography. A selected bibliography citing additional basic readings in each of the areas covered by the three parts—"Media," "Service," and "Young Adult Librarianship"—concludes the volume. [R: BL, 1 July 79, p. 1623; SLJ, Oct 79, p. 124]

1718. Varlejs, Jana, ed. **Young Adult Literature in the Seventies: A Selection of Readings.** Metuchen, N.J., Scarecrow, 1978. 452p. bibliog. $16.00. LC 78-6562. ISBN 0-8108-1134-0.

This anthology of approximately 60 short selections reprinted from popular professional periodicals in library science and education includes topics such as young adult reading interests, writing for teens, minorities in young adult literature, and censorship. It is representative of the literature appearing in journals such as the four most frequently used (*English Journal,* the *Arizona English Bulletin, Top-of-the-News,* and *Wilson Library Bulletin*); and it gathers together information and opinions about material for young adults. One problem, of course, is the time lag between the original publication of the young adult titles, reference to the titles in a published article, and the collection of articles in the anthology—most of the young adult titles mentioned were written in the early 1970s. The tone of most of the pieces is that of the after-dinner speech delivered often in the first person at workshops for secondary English teachers. Enjoyable and informative, they perhaps will appeal to the intended audience—the parent and the "professional" (presumably the professional English or reading teacher or librarian serving youth). The academician will miss the meat of solid literary analysis, criticism, or research, however.

The focus is on the junior level. Most authors have a thesis and discuss a number of titles by way of illustration. Some include bibliographies. Represented are some solid thinkers and good writers, such as Lou Willett Stanek; some memorable stylists, such as Lillian Shapiro; and some professional writers who add flavor and authenticity to casual observations, such as Nat Hentoff. There is more than ample representation of the Arizona school spawned by Ken Donelson. The ten categories are well chosen by the editor and some of the introductions (ranging from two paragraphs to two pages) alert the reader to points made by the contributors. Better than Dennis Thomison's *Readings about Adolescent Literature* (Scarecrow, 1970), this is comparable to Richard A. Meade and Robert C. Small's *Literature for Adolescents: Selection and Use* (Merrill, 1973). [R: BL, 15 Nov 78, p. 541]

JoAnn V. Rogers

56 Technical Services

1719. Applebaum, Edmond L., ed. **Reader in Technical Services.** Washington, D.C., NCR/ Microcard Editions, 1973. 266p. (Reader Series in Library and Information Science). o.p. LC 72-87717. ISBN 0-910972-21-4.

A good selection of 29 articles and papers on various aspects of technical services, starting with historical material ("Selections from the Proceedings of the First Conference of the American Library Association"). This reader offers separate sections on acquisitions, bibliographic control, cooperative and centralized processing systems, and "the future" (primarily articles describing MARC, microform bibliography, and the *British National Bibliography*). [R: LJ, 1 Sept 73, p. 2409]

1720. Bennett, Frederick. **Cataloguing in Practice: The Organisation of Book Acquisition in Libraries.** Hamden, Conn., Linnet Books, 1972. 74p. illus. index. o.p. ISBN 0-208-01181-1.

This simplified version of the standard procedures in British libraries provides brief explanations for most technical services areas. The 11 chapters, some of them two or three pages long, cover such topics as book selection and ordering methods, principles of cataloging, card reproduction methods, etc. In addition, there are two chapters dealing with acquisitions in school and special libraries. Because most of our texts for library technicians are much more sophisticated in their treatment of the individual routines, it is rather hard to envision the potential market for this little book. [R: LJ, 1 Feb 73, p. 396] Bohdan S. Wynar

1721. Bernhardt, Frances Simonsen. **Introduction to Library Technical Services.** New York, H. W. Wilson, 1979. 328p. illus. bibliog. index. $20.00. LC 79-12630. ISBN 0-8242-0637-1.

The title of this work is somewhat misleading. The preface states that the book was written more specifically as a textbook for a course in technical services in a two-year library media technology program, and will offer little for the professional librarian. The 18 chapters cover such topics as publishing; book selection; acquisition processes; cataloging (based on *AACR1*; a brief summary of *AACR2* is included in the appendix); maintenance of records; serials; the vertical file; etc. Most librarians are familiar with Bloomberg and Evans's *Introduction to Technical Services for Library Technicians* (third edition, Libraries Unlimited, 1976); in comparing both books, Bernhardt's text breaks no new ground. As a matter of fact, the material is occasionally presented in a rather simplistic form (e.g., the discussions of "Aids to Book Selection" [*Subject Guide to Books in Print* is useful in retrospective book selection] and approval plans). The several chapters on cataloging rules are obsolete, being based on *AACR1*. In addition, the brief summary of *AACR2* is too short to be meaningful. [R: BL, 15 Apr 80, p. 1176; C&RL, May 80, p. 265; LJ, 15 Feb 80, p. 488] Bohdan S. Wynar

1722. Bloomberg, Marty, and G. Edward Evans. **Introduction to Technical Services for Library Technicians.** 4th ed. Littleton, Colo., Libraries Unlimited, 1981. 363p. illus. bibliog. index. (Library Science Text Series). $28.00; $20.00pa. LC 81-798. ISBN 0-87287-228-9; 0-87287-248-3pa.

In addition to their thorough treatment of acquisition work, bibliographic verification, order procedures, and gifts and exchange processes, the authors have completely reworked their extensive treatment of descriptive and subject cataloging to bring it in line with the second edition of the *Anglo-American Cataloguing Rules (AACR2)*. This section is illustrated with numerous examples. The text now also treats computers and library automation and their effect on technical services, as well as the advent of networks, cooperatives, and automated systems. Also new to this edition are the review questions in each chapter, which are designed to reinforce the most significant elements of technical services. In this edition Bloomberg and Evans introduce — and place into context — technical service skills that can be developed through work experience, in-service training, classroom instruction, or a combination of these methods. For reviews of the first (1971), second (1974), and third (1976) editions, see *ARBA* 72 (entry 115); *ARBA* 75 (entry 247); and *ARBA* 77 (entry 269).

1723. Corbin, John B. **A Technical Services Manual for Small Libraries.** Metuchen, N.J., Scarecrow, 1971. 206p. illus. bibliog. index. $15.00. LC 70-156885. SBN 8108-0388-7.

Usually, when the title indicates that a manual is designed for small libraries, the reader expects to find a rather uncomplicated work describing simple but at the same time well-designed procedures pertaining to the organization of technical services. Although this is the author's aim, he does not always succeed. For example, in his discussion on choice of vendors, he makes no new discoveries but enumerates a number of factors to be taken into consideration (such as discounts, the time element, the quality of billing, or even "the courtesy shown the library by the jobber"). What he apparently forgets is the role of "shorts." Some jobbers may provide a better discount, more efficient deliveries, etc., but will not cover even some well-known publishers because of disagreements as to discount schedules. In other words, how well would they "deliver," how many imprint titles can they produce for, say, an ordinary order of 500 books? There are hundreds of articles on this subject, as well as a book by Melcher published by ALA. Corbin's comment that not all titles can be ordered through jobbers is correct. But he then states (p. 45): "When a publisher refuses to sell to a jobber, the librarian has no choice but to order 'direct.' " Well, not many publishers "refuse." This is a rather complex problem, and if the author is not familiar with the book market in all necessary details, it is much better not to mention it. One can find other examples similar to the above. In examining the appended bibliography one is under the impression that sources listed here are rather limited. Why not mention other manuals or even some of the most important articles on this subject? Some comments in the annotations are rather puzzling. Since when is Akers's *Simple Library Cataloging* a companion volume to Mann's work published in 1943? Some entries are simply obsolete, e.g., the listing for Rufsvold's well-known work (p. 194). In short, an unfinished product. [R: LJ, 1 Jan 72, p. 46]

Bohdan S. Wynar

1724. Dougherty, Richard M., and Lawrence E. Leonard. **Management and Costs of Technical Processes: A Bibliographical Review, 1876-1969.** Metuchen, N.J., Scarecrow, 1970. 145p. o.p. LC 72-14738. SBN 8108-0320-8.

An unannotated, 850-entry classified bibliography, with brief historical essay on library cost studies, author index, cross-references, and a few scope notes. Under 55 subject headings, works are listed on technical processing costs — catalog, ordering, preparation, reclassification, serials handling, card reproduction, book catalogs, etc. — cost study methodology, work simplification, system design and analysis, and evaluation of library activities. Each subject is subarranged by historical (1876-1945) and current (1946-1969). Recommended items are marked by a dagger, methodological techniques by an asterisk, and unexamined citations by a zero. Provides adequate coverage of sparsely-treated areas of library science. A list of sources consulted and a general index would have helped. [R: C&RL, Mar 71, p. 148; CLW, Oct 71, p. 107; LRTS, Summer 71, p. 421; RQ, Spring 71, p. 267]

Richard Palmer

1725. Dougherty, Richard M., and Joan M. Maier, eds. **Centralized Processing for Academic Libraries: The Final Report (Phase III, January 1-June 30, 1969) of the Colorado Academic Libraries Book Processing Center: The First Six Months of Operation.** Metuchen, N.J., Scarecrow, 1971. 254p. LC 73-155716. ISBN 0-8108-0381-X.

The final report of an experimental centralized acquisition and cataloging project undertaken by several Colorado academic libraries in 1969. The report is well written and documented with a plethora of technical information in text and tables. Fundamentally management rather than people oriented, it records details of an important experiment in library cooperation. [R: C&RL, Nov 72, p. 490; LJ, 1 Apr 72, p. 1249; RQ, Summer 72, p. 385]

1726. Magrill, Rose Mary, and Constance Rinehart, comps. **Library Technical Services: A Selected, Annotated Bibliography.** Westport, Conn., Greenwood Press, 1977. 238p. index. $29.95. LC 76-27130. ISBN 0-8371-9286-2.

This highly selective bibliography covers seven aspects of technical services: administrative organization, acquisitions, organization of materials, maintenance, circulation, serials, and special materials. Out of the total 1,274 entries (books and periodical articles), over 60 percent were published since 1970. Materials in foreign languages are excluded, as are books and articles that pertain to cataloging and classification (unless they discuss administrative procedures). All entries are briefly annotated, and the arrangement under specific topics is in chronological order, beginning with the oldest imprints. A major weakness of this bibliography is the intentional exclusion of bibliographic aids for such topics as acquisitions, gifts and exchanges, serials, microforms, etc., which are necessary to students of technical services. All in all, this is a satisfactory work, one that will provide a starting point for the uninitiated. [R: C&RL, Sept 77, p. 429; LJ, Aug 77, p. 1586]

1727. Slote, Stanley J. **Weeding Library Collections — II.** 2nd rev. ed. Littleton, Colo., Libraries Unlimited, 1982. 198p. illus. bibliog. index. $23.50. LC 81-20724. ISBN 0-87287-283-1.

In this work, Stanley J. Slote, a recognized authority on weeding library collections, builds upon and expands the material presented in his 1975 publication, *Weeding Library Collections* (see *ARBA* 76, entry 203). Part 1, discussing the broad background of weeding and weeding practice, provides the context for part 2, which is a step-by-step guide to the three preferred methods of weeding — the Book Card Method, the Spine-Marking Method, and the Historical Reconstruction Method. The methods described are applicable to all kinds of materials in all kinds of libraries. Sample forms used for weeding are included in an appendix and can be duplicated for library use. [R: C&RL, Sept 82, pp. 412-14; C&RL, June 82, p. 217; JAL, Sept 82, pp. 232-33; LJ, 1 Oct 82, p. 1831; SLJ, Oct 82, p. 318]

1728. Urquhart, J. A., and N. C. Urquhart. **Relegation and Stock Control in Libraries.** London, Oriel Press; distr., Boston, Routledge and Kegan Paul, 1976. 154p. illus. bibliog. $25.00. ISBN 0-85362-162-4.

The British have a way with words that often makes the mundane seem elegant; never-theless, the process of weeding a library book collection remains the same whether it is called relegation or stock reduction. John and Nancy Urquhart have prepared a succinct report on a three-year weeding project (1973-1975) at Newcastle University. As one would expect, a study at a university library is primarily concerned with academic library weeding problems; however, some sections are relevant to other types of libraries. "Steady state" or "controlled growth" book budgets will help delay the inevitable storage problem, but the factors causing the minimum materials budget also mean no new storage areas, much less new buildings. Thus, at some point in time, weeding will have to take place. Very few librarians find this prospect pleasant, and for more than twenty years there have been attempts to find an easy solution to deciding which "weeds to pull." Unfortunately, the Urquhart report does not have easy answers, any more than did the preceding efforts.

Although it lacks easy answers, this worthwhile report raises one interesting idea — block weeding. Block weeding of monographs, assuming suitable "blocks" (segments of a subject field) can be identified, is suggested as one way of gaining space at significantly lower costs. The Urquharts' calculations indicate that it costs as much as 13 times more to weed one monograph title than to weed one periodical title. But the library that succeeds in finding monographic blocks will be lucky; there is no real discussion of how one would go about identifying such blocks.

Most of the Urquharts' findings, in part based upon statistics from a number of other British academic libraries, generally confirm the findings of previous weeding studies. They do, however, present some evidence suggesting that date due slip data may not be totally reliable for weeding decisions. Since so many prior studies have suggested that these data are the *most reliable*, we can only reserve judgment on the validity of their results in this area.

The last two-thirds of the report is made up of appendices of supporting statistical data, special subreports, and the original funding proposal. The bibliography covers all the major works on weeding up to the date of publication. A necessary addition to any large library science collection; worthwhile reading for anyone interested in the problem of "relegation." [R: LJ, 1 May 77, p. 995]

G. Edward Evans

Author/Title Index

Reference is to entry number.

AACR 2: an introduction ..., 589
AACR 2 and the catalog, 594
AACR 2 decisions and rule interpretations, 2nd ed., 581
AACR 2 goes public, 575
AACR 2 headings, 576
AACR 2 headings: a five-year projection of their impact on catalogs, 584
AACR 2 seminar papers, 591
Aaron, S. L., 260, 289
ABC of BASIC: an introduction to programming for librarians, 501
ABC's of library promotion, 1380
Abell, M. D., 1274
Abridged Dewey decimal classification and relative index, 618
Abstracting and indexing, 1065
Abstracting and indexing career guide, 1067
Abstracting and indexing services in perspective, 1064
Abstracts and abstracting services, 1059
Academic change and the library function, 220
Academic librarianship, 209
Academic libraries by the year 2000, 192
Academic library: essays in honor of Guy R. Lyle, 183
Academic library buildings, 356
Academic library facilities and services for the handicapped, 1663
Academic research and library resources, 733
Access to library collections, 1489
Access to periodical resources, 1403
Accuracy of telephone reference/information services in academic libraries, 1544
Achieving accountability, 1319
Acquisition and provision of foreign books ..., 758

Acquisition of foreign materials for U.S. libraries, 2nd ed., 757
Acquisition of library materials, 752
Acquisitions: where, what, and how, 745
Acquisitions from the Third World, 759
Acronyms & abbreviations in library & information work, 2nd ed., 98
Adamovich, S. G., 455
Adams, S., 813
Administering the school library media center, 1330
Administration of a public affairs library, 1344
Administration of government documents collections, 937
Administration of the college library, 4th ed., 1281
Administration of the small public library, 2nd ed., 1312
Administrative aspects of education for librarianship, 910
Adopting the Library of Congress classification system, 634
Adult learners, learning and public libraries, 1624
Adults and the Pratt library, 1705
Advances in librarianship, 104
Advances in library administration and organization ..., 105
Advances in understanding approval and gathering plans ..., 755
Adventuring with books, 790
Afflerbach, L., 507
African libraries, 816
Age of Jewett, 986
Ahead of its time: the engineering societies library, 1038
Ainsworth Rand Spofford: bookman and librarian, 982

Akers' simple library cataloging, 7th ed., 530
ALA filing rules, 683
ALA glossary of library and information science, 87
ALA survey of librarian salaries, 928
ALA world encyclopedia of library and information services, 81
ALA yearbook, 106
Alexander, A. J., 1306
Alfred William Pollard: a selection of his essays, 999
Allan, A., 704
Allardyce, A., 88
Allen, C. G., 89
Allen, K., 224
Allen, K. W., 1275
Allen, L., 1275
Allen, W. C., 1605
Alley, B., 1224
Allison, A. M., 704
ALMS: a budget based library management system, 1232
Alternative materials in libraries, 776
Alternatives to traditional library services, 1543
Altman, E., 1297-98, 1303
Amadi, A. O., 816
Aman, M. M., 527, 672, 832
Amelia Gayle Gorgas: a biography, 989
American libraries as centers of scholarship, 1551
American library development 1600-1899, 972
American library directory, 111
American library history: a bibliography, 976
American library laws, 5th ed., 95
American library philosophy, 38
American library resources: a bibliographical guide, 138
American library resources: cumulative index, 145
American overseas library technical assistance, 1043
American reference books annual 1984, 61
American Society for Information Science, 62
Analysis of information systems, 2nd ed., 1090
Analysis of meaning, 1105
Analysis of vocabulary control in Library of Congress classification and subject headings, 665
Analytical access: history, resources, needs, 561
Anatomy of censorship, 718
Anderson, A. J., 711
Anderson, B. L., 300
Anderson, D., 573
Anderson, E. L., 336
Anderson, L., 339
Anderson, M. D., 1054
Anderson, P. H., 261
Angione, P. V., 920
Anglo-American cataloging rules: one year later, 582

Anglo-American cataloguing rules, 2nd ed., 577
Anglo-American cataloguing rules: revisions, 2nd ed., 578
Anglo-American cataloguing rules 1967: an introduction, 567
Angoff, A., 1354
Annotated bibliography of automation in libraries and information systems, 486
Annotated bibliography of automation in libraries 1975-78, 485
Annual review of information science and technology, 107
Annual statistics of medical school libraries in the United States and Canada, 4th ed., 312
Anthony, L. J., 280, 488
Apostles of culture: the public library ..., 1017
Apple, N., 1034
Applebaum, E. L., 1719
Applications of minicomputers to library and related problems, 496
Applications of operations research models to libraries, 1348
Applying the new copyright law, 889
Approach to classification, 611
Approval plans and academic libraries, 754
Arab states author headings, 672
Arab world: libraries and librarianship, 811
Architectural strategy for change, 359
Archive-library relations, 378
Archives and manuscript repositories in the USSR, 142
Archives and other special collections ..., 383
Area specialist bibliographer, 1464
Armour, R., 1051
Arnold, D. V., 1085
Art of the librarian: a collection of original papers, 186
Artandi, S., 435
As much to learn as to teach, 187
Ash, L., 155
Ashworth, W., 291
Asian libraries and librarianship, 810
ASLA report on interlibrary cooperation, 1402
Aslib directory, vol. 2, 301
Aspects of library development planning, 837
Assistance to libraries in developing nations ..., 839
Association for Asian Studies, 158
Association of American Library Schools library education statistical report, 1982, 904
Association of American Library Schools 1915-1968, 1044
Atherton, P., 1436. *See also* Cochrane, P. A.
Atkins, T. V., 658
Atkinson, F., 1, 777
Atkinson, R., 1136

Audiovisual librarianship, 393
Audiovisual media and libraries, 415
Aufdendamp, J. A., 1345
Australian and New Zealand library resources, 826
Australian libraries, 3rd ed., 825
Author index to Library of Congress classification, 626
Authority control: the key to tomorrow's catalog, 549
Author-number index to the L. C. classification schedules, vol. 1, 635
Authors and titles: an analytical study ..., 556
Author's guide to journals in library & information science, 77
Author's guide to the copyright law, 891
Automated library circulation systems, 1487
Automated library circulation systems 1979-80, 2nd ed., 1486
Automatic keyword classification for information retrieval, 1075
Automating library acquisitions, 489
Automation in libraries, 2nd ed., 446
AV cataloging and processing simplified, 544
Avram, H. D., 1405

Back to the books, 1136
Background readings in building library collections, 2nd ed., 737
Badough, R. M., 71
Baecker, E. K., 550
Baeckler, V. V. W., 1355-57
Bahr, A. H., 351, 432, 1387, 1442, 1486
Bailey, M. J., 1252, 1346
Baker, A., 1647
Baker, D. P., 1627, 1683
Baker, J. P., 854
Baker, L. R., 824
Baker, R. K., 1161
Bakewell, K. G. B., 528, 534
Balmforth, C. K., 436
Banks, P. N., 870
Banned books, 387 B.C. to 1978 A.D., 4th ed., 719
Bantly, H. A., 1127, 1157
Barber, P., 1381
Barefoot librarian, 823
Barnes, D. L., 1183
Barnes, M., 1714
Barr, K., 181
Barr, L. J., 63
Basic library skills, 1182
Basic reference sources: a self-study manual, 3rd ed., 1525
Basic statistics for librarians, 2nd ed., 1558
Basics of librarianship, 2nd ed., 3
Basics of online searching, 1444

Baskin, B. H., 1658, 1677
Basler, B. K., 313
Basler, R. P., 199
Basler, T. G., 313
Basova, I. M., 1093
Bassam, B., 1041
Batty, C. D., 614-15
Batty, D., 47 ·
Bauer, C. F., 1648
Baumann, C. H., 352
Baumol, W. J., 237
Beacon, R., 281
Beasley, K. E., 1303
Beaubien, A. K., 1126
Beaumont, J., 491
Beazley, R. M., 238
Becker, J., 441, 1419
Beckman, M., 361
Bedford, D. D., 872
Beeler, R. J., 1137
Beenham, R., 3
Bell, I. W., 1640
Bell, M. V., 122
Bellassai, M. C., 1307, 1403
Bender, D. R., 1683
Benefit-cost analysis of alternative library delivery systems, 1242
Bennett, F., 1720
Bennie, F., 1320
Bentinck-Smith, W., 1005
Berelson, B., 241
Berger, P., 66
Berman, S., 520, 662
Bernhardt, F. S., 1721
Bernier, C. L., 1055
Berry, J. N., 174
Bertalan, F. J., 781
Best reference books, 1970-1980, 123
Besterman, T., 64
Bettelheim, J., 311
Better libraries create better cities ..., 249
Between M.L.S. and Ph.D.: a study ..., 922
Beyond my expectation, 992
Bibliographic control, 2nd ed., 503
Bibliographic control of microforms, 1395
Bibliographic control of nonprint media, 405
Bibliographic control of official publications, 946
Bibliographic instruction: a handbook, 1131
Bibliographic instruction in academic libraries, 1154
Bibliographic record and information technology, 467
Bibliographical survey of UDC editions, 642
Bibliography: tiger or fat cat? 504
Bibliography and reading, 188
Bibliography for beginners, 2nd ed., 1172
Bibliography, library science, and reference books, 64

Bibliotherapy in rehabilitation, educational, and mental health settings, 519
Bibliotherapy sourcebook, 517
Bidmead, M., 456
Biebel, S. C., 688
Billings, R. G., 1321
Biographical subject index to the Library of Congress classification ..., 636
Biographical-bibliographical directory of women librarians, 172
Biomedical subject headings, 676
Bird, J., 1314
Birge, L. E., 1623
Biskup, P., 825
Black librarian in America, 177
Blagden, J., 1235
Blazek, R., 1184, 1319
Bliss bibliographic classification, 2nd ed., 612
Blixrud, J. C., 579
Blomquist, L. L., 1498
Bloomberg, M., 616, 1480, 1722
Bloomfield, B. C., 758
Bloomfield, M., 1162
Bloomquist, H., 314
Blunt, A., 337
Boaz, M., 895, 1086, 1218
Bobinski, G. S., 168
Bodart, J., 1706
Bogart, G. L., 124, 126, 128, 131, 134
Boll, J. J., 563-64
Bolté, C. G., 1347
Bomar, C. P., 1322
Bommer, M. R. W., 1203
Bonn, G. S., 12
Book catalogs, 682
Book for a sixpence, 1021
Book indexing, 1054
Book mark 51 & 52: fifth anniversary, 1042
Book numbers: a historical study, 648
Book numbers: history, principles, and application, 649
Book selection: an introduction ..., 3rd ed., 769
Book selection: principles and procedures, 766
Book selection and intellectual freedom, 725
Book selection policies in American libraries, 765
Book theft and library security systems, 1981-82, 351
Bookbinding & conservation by hand, 866
Bookbinding and the conservation of books, 869
Books afloat & ashore, 1039
Books are for use, 1568
Books behind bars, 1700
Books by mail: a handbook for librarians, 94
Books for college libraries: a core collection ..., 2nd ed., 782
Books for junior college libraries, 783

Books for public libraries, 3rd ed., 785
Books for sammies, 975
Books for secondary school libraries, 6th ed., 788
Books for you: a booklist for senior high students, 1710
Books in other languages 1979, 780
Books in our time: essays by Lawrence S. Thompson, 207
Books in stir, 1699
Books, libraries and electronics, 457
Books, libraries, and research, 1174
Bookstein, A., 509, 1108
Booktalk! 1706
Booms, B. H., 1242
Booth, R. E., 1266
Borchardt, D. H., 90
Borko, H., 896, 1055
Borkowski, M. V., 1467
Bosmajian, H., 712
Boss, R. W., 489, 494, 1122, 1388, 1575
Bowers, M. K., 1185
Bowker annual of library & book trade information, 108
Boxes for the protection of rare books, 855
Boyer, C. J., 765
Boyle, D., 386, 1378
Braden, I. A., 225
Bradley, C. J., 338
Bradshaw, C. I., 677, 1163
Bramley, G., 897, 1654
Branch library service, 1308
Branscomb, H., 226
Branscomb, L. C., 1276
Brautigam, P., 1427
Braverman, M., 1012
Brawne, M., 353
Breivik, P. S., 210, 1123, 1143
Brenni, V. J., 508
Brewer, M. L., 1323
Brewster, B. J., 1043
British and Irish library resources, 139
British archives, 140
British information services not available online, 1447
British librarianship and information science, 1966-1970, 851
British librarianship today, 847
British library history: bibliography 1973-1976, 977
Brittain, J. M., 1500
Broadus, R. N., 242, 739
Broderick, D., 740, 1628
Brodie, A. H., 977
Brooks, J., 355
Brooks, J. S., 1481
Brophy, P., 498
Brough, K. J., 1006
Broughton, V., 612

Brown, A. G., 599
Brown, A. L., 1353
Brown, C. D., 1599, 1608
Brown, E. F., 1225, 1247, 1684
Brown, J. W., 387
Brown, L. G., 789
Brown, M. J., 1450
Brown, M. R., 855
Brown, R., 1300
Brown, R. B., 1640
Brown, R. E., 1299
Bruemmer, A., 1220
Brug, S., 738
Bruntjen, S., 980
Bryan, H., 211
Bryant, E. C., 1243
BSO, broad system of ordering, 1070
BSO manual: the development, rationale and use ..., 1593
Buchanan, B., 1066
Buchinski, E. J., 1405
Buckman, T. R., 819, 1223
Budgetary control in academic libraries, 1284
Budgeting techniques for libraries and information centers, 1228
Building a great library: the Coolidge years at Harvard, 1005
Building library collections, 6th ed., 740
Building library collections: policies and practices ..., 770
Bundy, M. L., 243, 1301, 1543
Burgdorf, A. B., 1183
Burge, E. J., 1624
Burke, J. G., 1629
Burkett, J., 840, 1431
Burlingame, D. F., 227, 388
Burton, S., 1199
Burwell, H. P., 112
Bush, C. G., 877
Busha, C. H., 713-15, 1547-48
Butchart, I., 391
Butler, B., 448
Butler, L. A., 272
Butler, P., 1526
Buying new technology, 458
Byerly, G., 1446
Byrd, P., 1164

Cabeceiras, J., 400
Cadwallader, L. H., 1056
CAIN online user's guide, 709
Calderhead, P., 304
Calvert, S. J., 103
Cammack, F. M., 1144
Campbell, A., 1468
Campbell, D. J., 292
Campbell, H. C., 244, 827, 1432

Campbell, M. J., 305
Canadian libraries, 2nd ed., 827
Canadian libraries in their changing environment, 829
Canadian library directory, 308
Canadian selection: books and periodicals ... 1977-1979 supplement, 130
Canadian subject headings, 2nd ed., 673
Cannan, J. P., 557
Cannons' bibliography of library economy, 1876-1920: an author index with citations, 69
Carabelli, A., 836
Card catalog, current issues: readings and selected bibliography, 681
Career profiles and sex discrimination in the library profession, 930
Carey, R. J. P., 1358
Cargill, J. S., 753, 1224
Carl H. Milam and the American Library Association, 1003
Carl H. Milam and the United Nations Library, 1031
Carmel, M., 321
Carothers, D. F., 684
Carpenter, M., 560
Carpenter, R. L., 1556
Carrington, D. K., 429
Carroll, D. E., 437
Carroll, F. L., 284, 1029
Carson, B., 288
Carter, G. A., 380
Casciero, A. J., 389
Case, R. N., 262
Case for Bliss: modern classification practice ..., 613
Case for faculty status for academic librarians, 1276
Case method in teaching library management, 1207
Case studies in library/media management, 1337
Casey, J., 1412
Cassata, M. B., 910, 1359
Cataloging and classification, 529
Cataloging and classification: a workbook, 2nd ed., 536
Cataloging and classification of non-Western materials, 527
Cataloging machine-readable data files, 583
Cataloging nonbook materials, 542
Cataloging of audiovisual materials, 545-46
Cataloging phonorecordings, 430
Cataloging service bulletin index: No. 1-16, 526
Cataloging with copy, 531
Cataloguing, 534
Cataloguing: theory and practice, 4th ed., 540
Cataloguing in practice, 1720

Cataloguing practice, 2nd ed., 539
*Catholic subject headings: a modification of
    the 5th ed.*, 674
CATV and its implications for libraries, 434
Cave, R., 377
Celebrating with books, 1642
Censorship in the eighties, 713
Censorship, libraries, and the law, 712
Censorship litigation and the schools, 716
*Centralised processing for academic
    libraries ...*, 1725
Century of service, 964
*Certification model for professional school
    media personnel*, 925
Challenge for academic libraries, 1152
Champion of a cause: essays and addresses ...,
    203
Chan, L. M., 529, 624, 663
Chandler, G., 831, 841
Chandna, K., 85
Changing environment of libraries, 13
*Changing information concepts and
    technologies*, 459
*Changing role of the special librarian in
    history*, 306
Changing times: changing libraries, 12
Chaplin, A. H., 1457
Chapman, E. A., 1248, 1250
Charles Ammi Cutter: library systematizer,
    981
Chen, C., 315, 1219, 1226, 1236, 1348,
    1426, 1501
Chen, S. P. J., 700
Cheney, F. N., 1516
Chenhall, R. G., 650
Chernik, B. E., 1469
Chernyi, A. I., 1093
Cherry, S. S., 433
Chibnall, B., 403
Chickering, R. B., 884
Childers, T., 1532, 1685
Children in libraries, 717
Children using media, 1631
Children's catalog, 1981, 124
Children's librarianship, 1633
Children's library service: school or public?
    1629
Children's media market place, 2nd ed., 1637
Children's services of public libraries, 1634
Chirgwin, F. J., 1470
Chisholm, M. E., 394, 926
Chismore, W. D., 651
Choice of main and added entries, 3rd ed., 585
Choice of subject headings, 3rd ed., 660
Choosing an automated library system, 475
Chorba, R. W., 1203
Christ, J. M., 212, 657
Christian, R., 1581
Christian, R. W., 1436

Christianson, E., 1349
Church and synagogue libraries, 333
Cibbarelli, P., 1582
*CILA: a new approach to problems in the
    acquisition of Latin American
    library materials*, 760
*Citation indexing: its theory and
    application ...*, 1073
Clack, D. H., 580
Clark, A. S., 1557
Clark, R. L., 378
Clarke, D. A., 759
Clarke, J. M., 1657
Clason, W. E., 82
*Classics and other selected readings in medical
    librarianship*, 318
Classification: for use with LC or Dewey, 600
Classification and indexing in science, 3rd ed.,
    1083
Classification and indexing in the humanities,
    602
*Classification and subject index for cataloguing
    and arranging ...*, 617
Classification in the 1970's, 603
Classification in the 1970s: a second look,
    604
Classification of educational subject matter,
    651
*Classification system of Jacques-Charles
    Brunet*, 653
*Classified index to persons in the Library of
    Congress classification ...*, 637
*Classified Library of Congress subject
    headings*, 2nd ed., 669
Cleary, F. D., 1165
Cleaver, B. P., 1473
Cleveland, A. D., 1057
Cleveland, D. B., 1057
Cleverdon, C., 1058
Client-centered academic library, 1283
Clifford, A., 1506-7
Clifton, J. A., 438
Cline, H. F., 460, 770-71
*Clinic on library applications of data
    processing*, 437
Clinton, A., 416
Closing the catalog, 693
Closurdo, J. C., 1221
Clough, E., 1688
Clouston, J. S., 760
Coates, E., 1070, 1593
*COBOL programming: an introduction for
    librarians*, 498
Coburn, L., 1324
Cochrane, P. A., 664, 1443-44. *See also*
    Atherton, P.
Codlin, E. M., 301
Cohen, A., 354
Cohen, E., 354

Cole, J. Y., 323, 982, 1030
Collaborative library systems development, 440
Collection development: the selection of materials for libraries, 743
Collection development and acquisitions, 738
Collection development and public access of government documents, 955
Collection development in libraries, 736
Collection development policies and practices in academic libraries, 771
Collection development policy, 806
Collection program in elementary and middle schools, 775
Collective bargaining and the academic librarian, 1294
Collective bargaining in higher education, 1274
Collective bargaining in libraries, 1269
Collective bargaining procedures for public library employees, 1315
College learning resource center, 227
College learning resources programs, 228
College librarianship, 233
College libraries: guidelines for professional services and resource provision, 3rd ed., 229
College library: a collection of essays, 232
Collier, C., 137
Collins, M., 339
Collison, R. L., 1059-60, 1502
Collister, E. A., 867
Colyer, M. A., 1447
Comaromi, J. P., 619, 621, 648
Combined school/public libraries: a survey ..., 283
Commonsense cataloging, 3rd ed., 537
Communicate! a librarian's guide to interpersonal relations, 1262
Communicating public access to government information, 956
Communication: an introduction to the history of writing, printing, books and libraries, 4th ed., 1049
Communication knowledge and the librarian, 25
Communication research in library and information science, 29
Communication, the essence of science, 23
Communication throughout libraries, 1271
Community college library, 235
Community college library instruction, 1144
Community elite and the public library, 786
Community information services in libraries, 1512
Community information, 1490
Comparative and international library science, 798
Comparative evaluation of ... access to periodical literature, 1619

Comparative historical analysis of three associations of professional schools, 1045
Comparative librarianship: essays in honor of Professor D. N. Marshall, 182
Comparison of Panizzi's 91 rules and the AACR of 1967, 569
Complete book of forms for managing the school library media center, 1342
Complete guide to the new copyright law, 885
"The complete librarian" and other essays, 205
Composite MARC format, 703
Comprehensive program of user education for the General Libraries ..., 1145
Computer basics for librarians and information scientists, 466
Computer systems in the library: a handbook ..., 454
Computer-based library and information systems, 2nd ed., 444
Computer-based reference service, 1509
Computer-output microfilm: its library applications, 1396
Computer-readable data bases, 1588
Computerised systems in library and information services, 493
Computerizing the card catalog in the university library, 699
Computers and systems: an introduction for librarians, 439
Computers and the UDC, 643
Computers for libraries, 480
Computers in information data centers, 438
Computing in LASER, 478
Conant, R. W., 245, 898
Conant report: a study of the education of librarians, 898
Concepts and subject headings: their relation in information retrieval ..., 657
Concise AACR 2, 2nd ed., 553
Concise guide to library research, 1180
Conference on interlibrary communications and information networks, 1419
Conroy, B., 912
Conservation of archival and library materials, 867
Conservation of library materials, 2nd ed., 856
Conservation of library materials ... vol. II, bibliography, 2nd ed., 857
Conservation survey manual, 859
Conservation treatment procedures, 862
Construction and adaptation of the unit card, 586
Contemporary problems in technical library and information center management, 1352
Continuing education resource book, 918
Continuing library education: an interdisciplinary approach, 917

Continuing library education: needs assessment ..., 920
Continuing professional education in librarianship and other fields, 916
Cook, C. D., 581
Cook, J., 263
Cook, M. G., 1167
Cooper, A., 152
Cooperation between types of libraries, 1940-1968, 1418
Cooperation in library service to children, 1630
Cooperative resources development: a resort on ..., 749
Cooperative services: a guide to policies and procedures in library systems, 1406
Cope, G. E., 705
Coping with OCLC cataloging subsystem, 2nd ed., 705
Coplan, K., 417, 1360
Copyright and library materials for the handicapped, 1656
Copyright and photocopying, 882
Copyright book, 2nd ed., 892
Copyright dilemma: proceedings of a conference ..., 894
Copyright handbook, 2nd ed., 887
Copyright law symposium, 886
Corbin, J., 461, 1723
Core Media collection for elementary schools, 789
Cornog, M., 1064, 1067
Corporate authorship, 560
Corporate headings: their use in library catalogs ..., 562
Correy, T., 1491
Corrigan, J. T., 264, 582, 1715
Corry, E., 1124
Cost analysis of library functions, 1245
Costa, B., 490
Costa, M., 490
Coughlin, C. M., 30
Coughlin, R. E., 1302
Course-related library and literature-use instruction, 1148
Covey, A. A., 1503
Cowley, J., 230, 1253
Cox, N. S. M., 436
Cram, M. D., 1675
Cramer, C. H., 1013
Crawford, S., 316
Creating a school media program, 266
Creps, J. E., 1106
Creth, S., 1254
Criteria for planning the college and university learning resources center, 1287
Cronin, B., 899, 1374
Cross-reference index, 2nd ed., 658
Crowe, L., 1497
Crowley, T., 248, 1532

Cultural pluralism and children's media, 1638
Cummings, C. S., 172
Cunha, D. G., 856-58
Cunha, G. M., 856-59, 871
Curley, A., 530, 740
Current concepts in library management, 1218
Current problems in reference service, 1518
Current trends in library automation, 462
Current trends in reference services, 1513
Curriculum alternatives, 262
Custead, P. W., 700
Custer, B. A., 620
Cutler, W., 983
Cutting library costs, 1225
Cylke, F. K., 1671

Daily, J. E., 535
Daily, J. E., 404, 430, 669, 718
Dain, P., 1014
Daiute, R. J., 1237
Dale, D. C., 1031-32
Dance resources in Canadian libraries, 137
Dandurand, G., 316
Daniel, E. H., 395, 1091
Danky, J. P., 776
Danton, J. P., 180, 795, 922
Darnay, B. T., 302
Data gathering ... for performance measures in public libraries, 1298
Data handling for science and technology, 1596
Database: a bibliography, vol. 1, 1452
Davidson-Arnott, F., 231
Davie, J. F., 1667
Davies, D. W., 1015
Davies, R. A., 265
Davinson, D., 503, 1504, 1600
Davis, C. H., 499, 1569, 1592
Davis, C. M., 1655
Davis, D. G., 135, 976, 1044-45
Davis, E. A., 1655
Dawson, I., 1468
Dear faculty: a discovery method guidebook ..., 1193
Debons, A., 1087, 1458
Decade of censorship in America, 732
Decision making ..., 1311
Decision making for library management, 1203
DeCosin, M., 1144
Defending intellectual freedom, 726
Defusing censorship, 722
DeHart, F., 1255
Delaney, J. J., 1325
DeLoach, M. L., 1691
De Prospo, E. R., 1303
Dequin, H. C., 1678
Dersham, L. D., 625
Descriptive cataloging in a new light, 566

Descriptive catalogue: a students' introduction, 2nd ed., 573
Design of information systems for human beings, 1095
Designing and space planning for libraries, 354
Deterioration and preservation of library materials, 874
Deunette, J., 814
Developing a successful elementary school media center, 267
Developing career information centers, 1527
Developing collections of U.S. government publications, 938
Developing computer-based library systems, 461
Developing consumer health information services, 1545
Developing libraries in Brazil, 853
Developing library and information services, 1689
Developing library collections, 741
Developing microform reading facilities, 1388
Developing multi-media libraries, 411
Developing public library systems and services, 1432
Development of library collections of sound recordings, 778
Development of special libraries, 293
Development of the Chinese collection in the Library of Congress, 325
Development of university libraries in Papua New Guinea, 824
Development plans and planning, 1216
Deveny, M. A., 125
DeWath, N. V., 1307
Dewe, A., 485, 814, 1447, 1451
Dewey, M., 618-20
Dewey decimal classification and relative index, 19th ed., 620
Dewey decimal classification, 19th ed., 620
Dewey decimal classification, 19th edition: study manual, 622
Dewey decimal classification: 301-307 Sociology expanded version based on ed. 19, 619
Dewey to LC conversion tables, 607
Diary of a village library, 1023
Diaz, A. J., 1389
Dickinson, E. M., 1258
Dictionary of acronyms and abbreviations ..., 85
Dictionary of American library biography, 168
Dictionary of library and educational technology, 396
Dimensions of comparative librarianship, 795
Directions for the decade, 1149
Directorship by objectives, 1260
Directory of Chinese libraries, 807
Directory of continuing education opportunities for library ... personnel 1977, 2nd ed., 913

Directory of ethnic studies librarians, 173
Directory of fee-based information services, 112
Directory of Friends of Libraries groups in the U.S., 1361
Directory of government document ..., 3rd ed., 948
Directory of health sciences libraries ..., 316
Directory of information management ..., 1582
Directory of institutions offering programs ..., 5th ed., 906
Directory of libraries and special collections ..., U.S.S.R., 159
Directory of library associations in Canada, 3rd ed., 113
Directory of library consultants, 174
Directory of library networks ... 1980, 1417
Directory of library reprographic services, 8th ed., 881
Directory of medical and health care libraries, 5th ed., 320
Directory of medical libraries in the British Isles, 4th ed., 317
Directory of online information resources, 1448
Directory of outreach services in public libraries, 1668
Directory of recorded specialties, 398
Directory of special libraries ..., 9th ed., 302
Directory of the Black Caucus ..., 2nd ed., 175
Directory of UK library school teachers, 3rd rev. ed., 905
Disabled child in the library, 1680
Disadvantaged and library effectiveness, 1686
Disasters: prevention and coping, 872
Discovering books and libraries, 1165
Distributed computing and the electronic library, 495
Divilbiss, J. L., 463-65
Do we really need libraries? 1235
Document retrieval: sources & services, 1579
Document retrieval systems, 1563
Documentation of the United Nations system, 940
Dodd, S. A., 583
Doing library research, 1161
Dolnick, S., 1361
Donelson, K. L., 1710
Donnelly, F. D., 1033
Donohue, J. C., 514, 1508
Dosa, M. L., 984
Dougherty, R. M., 1204, 1498, 1724-25
Douglas C. McMurtrie: bibliographer and historian ..., 980
Dowell, A. T., 531, 584
Downing, M. H., 532
Downs, R. B., 138-39, 826, 1168
Doyle, J. M., 1517
Drake, M. A., 1482
Dranov, P., 1483
Draper, J., 355

Drazniowsky, R., 328
Dreyfuss, R. H., 883
Drob, H. A., 1287
Drott, M. C., 1333
Drum, C. A., 1164
DuBois, P. Z., 985
Ducote, R. L., 65
Duda, F., 1254
Du Mont, R. R., 1016
Dunkel, P. M., 920
Dunkin, P. S., 31, 504, 521
Dunlap, A., 675
Dunlap, L. W., 958
Durey, P., 1277
Dwoskin, R. P., 929
Dyer, E. R., 66, 1630, 1638
Dynamic information and library processing,
    453

*East central and southeast Europe: a
    handbook ...*, 160
Eastern Europe and Russia/Soviet Union, 162
Eastlick, J. T., 13, 1214
Eaton, N. L., 765
Eckard, H. M., 1251, 1417
Economic analysis of public library services,
    1306
Economics of academic libraries, 237
Economics of approval plans ..., 756
Economics of library automation, 463
Edsall, M. S., 1362
Educating the library user, 1128
Education and training ..., 923
Education and training of users ..., 1160
Education for librarianship, 924
Education inside the library-media center, 1188
Education of library-information professionals,
    899
Educational media selection centers, 276
Edwards, M., 1707
Edwards, R. J., 914
Edwards, R. M., 1459
*Effective library: report of the Hillingdon
    project ...*, 1314
Eldridge, L., 1672
Electronic document delivery, 477
Electronic library, 1581
Electronic library, 460
Elementary school libraries, 2nd ed., 271
Elementary school library, 1323
Elementary school library collection, 15th ed.,
    793
Elements of bibliography, 505
Elkins, E. A., 1520
Ellsworth, D., 559
Ellsworth, D. J., 959, 1478
Ellsworth, R. E., 200, 356-57
Ellsworth on Ellsworth, 200

Elrod, J. M., 585-86, 600, 629, 660, 685
*Elsevier's dictionary of library science,
    information and documentation*, rev.
    ed., 82
Ely, D. P., 926
Emergence of maps in libraries, 331
Emerging field of sociobibliography, 507
Emery, R., 1256
Emmens, C. A., 764, 1637
*Encyclopedia of information systems and
    services, 6th ed.*, 114
*Encyclopedia of library and information
    science*, 83
End of libraries, 484
Engelbarts, R., 176, 1699
England, C., 52, 1631
Enright, B. J., 390
ERIC Clearinghouse on library and
    information sciences, 62
*ERIC information analysis product in two
    parts*, 664
Ernestus, H., 848
Ernst, W. B., 944, 1407
Escreet, P. K., 565
Essays for Ralph Shaw, 195
Essays in Hispanic bibliography, 208
Essays on bibliography, 508
Essays on information and libraries, 181
Essential problems in terminology ..., 1099
Estabrook, L., 32, 930
Estes, G. E., 358
Etherington, D., 855, 869
Ethnic collections in libraries, 1691
EURIM 3: a European conference ..., 814
EURIM II: a European conference ..., 1096
Evaluating bibliographic instruction, 1146
*Evaluating information retrieval systems: the
    PROBE program*, 1595
Evaluating library use instruction: papers ...,
    1137
Evaluating media programs, 1326
Evaluation of alternative curricula, 915
*Evaluation of information services and
    products*, 1243
Evaluation of micropublications, 1400
*Evaluation techniques for school library/media
    programs*, 1343
Evans, A. J., 1160
Evans, C., 1492
Evans, G. E., 741, 1205, 1722
Evans, H., 419
Examples illustrating AACR 2, 590
Excellence in school media programs, 184
*Exchange of bibliographic data and the
    MARC format*, 701
Expanding media, 386
Experience of management, 1210
Experiencing display, 1369
Eyre, J., 439

Fachan, K. W., 738
*Factors affecting the renewal of periodical
  subscriptions*, 1611
Faculty involvement in library instruction, 1155
*Faculty of library science, University of
  Toronto ... 1911-1972*, 1041
Faculty status for academic librarians, 1278
Faculty status for librarians, 1287
Faibisoff, S., 12
Fair, J. H., 1390
Fair garden and the swarm of beasts, 1707
Fang, J. R., 115
Farber, E. I., 183
Farewell to Alexandria, 1279
Faria, Anthony, 1175
Fasana, P. J., 440, 680
Fasick, A. M., 1631
Fax and Teletext, 474
Fayen, E. G., 690, 1562
Fear of the word: censorship and sex, 727
*Feasibility of maintaining ... data archives
  through ERIC*, 1597
Federal and state government publications ...,
  950
Federal role in library and information services,
  1117
Fee-based information services, 1575
Feinberg, H., 682, 1061, 1071
Fenichel, C. H., 1439
Fenton, A. D., 791
Ferguson, D. K., 696
Ferguson, J., 842
Ferragamo, R. C., 1391
*FIAF classification scheme for ... film and
  television*, 654
Fiction catalog, 10th ed., 126
Fiction librarianship, 777
FID publications, 67
Field, C. W., 153
Fields, D. C., 227
*File management and information retrieval
  systems*, 1570
Files on parade: a memoir, 997
Filing in the public catalog and shelf list,
  3rd ed., 685
Filing rules: a three-way divided catalog, 689
Filing rules for author and title catalogs, 686
Film cataloging, 420
Film user's handbook, 427
*Final report on "Databases suitable for users
  of environmental information,"* 1598
Financial planning for libraries (Martin), 1231
Financial planning for libraries (Prentice), 1233
Find out who your friends are, 1375
Fine, S., 1527
Finer, R., 1529
Fjallbrant, N., 1169
*Focusing library services on the economic
  community*, 1495
Folcarelli, R. J., 1391

Foos, D. D., 1625
For Congress and the nation, 1030
For the people: fighting for public libraries, 255
Ford, S., 752
Format recognition process for MARC records,
  702
Fosdick, H., 466, 500
Foskett, A. C., 609, 644, 1072
Foskett, D. J., 796, 1118
Foster, D. L., 421, 522
Foster, J., 140
Fothergill, R., 391
Foundations of education for librarianship, 902
Foundations of the public library, 1028
Fox, N. J., 590
Francis, S., 843
Franck, M., 507
Franklin, L. C., 1363
Frase, R. W., 1125
Freedman, J. L., 1127, 1157
Freedman, M. J., 473, 678
Freedom of access to library materials, 730
Freedom versus suppression and censorship,
  714
Freeman, P., 285, 1327
Freezing card catalogs, 691
Freides, T. K., 1534
From press to people, 943
Frost, C. O., 542
Fry, B. M., 936
Fundamental reference sources, 2nd ed., 1516
Funding alternatives for libraries, 1123
Furnishing the library interior, 371
Furth, S. E., 1585
Fusonie, A., 340
Fussler, H. H., 213, 509
Futas, E., 744
Future of card catalogs, 692
*Future of general adult books and readings in
  America*, 1703
Future of the catalog: the library's choices, 680
Future of the main urban library, 250
Future of the National Library of Canada, 828

Gabriel, M. R., 1392-93
Galin, S., 127
Galvin, T. J., 184, 214, 469, 1103, 1422-23, 1518
Gaming in the media center made easy, 1640
Gandert, S. R., 860
Gapen, D. K., 693
Garde, P. K., 797
Gardner, F. M., 1112
Gardner, R. K., 742
Garfield, E., 1073
Garrison, D., 1017
Garrison, G., 1493
Garry, C., 829
Garry, L. S., 829

Garvey, M., 1364-65
Garvey, W. D., 23
Gates, J. K., 2, 1170
Gaver, M. V., 1328
Gebhardt, W., 141
Gechman, M., 1585
Gee, R. D., 1587
Gellatly, P., 1614
General classification systems in a changing world, 601
Generic book, 50
Genzel, P., 762
Geographical name index to the Library of Congress classification ..., 638
George, M. W., 1126
Gerard, D., 14, 33
Getting books to children, 1635
Getting ready for the AACR 2: the cataloger's guide, 588
Getz, M., 246
Gibson, E. B., 1123
Gibson, R. W., Jr., 1420
Gifts and exchange manual, 761
Gilbert, K. D., 379
Gilchrist, A., 1074
Gilder, L., 152
Gill, L., 613
Gill, S. L., 1570
Gillespie, J. T., 266, 1187, 1329-30, 1711
Gillespie, P. D., 1594
Gilreath, C. L., 709
Giuliano, V., 1114
Gleaves, E. S., 185
Glogau, L., 267
Glossary of indexing terms, 1066
GO, PEP, and POP, 1357
Godden, I. P., 738
Going, M. E., 1657
Goldberg, R. L., 1238
Goldhor, H., 924, 1316
Goldman, E., 1321
Goldstein, H., 978, 1119
Goodell, J. S., 1239
Goodman, D. M., 825
Goodrum, C. A., 324
Gordon, C., 1171
Gore, D., 201, 694, 755-56, 1172, 1279, 1607
Gorman, K. A., 1237
Gorman, M., 553, 577
Gough, C., 1240
Gover, H. R., 1173
Government documents in the library literature 1909-1974, 951
Government publications: their role ..., 936
Grannis, C. B., 719
Grant money and how to get it, 1122
Grants for libraries, 1124
Gray, K., 1105
Gray, L. M., 1403

Great Britain's National Lending Library, 849
Great libraries, 962
Green, S. S., 1018
Greenberg, A. M., 626
Greene, E., 1647
Greenfieldt, J., 131
Gregory, R. W., 1407
Grieder, T., 745
Griffith, B. C., 1097
Grimes, G. H., 1517
Grimsted, P. K., 142
Grogan, D., 1505, 1519
Grolier, E. de, 309
Grosch, A. N., 495
Group crafts for teachers and librarians on limited budgets, 1643
Grove, P. S., 405, 408
Growth of medical information systems in the U.S., 319
Guide for an agricultural library survey for developing countries, 836
Guide for the conversion of school libraries into media centers, 1331
Guide to academic libraries in the U.S. for students of English as a second language, 1164
Guide to basic reference materials for Canadian libraries, 7th ed., 52
Guide to better bulletin boards, 417
Guide to British documents ... Virginia library, 952
Guide to computer literature, 2nd ed., 450
Guide to information science, 1569
Guide to libraries and reference books: an introduction ..., 1177
Guide to online databases, 1449
Guide to personal indexes using edge-notched, uniterm and peek-a-boo cards, 2nd ed., 1072
Guide to Polish libraries and archives, 844
Guide to published library catalogs, 149
Guide to reference books, 9th ed., 54
Guide to reference books for school media centers, 2nd ed., 794
Guide to reference books, second supplement, 9th ed., 56
Guide to reference books, supplement, 9th ed., 55
Guide to reference material: vol. 3, 3rd ed., 57
Guide to research in American library history, 960
Guide to the availability of theses, 90
Guide to the development of educational media selection centers, 1322
Guide to the Library of Congress classification, 628

Guide to the research collections of the New York Public Library, 167
Guide to the use of libraries and information sources, 5th ed., 1170
Guide to Yugoslav libraries and archives, 808
Guidelines for audiovisual materials and services for large public libraries, 409
Guidelines for collection development, 767
Guidelines for handling library orders for in-print monographic publications, 746
Guidelines for library automation, 447
Guidelines for library cooperation: development of academic library consortia, 1411
Guides to educational media, 4th ed., 397
Guilmette, P., 137
Gulker, V., 1700
Gurney, G., 1034
Gustafson, K. L., 1549
Guyton, T. L., 1257

Hagler, R., 467, 587
Haglund, E. J., 286
Haight, A. L., 719
Hale, B. M., 1535
Hall, B., 1652
Hall, J. L., 1450-51, 1583
Halldór Hermannsson, 190
Halm, J. V., 293
Hamburg, M., 1249
Hamburger, R., 571-72
Hamilton, B. A., 187, 1408
Hamilton, L. K., 627
Hamlin, A. T., 1007
Hamlin, M., 1642
Hammer, D. P., 34
Handbook for AACR 2, 592
Handbook for school media personnel, 2nd ed., 279
Handbook for storytellers, 1648
Handbook of black librarianship, 91
Handbook of comparative librarianship, 2nd ed., 805
Handbook of data processing for libraries, 2nd ed., 441
Handbook of library regulations, 99
Handbook of special librarianship and information work, 5th ed., 290
Handbook on the international exchange of publications, 763
Handicapped librarian: a study in barriers, 1465
Hanna, P. B., 1494
Hannaford, W. E., 344
Hannam, H., 161
Hannigan, J. A., 358
Happy bookers, 1051
Hardesty, L. L., 1147

Harig, K. J., 919
Harleston, R. M., 937
Harmon, R. B., 505
Haro, R. P., 1689
Harris, J. L., 661
Harris, J. S., 344
Harris, K. H., 1658, 1677
Harris, M. H., 960-61, 965, 976, 983, 986
Harris, M. L., 286
Harris, P. R., 720
Harrison, K. C., 1366
Harrison, A. W., 867
Harrison, C., 3
Harrison, H. P., 422
Harrod, L. M., 84, 1062
Hart, T. L., 1157
Harter, S. P., 1548
Hartman, S., 884
Hartner, E. P., 1440
Hartsfield, A. M., 1119
Harvey, J. A., 720
Harvey, J. F., 333, 798
Harvey, J. H., 1258
Harvey, J. M., 1350
Harvey, S., 1455
Haskell, P. C., 373
Hauer, M. G., 1174
Haycock, K., 670
Hayes, R. M., 441, 1404
Healey, J. S., 987
Health sciences librarianship, 313
Heaps, H. S., 1571
Hebert, F., 1656
Hede, A. A., 1520
Hefley, B. F., 454
Heidbreder, M. A., 276, 1322
Heiliger, E. W., 442
Heilprin, L. B., 882
Heim, K. M., 930, 934, 1475, 1478
Heinritz, F. J., 1204
Held, R. E., 1019
Helgeson, D., 438
Helping people take control, 243
Henderson, K. L., 443, 610
Henderson, P. B., 442
Hendrickson, L., 1131
Hendry, J. D., 1020
Henley, J. P., 444
Hensel, E., 747
Herling, E. B., 964
Herner, S., 1584
Hernon, P., 116, 938, 941, 955-57, 1394, 1501
Herring, J. E., 268
Hewitt, A., 800
Hickerson, H. T., 1454
Hickey, D. J., 523, 747
Hicks, W. B., 411
High interest books for teens, 1713
Higham, N., 215

Hill, D., 424
Hill, Q. M., 651
Hillard, J. M., 1521
Historical introduction to library education, 1048
History of a hoax, 1053
History of libraries in the Western world, 965
History of the American Library Association, 973
History of the National Library of Medicine, 1037
History of the New York Society Library, 1036
History of the Principles of Librarianship, 9
History of the public library in Vigo County 1816-1975, 1024
Hoadley, I. B., 1557
Hobbs, J. L., 380
Hobson, A., 962
Hoffman, H. H., 533, 566, 687, 1559
Hoffmann, C. F. B., 588
Hoffmann, F. W., 778
Hogan, S. A., 1126
Hogan, T. H., 1439
Hollowell, J. S., 519
Holroyd, G., 1213
Holt, R. M., 359, 1495
Holte, S., 123
Hoole, W. S., 202
Hoover, R. E., 1441-42
Horecky, P. L., 160
Horner, J., 543
Horsnell, V., 1102
Hospital libraries and work with the disabled in the community, 1657
Hospital literature subject headings, 2nd ed., 675
Hostrop, R. W., 1188
Houghton, B., 1035
Houser, L., 900
How to catalog a rare book, 2nd ed., 521
How to determine author and title entries according to AACR, 570
How to do library research, 2nd ed., 1168
How to find out: printed and on-line sources, 5th ed., 1515
How to find what you want in the library, 1171
How to register a copyright and protect your creative work, 884
How to start an audiovisual collection, 401
How to use a library: a guide for literature searching, 1162
How to use the business library, 4th ed., 1175
Howard, E. N., 1241
Howell, J. B., 143
Hu, S. C., 325
Hu, T., 1242
Hubbard, W. J., 1488
Huck-Tee, L., 823

Hug, W. E., 35, 269
Hulbert, J. A., 4
Human resource management in small libraries, 1265
Humanities: a selective guide to information sources, 1539
Hunter, E. J., 501, 534, 567, 589-90
Huq, A. M. A., 832
Hutcherson, J., 1649
Hyman, R. J., 561, 679, 1489

Ideas and the university library, 204
IFLA directory 1980/81, 117
IFLA's first fifty years, 799
Illustrated guide to the Anglo-American cataloging rules, 571
Illustrated guide to the International Standard Bibliographic Description for monographs, 572
Illustrative computer programming for libraries, 2nd ed., 499
ILO Thesaurus, 652
Immroth's guide to the Library of Congress classification, 624
Immroth, J. P., 535, 628, 665, 988
Impact of new technology on libraries and information centres, 468
Impact of the environmental sciences ..., 341
Improving access to library resources, 1498
Improving library instruction: how to teach ..., 1150
Improving library service to physically disabled persons, 1659
Improving state aid to public libraries, 1113
Improving the quality of reference service ..., 941
Ina Coolbirth: librarian and laureate of California, 998
Index to Festschriften in librarianship 1967-1975, 180
Index to research in school librarianship, 1960-1974, 285
Index to the cataloging service bulletin of the L.C. See Olson, N. B.
Index to the L.C. cataloging service bulletin. See Olson, N. B.
Index to the Library of Congress classification, 629
Index to user studies, 1499
Indexers on indexing, 1062
Indexes and indexing: guide to the indexing of books, and collections ..., 1060
Indexing and abstracting: an international bibliography, 1069
Indexing concepts and methods, 1055
Indexing languages and thesauri, 1082
Indexing specialized formats and subjects, 1061
Indexing, the art of: a guide ..., 1063

Indian library literature: an annotated bibliography, 812
Industrial information systems: a manual ..., 1101
Influence of Angus Snead MacDonald ... on library architecture, 352
Influence of librarians in liberal arts colleges in selected decision making areas, 1295
Influencing students toward media center use, 1184
Informatics 3: proceedings of a conference ..., 1102
Information age: its development, its impact, 34
Information and its users, 1500
Information and library science source book, 76
Information brokers, 1546
Information economics: costs and prices ..., 1576
Information for academic library decision making, 1089
Information for science and technology: the international scene, 813
Information for the community, 1508
Information for the 1980's: final report of the White House conference ..., 1979, 15
Information management and organisational change, 1098
Information management, machine-readable records, and administration, 1094
Information needs of the 80s, 20
Information of the image, 42
Information professional: survey of an emerging field, 1458
Information retrieval, 2nd ed., 1580
Information retrieval: computational and theoretical aspects, 1571
Information retrieval and documentation in chemistry, 1592
Information retrieval, British and American, 1533
Information retrieval on-line, 1562
Information retrieval systems, 1572
Information science: search for identity, 1087
Information science and computer basics: an introduction, 449
Information searching: a handbook for ... instructional programs, 1127
Information seeking, 1501
Information service in public libraries, 1532
Information services: economics, management, and technology, 1106
Information society: issues and answers, 16
Information storage and retrieval systems for individual researchers, 1560
Information systems, 1565
Information systems and networks: eleventh annual symposium ..., 1590
Information systems, COINS IV, 1591

Information systems, services, and centers, 1567
Information technology, 469
Information worker: identity, image and potential, 1462
Informational interviews and questions, 1531
Information-poor in America, 1685
Ingram, K. E., 833
INIS: authority list for corporate entries ..., 551
INIS: descriptive cataloguing samples, 568
Initial considerations for a nationwide data base, 1405
Inouye, J., 629
Instruction in school media center use, 1158
Instructional design and the media program, 269
Insurance manual for libraries, 365
In-service training in British libraries, 914
Intellectual freedom manual, 2nd ed., 721
Intellectual freedom primer, 715
Interface: library automation ..., 436
Intergrative mechanisms in literature growth, 1550
Interior design for libraries, 355
Interlibrary loan involving academic libraries, 1429
Interlibrary loan policies directory, 1427
Interlibrary loan procedures manual, 1426
Interlibrary loan procedures manual (Thomson), 1430
International agricultural librarianship, 340
International and area studies librarianship, 804
International Association of Music Libraries: United Kingdom branch, 431
International bibliography of the book trade and librarianship, 12th ed., 68
International book and library activities, 803
International directory of acronyms ..., 120
International guide to library, archival, and ..., 2nd ed., 115
International handbook of contemporary developments ..., 92
International librarianship: surveys of ..., 831
Into the information age, 1114
Introducing books: a guide for middle grades, 1187
Introduction to automated literature searching, 1440
Introduction to A V for technical assistants, 389
Introduction to cataloging and classification (Downing), 5th ed., rev. and enl., 532
Introduction to cataloging and classification (Wynar), 7th ed., 541
Introduction to cataloging, vol. I, descriptive cataloging ..., 563
Introduction to cataloging, vol. II, ..., 564
Introduction to chain indexing, 1084
Introduction to classification and number building in Dewey, 616

Introduction to computer-based library systems, 483

Introduction to computers in information science, 435

Introduction to index language construction, 1079

Introduction to indexing and abstracting, 1057

Introduction to information science, 1092

Introduction to librarianship, 2nd ed., 1

Introduction to library science: basic elements ..., 8

Introduction to library service: a textbook, 4

Introduction to library services ..., 1474

Introduction to library services for library technicians, 1469

Introduction to library technical services, 1721

Introduction to minicomputers in federal libraries, 497

Introduction to PL/I programming for library ..., 502

Introduction to PRECIS for North American usage, 1081

Introduction to public services ..., 3rd ed., 1480

Introduction to quantitative research methods ..., 1559

Introduction to reference work, 4th ed., 1522

Introduction to serials management, 1603

Introduction to Soviet national bibliography, 513

Introduction to subject indexing, 2nd ed., 599

Introduction to technical services ..., 4th ed., 1722

Introduction to the Anglo-American cataloguing rules, 565

Introduction to the 18th ed. of the Dewey decimal classification, 614

Introduction to the 19th ed. of the Dewey decimal classification, 615

Introduction to UDC, 646

Introduction to United States public documents, 3rd ed., 942

Introduction to university library administration, 3rd ed., 1292

Inventory of bibliographic data bases in Canadian degree-granting institutions, 1453

Involving the school library media specialist ..., 1473

Irvine, B. J., 425

Isaacson, R. H., 124, 128, 134

ISBD(A), 511

ISBD(PM), 512

Issues and involvement: Alberta L. Brown lectures ..., 295

Issues in children's book selection, 773

Issues in library administration, 1223

Issues in personnel management in academic libraries, 1285

Itself an education ..., 605

Jackson, E. B., 294, 1101

Jackson, M. M., 92

Jackson, R. L., 1101

Jackson, S. L., 963-64

Jackson, W. V., 144, 911

Jaffe, J., 1245

Jahoda, G., 1560, 1659

Japanese and U.S. research libraries ..., 821

Jay, H. L., 1189

Jefferson, A. A., 833

Jefferson, G., 232, 1433

Jeffreys, A., 186

Jeffries, S. R., 1695

Jenkins, H. R., 1304

Jennison, P. S., 1703

Jirjees, J. M., 1544

Job dimensions and educational needs in librarianship, 932

Jobin, P., 295

Jobs in instructional media, 935

Joetta Community Library: a simulation exercise ..., 1299

John E. Fogarty: political leadership for library development, 987

Johns, C. J., 99

Johnson, D. W., 1611

Johnson, E. D., 965, 1049

Johnson, E. R., 1280

Johnson, F., 1639

Johnson, H. W., 1175

Johnson, J. T., 544

Johnson, R. D., 1008

Johnston, D. F., 887

Johnston, M. T., 989

Jonassen, D. H., 392

Joncich, M. J., 1244

Jones, F. M., 722

Jones, H. G., 939

Jones, K. P., 1102

Jones, K. S., 1075

Jones, M. H., 597

Jordan, A. H., 69

Jordan, A. T., 852

Jordan, M., 69

Jordan, R. T., 1496

Josey, E. J., 16, 91, 177, 216, 931, 964, 1115, 1690-91

Jovanović, S., 808

Joy of cataloging, 520

Juergens, B., 693

Junior college library collection, 781

Junior high school library catalog, 4th ed., 128

Justin Winsor: scholar-librarian, 983

Kaltreider, L. W., 1242

Kambayashi, Y., 1452

Kaplan, L., 445

Karetzky, S., 966
Karlgren, H., 1554
Karpisek, M. E., 1190
Karrenbrock, M. H., 1680
Kaser, D., 1021
Kaske, N. K., 1204
Kathman, M. D., 218
Katz, B., 109, 129, 1506-7, 1609
Katz, E., 21
Katz, L. S., 129
Katz, W. A., 743, 1176, 1522
Katzel, R., 1177
Katzenberger, P., 1594
Kaula, P. N., 360, 820
Kay, M., 1554
Kazlauskas, E. J., 1582
Keeling, D. F., 977
Keenan, S., 1160
Keep, A. B., 1036
Keeping track of what you spend, 1224
Keller, C. D., 145, 1168
Kemp, D. A., 48
Kemp, E. C., 381
Kemper, R. E., 1259-60
Kent, A., 83, 469, 1103, 1227, 1421-23
Kent, R., 93
Kesner, R. M., 1094
Key, J. D., 318
Key papers in information science, 1097
Key papers in the economics of information, 1104
Keys, C., 1669
Keys, T. E., 318
Keys to library research on the graduate level, 1173
Kies, C., 1367-68
Kiewitt, E. L., 1595
Kilgour, F. G., 70
Kim, C. H., 94
Kim, U. C., 750
Kimber, R. T., 446
Kimbrough, J., 694
Kimmel, M. M., 184
King, D. W., 24, 1104, 1243
Kirk, T., 1148
Kirkendall, C. A., 1138, 1149-51, 1201
Kirtland, M., 664
Knievel, H. A., 1406
Knight, G. N., 1063
Knight, H. M., 1191
Knowing books and men; knowing computers, too, 206
Knowledge and its organization, 47
Kochen, M., 1508, 1550, 1561
Koenig, M. E. D., 1228
Kohn, R., 1369-70
Koops, W. R. H., 799
Kortendick, J. J., 932
Kramer, M. W., 1696

Kramer-Greene, J., 1001
Kraus, D. H., 815
Krause, E., 267
Kronus, C. L., 1497
Krueger, D., 491
Krummel, D. W., 1371
Krupskaia and Soviet Russian librarianship, 995
Krzys, R., 800
Kuehn, J., 1597
Kuhlthau, C. C., 1192
Kumar, K., 5, 834
Kunz, W., 1088
Kwan, C. H., 641

Ladd, D. P., 1393
Ladendorf, J. M., 306
Ladenson, A., 95, 1116
LaFleur, L., 1379, 1484
LaHood, C. G., 876
Lancaster, F. W., 36, 470-72, 496, 1076, 1244, 1562, 1572-74
Lancour, H., 83
Landau, T., 170
Landmarks of library literature, 1876-1976, 959
Lane, A. H., 761
Lane, M. T., 949
Lang, J. P., 133, 630-31
Lang, V., 656
Langmead, S., 361
Langridge, D., 611
Langridge, D. W., 599, 602
Larouche, I., 809
Larsgaard, M., 329
Larson, L., 1357
Lathem, E. C., 1551
Laugher, C. T., 1022
Law librarianship, 337
Lawhun, K. S., 1579
Lawrence, C., 1649
Lawrence, G. S., 696
Layne, E. N., 255
LC rule interpretations of AACR 2, 1978-1982 cumulated ed., 598
Leach, S. G., 63
Learning centers: development and operation, 1320
Learning resource centers: best of ERIC, 65
Learning resource centers: selected readings, 272
Learning resource centers in community colleges ..., 1293
Learning the library, 1126
Lee, J., 81, 171, 187
Lee, S. H., 1152-53, 1229-30, 1528, 1610
Leerburger, B. A., 1372
Lehnus, D. J., 554, 569-70, 649

LeLieuvre, R. B., 1376
Lembo, D., 1187
Lemos, A. A., 835
Lendvay, O., 342
Lengenfelder, H., 118
Leonard, L. E., 1724
Leopold, C. C., 270
Lester, M. A., 950
Let's read together, 4th ed., 1636
*Letters for the international exchange of
   publications*, 88
Lewanski, R. C., 146, 162, 844
Lewis, S., 407
*Librarian: selections from the column of that
   name*, 970
Librarian and the patient, 1661
Librarian authors: a bibliography, 176
*Librarian speaking: interviews with university
   librarians ...*, 217
Librarians' affirmative action handbook, 1258
Librarians and labor relations, 1263
Librarians and online services, 1436
Librarians as professionals, 1463
*Librarians, censorship, and intellectual
   freedom ...*, 720
*Librarians' glossary of terms used in
   librarianship ...*, 84
Librarian's handbook, 100
Librarians of Congress, 1802-1974, 990
Librarians phone book, 169
Librarians' psychological commitments, 1255
*Librarians serving disabled children and young
   people*, 1678
Librarianship, 7
*Librarianship: an introduction to the
   profession*, 1
*Librarianship and literature: essays in honour
   of Jack Bafford*, 189
Librarianship and the Third World, 832
Libraries: architecture and equipment, 353
Libraries and archives in France: a handbook,
   850
*Libraries & culture: proceedings of library
   history seminar VI, 19-22 Mar. 1980,
   Austin, Tex.*, 979
*Libraries and librarians in an age of
   electronics*, 470
Libraries and librarianship in the West, 963
*Libraries and neighborhood information
   centers*, 1497
Libraries and the arts, 14
Libraries and the arts and humanities, 1347
Libraries and the challenge of change, 833
Libraries and the life of the mind in America, 17
Libraries and work sampling, 1239
Libraries and young adults, 1717
Libraries as communication systems, 27
*Libraries designed for users: a planning
   handbook*, 362

*Libraries, documentation and bibliography in
   the USSR*, 841
Libraries for professional practice, 304
Libraries for small museums, 339
Libraries for teaching, libraries for research,
   1008
*Libraries for the blind: an international
   study ...*, 1675
Libraries for today and tomorrow, 37
Libraries in American periodicals before 1876,
   63
Libraries in colleges of education, 2nd ed., 234
Libraries in East Africa, 818
Libraries in France, 842
*Libraries in higher education: the user
   approach ...*, 230
Libraries in post-industrial society, 32
Libraries in Senegal, 817
Libraries in society: a reader, 33
Libraries in the Federal Republic of Germany,
   848
Libraries in the political process, 1115
Libraries in the political scene, 984
Libraries in the U.S.S.R., 843
*Libraries, museums & art galleries yearbook
   1971*, 343
*Libraries of Stanford University collection ...,
   1980*, 772
Libraries, publishers and photocopying, 877
Library access for the handicapped: a guide ...,
   1662
Library acquisition policies and procedures,
   2nd ed., 744
*Library acquisitions: a classified guide to the
   literature and reference tools*, 2nd ed.,
   751
*Library and archives conservation: 1980s and
   beyond*, 858
*Library and archives conservation: the Boston
   Athenaeum's ...*, 871
Library and information CumIndex, 70
*Library and information manager's guide to
   online services*, 1442
*Library and information networks in the United
   Kingdom*, 1431
*Library and information networks in Western
   Europe*, 840
Library and information science, 71
*Library and information science education
   in the Americas*, 911
*Library and information sciences: an ERIC
   bibliography*, 62
*Library and information services for
   handicapped individuals*, 2nd ed., 1667
*Library and information services for special
   groups*, 1692
*Library and information studies in the United
   Kingdom and Ireland*, 78
Library and library-related publications, 116

Library and media: marriage or divorce, 388
Library and resource center in Christian education, 334
Library and the contemporary arts, 1483
Library as a learning service center, 40
Library assistant's manual, 2nd ed., 1470
Library at Mount Vernon, 1029
Library automation — computerized serials control, 1618
Library automation: experience, methodology, and technology ..., 442
Library automation: five case studies, 473
Library automation: the state of the art II, 448
Library automation, a state of the art review, 451
Library automation as a source of management information, 471
Library automation systems, 452
Library bibliographies and indexes, 79
Library budgeting: critical challenges for the future, 1229
Library building: innovation for changing needs, 376
Library buildings: planning and design ..., 360
Library cataloging, 535
Library clerical workers and pages, 1472
Library collections: their origin, selection, and development, 742
Library community services, 2nd ed., 1491
Library connection: essays written in praise of public libraries, 1373
Library conservation: preservation in perspective, 854
Library co-operation, 1433
Library data collection handbook, 1251
Library displays: their purpose, construction and use, 1364
Library education, 903
Library education in Italy, 846
Library funding and public support, 1125
Library guiding, 1358
Library history, 968
Library history: an examination guidebook, 969
Library humor: a bibliothecal miscellany to 1970, 1052
Library in the independent school, 261
Library in the university, 215
Library instruction: a bibliography, 1135
Library instruction and faculty development, 1156
Library instruction for librarians, 1133
Library instruction guide: suggested courses ..., 4th ed., 1159
Library instruction in the elementary school, 1185
Library instruction in the seventies, 1130
Library issues: the sixties, 39
Library law and legislation in the United States, 1116

Library leadership, 1460
Library life — American style, 41
Library lighting, 364
Library lit: the best of, 109
Library literature, 80
Library management, 2nd ed., 1214
Library management: a bibliography with abstracts, 1217
Library management; behavior-based personnel systems, 1259
Library management cases, 1206
Library management in review, 1220
Library management, volume I: papers from the management workshops ..., 1221
Library management without bias, 1219
Library manager's guide to automation, 494
Library manual, 5
Library media center problems: case studies, 1324
Library media programs and the special learner, 1683
Library media specialist in curriculum development, 278
Library networks, 1981-82, 1410
Library of Congress, 324
Library of Congress: a picture story ..., 1034
Library of Congress as the national bibliographic center, 326
Library of Congress cataloging service bulletins 1-125, 525
Library of Congress classification: class K, subclass KF ..., 625
Library of Congress classification adapted for ..., 640
Library of Congress classification schedules, 633
Library of Congress classification schedules: a cumulation ..., 632
Library of Congress filing rules, 688
Library of Congress in perspective, 323
Library of Congress shelflist: a user's guide ..., 627
Library of Congress subject headings, 663
Library of Congress subject headings, 9th ed., 668
Library operations research, 1237
Library orientation: papers presented ... at Eastern Michigan University, 1153
Library photocopying in the United States, 875
Library planning and decision-making systems, 1249
Library power, 10
Library practice in hospitals: a basic guide, 314
Library problems in science and technology, 1538
Library problems in the humanities, 1541
Library programs: how to select, plan and produce them, 2nd ed., 1379
Library promotion handbook, 1362

*Library public relations: a practical
    handbook*, 1365
Library resource sharing: proceedings of ...,
    1422
Library resources in Scotland, 157
Library resources market place: LRMP 1980,
    96
Library response to urban change, 248
Library science dissertations, 1973-1981, 75
Library science research, 1974-1979, 73
*Library science research reader and
    bibliographic guide*, 1547
Library searching: resources and strategies,
    1530
*Library service for the blind and physically
    handicapped*, 1671
*Library service to children: an international
    survey*, 1632
Library service to schools, 3rd ed., 274
Library service to schools and children, 273
Library service to the disadvantaged, 1684
Library service to the Spanish speaking, 1693
Library services for the handicapped adult,
    1664
Library services to developmentally disabled ...,
    1679
*Library services to the blind and physically
    handicapped*, 1676
Library services to the disadvantaged, 1687
*Library skills: a handbook for teachers and
    librarians*, 1186
*Library staff development and continuing
    education*, 912
Library statistics of colleges and universities,
    239
*Library statistics of colleges and universities,
    1976 institutional data*, 238
*Library statistics of colleges and universities,
    1982 institutional data*, 240
Library systems analysis guidelines, 1248
*Library systems evaluation guide, vol. 1. serials
    control*, 1613
Library technical assistant's handbook, 1467
Library technical services: a ... bibliography,
    1726
Library technician at work: theory and practice,
    1468
Library trustee: a practical guidebook, 1317
Library work with children, 1628
*Library's public: a report of the public library
    inquiry*, 241
Library-centered approach to learning, 1134
*Library-information science: bibliographies,
    guides ...*, 72
Library/media manual, 1195
LiBretto, E. V., 1708
Liebaers, H., 991
Lieberman, I., 907
Liesener, J. W., 1332

Lighthall, L. I., 670
Lilley, D. B., 71
Lindberg, D. A., 319
Lindberg, J., 1178
Line, J., 801
Line, M., 181, 801
Linton, W. D., 320
Lipscomb, E. J., 989
Lipsman, C. K., 1686
List: library and information science today, 110
Literacy and the nation's libraries, 97
Literary and library prizes, 10th ed.,
    103
*Literature and bibliography of the social
    sciences*, 1534
Literature and bibliometrics, 516
Little, A. D., 1619
Little brief authority: a manual ..., 550
Litton, G., 800
Lloyd, G., 1070, 1593
Local government records: an introduction ...,
    939
Local history and the library, 2nd ed.,
    380
*Local history collections: a manual for
    librarians*, 101
Local power and the community library,
    1241
Local public library administration, 2nd ed.,
    1297
Local studies librarianship, 384
Lock, R. N., 6
Lockwood, D. L., 1135
Loertscher, D. V., 1343
Lolley, J., 1179
London classification of business studies, 2nd
    ed., 656
Long, M., 1536
Loo, S., 1222
Loosjes, T. P., 506
Lord, C. M., 1023
Lorković, T., 513
*Louis Shores, author-librarian: a
    bibliography*, 197
Lowell, H. P., 859
Lowell, M. H., 1206-7
Lowrey, A. M., 262
Lowrie, J. E., 271, 802
Lubans, J., 1128-29, 1250
Lunati, R., 766
Lundeen, G. W., 499
Lundy, K. R., 1476
Lushington, N., 362
Lyders, R., 312
Lyle, G. R., 217, 992, 1281
Lyman, H. H., 97, 1704
Lynam, P., 1552
Lynch, B. P., 214
Lynch, M. J., 928, 1251

Maack, M. N., 817
MacCafferty, M., 72, 474, 486, 723, 1105, 1139
MacDonald, A. R., 1351
Macdonald, J., 407
Mackee, M., 805
MacLean, I. A., 1453
MacLeish, A., 203
Macon, M., 1681
Magazine selection: how to build ..., 1609
Magazines for libraries, 4th ed., 129
Magnotti, S., 73
Magrill, R. M., 1726
Maidment, W. R., 7
Maier, E., 1175
Maier, J. M., 1725
Mainstreamed library, 1658
Mainstreaming in the media center, 1682
Mainstreaming library service for disabled people, 1655
Major classification systems, 610
Major libraries of the world, 154
Making of a code: the issues underlying AACR 2, 580
Making of a library: the academic library in transition, 222
Making self-teaching kits for library skills, 1190
Malinconico, S. M., 678, 680
Malinowsky, H. R., 1537
Malley, I., 1169
Maloney, R. K., 1261
Maltby, A., 603-4, 613
Management and costs of technical processes, 1724
Management by design, 1222
Management for librarians, 1209
Management of a public library, 1304
Management of information analysis centers ..., 1589
Management of libraries and information centers, 1207
Management of library networks, 1415
Management of serials automation, 1614
Management of the information department, 1085
Management problems in serials work, 1607
Management process: a selection of readings for librarians, 1208
Management techniques for librarians, 1205
Managers view information, 1351
Managing the catalog department, 2nd ed., 522
Managing the library fire risk, 2nd ed., 366
Managing the modern school library, 1334
Managing the serials explosion, 1622
Mancall, J. C., 1333
Manheimer, M. L., 536, 669, 706
Mann, S. H., 1280
Mann, T., Jr., 735

Manning, R. W., 591
Manual for accessioning, arrangement ..., 2nd ed., 382
Manual for prison law libraries, 1702
Manual of AACR 2 examples, 597
Manual of AACR 2 examples for microforms, 596
Manual of AACR 2 examples tagged and coded ..., 579
Manual of business library practice, 305
Manual of cataloguing practice, 528
Manual of European languages for librarians, 89
Manual of library economy: a conspectus ..., 6
Manual on KF: the Library of Congress classification, 641
Manual on the use of the Dewey decimal classification: ed. 19, 621
Manuscript solicitations for libraries ..., 381
Many faces of information science, 1111
Map collections in the U.S. and Canada, 429
Map librarian in the modern world, 332
Map librarianship, 2nd ed., 330
Map librarianship: an introduction, 329
Map librarianship: readings, 328
Maranjian, L., 1575
March of library science, 196
Marchant, M. P., 1282
Marcus, M., 237
Margrabe, M., 413
Marino, S., 1179
Marketing of library and information services, 1374
Marketing the library, 1372
Markey, K., 1443
Markuson, B. E., 447, 1409
Marshall, F. D., 287, 1334
Marshall, J. D., 197, 1461
Marshall, J. K., 666
Martell, C. R., 1283
Martin, A. B., 257
Martin, B., 288
Martin, L. A., 248, 1705
Martin, M. S., 1231, 1284-85
Martin, S. K., 448, 1410
Martin, W., 1687
Martyn, J., 1598
Marulli, L., 940
Maruskin, A. F., 707
Mason, E., 363
Mason, M. G., 1117
Mason, R. M., 1106
Mason on library buildings, 363
Mass communications: selected readings for librarians, 26
Massman, V. F., 218, 1286
Masters, D. C., 133
Matarazzo, J. M., 1538
Mathai, A., 40

Mathews, A. J., 1262
Mathews, V. H., 37
Mathies, M. L., 1509
Matthews, J. R., 475, 695, 696
Matthis, R. E., 634
Matzek, R. A., 1424
Maurice Falcolm Tauber: a bibliography, 198
Maurstad, B. L., 1483
Maxwell, M. F., 592
Mayes, P., 1606
McCallum, S. H., 1405
McCarn, D. B., 697
McCarthy, C., 853
McClaskey, M. J., 594
McClellan, A. W., 18
McClure C. R., 941, 1089, 1212
McCormick, M., 53, 1523
McCormick, M. G., 888
McCrimmon, B., 38, 967
McCullough, K., 754
McDonald, D. D., 877
McDonough, I. R., 1024
McGarry, K. J., 25-26
McIlwaine, I., 188
McIlwaine, J., 188
McInnis, R. G., 1510
McKeon, D. B., 653
McLean, I., 130
McMichael, B., 334
McMullen, H., 63
McQuitty, B. J., 155
McShean, G., 724
Meacham, M., 1029
Meadow, C. T., 1090, 1444
Meadows, A. J., 1620
Measurement and evaluation of library services, 1244
Measuring student information use, 1333
Mechanized in-house information systems, 481
Media and the young adult, 1712
Media center facilities design, 358
Media in the library, 395
Media indexes and review sources, 394
Media personnel in education, 926
Media program in the elementary and middle schools, 1325
Media programs: district and school, 1335
Media selection handbook, 402
Mediamobiles: views from the road, 1378
Medical librarianship, 321
Meeting the needs of the handicapped, 1665
Melcher, D., 748
Melcher on acquisition, 748
Melin, N. J., 1602, 1617
Melvil Dewey: his enduring presence in librarianship, 1004
Melvil Dewey: the man and the classification, 1001
Melville, A., 165

Menzenska, Sister M. J., 383
Merrill, I. R., 1287
Merritt, L. C., 725
Metcalf, K. D., 364, 993
Metcalfe, J., 1533
Methods of analysis and evaluation of information needs, 1088
Methods of financing interlibrary loan services, 1425
Metropolitan library, 245
Mews, H., 1198
Meyers, G. E., 365
Michael Sadleir 1888-1957, 1002
Michael, M. E., 916
Micro handbook for small libraries and media centers, 490
Microcomputers for libraries, 491
Microcomputers in libraries, 492
Microform connection, 1391
Microform handbook, 1386
Microform librarianship, 1399
Microform librarianship, 2nd ed., 1399
Microform revolution in libraries, 1393
Microforms: the librarian's view 1978-79, 1387
Microforms and government information, 1394
Microforms in libraries: a reader, 1389
Microforms management in special libraries, 1390
Micrographics, 1397
Micrographics handbook, 1398
Micrographics 1900-1977, 1392
Microprocessors and intelligence, 488
Middle class attitudes and public library use, 1492
Middleton, B. C., 861
Miksa, F. L., 981, 1050
Miles, W. D., 1037
Milestones in cataloging, 554
Milestones to the present, 978
Miller, G. B., Jr., 244, 736
Miller, J. K., 889, 890
Miller, R. E., 537
Miller, S., 418
Miller, W., 233
Miller, W. G., 155
Mills, J., 599, 612
Mills, W. N., 362, 1305
Milne, A. T., 189
Miniaturised communications, 1401
Mitchell, B. J., 1232, 1245
Mitchell, P. M., 190
Mitchell, R. K., 449
Model continuing education recognition system ..., 919
Model for service to the elderly, 1695
Model school district media program, 1329
Modern branch libraries and libraries in systems, 1247
Modern news library, 350

Modern school library, 2nd ed., 277
Molz, K., 245
Monroe, M. E., 515
Montgomery, A. C., 98
Montgomery, K. L., 1563
Montgomery, P. K., 1196
Moon, E., 39
Moore, V., 1650
Moran, L., 340
More case studies in reference work, 1519
Morehead, J., 901, 942
Morris, J., 366
Morris, J. M., 1154, 1530
Morris, L. R., 1427
Morris, R. J. B., 1025
Morrow, C. C., 862-63
Morse, G. W., 689, 1180
Moses, H. A., 519
Mosher, P. H., 772
Mostly in the line of duty, 991
Mott, T. H., 502
Moulds, M., 654
Mount, E., 296, 345, 367, 1038
Muench, E. V., 676
Mugnier, C., 1471
Multimedia library: materials selection and use, 400
Multitype library cooperation, 1408
Murfin, M. E., 1514
Murphy, M., 99, 295
Muse and the librarian, 199
Music resources in Canadian collections, 147
Musicians and libraries in the United Kingdom, 1536
Musiker, R., 297
Myers, J. N., 872
Myers, M., 1477
Myers, M. J., 1544

Nadarajah, R., 823
Nadler, M., 401
Nakata, Y., 943-44
Nancy Pollette's E is for everybody, 2nd ed., 1641
National Agricultural Library catalog: indexes for 1971-1975, 166
National and international library planning, 1434
National inventory of library needs, 1975, 19
National libraries, 801
National library and information services: a handbook for planners, 1118
National Library of Canada, 1033
National Library of Canada: a bibliography, 809
National Library of India, 820
National Library of Medicine classification: a scheme ..., 655

National periodicals center: technical development plan, 1621
National science information systems ... in Bulgaria, Czechoslovakia, Hungary ..., 815
Nationwide provision and use of information, 1107
Natural language in information science, 1554
Nature and future of the catalog, 678
Nature of knowledge, 48
Needham, C. D., 538
Needham, W. L., 1659
Neglected resource, 307
Negotiating for computer services, 464
Nelson, B. R., 149
Nemeyer, C. A., 1322
Network concepts: four points of view, 1424
Networks for networkers, 1409
Neuburg, V. E., 994
Neufeld, M. L., 1064, 1067
Neveling, U., 86
New, P. G., 188, 878
New academic library buildings/II, 368
New copyright U.S.A., 893
New dimensions for academic library service, 216
New directions for young adult services, 1708
New governance structure for OCLC, 708
New horizons for academic libraries, 221
New information technologies—new opportunities, 476
New librarianship: a challenge for change, 45
New library buildings, 1974 issue, 369
New library design: guidelines to planning academic library buildings, 361
New library key, 1167
New media and the library in education, 390
New perspectives for reference service in academic libraries, 1510
New technology and documents librarianship, 957
New trends in documentation and information, 1109
New York Academy of Medicine Library collection ..., 779
New York Public Library: a history of ..., 1014
New York Times guide to reference materials, 53
Newhall, J. E., 335
Newhouse, J. P., 1306
Newkirk, L. I., 1434
Newspaper indexing for historical societies, 1077
Newspaper libraries in the U.S. and Canada, 2nd ed., 336
NFAIS membership directory, 1981, 1068
Nicholas, D., 516
Nichols, H., 330, 384
Nickel, M. L., 1336

Nickels, B. A., 132
Nitecki, J. Z., 881
No choice: library services for the mentally handicapped, 1660
Noel, W., 1656
Nomenclature for museum cataloging, 650
Nonbook materials: the organization of ..., 2nd ed., 407
Non-book materials in libraries: a practical guide, 391
Nonbook media, 392
Nonprint cataloging for multimedia collections, 547
Nonprint media in academic libraries, 408
Nonprint media information networking, 387
Non-theatrical film distributors, rev. ed., 764
Nordling, J. A., 1193
Noreault, T., 1597
Norman, A. R. D., 477
North American film and video directory, 399
North American library education ..., 908
Novak, G., 370
Novalis, C. M., 1412
"NOW" library: a stations approach media center teaching kit, 413
Nunn, G. R., 810
Nyren, K., 39, 368

Oak from an acorn, 1040
Oberman-Soroka, C., 1140
Oboler, E. M., 204, 726-28
Occupational definitions for school library media personnel, 1339
OCLC: a national library network, 704
OCLC: an introduction to searching and input, rev. ed., 706
OCLC: its governance, function, financing, and technology, 707
O'Connell, M. R., 868
Of books and men, 1011
Of, by and for librarians, 1461
Ogden, L. K., 855
O'Hara, F. J., 945
Oldfield, P., 1470
Ollé, J. G., 968-69
Olsen, H. A., 1104
Olson, E. E., 1425
Olson, N. B., 526, 545-46, 635-39
On documentation of scientific literature, 506
On equal terms: a thesaurus for non-sexist indexing and cataloging, 666
On this day: a collection of everyday learning events and activities ..., 286
1-2-3 guide to libraries, 5th ed., 1191
101 media center ideas, 1644
On-line age: plans and needs ..., 1455
Online bibliographic databases, 3rd ed., 1450

Online bibliographic searching: a learning manual, 1426
On-line bibliographic services—where we are, where we're going, 1456
Online catalog: improving public access to library materials, 690
On-line cataloging, 698
On-line cataloging and circulation at Western Kentucky University, 700
Online catalogs: requirements, characteristics and costs, 697
On-line information retrieval 1965-1976, 1583
Online information retrieval 1976-79, 1451
Online reference and information retrieval, 1445
On-line revolution in libraries: proceedings ..., 1103
Online search strategies, 1441
Online searching: a dictionary and bibliographic guide, 1446
Online searching: a primer, 1439
Online terminal/microcomputer guide & directory, 1982-83, 3rd ed., 487
Ontap: online training and practice manual for ERIC data base searchers, 2nd ed., 1443
Open admissions and the academic library, 210
Open shelves and open minds, 1013
Operations research: a tool for library management, 1246
Operations research: implications for libraries, 1108
Opportunities for minorities in librarianship, 931
Opportunities in library and information science, 934
Options for the 80s, 218
Oral antecedents of Greek librarianship, 974
O'Reilly, M. I., 1263
O'Reilly, R. C., 1263
Organisation of media, 403
Organization and administration of the learning resources center in the community college, 1275
Organization and staffing of the libraries of Columbia University, 1288
Organization development for academic libraries, 1280
Organization of information systems for government ... administration, 309
Organization of the library profession, 1457
Organizing a local government documents collection, 944
Organizing knowledge in libraries, 2nd ed., 538
Organizing nonprint materials: a guide for librarians, 404
Organizing the library's support, 1371
Origins of American academic librarianship, 1009
Orne, J., 191
Orr, J. M., 27

Osborn, J., 622
Osburn, C. B., 733
Ostrander, R. E., 1260
Out of the dinosaurs, 1035
Output measures for public libraries, 1318
Outreach: library services for the institutionalized ..., 1654

Page, J., 1594
Painter, A. F., 524
Palmer, B. I., 605
Palmer, R. C., 1359, 1445
Palmer, R. P., 699
Palmini, C., 249
Palmour, V. E., 1307, 1403, 1425, 1428
Pantelidis, V. S., 811
Paperback books for young people, 1711
Papers: communication's changing ..., 28
Paraprofessional and nonprofessional staff ..., 1349
Paraprofessional and the professional job structure, 1471
Parker, D., 836
Parker, J. S., 837
Parliament and the public libraries, 1025
Participative management in academic libraries, 1282
Participatory management in libraries, 1268
Pascarelli, A. M., 779
Passmore, R., 1462
Pastine, M., 116
Pathfinder: an operational guide ..., 1327
Patrick, R. J., 1411-12
Patrinostro, F. S., 845
Patton, W. L., 891
Paul Leicester Ford: an American man of letters, 985
Pearlman, D., 1660
Pearson, E. L., 970
Pearson, N. P., 272
Peeples, K. E., 931
Pellowski, A., 1651
Pemberton, J. E., 946
Penland, P. R., 40
Penna, C. V., 838, 1118
Pennell, H. B., 1375
People make it happen, 1494
Peoplework: communications dynamics for librarians, 1376
Performance measures for public libraries, 1303
Perica, E., 1077
Periodicals administration in libraries, 1606
Periodicals collection, 1600
Periodicals for school media programs, 792
Perkins, D. L., 767
Perkins, J. W., 640, 1308
Perreault, J., 646-47

Person, R. J., 1208
Personal documentation for professionals, 1578
Personnel administration in libraries, 1254
Personnel development in libraries: proceedings ..., 1261
Personnel management, 1207
Personnel management in libraries, 1253
Personnel policies in libraries, 1273
Personnel utilization in libraries, 1266
Peterson, A. R., 1693
Peterson, C. S., 791, 1652
Peterson, V. E., 1159
Petrie, J., 1682
Pezzanite, F. A., 497
Phillips, E. B., 737
Phinney, E., 1661
Phonograph record libraries, 2nd ed., 431
Photocopying in libraries: the librarians speak, 880
Pickett, D. C., 754
Picture file: a manual ..., 2nd ed., 424
Picture indexing for local history materials, 379
Picture librarianship (Evans), 419
Picture librarianship (Harrison), 423
Picture searching: techniques and tools, 428
Pierce, W. S., 371
Pillon, N. B., 1716
Piper, P. L., 641
Pirie, J. W., 783
Pitkin, G. M., 1615
Plaister, J. M., 478
Planning and design of library buildings, 2nd ed., 375
Planning and operating media centers, 414
Planning barrier free libraries, 372
Planning for library conservation, 864
Planning library workshops and institutes, 921
Planning manual for academic library buildings, 357
Planning of library and documentation services, 2nd ed., 838
Planning process for public libraries, 1307
Planning the library instruction program, 1143
Planning the special library, 367
Planning, programming, budgeting systems in academic libraries, 1296
Planning-programming-budgeting systems (PPBS), 1230
Platt, P., 234
Plotnik, A., 41
Polette, N., 1641-42
Policies and guidelines developed for community ..., 231
Policies of publishers: a handbook ... 1978, 750
Pollet, D., 373
Poole, H., 192
Pope, M., 729
Pope, S. E., 555, 1384
Portrait of librarianship in developing societies, 835

Posey, E. D., 754
Post, J., 1685
Poster ideas and bulletin board techniques, 2nd ed., 1360
Potter, W. G., 1616
Powell, J. W., 1376
Powell, R. R., 1525
Power, politics, and print, 967
PR for pennies: low-cost library public relations, 1355
Practical approach to serials cataloging, 558
Practical approval plan management, 753
Practical reference work, 1505
Prasher, R. G., 74, 812
Pratt, A. D., 42
Pratt, G., 1455, 1576
PRECIS: a workbook for students of librarianship, 1080
PRECIS index system: principles ..., 1078
Prejudices and antipathies: a tract on the LC subject heads ..., 662
Prentice, A. E., 1233, 1309-10
Preschool story hour, 2nd ed., 1650
Presenting the library service, 1382
Preservation challenge, 863
Preservation of library materials, 873
Preserving library materials: a manual, 865
Preslan, K., 1643
Price, P. P., 250, 803
Primer for agricultural libraries, 2nd ed., 342
Principal's handbook on the school library media center, 288
Principles of indexing and filing, 1056
Principles of information retrieval, 1561
Principles of librarianship, 11
Print for the visually handicapped reader, 1674
Printed ephemera, 416
Prints in the public library, 421
Priorities for academic libraries, 214
Pritchard, A., 450
Private law library, 347
Problems and failures in library automation, 472
Problems in bibliographic access to non-print materials, 406
Problems in developing academic library collections, 734
Problems in intellectual freedom and censorship, 711
Problems in library management, 1202
Problems in library public relations, 1367
Problems in organizing library collections, 523
Problems in school media management, 1341
Problems in university library management, 1289
Problems of document delivery for the EURONET user ..., 1594
Proceedings of a workshop on collection development ..., 1980, 768

Proceedings of the 1970 clinic on library associations ..., 443
Process for developing a competency based educational program ..., 927
Process of managing, 1207
Professional and non-professional duties in libraries, 2nd ed., 1264
Professional librarian's reader in library automation ..., 479
Professional negotiations for media/library professionals, 1321
Progress in documentation, 1577
Progress in educating the library user, 1129
Project progress: a study of Canadian public libraries, 830
Projecting a positive image through public relations, 1368
Prospects for change in bibliographic control, 509
Prostano, E. T., 415, 1337-38
Prostano, J. S., 415, 1337-38
Protecting your collection, 860
Ptacek, W., 1313
Public access to library automation, 465
Public access to online catalogs, 695
Public librarian as adult learners' advisor, 1626
Public librarianship: a reader, 251
Public libraries: an economic view, 246
Public libraries: smart practices in personnel, 1313
Public libraries and new directions for adult services, 252
Public libraries as culture and social centers, 1015
Public libraries in cooperative systems, 1407
Public libraries in the urban metropolitan setting, 244
Public library: circumstances and prospects, 254
Public library administration, 1300
Public library administrator and his situation, 1301
Public library and federal policy, 1121
Public library catalog, *1983*, 8th ed., 131
Public library finance, 1309
Public library in non-traditional education, 1481
Public library in perspective, 258
Public library legislation: a comparative study ..., 1112
Public library movement in the United States 1853-1893, 1018
Public library policy, 253
Public library service for ethnic minorities in Great Britain, 1688
Public library subject headings for 16mm motion pictures, 426
Public library trustee, 1310

Public library user fees, 1485
Public relations for librarians, 2nd ed., 1366
Public relations for libraries: essays ..., 1354
Public relations for public libraries, 1377
Public, school, and academic media centers, 66
Publications on theoretical foundations of information science, 1093
Pulis, J. F., 180
Puppetry library, 344
Purcell, G. R., 938
Purchasing library materials in public and school libraries, 747
Putting library instruction in its place, 1151

Quantitative measurement and dynamic library service, 1236
Quantitative methods in librarianship, 1557
Quarmby, J., 1688
Quien es quien: a who's who of Spanish heritage ..., 179
Quiet world, 1000
Quinly, W. J., 548
Quinn, K. T., 1220
Quirk, D., 1234

Rader, H. B., 1130, 1155
Raffin, M. R., 1462
Raikes, D., 1388
Ramsden, M. J., 1079-80
Random recollections of an anachronism, 993
Ranganathan, S. R., 539
Rare book librarianship, 2nd ed., 377
Rath, F. L., 868
Ratios of staff to users, 1270
Rawles, B. A., 1265
Rawski, C. H., 193
Ray, C., 273, 1632
Ray, S. G., 274, 1633, 1714
Raymond, B., 995
Rayward, W. B., 254, 996
Reaching young people through media, 1716
Reader in American library history, 961
Reader in classification and descriptive cataloging, 524
Reader in comparative librarianship, 796
Reader in government documents, 945
Reader in library and information services, 1091
Reader in library communication, 1359
Reader in library cooperation, 1413
Reader in library management, 1211
Reader in library services and the computer, 445
Reader in library systems analysis, 1250
Reader in library technology, 455
Reader in medical librarianship, 322
Reader in music librarianship, 338

Reader in technical services, 1719
Reader in undergraduate libraries, 236
Reader instruction in colleges and universities, 1198
Reader, the library, and the book, 18
Reading and the adult new reader, 1704
Reading guidance and bibliotherapy ..., 515
Reading research and librarianship, 966
Reading the Russian language, 93
Readings in library history, 958
Ready, W. B., 997
Recommendations for audiovisual materials and services, 410
Recommended reference books for ... centers 1984, 136
Recommended reference books in paperback, 125
Recurring library issues: a reader, 30
Redferb, B., 1213
Reed, J., 1220
Rees, A., 1352, 1545
Reeves, W. J., 1463
Reference and information services: a new reader, 1506
Reference and online services handbook, 1507
Reference and subscription books reviews, 132
Reference as the promotion of free inquiry, 1511
Reference books: a brief guide, 122
Reference books: how to select and use them, 127
Reference books for children, 791
Reference books in special media, 1669
Reference books in the social sciences and humanities, 4th ed., 135
Reference function of the library: papers ..., 1526
Reference readiness: a manual ..., 2nd ed., 1520
Reference resources: a systematic approach, 1517
Reference service, 1504
Reference service: a perspective, 1528
Reference services: an annotated bibliographic guide, 1514
Reference services and library education, 185
Reference sources for small and medium-sized libraries, 4th ed., 133
Reference work in the humanities, 1540
Reference work in the public library, 1524
Referral centres and services: a review, 1529
Reflections of tomorrow, 259
Reform and reaction: the big city public library ..., 1016
Reform and renewal in higher education, 1138
Rehrauer, G., 427
Reich, D. L., 1481
Reichmann, F., 1395
Reilly, J. A., 1626

Reisinger, J. C., 497
*Relationship of the library to instructional
    systems*, 264
Relegation and stock control in libraries, 1728
Religious archives: an introduction, 385
Renford, B., 1131
Report of the register of copyrights, 879
*Report of the task force on library and
    information services to cultural
    minorities*, 1694
Report on library cooperation 1982, 4th ed.,
    1416
*Reprographic services in libraries:
    organization ...*, 876
Reprography for librarians, 878
Requiem for the card catalog, 694
Research and the practitioner, 1552
Research collections in Canadian libraries ...,
    148, 150-51
Research for school media specialists, 1549
*Research librarianship: essays in honor of
    Robert B. Downs*, 191
*Research libraries and collections in the United
    Kingdom*, 152
Research libraries and technology, 213
Research library cooperation in the Caribbean,
    852
*Research methods in librarianship:
    techniques ...*, 1548
*Research methods in librarianship, historical
    and bibliographical methods*, 1553
Research methods in library science, 1555
Resource notebook on staff development, 1267
Resource sharing in libraries, 1421
*Resource sharing of libraries in developing
    countries*, 1435
*Resources of research libraries: a selected
    bibliography*, 144
Restoration of leather bindings ..., 861
Retrieval of information in the humanities ...,
    1542
Reviewing of reference books: an evaluation,
    1503
Revolting librarians, 21
Reynolds, M. M., 1091, 1413
Rhodehamel, J. D., 998
Rhodes, R. G., 1160
Rice, B., 1377
Rice, J., Jr., 1132
Rice, S. A., 1056
Richardson, J., 1046, 1537
Richardson, S. K., 792, 1634
Richmond, P. A., 1081
Ricking, M., 1266
Rider, A. D., 971
Rigby, M., 643
Riggs, D. E., 1460
Right to read and the nation's libraries, 43
Rights of the public employee, 929

Rinehart, C., 1726
Ring, D. F., 1026
Rise of the public library in California, 1019
Ristow, W. W., 331
Ritchie, M., 516
Rittel, H. W. J., 1088
Rizzo, J. R., 1209
Roberts, A. F., 1133
Roberts, D., 1378
Roberts, M. T., 869
Roberts, N., 1144
Roberts, S., 152
Robotham, J., 730
Robotham, J. S., 1379
Rockwood, D. S., 233
Roderer, N. K., 1104, 1425
Rodger, E. J., 1318
Rogers, A. R., 1539
Rogers, F., 1027
Rogers, J. V., 547, 1717
Rogers, R. D., 1290
Rojnić, M., 808
*Role of the beginning librarian in university
    libraries*, 1459
Role of the humanities in the public library,
    242
Role of the library in an electronic society, 36
*Role of the Library of Congress in the evolving
    national network*, 327
*Role of the school library media program in
    networking*, 1414
Role of the state library in adult education,
    1625
Role of women in librarianship 1876-1976,
    1478
Role playing, 1207
*Ronald Brunlee McKerrow: a selection of his
    essays*, 988
Roney, R. G., 389, 906
Roper, F. W., 999
Rosenberg, J. A., 1267
Rosenberg, K. C., 396
Rosenthal, C., 417
Rossmassler, S. A., 1596
Rossoff, M., 275
Rouse, S. H., 1415
Rouse, W. B., 1415
Routines for research, 1178
Rowell, J., 276
Rowley, J. E., 480-81, 1065, 1246
Rowley, P. J., 1246
Roxas, S. A., 846
Rubin, R. J., 517-18, 1701
Rufsvold, M. I., 397
Running a message parlor, 724
*Running out of space – what are the
    alternatives?* 370
Rush, J. E., 1569, 1592
Russell, J. R., 873

Russell, K. W., 606
Russian for librarians, 102
Ryans, C. C., 681

Sable, M. H., 804
Sachse, G., 947
Saffady, W., 1396-97
Sage, M., 917
Sager, D. J., 1268
Salmon, S. R., 451-52
Salton, G., 453
Samore, T., 757
Sample cataloguing forms, 3rd ed., 595
Sampler of forms for special libraries, 298
Samuels, A. R., 1212
SantaVicca, E. F., 1540
Saracevic, T., 1092
Sarkissian, A., 1713
Saul, M., 748
Saunders, H. E., 277
Saunders, W. L., 847
Savage, H., 525, 632-33
Sayre, J. L., 571-72
Scales, P. R., 289
Scarborough, M., 1477
Schad, J. G., 734
Schauder, D. E., 1675
Schlachter, Gail A., 75, 194
Schlipf, F. A., 1269
Schmierer, H. F., 509
Schnare, R. E., 859
Schneider, J. H., 1585
Scholar-librarian and literary maverick, 202
Scholar's workshop, 1006
School and public library media programs for children ..., 1627
School librarian as educator, 1197
School librarian's encyclopedic dictionary, 287
School librarian's grade-by-grade activities program, 1192
School librarianship, 263, 268
School libraries: international developments, 802
School libraries worth their keep, 270
School library and educational change, 275
School library and media center acquisitions policies and procedures, 774
School Library Manpower Project, 1339-40
School library media annual, 1985, 289
School library media center, 3rd ed., 1338
School library media program: instructional force for excellence, 3rd ed., 265
School library media services to the handicapped, 1681
School library personnel task analysis survey, 1340
School library volunteer, 282
School media center: a book of readings, 281

Schorr, A. E., 951
Schrader, A. M., 900
Schultz, C. K., 1586
Schulzetenberg, A. C., 227
Schumacher, A., 1216
Schuman, P. G., 44
Schuster, M., 1134
Schutze, G., 76
Schwartz, B. A., 1199
Schwuchow, W., 1088, 1426
Science and engineering literature, 1537
Scientific and technical libraries, 2nd ed., 1353
Scientific journal, 1620
Scientific management of library operations, 2nd ed., 1204
SCOLMA directory of libraries and special collections on Africa, 4th ed., 161
Search for a scientific profession, 900
Sears list of subject headings, 12th ed., 671
Sears list of subject headings: Canadian companion, 2nd ed., 670
Second-hand knowledge, 51
Selected bibliography on the aging, and the role of ..., 1696
Selected federal computer-based information systems, 1584
Selected U.S. government series, 953
Selecting materials for children and young adults: a bibliography ..., 787
Selecting materials for libraries, 2nd ed., 739
Selective bibliography on the conservation ..., 870
Self-instruction manual for filing catalog cards, 684
Sellen, B. C., 933
Senghas, D. C., 550
Senior high school library catalog, 12th ed., 134
Serial cataloging: a comparison of AACR 1 and 2, 557
Serials: acquisition and maintenance, 1608
Serials automation for acquisition and inventory control, 1616
Serials automation in the United States, 1615
Serials collection: organization and administration, 1602
Serials collection development: choices and strategies, 1610
Serials management and microforms: a reader, 1604
Serials management in an automated age, 1617
Serials publications in large libraries, 1605
Service imperative for libraries, 194
Services of secondary school media centers, 1328
Serving adult learners, 1623
Serving physically disabled people, 1666

Serving the older adult, 1697
Serving youth, 1709
Settel, B., 710
Sewell, P. H., 1118
Sewell, W., 322
Sex and the undecided librarian, 729
Seymour, W. N., 255
Shaffer, K. R., 699, 1210, 1311
Shaping library collections for the 1980s, 735
Shapiro, B. J., 173
Shapiro, L. L., 1194, 1709
SHARE: a directory ..., 3rd ed., 178
Shaughnessy, T., 248
Shaw, M., 593
Shaw, R. V., 428
Sheahan, E., 919
Sheehy, E. P., 54-56
Shelf access in libraries, 679
Sheppard, J., 140
Shera, J. H., 8, 49, 168, 205-6, 902, 1028
Sheridan, R. N., 1703
Sherman, S., 1380
Sherrod, J., 1590
Shields, G., 730
Shields, G. R., 1629
Shiflett, O. L., 1009
Shimmon, R., 1211
Shirey, D., 1343
Shockley, A. A., 91
Shonyo, C., 1217
Shore, E., 776
Shores, L., 50, 393, 903, 1000, 1511
Shreve, I. M., 1353
Shrinking library dollar, 1234
Sign systems for libraries, 373
Silverman, E., 1644-45
Simandl, D., 1070, 1593
Simkin, F., 749
Simmons, P., 467
Simonton, W., 594
Simpson, I. S., 1558
Simsova, S., 805
Simulation activities in library, communication and information science, 1384
Simulation teaching of library administration, 1215
Sinclair, D., 1312
Sinkankas, G. M., 667
Sinnot, L. T., 460, 770-71
Sirkin, A. F., 1616
Sistema de clasificación decimal, 623
Sive, M. R., 402
68 great ideas, 1381
Skallerup, H. R., 1039
SLA triennial salary survey, 299
Slamecka, V., 815
Slater, M., 307, 1270, 1552
Slavens, T. P., 1531, 1541-42
Slide libraries, 425

Sloane, R., 347
Slocum, R. B., 595
Slote, S. J., 1727
Small library cataloging, 533
Small technical libraries, 292
Smith, C., 1398
Smith, J. B., 1549
Smith, J. I., 1692
Smith, L. C., 476
Smith, L. S., 558, 1599
Smith, M. D., 1040
Smith, P. A., 738
Smith, R. D., 874
Smith, S. J., 944
Smith-Burnett, G. C. K., 232
Snow, P., 163
Social history of branch library development ..., 1020
Social responsibilities and libraries, 44
Sociological foundations of librarianship, 49
Soergel, D., 1082
Soroka, M. C., 854
Sourcebook of library technology, 482
Sourcebook on health sciences librarianship, 315
Sources, organization, utilization of international documentation, 510
South Asian library resources in North America, 158
South Asian library resources in North America: papers from the Boston conference, 1974, 158
Southeastern conference on approaches to bibliographic instruction, proceedings, 1140
Sparkle! PR for library staff, 1356
Speaking out, 1672
Special cataloguing with particular reference to music, film, maps ..., 543
Special child in the library, 1677
Special collections in children's literature, 153
Special collections in German libraries, 141
Special collections in libraries of the Southeast, 143
Special collections in the Library of Congress, 165
Special librarian as a supervisor or middle manager, 1346
Special librarianship, 291
Special librarianship: a new reader, 294
Special libraries: a general survey ..., 297
Special libraries: a guide for management with revisions through 1974, 1345
Special libraries and information centers, 296
Special libraries and information centres in Canada: a directory, 300
Special library role in networks, 1420
Sperr, I. L., 1064

Spielberg, P., 127
Spiller, D., 769
SPINDEX users conference, 1454
Spirit of inquiry, 1046
Spirt, D. L., 266, 1195, 1330
Spyers-Duran, P., 694, 735, 755-56, 1607
Srikantaiah, T., 1240, 1559
St. Angelo, D., 1119
Stack management, 1488
Staff communications in libraries, 1256
Staff management in university and college libraries, 1277
Standards for cataloging nonprint materials, 4th ed., 548
Standards for library service: an international survey, 46
Standards for public libraries, 247, 256
Standards of service for the Library of Congress network ... handicapped, 1670
Start early for an early start, 1639
State aid: a survey report, 1120
State library agencies: a survey project report 1983, 6th ed., 349
State library policy: its legislative and environmental contexts, 1119
State publications and depository libraries, 949
Statement of principles adopted at the international conference ..., 574
Statistical methods for librarians, 1556
Status of women in librarianship, 1475
Steady-state, zero-growth and the academic library, 1291
Steele, C., 154, 1291
Stenstrom, R. H., 1418
Stephenson, R. W., 429
Steps to service, 1336
Stereotype and status: librarians in the U.S., 1466
Stevens, B. H., 1302
Stevens, N. B., 77
Stevens, N. D., 77, 195, 959, 1052, 1271
Stevens, R. D., 821
Stevens, R. E., 135, 1272, 1524, 1553
Stevenson, G., 1001
Stibic, V., 1578
Stimulating student search, 1189
Stirling, J. F., 219
Stoakley, R., 1382
Stoffel, L. L., 1407
Stoffle, C. J., 937
Stokes, R., 1002
Stone, E. W., 918-19, 932, 972
Stone, W. C., 220
Story of a small town library, 1027
Story of books and libraries, 971
Story programs: a source book of materials, 1652
Storytelling: art and technique, 1647

Storytelling for teachers and school library media specialists, 1649
Strategies for change in information programs, 35
Strategies for library administration, 1212
Strategies for meeting the information needs of society in the year 2000, 1086
Strategy for public library change, 257
Strauss, L. J., 1353
Strawn, R. R., 1200
Strizich, M. D., 1579
Strom, M. G., 1676
Strong, W. S., 892
Structure and governance of library networks, 1423
Structured PL/I programming for textual and library processing, 500
Struminger, S. A. L., 502
Studies in creative partnership, 1026
Studies in indexing and cataloging, 1058
Studies in library management, 1213
Studies in the international exchange of publications, 762
Study in the syndetic structure of the Library of Congress list of subject headings, 667
Study of combined school-public libraries, 260
Study of library cooperatives ... and demonstration projects, 1412
Study skills for information retrieval, 1183
Stueart, R. D., 20, 209, 221, 736, 1214, 1464
Subject access: report of a meeting sponsored by the council on library resources, 606
Subject analysis: computer application ..., 661
Subject approach to information, 4th ed., 609
Subject authorities: a guide to subject cataloging, 552
Subject bibliography of the social sciences and humanities, 1535
Subject collections: a guide ..., 6th ed., 155
Subject collections in European libraries, 2nd ed., 146
Subject cross reference guide, 659
Subject description of books: a manual of procedures ..., 710
Subject in the dictionary catalog from Cutter to the present, 1050
Subject keyword index to the Library of Congress classification ..., 639
Subject retrieval in the seventies, new directions, 608
Suelflow, A. R., 385
Suffolk parochial libraries: a catalogue, 156
Suitable for children? 731
Sullivan, M., 1267
Sullivan, P., 934, 1003, 1313, 1341
Sullivan, R. C., 876
Supervision of employees in libraries, 1272
Supervisory and middle managers in libraries, 1252

Survey of automated activities in the libraries of the Soviet Union, 845
Survey of commercially available computer-readable bibliographic data bases, 1585
Survey of library service in local correctional facilities, 1698
Sutherland, Z., 717
Suzuki, Y., 819, 1223
Sviridov, F. A., 1093
Swank, R. C., 821
Swanson, D. R., 1108
Swanson, E., 579, 596-97
Swanson, G. L., 607
Swartzburg, S. G., 865
Swihart, S. J., 454
Sykes, P., 258
System for inter-library communication, 1404
Systematic process for planning media programs, 1332
Systems analysis in libraries: a question and answer approach, 1240
Systems approach to library program development, 1238
Szigethy, M. C., 198

Taieb, F., 1302
Tait, J. A., 157, 556, 573
Tales of Melvil's mouser ..., 31
Tanis, N. E., 734, 1245
Tannenbaum, A. C., 1391
Tarakan, S. L., 398
Targets for research in library education, 896
Tauber, M. F., 682
Taylor, D., 634
Taylor, D. C., 1622
Taylor, H., 1098
Taylor, L. J., 100
Taylor, M. M., 774
Taylor, M. T., 1525
Taylor, P. J., 1109
Taylor, R. S., 222
Taylor, W. D., 1473
Tayyeb, R., 85
Teaching for better use of libraries, 1142
Teaching library media skills, 1196
Teaching library skills in freshman English, 1199
Teaching library use: a guide for library instruction, 1132
Teaching library use competence, 2nd ed., 1201
Teaching role of the school media specialist, 280
Teaching with books, 226
Teaching yourself in libraries, 1194
Teague, S. J., 1399

Technical services manual for small libraries, 1723
Techniques of information retrieval, 1566
Technology and copyright, 2nd ed., 883
Tedd, L. A., 483
Telecommunications and libraries, 24
Telling stories to children, 1653
Ten-year supplement to abridged UDC editions, 1958-1968, 645
Tenopir, C., 1582
Tepper, K., 1370
Terminologie de la documentation, 86
Terwillegar, J. C., 537
Tessier, J. A., 1597
Thawley, J. D., 90
Theological library manual, 335
Theoretical problems of informatics, 1100
Theories of bibliographic education, 1141
Theory and practice in library education, 901
Thesaurus in retrieval, 1074
Thesaurus of information science terminology, 1586
Thesaurus-making, 1587
30,000 libraries: a practical guide, 1166
Thomas Bray's grand design: libraries of the Church of England in America, 1022
Thomas Frognall Dibdin: selections, 994
Thomas, C. H., 1663-65
Thomas, J. L., 1646, 1649, 1663-65
Thomasen, C. E., 434
Thomason, N. W., 278
Thomison, D., 973
Thompson, E. T., 101
Thompson, G., 375
Thompson, J., 9-10, 484, 1001, 1292
Thompson, L. S., 207-8
Thomson, S. K., 1293, 1429-30
Tillin, A., 411
Tillin, A. M., 548
Time-lag in cataloging, 555
Title derivative indexing techniques, 1071
To free the mind, 728
To know a library: essays and annual reports, 201
Today's youth/today's librarian, 1715
Tomorrow's library: direct access ..., 1496
Tonks, P., 439
Toor, R., 1342
Topics, terms, and research techniques, 1200
Toshokan: libraries in Japanese society, 822
Total community library service, 1493
Totten, H. L., 910
Totterdell, B., 1314
Tou, J. T., 1591
Toward a national serials data program, 1612
Toward a philosophy of educational librarianship, 212
Toward a theory of librarianship: papers in honor of Jesse Hauk Shera, 193

*Toward the improvement of library
    education*, 895
Towards a theory for UDC, 647
*Transportation libraries in the U.S. and
    Canada*, 348
Trash into treasure, 1645
Trejo, A. D., 179
Trezza, A. F., 376
Trinkner, C. L., 1142
Tseng, H. P., 893
Tseng, S. C., 598
Tsukamoto, J. T., 1156
Tsuneishi, W. M., 819, 1223
Tucker, J. M., 185
Tucker, N., 731
Tucker, N. P., 871
Turick, D., 1512
Turner, A. C., 629
Turner, P. M., 279
Turning kids on to print using nonprint, 1646
Turock, B. J., 1697
Turow, J., 1635
Tuttle, M., 1603

UK online search services, 1438
Undergraduate library, 225
Understanding scientific literatures, 514
Union lists, 559
Unionization: the viewpoint of librarians, 1257
UNISIST: report on the feasibility, 1110
United Nations family of libraries, 797
United Nations library, 1032
*United States: a guide to library holdings in
    the UK*, 163
U.S. copyright documents, 890
*U.S. government publications for small and
    medium-sized public libraries*, 947
*U.S. government publications for the school
    media center*, 954
U.S. prison library services, 1701
*Universal decimal classification: the history,
    present status and future prospects ...*,
    644
*Universe of information: the work of Paul
    Otlet ...*, 996
*University and research libraries in Japan and
    the United States*, 819
University librarianship, 219
University libraries in Britain, 211
University library administration, 1290
University library history, 1010
University library in the United States, 1007
University science and engineering libraries,
    2nd ed., 345
*Urban analysis for branch library system
    planning*, 1302
Urquhart, D., 11
Urquhart, J. A., 1728

Urquhart, N. C., 1728
*Use, mis-use and non-use of academic
    libraries*, 223
Use of community college libraries, 224
*Use of computers in libraries and information
    centres*, 456
*Use of computers in literature searching and
    related reference activities in
    libraries*, 1574
*Use of library materials: the University of
    Pittsburgh study*, 1227
*Use of slide/tape presentations in academic
    libraries*, 1147
*User education: toward a better use of
    information resources*, 1139
User education in libraries, 1169
User fees: a practical perspective, 1482
Usherwood, B., 1383
Using AACR 2: a diagrammatic approach, 593
*Using bibliotherapy: a guide to theory and
    practice*, 518
Using libraries: an informative guide ...,
    3rd ed., 1181
Using online catalogs: a nationwide survey, 696
Using the library: the card catalog, 677

Vaillancourt, P. M., 120
Van House, N. A., 1485
Van Orden, P., 737, 775
van Rijsbergen, C. J., 1564, 1580
Van Zant, N. P., 953
Vandercook, S., 952
Vandergrift, K. E., 280
Vann, S. K., 1004, 1047
Vanwijngaerden, F., 763
Varlejs, J., 530, 1718
Vasu, E. S., 1556
Vavrek, B., 1513
Veaner, A., 440
Veillette, P. D., 747
Veit, F., 235
Velleman, R. A., 1666
Velucci, M. J., 1584
Venkatappaiah, V., 196
Vernon, K. D. C., 656
Verona, E., 562, 574
Vertical file and its satellites ..., 2nd ed.,
    418
Vervliet, H. D. L., 1435
Vickery, B. C., 1083, 1565-66
Video in libraries: a status report, 2nd ed., 432
Video involvement for libraries, 433
Vignone, J. A., 1315
Virgo, J. A., 920
Visible library, 1383
Viswanathan, C. G., 540
*Vocabulary control for information
    retrieval*, 1076

*Vocational-technical periodicals for
    community college libraries*, 784
Von Busse, G., 848
Vosper, R., 1434

Waldhart, E. S., 29
Waldhart, T. J., 29
Walford, A. J., 57-60
Walford's concise guide to reference material,
    58
Walford's guide to reference material, vol. 1,
    4th ed., 59
Walford's guide to reference material, vol. 2,
    4th ed., 60
Walker, D. E., 1554
Walker, G., 863
Walker, G., 102, 159
Walker, H. T., 1196
Walker, R., 1552
Wallace, M., 347
Wallenius, A. B., 818
Walling, R., 183
Wallington, C. J., 935
Wallis, H., 332
Walsh, P. M., 1604
Walton, J. M., 1524
Ward, P. L., 281
Wareham, N. L., 1416
Warncke, R., 921
Warnken, K., 1546
Warren, G. G., 1465
Wasserman, P., 45, 79, 1301
Wassom, E. E., 700
Watson, D. G., 1596
Watson, P. G., 849, 1456, 1509
Weatherford, J. W., 1294
Weber, D. C., 1290
Weber, H., 616
Weber, O. S., 103, 399
Wedgeworth, R., 81, 106
Weeding library collections-II, 2nd ed., 1727
Wehmeyer, L. B., 282, 1197
Weibel, K., 1478
Weihs, J., 407
Weingand, D. E., 259, 1479
Weisburg, H. K., 1342
Weisman, H. M., 1567
Weiss, E. C., 1111
Welch, T. F., 821-22
Wellisch, H., 608, 1069
Wellisch, J. B., 1121
Welsch, E. K., 850
Werner, O. J., 1702
Wersig, G., 86
Wertheimer, L., 780
West, C., 21
Westby, B. M., 671
Wexler, M., 267

What black librarians are saying, 1690
What else you can do with a library degree, 933
What happens in library filing? 687
Whatley, H. A., 851
Whatmore, G., 350
Wheeler, J. L., 1316
*Wheeler and Goldhor's practical administration
    of public libraries*, 1316
Where to find what, 1521
Where's that rule? 587
Whitbeck, G. W., 1295
Whitby, T. J., 513
White, B. H., 184
White, C. M., 1048
White, H. S., 894
White, M. L., 790
*White house conference on library and
    information services, 1979*, 22
Whitestone, P., 880, 1234
Whittaker, K., 1181
*Who's who in librarianship and information
    science*, 2nd ed., 170
Who's who in library and information services,
    171
Who's who in special libraries, 1985-86, 303
Who-what-when-where-how-why made easy,
    1523
Wieder, J., 799
Wiegand, W. A., 1053
Wijasuriya, D. E. K., 823
Wilkinson, B. R., 236
Williams, B. J. S., 1401
Williams, H. L., 493
Williams, J. G., 669, 1384
Williams, M. E., 1588
Williams, N. Z., 1156
Williams, S. L., 116
Williams, S. P., 167
Williams, W. J., 1516
Williams & Wilkins Case, 888
Williamson, W. L., 839
Williamson reports of 1921 and 1923, 1047
Willis, R. E., 867
Willis, S. O., 1323
Wilson, P., 51, 786, 1466
Wilson, T. D., 608, 1084
Winger, H. W., 874
Winkel, L., 793
Winkler, P. W., 577
Winning the money game, 1385
Wisdom, A. C., 1474
Withers, F. N., 46
Wittig, A. J., 954
Wittkopf, B. J., 1164
Wolf, C. E., 1182
Wolf, R., 1182
Women and library management, 1479
*Women in librarianship: Melvil's rib
    symposium*, 1477

Women view librarianship, 1476
Wood, R. F., 998
Woods, L. B., 732
Woodward, A. M., 1611
Woolard, W. L. B., 283
Woolls, B., 1343, 1409
*Working bibliography of commercially
    available audiovisual materials ...*, 907
*Workshop for Japanese collection librarians in
    American research libraries*, 164
World directory of administrative libraries, 310
World guide to libraries, 6th ed., 118
World guide to library schools and training ...,
    2nd ed., 909
*World guide to technical information and
    documentation services*, 121
World librarianship: a comparative study, 800
World of storytelling, 1651
World trends in library education, 897
Worldwide directory of federal libraries, 311
Wright, A. E., 1472
Wright, H. C., 973
Wright, H. K., 132
Wright, K. C., 1667
Wright, L. B., 1011
Wynar, B. S., 61, 123, 136, 168, 541, 751, 1555
Wynar, C. G., 794

Wynar, L. R., 1514

Yaakov, J., 126
You can do it: a PR manual for librarians, 1370
Young adult literature in the seventies, 1718
Young, A. P., 975
Young, H., 87, 1296
Young, L. S., 866
Young, M. J., 497
Young, M. L., 980
Young, V. G., 1317
Your library: a reference guide, 1176
Your library: what's in it for you? 1179
Your search key to L.C., student's ed., 630
Your search key to L.C., teacher's ed., 631
Youth library work, 2nd ed., 1714
Youth, society, and the public library, 1012
Yska, G., 1598

Zaccaria, J. S., 519
Zachert, M. J. K., 1215
Zero-based budgeting in library management,
    1226
Ziskind, S., 1653
Zögner, L., 332
Zunde, P., 815
Zweizig, D., 1318

Subject Index

AACR, 556, 565, 567, 569-71, 573
AACR2, 553, 575-98
Abstracting
  general works, 1057, 1059, 1064-65
  reference works, 1067-69
Acquisitions. *See also* Technical services:
    acquisitions
  general works, 744-49
  approval plans, 753-56
  foreign materials, 757-60
  gifts and exchanges, 761-63
  introductory texts and manuals, 752
  nonbook materials, 764
  reference works, 750-51
  serials, 1608-11
  technical services, 1720, 1725
Abbreviations and acronyms, 98
Administration. *See* Management
Adult learners, 1623-26, 1703-5
Africa, 297, 816-18
Agricultural libraries, 166, 340, 342
Anglo-American cataloging rules. See AACR
Anglo-American cataloguing rules, second
    edition. See AACR2
Annuals and yearbooks, 104-10
Approval plans, 753-56
Architecture, 352-57, 359-63, 367-69, 375-76
Archives, 378, 381-82, 385, 858, 860, 867, 871
Asheim, Lester, 187
Asia, 810
ASIS (American Society for Information
    Science), 1097, 1104, 1106
Aslib, 301, 1095-96, 1098, 1102, 1105, 1107
Audiovisual and other media
  general works, 386-92, 1646
  in academic libraries, 408
  bibliographic control, 405-6
  bulletin boards, 417
  cataloging and classification, 542-48
  collection development, 400-402
  ephemera, 416, 418
  film, 420, 422, 426-27

maps, 429
  organization, 403-4, 407
  phonorecords, 430-31
  pictures, 419, 421, 423-24,
    428
  in public libraries, 409-10
  reference works, 394-99
  in school library media centers,
    411-15
  slides, 425
  video, 432-34
Australia, 825-26
Authority control, 549-52
Autobiography. *See also* Biography
  Liebaers, Herman, 991
  Lyle, Guy R., 992
  Metcalf, Keyes DeWitt, 993
  Milam, Carl H., 1031
  Ready, William B., 997
  Shores, Louis, 1000
Automation in libraries, 452-53, 470, 474, 484.
    See also Microcomputer use;
    Minicomputer use; Programming
    languages
  circulation systems, 1486-87
  data processing, 437, 441, 443
  handbooks, 454, 461, 475
  hardware, 487
  introductory works, 435, 439,
    444, 449-50, 466, 480-81,
    483
  online cataloging, 690-710
  online searching, 1436-56
  proceedings, symposia, reports, and essays,
    436-38, 440, 442-43, 445, 447-48, 451,
    455-60, 462-64, 468-69, 471-73,
    476-79, 482
  public access, 465
  reference services, 1507, 1509
  reference works, 485-86
  serials, 1612-18
  textbooks, 446, 467

Basler, Roy P., 199
Bibliographic control
  general works, 503
  International Standard Bibliographic
    Description (Antiquarian), ISBD(A),
    511
  International Standard Bibliographic
    Description, Monographs, (ISBD),
    572
  International Standard Bibliographic
    Description, Printed Music,
    ISBD(PM), 512
  microforms, 1395
  proceedings, symposia, and essays, 509
Bibliographic instruction, 1126, 1131, 1136,
  1140-41, 1146, 1154
Bibliographies
  general, 62-64, 68-72, 76, 78-79
  ERIC, 62, 65
  FID, 67
  learning resource centers, 65-66
Bibliography
  general works, 504-6
  proceedings, symposia, and essays, 507-8, 510
  Soviet national, 513
Bibliotherapy, 514-19
Biographical works
  authors, 176
  blacks, 175, 177
  comprehensive, 168-71
  consultants, 174
  ethnic studies, 173
  Hispanics, 179
  special libraries, 303
  women, 172, 178
Biography. *See also* Autobiography
  Coolbrith, Ina, 998
  Cutter, Charles Ammi, 981
  Dewey, Melvil, 1001, 1004
  Dibdin, Thomas Frognall, 994
  Fogarty, John E., 987
  Ford, Paul Leicester, 985
  Gorgas, Amelia Gayle, 989
  Jewett, Charles Coffin, 986
  Krupskaia, Nadezhda, 995
  Leyh, Georg, 984
  Librarians of Congress, 990
  MacDonald, Angus Snead, 352
  McKerrow, Ronald Brunlees, 988
  McMurtrie, Douglas C., 980
  Milam, Carl H., 1003
  Otlet, Paul, 996
  Pollard, Alfred William, 999
  Sadleir, Michael, 1002
  Spofford, Ainsworth Rand, 982
  Winsor, Justin, 983
Blacks, 91, 175, 177, 1690
Bliss, 612-13
Book numbers, 648-49

Broad System of Ordering (BSO), 1070
Budgeting and finance, 1224-34
Bulletin boards, 417
Business and industrial libraries, 304-7

Canada, 52, 113, 130, 137, 147-48, 150-51,
  155, 300, 308, 336, 809, 827-30, 900,
  908, 964, 1033, 1041, 1453
Caribbean, 852
Catalog maintenance
  general works, 677-82
  filing, 683-89
Cataloging. *See also* Classification
  general works, 520, 522, 524
  AACR, 556, 565, 567, 569-71, 573
  AACR2, 553, 575-98
  analytics, 561
  audiovisual materials, 542-48
  authority control, 549-52
  corporate authors, 560, 562
  introductory texts and manuals, 527-37,
    539-41, 563-74
  Library of Congress service, 525-26
  rare books, 521
  research, 553-56
  serials, 557-59
Censorship and intellectual freedom
  general works, 711-13, 715, 718-30
  public libraries, 714, 717, 731
  school library media centers, 716-17,
    731-32
  sex, 727, 729
Cheney, Frances Neel, 185
Children's library services
  general works, 1627-35
  disabled, 1677-82
  international, 1632
  media skills and curriculum enrichment,
    1640-46
  proceedings, symposia, and essays,
    1638-39
  reference works, 1636-37
  storytelling, 1647-53
China, Republic of, 807
Church libraries. *See* Theological collections
  and church and synagogue libraries
Circulation systems, 1486-89
Classification. *See also* Cataloging; Subject
  headings
  general works, 523-24, 599-608
  Bliss, 612-13
  book numbers, 648-49
  Brunet, 653
  Dewey Decimal, 600, 607, 614-23
  International Labour Office, 652
  introductory texts and manuals, 527, 529,
    532, 536, 538, 541, 609-11
  Library of Congress, 600, 607, 624-41

National Library of Medicine, 655
other schemes, 650-51, 656
Universal Decimal, 642-47
Collected writings
Basler, Roy P., 199
Ellsworth, Ralph E., 200
Gore, Daniel, 201
Hoole, William S., 202
MacLeish, Archibald, 203
Oboler, Eli M., 204
Shera, Jesse H., 205-6
Shores, Louis, 197
Tauber, Maurice F., 198
Thompson, Lawrence S., 207-8
Collection development, 806. *See also*
Selection aids; Selection process
general works, 733-37
acquisitions, 1608-11
audiovisual media, 400-402
introductory texts and manuals, 739-43
reference works, 738
Collective bargaining, 1269, 1274, 1294, 1315.
See also Unions
College and university libraries, 209-36, 1191,
1198-1201
audiovisual and other media in, 408
collection development, 733-34, 770-72
disabled users, 1663
history, 1005-11
Japanese, 819, 821
library instruction, 1143-56
management, 1274-96
networking and resource sharing, 1411,
1428-29
personnel, 1459
reference services, 1510, 1544
selection aids, 781-84
statistics, 237-40
Communications, 23-29
Community services, 1490-97
Comparative and international
librarianship
general works, 182, 795-805
Africa, 816, 818
Asia, 810
Australia, 825-26
Brazil, 853
Canada, 809, 827-30
Caribbean, 852
China, Republic of, 807
Europe, 840
France, 842, 850
Great Britain, 847, 849, 851,
1431
IFLA, 1435
India, 812, 820
Italy, 846
Japan, 819, 821-22
Middle East, 811

networking and resource sharing, 813-15,
1431-35, 1594
New Zealand, 826
Papua New Guinea, 824
Poland, 844
reference services, 1533
reference works, 807-12
Senegal, 817
Southeast Asia, 823
Third World, 831-39, 1435
UNESCO, 1435
USSR, 841, 843, 845, 995
West Germany, 848
Yugoslavia, 808
Conservation and preservation
general works, 854-66
proceedings and seminars, 871-74
reference works, 867-70
Continuing education, 912-21
Coolbrith, Ina, 998
Copyright, 875, 877, 879, 882-94, 1656. *See
also* Reprography
Current issues, 30-46
Curriculum studies, 922-24
Cutter, Charles Ammi, 981

Databases. *See* Online searching:
databases; Retrieval systems:
databases
Descriptive cataloging. *See* Cataloging
Dewey, Melvil, 1001, 1004
Dewey Decimal Classification, 600, 607,
614-23
Dibdin, Thomas Frognall, 994
Dictionaries, 82, 84-87
Directories
Canadian, 113, 300, 308
international, 112, 114-18, 120-21, 310-11
special libraries, 300-302
U.S., 111
Disabled users
general works, 1654-67
blind and physically handicapped, 1654,
1659, 1662, 1666, 1670-76
children and young adults, 1677-82
reference works, 1668-69
Disadvantaged users, 1683-87
Dissertations and theses, 75, 90
Downs, Robert B., 191

Education
general works, 895-903
Canada, 900, 908, 1041
continuing, 912-21
curriculum studies, 922-24
Great Britain, 905, 914
history, 1041-48

Education *(continued)*
  Latin America, 911
  proceedings and symposia, 910-11
  reference works, 904-9
  school media personnel, 925-27
  Third World, 923
Elderly, 1695-97
Ellsworth, Ralph E., 200
Employment, 928-35. *See also* Professional
  status
Encyclopedias, 81, 83
Ephemera, 416, 418
Essays, 18, 21
Ethnic minorities, 1688-94
Europe, 146, 840
Evaluating and measurement, 1235-46,
  1303, 1318-19, 1326, 1328, 1343

Facilities and equipment, 351, 353, 358,
  364-66, 370-74
Fast, Elizabeth T., 184
Federal Republic of Germany, 141, 848
Festschriften
  Asheim, Lester, 187
  Cheney, Frances Neel, 185
  Downs, Robert B., 191
  Fast, Elizabeth T., 184
  Gladstone, Joan M., 186
  Hermannsson, Halldór, 190
  indexes, 180
  Kaula, P. N., 196
  Lyle, Guy R., 183
  Marshall, D. N., 182
  Monroe, Margaret E., 194
  Orne, Jerrold, 192
  Pafford, Jack, 189
  Shaw, Ralph, 195
  Shera, Jesse H., 193
  Staveley, Ronald, 188
  Urquhart, Donald, 181
FID (Federation Internationale de
  Documentation), 1088, 1093, 1099,
  1100, 1109
Filing rules, 683-89
Film, 420, 422, 426-27
Fogarty, John E., 987
Ford, Paul Leicester, 985
Funding, 1120, 1122-25, 1385

Gifts and exchanges, 761-63
Gladstone, Joan M., 186
Gore, Daniel, 201
Gorgas, Amelia Gayle, 989
Government libraries, 308-11
Government publications
  general works, 936-37, 941, 945-46, 1394
  British, 952

  local, 939, 944
  proceedings, 955-57
  reference works, 948, 951
  state, 949-50
  UN, 940
  U.S., 938, 942-43, 947, 950, 953-54
Great Britain, 78, 98, 139-40, 152, 156, 847,
  849, 851, 905, 914, 952, 967, 969, 977,
  1431, 1438, 1447, 1533, 1536, 1633,
  1688, 1728

Handbooks and manuals, 100
  books by mail, 94
  foreign language, 89, 93, 102
  international correspondence, 88
  international developments, 92
Handicapped users. *See* Disabled users
Health sciences libraries, 312-22
Hermannsson, Halldór, 190
Hispanics, 179
History
  general works, 958, 962-63, 965-66, 968, 971
  biography, 980-1004
  British, 967, 969, 977
  Canadian, 964, 1033
  college and university libraries, 1005-11
  Greek, 974
  library education, 1041-48
  National Library of Canada, 1033
  private libraries, 1029, 1036, 1040
  proceedings, 978-79
  public libraries, 1012-28
  publishing, 1049
  special libraries, 1030, 1034-35, 1037-38
  subject headings, 1050
  UN library, 1031-32
  U.S., 959-60, 961, 964, 970, 972-73, 975-76
Hoole, William S., 202
Humor, 1051-53

IFLA. *See* International Federation of Library
  Associations and Institutions
Indexes, 80
Indexing
  general works, 1054-58, 1060-65
  automatic keyword classification, 1075
  BSO (Broad System of Ordering), 1070
  chain, 1084
  citation, 1073
  of newspapers, 1077
  personal, 1072
  PRECIS, 1078, 1080-81
  reference works, 1066-69
  in sciences, 1083
  title derivative, 1071
  vocabulary control, 1074, 1076, 1079,
  1082

India, 812, 820
Information management
  general works, 1085-92
  ASIS, 1097, 1104, 1106
  Aslib, 1095-96, 1098, 1102, 1105, 1107
  FID, 1088, 1093, 1099, 1100, 1109
  proceedings, symposia, and essays, 1095-1111
  reference works, 1093-94
  UNESCO, 1088, 1110
Information retrieval, 1074-76
Information science, 34-35
Information services, 112, 114
Information systems and networks, 813-15
Interlibrary loan, 1425-30
International Federation of Library
      Associations and Institutions (IFLA),
      117, 253, 799, 1435
International Standard Bibliographic
      Description (Antiquarian), ISBD(A), 511
International Standard Bibliographic
      Description, Monographs, (ISBD), 572
International Standard Bibliographic
      Description, Printed Music, ISBD(PM),
      512
Introductory works, 1-11
ISBD. *See* International Standard Bibliographic
      Description, Monographs
ISBD(A). *See* International Standard
      Bibliographic Description (Antiquarian)
ISBD(PM). *See* International Standard
      Bibliographic Description, Printed
      Music

Japan, 819, 821
Jewett, Charles Coffin, 986

Kaula, P. N., 196
Krupskaia, Nadezhda, 995

Latin America, 853, 911
Law libraries, 337, 341, 347
Learning resource centers, 65-66, 272. *See also*
      School library media centers
Legislation and public policy, 95, 1112-21
Leyh, Georg, 984
Libraries and society, 32-33, 36-37, 40-45, 241,
      243-44, 248-49, 252, 255, 258-59
Library cooperation. *See* Networking and
      resource sharing
Library education. *See* Education
Library holdings
  British and Irish, 139-40, 152, 156
  Canadian, 137, 147-48, 150-51, 155
  comprehensive, 137-57
  European, 146
  international, 154

Library of Congress, 165
National Agricultural Library, 166
New York Public Library, 167
regional studies, 158-64
Scottish, 157
Soviet, 142
U.S., 138, 143-45, 153, 155
West German, 141
Library instruction
  general works, 1126-34
  college and university libraries, 1143-56
  proceedings, symposia, and essays, 1136-42
  reference works, 1135
  school library media centers, 1157-59
  UNISIST, 1160
Library of Congress, 165, 323-36, 525-26,
      990, 1030, 1034
Library of Congress Classification, 600, 607,
      624-41
Library of Congress Subject Headings, 662-69
Library orientation guides
  general works, 1161-82
  college and university libraries, 1191,
      1198-1201
  school library media centers, 1183-90,
      1192-97
Library philosophy, 10, 38
Library resources, 96
Library science
  current issues, 31-46
  introductory works, 1-11
  theoretical foundations, 47-51
Library service, 46
Liebaers, Herman, 991
Local history collections, 101, 379-80,
      384
Lyle, Guy R., 183, 992

MacDonald, Angus Snead, 352
MacLeish, Archibald, 203
Management
  general works, 1202-15
  budgeting and finance, 1224-34
  college and university libraries, 1274-96
  evaluating and measurement, 1235-46, 1303,
      1318-19, 1326, 1328, 1343
  planning and decision-making systems,
      1247-51
  proceedings, symposia, and essays,
      1218-23
  public libraries, 1297-1318
  reference works, 1216-17
  school library media centers, 1319-43
  special libraries, 1344-53
  staffing personnel, 1252-73
Manuscripts, 381-82, 860
Map libraries, 328-32, 429
MARC, 701-3

Marketing and promotion, 1357-64, 1369, 1371-76, 1378, 1380-82, 1384-85. *See also* Public relations
Marshall, D. N., 182
Mason, Ellsworth, 363
McKerrow, Ronald Brunlees, 988
McMurtrie, Douglas C., 980
Measurement. *See* Evaluating and measurement
Medical libraries. *See* Health sciences libraries
Metcalf, Keyes DeWitt, 993
Microcomputer use, 488-93
Microforms
   general works, 1386-95, 1397-1401
   microfilm, 1396
   serials, 1604
Milam, Carl H., 1003, 1031
Minicomputer use, 494-97
Monroe, Margaret E., 194
Museum libraries, 339, 343
Music libraries, 338

National Agricultural Library, 166
National Library of Canada, 1033
National Library of Medicine, 655, 1037
Networking and resource sharing
   general works, 1402-16
   college and university libraries, 1411, 1428-29
   EURONET, 1594
   interlibrary loan, 1425-30
   international, 1431-35, 1455
   proceedings, symposia, and essays, 1419-24
   public libraries, 1407
   reference works, 1417-18
   school library media centers, 1414
New Zealand, 826
Newspaper and broadcasting libraries, 336, 350
Nonprint materials. *See* Audiovisual and other media

Oboler, Eli M., 204
OCLC, 704-8
Online cataloging and automation
   general works, 690-700
   MARC, 701-3
   OCLC, 704-8
   other systems, 709-10
Online retrieval systems. *See* Retrieval systems: online
Online searching
   general works, 1436-45
   databases, 1448-50, 1452-53
   proceedings, 1454-56
   reference works, 1446-53
Orientation guides. *See* Library orientation guides
Orne, Jerrold, 192
Otlet, Paul, 996

Pafford, Jack, 189
Paraprofessionals, 1467-72
Periodicals. *See* Serials
Personnel. *See* Professional status; Staffing and personnel
Phonorecords, 430-31
Pictures, 419, 421, 423-24, 428
Planning and decision-making systems, 1247-51
Pollard, Alfred William, 999
PRECIS, 1078, 1080-81
Prisoners, 1698-1702
Prizes, 103
Proceedings, 12-13, 15-17, 20
Professional status
   general works, 1264, 1276, 1278, 1286, 1457-66
   paraprofessionals, 1467-72
   school library media centers, 1473-74
   special libraries, 1349
   women, 1475-79
Programming languages, 498-502
Promotion. *See* Marketing and promotion; Public relations
Public libraries, 241-59, 1373, 1377
   adult learners, 1623-24, 1626
   audiovisual and other media in, 409-10
   and children, 1627-31, 1634
   community services, 1492, 1494
   disabled users, 1662, 1668
   elderly users, 1695
   funding, 1113, 1120
   history, 1012-29
   legislation, 1112
   management, 1297-1318
   networking and resource sharing, 1407, 1432
   public policy, 1121
   public services, 1481, 1485
   reference services, 1532
   selection aids, 785-86
   young adults, 1708
Public policy. *See* Legislation and public policy
Public relations, 1354-56, 1365-68, 1370, 1377, 1383. *See also* Marketing and promotion
Public services
   general works, 1480-85
   circulation systems, 1486-89
   community services and information, 1490-97
   user studies, 1498-99
Publishers and publishing, 1049, 1620, 1622, 1711

Rare books, 377, 521, 855, 860
Ready, William B., 997

Reference services
  general works, 1500-13, 1546
  alternative approaches, 1543
  consumer services, 1545
  introductory texts and manuals, 1515-25
  proceedings and essays, 1526-28
  reference strategies, 1529-31
  reference works, 1514
  research studies, 1532-33
  subject approaches, 1534-42
  telephone services, 1544
Reference sources, 52-61, 122-23, 125, 127,
    132-33, 135-36, 1503, 1515-17, 1525
Reports, 19, 22
Reprography, 875-80, 881-82. *See also*
    Copyright
Research
  general works, 73, 105, 110, 285, 896,
    1547-55
  school library media centers, 1549
  statistical methods, 1556-59
Research libraries. *See* College and university
    libraries
Research studies, 1532-33
Resource sharing. *See* Networking and resource
    sharing
Retrieval systems
  general works, 1560-61, 1563-70, 1572,
    1575-80
  Broad System of Ordering (BSO), 1593
  databases, 1581-83, 1585, 1588, 1598
  ERIC, 1597
  EURONET, 1594
  online, 1562, 1571, 1573-74, 1581, 1583-85
  PROBE, 1595
  proceedings and symposia, 1589-91
  reference works, 1581-88
  subject approaches, 1592, 1596

Sadleir, Michael, 1002
School library media centers. *See also* Learning
    resource centers
  general works, 260-83, 802, 1627, 1629-30,
    1709
  activities, 286
  audiovisual and other media, 411-15
  collection development, 773-75
  disabled children and young adults, 1681-82
  disadvantaged users, 1683
  education of personnel, 915, 925-27
  instructional design, 264, 269
  library instruction, 1157-59
  management, 1319-43
  materials, 1638
  media skills and curriculum enrichment,
    1640-46
  networking and resource sharing, 1414
  orientation guides, 1183-90, 1192-97

  personnel, 1473-74
  reference works, 284-89
  research, 1549
  selection aids, 787-94, 954
Science and engineering libraries, 345
Sears list, 670-71
Selection aids. *See also* Selection process
  college and university libraries, 781-84
  fiction, 126
  magazines, 129
  public libraries, 130-31, 785-86
  reference, 52-61, 122-23, 125, 127, 132-33,
    135-36, 1503, 1515-17, 1525
  school library media centers, 124, 128,
    134, 136, 787-94
Selection process. *See also* Collection
    development; Selection aids
  general works, 765-69
  alternative press materials, 776
  college and university libraries, 733-34,
    770-72
  fiction, 777
  foreign materials, 780
  medical literature, 779
  phonorecords, 778
  school library media centers, 773-75
Serials
  general works, 77, 1403, 1599-1604, 1621
  access, 1619
  acquisitions, 129, 1608-11
  automation, 1612-18
  proceedings, symposia, and essays, 1605-7
  publication, 1620, 1622
Shaw, Ralph, 195
Shera, Jesse H., 193, 205-6
Shores, Louis, 197, 1000
SLA. *See* Special Libraries Association
Slides, 425
Southeast Asia, 823
Soviet national bibliography, 513
Special libraries and collections
  general works, 155, 159, 161, 290-99,
    382-83, 1390
  agricultural, 166, 340, 342
  business and industrial, 304-7
  Canadian, 300, 308, 1033
  children's literature, 153
  government, 308-11
  health sciences, 312-22
  history, 101, 379-80, 384, 1029-40
  law, 336, 341, 347
  Library of Congress, 165, 323-27
  management, 1344-53
  manuscript solicitation, 381
  map, 328-32, 429
  museums, 339, 343
  music, 338
  newspaper and broadcasting, 336, 350
  puppetry, 344

Special libraries and collections *(continued)*
  rare books, 377
  reference works, 300-303
  science and engineering, 345
  South Africa, 297
  state agencies, 349
  technical, 292
  theological, 333-35, 385
  transportation, 348
Special Libraries Association (SLA), 299
Special user groups, 1698-1702
  adult learners, 1623-26, 1703-5
  children, 1627-53
  disabled, 1654-81
  disadvantaged, 1683-87
  elderly, 1654, 1695-97
  ethnic minorities, 1688-94
  young adults, 1706-18
Spofford, Ainsworth Rand, 982
Staffing and personnel, 1252-73. *See also*
    Volunteers
Statistics, 237-40, 1556-59
Staveley, Ronald, 188
Storytelling, 1647-53
Subject headings
  general works, 657
  Arab states authors, 672
  biomedical, 676
  Canadian, 673
  Catholic, 674
  history, 1050
  hospital literature, 675
  introductory texts and manuals, 660-61
  Library of Congress, 662-69
  reference works, 658-59
  Sears, 670-71
Symposia, 14
Synagogue libraries. *See* Theological collections
    and church and synagogue libraries

Tauber, Maurice F., 198
Technical services
  general works, 1719, 1724, 1726

  acquisitions, 1720, 1725
  introductory texts and manuals, 1721-23
  weeding, 1727-28
Telecommunications, 24
Theological collections and church and
    synagogue libraries, 333-35, 385
Theoretical foundations, 47-51
Third World, 831-39, 923, 1435
Thompson, Lawrence S., 207-8

UDC. *See* Universal Decimal Classification
UNESCO, 1088, 1110, 1435
Union of Soviet Socialist Republics, 142, 513,
    841, 843, 845, 995
Unions, 1257, 1263, 1321. *See also* Collective
    bargaining
UNISIST, 1160
United Nations, 940, 1031-32. *See also*
    UNESCO
Universal Decimal Classification, 642-47
University libraries. *See* College and university
    libraries
Urquhart, Donald, 181
User studies, 1498-99

Video, 432-34
Volunteers, 282. *See also* Staffing and
    personnel

West Germany. *See* Federal Republic of
    Germany
Winsor, Justin, 983
Women, 172, 178, 1475-79

Yearbooks. *See* Annuals and yearbooks
Young adult library services
  general works, 1706-9
  proceedings and symposia, 1714-18
  reference works, 1710-13